7th BRIEF CANADIAN EDITION

BUSINESS COMMUNICATION
PROCESS & PRODUCT

Dr. Mary Ellen Guffey
Emerita Professor of Business
Los Angeles Pierce College

Dr. Dana Loewy
Emerita Lecturer, Business Communication
California State University, Fullerton

Esther Griffin
Liberal Arts Professor
Georgian College

CENGAGE

Australia • Brazil • Canada • Mexico • Singapore • United Kingdom • United States

***Business Communication: Process and Product*, Seventh Brief Canadian Edition**

Dr. Mary Ellen Guffey, Dr. Dana Loewy, and Esther Griffin

Sr. Director, Product: Jackie Wood

Sr. Portfolio Manager: Lenore Taylor-Atkins

Product Marketing Manager: Sydney Pope

Director, Content and Production: Toula DiLeo

Content Development Manager: Catherine Gillespie-Lopes

Sr. Content Production Manager: Imoinda Romain

Sr. IP Analyst: Christine Myaskovsky

Production Service: MPS Limited

Copy Editor: Dawn Hunter

Compositor: MPS Limited

Text Designer: Cathy Mayer

Cover Designer: John Montgomery

Library and Archives Canada Cataloguing in Publication:

Title: Business communication : process & product / Dr. Mary Ellen Guffey (Emerita Professor of Business, Los Angeles Pierce College), Dr. Dana Loewy (Emerita Lecturer, Business Communication, California State University, Fullerton), Esther Griffin (Liberal Arts Professor, Georgian College).

Names: Guffey, Mary Ellen, author. | Loewy, Dana, author. | Griffin, Esther, author.

Description: 7th brief Canadian edition. | Includes bibliographical references and index.

Identifiers: Canadiana (print) 20210114894 | Canadiana (ebook) 20210114959 | ISBN 9780176910181 (softcover) | ISBN 9780176910280 (PDF)

Subjects: LCSH: Business communication—Textbooks. | LCSH: Business writing—Textbooks. | LCGFT: Textbooks.

Classification: LCC HF5718.3 .G82 2021 | DDC 651.7—dc23

ISBN-13: 978-0-17-691018-1
ISBN-10: 0-17-691018-2
Ebook ISBN-13: 978-0-17-691028-0
Ebook ISBN-10: 0-17-691028-X

Cengage Canada
333 Bay Street, #2400
Toronto, ON M5H 2T6
Canada

Cengage is a leading provider of customized learning solutions with employees residing in nearly 40 different countries and sales in more than 125 countries around the world. Find your local representative at **www.cengage.com.**

To learn more about Cengage platforms and services, register or access your online learning solution, or purchase materials for your course, visit **www.cengage.ca.**

Printed in Canada
Print Number: 01 Print Year: 2021

BUSINESS COMMUNICATION: PROCESS & PRODUCT

7TH BRIEF CANADIAN EDITION

Dear Business Communication Student:

The seventh brief Canadian edition of ***Business Communication: Process and Product*** prepares you for a career in an increasingly digital and global workplace. Coauthors Dr. Mary Ellen Guffey and Dr. Dana Loewy have once again revised their award-winning book to help prepare students for a career in a complex mobile, social, and global workplace and to help students successfully navigate this vast networked environment. Esther Griffin has updated the text with new Canadian case studies, concept checks, examples, and references to make its content even more relevant.

Students will learn how social media networks and mobile technology function in the workplace and how they can strengthen their professional communication and critical thinking skills. All the features that have made this award-winning textbook so successful for three decades have been updated in this edition.

In addition to solid instruction in writing skills, which employers continue to demand, the seventh Canadian edition brings you numerous enhancements, a few of which are highlighted here:

- **MindTap.** This multimedia learning experience helps students apply what they are learning through dynamic assignments that they use to build a professional portfolio. Alongside the enhanced ebook, MindTap provides a variety of multimedia: animated model documents, video cases, and interviews with industry professionals who contextualize core concepts and help students understand the connection between what they are learning and how it impacts their future careers. Study tools include chapter quizzes, downloadable documents, PowerPoint slides, and flashcards. Students walk away from MindTap having applied what they have learned through a variety of activity types, including writing assignments and oral presentations. All written assignments can then be uploaded into their Pathbrite e-portfolio, which students have access to even after their access to MindTap has expired.
- **Integrated digital technologies.** The professional use of social media networks and mobile technology requires that you know best practices. This edition provides the latest advice to guide you in using these digital technologies safely and effectively in the workplace. You'll find best practices for texting, instant messaging, blogging, collaborating with wikis, and networking with social media in business today.
- **Focus on employability and soft skills.** Each chapter highlights and develops the employability and soft skills that employers demand. You will learn how to identify your strengths and areas for improvement, and through critical thinking and practice, hone your skills.
- **Latest trends in job searching.** Chapter 15 presents the most current trends, technologies, and practices affecting the job search, résumés, and cover letters. You will learn how to build a personal brand, how to network, and how to write customized résumés and create an effective LinkedIn profile.
- **Hottest trends in job interviewing.** Chapter 16 provides countless tips on how to interview successfully in today's highly competitive job market, including one- and two-way video interviewing.

We wish you well in your course! As always, we welcome your comments and suggestions as you use the No. 1 business communication franchise in North America and abroad.

Cordially,

Mary Ellen Guffey ***Dana Loewy*** ***Esther Griffin***

About the Authors

Dr. Mary Ellen Guffey

A dedicated professional, Mary Ellen Guffey has taught business communication and business English topics for over 35 years. She received a bachelor's degree, *summa cum laude,* from Bowling Green State University, a master's degree from the University of Illinois, and a doctorate in business and economic education from the University of California, Los Angeles (UCLA). She has taught at the University of Illinois, Santa Monica College, and Los Angeles Pierce College.

Now recognized as the world's leading business communication author, Dr. Guffey corresponds with instructors around the globe who are using her books. She is the founding author of the award-winning *Business Communication: Process and Product*, the leading business communication textbook in this country. She also wrote *Business English*, which serves more students than any other book in its field; *Essentials of College English*; and *Essentials of Business Communication*, the leading text/workbook in its market. Dr. Guffey is active professionally, serving on the review boards of *Business and Professional Communication Quarterly* and the *Journal of Business Communication*, publications of the Association for Business Communication. She participates in national meetings, sponsors business communication awards, and is committed to promoting excellence in business communication pedagogy and the development of student writing skills.

Dr. Dana Loewy

Dana Loewy has been teaching business communication at California State University, Fullerton since 1996. She enjoys introducing undergraduates to business writing and honing the skills of graduate students in managerial communication. Most recently, she has also taught various German courses and is a regular guest lecturer at Fachhochschule Nürtingen, Germany. In addition to completing numerous brand-name consulting assignments, she is a certified business etiquette consultant. Dr. Loewy has collaborated with Dr. Guffey on recent editions of *Business Communication: Process and Product* as well as on *Essentials of Business Communication.*

Dr. Loewy holds a master's degree from Bonn University, Germany, and earned a PhD in English from the University of Southern California. Fluent in several languages, among them German and Czech, her two native languages, Dr. Loewy has authored critical articles in many areas of interest—literary criticism, translation, business communication, and business ethics. Before teaming up with Dr. Guffey, Dr. Loewy published various poetry and prose translations, most notably *The Early Poetry of Jaroslav Seifert* and *On the Waves of TSF.* Active in the Association for Business Communication, Dr. Loewy focuses on creating effective teaching and learning materials for undergraduate and graduate business communication students.

Adapting Author: Esther Griffin

For over 20 years, Esther Griffin has taught business communications both online and face-to-face at Georgian College in Barrie, Ontario. This hands-on experience, as well as her background as an employment specialist and her MA in education, specializing in college curriculum development, has kept her current and engaged in her field. She also holds an MFA in creative writing and is an award-winning fiction author. Having worked as adapting author of *Business Communication: Process and Product*, Sixth Brief Canadian Edition, Professor Griffin is thrilled to join the Cengage team as adapting author of the seventh brief Canadian edition. She believes that with technology and global trends rapidly affecting the workplace, strong communication skills are more important than ever. Professor Griffin encourages students to keep their employability skills sharp by using this textbook in the classroom and beyond.

Brief Contents

Contents

Dimitar Gorgev/Alamy Stock Photo

Westend61/Getty Images

UNIT 4 Reports, Proposals, and Presentations

CHAPTER 11

Reporting in the Workplace 272

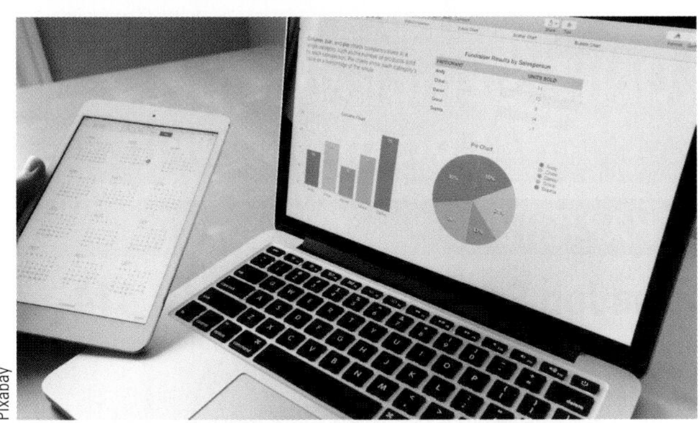

Pixabay

CHAPTER 12

Informal Business Reports 310

RF._.studio

CHAPTER 13

Proposals, Business Plans, and Formal Business Reports 346

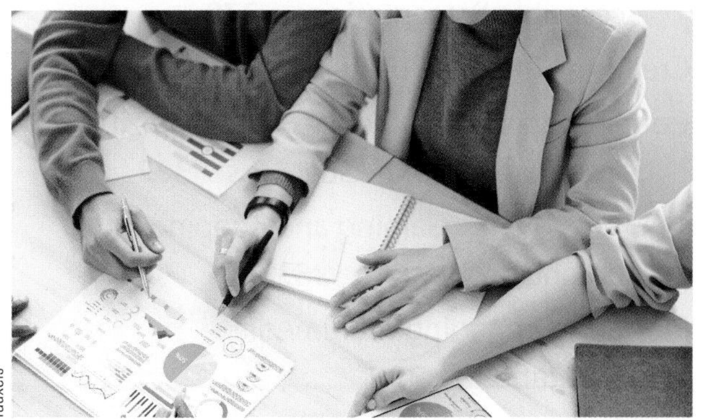

fauxels

CHAPTER 14

Business Presentations 378

Atstock Productions/Shutterstock

UNIT 5 Employment Communication

CHAPTER 15

The Job Search and Résumés 414

SFIO CRACHO/Shutterstock

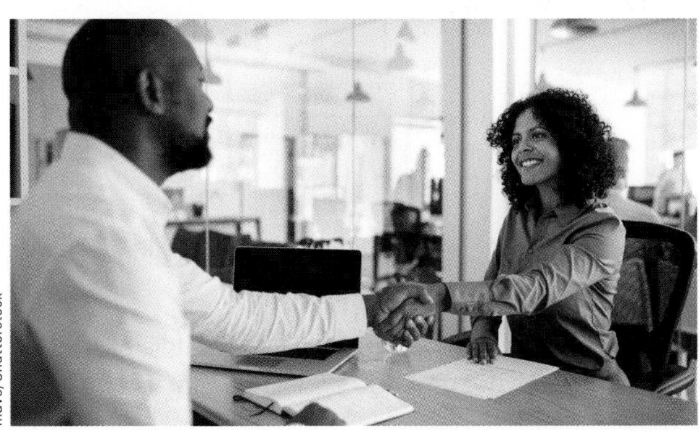

mavo/Shutterstock

Introduction

Business Communication: Process and Product offers the most up-to-date and best researched text on the market. The seventh brief Canadian edition includes interactive student resources and comprehensive coverage of workplace technology. This innovative coverage enhances the hallmark features of this textbook: the 3-x-3 writing process, Canadian case studies, and abundant use of model documents. This edition also features robust online support for courses, so whether your course is in-person, hybrid, or fully online, *Business Communication: Process and Product* has a solution for you.

MEETING EMPLOYER EXPECTATIONS

Survey after survey reveals that employers are seeking new hires with these key skills:

- Written and oral communication skills
- Critical thinking and analytical reasoning
- Ethical decision making
- Teamwork skills
- Professionalism

Business Communication: Process and Product, Seventh Brief Canadian Edition, covers the following topics that are indispensable for the workplace:

- Expert writing techniques geared to developing your writing skills plus interactive documents for analysis, authentic model documents, and engaging activities in which you apply your skills
- Presentation skills featuring contemporary examples, including coverage of smartphone best practices, to prepare you for the realities of workplace communication and technology
- Critical thinking questions and activities in every chapter to stimulate and develop skills
- Ethics Checks in addition to guidance and tools provided through discussion questions and ethical dilemma scenarios
- Teamwork skills with a heavy emphasis on professionalism and etiquette in the workplace so that you will know how to meet employer expectations
- Two employment chapters that present the latest trends in job searching, interviewing, and résumé writing, along with current, effective résumé models, tips for mobile devices and apps, and LinkedIn advice

SOCIAL MEDIA NETWORKS AND MOBILE TECHNOLOGY

Trusted authors Mary Ellen Guffey and Dana Loewy and adapting author Esther Griffin understand social and mobile! The authors address workplace use of social media and communication technology in a chapter solely dedicated to best practices on the job. Because these skills are fundamental in the contemporary world of work, social media and communication technology are integrated in each chapter. Every chapter reflects the pervasive influence of communication technology on business writing. This state-of-the-art coverage makes it clear that writing is more important than ever in the digital world.

FEATURES

The 3-x-3 writing process provides students with a proven three-step strategy for developing effective communication.

Model documents enable students to better understand strategies highlighted in the text.

Concept Checks are now featured in every chapter for each learning objective. These critical thinking questions and activities allow students to review and process information as they work through each chapter.

Spotlight on Communication (Canadian case studies) begin and end every chapter and create opportunities to stimulate vigorous in-class or online discussion of topics.

Case Connections (brief Canadian case studies) are now included in every chapter and feature additional critical thinking questions to further engage students with the chapter's concepts.

MindTap Callouts point students to online video interviews with Canadian industry professionals to support concepts discussed in the text.

End-of-chapter activities offer the most complete, descriptive, understandable, and relevant activities on the market.

Coverage of the latest digital media illustrates the professional uses of Twitter, LinkedIn, instant messages, podcasts, blogs, and wikis in numerous figures and model documents. Integrated coverage and applications of the latest digital technologies and mobile devices emphasize best practices and help students understand the difference between professional and social applications.

Focus on soft skills provides up-to-date guidance on acceptable professional behaviour and business etiquette for today's digital workplace.

Extensive coverage of interview types includes online, video, and virtual interviews, ensuring that students are better prepared for entering the workforce.

The **Style Guide for Business Communication: Process and Product** is included in the textbook as appendixes that offer students a quick and easy reference for grammar and mechanics, as well as documentation formatting. These appendixes contain a Guide to Documentation Formats, the Grammar and Mechanics Guide, and the answers to the end-of-chapter Grammar and Mechanics reviews.

NEW TO THE EDITION

- **New Concept Check** sections have been added to every chapter so students can review content and test their knowledge as they progress through the textbook.
- **New Case Connections** provide more opportunity for critical thinking as students analyze Canadian case studies and apply concepts.
- **Updated Spotlight on Communication boxes in every chapter** explore relevant communication strategies and challenges at organizations across Canada, including Editors Canada, Makivik Corporation, Immersive Tech, and The David Suzuki Foundation.

- **MindTap callouts** point students to online video interviews with Canadian industry professionals to support concepts discussed in the text.
- **Increased Canadian content** includes updated research and statistics, new figures, more Indigenous content, and the pandemic's impact.
- **Bias-free language** has been integrated throughout the textbook for inclusivity and is highlighted as a best-practice in chapter content and the Grammar and Mechanics Guide.
- **New end-of-chapter activities** will help students develop workplace writing, presenting, team, and social media skills.

INSTRUCTOR'S RESOURCES

The *Process and Product* Instructor's Resource Centre

On this password-protected site, instructors will find all their supplements in one convenient and easy-to-use place, including instructor's manual, PowerPoints, solutions, cases, additional exercises and handouts, simulations, grammar support, and much, much more. Go to login.cengage.com to access the ultimate tools for customizing lectures and presentations.

Test Bank: This resource includes more than 900 multiple-choice questions written according to guidelines for effective construction and development of higher-order questions. Also included are 460 true/false questions, 300 completion questions, and 75 essay questions.

The test bank is available in a new cloud-based platform. Cognero® is a secure online testing system that allows you to author, edit, and manage test bank content from any place you have Internet access. No special installations or downloads are needed, and the desktop-inspired interface, with its drop-down menus and familiar, intuitive tools, allows you to create and manage tests with ease. You can create multiple test versions in an instant and import or export content into other systems. Tests can be delivered from your learning management system, your classroom, or wherever you choose.

PowerPoint: Microsoft® PowerPoint® lecture slides for every chapter have been created. There is an average of 40 slides per chapter, many featuring key figures, tables, and photographs from *Business Communication: Process and Product*. Principles of clear design and engaging content have been incorporated throughout, making it simple for instructors to customize the deck for their courses.

Image Library: This resource consists of digital copies of figures, short tables, and photographs used in the book. Instructors may use these JPEGS to customize the PowerPoint or create their own PowerPoint presentations.

Instructor's Manual: This resource is organized according to the textbook chapters and addresses key educational concerns, such as typical obstacles students face and how to address them. Other features include in-class and online activities, discussion starters, technology links, solutions and answer keys, and much more.

MindTap

MindTap is the digital learning solution that powers students from memorization to mastery. It gives instructors complete control of their course—to provide engaging content, challenge every individual, and build student confidence. Instructors can customize interactive syllabi to emphasize priority topics as well as add their own material or notes to the ebook as desired. This outcome-driven application gives instructors the tools needed to empower students and boost both understanding and performance.

STUDENT RESOURCES

MindTap

Modern students require modern solutions. MindTap is a flexible, all-in-one teaching and learning platform that includes the full ebook, a customizable learning path, and various course-specific activities that drive student engagement and critical thinking. The MindTap that accompanies this textbook includes the following:

- Animated model documents
- Video cases and interviews with Canadian industry professionals
- Aplia™ offers high-quality, auto-graded assignments that ensure students put forth effort on a regular basis throughout the term.
- Study tools like practice quizzes, chapter PowerPoint summaries, and flashcards
- ReadSpeaker will read the text aloud.
- Highlight the text and make notes in the MindTap Reader. Notes will flow into Evernote, the electronic notebook app that is accessible anywhere when it's time to study for the exam.
- All written assignments can be uploaded into Pathbrite, our e-portfolio app. Access to Pathbrite continues after the MindTap access expires.

Visit cengage.ca to start using MindTap. Enter the Online Access Code from the card included with the textbook. If a code card is *not* provided, instant access can be purchased at CengageBrain.com.

Appreciation for Support

I am very pleased to introduce the updated content of the seventh brief Canadian edition of *Business Communication: Process and Product.* The Cengage Canada team owes a huge debt of gratitude to Dr. Mary Ellen Guffey, whose exceptional market-driven texts and ancillaries, now written in conjunction with Dr. Dana Loewy, form the foundation and framework of the Canadian edition.

I'd like to extend a warm thank you to the amazing team of professionals at Cengage Canada, including Imoinda Romain, Lenore Taylor-Atkins, Catherine Gillespie-Lopes, Alexis Hood, as well as to copyeditor Dawn Hunter. Their expertise and guidance have been invaluable during the development of this edition.

Our team appreciates those instructors and students who continue to choose *Business Communication: Process and Product*, especially those who provide both formal and informal feedback. No successful textbook reaches a No. 1 position without a great deal of help. The Cengage Canada team is grateful to the reviewers and other experts who contributed their pedagogic and academic expertise to shaping *Business Communication: Process and Product.* Those who had a specific impact on the content of this edition include the following:

Lisa Deighan, *New Brunswick Community College*

Chelsea Budd, *Saskatchewan Polytechnic*

Candice Dyck, *College of New Caledonia*

Edie Lowes, *Okanagan College*

Marina Arkley, *Seneca College*

I want to extend my gratitude to the faculty and students who provided their wisdom and support during the writing of this edition. Thank you also to my children for their love and strength.

Esther Griffin

UNIT 1

Communication Foundations

CHAPTER 1
Business Communication in the Digital Age

CHAPTER 2
Professionalism: Team, Meeting, Listening, Nonverbal, and Etiquette Skills

CHAPTER 3
Intercultural Communication

IN UNIT 1, YOU WILL DEVELOP THE FOLLOWING EMPLOYABILITY SKILLS:

EMPLOYABILITY AND SOFT SKILLS	
Oral and Written Communication	✓
Information Management	✓
Critical Thinking	✓
Problem Solving	✓
Active Listening	✓
Professional Work Behaviours	✓
Goal-Setting	✓
Agility	✓
Adaptability	✓
Personal and Social Responsibility	✓
Ethical Decision Making	✓
Engagement	✓
Innovation and Creativity	✓
Learning Worker Attitude	✓
Team Building	✓
Accountability	✓
Project Collaboration	✓
Online Tools and Social Media[1]	✓

CHAPTER 1

Business Communication in the Digital Age

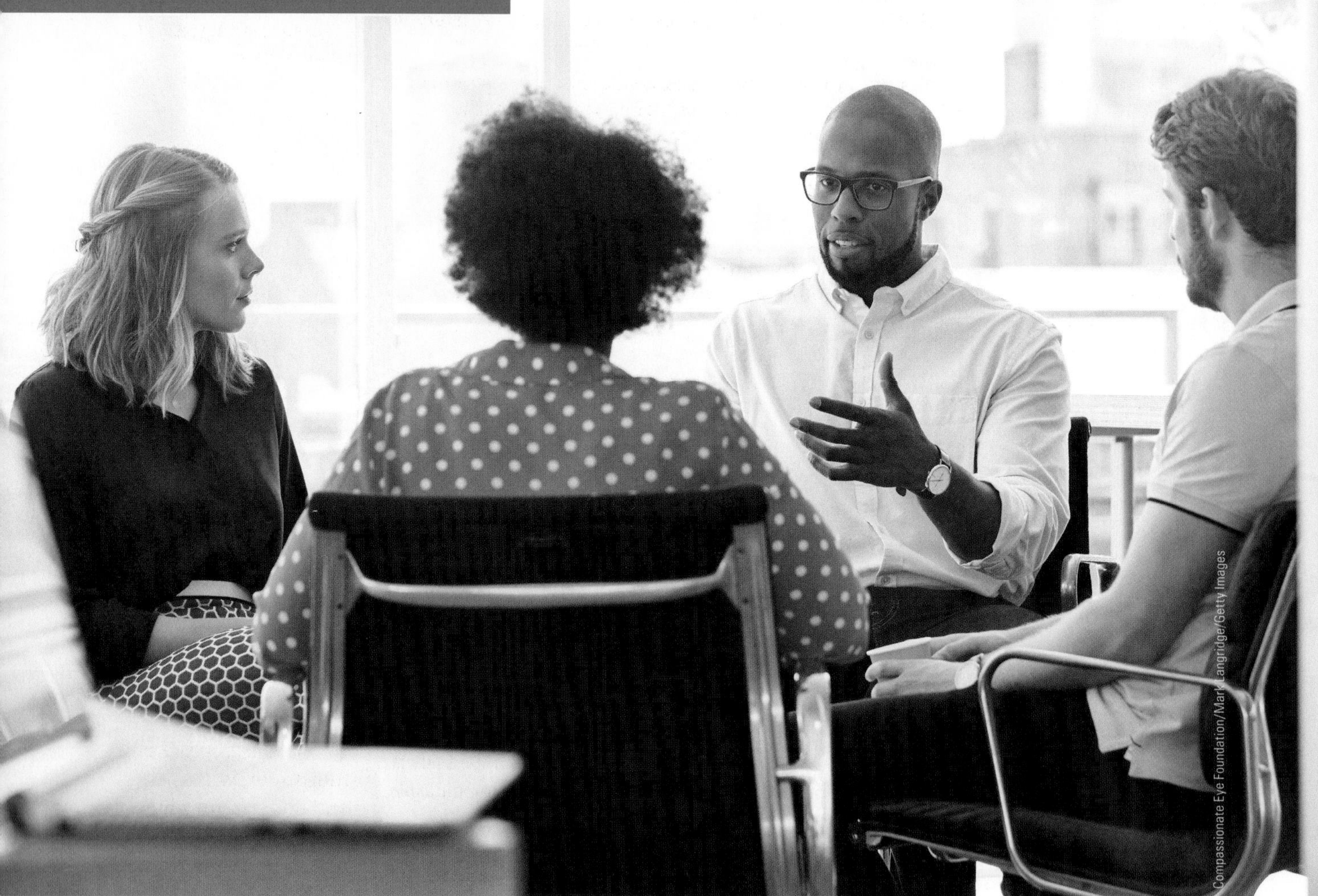
Compassionate Eye Foundation/Mark Langridge/Getty Images

LEARNING OBJECTIVES

After studying this chapter, you should be able to

1 Explain how communication skills fuel career success, and understand why writing skills are vital in a digital, mobile, and social-media-driven workplace.

2 Identify the skills for success in the hyperconnected 21st-century workplace and competitive job market.

3 Describe significant trends and technologies in today's dynamic work environment.

4 Understand the nature of communication and its barriers.

5 Examine critically the flow of communication in organizations, explain the importance of effective media choices, and understand how to overcome typical barriers to organizational communication.

6 Analyze ethics in the workplace, understand the goals of ethical business communicators, and choose the tools for doing the right thing.

SPOTLIGHT ON COMMUNICATION: PART 1

Canadian Tire and Myant Inc.—Smart Technology and Innovation

Founded in 1922, Canadian Tire is seen by many as a Canadian institution—it even has its own money. And at a time when so many Canadian companies are being sold to U.S. owners, Canadian Tire is still wholly ours![2] Canadian Tire remains competitive by forming industry partnerships and responding to the evolving market.

Reprinted courtesy of Myant

Canadian Tire Corporation (CTC) recently partnered with Myant Inc., a textile computing company, to offer "wearable computing and smart textiles" at all its retail stores.[3] Myant's innovative technology is integrated into footwear and apparel with comfort and safety in mind:

> Myant knits sensors and actuators into everyday textiles, giving them the ability to sense and react to the human body. This continuous bidirectional interface to the human operating system will empower humanity to transform its capabilities and performance, help people proactively manage health and deliver treatment, and allow us to build better connections to our own selves and those around us.
>
> Myant believes that textiles are an ideal medium for interaction with the human body. While many technological advancements necessitate radical change in behavior to be widely adopted, textiles have the benefit of being familiar to all people across society, inconspicuously integrated into our daily lives, and pervasive across all environments.[4]

Tony Chahine, founder and CEO of Myant, shares his mission: "We have developed the capabilities required to design, engineer and manufacture connected textile solutions so that other innovators, be they large enterprises or small startups, can help deliver on the promise of Textile Computing."[5]

Responding to the market and adopting new technologies like Textile Computing has helped Canadian Tire maintain its position as Canada's biggest auto-parts and household-goods retailer.

CRITICAL THINKING

- How are Canadian Tire and Myant Inc. meeting the demands of today's marketplace?
- What skills do you think businesspeople need to succeed in today's workplace?

Communicating in the Digital World

LEARNING OBJECTIVE 1

Explain how communication skills fuel career success, and understand why writing skills are vital in a digital, mobile, and social-media-driven workplace.

What kind of workplace will you enter when you graduate, and which skills will you need to be successful in it? Expect a fast-paced, competitive, and highly connected digital environment. Communication technology provides unmatched mobility and connects individuals at any time and from anywhere in the world. Today's communicators interact by using multiple electronic devices and access information stored in remote cloud locations.

This mobility and instant access explain why increasing numbers of workers must respond quickly and be available practically around the clock. Progressive businesses have recognized the power of social media networks and seek to engage their customers and other stakeholders where they meet online. Communication no longer flows one way; rather, electronic media have empowered the public to participate and be heard. In this increasingly complex, networked environment, communication skills matter more than ever.[6] When competition for jobs is keen, job candidates with exceptional communication skills immediately stand out.

In this chapter, you will learn about communication skills in the digital era and about the changing world of work. Later you will study tools to help you negotiate ethical minefields and do the right thing. Each section covers the latest information about communicating in business and provides tips that will help you function effectively and ethically in today's workplace.

NOTE

Because this is a well-researched textbook, you will find small superscript numbers in the text. These announce information sources. Full citations are located in the Notes section at the end of each chapter.

Communication Skills: Your Pass to Success

Surveys of employers consistently show that communication skills are critical to effective job placement, performance, career advancement, and organizational success. In making hiring decisions, employers often rank communication skills among the most valued. Many job advertisements specifically ask for excellent oral and written communication skills. When executives were asked what they looked for in a job candidate, the top choices were general communication skills, interpersonal skills, and teamwork skills. The majority of employers also said that communication skills are at least as important as technical skills for entry-level and management positions.[7]

Writing skills are especially important today. Technology enables us to transmit messages more rapidly, more often, and more widely than ever before. Writing skills are also significant because many people work together but are not physically together. They stay connected through spoken and written messages.

Employability Skills

The Conference Board of Canada, an organization dedicated to evidence-based, not-for-profit applied research, has determined the employability skills required in the workplace: "Employability Skills 2000+ are the employability skills, attitudes, and behaviours you need to participate and progress in today's dynamic world of work."[8] This includes fundamental, personal management, and teamwork skills.[9]

This textbook is designed to build and strengthen many of the employability skills that you will require in the workplace. Special attention is given to writing skills because they are difficult to develop and increasingly significant in e-communication.

Writing in Today's Workplace

Writing matters more than ever because the online media require more of it, not less.[10] Ever since the digital revolution swept the workplace, most workers write their own messages. An important employer survey by Hart Research Associates supports this view. When hiring, employers look for a broader range of skills and place strong value on "written and oral communication skills, teamwork skills, ethical decision making, critical thinking, and the ability to apply knowledge in real-world settings."[11] Developing these skills in this course will help you stand out.

© Andrey_Kuzmin/Shutterstock

Job candidates with exceptional communication skills instantly stand out. Communication skills are critical to career success.

It's Up to You: Communication Skills Can Be Learned

By enrolling in a business writing class, you have already taken the first step toward improving or polishing your communication skills. The goals of this book include teaching you basic business communication skills, such as how to write an effective e-mail or a short message on a mobile device. You will also learn how to write a persuasive cover letter and résumé and how to make a memorable presentation.

Thriving in the challenging work world depends on many factors, some of which you cannot control. However, one factor that you do control is how well you communicate. You are not born with the abilities to read, listen, speak, and write effectively. These skills must be learned. This book and this course may well be the most important in your entire college or university curriculum because they will equip you with the skills most needed in today's fast-paced workplace.

Concept Check

1. In what ways can a lack of oral and written communication skills affect your performance on the job?
2. Individually or in teams, check the listings at an online job board such as Monster, Workopolis, CanadianCareers, or CollegeGrad. Follow the instructions to search job categories and locations. Find three to five job listings in your field of interest. Examine the skills requested. How often do the ads mention communication and teamwork skills? What tasks do the ads mention? Prepare a list of the most frequently requested skills. Discuss your findings with your team members.

Tools for Success in the 21st-Century Workplace

LEARNING OBJECTIVE 2

Identify the skills for success in the hyperconnected 21st-century workplace and competitive job market.

Information technology has changed how we work, play, and communicate in distinct ways. It has never been easier to access and share information via various digital media from a vast network of sources and to distribute it nearly instantly and to widespread audiences.[12] What hasn't changed is that our communication skills need time and effort to develop.

Achieving literacy in the digital age means not only using multimedia applications but also using technology thoughtfully and in a professional manner to achieve success. The 21st-century economy depends mainly on information and knowledge. Previously, in the Industrial Age, raw materials and physical labour were the key ingredients in the creation of wealth. Today, however, individuals in the workforce offer their knowledge, not their muscles. Knowledge workers (a term first coined by management guru Peter Drucker) are paid for their education and their ability to learn.[13]

More recently, we are hearing the term *learning worker* to describe those who not only have acquired knowledge through their diplomas and degrees but also have developed the knowledge of how to learn.[14]

As workplaces grow and change, "learning workers have the skills to learn as they go, adapt, and apply their learning to new situations and issues."[15] Learning workers position themselves to become organizational leaders, anticipating and adapting to industry changes, which makes them valuable, innovative employees.[16]

In such a demanding environment, continual, lifelong learning will make you more competitive and valuable to employers.[17] An adaptable, highly skilled workforce is well equipped to weather any economic climate, as well as global competition.

Why Should You Care?

As a worker in the digital age, you can expect to be generating, processing, and exchanging information. You will need to be able to transmit it effectively across various communication channels and multiple media. You might be called upon to use e-mail, electronic slide presentations, wikis, podcasts, or Facebook and other social media in a professional setting. With added job responsibilities, you will be expected to make sound decisions and solve complex problems.

In one report, Canadian employers identified the ability to adapt quickly to the job, as well as flexibility and on-demand availability, right behind skills and knowledge.[18] You are learning to think, read, and ask questions in a networked world that is accessed with computers, tablets, smartphones, wearable devices, and more. The avalanche of information that engulfs you daily requires you to evaluate all sources critically because information flows at a great speed, across various media, and in many directions.[19]

© Marish/Shutterstock

It has never been easier to access and share information via various digital media from a vast network of sources and to distribute it instantly to widespread audiences.

Thinking Critically in the Digital Age

Whether you work in *m-commerce* (mobile technology businesses), *e-commerce* (Internet-based businesses), or *brick-and-mortar commerce* (businesses with a physical location), nearly three out of four jobs will involve some form of mind work. Jobs that require thinking, brainpower, and decision-making skills are likely to remain plentiful. To be successful in these jobs, you will need to be able to think critically, make decisions, and communicate those decisions.

FIGURE 1.1 Osborn-Parnes Creative Problem-Solving Process

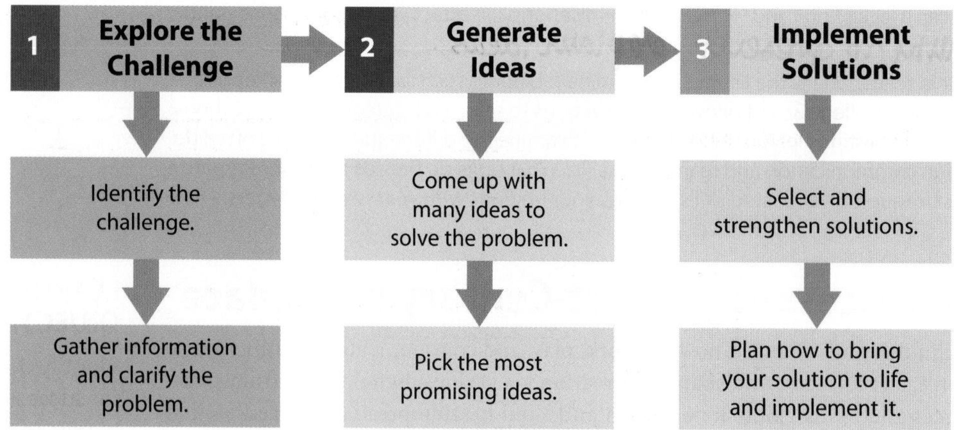

When your boss or team leader says, *What do you think we ought to do?* you want to be able to supply good ideas and demonstrate that you can think critically. This means having opinions that are backed by reasons and evidence. Faced with a problem or an issue, most of us do a lot of worrying before separating the issues or making a decision. Figure 1.1 provides a three-point plan to help you think critically and solve problems competently. Understanding the problem is essential and must come first. Generating and selecting the most feasible ideas is the intermediate step. Finally, the problem-solving model prompts you to refine, justify, and implement the solution. At the end of each learning objective and chapter in this text, you will find activities and problems that will help you develop and apply your critical-thinking skills.

Managing Your Career Well: Guarding Your Credibility

In the dynamic, highly competitive world of work, not even the most talented postsecondary graduate can afford to send out résumés, kick back, and wait to be discovered. You will need to be proactive and exercise greater control over your career than college and university graduates before you did.

In the networked professional environment of the digital era, you must manage and guard your reputation—at the office and online. How you present yourself in the virtual world, meaning how well you communicate and protect your *brand*, may very well determine how successful your career will be. Thoughtful blog posts, well-crafted messages on social media, and competent e-mails will help you make a positive impression.

Succeeding in a Competitive Job Market

In an unstable economy and a tight job market, you may rightly worry about finding work.[20] It's important to keep in mind that a prospective employee must meet the employer's fundamental criteria, including having the required major, course work, and grade point average (GPA). Employers then look for communication skills, a strong work ethic, the ability to work in a team, and initiative.[21] Similar results from another employer survey are summarized in Figure 1.2.

If you are able to communicate effectively about work that is increasingly complex and intellectually demanding, you will be more likely to secure employment even in a tough market. Job candidates needing remediation in basic skills will be last on the list of potential new hires.

FIGURE 1.2 Survey Shows the Skills Employers Want

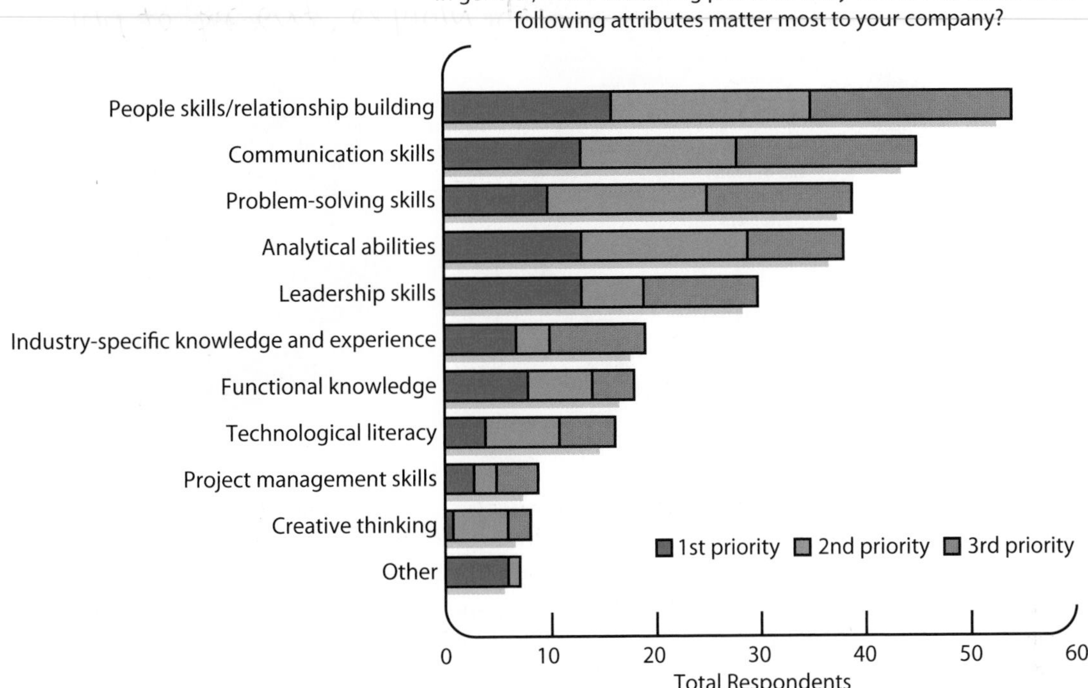

Source: *Preliminary survey report: the skill needs of major Canadian employers*. Copyright 2014. Taking Action for Canada: Jobs and Skills for the 21st Century, an initiative of the Canadian Council of Chief Executives (CCCE).

Concept Check

1. In what ways do you see yourself as a learning worker for your current or future employer?
2. Refer to the employability skills listed on the Unit 1 opening page. Write down your five strongest skills related to your chosen career field. How did you develop these skills? Now write down your five weakest skills related to your chosen career field. What can you do to strengthen these skills?

Trends and Challenges Affecting You in the Information Age Workplace

LEARNING OBJECTIVE 3

Describe significant trends and technologies in today's dynamic work environment.

Today's workplace is changing profoundly and rapidly. As a communicator in the workplace, you will undoubtedly be affected by many trends. Some of those trends include new communication technologies, such as social media; expectations of around-the-clock availability; and global competition. Other trends include flattened management hierarchies, the gig economy, team-based projects, a diverse workforce, and the mobile or virtual office. The following overview reveals how communication skills are closely tied to your success in a constantly evolving workplace.

Social Media and Changing Communication Technologies

Interacting with others on social media has become a daily necessity for many Canadians. Most larger organizations are completely plugged in and have created a positive presence with the help of both traditional and social media.

FIGURE 1.3 Some YouTube, Instagram, and Twitter Facts

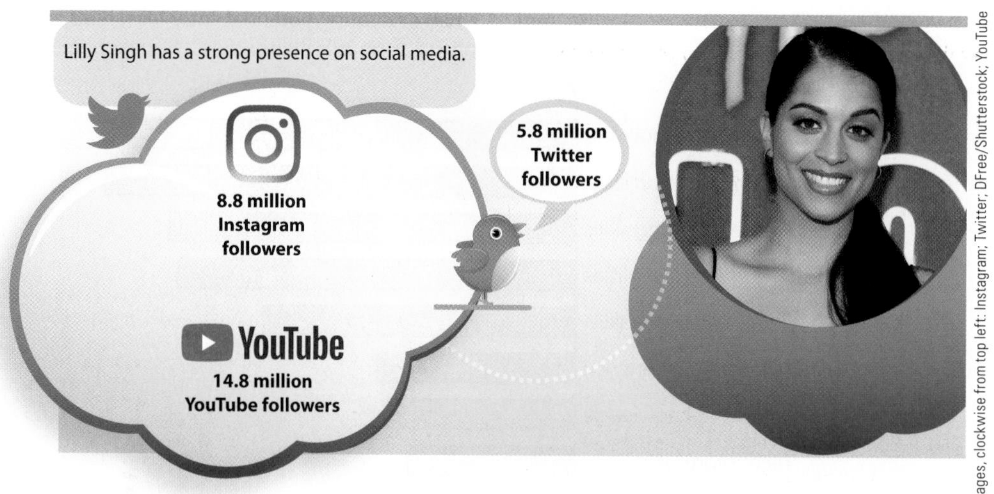

Go to section 1-3a in MindTap, where you can watch a video featuring Candice Wong, the owner of a physiotherapy clinic, discuss the importance of social media for her business.

Social Media Growth. Even the most reluctant late adopters of technology eye the explosive growth of social media networks in the last decade with some interest. After all, online communities continue to draw huge numbers of people from all over the world. Consider Lilly Singh, a YouTube influencer, whose career was built on having a strong social media presence, as Figure 1.3 illustrates. In 2019 WhatsApp had 1 billion users,[22] Facebook had 1.56 billion daily active users on average,[23] and Twitter had 330 million monthly active users.[24] Eighty-four percent of Canadian adults have a Facebook account, with 46 percent on LinkedIn and 42 percent on Twitter.[25] According to Statistics Canada, "nearly all Canadians under the age of 45 use the Internet every day" (see Figure 1.4).[26]

Word of Mouth. Positive and negative comments can travel instantly at the speed of a few mouse clicks. Because bad customer-service experiences can lead to lifelong grudges, tech-savvy companies are embracing digital tools to connect with consumers, invite feedback, and improve their products and services.[27] Figure 1.5 illustrates many new office and communication technologies you will use in today's workplace.

FIGURE 1.4 Canadians' Internet Usage

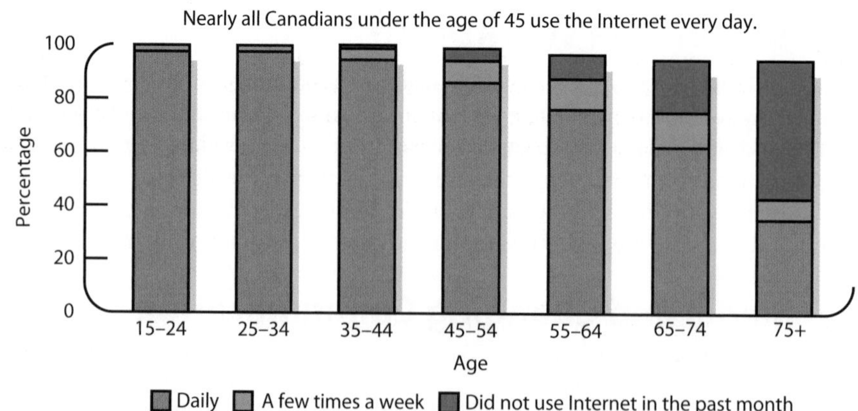

Source: Adapted from Statistics Canada. November 14, 2017. The Internet and Digital Technology. https://www150.statcan.gc.ca/n1/pub/11-627-m/11-627-m2017032-eng.htm (accessed August 31, 2020).
This does not constitute an endorsement by Statistics Canada of this product.

FIGURE 1.5 Communication and Collaborative Technologies

Communication Technologies at Work

Becoming familiar with communication technology can help you succeed on the job. Today's workplace is shaped by mobile devices, mobile apps, and social media networks. With today's tools you can exchange ideas, solve problems, develop products, forecast future performance, and complete team projects any time of the day or night from anywhere in the world.

ArthurStock/Shutterstock

Cloud Computing

Increasingly, applications and data are stored in remote locations online, instead of on costly in-house servers. Businesses and individuals use Dropbox, Google Drive, iCloud, and other cloud-based services to manage and store their data.

Telephony: VoIP

Internet protocol (VoIP) technology uses a broadband Internet connection, which eliminates telephone charges. Many businesses are opting for free or low-cost Internet telephony sites, such as Skype or FaceTime.

Mobile Apps and Digital Convergence

Mobile apps are the software that enables smartphones to run and accomplish amazing feats. Despite their size limitations, mobile apps rival the capabilities of full-fledged software applications. With mobile apps and connectivity between TVs and computers, technology is converging, consolidating into increasingly powerful devices.

Web Conferencing

With services such as GoToMeeting, WebEx, and Microsoft Live Meeting, all you need is a computer or a smart device and an Internet connection to hold a meeting (webinar) with customers or colleagues in real time. Web conferencing incorporates screen sharing, chats, slide presentations, text messaging, and application sharing.

Social Media

Tech-savvy companies use microblogging services, like Twitter, to issue up-to-date news, link to their blogs and websites, announce events and promotions, and track what is being said about their products. Businesses also use social networks such as Facebook and Instagram to interact with customers and build their brands.

Videoconferencing

Videoconferencing allows participants to meet in special conference rooms equipped with cameras and television screens where they can share applications, spreadsheets, and presentations. The technology extends from Internet applications, like Skype, Zoom, and Blue Jeans, to sophisticated software that delivers HD-quality audio and video.

Voice Recognition

Voice recognition software enables users to dictate up to 160 words a minute with accurate transcription. It also improves accessibility for workers with disabilities. Users can compose documents and e-mails, enter data, browse online, and control their devices—all by voice.

Electronic Presentations and Data Visualization

Business presentations in PowerPoint, Prezi, or Keynote can be projected from a laptop or tablet, or posted online. Sophisticated presentations may include animation, sound effects, digital photos, video clips, or hyperlinks to Internet sites.

Wearable Devices

The most recent trend in mobile computing is wearable devices. Fitbit, Google Glass, Apple Watch, and similar accessories do more than track fitness activities. They are powerful mobile devices in their own right that can sync with other smart electronics.

Blogs and Wikis

Businesses use blogs to keep customers and employees informed and to receive feedback. A wiki is a site that allows multiple users to collaboratively create and edit digital files and media. Wikis for business include Confluence, Socialtext, and Jive.

New Skills. A business communicator must develop a tool kit of new communication skills. You will want to know how to select the best communication channel, how to use each channel safely and effectively, and how to incorporate the latest technologies and search tools efficiently. All these topics are covered in this book.

Anytime, Anywhere: 24/7/365 Availability

Although the dizzyingly fast connectedness across time zones and vast distances offers businesses and individuals many advantages, it also comes with more responsibility.

Increased Availability. As you rise on the career ladder, you may be expected to work long hours without extra compensation. You're expected to be available practically at any time and from anywhere should a crisis strike at work. In the last two decades, the line between work and leisure has become increasingly blurry.

Anywhere Contact. In many industries, workers are expected to remain tethered to their workplaces with laptops, tablets, and smartphones around the clock and on weekends. The office of the future is mobile and always open.

The Global Marketplace and Competition

The rise of new communication technologies, the removal of trade barriers, advanced forms of transportation, and saturated local markets—all these developments have encouraged companies to move beyond familiar territories to emerging markets around the world. Small, medium, and large companies in North America and abroad have expanded overseas.

Diversity and Distance. People in other countries may practise different religions, follow different customs, live different lifestyles, and rely on different approaches in business. Now add the complications of multiple time zones, vast distances between offices, and different languages. No wonder global communicators can stumble.

Cultural Awareness and Skills Training. Successful communication in new markets requires developing new skills and attitudes. These include cultural awareness, flexibility, and patience. Because these skills and attitudes may be difficult to achieve, you will receive special communication training to help you deal with intercultural business transactions.

Shrinking Management Layers

In traditional companies information flows through many levels of managers. In response to intense global competition and other pressures, however, innovative businesses have for years been cutting costs and flattening their management hierarchies.

Flatter Organizations. This flattening means that fewer layers of managers separate decision makers from line workers. In flat organizations, in which the lines of communication are shorter, decision makers can react more quickly to market changes.

Communication Challenges. In the past authoritarian and hierarchical management structures did not require that every employee be a skilled communicator. Managers simply passed along messages to the next level. Today, however, frontline employees and managers participate in critical thinking and decision making. Corporate Travel Management Solutions, with its head office based in Concord, Ontario, has experienced rapid growth because of its flat management structure. CEO Tom Osovitzki states that "avoiding layers of middle management gives the company an edge over its bigger competitors, including Amex and Carlson Wagonlit Travel, because it can offer more personalized service." When frontline employees are empowered to make decisions, "issues get resolved in five minutes, not five days."[28] In flat organizations, nearly everyone is a writer and a communicator.

FIGURE 1.6 Agile Workers

Top Five Attributes of Agile Workers

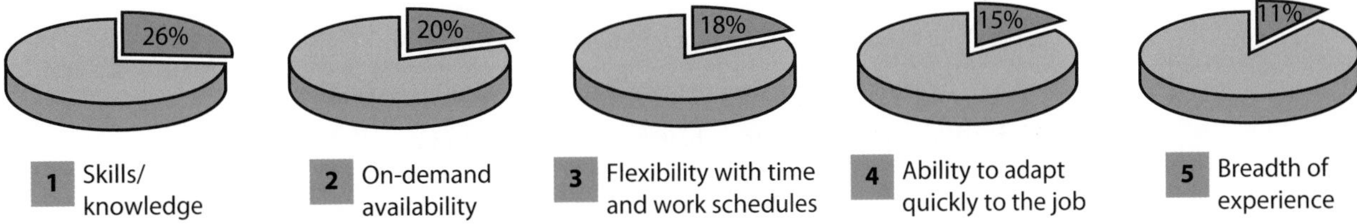

Source: Randstad. (n.d.). *Workforce 2025: The future of the world of work*. Retrieved from http://content.randstad.ca/hubfs/workforce2025/Workforce-2025-Randstad-Part1.pdf. Courtesy of Randstad Canada.

The Gig Economy and Agile Workers

Not unlike musicians who travel from city to city doing *gigs*, today's workers can be expected to work contract to contract with various employers and organizations as part of the *gig economy*. To thrive in the gig economy, Canadians need to become agile workers.

Agile Workers. Workforce agility is "the ability of employees and organizations to remain steadfast and maintain productivity in the face of change."[29] To adapt to change, many employers opt for a staffing model that includes nontraditional workers (self-employed, independent contractors, and contingent workers) who are agile and adaptable. Currently, nontraditional workers make up 30 percent of the workplace, and this contributes to the gig economy. Agile workers need to possess knowledge and skills, but they also need to be well organized and adaptable with a breadth of experience (see Figure 1.6).[30]

ETHICS CHECK

Too Connected?

Office workers use smartphones, e-mail, voice mail, and text messaging. Many are literally always on call and feel overwhelmed. What are the limits of connectedness, and what is the expected response time for various media?

Collaborative Environments and Teaming

Teamwork has become a reality in business. Many companies have created cross-functional teams to empower employees and boost their involvement in decision making. Such stable teams of people have learned to work well together over time.

Cooperative Teams. Whether companies form standing or ad hoc teams, individuals must work together and share information. Working relationships can become strained when individuals don't share the same location, background, knowledge, or training. Some companies even hire communication coaches to help teams get along. Such experts work to develop interpersonal, negotiation, and collaboration techniques. However, companies would prefer to hire new workers who already possess these skills.

Growing Workforce Diversity

In addition to pervasive communication technology, advanced team management, and distant work environments, today's workplace is changing in yet another area.

Multilingual Society. In the most recent census, the number of Canadians who speak a language other than English or French at home rose to 7.6 million. This is up 14.5 percent since the 2011 census.[31] Statistics Canada predicts that by 2031 approximately one third of the people in the Canadian labour force will be foreign born.[32] For the population of Canadians who currently speak a language other than French or English, at least some of the time, the most prominent languages are Mandarin, Cantonese, Punjabi, Spanish, Tagalog, and Arabic.[33]

English and French bilingualism is at an all-time high at 18 percent of Canada's population. As well, the number of people speaking First Nations, Métis, and Inuit languages has grown by 3.1 percent over the past 10 years. There are over 70 Indigenous languages in Canada in 12 language groups.[34] With more Indigenous youth learning to speak their languages, 228,770 people are speaking Indigenous languages at home.[35]

Gender Perspectives. In Canada a woman earns 87 cents for each dollar a man earns.[36] Some of this can be attributed to the following:

- The over-representation of women in part-time work
- The labour market segmentation of women in low paying sectors
- Women's lack of representation in senior positions
- Bias and discrimination in the workplace
- Women's greater share of unpaid work[37]

However, according to statisticians, discrimination accounts for 10 to 15 percent of the gender wage gap.[38]

The gender wage gap increases for transgender women in Canada. While 71 percent have postsecondary credentials, 50 percent of transgender individuals earn $15,000 or less per year.[39]

Older Workers. In addition to the increasing numbers of women and members of minority groups, the workforce will see a big jump in older workers. The Canadian census recorded 1.1 million older workers in the labour market.[40] By 2021 workers 55 and older made up one quarter of the labour force.[41] Because of these and other demographic trends, businesses must create work environments that value and support all people.

Diversity. Teams made up of people with various experiences are more likely to create the products that consumers demand. Customers also want to deal with companies that respect their values. Communicating in this diverse work environment requires new attitudes and skills. Learning to cooperate and communicate successfully with diverse coworkers should be a major priority for all businesspeople.

Virtual and Nonterritorial Offices

You may have heard people refer to the *virtual office*, a workspace that's mobile and decentralized. Today's physical work environments are changing profoundly. Thanks largely to Internet and data access, millions of workers have flexible working arrangements so they can work at home, on the road, and at the customer's place of business.

Nonterritorial Workspaces. Approximately 1.7 million Canadians work from home, not including those who are self-employed.[42] To save on office real estate costs, a number of companies provide *nonterritorial* workspaces. Also known as *mobile platforms* and hot desks, these unassigned workspaces are up for grabs. The first to arrive gets the best desk and the corner window.[43]

Open, nonterritorial workspaces require a new kind of etiquette. Some companies have instituted rules on sharing open office space:

1. Don't hang around.
2. Limit chitchat.
3. Don't sneak up on anyone.
4. Don't eavesdrop or otherwise spy on others.
5. Speak in a soft voice.
6. Wear headphones.

Victor Metelskiy/Shutterstock

Open-Plan Spaces. Even in more traditional offices, employees work in open-plan spaces with flexible workstations, shared conference rooms, and boomerang-shaped desks that save space and discourage territorial behaviour while encouraging casual interaction and spontaneous collaboration.

Global Pandemic Impact

Job Losses. When the COVID-19 pandemic locked down businesses and forced individuals to stay home to reduce the spread of the virus, Canada reported 1 million job losses in the first month alone. The highest number of losses came from the hospitality, food, and retail sectors. In addition, education, law, community, arts, culture, sports, and trades sectors were greatly affected.[44] Businesses and organizations had to adapt to a modified delivery of services and ensure the safety of their workers and customers as the economy slowly reopened. The impact of the pandemic on workplaces will be felt for years to come.

Remote Workers. As Canadians adapt to life during a pandemic, many are working from home. A study shows that "the number of Canadians working from home has grown seven-fold."[45] Before the pandemic, 7 percent of Canadians worked from home, and within the first few months of the pandemic, 52 percent of Canadians reported they were working remotely.[46] As a result, communication technology and online business skills are more important than ever. Look back at Figure 1.5 for a list of communication technologies that are in demand.

Concept Check

1. How has the global pandemic affected work practices in Canada?
2. Refer to Figure 1.5. Within the next five years, what technologies do you think will dominate the workplace? Write a list of the top three technologies. Do you have these technological skills?

Understanding the Nature of Communication

LEARNING OBJECTIVE 4

Understand the nature of communication and its barriers.

The digital revolution with electronic transmission of messages has profoundly changed the way we live our lives, do business, and communicate. As the world becomes increasingly interconnected, people are sending more and more messages. However, even as we have gotten used to e-mail, instant messaging (IM), texting, Twitter, and other interactive media, the nature of communication remains unchanged. No matter how we create or send our messages, the basic communication process consists of the same elements. It starts with an idea that must be transmitted.

In its simplest form, communication may be defined as the *transmission of information and meaning from a sender to a receiver.* The crucial element in this definition is *meaning.* The process is successful only when the receiver understands an idea as the sender intended it. How does an idea travel from one person to another? It involves a sensitive process, as shown in Figure 1.7. This process can easily be sidetracked, resulting in miscommunication. The process of communication, however, is successful when both the sender and the receiver understand the process and how to make it work effectively. In our discussion, we concentrate on professional communication in the workplace so that you can be successful as a business communicator in your career.

Sender Has an Idea

The communication process begins when the sender has an idea. The form of the idea may be influenced by complex factors surrounding the sender. These factors may include mood, frame of reference, background, culture, and physical makeup, as well as the context of the situation and many other factors. Senders shape their ideas based on their own experiences and assumptions. To communicate most effectively, a sender must begin by clarifying the idea and purpose. What exactly does the sender want to achieve? How is the message likely to be received? When senders know their purpose and anticipate the expected response, they are better able to shape successful messages.

Sender Encodes the Idea

The next step in the communication process involves *encoding.* This means converting the idea into words or gestures that will convey meaning. A major problem in communicating any message verbally is that words have different meanings for different people. Recognizing how easy it is to be misunderstood, skilled communicators choose familiar, concrete words. In choosing proper words and symbols, senders must be alert to the receiver's communication skills, attitudes, background, experiences, and culture.

FIGURE 1.7 The Communication Process

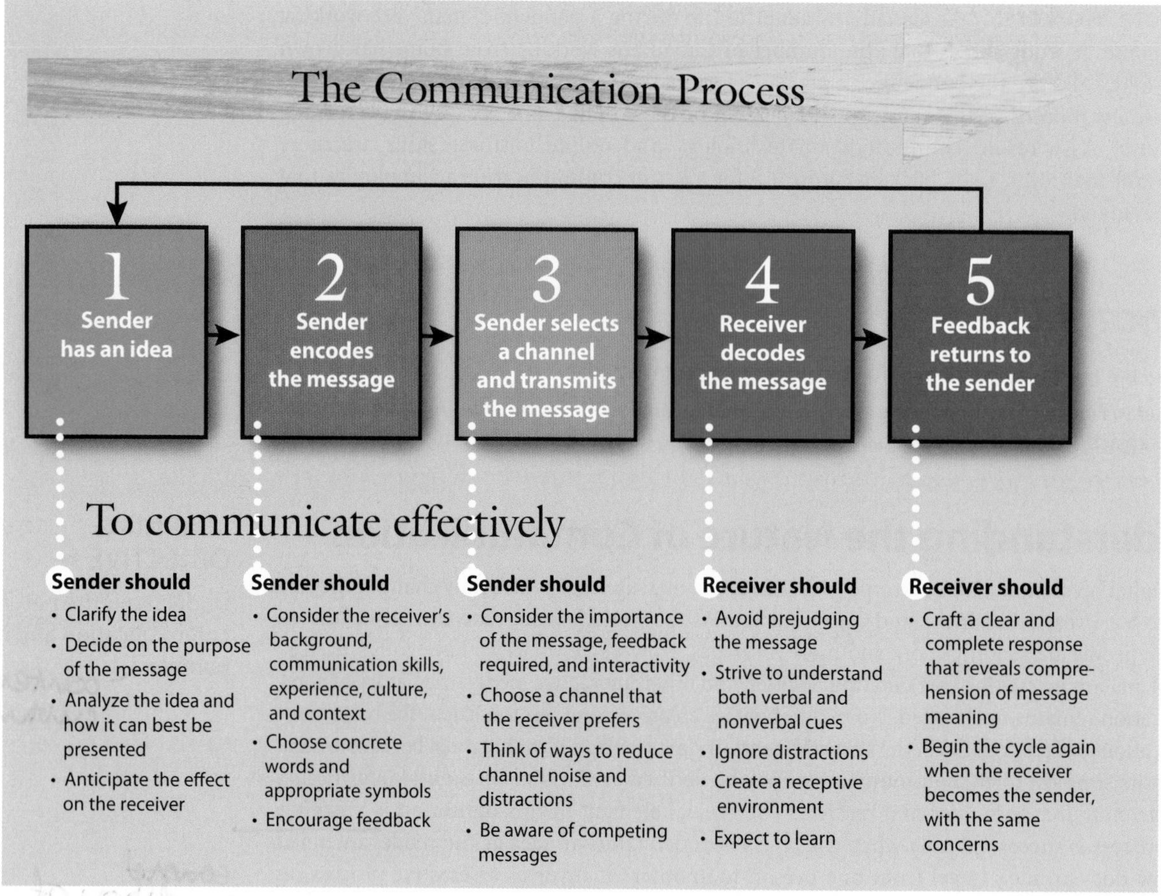

The Communication Process
1 Sender has an idea
2 Sender encodes the message
3 Sender selects a channel and transmits the message
4 Receiver decodes the message
5 Feedback returns to the sender
To communicate effectively
Sender should
• Clarify the idea
• Decide on the purpose of the message
• Analyze the idea and how it can best be presented
• Anticipate the effect on the receiver
Sender should
• Consider the receiver's background, communication skills, experience, culture, and context
• Choose concrete words and appropriate symbols
• Encourage feedback
Sender should
• Consider the importance of the message, feedback required, and interactivity
• Choose a channel that the receiver prefers
• Think of ways to reduce channel noise and distractions
• Be aware of competing messages
Receiver should
• Avoid prejudging the message
• Strive to understand both verbal and nonverbal cues
• Ignore distractions
• Create a receptive environment
• Expect to learn
Receiver should
• Craft a clear and complete response that reveals comprehension of message meaning
• Begin the cycle again when the receiver becomes the sender, with the same concerns

International messages require even more care. The most successful messages use appropriate words, gestures, and symbols selected specifically to match the situation. Good messages also encourage feedback and make it easy for the receiver to respond.

Sender Selects a Channel and Transmits the Message

The medium over which the message travels is the *channel*. Messages may be delivered by computer, wireless network, smartphone, social media, website, letter, memorandum, report, announcement, picture, spoken word, or some other channel. Today's messages are increasingly carried over digital networks with much opportunity for distraction and breakdown. Receivers may be overloaded with incoming messages or unable to receive messages clearly on their devices. Only well-crafted messages may be accepted, understood, and acted on.

Anything that interrupts the transmission of a message in the communication process is called *noise*. Channel noise may range from a weak Internet signal to sloppy formatting and typos in e-mail messages. Noise may even include the annoyance a receiver feels when the sender chooses an improper channel for transmission or when the receiver is overloaded with messages and information.

Receiver Decodes the Message

The individual for whom the message is intended is the *receiver*. Translating the message from its symbol form into meaning involves *decoding*. Only when the receiver understands the meaning intended by the sender—that is, successfully decodes the message—does communication take place. Such success is often difficult to achieve because of a number of barriers that block the process.

No two people share the same life experiences or have the same skills. Decoding can be disrupted internally by the receiver's lack of attention or by bias against the sender or by competing messages. It can be disrupted externally by loud sounds or illegible words. Decoding can also be sidetracked by semantic obstacles, such as misunderstood words or emotional reactions to certain terms.

On the receiving end, successful decoding is more likely to be achieved when the receiver creates a receptive environment and ignores distractions. Alert receivers strive to understand both verbal and nonverbal cues, avoid prejudging the message, and expect to learn something.

Feedback Returns to the Sender

o01shorty10o/istock by Getty Images

The idea of sunglasses for cool dogs could receive both judgmental and evaluative feedback.

The verbal and nonverbal responses of the receiver create *feedback*, a vital part of the communication process. Feedback helps the sender know that the message was received and understood. Senders can encourage feedback by asking questions such as *Am I making myself clear?* and, *Is there anything you don't understand?* Senders can further improve feedback by timing the delivery appropriately and by providing only as much information as the receiver can handle.

In the business world, receivers improve the communication process by providing clear, descriptive, and nonjudgmental feedback. Here's a descriptive response: *I understand you want to sell sunglasses for cool dogs, and you would call them Doggles.*[47] Here's an evaluative response: *Your business ideas are always far-fetched!* An evaluative response is judgmental and doesn't tell the sender whether the receiver actually understood the message. When the receiver returns feedback, this person then becomes the sender of a new cycle of communication with all the same concerns as the original sender.

Barriers That Create Misunderstanding

Go to Chapter 1 in MindTap, where you can watch a video featuring Candice Wong, the owner of a physiotherapy clinic, discuss the importance of job applicants having a professional social media presence.

The communication process is successful only when the receiver understands the message as intended by the sender. It sounds quite simple. Yet it's not. How many times have you thought that you delivered a clear message only to learn later that your intentions were misunderstood?

You can improve your chances of communicating successfully by learning to recognize barriers that are known to disrupt the process. Some of the most significant barriers for individuals are bypassing, differing frames of reference, lack of language skill, and distractions.

Bypassing. An important barrier to clear communication involves words. Each of us attaches a little bundle of meanings to every word, and these meanings are not always similar. Bypassing happens when people miss each other with their meanings.[48] Bypassing can lead to major miscommunication because people assume that meanings are contained in words. In fact, meanings are in people. For communication to be successful, the receiver and sender must attach the same symbolic meanings to their words. One study revealed a high likelihood of miscommunication when people use common but vague words, such as *probably, always, never, usually, often, soon,* and *right away.* What do these words really mean?[49]

Differing Frames of Reference. Another barrier to clear communication is your *frame of reference*. Everything you see and feel in the world is translated through your individual frame of reference. Your unique frame is formed by a combination of your experiences, education, culture, expectations, personality, and other elements. As a result, you bring your own biases and expectations to any communication situation. Because your frame of reference is different from everyone else's, you will never see things exactly as others do. Wise business communicators strive to prevent miscommunication by being alert to both their own frames of reference and those of others.

Lack of Language Skill. No matter how extraordinary the idea is, it won't be understood or fully appreciated unless the communicators involved have an adequate vocabulary and

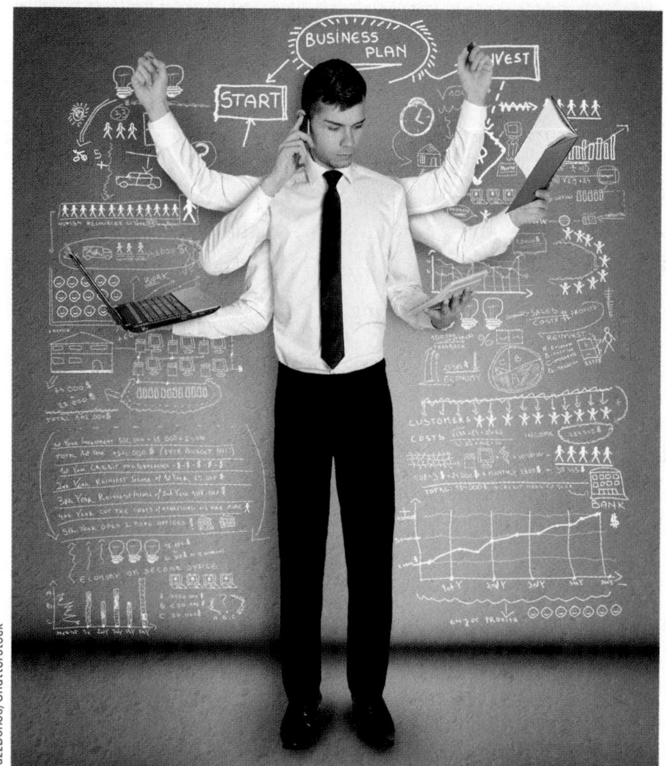

FuzzBones/Shutterstock

Studies have found that people who combine texting, video, phone, and other activities perform tasks significantly worse than non-multitaskers. According to researchers, our brains can do two things at once, but they can't do them very well. In particular, recall, focus, and attention become impaired by information overload.[51]

skill in oral and written expression. Using unfamiliar words, jargon, and unrecognizable abbreviations can seriously impede the transmission of meaning. You will learn more about using plain language and familiar words in Chapter 4.

Distractions. Other barriers include emotional interference, physical distractions, and digital interruptions. Shaping an intelligent message is difficult when one is feeling joy, fear, resentment, hostility, sadness, or some other strong emotion. To reduce the influence of emotions on communication, both senders and receivers should focus on the content of the message and try to remain objective.

Physical distractions, such as faulty acoustics, noisy surroundings, or a poor mobile connection, can disrupt oral communication. Similarly, sloppy appearance, poor printing, careless formatting, and typographical or spelling errors can disrupt written messages. Knowledge workers are increasingly distracted by multitasking, information overload, conflicting demands, and the need to be constantly available digitally. Clear communication requires focusing on what is important and shutting out interruptions.[50]

Overcoming Communication Obstacles

Careful communicators can conquer barriers in a number of ways. To communicate successfully, recognize that the entire process is sensitive and susceptible to breakdown. Like a defensive driver anticipating problems on the road, a good communicator anticipates problems in encoding, transmitting, and decoding a message.

- Effective communicators focus on the receiver's environment and frame of reference, considering questions such as *How is that individual likely to react to my message?*
- Misunderstandings are less likely if you arrange your ideas logically and use words precisely, creating an environment for useful feedback.
- In oral communication this means asking *Do you have any questions?* and encouraging listeners to repeat instructions or paraphrase ideas.
- In written communication it also means providing access: *Here's my phone number so that you can give me your response immediately.*
- In addition to expressing yourself well, successful communication is listening and providing feedback that describes rather than evaluates.

CENGAGE

MINDTAP

Check out section 1-4g in MindTap, where you can watch a video featuring Mike Stiers, a cloud and infrastructure engineer, discuss the importance of the communication process when sending email messages.

Concept Check

1. What is the definition of *communication*?
2. Consider a time when you were misunderstood. What were the barriers to communication? How did you overcome the misunderstanding?

Information Flow and Media Choices in Today's Workplace

LEARNING OBJECTIVE 5

Examine critically the flow of communication in organizations, explain the importance of effective media choices, and understand how to overcome typical barriers to organizational communication.

You may want to connect with friends and family for a specific reason or just for fun. However, businesspeople usually communicate strategically—that is, purposefully, hoping to achieve a particular outcome. Business communication functions can be summarized in three simple categories: (a) to inform, (b) to persuade, and (c) to promote goodwill. Most business messages have one of these functions as their purpose. Informing or sharing information is perhaps the most common communication function in all organizations today.

As discussed earlier, social media, flattened management structures, mobility, interactivity, and mobile devices have all changed the way we communicate at work. One major shift is away from one-sided, slow forms of communication, such as hard-copy memos and letters, to interactive, instant, less paper-based communication. On the job you will have an array of media to help you share information and stay connected both internally and externally. You will need to know which medium is most suitable to accomplish your goal and be able to distinguish between formal and informal channels.

Internal and External Communication

Despite the range of interactive technologies, businesspeople are still working with two basic forms of communication: oral and written. Each has advantages and disadvantages, as summarized in Figure 1.8. These general rules apply whether the communication is directed at audiences inside the organization or outside.

FIGURE 1.8 Comparing Forms of Organizational Communication

Communication	Deliverables/Form	Advantages	Disadvantages
Paper-based (hard copy)	Memos, letters, employee newsletters, brochures, performance appraisals, pay-packet enclosures, agendas and minutes, internal and external reports, questionnaires	Creates a permanent record, is convenient to distribute, may be economical, promotes comprehension and recall, allows precise and uniform expression, gives audience flexibility in when and how to receive content	Leaves a paper trail, requires skill and effort to produce, lacks verbal cues and warmth, cannot be immediately adjusted to audience feedback, may seem impersonal
Digital (soft copy)	E-mail, newsletters, brochures, instant messages, websites, intranets, blogs, social media posts, agendas and minutes, internal and external reports, questionnaires	In addition to all the advantages of paper output, is more economical than paper, can be mass produced and distributed, allows mobile access anytime and anywhere	Leaves a permanent digital footprint, can lead to public embarrassment on a massive scale, may be inaccessible to unplugged audiences, is subject to malfunctions
Oral	Telephone calls, face-to-face conversations, in-person meetings, conferences, team addresses, seminars, workshops, training sessions, roundtables, teleconferences	Provides immediate feedback, can be adjusted to the audience, can be delivered quickly, supplies nonverbal cues, may create a warm feeling, can be powerful	Lacks a permanent record (unless recorded), may contain careless or imprecise expression, may be inappropriate for formal or complex ideas, does not promote easy recall

Internal communication includes exchanging ideas and messages with superiors, co-workers, and subordinates. When those messages must be written, you will probably choose e-mail—the most prevalent communication channel in the workplace today. Brief messages and status updates may be conveyed by text message or IM, especially when the writer is travelling.

External communication is also handled by e-mail in most routine cases. When you are communicating externally with customers, suppliers, the government, and the public, e-mail correspondence is generally appropriate. Hard-copy letters sent by traditional "snail mail" are becoming increasingly rare, especially under time constraints. However, some businesses do create signed paper documents to be faxed, or they scan and e-mail them.

Media Richness and Social Presence

Many Canadian companies are using social media to improve their marketing and customer outreach plans. A recent social media usage study revealed that approximately 56 percent of Canadians follow companies and their products on social media.[52]

Business communicators must be able to choose from a wide range of communication channels most suitable to eliciting the desired outcome. How workers choose the appropriate medium to avoid ambiguity, confusing messages, and misunderstandings has long been studied by researchers. Media richness theory and the concept of social presence are particularly useful for evaluating the effectiveness of old and new media in a given situation.

Media Richness. Daft and Lengel's media richness theory attempts to classify media in organizations according to how much clarifying information they are able to convey from a sender to a recipient.[53] The more helpful cues and immediate feedback the medium provides, the richer it is; face to face and on the telephone, managers can best deal with complex organizational issues. For routine, unambiguous problems, however, media of lower richness, such as memos, reports, and other written communication, usually suffice. Figure 1.9 displays contemporary and traditional media based on their richness and, hence, their likely communication effectiveness.

Ideally, senders would choose the richest medium necessary to communicate the message to the recipient with as little ambiguity as possible. Because a rich medium (such as a face-to-face conversation) is not always available, communicators must often use leaner media (e.g., e-mail) that may not be as effective in reducing ambiguity and decreasing the risk of miscommunication. Just think how hard it is to know whether a text or an e-mail is sarcastic.

Social Presence. *Social presence* has come to mean the degree to which people are engaged online and ready to connect with others. As proposed by Short, Williams, and Christie,[54] however, social presence is the degree of *salience* (being there) between a sender and receiver using a communication medium. Media with high social presence convey warmth and are personal. Social presence is greatest face-to-face and less so in mediated and written communication, such as phone conversations and text messages. Likewise, social presence is greater in synchronous communication (live chat, IM) than in asynchronous communication (e-mail, forum post) that is rather impersonal.

Face to face we receive many more signals than just speech. For example, nonverbal cues, emotional disposition, and voice inflection help us interpret a message correctly. In real time, we can ask the author of a message to clarify—something we cannot do as easily when the message arrives with a delay and is enabled by technology. You could say that social presence means how much awareness of the sender is conveyed along with the message. Communication can succeed as long as the chosen communication medium offers enough social presence to complete the task.[55]

Formal Communication Channels

Information within organizations flows through formal and informal communication channels. A free exchange of information helps organizations respond rapidly to changing markets, boost efficiency and productivity, build employee morale, serve the public, and take full advantage of workers' ideas. Official information within an organization typically flows through formal channels in three directions: downward, upward, and horizontally, as shown in Figure 1.10.

FIGURE 1.9 Media Richness and Communication Effectiveness

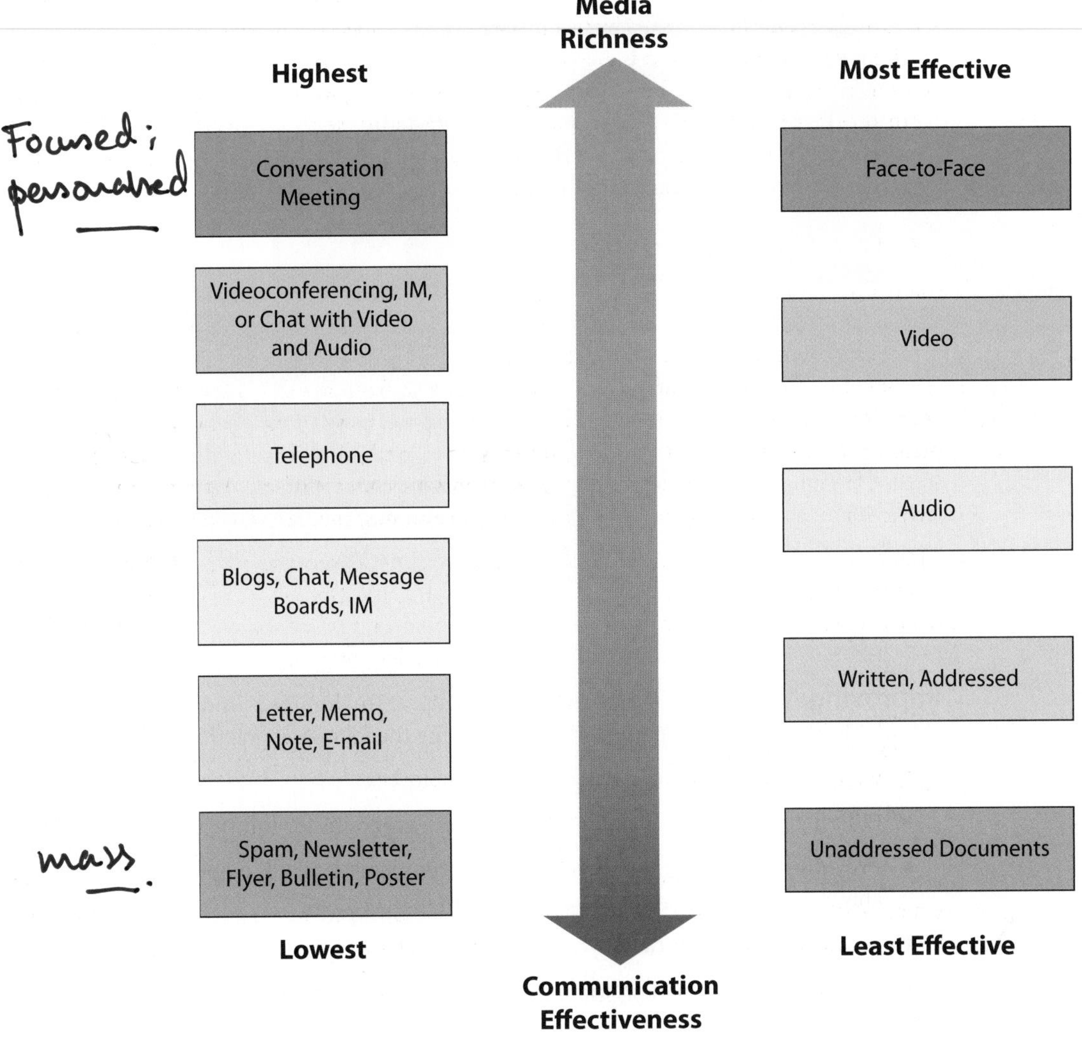

Formal channels of communication generally follow an organization's chain of command. That is, a message originates with executives and flows down through managers to supervisors and finally to lower-level employees. Many organizations have formulated communication policies that encourage regular open communication through newsletters, the corporate intranet, official messages, company-provided social networks, and blogs. Free-flowing, open communication invigorates organizations and makes them successful. Barriers, however, can obstruct the flow of communication, as summarized in Figure 1.11, and must be overcome if the organization is to thrive.

Improving Downward Information Flow. To improve communication and to compete more effectively, many of today's managers are making changes:

- Reengineering their companies into smaller operating units and work teams
- Speaking directly to employees, keeping them informed about how well the company is doing and what new projects are planned
- Providing timely company publications, announcements, meetings, videos, and podcasts

FIGURE 1.10 Information Flow in Organizations

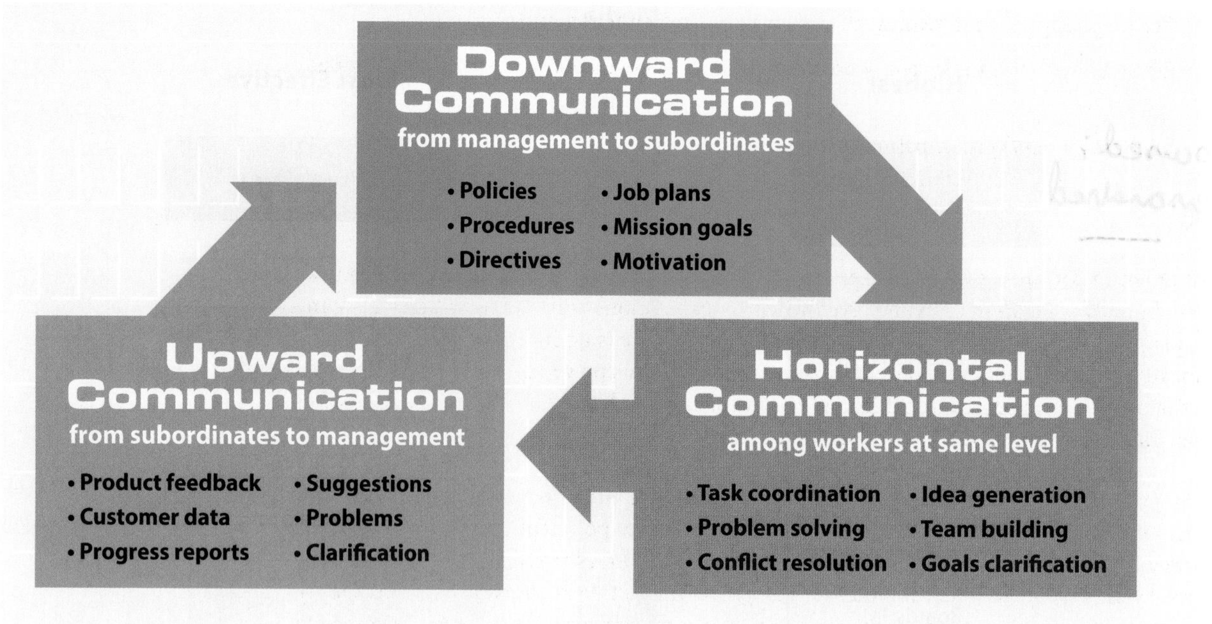

Downward Communication
from management to subordinates
• Policies
• Procedures
• Directives
• Job plans
• Mission goals
• Motivation
Upward Communication
from subordinates to management
• Product feedback
• Customer data
• Progress reports
• Suggestions
• Problems
• Clarification
Horizontal Communication
among workers at same level
• Task coordination
• Problem solving
• Conflict resolution
• Idea generation
• Team building
• Goals clarification

Improving Upward Information Flow. To improve the upward flow of communication, some companies are implementing the following practices:

- Hiring communication coaches to train employees
- Offering regular staff meetings and incentive programs for information sharing
- Providing a trusting, nonthreatening environment in which employees can comfortably share their observations and ideas with management
- Setting up hotlines for anonymous feedback to management
- Installing ombudsman programs (mediators who resolve problems fairly)

FIGURE 1.11 Barriers Blocking the Flow of Communication in Organizations

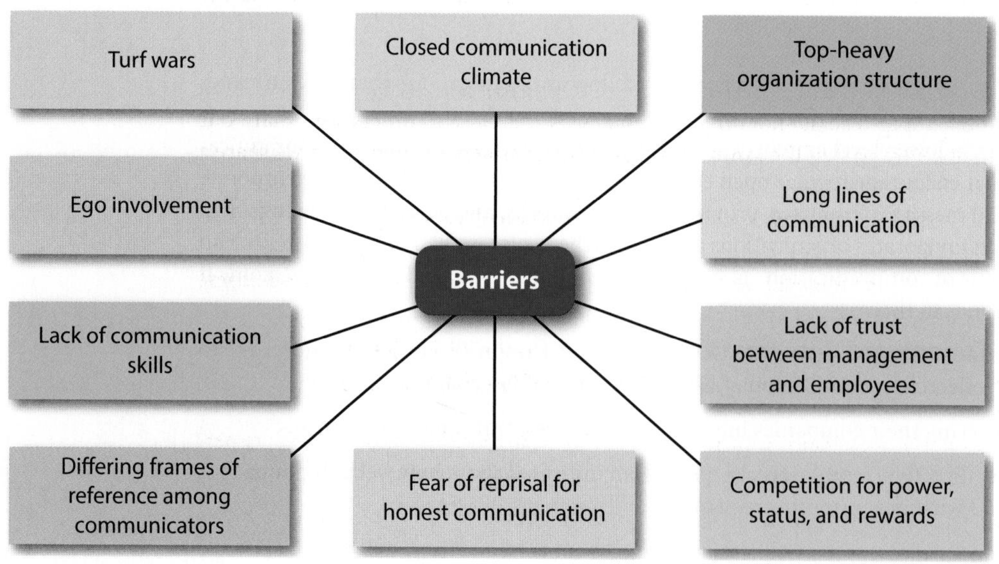

Improving Horizontal Information Flow. To improve horizontal communication, companies are providing additional support:

- Training employees in teamwork and communication techniques
- Establishing reward systems based on team achievement rather than individual achievement
- Encouraging full participation in team functions

Informal Communication Channels

Most organizations today share company news through consistent formal channels, such as e-mail and staff meetings. However, even within organizations with consistent formal channels, people still gossip about company news. The *grapevine* is an informal channel of communication that carries organizationally relevant gossip. This powerful but informal channel functions through social relationships. At one time gossip took place mostly around the water cooler. Today, however, gossip travels much more rapidly online.

Using the Grapevine Productively. Researchers studying communication flow within organizations know that the grapevine can be a powerful, pervasive source of information. In some organizations it can account for as much as two thirds of an employee's information. Is this bad? Well, yes and no. The grapevine can be a fairly accurate and speedy source of organization information; however, grapevine information is often incomplete because it travels in headlines. When employees obtain most of their company news from the grapevine, management is not releasing sufficient information through formal channels.

Managers can use the grapevine productively by doing the following:

- Respecting employees' desire to know
- Increasing the amount of information delivered through formal channels
- Sharing bad and good news
- Monitoring the grapevine
- Acting promptly to correct misinformation[56]

As opposed to the offline grapevine, online consumer-generated comments provide a very public glimpse of what employees and the public are thinking. High-profile leaks travel fast, and their accuracy can be verified more easily than rumours in an offline grapevine. Companies that actively monitor social media are better able to correct inaccuracies and misperceptions. Through formal and informal channels of communication, smart companies keep employees and the public informed.

Responding Ethically to Office Gossip. To many of us, gossip is fun and even entertaining. It encourages social bonding and makes us feel close to others who share our trust. We feel that we are part of the group and that we can influence others when we share a significant tidbit.

However, not all gossip is harmless. Someone known as an office gossip can be viewed as untrustworthy and unpromotable. Even more damaging, malicious gossip spread in e-mails, via text messages, or on social media sites can be used in defamation cases. It can also become evidence against employers in supporting charges of harassment or maintaining a hostile work environment. Unfounded gossip can ruin careers and harm companies. In addition, employers look upon gossip as a productivity drain. The time spent gossiping reduces the time spent working.

How can you respond ethically to gossip or reduce its occurrence? Workplace ethics expert Nan DeMars offers several helpful pointers, reproduced here from her Office Ethics website:

- **Run, don't walk, away from anyone who starts to gossip.** Even if you don't contribute to the conversation, just being present indicates consent.

- **End rumours about others.** If you overhear something that is untrue, step up and say so. People will respect your integrity.
- **Attack rumours about yourself.** Be aggressive and determine who originated the remark, if possible. Always follow up with documentation explaining what really happened.
- **Keep confidences.** Become known as someone who is close-mouthed.
- **Limit the personal tidbits you share about yourself and keep them on the light side.** Too much information may be blown out of proportion or become tempting to someone else to expand. Trust only those who have demonstrated trustworthiness and earned your confidence.
- **Avoid any form of coworker belittlement.** Today's coworker may be tomorrow's senior vice president.
- **Build coworkers up; don't tear them down.** If you must use the grapevine, use it to praise coworkers. They will remember.[57]

Concept Check

1. List three ways that managers can improve the downward flow of communication.
2. Consider the following scenario: Jon Bender, a managing partner at an executive search firm, was surprised to receive a nasty, gossipy e-mail about himself. He was obviously not the intended receiver. Instead of shooting back an equally incendiary message, he decided to talk with the sender. He said, "You're upset. Let's talk about it, but it's not appropriate in an e-mail."[58] In groups, discuss Mr. Bender's response to gossip about himself. Did he do the right thing? How would you have reacted? Although gossip is generally considered unacceptable and a negative force, it can be a tool for managers and employees. Make a list of at least four benefits and four negative consequences of workplace gossip. Be prepared to explain and defend each item.

CASE CONNECTIONS

Loblaws and the Loop Initiative

Martin Good/Shutterstock

According to Statistics Canada in the most recent census, Canadians generate 25 million tons of waste for disposal per year.[59] Most of this waste is due to the way our consumables are packaged, and Loblaws is partnering with TerraCycle, a recycling company, and their Loop initiative to help tackle the issue.

> There is too much plastic waste," said Loblaw executive chairman Galen Weston in a news release. "Our industry is part of the problem and we can be part of the solution. Our partnership with Loop is a powerful example of entrepreneurial innovators working with like-minded large enterprise to bring a meaningful solution to a real problem."[60]

The Loop initiative offers products in reusable containers. It delivers items, then collects and cleans the containers for reuse. Loblaws will pilot the program to online shoppers first before it offers the service in-store.[61]

- The Loop Initiative responds to the climate emergency in Canada. How can other Canadian companies incorporate ethical decision making regarding the environment into their daily business practices?

Ethics in the Workplace Is Needed More Than Ever

LEARNING OBJECTIVE 6

Analyze ethics in the workplace, understand the goals of ethical business communicators, and choose the tools for doing the right thing.

Ethics continues to be a hot topic in business and political circles. Recent media reports seem to have an increased focus on workplace or business ethics. Reports cover not only issues of workplace corruption, fraud, influence peddling, and cronyism but also ethical questions relating to policies on human rights, animal welfare, genetic engineering, relations with developing nations, and the environment.[62] As a business communicator, you should understand basic ethical principles so that you can make logical decisions when faced with dilemmas in the workplace. Professionals in any field must deal with moral dilemmas on the job. However, just being a moral person and having sound personal ethics may not be sufficient to handle the ethical issues that you may face in the workplace.

The topic of ethics could fill this entire book. However, we will examine aspects that specifically concern you as a business communicator in today's workplace.

Defining Ethics

Ethics refers to conventional standards of right and wrong that prescribe what people should do. These standards usually consist of rights, obligations, and benefits to society. They also include virtues, such as fairness, honesty, loyalty, and concern for others. Ethics is about having values and taking responsibility. Ethical individuals are expected to follow the law and refrain from theft, murder, assault, slander, and fraud. Figure 1.12 depicts some of the influences that form our awareness of ethics and help us develop a value system that guides our ethical decisions. In the following discussion, we examine ethics in the workplace, study goals of ethical business communicators, and learn tools for doing the right thing.

On the job you will face many dilemmas, and you will want to react ethically. Determining the right thing to do, however, is not always an easy task. No solid rules guide us. For some people, following the law seems to be enough. They think that anything legal must also be ethical or moral. Most people, however, believe that ethical standards rise to a higher level. What are those standards? Although many ethical dilemmas have no right answer, one solution is often better than another. In deciding on that solution, keep in mind the goals of ethical business communicators.

Doing What Ethical Communicators Do

Taking ethics into consideration can be painful in the short term. In the long term, however, ethical behaviour makes sense and pays off. Dealing honestly with colleagues and customers develops trust and builds strong relationships. The following guidelines can help you set specific ethical goals. Although these goals hardly constitute a formal code of conduct, they will help you maintain a high ethical standard.

Abiding by the Law. Know the laws in your field and follow them. Particularly important for business communicators are issues of copyright law. Don't assume that Internet items are in the public domain and free to be used or shared. Internet items are covered by copyright laws. According to Canadian copyright law, "copyright exists automatically when an original work or other subject matter is created." Canadians do not need to register to be protected, so it is safe to assume that all text, visual, and audio materials you access are copyrighted.[63]

If you are in accounting, financial management, investing, or corporate management, you should be aware of the restrictions set forth by legal and professional organizations. Whatever your field, become familiar with its regulations.

Telling the Truth. Ethical business communicators do not intentionally make statements that are untrue or deceptive. We become aware of dishonesty in business when violators break laws, notably in advertising, packaging, and marketing.

FIGURE 1.12 The Context of Ethical Decision Making

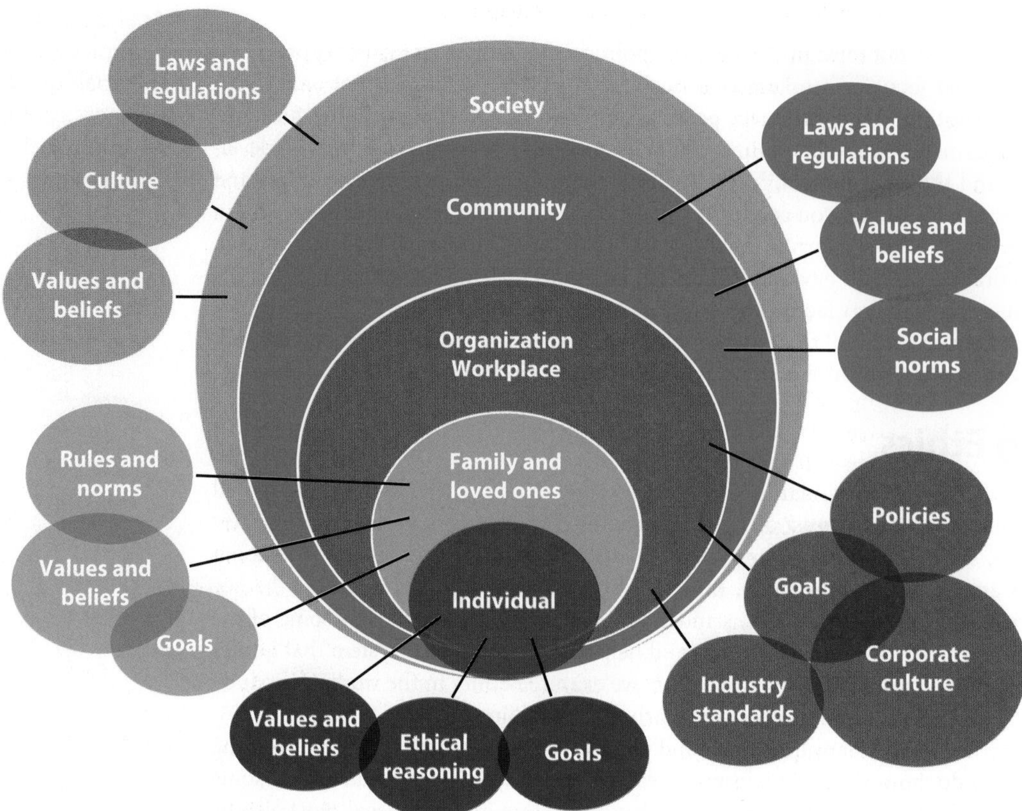

Various influences shape an individual's value system and affect ethical decision making. Most of us exist in a family, a workplace, one or several communities, and society at large. Each of these environments may emphasize different norms. Not surprisingly, sometimes the various rules and beliefs clash, causing ethical dilemmas that need to be resolved.

Labelling Opinions. Sensitive communicators know the difference between facts and opinions. Facts are verifiable and often are quantifiable; opinions are beliefs held with confidence but without substantiation. Assertions that cannot be proved are opinions, and stating opinions as if they were facts is unethical.

Being Objective. Ethical business communicators recognize their own biases and strive to keep them from distorting a message. Suppose you are asked to investigate laptop computers and write a report recommending a brand for your office. As you visit stores, you discover that an old high school friend is selling Brand X. Because you always liked this individual and have faith in his judgment, you may be inclined to tilt your recommendation in his direction. However, it is unethical to misrepresent the facts in your report or to put a spin on your arguments based on friendship. To be ethical, you could note in your report that you have known the person for ten years and that you respect his opinion. Honest reporting means presenting the whole picture and relating all facts fairly.

Communicating Clearly. Ethical business communicators feel an obligation to write clearly so that receivers understand easily and quickly. Some organizations have even passed *plain English* (also called *plain language*) policies that require policies, warranties, and contracts to be written in language comprehensible to average readers. Plain language means short sentences, simple words, and clear organization. Communicators who intentionally obscure the meaning with long sentences and difficult words are being unethical.

Using Inclusive Language. Ethical business communicators use language that includes rather than excludes. They avoid expressions that discriminate against individuals or groups on the basis of their sex, gender identity, ethnicity, disability, race, sexual orientation, or age. Language is discriminatory when it stereotypes, insults, or excludes people. You will learn more about how to use inclusive, bias-free language in Chapter 4.

Giving Credit. Ethical communicators give credit for ideas by (a) referring to originators' names within the text; (b) using quotation marks; and (c) documenting sources with endnotes, footnotes, or internal references. You will learn more about how to do this in Chapter 11. In school or on the job, stealing ideas, words, graphics, or any other original material is unethical.

In addition to legal and regulatory restrictions in their fields, many professionals uphold their own rigorous rules of conduct; for example, physicians, psychologists, and accountants follow standards of professional ethics much higher than the restrictions imposed by law.

Choosing Tools for Doing the Right Thing

It's easy to fall into ethical traps because of natural self-interest and the desire to succeed. In composing messages or engaging in other activities on the job, business communicators can't help being torn by conflicting loyalties. Do we tell the truth and risk our jobs? Do we show loyalty to friends even if it means bending the rules? Should we be tactful or totally honest? Is it our duty to make a profit or to be socially responsible?

Acting ethically means doing the right thing given the circumstances. Each set of circumstances requires analyzing issues, evaluating choices, and acting responsibly. Resolving ethical issues is never easy, but the task can be made less difficult if you know how to identify key issues. The five questions in Figure 1.13 may help you resolve most ethical dilemmas. The checklist begins by asking whether an action is legal. You should go forward only if the action complies with the law. If it does, then test the ethical soundness of your plan by asking the remaining questions: Would you proceed if you were on the receiving end of the action, and can you rule out different options? Even if the answer is *yes*, consider then how a trusted mentor or your family, friends, and coworkers would view your decision.

Perhaps the best advice in ethical matters is contained in the Golden Rule: Treat others the way you want to be treated yourself. The principle of reciprocity has a long tradition and exists in most religions and cultures. The ultimate solution to all ethics problems is treating others fairly and doing what is right to achieve what is good. In succeeding chapters, you will find additional discussions of ethical questions as they relate to relevant topics.

FIGURE 1.13 Five Questions to Guide Ethical Decisions

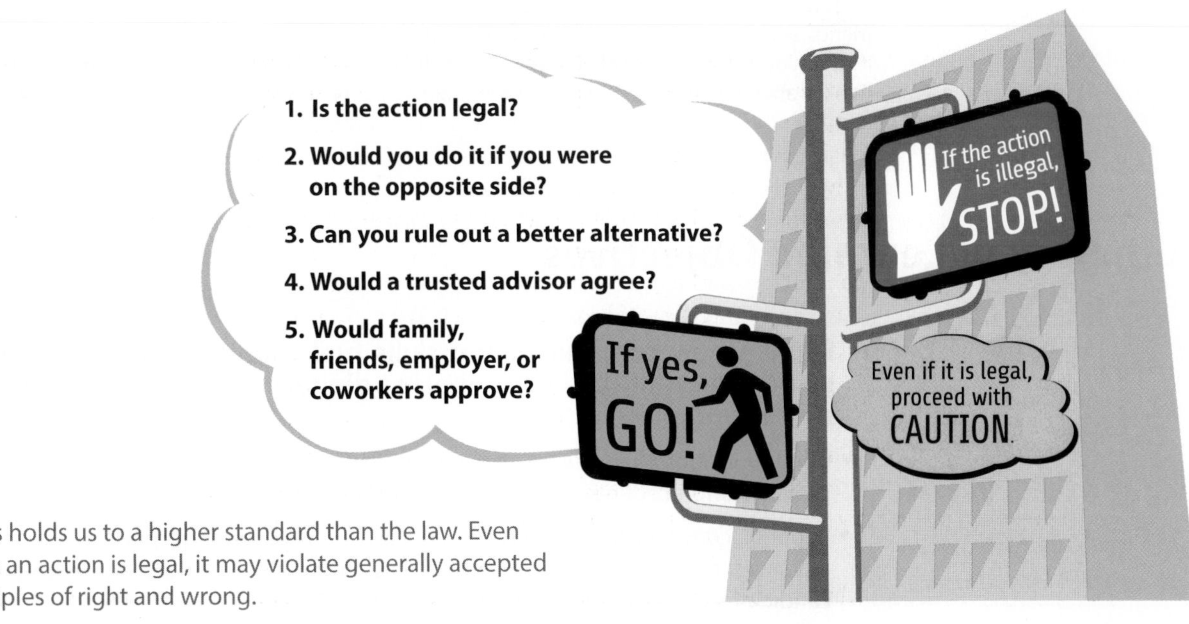

1. Is the action legal?
2. Would you do it if you were on the opposite side?
3. Can you rule out a better alternative?
4. Would a trusted advisor agree?
5. Would family, friends, employer, or coworkers approve?
If the action is illegal, STOP!
If yes, GO!
Even if it is legal, proceed with CAUTION.

Ethics holds us to a higher standard than the law. Even when an action is legal, it may violate generally accepted principles of right and wrong.

Concept Check

1. Why are ethics in the workplace needed now more than ever?
2. Professionals in any field deal with moral dilemmas on the job. However, just being a moral person and having sound personal or professional ethics may not be sufficient to handle the ethical issues you may face in the workplace. Consider the following ethical dilemmas:
   a. **Presentation** You are rushing to prepare a presentation. On the Internet you find perfect wording and great graphics. Should you lift the graphics and wording but change a few words? You figure that if it is on the Internet, it must be in the public domain.
   b. **Customer e-mail** You are replying to an e-mail from a customer who is irate over a mistake you made. Should you blame it on a computer glitch, point the finger at another department, or take the blame and risk losing this customer's trust and possibly your job?

For each scenario, consider the five questions to guide ethical decisions, as shown in Figure 1.13.

SPOTLIGHT ON COMMUNICATION: PART 2

Canadian Tire Revisited

CRITICAL THINKING

- As a consumer, how do you prefer to learn about a company's loyalty program? Refer to Figure 1.9, and consider media richness and communication effectiveness.
- Compare the loyalty programs you participate in. Which one has better customer benefits? Why?

Morgan Modjeski/CBC Licensing

What cards do you carry in your wallet? If you have at least one loyalty card, you are part of the over 90 percent of Canadian consumers who are enrolled in a loyalty marketing program. In fact, Canadians carry an average of four loyalty cards each.[64] Loyalty cards and related programs are designed to reach shoppers and encourage frequent dealing with the company.

To stay current, Canadian Tire needed to expand its loyalty program to include a digital option. With the introduction of its "Triangle Rewards" loyalty card, the company lets customers collect digital Canadian Tire money and stay connected on the go with the Triangle App. However, to appeal to its loyal customer base, it still offers its iconic paper Canadian Tire money for customers who pay with cash or debit.[65] And Canadian Tire money can really add up!

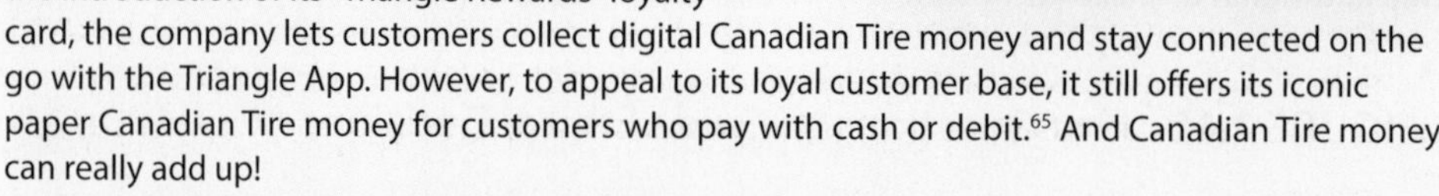

Tomas Terfloth, a Saskatoon man, bought a canoe with Canadian Tire money. With the help of friends and strangers on social media, Terfloth raised $941 in Canadian Tire money. He brought it to his local store in a briefcase, delighting the cashier and customers alike. "I don't think I can think of anything more Canadian," Terfloth said. "I don't know if it could have happened anywhere else."[66]

Summary of Learning Objectives

1 Explain how communication skills fuel career success, and understand why writing skills are vital in a digital, mobile, and social-media-driven workplace.

- Communication skills matter more than ever before as communication technology provides unprecedented mobility, and workers write more, not less.
- Superior communication skills are critical to job placement, performance, career advancement, and organizational success; they can set you apart from other candidates.

- Workers must write their own messages and use fast communication channels, such as social media, that connect vast numbers of people.
- Writing skills can be learned; they are not inherent.

2 Identify the skills for success in the hyperconnected 21st-century workplace and competitive job market.

- Accessing and sharing various digital media from a vast network of sources and distributing them nearly instantly to widespread audiences has never been easier.
- Expect to be a knowledge and learning worker who must think critically and develop opinions backed by evidence.
- You are learning to think, read, and ask questions in a networked world in which employers demand professionalism.
- Because technologies are constantly evolving and you will work for multiple employers, you must be flexible and engage in lifelong learning to be competitive.

3 Describe significant trends and technologies in today's dynamic work environment.

- The trends affecting today's workers include new communication technologies, such as social media, expectations of around-the-clock availability, and global competition.
- Flattened management hierarchies, the gig economy, team-based projects, a diverse workforce, and the virtual office operating practically 24/7/365 are other significant trends.
- Workers need new skills and attitudes as potential telecommuters and to collaborate successfully as team members in workplaces that are increasingly diverse.
- Businesspeople need to have strong communication skills to make effective decisions and stay connected across time zones and vast distances.

4 Understand the nature of communication and its barriers.

- The sender encodes (selects) words or symbols to express an idea in a message and sends it verbally or nonverbally over a channel (such as an e-mail or a phone call).
- The receiver decodes (interprets) the message and may respond with feedback, informing the sender of the effectiveness of the message.
- Miscommunication may be caused by barriers such as bypassing, differing frames of reference, lack of language skills, and distractions.

5 Examine critically the flow of communication in organizations, explain the importance of effective media choices, and understand how to overcome typical barriers to organizational communication.

- The mobile digital workplace is unthinkable without e-mail, IM, company intranets, corporate websites, audio and video podcasts, and videoconferences.
- Internal communication involves superiors, coworkers, and subordinates, whereas external communication includes customers, suppliers, government agencies, and the public.
- Media richness and social presence describe the communication media most suitable to avoid ambiguity in any workplace interaction.
- Formal channels of communication follow an organization's rank order; informal channels, such as the grapevine, deliver unofficial news among coworkers.

6 **Analyze ethics in the workplace, understand the goals of ethical business communicators, and choose the tools for doing the right thing.**

- *Ethics* describes standards of right and wrong that prescribe what people should do and includes virtues such as fairness, honesty, and loyalty.
- The goals of ethical communicators include abiding by the law, telling the truth, labelling opinions, being objective, communicating clearly, using inclusive language, and giving credit.
- To do the right thing, ask these questions: (a) Is the action legal? (b) Would you do it if you were on the opposite side? (c) Can you rule out a better alternative? (d) Would a trusted advisor agree? and (e) Would your family, friends, employer, or coworkers approve?

Chapter Review

1. What employability skills are Canadian employers looking for in an employee? (Obj. 1)
2. Why are critical thinking skills increasingly important in today's workplace? (Obj. 2)
3. How are tech-savvy companies using social media and other digital tools? (Obj. 3)
4. What is the gig economy, and why are employers seeking agile workers? (Obj. 3)
5. Describe the five steps in the process of communication. (Obj. 4)
6. Name and explain four barriers to communication. What other barriers have you experienced? (Obj. 4)
7. What are five advantages of oral communication within an organization? (Obj. 5)
8. Compare formal and informal channels of communication within organizations. Which is more valuable to employees? (Obj. 5)
9. What are seven goals of ethical business communicators? (Obj. 6)
10. When you are faced with a difficult ethical decision, what questions should you ask yourself? (Obj. 6)

Critical Thinking

1. Can workers today be successful if their writing is and remains poor? What could be the career fallout for someone who is unwilling or unable to train to become a better communicator? (Obj. 1)
2. Sharing on various digital media impulsively can lead to embarrassment and worse. Have you or has someone you know ever regretted posting a comment, photo, or other digital media online? What happened as a result of the post? (Obj. 2)
3. Some experts believe that although computer technology is improving our lives in many ways, it might be impairing our ability to think critically by putting answers at our fingertips. What do you think? (Obj. 3)
4. Critics complain that texting and instant messaging lead to textspeak, poor writing characterized by acronyms, abbreviations, and emoticons. Others have claimed that emoji help supply important missing cues in lean media channels that are "toneless" otherwise.[67] What do you think? (Obj. 5)
5. **Ethical Issue:** Your company urgently needs a revenue-producing project. Should you submit a proposal that unrealistically suggests a short completion schedule to ensure that you get the job? Provide a rationale for your decision. (Obj. 6)

Activities

1.1 Assessing Communication Skills Online: Evaluate Your Skills (Objs. 1–3)

Web

This course can help you dramatically improve your business communication skills. How much do you need to improve? This assessment exercise enables you to evaluate your skills with specific standards in four critical communication skill areas: writing, reading, speaking, and listening. How well you communicate will be an important factor in your future career—particularly if you are promoted into management, as many college and university graduates are.

YOUR TASK For each of the following skills, select a number from 1 (indicating low ability) to 5 (indicating high ability) that best reflects your perception of yourself. Be honest in rating yourself. Think about how others would rate you. When you finish, see a rating of your skills. Complete this assessment online to see your results automatically!

Writing Skills	**Low**				**High**
1. Possess basic spelling, grammar, and punctuation skills	1	2	3	4	5
2. Am familiar with proper e-mail, memo, letter, and report formats for business documents	1	2	3	4	5
3. Can analyze a writing problem and quickly outline a plan for solving the problem	1	2	3	4	5
4. Am able to organize data coherently and logically	1	2	3	4	5
5. Can evaluate a document to determine its probable success	1	2	3	4	5
Reading Skills					
1. Am familiar with specialized vocabulary in my field, as well as general vocabulary	1	2	3	4	5
2. Can concentrate despite distractions	1	2	3	4	5
3. Am willing to look up definitions whenever necessary	1	2	3	4	5
4. Am able to move from recreational to serious reading	1	2	3	4	5
5. Can read and comprehend college-level material	1	2	3	4	5
Speaking Skills					
1. Feel at ease in speaking with friends	1	2	3	4	5
2. Feel at ease in speaking before a group of people	1	2	3	4	5
3. Can adapt my presentation to the audience	1	2	3	4	5
4. Am confident in pronouncing and using words correctly	1	2	3	4	5
5. Sense that I have credibility when I make a presentation	1	2	3	4	5
Listening Skills					
1. Spend at least half the time listening during conversations	1	2	3	4	5
2. Am able to concentrate on a speaker's words despite distractions	1	2	3	4	5
3. Can summarize a speaker's ideas and anticipate what's coming during pauses	1	2	3	4	5
4. Provide proper feedback, such as nodding, paraphrasing, and asking questions	1	2	3	4	5
5. Listen with the expectation of gaining new ideas and information	1	2	3	4	5

Total your score in each section. How do you rate?

22–25	Excellent! You have indicated that you have exceptional communication skills.
18–21	Your score is above average, but you could improve your skills.
14–17	Your score suggests that you have much room for improvement.
5–13	You recognize that you need serious study, practice, and follow-up reinforcement.

Where are you strongest and weakest? Are you satisfied with your present skills? The first step to improvement is recognition of a need. The second step is making a commitment to improve. The third step is following through, and this course will help you do that.

1.2 Social Media Inventory (Objs. 1–5)

Communication Technology | E-mail | Social Media

The millennials (those born after 1985) do not remember a time without computer technology and cell phones in wide use. People born in the 1990s and since have only known a society that depends on the Internet and mobile technology. Social media are second nature to most young people.

> You too may live, learn, work, play, network, and shop in the digital world; your daily life depends on technology because your electronics are increasingly networked.

YOUR TASK Take stock of your Internet, social media, and other technology use. First establish useful criteria—for example, categories such as consumer electronics, social networking sites, preferred modes of communication with friends and family, and so forth. Within each category, list the technology you use most frequently. For instance, for social media networks, indicate your use of Facebook, Instagram, Snapchat, Twitter, YouTube, Hulu, LinkedIn, and more. How do you use each? How often do you access these sites per day and on which tools (e.g., smartphone, tablet, laptop)? How much do you text every day? Your instructor may ask you to create at least three categories, record your responses in writing, and compare your lists with a group of classmates. Your instructor may ask you to summarize your observations about how plugged in you and your classmates are in a post on a discussion board or in an e-mail.

1.3 Introducing Yourself (Objs. 1, 2)

Communication Technology | E-mail | Social Media

Your instructor wants to know more about you, your motivation for taking this course, your career goals, and your writing skills.

YOUR TASK Send an e-mail or write a memo of introduction to your instructor. See Chapters 7 and 8 for tips on preparing an e-mail message. In your message include the following:

a. Your reasons for taking this class

b. Your career goals (both temporary and long term)

c. A brief description of your employment, if any, and your favourite activities

d. An assessment and a discussion of your current communication skills, including your strengths and weaknesses

Alternatively, your instructor may ask you to (a) create a profile for LinkedIn, the business-oriented social networking site, or (b) develop a profile within a learning-management system (e.g., Blackboard and Moodle) to introduce yourself to your classmates. If yours is a small class, your instructor may challenge you to compose your introduction in Twitter posts of 140 or fewer characters.

1.4 Small-Group Presentation: Introducing Team Members (Objs. 1, 2)

Team

Many business organizations today use teams to accomplish their goals. To help you develop speaking, listening, and teamwork skills, your instructor may assign team projects. One of the first jobs in any team is selecting members and becoming acquainted.

YOUR TASK Your instructor will divide your class into small groups or teams. At your instructor's direction, either (a) interview another group member and introduce that person to the group or (b) introduce yourself to the group. Think of this as an informal interview for a team assignment or a job. You will want to make notes from which to speak. Your introduction should include information such as the following:

a. Where did you grow up?

b. What work and extracurricular activities have you engaged in?

c. What are your interests and talents? What are you good at doing?

d. What are your professional and personal goals? Where do you expect to be five years from now?

e. Name one thing about you that others might not guess when first meeting you.

To develop listening skills, team members should practise good listening techniques (see Chapter 2) and take notes. They should be prepared to discuss three important facts and remember details about each speaker.

Alternatively, you could be asked to write a short professional biographical blurb after your interview of a group member. After feedback to ensure that it is correct, discuss with your partner or the whole group whether the bio would be attractive to employers looking for communication skills and other employability skills as presented in this chapter.

1.5 Writing Skills: But My Job Won't Require Writing! (Objs. 1–3)

Team

Some job candidates experience a disconnect between what they expect to be doing in their career fields and what they actually will do.

YOUR TASK In teams or as a class, discuss the accuracy of the following statements. Are they myths or facts?

a. No one really writes anymore. They just text and send e-mails.

b. Because I'm in a technical field, I will work with numbers, not words.

c. Administrative assistants will clean up my writing problems.

d. Today's sophisticated software programs can fix any of my writing mistakes.

1.6 Oral or Written Communication: How Rich Must the Media Be? (Obj. 5)

YOUR TASK First decide whether the following messages need to be communicated orally or in writing. After consulting the media richness diagram in Figure 1.9, consider how rich the medium must be in each communication situation to convey the message most appropriately and reliably. You may want to choose channels such as e-mail, letter, report, texting, instant messaging, telephone call, live chat, teleconferencing, face-to-face conversation, or team meeting. Describe the advantages and disadvantages of each choice.

a. You are returning with the senior auditor from a client visit to company headquarters, where you must attend an important department meeting. It looks as though you will be at least 15 minutes late. What are your options?

b. Maya, the information technology vice president, must tell employees about a new company social media policy. She has two employees in mind who particularly need this information.

c. As a manager in your Human Resources Department, you must terminate three employees in a companywide initiative to reduce costs.

Grammar and Mechanics | *Review 1*

Each chapter includes an exercise based on Appendix B, Grammar and Mechanics Guide. This appendix is a business communicator's condensed guide to language usage, covering 54 of the most misused language elements. It also includes a list of frequently misspelled words and a list of confusing words. In the first ten chapters, each exercise will focus on a specific set of grammar/mechanics guidelines. In the last six chapters, the exercises will review all the guidelines plus spelling and confusing words.

Sentence Structure

Study Guides 1 to 3 are about sentence structure in Appendix B, beginning on page B-1. Some of the following numbered word groups have sentence faults. On a sheet of paper or on your computer, indicate whether each word group is (a) correctly punctuated, (b) a fragment, (c) a comma splice, or (d) a run-on. If incorrect, write a correct version. Also identify the fault and the relevant guide. Avoid adding new phrases or rewriting in your own words. When you finish, compare your responses with the key in Appendix C.

EXAMPLE: The message was meant to inform, however it confused instead.

REVISION: The message was meant to inform; however, it confused instead. [c, Guide 3, Comma splice]

1. Because you will be entering a fast-paced, competitive, and highly connected digital environment. Communication and technology skills are critical to your career success.
2. Such skills are particularly significant now. When competition is keen.
3. Many qualified people will apply for openings, however candidates with exceptional communication skills will immediately stand out.
4. Although we cannot predict the kinds of future jobs that will be available, they will undoubtedly require brainpower and education.
5. In traditional companies decisions must move through many levels of managers, in flat organizations decisions can be made more quickly.
6. Millions of workers no longer report to nine-to-five jobs. Thanks largely to advances in new technologies and wireless Internet access.
7. Nearly all potential employers said that being able to think critically, communicate clearly, and solve complex problems is more important than a candidate's program of study.
8. The grapevine can be a powerful source of information. Although it increasingly operates informally through social media.
9. Ethical companies experience less litigation, and they also are the target of less government regulation.
10. Even when an action is legal. It may violate generally accepted principles of right and wrong.

Notes

[1] Based on Conference Board of Canada. (2020). *Employability skills.* https://www.conferenceboard.ca/edu/employability-skills.aspx

[2] Middleton, A. (2006, April 17–24). The great Canadian brand. *Marketing*, p. 12.

[3] Canadian Tire Corporation. (2019, May 24). *Canadian Tire Corporation announces strategic partnership with Myant Inc. to bring smart technology and innovation to key performance and safety apparel and footwear* [Press release]. https://corp.canadiantire.ca/English/media/news-releases/press-release-details/2019/Canadian-Tire-Corporation-Announces-Strategic-Partnership-with-Myant-Inc-to-Bring-Smart-Technology-and-Innovation-to-Key-Performance-and-Safety-Apparel-and-Footwear/default.aspx

[4] Myant. (2020). *Textiles that unlock human potential.* https://myant.ca/vision/

[5] Ibid.

[6] Canavor, N. (2012). *Business writing in the digital age.* Sage. See also National Writing Project, with DeVoss, D. N., Eidman-Aadahl, E., & Hicks, T. (2010). *Because digital writing matters.* Jossey-Bass.

[7] *Back-to-school wake-up call: Gen Y, employers diverge on importance of knowledge economy skills* [Press release]. (n.d.). http://www.newswire.ca/en/story/585427/back-to-school-wake-up-call-gen-y-employers-diverge-on-importance-of-knowledge-economy-skills; Engineers Canada and Canadian Council of Technicians and Technologists. (2008). *2007 engineering and technology employer survey.* http://wwest.mech.ubc.ca/files/2010/10/2007-Employer-Survey-Report1.pdf; Hamilton, D. (2005). *BCIT survey highlights importance of oral communication skills.* http://johnkeithcommunications.com/listening/prof/BCITGradSurvey.html8 Conference Board of Canada. (2016). *Employability skills 2000+.* http://www.conferenceboard.ca/Libraries/EDUC_PUBLIC/esp2000.sflb

[9] Ibid.

[10] Canavor, N. (2012). *Business writing in the digital age.* Sage, pp. 1–3; National Writing Project, with DeVoss, D. N., Eidman-Aadahl, E., & Hicks, T. (2010). *Because digital writing matters.* Jossey-Bass, pp. 1–5.

[11] Hart Research Associates. (2015, January 20). *Falling short? College learning and career success.* American Association of Colleges & Universities. https://www.aacu.org/sites/default/files/files/LEAP/2015employerstudentsurvey.pdf

[12] National Writing Project, with DeVoss, D. N., Eidman-Aadahl, E., & Hicks, T. (2010). *Because digital writing matters.* Jossey-Bass, p. 7.

[13] Drucker, P. (1989, May). New realities, new ways of managing. *Business Month*, pp. 50–51. National Writing Project, with DeVoss, D. N., Eidman-Aadahl, E., & Hicks, T. (2010). *Because digital writing matters.* Jossey-Bass, p. 150.

[14] Morgan, J. (2016, June 7). Say goodbye to knowledge workers and welcome to learning workers. *Forbes.* https://www.forbes.com/sites/jacobmorgan/2016/06/07/say-goodbye-to-knowledge-workers-and-welcome-to-learning-workers/#7243005c2f93

[15] Ibid.

[16] Ibid.

[17] Ibid.

[18] Randstad. (n.d.). *Workforce 2025: the future of the world of work.* http://content.randstad.ca/hubfs/workforce2025/Workforce-2025-Randstad-Part1.pdf

[19] National Writing Project, with DeVoss, D. N., Eidman-Aadahl, E., & Hicks, T. (2010). *Because digital writing matters.* Jossey-Bass, p. 150.

[20] Shierholz, H., & Edwards, K. A. (2011, April 20). *The class of 2011: Young workers face a dire labor market without a safety net.* Economic Policy Institute, Briefing Paper 306. http://www.epi.org/publication/bp306-class-of-2011

[21] Koncz, A. (2009, January 29). *Employers cite qualities, attributes of "perfect" job candidate*

[NACE Web press release]. http://www.naceweb.org
[22] WhatsApp. (2019). *About Whatsapp*. https://www.whatsapp.com/about/
[23] Facebook. (2019). *Newsroom*. https://newsroom.fb.com/company-info/
[24] Zephoria Digital Marketing. (2019, July). *Top 10 Twitter statistics*. https://zephoria.com/twitter-statistics-top-ten/
[25] CBC Radio. (2018, July 8). *How does your social media use stack up against other Canadians?* https://www.cbc.ca/radio/spark/how-does-your-social-media-use-stack-up-against-other-canadians-1.4712470
[26] Statistics Canada. (2017, November 14). *The Internet and digital technology*. https://www150.statcan.gc.ca/n1/pub/11-627-m/11-627-m2017032-eng.htm
[27] Roberts, I. (2011, March 30). *Consumer boycotts: How bad brand experience can turn into lifelong grudges*. http://experiencematters.criticalmass.com
[28] Bosanac, A. (2015, September 21). How flat hierarchies help companies stay nimble and grow faster. *Canadian Business*. https://www.canadianbusiness.com/innovation/how-flat-hierarchies-help-companies-stay-nimble-and-grow-faster/
[20] Randstad. (n.d.). *Workforce 2025: The future of the world of work*. Retrieved from http://content.randstad.ca/hubfs/workforce2025/Workforce-2025-Randstad-Part1.pdf
[30] Ibid.
[31] CBC News. (2017, August 2). *2016 census: Highlights of latest data on language, marital status, households*. https://www.cbc.ca/news/politics/census-family-language-highlights-1.4231841
[32] Statistics Canada. (2011, August 17). Study: Projected trends to 2031 for the Canadian labour force. *The Daily*. http://www.statcan.gc.ca/daily-quotidien/110817/dq110817b-eng.htm
[33] CBC News. (2017, August 2). *2016 census: Highlights of latest data on language, marital status, households*. https://www.cbc.ca/news/politics/census-family-language-highlights-1.4231841
[34] McIvor, O. (2018). *Indigenous languages in Canada: What you need to know*. https://en.ccunesco.ca/-/media/Files/Unesco/Resources/2018/09/IndigenousLanguagesCCUNESCO.pdf
[35] CBC News. (2017, August 2). *2016 census: Highlights of latest data on language, marital status, households*. https://www.cbc.ca/news/politics/census-family-language-highlights-1.4231841
[36] Nath, I. (2018, February 8). For transgender women, the pay equity gap is even wider. *Maclean's*. https://www.macleans.ca/society/for-transgender-women-the-pay-equity-gap-is-even-wider/
[37] Government of Canada. (2018, October 29). *Government of Canada introduces historic proactive pay equity legislation*. https://www.canada.ca/en/employment-social-development/news/2018/10/government-of-canada-introduces-historic-proactive-pay-equity-legislation.html
[38] Pay Equity Commission. (2019). What is the gender wage gap? Retrieved from http://www.payequity.gov.on.ca/en/GWG/Pages/what_is_GWG.aspx
[39] Nath, I. (2018, February 8). For transgender women, the pay equity gap is even wider. *Maclean's*. https://www.macleans.ca/society/for-transgender-women-the-pay-equity-gap-is-even-wider/
[40] Statistics Canada. (2017, November 29). *Working seniors in Canada*. https://www12.statcan.gc.ca/census-recensement/2016/as-sa/98-200-x/2016027/98-200-x2016027-eng.cfm41 Statistics Canada. (2011, August 17). Study: Projected trends to 2031 for the Canadian labour force. *The Daily*. http://www.statcan.gc.ca/daily-quotidien/110817/dq110817b-eng.htm
[42] Marowits, R. (2016, May 23). *Telecommuting growing as companies look to save money, respond to employees*. CBC News. https://www.cbc.ca/news/business/telecommuting-growing-as-companies-look-to-save-money-respond-to-employees-1.3596420
[43] Silverman, R. E., & Sidel, R. (2012, April 17). Warming up to the officeless office. *Wall Street Journal*. http://online.wsj.com/article/SB10001424052702304818404577349783161465976.html; Holland, K. (2008, September 28). The anywhere, anytime office. *New York Times*, p. 14.
[44] Evans, P. (2020, April 9). *Canada lost more than 1 million jobs last month as COVID-19 struck*. CBC News. https://www.cbc.ca/news/business/canada-jobs-march-covid-19-1.5527359
[45] Canadian Internet Registration Authority. (2020, April 14). *"COVID-19 has changed everything": New survey shows the number of Canadians working from home has grown seven-fold*. https://www.cira.ca/newsroom/state-internet/covid-19-has-changed-everything-new-survey-shows-number-canadians-working
[46] Ibid.
[47] Li, L. (n.d.). *10 stupid business ideas that made millions*. http://www.entrepreneursforachange.com/10-stupid-business-ideas-that-made-millions
[48] Sullivan, J., Karmeda, N., & Nobu, T. (1992, January/February). Bypassing in managerial communication. *Business Horizons*, *34*(1), 72.
[49] Brewer, E., & Holmes, T. (2009, October). Obfuscating the obvious: Miscommunication issues in the interpretation of common terms. *Journal of Business Communication, 46*(4), 480–496.
[50] McGirt, E. (2006, March 20). Getting out from under: Beset by interruptions, information overload, and irksome technology, knowledge workers need help: A survival guide. *Fortune*, p. 8. See also Simperl, E., Thurlow, I., et al. (2010, November 1). Overcoming information overload in the enterprise: The active approach. *Internet Computing, 14*(6). https://doi.org/10.1109/MIC.2010.146
[51] Photo essay based on Keim, B. (2009, August 24). Multitasking muddles brains, even when the computer is off. *Wired*. http://www.wired.com; Gorlick, A. (2009, August 24). Media multitaskers pay mental price, Stanford study shows. *Stanford News*. http://news.stanford.edu; Nauert, R. (2011, May 3). Multitasking is distracting. *Psych Central*. http://psychcentral.com
[52] McKinnon, M. (2018, July 17). *2018 social media use in Canada*. Canadian's Internet Business. Retrieved from https://canadiansinternet.com/2018-social-media-use-canada/
[53] Daft, R. L., & Lengel, R. H. (1983, May). *Information richness: A new approach to managerial behavior and organization design* [Technical report], p. 13. http://www.dtic.mil/cgi-bin/GetTRDoc?AD=ADA128980; Daft, R. L., & Lengel, R. H. (1986). Organizational information requirements, media richness and structural design. *Management Science*, 32(5), 560. http://search.ebscohost.com
[54] Short, J., Williams, E., & Christie, B. (1976). *The social psychology of telecommunications*. John Wiley.
[55] Discussion based in part on Kaplan, A., & Haenlein, M. (2010). Users of the world unite! The challenges and opportunities of social media. *Business Horizons*, 53, pp. 59–69. http://michaelhaenlein.com/Publications/publications.htm
[56] Goman, C. K. (2006, June). *I heard it through the grapevine*. Paper presented at the International Association of Business Communicators, Vancouver, Canada.
[57] DeMars, N. (2008). *What you can do when you're the latest topic on the rumour mill*. http://www.office-ethics.com/columns/gossip.html
[58] Armour, S. (2007, September 7). Did you hear the real story about office gossip? *USA Today*, p. 1B.
[59] Recycling Council of Ontario. (2019). *Waste statistics: how much Canada throws out*. https://rco.on.ca/canada-waste-statistics/
[60] Rubin, J. (2019, June 6). Loblaws to sell products in reusable containers in Toronto-area trial. *The Star*. https://www.thestar.com/business/2019/06/06/loblaws-to-sell-products-in-reusable-containers-in-toronto-area-trial.html
[61] Ibid.
[62] Saner, M., & von Baeyer, C. (2005). *Workplace and policy ethics: A call to end the solitudes* (Policy Brief No. 24). Institute On Governance. http://-workplaceethics.ca/brief24.pdf
[63] Government of Canada. (2017). *What is copyright?* https://www.ic.gc.ca/eic/site/cipointernet-internetopic.nsf/eng/wr03719.html?Open&wt_src=cipo-cpyrght-main
[64] Jackson, B. (2015, March 31). *Canadians' love of loyalty rewards is swayed most by this digital channel*. Itbusiness. http://www.itbusiness.ca/news/canadians-love-of-loyalty-rewards-is-swayed-most-by-this-digital-channel/54790
[65] Cazzin, J. (2018, April 9). What Canadian Tire's loyalty changes mean to you: Can I still use my Canadian Tire money? *Maclean's*. https://www.macleans.ca/economy/money-economy/what-canadian-tires-loyalty-changes-mean-to-you/
[66] Modjeski, M. (2019, June 28). *Only in Canada: Saskatoon man buys canoe with briefcase full of Canadian Tire cash*. CBC News. https://www.cbc.ca/news/canada/saskatoon/saskatoon-canoe-candian-tire-money-1.5193298
[67] Will Schwalbe quoted in Lam, B. (2015, May 15). Why emoji are suddenly acceptable at work. *The Atlantic*. http://www.theatlantic.com/business/archive/2015/05/why-emoji-aresuddenly-acceptable-at-work/393191

CHAPTER 2

Professionalism: Team, Meeting, Listening, Nonverbal, and Etiquette Skills

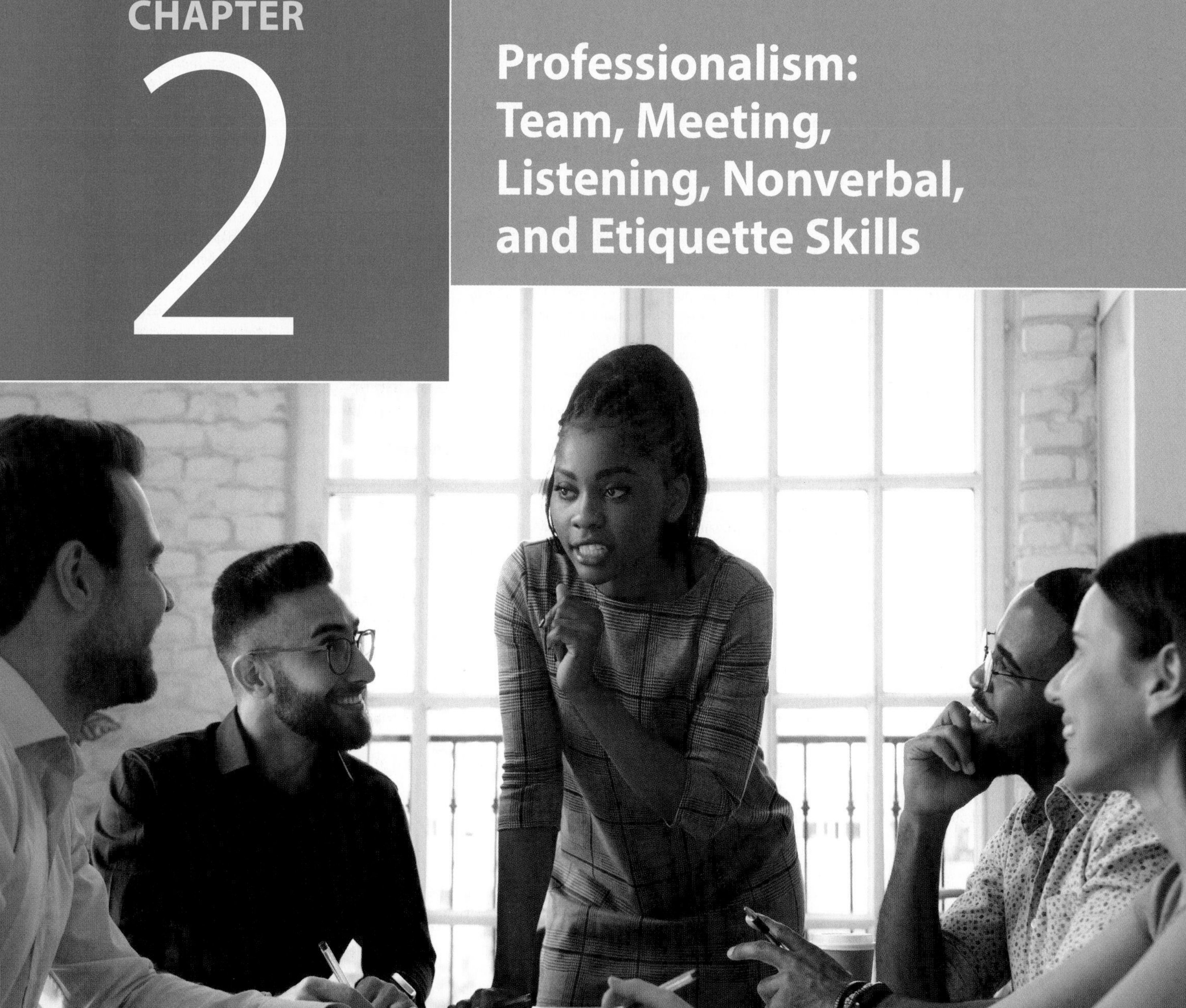

fizkes/Shutterstock

LEARNING OBJECTIVES

After studying this chapter, you should be able to

1 Understand the importance of teamwork in the workplace, and explain how you can contribute positively to team performance.

2 Discuss effective practices and technologies for planning and participating in face-to-face meetings and virtual meetings.

3 Explain and apply active listening techniques.

4 Understand how effective nonverbal communication can help you advance your career.

5 Improve your competitive advantage by developing professionalism and business etiquette skills.

SPOTLIGHT ON COMMUNICATION: PART 1

Makivik Corporation—Building Communities

Makivik Corporation

Makivik Corporation is an Inuit-run nonprofit organization. In Inukitut, *Makivik* means "to rise up," and the organization's commitment is to "to foster, promote, protect and assist in preserving the Inuit way of life, values and traditions."[1] Makivik Corporation works to generate jobs, build the economy, improve housing conditions, and protect the natural environment and Inuit language and culture in the Nunavik communities it serves.[2] In 1990 Makivik Corporation purchased the northern airline First Air, and contributed $40 million each year to the northern Canada's economy, honouring Makivik's commitment to Inuit communities.[3]

In 2019 Makivik Corporation announced its partnership with Inuvialuit Regional Corporation, another Inuit-run organization, to merge First Air and Canadian North airlines: "As Northern airlines that are dedicated to the well-being of the communities they serve, First Air and Canadian North have shared the same vital mission—to bridge vast distances, bring people together and deliver important goods—always with friendly and helpful customer service."[4]

The integration of the two airlines took two years to plan and coordinate in order to maintain the quality and safety of their services. As the companies began the initial phases of organizational change, Chris Avery, president and CEO, who serves as leader of the merged organization, stated, "We understand that our actions touch many lives, so we will maintain a 'community-first' approach throughout this integration, which includes carefully considering the essential needs of our customers when making decisions, communicating clearly and listening for feedback."[5]

All employees formed a new team under the unified Canadian North banner. Together, under this new branding, the airline is committed to growing strong communities in the North.

CRITICAL THINKING

- Makivik Corporation's commitment is reflected in Canadian North's values statement: "Safety, Integrity, Teamwork, Innovation, Service, Excellence, Community, Respect."[6] How do an organization's values contribute to the success of its teams?
- The president and CEO of Canadian North emphasizes the importance of "communicating clearly and listening for feedback." Why are these communication skills so important during times of organizational change?

https://canadiannorth.com

www.makivik.org

Adding Value to Professional Teams

LEARNING OBJECTIVE 1

Understand the importance of teamwork in the workplace, and explain how you can contribute positively to team performance.

Most businesses seek employees who can get along and deliver positive results that increase profits and boost their company's image. As a budding business professional, you have a stake in acquiring skills that will make you a strong job applicant and a valuable employee.

What Do Employers Want?

Employers are typically interested in four key areas: education, experience, hard skills, and soft skills. Hard skills refer to the technical skills in your field. Soft skills, however, are vital. Desirable competencies include not only oral and written communication skills but also active listening skills, appropriate nonverbal behaviour, and proper business etiquette. According to the Conference Board of Canada's Employability Skills 2000+, employers want employees who "listen and ask questions to understand and appreciate the points of view of others."[7] In addition, employers want efficient and productive team members. They want managers and employees who are comfortable with diverse audiences, listen actively to customers and colleagues, make eye contact, and display good workplace manners. These soft skills are immensely important not only to being hired but also to being promoted.

Hiring managers expect you to have technical expertise in your field and know the latest communication technology. Such skills and an impressive résumé may get you in the door. However, your long-term success depends on how well you communicate with your boss, coworkers, and customers and whether you can be an effective and contributing team

In MindTap, go to the "Chapter Overview: Business Communication in the Digital Age" video in Chapter 1 and watch it now.

member. Even in technical fields, such as accounting and finance, employers are looking for soft skills.

As we discussed in Chapter 1, the workplace is changing. Collaboration is the rule today, and an overwhelming majority of white-collar professionals (82 percent) need to partner with others to complete their work.[8] This chapter focuses on the soft skills workers must have to be successful in the workplace: team, meeting, listening, nonverbal, and etiquette skills.

Excelling in Teams

In today's workplace teamwork is more important than ever. When the Business Council of Canada released its report *Developing Canada's Future Workforce: A Survey of Large Private-Sector Employers*, the results showed that the soft skills most in demand included collaboration and teamwork, communication skills, problem-solving skills, and people and relationship-building skills. Even though educational credentials are important to employers, companies are "increasingly focused on finding people who can work in teams, solve complex problems, and show a willingness to learn."[9]

You might find yourself a part of a work team, project team, customer support team, supplier team, design team, planning team, functional team, cross-functional team, or some other group. All these teams are formed to accomplish specific goals. Businesses are constantly looking for ways to do jobs better at less cost. They are forming teams for the following reasons:

- **Better decisions.** Decisions are generally more accurate and effective because group members contribute different expertise and perspectives.
- **Faster response.** When action is necessary to respond to competition or to solve a problem, small groups and teams can act rapidly.
- **Increased productivity.** Because they are often closer to the action and to the customer, team members can see opportunities for improving efficiency.
- **Greater buy-in.** Decisions arrived at jointly are usually better received because members are committed to the solution and are more willing to support it.
- **Less resistance to change.** People who have input into decisions are less hostile, aggressive, and resistant to change.
- **Improved employee morale.** Personal satisfaction and job morale increase when teams are successful.
- **Reduced risks.** Responsibility for a decision is diffused on a team, thus carrying less risk for any individual.

Despite the current popularity of teams, however, they are not a solution for all workplace problems, particularly if such groups are dysfunctional. Recent studies suggest that organizations must strike a balance between solo effort—in highly creative endeavours—and collective action. "The most spectacularly creative people" are often introverted and prefer to work alone, which is when they do their best and most innovative work.[10] However, in most models of future organizations, teams—not individuals—function as the primary performance units.

Collaborating in Virtual Teams

With over 1.7 million Canadians working from home, virtual teams are here to stay.[11] The days when you could expect to work with a colleague who sat near you are long gone. Today you can expect to collaborate with fellow workers in other cities and even in other countries. Work is increasingly viewed as *what you do* rather than a place you go. Because of the rising prices in the real estate market, more Canadian businesses are looking to reduce costly office space expenses; likewise, many Canadians cannot afford housing in large urban areas and appreciate flexible work arrangements.[12] And with more Canadians working from home as a result of the global pandemic, collaborating in virtual teams is becoming the norm.

In some organizations, remote coworkers may be permanent employees from the same office or may be specialists called together for special projects. Regardless of the assignment, virtual teams can benefit from shared views, skills, and diversity.

Understanding the Four Phases of Team Development

Although formed for various purposes, teams normally go through predictable phases as they develop. Psychologist B. A. Tuckman identified four phases: *forming*, *storming*, *norming*, and *performing*, as Figure 2.1 illustrates.[13] Some groups get lucky and move quickly from forming to performing. But most struggle through disruptive, although ultimately constructive, team-building stages.

Forming. During the first stage, individuals get to know one another. They often are overly polite and feel a bit awkward. As they search for similarities and attempt to bond, they begin to develop trust in each other. Members discuss fundamental topics, such as why the team is necessary, who "owns" the team, whether membership is mandatory, how large the team should be, and what talents members can contribute. A leader functions primarily as a traffic director. Groups and teams should resist the efforts of some members to dash through the first stages and race to the performing stage. Moving slowly through the stages is necessary to build a cohesive, productive unit.

Storming. During the second phase, members define their roles and responsibilities, decide how to reach their goals, and iron out the rules governing how they interact. Unfortunately, this stage often produces conflict, resulting in *storming*. Good leaders, however, should step in to set limits, control the chaos, and offer suggestions. Leaders will be most successful if they coach the team, rather than police it. Teams composed of dissimilar personality types may take longer to progress through the storming phase. Tempers may flare, sleep may be lost, and leaders may be deposed. But most often the storm passes, and a cohesive group emerges.

Norming. During the *norming* stage, tension subsides, roles are clarified, and information begins to flow among members. The group periodically checks its agenda to remind itself of its progress toward its goals. People are careful not to shake the hard-won camaraderie and formation of a single-minded purpose. Formal leadership is unnecessary because everyone takes on leadership functions. Important data are shared with the entire group, and interdependence becomes typical. The group or team begins to move smoothly in one direction. Figure 2.1 shows how a team might proceed through the four phases while solving a problem and reaching a decision.

FIGURE 2.1 Four Phases of Team Development in Decision Making

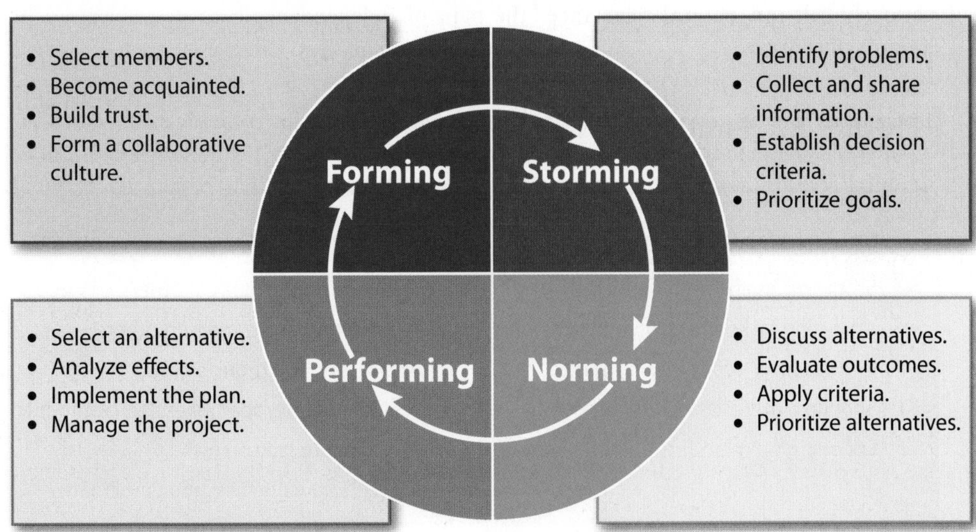

Performing. In Tuckman's team growth model, some groups never reach the final stage of *performing.* For those that survive the first three phases, however, the final stage is gratifying. Group members have established routines and a shared language. They develop loyalty and a willingness to resolve all problems. A "can-do" mentality pervades as they progress toward their goal. Fights are clean, and members continue working together without grudges. Best of all, information flows freely, deadlines are met, and production exceeds expectations.

Identifying Positive and Negative Team Behaviour

Team members who are committed to achieving the group's purpose contribute by displaying positive behaviour. How can you be a good team member?

- Establish rules and abide by them.
- Analyze tasks and define problems so that the team can work toward solutions.
- Offer information and try out ideas on the group to stimulate discussion.
- Show interest in others' ideas by listening actively.
- Seek to involve silent members.
- Encourage a warm, supportive climate by praising and agreeing with others.
- Review significant points and move the group toward its goal by synthesizing points of understanding.

Not all groups, however, have members who contribute positively. Negative behaviour is shown by those who constantly put down the ideas and suggestions of others. They insult, criticize, and aggress against others. They waste the group's time with unnecessary recounting of personal achievements, irrelevant topics, excessive joke-telling, inappropriate comments, and disruptive antics. Also disturbing are team members who withdraw and refuse to be drawn out. They have nothing to say, either for or against ideas being considered. To be a productive and welcome member of a group, be prepared to perform the positive tasks described in Figure 2.2. Avoid the negative behaviours.

ETHICS CHECK

The Cost of Groupthink

Without the consent of the Halifax regional counsel, senior officials advanced money to a concert promoter before two summer concerts. Because they had an "overwhelming desire" to bring concerts to the Halifax Common, the officials ignored warning signs. When ticket sales were poor, the city was left with the bill. An auditor found a "groupthink" mentality responsible for costing the municipality of Halifax nearly $360,000 and suggested ethics training for managers and councillors.[14] What factors can contribute to a groupthink mentality?

Combating Groupthink

Conflict is normal in team interactions, and successful teams are able to resolve it using the methods you just learned. But some teams avoid conflict. They smooth things over and in doing so may fall victim to *groupthink.* This is a term coined by theorist Irving Janis to describe faulty decision-making processes by team members who are overly eager to agree with one another.[15] Apparently, when we deviate from a group, we fear rejection. Scientists variously call this natural reluctance "the pain of independence"[16] or describe it as "the hazards of courage."[17]

FIGURE 2.2 Positive and Negative Group Behaviours

Positive Group Behaviours

- ✓ Setting rules and abiding by them
- ✓ Analyzing tasks and defining problems
- ✓ Contributing information and ideas
- ✓ Showing interest by listening actively
- ✓ Encouraging members to participate

Negative Group Behaviours

- ✗ Blocking the ideas of others
- ✗ Insulting and criticizing others
- ✗ Wasting the group's time
- ✗ Making improper jokes and comments
- ✗ Failing to stay on task
- ✗ Withdrawing, failing to participate

Several conditions can lead to groupthink: team members with similar backgrounds, a lack of systematic procedures, a demand for a quick decision, and a strong leader who favours a specific outcome. Symptoms of groupthink include pressure placed on any member who argues against the group's mutual beliefs, self-censorship of thoughts that stray from the group's agreement, collective efforts to rationalize, and an unquestioned belief in the group's moral authority. Teams suffering from groupthink fail to check alternatives, are biased in collecting and evaluating information, and ignore the risks of the preferred choice. They may also neglect to work out a contingency plan in case the preferred choice fails.[18]

Effective teams avoid groupthink by striving for team diversity—in age, gender, background, experience, and training. They encourage open discussion, search for relevant information, evaluate many alternatives, consider how a decision will be implemented, and plan for contingencies in case the decision doesn't work out.

Reaching Group Decisions

The way teams reach decisions greatly affects their morale and commitment, as well as the implementation of any team decision. In Western culture the majority usually rules, but other methods, five of which are discussed here, may be more effective. As you study these methods, think about which would be best for routine decisions and which would be best for dealing with emergencies.

- **Majority.** Group members vote and a majority wins. This method results in a quick decision but may leave an alienated minority uncommitted to implementation.
- **Consensus.** Discussion continues until all team members have aired their opinions and, ultimately, agree. This method is time-consuming; however, it produces creative, high-quality discussion and generally elicits commitment by all members to implement the decision.
- **Minority.** Typically, a subcommittee investigates and makes a recommendation for action. This method is useful when the full group cannot get together to make a decision or when time is short.
- **Averaging.** Members haggle, bargain, wheedle, and negotiate to reach a middle position, which often requires compromise. With this method, the opinions of the least knowledgeable members may cancel the opinions of the most knowledgeable.
- **Authority rule with discussion.** The leader, boss, or manager listens to team members' ideas, then makes the final decision. This method encourages lively discussion and results in participatory decision making. However, team members must have good communication skills. This method also requires a leader who is willing to make decisions.

Defining Successful Teams

The use of teams has been called the solution to many ills in today's workplace.[19] Many teams, however, do not work well together. In fact, some teams can actually increase frustration, lower productivity, and create employee dissatisfaction. Experts who have studied team workings and decisions have discovered that effective teams share some or all of the following characteristics.

Stay Small and Embrace Diversity.

Teams may range from 2 to 25 members, although 4 or 5 is optimal for many projects. Teams smaller than ten members tend to agree more easily on a common objective and form more cohesive units.[20] For the most creative decisions, teams generally have members who differ in age, gender, ethnicity, social background, training, and experience. The key business advantage of diversity is the ability to view a project and its context from multiple perspectives. Many of us tend to think that everyone in the world is like us because we know only our own experience. Teams with members from different ethnicities and cultures can look at projects beyond the limited view of one culture.

ETHICS CHECK

Members Riding Team's Coattails

Teamwork is a staple in college and university classes today and usually works well for students and their instructors. However, occasionally a rogue member will take advantage of a group and barely collaborate. How do you deal with a student who does sloppy work, misses team meetings, and fails to respond to calls or e-mails?

Agree on Purpose. An effective team begins with a purpose. Working from a general purpose to specific goals typically requires a huge investment of time and effort. Meaningful discussions, however, motivate team members to buy in to the project.

Agree on Procedures. The best teams develop procedures to guide them. They set up intermediate goals with deadlines. They assign roles and tasks, requiring all members to contribute equivalent amounts of real work. They decide how they will reach decisions by using one of the strategies discussed earlier. Procedures are continually evaluated to ensure movement toward the attainment of the team's goals.

Confront Conflict. Poorly functioning teams avoid conflict, preferring to sulk, gossip, or bicker. A better plan is to acknowledge conflict and address the root of the problem openly by using the six-step plan outlined in Figure 2.3. Although it may feel emotionally risky, direct confrontation saves time and enhances team commitment in the long run. To be constructive, however, confrontation must be task oriented, not person oriented. An open airing of differences, in which all team members have a chance to speak their minds, should centre on the strengths and weaknesses of the various positions and ideas—not on personalities. After hearing all sides, team members must negotiate a fair settlement, no matter how long it takes.

Communicate Effectively. The best teams exchange information and contribute ideas freely in an informal environment, often facilitated by technology. Team members speak and write clearly and concisely, avoiding generalities. They encourage feedback. Listeners become actively involved, read body language, and ask clarifying questions before responding. Tactful, constructive disagreement is encouraged. Although a team's task is taken seriously, successful teams are able to inject humour into their face-to-face interactions.

Be cautious with humour, however, as its use can vary between cities, provinces, and territories. For example, East Coast Canadians' sensitivities are tougher, and they often use humour that can be self-effacing. Canadians from different regions may have a less tolerant threshold for humour.[21]

Collaborate Rather Than Compete. Effective team members are genuinely interested in achieving team goals instead of receiving individual recognition. They

FIGURE 2.3 Six Steps for Dealing With Conflict

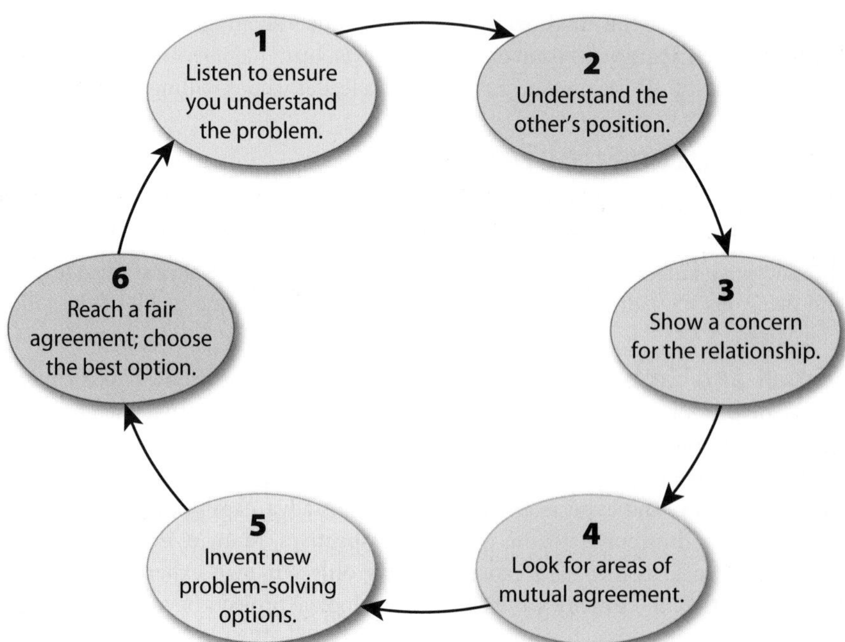

CHECKLIST

Developing Team Effectiveness

- **Establish small teams.** Smaller teams function more efficiently and more effectively than larger teams.
- **Encourage diversity.** Innovative teams typically include members who differ in age, gender, ethnicity, and background. Team members should possess the necessary technical expertise, problem-solving skills, and interpersonal skills.
- **Determine the purpose, procedures, and roles.** Members must understand the task at hand and what is expected of them. Teams function best when operating procedures are ironed out early and each member assumes a specific role.
- **Acknowledge and manage conflict.** Conflict is productive when it motivates a team to search for new ideas, increase participation, delay premature decisions, or discuss disagreements. Keep conflict centred on issues rather than on people.
- **Cultivate effective communication skills.** Productive team members articulate ideas clearly and concisely, recognize nonverbal cues, and listen actively.
- **Advance an environment of open communication.** Teams are most productive when members trust each other and feel free to discuss all viewpoints openly in an informal atmosphere.
- **Encourage collaboration and discourage competition.** Sharing information in a cooperative effort to achieve the team purpose must be more important than competing with other members for individual achievement.
- **Share leadership.** Members with the most expertise should lead at various times during the project's evolution.
- **Strive to make fair decisions.** Effective teams resolve problems without forcing members into a win–lose situation.
- **Lighten up.** The most successful teams take their task seriously, but they are also able to laugh at themselves and interject humour to enliven team proceedings.
- **Continually assess performance.** Teams should establish checkpoints along the way to determine whether they are meeting their objectives and adjust procedures if progress is unsatisfactory.

contribute ideas and feedback unselfishly. They monitor team progress, including what's going right, what's going wrong, and what to do about it. They celebrate individual and team accomplishments.

Accept Ethical Responsibilities. Teams as a whole have ethical responsibilities to their members, to their larger organizations, and to society. Members have a number of specific responsibilities to each other. As a whole, teams have a responsibility to represent the organization's view and respect its privileged information. They should not discuss with outsiders any sensitive issues without permission. In addition, teams have a broader obligation to avoid advocating actions that would endanger members of society at large.

Share Leadership. Effective teams often have no formal leader. Instead, leadership rotates to those with the appropriate expertise as the team evolves and moves from one phase to another. Many teams operate under a democratic approach. This approach can achieve buy-in to team decisions, boost morale, and create fewer hurt feelings and less resentment. In times of crisis, however, a strong team member may need to step up as a leader.

The Checklist above summarizes effective techniques for developing successful teams.

Concept Check

1. What are the business advantages of establishing working teams with diverse members?
2. Suppose you are working on a team that has one or two dominant individuals who make most of the decisions and who sometimes don't consider your ideas. Instead of giving up and not participating, what could you do that would be more helpful to the team and to your career?

LEARNING OBJECTIVE 2

Discuss effective practices and technologies for planning and participating in face-to-face meetings and virtual meetings.

Planning and Participating in Face-to-Face and Virtual Meetings

As you prepare to join the workforce, expect to attend meetings—lots of them! Estimates suggest that workers on average spend four hours a week in meetings and consider more than half that time to be wasted.[22] Managers spend even more time in meetings. In one survey managers considered over a third of meeting time unproductive and reported that two thirds of meetings fell short of their stated objectives.[23]

Meetings consist of three or more people who assemble to pool information, solicit feedback, clarify policy, seek consensus, and solve problems. However, as growing numbers of employees work at distant locations, meetings have changed. People are meeting regularly, but not always face to face. To be able to exchange information effectively and efficiently, you should know how to plan and participate in face-to-face and other kinds of meetings.

Making Face-to-Face Meetings Productive

As inevitable and commonplace as meetings are, most workers dread them. In spite of their bad reputation, if meetings are well run, workers actually want more, not fewer, of them.[24] Our task, then, as business communicators is to learn how to make them more efficient, satisfying, and productive.

Although meetings are disliked, they can be career critical. At meetings, judgments are formed and careers are made or blunted.[25] Therefore, instead of treating them as thieves of your valuable time, try to see them as golden opportunities to demonstrate your leadership, communication, and problem-solving skills. So that you can make the most of these opportunities, this section outlines techniques for planning and conducting successful meetings.

Determining the Purpose of a Meeting

A face-to-face meeting provides the most nonverbal cues and other signals that help us interpret the intended meaning of words. Thus, an in-person meeting is the richest of available media. No meeting should be called unless it is important, can't wait, and requires an exchange of ideas. If people are merely being informed, send an e-mail, a text message, a memo, or a letter. Leave a telephone or voice mail message, but don't call a costly meeting. Remember, the real expense of a meeting is the lost productivity of all the people attending. To decide whether the purpose of the meeting is valid, consult the key people who will be attending. Ask them what outcomes they want and how to achieve those goals. This consultation also sets a collaborative tone and encourages full participation.

Selecting Meeting Participants. The purpose of the meeting determines the number of participants, as shown in Figure 2.4. If the meeting purpose is motivational, such as an awards ceremony for top sales reps, then the number of participants is potentially unlimited.

FIGURE 2.4 Meeting Purpose and Number of Participants

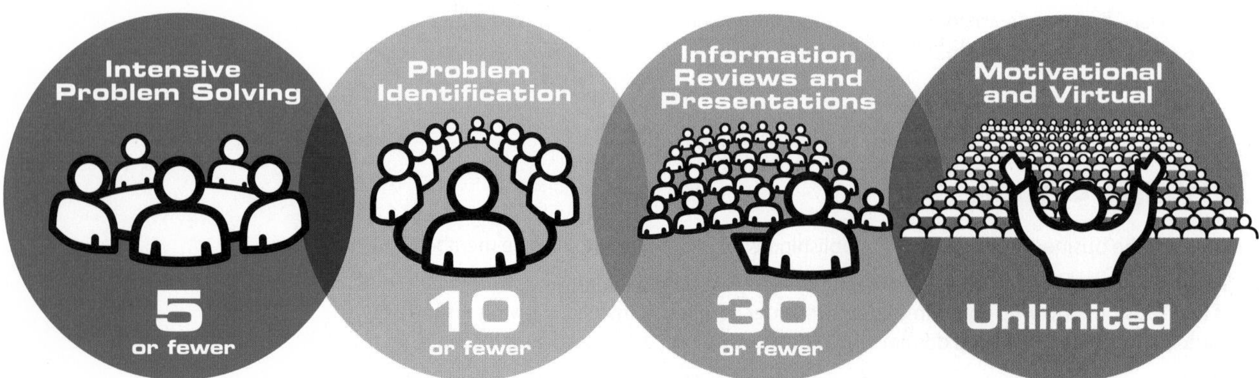

However, for productive results at a meeting, the best number is five to ten participants, as studies suggest.[26]

Ideally, decision makers and people with the information necessary to make the decision should attend. Also attending should be people who will be responsible for implementing the decision and representatives of groups who will benefit from the decision.

Using Digital Calendars to Schedule Meetings. Finding a time when everyone can meet is often difficult. Fortunately, digital calendars now make the task quicker and more efficient. Two of the most popular digital calendar programs are Google Calendar and Yahoo Calendar. Microsoft Outlook also provides a calendar. Online calendars enable you to make appointments, schedule meetings, and keep track of daily activities. To schedule meetings, you enter a new meeting request and add the names of attendees. You select a date, enter a start and end time, and list the meeting subject and location. Then the meeting request goes to each attendee. Later you check the attendee availability tab to see a list of all meeting attendees. As the meeting time approaches, the program automatically sends reminders to attendees.

Distributing an Agenda and Other Information. At least two days before a meeting, distribute an agenda of topics to be discussed. Also include any reports or materials that participants should read in advance. For continuing groups, you might also include a copy of the minutes of the previous meeting. To keep meetings productive, limit the number of agenda items. Remember, the narrower the focus, the greater the chances for success. A good agenda, as illustrated in Figure 2.5, covers the following information:

- Date and place of meeting
- Start time and end time
- Brief description of each topic, in order of priority, including the names of individuals who are responsible for performing some action

FIGURE 2.5 Typical Meeting Agenda

AGENDA
Quantum Travel International
Staff Meeting
September 18, 2020
10 to 11 a.m.
Conference Room

		Person	Proposed Time
I.	Call to order; roll call		
II.	Approval of agenda		
III.	Approval of minutes from previous meeting		
IV.	Committee reports		
	A. Social media news update	Jared	5 minutes
	B. Tour packages	Lakisha	10 minutes
V.	Old business		
	A. Equipment maintenance	John	5 minutes
	B. Client escrow accounts	Alicia	5 minutes
	C. Internal newsletter	Adrienne	5 minutes
VI.	New business		
	A. New accounts	Garth	5 minutes
	B. Pricing policy for Asian tours	Minh	15 minutes
VII.	Announcements		
VIII.	Chair's summary, adjournment		

- Proposed allotment of time for each topic
- Any premeeting preparation expected of participants

Managing the Meeting. Whether you are the meeting leader or a participant, it is important to act professionally during the meeting. Meetings can be more efficient and productive if leaders and participants recognize how to get the meeting started, establish ground rules, move the meeting along, and handle conflict.

Getting Started and Establishing Ground Rules

To avoid wasting time and irritating attendees, always start meetings on time—even if some participants are missing. For the same reasons, don't give a quick recap to anyone who arrives late. Open the meeting with a three- to five-minute introduction that includes the following:

- Goal and length of the meeting
- Background of topics or problems
- Possible solutions and constraints
- Tentative agenda
- Ground rules to be followed

Typical ground rules are communicating openly, being supportive, listening carefully, participating fully, confronting conflict frankly, silencing cell phones and other digital devices, and following the agenda. The next step is to assign one attendee to take minutes and one to act as a recorder. The minute-taker records all key points and notes all action items. The recorder uses a computer and projector or stands at a flipchart or whiteboard to list the main ideas being discussed and agreements reached.

Moving the Meeting Along. An effective leader lets others talk and tries to involve all participants. If the group has one member who dominates, the leader might say, *Thanks, Gary, for that perspective, but please hold your next point while we hear how Rachel would respond to that.* This technique also encourages quieter participants to speak up.

To avoid allowing digressions to sidetrack the group, try generating a *parking lot* list. This is a list of important but divergent issues that should be discussed later. Another way to handle digressions is to say, *Folks, we're going astray here. Please forgive me for pressing on, but let's return to the central issue of ____.* It is important to adhere to the agenda and the schedule. Equally important, when the group seems to have reached a consensus, is to summarize the group's position and check to see whether everyone agrees.

Participating Actively and Productively. Meetings are an opportunity for you to showcase your abilities and boost your career. To get the most out of the meetings you attend, try these techniques:[27]

- **Arrive early.** You show respect and look well organized when you arrive a little early.
- **Come prepared.** Bring the agenda and any distributed materials. Study the topics and be ready with questions, comments, and good ideas.
- **Have a positive attitude.** Use positive body language; speak energetically.
- **Contribute respectfully.** Wait your turn to speak; raise your hand to be recognized.
- **Wait for others to finish.** Show respect and good manners by not interrupting.
- **Keep your voice calm and pleasant yet energetic.** Avoid showing anger as this focuses attention on your behaviour rather than on your ideas.
- **Give credit to others.** Gain allies and enhance your credibility by recognizing others in front of peers and superiors.
- **Use your cell phone, tablet, and laptop only for meeting-related tasks.** Focus your attention on the meeting, not on answering e-mails or texting on your phone.

- **Help summarize.** Assist the meeting leader by reviewing points you have noted.
- **Express your views IN the meeting.** Build trust by not holding postmeeting sidebars that involve criticism and judgments.
- **Follow up.** Send the signal that you are efficient and caring by completing the actions assigned to you.

Handling Conflict in Meetings. As you learned earlier, conflict is natural and even desirable. It can also cause awkwardness and uneasiness. Canadians typically dislike confrontation; however, they respond well to genuine attempts to remedy conflict.[28]

In meetings, conflict typically develops when people feel unheard or misunderstood. If two people clash, the best approach is to encourage each to make a complete case while group members give their full attention. Let each one question the other. Then, the leader should summarize what was said, and the participants should offer comments. The group may modify a recommendation or suggest alternatives before reaching consensus on a direction to follow.

Concluding and Following Up. End the meeting at the agreed time or sooner. The leader should summarize all decisions, assigned tasks, and deadlines. It may be necessary to ask attendees to volunteer to complete action items. All participants should understand what was accomplished. One effective technique that encourages full participation is *round-robin*. Team members take turns summarizing briefly their interpretation of what was decided and what happens next. Of course, this closure technique works best with smaller groups. The leader should conclude by asking the group to set a time for the next meeting and assure the group that a report will follow. Finally, the leader should thank participants for attending.

Meeting minutes should be distributed within a couple of days of the meeting. Software enables you to follow a structured template that includes brief meeting minutes, key points and decisions, and action items. The leader needs to ensure that decisions are executed. The leader may need to call participants to remind them of their assignments and also to solicit help if necessary.

Respecting Cultural Diversity

As you schedule and organize meetings with diverse groups, allow time for research to prepare for cultural differences. Have you considered days of religious observance? Are there ceremonies or traditions that need to be honoured when people from the community come together? For example, when travelling to Indigenous communities for meetings, plan for delays. Rather than arriving just in time for the meeting and leaving immediately after, it is expected that you will spend some time in the community. It is also important to provide options for meeting dates. If there has been a recent death in the community, funerals and wakes will take precedence and may last for days.[29] For more tips on meetings with Indigenous peoples, visit the Indigenous Corporate Training, Inc. website for free resources and e-books.

Preparing for Virtual Meetings

One of the major trends in today's workplace is the rise of virtual meetings instead of face-to-face meetings. *Virtual meetings* are gatherings of participants who are connected technologically. As travel costs rise and companies slash budgets, many organizations are cutting back on meetings that require travel.[30] Within the first month of the global pandemic, the demand for virtual meeting platforms, like WebEx, more than doubled.[31] Many executives say they will not return to their previous workplace practices: "The way we work is going to change forever. Employers are going to be able to hire workers from wider geographic areas because staff won't have to come to the office as much."[32]

nattrass/iStock/Getty Images

Steady improvement in telecommunications networks, software, and computer processing continues to fuel the shift to virtual meetings. These meetings have many purposes, including training employees, making sales presentations, coordinating team activities, and talking to customers.

Although the same good meeting management techniques discussed for face-to-face meetings prevail, additional skills and practices are important in virtual meetings. The following best practices recommended by experienced meeting facilitators will help you address premeeting issues such as technology glitches, scheduling across time zones, and language challenges.[33] Creating ground rules, anticipating limited media richness, managing turn-taking, and humanizing the interaction with remote members all achieve the best results during virtual meetings.

- **Select the most appropriate technology.** Decide whether audio- or videoconferencing is needed. Choose the appropriate program or application.
- **Ensure that all participants are able to use the technology.** Coach attendees who may need help before the session begins.
- **Encourage participants to log in 15 minutes early.** Some programs require downloads and installations that can cause immense frustration if not done early.
- **Be aware of different time zones.** Canada has six primary time zones: Pacific, Mountain, Central, Eastern, Atlantic, and Newfoundland. Each zone is one hour apart, except for Newfoundland, which is half an hour apart.[34] Use Coordinated Universal Time (UTC) to minimize confusion resulting from mismatched local times. Avoid spanning a lunch hour or holding someone overtime.
- **Rotate your meeting time to be fair to all dispersed group members.** Ensure that everyone shares the burden of an inconvenient time.[35]
- **Decide what language to use.** If the meeting language may be difficult for some participants, think about using simple expressions and repeating major ideas. Always follow up in writing.
- **Explain how questions may be asked and answered.** Many meeting programs allow participants to virtually raise their hands using an icon on the computer screen and to type in their questions.
- **Ensure it is clear who is speaking in audioconferences.** Ask participants to always say their names before beginning to comment.
- **Remind the group to silence all electronic alerts and alarms.** Ask participants to mute ringers and buzzers and control background noise, or you may also hear dogs barking, telephones ringing, and toilets flushing.
- **Don't multitask.** Giving your full attention is critical, including not texting and checking e-mail.
- **Anticipate the limitations of virtual technology.** Given the lack of nonverbal cues, be as precise as possible. Use simple language and summarize the discussion often. Confirm your understanding of the discussion. Project an upbeat, enthusiastic, and strong voice.
- **Manage turn-taking.** Ask questions of specific people. Invite each participant to speak for 30 seconds without interruption. Avoid asking vague questions such as, *Does everyone agree?*
- **Humanize virtual meetings.** Build camaraderie and trust. Leave time for small talk to establish a warm environment. Build trust and interest by logging in early and greeting others as they join.

fizkes/Shutterstock

The benefits of videoconferencing are so wide-ranging that telepresence applications are replacing business travel, doctor's visits, and even courtroom appearances. What are the advantages of videoconferencing compared with face-to-face meetings?

CHECKLIST

Planning and Participating in Productive Meetings

Before the Meeting

- **Consider alternatives.** Unless a topic is important and pressing, avoid calling a meeting.
- **Invite the right people.** Invite people who have information and authority to make the decision and implement it.
- **Distribute an agenda.** Include the date and place, the starting and ending time, brief topic descriptions with time allotments, and the names of the people assigned action items.
- **Use a calendar program.** If available, use calendaring software to set a meeting date, issue invitations, and send the agenda.
- **Train participants on technology.** Especially for virtual meetings, be sure participants are comfortable with the conferencing software.

During the Meeting

- **Start on time and introduce the agenda.** Discuss the goal and length of the meeting, propose a tentative agenda, and clarify the ground rules for the meeting.
- **Appoint a note-taker and a recorder.** Ask one attendee to take notes of the proceedings, and ask another person to record discussion topics on a flipchart or whiteboard.
- **Encourage participation.** Ensure that all participants' views are heard and that no one monopolizes the discussion. Avoid digressions by steering the group back to the topics on the agenda.
- **Confront conflict frankly.** Encourage people who disagree to explain their positions completely. After discussion, the group may suggest alternatives before agreeing on a plan of action.
- **Summarize along the way.** When the group seems to reach a consensus, summarize and see whether all members agree.

Ending the Meeting and Following Up

- **Review meeting decisions.** At the end of the meeting, consider using round-robin to be sure everyone understands what has been decided. Discuss action items and a completion schedule.
- **Distribute minutes of the meeting.** A few days after the meeting, distribute the minutes.
- **Remind people of action items.** Follow up by calling people to see whether they are completing the actions recommended at the meeting.

Although many acknowledge that virtual meetings may not be as effective as face-to-face meetings,[36] virtual meetings are here to stay. Learning to plan and participate in them professionally will enhance your career as a business communicator. The Checklist above summarizes helpful techniques for both face-to-face and virtual meetings.

Concept Check

1. Why is it important to invite the right people to a meeting?
2. With the increase in virtual meetings because of COVID-19, many experts report that workers are experiencing *Zoom fatigue*. With the pivot to remote work, people are noticing physical symptoms, like dry and sore eyes, as well as emotional exhaustion.[37] Research Zoom fatigue, and list three factors that contribute to this condition. What can workers do to decrease this fatigue?

Listening in the Workplace

LEARNING OBJECTIVE 3

Explain and apply active listening techniques.

As you learned earlier, workers are communicating more than ever before, largely because of the Internet, social media, teamwork, global competition, and an emphasis on customer service. A vital ingredient in every successful workplace is high-quality communication, and three quarters of high-quality communication involves listening.[38]

Listening skills are important for career success, organization effectiveness, and worker satisfaction. Numerous studies and experts report that good listeners make good managers and that good listeners advance more rapidly in their organizations.[39] Listening is especially important in the workplace because we spend so much time doing it. Although estimates vary,

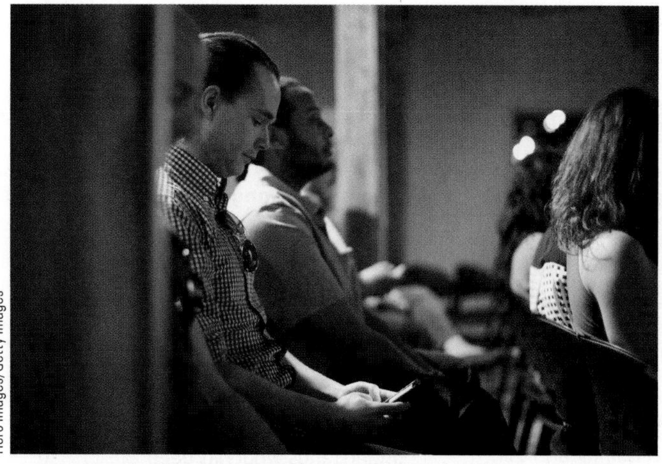

Most of us can probably recall a situation in which smart portable electronics created a distraction, making listening difficult.

most workers spend 30 to 45 percent of their communication time listening.[40] Executives spend 60 to 70 percent of their communication time listening.[41]

In this section, we explore the importance of listening, the kinds of listening required in the workplace, and ways to improve listening skills. Although many of the tips for improving your listening skills will be effective in your personal life, our discussion centres primarily on workplace and employment needs.

Poor Listening Habits

Although executives and employees devote the bulk of their communication time to listening, research suggests that they're not very good at it. In fact, most of us are poor listeners. Some estimates indicate that only half of the oral messages heard in a day are completely understood.[42] Experts say that we listen at only 25 percent efficiency. In other words, we ignore, forget, distort, or misunderstand 75 percent of everything we hear.

Poor listening habits may result from several factors. Lack of training is one significant factor. Few schools give as much emphasis to listening as they do to the development of reading, speaking, and writing skills. In addition, our listening skills may be less than perfect because of the large number of competing sounds and stimuli in our lives that interfere with concentration. Finally, we are inefficient listeners because we are able to process speech much faster than others can speak. Although most speakers talk at about 125 to 175 words per minute, listeners can listen at 450 words per minute.[43] The resulting lag time fosters daydreaming, which clearly reduces listening efficiency.

Types of Workplace Listening

On the job you can expect to be involved in many types of listening. These include listening to supervisors, to colleagues, and to customers. If you are an entry-level employee, you will probably be most concerned with listening to superiors. But you also must develop skills for listening to colleagues and team members. As you advance in your career and enter the ranks of management, you will need skills for listening to subordinates. Finally, the entire organization must listen to customers, employees, government agencies, all stakeholders, and the public at large to compete in today's service-oriented economy.

As you can see in Figure 2.6, employees trained in listening techniques are far more likely to elicit customer feedback and promote goodwill.

Improving Workplace Listening

Listening on the job is more difficult than listening in college or university classes in which experienced professors present well-organized lectures and repeat important points. Workplace listening is more challenging because information is often exchanged casually or under time pressure. It may be disorganized, unclear, and cluttered with extraneous facts. Moreover, your fellow workers are usually your friends. Because they are familiar with you, they may not be as polite and respectful as they are with strangers. Friends tend to interrupt, jump to conclusions, and take each other for granted.

According to Statistics Canada, over 20 percent of Canadians speak an immigrant language at home. This is up 14.7 percent since the last census.[44] Listening in groups or listening to speakers for whom English is an additional language (EAL) or second language (ESL) further complicates the listening process. In groups more than one person talks at once, and topics change rapidly. Group members are monitoring both verbal and nonverbal messages to learn what relates to their group roles. Listening to EAL/ESL speakers often creates special challenges. Chapter 3 presents suggestions for communicating across cultures.

FIGURE 2.6 Listening to Customers: Comparing Trained and Untrained Listeners

Untrained Listeners	Trained Listeners
✗ Tune out some of what the customer is saying because they know the answer	✓ Defer judgment; listen for the customer's feelings and assess the situation
✗ Focus on style; mentally dismiss grammar, voice tone, and speech mannerisms	✓ Pay most attention to content, not to appearances, form, or other surface issues
✗ Tend to listen mainly for facts and specific bits of information	✓ Listen completely, trying to really understand every nuance
✗ Attempt to take in everything being said, including exaggerations and errors ("fogging"), only to refute each comment	✓ Listen primarily for the main idea and avoid replying to everything, especially sidetracking issues
✗ Divide their attention among two or more tasks because listening is automatic	✓ Do one thing at a time, realizing that listening is a full-time job
✗ Tend to become distracted by emotional words, have difficulty controlling anger	✓ Control their anger and refuse to fight fire with fire
✗ Interrupt the customer	✓ Are silent for a few seconds after speakers finish to let them complete their thought
✗ Give few, if any, verbal responses	✓ Give affirming statements and invite additional comments

CASE CONNECTIONS

The Gig Economy

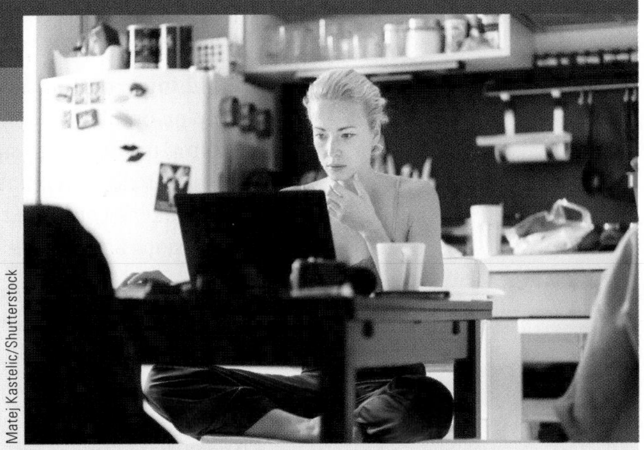
Matej Kastelic/Shutterstock

As discussed in Chapter 1, with more employers looking for contract and short-term on-demand workers, the gig economy in Canada continues to grow. Employers from all industries seek workers with specialization that can complement their existing teams, and many self-employed Canadians enjoy the flexibility of the gig economy.[45] Bank of Montreal (BMO) Wealth Management commissioned a report with the following results:

> The survey asked respondents of their reasons for becoming self-employed. Voluntarily making the choice was the most popular reason (cited by 60% of respondents), followed by needing a new challenge or change (49%), and to find purpose after a previous business venture (19%). More men than women (55% vs. 43%) needed a new challenge, and more millennials voluntarily made the choice (62%) compared to generation-Xers (58%) and boomers (54%). Another interesting (but perhaps predictable) result from this survey question was that more boomers felt they needed to supplement their retirement income (31%) than did generation-Xers (10%) or millennials (9%).[46]

Even with these results, many Canadians don't prefer contract work but feel it is their only option due to a lack of full-time permanent jobs.

- What are the pros and cons of the gig economy?
- How can you make the most of the gig economy with your skills and expertise?

Ten Keys to Building Powerful Listening Skills

Despite the complexities and challenges of workplace listening, good listeners on the job must remember that their goal is to listen carefully and to *understand* what is being said so that they can do their work well. The following recommendations can help you improve your workplace listening effectiveness.

1. **Control external and internal distractions.** Move to an area where you can hear without conflicting noises or conversations. Block out surrounding physical distractions. Internally, try to focus totally on the speaker. If other projects are on your mind, try not to think about them. When you are emotionally charged, whether angry or extremely happy, it is a good idea to postpone any serious listening.
2. **Become actively involved.** Show that you are listening closely by leaning forward and maintaining eye contact with the speaker. Don't fidget or try to complete another task at the same time you are listening. Listen to more than the spoken words. How are they said? What implied meaning, reasoning, and feelings do you hear behind the spoken words? Does the speaker's body language (eye contact, posture, movements) support or contradict the main message?
3. **Separate facts from opinions.** Facts are truths known to exist; for example, *PartSource, Mark's Work Wearhouse, and Canadian Tire Financial Services are all included under Canadian Tire Corporation, Ltd.* Opinions are statements of personal judgments or preferences; for example, *Canadian Tire has the best choice of household goods.* Some opinions are easy to recognize because speakers preface them with statements such as, *I think, It seems to me*, and *As far as I'm concerned.*[47] Often, however, listeners must evaluate assertions to decide their validity. Good listeners consider whether speakers are credible and speaking within their areas of competence. They do not automatically accept assertions as facts.
4. **Identify important facts.** Speakers on the job often intersperse important information with casual conversation. Unrelated topics pop up—ball scores, a customer's weird request, a computer glitch. Your task is to select what's crucial and register it mentally. What step is next in your project? Who does what? What is your role?
5. **Avoid interrupting.** While someone else has the floor, do not interrupt with a quick reply or opinion. Don't signal nonverbal disagreement, such as with negative head shaking, rolling eyes, sarcastic snorting, or audible sighs. Good listeners let speakers have their say. Interruptions are not only impolite but also prevent you from hearing the speaker's complete thought. Listeners who interrupt with their opinions sidetrack discussions and cause hard feelings.
6. **Ask clarifying questions.** Good listeners wait for the proper moment and then ask questions that do not attack the speaker. Instead of saying, *But I don't understand how you can say that*, a good listener seeks clarification with statements such as, *Please help me understand by explaining more about. . . .* Use *open questions* (those without set answers) to draw out feelings, motivations, ideas, and suggestions. Use *closed questions* (those that require a choice among set answers) to identify key factors in a discussion.[48]
7. **Paraphrase to increase understanding.** To make sure you understand a speaker, rephrase and summarize a message in your own words. Be objective and nonjudgmental. Remember, your goal is to understand what the speaker has said—not to show how mindless the speaker's words sound when parroted. Remember, too, that other workplace listeners will also benefit from a clear summary of what was said.
8. **Capitalize on lag time.** While you are waiting for a speaker's next idea, use the time to review what the speaker is saying. Separate the central idea, key points, and details. Use lag time to silently rephrase and summarize the speaker's message. Another effective trick for keeping your mind from drifting is to try to guess what a speaker's next point will be. Most important, keep your mind focused on the speaker's ideas—not on all the other work waiting for you.

CHECKLIST

Improving Listening

- **Stop talking.** Accept the role of listener by concentrating on the speaker's words, not on your response.
- **Work hard at listening.** Become actively involved; expect to learn something.
- **Block out competing thoughts.** Concentrate on the message. Don't daydream during lag time.
- **Control the listening environment.** Move to a quiet area where you won't be interrupted by calls, texts, or visitors.
- **Maintain an open mind.** Know your biases and be tolerant of differences. Encourage the speaker with comments such as, *Yes, I see*, and *Okay.* Look alert by leaning forward.
- **Paraphrase the speaker's ideas.** Silently repeat the details in your own words. In conversation, sum up the main points to confirm what was said.
- **Listen between the lines.** Observe nonverbal cues and interpret the feelings of the speaker: What is really being said?
- **Distinguish between facts and opinions.** Know the difference between factual statements and opinions stated as assertions.
- **Capitalize on lag time.** Use spare moments to organize, review, anticipate, challenge, and weigh the evidence.
- **Use memory devices.** If the information is important, develop acronyms, links, or rhymes to help you remember it.
- **Take selective notes.** If you are hearing instructions or important data, record the major points; then verify them with the speaker.

9. **Take notes to ensure retention.** If you have a hallway conversation with a colleague and don't have a pen or smart electronic device handy, make a mental note of the important items. Then record them as soon as possible. Even with seemingly easily remembered facts or instructions, jot them down to ease your mind and also to be sure you understand them correctly. Two weeks later you will be glad you did. Be sure you have a good place to store notes about various projects, such as file folders, notebooks, or digital files.
10. **Be aware of gender differences.** As a generalization, men tend to listen for facts, whereas women tend to perceive listening as an opportunity to connect with the other person on a personal level.[49] Men tend to use interrupting behaviour to control conversations, while women generally interrupt to communicate assent, to elaborate on an idea of another group member, or to participate in the topic of conversation. Female listeners tend to be attentive, provide steady eye contact, remain stationary, and nod their heads.[50] Male listeners are less attentive, provide sporadic eye contact, and move around. Being aware of these tendencies will make you a more sensitive and knowledgeable listener. Keep an open mind while you listen; some people are nonbinary, and communication styles will vary from the binary gender generalizations discussed above.

Concept Check

1. Employees trained in listening techniques are far more likely to elicit positive customer feedback and promote goodwill. Name five techniques that trained listeners use.
2. Consider a situation in your family, in your circle of friends, in high school, at college, during an internship, or at work that shows the potential risks of poor listening skills. How could the resulting misunderstandings or other negative consequences have been prevented? Which techniques would have helped avert the undesirable outcome?

Communicating Nonverbally

LEARNING OBJECTIVE 4

Understand how effective nonverbal communication can help you advance your career.

Understanding messages often involves more than merely listening to spoken words. Nonverbal cues also carry powerful meanings. Nonverbal communication includes all unwritten and unspoken messages, both intentional and unintentional. Eye contact, facial expressions, body movements, space, time, distance, appearance—all these nonverbal cues influence the way a message is interpreted, or decoded, by the receiver.

Nonverbal communication includes all unwritten and unspoken messages, whether intended or not. These silent signals have a strong effect on receivers. However, understanding them is not simple. Does a downward glance indicate modesty? Fatigue? Does a constant stare reflect coldness? Dullness? Aggression? Do crossed arms mean defensiveness, withdrawal, or just that the person is shivering?

In one experiment, speakers delivered a positive message but averted their eyes as they spoke. Listeners perceived the overall message to be negative. Moreover, listeners thought that gaze aversion suggested lack of affection, superficiality, lack of trust, and nonreceptivity.[51] The lesson to be learned here is that effective communicators must be certain that all their nonverbal messages reinforce their spoken words and their professional goals. To make sure that you're on the right track to nonverbal communication competency, let's look at the specific forms of nonverbal communication.

Your Body Sends Silent Messages

Each of us sends and receives thousands of nonverbal messages daily in our business and personal lives. Although the following discussion covers many forms of nonverbal communication, we will be especially concerned with workplace applications. As you learn about the silent messages you send, think about how you can use these nonverbal cues positively in your career.

Eye Contact. The eyes have been called the windows to the soul. Even if communicators can't look directly into the soul, they consider the eyes to be the most accurate predictor of a speaker's true feelings and attitudes. Most of us cannot look another person straight in the eyes and lie. As a result, in Canadian culture we tend to believe people who look directly at us. Sustained eye contact suggests trust and admiration; brief eye contact signifies fear or stress. Prolonged eye contact or staring, however, can be intrusive and intimidating.

Good eye contact enables the message sender to determine whether a receiver is paying attention, showing respect, responding favourably, or feeling distress. From the Canadian receiver's perspective, good eye contact reveals the speaker's sincerity, confidence, and truthfulness. However, nonverbal cues, including eye contact, have different meanings in different cultures. In some Indigenous cultures, continuous eye contact is not expected; instead, the listener is more focused on the speaker's words.[52] Chapter 3 presents more information about the cultural influence of nonverbal cues.

Facial Expressions. The expression on a communicator's face can be almost as revealing of emotion as the eyes. Experts estimate that the human face can display more than 250,000 expressions.[53] To hide their feelings, some people can control these expressions and maintain so-called poker faces. Most of us, however, display our emotions openly. Raising or lowering the eyebrows, squinting the eyes, swallowing nervously, clenching the jaw, smiling broadly—these voluntary and involuntary facial expressions can add to or entirely replace verbal messages.

Check out section 2-4a in MindTap, where you can watch a video featuring Candice Wong, the owner of a physiotherapy clinic, discuss the importance of reading body and verbal language to create a safe space.

Posture and Gestures. An individual's general posture can convey anything from high status and self-confidence to shyness and submissiveness. Leaning toward a speaker suggests attentiveness and interest; pulling away or shrinking back denotes fear, distrust, anxiety, or disgust. Similarly, gestures can communicate entire thoughts via simple movements. But remember that these nonverbal cues may have vastly different meanings in different cultures.

In the workplace you can make a good impression by controlling your posture and gestures. When speaking, make sure your upper body is aligned with the person to whom you're talking. Erect posture sends a message of confidence, competence, diligence, and strength.

Time, Space, and Territory Send Silent Messages

In addition to nonverbal messages transmitted by your body, three external elements convey information in the communication process: time, space, and territory.

Time. How we structure and use time tells observers about our personality and attitudes. For example, when a banking executive gives a visitor a prolonged interview, she signals her respect for, interest in, and approval of the visitor or the topic being discussed. By sharing her valuable time, she sends a clear nonverbal message. In the workplace you can send positive nonverbal messages by being on time for meetings and appointments, staying on task during meetings, and giving ample time to appropriate projects and individuals.

Space. How we arrange things in the space around us tells something about ourselves and our objectives. Whether the space is a dorm room, an office, or a department, people reveal themselves in the design and grouping of furniture within that space. Generally, the more formal the arrangement, the more formal and closed the communication environment.

Territory. Each of us has certain areas that we feel are our own territory, whether it is a specific spot or just the space around us. For example, veteran employees may feel that certain work areas and tools belong to them. We all maintain zones of privacy in which we feel comfortable. When waiting in public lines, Canadians require a minimum of 35 centimetres (14 inches) of space.[54] If someone violates that territory, we feel uncomfortable and defensive and may step back to reestablish our space. However, this can vary across provinces and territories. For example, people in Québec may not need as much personal space, and touching is more common.[55]

In the workplace, be aware of the territorial needs of others and don't invade their space. Figure 2.7 categorizes the four zones of social interaction among North Americans, as formulated by anthropologist Edward T. Hall.

Appearance Sends Silent Messages

Eye Appeal of Business Documents. The way an e-mail, a letter, a memo, or a report looks can have either a positive or a negative effect on the receiver. Sloppy e-mails send a nonverbal message that you are in a terrific hurry or that you do not care about the receiver. Envelopes—through their postage, stationery, and printing—can suggest that the messages they carry are routine, important, or junk mail. Letters and reports can look neat, professional, well organized, and attractive—or just the opposite.

FIGURE 2.7 Four Space Zones for Social Interaction

Intimate Zone (0.3 to 0.5 metres)

Personal Zone (0.5 to 1.3 metres)

Social Zone (1.3 to 3.5 metres)

Public Zone (3.6 metres or more)

Photos, L to R: lewkmiller/istock via Getty Images; Dean Mitchell/istock via Getty Images; monkeybusinessimages/istock via Getty Images; © Kablonk Royalty-Free/Inmagine

In succeeding chapters you will learn how to create documents that send positive nonverbal messages through their appearance, format, organization, readability, and correctness.

Personal Appearance. The way you look—your clothing, grooming, and posture—transmits an instant nonverbal message about you. Based on what they see, viewers make quick judgments about your status, credibility, personality, and potential. Business communicators who look the part are more likely to be successful in working with supervisors, colleagues, and customers. Because appearance is such a powerful force in business, some aspiring professionals are turning for help to image consultants (who charge up to $500 an hour!).

What do image consultants say? They suggest investing in appropriate, professional-looking clothing and accessories. Remember that quality is more important than quantity. Avoid flashy garments, clunky jewellery, garish makeup, and overpowering colognes. Pay attention to good grooming, including a neat hairstyle, body cleanliness, polished shoes, and clean nails. Project confidence in your posture, both standing and sitting.

While body art in the form of tattoos and piercings has become the norm for many Canadians, not all employers are enthusiastic about this form of expression. Think twice before displaying tattoos and piercings at work without learning your employer's policies first. Respect the work environment and understand that some workplaces may require you to cover up tattoos or remove certain piercings before dealing with customers.

In recent years, casual dress days have become popular at many workplaces. Be aware, though, that casual clothes change the image you project and also may affect your work style. See the accompanying Career Coach box regarding the pros and cons of casual apparel.

In the preceding discussion of nonverbal communication, you learned that each of us sends and responds to thousands of nonverbal messages daily in our personal and work lives. You can harness the power of silent messages by reviewing Figure 2.8 and by studying the tips in the Checklist that ends this section.

FIGURE 2.8 Sending Positive Nonverbal Signals in the Workplace

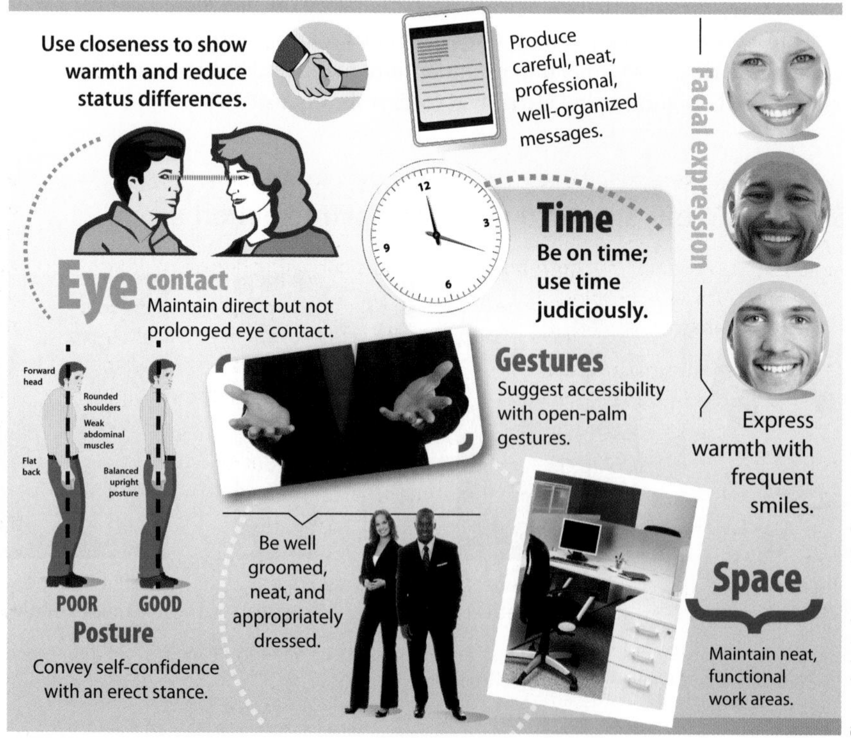

Use closeness to show warmth and reduce status differences.
Produce careful, neat, professional, well-organized messages.
Facial expression
Eye contact
Maintain direct but not prolonged eye contact.
Time
Be on time; use time judiciously.
Forward head
Rounded shoulders
Weak abdominal muscles
Flat back
Balanced upright posture
Gestures
Suggest accessibility with open-palm gestures.
Express warmth with frequent smiles.
Be well groomed, neat, and appropriately dressed.
POOR
GOOD
Posture
Convey self-confidence with an erect stance.
Space
Maintain neat, functional work areas.

Photos, clockwise from top right: PhotoMediaGroup/Shutterstock.com; © Terry Schmidbauer/Shutterstock.com; © Robert Kneschke/Shutterstock.com; terekhov igor/Shutterstock.com; Ken Hurst/Shutterstock.com; © Piotr Marcinski/Shutterstock.com; © Nickolay Stanev/Shutterstock.

CAREER COACH

Perils of Casual Apparel in the Workplace

Your choice of work clothes sends a strong nonverbal message about you. It also affects the way you work. Some surveys suggest that the pendulum is swinging back to more conservative attire in the workplace,[56] although employers and employees have mixed feelings about what to wear to work.

What Critics Are Saying

Some employers oppose casual dress because, in their opinion, too many workers push the boundaries of what is acceptable. They contend that absenteeism, tardiness, and flirtatious behaviour have increased since dress-down policies began to be implemented. Relaxed dress codes also lead to reduced productivity and lax behaviour. Image counsellor Judith Rasband claimed that the general casualization of North America has resulted in an overall decline in civility. "Manners break down, you begin to feel down, and you're not as effective," she said.[57] Others fear that casual attire undermines the authority and credibility of executives, particularly females and members of minority groups.[58] Moreover, customers are often turned off by casually attired employees.[59]

What Supporters Are Saying

Supporters argue that comfortable clothes and relaxed working environments lift employee morale, increase employee creativity, and improve internal communication. Employees appreciate reduced clothing-related expenses, while employers use casual dress as a recruitment and retention tool. Because employees seem to love casual dress, nine out of ten employers have adopted casual-dress days for at least part of the workweek—even if it is just on Fridays during the summer.

What Employees Need to Know

The following suggestions, gleaned from surveys and articles about casual-dress trends in the workplace, can help you avoid casual-attire blunders.

- For job interviews, dress conservatively or call ahead to ask the interviewer or the receptionist what is appropriate.
- Find out what your company allows. Ask whether a dress-down policy is available. Observe what others are wearing on casual-dress days.
- If your company has no casual-attire policy, volunteer to work with management to develop relevant guidelines, including illustrations of suitable casual attire.
- Avoid wearing the following items: T-shirts, sandals, flip-flops, shoes without socks, backless dresses, tank tops, shorts, miniskirts, yoga pants, athletic shoes, hiking boots, and baseball caps.[60]
- When meeting customers, dress as well as or better than they do.

CHECKLIST

Techniques for Improving Nonverbal Communication Skills in the Workplace

- **Establish and maintain eye contact.** Remember that in North America appropriate eye contact signals interest, attentiveness, strength, and credibility. However, be mindful of cultural differences.
- **Use posture to show interest.** Encourage interaction by leaning forward, sitting or standing up straight, and looking alert.
- **Probe for more information.** When you perceive nonverbal cues that contradict verbal meanings, politely seek additional clues (*I'm not sure I understand, Please tell me more about . . .*, or *Do you mean that . . . ?*).
- **Interpret nonverbal meanings in context.** Make nonverbal assessments only when you understand a situation or a culture.
- **Associate with people from diverse cultures.** Learn about other cultures to widen your knowledge and tolerance of intercultural nonverbal messages.
- **Reduce or eliminate physical barriers.** Move out from behind a desk or lectern; arrange meeting chairs in a circle.
- **Improve your decoding skills.** Watch facial expressions and body language to understand the complete verbal and nonverbal message being communicated.
- **Appreciate the power of appearance.** Keep in mind that the appearance of your business documents, your business space, and yourself sends immediate positive or negative messages to others.
- **Observe yourself on video.** Ensure that your verbal and nonverbal messages are in sync by recording and evaluating yourself making a presentation.
- **Enlist friends and family.** Ask friends and family members to monitor your conscious and unconscious body movements and gestures to help you become a more effective communicator.

Concept Check

1. What are five ways to avoid casual-attire blunders in the workplace?
2. Gestures play an important role when people communicate. Because culture shapes the meaning of gestures, miscommunication and misunderstanding can easily result in international situations. Use the Internet to research the meanings of selected gestures. Make a list of ten gestures (other than those discussed in the text) that have different meanings in different countries. Consider the fingertip kiss, nose thumb, eyelid pull, nose tap, head shake, and other gestures. How are the meanings different in other countries?

LEARNING OBJECTIVE 5

Improve your competitive advantage by developing professionalism and business etiquette skills.

Developing Professionalism and Business Etiquette Skills at the Office and Online

What exactly is professionalism? Your future employer will expect you to possess soft skills in addition to your technical knowledge. Soft skills are the hallmark of a professional. They are essential career attributes that include the ability to communicate, work well with others, solve problems, make ethical decisions, and appreciate diversity.[61] These soft skills, as outlined in Canada's Employability Skills 2000+, are desirable in all business sectors and job positions.[62] In the digital age, professionalism also means maintaining a positive online presence, a subject we discuss in Chapters 1 and 5.

Etiquette is more about attitude than about formal rules of behaviour. Attitude is a desire to show others consideration and respect. Good manners and a businesslike, professional demeanour are among the top soft skills that employers seek in job candidates. Employers prefer courteous and professional job candidates over those who lack these skills and traits. But can you really learn how to be courteous, civil, and professional? Of course! This section gives you a few pointers.

Understanding Professionalism

Not everyone who seeks a job is aware of the employer's expectations. Some new hires have no idea that excessive absenteeism or tardiness is grounds for termination. Others are surprised to learn that they are expected to devote their full attention to their duties when on the job. Many employees don't realize that they are sabotaging their careers when they sprinkle their conversation with *like, literally,* and uptalk (a singsong speech pattern that makes declarative statements sound like questions).

Projecting and maintaining a professional image can make a real difference in helping you obtain the job of your dreams. Once you get that job, you are more likely to be taken seriously and much more likely to be promoted if you look and sound professional. Do not send the wrong message with unwitting or unprofessional behaviour. Figure 2.9 reviews seven areas you will want to check to be sure you are projecting professionalism.

Gaining an Etiquette Edge

An awareness of courtesy and etiquette can give you a competitive edge in the job market. Etiquette, civility, and goodwill efforts may seem out of place in today's fast-paced, high-tech offices. However, when two candidates have equal qualifications, the one who appears to be more polished and professional is more likely to be hired and promoted.

As workloads increase and face-to-face meetings decline, bad manners and incivility are becoming alarmingly common in the North American workplace.[63] Employers, of course, suffer from the resulting drop in productivity and exodus of talent. Employees, too, suffer. They worry about incidents, think about changing jobs, and cut back their efforts on the job. It is not hard to understand why employers are looking for people who are courteous, polite, respectful, and well-mannered.

FIGURE 2.9 Projecting Professionalism When You Communicate

Unprofessional		Professional
Slang, uptalk, *like* as a filler, poor grammar, and profanity	Speech	A composed tone and correct grammar to sound educated and credible
Sloppy messages with incomplete sentences, misspelled words, exclamation points, and IM slang	E-mail	Concise messages with subjects, verbs, correct punctuation marks and spelling, and no IM slang
E-mail addresses that sound cute or like a chat room nickname, such as *supasnugglykitty@yahoo.com*	Internet	E-mail addresses with a positive, businesslike expression or a name, such as *jsmith@yahoo.com*
Outgoing messages with loud background music, weird sounds, or a joke message	Voicemail	Outgoing messages that state a name or phone number and instructions for leaving a message
Television or music playing noisily in the background when answering the phone	Telephone	A quiet background when answering the telephone, especially for a prospective employer's call
Use of electronics during business meetings or during conversations with fellow employees; loud conversations (cell yell) that others overhear	Devices	Silencing of phone and message notifications, both audible and vibrate, during meetings; use of smart devices only for meeting-related purposes
Sending and receiving of text messages during meetings, allowing texting to interrupt face-to-face conversations, or texting when driving	Texting	Sending of appropriate business text messages only when necessary (perhaps when a cell phone call would disturb others)

Good manners convey a positive image of an organization. People like to do business with those who show respect and treat others politely. Most of us also like to work in a pleasant environment. Considering how much time North Americans spend at work, it makes sense that people prefer an agreeable environment to one that is rude and uncivil.

Consider the following simple pointers to polish your social competencies:

- **Use polite words.** Be generous with words and phrases such as *please*, *thank you*, and *you're welcome*.
- **Express sincere appreciation and praise.** Tell coworkers how much you appreciate their efforts. Written and specific thank-you notes are even better than saying thanks.
- **Be selective in sharing personal information.** Avoid talking about health concerns, personal relationships, or finances in the office.
- **Don't put people down.** If you have a reputation for criticizing people, your coworkers will begin to wonder what you are saying behind their backs.
- **Respect coworkers' space.** Turn down the ringer on your business phone, minimize the use of speakerphones, and turn your personal cell phone down or off during business hours. Avoid wearing heavy perfumes or bringing strong-smelling food.
- **Rise above others' rudeness.** Don't use profanity or participate in questionable joke-telling.
- **Be considerate when sharing space and equipment with others.** Clean up after yourself.

- **Choose the high road in conflict.** Avoid letting discussions degenerate into shouting matches. Keep your voice calm and focus on the work rather than on personality differences.
- **Disagree agreeably.** You may not agree with everyone, but you should respect their opinions.

CENGAGE

MINDTAP

Check out section 2-5b in MindTap, where you can watch videos featuring Taylor Roberts, the general manager of Dynapole, discuss how to introduce yourself over the phone and how to speak in a businesslike manner.

Concept Check

1. When is it appropriate to send and receive text messages while at work?
2. Test your etiquette IQ: New communication platforms and casual workplace environments have blurred the lines of appropriateness, leaving workers wondering how to navigate uncharted waters. Indicate whether the following statements are true or false and discuss why in groups.
   a. If a business meeting is long and you are not directly involved, it is acceptable for you to perform minor grooming tasks such as combing your hair, applying lipstick, or clipping your fingernails—as long as you do it discreetly.
   b. Even though you may be working on a team project together, you should not open the closed door of a coworker's office without knocking first.

SPOTLIGHT ON COMMUNICATION: PART 2

Makivik Corporation Revisited

CRITICAL THINKING

- During a time of global crisis, why are professional public statements from leadership important for both employees and customers?
- Canadian North continued to operate during the pandemic with strict regulations in place, such as all passengers wearing face coverings. Consider other ways that companies and organizations adapted to the pandemic. How well were these changes communicated to their customers?

https://canadiannorth.com

In 2020 when the global pandemic reached Canada, the airline industry was hit hard as few people were travelling and flights were suspended. However, because Canadian North provides essential cargo delivery and customer transport to remote areas within northern Canada, it continued flights with dedication to its communities:

Joel Serre/Shutterstock

> The communities we serve in Canada's Arctic for the most part have no roads, we are the roads for them. Throughout this COVID-19 pandemic our front-line staff have been providing essential services to our communities to ensure they continue to receive their food, medical supplies and other important goods while also being able to travel to their medical appointments. When people need to travel it's our job to ensure we provide safe and clean service to those who need it.
>
> Without our amazing crew and employees, we wouldn't be able to ensure these essential services continue. We're tremendously lucky to have the employees we have that understand our role every day and especially in a situation like this one.[64]

Chris Avery, president and CEO of Canadian North, acknowledged the significant challenges the airline was facing: "Canadian North and all other airlines are experiencing a sudden and significant decrease in passenger demand. This represents a severe reduction in the revenue that we rely on to operate our business. . . . While there is no clear end in sight to these challenges, Canadian North will continue to provide essential passenger and cargo services to the people, communities and organizations we serve, regardless of these circumstances."[65] This response demonstrates Makivik Corporation's commitment to its people and communities.

Summary of Learning Objectives

1 Understand the importance of teamwork in the workplace, and explain how you can contribute positively to team performance.

- Teams are popular because they lead to better decisions, faster responses, increased productivity, greater buy-in, less resistance to change, improved morale, and reduced risks.
- The four phases of team development are forming, storming, norming, and performing.
- Positive group behaviours include establishing and following rules, resolving differences, being supportive, praising others, and summarizing points of understanding.
- Negative behaviours include having contempt for others, wasting the team's time, and withdrawing.
- Successful teams are small and diverse, agree on a purpose and procedures, confront conflict, communicate well, don't compete but collaborate, are ethical, and share leadership.

2 Discuss effective practices and technologies for planning and participating in face-to-face meetings and virtual meetings.

- Before a meeting businesspeople determine its purpose and location, choose participants, use a digital calendar, and distribute an agenda.
- Experienced meeting leaders establish ground rules, move the meeting along, and confront any conflict; they end the meeting on time, make sure everyone is heard, and distribute meeting minutes promptly.
- Virtual meetings demand specific procedures to handle questions, noise, lack of media richness, and turn-taking. Because they are impersonal, virtual meetings benefit from building camaraderie and trust.

3 Explain and apply active listening techniques.

- Most of us are poor listeners; as untrained listeners, we are easily distracted.
- Career and organizational success depend on active listening.
- Effective listeners control distractions, show active involvement, separate facts from opinions, identify important facts, refrain from interrupting, ask clarifying questions, paraphrase, take advantage of lag time, take notes to ensure retention, and consider gender differences.

4 Understand how effective nonverbal communication can help you advance your career.

- Be aware of nonverbal cues, such as eye contact, facial expression, and posture, that send silent, highly believable messages.
- Understand that how you use time, space, and territory is interpreted by the receiver, who also reads the eye appeal of your business documents and your personal appearance.
- Build solid nonverbal skills by keeping eye contact, maintaining good posture, reducing physical barriers, improving your decoding skills, and probing for more information.
- Interpret nonverbal meanings in context, learn about other cultures, and understand the impact of appearance—of your documents, your office space, and yourself.

5 **Improve your competitive advantage by developing professionalism and business etiquette skills.**

- Professionalism, good business etiquette, developed soft skills, social intelligence, polish, and civility are desirable workplace behaviours that are complemented by a positive online presence.
- Essential career attributes are the ability to communicate, working well with others, solving problems, making ethical decisions, and appreciating diversity.
- Good workplace behaviour includes using polite words, giving sincere praise, respecting coworkers' space, rising above others' rudeness, taking the high road in conflict, and disagreeing agreeably.

Chapter Review

1. What are *soft skills*, and why are they increasingly important in the knowledge-based economy of the digital era? (Obj. 1)
2. Describe the four phases of team development in decision making. (Obj. 1)
3. What are virtual teams, and how can they reduce misunderstandings among participants? (Obj. 1)
4. List three ground rules for meetings. As part of your answer, discuss why it is important to establish these ground rules before the meeting. (Obj. 2)
5. What are the symptoms of groupthink? (Obj. 2)
6. Discuss five ways to achieve the best results during a virtual meeting. (Obj. 2)
7. According to experts, we ignore, forget, distort, or misunderstand 75 percent of everything we hear. Why are we such poor listeners? (Obj. 3)
8. List ten techniques for improving nonverbal communication skills in the workplace. Be prepared to discuss each. (Obj. 4)
9. What five specific behaviours do you think would be most important in giving you an etiquette edge in your business career? (Obj. 5)
10. List five unprofessional workplace behaviours that could put your career in jeopardy. (Obj. 6)

Critical Thinking

1. Author and teamwork critic Susan Cain claims that research "strongly suggests that people are more creative when they enjoy privacy and freedom from interruption." In her book *Quiet: The Power of Introverts in a World That Can't Stop Talking*, in articles, and public appearances, Cain cautions against the current emphasis on teamwork in the workplace. Cain cites studies by psychologists Mihaly Csikszentmihalyi and Gregory Feist, according to whom "the most spectacularly creative people in many fields are often introverted. . . . They are not joiners by nature."[66] How would you, as a critical thinker, respond to these statements? (Obj. 1)
2. What kinds of conflict could erupt during the storming phase of team development? Should conflict be avoided? Explain. (Obj. 2)
3. What workplace distractions contribute to poor listening? (Obj. 3)
4. What arguments could you give for or against the idea that body language is a science with principles that can be interpreted accurately by specialists? (Obj. 4)
5. **Ethical Issue:** After much discussion and even conflict, your workplace team has finally agreed on Plan B, but you are firmly convinced that Plan A is a much better option. Your team is presenting Plan B to the whole department and company executives are present. A vice president asks you for your opinion. Should you (a) keep your mouth shut, (b) try to persuade the team to adopt Plan A, (c) explain why you believe Plan A is a better plan, (d) tell the VP and all present that Plan B is not your idea, or (e) discuss one or two points you can agree on in Plan B?[67] (Objs. 1, 2, 5)

Activities

2.1 Soft Skills: Personal Strengths Inventory (Obj. 1)

Web

When hiring workers, employers look for hard skills, which are those we learn, such as mastery of software applications or accountancy procedures, and soft skills. Soft skills are personal characteristics, strengths, or other assets a person possesses. Studies have divided soft skills into four categories:

- Thinking and problem solving
- Oral and written communication
- Personal qualities and work ethic
- Interpersonal and teamwork

YOUR TASK Using the preceding categories to guide you, identify your own soft skills, paying attention to those attributes you think a potential employer would value. Prepare lists of at least four items in each of the four categories. For example, as evidence of problem solving, you might list a specific workplace or student problem you recognized and solved. You will want to weave these words and phrases into cover letters and résumés, which are covered in Chapter 15.

2.2 Resolving Workplace Conflicts: Apply a Plan (Obj. 1)

Team

Although conflict is a normal part of every workplace, if unresolved, it can create hard feelings and reduce productivity.

YOUR TASK Analyze the following scenarios. In teams discuss each scenario and apply the six-step procedure for dealing with conflict outlined in Figure 2.3. Choose two of the scenarios to role-play, with two of your team members taking roles.

a. Meghan, an accountant, cannot complete her report until Matt, a salesperson, provides her with all the necessary numbers and documentation. Meghan thinks that Matt is a procrastinator who forces her to deliver a rush job, thus causing her great stress and increasing the likelihood of error. Matt believes that Meghan is exerting pressure on both of them and setting unrealistic deadlines. As the conflict intensifies, productivity decreases.

b. The author of a lengthy report refuses to collaborate with a colleague on future projects because she believes that her colleague's review of her document was superficial, short, and essentially useless. The report author is angry at the lack of attention her 25-page paper received.

c. A manager and his assistant plan to attend a conference together at a resort location. Six weeks before the conference, the company announces a cutback and limits conference attendance to one person. The assistant, who has developed a presentation specifically for the conference, feels that he should be the one to attend. Travel arrangements must be made immediately.

2.3 Stand-Up Meetings: Keeping Business Meetings Short and Sweet (Obj. 2)

Communication Technology E-mail

Team

Here is an idea to shorten tedious meetings: Ban sitting down! A growing number of tech companies hold mandatory morning meetings in which nonwork chatter is frowned upon and all participants must stand. Called the huddle in one company and a daily scrum in another, these regular stand-up meetings last no longer than 15 minutes. At one company, if someone starts rambling, an employee holds up a rubber rat. A Microsoft development team determines the next speaker by tossing around a rubber chicken called Ralph. Other gimmicks include passing around a 4.5 kilogram (10 pound) medicine ball to literally keep the meeting moving. Other methods to speed up the proceedings include holding meetings just before lunch or gathering in cold stairwells.[68]

> It turns out that the practice of holding meetings standing up dates back to some military commanders in World War I. A researcher who conducted a study of stand-up meetings found that they were about a third shorter than sit-down meetings, and the quality of decision making did not suffer at all. A recent survey of more than 6,000 global tech workers found that 78 percent held daily stand-up meetings.[69]

YOUR TASK As a team, brainstorm all possible applications of quick stand-up meetings. What types of businesses could benefit from such meetings? How would you ensure on-time arrival, participation, and order during the meeting, and turn-taking? What type of sanctions would you impose for violations? If your instructor directs, write an e-mail to persuade your current or past boss to adopt stand-up meetings.

2.4 Listening: An In-Person or Virtual Social Media Interview (Obj. 3)

Communication Technology

Social Media Team

How much and to whom do businesspeople listen?

YOUR TASK Interview a businessperson about his or her workplace listening. Connect with a worker in your circle of friends, family, and acquaintances; in your campus network; at a prior or current job; or via LinkedIn or Facebook. Come up with questions to ask about listening—for example: (a) How much active listening do you practise daily? (b) To whom do you listen on the job? (c) How do you know that others are listening or not listening to you? (d) Can you share anecdotes of poor listening that led to negative outcomes? and (e) Do you have tips for better listening?

2.5 The Silent Language of Tattoos: How Much Self-Expression on the Job? (Obj. 4)

Team

Tattoos and piercings have gained in popularity among young Canadians over the last two decades. Recent findings by a Harris Poll and Pew Research Center suggest that nearly 40 percent of 18- to 29-year-olds and about one third of 30- to 45-year-olds sport tattoos. Even so, body art is still not universally accepted.[70]

Career expert Andrea Kay warns that acceptance among hiring managers varies by industry. She says that recruiters in the technology and retail fields may be more forgiving than those in banking and law. Tattoos and piercings send a strong message, and Kay cautions that if they make people at work uncomfortable, such decorations are detrimental. She has the following advice for job seekers: "People have adjusted their thinking in what is acceptable, but it still comes down to the impression you want to make on the people you're dealing with in your business."[71] Many workplaces today have policies covering body adornment, some requiring employees with customer contact to conceal such decorations.

YOUR TASK In teams or in class, discuss tattoos as a form of self-expression in the workplace. Gauge the attitudes toward tattoos and piercings in your class. Consider the limits to self-expression on the job. Think about casual clothing or blogging and tweeting about your employer. What is different? What are some of the similarities among these forms of self-expression? What types of nonverbal cues do body adornments send? Summarize your discussion orally or in an e-mail to your instructor. Alternatively, your instructor may ask you to post your responses to a Blackboard discussion board or some other forum that allows individual postings.

2.6 Business Etiquette: Breaking the Smartphone Habit in Meetings (Obj. 5)

Team

Increasingly, many professionals are tired of disruptions caused by smart phones during meetings. Nancy Flynn, executive director of the ePolicy Institute and author of *The Handbook of Social Media*, has this suggestion: "Require employees to turn off mobile devices during business-related meetings, seminars, conferences, luncheons and any other situation in which a ringing phone or tapping fingers are likely to disrupt proceedings or interrupt a speaker's or participant's train of thought."[72]

YOUR TASK Organizations are beginning to establish policies on smartphone use in meetings. Assume that your team has been asked to develop such a policy. Your boss would like your team to develop a one-page policy that includes a set of guidelines that spell out exactly how smart phones should and should not be used in the workplace.

Grammar and Mechanics | *Review 2*

Verbs

Review Guides 4 to 10 in Appendix B, Grammar and Mechanics Guide, beginning on page B-1. On a sheet of paper or on your computer, revise the following sentences to correct errors in verb use. For each error that you locate, write the guide number that deals with this usage. If a sentence is correct, write *C*. When you finish, compare your responses with the key in Appendix C.

EXAMPLE: If I was in charge, I would have handled the matter differently.

REVISION: If I were in charge, I would have handled the matter differently. [Guide 5]

1. Have you spoke with the other member of the virtual team?
2. During job interviews one of the most frequently requested soft skills are writing proficiency.
3. Jeremy said he wished he was president for just one day.
4. Better decisions and faster response time explains why companies are using teams.
5. Either the team leader or the manager are going to schedule the meeting.
6. Conflict and disagreement is normal and should be expected in team interactions.
7. Everything in the company's e-mails and written records were made public during the trial.
8. A committee of faculty and students are examining strategies to improve campus interviewing.
9. Each of the employees was given the opportunity to chose a team to join.
10. When two candidates have equal qualifications, the one who appears to be more polished and professional is more likely to be hired and promoted.

Notes

[1] Makivik Corporation. (2019). *Corporate*. https://www.makivik.org/corporate/

[2] First Air. (2019). *Executives & ownership*. https://firstair.ca/about/executives-ownership/

[3] First Air. (2019). *Media kit*. https://firstair.ca/about/media-kit/

[4] First Air. (2019, July 10). *First Air and Canadian North embark on transformative journey to build strong, unified new Northern airline*. https://firstair.ca/about/latest-news/

[5] First Air. (2019, July 10). *First Air and Canadian North embark on transformative journey to build strong, unified new Northern airline*. https://firstair.ca/about/latest-news/

[6] Canadian North. (2020, June). About Canadian North. https://canadiannorth.com/about/our-mission/

[7] Conference Board of Canada. (2016). Employability Skills 2000+. http://www.conferenceboard.ca/Libraries/EDUC_PUBLIC/esp2000.sflb

[8] Lechner, A. (2012, April 18). Better teamwork through better workplace design. *Harvard Business Review*. http://blogs.hbr.org/cs/2012/04/better_teamwork_through_office.html

[9] Hewitt, A. (2016, March). *Developing Canada's future workforce: A survey of large private-sector employers*. Business Council of Canada. http://thebusinesscouncil.ca/wp-content/uploads/2016/03/Developing-Canadas-Future-Workforce.pdf

[10] Cain, S. (2012, January 13). The rise of the new groupthink. *New York Times*. http://www.nytimes.com/2012/01/15/opinion/sunday/the-rise-of-the-new-groupthink.html?pagewanted=all

[11] Marowits, R. (2016, May 23). *Telecommuting growing as companies look to save money, respond to employees*. CBC News. https://www.cbc.ca/news/business/telecommuting-growing-as-companies-look-to-save-money-respond-to-employees-1.3596420

[12] Weikle, B. (2018, November 4). *Telecommuting on the rise to meet challenges of real estate market, labour shortage*. CBC News. https://www.cbc.ca/news/business/telecommuting-on-rise-1.4887564

[13] Discussion of Tuckman's model based on Robbins, H. A., & Finley, M. (1995). *Why teams don't work*. Peterson's/Pacesetter Books, Chapter 22.

[14] CBC News. (2011, June 7). *"Groupthink" cited in concert cash audit*. http://www.cbc.ca/news/canada/nova-scotia/groupthink-cited-in-concert-cash-audit-1.985178

[15] Discussion of conflict and groupthink based on Toledo, R. (2008, June). *Conflict is everywhere*. PM Network. http://search.ebscohost.com; McNamara, P. (2003, August/September). Conflict resolution strategies. *OfficePro*, p. 25; Weiss, W. (2002, November). Building and managing teams. *SuperVision*, p. 19; Eisenhardt, K. (1997, July/August). How management teams can have a good fight. *Harvard Business Review*, pp. 77–85; Brockmann, E. (1996, May). Removing the paradox of conflict from group decisions. *Academy of Management Executives*, pp. 61–62; Beebe, S., & Masterson, J. (1999). *Communicating in small groups*. New York: Longman, pp. 198–200.

[16] Emory University neuroscientist Gregory Berns quoted in Cain, S. (2012, January 13). The rise of the new groupthink. *New York Times*. http://www.nytimes.com/2012/01/15/opinion/sunday/the-rise-of-the-new-groupthink.html?pagewanted=all

[17] J. Richard Hackman quoted in Coutu, D. (2009, May). Why teams don't work. *Harvard Business Review, 87*(5), 105. http://search.ebscohost.com

[18] Janis, I. L. (1982). *Groupthink: Psychological studies on policy decisions and fiascos*. Houghton Mifflin. See also Miranda, S. M., & Saunders, C. (1995, Summer). Group support systems: An organization development intervention to combat groupthink. *Public Administration Quarterly, 19*, 193–216. http://search.ebscohost.com

[19] Amason, A. C., Hochwarter, W. A., Thompson, K. R., & Harrison, A. W. (1995, Autumn). Conflict: An important dimension in successful management teams. *Organizational Dynamics, 24*, 1. http://search.ebscohost.com

[20] Holtzman, Y., & Anderberg, J. (2011). Diversify your teams and collaborate: Because great minds don't think alike. *Journal of Management Development, 30*(1), 79. https://doi.org/10.1108/02621711111098389; Katzenbach, J., & Smith, D. (1994). *Wisdom of teams*. New York: HarperBusiness, p. 45.

[21] Global Affairs Canada. (2017). *Cultural information—conversations*. https://www.international.gc.ca/cil-cai/country_insights-apercus_pays/ci-ic_ca.aspx?lang=eng#cn-10

[22] Phillips, A. (2012, May 9). *Wasted time in meetings costs the UK economy £26 billion*. http://www.businessrevieweurope.eu/business_leaders/wasted-time-in-meetings-costs-the-uk-economy-26-billion; Herring, H. B. (2006, June 18). Endless meetings: The black holes of the workday. *New York Times*. http://www.nytimes.com

[23] Rogelberg, S. G., Shanock, L. R., & Scott, C. W. (2012). Wasted time and money in meetings: Increasing return on investment. *Small Group Research, 43*(2), 237. https://doi.org/10.1177/1046496411429170

[24] Rogelberg, S. G., Shanock, L. R., & Scott, C. W. (2012). Wasted time and money in meetings: Increasing return on investment. *Small Group Research, 43*(2), 237. https://doi.org/10.1177/1046496411429170

[25] Wuorio, J. (2010). *8 ways to show speaking skills in a meeting*. Microsoft Business. http://www.microsoft.com/business/en-us/resources/management/leadership-training/8-ways-to-show-speaking-skills-in-a-meeting.aspx?fbid=O3xpKd4lO4M

[26] Axtell, P. (2018, June 22). The most productive meetings have fewer than 8 people. *Harvard Business Review*. https://hbr.org/2018/06/the-most-productive-meetings-have-fewer-than-8-people

[27] Based on Egan, M. (2006, March 13). Meetings can make or break your career. *Insurance Advocate, 117*, 24.

[28] Global Affairs Canada. (2017). *Cultural information—Communication style*. https://www.international.gc.ca/cil-cai/country_insights-apercus_pays/ci-ic_ca.aspx?lang=eng#cn-10

[29] Murray, K. (2015, April 16). *Reflecting on death: First Nations people*. Life and Death Matters. https://www.lifeanddeathmatters.ca/reflecting-on-death-first-nations-people/

[30] Lohr, S. (2008, July 22). As travel costs rise, more meetings go virtual. *New York Times*. http://www.nytimes.com

[31] King, I. (2020, March 24). *Cisco sees demand surge for Webex, Zoom's larger rival*. Bloomberg. https://www.bloomberg.com/news/articles/2020-03-23/cisco-sees-video-demand-surge-for-webex-zoom-s-larger-rival

[32] King, I. (2020, March 24). *Cisco sees demand surge for Webex, Zoom's larger rival*. Bloomberg. https://www.bloomberg.com/news/articles/2020-03-23/cisco-sees-video-demand-surge-for-webex-zoom-s-larger-rival

[33] Schlegel, J. (2012). *Running effective meetings: Types of meetings*. Salary.com. http://www.salary.com/runningeffectivemeetings-6; Cohen, M. A., Rogelberg, S. G. Allen, J. A., & Luong, A. (2011). Meeting design characteristics and attendee perceptions of staff/team meeting quality. *Group Dynamics: Theory, Research, and Practice, 15*(1), 100–101; Schindler, E. (2008, February 15). *Running an effective teleconference or virtual meeting*. CIO. http://www.cio.com. See also Brenowitz, R. S. (2004, May). Virtual meeting etiquette. *Innovative Leader*, Article 601. http://www.winstonbrill.com

[34] *Time zones in Canada*. (2017). https://www.timeanddate.com/time/zone/canada

[35] Tips on meetings: Two rules for making global meetings work. (2011, April 11). *Harvard Business Review*. http://hbr.org/web/management-tip/tips-on-meetings

[36] Fox, J. (2014, October 8). Why virtual conferences will not replace face-to-face meetings. *International Meetings Review*. http://www.internationalmeetingsreview.com/research-education/why-virtual-conferences-will-not-replace-face-face-meetings-100145

[37] Daigle, T. (2020, May 27). *"Zoom fatigue" is setting in: What it is and how to prevent it*. CBC News. https://www.cbc.ca/news/technology/zoom-fatigue-is-setting-in-1.5585933

[38] Rowh, M. (2006, April/May). Listen up! Tune out distractions, and tune in to people. Here's how listening skills help lead to success. *Career World, 34*(6), 22. http://search.ebscohost.com; Robbins, H., & Finley, M. (1995). *Why teams don't work*. Peterson's/Pacesetter Books, p. 123.

[39] Pellet, J. (2003, April). Anatomy of a turnaround guru. *Chief Executive*, 41; Mounter, P. (2003). Global internal communication: A model. *Journal of Communication Management, 3*, 265; Feiertag, H. (2002, July 15). Listening skills, enthusiasm top list of salespeople's best traits. *Hotel and Motel Management*, 20; Goby, V. P., & Lewis, J. H. (2000, June). The key role of listening in business: A study of the Singapore insurance industry. *Business Communication Quarterly, 63*, 41–51; Cooper, L. O. (1997, December). Listening competency in the workplace: A model for training. *Business Communication Quarterly, 60*, 75–84; Penley, L. E., Alexander, E. R., Jerigan, I. E., & Henwood, C. I. (1997). Communication abilities of managers: The relationship to performance. *Journal of Management, 17*, 57–76.

[40] Harris, T. W. (1989, June). Listen carefully. *Nation's Business*, p. 78.

[41] Steil, L. K., Barker, L. I., & Watson, K. W. (1983). *Effective listening: Key to your success*. Addison-Wesley; Harris, J. A. (1998, August). Hear what's really being said. *New Zealand Management, 45*, 18.

[42] Nelson, E., & Gypen, J. (1979, September/October). The subordinate's predicament. *Harvard Business Review*, 133.

[43] International Listening Association. (2009). Listening and speech rates. http://www.listen.org

[44] Statistics Canada. (2016). *Immigrant languages in Canada*. https://www150.statcan.gc.ca/n1/en/pub/11-627-m/11-627-m2017025-eng.pdf?st=JXRfoKdw

[45] BMO Wealth Management. (2018, July). *The gig economy: Achieving financial wellness with confidence*. https://www.bmo.com/assets/pdfs/wealth/bmo_gig_economy_report_en.pdf

[46] Statistics Canada. (2016). *Immigrant languages in Canada*. https://www150.statcan.gc.ca/n1/en/pub/11-627-m/11-627-m2017025-eng.pdf?st=JXRfoKdw

[47] Wolvin, A., & Coakley, C. G. (1996). *Listening* (5th ed.). McGraw-Hill, pp. 136–137.

[48] Effective communication. (1994, November). *Training Tomorrow*, 32–33.

[49] Wood, J. T. (2003). *Gendered lives: Communication, gender, and culture* (5th ed.). Wadsworth, pp. 119–120; Anderson, K. J., & Leaper, C. (1998, August). Meta-analyses of gender effects on conversational interruption: Who, what, when, where, and how. *Sex Roles: A Journal of Research*, 225; Booth-Butterfield, M. (1984). She hears: What they hear and why. *Personnel Journal, 44*, 39.

[50] Tear, J. (1995, November 20). They just don't understand gender dynamics. *Wall Street Journal*, p. A12; Wolfe, A. (1994, December 12). She just doesn't understand. *New Republic*, 26–34.

[51] Burgoon, J., Coker, D., & Coker, R. (1986). Communication explanations. *Human Communication Research*, 463–494.

[52] Indigenous Corporate Training, Inc. (2012, April 11). *Eye contact and aboriginal peoples*. https://www.ictinc.ca/blog/eye-contact-and-aboriginal-peoples

[53] Birdwhistel, R. (1970). *Kinesics and context*. University of Pennsylvania Press.

[54] Global Affairs Canada. (2017). *Cultural information—Conflicts in the workplace*. https://www.international.gc.ca/cil-cai/country_insights-apercus_pays/ci-ic_ca.aspx?lang=eng#cn-10

[55] Global Affairs Canada. (2017). *Cultural information—Conflicts in the workplace*. https://www.international.gc.ca/cil-cai/country_insights-apercus_pays/ci-ic_ca.aspx?lang=eng#cn-10

[56] Finney, P. (2007, October 23). Redefining business casual. *New York Times*. http://search.ebscohost.com. See also Osterman, R. (2006, March 20). Casual loses its cool in business: More employers are trying to tighten up workplace clothing standards. *Sacramento Bee*. http://search.ebscohost.com; Business casual: Out of style? (2005, May). *HR Focus*, 9. http://search.ebscohost.com

[57] Wilkie, H. (2003, Fall). Professional presence. *Canadian Manager*, 14; Kaplan-Leiserson, L. (2000, November). Casual dress/back to business attire. *Training & Development*, 38–39.

[58] Kennedy, M. M. (1997, September–October). Is business casual here to stay? *Executive Female*, 31.

[59] Wood, N., & Benitez, T. (2003, April). Does the suit fit? *Incentive*, p. 31.

[60] Business casual out of style. (2005, May). *HR Focus, 82*, 16. http://search.ebscohost.com; Egodigwe, L. (2003, March). Here come the suits. *Black Enterprise, 33*, 59. http://search.ebscohost.com; Summerson, C. (2002, November 18). The suit is back in business. *BusinessWeek*, p. 130.

[61] Mitchell, G. A., Skinner, L. B., & White, B. J. (2010). Essential soft skills for success in the twenty first-century workforce as perceived by business educators. *The Delta Pi Epsilon Journal, 52*(1). http://www.faqs.org/periodicals/201001/2036768821.html

[62] McEwen, B. C. (2010). Cross-cultural and international career exploration and employability skills. *National Business Education Association Yearbook 2010: Cross-Cultural and International Business Education, 48*, 142.

[63] Chao, L. (2006, January 17). Not-so-nice costs. *Wall Street Journal*, p. B1.

[64] Valberg, M. [@planethopecanada]. (2020, June 6). This is Captain Peter Black and flight attendant Veronica Vasquez [Photograph]. Instagram. https://www.instagram.com/p/CBF_OgAlo-A/

[65] Canadian North. (2020, March). *An update on our response to the Coronavirus (COVID-19)*. https://canadiannorth.com/coronavirus/

[66] Cain, S. (2012, January 13). The rise of the new groupthink. *New York Times*. http://www.nytimes.com/2012/01/15/opinion/sunday/the-rise-of-the-new-groupthink.html?pagewanted=all

[67] Based on Worth, R. (Ed.). (2004). *Professional ethics and etiquette* (2nd ed.). Ferguson.

[68] Silverman, R. E. (2012, February 2). No more angling for the best seat; more meetings are stand-up jobs. *Wall Street Journal*. http://www.wsj.com/articles/SB10001424052970204652904577193460472598378

[69] Silverman, R. E. (2012, February 2). No more angling for the best seat; more meetings are stand-up jobs. *Wall Street Journal*. http://www.wsj.com/articles/SB10001424052970204652904577193460472598378

[70] Scenario based on Greenblatt, A. (2014, February 21). *Job seekers still have to hide tattoos (from the neck up)*. National Public Radio. http://www.npr.org/2014/02/21/280213268/job-seekers-still-have-to-hide-tattoos-from-the-neck-up; Schepp, D. (2010, July 26). *People@work: How to job hunt with tattoos*. DailyFinance.com. http://www.dailyfinance.com/story/careers/ tattoos-job-hunt-interviews-career/19566567

[71] Schepp, D. (2010, July 26). *People@work: How to job hunt with tattoos*. DailyFinance.com. http://www.dailyfinance.com/ story/careers/tattoos-job-hunt-interviews-career/19566567

[72] O'Brien Coffey, J. (2011, September). How to manage smartphones at meetings. *Executive Travel Magazine*. http://www.executivetravelmagazine.com/articles/how-to-manage-smartphones-at-meetings

Intercultural Communication

CHAPTER 3

Ariel Skelley/DigitalVision/Getty Images

LEARNING OBJECTIVES

After studying this chapter, you should be able to

1 Understand the powerful effects of globalization and the major trends fuelling it.

2 Define *culture*, name its primary characteristics, and explain the five key dimensions of culture.

3 Discuss strategies for enhancing intercultural effectiveness and communication techniques.

4 Explain the advantages and challenges of workforce diversity, and address approaches for improving communication among diverse workplace audiences.

SPOTLIGHT ON COMMUNICATION: PART 1

Federation of Black Canadians

The Federation of Black Canadians (FBC) was established in 2017 to affect change across Canada. FBC is a nonprofit organization that collaborates with other organizations to advance "the social, economic, political and cultural interests of Canadians of African descent."[1] Through identifying challenges that Black Canadians experience, the FBC aims to create conversations and opportunities for growth:[2]

Christina Morillo

> Black communities across Canada are diverse, resilient, creative, and multifaceted. For the first time in Canada's history, there are over 1,000,000 Black Canadians who call Canada home. With that number projected to double by 2036, the Federation of Black Canadians is working hard to partner with people and organizations across Canada to advance the interests of Black Canadians. We want to ensure that as our communities grow, we unlock the opportunities that will help build a promising future, building on and celebrating our diverse heritages, histories, cultures, and contributions to Canada.[3]

FBC's priorities are health, economic security, the addressing of anti-Black racism, community building, higher education, and criminal justice reform.[4] Through its work FBC addresses systemic barriers in order to build stronger communities and opportunities for youth and families.[5]

CRITICAL THINKING

- What challenges do Black Canadians face in our society? How can organizations like FBC make a difference in their lives?
- For the Federation of Black Canadians to grow as an organization, it needs to establish partnerships with other organizations and communities across Canada. What characteristics and dimensions of culture need to be considered when establishing partnerships across different cultures and subcultures?

LEARNING OBJECTIVE 1

Understand the powerful effects of globalization and the major trends fuelling it.

The Growing Importance of Intercultural Communication

The *global village* predicted many years ago is here, making intercultural communication skills ever more important. You may face intercultural differences in your current or future jobs. Your employers, coworkers, or customers could very well be from other countries and cultures. You may travel abroad for your employer or on your own. Learning more about the powerful effect that culture has on behaviour will help you reduce friction and misunderstanding in your dealings with people from other cultures. Before examining strategies for helping you overcome intercultural obstacles, let's take a closer look at globalization and the trends fuelling it.

In MindTap, go to "Chapter Overview: Intercultural Communication" in Chapter 3 and watch it now.

Markets Go Global

Doing business beyond borders is now commonplace. Not only are Canadian businesses expanding their markets beyond our borders, but acquisitions, mergers, alliances, and buyouts are also obscuring the nationality of many companies.

To succeed in today's interdependent global village, multinational companies are increasingly finding it necessary to adapt to other cultures. Even a locally successful company like Tim Hortons has expanded its franchise to overseas markets. Its newest store opened in Shanghai, China, where the market is poised for growth.[6]

But for overseas expansion to thrive, several factors must be considered.

Major Trends Fuel Globalization

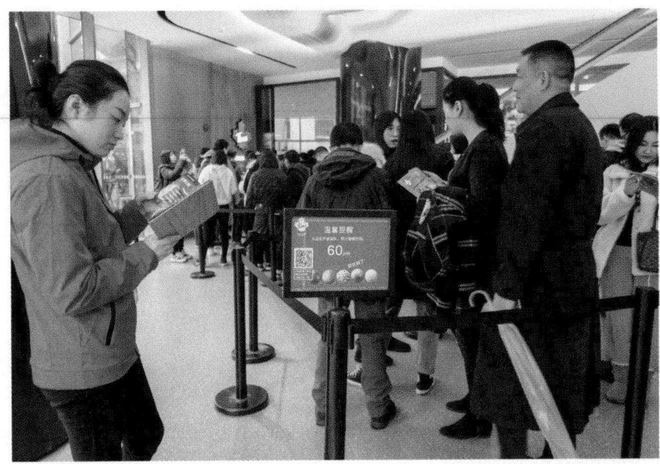
Imaginechina Limited/Alamy Stock Photo

In 2019 Tim Hortons opened its first store in China. Tim Hortons already has chains in the Philippines, United States, Middle East, Scotland, England, and Wales.[7] How can a company like Tim Hortons maintain its Canadian identity while pursuing the global market?

Why are Canadian businesses and those of other countries rushing to expand around the world? What is causing this dash toward the globalization of markets and blurring of national identities? Many companies are increasingly looking overseas as domestic markets mature. They can no longer expect double-digit sales growth at home. As summarized in Figure 3.1, aside from shrinking domestic markets, several trends fuel global expansion, including favourable trade agreements, growing numbers of middle-class consumers in emerging nations, transportation advancements, and increasingly sophisticated information and communication technologies.

Favourable Trade Agreements. A significant factor in the expansion of global markets is the passage of favourable trade agreements. In 2018 the new Canada-United States-Mexico Agreement (CUSMA) was signed, which replaced the North American Free Trade Agreement (NAFTA). This new agreement will continue to strengthen the economies between Canada, the United States, and Mexico.[8] Additional trade agreements significantly open global markets to imports and exports.

An Emerging Global Middle Class. Parts of the world formerly considered developing now boast robust middle classes. Once known only for cheap labour, many countries with emerging economies are now seen as promising consumer markets. Estimates suggest that 70 percent of world growth over the next few years will come from emerging

FIGURE 3.1 Trends Fuelling Globalization

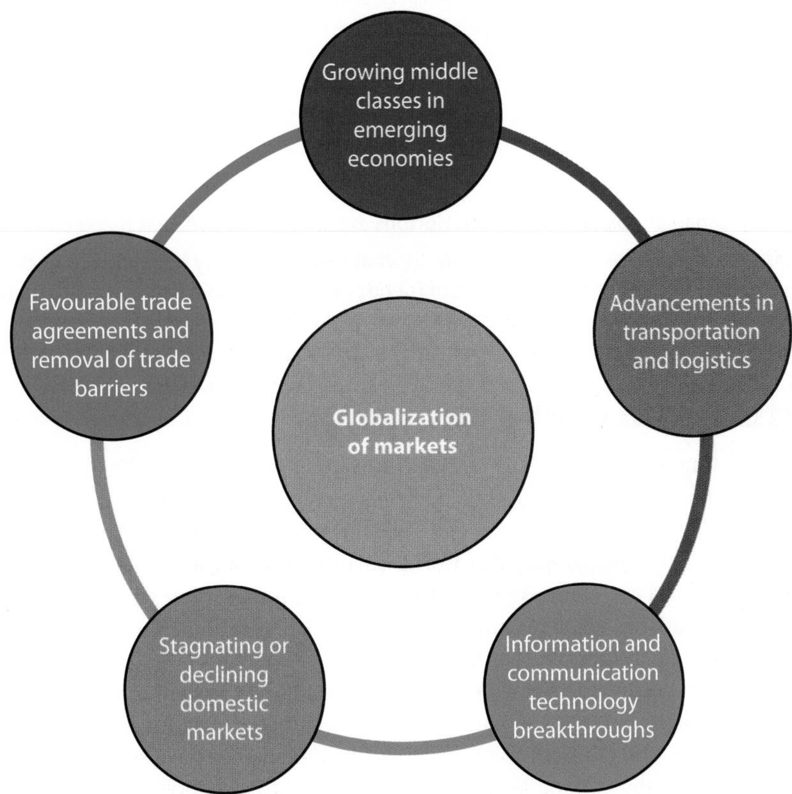

markets. By 2030 the global middle class will more than double, from 2 billion today to 4.9 billion, two thirds of whom will reside in the Asia-Pacific region.[9]

Check out section 3-1b in MindTap, where you can watch a video featuring Léonicka Valcius, a book publishing professional, discuss the importance of communicating with clients overseas.

Advancements in Transportation and Logistics. Amazing advancements in transportation and logistics technology are major contributors to the development of our global interconnectivity. Supersonic planes carry goods and passengers to other continents overnight and are so fast and reliable that most of the world is becoming an open market.

Breakthroughs in transportation technology also push the drive toward globalization. For example, digital wireless sensor telemetry keeps shippers informed of vital information en route.[10] Senders can track the destination, the speed of movement, and even the temperature of a shipment's environment.

Growing Reach of Information and Communication Technologies. Probably the most significant factor fuelling globalization is the development of information and communication technologies. These technologies have changed the way we live and do business with the help of the Internet, wireless networks, smartphones, mobile electronic devices, and other communication media. High-speed, high-capacity, and relatively low-cost communications have opened new global opportunities that make geographic location virtually irrelevant for many activities and services.

Domestic Workforce Is Becoming Increasingly Diverse

As world commerce mingles more and more, another trend gives intercultural communication importance: people are on the move. Lured by the prospects of peace, prosperity, education, or a fresh start, people from many cultures are moving to countries promising to fulfill their dreams. For generations the two most popular destinations have been Canada and the United States.

Cultural diversity is increasingly the norm. As Canada's multiethnic neighbourhoods, multinational companies, and intercultural workforce grow, we can expect some changes to happen smoothly. Other changes will involve conflict and resentment, especially for people losing their positions of power and privilege. Learning to accommodate and manage intercultural change is an important part of the education of any business communicator.

Concept Check

1. Why are Canadian companies like Tim Hortons expanding into overseas markets?
2. Consider the social media you use daily. In what ways could they help you connect with people outside your immediate circle of friends or family, people from other, perhaps unfamiliar cultures? Would you find it useful?

LEARNING OBJECTIVE 2

Define *culture,* name its primary characteristics, and explain the five key dimensions of culture.

Culture and Communication

Comprehending the verbal and nonverbal meanings of a message is difficult even when communicators share the same culture. When they come from different cultures, special sensitivity and skills are necessary. True, global business, new communication technologies, the Internet, and social media span the world, shrinking distances. However, cultural differences still exist and can cause significant misunderstandings, even within our own country. According to Statistics Canada, in addition to English and French, Canadians speak more than 200 languages as their mother tongue.[11]

For our purposes, *culture* may be defined as the complex system of values, traits, morals, and customs shared by a society. Culture is a powerful operating force that moulds the way we think, behave, and communicate. Even within Canada, we have subcultures of different traditions, beliefs, and colloquialisms. The objective of this chapter is to broaden your view of culture and open your mind to flexible attitudes so that you can avoid frustration when cultural adjustment is necessary.

Characteristics of Culture

Consider how culture in Canada varies across provinces and territories. Canada is a bilingual country, and Québec, the only majority-French-speaking province, has its own proud heritage.[12] Canada is also culturally rich with Indigenous (First Nations, Métis, and Inuit) communities.[13] Every county or region within a country has a unique common heritage, joint experience, or shared learning. This shared background creates the culture of a region, country, or society.

Despite globalization, interculturalism, and extensive social networking, we should expect to make adjustments and adopt new attitudes. However, first we must understand some basic characteristics of culture.

Culture Is Learned. The rules, values, and attitudes of a culture are learned and passed down from generation to generation. For example, in many Middle Eastern and some Asian cultures, same-sex people may walk hand in hand in the street, but opposite-sex people may not do so. In Arab cultures conversations are sometimes held nose to nose. However, in Western cultures if a person stands too close, one may react as if violated. Cultural rules of behaviour learned from your family and society are conditioned from early childhood.

Cultures Are Inherently Logical. The rules in any culture reinforce that culture's values and beliefs. They act as normative forces. Although current cultural behaviour may not always make sense to you, nearly all serious rules and values originate in deep-seated beliefs. Rules about exposing teeth or how close to stand are linked to values about sexuality, aggression, modesty, and respect. Acknowledging the inherent logic of a culture is extremely important when encountering behaviour that differs from one's own cultural norms.

Culture Is the Basis of Self-Identity and Community. Culture is the basis for how we tell the world who we are and what we believe. People build their identities through cultural overlays to their primary culture. When Canadians make choices in education, career, place of employment, and life partner, they consider certain rules, manners, ceremonies, beliefs, languages, and values. These considerations add to their total cultural outlook and are major expressions of their self-identity.

Culture Combines the Visible and Invisible. To outsiders, the way we act—those things that we do in daily life and work—are the most visible parts of our culture. On the surface we recognize numerous signs of culture, including the words we use, our body language and gestures, the way we dress, and our outward behaviour. Under the surface, however, lie unspoken rules governing what is seen. These unspoken and often unconscious rules are determined by our beliefs and values, attitudes and biases, feelings and fears, and upbringing. The invisible structure of culture vastly outweighs the visible, as illustrated by the iceberg concept shown in Figure 3.2.

Culture Is Dynamic. Over time cultures change. Changes are caused by advancements in technology and communication, as discussed earlier. Local differences are modified or slowly erased. Change is also caused by events such as migration, natural disasters, and wars. One major event in this country was the exodus of people from farms. When families moved to cities, major changes occurred in the way family members interacted. Attitudes, behaviours, and beliefs change in open societies more quickly than in closed societies.

ETHICS CHECK

Cultural Change: From Sexist to Gender-Neutral Language

Changes in language now dictate gender neutrality to avoid stereotyping. In business, the honorific *Ms.* is used for all women, regardless of their marital status. More recently, the gender-neutral honorific *Mx.* has become more widely accepted.[14] Does language reflect just the current culture, or does it have the power to effect change?

Dimensions of Culture

The more you know about culture in general and your own culture in particular, the better you will be able to adopt an intercultural perspective. In this book, it is impossible to describe fully the infinite facets of culture, but we can outline some key dimensions of culture identified by social scientists.

FIGURE 3.2 Culture Combines the Visible and Invisible

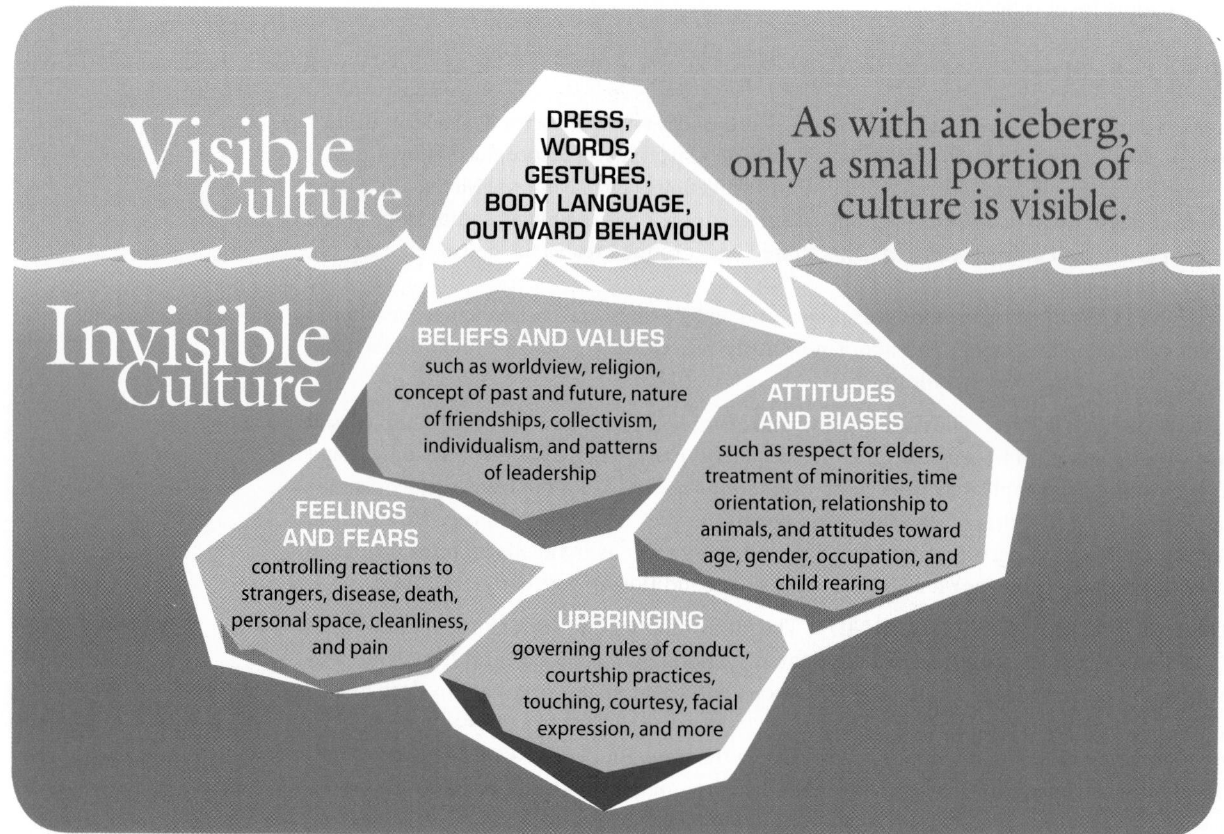

So that you will better understand your culture and how it contrasts with other cultures, we will describe five key dimensions of culture: context, individualism, time orientation, power distance, and communication style.

High and Low Context. Context is probably the most important cultural dimension and also the most difficult to define. It is a concept developed by cultural anthropologist Edward T. Hall. In his model context refers to the stimuli, environment, or ambience surrounding an event.

- **Low-context.** Communicators in low-context cultures (such as those in North America, Scandinavia, and Germany) depend little on the context of a situation and shared experience to convey their meaning. They assume that messages must be explicit, and listeners rely exclusively on the written or spoken word.
- **High-context.** In high-context cultures (such as those in Japan, China, and Middle Eastern countries), much is left unsaid because the listener is assumed to be already "contexted" and does not require much background information.[15] To identify low- and high-context countries, Hall arranged them on a continuum, as shown in Figure 3.3.[16]

Low-context cultures tend to be logical, analytical, and action oriented. Business communicators stress clearly articulated messages that they consider to be objective, professional, and efficient. High-context cultures are more likely to be intuitive and contemplative. Communicators in high-context cultures pay attention to more than the spoken or written words. They emphasize interpersonal relationships, nonverbal expression, physical setting, and social setting. Thus, in high-context cultures communication cues are transmitted by posture, voice inflection, gestures, and facial expression. Establishing relationships is an important part of communicating and interacting.

FIGURE 3.3 Comparing Low- and High-Context Cultures

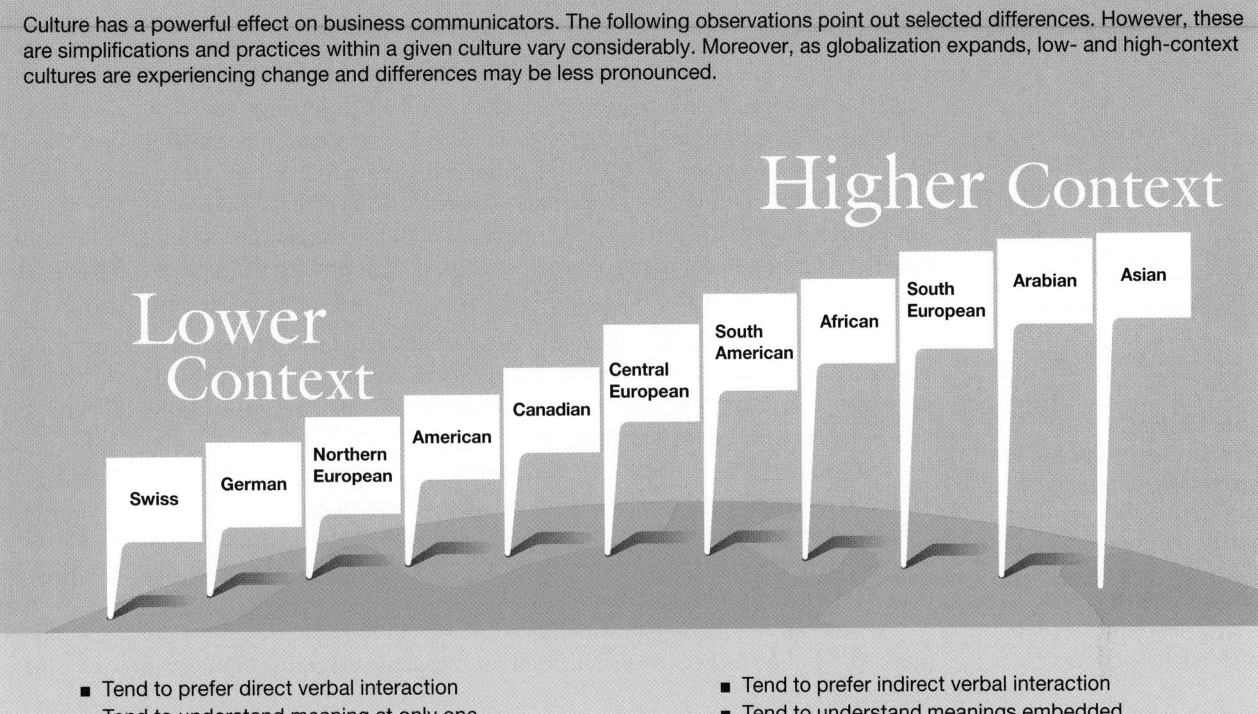
Culture has a powerful effect on business communicators. The following observations point out selected differences. However, these are simplifications and practices within a given culture vary considerably. Moreover, as globalization expands, low- and high-context cultures are experiencing change and differences may be less pronounced.
Higher Context
Lower Context
Swiss
German
Northern European
American
Canadian
Central European
South American
African
South European
Arabian
Asian

- Tend to prefer direct verbal interaction
- Tend to understand meaning at only one sociocultural level
- Are generally less proficient in reading nonverbal cues
- Value individualism
- Rely more on logic
- Say *no* directly
- Communicate in highly structured, detailed messages with literal meanings
- Give authority to written information

- Tend to prefer indirect verbal interaction
- Tend to understand meanings embedded at many sociocultural levels
- Are generally more proficient in reading nonverbal cues
- Value group membership
- Rely more on context and feeling
- Talk around point, avoid saying *no*
- Communicate in sometimes simple, sometimes ambiguous messages
- Understand visual messages readily

In terms of thinking patterns, low-context communicators tend to use *linear logic*. They proceed from Point A to Point B to Point C and finally arrive at a conclusion. High-context communicators, however, may use *spiral logic*, circling around a topic indirectly and looking at it from many tangential or divergent viewpoints. A conclusion may be implied but not argued directly.

Individualism and Collectivism. An attitude of independence and freedom from control characterizes individualism. Members of low-context cultures, particularly North Americans, tend to value individualism. They believe that initiative and self-assertion result in personal achievement. They believe in individual action and personal responsibility, and they desire a large degree of freedom in their personal lives.

Members of high-context cultures are more collectivist. They emphasize membership in organizations, groups, and teams; they encourage acceptance of group values, duties, and decisions. They typically resist independence because it fosters competition and confrontation instead of consensus. In group-oriented cultures, self-assertion and individual decision making are discouraged. Business decisions are often made by all who have competence in the matter under discussion. Many cultures, of course, are quite complex and cannot be characterized as totally individualistic or group oriented.[17]

Time Orientation. North Americans consider time a precious commodity to be conserved. They correlate time with productivity, efficiency, and money. Keeping people waiting for business appointments is considered a waste of time and also rude. In other cultures time may be perceived as an unlimited and never-ending resource to be enjoyed. Basic concepts of time can make international mergers more difficult.

Power Distance. One important element of culture is power distance, a concept first introduced by influential social psychologist Geert Hofstede. The Power Distance Index measures how people in different societies cope with inequality and how they relate to more powerful individuals. In high-power-distance countries, subordinates expect formal hierarchies and embrace relatively authoritarian, paternalistic power relationships. In low-power-distance cultures, however, subordinates consider themselves as equals of their supervisors. They confidently voice opinions and participate in decision making. Relationships between high-powered individuals and people with little power tend to be more democratic, egalitarian, and informal.[18]

CENGAGE

MINDTAP

Go to section 3-2b in MindTap, where you can watch a video featuring Jarrod Hann, VP sales, Xello, discuss the importance of appreciating culture differences when establishing contracts with international partners.

Communication Style. People in low- and high-context cultures tend to communicate differently with words. For example, many North Americans tend to take words literally, whereas South Americans sometimes speak with extravagant or poetic figures of speech that may be misinterpreted if taken literally.[19]

In communication style North Americans value straightforwardness, are suspicious of evasiveness, and distrust people who might have a "hidden agenda."[20] North Americans also tend to be uncomfortable with silence and impatient with delays. Some overseas businesspeople have learned that the longer they drag out negotiations, the more concessions impatient North Americans are likely to make.

As you can see, high-context cultures differ from low-context cultures in many dimensions. These differences can be significant for companies engaging in international business.

Concept Check

1. What are the differences between visible and invisible culture?
2. If you live in Summerside, Prince Edward Island, and have a conference call scheduled with a prospective business partner in Yellowknife, Northwest Territories, how might you prepare?

LEARNING OBJECTIVE 3

Discuss strategies for enhancing intercultural effectiveness and communication techniques.

Becoming Interculturally Proficient

Being aware of your own culture and how it contrasts with others is an important first step in achieving intercultural proficiency. Another step involves recognizing barriers to intercultural accommodation and striving to overcome them. Some of these barriers occur quite naturally and require conscious effort to surmount. Becoming interculturally competent will make your personal life more satisfying and your work life more productive, gratifying, and effective.

Strategies for Improving Your Intercultural Effectiveness

Remember that culture is learned. Developing cultural competence often involves changing attitudes. Through exposure to other cultures and through training, such as you are receiving in this course, you can learn new attitudes and behaviours that help bridge gaps between cultures. The following are some suggestions to help you boost your intercultural savvy.

Building Cultural Self-Awareness. Begin to think of yourself as a product of your culture, and understand that your culture is just one among many. Try to stand outside and look at yourself. Do you see any reflex reactions and automatic thought patterns that are a result of your upbringing? These may be invisible to you until challenged by difference. Remember, your culture was designed to help you succeed and survive in a certain environment. Be sure to keep what works and yet be ready to adapt as environments change. Flexibility is an important survival skill.

Recognizing Canadian Subcultures. Many subcultures exist within Canada—between provinces and territories, urban and rural communities within the same region, and even within the same city. A *subculture* is defined as "an ethnic, regional, economic, or social group exhibiting characteristic patterns of behavior sufficient to distinguish it from others within an embracing culture or society."[21] Many subculture traits are evident in the language we use. The following are examples of slang and terms used across Canada.

- **Canadian regional slang.** If you haven't travelled across Canada, you might be surprised to learn that slang varies widely across the country. Bypassing can occur if you aren't familiar with differences in Canadian regional slang. For example, while most of Canada refers to a hooded sweatshirt as a *hoodie*, people in Saskatchewan refer to it as a *bunnyhug*. And while most Canadians would refer to a bad mood as being *cranky*, residents of Newfoundland and Labrador use the word *crooked*.[22]

- **Canadian terms.** Terms can differ across the country as well. The terms *cabin* and *cottage* are used to describe a summer home in most of Canada; however, in northern Ontario it is called a *camp*, in Québec it is called a *chalet*, and in Cape Breton it is called a *bungalow*. While the terms *grades* and *marks* are both widely used in Canada, residents of British Columbia and Québec strongly prefer *grades*, while residents of Newfoundland and Labrador prefer *marks*.[23]

Curbing Ethnocentrism. The belief in the superiority of one's own race is known as *ethnocentrism*, a natural attitude inherent in all cultures. If you were raised in North America, many of the dimensions of culture described previously probably seem "right" to you. For example, it is only logical to think that time is money and you should not waste it. Everyone knows that, right? That is why a North American businessperson in an Arab or Asian country might feel irritated at time spent over coffee or other social rituals before any "real" business is transacted. In these cultures, however, time is viewed differently. Moreover, personal relationships must be established and nurtured before credible negotiations may proceed.

Ethnocentrism causes us to judge others by our own values. We expect others to react as we would, and they expect us to behave as they would. Misunderstandings naturally result. A North American smiling broadly, joking, and excitedly presenting a proposed project to German business partners will be perceived as lacking credibility. In turn German businesspersons who respond soberly and ask direct, probing questions will appear rude and humourless. These automatic ethnocentric responses can be reduced through knowledge of other cultures and the development of increased intercultural sensitivity.

Without intercultural sensitivity, ethnocentric attitudes can develop into discriminatory behaviour and xenophobia. During the COVID-19 pandemic, Asian Canadians reported a rise in racist acts toward their communities. Because the virus originated in China, Chinese values and culture came under attack. This created undue hardship and distress for individuals and businesses.[24] When you strive to learn about other cultures, you will curb ethnocentrism.

Understanding Generalizations and Stereotyping. Most experts recognize that it is impossible to talk about cultures without using mental categories, representations, and generalizations to describe groups. These categories are sometimes considered *stereotypes*. Because the term *stereotype* has a negative meaning, intercultural authors Varner and Beamer suggested that we distinguish between *stereotype* and *prototype*.

- **Stereotype.** A *stereotype* is an oversimplified behavioural pattern applied uncritically to groups. Although they may be exaggerated and overgeneralized beliefs when applied to groups of people, stereotypes are not always entirely false.[25] Often they contain a grain of truth. When a stereotype develops into a rigid attitude and when it is based on erroneous beliefs or preconceptions, however, then it should be called a *prejudice*.

- **Prototype.** Varner and Beamer recommended using the term *prototype* to describe "mental representations based on general characteristics that are not fixed and rigid, but rather are open to new definitions."[26] Prototypes, then, are dynamic and change with fresh experience. Prototypes based on objective observations usually have a considerable amount of truth in them. That is why they can be helpful in studying culture. For example, South American businesspeople often talk about their families before getting down to business. This prototype is generally accurate, but it may not universally apply, and it may change over time.

- **Generalizations.** Some people object to making any generalizations about cultures whatsoever. It is wise to remember, however, that whenever we are confronted with something new and unfamiliar, we naturally strive to categorize the data to make sense out of them. In categorizing these new data, we are making generalizations. Significant intellectual discourse and science would be impossible without generalizations. Unfounded generalizations about people and cultures, of course, can lead to bias and prejudice. However, for our purposes, when we discuss cultures, it is important to use generalizations and describe cultural prototypes.

Being Open-Minded. One desirable attitude in achieving intercultural proficiency is that of *tolerance*. Closed-minded people cannot look beyond their own ethnocentrism. But as global markets expand and as our own society becomes increasingly multiethnic, tolerance becomes especially significant.

- **Empathy.** To improve tolerance, you will want to practise *empathy*. This means trying to see the world through another's eyes. It means being less judgmental and more eager to seek common ground.
- **Patience.** Being tolerant also involves patience. If a speaker for whom English is an additional language (EAL) is struggling to express an idea in English, Canadians must avoid the temptation to finish the sentence and provide the word that they presume is wanted. When we put words into their mouths, many EAL speakers often smile and agree out of politeness, but our words may in fact not express their thoughts.
- **Silence.** Remaining silent is another means of exhibiting tolerance. Instead of filling every lapse in conversation, Canadians, for example, should recognize that some cultures deliberately use periods of silence for reflection and contemplation. As well, many Indigenous Peoples value "appreciating silences." Listening is important to their cultures, as is giving each person time to finish speaking.[29]

Saving Face. In business transactions North Americans often assume that economic factors are the primary motivators of people. It is wise to remember, though, that strong cultural influences are also at work. *Saving face*, for example, is important in many parts of the world. *Face* refers to the image people hold in their social network. Positive comments raise a person's social standing, but negative comments lower it.

People in low-context cultures are less concerned with face. Instead they value honesty and directness and generally come right to the point and tell it like it is. Members of high-context cultures, on the other hand, are more concerned with preserving social harmony and saving face. They are indirect and go to great lengths to avoid giving offence by saying *no*.

Masterfile

In Québec many people, including business associates, greet each other with *la bise* or "the French double-kiss" on each cheek.[27] This practice is less common in other provinces and territories.[28] What are the greeting customs in your home town?

Successful Nonverbal Intercultural Communication

Verbal skills in another culture can generally be mastered if someone studies hard enough. But nonverbal skills are much

CASE CONNECTIONS

SaskTel: One of Canada's Best Diversity Employers

SaskTel

Courtesy of SaskTel

SaskTel, with its head office located in Regina, is the top information and communications technology (ICT) company in Saskatchewan. Its ICT services include Internet, wireless data, maxTV, cloud-based, security monitoring, and consulting, and it employs over 3,600 full-time equivalent employees.[30] In 2020 SaskTel was recognized as one of Canada's best diversity employers for the following reasons:

> SaskTel's Indigenous recruitment strategy aims to increase the number of Indigenous employees in the workforce through partnerships with community organizations and post-secondary institutions, career fair attendance, and participation in networking events.
>
> SaskTel also maintains a hiring strategy for persons with disabilities and conducts information sessions and pre-employment workshops with community partners.
>
> Additionally, the organization created the Supported Employment program for candidates with cognitive disabilities in partnership with community-based organizations and is a participant in the "4 to 40" program, which connects individuals with intellectual disabilities to employers who embrace a flexible four-to 40-hour work week.[31]

SaskTel was also recognized as one of the top employers for young people and as one of Canada's greenest companies.

- Consider the diversity strategies SaskTel uses, as listed above. How do these strategies benefit both the company and its customers?

more difficult to learn. Nonverbal behaviour includes the areas described in Chapter 2, such as eye contact, facial expressions, posture, gestures, and the use of time, space, and territory. Fortunately, you can learn techniques to boost your intercultural competence.

How Nonverbal Cues Affect Communication.

- **Deciphering body language.** The messages sent by body language and the way we arrange time and space have always been open to interpretation. Deciphering nonverbal communication is difficult for people who are culturally similar, and it is even more complex when cultures differ. If you've ever had to talk with someone who does not share your language, you probably learned quickly to use gestures to convey basic messages. Because gestures can create very different reactions in different cultures, we must be careful in using and interpreting them. In Canada, for example, many anglophone Canadians feel uncomfortable with strong displays of emotions, especially from people they've just met. However, in Québec and many immigrant communities, displays of emotion are often freely made.[32]
- **Increasing awareness.** Striving to associate with people from different cultures can further broaden your intercultural savvy. Numerous lists of cultural dos and don'ts have been compiled. However, learning all the nuances of nonverbal behaviour in other cultures is impossible; such lists are merely the tip of the cultural iceberg (see Figure 3.2).

Techniques for Achieving Intercultural Competence.

- **Avoid judgment.** Nonjudgmental attitudes go a long way in preventing defensive reactions from communicators. As you will learn in Chapter 4 about the process of communication, descriptive feedback is more effective than judgmental feedback. *Descriptiveness* refers to the use of concrete and specific feedback.[33] For example, using objective terms to describe the modest attire of Muslim women is more effective than judgementally describing it as oppressive to women.

- **Show support.** Most important in achieving effective communication is *supportiveness.* This attitude requires us to support others positively with head nods, eye contact, facial expressions, and physical proximity.[34]
- **Follow their lead.** When interacting with businesspeople in other cultures, you would be wise to follow their lead. If they avoid intense eye contact, don't stare. Until you are knowledgeable about the meaning of gestures, it is probably a good idea to keep yours to a minimum.

While intercultural competence in nonverbal behaviour may never be totally attained, sensitivity, nonjudgmentalism, and tolerance go a long way toward improving interactions.

Improving Conversations in Intercultural Environments

Although it is advantageous to speak an additional language fluently, many Canadians lack that skill. Fortunately, global business transactions are increasingly conducted in English. English has become the language of technology, the language of film, and the language of business even for traditionally non-English-speaking countries.[35] However, Canadians and others who communicate with EAL/ESL speakers are more likely to be understood if they observe a few polite and helpful suggestions.

Enhancing Oral Communication. Canadians abroad make a big mistake in thinking that EAL speakers can always follow the conversation. Comprehension can be fairly superficial. Even when they use English, foreign nationals appreciate your learning greetings and a few phrases in their language. Learning the words for *please, yes,* and *thank you* is better than relying on gestures. It's also wise to speak slowly, use simple English, opt for short sentences, and avoid long, complex words. Following are additional suggestions to improve oral intercultural communication:

- **Observe eye messages.** Be alert to a glazed expression or wandering eyes. These tell you that the listener is lost.
- **Encourage accurate feedback.** Ask probing questions, and encourage the listener to paraphrase what you say. Do not assume that a *yes,* a nod, or a smile indicates comprehension.
- **Accept blame.** If a misunderstanding results, graciously accept the blame for not making your meaning clear.
- **Listen without interrupting.** Curb your desire to finish sentences or to fill out ideas for the speaker. Keep in mind that North Americans abroad are often accused of listening too little and talking too much.
- **Smile when appropriate.** The smile is often considered the single most understood and most useful form of communication. However, in some cultures excessive smiling may seem insincere.
- **Follow up in writing.** After conversations or oral negotiations, confirm the results and agreements with written messages. For proposals and contracts, hire a professional translator.

Because Canada has such a diverse workforce, it is best to avoid using acronyms, technical terms, and colloquialisms. Acronyms and technical terms may not be understood, and many popular colloquialisms have connotations that may offend.[36]

Improving Written Communication. In sending letters, e-mails, and other documents to businesspeople in other cultures, try to adjust your writing style and tone. For example, in cultures where formality and tradition are important, be scrupulously polite. Don't even think of sharing the latest joke. Humour translates very poorly and can cause misunderstanding and negative reactions. Familiarize yourself with customary channels of communication. Are letters and e-mails common? Would a direct or an indirect organizational pattern be more effective? The following additional suggestions can help you prepare successful written messages for intercultural audiences.

- **Use short sentences and short paragraphs.** Sentences with fewer than 20 words and paragraphs with fewer than eight lines are most readable.
- **Observe titles and rank.** Use last names, titles, and other signals of rank and status. Send messages to higher-status people and avoid sending copies to lower-rank people.
- **Avoid ambiguous expressions.** Include relative pronouns (*that, which, who*) for clarity in introducing clauses. Stay away from contractions (especially ones like *Here's the problem*). Avoid idioms and figurative clichés (*once in a blue moon*), slang (*my presentation really bombed*), acronyms (*ASAP*, for *as soon as possible*), abbreviations (*BTW*, for *by the way*), jargon (*input, bottom line*), and sports references (*play ball, slam dunk, ballpark figure*). Use action-specific verbs (*purchase a printer* rather than *get a printer*).
- **Strive for clarity.** Avoid words that have many meanings (the word *light* has 18 meanings). If necessary, clarify words that may be confusing. Replace two-word verbs with clear single words (*return* instead of *bring back*; *delay* instead of *put off*; *maintain* instead of *keep up*).
- **Use correct grammar.** Be careful about misplaced modifiers, dangling participles, and sentence fragments. Use conventional punctuation.
- **Cite numbers carefully.** In citing numbers use figures (*12*) instead of spelling them out (*twelve*). Always convert dollar figures into local currency. Avoid using figures to express the month of the year. In North America, for example, June 12, 2020, might be written as 6/12/20, whereas in Europe the same date might appear as 12.6.20.

The following Checklist summarizes suggestions for improving communication with intercultural audiences.

CHECKLIST

Achieving Intercultural Proficiency

- **Examine your own culture.** Study your customs, biases, and views and how they differ from those in other societies, including differences within Canadian subcultures. Work to better understand and accept the values and behaviour of other cultures.
- **Explore other cultures.** Education can help you alter cultural misconceptions, reduce fears, and minimize misunderstandings. Knowledge of other cultures opens your eyes and enriches your life.
- **Curb ethnocentrism.** Avoid judging others by your personal views. Overcome the view that other cultures are incorrect, defective, or primitive.
- **Treat each individual you meet as a prototype.** Be open to adjusting your perceptions of other cultures. To avoid stereotypes and prejudice, treat people as unique individuals, not as typical representatives of an entire group.
- **Observe nonverbal cues in your culture.** Become more alert to the meanings of eye contact, facial expressions, posture, gestures, and the use of time, space, and territory. How do they differ in other cultures?
- **Embrace nonjudgmentalism.** Strive for objectivity. Learn to accept unfamiliar behaviour as different, rather than as right or wrong.
- **Be aware of culture when using communication technology.** Don't expect that individuals from other cultures think and act the same way you do. Try to reach out to others over common interests.
- **Use plain English.** Speak and write in short sentences using simple words and standard English. Eliminate puns, slang, jargon, acronyms, abbreviations, and any words that cannot be easily translated.
- **Encourage accurate feedback.** Ask probing questions and listen attentively without interrupting. Do not assume that a *yes* or a smile indicates agreement or comprehension.
- **Adapt to local preferences.** Write to reflect the reader's culture, if appropriate. Express currency in local figures. Write out months of the year for clarity.

Concept Check

1. In groups, discuss subcultures that exist within Canada. What are the differences in language and customs within your own province, territory, or city? For fun, conduct a Google search for "Canadian slang words from different provinces and territories" and review the result with your group.
2. Identify a situation in which you were aware of ethnocentrism in your own actions or those of friends, family members, or colleagues. In general terms, describe what happened. What made you think the experience involved ethnocentrism?

LEARNING OBJECTIVE 4

Explain the advantages and challenges of workforce diversity, and address approaches for improving communication among diverse workplace audiences.

Workforce Diversity: Benefits and Challenges

While Canadian companies are expanding global operations and adapting to a variety of emerging markets, the domestic workforce is also becoming more diverse. This diversity has many dimensions—race, ethnicity, age, religion, gender, national origin, physical ability, and countless other qualities. No longer, say the experts, will the workplace be predominantly Anglo-oriented or male. In addition, the average age of the Canadian population has been rising in recent decades, and people over 65 years of age are one of the fastest-growing segments of the population.[37] Trends suggest that many of these older people will remain in the workforce. Because of technological advances, more people with disabilities are also joining the workforce.

Diversity and Its Advantages

As society and the workforce become more diverse, successful interactions and communication among the various identity groups bring distinct advantages.

Consumers. A diverse staff is better able to read trends and respond to the increasingly diverse customer base in local and world markets. Teams made up of people with different experiences are better equipped to create products that these markets require. Consumers also want to deal with companies that respect their values and reflect them.

Business Organizations. Companies that set aside time and resources to cultivate and capitalize on diversity will suffer fewer discrimination lawsuits, fewer union clashes, and less government regulatory action. Most important, though, is the growing realization among organizations that diversity is a critical bottom-line business strategy to improve employee relationships, strengthen work teams, and increase productivity. Developing a diverse staff that can work together is one of the biggest challenges facing business organizations today.

Diversity and Discord

Diversity can be a positive force within organizations. However, all too often it can also cause divisiveness, discontent, and clashes. Many of the identity groups have legitimate concerns, and organizations need to ensure equality for all employees.

- Many women experience the *glass ceiling*, that invisible barrier of attitudes, prejudices, and "old boy networks" blocking them from reaching important corporate positions.
- Issues of sexual harassment, unequal wages, and sexism still exist in some Canadian workplaces.
- Transgender people experience workplace discrimination, lower wages, and fewer advancement opportunities.
- Older employees feel that the deck is stacked in favour of younger employees.
- Members of minority groups feel discriminated against in hiring, retention, wages, and promotions.

CAREER COACH

He Said, She Said: Gender Talk and Gender Tension

Has the infiltration of gender rhetoric done great damage to the workplace? Are men and women experiencing misunderstandings caused by stereotypes of so-called masculine and feminine attitudes?[38] Judging from workplace surveys, gender differences are fading: 33 percent of North American adults prefer a male boss and 20 percent prefer a female leader, but a whopping 46 percent have no preference.[39]

Deborah Tannen's book *You Just Don't Understand: Women and Men in Conversation*, as well as John Gray's *Men Are From Mars, Women Are From Venus*, caused an avalanche of discussion (and some hostility) by comparing the communication styles of men and women.

Gender theorists suggest that one reason women can't climb above the glass ceiling is that their communication style is less authoritative than that of men. Compare the following observations (greatly simplified) from gender theorists:

	Women	Men
Object of talk	Establish rapport, make connections, negotiate inclusive relationships	Preserve independence, maintain status, exhibit skill and knowledge
Listening behaviour	Attentive, steady eye contact; remain stationary; nod head	Less attentive, sporadic eye contact; move around
Pauses	Frequent pauses, giving chance for others to take turns	Infrequent pauses; interrupt each other to take turns
Small talk	Personal disclosure	Impersonal topics
Focus	Details first, pulled together at end	Big picture
Gestures	Small, confined	Expansive
Method	Questions, apologies; "we" statements; hesitant, indirect, soft speech	Assertions; "I" statements; clear, loud, take-charge speech

These observations do not use gender neutral language or include people who are nonbinary. A nonbinary person is one "who identifies with or expresses a gender identity that is neither entirely male nor entirely female."[40] How can nonbinary communication styles be factored into gender theory?

- Individuals with disabilities feel that their limitations should not hold them back, and they fear that their potential is often prejudged.
- People of different religions feel their beliefs are not respected.

Improving Communication Among Diverse Workplace Audiences

Harmony and acceptance do not happen automatically when people who are dissimilar work together. This means that organizations must commit to diversity. Harnessed effectively, diversity can enhance productivity and propel a company to success. Mismanaged, it can become a tremendous drain on a company's time and resources. The following suggestions can help you and your organization find ways to improve communication and interaction.

- **Seek training.** Especially if an organization is experiencing diversity problems, awareness-raising sessions may be helpful. Spend time reading and learning about workforce diversity and how it can benefit organizations. Look upon diversity as an opportunity, not a threat. Intercultural communication, team building, and conflict resolution are skills that can be learned in diversity training programs.
- **Understand the value of differences.** Diversity makes an organization innovative and creative. Sameness fosters an absence of critical thinking called groupthink, as discussed in Chapter 2. Even smart people working collectively can make poor decisions if they do not see the situation from different perspectives.[41] Diversity in problem-solving groups encourages independent and creative thinking.

- **Make fewer assumptions.** Be careful of seemingly insignificant, innocent workplace assumptions. For example, don't assume that everyone wants to observe the holidays with a Christmas party and a decorated tree. Celebrating only Christian holidays in December and January excludes those who honour Hanukkah, Kwanzaa, and the Lunar New Year.
- **In workplace discussions don't assume anything about others' sexual orientation or attitude toward marriage.** For invitations, avoid phrases such as *managers and their wives. Spouses* or *partners* is more inclusive. Valuing diversity means making fewer assumptions that everyone is like you or wants to be like you.
- **Build on similarities.** Look for areas in which you and others not like you can agree or at least share opinions. Be prepared to consider issues from many perspectives, all of which may be valid. Accept that there is room for different points of view to coexist peacefully. Although you can always find differences, it is much harder to find similarities. Look for common ground in shared experiences, mutual goals, and similar values.[42] Concentrate on your objective even when you may disagree on how to reach it.

Concept Check

1. How does having a diverse staff benefit customers?
2. In your own experience, how accurate are characterizations that gender theorists make about differences between men and women? Support your views.

SPOTLIGHT ON COMMUNICATION: PART 2

Federation of Black Canadians Revisited

CRITICAL THINKING

- As a student, what can you do to improve your intercultural proficiencies? How can you help to combat anti-Black, -Indigenous, and -people-of-colour (BIPOC) racism in Canada?
- What can employers and governments do to create true equity in Canada's workplaces and communities?

The Federation of Black Canadians lends its support to other groups and organizations, like Black Lives Matter, to create a better Canada. FBC organizes petitions and creates partnerships to motivate corporations and governments to acknowledge and combat systemic racism.[43] For example, Black Canadians experienced higher rates of COVID-19 because of socioeconomic inequalities:

Josie Desmarais/iStock

> The Federation of Black Canadians is gravely concerned about the recent socioeconomic COVID-19 findings and data trends from the City of Toronto. Black people and people of colour make up 83% of reported COVID-19 cases in Toronto. The data shows that Black people make up 21 percent of reported cases in the city, while making up only nine percent of the overall population.
>
> During this time of grave uncertainty, the Federation of Black Canadians along with everyone in our nation is doing what we can to support one another as it relates to the immediate emergency and long-term impacts of COVID-19. Unfortunately, the reality is that COVID-19 has disproportionately affected the Black community. This is a result of structural and systemic racism, which has profoundly affected the fairness and equitable access to health care services, housing, fair treatment in the justice system and access to education. Black people in Canada continue to suffer the social, political, and economic impacts of colonization, slavery, and over-policing, and this pandemic has only heightened and worsened the challenges already faced by our community.[44]

FBC created an online petition urging all levels of government to collect race-based data, stating the following: "The collection and reporting of race-based data during this pandemic is a critical component in understanding and addressing anti-Black racism in Canada."[45]

Summary of Learning Objectives

1 Understand the powerful effects of globalization and the major trends fuelling it.

- Intercultural competency is needed to contend with several major trends. Shrinking domestic markets have prompted movement toward globalized markets free of trade barriers.
- Communication and information technologies extend the global reach of business.
- In emerging economies, the middle class is growing.
- The domestic workforce is becoming increasingly diverse as immigrants settle in Canada.

2 Define *culture*, name its primary characteristics, and explain the five key dimensions of culture.

- *Culture* is the complex system of values, traits, morals, and customs shared by a society.
- Significant characteristics of culture include the following: (a) culture is learned, (b) cultures are inherently logical, (c) culture is the basis of self-identity and community, (d) culture combines the visible and invisible, and (e) culture is dynamic.
- Members of low-context cultures (e.g., North America, Scandinavia, and Germany) and high-context cultures (e.g., Japan, China, and Arab countries) communicate differently.
- Other key dimensions of culture include individualism, time orientation, power distance, and communication style.

3 Discuss strategies for enhancing intercultural effectiveness and communication techniques.

- To function effectively in a global economy, we must learn about other cultures and be willing to change our attitudes once we become aware of our own cultural assumptions and biases.
- *Ethnocentrism* refers to the belief that one's own culture is superior to all others and holds all truths; to overcome stereotypes and become more tolerant, we need to practise empathy.
- Nonverbal miscommunication can be avoided by recognizing that body language, such as eye contact, posture, gestures, use of time, space, and territory, is largely culture dependent.
- To improve intercultural written messages, communicators accommodate the reader in organization, tone, and style.

4 Explain the advantages and challenges of workforce diversity, and address approaches for improving communication among diverse workplace audiences.

- A diverse workforce can benefit consumers and business organizations.
- To foster harmony and communication in diverse workplaces, many organizations develop diversity training programs.
- Workers are tasked with understanding and accepting the value of differences; they should not expect conformity, should make fewer assumptions about others, and should look for common ground.

Chapter Review

1. Which important trends fuel globalization? (Obj. 1)
2. Which significant changes in the workforce can we expect over the next 40 years? (Obj. 1)
3. List the five main characteristics of culture. (Obj. 2)
4. What is a *subculture*? (Obj. 3)
5. How do terms and slang differ within Canada's provinces and territories? (Obj. 3)
6. Name four or more strategies for bridging the gap between cultures and achieving intercultural proficiency. (Obj. 3)
7. Explain the difference between a stereotype and a prototype. (Obj. 3)
8. When interacting with people who do not use your language, why is it important to learn the words for *please*, *yes*, and *thank you* rather than rely on gestures? (Obj. 3)
9. Describe at least five ways you can improve written communication with someone who speaks another language. (Obj. 3)
10. Name three examples of inequalities that may exist in some diverse workplaces. (Obj. 4)

Critical Thinking

1. When we travel or work abroad, we tend to be perceived not so much as individuals but as members of racial, ethnic, or national groups. For example, when visiting Europe, Americans can expect to be questioned on U.S. foreign policy, military actions, and economic influence. How can you ensure that you function as an effective ambassador of your country when working and travelling overseas? (Objs. 1, 3, 5)
2. If the rules, values, and attitudes of a culture are learned, can they be unlearned? Explain. (Obj. 2)
3. It is quite natural to favour one's own country over a foreign one. To what extent can ethnocentrism be considered a normal reaction, and when could it become destructive and unproductive? Provide examples to support your answer. (Objs. 2, 3)
4. Some economists and management scholars argue that statements such as *diversity is an economic asset* or *diversity is a new strategic imperative* are unproved and perhaps unprovable assertions. Should social responsibility or market forces determine whether an organization strives to create a diverse workforce? Why? (Obj. 4)
5. **Ethical Issue:** You are part of the hiring committee for a hardware engineer position at your company. The two other hiring committee members are both men, and during the interviews you observe that they are dismissive to a woman candidate. They rush her through the questions and talk over her responses. When you confront them about it, they brush you off and say she isn't qualified. You know this isn't true; she has strong qualifications for the position. What should you do next? (Obj. 4)

Activities

3.1 Minding One's Intercultural Social Media Manners (Objs. 1–3)

Intercultural   Social Media

Consider your worst, most embarrassing intercultural blunder and then imagine it amplified a thousandfold or millionfold for everyone to see. Social networking is instant and, once released, it can't be recalled. What follows is a partial list of extremely awkward social media slipups with intercultural implications.[46]

YOUR TASK Consider the gravity of each offence; individually or in groups discuss each for its "takeaway," the lesson to be learned from it. Contribute your own intercultural blunders that you or someone you know has experienced. Explain the lessons learned.

a. Red Cross social media specialist Gloria Huang sent out the following tweet from the organization's Twitter account @RedCross: "Ryan found two more 4 bottle packs of Dogfish Head's Midas Touch beer ... when we drink we do it right #gettngslizzerd." The late-night tweet stayed up for an hour. Huang's boss, Wendy

Harman, fielded calls in the middle of the night and took the tweet down.

b. Home improvement chain Lowe's allowed a discussion on its Facebook page to get out of hand after withdrawing its advertising from a TLC reality show about Muslim families. The 23,000 comments on Facebook that followed were mostly critical of the company, but some praised the home improvement giant. Only when the media picked up the story did the company respond to offensive and racist posts by deleting all the messages and explaining its late intervention as "respect for the transparence of social media."

c. Australian airline Qantas tried to lure its customers with gift packs to describe their "dream luxury in-flight experience." However, this promotion coincided with grounded flights in response to ongoing strikes, and the passengers took to venting and griping, not praising.

3.2 Learning About Other Countries (Objs. 2, 4)

Intercultural Web

When meeting businesspeople from other countries, you will feel more comfortable if you know the basics of business etiquette and intercultural communication, such as greetings, attire, or dos and don'ts. On the Web you will find many resources, some more reliable than others.

YOUR TASK Use a browser to search for *international business etiquette*. Choose a few websites from the result and explore them to answer the following questions:

a. How do people greet each other in Australia, India, Japan, Korea, the Netherlands, and Spain?

b. In what countries is it important to keep a certain distance from the person you are greeting?

c. In what countries is a kiss an appropriate greeting?

3.3 Learn to Speak a Foreign Language or Just a Few Phrases With Livemocha, Busuu, or Duolingo (Objs. 2, 3)

E-mail Intercultural

Social media have taken the world by storm; therefore, it's not surprising that social networks have formed around various interests and pursuits. At least two major social networks have united people eager to learn or practice a foreign language online. A few of the most popular include Livemocha, busuu, and Duolingo. They offer free basic instruction and premium fee-based content in a number of popular languages.

YOUR TASK Compare the two online language learning communities. Consider these and similar questions: How many languages do they support? How do they operate, and how much do they cost? What features do they offer? How many users do they have? Learn a few phrases in a language that interests you and report back to class. Your instructor may ask you to summarize your findings in writing, in either an e-mail or an online post.

3.4 Negotiating Traps (Objs. 2, 3)

Intercultural

Businesspeople often have difficulty reaching agreement on the terms of contracts, proposals, and anything that involves bargaining. They have even more difficulty when the negotiators are from different cultures.

YOUR TASK Discuss the causes and implications of the following common mistakes made by Canadians in their negotiations with people in other countries.

a. Assuming that a final agreement is set in stone

b. Thinking that an interpreter is always completely accurate

c. Ignoring or misunderstanding the significance of rank

3.5 Examining Cultural Stereotypes (Objs. 2, 3)

Intercultural Team Web

As you have learned in this chapter, generalizations are necessary as we acquire and categorize new knowledge. As long as we remain open to new experiences, we won't be stymied by rigid, stereotypical perceptions of other cultures. Almost all of us are at some point in our lives subject to stereotyping by others, whether we are immigrants, women, members of minority groups or of certain professions, Canadians abroad, and so forth. Generally speaking, negative stereotypes sting. However, even positive stereotypes can offend or embarrass because they fail to acknowledge the differences among individuals.

YOUR TASK Think about a nation or culture about which you have only a hazy idea. Jot down a few key traits that come to mind. For example, you may not know much about the Netherlands and the Dutch people. You can probably think of gouda cheese, wooden clogs, Heineken beer, tulips, and windmills. Anything else? Then consider a culture with which you are very familiar, whether it is yours or that of a country you have visited or studied. In one column, write down a few stereotypical perceptions that are positive. Then, in another column record negative stereotypes you associate with that culture. Share your notes with your team or the whole class, as the instructor directs. How do you respond to others' descriptions of your culture? Which stereotypes irk you and why? For a quick fact check and overview at the end of this exercise, google the *CIA World Factbook* or *BBC News Country Profiles*.

3.6 Make Yourself at Home: Ambiguous Expressions Invite New Friends (Obj. 3)

Intercultural

To end conversations, North Americans often issue casual invitations to new acquaintances and even virtual strangers, such as *Visit me when you come to Victoria*, or *Come on over anytime*. However, nonnative speakers and visitors may misinterpret such casual remarks. They may embarrass their hosts and suffer disappointment by taking the offhand invitation literally and acting on it. Those interacting across cultures would be wise to avoid using expressions that have multiple meanings.

YOUR TASK Assume you are a businessperson engaged in exporting and importing. As such, you are in constant communication with suppliers and customers around the world. In messages sent abroad or in situations with nonnative speakers of English at home, what kinds of ambiguous expressions should you avoid? In teams or individually, list three to five original examples of idioms, slang, acronyms, sports references, abbreviations, jargon, and two-word verbs. Which phrases or behaviour could be taken literally by a person from a different culture?

Grammar and Mechanics | *Review 3*

Pronouns

Review Guides 11 to 18 about pronoun usage in Appendix B, Grammar and Mechanics Guide, beginning on page B-1. On a sheet of paper or on your computer, revise the following sentences to correct errors in pronouns. For each error that you locate, write the guide number that deals with this usage. Some sentences may have two errors. If a sentence is correct, write *C*. When you finish, compare your responses with the key in Appendix *C*.

EXAMPLE: My friend and me are both looking for jobs.

REVISION: My friend and I are both looking for jobs. [Guide 12]

1. Please send texts to my manager and I so that she and I both understand the situation.
2. Except for Mark and I, all the sales reps attended the team meeting.
3. Google encourages developers to create apps and games for families and children using it's new program.
4. Most of we consumers remember when fruits and vegetables were available only in season.
5. Send the report to the administrative assistant or myself when it's finished.
6. All employees have a right to see they're personnel folder.
7. Lunches will be delivered to whomever ordered them.
8. Most reservations were made in time, but your's and her's missed the deadline.
9. Just between you and me, who do you think will be our new manager?
10. It must have been her who sent the e-mail to Jason and me.

Notes

[1] Federation of Black Canadians. (2020). *About.* https://fbcfcn.ca/about

[2] Ibid.

[3] Ibid.

[4] Ibid.

[5] Ibid.

[6] Tim Hortons. (2019). *Tim Hortons opens first restaurant in Shanghai, China.* https://www.timhortons.com/ca/en/corporate/news-release.php?id=11415

[7] Ibid.

[8] Government of Canada. (2019). *A new Canada-United States-Mexico agreement.* https://www.international.gc.ca/trade-commerce/trade-agreements-accords-commerciaux/agr-acc/cusma-aceum/index.aspx?lang=eng

[9] Ernst & Young. (2013, April 25). *Entering the global middle class: Hitting the sweet spot.* http://www.ey.com/GL/en/Issues/Driving-growth/middle-class-growth-in-emerging-markets

[10] Vossos, T. (2011, April 3). *The effect of advancements in transportation technology on global business.* http://www.ehow.com/info_8160779_effects; Gouvernement du Québec. (2016). *Québec portal: Culture.* http://www.gouv.qc.ca/EN/LeQuebec/Pages/Culture.aspxGovernment of Canada

[11] Statistics Canada. (2011). *Immigration and ethnocultural diversity in Canada.* https://www12.statcan.gc.ca/nhs-enm/2011/as-sa/99-010-x/99-010-x2011001-eng.cfm#a5

[12] Gouvernement du Québec. (2016). *Québec portal: Culture.* http://www.gouv.qc.ca/EN/LeQuebec/Pages/Culture.aspx

[13] Government of Canada. (2016). *Aboriginal peoples and communities*. Indigenous and Northern Affairs Canada. https://www.aadnc-aandc.gc.ca/eng/1100100013785/1304467449155-transportation-technology-global-business.html

[14] Rosman, K. (2015, June 5). Me, Myself and Mx. *New York Times*. http://www.nytimes.com/2015/06/07/style/me-myself-and-mx.html?_r=0

[15] Hall, E. T., & Hall, M. R. (1990). *Understanding cultural differences*. Yarmouth, ME: Intercultural Press, pp. 183–184.

[16] Figure based on Chaney, L. H., & Martin, J. S. (2011). *Intercultural business communication* (5th ed.). Upper Saddle River, NJ: Prentice Hall, Chapter 5; J. Chung's analysis appearing in Chen, G. M., & Starosta, W. J. (1998). *Foundations of intercultural communication*. Allyn and Bacon, p. 51; O'Hara-Devereaux, M., & Johansen, R. (1994). *Globalwork: Bridging culture and time*. San Francisco: Jossey-Bass, p. 55.

[17] Gallois, C., & Callan, V. (1997). *Communication and culture*. Wiley, p. 24.

[18] Ibid., p. 29.

[19] Copeland, L., & Griggs, L. (1985). *Going international*. Penguin, p. 108.

[20] Ibid., p. 12.

[21] Merriam-Webster. (n.d.). Definition of subculture. In *Merriam-Webster.com dictionary*. Retrieved June 4, 2019, from https://www.merriam-webster.com/dictionary/subculture

[22] Zamon, R. (2017, August 25). *The differences in Canadian slang show the country's real divides*. Huffington Post. https://www.huffingtonpost.ca/2017/08/25/canadian-slang-differences_a_23185575/

[23] Ibid.

[24] Gill, R. (2020, June 7). Asian communities across Canada report rising racist behaviour during COVID-19 crisis. *Global News*. https://globalnews.ca/news/7033253/coronavirus-asian-racism-crisis-canada/

[25] Chen, G. M., & Starosta, W. J. (1998). *Foundations of intercultural communication*. Allyn and Bacon, p. 40.

[26] Varner, I., & Beamer, L. (2001). *Intercultural communication in the global workplace*. McGraw-Hill Irwin, p. 18.

[27] *La bise, or the French double-kiss: a guide to greeting in Quebec*. (2014, November 28). The Main. http://www.themainmtl.com/2014/11/guide-french-double-kiss-bise/

[28] Government of Canada. (2016). *Cultural information: Communication styles*. Global Affairs Canada. https://www.international.gc.ca/cil-cai/country_insights-apercus_pays/ci-ic_ca.aspx

[29] Aboriginal Construction Careers. (2010). *What is culture and why does it matter?* Retrieved from http://www.aboriginalconstructioncareers.ca/toolkit/what-culture-and-why-does-it-matter

[30] SaskTel. (2019). *Our company*. https://www.sasktel.com/about-us/our+company

[31] Leung, K., & Leung, S. (2020, March 5). SaskTel: Recognized as one of Canada's best diversity employers (2020). *Mediacorp Canada*. https://reviews.canadastop100.com/top-employer-sasktel. Reprinted courtesy of Mediacorp Canada.

[32] Government of Canada. (2016). *Cultural information: Display of emotion*. Global Affairs Canada. https://www.international.gc.ca/cil-cai/country_insights-apercus_pays/ci-ic_ca.aspx?lang=eng#cn-2

[33] Hammer, M. R. (1993). Quoted in Chen and Starosta's *Foundations of intercultural communication*. Allyn & Bacon, p. 247.

[34] Ibid.

[35] Weber, G. (2004, May). English rules. *Workforce Management*, pp. 47–50; Desai, D. (2008). Globalization and the English skills gap. *Chief Learning Officer, 7*(6), 62–63. http://search.ebscohost.com; Dvorak, P. (2007, November 5). Plain English gets harder in global era. *Wall Street Journal*. http://search.ebscohost.com

[36] Joseph, B. (2014, March 24). Six "must don'ts" for an effective First Nations engagement strategy. *Working Effectively with Indigenous Peoples*. http://www.ictinc.ca/blog/six-must-donts-effective-first-nations-engagement-strategy

[37] Zikmund, W. G., D'Amico, M., Browne, P., Anthony, D., Monk, J., & Donville, L. (2008). *Effective marketing* (1st Canadian ed.). Nelson Education.

[38] Career Coach (He Said, She Said) based on Basow, S. A., & Rubenfeld, K. (2003, February). Troubles talk: Effects of gender and gender-typing. *Sex Roles, 183*. http://www.springerlink.com/content/rm75xx843786037q/fulltext.pdf; Wood, J. T. (2002). *Gendered lives*. Wadsworth, p. 119; Tear, J. (1995, November 20). They just don't understand gender dynamics. *Wall Street Journal*, p. A12. http://www.dowjones.com/factiva; Roiphe, A. (1994, October). Talking trouble. *Working Woman*, pp. 28–31; Stuart, C. (1994, February). Why can't a woman be more like a man? *Training Tomorrow*, pp. 22–24; Wolfe, A. (1994, December 12). She just doesn't understand. *New Republic, 211*(24), 26–34.

[39] Smith, J. (2015, April 3). Study finds women are better bosses than men—here's why. *Business Insider*. http://www.businessinsider.com/why-women-are-bettermanagers-than-men-2015-4

[40] Merriam-Webster. (n.d.). Definition of nonbinary. In *Merriam-Webster.com dictionary*. Retrieved June 24, 2020, from https://www.merriam-webster.com/dictionary/nonbinary

[41] Schwartz, J., & Wald, M. L. (2003, March 9). Smart people working collectively can be dumber than the sum of their brains. Appeared originally in *New York Times*. http://www.mindfully.org/Reform/2003/Smart-People-Dumber9mar03.htm

[42] White, M. D. (2002). *A short course in international marketing blunders*. World Trade Press, p. 46.

[43] Federation of Black Canadians. (2020, July 31). *The Federation of Black Canadians seeks dedicated government wide Covid19 measure for Black Canadians*. https://fbcfcn.ca/news/dedicated_government_support

[44] Ibid.

[45] Ibid.

[46] Scenario based on Berens, C. (n.d.). *Top 12 social media blunders of 2011*. Inc. http://www.inc.com/ss/caitlin-berens/top-12-social-media-blunders-2011#3 and on Wasserman, T. (2011, February 16). *Red Cross does PR disaster recovery on rogue tweet*. Mashable.com. http://mashable.com/2011/02/16/red-cross-tweet

UNIT 2

The Writing Process

CHAPTER 4
Planning Business Messages

CHAPTER 5
Organizing and Drafting Business Messages

CHAPTER 6
Revising Business Messages

IN UNIT 2, YOU WILL DEVELOP THE FOLLOWING EMPLOYABILITY SKILLS:

EMPLOYABILITY AND SOFT SKILLS	
Oral and Written Communication	✓
Information Management	✓
Critical Thinking	✓
Problem Solving	✓
Active Listening	✓
Professional Work Behaviours	✓
Goal-Setting	✓
Agility	✓
Adaptability	✓
Personal and Social Responsibility	✓
Ethical Decision Making	✓
Engagement	✓
Innovation and Creativity	✓
Learning Worker Attitude	✓
Team Building	✓
Accountability	✓
Project Collaboration	✓
Online Tools and Social Media[1]	✓

CHAPTER 4

Planning Business Messages

Andrey_Popov/Shutterstock

LEARNING OBJECTIVES

After studying this chapter, you should be able to

1 Summarize the 3-x-3 writing process and explain how it guides a writer.

2 Analyze the purpose of a message, anticipate its audience, and select the best communication channel.

3 Employ expert writing techniques and professional language skills.

4 Understand how teams approach collaborative writing projects.

SPOTLIGHT ON COMMUNICATION: PART 1

Wuxly Movement: Live Warm

Courtesy of Wuxly Movement

Wuxly Movement is a Canadian company dedicated to creating animal-free and sustainable outerwear. Its line of jackets has been created to endure tough Canadian winters while maintaining the company's progressive vision. The company employs strict fair labour practices, and through local production, it contributes to Canadian communities. Its products have been tested in every province and territory of Canada, as well as around the world.[2]

James Yurichuk and Anthony DeBartolo created Wuxly Movement to bring animal-free options to Canada and to minimize the environmental impact of production:

> The Earth is our home, and at Wuxly they ensure it's treated that way. When selecting fabrics, they gravitate towards those that provide top performance and minimal ecological impact. The local production limits the carbon footprint, and their commitment to reducing CO_2 emissions further supports wildlife. Wuxly proudly sources their VeganTech Shells from a 100-year old company in Montreal, Quebec. Every ounce of water that leaves the facility is clean, after being tested and treated for any water pollution. Plus, they use the heat from the dyeing process to help power the facility. As you can tell, they're on a constant mission to make their production, products, and packaging as green as possible.[3]

Wuxly's headquarters is located in downtown Toronto, Ontario, and the brand is available in 21 stores across Canada, as well as in New York.[4] In addition to Wuxly's strong ecommerce presence, "Ontario's thriving film industry made over 50 requests in the past year for heavy duty jackets" for its production teams. With the demand for animal-free and sustainable products on the rise, Wuxly Movement is poised for growth.[5]

CRITICAL THINKING

- Wuxly Movement's brand is committed to animals, fair labour, and sustainability. As the company composes messages to its customers, anticipating its primary audience is essential. Write an audience profile for the brand, detailing potential characteristics of the consumer.
- When marketing its brand, Wuxly knows its primary audience is already interested in its products. What expert writing techniques can Wuxly use to attract secondary audiences to the brand?

Using the 3-x-3 Writing Process as a Guide

LEARNING OBJECTIVE 1

Summarize the 3-x-3 writing process and explain how it guides a writer.

Today's new media and digital technologies enable you to choose from innumerable communication channels to create, transmit, and respond to messages. Nearly all communication, however, revolves around writing. Whether you are preparing a message that will be delivered digitally, orally, or in print, that message requires thinking and writing. Many of your messages will be digital. A *digital message* may be defined as one that is generated, stored, processed, and transmitted electronically by computers using strings of positive and nonpositive binary code (0s and 1s). That definition encompasses many messages, including e-mail, Facebook posts, tweets, and other messages.

For our purposes we will focus primarily on messages exchanged on the job. Because writing is central to all business communication, this chapter presents a systematic plan for preparing business messages in the digital age.

Defining Your Business Writing Goals

One thing you should immediately recognize about business writing is that it differs from other writing you have done. In preparing high school or postsecondary compositions and term papers, you probably focused on discussing your feelings or displaying your knowledge. Your instructors wanted to see your thought processes and assurance that you had internalized the subject matter. Business writing is definitely not like that. It also differs from personal texts you may exchange with your friends and family to stay connected and express your feelings. In the workplace you will want your writing to be the following:

- **Purposeful.** You will be writing to solve problems and convey information. You will have a definite strategy to fulfill in each message.
- **Economical.** You will try to present ideas clearly but concisely. Length is not rewarded.
- **Audience oriented.** You will concentrate on looking at a problem from the perspective of the audience instead of seeing it from your own.

These distinctions actually ease your task. Writing consultants and businesspeople complain that many postsecondary graduates entering industry have a conscious—or perhaps unconscious—perception that quantity enhances quality. Whether you are presenting your ideas in print, online, or in person, conciseness and clarity are what count in business.

The ability to prepare purposeful, concise, and audience-centred messages does not come naturally. Very few people, especially beginners, can sit down and draft an effective e-mail message, letter, or report without training. However, following a systematic process, studying model messages, and practising the craft can make nearly anyone a successful business writer or speaker.

CENGAGE

MINDTAP

Check out section 4-1b in MindTap, where you can watch a video featuring Courtney Thorne, an editor, discuss how to draft and tailor an e-mail for the receiver.

Introducing the 3-x-3 Writing Process

Regardless of what you are writing, the process will be easier if you follow a systematic plan. The 3-x-3 writing process breaks the entire task into three phases: *prewriting*, *drafting*, and *revising*, as shown in Figure 4.1.

FIGURE 4.1 The 3-x-3 Writing Process

1 Prewriting	2 Drafting	3 Revising
Analyze • What is your purpose? • What do you want the receiver to do or believe? • What channel should you choose: face-to-face conversation, group meeting, e-mail, memo, letter, report, blog, wiki, tweet, etc.?	**Research** • Gather data to provide facts. • Search company files, previous correspondence, and the Internet. • What do you need to know to write this message? • How much does the audience already know?	**Edit** • Edit your message to be sure it is clear, concise, conversational, and readable. • Revise to eliminate wordy fillers, long lead-ins, redundancies, and trite business phrases. • Develop parallelism. • Consider using headings and numbered and bulleted lists for quick reading.
Anticipate • Profile the audience. • What does the receiver already know? • Will the receiver's response be neutral, positive, or negative? How will this affect your organizational strategy?	**Organize** • Organize direct messages with the big idea first, followed by an explanation in the body and an action request in the closing. • For persuasive or negative messages, use an indirect, problem-solving strategy.	**Proofread** • Take the time to read every message carefully. • Look for errors in spelling, grammar, punctuation, names, and numbers. • Check to be sure the format is consistent.
Adapt • What techniques can you use to adapt your message to its audience? • How can you promote feedback? • Strive to use positive, conversational, and courteous language.	**Draft** • Prepare a first draft, usually quickly. • Focus on short, clear sentences using the active voice. • Build paragraph coherence by repeating key ideas, using pronouns, and incorporating appropriate transitional expressions.	**Evaluate** • Will this message achieve your purpose? • Does the tone sound pleasant and friendly rather than curt? • Have you thought enough about the audience to be sure this message is appealing? • Did you encourage feedback?

To illustrate the writing process, let's say that you own a popular Tim Hortons franchise. At rush times, customers complain about the chaotic multiple waiting lines to approach the service counter. Customer arguments over cutting in line are also increasing. You want to convince other franchise owners that an order-ahead mobile app system would work better. Instead of phoning the other owners, you want to present a serious argument with good points that they will remember and be willing to act on when they gather for their next district meeting. You decide to send a persuasive e-mail that you hope will win their support.

Prewriting. The first phase of the writing process prepares you to write. It involves *analyzing* the audience and your purpose for writing. The audience for your message will be other Tim Hortons franchise owners, some highly educated and others not. Your purpose in writing is to convince them that a change in policy would improve customer service. You think that an order-ahead system, like the ordering app Starbucks uses, would reduce chaos and make customers happier because they would not have to worry about where they are in line.

Prewriting also involves *anticipating* how your audience will react to your message. You are sure that some of the other owners will agree with you, but others might fear new technologies. In *adapting* your message to the audience, you try to think of the right words and the right tone that will win approval.

Drafting. The second phase involves researching, organizing, and then drafting the message. In *researching* information for this message, you would probably investigate other kinds of businesses that use mobile apps for customers. You might check your competitors. What are other coffee shops doing? You might do some calling to see whether other franchise owners are interested in an order-ahead system. Before writing to the entire group, you might brainstorm with a few owners to see what ideas they have for solving the problem.

After you have collected enough information, you would focus on *organizing* your message. Should you start out by offering your solution? Or should you work up to it slowly, describing the problem, presenting your evidence, and then ending with the solution? The final step in the second phase of the writing process is actually *drafting* the letter. At this point many writers write quickly, realizing that they will polish their ideas when they revise.

Revising. The third phase of the process involves editing, proofreading, and evaluating your message. After writing the first draft, you will spend considerable time *editing* the message for clarity, conciseness, tone, and readability. Could parts of it be rearranged to make your point more effectively? This is the time when you look for ways to improve the organization and tone of your message. Next, you will spend time *proofreading* carefully to ensure correct spelling, grammar, punctuation, and format. The final phase involves *evaluating* your message to decide whether it accomplishes your goal.

Pacing the Writing Process

The time you spend on each phase of the writing process varies depending on the complexity of the problem, the purpose, the audience, and your schedule. On average, you should expect to spend about 25 percent of your time prewriting, 25 percent drafting, and 50 percent revising.

These are rough guides, yet you can see that good writers spend most of their time on the final phase of revising and proofreading. Much depends, of course, on your project, its importance, and your familiarity with it. Beginning business writers often follow the writing process closely. With experience, though, they will become like other good writers and presenters who alter, compress, and rearrange the steps as needed. Refer to Figure 4.2 for the recursive nature of writing. What is critical to remember, though, is that revising is a major component of the writing process even if the message is short.

ETHICS CHECK

Contract Cheating

In Canada an academic black market exists where students can contract someone to write their papers for them. These online services charge per page and "offer completely original content, based on the assignment instructions and criteria."[6] To combat cheating, colleges and universities are working to increase students' awareness about academic integrity and are stiffening plagiarism consequences. Beyond lost degrees, what do students miss by buying assignments?

FIGURE 4.2 Scheduling the Writing Process

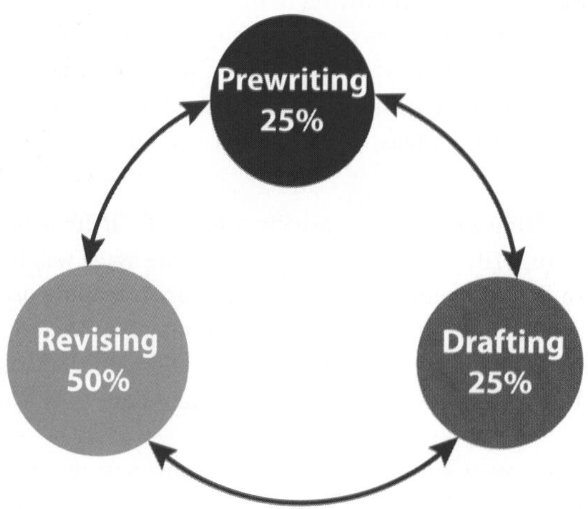

Although the writing process looks like a linear set of steps, it actually is recursive, enabling writers to revise their work continually as they progress. However, careful planning can avoid wasted time and frustration caused by rethinking and reorganizing during drafting.

Concept Check

1. Why is it recommended to prepare your first draft quickly?
2. Have you ever tried to make your writing longer than it needed to be? For example, did you count the words in what you wrote to meet a minimum word count? In pairs, discuss why some students overwrite for their assignments.

LEARNING OBJECTIVE 2

Analyze the purpose of a message, anticipate its audience, and select the best communication channel.

Analyzing and Anticipating the Audience

Surprisingly, many people begin writing and discover only as they approach the end of a message what they are trying to accomplish. If you analyze your purpose before you begin, you can avoid having to backtrack and start over. The remainder of this chapter covers the first phase of the writing process: analyzing the purpose for writing, anticipating how the audience will react, and adapting the message to the audience.

Determining Your Purpose

As you begin to compose a workplace message, ask yourself two important questions: (a) Why am I sending this message? and (b) What do I hope to achieve? Your responses will determine how you organize and present your information.

Your message may have primary and secondary purposes. The primary purposes for sending business messages are typically to inform and to persuade. A secondary purpose is to promote goodwill. You and your organization want to look good in the eyes of your audience.

Many business messages do nothing more than *inform*. They explain procedures, announce meetings, answer questions, and transmit findings. Such messages are usually developed directly. Some business messages, however, are meant to *persuade*. These messages sell products, convince managers, motivate employees, and win over customers. Persuasive messages are often developed indirectly. Direct and indirect strategies will be presented in Chapter 5 and subsequent chapters.

FIGURE 4.3 Asking the Right Questions to Profile Your Audience

Primary Audience

- Who is my primary reader or listener?
- What are my personal and professional relationships with this person?
- What position does this person hold in the organization?
- How much does this person know about the subject?
- What do I know about this person's education, beliefs, culture, and attitudes?
- Should I expect a neutral, positive, or negative response to my message?

Secondary Audience

- Who might see or hear this message in addition to the primary audience?
- How do these people differ from the primary audience?
- Do I need to include more background information?
- How must I reshape my message to make it understandable and acceptable to others to whom it might be forwarded?

Anticipating and Profiling the Audience

A good writer anticipates the audience for a message: What is the reader or listener like? How will that person react to the message? Although we can't always know exactly who the receiver is, it is possible to imagine some of that person's characteristics.

Profiling your audience is a pivotal step in the writing process. The questions in Figure 4.3 will help you profile your audience. How much time you devote to answering these questions depends on your message and its context.

- **An analytical report** that you compose for management or **an oral presentation** before a big group would, of course, demand considerable time profiling the audience.
- **An e-mail message** to a coworker or a message to a familiar supplier might require only a few moments of planning.
- **A blog post** on an important topic to be posted to a company website would require you to think about the local, national, and international audiences that might read that message.
- **Brief messages on social media** should make you think about who will read the messages. How much of your day and life do you want to share? Will customers and business partners be reading your posts?

No matter how short your message is, though, remember that your receivers will be thinking, *What's in it for me?* (*WIIFM*). WIIFM is one of the most important writing tips you can take away from this book.

Go to section 4-2b in MindTap, where you can watch a video featuring Mike Stiers, a cloud and infrastructure engineer, discuss the importance of planning your message carefully before sending it out.

Making Choices Based on the Audience Profile

Profiling your audience helps you make decisions about shaping the message. You will discover what language is appropriate, whether you are free to use specialized technical terms, whether you should explain the background, and so on. Profiling the audience helps you decide whether your tone should be formal or informal. Profiling helps you consider whether the receiver is likely to respond positively or negatively to your message, or be neutral about it.

Another consideration in profiling your audience is the possibility of a secondary audience. For example, let's say you start to write an e-mail message to your supervisor, Shruti, describing a problem you are having. Halfway through the message, you realize that Shruti will probably forward this message to her boss, the vice president. Considering the vice president as a secondary audience, you carefully revise your message in the following ways:

- Use a more formal tone.
- Remove your inquiry about Shruti's family.
- Reduce your complaints and tone down negative language.
- Provide more background information.

Analyzing the task and anticipating the audience help you adapt your message so it will be effective for both primary and secondary receivers.

Selecting the Best Channel

After identifying the purpose of your message, you will want to select the most appropriate communication channel. Your decision to send an e-mail message, schedule a videoconference, or use some other channel depends on some of the following factors:

- Importance, confidentiality, and sensitivity of the message
- Amount and speed of feedback and interactivity required
- Necessity of a permanent record
- Cost of the channel
- Degree of formality desired
- Receiver's preference and level of technical expertise

In addition to these practical issues, you will also consider how "rich" the channel is, as shown in Figure 4.4. As discussed in Chapter 1, a richer medium, such as a face-to-face conversation, permits more interactivity and feedback. A leaner medium, such as a letter or an e-mail, presents a flat, one-dimensional message. Richer media enable the sender to provide more verbal and visual cues and to tailor the message to the audience.

Choosing the wrong medium can result in a message that is less effective or even misunderstood. If, for example, marketing manager Jin must motivate the sales force to increase sales in the fourth quarter, he is unlikely to achieve his goal if he merely posts an announcement on the office bulletin board, writes a memo, or sends an e-mail. Jin could be more persuasive with a richer channel, such as individual face-to-face conversations or a group meeting to stimulate sales. For sales reps on the road, a richer medium would be a videoconference. In choosing channels, keep in mind two tips: (a) use the richest medium available and (b) employ richer media for more persuasive or personal communications.

Concept Check

1. Why is it important to always consider a secondary audience when composing a message?
2. After searching an alumni database, you decide to e-mail a professional who is working in the career you hope to enter. Your goal in writing to this professional is to obtain firsthand information about this person's career and to receive career advice. However, you know nothing about this person. How could you profile the receiver to help you shape your message? What audience benefits could you use to persuade the receiver? What channel would you choose to deliver your message?

FIGURE 4.4 Comparing Rich and Lean Communication Channels

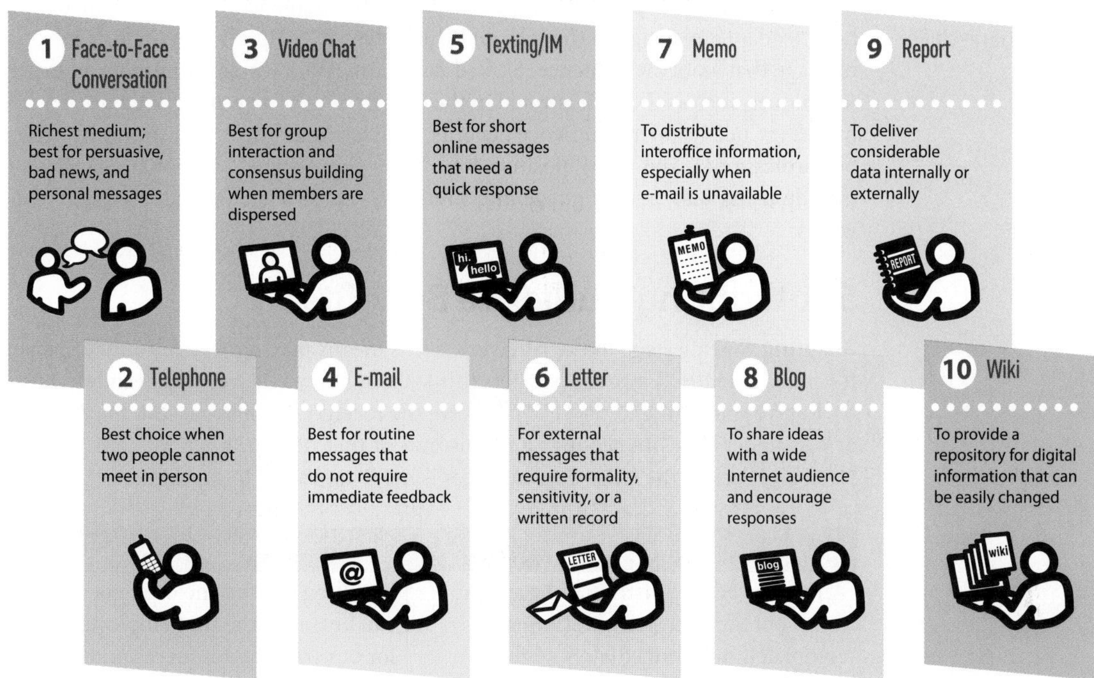

Ten Levels of Richness in Today's Workplace Communication Channels—Richest to Leanest
1 Face-to-Face Conversation
Richest medium; best for persuasive, bad news, and personal messages
2 Telephone
Best choice when two people cannot meet in person
3 Video Chat
Best for group interaction and consensus building when members are dispersed
4 E-mail
Best for routine messages that do not require immediate feedback
5 Texting/IM
Best for short online messages that need a quick response
hi.
hello
6 Letter
For external messages that require formality, sensitivity, or a written record
LETTER
7 Memo
To distribute interoffice information, especially when e-mail is unavailable
MEMO
8 Blog
To share ideas with a wide Internet audience and encourage responses
blog
9 Report
To deliver considerable data internally or externally
REPORT
10 Wiki
To provide a repository for digital information that can be easily changed
wiki

CASE CONNECTIONS

Hilroy: A Canadian Staple

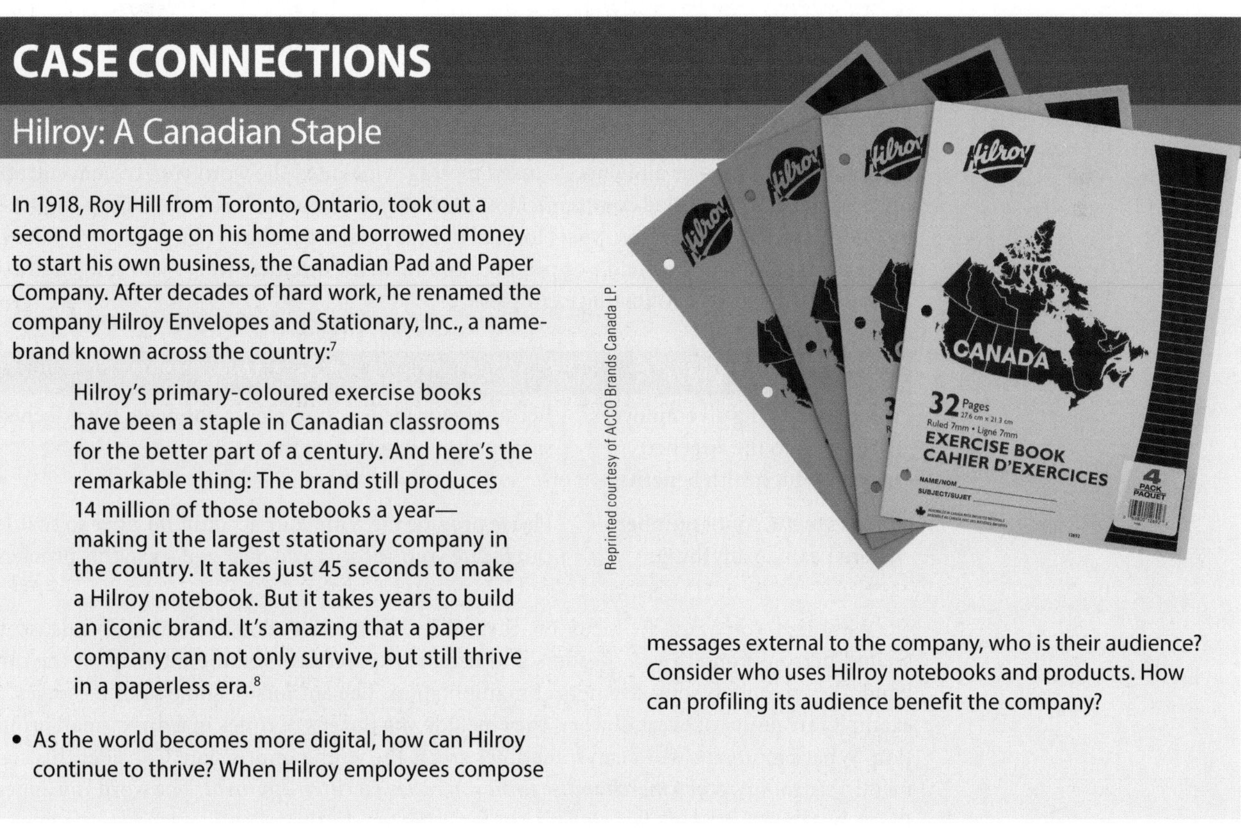

Hilroy
CANADA
32 Pages
EXERCISE BOOK
CAHIER D'EXERCICES
4 PACK PAQUET

Reprinted courtesy of ACCO Brands Canada LP.

In 1918, Roy Hill from Toronto, Ontario, took out a second mortgage on his home and borrowed money to start his own business, the Canadian Pad and Paper Company. After decades of hard work, he renamed the company Hilroy Envelopes and Stationary, Inc., a name-brand known across the country:[7]

> Hilroy's primary-coloured exercise books have been a staple in Canadian classrooms for the better part of a century. And here's the remarkable thing: The brand still produces 14 million of those notebooks a year—making it the largest stationary company in the country. It takes just 45 seconds to make a Hilroy notebook. But it takes years to build an iconic brand. It's amazing that a paper company can not only survive, but still thrive in a paperless era.[8]

- As the world becomes more digital, how can Hilroy continue to thrive? When Hilroy employees compose messages external to the company, who is their audience? Consider who uses Hilroy notebooks and products. How can profiling its audience benefit the company?

LEARNING OBJECTIVE 3

Employ expert writing techniques and professional language skills.

Using Expert Writing Techniques to Adapt to Your Audience

After analyzing the purpose and anticipating the audience, writers begin to think about how to adapt a message to the task and the audience. Adaptation is the process of creating a message that suits the audience. Skilled communicators employ a number of expert writing techniques, such as those illustrated in the two versions of an e-mail in Figure 4.5. These techniques include featuring audience benefits, cultivating a "you" view, sounding conversational but professional, and using positive, courteous expression. Additional adaptive techniques include using bias-free language and preferring plain language with familiar but vigorous words.

Spotlighting Audience Benefits

Adapting your message to the receiver's needs means putting yourself in that person's shoes. It's called *empathy.* Empathic senders think about how a receiver will decode a message. They try to give something to the receiver, solve the receiver's problems, save the receiver's money, or just understand the feelings and position of that person. Keep WIIFM in mind. Which version of each of the following messages is more appealing to the audience?

Sender Focus	Audience Focus
All employees are instructed herewith to fill out the enclosed questionnaire completely and immediately so that we can allocate our training resource funds to employees.	By filling out the enclosed questionnaire, you can be one of the first employees to sign up for our training resource funds.
Our warranty becomes effective only when we receive an owner's registration.	Your warranty begins working for you as soon as you return your owner's registration.

Developing the "You" View

Notice that the previous audience-focused messages included the word *you*. In concentrating on receiver benefits, skilled communicators naturally develop the "you" view. They emphasize second-person pronouns (*you, your*) instead of first-person pronouns (*I/we, us, our*). Whether your goal is to inform, persuade, or promote goodwill, the catchiest words you can use are *you* and *your.* Compare the following examples.

"I/We" View	"You" View
We are requiring all employees to respond to the attached survey about health benefits.	Because your ideas count, please complete the attached survey about health benefits.
I need your account number before I can do anything.	Please provide me with your account number so that I can locate your records and help you solve this problem.

Although you want to focus on the reader or listener, don't overuse or misuse the second-person pronoun *you*. Readers and listeners appreciate genuine interest; on the other hand, they resent obvious attempts at manipulation. The authors of some sales messages, for example, are guilty of overkill when they include *you* dozens of times in a direct-mail promotion. What's more, the word can sometimes create the wrong impression. Consider this statement: *You cannot return merchandise until you receive written approval.* The word *you* appears twice, but the reader may feel singled out for criticism. In the following version, the message is less personal and more positive: *Customers may return merchandise with written approval.*

FIGURE 4.5 Applying Expert Writing Techniques to Improve an E-mail Message

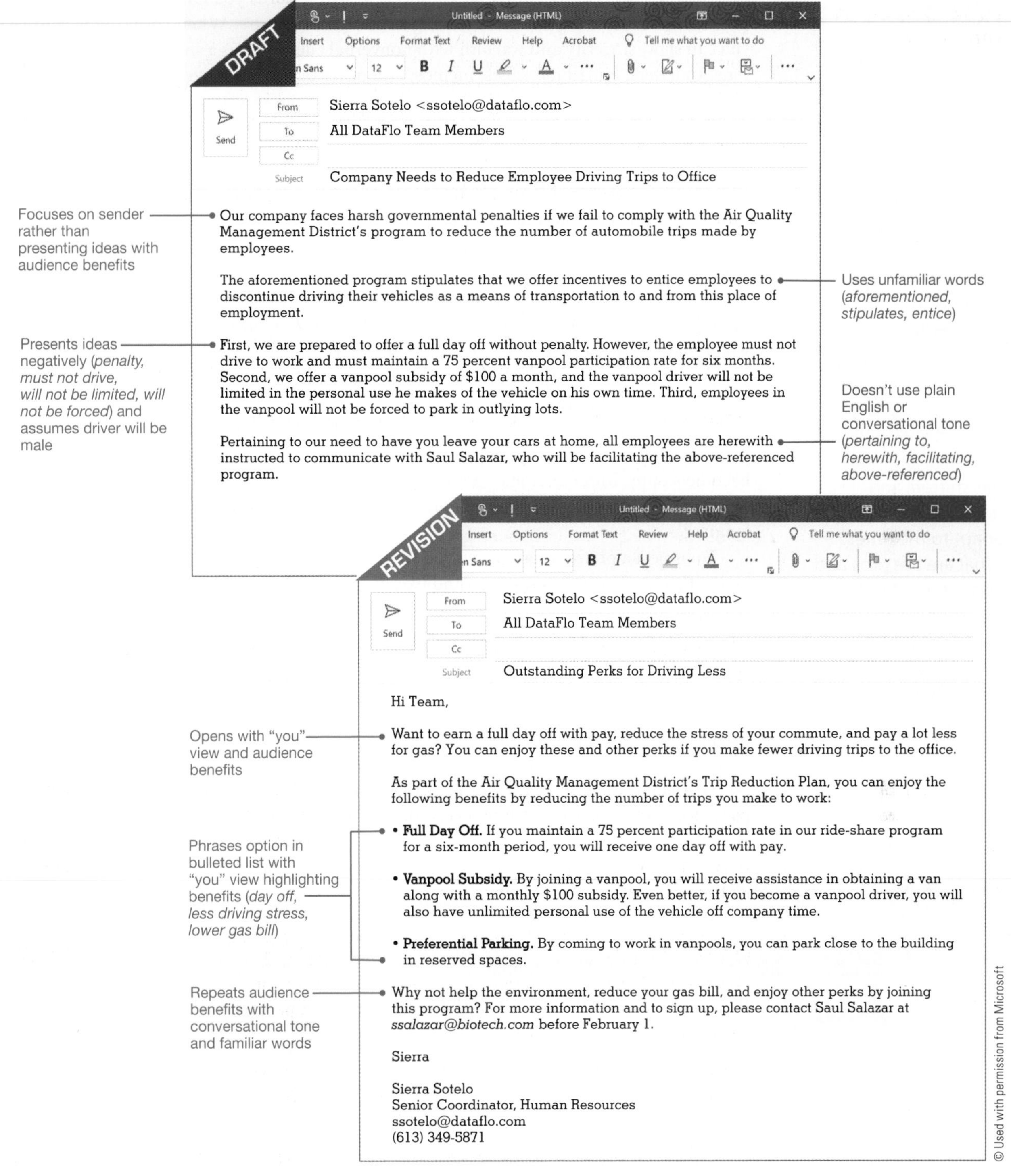

DRAFT
Untitled - Message (HTML)
From
Sierra Sotelo <ssotelo@dataflo.com>
To
All DataFlo Team Members
Cc
Subject
Company Needs to Reduce Employee Driving Trips to Office
Focuses on sender rather than presenting ideas with audience benefits
Our company faces harsh governmental penalties if we fail to comply with the Air Quality Management District's program to reduce the number of automobile trips made by employees.
The aforementioned program stipulates that we offer incentives to entice employees to discontinue driving their vehicles as a means of transportation to and from this place of employment.
Uses unfamiliar words (aforementioned, stipulates, entice)
Presents ideas negatively (penalty, must not drive, will not be limited, will not be forced) and assumes driver will be male
First, we are prepared to offer a full day off without penalty. However, the employee must not drive to work and must maintain a 75 percent vanpool participation rate for six months. Second, we offer a vanpool subsidy of $100 a month, and the vanpool driver will not be limited in the personal use he makes of the vehicle on his own time. Third, employees in the vanpool will not be forced to park in outlying lots.
Pertaining to our need to have you leave your cars at home, all employees are herewith instructed to communicate with Saul Salazar, who will be facilitating the above-referenced program.
Doesn't use plain English or conversational tone (pertaining to, herewith, facilitating, above-referenced)
REVISION
Untitled - Message (HTML)
From
Sierra Sotelo <ssotelo@dataflo.com>
To
All DataFlo Team Members
Cc
Subject
Outstanding Perks for Driving Less
Hi Team,
Opens with "you" view and audience benefits
Want to earn a full day off with pay, reduce the stress of your commute, and pay a lot less for gas? You can enjoy these and other perks if you make fewer driving trips to the office.
As part of the Air Quality Management District's Trip Reduction Plan, you can enjoy the following benefits by reducing the number of trips you make to work:
Phrases option in bulleted list with "you" view highlighting benefits (day off, less driving stress, lower gas bill)
• Full Day Off. If you maintain a 75 percent participation rate in our ride-share program for a six-month period, you will receive one day off with pay.
• Vanpool Subsidy. By joining a vanpool, you will receive assistance in obtaining a van along with a monthly $100 subsidy. Even better, if you become a vanpool driver, you will also have unlimited personal use of the vehicle off company time.
• Preferential Parking. By coming to work in vanpools, you can park close to the building in reserved spaces.
Repeats audience benefits with conversational tone and familiar words
Why not help the environment, reduce your gas bill, and enjoy other perks by joining this program? For more information and to sign up, please contact Saul Salazar at ssalazar@biotech.com before February 1.
Sierra
Sierra Sotelo
Senior Coordinator, Human Resources
ssotelo@dataflo.com
(613) 349-5871

Another difficulty in emphasizing the "you" view and de-emphasizing *we/I* is that it may result in an overuse of the passive voice. For example, to avoid *We will give you* (active voice), you might write *You will be given* (passive voice). The active voice in writing is generally preferred because it identifies who is doing the acting. You will learn more about active and passive voice in Chapter 5.

ETHICS CHECK

Time to Spell Out the F-word?

Many journalists have started to question the censorship of swear words in traditional newspapers. Newspapers like the *Toronto Star* have profanity policies in place. For example, out of respect for their readers, they use dashes to omit letters in the f-word. Some argue that society's comfort level with offensive language has shifted, and newspapers should adapt to the times.[9] What are the pros and cons of traditional newspapers adjusting their standards to reflect the online media culture?

In recognizing the value of the "you" attitude, however, you don't have to sterilize your writing and totally avoid any first-person pronouns or words that show your feelings. You can convey sincerity, warmth, and enthusiasm by the words you choose. Don't be afraid of phrases such as *I'm happy* or *We're delighted*, if you truly are. When speaking face to face, you can show sincerity and warmth with nonverbal cues, such as a smile and a pleasant voice tone. In letters, e-mail messages, memos, and other digital messages, however, only expressive words and phrases can show your feelings. These phrases suggest hidden messages that say *You are important, I hear you*, and *I'm honestly trying to please you.*

Sounding Conversational but Professional

Most of the business messages you write replace conversation. Thus, they are most effective when they convey an informal, conversational tone instead of a formal, pretentious tone. Just how informal you can be depends greatly on the workplace. At Google casual seems to be preferred. In a short message to users describing changes in its privacy policies, Google wrote, "We believe this stuff matters."[10] In more traditional organizations, that message probably would have been more formal. The dilemma for you, then, is knowing how casual to be in your writing. We suggest that you strive to be conversational but professional, especially until you learn what your organization prefers.

E-mail, instant messaging, chat, and other short messaging channels enable you and your coworkers to have spontaneous conversations. Don't, however, let your messages become sloppy, unprofessional, or even dangerous. You will learn more about the dangers of e-mail and other digital channels later. At this point, though, we focus on the tone of the language.

To project a professional image, you want to sound educated and mature. The overuse of expressions such as *hey, you know*, and *like*, as well as reliance on unnecessary abbreviations (*BTW* for *by the way*), make a businessperson sound like a teenager. Professional messages do not include texting-style abbreviations, slang, sentence fragments, and chitchat. We urge you to strive for a warm, conversational tone that avoids low-level diction. Levels of diction, as shown in Figure 4.6, range from unprofessional to formal.

Although some writers are too casual, others are overly formal. To impress readers and listeners, they use big words, long sentences, legal terminology, and third-person constructions. Stay away from expressions such as *the undersigned, the writer*, and *the affected party.* You will sound friendlier with familiar pronouns, such as *I, we*, and *you*. The following examples illustrate a professional yet conversational tone:

FIGURE 4.6 Levels of Diction

Unprofessional (low-level diction)	Conversational (middle-level diction)	Formal (high-level diction)
badmouth	criticize	denigrate
guts	nerve	courage
pecking order	line of command	dominance hierarchy
ticked off	upset	provoked
rat on	inform	betray
rip off	steal	expropriate
If we just hang in there, we'll snag the contract.	If we don't get discouraged, we'll win the contract.	If the principals persevere, they will secure the contract.

Unprofessional	Professional
Hey, boss. Firewall now installed!! Lmk before announcing it.	Mr. Smith, our new firewall software is now installed. Please let me know before announcing it.
This report is basic. And the figures are garbage, tbh. Show me some real stats.	Because the figures in this report seem inaccurate, please submit the source statistics.

Overly Formal	Conversational
All employees are herewith instructed to return the appropriately designated contracts to the undersigned.	Please return your contracts to me.
Pertaining to your order, we must verify the sizes that your organization requires prior to consignment of your order to our shipper.	We will send your order as soon as we confirm the sizes you need.

Being Positive Rather Than Negative

You can improve the clarity, tone, and effectiveness of a message if you use positive rather than negative language. Positive language generally conveys more information than negative language does. Moreover, positive messages are uplifting and pleasant to read. Positive wording tells what *is* and what *can be done* rather than what *isn't* and what *can't be done.* For example, *Your order cannot be shipped by January 10* is not nearly as informative as *Your order will be shipped January 15.* An office supply store adjacent to an ice cream parlour posted a sign on its door that reads *Please enjoy your ice cream before you enjoy our store.* That sounds much more positive and inviting than *No food allowed!*[11]

Using positive language also involves avoiding negative words that create ill-will. Some words appear to blame or accuse your audience. For example, opening a letter to a customer with *You claim that* suggests that you don't believe the customer. Other loaded words that can get you in trouble are *complaint, criticism, defective, failed, mistake,* and *neglected.* Also avoid phrases such as *you apparently are unaware of, you did not provide, you misunderstood,* and *you don't understand.* Often you may be unconscious of the effect of these words. Notice in the following examples how you can revise the negative tone to create a more positive impression.

Negative	Positive
This plan definitely cannot succeed if we don't obtain management approval.	This plan definitely can succeed if we obtain management approval.
You failed to include your credit card number, so we can't mail your order.	We look forward to completing your order as soon as we receive your credit card number.

Expressing Courtesy

Maintaining a courteous tone involves not just guarding against rudeness but also avoiding words that sound demanding or preachy. Expressions such as *you should, you must,* and *you have to* cause people to instinctively react with *Oh, yeah?* One remedy is to turn these demands into rhetorical questions that begin with *Will you please . . .* Giving reasons for a request also softens the tone.

Even when you feel justified in displaying anger, remember that losing your temper or being sarcastic will seldom accomplish your goals as a business communicator: to inform, to persuade, and to create goodwill. When you are irritated, frustrated, or infuriated, keep cool and try to defuse the situation. In dealing with customers in telephone conversations, use polite phrases, such as *I would be happy to assist you with that*, *Thank you for being so patient*, and *It was a pleasure speaking with you*.

Less Courteous	More Courteous and Helpful
Can't you people get anything right? This is the second time I've written!	Please credit my account for $340. My latest statement shows that the error noted in my letter of May 15 has not yet been corrected.
Stewart, you must complete all performance reviews by Friday.	Stewart, will you please complete all performance reviews by Friday.

As a new or young employee who wants to fit in, don't fail to be especially courteous to older employees and important people in superior positions.[12] To make a great impression and show respect, use good manners in person and in writing. For example, don't be presumptuous by issuing orders or setting the time for a meeting with a superior. Use first names only if given permission to do so. In your messages be sure to proofread meticulously even if the important person to whom you are writing sends careless, error-filled messages.[13]

Employing Bias-Free Language

In adapting a message to its audience, be sure your language is sensitive and *bias free*. Few writers set out to be offensive. Sometimes, though, we all say things that we never thought might be hurtful. The real problem is that we don't think about the words that stereotype groups of people, such as *the boys in the mail room* or *the girls in the front office*. Be cautious about expressions that might be biased in terms of gender, race, ethnicity, age, or disability.

Generally, you can avoid gender-biased language by choosing alternative language for words involving *man* or *woman*, by using plural nouns and pronouns, or by changing to a gender-free word (*person* or *representative*). Avoid the *his or her* option whenever possible. It's wordy and conspicuous and doesn't consider nonbinary people. With a little effort, you can usually find a construction that is graceful, grammatical, and unselfconscious.

Specify age only if it is relevant, and avoid expressions that are demeaning or subjective (such as *the old guy*). To avoid disability bias, do not refer to an individual's disability unless it is relevant. When necessary, use terms that do not stigmatize individuals with disabilities. The real key to bias-free communication, though, lies in your awareness and commitment. Be on the lookout to ensure that your messages do not exclude, stereotype, or offend people. Many everyday expressions carry negative connotations that you may not realize. For example, idioms like *low man on the totem pole* and *circle the wagons* not only are confusing to many individuals in Canada's diverse workforce but are offensive to Indigenous people.[14] The following examples give you a quick look at a few problem expressions and possible replacements.

Gender Biased	Improved
male nurse, cleaning woman	nurse, cleaner
waiter/waitress, stewardess	server, flight attendant
the doctor . . . he	doctors . . . they
the teacher . . . she	teachers . . . they
executives and their wives	executives and their spouses
businessman, salesman	businessperson, sales representative
Each employee had his picture taken.	Each employee had a picture taken. All employees had their pictures taken.

Racially or Ethnically Biased	Improved
An Indian accountant was hired.	An accountant was hired.
James Lee, a Chinese Canadian, applied.	James Lee applied.

Age Biased	Improved
The law applied to old people.	The law applied to people over 65.
Sally Kay, 55, was transferred.	Sally Kay was transferred.

Disability Biased	Improved
afflicted with arthritis, suffering from arthritis, crippled by arthritis	has arthritis
confined to a wheelchair	uses a wheelchair

Preferring Plain Language and Familiar Words

In adapting your message to your audience, use plain language and familiar words that you think audience members will recognize. Don't, however, avoid a big word that conveys your idea efficiently and is appropriate for the audience. Your goal is to shun pompous and pretentious language. Instead, use "GO" words. If you mean *begin*, don't say *commence* or *initiate*. If you mean *pay*, don't write *compensate*. By substituting everyday, familiar words for unfamiliar ones, as shown here, you help your audience comprehend your ideas quickly.

Unfamiliar	Familiar
interrogate	question
materialize	appear
obfuscate	confuse
remuneration	pay, salary
terminate	end

At the same time, be selective in your use of jargon. *Jargon* describes technical or specialized terms within a field. These terms enable insiders to communicate complex ideas briefly, but to outsiders they mean nothing. Human resources professionals, for example, know precisely what's meant by *cafeteria plan* (a benefits option program), but most of us would be thinking about lunch. Geologists refer to *plate tectonics*, and physicians discuss *metastatic carcinomas*. These terms mean little to most of us. Use specialized language only when the audience will understand it. In addition, don't forget to consider secondary audiences: Will those potential receivers understand any technical terms used?

Using Precise, Vigorous Words

Strong verbs and concrete nouns give receivers more information and keep them interested. Don't overlook the thesaurus (or the thesaurus program on your computer) for expanding your word choices and vocabulary. Whenever possible, use specific words, as shown here.

Imprecise, Dull	More Precise
a change in profits	a 25 percent hike in profits; a 10 percent plunge in profits
to say	to promise, confess, understand, allege, assert, assume, judge
to think about	to identify, diagnose, analyze, probe, examine, inspect

The Checklist reviews important elements in the first phase of the 3-x-3 writing process. As you review these tips, remember the three basics of prewriting: analyzing, anticipating, and adapting.

CHECKLIST

Adapting a Message to Its Audience

- **Identify the message purpose.** Why are you writing and what do you hope to achieve? Consider both primary and secondary audiences.
- **Select the most appropriate channel.** Consider the importance, feedback, interactivity, cost, formality, sensitivity, and richness of the options.
- **Profile the audience.** What is your relationship with the receiver? How much does the receiver know or need to know?
- **Focus on audience benefits.** Phrase your statements from the reader's view. Concentrate on the "you" view.
- **Avoid gender, racial, age, and disability bias.** Use bias-free words. Instead of *new 22-year-old employee,* say *new employee.*
- **Be conversational but professional.** Strive for a warm, friendly tone that is not overly formal or familiar. Avoid slang and low-level diction.
- **Express ideas positively rather than negatively.** Instead of *We can't ship until June 1,* say *We can ship on June 1.*
- **Use short, familiar words.** Avoid big words and technical terms unless they are appropriate for the audience (*end*, not *terminate*).
- **Search for precise, vigorous words.** Use a thesaurus if necessary to find strong verbs and concrete nouns (*announces* instead of *says, brokerage* instead of *business*).

Concept Check

1. Consider a time when you heard someone use biased language. Discuss how this biased language affected your opinion of the individual or the organization.
2. Negative phrases can often be rewritten to sound positive. Rewrite the following sentences to sound positive:
   a. Your e-mail from May 30 claims that you did not receive your order.
   b. Do you have any complaints?
   c. You cannot park in Lot E until April 12.

LEARNING OBJECTIVE 4

Understand how teams approach collaborative writing projects.

Sharing the Writing in Teams

As you learned in Chapter 2, many of today's workers collaborate in teams to deliver services, develop products, and complete projects. It is almost assumed that today's progressive organizations will employ teams in some capacity to achieve their objectives. Because much of a team's work involves writing, you can expect to be putting your writing skills to work as part of a team.

When Is Team Writing Necessary?

Collaboration on team-written documents is necessary for projects that (a) are big, (b) have short deadlines, and (c) require the expertise or consensus of many people. Businesspeople sometimes also collaborate on short documents, such as memos, letters, information briefs, procedures, and policies. More often, however, teams work together on big documents and presentations.

Why Are Team-Written Documents Better?

Team-written documents and presentations are standard in most organizations because collaboration has many advantages. Most important, collaboration usually produces a better product because many heads are better than one. In addition, team members and organizations benefit from team processes. Working together helps socialize members. They learn more about the organization's values and procedures. Members are able to break down functional barriers, and they improve both formal and informal chains of communication.

Additionally, they buy in to a project when they are part of its development. Members of effective teams are eager to implement their recommendations.

How Are Team-Written Documents Divided?

With big writing projects, teams may not actually function together for each phase of the writing process. Typically, team members gather at the beginning to brainstorm. They iron out answers to questions about the purpose, audience, content, organization, and design of their document or presentation. They develop procedures for team functioning, as you learned in Chapter 2. Then, they often assign segments of the project to individual members.

In Phase 1 of the writing process, teams work together closely as they discuss the project and establish their purpose. In Phase 2 members generally work separately when they conduct research, organize their findings, and compose a first draft. During Phase 3 some teams work together to synthesize their drafts and offer suggestions for revision. Other teams appoint one person to proofread and edit and another to prepare the final document. The revision and evaluation phase might be repeated several times before the final product is ready for presentation. Sharing the entire writing process, illustrated in Figure 4.7, means that all team members contribute their skills during the three phases.

What Digital Collaboration Tools Support Team Writing?

One of the most frustrating tasks for teams is writing shared documents. Keeping the various versions straight and recognizing who made what comment can be difficult. Fortunately, digital collaboration tools are constantly being developed and improved. During the planning stage, teams will decide on the following tools to support their writing project:

- **E-mail.** E-mail remains a popular tool for online asynchronous (intermittent data transmission) collaboration. As projects grow more complex, however, e-mail becomes an ineffective tool, especially for teams of people who are not working near each other.
- **Instant messaging and texting.** Instant messaging and texting are helpful in initiating a quick group discussion and allow members to clear up minor matters immediately.

FIGURE 4.7 Sharing the Writing of Team Documents

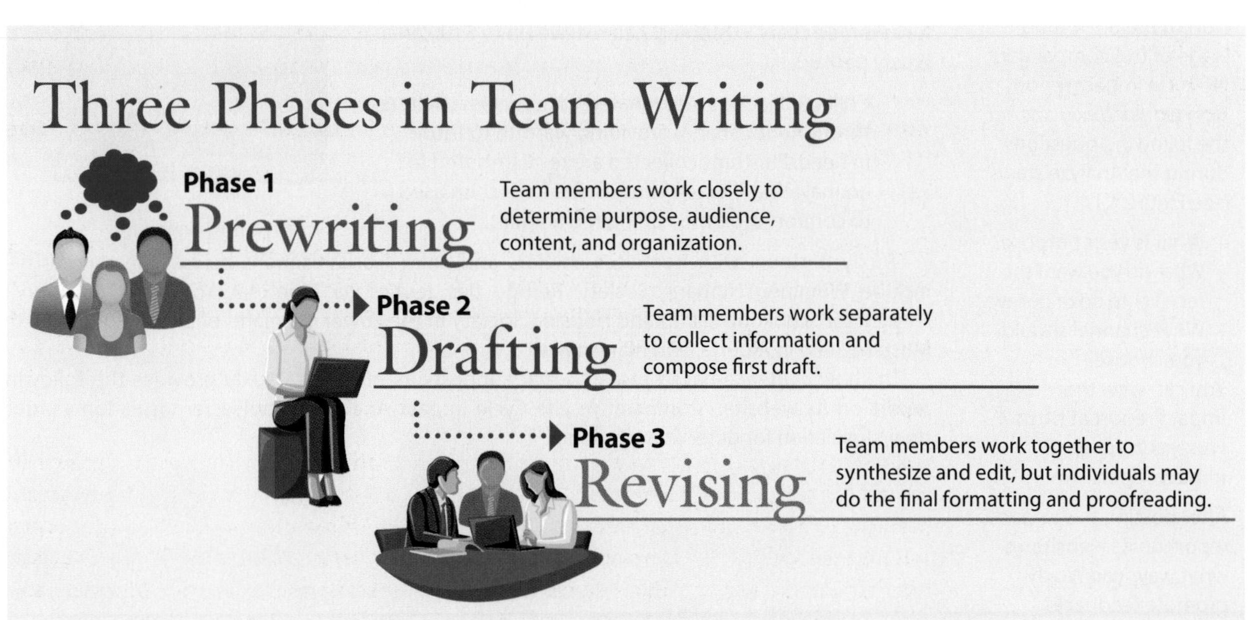

Three Phases in Team Writing
Phase 1
Prewriting
Team members work closely to determine purpose, audience, content, and organization.
Phase 2
Drafting
Team members work separately to collect information and compose first draft.
Phase 3
Revising
Team members work together to synthesize and edit, but individuals may do the final formatting and proofreading.

Images, left to right: iadams/Fotolia LLC; denis_pc/Fotolia LLC; denis_pc/Fotolia LLC.

- **Wikis.** A *wiki* is a website that allows multiple users to create, revise, and edit their own documents, as well as contribute ideas to others. A wiki facilitates teamwork because members can make comments and monitor the progress of a project. You'll learn more about wikis in Chapter 7.
- **Track Changes and other tools.** MS Word includes Track Changes and Comment features that enable collaborators working on the same document to identify and approve edits made by team members. See the Plugged In box in Chapter 6 for more information about revising team documents.
- **Web and telephone conferencing.** When teams are unable to meet in person and need to share information and make decisions in real time, conferencing tools such as Zoom and BlueJeans work well.
- **Collaboration software.** For simple projects, collaboration software, such as Google Docs, permits teams to work on text documents, spreadsheets, and presentations either in real time or at different times. Multiple team members can edit and share Web pages, MS Word documents, or PDF (portable document format) files. Another popular collaboration tool is Dropbox, which offers cross-platform file sharing and online backup.

Concept Check

1. What is the best way to distribute tasks when working on a team-written document?
2. Think back to the last time you were involved in a team project. What did the team do that resulted in an efficient working process and a successful product, or an inefficient working process and an unsuccessful product?

SPOTLIGHT ON COMMUNICATION: PART 2

Wuxly Movement Revisited

CRITICAL THINKING

- During the prewriting stage of this comparative life cycle impact report, how would Wuxly answer the following questions during the Analyze stage (see Figure 4.1):
  - What is your purpose?
  - What do you want the receiver to do or believe?
  - What channel should you choose?

  You can view the impact report at https://wuxly.com/pages/impact-report.
- After posting this impact report on its website, in what ways can Wuxly promote feedback?

As a customer incentive, Wuxly Movement offers a Live Warm Trade Up program. By trading in their down-filled or fur-trimmed coats, customers can receive up to $100 off a Wuxly parka:[15]

Courtesy of Wuxly Movement

> Collected jackets are donated to homeless shelters throughout Canada, providing warmth to those in need. Fur-trims collected are re-distributed to animal rehabilitation centres; the fur is then used to comfort orphaned or injured animals.[16]

Wuxly partners with homeless shelters and animal organizations across Canada. Partners include Winnipeg Humane Society, Refuge des Jeunes de Montréal, Youth in Transition in Fredericton, Lookout Health and Housing Society in the Lower Mainland of British Columbia, the Mustard Seed in Alberta, and many more.[17]

To show evidence-based research that supports its products, Wuxly provides the following report on its website: "Comparative Life Cycle Impact Analysis of polyester insulation vs. duck down insulation for outerwear clothing."[18]

Summary of Learning Objectives

1 Summarize the 3-x-3 writing process and explain how it guides a writer.

- The 3-x-3 writing process helps writers by providing a systematic plan for writing efficient and effective messages.
- Phase 1 of the 3-x-3 writing process (prewriting) involves analyzing the message, anticipating the audience, and considering ways to adapt the message to the audience.
- Phase 2 (drafting) involves researching, organizing, and drafting the message.
- Phase 3 (revising) includes editing, proofreading, and evaluating the message.

2 Analyze the purpose of a message, anticipate its audience, and select the best communication channel.

- Before drafting, communicators must determine their purpose for writing and select the best communication channel.
- Communicators must also visualize both the primary and the secondary audiences, which helps them choose the most appropriate language, tone, and content for a message.
- Senders consider that receivers will usually be thinking, *What's in it for me?* (*WIIFM*).

3 Employ expert writing techniques and professional language skills.

- Skilled communicators consider audience benefits and look at a message from the receiver's perspective, applying the "you" view without attempting to manipulate.
- Expert writing techniques also include using conversational but professional language along with positive language and a courteous tone.
- Writers should also avoid language that excludes, stereotypes, or offends people.
- Plain language, familiar terms, strong verbs, and concrete nouns improve readability and effectiveness.

4 Understand how teams approach collaborative writing projects.

- Workplace projects involving the expertise of many people often require team writing.
- During Phase 1 (prewriting) of the writing process, teams usually work together in brainstorming and working out their procedures and assignments.
- During Phase 2 (drafting) individual members research and write their portions of the project report or presentation.
- During Phase 3 (revising) teams may work together using digital collaboration tools to combine and revise their drafts.

Chapter Review

1. What is the definition of a *digital message*? (Obj. 1)
2. Describe the components in each stage of the 3-x-3 writing process. Approximately how much time is spent on each stage? (Obj. 1)
3. How does profiling the audience help a business communicator prepare a message? (Obj. 2)
4. What factors should writers consider in selecting an appropriate channel to deliver a message? (Obj. 2)
5. What is the "you" view? When can the use of *you* backfire? (Obj. 3)
6. Why is it important to avoid texting-style abbreviations in your business messages? (Obj. 3)

7. How can you improve the clarity, tone, and effectiveness of your message? (Obj. 3)
8. What is the best way to avoid gender-biased language in your writing? (Obj. 3)
9. How do teams collaborate during the three phases of the writing process? (Obj. 4)
10. What is *collaboration software*, and how can it benefit team writing projects? (Obj. 4)

Critical Thinking

1. Because of today's new media and technologies, many of your messages will be digital. In what ways does this make your writing skills more important than ever? (Obj. 1)
2. Why do you think employers prefer messages that are not written like high school, university, or college essays? (Obj. 1)
3. Why is it important to consider a secondary audience when composing a message? (Obj. 2)
4. Some businesspeople use big words to impress readers. In what ways can using high-level diction backfire on the writer? (Obj. 3)
5. **Ethical Issue:** After a workplace project was completed, you were upset. You and two other team members did all the work, but two freeloaders are sharing in the credit. Should you report the freeloaders to the manager? Explain your decision. (Obj. 4)

Activities

4.1 Analyzing Audiences (Obj. 2)

YOUR TASK Using the questions in Figure 4.3, write a brief analysis of the audience for each of the following communication tasks. What kind of reaction should you expect from the primary reader and any secondary readers?

a. As an administrator at the municipal water department, you must write a letter to water users explaining that the tap water may taste and smell bad; however, it poses no threats to health.

b. As a new graduate, you are preparing a cover message to accompany your résumé for a job that you saw listed on a company website. You are confident that your qualifications match the job description.

c. You are about to send an e-mail to your regional sales manager describing your visit to a new customer who is demanding special discounts.

4.2 Audience Benefits and the "You" View (Obj. 3)

YOUR TASK Revise the following sentences to emphasize the perspective of the audience and the "you" view.

a. Our social media engineers are excited to announce a new free app called Fan Boosters that we believe will get fans to share, like, and subscribe to your content.

b. To help us process your order with our new database software, we need you to go to our website and fill out the customer information required.

c. We are now offering RapidAssist, a software program we have developed to provide immediate technical support through our website to your employees and customers.

4.3 Conversational but Professional (Obj. 3)

YOUR TASK Revise the following to make the tone conversational yet professional.

a. Pertaining to your request, the above-referenced items (printer toner and supplies) are being sent to your Oakdale office, as per your telephone conversation of April 1.

b. BTW, Angela went ballistic when the manager accused her of ripping off office supplies.

c. To facilitate ratification of this agreement, your negotiators urge that the membership respond in the affirmative.

4.4 Bias-Free Language (Obj. 3)

YOUR TASK Revise the following sentences to reduce gender, racial, ethnic, age, and disability bias.

a. The conference will offer special excursions for the wives of executives.

b. Does each salesman have his own smartphone loaded with his special sales information?

c. Media Moguls hired Amanda Love, an Indigenous Canadian, for the position of social media coordinator.

4.5 Plain Language and Familiar Words (Obj. 3)

YOUR TASK Revise the following sentences to use plain language and familiar words.

a. To expedite ratification of the agreement, we beseech you to vote in the affirmative.

b. The seller tried to obfuscate the issue by mentioning closing and other costs.

c. Even after officers interrogated the suspect, solid evidence failed to materialize.

4.6 Precise, Vigorous Words (Obj. 3)

YOUR TASK From the choices in parentheses, select the most precise, vigorous words.

a. Management is predicting a (*change, difference, drop*) in earnings after the first of the year.

b. We plan to (*acknowledge, announce, applaud*) the work of outstanding employees.

c. If necessary, we will (*review, change, reduce*) overtime hours to (*fix, balance, rework*) the budget.

Grammar and Mechanics | *Review 4*

Adjectives and Adverbs

Review Guides 19 to 20 about adjectives and adverbs in Appendix B, Grammar and Mechanics Guide, beginning on page B-1. On a sheet of paper or on your computer, revise the following sentences to correct errors in adjectives and adverbs. For each error that you locate, write the guide number that deals with this usage. Some sentences may have two errors. If a sentence is correct, write *C*. When you finish, compare your responses with the key in Appendix C.

1. The ability to prepare a purposeful, concise, and audience-centred message does not come natural to most people.
2. Christie thought she had done good in her performance review.
3. The team wiki enables everyone to see the most up to the minute status information.
4. All of our newly-created team documents can be posted quick to the wiki.
5. We all felt badly when one member lost her laptop and had no backup.
6. The 3-x-3 writing process provides step by step instructions for preparing messages.
7. Everyone likes the newly-revamped website and its up-to-date links.
8. Our project ran smooth after Justin reorganized the team.
9. Locally installed online collaboration tools are easy-to-use and work well.
10. Well written business messages sound conversational but professional.

Notes

[1] Based on Conference Board of Canada. (2020). *Employability skills.* https://www.conferenceboard.ca/edu/employability-skills.aspx

[2] allTRUEist. (n.d.). Wuxly Movement. https://www.alltrueist.com/pages/about-wuxly-movement

[3] Ibid.

[4] Siwak, H. (2019, June 5). Animal-free brand "Wuxly Movement" seeks to dominate Canadian outerwear market. *Retail Insider.* https://www.retail-insider.com/retail-insider/2019/6/animal-free-outerwear-brand-wuxly-movement-sees-growth-in-canadian-market

[5] Ibid.

[6] Eaton, S. E. (2017, October 18). Universities unite against the academic black market. *University Affairs.* https://www.universityaffairs.ca/opinion/in-my-opinion/universities-unite-academic-black-market/

[7] CBC Radio. (2019, May 23). *How this Canadian-born paper company thrives in a paperless era.* https://www.cbc.ca/radio/undertheinfluence/how-this-canadian-born-paper-company-thrives-in-a-paperless-era-1.5146339

[8] Ibid. CBC Licensing.

[9] English, K. (2014, April 4). Is it time for the *Star* to spell out swear words? *Toronto Star.* https://www.thestar.com/opinion/public_editor/2014/04/04/is_it_time_for_the_star_to_spell_out_swear_words_public_editor.html

[10] Google. (2012, January 30). E-mail message to Mary Ellen Guffey.

[11] Be positive. (2009, March). *Communication Briefings*, p. 5. Adapted from Brandi, J. (n.d.). *Winning at customer retention*. Customer Coach. http://www.customercarecoach.com

[12] Canavor, N. (2012). *Business writing in the digital age*. SAGE, p. 52.

[13] Ibid.

[14] Indigenous Corporate Training, Inc. (2019). *23 tips on what not to say or do when working effectively with Indigenous peoples.* https://www.ictinc.ca

[15] Wuxly Movement. (2019). *Live warm trade up program.* https://wuxly.ca/pages/trade-up

[16] Ibid.

[17] Wuxly Movement. (2019). *Partners*. https://wuxly.ca/pages/partners

[18] Wuxly Movement. (2019). *Impact report.* https://wuxly.ca/pages/impact-report

CHAPTER 5

Organizing and Drafting Business Messages

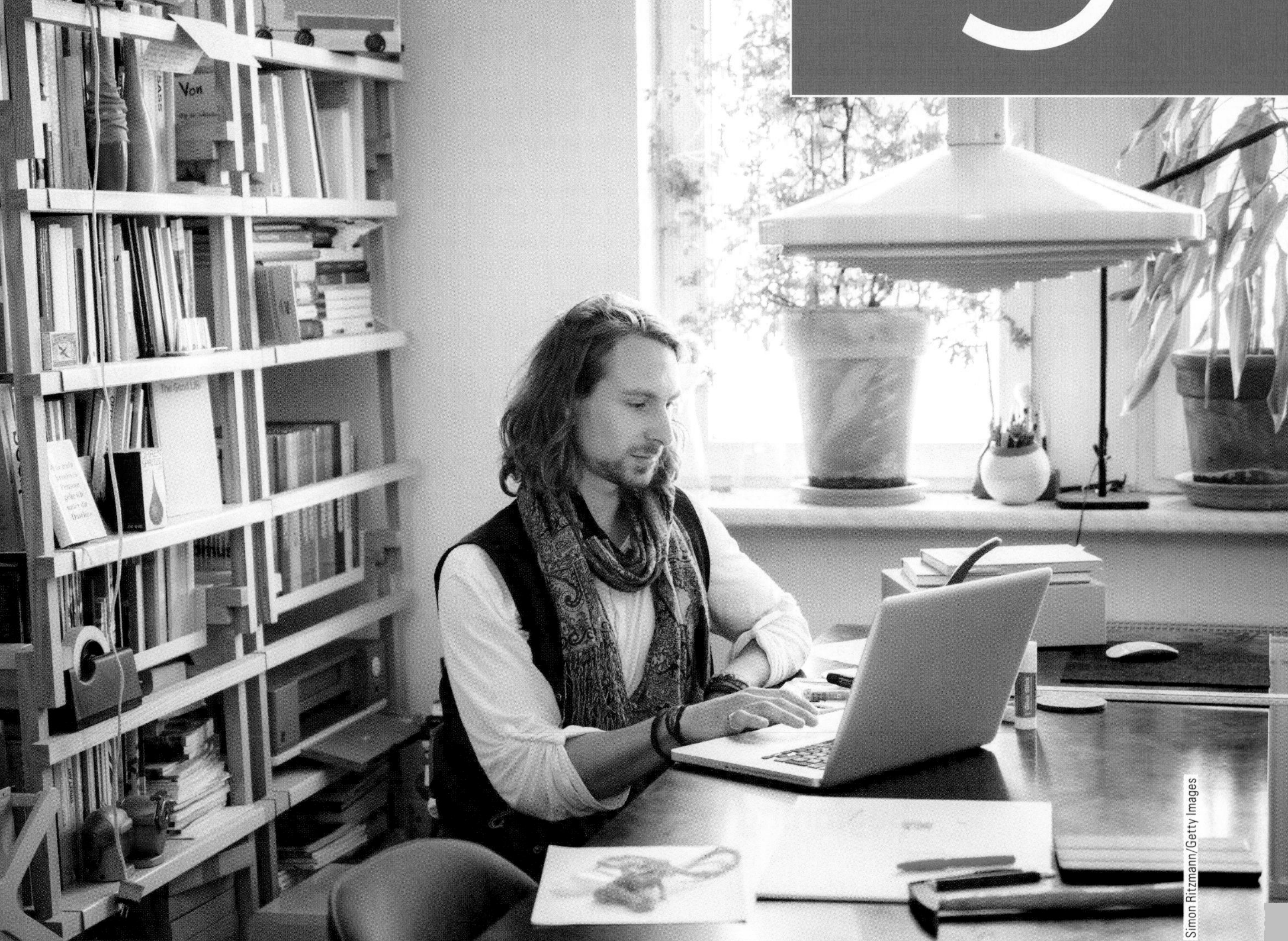

Simon Ritzmann/Getty Images

LEARNING OBJECTIVES

After studying this chapter, you should be able to

1 Apply Phase 2 of the 3-x-3 writing process, which begins with research to collect background information.

2 Explain how to generate and organize ideas resulting from brainstorming, brainwriting, and social media techniques.

3 Compose the first draft of a message by using a variety of sentence types and avoiding common sentence errors.

4 Improve your writing techniques by carefully constructing sentences.

5 Draft well-organized paragraphs and use techniques for achieving paragraph coherence.

6 Enhance readability by understanding document design.

SPOTLIGHT ON COMMUNICATION: PART 1

Wordsmith Associates Communications Consultants Inc.: One Company's Passion for Simplicity

CRITICAL THINKING

- In what ways can effective sentences and well-organized paragraphs create simplicity and clarity in a message?
- Whether you are preparing a presentation or composing a business letter, why is it important to customize every word to relate to a specific purpose and audience?

Courtesy of Wordsmith

Wordsmith has offices in Calgary, Alberta. Over the past 35 years, about 40,000 participants have been through Wordsmith's workshops to learn the importance of using *plain language* and the methods to create it. The workshops, conducted in most provinces and all three territories, have helped businesses, governments, lawyers, and other professional writers to truly connect to their audiences through messages that are immediately clear and understandable.[1]

Misunderstandings can create disastrous results, legal problems, and costly mistakes. In the areas of finance, health, education, and government, where readers may not know technical or insider terms and phrases, it is especially important to write at a level that everyone can understand.

Wordsmith teaches writers a process that is based on a deep understanding of their audience and their purpose. Writers analyze the purposes of their documents, for example, to provide or collect information, to recommend, or to explain a process. Then they identify their audience, considering how they want to use the document and taking into account related factors such as experience, education, cultural background, and age.

Wordsmith recommends thinking content through before writing, to make the process faster and the end product clearer. The final step of the process is to edit, often including a review by a practice reader. In this way, Wordsmith takes seriously the usability of a document, the same way you might test usability of software or a steering wheel.

Wordsmith's team also edits documents to make messages clear by customizing every word to relate to the specific purpose and audience. Focusing on the reader and the benefits to the reader creates a spirit of cooperation and results in higher sales and more business.[2] People respond positively to words and phrases that make sense to them.

This approach applies to all types of communication: e-mails, letters, reports, proposals, forms, books, and speeches. Helping writers achieve simplicity and clarity creates a bond of trust between service providers and customers, between government and citizens, between legal professionals and clients, and between writers and readers. When the writer edits for clarity and simplicity, the readers appreciate the effort to make their lives easier.

LEARNING OBJECTIVE 1

Apply Phase 2 of the 3-x-3 writing process, which begins with research to collect background information.

Beginning With Research

Business leaders strive to solve problems and make decisions by gathering information, generating ideas, and organizing those ideas into logical messages that guide their organizations. As reviewed in Figure 5.1, these activities are part of the second phase of the 3-x-3 writing process: researching, organizing, and drafting.

A smart businessperson gathers background information before drafting a message. We call this process *research*. While this is a rather formal-sounding term, *research* simply means collecting information about a certain topic. This is an important step in the writing process because that information helps the writer shape the message. Discovering significant information after a message is half completed often means having to start over and reorganize. To avoid frustration and inaccurate messages, writers collect information that answers several questions:

- What does the receiver need to know about this topic?
- Does the receiver need to respond or take action? If so, how and when?
- What will happen if the receiver doesn't respond as anticipated?

FIGURE 5.1 The 3-x-3 Writing Process

1 Prewriting	2 Drafting	3 Revising
Analyze: Decide on the message purpose. What do you want the receiver to do or believe?	**Research:** Gather background data by searching files and the Internet.	**Edit:** Eliminate wordy fillers, long lead-ins, redundancies, and trite business phrases. Strive for parallelism, clarity, conciseness, and readability.
Anticipate: What does the audience already know? How will it receive this message?	**Organize:** Arrange direct messages with the big idea first. For persuasive or negative messages, use an indirect, problem-solving strategy.	**Proofread:** Check carefully for errors in spelling, grammar, punctuation, and format.
Adapt: Think about techniques to present this message most effectively. Consider how to elicit feedback.	**Draft:** Prepare the first draft, using active-voice sentences, coherent paragraphs, and appropriate transitional expressions.	**Evaluate:** Will this message achieve your purpose? Is the tone pleasant? Did you encourage feedback?

Whenever your communication problem requires additional information, you must conduct informal or formal research.

What Are Informal Research Methods?

Many routine tasks—such as drafting e-mails, memos, letters, informational reports, and oral presentations—require information that you can collect informally. Where can you find information before starting a project? The following techniques are useful in informal research:

- **Search your company's files.** If you are responding to an inquiry or drafting a routine message, you often can find background information, such as previous correspondence, in your own files or the company's digital and manual files.
- **Talk with the boss.** Get information from the individual making the assignment. What does that person know about the topic? What slant should you take? What other sources would that person suggest? You might also consult colleagues.
- **Interview the target audience.** Consider talking with individuals at whom the message is aimed. They can provide clarifying information that tells you what they want to know and how you should shape your remarks. Suggestions for conducting more formal interviews are presented in Chapter 11.
- **Conduct an informal survey.** Gather unscientific but helpful information through questionnaires, telephone surveys, or online surveys. In preparing a report predicting the success of a proposed company fitness centre, for example, circulate a questionnaire asking for employee reactions.

What Are Formal Research Methods?

Long reports and complex business problems generally require formal research methods. Let's say you are part of the management team at a major retailer, and you have been asked to help launch a new store. Or let's assume you must write a term paper for a college or university class. Both tasks require more data than you have in your head or at your fingertips. To conduct formal research, consider the following research options:

- **Access electronic sources.** Postsecondary and public libraries provide databases that permit access to a wide array of reputable books, journals, magazines, newspapers, and other online literature. Reputable websites, like Statistics Canada and CBC Archives,

ETHICS CHECK

Should Spelling Evolve?

In the age of digital communication, some argue that spelling should evolve to make the language of texting acceptable. The writers at the *Toronto Star* disagree: "Misspellings and typos in the newspaper and online can provoke more passionate reader indignation than just about any other journalistic transgression." What are the arguments for and against the evolution of spelling?[3]

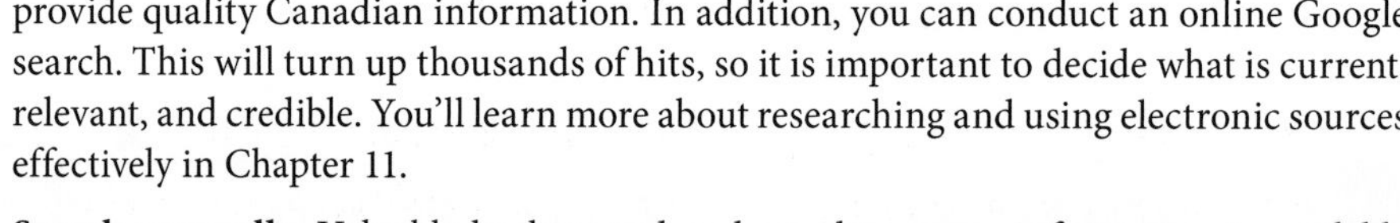

provide quality Canadian information. In addition, you can conduct an online Google search. This will turn up thousands of hits, so it is important to decide what is current, relevant, and credible. You'll learn more about researching and using electronic sources effectively in Chapter 11.

- **Search manually.** Valuable background and supplementary information is available through manual searching of resources in public and postsecondary libraries. These traditional sources include books, encyclopedias, newspapers, magazines, and journals.
- **Investigate primary sources.** To develop first-hand, primary information for a project, go directly to the source. You can search blogs, newsfeeds, and other social media pages. Formal research often includes using questionnaires, conducting interviews and focus groups, observing, and experimenting. Because formal research techniques are particularly necessary for reports, you will study resources and techniques more extensively in Unit 4.

Check out Chapter 5 in MindTap, where you can watch a video featuring Mike Stiers, a cloud and infrastructure engineer, discuss the importance of research.

Concept Check

1. Discuss the difference between informal and formal research methods.
2. Your boss has asked you to write a report about the effectiveness of the new lunch schedule policy. What type of research method should you begin with, and why?

LEARNING OBJECTIVE 2

Explain how to generate and organize ideas resulting from brainstorming, brainwriting, and social media techniques.

Generating Ideas and Organizing Information

Not all information for making decisions is available through research. Often fresh ideas to solve problems must be generated. For example, how can we expand our business into mobile technologies? How can we cut costs without losing market share? Should we radically reinvent our website? For years organizations have tried to solve problems and generate ideas in group discussions. Two methods have prevailed.

Brainstorming and Brainwriting

Traditionally, groups have generated ideas by *brainstorming*, which may be defined as the spontaneous contribution of ideas from members of a group. A group gathers to solve a problem, and every member strives to present as many ideas as possible. Teams also use digital brainstorming tools, like Bubbl.us, Mindomo, or IdeaFlip. The emphasis is on quantity, not quality. The ideas are then evaluated, and the best are selected. Critics, however, charge that brainstorming in this traditional format doesn't work. It results in the "loudmouth meeting-hog phenomenon," in which one extrovert dominates the conversation.[4]

Not only can one person dominate the session, but early ideas tend to sway the group. "It's called anchoring, and it crushes originality," claimed Professor Leigh Thompson in a Fast Company interview.[5] Brainstorming often favours first ideas, thus promoting groupthink and limiting fresh avenues of thought.

To deal with the shortcomings of traditional brainstorming, some critics champion *brainwriting*. This creativity technique involves writing out ideas rather than speaking them.[6]

Supporters claim that brainwriting generates far more creative ideas than traditional brainstorming. Its emphasis is on writing first and discussing afterward. Notice in Figure 5.2 that brainstorming and brainwriting have much in common. The chief difference is in how the ideas are presented: orally or in writing. Brainstorming can be a wild affair with visionary off-the-wall suggestions, whereas brainwriting is quieter and more thoughtful. Both techniques, however, end in the same place—with the selection of the best ideas.

FIGURE 5.2 Comparing Brainstorming and Brainwriting to Solve Problems

Brainstorming

- Clarify the problem and explain its background.
- Establish a time limit for the session.
- Set a goal, such as 100 ideas.
- Require everyone to contribute or improve the ideas of others.
- Emphasize quantity, not quality.
- No criticism.
- Write ideas on flipcharts or on sheets of paper on the walls.
- Organize, classify, and rank the ideas.
- Choose the best ideas.

Brainwriting

- Define the problem and explain its background.
- Before or at the meeting, emphasize writing out ideas.
- In a group circle, present ideas. Or participants may write their ideas anonymously on sheets hung on walls.
- Classify the ideas into groups, deleting repetitions.
- Discuss the merits of each idea.
- Vote to select the best ideas.

LvNL/Shutterstock.com

Crowdsourcing, Crowdstorming, and Crowdfunding

Closely related to brainstorming and brainwriting are three collaborative efforts with similar-sounding names that arose with the spread of social media networks. *Crowdsourcing* describes the practice of requesting ideas or services online from unknown crowd members rather than from traditional employees or contractors. Crowdsourcing has become an appealing and inexpensive method of tapping into the collective knowledge of consumers. Coca-Cola, for instance, invited its 50 million Facebook fans to offer ideas to "promote positivity both online and in the real world."[7]

Crowdstorming moves beyond crowdsourcing by requiring the crowd to evaluate and filter the ideas into a viable product or plan. Constantly evolving, crowdstorming patterns are moving from simple searches for ideas to more complex interactions in which internal or external groups take on specialized tasks.

CASE CONNECTIONS

Plagiarism and Team Writing

A recent study shows that at the top ten Canadian universities where students admit to cheating on assignments, an average of 63 percent of these students admitted to "collaborating on an assignment when the instructor requested individual work."[8] With the rise of plagiarism, schools have had to implement new policies to deal with team cheating. When all members of the team admit to cheating, they are all penalized, but what about cases when only one member of the team cheats?[9] One university's policy states the following:

> "If any member of a team engages in plagiarism, all team members can be penalized, since each member shares responsibility for verifying the integrity of an assignment before it is handed in to the teacher," it writes. "The same principle of verifying integrity also applies to academic articles with multiple authors."[10]

Jacob Lund/Shutterstock

- Discuss the university's policy for plagiarism. During the three phases in team writing, what can members do to ensure that the final document hasn't been plagiarized by anyone?

Crowdfunding is the practice of soliciting contributions, usually through the Internet, from a group of friends or strangers to finance a project, cause, or business venture. Capitalizing on the convenience of the Internet, the crowdfunding economy has exploded with requests to fund everything from fertility treatments to film projects and vacations.[11] Musicians, filmmakers, and artists have raised huge amounts that not only finance projects but also raise awareness of worthy causes.

Grouping Ideas to Show Relationships

After collecting data and generating ideas, writers must find some way to organize their information. Organizing includes two processes: grouping and strategizing. Skilled writers group similar items together. Then they place ideas in a strategic sequence that helps the reader understand relationships and accept the writer's views. Unorganized messages that jump from one thought to another fail to emphasize important points. Puzzled readers can't see how the pieces fit together, and they become frustrated and irritated. Many communication experts regard poor organization as the greatest failing of business writers. Two simple techniques can help writers organize data: the scratch list and the outline.

Using Lists and Outlines. In developing simple messages, some writers make a quick scratch list of the topics they want to cover. Next they compose a message at their computers directly from the scratch list. Most writers, though, need to organize their ideas—especially if the project is complex—into a hierarchy, such as an outline. The benefit of preparing an outline is that it gives writers a chance to organize their thoughts before becoming bogged down in word choice and sentence structure. Figure 5.3 shows the format for a typical outline.

Typical Document Components. How you group ideas into components depends on your topic and your channel of communication. Business documents usually contain typical components arranged in traditional strategies, as shown in Figure 5.4. Notice that an e-mail, a memo, or a letter generally is organized with an *opening*, a *body*, and a *closing*. Instructions for writing a procedure, such as how to use the company wiki, would proceed through a number of steps. The organizational plan for an informational report usually includes an introduction, facts, and a summary. However, the plan for an analytical report includes an introduction/

FIGURE 5.3 Format for an Outline

Title: Major Idea or Purpose

I. First major component
    A. First subpoint
        1. Detail, illustration, evidence
        2. Detail, illustration, evidence
        3. Detail, illustration, evidence
    B. Second subpoint
        1.
        2.
II. Second major component
    A. First subpoint
        1.
        2.
    B. Second subpoint
        1.
        2.
        3.

Tips for Making Outlines

- Define the main topic in the title.
- Divide the main topic into major components or classifications (preferably three to five).
- Break the components into subpoints.
- Don't put a single item under a major component; if you have only one subpoint, integrate it with the main item above it or reorganize.
- Strive to make each component exclusive (no overlapping).
- Use details, illustrations, and evidence to support subpoints.

FIGURE 5.4 Typical Major Components in Business Outlines

E-mail, Memo, Letter	Procedure	Informational Report	Analytical Report	Proposal
I. Opening II. Body III. Closing	I. Step 1 II. Step 2 III. Step 3 IV. Step 4	I. Introduction II. Facts III. Summary	I. Introduction/problem II. Facts/findings III. Conclusions IV. Recommendations (if requested)	I. Introduction II. Proposed solution III. Staffing IV. Schedule, costs V. Authorization

problem, facts/findings, conclusions, and recommendations (if requested). The plan for a proposal includes an introduction, a proposed solution, staffing, a schedule and/or costs, and authorization.

Later in this book, you will be introduced to all the business documents outlined here, and you will learn how to expertly draft all their parts.

Organizing Ideas Into Strategies

Thus far, you have seen how to collect information, generate ideas, and prepare an outline. How you order the information in your outline, though, depends on the strategy you choose. Two organizational strategies provide plans of action for typical business messages: the direct strategy and the indirect strategy. The primary difference between the two strategies is where the main idea is placed. In the direct strategy, the main idea comes first, followed by details, explanation, or evidence. In the indirect strategy, the main idea follows the details, explanation, and evidence. The strategy you select is determined by how you expect the audience to react to the message, as illustrated in Figure 5.5.

Direct Strategy for Receptive Audiences. In preparing to write any message, you need to anticipate the audience's reaction to your ideas and frame your message accordingly. When you expect the reader to be pleased, mildly interested, or, at worst, neutral, use the direct strategy. That is, put your main point—the purpose of your message—in the first or

FIGURE 5.5 Audience Response Determines Direct or Indirect Strategy

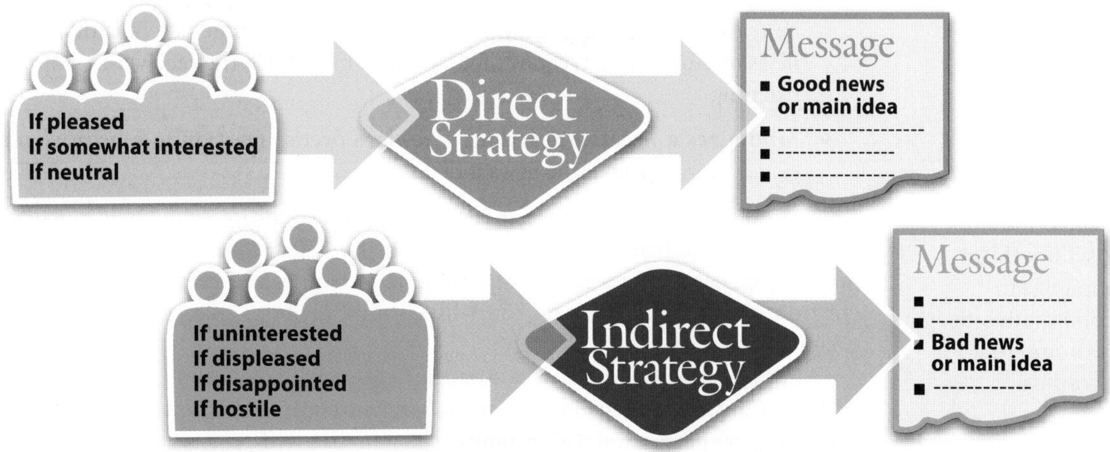

Go to section 5-2d in MindTap, where you can watch a video featuring Taylor Roberts, general manager of Dynapole, discuss crafting messages for a receptive audience.

second sentence. As quickly as possible, tell why you are writing. Compare the direct and indirect strategies in the following e-mail openings. Notice how long it takes to get to the main idea in the indirect opening.

Indirect Opening	Direct Opening
Our company has been concerned with attracting better-qualified prospective job candidates. For this reason, the Management Council has been gathering information about an internship program for college students. After considerable investigation, we have voted to begin a pilot program starting next fall.	The Management Council has voted to begin a college internship pilot program next fall.

Explanations and details follow the direct opening. What's important is getting to the main idea quickly. This direct method, also called *frontloading*, has at least three advantages:

- **Saves the reader's time.** Many of today's businesspeople can devote only a few moments to each message. Messages that take too long to get to the point may lose their readers along the way.
- **Sets a proper frame of mind.** Learning the purpose up front helps the reader put the subsequent details and explanations in perspective. Without a clear opening, the reader may be thinking, "Why am I being told this?"
- **Reduces frustration.** Readers forced to struggle through excessive verbiage before reaching the main idea become frustrated. Poorly organized messages create a negative impression of the writer.

Typical business messages that follow the direct strategy include routine requests and responses, orders and acknowledgments, nonsensitive memos, e-mails, informational reports, and informational oral presentations. All these tasks have one element in common: none has a sensitive subject that will upset the reader.

Indirect Strategy for Unreceptive Audiences. When you expect the audience to be uninterested, unwilling, displeased, or perhaps even hostile, the indirect strategy is more appropriate. In this strategy you reveal the main idea only after you have offered an explanation and evidence. This approach works well with three kinds of messages: (a) bad news, (b) ideas that require persuasion, and (c) sensitive news, especially when it is being transmitted to superiors. The indirect strategy has these benefits:

- **Respects the feelings of the audience.** Bad news is always painful, but the trauma can be lessened by preparing the receiver for it.
- **Facilitates a fair hearing.** Messages that may upset the reader are more likely to be read when the main idea is delayed. Beginning immediately with a piece of bad news or a persuasive request, for example, may cause the receiver to stop reading or listening.
- **Minimizes a negative reaction.** A reader's overall reaction to a negative message is generally improved if the news is delivered gently.

Typical business messages that could be developed indirectly include e-mails, memos, and letters that refuse requests, deny claims, and disapprove credit. Persuasive requests, sales letters, sensitive messages, and some reports and oral presentations may also benefit from the indirect strategy. You will learn more about using the indirect strategy in Chapters 9 and 10.

Although direct and indirect strategies cover many communication problems, every business transaction is distinct. Some messages are mixed: part good news, part bad; part goodwill, part persuasion. In upcoming chapters you will practise applying the direct and

ETHICS CHECK

How Sweet It Is

The makers of artificial sweetener Equal sued competitor Splenda because the latter claimed that Splenda was "made from sugar." In reality Splenda's core ingredient is made from sucralose, a nonnutritive synthetic compound manufactured in laboratories. Although Splenda contains a sugar molecule, sucralose is not the same as sucrose, the technical name for pure table sugar, despite its similar-sounding name. Is it unethical for companies to intentionally advertise using wording that would confuse consumers?[12]

indirect strategies in typical situations. Then, you will have the skills and confidence to evaluate communication problems and vary these strategies depending on the goals you want to achieve.

Concept Check

1. This section describes brainstorming and brainwriting as techniques for generating ideas. Explore the Internet for other methods such as freewriting, looping, listing, clustering, and reporters' questions. Select a method that appeals to you, and explain why it would be effective.
2. The direct opening for messages is the preferred strategy for Western cultures. Other cultures may find the direct strategy rude. Discuss cultural considerations when using the direct strategy.

Composing the First Draft With Effective Sentences

LEARNING OBJECTIVE 3

Compose the first draft of a message by using a variety of sentence types and avoiding common sentence errors.

Once you have researched your topic, organized the data, and selected a strategy, you're ready to draft your message. As you begin writing, think about what style fits you best. Some experts suggest that you write quickly (freewriting). Get your thoughts down now and refine them in later versions. As you take up each idea, imagine that you are talking to the reader. If you can't think of the right word, insert a substitute or type *find perfect word later.* Freewriting works well for some writers, but others prefer to move more slowly and think through their ideas more deliberately. Whether you are a speedy or a deliberate writer, keep in mind that you are writing the first draft. You will have time later to revise and polish your sentences.

Achieving Variety With Four Sentence Types

Messages that repeat the same sentence pattern soon become boring. To avoid monotony and to add spark to your writing, use a variety of sentence types. You have four sentence types from which to choose: simple, compound, complex, and compound-complex.

Simple Sentence.

A simple sentence contains one complete thought (an independent clause) with a subject and predicate verb:

The entrepreneur saw an opportunity.

Compound Sentence.

A compound sentence contains two complete but related thoughts. These thoughts may be joined by (a) a coordinating conjunction, such as *and, but,* or *or*; (b) a semicolon; or (c) a conjunctive adverb, such as *however, consequently,* and *therefore.* Note the important placement of commas when using coordinating conjunctions and conjunctive adverbs:

The entrepreneur saw an opportunity, and she responded immediately.
The entrepreneur saw an opportunity; she responded immediately.
The entrepreneur saw an opportunity; consequently, she responded immediately.

Complex Sentence.

A complex sentence contains an independent clause (a complete thought) and a dependent clause (a thought that cannot stand by itself). Dependent clauses are often introduced by words such as *although, since, because, when,* and *if.* When dependent clauses precede independent clauses, they are always followed by a comma:

When the entrepreneur saw the opportunity, she responded immediately.

Compound-Complex Sentence.

A compound-complex sentence contains at least two independent clauses and one dependent clause:

> *When the entrepreneur saw the opportunity, she responded immediately; however, she needed capital.*

Avoiding Three Common Sentence Faults

As you craft your sentences, beware of three common traps: fragments, run-on (fused) sentences, and comma-splice sentences. If any of these faults appears in a business message, the writer immediately loses credibility.

One of the most serious errors a writer can make is punctuating a **fragment** as if it were a complete sentence. A fragment is usually a broken-off part of a complex sentence or a dependent clause. Fragments often can be identified by the words that introduce them—words such as *although, as, because, even, except, for example, if, instead of, since, such as, that, which,* and *when.* These words introduce dependent clauses. Make sure such clauses always connect to independent clauses.

Fragment	Revision
Because most transactions require a permanent record. Good writing skills are critical.	Because most transactions require a permanent record, good writing skills are critical.
The recruiter requested a writing sample. Even though the candidate seemed to communicate well.	The recruiter requested a writing sample even though the candidate seemed to communicate well.

A second serious writing fault is the **run-on (fused)** sentence. A sentence with two independent clauses must be joined by a comma *and* a coordinating conjunction (*and, or, nor, but*) or by a semicolon (;) or separated into two sentences. Without a comma before the coordinating conjunction, it is still a run-on sentence.

Run-On Sentence	Revision
Many job seekers prepare traditional résumés some also use websites as electronic portfolios.	Many job seekers prepare traditional résumés, but some also use websites as electronic portfolios.
One candidate sent an e-mail résumé another sent a link to her Web portfolio.	One candidate sent an e-mail résumé; another sent a link to her Web portfolio.

A third sentence fault is a **comma splice**. It results when a writer joins (splices together) two independent clauses with a comma. Independent clauses may be joined with a comma *and* a coordinating conjunction (*and, or, nor, but*) or a semicolon *and* a conjunctive adverb (*however, consequently, therefore,* and others). You can also fix a comma splice by replacing the comma with a period. To rectify a comma splice, try one of the possible revisions shown here:

Comma Splice	Revisions
Some employees prefer their desktop computers, others prefer their tablets.	Some employees prefer their desktop computers, but others prefer their tablets.
Tablets are useful during meetings, they are convenient for note-taking.	Tablets are useful during meetings. They are convenient for note-taking.
Management has discussed replacing all tablets with smartphones next year, employees will have an opportunity to provide input on the decision.	Management has discussed replacing all tablets with smartphones next year; however, employees will have an opportunity to provide input on the decision.

Favouring Short Sentences

Because your goal is to communicate clearly, you should strive for sentences that average 20 words. Some sentences will be shorter; some will be longer. The American Press Institute reports that reader comprehension drops off markedly as sentences become longer.[13] Therefore, in crafting your sentences, think about the relationship between sentence length and comprehension.

Sentence Length	Comprehension Rate
8 words	100%
15 words	90%
19 words	80%
28 words	50%

Instead of stringing together clauses with *and*, *but*, and *however*, break some of those complex sentences into separate sentences. Business readers want to grasp ideas immediately. They can do that best when thoughts are separated into short sentences. On the other hand, too many monotonous short sentences may bore or even annoy the reader. Strive for a balance between longer sentences and shorter ones. Your grammar- and spell-checker can show you readability statistics that flag long sentences and give you an average sentence length. Software programs like Grammarly can provide an even more advanced check of your writing. Grammarly's AI-powered writing assistant can help you with e-mails, messages, documents, and social media.[14]

Concept Check

1. In your opinion, how many business managers know what a comma splice is? If some managers don't know what a comma splice is, then is it critical that you avoid comma splices in your writing? Explain.
2. For each of the following sentences, select the number that identifies its type:
   1. Simple sentence
   2. Compound sentence
   3. Complex sentence
   4. Compound-complex sentence

a. Bottled water consumption rose 2.2 percent in volume last year.

b. Because North Americans are increasingly health conscious, they are drinking more bottled water than ever before.

c. North Americans are drinking fewer soft drinks, and Coca-Cola and PepsiCo are being hit hard.

d. Sales volume across the entire beverage industry slid last year; however, smaller players, such as Monster Beverage and Red Bull, expanded their market share because they appealed to younger drinkers.

Developing Business Writing Techniques

LEARNING OBJECTIVE 4

Improve your writing techniques by carefully constructing sentences.

You can significantly improve your messages by working on a few writing techniques. These techniques are emphasizing important ideas, employing the active and passive voice effectively, using parallelism, and preventing dangling and misplaced modifiers.

Emphasizing Important Ideas

Some ideas are more important than others. You can stress prominent ideas *mechanically* by underscoring, italicizing, or boldfacing, which will be discussed later in this chapter. You can also stress important ideas *stylistically* by employing one of the following methods:

- **Use vivid words.** Vivid words are emphatic because the reader can picture ideas clearly.

General	Vivid
The way we socialize is changing.	Instagram has dramatically changed the way people socialize online.

- **Label the main idea.** If an idea is significant, tell the reader.

Unlabelled	Labelled
Explore the possibility of an Instagram fan page, but also consider security.	Explore the possibility of an Instagram fan page, but, *most important*, consider security.

- **Place the important idea first or last.** Ideas have less competition from surrounding words when they appear first or last in a sentence.

Main Idea Lost	Main Idea Emphasized
Profit-sharing plans are more effective in increasing *productivity* when they are linked to individual performance rather than to group performance.	*Productivity* is more likely to be increased when profit-sharing plans are linked to individual performance rather than to group performance.

- **Give the important idea the spotlight.** Don't dilute the effect of the idea by making it share the spotlight with other words and clauses. Instead, put it in a simple sentence or in an independent clause.

Main Idea Lost	Main Idea Clear
Although you are the first trainee that we have hired for this program, we have interviewed many candidates and expect to expand the program in the future. (The main idea is lost in a dependent clause.)	You are the first trainee that we have hired for this program. (This simple sentence contains the main idea.)

- **De-emphasize when necessary.** To de-emphasize an idea, such as bad news, try one of the following stylistic devices:

Emphasizes Harsh Statement	De-emphasizes Harsh Statement
Our records indicate that you were recently fired.	Our records indicate that your employment status has recently changed.

Using the Active and Passive Voice Effectively

In active-voice sentences, the subject (the actor) performs the action. In passive-voice sentences, the subject receives the action. Active-voice sentences are more direct because they reveal the performer immediately. They are easier to understand and usually shorter. Most business writing should be in the active voice. However, passive voice is useful to (a) emphasize an action rather than a person, (b) de-emphasize negative news, and (c) conceal the doer of an action.

Active Voice	Passive Voice
Actor → Action Justin must submit a tax return.	Receiver ← Action The tax return was submitted [by Justin].
Actor → Action Officials reviewed all tax returns.	Receiver ← Action All tax returns were reviewed [by officials].
Actor → Action We cannot make cash refunds.	Receiver ← Action Cash refunds cannot be made.
Actor → Action Our CPA made a big error in the budget.	Receiver ← Action A big error was made in the budget.

Using Parallelism

Parallelism is a skillful writing technique that involves balanced writing. Sentences written so that their parts are balanced or parallel are easy to read and understand. To achieve parallel construction, use similar structures to express similar ideas. For example, the words *computing, coding, recording,* and *storing* are parallel because the words all end in *-ing.* To express the list as *computing, coding, recording,* and *storage* is disturbing because the last item is not what the reader expects. Try to match nouns with nouns, verbs with verbs, and clauses with clauses. Avoid mixing active-voice verbs with passive-voice verbs. Your goal is to keep the wording balanced in expressing similar ideas.

Lacks Parallelism	Illustrates Parallelism
The policy affected all vendors, suppliers, and *those involved with consulting.*	The policy affected all vendors, suppliers, and *consultants.* (Matches nouns)
Our primary goals are to increase productivity, reduce costs, and *the improvement of product quality.*	Our primary goals are to increase productivity, reduce costs, and *improve product quality.* (Matches verbs)
Shelby audits all accounts lettered A through L; accounts lettered M through Z are audited by Andrew.	Shelby audits all accounts lettered A through L; Andrew audits accounts lettered M through Z. (Matches clauses)
Our ads have three objectives:	Our ads have three objectives:
1. We want to increase product use.	1. Increase product use.
2. Introduce complementary products.	2. Introduce complementary products.
3. Our corporate image will be enhanced.	3. Enhance our corporate image. (Matches verbs in listed items)

Escaping Dangling and Misplaced Modifiers

For clarity, modifiers must be close to the words they describe or limit. A modifier dangles when the word or phrase it describes is missing from its sentence—for example, *After working overtime, the report was finally finished.* This sentence says the report was working overtime. Revised, the sentence contains a logical subject: *After working overtime, we finally finished the report.*

Introductory verbal phrases are particularly dangerous; be sure to follow them immediately with the words they logically describe or modify. Try this trick for detecting and remedying many dangling modifiers. Ask the question *Who?* or *What?* after any introductory phrase. The words immediately following should tell the reader who or what is performing the action. Try the *Who?* test on the two danglers here:

CHECKLIST

Drafting Effective Sentences

For Effective Sentences

- **Use a variety of sentence types.** To avoid monotony, include simple, compound, complex, and occasionally compound-complex sentences in your writing.
- **Avoid common sentence faults.** To avoid run-on sentences, do not join two clauses without appropriate punctuation. To avoid comma splices, do not join two clauses with a comma. To avoid fragments, be sure to use periods only after complete sentences.
- **Control sentence length.** Use longer sentences occasionally, but rely primarily on short and medium-length sentences.
- **Emphasize important ideas.** Place main ideas at the beginning of short sentences for emphasis.
- **Apply active- and passive-voice verbs strategically.** Use active-voice verbs (*She sent the e-mail* instead of *The e-mail was sent by her*) most frequently; they immediately identify the doer. Use passive-voice verbs to emphasize an action, to be tactful, or to conceal the performer.
- **Employ parallelism.** Balance similar ideas (*biking, jogging, and walking* instead of *biking, jogging, and to walk*).
- **Eliminate dangling and misplaced modifiers.** Be sure that introductory verbal phrases are followed by the words that can logically be modified. Position the modifier closer to the word(s) it describes or limits.

Dangling Modifier	Clear Modification
Skilled at graphic design, the contract went to Design One.	Skilled at graphic design, Design One won the contract.
Working together as a team, the project was finally completed.	Working together as a team, we finally completed the project.

A modifier is misplaced when the word or phrase it describes is not close enough to be clear—for example, *Firefighters rescued a dog from a burning car that had a broken leg.* Obviously, the car did not have a broken leg. The solution is to position the modifier closer to the word(s) it describes or limits: *Firefighters rescued a dog with a broken leg from a burning car.*

Misplaced Modifier	Clear Modification
The recruiter interviewed candidates who had excellent computer skills in the morning.	In the morning the recruiter interviewed candidates with excellent computer skills.

Concept Check

1. Business writing is more forceful when it uses active-voice verbs. Revise the following sentences so that verbs are in the active voice. Put the emphasis on the doer of the action. Add subjects if necessary.

   EXAMPLE: Antivirus software was installed on her computer.

   REVISION: Madison installed antivirus software on her computer.

   a. Reliable data about how workers do their jobs are difficult to collect.
   b. Companies were warned by managers that privacy issues and making sense of the data were equally perplexing issues.
   c. Laws are being considered to restrict gathering workers' data without their knowledge.

2. Revise the following sentences to avoid dangling and misplaced modifiers.

   a. While interviewing applicants, questions are often asked by recruiters about qualifications.
   b. To be reimbursed, the enclosed application must be filled out and returned.
   c. Angered by autodialled and prerecorded calls and texts, complaints deluged PayPal.

Building Well-Organized Paragraphs

LEARNING OBJECTIVE 5

Draft well-organized paragraphs and use techniques for achieving paragraph coherence.

A *paragraph* is a group of sentences about one idea. To avoid muddled paragraphs, writers should be able to recognize basic paragraph elements, conventional sentence patterns, and ways to organize sentences by using one of three classic paragraph plans. They must also be able to polish their paragraphs by building coherence and using transitional expressions.

Well-constructed paragraphs discuss only one topic. A *topic sentence* reveals the primary idea in a paragraph and usually, but not always, appears first. Paragraphs may be composed of three kinds of sentences:

Topic Sentence	Expresses the primary idea of the paragraph
Supporting Sentence	Illustrates, explains, or strengthens the primary idea
Limiting Sentence	Opposes the primary idea by suggesting a negative or contrasting thought; may precede or follow the topic sentence

These sentences may be arranged in any of three classic paragraph plans: direct, pivoting, and indirect.

Using the Direct Paragraph Plan to Define, Classify, Illustrate, or Describe

Paragraphs using the direct plan begin with the topic sentence, followed by supporting sentences. Most business messages use this paragraph plan because it clarifies the subject immediately. This plan is useful whenever you must define (a new product or procedure), classify (parts of a whole), illustrate (an idea), or describe (a process). Start with the topic sentence; then strengthen and amplify that idea with supporting ideas, as shown here:

Topic Sentence	A social audit is a report on the social performance of a company.
Supporting Sentence	Such an audit may be conducted by the company itself or by outsiders who evaluate the company's efforts to produce safe products, engage in socially responsible activities, and protect the environment. Many companies publish the results of their social audits in their annual reports. LBG Canada, for example, devotes a major portion of its annual report to its social audit. The report discusses LBG's efforts to support environmental restoration. Moreover, it describes workplace safety, employment equality, and peace programs.

You can alter the direct plan by adding a limiting sentence if necessary. Be sure, though, that you follow with sentences that return to the main idea and support it, as shown here:

Topic Sentence	Flexible work scheduling could immediately increase productivity and enhance employee satisfaction in our entire organization.
Limiting Sentence	Such scheduling, however, is impossible for all employees.
Supporting Sentences	Managers would be required to maintain their regular hours. For many other employees, though, flexible scheduling permits extra time to manage family responsibilities. Feeling less stress, employees are able to focus their attention better at work; hence they become more relaxed and more productive.

Using the Pivoting Paragraph Plan to Compare Ideas

Paragraphs using the pivoting plan start with a limiting sentence that offers a contrasting or negative idea before delivering the topic sentence. Notice in the following example how two limiting sentences about drawbacks to foreign service careers open the paragraph; only then do the topic and supporting sentences describing rewards in foreign service appear. The pivoting plan is especially useful for comparing ideas. In using the pivoting plan, be sure to emphasize the turn in direction with an obvious *but* or *however.*

Limiting Sentences	Foreign service careers are certainly not for everyone. Many representatives are stationed in remote countries where harsh climates, health hazards, security risks, and other discomforts exist.
Topic Sentence	However, careers in the foreign service offer rewards for the special people who qualify.
Supporting Sentences	Foreign service employees enjoy the pride and satisfaction of representing Canada abroad. They enjoy frequent travel, enriching cultural and social experiences in living abroad, and action-oriented work.

Using the Indirect Paragraph Plan to Explain and Persuade

Paragraphs using the indirect plan start with the supporting sentences and conclude with the topic sentence. This useful plan enables you to build a rationale, a foundation of reasons, before hitting the audience with a big idea—possibly one that is bad news. It enables you to explain your reasons and then in the final sentence draw a conclusion from them. In the following example, the vice president of a large accounting firm begins by describing the trend toward casual dress and concludes with a recommendation that his firm change its dress code. The indirect plan works well for describing causes followed by an effect.

Supporting Sentences	According to a recent poll, more than half of all white-collar workers are now dressing casually at work. Many high-tech engineers and professional specialists have given up suits and ties, favouring khakis and sweaters instead. In our own business, our consultants say they stand out like "sore thumbs" because they are attired in traditional buttoned-down styles, while the businesspeople they visit are usually wearing comfortable, casual clothing.
Topic Sentence	Therefore, I recommend that we establish an optional business casual policy allowing consultants to dress down, if they want, as they perform their duties both in and out of the office.

In coming chapters you will learn more techniques for implementing direct and indirect writing strategies when you draft e-mails, memos, letters, reports, and other business messages, as well as prepare oral presentations.

Developing Paragraph Coherence

Paragraphs are coherent when ideas cohere—that is, when the ideas stick together and when one idea logically leads to the next. Well-written paragraphs take the reader through a number of steps. When the author skips from Step 1 to Step 3 and forgets Step 2, the reader is lost. Several techniques will help you keep the reader in step with your ideas.

Sustaining the Key Idea. Repeating a key expression or using a similar one throughout a paragraph helps sustain a key idea. In the following example, notice that the repetition of *guest* and *VIP* connects ideas.

> *Our philosophy holds that every customer is really a guest. All new employees are trained to treat guests in our theme parks as VIPs. We take great pride in respecting our guests. As VIPs, they are never told what they can or cannot do.*

FIGURE 5.6 Transitional Expressions That Build Coherence

To Add or Strengthen	To Show Time or Order	To Clarify	To Show Cause and Effect	To Contradict	To Contrast
additionally	After	for example	accordingly	actually	as opposed to
accordingly	before	for instance	as a result	but	at the same time
again	earlier	I mean	Consequently	however	by contrast
also	finally	in other words	for this reason	in fact	conversely
beside	First	put another way	Hence	instead	on the contrary
indeed	meanwhile	that is	So	rather	on the other hand
likewise	Next	this means	therefore	still	previously
moreover	Now	thus	Thus	yet	similarly

Dovetailing Sentences. Sentences are "dovetailed" when an idea at the end of one connects with an idea at the beginning of the next. Dovetailing sentences is especially helpful with dense, difficult topics. It is also helpful with ordinary paragraphs, such as the following.

> *New guides learn about the theme park and its facilities. These facilities include telephones, food services, bathrooms, and attractions, as well as the location of offices. Knowledge of offices and the internal workings of the company is required of all staffers.*

Including Pronouns. Familiar pronouns, such as *we, they, he, she,* and *it,* help build continuity, as do demonstrative pronouns, such as *this, that, these,* and *those.* These words confirm that something under discussion is still being discussed. However, be careful with such pronouns. They often need a noun with them to make their meaning clear. In the following example, notice how confusing the pronoun *this* would be if the word *training* were omitted.

> *All new park employees receive a two-week orientation. They learn that every staffer has a vital role in preparing for the show. This training includes how to maintain enthusiasm.*

Employing Transitional Expressions. Transitional expressions are another excellent device for showing connections and achieving paragraph coherence. These words act as verbal road signs to readers and listeners. Transitional expressions enable the receiver to anticipate what's coming, reduce uncertainty, and speed comprehension. They signal that a train of thought is moving forward, being developed, possibly detouring, or ending. As Figure 5.6 shows, transitions can add or strengthen a thought, show time or order, clarify ideas, show cause and effect, contradict thoughts, and contrast ideas. Look back at the examples of direct, pivoting, and indirect paragraphs to see how transitional expressions and other techniques build paragraph coherence. Remember that coherence in communication rarely happens spontaneously; it requires effort and skill.

Controlling Paragraph Length

Although no rule regulates the length of paragraphs, business writers recognize that short paragraphs are more attractive and readable than longer ones. Paragraphs with eight or fewer lines look inviting. If a topic can't be covered in eight or fewer printed lines (not sentences), consider breaking it up into smaller segments.

The following Checklist summarizes key points in preparing meaningful paragraphs.

CHECKLIST

Preparing Meaningful Paragraphs

- **Develop one idea.** Each paragraph should include a topic sentence plus supporting and limiting sentences to develop a single idea.
- **Use the direct plan.** To define, classify, illustrate, and describe, start with the topic sentence followed by supporting sentences.
- **Use the pivoting plan.** To compare ideas, start with a limiting sentence; then, present the topic sentence followed by supporting sentences.
- **Use the indirect plan.** To explain reasons or causes first, start with supporting sentences. Build to the conclusion with the topic sentence at the end of the paragraph.
- **Build coherence with linking techniques.** Hold ideas together by repeating key words, dovetailing sentences (beginning one sentence with an idea from the end of the previous sentence), and using appropriate pronouns.
- **Provide road signs with transitional expressions.** Use verbal signals to help the audience know where the idea is going. Words and phrases such as *moreover, accordingly, as a result*, and *therefore* function as idea pointers.
- **Limit paragraph length.** Remember that paragraphs with eight or fewer printed lines look inviting. Consider breaking up longer paragraphs if necessary.

Concept Check

1. What is *paragraph coherence*, and how is it achieved?
2. Revise the following wordy and poorly organized paragraph. Add a topic sentence. Correct problems with pronouns, parallelism, and misplaced or dangling modifiers. Add transitional expressions if appropriate.

   You may be interested in applying for a new position within the company. The Human Resources Department maintains these lists, and you may see which jobs are available immediately. The positions are at a high level. Current employees may apply immediately for open positions in production, for some in marketing, and jobs in administrative support are also available. To make application, these positions require immediate action. Come to the Human Resources Department. On the company intranet you can see the lists showing the open positions, what the qualifications are, and job descriptions are shown. Many of the jobs are now open. That's why we are sending this now. To be hired, an interview must be scheduled within the next two weeks.

LEARNING OBJECTIVE 6

Enhance readability by understanding document design.

Applying Document Design to Enhance Readability

Well-designed documents improve your messages in two important ways. First, they enhance readability and comprehension. Second, they make readers think you are a well-organized and intelligent person. Significant design techniques to improve readability include the appropriate use of white space, margins, typefaces, numbered and bulleted lists, and headings for visual impact.

Employing White Space

Empty space on a page is called *white space*. A page crammed full of text or graphics appears busy, cluttered, and unreadable. To increase white space, use headings, bulleted or numbered lists, and effective margins. Remember that short sentences (20 or fewer words) and short paragraphs (eight or fewer printed lines) improve readability and comprehension. As you organize and draft your message, think about shortening long sentences. Consider breaking up long paragraphs into shorter chunks.

Understanding Margins and Text Alignment

Margins determine the white space on the left, right, top, and bottom of a block of type. They define the reading area and provide important visual relief. Business letters and memos usually have side margins of 2.5 to 3 centimetres.

Your word processing program probably offers four forms of margin alignment: (a) lines align only at the left, (b) lines align only at the right, (c) lines align at both left and right (*justified*), and (d) lines are centred. Nearly all text in Western cultures is aligned at the left and reads from left to right. The right margin may be either *justified* or *ragged right*. The text in books, magazines, and other long works is often justified on the left and right for a formal appearance.

Justified text, however, may require more attention to word spacing and hyphenation to avoid awkward empty spaces or "rivers" of spaces running through a document. When right margins are *ragged*—that is, without alignment or justification—they provide more white space and improve readability. Therefore, you are best served by using left-justified text and ragged-right margins without justification. Centred text is appropriate for headings and short invitations but not for complete messages.

Check out section 5-6f of MindTap, where you can watch a video featuring Debi Rampersad, a financial industry manager, discuss how to consider design while crafting your message.

Choosing Appropriate Typefaces

Business writers today may choose from a number of typefaces on their word processors. A typeface defines the shape of text characters. A wide range of typefaces is available for various uses. Some are decorative and useful for special purposes. For most business messages, however, you should choose from *serif* or *sans serif* categories.

Serif typefaces have small features at the ends of strokes. The most common serif typeface is Times New Roman. Other popular serif typefaces are Century, Georgia, and Palatino. Serif typefaces suggest tradition, maturity, and formality. They are frequently used for body text in business messages and longer documents. Because books, newspapers, and magazines favour serif typefaces, readers are familiar with them.

Sans serif typefaces include Arial, Calibri, Gothic, Tahoma, Helvetica, and Univers. These clean characters are widely used for headings, signs, and material that does not require continuous reading. Web designers often prefer sans serif typefaces for simple, pure pages. For longer documents, however, sans serif typefaces may seem colder and less accessible than familiar serif typefaces.

fizkes/Shutterstock

Despite the wonderful possibilities available on your word processor, don't get carried away with fancy typefaces. All-purpose sans serif and traditional serif typefaces are most appropriate for your business messages, especially résumés. Generally, use no more than two typefaces within one document.

Understanding Type Font, Sizes, and Listing Techniques

Font refers to a specific style (such as *italic*) within a typeface family (such as Times New Roman). Most typeface families offer various fonts such as CAPITALIZATION, SMALL CAPS, **boldface**, *italic*, and underline, as well as less common fonts such as outline and shadow.

Font styles are a mechanical means of adding emphasis to your words. ALL CAPS, SMALL CAPS, and **bold** are useful for headings, subheadings, and single words or short phrases in the text. ALL CAPS, HOWEVER, SHOULD NEVER BE USED FOR LONG STRETCHES OF TEXT BECAUSE ALL THE LETTERS ARE THE SAME HEIGHT, MAKING IT

Check out section 5-6f in MindTap, where you can watch a video about improving the readability of your documents.

DIFFICULT FOR READERS TO DIFFERENTIATE WORDS. In addition, excessive use of all caps feels like shouting and irritates readers. **Boldface**, *italics*, and underlining are effective for calling attention to important points and terms. Be cautious, however, when using fancy or an excessive number of font styles. Don't use them if they will confuse, annoy, or delay readers.

During the drafting process, think about type size. Readers are generally most comfortable with 11- to 12-point type for body text. Smaller type enables you to fit more words into a space but makes text look dense and unappealing. Slightly larger type makes material more readable. Overly large type (14 points or more) looks amateurish and out of place for body text in business messages. Larger type, however, is appropriate for headings.

Numbering and Bulleting Lists for Quick Comprehension

One of the best ways to ensure rapid comprehension of ideas is through the use of numbered or bulleted lists. Lists provide high *skim value*. This means that readers can browse quickly and grasp main ideas. By breaking up complex information into smaller chunks, lists improve readability, understanding, and retention. They also force the writer to organize ideas and write efficiently. Figure 5.7 shows how breaking up dense text improves readability.

As you draft your message, look for ideas that could be converted to lists, and follow these techniques to make your lists look professional:

- **Numbered lists.** Use for items that represent a sequence or reflect a numbering system.
- **Bulleted lists.** Use to highlight items that don't necessarily show a chronology.
- **Capitalization.** Capitalize the initial word of each line.
- **Punctuation.** Add end punctuation only if the listed items are complete sentences.
- **Parallelism.** Make all the lines consistent; for example, start each with a verb.

In the following examples, notice that the list on the left presents a sequence of steps with numbers. The bulleted list does not show a sequence of ideas; therefore, bullets are appropriate. Also notice the parallelism in each example. In the numbered list, each item begins with a verb. In the bulleted list, each item follows an adjective/noun sequence. Business readers appreciate lists because they focus attention. Be careful, however, not to use so many that your messages look like grocery lists.

Numbered List	Bulleted List
Our recruiters follow these steps when hiring applicants:	To attract upscale customers, we feature the following:
1. Examine the application.	• Quality fashions
2. Interview the applicant.	• Personalized service
3. Check the applicant's references.	• Generous return policy

Adding Headings for Visual Impact

Headings are an effective tool for highlighting information and improving readability. They encourage the writer to group similar material together. Headings help the reader separate major ideas from details. They enable a busy reader to skim familiar or less important information. They also provide a quick preview or review. Headings appear most often in reports, which you will study in greater detail in Chapters 11, 12, and 13. However, main headings, subheadings, and category headings can also improve readability in e-mails, memos, and letters. In the following example, they are used with bullets to summarize categories:

FIGURE 5.7 Document Design Improves Readability

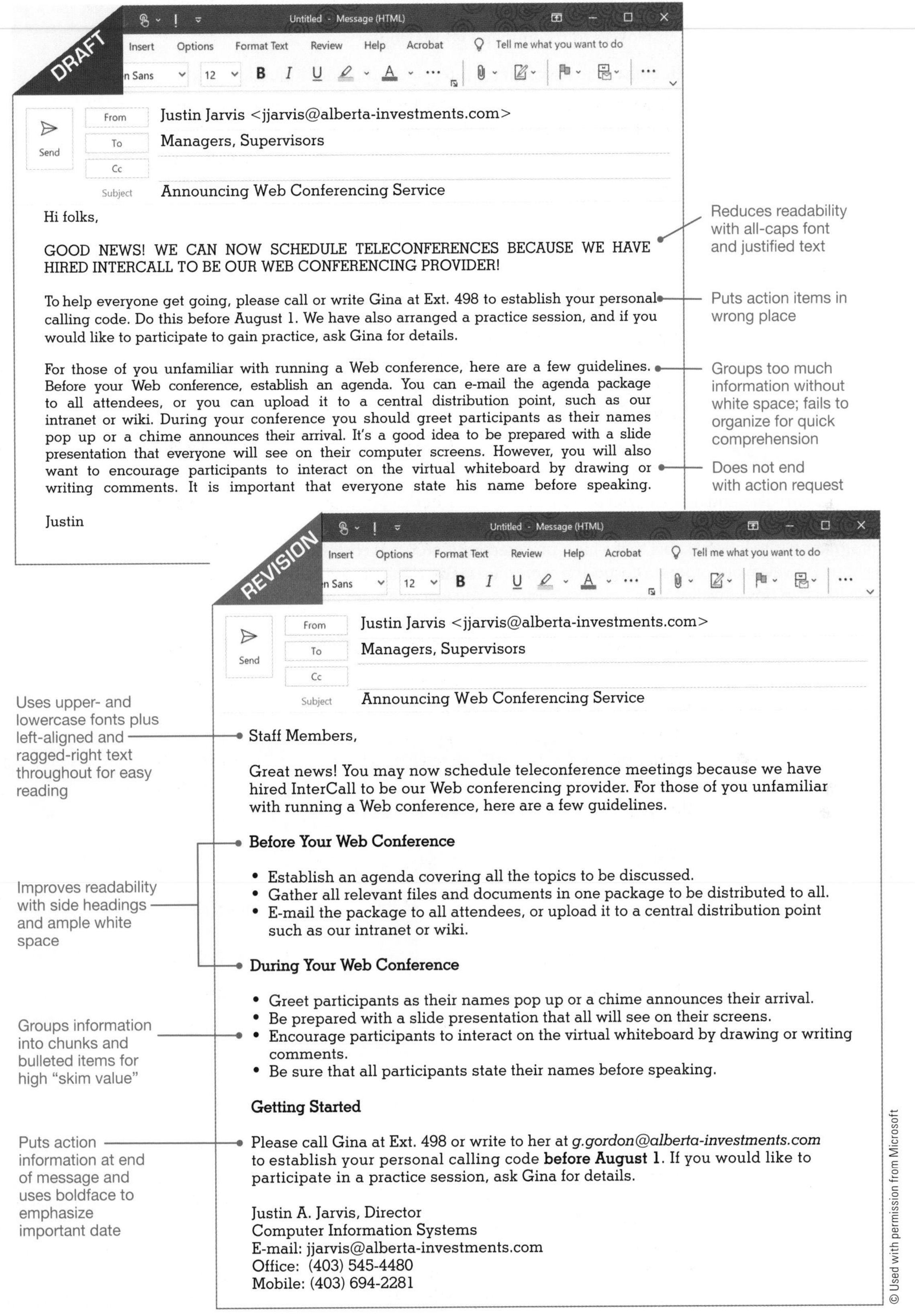

DRAFT
Untitled - Message (HTML)
Insert Options Format Text Review Help Acrobat Tell me what you want to do
Send
From Justin Jarvis <jjarvis@alberta-investments.com>
To Managers, Supervisors
Cc
Subject Announcing Web Conferencing Service
Hi folks,
GOOD NEWS! WE CAN NOW SCHEDULE TELECONFERENCES BECAUSE WE HAVE HIRED INTERCALL TO BE OUR WEB CONFERENCING PROVIDER!
To help everyone get going, please call or write Gina at Ext. 498 to establish your personal calling code. Do this before August 1. We have also arranged a practice session, and if you would like to participate to gain practice, ask Gina for details.
For those of you unfamiliar with running a Web conference, here are a few guidelines. Before your Web conference, establish an agenda. You can e-mail the agenda package to all attendees, or you can upload it to a central distribution point, such as our intranet or wiki. During your conference you should greet participants as their names pop up or a chime announces their arrival. It's a good idea to be prepared with a slide presentation that everyone will see on their computer screens. However, you will also want to encourage participants to interact on the virtual whiteboard by drawing or writing comments. It is important that everyone state his name before speaking.
Justin
Reduces readability with all-caps font and justified text
Puts action items in wrong place
Groups too much information without white space; fails to organize for quick comprehension
Does not end with action request
REVISION
Untitled - Message (HTML)
Insert Options Format Text Review Help Acrobat Tell me what you want to do
Send
From Justin Jarvis <jjarvis@alberta-investments.com>
To Managers, Supervisors
Cc
Subject Announcing Web Conferencing Service
Staff Members,
Great news! You may now schedule teleconference meetings because we have hired InterCall to be our Web conferencing provider. For those of you unfamiliar with running a Web conference, here are a few guidelines.
Before Your Web Conference
• Establish an agenda covering all the topics to be discussed.
• Gather all relevant files and documents in one package to be distributed to all.
• E-mail the package to all attendees, or upload it to a central distribution point such as our intranet or wiki.
During Your Web Conference
• Greet participants as their names pop up or a chime announces their arrival.
• Be prepared with a slide presentation that all will see on their screens.
• Encourage participants to interact on the virtual whiteboard by drawing or writing comments.
• Be sure that all participants state their names before speaking.
Getting Started
Please call Gina at Ext. 498 or write to her at g.gordon@alberta-investments.com to establish your personal calling code before August 1. If you would like to participate in a practice session, ask Gina for details.
Justin A. Jarvis, Director
Computer Information Systems
E-mail: jjarvis@alberta-investments.com
Office: (403) 545-4480
Mobile: (403) 694-2281
Uses upper- and lowercase fonts plus left-aligned and ragged-right text throughout for easy reading
Improves readability with side headings and ample white space
Groups information into chunks and bulleted items for high "skim value"
Puts action information at end of message and uses boldface to emphasize important date
© Used with permission from Microsoft

Category Headings
Our company focuses on the following areas in the employment process:

- **Attracting applicants.** We advertise for qualified applicants, and we also encourage current employees to recommend good people.
- **Interviewing applicants.** Our specialized interviews include simulated customer encounters, as well as scrutiny by supervisors.
- **Checking references.** We investigate every applicant thoroughly. We contact former employers and all listed references.

In Figure 5.7 the writer was able to convert a dense, unappealing e-mail message into an easier-to-read version by applying document design. Notice that the all-caps font in the first paragraph makes its meaning difficult to decipher. Justified margins and lack of white space further reduce readability. In the revised version, the writer changed the all-caps font to upper- and lowercase and also used ragged-right margins to enhance visual appeal. One of the best document design techniques in this message is the use of headings and bullets to help the reader see chunks of information in similar groups. You can make any message more readable by applying the document design techniques presented here.

Concept Check

1. What is *high skim value*, and how can you achieve it?
2. Create an introductory sentence and a bulleted list from the following wordy paragraph: This information is to let you know that a high-powered MBA program costs hundreds of dollars an hour. However, our program covers the same information. That information includes entrepreneurship tips as well as how to start a business. You will also learn information about writing a business plan and understanding taxes. In addition, our MBA program covers how to go about writing a marketing feasibility study. Another important topic that our program covers is employment benefits plans.

SPOTLIGHT ON COMMUNICATION: PART 2

Wordsmith Revisited

Wordsmith has identified common writing problems that exist in most organizations:

Pressmaster/Shutterstock

- Many documents are twice as long as they need to be.
- Writers work hard, in isolation, without achieving the mastery (or confidence) that makes writing easier.
- Hide-and-seek messages make management and other readers work hard to extract information.
- High-value, time-pressured executives expend too much brain power editing documents.
- Documents boomerang between writers and reviewers multiple times, delaying delivery and creating stress.
- Documents are often not clear and usable for the end reader, despite the human and organizational cost to create them.[15]

With so much writing taking place in the workplace, these common writing problems can have a negative impact on business. Organizations that invest in employees who write well, and provide training opportunities for writing skills development, position themselves for success.

CRITICAL THINKING

- In what ways can offering writing-techniques training for employees save organizations time and money?
- Watch the video "Thinking Differently About Writing at Work," located on Wordsmith's website: https://wordsmith.ca/about-us/. In what ways do we need to change the way we think about writing?

http://wordsmith.ca

Summary of Learning Objectives

1 Apply Phase 2 of the 3-x-3 writing process, which begins with research to collect background information.

- The second phase of the writing process includes researching, organizing, and drafting.
- Informal research may include looking in the company's files, talking with your boss, interviewing target audiences, and conducting informal surveys.
- Formal research may involve searching electronically or manually and investigating primary sources.

2 Explain how to generate and organize ideas resulting from brainstorming, brainwriting, and social media techniques.

- Brainstorming and brainwriting are techniques that develop ideas; crowdsourcing, crowdstorming, and crowdfunding also disseminate and act on collective knowledge.
- To prepare an outline, divide the main topic into three to five major components; break the components into subpoints consisting of details, illustrations, and evidence.
- The direct strategy organizes information with the main idea first and is useful when audiences will be pleased, mildly interested, or neutral.
- The indirect strategy places the main idea after explanations and is useful when audiences will be unwilling, displeased, or hostile.

3 Compose the first draft of a message by using a variety of sentence types and avoiding common sentence errors.

- Compose your first draft quickly, using freewriting, but plan to revise.
- Employ a variety of sentence types including simple, complex, compound, and compound-complex.
- Avoid fragments, comma splices, and run-on sentences.
- Remember that short sentences are the most effective (20 or fewer words).

4 Improve your writing techniques by carefully constructing sentences.

- Emphasize an important idea by strategically placing it within the sentence.
- Most sentences should be written in the active voice, where the subject is the doer of the action.
- The passive voice is useful to de-emphasize negative news, to emphasize an action rather than the doer, and to conceal the doer of an action.
- Skillful writing uses parallelism for balanced construction and avoids dangling and misplaced modifiers.

5 Draft well-organized paragraphs and use techniques for achieving paragraph coherence.

- Well-constructed paragraphs discuss only one topic and may be composed of a topic sentence, supporting sentence, and limiting sentence.
- Sentences may be arranged in direct, pivoting, or indirect paragraph plans.
- Paragraphs are more coherent when the writer uses techniques to link ideas, like employing transitional expressions.
- Paragraphs with eight or fewer lines look the most attractive.

6 Enhance readability by understanding document design.

- Well-designed messages enhance readability and comprehension by using ample white space, appropriate side margins, and ragged-right (not justified) margins.
- Serif typefaces (such as Times New Roman) are often used for body text, and sans serif typefaces (such as Arial) are often used for headings and signs.
- Numbered and bulleted lists provide high *skim value* in messages.
- Headings add visual impact and aid readability in business messages, as well as in reports.

Chapter Review

1. Describe the three parts of the second phase of the writing process. (Obj. 1)
2. Explain the difference between brainstorming and brainwriting (Obj. 2)
3. When is the indirect strategy appropriate, and what are the benefits of using it? (Obj. 2)
4. What is the difference between a compound and a complex sentence? Provide an original example of each. (Obj. 3)
5. List four techniques for emphasizing important ideas in sentences. (Obj. 4)
6. Describe three paragraph plans. Identify the uses for each. (Obj. 5)
7. Describe three kinds of sentences used to develop ideas in paragraphs. (Obj. 5)
8. What is the benefit of dovetailing sentences within a paragraph? (Obj. 5)
9. How do bulleted and numbered lists improve readability? (Obj. 6)
10. Should headings be used in correspondence, such as e-mail, memos, and letters? (Obj. 6)

Critical Thinking

1. Some critics complain that crowdfunding projects, such as requesting funds to pay college tuition, are essentially begging. How do you see it? (Obj. 2)
2. Have you experienced "loudmouth meeting-hog phenomenon" during group brainstorming? In what ways is brainwriting a better method to foster creativity in large groups? (Obj. 2)
3. Why is audience analysis so important in the selection of the direct or indirect strategy of organization for a business message? (Obj. 2)
4. Because business writing should have high skim value, why not write everything in bulleted lists? (Obj. 6)
5. **Ethical Issue:** Discuss the ethics of the indirect strategy of organization. Is it manipulative to delay the presentation of the main idea in a message? (Obj. 2)

Activities

5.1 Brainstorming: Solving a Problem on Campus (Objs. 1, 2)

Team

YOUR TASK In teams of three to five, analyze a problem on your campus such as the following: insufficient parking on campus, unavailable classes, closed campus facilities for students taking evening or weekend classes, unrealistic diploma or degree requirements, a lack of student intern programs, an inadequate registration process, too few healthy and affordable food choices, a lack of charging stations for electric vehicles, and so forth. Use brainstorming techniques to generate ideas that clarify the problem, and explore its solutions. Either individually or as a team, organize the ideas into an outline with three to five main points and numerous subpoints. Assume that your ideas will become part of a message to be sent to an appropriate campus official or to your campus newspaper. Remember, however, your role as a student. Be polite, positive, and constructive—not negative, hostile, or aggressive.

5.2 Brainstorming: Solving a Problem at Work (Objs. 1, 2)

E-mail

YOUR TASK Analyze a problem that exists where you work or go to school such as noisy work areas, an overuse of express mail services, understaffing during peak customer service hours, poor scheduling of employees, inappropriate cell phone use, an inferior or inflexible benefits package, outdated equipment, time wasted on social media instead of working, or one of the campus problems listed in **Activity 5.1**. Select a problem about which you have some knowledge. Organize the ideas into an outline with three to five main points and numerous subpoints. Be polite, positive, and constructive. E-mail the outline to your boss (your instructor). Include an introduction (such as *Here is the outline you requested regarding . . .*). Include a closing that offers to share your outline if your boss would like to see it.

5.3 Sentence Faults (Obj. 3)

YOUR TASK In the following, identify the sentence fault (fragment, run-on, comma splice). Then revise to remedy the fault.

a. Although PepsiCo signed Beyoncé to endorse its soft drinks. Sales continued to plummet.

b. In the beverage industry, the latest sales declines are astonishing. But not surprising.

c. Sugar-filled soft-drink sales have been declining for nine straight years, however diet drinks are not far behind.

d. Coca-Cola hired a creative director PepsiCo tried a new bottle design.

e. Health concerns are not the only problem, soft-drink makers are also facing a boom in alternative beverages.

5.4 Passive Voice (Obj. 4)

YOUR TASK When indirectness or tact is required, use passive-voice verbs. Revise the following sentences so that they are in the passive voice.

EXAMPLE: Travis did not submit the proposal before the deadline.

REVISION: The proposal was not submitted before the deadline.

a. We discovered the error too late to correct the annual report.

b. We cannot ship your order for smart surge protectors until May 5.

c. The government first issued a warning regarding the use of this pesticide more than 15 months ago.

5.5 Parallelism (Obj. 4)

YOUR TASK Revise the following sentences so that their parts are balanced.

a. (Hint: Match verbs.) To improve your listening skills, you should stop talking, your surroundings should be controlled, be listening for main points, and an open mind must be kept.

b. (Hint: Match verb phrases.) Job seekers use the Internet to find job opportunities, market themselves to companies, showcase their skills, and they hope to be able to land that dream job.

c. (Hint: Match adjectives.) Recent graduates are seeking jobs that are stimulating and a challenge.

5.6 Organizing Paragraph Sentences (Obj. 5)

YOUR TASK In a memo to the college president, the athletic director argues for a new stadium scoreboard. One paragraph will describe the old scoreboard and why it needs to be replaced. Study the following list of ideas for that paragraph.

1. The old scoreboard is a tired warhorse that was originally constructed in the 1970s.
2. It is now hard to find replacement parts when something breaks.
3. The old scoreboard is not energy efficient.
4. Coca-Cola has offered to buy a new sports scoreboard in return for exclusive rights to sell pop on campus.
5. The old scoreboard should be replaced for many reasons.
6. It shows only scores for football games.
7. When we have soccer games or track meets, we are without a functioning scoreboard.

   a. Which sentence should be the topic sentence?

   b. Which sentence(s) should be developed in a separate paragraph?

   c. Which sentences should become support sentences?

Commas

Review Guides 21 to 26 about commas in Appendix B, Grammar and Mechanics Guide, beginning on page B-1. On a sheet of paper or on your computer, revise the following sentences to correct errors in comma usage. For each error that you locate, write the guide number and abbreviation that deals with this usage. The more you recognize the reasons, the better you will learn these punctuation guidelines. If a sentence is correct, write *C*. When you finish, compare your responses with the key in Appendix C.

Guide 21, CmSer (Comma series)

Guide 22, CmIntr (Comma introductory, addresses, geographical names, etc.)

Guide 23, CmConj (Comma conjunction)

Guide 24, CmDate (Comma, dates)

Guide 26, CmNo (Unnecessary comma)

EXAMPLE: When we use company e-mail we know our messages are monitored.

REVISION: When we use company **e-mail, we** know our messages are monitored. [Guide 22, CmIntr]

1. Informal research methods include looking in the files talking with your boss and interviewing the target audience.
2. When we use company e-mail we realize that our messages are monitored.
3. By learning to distinguish between dependent and independent clauses you will be able to avoid serious sentence faults.
4. Active-voice verbs are best in most business messages but passive-voice verbs are useful when sensitivity is required.
5. We hired Davida Michaels who was the applicant with the best qualifications as our new social media manager.
6. Our business was incorporated on August 1, 2008 in Calgary Alberta.
7. The new social media business by the way is flourishing and is expected to show a profit soon.
8. After he graduates Dustin plans to move to Victoria and find work there.
9. Last fall our company introduced policies regulating the use of cell phones texting and e-mail on the job.
10. The problem with many company telecommunication policies is that the policies are self-policed and never enforced.

Notes

[1] Wordsmith Associates Communications Consultations, Inc. (2017). *Plain language training, writing, and auditing*. https://wordsmith.ca/

[2] Ibid.

[3] English, K. (2012, February 10). Does correct spelling matter to journalists? *Toronto Star*. https://www.thestar.com/opinion/public_editor/2012/02/10/does_correct_spelling_matter_to_journalists.html

[4] Greenfield, R. (2014, July 29). *Brainstorming doesn't work; try this technique instead*. Fast Company. http://www.fastcompany.com/3033567/agendas/brainstorming-doesntwork-try-this-technique-instead

[5] Ibid.

[6] Russell, M. (2013). *Brainwriting: A more perfect brainstorm*. Innovation Management. http://www.innovationmanagement.se/imtool-articles/brainwriting-a-more-perfect-brainstorm

[7] Moye, J. (2015, January 26). #MakeItHappy: Coca-Cola's big game ad to champion online positivity. *Coca-Cola Journey*. http://www.coca-colacompany.com/stories/makeithappy-coca-colas-big-game-ad-to-champion-online-positivity

[8] Hutchins, A. (2017, March 30). Universities' new rules for cheating: Three students complete a group assignment. One cheats. Should they all be punished? *Maclean's*. https://www.macleans

.ca/education/universities-new-rules-for-cheating/

[9] Ibid.

[10] Ibid.

[11] Press, G. (2015, February 16). 15 Most-funded crowdfunding projects on Kickstarter and Indiegogo. *Forbes*. http://www.forbes.com/sites/gilpress/2015/02/16/15-mostfunded-crowdfunding-projects-on-kickstarterand-indiegogo. See also Briody, G. (2013, May 14). Crowdfunding: Why strangers will pay your tuition. *Fiscal Times*. http://www.thefiscaltimes.com/Articles/2013/05/14/Crowdfunding-Why-Strangers-Will-Pay-Your-Tuition

[12] Hull, J. S. (2007). *Splenda hearings*. http://www.janethull.com/newsletter/0607/splenda_hearings.php

[13] Goddard, R. W. (1989, April). Communication: Use language effectively. *Personnel Journal*, 32.

[14] Grammarly. (2019). https://www.grammarly.com/

[15] Wordsmith Associates. (2019). *Changing culture*. https://wordsmith.ca/changing-culture/

CHAPTER 6

Revising Business Messages

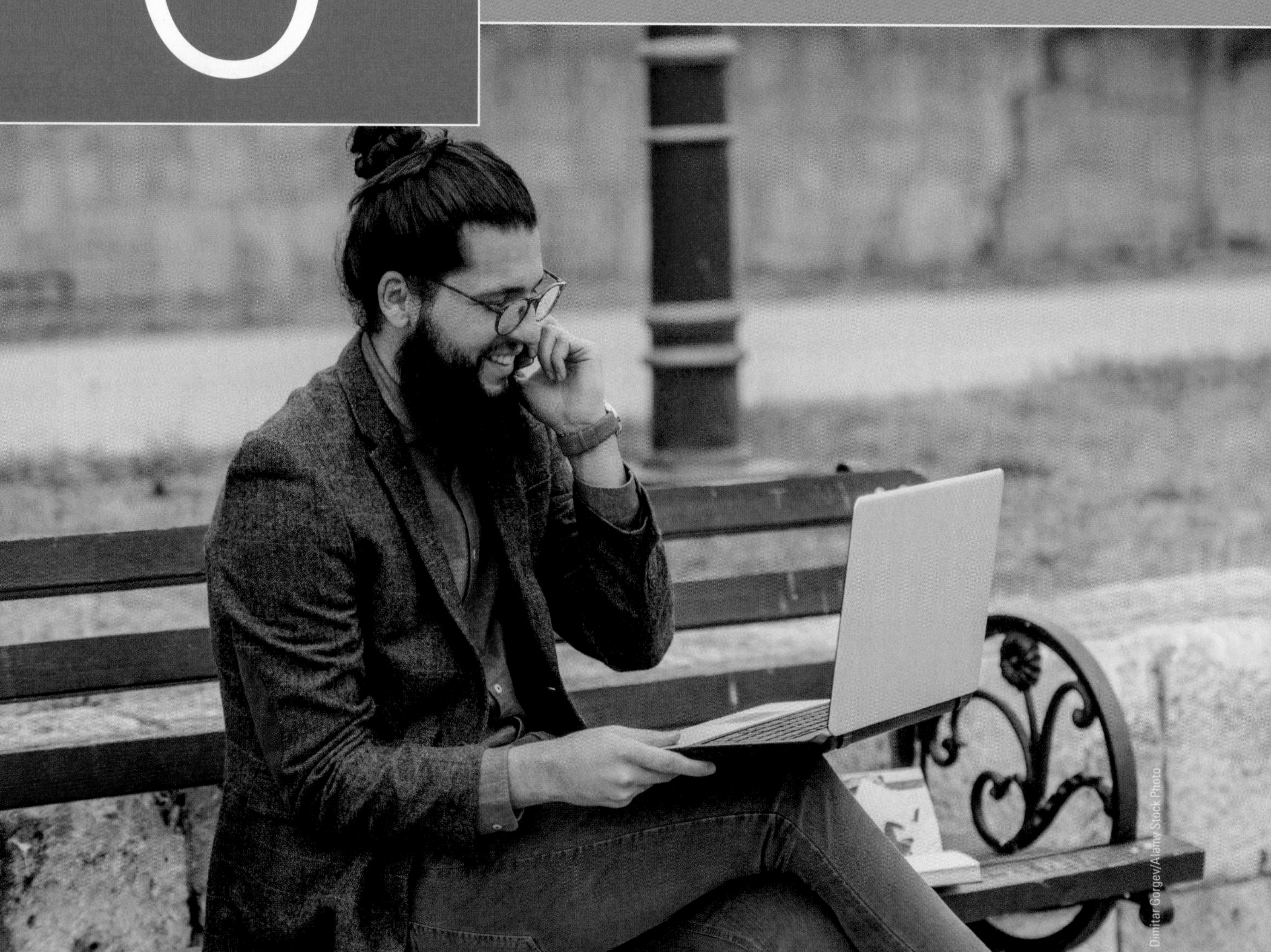

Dimitar Gorgev/Alamy Stock Photo

LEARNING OBJECTIVES

After studying this chapter, you should be able to

1. Polish business messages by revising for conciseness.
2. Improve clarity in business messages.
3. Recognize proofreading problem areas, and apply effective techniques to catch mistakes.
4. Evaluate a message to judge its effectiveness.

SPOTLIGHT ON COMMUNICATION: PART 1

Editors Canada: The Importance of Editing

Editors Canada is a not-for-profit organization run primarily by volunteers. Editors Canada provides access to over 1,300 editors across Canada who work with "individuals and organizations in the corporate, technical, government, not-for-profit, academic and publishing sectors across the country and around the world in English and French."[1]

Reprinted courtesy of Editors Canada

Local branches (or twigs) provide professional development opportunities to its members and the community, including seminars, speakers, networking, and mentorships. Organizations and individuals looking to hire an editor can post an ad for free on the Editors Canada online job board.[2]

Editors Canada defines editorial skills as follows:

> Editing involves carefully reviewing material before it is published and suggesting or making changes to correct or improve it. The editor must communicate clearly and tactfully with all team members, and clearly mark and convey changes, suggestions, and directions. In all cases, the editor should strive to make all changes without altering intended meaning or introducing errors.
>
> The editor should also be aware of the legal and ethical dimensions of the publishing process, including issues involving copyright, plagiarism, libel, privacy protection, and confidentiality, and the need to address biased, non-inclusive, and offensive material.[3]

Skilled editors not only save organizations and individuals time and money but also make them look professional.

CRITICAL THINKING

- Why is it important for an editor to have legal and ethical awareness of the publishing process, in addition to technical skills?
- How can your developing strong editing skills benefit your employer?

Stopping to Revise: Applying Phase 3 of the Writing Process

LEARNING OBJECTIVE 1

Polish business messages by revising for conciseness.

In this fast-paced era of e-mailing, texting, and tweeting, the idea of stopping to revise a message seems almost alien to productivity. What? Stop to proofread? No time! However, sending quick but sloppy business messages not only fails to enhance productivity but also often produces the opposite result. Those unprofessional messages can be confusing and frustrating. They often set into motion an annoying flurry of back-and-forth queries and responses seeking clarification. To avoid messages that waste time, create confusion, and reduce your credibility, take time to slow down and revise—even for short messages.

The final phase of the 3-x-3 writing process focuses on editing, proofreading, and evaluating. Although the drafting process differs depending on the person and the situation, this final phase should occupy a significant share of the total time you spend on a message. As you learned earlier, some experts recommend devoting about half the total writing time to the third phase of the writing process.[4]

Rarely is the first or even second version of a message satisfactory. The revision stage is your chance to make sure your message says what you mean and makes you look good. Whether you revise immediately or after a break, you will want to examine your message critically. You should be especially concerned with ways to improve its conciseness, clarity, and readability.

Polishing Your Message by Revising for Conciseness

In business, time is indeed money. Translated into writing, this means that concise messages save reading time and, thus, money. In addition, messages that are written directly and efficiently are

CENGAGE

MINDTAP

Check out section 6-1a in MindTap, where you can watch a video featuring Debi Rampersad, a financial industry manager, discuss the importance of making your message clear and concise.

easier to read and comprehend. In the revision process, look for shorter ways to say what you mean. Examine every sentence that you write. Could the thought be conveyed in fewer words? Your writing will be more concise if you remove excessive expressions, drop unnecessary introductory words, get rid of redundancies, and purge empty words.

Removing Excessive Expressions

As you revise, focus on removing excessive expressions. This takes conscious effort. For example, notice the excessive phrases in this sentence: *Due to the fact that sales are booming, profits are good.* It could be said more concisely: *Because sales are booming, profits are good.* Many excessive expressions can be shortened to one concise word, as shown here and illustrated in Figure 6.1. Notice in this figure how you can revise digital documents with strikethrough formatting and colour. If you are revising print documents, use popular proofreading marks.

Excessive	Concise
as a general rule	generally
at a later date	later
at this point in time	now, presently
despite the fact that	although
due to the fact that, inasmuch as, in view of the fact that	because
feel free to	please
in all probability	probably
in the event that	if
until such time as	until
with regard to	about

Omitting Long Lead-Ins

Concise sentences avoid long lead-ins with unnecessary introductory words. Consider this sentence: *I am sending you this e-mail to announce that we have hired a new manager.* It's more concise and direct without the long lead-in: *We have hired a new manager.* The main idea of the sentence often follows the words *that* or *because*, as shown in the following:

Wordy	Concise
We are sending this announcement to let everyone know that we expect to change Internet service providers within six weeks.	We expect to change Internet service providers within six weeks.
This is to inform you that you may find lower airfares on our website.	You may find lower airfares on our website.

Purging *There Is/Are* and *It Is/Was* Fillers

In many sentences the expressions *there is/are* and *it is/was* are unnecessary fillers. In addition to taking up space, these fillers delay getting to the point of the sentence. Eliminate them by recasting the sentence. Many—but not all—sentences can be revised so that fillers are unnecessary.

FIGURE 6.1 Revising Digital and Print Documents

Revising Digital Documents Using Strikethrough and Colour

~~This is a short note to let you know that, as~~ As you requested, I ~~made an investigation of~~ investigated several of our competitors' websites. Attached ~~hereto~~ is a summary of my findings. ~~of my investigation.~~ I was ~~really~~ most interested in ~~making a comparison of the employment of strategies for~~ comparing marketing strategies as well as ~~the use of~~ navigational graphics ~~used~~ to guide visitors through the sites. ~~In view of the fact that~~ Because we will be revising our own website ~~in the near future~~ soon, I was ~~extremely~~ intrigued by the organization, ~~kind of~~ marketing tactics, and navigation at each ~~and every~~ site I visited.

When revising digital documents, you can use simple word processing tools such as strikethrough and colour. In this example, strikethroughs in red identify passages to be deleted. The strikethrough function is located on the **Font** tab. We used blue to show inserted words, but you may choose any colour you prefer.

Revising Printed Documents Using Proofreading Symbols

When revising printed documents, use standard symbols to manually show your revisions.

~~This is a short note to let you know that,~~ as you requested, I ~~made an~~ investigat~~ion of~~ several of our competitors' websites. Attached ~~hereto~~ is a summary of my findings ~~of my investigation.~~ I was ~~really~~ most interested in ~~making a comparison of the employment of~~ strategies ~~for marketing~~ as well as ~~the use of~~ navigational graphics ~~used~~ to guide visitors through the sites. ~~In view of the fact that~~ we will be revising our own website ~~in the near future,~~ I was ~~extremely~~ intrigued by the organization, ~~kind of~~ marketing tactics, and navigation at each ~~and every~~ site I visited.

Popular Proofreading Symbols

- Delete
- Capitalize
- Insert
- Insert comma
- Insert period
- Start paragraph

Wordy	Concise
There are more women than men enrolled in college today.	More women than men are enrolled in college today.
It was a Facebook post that revealed the news.	A Facebook post revealed the news.

Rejecting Redundancies

Expressions that repeat meaning or include unnecessary words are redundant. Saying *unexpected surprise* is like saying *surprise surprise* because *unexpected* carries the same meaning as *surprise*. Excessive adjectives, adverbs, and phrases often create redundancies and wordiness. Redundancies do not add emphasis, as some people think. Instead, they identify a writer as careless. As you revise, look for redundant expressions such as the following:

Redundant	Concise
absolutely essential	essential
basic fundamentals	fundamentals *or* basics
big in size	big
combined together	combined
exactly identical	identical
each and every	each *or* every
new beginning	beginning
refer back	refer
PIN number	PIN

Editing Empty Words

Familiar phrases roll off the tongue easily, but many contain expendable parts. Be alert to these empty words and phrases: *case, degree, the fact that, factor, instance, nature,* and *quality.* Notice how much better the following sentences sound when we remove all the empty words:

~~In the case of~~ Twitter~~, it~~ increased users but lost share value.

Because of ~~the degree of~~ support from upper management, the plan worked.

We are aware ~~of the fact~~ that new products soar when pushed by social networking.

She chose a career in a field that was analytical ~~in nature~~.

Student writing in that class is excellent ~~in quality~~.

Also avoid saying the obvious. In the following examples, notice how many unnecessary words we can omit through revision:

~~When it arrived~~, I cashed your cheque immediately. (Announcing the cheque's arrival is unnecessary. That fact is assumed in its cashing.)

As consumers learn more about ingredients ~~and as they become more knowledgeable~~, they are demanding fresher foods. (Avoid repeating information.)

Look carefully at clauses beginning with *that, which,* and *who.* They can often be shortened without loss of clarity. Search for phrases such as *it appears that.* These phrases often can be reduced to a single adjective or adverb, such as *apparently.*

Changing the name of a ∧ successful company ~~that is successful~~ is always risky.

All employees ~~who are among those~~ completing the course will be reimbursed.

Our ∧ final proposal, ~~which was~~ slightly altered ~~in its final form~~, won approval.

We plan to schedule ∧ weekly meetings ~~on a weekly basis~~.

Microblogging and Conciseness

Microblogging is a term you probably haven't heard very often, but chances are you have posted a microblog message today. As its name suggests, microblogging consists of short messages exchanged on social media networks, such as Facebook, Instagram, and Twitter.

Businesses are eagerly joining these microblogging networks to hear what's being said about them and their products. When they hear complaints, they can respond immediately and often solve customer problems. Companies are also using microblogging to make announcements, promote goodwill, and sell their products.

Enterprise Microblogging. Recognizing the usefulness of microblogging but desiring more confidentiality and security, some companies prefer to keep their messages

ETHICS CHECK

Bending Grammar in Advertisements

Many marketers use incorrect grammar in advertisements on purpose because they feel it sounds more casual, concise, clever, or attention-grabbing, like Apple's "Think Different" campaign. Ford Canada stirred up consumer controversy with their slogan "Go Further." *Farther* is a measurable distance, while *further* is for metaphorical distance.[5] Ford defended their slogan by stating: "Go Further means going where no one expects a car company to go by delivering the best in Quality, Green, Safe and Smart products."[6] What should companies consider before bending grammar rules or using ambiguous language in their slogans?

internal. *Enterprise microblogging* enables companies using special platforms to collaborate, share information, and communicate privately within their organizations.

Examples of Company Twitter Messages. Regardless of the microblogging platform, conciseness is critical. Your messages must be short—without straying too far from conventional spelling, grammar, and punctuation. Sound difficult? It is, but it can be done, as shown in the following 140-character examples of workplace tweets:

Trademarks of Canadian Tire Corporation, Limited used under license

Replying to Customer
@CanadianTire

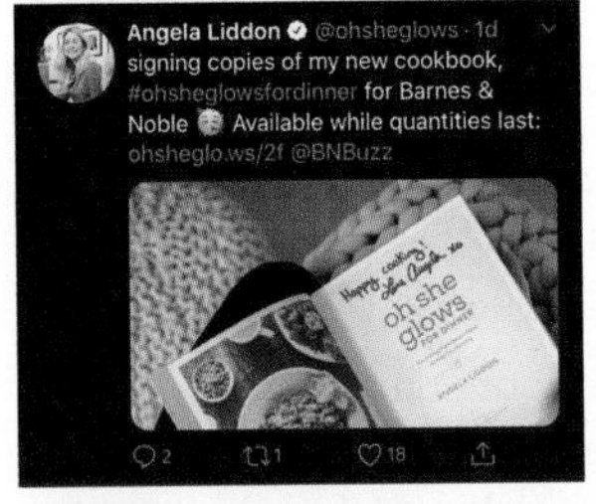

Oh She Glows

Sharing Information
@ohsheglows

Canadian North Airlines

Making an Announcement
@CanadianNorth

Tips for Writing Concise, Effective Tweets. Your microblogging messages will be most effective if you follow these tips:

- Include only main ideas focused on useful information.
- Choose descriptive but short words.
- Personalize your message if possible.

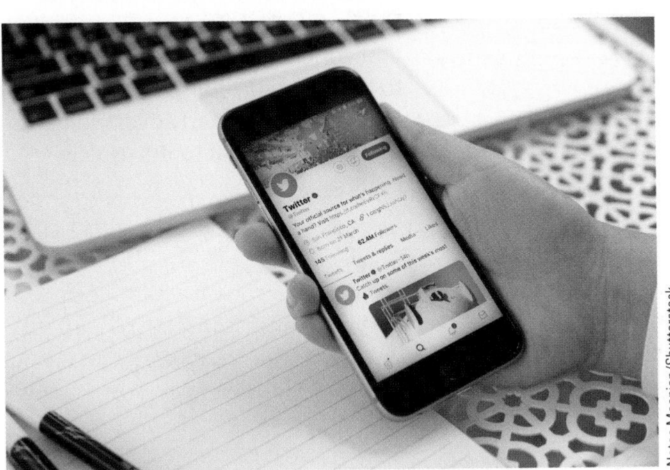

Natee Meepian/Shutterstock

To find out what makes a tweet good or bad, university researchers asked 1,400 Twitter users to rate thousands of tweets. The study found that tweets rated as good typically conveyed useful information or humour, or even posed questions to followers. Tweets rated as bad typically contained status updates, cryptic messages, negativity, or hashtag clutter.[7]

- Be prepared to draft several versions striving for conciseness, clarity, and, yes, even correctness.

It's like playing a game: can you get your message across in only 140 characters? You'll learn more about microblogging in Chapter 7.

Concept Check

1. Why is it important to devote half of your total writing time to Phase 3 of the writing process?
2. Revise the following sentences to remove excessive expressions.
   a. In the event that interest rates increase, we will begin investing in the very near future.
   b. We cannot fill the order until such time as payment is received for previous shipments.
   c. As a general rule, we would not accept the return; however, we will in all probability make an exception in this case.

LEARNING OBJECTIVE 2

Improve clarity in business messages.

Improving Message Clarity

One of the most important tasks in revising is assessing the clarity of your message. A clear message is one that is immediately understood. Employees, customers, and investors increasingly want to be addressed in a clear and genuine way. Fuzzy, long-winded, and unclear writing prevents comprehension. Readers understand better when information is presented clearly and concisely, as illustrated in Figure 6.2. Numerous techniques can improve the clarity of your writing: applying the KISS formula (keep it short and simple), slashing trite business phrases, cutting clichés and buzzwords, rescuing buried verbs, and eliminating intensifiers.

Keep It Short and Simple

To achieve clarity, resist the urge to show off or be fancy. Remember that as a business writer your goal is to *express*, not *impress*. One way to achieve clear writing is to apply the familiar KISS formula. Use active-voice sentences that avoid indirect, pompous language.

FIGURE 6.2 Conciseness Improves Clarity in Understanding Drug Facts

People who correctly quantified a heart drug's benefits after reading concise fact box.

People who correctly quantified a heart drug's benefits after reading the company's long ad.

Consumers understand drug effects better when the information is presented concisely and clearly. A Dartmouth University study revealed that concise fact boxes were superior to the tiny-type, full-page DTC (direct-to-consumer) advertisements that drug manufacturers usually publish.

Source: Based on Rubin, R. (2009, February 7). Concise drug-facts boxes vs. "brief" summaries. *USA Today*, p. D7.

Wordy and Unclear	Improved
Employees have not been made sufficiently aware of the potentially adverse consequences regarding the use of these perilous chemicals.	Warn your employees about these dangerous chemicals.
In regard to the matter of obtaining optimal results, it is essential that employees be given the implements that are necessary for jobs to be completed satisfactorily.	To get the best results, give employees the tools they need to do the job.

Slashing Trite Business Phrases

To sound businesslike, some business writers repeat the same stale expressions that others have used over the years. Your writing will sound fresher and more vigorous if you eliminate these trite phrases or find more original ways to convey the idea.

Trite Phrase	Improved
as per your request	as you requested
enclosed please find	enclosed is
every effort will be made	we'll try
in receipt of	have received
please do not hesitate to	please
thank you in advance	thank you
with reference to	about

Cutting Clichés

Clichés are expressions that have become exhausted by overuse. Many cannot be explained, especially to those who are new to our culture. Clichés lack not only freshness but also clarity. Instead of repeating clichés such as the following, try to find another way to say what you mean.

below the belt	last but not least
better than new	make a bundle
easier said than done	quick as a flash
exception to the rule	pass with flying colours
good to go	stand your ground
first and foremost	think outside the box

Changing Slang and Buzzwords

Slang is composed of informal words with arbitrary and extravagantly changed meanings. Slang words quickly go out of fashion because they are no longer appealing when everyone begins to understand them. If you want to sound professional, avoid using slang expressions like *literally*, *ghosted*, and *cringe-worthy*, and social media slang such as *IMO* (in my opinion), *SMH* (shaking my head), and *TL;DR* (too long; didn't read).

Buzzwords are technical expressions that have become fashionable and often are meant to impress rather than express. Business buzzwords include empty terms, such as *optimize*, *impactful*, *innovative*, *leveraging*, *right-size*, and *paradigm shift*. Countless businesses today

Check out section 6-2d in MindTap, where you can watch a video featuring Léonicka Valcius, a book publishing professional, discuss the importance of avoiding buzzwords and jargon in your writing.

use vague rhetoric, such as *cost effective, positioned to perform, solutions-oriented,* and *value-added services with end-to-end fulfillment.*

Consider the following statement by a government official who had been asked why his department was dropping a proposal to lease offshore oil lands: *The administration has an awful lot of other things in the pipeline, and this has more wiggle room so they just moved it to the back burner.* He added, however, that the proposal might be offered again since *there is no pulling back because of hot-potato factors.* What exactly does this mean?

Rescuing Buried Verbs

Buried verbs are those that are needlessly converted to wordy noun expressions. This happens when verbs such as *acquire, establish,* and *develop* are made into nouns such as *acquisition, establishment,* and *development.* Such nouns often end in *-tion, -ment,* and *-ance.* Sometimes called *zombie nouns* because they cannibalize and suck the life out of active verbs,[8] these nouns increase sentence length, slow the reader, and muddy the thought. Notice how you can make your writing cleaner and more forceful by avoiding buried verbs and zombie nouns:

Buried Verbs	Unburied Verbs
conduct a discussion of	discuss
engage in the preparation of	prepare
give consideration to	consider
make an assumption of	assume
perform an analysis of	analyze
reach a conclusion that	conclude

Eliminating Intensifiers

Occasionally, we show our exuberance with words such as *very, definitely, quite, completely, extremely, really, actually,* and *totally.* These intensifiers can emphasize and strengthen your meaning. Overuse, however, sounds unbusinesslike. Control your enthusiasm and guard against excessive use.

Overused Intensifiers	Businesslike
The manufacturer was *extremely* upset to learn that its smartphones were *definitely* being counterfeited.	The manufacturer was upset to learn that its smartphones were being counterfeited.
We *totally* agree that we *actually* did not give his proposal a *very* fair trial.	We agree that we did not give his proposal a fair trial.

Concept Check

1. Revise the following sentences to avoid confusing clichés, slang, buzzwords, and wordiness.
   a. Although our last presentation bombed, we think that beyond the shadow of a doubt our new presentation will fly.
   b. If you will refer back to the budget, you will see that there are provisions that prevent blowing the budget.
   c. The team leader didn't know that we were literally starving and getting very hangry b/c someone 4got to order lunch.

2. Revise the following to recover buried verbs.
   a. After making an investigation, the fire department reached the conclusion that the blaze was set intentionally.
   b. Web-based customer service certainly causes a reduction in overall costs.
   c. When used properly, zero-based budgeting can bring about a reduction in overall costs.

CASE CONNECTIONS

Kinova Robotics: Assistive Robotics

Courtesy of Kinova

Kinova Robotics has been named one of Growth 500's fastest-growing companies in Canada,[9] as well as one of *Robotics Business Review*'s top 50 "innovative and disruptive companies for commercial and industrial robotics."[10] Located in Boisbriand, Québec, Kinova launched its first robotic arm in 2006 and now produces "next-generation medical robotics that complement and extend human capabilities."[11] Kinova products are used in academic and industrial research, industrial and professional robots, and medical and assistive robots:

> Whether you're seeking greater control over your daily life or you're looking to lead the charge for innovation in your industry for years to come, Kinova can customize solutions to help you meet your specific needs. All of our products are designed to augment human capability in any environment—at home, in research labs and medical facilities, in manufacturing plants, and many more. Our robotics always put the human at the forefront, meaning the individual is always in control of the technology, and the technology always complements the individual. Together, extraordinary results are always within reach.[12]

Kinova's assistive technologies are changing the lives of people with disabilities. Their robotics make independence possible, assisting with daily activities like eating, brushing teeth, and using the computer.[13]

- Many people fear that as robotics and Artificial Intelligence (AI) technologies advance, they will replace human jobs and functions. Kinova's innovations demonstrate how robotics can assist humans rather than replace them. In what ways do assistive technologies complement and better the lives of Canadians?

Proofreading to Catch Errors

LEARNING OBJECTIVE 3

Recognize proofreading problem areas, and apply effective techniques to catch mistakes.

Even the best writers make mistakes. The problem, however, is not making the mistakes; the real problem is not finding and correcting them. Documents with errors affect your credibility and the success of your organization, as illustrated in Figure 6.3.

Once you have the message in its final form, it's time to proofread. Don't proofread earlier because you may waste time checking items that eventually are changed or omitted. Important messages—such as those you send to management or to customers or turn in to instructors for grades—deserve careful revision and proofreading. When you finish a first draft, plan for a cooling-off period. Put the document aside and return to it after a break, preferably after 24 hours or longer. Proofreading is especially difficult because most of us read what we think we wrote. That's why it's important to look for specific problem areas, as detailed in Figure 6.4.

FIGURE 6.3 Why Proofread? In Business, Accuracy Matters

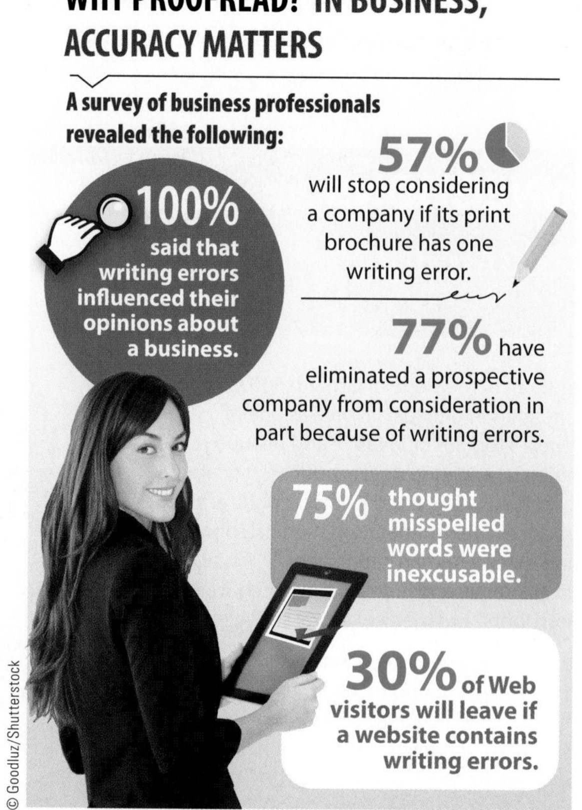

Source: Based on PenroseMcNab Consulting. (2010). Poor grammar and business. http://www.penrosemcnab.com/theproblem.htm. © PenroseMcNab Consulting.

What to Watch for in Proofreading

Careful proofreaders check for problems in the following areas:

- **Spelling.** Now is the time to consult the dictionary. Is *recommend* spelled with one or two c's? Do you mean *affect* or *effect*? Use your computer spell-checker, but don't rely on it totally. Check closely for Canadian spellings, like *honour, colour, centre*, and *behaviour.* In Microsoft Word you can set your spell-checker for Canadian settings, as most come with U.S. spelling as a default.
- **Grammar.** Locate sentence subjects; do their verbs agree with them? Do pronouns agree with their antecedents?
- **Punctuation.** Make sure that introductory clauses are followed by commas. In compound sentences put commas before coordinating conjunctions (*and, or, but, nor*). Double-check your use of semicolons and colons.
- **Names and numbers.** Compare all names and numbers with their sources because inaccuracies are not always obvious. Especially verify the spelling of the names of individuals receiving the message. Misspelling a name can make you look sloppy or unprofessional.
- **Format.** Be sure that your document looks balanced on the page. If you indent paragraphs, be certain that all are indented. Review the tips presented in Chapter 5.

FIGURE 6.4 Partially Revised First Draft

Reduces wordiness throughout

The first two paragraphs show revisions. Your task is to finish the revision.

DRAFT

Date: May 9, 2020
To: Taco Bell Management Council
From: Dustin Ortiz, Culinary Product Manager
Subject: ~~New Ideas~~ Eating Trends and New Menu Options

Improves subject line

Revises trite expression (*as per your request*) and uses first-person pronoun

Converts four-word phrase (*that serve fast food*) to adjective (*fast-food*)

Shortens wordy noun phrase (*represents a summary*) to more efficient verb (*summarizes*)

As ~~per your~~ you requested, ~~the writer is~~ I am submitting the following ideas based on ~~his~~ my ~~personal~~ observation and research ~~in regard to~~ about eating trends in fast-food restaurants ~~that serve fast-food~~. ~~As you suggested, I am also offering b~~Below is a rough outline of possible concepts to ~~enlarge and~~ expand Taco Bell's menu reflecting ~~these aforementioned~~ current eating trends. ~~This is to inform you that t~~This memo ~~represents a summary of~~ summarizes the findings ~~that I have extracted~~ from my longer report to be presented at your next Management Council meeting.

Deletes *and foremost* to avoid cliché; reduces excessive exuberance (*much more*)

Develops parallelism (*flavour, portability, ease of production*)

Unburies verb by changing *made an observation* to *observed*

First ~~and foremost~~, I ~~would like to~~ will focus on new menu items that are ~~more~~ fresher, ~~and much~~ more sophisticated, ~~And~~ and ~~with more~~ locally grown ~~items~~. However, I know that these items must also meet Taco ~~Bells~~ Bell's strict criteria: high-quality flavour, ~~they must be portable~~ portability, and ~~they must be easily produced~~ ease of production. In ~~an~~ a recovering economy ~~that is recovering~~, our restaurant ~~can and most certainly~~ should offer value as well as tasty food ~~that tastes very good~~. From my ~~personal~~ firsthand experience ~~that I gained firsthand~~ as a chef and from current reading and research, I have ~~made an observation of~~ observed numerous eating trends.

In the remaining report, edit to reduce wordiness and correct errors

Taking a Look at Trends in Fast-Food Eating Preferences

As you probably know, Mexican cuisine is increasingly popular from coast to coast, but today's customers—especially Generation Z—want much more intense flavours. With locally sourced ingredients. There are four trends that are most appropriate for us to take action on as we revamp the Taco Bell menu.

Use bulleted list with headings to improve readability in this paragraph

The first deals with the matter of **high-protein items**. A lot of recent research reveals that 42 percent of all Generation Z as well as more then half of all adults think that it is important to eat more protein. A second trend deals with **spices**. Consumers are appreciating much more highly spiced foods and hot sauces. Spicy Thai and other ethnic dishes are growing in popularity. A third trend has to do with **freshness**. As consumers become more knowledgeable and more discriminating they are making a demand for fresher ingredients. Which are often locally grown. A fourth trend has to do with **small portions**. Trend watchers say that 35 percent of all meals that are eaten by Generation Z are snacks, thus suggesting small portions.

A Few Ideas for New Menu Options

Revise wordy phrases (*Despite the fact that*)

Despite the fact that my full report contains a number of additional trends and menu ideas, here are three significant menu concepts that are significant and important:

Consider a bulleted or numbered list to improve this dense paragraph

First, I am totally of the opinion that we should add a **PowerProtein Menu**. Reflecting the trend toward more protein, I suggest that we could be offering high-protein breakfast items such as steak burritos and Greek yogurt with granola. Second, I would like to recommend a **Fresh-Flavoured Salsa Bar**. To appeal to those desiring fresh flavours, we could offer homemade exotic salsas. With locally sourced ingredients for bold flavours and textures. Third, to cater to snackers, I suggest **Small Plate** items. We could offer grilled sweet potato nachos with crumbled cojito and gooey cheese sauce on top. Other small plates might offer jalapeno pepper quinoa bites that are cheesy and spicy along with sharable snacks such as rolled chicken tacos.

Convert buried verbs (*have a discussion*) and reduce other wordiness

I would be more than delighted and happy to have a discussion of these ideas with you in greater detail and have a demonstration of them in the kitchen. Please accept my humble thanks for this opportunity to work with you in expanding our menu to ensure that Taco Bell remains tops in Mexican cuisine.

How to Proofread Routine Documents

Most routine documents require a light proofreading. If you read on screen, use the down arrow to reveal one line at a time. This focuses your attention at the bottom of the screen. A safer proofreading method, however, is reading from a printed copy. Regardless of which method you use, look for typos and misspellings. Search for easily confused words, such as *to* for *too* and *then* for *than*. Read for missing words and inconsistencies. For handwritten or printed messages, use standard proofreading marks, shown briefly in Figure 6.1 or completely on the inside front cover of this book. For digital documents and collaborative projects, use the simple word processing tools also shown in Figure 6.1, or use the Comment and Track Changes functions described in the Plugged In box later in this chapter.

How to Proofread Complex Documents

Long, complex, or important documents demand careful proofreading. Apply the previous suggestions but also add the following techniques:

- **Print a copy,** preferably double-spaced, and set it aside for at least a day. You will be more alert after a breather.
- **Allow adequate time to proofread carefully.** A common excuse for sloppy proofreading is lack of time.
- **Be prepared to find errors.** Psychologically, we don't expect to find errors, and we don't want to find them. You can overcome this obstacle by anticipating errors and congratulating, not criticizing, yourself each time you find one.
- **Read the message at least twice**—once for word meanings and once for grammar and mechanics. For very long documents (book chapters and long articles or reports), read a third time to verify consistency in formatting.
- **Reduce your reading speed.** Concentrate on individual words rather than ideas.
- **For documents that must be perfect,** enlist a proofreading buddy. Have someone read the message aloud. Spell names and difficult words, note capitalization, and read punctuation.
- **Use the standard proofreading marks** shown on the inside front cover to indicate changes.

Many of us struggle with proofreading our own writing because we are seeing the same information over and over. We tend to see what we expect to see as our eyes race over the words without looking at each one carefully. We tend to know what is coming next and glide over it. To change the appearance of what you are reading, you might print it on a different-coloured paper or change the typeface. If you are proofing on screen, enlarge the page view or change the background colour of the screen.

ETHICS CHECK

Overly Helpful

Students sometimes visit writing centres to receive useful advice and help. However, some well-meaning tutors take over, revising documents until they don't resemble the original student work. Instructors worry that the resulting documents amount to cheating. Yet in the workplace today, writers must collaborate, and individual authorship is often not relevant. How much assisted revision is acceptable in a postsecondary setting versus in the workplace?

How to Edit Team Writing

When your team is preparing a report or presentation and members create different sections, you will probably be expected to edit or respond to the writing of others. Remember that no one likes to be criticized, so make your statements specific, constructive, and helpful. Use MS Word Track Changes and Comment feature to identify and approve edits made by team members. See the accompanying Plugged In box for how to use collaborative tools. The following suggestions will help you edit team writing:

- Begin your remarks with a positive statement. What can you praise? Do you like the writer's conversational tone, word choice, examples, directness, or conciseness?
- Do you understand the writer's purpose? If not, be specific in explaining what you don't understand.
- Is the material logically organized? If not, how could it be improved?
- What suggestions can you make to improve specific ideas or sections?

PLUGGED IN

Using Track Changes and Other Editing Tools to Revise Collaborative Documents

Collaborative writing and editing projects are challenging. Fortunately, Microsoft Word offers useful tools to help team members edit and share documents electronically. Two simple but helpful editing tools are **Text Highlight Colour** and **Font Colour.** These tools, which are found on the **Home** tab in the MS Office suite, enable reviewers to point out errors and explain problematic passages through the use of contrast. However, some projects require more advanced editing tools such as **Track Changes** and **Comment**.

- **Track Changes.** To suggest specific editing changes to other team members, **Track Changes** is handy. The revised wording is visible on screen, and deletions show up in the text or in callout balloons that appear in the right-hand margin (see Figure 6.5). Team members suggest revisions that are identified and dated. The original writer may accept or reject these changes. **Track Changes** is located on the **Review** tab.
- **Comment.** Probably the most useful editing tool is the **Comment** function, also shown in Figure 6.5. This tool allows users to point out problematic passages or errors, ask or answer questions, and share ideas without changing or adding text. When more than one person adds comments, the comments appear in different colours and are identified by the writer's name and a date/time stamp. To use this tool in Word 2019, click **New Comment** from the drop-down **Review** tab. Then type your comment, which can be seen in the Web or print layout view (click **View** and **Print Layout** or **Web Layout**).
- **Completing a document.** When a document is finished, be sure to accept or reject all changes on the **Review** tab, a step that removes the tracking information.

FIGURE 6.5 Track Changes and Comment Feature in a Team Document

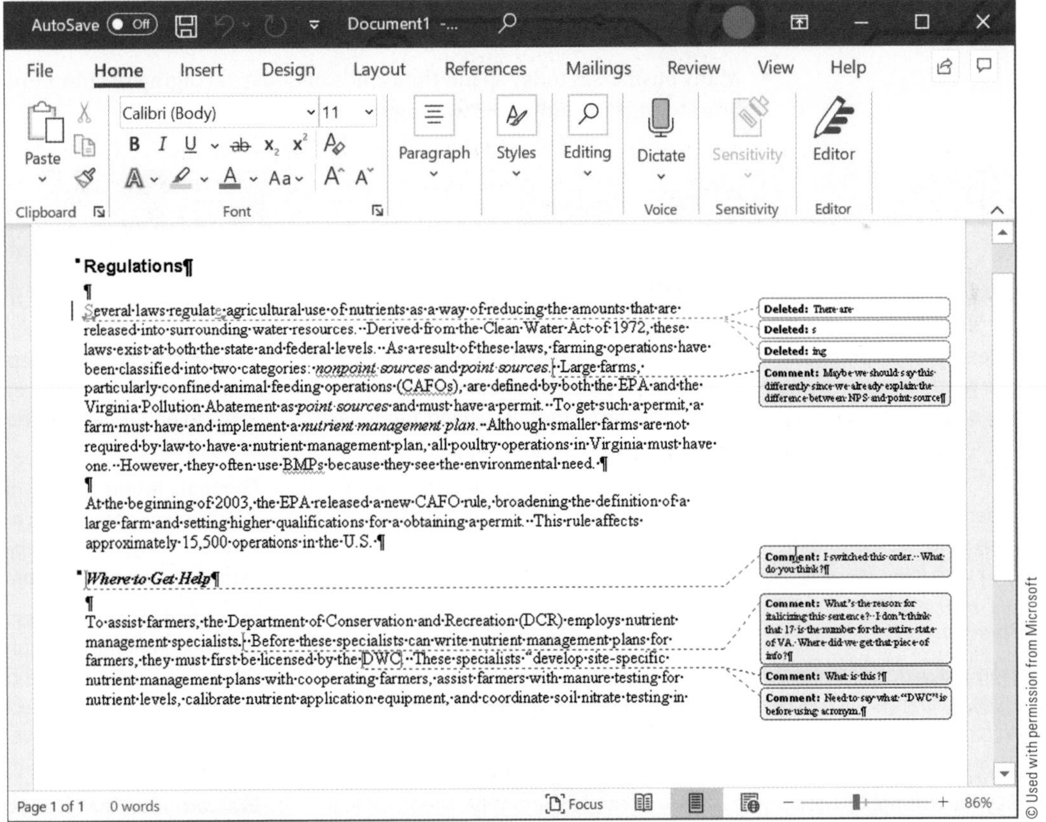

Team members can collaborate on shared documents with the **Track Changes** and **Comment** features in MS Word. Notice that **Track Changes** displays balloons to show deletions, comments, formatting changes, and the people who made the changes. See the Plugged In box for information on the usefulness of the **Track Changes** and **Comment** features when collaborating on team documents.

- Make polite statements such as *I would suggest . . . , You might consider . . . , How about doing this . . . ?*

Concept Check

1. Think about your own speaking and writing. Do you have some favourite redundancies that you use in spoken or written messages? What could you say that would be more precise?
2. Are you a good proofreader? Is it easier to find other people's errors than your own? Why? What are you good at finding? What do you frequently miss?

LEARNING OBJECTIVE 4

Evaluate a message to judge its effectiveness.

Evaluating the Effectiveness of Your Message

As part of applying finishing touches, take a moment to evaluate your writing. Remember that everything you write, whether for yourself or someone else, takes the place of a personal appearance. If you were meeting in person, you would be certain to dress appropriately and professionally. The same standard applies to your writing. Evaluate what you have written to be certain that it attracts the reader's attention. Is it polished and clear enough to convince the reader that you are worth listening to? How successful will this message be? Does it say what you want it to? Will it achieve your purpose? How will you know whether it succeeds?

The best way to judge the success of your communication is through feedback. Although any criticism is painful, try not to be defensive. The following three elements are the reasons this book and this course may be the most valuable in your entire curriculum:

- When your instructor evaluates your writing, look on these comments as valuable advice tailored to your specific writing weaknesses—and strengths.
- Many businesses today spend thousands of dollars bringing in communication consultants to improve employee writing skills.

CHECKLIST

Editing, Proofreading, and Evaluating

- **Remove excessive expressions.** Strive to reduce wordy phrases to single words (*as a general rule* becomes *generally; at this point in time* becomes *now*).
- **Avoid opening fillers and long lead-ins.** Revise sentences so that they don't start with fillers (*there is, there are, it is, it was*) and long lead-ins (*this is to inform you that*).
- **Reject redundancies.** Eliminate words that repeat meanings, such as *refer back*. Watch for repetitious adjectives, adverbs, and phrases.
- **Tighten your writing.** Check phrases that include *case, degree, the fact that, factor*, and other words and phrases that unnecessarily increase wordiness. Avoid saying the obvious.
- **Write concisely for microblogging.** Keep your messages short without sacrificing proper spelling, grammar, and punctuation.
- **Keep the message simple.** Express ideas directly. Don't show off or use fancy language.
- **Slash trite business phrases.** Keep your writing fresh, direct, and contemporary by skipping such expressions as *enclosed please find* and *pursuant to your request.*
- **Cut clichés or slang.** Avoid expressions that are overused and unclear (*below the belt, shoot from the hip*). Don't use slang, which is not only unprofessional but also often unclear to a wide audience.
- **Rescue buried verbs.** Keep your writing vigorous by not converting verbs to nouns (*analyze*, not *make an analysis of*).
- **Eliminate intensifiers.** Avoid overusing intensifiers such as *really, very, definitely, quite, completely, extremely, actually*, and *totally*.
- **Proofread for correctness.** Check spelling, grammar, and punctuation. Compare names and numbers with their sources. Double-check the format to be sure you have been consistent.
- **Evaluate your final product.** Will your message achieve its purpose? Could it be improved? How will you know whether it is successful?

- You are getting the same training in this course: instruction in the writing process, practice materials, and someone to guide you and evaluate your efforts.

The task of editing, proofreading, and evaluating, summarized in the Checklist provided on the previous page, is hard work. It demands objectivity and a willingness to cut, cut, cut. It's a great feeling when you realize your finished message is clear, concise, and effective.

Concept Check

1. How can you overcome defensiveness when your writing is criticized constructively?
2. What proofreading tasks can you safely ask a proofreading buddy to perform? What if that person is not a skilled writer?

SPOTLIGHT ON COMMUNICATION: PART 2

Editors Canada Revisited

CRITICAL THINKING

- What is the value in hiring a professional editor if the editor can't make corrections for you?
- What issues could arise if you hire an editor who isn't a member of Editors Canada?

Reprinted courtesy of Editors Canada

Members of Editors Canada often receive requests from students who want their assignments proofread. This becomes problematic as many editing services include substantive edits and corrections. While thorough edits are acceptable for workplace documents and personal works with credit given to the editor, these edits are not ethical for academic work that is being submitted for marks to earn a diploma or degree credential. All academic work must belong wholly to the student to avoid issues of plagiarism. To help members respond to student requests, Editors Canada created its "Guidelines for Ethical Editing of Student Texts."[14] Some highlights from the guidelines include the following:

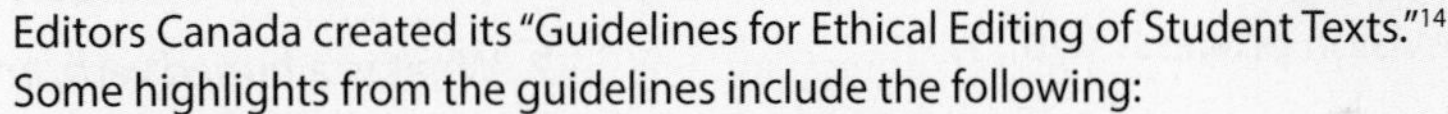

- Permission is needed from the student's instructor.
- There are limitations to the editing; the editor points out areas that need work but does not correct the student's work.
- The editor and student sign a contract, clearly stating the limitations of the editing.
- The editor records all suggestions with track changes and comments, and keeps clear records of edits and conversations with the student.[15]

By following these guidelines, the student and editor can work together while maintaining academic integrity.

Summary of Learning Objectives

1 Polish business messages by revising for conciseness.

- Concise messages make their points by using the fewest words.
- Revising for conciseness involves eliminating excessive expressions, opening fillers, redundancies, and empty words.
- Conciseness is especially important in revising microblogging messages as short as 140 characters.

2 **Improve clarity in business messages.**

- To be sure your messages are clear, apply the KISS formula: keep it short and simple.
- Avoid foggy, indirect, and pompous language.
- Do not include trite business phrases, clichés, slang, and buzzwords.
- Rescue buried nouns, and avoid overusing intensifiers that show exuberance.

3 **Recognize proofreading problem areas, and apply effective techniques to catch mistakes.**

- When proofreading, be especially alert to spelling, grammar, punctuation, names, numbers, and document format.
- Proofread routine documents immediately after completion; however, proofread complex documents after a breather.
- To do a good job, you should read from a printed copy, allow adequate time, reduce your reading speed, and read the document at least three times.
- Teams may use digital collaboration tools to work effectively together during the revising phase.

4 **Evaluate a message to judge its effectiveness.**

- Evaluate what you have written to be certain that it attracts the reader's attention.
- Welcome any advice from your instructor on how to improve your writing skills.

Chapter Review

1. Is revision still necessary in a digital age when workplace messages fly back and forth in seconds? What's involved in the revision process? (Obj. 1)
2. What is *microblogging*, and how do you make these messages effective? (Obj. 1)
3. What's wrong with using slang or buzzwords in microblogging messages? (Obj. 1)
4. Why should writers avoid familiar business phrases such as *as per your request* and *enclosed please find*? (Obj. 1)
5. What is the KISS formula? In what ways can it apply to business writing? (Obj. 2)
6. Why should writers avoid expressions such as *first and foremost* and *think outside the box*? (Obj. 2)
7. What is a *buried verb*, and how can you avoid these in your writing? (Obj. 2)
8. What are five specific items to check in proofreading? Be ready to discuss methods you find useful in spotting these errors. (Obj. 3)
9. List four or more effective techniques for proofreading complex documents. (Obj. 3)
10. What is the best way to judge the success of your communication? (Obj. 4)

Critical Thinking

1. A blogger recently asserted that "the pervasive use of e-mail for business has made the work of writing well even more difficult because it invites—relentlessly—hitting Send before you have thought through, organized, reviewed, and even rewritten your message."[16] Do you agree that the process of writing has become more difficult with e-mail? Explain. (Obj. 1)
2. Conciseness is valued in business. However, what issues arise if messages are too short? (Obj. 1)
3. In what ways should the proofreading process for routine documents differ from the process for complex documents? (Obj. 3)
4. In this age of rapid communication, how can you justify the time it takes to stop and revise a message? (Objs. 1–4)
5. **Ethical Issue:** What advice would you give in this ethical dilemma? Michiko is serving as interim editor

of the company newsletter. She receives an article written by the company president describing, in abstract and pompous language, the company's goals for the coming year. Michiko thinks the article will need considerable revising to make it readable. Attached to the president's article are complimentary comments by two of the company vice presidents. What action should Michiko take? (Obj. 2)

Activities

6.1 Long Lead-Ins (Obj. 1)

YOUR TASK Revise the following to eliminate long lead-ins.

a. This message is to let you know that I received your e-mail and its attachments.

b. This memo is to notify everyone that we will observe Monday as a holiday.

c. I am writing this letter to inform you that your homeowner's coverage expires soon.

6.2 Unnecessary *There Is/Are* and *It Is/Was* Fillers (Obj. 1)

YOUR TASK Revise the following to avoid unnecessary *there is/are* and *it is/was* fillers.

a. There are many businesses that are implementing strict e-mail policies for employees.

b. The manager says that there are many employees who did not return the health surveys.

c. It is my personal opinion that there are too many people dying while taking dangerous selfies.

6.3 Redundancies (Obj. 1)

YOUR TASK Revise the following to avoid redundancies.

a. Because the proposals are exactly identical, we need not check each and every item.

b. Some of the funniest animated gifs on Twitter, Tumblr, and Reddit combine together clips from movies or TV to produce comedic masterpieces.

c. Our supervisor requested that team members return back to the office.

6.4 Empty Words (Obj. 1)

YOUR TASK Revise the following to eliminate empty words.

a. Are you aware of the fact that social media can drive brand awareness and customer loyalty?

b. With such a degree of active participation in Facebook and Twitter, it's easy to understand why businesses are flocking to social sites.

c. We plan to schedule online meetings on a monthly basis.

6.5 Trite Business Phrases (Obj. 2)

YOUR TASK Revise the following sentences to eliminate trite business phrases.

a. As per your request, we will no longer send you e-mail offers.

b. Thank you in advance for considering our plea for community support.

c. Every effort will be made to send the original copies under separate cover.

d. Enclosed please find a cheque in the amount of $700.

e. In accordance with your wishes, we are responding forthwith to return your funds.

6.6 Investigating Writing in Your Field (Objs. 1–4)

How much writing is required by people working in your career area? The best way to learn about on-the-job writing is to talk with someone who has a job similar to the one you hope to have one day.

YOUR TASK Interview someone working in your field of study. Your instructor may ask you to present your findings orally or in a written report. Ask questions such as these: What kind of writing do you do? What kind of planning do you do before writing? Where do you get information? Do you brainstorm? Make lists? Do you compose on a computer or on your iPad? How many e-mail messages do you typically write in a day? How long does it take you to compose a routine one- or two-page memo, e-mail, or letter? Do you revise? How often? Do you have a preferred method for proofreading? When you have questions about grammar and mechanics, what or whom do you consult? Does anyone read your drafts and make suggestions? Can you describe your entire composition process? Do you ever work with others to produce a document? How does this process work? What makes writing easier or harder for you? Have your writing methods and skills changed since you left school?

Grammar and Mechanics | *Review 6*

Semicolons, Colons

Review Guides 27 to 30 about semicolons and colons in the Appendix B, Grammar and Mechanic Guide, beginning on page B-1. On a sheet of paper or on your computer, revise the following sentences to correct errors in semicolon and colon usage. Do not start new sentences. For each error that you locate, write the guide number that deals with this usage. The more you recognize the reasons, the better you will learn these punctuation guidelines. If a sentence is correct, write *C*. When you finish, compare your responses with the key in Appendix C.

EXAMPLE: Engineers produced a snazzy new product, however it had no exciting name.

REVISION: Engineers produced a snazzy new **product; however,** it had no exciting name. [Guide 27]

1. Companies find it difficult to name new products consequently they often hire specialists.
2. New product names must be interesting however many of the best names are already taken.
3. Branding a product is a creative endeavour, the name becomes a product's shorthand.
4. Global names must be appealing in such faraway places as Beijing China Montréal Canada and Dubai City United Arab Emirates.
5. One naming expert warned companies with the following comment "Be aware of global consequences. For example, Bimbo is the name of a Mexican baking conglomerate. However, the word in English has an unsavoury meaning."
6. Product and company names are developed by combining the following three linguistic elements morphemes, phonemes, and syntax.
7. One of the reasons company names such as Google and Apple work is that they are catchy, however they are also backed by high-quality products.
8. Some English sounds (such as L, V, F, and W) are considered feminine, others (such as X, M, and Z) are viewed as masculine.
9. Among the company officers judging new names were Anthony Simmons, vice president, Rachel Lohr, CFO, and Lavonne Jones, manager.
10. Tech specialists created a snazzy new app, however it lacked an exciting name.

Notes

[1] Editors Canada. (2019). *About Editors Canada*. https://www.editors.ca/about-editors-canada

[2] Editors Canada. (2019). *Hire an editor*. https://www.editors.ca/hire-editor-0

[3] Editors Canada. (2019). *Definitions of editorial skills*. https://www.editors.ca/node/11715

[4] Elbow, P. (1998). *Writing with power: Techniques for mastering the writing process*. Oxford University Press, p. 30.

[5] Chambers, B. (2014, September 17). *Advertisers attract attention with grammatical errors: Controversial grammar still gets consumers talking*. CBC News. http://www.cbc.ca/news/canada/advertisers-attract-attention-with-grammatical-errors-1.2764884

[6] Cohen, L. (2012, May 5). "Go further with Ford." Is Ford grammatically correct? Part 2, the response. *Word Feeder*. https://lescohen.wordpress.com/2012/12/05/go-further-with-ford-is-ford-grammatically-correct-part-2-the-response/

[7] Photo essay based on Fell, J. (2012, April 19). Want better Twitter results? Try these effective types of tweets. *Entrepreneur*. http://www.entrepreneur.com

[8] Sword, H. (2012, July 23). Zombie nouns. *Opinionator*. https://opinionator.blogs.nytimes.com/2012/07/23/zombie-nouns/

[9] Canadian Business. (2019). *Growth 500: Canada's fastest growing companies*. https://www.canadianbusiness.com/growth-500-2/2019-163-kinova/

[10] Kinova. (2019). *Kinova among 2019 RBR50 top innovative and disruptive companies for commercial and industrial robotics*. https://www.kinovarobotics.com/en/knowledge-hub/kinova-among-2019-rbr50-top-innovative-and-disruptive-companies-commercial-and

[11] Kinova. (2019). *Achieve extraordinary with our versatile robotic arms*. https://www.kinovarobotics.com/en

[12] Kinova. (2019). *Products*. https://www.kinovarobotics.com/en/products. Reprinted courtesy of Kinova.

[13] Kinova. (2018). *Dynamic arm supports*. https://www.kinovarobotics.com/en/products/assistive-technologies/dynamic-arm-supports

[14] Editors Canada. (2019). *Guidelines for ethical editing of student texts*. https://www.editors.ca/hire/guidelines-ethical-editing-student-texts

[15] Editors Canada. (2018). *Guidelines for ethical editing of undergraduate student texts*. https://www.editors.ca/sites/default/files/guidelines_editing_undergraduatestudenttexts_revised.pdf

[16] The trouble with email. (2015, September 13). *Business Today*. http://businesstodaync.com/the-troublewith-email

UNIT 3

Workplace Communication

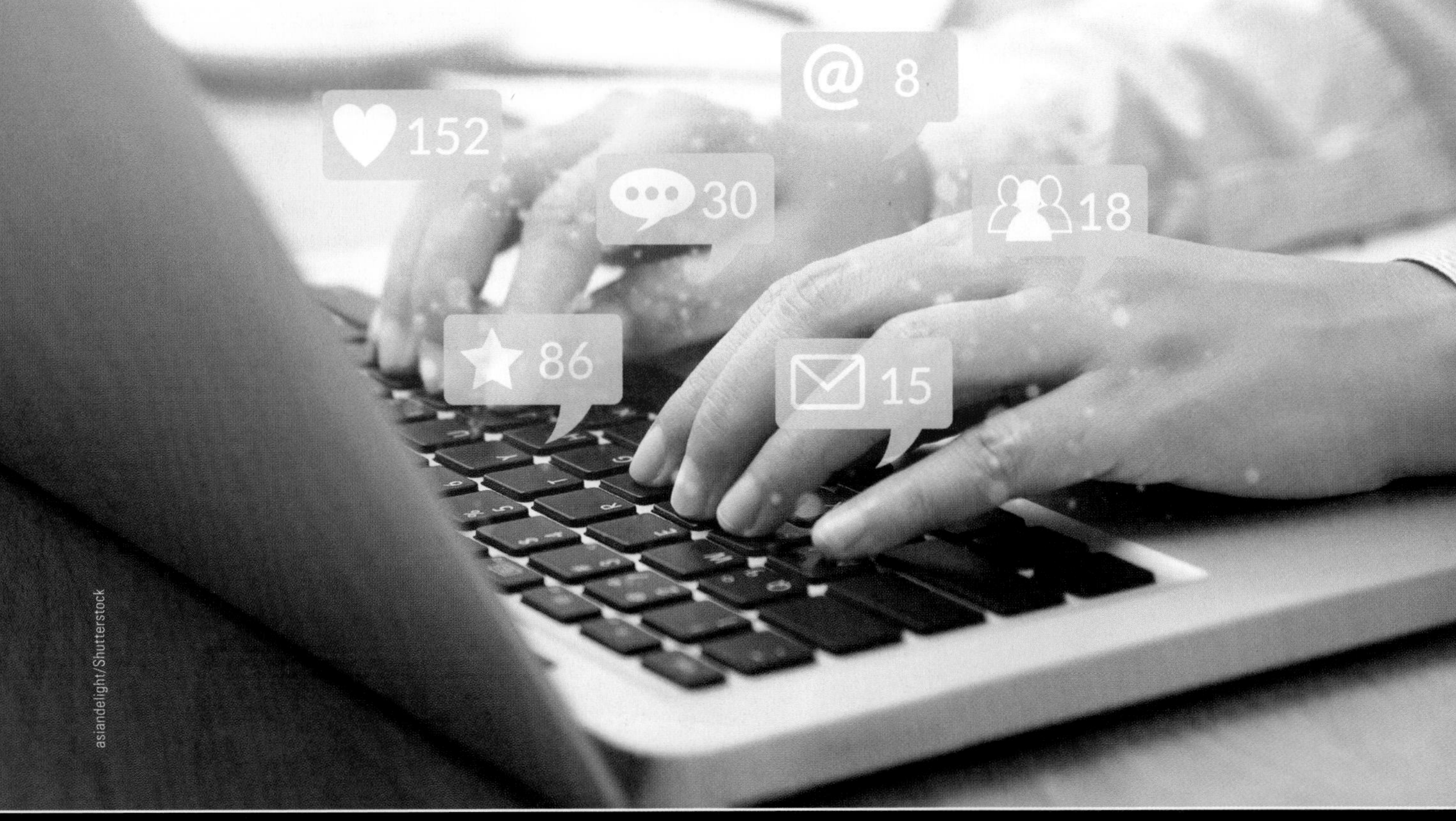

asiandelight/Shutterstock

CHAPTER 7
Short Workplace Messages and Digital Media

CHAPTER 8
Positive Messages

CHAPTER 9
Negative Messages

CHAPTER 10
Persuasive and Sales Messages

IN UNIT 3, YOU WILL DEVELOP THE FOLLOWING EMPLOYABILITY SKILLS:

EMPLOYABILITY AND SOFT SKILLS	
Oral and Written Communication	✓
Information Management	✓
Critical Thinking	✓
Problem Solving	✓
Active Listening	✓
Professional Work Behaviours	✓
Goal-Setting	✓
Agility	✓
Adaptability	✓
Personal and Social Responsibility	✓
Ethical Decision Making	✓
Engagement	✓
Innovation and Creativity	✓
Learning Worker Attitude	✓
Team Building	✓
Accountability	✓
Project Collaboration	✓
Online Tools and Social Media[1]	✓

CHAPTER 7

Short Workplace Messages and Digital Media

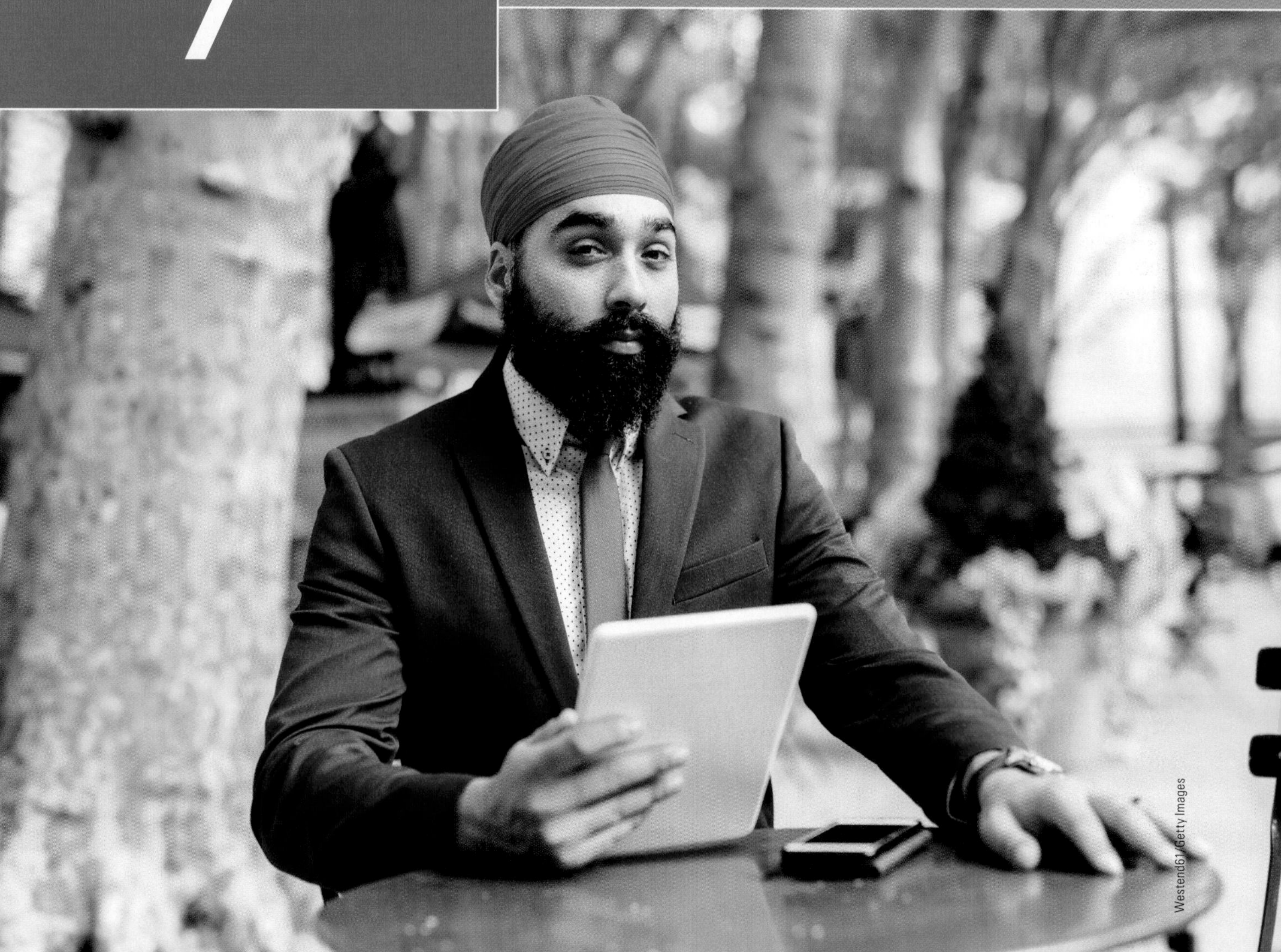

Westend61/Getty Images

LEARNING OBJECTIVES

After studying this chapter, you should be able to

1 Understand e-mail and the professional standards for its usage, structure, and format.

2 Explain workplace instant messaging and texting, as well as their liabilities and best practices.

3 Identify professional applications of podcasts and wikis, and describe guidelines for their use.

4 Describe how businesses use blogs to connect with internal and external audiences, and list best practices for professional blogging.

5 Define business uses of social networking.

SPOTLIGHT ON COMMUNICATION: PART 1

MobileSyrup

Rawpixel.com/Shutterstock

MobileSyrup is an online blog resource that provides information on mobile technology in Canada. Independently run, MobileSyrup's staff, reporters, and researchers are proudly Canadian. Their audience is Canadian "mobile enthusiasts," as well as consumers and professionals.[2] MobileSyrup averages 168 posts per week,[3] providing "daily market and industry news & reviews on smartphones, tablets, wearables, IoT and automotive."[4]

MobileSyrup post reviews of the latest mobile technologies, including games, apps, phones, tablets, computers, wearables, and virtual reality. Followers can even find out what shows and movies are coming and going from online streaming services, like Netflix and Amazon Prime.[5]

You can search the blog articles by category or type, sign up for MobileSyrup's newsletter, subscribe to its YouTube channel, or follow on Instagram, Facebook, or Twitter. And with over 75,000 Facebook fans and over 95,000 Twitter followers, thousands of Canadians are reading MobileSyrup's daily posts.[6]

CRITICAL THINKING

- While 51 percent of Canadians are still using desktops and laptops for online access, use of tablets, smartphones, and mobile devices is on the rise.[7] Given these points of access, why is it important for organizations to use a multimedia approach to convey information?
- MobileSyrup is a fully online organization. What are the advantages and disadvantages of not having a storefront office?

Writing E-mail Messages and Memos

LEARNING OBJECTIVE 1

Understand e-mail and the professional standards for its usage, structure, and format.

The world of communication is rapidly changing. The Internet has evolved from a mere repository of passively consumed information to Web 2.0—a dynamic, interactive, and highly networked environment. As discussed in previous chapters, communicators are increasingly switching to mobile devices. Messages are shorter and more frequent, and response time is much speedier.

This chapter explores short forms of workplace communication, beginning with e-mail and memos. Moving on to newer media, you will learn about workplace functions of instant messaging, text messaging, corporate blogs, podcasts, wikis, and social networking sites. Learning these workplace technologies and best practices can save you time, reduce mistakes, and help you excel as a professional.

E-mail: It's Here to Stay

Even with the rise of instant messaging, e-mail in the workplace is unlikely to go away. According to a Canadian survey, "people spend a total of 17 hours a week reading, responding and sending work emails both at work and at home."[8] The survey also revealed that per week "workers send and receive an average of 86 work-related emails at work and 25 from home."[9] According to another study, e-mail usage is on the rise. By 2021, 319.6 billion e-mails were being sent and received worldwide each day. This is up from 293.6 billion in 2019.[10] Because you can expect to use e-mail extensively to communicate at work, it's smart to learn how to do it efficiently and expertly.

Common Issues With E-mail

Although e-mail is recognized as the mainstay of business communication, it's not always done well. In addition to receiving confusing and poorly written e-mails, many people are overwhelmed with too many messages. Some of those messages are unnecessary, such as those that merely confirm receipt of a message or ones that express thanks. The use of "reply all" adds to the inbox, irritating those who have to plow through dozens of messages that barely relate to them. Others blame e-mail for eliminating the distinction between work life and home life. They feel an urgency to be available 24/7 and respond immediately.

Still other e-mail senders fail to recognize how dangerous e-mail can be. After deletion e-mail files still leave trails on servers within and outside organizations. Messages are also backed up on other servers, making them traceable and recoverable by forensic experts. Long-forgotten messages may turn up in court cases as damaging evidence. Even writers with nothing to hide should be concerned about what may come back to haunt them. Your best bet is to put nothing in an e-mail message that you wouldn't post on your office door. Also be sure that you know your organization's e-mail policy before sending personal messages.

CENGAGE

MINDTAP

Check out section 7-1c in MindTap, where you can watch a video featuring Taylor Roberts, general manager of Dynapole, discuss the value and pitfalls of e-mails.

Knowing When E-mail Is Appropriate

E-mail is appropriate for short, informal messages that request information and respond to inquiries. It is especially effective for messages to multiple receivers and messages that must be archived (saved). An e-mail is also appropriate as a cover document when sending longer attachments.

E-mail, however, is not a substitute for face-to-face conversations or telephone calls. These channels are much more successful if your goal is to convey enthusiasm or warmth, explain a complex situation, present a persuasive argument, or smooth over disagreements. One expert advises delivering messages in person when they "require a human moment"—that is, when they are emotional, require negotiation, and relate to personnel.[12]

Composing Professional E-mails

Professional e-mails are quite different from messages you may send to friends. Professional e-mails are well-constructed messages that involve all three stages of the writing process. They have compelling subject lines, appropriate greetings, well-organized bodies, and complete closing information.

Draft a Compelling Subject Line. The most important part of an e-mail is its subject line. It summarizes the central idea, providing quick identification for reading and filing. Avoid meaningless statements such as *Issue*, *Important*, or *Meeting*. Including the word *Free* is dangerous because it may trigger spam filters.

Summarize the purpose of the message clearly and make the receiver want to open the message. Try to include a verb (*Need You to Attend Montréal Trade Show*). It need not be a complete sentence, and it does not end with a period. Remember that in some instances the subject line can be the entire message (*Meeting Changed From May 3 to May 10*). Also be sure to adjust the subject line if the topic changes after repeated replies.

Include a Greeting. To help receivers see the beginning of a message and to help them recognize whether they are the primary or secondary receiver, include a greeting. The greeting sets the tone for the message and reflects your audience analysis. For friends and colleagues, try friendly greetings (*Hi, Julie*; *Thanks, Julie*; or *Good morning, Julie*). For more formal messages and those to outsiders, include an honorific and last name (*Dear Ms. Bélanger*).

Begin With a Strong Opening. Begin your e-mail by clearly stating the reason for writing. Your reader is most likely pressed for time and wants to get to the heart of your message quickly. Open your message with a professional and courteous tone.

Organize the Body for Readability and Tone. In the revision phase, ask yourself how you could make your message more readable. Did you group similar topics together? Could some information be presented with bulleted or numbered lists? Could you add side headings—especially if the message is more than a few paragraphs? Do you see any phrases or sentences that could be condensed? Get rid of wordiness, but don't sacrifice clarity. If a longer sentence is necessary for comprehension, then keep it. To convey the best tone, read the message aloud. If it sounds curt, it probably is.

ETHICS CHECK

Caught Cheating on Your Taxes

To crack down on Canadians cheating on their taxes, the Canada Revenue Agency (CRA) has started scrutinizing Facebook pages, Twitter feeds, and other social media. Because this information is publicly available, and the CRA has reported its use to the privacy commission, the agency is within its rights to access it. However, some privacy advocate groups feel the government should stay off social media.[11] If Canadians are making their social media feeds public, do you think they have waived their right to privacy?

FIGURE 7.1 Formatting an E-mail Request

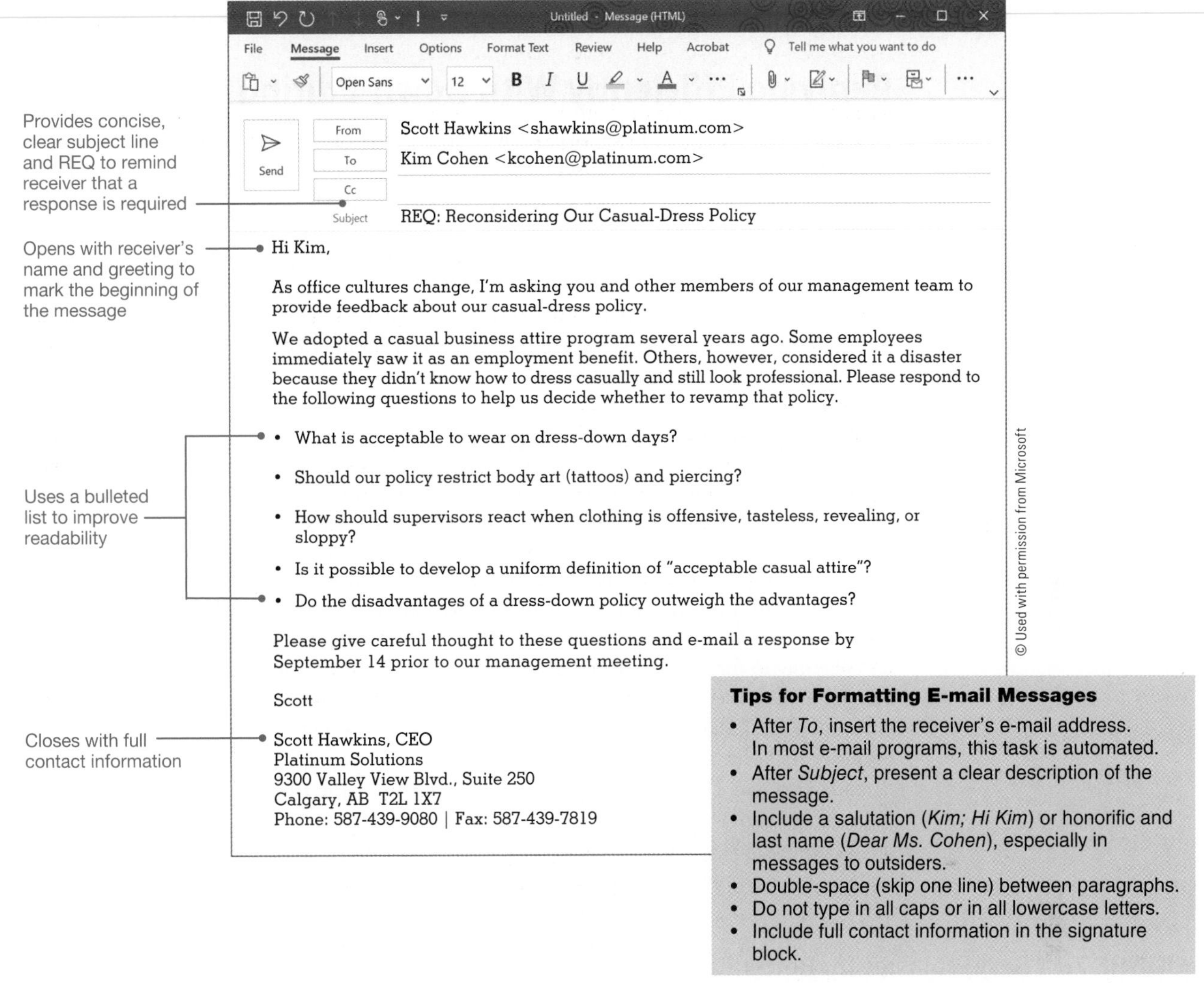

Untitled - Message (HTML)
File Message Insert Options Format Text Review Help Acrobat Tell me what you want to do
Open Sans 12
Provides concise, clear subject line and REQ to remind receiver that a response is required
Opens with receiver's name and greeting to mark the beginning of the message
Uses a bulleted list to improve readability
Closes with full contact information
© Used with permission from Microsoft

Send

From: Scott Hawkins <shawkins@platinum.com>

To: Kim Cohen <kcohen@platinum.com>

Cc:

Subject: REQ: Reconsidering Our Casual-Dress Policy

Hi Kim,

As office cultures change, I'm asking you and other members of our management team to provide feedback about our casual-dress policy.

We adopted a casual business attire program several years ago. Some employees immediately saw it as an employment benefit. Others, however, considered it a disaster because they didn't know how to dress casually and still look professional. Please respond to the following questions to help us decide whether to revamp that policy.

- What is acceptable to wear on dress-down days?
- Should our policy restrict body art (tattoos) and piercing?
- How should supervisors react when clothing is offensive, tasteless, revealing, or sloppy?
- Is it possible to develop a uniform definition of "acceptable casual attire"?
- Do the disadvantages of a dress-down policy outweigh the advantages?

Please give careful thought to these questions and e-mail a response by September 14 prior to our management meeting.

Scott

Scott Hawkins, CEO
Platinum Solutions
9300 Valley View Blvd., Suite 250
Calgary, AB T2L 1X7
Phone: 587-439-9080 | Fax: 587-439-7819

Tips for Formatting E-mail Messages

- After *To*, insert the receiver's e-mail address. In most e-mail programs, this task is automated.
- After *Subject*, present a clear description of the message.
- Include a salutation (*Kim; Hi Kim*) or honorific and last name (*Dear Ms. Cohen*), especially in messages to outsiders.
- Double-space (skip one line) between paragraphs.
- Do not type in all caps or in all lowercase letters.
- Include full contact information in the signature block.

Close Effectively. At the end of your message, include an action statement with due dates and requests. Although complimentary closes are unnecessary, you might include a friendly closing, such as *Many thanks* or *Warm regards*. Do include your name because messages without names become confusing when forwarded or when they are part of a long string of responses.

For most messages, include full contact information in a signature block that can be inserted automatically. Figure 7.1 illustrates a typical e-mail with proper formatting.

Time-Management Strategies

Managing your inbox can be a strain on productivity. The most important time-management strategy is checking your e-mail at set times, such as first thing in the morning and again after lunch or at 4 p.m. To avoid being distracted, be sure to turn off your audio and visual alerts. If mornings are your best working times, check your e-mail later in the day. Let your boss and colleagues know about your schedule for responding.

Another excellent time-saver is the "two-minute rule." If you can read and respond to a message within two minutes, then take care of it immediately. For messages that require more time, add them to your to-do list or schedule them on your calendar. To be polite, send a quick note telling the sender when you plan to respond.

Replying Efficiently With Down-Editing

When answering e-mail, a neat skill to develop is *down-editing*. This involves inserting your responses to parts of the incoming message. After a courteous opening, your reply message will include only the parts of the incoming message to which you are responding. Delete the sender's message headers, signature, and all unnecessary parts. Your responses can be identified with your initials, if more than one person will be seeing the responses. Another efficient trick is to use a different colour for your down-edits. It takes a little practice to develop this skill, but the down-edited reply reduces confusion, saves writing and reading time, and makes you look truly competent. Figure 7.2 shows a number of additional best practices for managing your e-mail.

Writing Interoffice Memos

In addition to e-mail, you should be familiar with another workplace document type, the interoffice memorandum. Although e-mail has largely replaced memos, you may still be called on to use the memo format in specific instances. Memos are necessary for important internal messages that (a) are too long for e-mail, (b) require a permanent record, (c) demand formality, or (d) inform employees who may not have access to e-mail. Within organizations, memos deliver changes in procedures, official instructions, and reports.

The memo format is particularly necessary for complex internal messages that are too long for e-mail. Prepared as memos, long messages are then delivered as attachments to e-mail cover messages. Memos seem to function better as permanent records than e-mail messages because the latter may be difficult to locate and may contain a trail of confusing replies. E-mails also may change the origination date whenever the file is accessed, thus making it impossible to know the original date of the message.

When preparing e-mail attachments, be sure that they carry sufficient identifying information. Because the cover e-mail message may become separated from the attachment, the

FIGURE 7.2 Best Practices for Better E-mail

Getting Started

- Don't write if another channel—such as IM, social media, or a phone call—might work better.
- Send only content you would want published.
- Write compelling subject lines, possibly with names and dates: *Jake: Can You Present at January 10 Staff Meeting?*

Replying

- Scan all e-mails, especially those from the same person. Answer within 24 hours or say when you will.
- Change the subject line if the topic changes. Check the threaded messages below yours.
- Practise down-editing; include only the parts from the incoming e-mail to which you are responding.
- Start with the main idea.
- Use headings and lists.

Observing Etiquette

- Obtain approval before forwarding.
- Soften the tone by including a friendly opening and closing.
- Resist humour and sarcasm. Without facial expressions and tone of voice, humour can be misunderstood.
- Avoid writing in all caps, which is like SHOUTING.

Closing Effectively

- End with due dates, next steps to be taken, or a friendly remark.
- Add your full contact information, including social media addresses.
- Edit your text for readability. Proofread for typos or unwanted auto-corrections.
- Double-check before hitting **Send.**

attachment must be fully identified. Preparing the e-mail attachment as a memo provides a handy format that identifies the date, sender, receiver, and subject.

Similarities in Memos and E-mails. Memos have much in common with e-mails. Both usually carry nonsensitive information that may be organized directly with the main idea first. Both have guide words calling for a subject line, a dateline, and the identification of the sender and receiver. To enhance readability, both should be organized with headings, bulleted lists, and enumerated items whenever possible.

E-mails and memos both generally close with (a) action information, dates, or deadlines; (b) a summary of the message; or (c) a closing thought. An effective memo or e-mail closing might be *Please submit your written report to me by June 15 so that we can review your data before our July planning session.* In more detailed messages, a summary of main points may be an appropriate closing. If no action request is made and a closing summary is unnecessary, you might end with a simple concluding thought (*I'm glad to answer your questions* or *This sounds like a useful project*).

You need not close messages to coworkers with goodwill statements such as those found in letters to customers or clients. However, some closing thought is often necessary to avoid sounding abrupt. Closings can show gratitude or encourage feedback with remarks such as *I sincerely appreciate your help* or *What are your ideas on this proposal?* Other closings look forward to what's next, such as *How would you like to proceed?* Avoid closing with overused expressions such as *Please let me know if I may be of further assistance.* These sound mechanical and insincere.

In Figure 7.3 notice how memos are formatted and how they can be created to improve readability with lists and white space. The Checklist offers tips for including professional content in your e-mail messages and memos.

CHECKLIST

Professional E-mail and Memos

Subject Line

- **Summarize the central idea.** Express concisely what the message is about and how it relates to the reader.
- **Include labels if appropriate.** Labels such as *FYI* (*for your information*) and *REQ* (*required*) help receivers recognize how to respond.
- **Avoid empty or dangerous words.** Don't write one-word subject lines such as *Help, Problem,* or *Free.*

Opening

- **State the purpose for writing.** Include the same information that is in the subject line, but expand it.
- **Highlight questions.** If you are requesting information, begin with the most important question, use a polite command (*Please answer the following questions about*...), or introduce your request courteously.
- **Supply information directly.** If responding to a request, give the reader the requested information immediately in the opening. Explain later.

Body

- **Explain details.** Arrange information logically. For detailed topics develop separate coherent paragraphs.
- **Enhance readability.** Use short sentences, short paragraphs, and parallel construction for similar ideas.
- **Apply document design.** If appropriate, provide bulleted or numbered lists, headings, tables, or other graphic devices to improve readability and comprehension.
- **Be cautious.** Remember that e-mail messages often travel far beyond their intended audiences.

Closing

- **Request action.** If appropriate, state specifically what you want the reader to do. Include a deadline, with reasons, if possible.
- **Provide a goodwill statement or a closing thought.** When communicating outside the company or with management, include a positive goodwill statement such as *Our team enjoyed working on the feasibility report, and we look forward to your feedback.* If no action request is necessary, end with a closing thought.
- **Avoid cliché endings.** Use fresh remarks rather than overused expressions such as If you have additional questions, please do not hesitate to call or Thank you for your cooperation.

FIGURE 7.3 Formatting a Memo That Responds to a Request

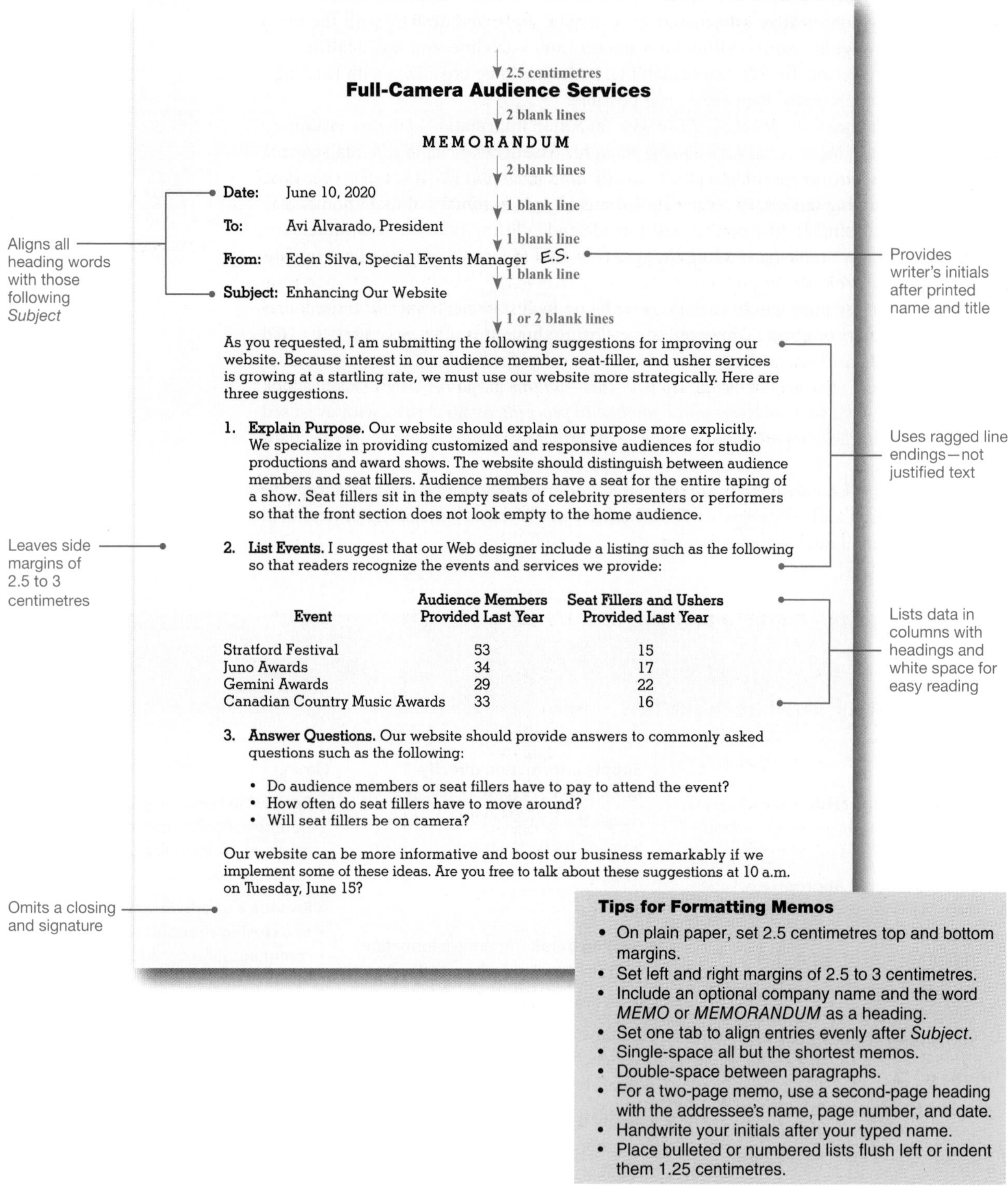

2.5 centimetres

Full-Camera Audience Services

2 blank lines

MEMORANDUM

2 blank lines

Date: June 10, 2020

1 blank line

To: Avi Alvarado, President

1 blank line

From: Eden Silva, Special Events Manager E.S.

1 blank line

Subject: Enhancing Our Website

1 or 2 blank lines

As you requested, I am submitting the following suggestions for improving our website. Because interest in our audience member, seat-filler, and usher services is growing at a startling rate, we must use our website more strategically. Here are three suggestions.

1. **Explain Purpose.** Our website should explain our purpose more explicitly. We specialize in providing customized and responsive audiences for studio productions and award shows. The website should distinguish between audience members and seat fillers. Audience members have a seat for the entire taping of a show. Seat fillers sit in the empty seats of celebrity presenters or performers so that the front section does not look empty to the home audience.

2. **List Events.** I suggest that our Web designer include a listing such as the following so that readers recognize the events and services we provide:

Event	Audience Members Provided Last Year	Seat Fillers and Ushers Provided Last Year
Stratford Festival	53	15
Juno Awards	34	17
Gemini Awards	29	22
Canadian Country Music Awards	33	16

3. **Answer Questions.** Our website should provide answers to commonly asked questions such as the following:

- Do audience members or seat fillers have to pay to attend the event?
- How often do seat fillers have to move around?
- Will seat fillers be on camera?

Our website can be more informative and boost our business remarkably if we implement some of these ideas. Are you free to talk about these suggestions at 10 a.m. on Tuesday, June 15?

Aligns all heading words with those following *Subject*
Provides writer's initials after printed name and title
Uses ragged line endings—not justified text
Leaves side margins of 2.5 to 3 centimetres
Lists data in columns with headings and white space for easy reading
Omits a closing and signature

Tips for Formatting Memos

- On plain paper, set 2.5 centimetres top and bottom margins.
- Set left and right margins of 2.5 to 3 centimetres.
- Include an optional company name and the word *MEMO* or *MEMORANDUM* as a heading.
- Set one tab to align entries evenly after *Subject*.
- Single-space all but the shortest memos.
- Double-space between paragraphs.
- For a two-page memo, use a second-page heading with the addressee's name, page number, and date.
- Handwrite your initials after your typed name.
- Place bulleted or numbered lists flush left or indent them 1.25 centimetres.

Concept Check

1. Why is clear and correct writing still needed, even in short posts and text messages?
2. In what ways can e-mail be dangerous, and how can you avoid these dangers?

Workplace Messaging and Texting

LEARNING OBJECTIVE 2

Explain workplace instant messaging and texting, as well as their liabilities and best practices.

Instant messaging (IM) and text messaging have become powerful communication tools among established businesspeople. Companies large and small now provide live online chats with customer-service representatives during business hours, in addition to the usual contact options, such as telephone and e-mail.

Text messaging, or texting, is another popular means for exchanging brief messages in real time. Increasingly, both instant and text messages are sent by smart handheld electronic devices as the use of such devices is skyrocketing. As of 2019 over 33.6 million Canadians subscribed to wireless services. Ninety percent of Canadians own smartphones, and by 2022 "mobile data traffic in Canada will be equivalent to 2x the volume of what the entire Canadian internet was in 2005."[13] Figure 7.4 shows how instant messaging can be used effectively at work.

Impact of Instant Messaging and Texting

Text messaging and IM are convenient alternatives to the telephone and are replacing e-mail for short internal communication. More than 7 billion IM accounts worldwide[14] attest to IM's popularity. In 2019, 47 percent of Canadians were online for instant messaging, which was up from 32 percent in 2016.[15]

FIGURE 7.4 Instant Message for Brief, Fast Communication

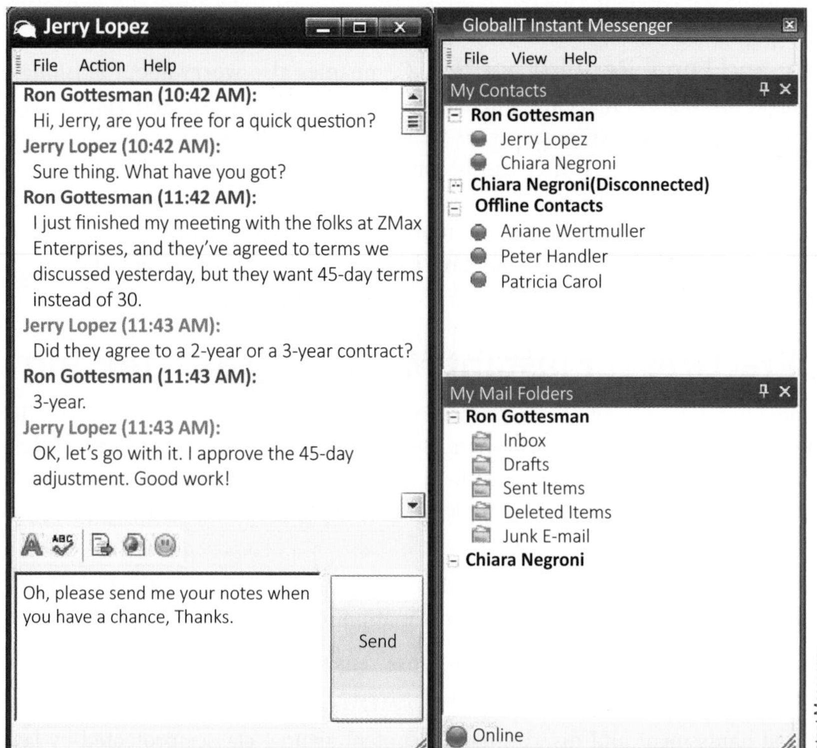

A brief IM exchange between a supervisor and a subordinate. Both are using a computer-based IM program.

Benefits of IM and Texting. The major attraction of instant messaging is real-time communication with colleagues anywhere in the world—so long as a cell phone signal or a Wi-Fi connection is available. Because IM allows people to share information immediately and make decisions quickly, its impact on business communication has been dramatic.

Like IM, texting can be a low-cost substitute for voice calls, delivering messages between private mobile phone users quietly and discreetly. Organizations around the world provide news alerts, financial information, and promotions to customers via text.

The immediacy of instant and text messaging has created many fans. Messaging avoids phone tag and eliminates the downtime associated with personal telephone conversations. Many people consider instant messaging and texting productivity boosters because they enable users to get answers quickly and allow multitasking.

Risks of IM and Texting. Despite the popularity of instant and text messaging among workers, some organizations forbid employees from using them for a number of reasons. Employers often consider instant messaging yet another distraction in addition to the telephone, e-mail, and the Internet. Some organizations also fear that employees using free consumer-grade instant messaging systems will reveal privileged information and company records. Large corporations are protecting themselves by taking instant messaging behind a firewall where they can log and archive traffic.

Liability Burden. A worker's improper use of mobile devices while on company business can expose the organization to staggering legal liability. All Canadian provinces and territories except Nunavut have some form of distracted driving/cell phone use legislation; thus employers should be aware of the possibility of being found liable for the harm caused by the negligent acts of an employee. If an employee is using a cell phone for a work-related purpose at the time of an accident, the employer could be held vicariously liable. Employers could also be found directly liable if employees are required or actively encouraged to use a phone for work purposes while driving.[16]

Organizations are fighting back to raise awareness and diminish liability. Many are instituting detailed e-policies, offering formal employee training, and using technology tools, such as monitoring, filtering, and blocking.

Security and Legal Requirements. Companies also worry about *phishing* (fraudulent schemes), viruses, malware (malicious software programs), and *spim* (IM spam). Like e-mail, instant and text messages, as well as all other electronic records, are subject to discovery (disclosure); that is, they can become evidence in lawsuits. Moreover, companies fear instant messaging and texting because the services necessitate that businesses track and store messaging conversations to comply with legal requirements. This task may be overwhelming. Finally, IM and texting have been implicated in inappropriate uses, such as bullying and sexting.

Best Practices for Instant Messaging and Texting

Aside from digital marketing, instant messaging and texting can save time and simplify communication with coworkers and customers. Before using IM or text messaging on the job, be sure you have permission. Do not download and use software without checking with your supervisor. If your organization does allow IM or texting, you can use it efficiently and professionally by following these guidelines:

- Adhere to company policies at all times: "netiquette" rules, code of conduct, ethics guidelines, and harassment and discrimination policies.[17]
- Don't use IM or text messages to disclose sensitive information: financial, company, customer, employee, or executive data.
- Avoid harassment and discriminatory content against classes protected by law (race, colour, religion, sex, sexual orientation, national origin, age, and disability).

- Be vigilant about the appropriateness of photos, videos, and art that you link to or forward.
- As with e-mail, don't say anything that would damage your reputation or that of your organization.
- Don't text or IM while driving a car. Pull over if you must read or send a message.
- Organize your contact lists to separate business contacts from family and friends.
- Avoid unnecessary chitchat, and know when to say goodbye. If personal messaging is allowed, keep it to a minimum.
- Keep your presence status up to date so that people trying to reach you don't waste their time. Make yourself unavailable when you need to meet a deadline.
- Beware of jargon, slang, and abbreviations, which, although they may reduce keystrokes, can be confusing and appear unprofessional.
- Use good grammar and proper spelling.

Text Messaging and Business Etiquette

Texting is quick and unobtrusive, and for routine messages it is often the best alternative to a phone call or an e-mail. In Canada, more people have "mobile phones (90.18%) than landlines (41.25%), while approximately one third of Canadian households rely exclusively on wireless services."[18] Given the popularity of text messaging, etiquette experts are taking note.[19] Figure 7.5 summarizes the suggestions they offer for the considerate and professional use of texting.

FIGURE 7.5 Texting Etiquette

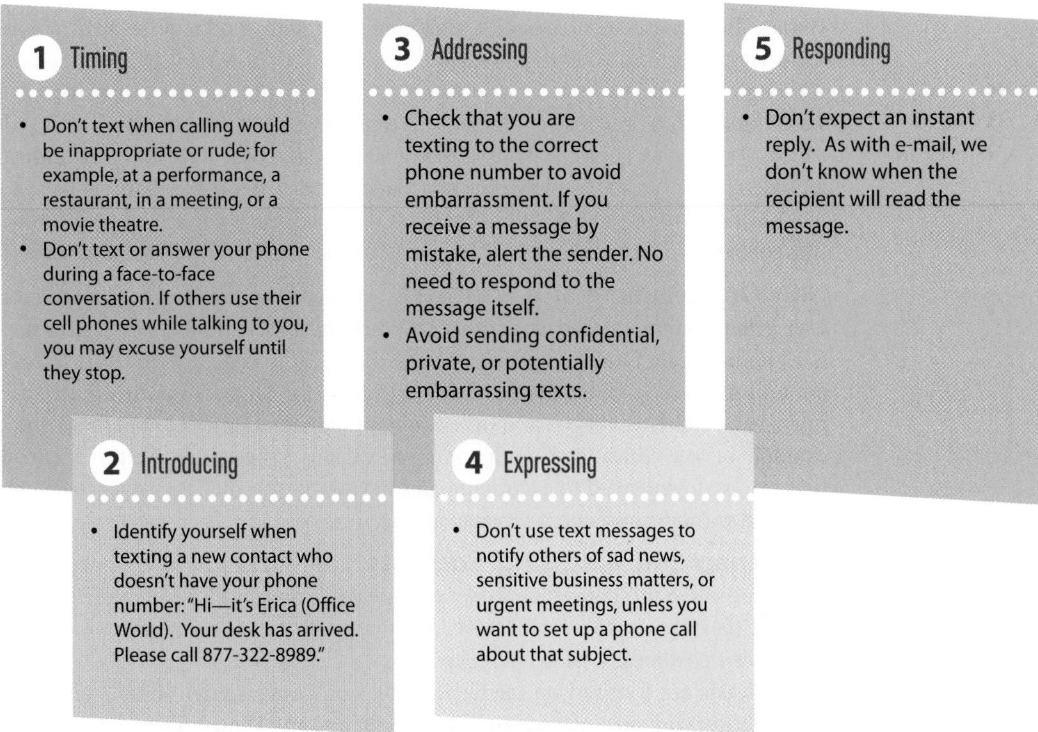

1 Timing
• Don't text when calling would be inappropriate or rude; for example, at a performance, a restaurant, in a meeting, or a movie theatre.
• Don't text or answer your phone during a face-to-face conversation. If others use their cell phones while talking to you, you may excuse yourself until they stop.
2 Introducing
• Identify yourself when texting a new contact who doesn't have your phone number: "Hi—it's Erica (Office World). Your desk has arrived. Please call 877-322-8989."
3 Addressing
• Check that you are texting to the correct phone number to avoid embarrassment. If you receive a message by mistake, alert the sender. No need to respond to the message itself.
• Avoid sending confidential, private, or potentially embarrassing texts.
4 Expressing
• Don't use text messages to notify others of sad news, sensitive business matters, or urgent meetings, unless you want to set up a phone call about that subject.
5 Responding
• Don't expect an instant reply. As with e-mail, we don't know when the recipient will read the message.

Concept Check

1. In Ontario, a legal case "resulted in an employer paying over one million dollars in damages after an employee who was found to be driving distracted caused an accident that resulted in catastrophic injuries to a 17-year-old girl. As the Canadian justice system and government start to take aim at distracted driving, the numbers of employers being fined for employee conduct behind the wheel will no doubt increase."[20] What can employers do to make sure their employees aren't driving distracted?
2. Consider the following statement: *As long as you use your own Facebook or Instagram account, it's okay to message friends and family while at work*. Do you agree or disagree with the statement? Explain your answer with specific examples.

LEARNING OBJECTIVE 3

Identify professional applications of podcasts and wikis, and describe guidelines for their use.

Making Podcasts and Wikis Work for Business

Far from being passive consumers, today's Internet users have the power to create Web content; interact with businesses and each other; review products, self-publish, or blog; contribute to wikis; or tag and share images and other files. Businesses often rightly fear the wrath of disgruntled employees and customers, or they curry favour with influential plugged-in opinion leaders, called *influencers*. Like Twitter, other communication technologies, such as podcasts and wikis, are part of the new user-centred virtual environment called Web 2.0.

The democratization of the Web has meant that in the online world, Internet users can bypass gatekeepers who filter content in the traditional print and visual media. Hence, even extreme views often reach audiences of thousands or even millions. The dangers are obvious. Fact-checking often falls by the wayside, buzz may become more important than truth, and a single keystroke can make or destroy a reputation. This section addresses prudent business uses of podcasts and wikis because you are likely to encounter these and other electronic communication tools on the job.

Business Podcasts or Webcasts

Perhaps because podcasts are more elaborate to produce and require quality hardware, their use is lagging behind other digital media. However, they have their place in the business world. Although the terms *podcast* and *podcasting* have caught on, they are somewhat misleading. The words *broadcasting* and *iPod* combined to create the word *podcast*; however, audio and video files can be played on any number of devices, not just Apple's iPod. *Webcasting* for audio and *vcasting* for video content would be more accurate. Podcasts can extend from short clips of a few minutes to 30-minute or longer digital files. Most are recorded, but some are live. Naturally, large video files gobble up a lot of memory, so they tend to be streamed on a website rather than downloaded.

How Organizations Use Podcasts. Podcasting has found its place among various user groups online. Major news organizations and media outlets podcast radio shows (e.g., CBC Radio/Radio Canada) and TV shows, from CTV to Global. Some businesses have caught on, and podcasts are also common in education. Students can access instructors' lectures, interviews, sporting events, and other content. Apple's iTunes U is perhaps the best-known example of free educational podcasts from various universities. Podcasts encoded as MP3 files can be downloaded to a computer, a smartphone, or an MP3 player to be enjoyed on the go, often without subsequent Internet access.

Delivering and Accessing Podcasts. Businesses have embraced podcasting for audio and video messages that do not require a live presence yet offer a friendly human face. Because they can broadcast repetitive information that does not require interaction, podcasts can replace costlier live teleconferences.

Podcasts are featured on media websites and company portals or shared on blogs and social networking sites, often with links to YouTube and Vimeo. They can usually be streamed or downloaded as media files. To browse and learn, check out CBC Radio at cbc.ca/radio/podcasts/ for podcasts in various categories.

FIGURE 7.6 Four Main Uses for Business Wikis

The global wiki
For companies with a global reach, a wiki is an ideal tool for information sharing between headquarters and satellite offices. Far-flung team members can easily edit their work and provide input to the home office and each other.
The wiki knowledge base
Teams or departments use wikis to collect and disseminate information to large audiences creating a database for knowledge management. For example, human resources managers may update employee policies, make announcements, and convey information about benefits.
Wikis for meetings
Wikis can facilitate feedback from employees before and after meetings and serve as repositories of meeting minutes. In fact, wikis may replace some meetings, yet still keep a project on track.
Wikis for project management
Wikis offer a highly interactive environment for project information with easy access and user input. All participants have the same information, templates, and documentation readily available.

Collaborating With Wikis

As discussed in Chapter 4, a wiki is a Web-based tool that employs easy-to-use collaborative software to allow multiple users collectively to create, access, and modify documents. Wikipedia, the well-known online encyclopedia, is one example. You will find wikis in numerous subject categories on the Internet. Wiki editors may be given varying access privileges and control over the material; however, many public wikis are open to anyone.

Two major advantages of wikis come to mind. First, wikis capitalize on *crowdsourcing*, which can be defined as the practice of tapping into the combined knowledge of a large community to solve problems and complete assignments. Second, working on the same content jointly eliminates the infamous problem of version confusion. Most wikis store all changes and intermediate versions of files so that users can return to a previous stage if necessary.

How Businesses Use Wikis. Enterprises using wikis usually store their internal data on an intranet, a private network. An enterprise-level wiki serves as an easy-to-navigate, efficient central repository of company information, complete with hyperlinks and keywords pointing to related subjects and media. The four main uses of wikis in business, shown in Figure 7.6,[21] range from providing a shared internal knowledge base to storing templates for business documents.

Popular simple-to-use wiki hosting services, called *wiki farms*, are PBworks, Fandom, Wikidot, and Ourproject.org. Some are noncommercial. Consider starting a wiki for your next classroom project requiring teamwork. Alternatively, explore Google Docs and Google Sites.

Concept Check

1. Visit CBC Radio's Podcast page at www.cbc.ca/radio/podcasts. Write a list of five podcasts that are related to your program of study or are of personal interest.
2. Why do colleges and universities restrict students from using Wikipedia as a source for their essays and reports?

LEARNING OBJECTIVE 4

Describe how businesses use blogs to connect with internal and external audiences, and list best practices for professional blogging.

Blogging for Business

The biggest advantage of business blogs is that they can potentially reach a vast audience. A blog is a website with journal entries on any imaginable topic. Blogs are usually written by one person, although most corporate blogs feature multiple contributors. Typically, readers leave comments. Businesses use blogs to keep customers, employees, and the public at large informed and to interact with them.

Innovative CEOs have realized that social media, including blogs, discussion forums, and wikis, allow employees to have input, and they cite two major benefits of embracing social media. First, it permits richer and more detailed feedback by allowing insights from diverse groups. Second, this social approach yields a cultural benefit by garnering more employee engagement. Results reveal that when teams are able to post and respond, they have greater ownership of their performance and communicate better with one another.[22]

Popular social media platforms such as Instagram and LinkedIn have added a blogging feature, a move that may precipitate the decrease of stand-alone blogs. Instead, corporate Twitter use is high in a field dominated by Facebook, as we will see in the last section of this chapter.

How Companies Blog

Like other social networking tools, corporate blogs help create virtual communities, build brands, and develop relationships. Specifically, companies use blogs for public relations, customer relations, crisis communication, market research, viral marketing, internal communication, online communities, and recruiting.

Public Relations, Customer Relations, and Crisis Communication. One of the prominent uses of blogs is to provide up-to-date company information to the press and the public. A company blog is a natural forum for late-breaking news, especially when disaster strikes. In addition, business bloggers can address rumours and combat misinformation. Although a blog cannot replace other communication channels in a public relations (PR) crisis or an emergency, it should be part of the overall effort to soothe the public's emotional reaction with a human voice of reason.

Market Research and Viral Marketing. Because most blogs invite feedback, they can be invaluable sources of opinion and bright ideas from customers, as well as from industry experts. In addition to monitoring visitor comments on their corporate blogs, large companies employ teams of social media experts and marketers who scrutinize the blogosphere for buzz and positive or negative postings about their organization and products.

The term *viral marketing* refers to the rapid spread of messages online. Marketers realize the potential of getting the word out about their products and services in the blogosphere, where their messages are often picked up by well-connected bloggers, *influencers,* who boast large audiences. Viral messages must be authentic and elicit an emotional response, but for that very reason they are difficult to orchestrate. Online denizens resent being co-opted by companies using overt hard-sell tactics.

Experts say that marketers must provide content that will resonate with lots of people who will then share it in small networks. This buzz is comparable to word of mouth offline.[23] For example, WestJet invited the residents of Fort McMurray, Alberta, to a Christmas party to take their minds off the fire that devastated their community. As part of WestJet's Christmas miracle, residents were surprised with gifts that parachuted from the sky, and each family received a keepsake to remember the night, plus a free flight. The video was posted on WestJet's website and YouTube and reached over a million views.[24]

Online Communities. Like Twitter, which can draw a loyal core following to businesses and brands, company blogs can attract a devoted community of participants. Such followers want to keep informed about company events, product updates, and other news. In turn, those enthusiasts can contribute new ideas.

Internal Communication. Blogs can be used to keep virtual teams on track and share updates on the road. Members in remote locations can stay in touch by smartphone and

FIGURE 7.7 Creating a Professional Blog

Identify your audience.

- As with any type of communication, you must know your audience to decide what to write to get people to read your blog. Will your blog stand out? Is it interesting?

Pick the right keywords.

- Emphasize potential search terms to rise to the top of search listings. An import business might stress the keywords *import*, *China*, *trade*, and industry-specific terms (*toys*).

Choose a hosting site.

- WordPress, Tumblr, and Blogger are popular platforms. Templates and other options will help you attract traffic. You will be able to track recent posts and message threads.

Work the blogroll. Blog often.

- Provide links to other quality blogs relevant to your business or industry to boost traffic. Chances are those bloggers will link back to you, and their readers too may visit your blog.
- Provide fresh content regularly. Stay current. Stale information puts off visitors. Post short, concise messages, but do so often.

Craft your message.

- Highlight your expertise and insights. Offer a fresh, unique perspective on subjects your audience cares about. Your writing should be intriguing and sincere.

Monitor traffic.

- If traffic slows, experiment with new topics while staying with your core business and expertise. Monitor the effectiveness of your hosting site in increasing your blog's visibility to search engines.

other devices, exchanging text, images, sound, and video clips. In many companies blogs have replaced hard-copy publications in offering late-breaking news or tidbits of interest to employees. Blogs can create a sense of community and stimulate employee participation.

To create a professional blog, consider the guidelines[25] in Figure 7.7.

CASE CONNECTIONS

Zoocasa

Zoocasa is a thriving online real estate brokerage that assists Canadians in finding the right home, faster. Lauren Haw, the CEO of Zoocasa, brings the following vision to the company: "We marry the ease and intelligence of technology with a full service real estate team to create a seamless experience."[26]

Zoocasa uses an online system that creates this versatile and seamless interface for its customers.[27]

As the role of the realtor shifts and the industry becomes more digital, this creates opportunities for innovative companies like Zoocasa. Because real estate has traditionally been a fragmented industry, Haw says it is Zoocasa's opportunity "to bring a cohesive and comprehensive search platform so Canadians can get all the info they want in one spot."[28]

- Zoocasa maintains a website blog and Facebook page, posting several times per week. How does building a strong social media presence benefit a company and its clients?

Blog Best Practices: Eight Tips for Master Bloggers

Much advice is freely accessible on the Internet, but this section offers guidelines culled from experienced bloggers and communication experts that will lead you to successful online writing. As with any public writing, your posts will be scrutinized; therefore, you want to make the best impression. Your blog posts can benefit from the journalistic pattern shown in Figure 7.8 by emphasizing the big news up front, supported with specifics and background information.

Craft a Catchy but Concise Title. The headline is what draws online readers to open your post. Some will be intriguing questions or promises. Online writers often use numbers to structure their posts. Here are some examples: *Six Apps You Don't Want to Miss; 5 Tips to Keep Spear Phishers Out of Your Inbox; How Many Lives Does a Brand Have?; Create Powerful Imagery in Your Writing.*

Ace the Opening Paragraph. The lead must deliver on the promise of the headline. Identify a need and propose to solve the problem. Ask a relevant question. Say something startling. Tell an anecdote or use an analogy to connect with the reader. The author of *How Many Lives Does a Brand Have?* opened with this:

> *It's said that cats have nine lives, but how many lives does a brand have? The answer, it seems, is definitely more than one. Recently, in Shanghai, a friend took me to one of the city's most sophisticated luxury malls. . . .*[30]

Provide Details in the Body. Mind the *So what?* and *What's in it for me?* questions. Use vivid examples, quotations and testimonials, or statistics. Structure the body with numbers, bullets, and subheadings. Use expressive action verbs (*buy* for *get*; *own* for *have*; *to travel* or *to jet* for *go*). Use conversational language to sound warm and authentic. Use contractions (*isn't* for *is not*).

Consider Visuals. Add visual interest with relevant images and diagrams. Keep paragraphs short and use plenty of white space around them. Aim to make the look simple and easy to scan.

ETHICS CHECK

Fired for Game Development

Former Canada Revenue Agency (CRA) employee David Gallant developed a computer game, "I Get This Call Every Day," that mocked the types of interactions in his job. Although the game was developed on Gallant's own time, and he was careful not to include any confidential information, CRA officials felt his conduct was "offensive and completely unacceptable." Gallant was subsequently fired.[29] Whose rights take precedence: the employee's or the employer's?

FIGURE 7.8 Writing a Captivating Blog

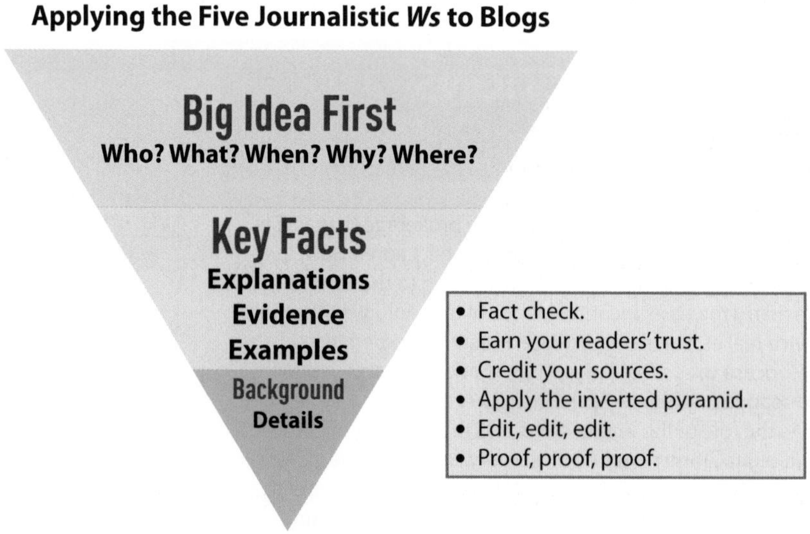

Applying the Five Journalistic *Ws* to Blogs

Big Idea First
Who? What? When? Why? Where?

Key Facts
Explanations
Evidence
Examples

Background
Details

- Fact check.
- Earn your readers' trust.
- Credit your sources.
- Apply the inverted pyramid.
- Edit, edit, edit.
- Proof, proof, proof.

FIGURE 7.9 Business Blog Article Illustrates Best Practices

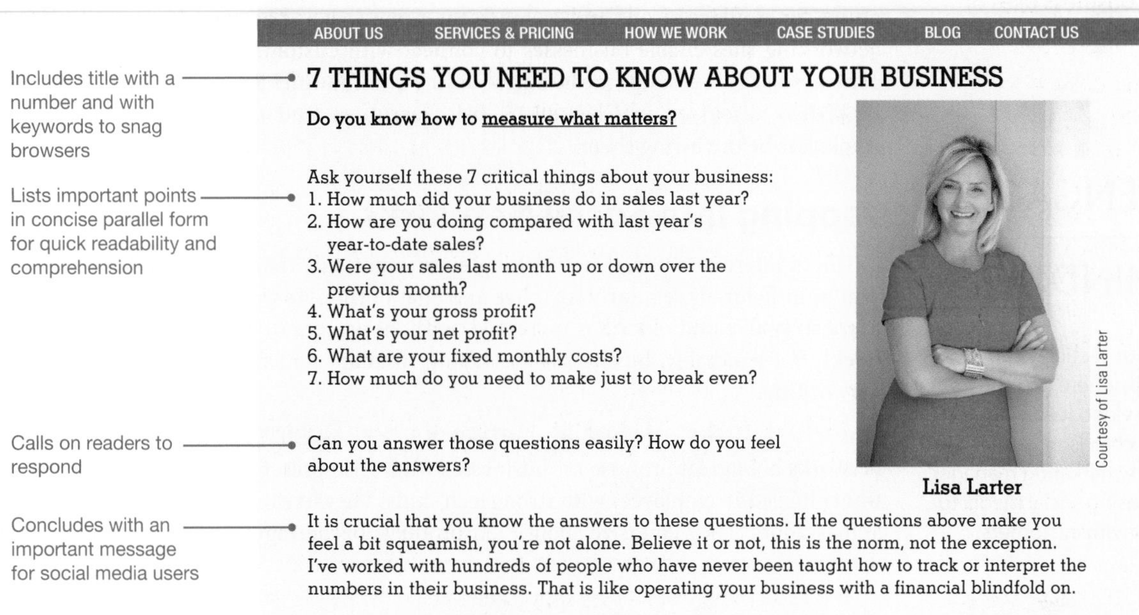

ABOUT US
SERVICES & PRICING
HOW WE WORK
CASE STUDIES
BLOG
CONTACT US
Includes title with a number and with keywords to snag browsers
7 THINGS YOU NEED TO KNOW ABOUT YOUR BUSINESS
Do you know how to measure what matters?
Ask yourself these 7 critical things about your business:
Lists important points in concise parallel form for quick readability and comprehension
1. How much did your business do in sales last year?
2. How are you doing compared with last year's year-to-date sales?
3. Were your sales last month up or down over the previous month?
4. What's your gross profit?
5. What's your net profit?
6. What are your fixed monthly costs?
7. How much do you need to make just to break even?
Calls on readers to respond
Can you answer those questions easily? How do you feel about the answers?
Courtesy of Lisa Larter
Lisa Larter
Concludes with an important message for social media users
It is crucial that you know the answers to these questions. If the questions above make you feel a bit squeamish, you're not alone. Believe it or not, this is the norm, not the exception. I've worked with hundreds of people who have never been taught how to track or interpret the numbers in their business. That is like operating your business with a financial blindfold on.

Source: https://lisalarter.com/7-things-need-know-business/

Include Calls to Action. Call on readers to do something or provide a take-away and gentle nudge at the end. Ask open-ended questions or tell the reader what to do: *So, be sure to ask about 360-degree security tactics that block outbound data theft attempts.*

Edit and Proofread. Follow the revision tips in Chapter 6 of this book. Cut any unneeded words or sentences and irrelevant ideas. Fix awkward, wordy, and repetitious sentences. The best blogs are error free.

Respond to Posts Respectfully. Build a positive image online by posting compelling comments on other bloggers' posts. Politely and promptly reply to comments on your site. If you disagree with a post, do so respectfully.

Learn From the Best. Visit popular blogs to see what you can adopt and make work for yourself (see Figure 7.9), but make sure to review the blogger's credentials. Lisa Larter outlines her extensive business experience in Ottawa, Ontario, and then in Annapolis Royal, Nova Scotia. Her appearance on *Oprah* will lend credibility to a select audience. Notice that Lisa Larter's blog[31] offers a catchy title with a number in it (*7 Things You Need to Know About Your Business*) on a popular topic that will attract readers. She shares helpful advice as easy-to-read numbered items. To motivate readers to respond, she asks questions (*Can you answer those questions easily? How do you feel about them?*).

Concept Check

1. Why is it important to make sure your blog is error-free?
2. What are the five journalistic Ws, and why should they be applied to writing a blog?

LEARNING OBJECTIVE 5

Define business uses of social networking.

Check out section 7-5a in MindTap, where you can watch a video featuring Karen Richardson, an associate marketing manager, discuss using social media to connect with customers.

Social Networking Sites

Popular social networking sites, such as Instagram, Facebook, and Twitter, are used by businesses for similar reasons and in much the same way as podcasts, blogs, and wikis. Social networking sites enable businesses to connect with customers and employees, share company news, and exchange ideas. Social online communities for professional audiences (e.g., LinkedIn), discussed in Chapter 15, help recruiters find talent and encounter potential employees before hiring them.

Tapping Into Social Networks

Business interest in social networking sites is not surprising if we consider that 88 percent of millennials regularly socialize and chat online. As well, the number of social media users sixty-five and older has increased, with 79 percent of baby boomers using Facebook weekly.[32] Predictably, businesses are trying to adapt and tap the vast potential of social networking.

Potential Risks of Social Networks for Businesses. Online public social networks hold great promise for businesses while also presenting some risk. Most managers want plugged-in employees with strong tech skills. They like to imagine their workers as brand ambassadors. They fantasize about their products becoming overnight sensations thanks to

CHECKLIST

Using Electronic Media Professionally: Dos and Don'ts

Dos: Know Workplace Policies and Avoid Private Use of Media at Work

- **Learn your company's rules.** Some companies require workers to sign that they have read and understood Internet and digital media use policies. Being informed is your best protection.
- **Avoid sending personal e-mail, instant messages, or texts from work.** Even if your company allows personal use during lunch or after hours, keep it to a minimum. Better yet, wait to use your own electronic devices away from work.
- **Separate work and personal data.** Keep information that could embarrass you or expose you to legal liability on your personal storage devices, on hard drives, or in the cloud, never on your office computer.
- **Be careful when blogging, tweeting, or posting on social networking sites.** Remember that posts are easily saved as a screenshot and shared. Negative posts can find their way to coworkers or even your supervisor.
- **Keep sensitive information private.** Use privacy settings, but don't trust the "private" areas on Facebook, Twitter, Flickr, and other social networks. Stay away from pornography, sexually explicit jokes, or inappropriate screen savers. Anything that might "poison" the work environment is a harassment risk and, therefore, prohibited.

Don'ts: Avoid Questionable Content, Personal Documents, and File Sharing

- **Don't spread rumours, gossip, or negative, defamatory comments.** Because all digital information is subject to discovery in court, avoid unprofessional content and conduct, including complaints about your employer, customers, and employees.[33]
- **Don't download or share cartoons, video clips, photos, or art.** Businesses are liable for any recorded digital content regardless of the medium used.[34]
- **Don't open attachments sent by e-mail.** Attachments with executable files or video files may carry viruses, spyware, or other malware (malicious programs).
- **Don't download free software or utilities to company machines.** Employees can unwittingly introduce viruses, phishing schemes, and other cyber "bugs."
- Don't store your music or photos on a company machine (or server), and don't watch streaming videos. Capturing precious company bandwidth for personal use is a sure way to be shown the door.
- **Don't share files, and avoid file-sharing services.** Clarify whether you may use Google Docs and other services that offer optional file sharing. Stay away from distributors of pirated files.

FIGURE 7.10 Guidelines for Safe Social Networking

Establish boundaries

Don't share information, images, and media online that you would not be comfortable sharing openly in the office.

Distrust privacy settings

Privacy settings don't guarantee complete protection from prying eyes. Facebook has come under fire for changing privacy settings and opening unwitting users profiles for the world to see.

Rein in your friends

One of your 500 Facebook friends may tag you in an inappropriate photograph. Tags make pictures searchable; an embarrassing college or university incident may resurface years later. Always ask before tagging someone.

Beware *"friending"*

Don't reject friend requests from some coworkers while accepting them from others. Snubbed colleagues may harbour ill feelings. Don't friend your boss unless he or she friends you first. Send friend requests only once.

Expect the unexpected

Recruiters now routinely check applicants' online presence. Some employers have gone so far as to demand that candidates disclose their Facebook log-in information. Facebook and lawmakers have criticized the practice.

viral marketing. However, they also fret about inappropriate social media use. Businesses take different approaches to the "dark side" of social networking:

- Some take a hands-off approach and encourage employee online activity.
- Some allow partial access by limiting what employees can do online. They may disable file sharing to protect sensitive information.
- Others have drafted detailed policies to cover all forms of self-expression online.

However, experts believe that organizations should embrace positive word-of-mouth testimonials from employees about their jobs, not quash them with rigid policies.[35] In North America, social media policies need to be guidelines, not rules, or they could violate labour laws under certain circumstances.[36]

Using Social Networking Sites and Keeping Your Job. Experts agree that, as with any public online activity, users of social networking sites would do well to exercise caution. Privacy is a myth, and sensitive information should not be shared lightly, least of all inappropriate photographs. Furthermore, refusing "friend" requests or "unfriending" individuals could jeopardize professional relationships. Consider the tips in Figure 7.10 provided by career counsellor Julie Powell[37] if you like to visit social networking sites and want to keep your job.

Concept Check

1. Consider the social networking sites you use. How well do you screen your friends and followers? Why is it important to carefully consider who you add, as well as who you follow?
2. How well do you protect your online privacy? Have you checked the privacy settings on your online accounts? Many people leave their accounts open to the public and freely allow others to tag them. In groups, discuss the importance of privacy settings on your accounts.

CENGAGE

MINDTAP

Check out section 7-5a in MindTap, where you can watch a video featuring Devon Close, a chartered professional accountant (CPA) and certified management accountant (CMA), discuss the positive and negative effects of social media.

SPOTLIGHT ON COMMUNICATION: PART 2

MobileSyrup Revisited

CRITICAL THINKING

- How can including podcasts in addition to other social media help companies increase revenue?
- Visit MobileSyrup's website (mobilesyrup.com) and click on Syrup Community to access their podcasts. How do the podcasts inform and entertain?

In addition to its daily blog, MobileSyrup offers SyrupCast as part of their Syrup Community. With over 200 episodes, these podcasts provide current information and reviews of mobile technology and more.[38] As the popularity of podcasts grows in Canada, more advertisers are investing in podcasts as part of their marketing strategy:[39]

Primakov/Shutterstock

> According to the Reuters Institute for the Study of Journalism, about a third (29%) of internet users in Canada listen to podcasts. A May 2019 study from Edison Research and Triton Digital found that 36% of consumers in Canada listened to podcasts monthly in 2019, up from 28% in 2018. Roughly half (45%) of respondents ages 35 to 54 said they listened to podcasts monthly, compared with 21% of consumers 55 and older.[40]

The most successful podcasts not only inform but entertain. This helps to generate a larger listening audience, and with more Canadians commuting, podcasts allow for convenient access to the information.[41]

Summary of Learning Objectives

1 Understand e-mail and the professional standards for its usage, structure, and format.

- E-mail is still the lifeblood of businesses, but instant messaging is gaining popularity.
- Office workers still send paper-based messages when they need a permanent record; want to maintain confidentiality; and need to convey formal, long, and important messages.
- E-mail and memo subject lines summarize the central idea, which is restated in the opening. The body provides details. The closing includes (a) action information and deadlines, (b) a summary, or (c) a closing thought.
- Careful e-mail users write concisely and don't send content they wouldn't want published.

2 Explain workplace instant messaging and texting, as well as their liabilities and best practices.

- Exchanging instant messages (IM) and text messages with customers, employees, and suppliers is fast, discreet, and inexpensive.
- Risks include productivity losses, leaked trade secrets, and legal liability from workers' improper use of digital media; fraud, malware, and spam pose additional risks.
- Best practices include following company policies, avoiding sensitive information, not sending inappropriate digital content, and using correct grammar and spelling.
- Text messages should observe proper timing, be addressed to the correct person, and identify the sender; savvy workers don't send sensitive news or expect an instant reply.

3 Identify professional applications of podcasts and wikis, and describe guidelines for their use.

- Business podcasts are digital audio or video files ranging from short clips to long media files.
- Applications that do not require a human presence (e.g., training videos) lend themselves to podcast recordings that users can stream or download on the go.
- Wikis enable far-flung team members to share information and build a knowledge base.
- Wikis can be used to replace meetings, manage projects, and document projects large and small.

4 Describe how businesses use blogs to connect with internal and external audiences, and list best practices for professional blogging.

- Blogs help businesses to keep customers, employees, and suppliers informed and to receive feedback.
- Online communities can form around blogs.
- Companies employ blogs for public relations and crisis communication, market research and viral marketing, internal communication, and recruiting.

5 Define business uses of social networking.

- Social media sites, such as Facebook and Twitter, allow firms to share company news; exchange ideas; and connect with customers, employees, other stakeholders, and the public.
- Companies boost their brand recognition, troubleshoot customer problems, and engage customers by using social media.
- Productivity losses, legal liability, leaking of trade secrets, and angry Internet users are potential risks of social media use at work.
- Workers should share only appropriate, work-related information, not post questionable content; they should activate and monitor their privacy options on social media sites.

Chapter Review

1. Discuss the benefits and drawbacks of using e-mail in the workplace. (Obj. 1)
2. Why is the subject line the most important part of an e-mail message? (Obj. 1)
3. List the similarities between memos and e-mail. (Obj. 1)
4. How can you use instant messaging and texting safely on the job? (Obj. 2)
5. How do organizations use podcasts, and how are they accessed? (Obj. 3)
6. What is a *wiki*, and what are its advantages to businesses? (Obj. 3)
7. Explain the best practices for creating and maintaining a professional blog. (Obj. 4)
8. What is *viral marketing*, and how can it benefit businesses? (Obj. 4)
9. How do businesses try to tap the vast potential of social networking? (Obj. 5)
10. What are five guidelines for safe social networking at work? (Obj. 5)

Critical Thinking

1. The Pew Research Center found that almost three quarters of millennials adjust their privacy settings to limit access to their information.[42] They safeguard their data for fear of identity theft even if the process is cumbersome, but the study found they worry much less about their privacy, for example, when companies sell their personal information. If facing the choice between safety and privacy, which would you choose? How concerned are you about privacy and security online? Do you watch your own privacy settings? (Objs. 1–5)
2. In her book *Alone Together*, professor Sherry Turkle argues that increasing dependence on technology leads to a consequent diminution in personal connections. "Technology is seductive when what it offers meets our human vulnerabilities. As it turns out, we are very vulnerable indeed. We are lonely but fearful of intimacy. Digital connections . . . may offer the illusion of companionship without the demands of friendship."[43] Do you agree that technology diminishes personal relationships rather than bringing us closer together? Do social media fool us into thinking that we are connected when in reality we bear none of the commitments and burdens of true friendship?
3. How could IM be useful in your career field? Does IM produce a permanent record? Do you think that common abbreviations such as *lol* and *imho* and all-lowercase writing are acceptable in text messages for business? (Obj. 2)
4. Why is it important that companies and organizations closely monitor their social media accounts? (Obj. 5)
5. **Ethical Issue:** Although they don't actually pay people to act as fans on social networks and entice their friends to do so as well, some marketers employ machines, called bots, to inflate the number of their fans and followers online. In developing countries businesses trafficking in fake profiles, the so-called click farms, are selling 1,000 followers for $10. Social networks try to respond by deleting fake accounts, and the likes earned in the process vanish too. Google has introduced an algorithm to eliminate spammers and other abusers of its systems, and Facebook and Twitter will probably follow suit.[44] Why do some businesses resort to such measures? What might be the consequences of faking fans? (Obj. 5)

Activities

7.1 Instant Messaging: Practising Your Professional IM Skills (Obj. 2)

Communication Technology | Social Media | Team | Web

Your instructor will direct this role-playing group activity. Using instant messaging, you will simulate one of several typical business scenarios—for example, responding to a product inquiry, training a new-hire, troubleshooting with a customer, or making an appointment. For each scenario, two or more students will chat professionally with only a minimal script to practise on-the-spot yet courteous professional interactions by IM. Your instructor will determine which software you will need and provide brief instructions to prepare you for your role in this exercise.

If you don't have instant messaging software on your computer or smart device yet, download the application first. WhatsApp, Facebook Messenger, QQ, WeChat, and Skype are just a few of the most popular apps. You may want to use a computer because downloading chat sessions is easier on a computer than on a smartphone.

YOUR TASK Log on to the IM or chat program your instructor chooses. Follow your instructor's directions closely as you role-play the business situation you were assigned with your partner or team. The scenario will involve two or more people who will communicate by instant messaging in real time.

7.2 Analyzing a Podcast (Obj. 3)

Communication Technology | Social Media | E-mail | Web

Review the list of interesting Podcasts you generated from CBC Radio: www.cbc.ca/radio/podcasts (Learning Objective 3, Concept Check, Question 1).

YOUR TASK Choose a CBC podcast that interests you. Listen to it or obtain a transcript on the website and study it for its structure. Is it direct or indirect? How is it presented? What style does the speaker adopt? How useful is the information provided? At your instructor's request, write an e-mail that discusses the podcast you analyzed. Alternatively, if your instructor allows, you could also send a very concise summary of the podcast by text message from your cell phone or a tweet to your instructor. Try limiting yourself to 140 characters to practice conciseness, although Twitter now allows longer messages.

7.3 Composing a Personal Blog Entry (Obj. 4)

Communication Technology | Social Media | E-mail | Web

Review the guidelines for professional blogging in this chapter. Find a recent social media–related study or survey, and target an audience of business professionals who may want to know more about social networking. Search for studies conducted by respected organizations and businesses such as Canada Internet Registration Authority (CIRA), Statistics Canada, and Government of Canada agencies, as applicable. As you plan and outline your post, follow the advice provided in this chapter. Although the goal is usually to offer advice, you could also weigh in with your opinion regarding a controversy. For example, do you agree with companies that forbid employees to use company-owned devices and networks for social media access? Do you agree that millennials and Generation Z are losing social skills because of excessive online connectivity?

YOUR TASK Compose a one-page blog entry in MS Word and submit it in hard copy. Alternatively, post it to the discussion board on the class course-management platform, or e-mail it to your instructor, as appropriate. Because you will be using outside sources, be careful to paraphrase correctly and cite your work. Visit Chapter 11 to review how to put ideas into your own words with integrity.

7.4 Twitter Communication Audit (Obj. 5)

Communication Technology | Social Media | E-mail | Web

YOUR TASK On Twitter read a number of business-related messages from reputable organizations, such as GM, Ford Motor Company, Kia Motors, Pepsi, or Coca-Cola. Look for apparent examples of successful customer-service interventions, promotional appeals, and special deals. Conversely, copy or make screenshots of conversations on Twitter that you deem unprofessional based on the principles discussed in this chapter. If your instructor directs, submit your findings with a brief commentary in memo form, as an e-mail, or as a post on a discussion board you may be using in your course. You may be asked to edit and rewrite some of the tweets you find.

7.5 What? You Tweeted THAT? (Obj. 5)

Communication Technology | Social Media | E-mail

The modern workplace is a potential digital minefield. The imprudent use of practically any online tool—whether e-mail, IM, texting, tweeting, blogging, or posting to Facebook—can land workers in hot water and even lead to dismissal. Here are three ways Twitter can get you fired for showing poor judgment:[45]

1. **Sending hate tweets about the boss**. Example: *My idiot boss said he put in for raises. I think he lies. He is known for that. His daddy owns the company.*
2. **Lying to the boss and bragging about it**. Example: *I so lied to my boss . . . I was late but I said I forgot my badge and got away with it.*
3. **Announcing the desire to quit**. Example: *So close to quitting my job right now. Sometimes I can't [expletive] stand this place [expletive] moron assistant plant manager I'm about to deck him.*

YOUR TASK Discuss each violation of Twitter best practices, or summarize in general why these tweets are potentially damaging to their authors. How could the Twitter users have handled their grievances more professionally? Comment on the style of these questionable tweets. If your instructor requests, summarize your observations in an e-mail message or an online post.

7.6 The Dark Side: Hooked on Social Media? (Obj. 5)

Social Media

Could you give up your electronic toys for 24 hours without "withdrawal symptoms"? Would you be able to survive a full day unplugged from all media? A class of 200 university students went media free for 24 hours and then blogged about the experience.[46]

> Some sounded like addicts going cold turkey: In withdrawal. Frantically craving. Very anxious. Extremely antsy. Miserable. Jittery. Crazy. One student lamented: I clearly am addicted and the dependency is sickening. In the absence of technology that anchors them to friends and family, students felt bored and isolated.
>
> The study reveals a paradigm shift in human interaction. A completely digital generation is viscerally wedded to electronic toys, so much so that technology has become an indispensable part of the young people's lives.

Perceived advantages: Electronically abstinent students stated that they spent more time on course work, took better notes, and were more focused. As a result, they said they learned more and became more productive. They also reported that they spent more time with loved ones and friends face to face. Life slowed down and the day seemed much longer to some.

YOUR TASK Discuss in class, in a chat, or in an online post the following questions: Have you ever unplugged? What was that experience like? Could you give up your cell phone, computer, or gaming console (no texting, no Facebook or IM) for a day or longer? What would you be doing instead? Is there any harm in not being able to unplug?

Grammar and Mechanics | *Review 7*

Apostrophes and Other Punctuation

Review Guides 31 to 38 about apostrophes and other punctuation in Appendix B, Grammar and Mechanics Guide, beginning on page B-1. On a sheet of paper or on your computer, revise the following sentences to correct errors in the use of apostrophes and other punctuation. For each error that you locate, write the guide number that deals with this usage. The more you recognize the reasons, the better you will learn these punctuation guidelines. If a sentence is correct, write *C*. When you finish, compare your responses with the key in Appendix C.

EXAMPLE: Facebook users accounts may be suspended if the rules are violated.

REVISION: Facebook **users**' accounts may be suspended if the rules are violated. [Guide 32]

1. In just one years time, James increased the number of his blog followers by 20 percent.
2. Many followers of James blog commented on the overuse of the Reply All button.
3. Would you please give me directions to your downtown headquarters?
4. Success often depends on an individuals ability to adapt to change.
5. My friend recommended an article titled Ten Tools for Building Your Own Mobile App.
6. You must replace the ink cartridge see page 8 in the manual, before printing.
7. Tyler wondered whether all sales managers databases needed to be updated.
8. (Direct quotation) The death of e-mail, said Mike Song, has been greatly exaggerated.
9. In just two years time, the number of people e-mailing on mobile devices nearly doubled.
10. The staffing meeting starts at 10 a.m. sharp, doesn't it.

Notes

[1] Based on Conference Board of Canada. (2020). *Employability skills*. https://www.conferenceboard.ca/edu/employability-skills.aspx

[2] MobileSyrup. (2019). *About MobileSyrup*. https://mobilesyrup.com/about-us/

[3] Feedspot. (2019, September 6). *Top 40 Canadian technology blogs and websites on the web*. https://blog.feedspot.com/canadian_technology_blogs/

[4] MobileSyrup. (2019). *About MobileSyrup*. https://mobilesyrup.com/about-us/

[5] MobileSyrup. (2019). *Reviews*. https://mobilesyrup.com/category/reviews/

[6] Feedspot. (2019, September 6). *Top 40 Canadian technology blogs and websites on the web*. https://blog.feedspot.com/canadian_technology_blogs/

[7] Canadian Internet Registration Authority. (2019). *2019 Canada's Internet factbook*. https://cira.ca/resources/corporate/factbook/canadas-internet-factbook-2019

[8] Dubé, D. E. (2017, April 21). *This is how much time you spend on work emails every day, according to a Canadian survey*. Global News. https://globalnews.ca/news/3395457/this-is-how-much-time-you-spend-on-work-emails-every-day-according-to-a-canadian-survey/

[9] Ibid.

[10] The Radicati Group. (2017, February). *Email statistics report, 2017–2021.* https://www.radicati.com/wp/wp-content/uploads/2019/01/Instant_Messaging_Statistics_Report,_2019-2023_Exceutive_Summary.pdf

[11] Thompson, E. (2017, January 19). *Canada Revenue Agency monitoring Facebook, Twitter posts of some Canadians.* CBC News. http://www.cbc.ca/news/politics/taxes-cra-facebook-big-data-1.3941416

[12] Lamb, S. E. (2015). *Writing well for business success.* St. Martin's Griffin, p. 139.

[13] Canadian Wireless Telecommunications Association. (2019). *Facts and figures: The Canadian market.* https://www.cwta.ca/facts-figures/

[14] The Radicati Group. (2019, February). *Instant messaging statistics report, 2019–2023.* https://www.radicati.com/wp/wp-content/uploads/2019/01/Instant_Messaging_Statistics_Report,_2019-2023_Exceutive_Summary.pdf

[15] Canadian Internet Registration Authority. (2019). *2019 Canada's Internet factbook.* https://cira.ca/resources/corporate/factbook/canadas-internet-factbook-2019

[16] Stevenson, G. (2016, August 16). *What employers and employees need to know about distracted driving.* Occupational Safety Group, Inc. https://osg.ca/what-employers-and-employees-need-to-know-about-distracted-driving/

[17] Flynn, N. (2012, May 23). *Social media rules: Policies and best practices to effectively manage your presence, posts and potential risks.* The ePolicy Institute. http://www.ohioscpa.com/docs/conference-outlines/8_social-media-rules.pdf?sfvrsn=4

[18] Canadian Wireless Telecommunications Association. (2019). *Facts and figures: The Canadian market.* https://www.cwta.ca/facts-figures/

[19] Based on the Emily Post Institute. (n.d.). *Text messaging: I love text messaging.* http://www.emilypost.com/home-and-family-life/133/391-text-messaging

[20] Ibid.

[21] The five main uses of wikis based on Nations, D. (2009). *The business wiki: Wiki in the workplace.* About.com: Web Trends. http://webtrends.about.com/od/wiki/a/business-wiki.htm

[22] Barton, D. (2013, July 15). The rise of the social CEO. *Canadian Business, 86*(11/12), 19.

[23] Kawczyk, J., & Steinberg, J. (2012, March 7). How content is really shared: Close friends, not "influencers." *Ad Age Digital.* http://adage.com/article/digitalnext/content-shared-closefriends-influencers/233147

[24] WestJet. (2016). *WestJet Christmas miracle: Fort McMurray strong.* https://www.westjet.com/en-ca/about-us/story/christmas-miracle

[25] Tips for Creating a Professional Blog based on Wuorio, J. (n.d.). *Blogging for business: 7 tips for getting started.* Microsoft Small Business Center. http://www.microsoft.com/smallbusiness/resources/marketing/online-marketing/small-business-blog.aspx#Smallbusinessblog

[26] Zoocasa. (2017). *Our story.* https://www.zoocasa.com/company/our-story

[27] Galang, J. (2016, October 28). *Zoocasa wants to tackle fragmented real estate customer journey with $1.35 million in funding.* http://betakit.com/zoocasa-wants-to-tackle-fragmented-real-estate-customer-journey-with-1-35-million-in-funding/

[28] Ibid.

[29] Kaszor, D. (2013, January 30). Download code: The game David S. Gallant got fired over is a perfect example of games as art. *Financial Post.* http://business.financialpost.com/2013/01/30/download-code-the-game-david-s-gallant-got-fired-over-is-a-perfect-example-of-games-as-art/

[30] Lindstrom, M. (2012, July 3). How many lives does a brand have? *Fast Company.* http://www.fastcompany.com/1841927/buyology-martin-lindstrom-lives-of-brands-china-marketing

[31] Larter, L. (2016, October 12). *7 things you need to know about your business.* https://lisalarter.com/7-things-need-know-business/

[32] McKinnon, M. (2019, June 30). *2019 report: social media use in Canada.* https://canadiansinternet.com/2019-report-social-media-use-canada/

[33] Villano, M. (2009, April 26). The online divide between work and play. *New York Times.* http://www.nytimes.com

[34] Ibid.

[35] Wright, A. D. (2012, February 3). *Social media policies slowly catch on worldwide.* Society for Human Resource Management. http://www.shrm.org/hrdisciplines/global/Articles/Pages/WorldwidePolicies.aspx

[36] Ibid.

[37] Villano, M. (2009, April 26). The online divide between work and play. New York Times. http://www.nytimes.com

[38] MobileSyrup. (2019). *SyrupCast.* https://mobilesyrup.com/category/syrup-community/

[39] Briggs, P. (2019, August 14). *Marketers in Canada turn to podcasts for brand awareness.* eMarketer. https://www.emarketer.com/content/the-rise-of-podcasting-in-canada-content-marketing

[40] Ibid. Reprinted courtesy of eMarketer.

[41] Ibid.

[42] Bryan, B. (2015, June 24). Millennials are more than happy to trade privacy for security. *Business Insider.* http://www. businessinsider.com/millennials-willing-to-trade-privacy-for-safety-online-2015-6

[43] Turkle, S. (2011). *Alone together: Why we expect more from technology and less from each other.* Basic Books, p. 1.

[44] Hutchinson, A. (2014, January 21). *The inevitable bite of buying followers and likes.* Social Media Today. http://www.socialmediatoday.com/content/inevitable-bite-buying-followers-and-likes

[45] *5 ways Twitter can get you fired.* (2009, October 8). Applicant.com. http://applicant.com/5-ways-twitter-can-get-you-fired

[46] Moeller, S. D. (2010). *24 hours: Unplugged.* http://withoutmedia.wordpress.com; Associated Press. (2009, September 6). Center tries to treat Web addicts. *New York Times.* http://www.nytimes.com

CHAPTER 8

Positive Messages

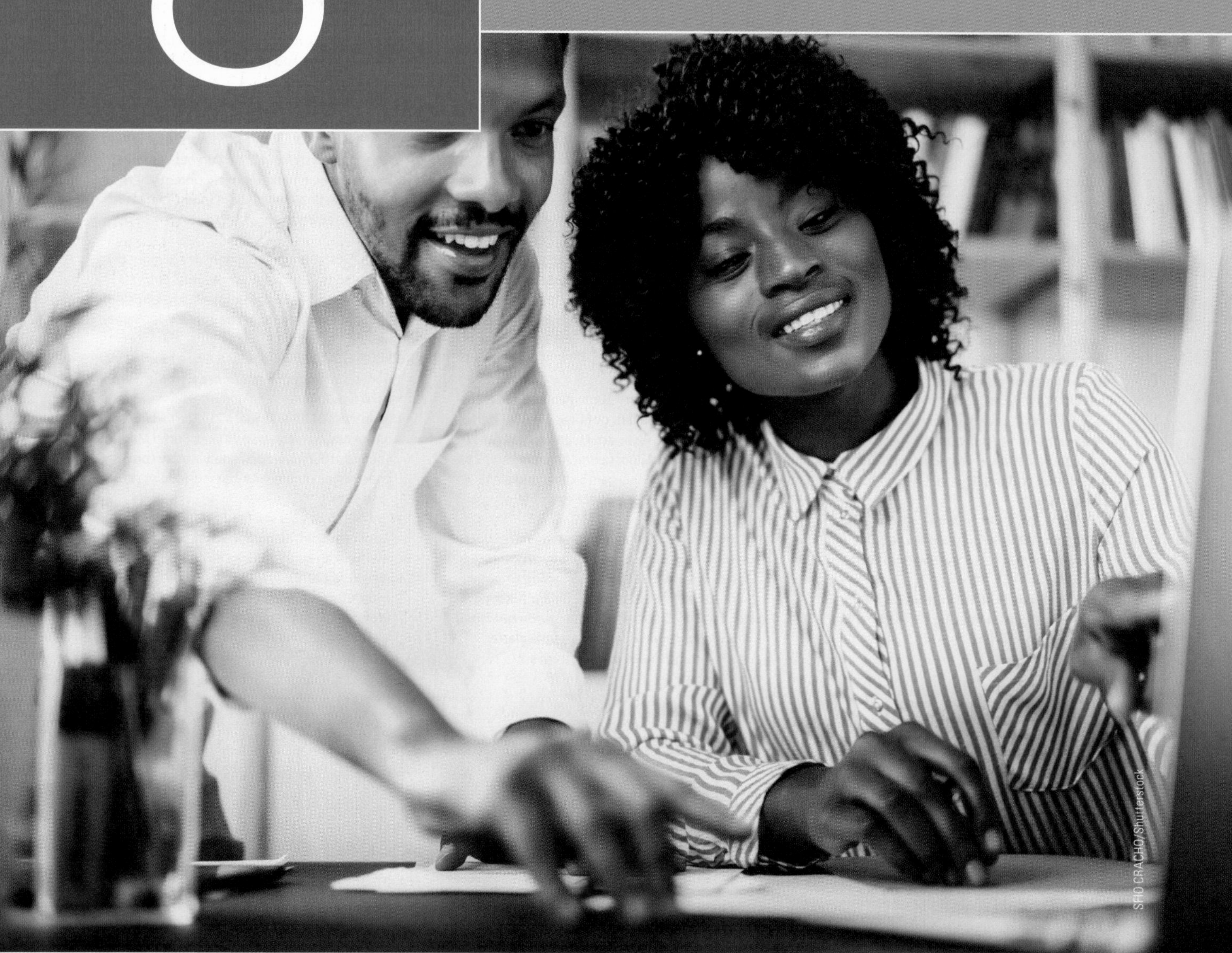

SFIO CRACHO/Shutterstock

LEARNING OBJECTIVES

After studying this chapter, you should be able to

1 Understand the channels through which positive messages travel and apply the 3-x-3 writing process.

2 Compose direct messages that make requests, respond to inquiries online and offline, and deliver step-by-step instructions.

3 Prepare messages that make direct claims and voice complaints.

4 Create adjustment messages that salvage customers' trust and promote further business.

5 Write special messages that convey kindness and goodwill.

SPOTLIGHT ON COMMUNICATION: PART 1

Raven Reads—Subscription Box

Courtesy of Raven Reads

Nicole McLaren ran an Indigenous-author book club that allowed Indigenous and non-Indigenous members to connect through literature. With the success of her book club, combined with her entrepreneurial spirit and the growing popularity of subscription boxes, Raven Reads was born. McLaren, who is of Métis, Cree, and European heritage, carefully curates each box to include engaging stories. Every season, subscribers receive a book by an Indigenous author, as well as "crafts, art, jewelry, giftware and other products made solely by Indigenous artisans," to share the history and culture of Indigenous peoples:[1]

> It has everything to do with reconciliation and the Truth and Reconciliation Commission's calls to action for all Canadians. It is meant to allow you to create a safe space for you to learn about other cultures, learn a little bit of history, and try out fascinating products by other Indigenous entrepreneurs from around the globe![2]

Raven Reads is not just for Canadians. They also ship subscription boxes to the United States and Europe. With about 500 boxes shipping every quarter, Raven Reads has a far reach.[3]

CRITICAL THINKING

- As an entrepreneur from a rural area with no storefront,[4] Nicole McLaren relies heavily on social media to grow her business. What are the best practices for responding to customers online?
- Each subscription box comes with a letter from the author. How does a letter add value to the box?

Neutral and Positive Messages: The Writing Process

LEARNING OBJECTIVE 1

Understand the channels through which positive messages travel and apply the 3-x-3 writing process.

In the workplace neutral and positive messages are routine and straightforward. Such routine messages include simple requests for information or action, replies to customers, and explanations to coworkers. Other types of positive messages are instructions, direct claims, and complaints.

E-mails, memos, and letters are the channels most frequently used. In addition, businesses today must listen and respond to social media. As discussed in Chapter 7, e-mail and social media are used to communicate within organizations and with outside audiences. At the same time, in some industries, memos continue to be an important channel of communication within an organization, while letters are a vital paper-based external channel.

This chapter focuses on routine, positive messages. These will make up the bulk of your workplace communication. Figure 8.1 has a quick review of the 3-x-3 writing process to help you apply it to positive messages. You will also learn when to respond by business letter and how to format one.

Understanding Business Letters

Despite the advent of e-mail, social networking, and other electronic communication technologies, in certain situations letters are still the preferred channel of communication for delivering messages *outside* an organization. Such letters go to suppliers, government agencies, other businesses, and, most important, customers. You may think that everybody is online, but with socioeconomic factors and lack of access because of geographical region, thousands of Canadians are offline.[5] Just as they are eager to connect with a majority of consumers online, businesses continue to give letters to customers a high priority because these messages, too, encourage product feedback, project a favourable image of the organization, and promote future business.

FIGURE 8.1 The 3-x-3 Writing Process

1 Prewriting	2 Drafting	3 Revising
Analyze • What is your purpose? • What do you want the receiver to do or believe? • What channel should you choose: face-to-face conversation, group meeting, e-mail, memo, letter, report, blog, wiki, tweet, etc.?	**Research** • Gather data to provide facts. • Search company files, previous correspondence, and the Internet. • What do you need to know to write this message? • How much does the audience already know?	**Edit** • Edit your message to be sure it is clear, concise, conversational, and readable. • Revise to eliminate wordy fillers, long lead-ins, redundancies, and trite business phrases. • Develop parallelism. • Consider using headings and numbered and bulleted lists for quick reading.
Anticipate • Profile the audience. • What does the receiver already know? • Will the receiver's response be neutral, positive, or negative? How will this affect your organizational strategy?	**Organize** • Organize direct messages with the big idea first, followed by an explanation in the body and an action request in the closing. • For persuasive or negative messages, use an indirect, problem-solving strategy.	**Proofread** • Take the time to read every message carefully. • Look for errors in spelling, grammar, punctuation, names, and numbers. • Check to be sure the format is consistent.
Adapt • What techniques can you use to adapt your message to its audience? • How can you promote feedback? • Strive to use positive, conversational, and courteous language.	**Draft** • Prepare a first draft, usually quickly. • Focus on short, clear sentences using the active voice. • Build paragraph coherence by repeating key ideas, using pronouns, and incorporating appropriate transitional expressions.	**Evaluate** • Will this message achieve your purpose? • Does the tone sound pleasant and friendly rather than curt? • Have you thought enough about the audience to be sure this message is appealing? • Did you encourage feedback?

Permanent Record. Whether you send a business letter will depend on the situation and the preference of your organization. Business letters are necessary when the situation calls for a permanent record. For example, when a company enters into an agreement with another company, business letters introduce the agreement and record decisions and points of understanding. Business letters deliver contracts, explain terms, exchange ideas, negotiate agreements, answer vendor questions, and maintain customer relations.

Confidential. Business letters are less likely than electronic media to be intercepted, misdirected, forwarded, retrieved, or otherwise inspected by unintended recipients. Also, business letters presented on company stationery carry a sense of formality and importance not possible with e-mail. They look important, as illustrated in Figure 8.2, a customer-welcoming letter in the popular block format.

Persuasive. Finally, business letters can persuade people to change their actions, adopt new beliefs, make donations, contribute their time, and try new products. Direct-mail letters remain a powerful tool to promote services and products, boost online and retail traffic, and enhance customer relations. You will learn more about writing persuasive and sales messages in Chapter 10.

FIGURE 8.2 Direct Letter Welcoming Customer—Block Style

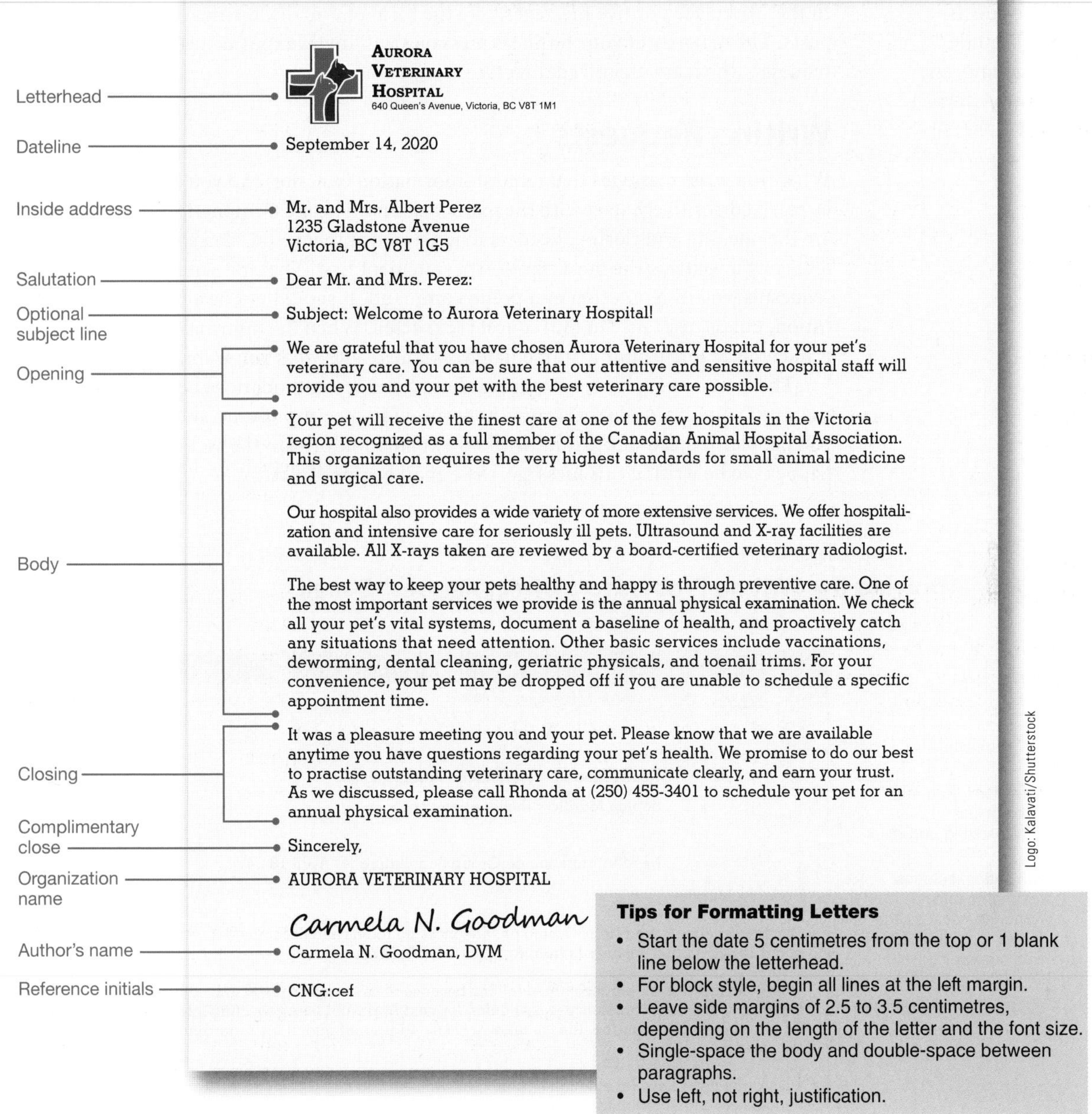

AURORA VETERINARY HOSPITAL
640 Queen's Avenue, Victoria, BC V8T 1M1

September 14, 2020

Mr. and Mrs. Albert Perez
1235 Gladstone Avenue
Victoria, BC V8T 1G5

Dear Mr. and Mrs. Perez:

Subject: Welcome to Aurora Veterinary Hospital!

We are grateful that you have chosen Aurora Veterinary Hospital for your pet's veterinary care. You can be sure that our attentive and sensitive hospital staff will provide you and your pet with the best veterinary care possible.

Your pet will receive the finest care at one of the few hospitals in the Victoria region recognized as a full member of the Canadian Animal Hospital Association. This organization requires the very highest standards for small animal medicine and surgical care.

Our hospital also provides a wide variety of more extensive services. We offer hospitalization and intensive care for seriously ill pets. Ultrasound and X-ray facilities are available. All X-rays taken are reviewed by a board-certified veterinary radiologist.

The best way to keep your pets healthy and happy is through preventive care. One of the most important services we provide is the annual physical examination. We check all your pet's vital systems, document a baseline of health, and proactively catch any situations that need attention. Other basic services include vaccinations, deworming, dental cleaning, geriatric physicals, and toenail trims. For your convenience, your pet may be dropped off if you are unable to schedule a specific appointment time.

It was a pleasure meeting you and your pet. Please know that we are available anytime you have questions regarding your pet's health. We promise to do our best to practise outstanding veterinary care, communicate clearly, and earn your trust. As we discussed, please call Rhonda at (250) 455-3401 to schedule your pet for an annual physical examination.

Sincerely,

AURORA VETERINARY HOSPITAL

Carmela N. Goodman

Carmela N. Goodman, DVM

CNG:cef

Tips for Formatting Letters

- Start the date 5 centimetres from the top or 1 blank line below the letterhead.
- For block style, begin all lines at the left margin.
- Leave side margins of 2.5 to 3.5 centimetres, depending on the length of the letter and the font size.
- Single-space the body and double-space between paragraphs.
- Use left, not right, justification.

Concept Check

1. Why is it important to have a permanent record for some messages?
2. Consider the last letter you received in the mail that was personally addressed to you. What message did the letter contain? Did the letter require a permanent record, confidentiality, or persuasion? Depending on the purpose of the message, in what ways was receiving a hard copy useful or not?

LEARNING OBJECTIVE 2

Compose direct messages that make requests, respond to inquiries online and offline, and deliver step-by-step instructions.

Routine Request, Response, and Instruction Messages

In the workplace positive messages take the form of e-mails, memos, letters, or social media posts. The majority of your business messages will involve routine requests and responses to requests, which are organized directly.

Writing Requests

When you write messages that request information or action and you think your request will be received positively, start with the main idea first. The most emphatic positions in a message are the opening and closing. Readers tend to look at them first. You should capitalize on this tendency by putting the most significant statement first. The first sentence of an information request is usually a question or a polite command. It should not be an explanation or justification, unless resistance to the request is expected. When the information or action requested is likely to be forthcoming, immediately tell the reader what you want.

The e-mail in Figure 8.3 inquiring about hotel accommodations begins immediately with the most important idea: Can the hotel provide meeting rooms and accommodations for 150 people? Instead of opening with an explanation of who the writer is or why the writer happens to be writing this message, the e-mail begins directly.

FIGURE 8.3 Applying the Writing Process to a Direct Request E-mail

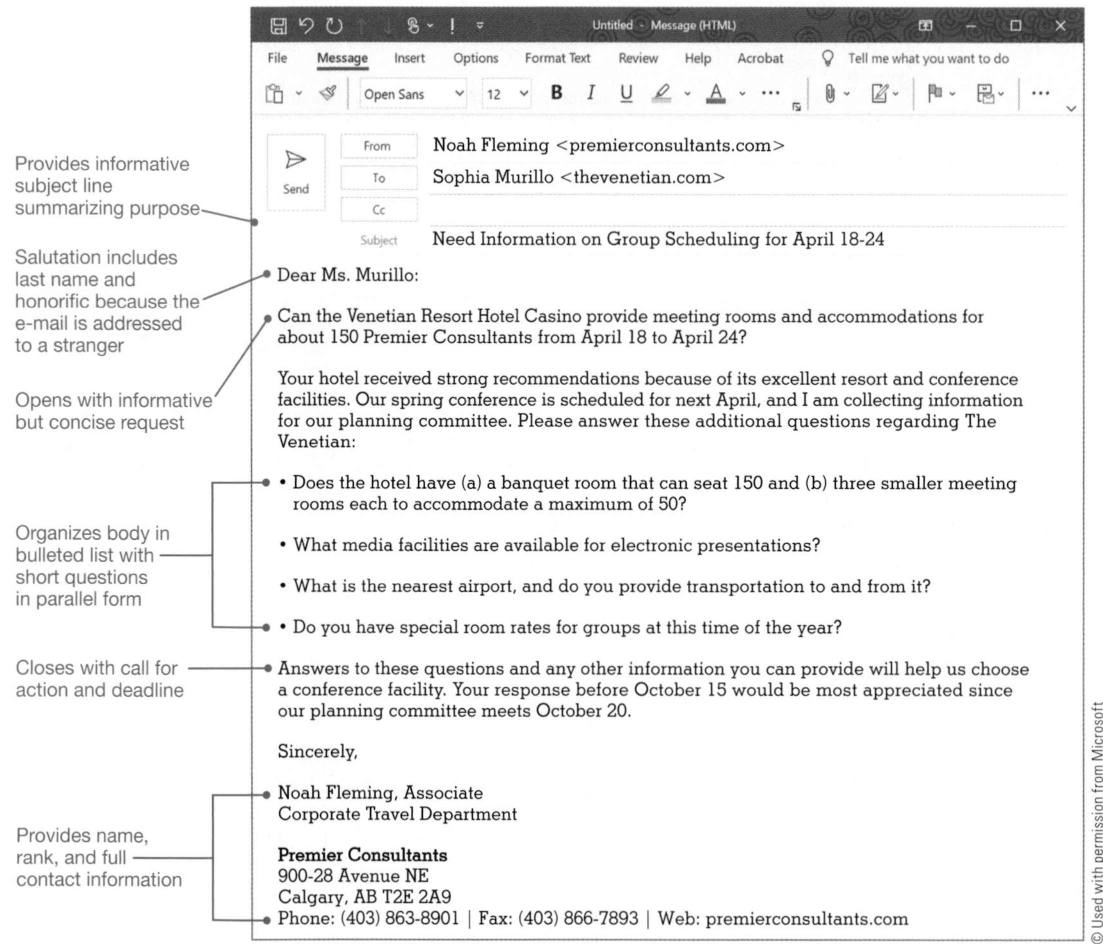

From: Noah Fleming <premierconsultants.com>

To: Sophia Murillo <thevenetian.com>

Cc:

Subject: Need Information on Group Scheduling for April 18-24

Dear Ms. Murillo:

Can the Venetian Resort Hotel Casino provide meeting rooms and accommodations for about 150 Premier Consultants from April 18 to April 24?

Your hotel received strong recommendations because of its excellent resort and conference facilities. Our spring conference is scheduled for next April, and I am collecting information for our planning committee. Please answer these additional questions regarding The Venetian:

- Does the hotel have (a) a banquet room that can seat 150 and (b) three smaller meeting rooms each to accommodate a maximum of 50?
- What media facilities are available for electronic presentations?
- What is the nearest airport, and do you provide transportation to and from it?
- Do you have special room rates for groups at this time of the year?

Answers to these questions and any other information you can provide will help us choose a conference facility. Your response before October 15 would be most appreciated since our planning committee meets October 20.

Sincerely,

Noah Fleming, Associate
Corporate Travel Department

Premier Consultants
900-28 Avenue NE
Calgary, AB T2E 2A9
Phone: (403) 863-8901 | Fax: (403) 866-7893 | Web: premierconsultants.com

Polite Command in the Opening. If several questions must be asked, you have two choices. You can ask the most important question first, as shown in Figure 8.3, or you can begin with a summary statement, such as *Please answer the following questions about providing meeting rooms and accommodations for 150 people from April 18 through April 24.* Avoid beginning with *Will you please. . . .* Although such a statement sounds like a question, it is actually a disguised command. Because you expect an action rather than a reply, you should punctuate this polite command with a period instead of a question mark. To avoid having to choose between a period and a question mark, just omit *Will you* and start with *Please answer.*

Providing Details. The body of a message that requests information or action provides necessary details. Remember that the quality of the information obtained from a request depends on the clarity of the inquiry. If you analyze your needs, organize your ideas, and frame your request logically, you are likely to receive a meaningful answer that doesn't require a follow-up message. Whenever possible, focus on benefits to the reader (*To ensure that you receive the exact sweater you want, send us your colour choice*). To improve readability, itemize appropriate information in bulleted or numbered lists. Notice that the questions in Figure 8.3 are bulleted, and they are parallel.

Closing With Appreciation and a Call for Action. In the closing of your message, tell the reader courteously what is to be done. If a date is important, set an end date to take action and explain why. Avoid simply ending the message with *Thank you*, which forces the reader to review the contents to determine what is expected and when. You can save the reader's time by spelling out the action to be taken. Avoid other overused endings such as *Thank you for your cooperation* (trite), *Thank you in advance for . . .* (trite and presumptuous), and *If you have any questions, do not hesitate to call me* (suggests that you didn't make yourself clear). Show appreciation in a fresh and efficient manner:

- Hook your thanks to the end date (Thanks for returning the questionnaire before May 5, when we will begin tabulation).
- Connect your appreciation to a statement developing reader benefits (We are grateful for the information you will provide because it will help us serve you better).
- Briefly describe how the information will help you (I appreciate this information, which will enable me to . . .).
- When possible, make it easy for the reader to comply with your request (Note your answers on this sheet and return it in the postage-paid envelope or Here is my e-mail address so that you can reach me quickly).

ETHICS CHECK

Surprising the Boss

Kyra Montes uses e-mail for nearly all messages. She is ecstatic over a new job offer and quickly sends an e-mail to her manager announcing that she is leaving. He did not know she was looking for a new position. Is this an appropriate use of e-mail?

Responding to Requests

Often your messages will respond directly and favourably to requests for information or action. A customer wants information about a product, an employee inquires about a procedure, or a manager requests your input on a marketing campaign. In complying with such requests, you will want to apply the same direct strategy you used in making requests.

Subject Line. A customer reply e-mail that starts with an effective subject line, as shown in Figure 8.4, helps the reader recognize the topic immediately. The subject line refers in abbreviated form to previous correspondence or summarizes a message (*Subject: Your July 12 Inquiry About WorkZone Software*). Using a subject line to refer to earlier correspondence emphasizes the main idea.

Opening. In the first sentence of a direct reply e-mail, deliver the information the reader wants. Avoid wordy, drawn-out openings (*I am responding to your e-mail of December 1, in which you request information about . . .*). More forceful and more efficient is an opener that answers the inquiry (*Here is the information you wanted about . . .*). When agreeing to a request for action, announce the good news promptly (*Yes, I will be happy to speak to your business communication class on the topic of . . .*).

FIGURE 8.4 Customer Response E-mail

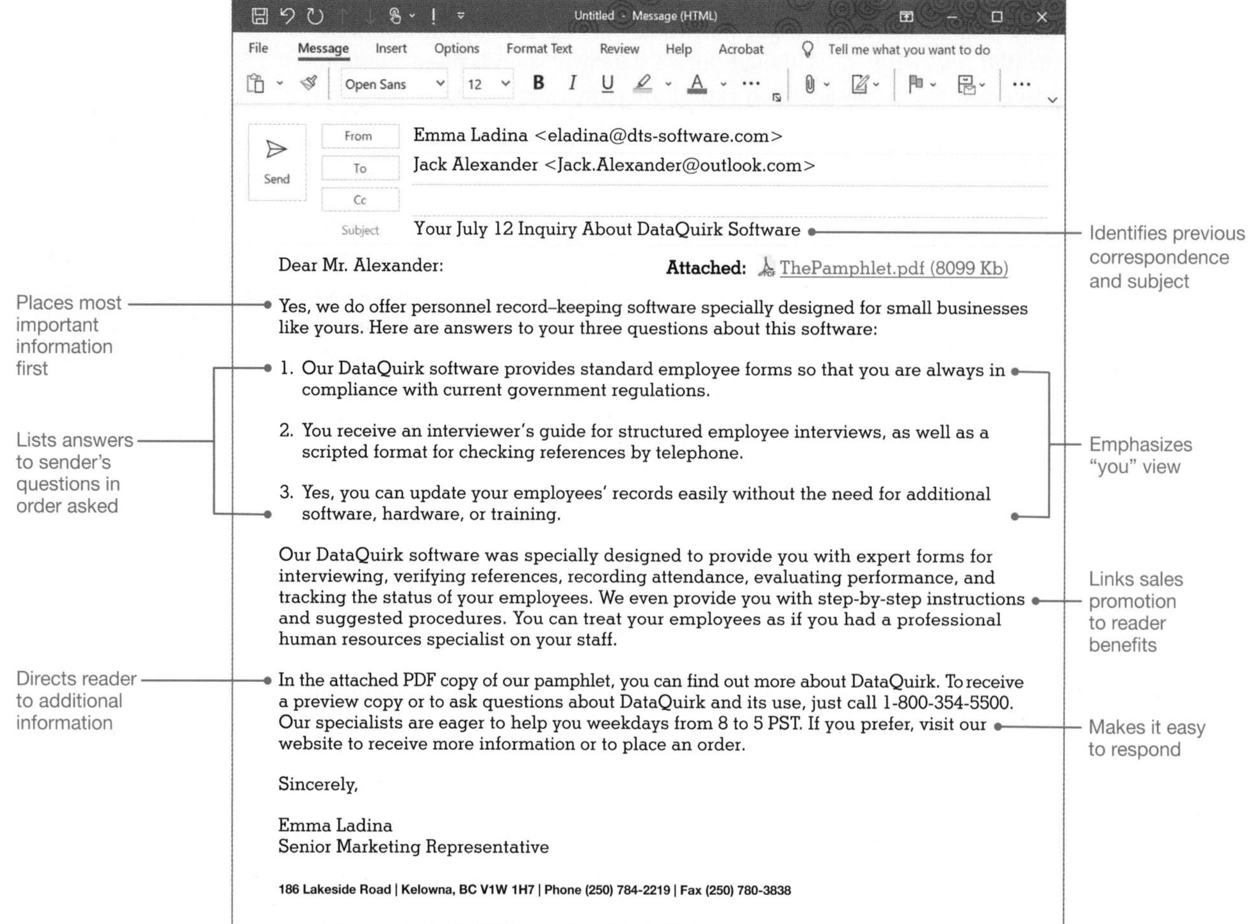

Body. In the body of your response, supply explanations and additional information. Because an e-mail, like any other document written for your company, may be considered a legally binding contract, be sure to check facts and numbers carefully. Exercise caution when using a company e-mail address or anytime you are writing for your employer online. If a policy or procedure needs authorization, seek approval from a supervisor or an executive before writing the message.

When customers or prospective customers inquire about products or services, your response should do more than merely supply answers. Try to promote your organization and products. Be sure to present the promotional material with attention to the "you" view and to reader benefits (*You can use our standardized tests to free you from time-consuming employment screening*).

Closing. In concluding a response message, refer to the information provided or to its use. (*The attached list summarizes our recommendations. We wish you all the best in redesigning your social media presence.*) If further action is required, help the reader with specifics (*The Small Business Administration publishes a number of helpful booklets. Its Internet address is . . .*). Avoid signing off with clichés (*If I may be of further assistance, don't hesitate to . . .*).

The following Checklist reviews the direct strategy for information or action requests and replies to such messages.

CHECKLIST

Writing Direct Requests and Responses

Requesting Information or Action

- **Open by stating the main idea.** To elicit information, ask a question or issue a polite command (*Please answer the following questions . . .*).
- **Explain and justify the request.** In the body arrange information logically in parallel form. Clarify and substantiate your request.
- **Request action in the closing.** Close a request by summarizing exactly what is to be done, including dates or deadlines. Express appreciation. Avoid clichés (*Thank you for your cooperation*).

Responding to Requests

- **Open directly.** Immediately deliver the information the receiver wants. Avoid wordy, drawn-out openings. When agreeing to a request, announce the good news immediately.
- **Supply additional information.** In the body provide explanations and expand initial statements. For customer letters promote products and the organization.
- **Conclude with a cordial statement.** Refer to the information provided or its use. If further action is required, describe the procedures and give specifics. Avoid clichés (*If you have questions, please do not hesitate to let me know*).

Reacting to Customer Comments Online

We live in an age when vocal individuals can start a firestorm of criticism online or become powerful brand ambassadors who champion certain products. Therefore, businesses must listen to social media comments about themselves and, if necessary, respond.

Figure 8.5 shows a social media response flowchart, now increasingly common in for-profit and nonprofit organizations alike. Businesses can't control the conversation without disabling the comments section, but they can respond in a way that benefits customers, prevents the problem from snowballing, and shines a positive light on the organization.

Embracing Customer Comments. Customer reviews online are opportunities for savvy businesses to improve their products or services and may serve as a free and efficient crowdsourced quality-control system.

Adopting Best Practices for Responding to Online Posts. Social media experts say that not every online comment merits a response. They recommend responding to posts only when you can add value—for example, by correcting false information or providing customer service. Additional guidelines for professional responses to customer comments are summarized in Figure 8.6.

CENGAGE

MINDTAP

Check out section 8-2c in MindTap, where you can watch a video featuring Karen Richardson, an associate marketing manager, discuss responding positively to online commentary.

Composing Instruction Messages

Instruction messages describe how to complete a task. You may be asked to write instructions about how to repair a paper jam in the photocopier, order supplies, file a grievance, or hire new employees. Instructions are different from policies and official procedures, which establish rules of conduct to be followed within an organization. We are most concerned with creating messages that clearly explain how to complete a task.

Like requests and responses, instruction messages follow a straightforward, direct approach. Before writing instructions for a process, be sure you understand the process completely. Practise doing it yourself. If you are asked to prepare a list of instructions that is not part of a message, include a title such as *How to Clear Paper Jams.* Include an opening paragraph explaining why the instructions are needed.

FIGURE 8.5 Social Media Response Flowchart

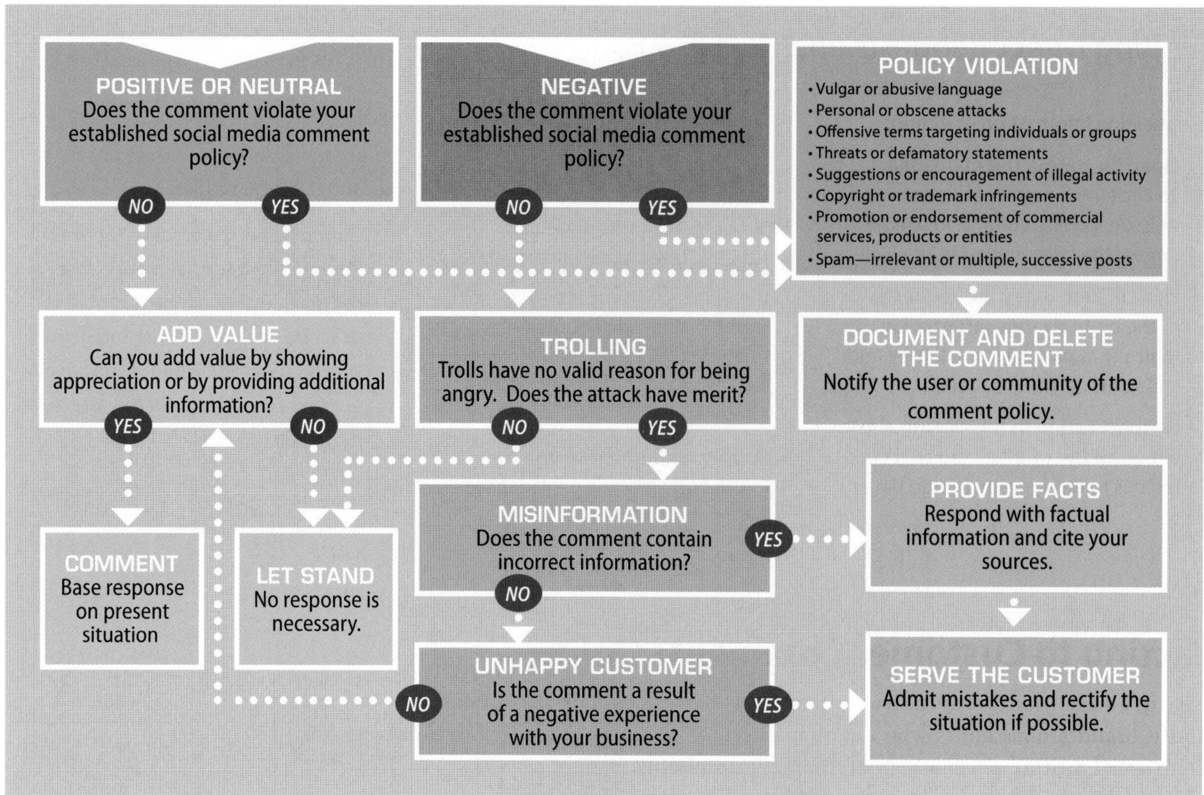

To help their employees make a prudent decision about whether and how to respond to online posts, companies are creating decision trees and diagrams such as the one shown here.[6]

Source: Courtesy of Amanda Ford

FIGURE 8.6 Responding to Customers Online

Be positive.

- Respond in a friendly, upbeat, yet professional tone.
- Correct mistakes politely.
- Do not argue, insult, or blame others.

Be honest.

- Own up to problems and mistakes.
- Inform customers when and how you will improve the situation.

Be transparent.

- State your name and position with the business.
- Personalize and humanize your business.

Be helpful.

- Point users to valuable information on your website or other approved websites.
- Follow up with users when new information is available.

As businesses increasingly interact with their customers and the public online, they are developing rules of engagement and best practices.[7]

Source: Courtesy of Amanda Ford

Opening. A message that delivers instructions should open with an explanation of why the procedure or set of instructions is necessary.

Creating Step-by-Step Instructions. The body of an instruction message should use plain English and familiar words to describe the process. Your messages explaining instructions will be most readable if you follow these guidelines:

- Divide the instructions into steps.
- List the steps in the order in which they are to be carried out.
- Arrange the items vertically with numbers.
- Begin each step with an action verb using the imperative (command) mood rather than the indicative mood.

Indicative Mood	Imperative Mood
The contract should be sent immediately.	Send the contract immediately.
The first step involves downloading the app.	Download the app first.

Closing. In the closing of a message issuing instructions, try to tie following the instructions to benefits to the organization or individual.

Revising a Message That Delivers Instructions

Figure 8.7 shows the first draft of an interoffice memo written by Brian Belmont. His memo was meant to announce a new method for employees to follow in requesting equipment repairs. However, the tone was negative, the explanation of the problem rambled, and the new method was unclear. Finally, Brian's first memo was wordy and filled with clichés (*do not hesitate to call*).

Polite Subject Line. In the revision, Brian improved the tone considerably. The front-loaded main idea is introduced with a *please*, which softens an order. The subject line specifies the purpose of the memo. Instead of dwelling on past procedures and failures (*we are no longer using* and *many mix-ups in the past*), Brian revised his message to explain constructively how reporting should be handled.

Action Verbs. Brian realized that his original explanation of the new procedure was confusing. To clarify the instructions, he itemized and numbered the steps. Each step begins with an action verb in the imperative (command) mood (*Log in*, *Indicate*, *Select*, *Identify*, and *Print*). It is sometimes difficult to force all the steps in a list into this kind of command language. Brian struggled, but he finally found verbs that worked.

Parallelism. Why should you go to so much trouble to make lists and achieve parallelism? Because readers can comprehend what you have said much more quickly. Parallel language also makes you look professional and efficient.

Positive Tone. In writing messages that deliver instructions, be careful of tone. Today's managers and team leaders seek employee participation and cooperation. These goals can't be achieved, though, if the writer sounds like a dictator or an autocrat. Avoid making accusations and assigning blame. Rather, explain changes, give reasons, and suggest benefits to the reader. Assume that employees want to contribute to the success of the organization and to their own achievement. Notice in the revision in Figure 8.7 that Brian tells readers that they will save time and reduce mix-ups if they follow the new method.

FIGURE 8.7 Memo Explaining Instructions

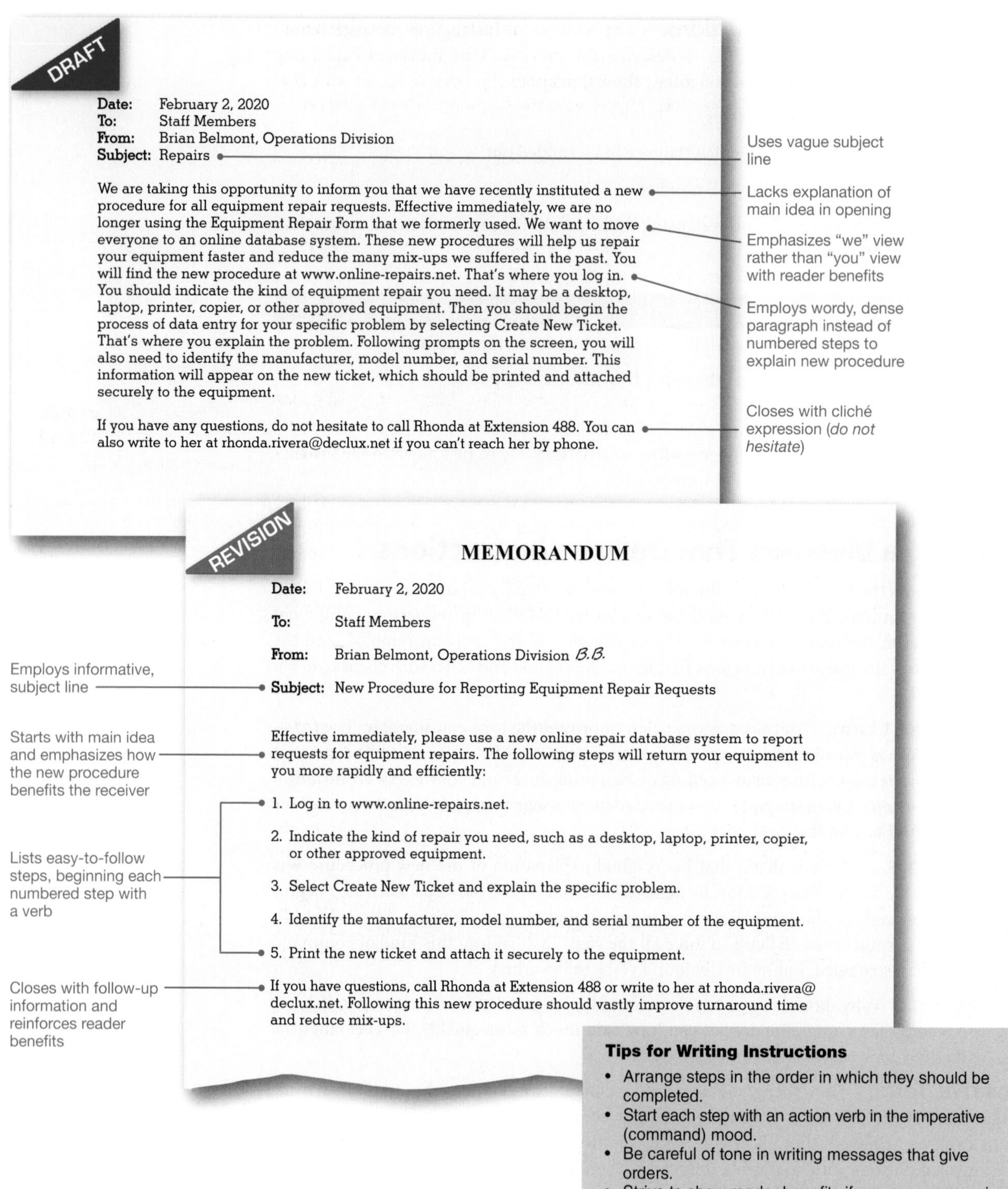

DRAFT

Date: February 2, 2020
To: Staff Members
From: Brian Belmont, Operations Division
Subject: Repairs

We are taking this opportunity to inform you that we have recently instituted a new procedure for all equipment repair requests. Effective immediately, we are no longer using the Equipment Repair Form that we formerly used. We want to move everyone to an online database system. These new procedures will help us repair your equipment faster and reduce the many mix-ups we suffered in the past. You will find the new procedure at www.online-repairs.net. That's where you log in. You should indicate the kind of equipment repair you need. It may be a desktop, laptop, printer, copier, or other approved equipment. Then you should begin the process of data entry for your specific problem by selecting Create New Ticket. That's where you explain the problem. Following prompts on the screen, you will also need to identify the manufacturer, model number, and serial number. This information will appear on the new ticket, which should be printed and attached securely to the equipment.

If you have any questions, do not hesitate to call Rhonda at Extension 488. You can also write to her at rhonda.rivera@declux.net if you can't reach her by phone.

Uses vague subject line
Lacks explanation of main idea in opening
Emphasizes "we" view rather than "you" view with reader benefits
Employs wordy, dense paragraph instead of numbered steps to explain new procedure
Closes with cliché expression (*do not hesitate*)

REVISION

MEMORANDUM

Date: February 2, 2020

To: Staff Members

From: Brian Belmont, Operations Division *B.B.*

Subject: New Procedure for Reporting Equipment Repair Requests

Effective immediately, please use a new online repair database system to report requests for equipment repairs. The following steps will return your equipment to you more rapidly and efficiently:

1. Log in to www.online-repairs.net.
2. Indicate the kind of repair you need, such as a desktop, laptop, printer, copier, or other approved equipment.
3. Select Create New Ticket and explain the specific problem.
4. Identify the manufacturer, model number, and serial number of the equipment.
5. Print the new ticket and attach it securely to the equipment.

If you have questions, call Rhonda at Extension 488 or write to her at rhonda.rivera@declux.net. Following this new procedure should vastly improve turnaround time and reduce mix-ups.

Employs informative, subject line
Starts with main idea and emphasizes how the new procedure benefits the receiver
Lists easy-to-follow steps, beginning each numbered step with a verb
Closes with follow-up information and reinforces reader benefits

Tips for Writing Instructions

- Arrange steps in the order in which they should be completed.
- Start each step with an action verb in the imperative (command) mood.
- Be careful of tone in writing messages that give orders.
- Strive to show reader benefits if you are encouraging the use of the procedure.

Concept Check

1. Conduct research regarding costly mistakes that resulted from unclear instructions. What is the most costly mistake you discovered?
2. Imagine that your employer put you in charge of managing the organization's Facebook page for a week. Refer to Figure 8.5 as you consider responses to the following online posts, and draft responses:
   a. I love your new full-figure advertising campaign. It's great that your company supports people of all sizes. Keep up the great work!
   b. I've been waiting weeks for my order. Such bad customer service.
   c. The cashiers spend more time on their cell phones than serving customers. Next time I'm going to give them a piece of my mind!

Direct Claims and Complaints

LEARNING OBJECTIVE 3

Prepare messages that make direct claims and voice complaints.

In business things can and do go wrong—promised shipments are late, warrantied goods fail, and service is disappointing. When you as a customer must write to identify or correct a wrong, the message is called a *claim*. Straightforward claims are those to which you expect the receiver to agree readily.

Increasingly, consumers resort to telephone calls, they e-mail their claims, or—as we have seen—they vent their peeves in online posts. This is why even in an age of digital communication, claims written as letters are taken more seriously than telephone calls or e-mails. Letters also more convincingly establish a record of what happened. Regardless of channel, straightforward claims use a direct approach. Claims that require a persuasive response are presented in Chapter 10.

Opening a Claim With a Clear Statement

When you, as a customer, have a legitimate claim, you can expect a positive response from a company. Smart businesses want to hear from their customers. They know that retaining a customer is far less costly than recruiting a new customer.

Open your claim with a compliment, a point of agreement, a statement of the problem, a brief review of action you have taken to resolve the problem, or a clear statement of the action you want. You might expect a replacement, a refund, a new product, credit to your account, correction of a billing error, free repairs, free inspection, or cancellation of an order. When the remedy is obvious, state it immediately (*Please correct an erroneous double charge of $59 to my credit card for LapLink migration software. I accidentally clicked the Submit button twice*). When the remedy is less obvious, you might ask for a change in policy or procedure or simply for an explanation (*Because three of our employees with confirmed reservations were refused rooms September 16 in your hotel, would you please clarify your policy regarding reservations and late arrivals*).

Explaining and Supporting a Claim

In the body of a claim message, explain the problem and justify your request. Provide the necessary details so that the difficulty can be corrected without further correspondence. Avoid becoming angry or trying to assign blame. Bear in mind that the person reading your message is seldom responsible for the problem. Instead, state the facts logically, objectively, and unemotionally; let the reader decide on the causes. If you choose to send a letter by postal mail, include copies of all pertinent documents, such as invoices, sales slips, catalogue descriptions, and repair records. Of course, those receipts and other documents can also be scanned and attached to an e-mail.

If using paper mail, send copies and *not* your originals, which could be lost. When service is involved, cite the names of individuals you spoke to and the dates of calls. Assume that a company honestly wants to satisfy its customers—because most do. When an alternative remedy exists, spell it out (*If you are unable to offer store credit, please apply the second amount of $59 to your TurboSpeed software and a LapLink USB cable that I would like to buy too*).

Concluding With an Action Request

End a claim message with a courteous statement that promotes goodwill and summarizes your action request. If appropriate, include an end date (*I hope you understand that mistakes in ordering online sometimes occur. Because I have enjoyed your prompt service in the past, I hope that you will be able to issue a refund or store credit by May 2*).

Finally, in making claims, act promptly. Delaying claims makes them appear less important. Delayed claims are also more difficult to verify. By taking the time to put your claim in writing, you indicate your seriousness. A written claim starts a record of the problem, should later action be necessary. Be sure to save a copy of your message whether paper or electronic.

Completing the Message and Revising

When Jade Huggins received a statement showing a charge for a three-year service warranty that she did not purchase, she was furious. She called the store but failed to get satisfaction. She decided against voicing her complaint online because she wanted a quick resolution and doubted that a social media post would be noticed by the small business. She chose to write an e-mail to the customer service address featured prominently on the MegaMedia website.

You can see the first draft of her direct claim e-mail in Figure 8.8. This draft gave her a chance to vent her anger, but it accomplished little else. The tone was belligerent, and it assumed that the company intentionally mischarged her. Furthermore, it failed to tell the reader how to remedy the problem. The revision, also shown in Figure 8.8, tempered the tone, described the problem objectively, and provided facts and numbers. Most important, it specified exactly what Jade wanted done.

Posting Complaints and Reviews Online

Social media experts advise that consumers exhaust all other options for claims and complaints with the company before venting online.[8] Just as you probably wouldn't complain to the Better Business Bureau without giving a business at least one chance to respond, you shouldn't express dissatisfaction just to let off steam. Although it may feel good temporarily to rant, most businesses want to please their customers and welcome an opportunity to right a wrong. A well-considered message, whether a letter or an e-mail, allows you to tell the full story and is more likely to be heard.

Two other reasons may dissuade you from letting loose in ill-conceived online comments.

1. Social media posts have a way of ending up in the wrong hands. As always, think whether people you respect and prospective employers would approve. Even anonymous posts can be tracked back to the writer. Moreover, nasty "cyber chest-pounding" might not be taken seriously, and your remarks could be deleted.[10]
2. Businesses and professionals can take individuals to court for negative comments online.

Online negativity is on the rise in Canada, and businesses are wise to be cautious when providing opportunities for online comments and feedback. Because of the increase in online negativity, Canada has implemented a Digital Charter to help combat online hate speech and misinformation.[11] (See Case Connections below.) It's not surprising that the *Toronto Star* decided to remove the comments section from its online articles because of inappropriate posts.[12] Because it is a company's right and responsibility to intervene or shut down unsuitable content, it is important that your messages be respectful and well composed if you want a response or resolution. The tips in Figure 8.9, gleaned from *Consumer Reports*, will allow you to exercise your right to free speech while remaining professional when critiquing a product or service online.

ETHICS CHECK

How Authentic Are Customer Reviews Online?

Not all online customer critiques can be trusted, particularly when so many are anonymous. Bell Canada had to pay $1.25 million in fines after its employees posted positive reviews of their free MyBell Mobile app.[9] As consumers, how much stock should we put in online reviews?

FIGURE 8.8 Direct Claim E-mail

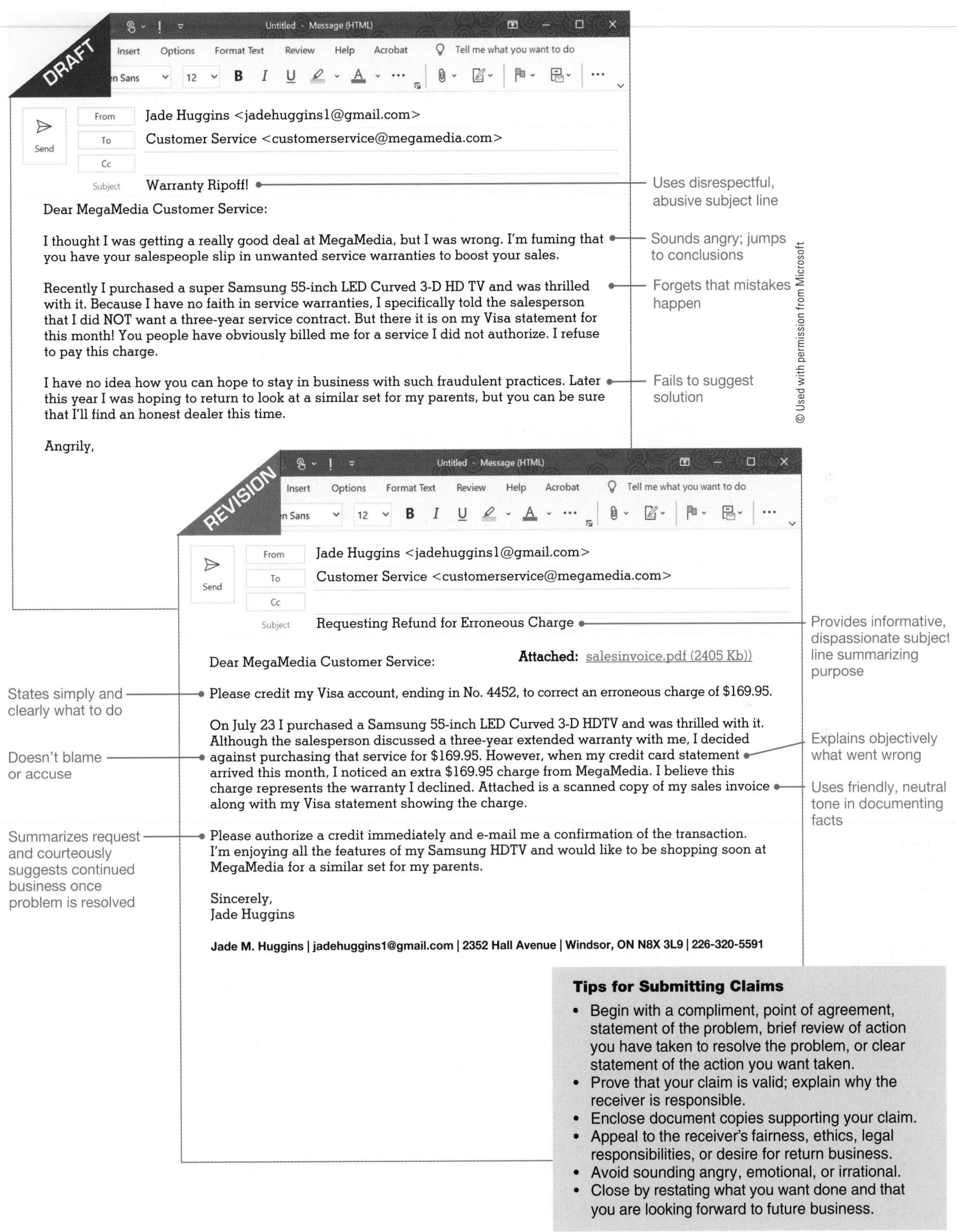

DRAFT
Untitled - Message (HTML)
Insert Options Format Text Review Help Acrobat Tell me what you want to do
From Jade Huggins <jadehuggins1@gmail.com>
To Customer Service <customerservice@megamedia.com>
Cc
Subject Warranty Ripoff!
Uses disrespectful, abusive subject line
Dear MegaMedia Customer Service:
I thought I was getting a really good deal at MegaMedia, but I was wrong. I'm fuming that you have your salespeople slip in unwanted service warranties to boost your sales.
Sounds angry; jumps to conclusions
Recently I purchased a super Samsung 55-inch LED Curved 3-D HD TV and was thrilled with it. Because I have no faith in service warranties, I specifically told the salesperson that I did NOT want a three-year service contract. But there it is on my Visa statement for this month! You people have obviously billed me for a service I did not authorize. I refuse to pay this charge.
Forgets that mistakes happen
I have no idea how you can hope to stay in business with such fraudulent practices. Later this year I was hoping to return to look at a similar set for my parents, but you can be sure that I'll find an honest dealer this time.
Fails to suggest solution
Angrily,
© Used with permission from Microsoft
REVISION
Untitled - Message (HTML)
Insert Options Format Text Review Help Acrobat Tell me what you want to do
From Jade Huggins <jadehuggins1@gmail.com>
To Customer Service <customerservice@megamedia.com>
Cc
Subject Requesting Refund for Erroneous Charge
Provides informative, dispassionate subject line summarizing purpose
Dear MegaMedia Customer Service:
Attached: salesinvoice.pdf (2405 Kb))
States simply and clearly what to do
Please credit my Visa account, ending in No. 4452, to correct an erroneous charge of $169.95.
On July 23 I purchased a Samsung 55-inch LED Curved 3-D HDTV and was thrilled with it. Although the salesperson discussed a three-year extended warranty with me, I decided against purchasing that service for $169.95. However, when my credit card statement arrived this month, I noticed an extra $169.95 charge from MegaMedia. I believe this charge represents the warranty I declined. Attached is a scanned copy of my sales invoice along with my Visa statement showing the charge.
Doesn't blame or accuse
Explains objectively what went wrong
Uses friendly, neutral tone in documenting facts
Summarizes request and courteously suggests continued business once problem is resolved
Please authorize a credit immediately and e-mail me a confirmation of the transaction. I'm enjoying all the features of my Samsung HDTV and would like to be shopping soon at MegaMedia for a similar set for my parents.
Sincerely,
Jade Huggins
Jade M. Huggins | jadehuggins1@gmail.com | 2352 Hall Avenue | Windsor, ON N8X 3L9 | 226-320-5591

Tips for Submitting Claims

- Begin with a compliment, point of agreement, statement of the problem, brief review of action you have taken to resolve the problem, or clear statement of the action you want taken.
- Prove that your claim is valid; explain why the receiver is responsible.
- Enclose document copies supporting your claim.
- Appeal to the receiver's fairness, ethics, legal responsibilities, or desire for return business.
- Avoid sounding angry, emotional, or irrational.
- Close by restating what you want done and that you are looking forward to future business.

FIGURE 8.9 Guidelines for Writing Online Reviews and Complaints

Establish your credibility.

- Zero in on your objective and make your comment as concise as possible.
- Focus only on the facts and be able to support them.

Consider online permanence.

- Know that your review may be posted indefinitely, even if you change your mind and modify a post later.

Check posting rules.

- Understand what's allowed by reading the terms and conditions on the site.
- Keep your complaint clean, polite, and to the point.

Accept offers to help.

- Reply if a business offers to help or discuss the problem; update your original post as necessary.

Provide balanced reviews.

- To be fair, offset criticism with positives to show that you are a legitimate consumer.
- Suggest improvements even in glowing reviews; all-out gushing is suspicious and not helpful.

Refuse payment for favourable critiques.

- Never accept payment to change your opinion or your account of the facts.
- Comply with requests for a review if you are a satisfied customer.

Concept Check

1. After leaving voicemail messages and writing an e-mail, you still haven't heard back from a company about a product you were charged for but never received. You've decided to post a claim on the company's Twitter page. In 280 characters or less, draft an online claim based on the guidelines presented in Figure 8.9.
2. Why should you avoid anger or blame in claim messages?

LEARNING OBJECTIVE 4

Create adjustment messages that salvage customers' trust and promote further business.

Adjustment Messages

When a company receives a claim and decides to respond favourably, the message is called an *adjustment.* Most businesses make adjustments promptly: they replace merchandise, refund money, extend discounts, send coupons, and repair goods. Businesses make favourable adjustments to legitimate claims for two reasons:

1. Consumers are protected by contractual and tort law for recovery of damages.
2. Most organizations genuinely want to satisfy their customers and retain their business.

In responding to customer claims, you must first decide whether to grant the claim. Unless the claim is obviously fraudulent or excessive, you will probably grant it. When you say *yes,* deliver the good news by using the direct strategy. When your response is *no,* the indirect strategy might be more appropriate. Chapter 9 discusses the indirect strategy for conveying negative news. You have three goals in adjustment messages:

- Rectifying the wrong, if one exists
- Regaining the confidence of the customer
- Promoting further business

CASE CONNECTIONS

Canada's Digital Charter

Nicolo Campo/Agf/Shutterstock

Navdeep Singh Bains, Minister of Innovation, Science and Economic Development

Canada's economy relies on digital technology. With e-commerce and the use of social media on the rise, Canadians need to "trust that their privacy is protected, that their data will not be misused, and that companies operating in this space communicate in a simple and straightforward manner with their users."[13] The following are the ten principles of the Digital Charter:

1. Universal Access:

   All Canadians will have equal opportunity to participate in the digital world and the necessary tools to do so, including access, connectivity, literacy and skills.

2. Safety and Security:

   Canadians will be able to rely on the integrity, authenticity and security of the services they use and should feel safe online.

3. Control and Consent:

   Canadians will have control over what data they are sharing, who is using their personal data and for what purposes, and know that their privacy is protected.

4. Transparency, Portability and Interoperability:

   Canadians will have clear and manageable access to their personal data and should be free to share or transfer it without undue burden.

5. Open and Modern Digital Government:

   Canadians will be able to access modern digital services from the Government of Canada, which are secure and simple to use.

6. A Level Playing Field:

   The Government of Canada will ensure fair competition in the online marketplace to facilitate the growth of Canadian businesses and affirm Canada's leadership on digital and data innovation, while protecting Canadian consumers from market abuses.

7. Data and Digital for Good:

   The Government of Canada will ensure the ethical use of data to create value, promote openness and improve the lives of people—at home and around the world.

8. Strong Democracy:

   The Government of Canada will defend freedom of expression and protect against online threats and disinformation designed to undermine the integrity of elections and democratic institutions.

9. Free from Hate and Violent Extremism:

   Canadians can expect that digital platforms will not foster or disseminate hate, violent extremism or criminal content.

10. Strong Enforcement and Real Accountability:

    There will be clear, meaningful penalties for violations of the laws and regulations that support these principles.[14]

How will the Digital Charter improve the ways Canadians conduct business and live their lives?

Revealing Good News Up Front in an Adjustment Message

The primary focus of an adjustment message is on how you are complying with the request, how the problem occurred, and how you are working to prevent its recurrence. Instead of beginning with a review of what went wrong, present the good news in an adjustment message immediately. When Kimberly Lu responded to the claim letter from customer Optima Ventures about a missing shipment, her first draft, shown at the top of Figure 8.10, was angry. No wonder. Optima Ventures apparently had provided the wrong shipping address, and the goods were returned. Once Kimberly and her company decided to send a second shipment and comply with the customer's claim, however, she had to give up the anger. Her goal was to regain the goodwill and the business of this customer. The improved version of her letter announces that a new shipment will arrive shortly.

FIGURE 8.10 Customer Adjustment Letter

DRAFT

Dear Sir:

Your complaint letter dated May 15 has reached my desk. I assure you that we take all inquiries about missing shipments seriously. However, you failed to supply the correct address.

> Fails to reveal good news immediately and blames customer

After receiving your complaint, our investigators looked into your problem shipment and determined that it was sent immediately after we received the order. According to the shipper's records, it was delivered to the warehouse address given on your stationery: 66B Industrial Lane, Toronto, ON M4S 1G9. Unfortunately, no one at that address would accept delivery, so the shipment was returned to us. I see from your current stationery that your company has a new address. With the proper address, we probably could have delivered this shipment.

> Creates ugly tone with negative words and sarcasm

Although we feel that it is entirely appropriate to charge you shipping and restocking fees, as is our standard practice on returned goods, in this instance we will waive those fees. We hope this second shipment finally catches up with you at your current address.

> Sounds grudging and reluctant in granting claim

Sincerely,

REVISION

DAP Digit-All Purveyors
601 Scottsdale Road
Guelph, ON N1C 3E7

Phone: (519) 488-2202
Fax: (519) 489-3320
Web: www.digit-all-purveyors.com

May 22, 2020

Mr. Richard Lopez
Optima Ventures
1432 Front Street
Toronto, ON M6V 2J8

Dear Mr. Lopez:

> Uses customer's name in salutation

Subject: Your May 17 Letter About Your Purchase Order

Your second shipment of the Blu-ray players, video game consoles, and other electronics that you ordered April 18 is on its way and should arrive on May 29.

> Announces good news immediately

The first shipment of this order was delivered May 3 to 66B Industrial Lane, Toronto, ON M4S 1G9. When no one at that address would accept the shipment, it was returned to us. Now that I have your letter, I see that the order should have been sent to 1432 Front Street, Toronto, ON M6V 2J8. When an order is undeliverable, we usually try to verify the shipping address by telephoning the customer. Somehow the return of this shipment was not caught by our normally painstaking shipping clerks. You can be sure that I will investigate shipping and return procedures with our clerks immediately to see if we can improve existing methods.

> Regains confidence of customer by explaining what happened and by suggesting plans for improvement

Your respect is important to us, Mr. Lopez. Although our rock-bottom discount prices have enabled us to build a volume business, we don't want to be so large that we lose touch with valued customers like you. Over the years our customers' respect has made us successful, and we hope that the prompt delivery of this shipment will retain yours.

> Closes confidently with genuine appeal for customer's respect

Sincerely,

Kimberly Lu

Kimberly Lu
Distribution Manager

c Taylor Nelson
Shipping Department

If you decide to comply with a customer's claim, let the receiver know immediately. Don't begin your letter with a negative statement (*We are very sorry to hear that you are having trouble with your dishwasher*). This approach reminds the reader of the problem and may rekindle the heated emotions or unhappy feelings experienced when the claim was written. Instead, focus on the good news. The following openings for various letters illustrate how to begin a message with good news:

> *You're right! We agree that the warranty on your American Standard Model UC600 dishwasher should be extended for six months.*
> *The enclosed cheque for $325 demonstrates our desire to satisfy our customers and earn their confidence.*

In announcing that you will make an adjustment, do so without a grudging tone—even if you have reservations about whether the claim is legitimate. Once you decide to comply with the customer's request, do so happily. Avoid half-hearted or reluctant responses (*Although the American Standard dishwasher works well when used properly, we have decided to allow you to take yours to A-1 Appliance Service for repair at our expense*).

Explaining Compliance in the Body of an Adjustment Message

In responding to claims, most organizations sincerely want to correct a wrong. They want to do more than just make the customer happy. They want to stand behind their products and services; they want to do what is right.

- In the body of the message, explain how you are complying with the claim. Seek to regain the confidence of the customer.
- Expect that a customer who has experienced a difficulty may have lost faith in your organization. Rebuilding that faith is important for future business.
- Notice in Figure 8.10 that the writer promises to investigate shipping procedures to see whether improvements might prevent future mishaps.
- Remember that rational and sincere explanations will do much to regain the confidence of unhappy customers. Avoid emphasizing negative words, such as *trouble*, *regret*, *misunderstanding*, *fault*, *defective*, *error*, *inconvenience*, and *unfortunately*.
- Keep your message positive and upbeat.

Deciding Whether to Apologize

Whether to apologize is a debatable issue. Lawyers generally discourage apologies, fearing that they admit responsibility and will trigger lawsuits. However, both judges and juries tend to look on apologies favourably. As Canadians, we are known for our readiness to say sorry, even if someone else is clearly at fault.[15] Some Canadian provinces have passed an *Apology Act*, "which makes it easier for people to say sorry for their actions without worry that their words will be used against them in a civil suit."[16] Supporters of this law believe it will lead to fewer court cases over damages by allowing those who want only an apology to get what they want without going to court.[17] If you feel that an apology is appropriate, do it early and briefly. You will learn more about delivering effective apologies in Chapter 9 when we discuss negative messages.

Using Sensitive Language in Adjustment Messages

The language of adjustment messages must be particularly sensitive because customers are already upset. Here are some don'ts:

- Don't use negative words.
- Don't blame customers—even when they may be at fault.
- Don't blame individuals or departments within your organization; it's unprofessional.
- Don't make unrealistic promises; you can't guarantee that the situation will never recur.

CHECKLIST

Direct Claim, Complaint, and Adjustment Messages

Messages That Make Claims and Voice Complaints

- **Begin directly with the purpose.** Present a clear statement of the problem or the action requested, such as a refund or an explanation. Add a compliment if you have been pleased in other respects.
- **Explain objectively.** In the body tell the specifics of the claim. Consider reminding the receiver of ethical and legal responsibilities, fairness, and a desire for return business. Provide copies of necessary documents.
- **Conclude by requesting action.** Include an end date, if important. Add a pleasant, forward-looking statement. Keep a copy of the message.
- **Exercise good judgment.** Online postings are permanent. Make your comments concise and focus only on the facts. Respect posting rules and be polite. Provide balanced reviews. Shun anonymity.

Messages That Make Adjustments

- **Open with approval.** Comply with the customer's claim immediately. Avoid sounding grudging or reluctant.
- **In the body, win back the customer's confidence.** Explain the cause of the problem. Apologize if you feel that you should, but do so early and briefly. Avoid negative words, accusations, and unrealistic promises.
- **Close positively.** Express appreciation to the customer for writing, extend thanks for past business, anticipate continued patronage, refer to your desire to be of service, or mention a new product if it seems appropriate.

Showing Confidence in the Closing

End positively by expressing confidence that the problem has been resolved and that continued business relations will result. You might mention the product in a favourable light, suggest a new product, express your appreciation for the customer's business, or anticipate future business. It's often appropriate to refer to the desire to be of service and to satisfy customers. Notice how the following closings illustrate a positive, confident tone:

> *You were most helpful in informing us of this situation and permitting us to correct it. We appreciate your thoughtfulness in writing to us.*
>
> *Thanks for writing. Your satisfaction is important to us. We hope that this refund cheque convinces you that service to our customers is our No. 1 priority. Our goals are to earn your confidence and continue to justify that confidence with quality products and excellent service.*

Although the direct strategy works for many requests and replies, it obviously won't work for every situation. With more practice and experience, you will be able to alter the pattern and apply the writing process to other communication problems. See the Checklist above for a summary of what to do when you must write claim and adjustment messages.

Concept Check

1. When responding favourably to a request that you are not thrilled to grant, why is it important in business to nevertheless sound gracious or even agreeable?
2. Do you agree that saying sorry for a mishap in doing business is difficult? Even aside from fears of litigation, some businesspeople struggle with apologizing properly. Have you experienced situations in which saying sorry was difficult? What makes an apology effective?

LEARNING OBJECTIVE 5

Write special messages that convey kindness and goodwill.

Goodwill Messages

Many communicators are intimidated when they must write goodwill messages expressing thanks, recognition, and sympathy. Finding the right words to express feelings is often more difficult than writing ordinary business documents. That is why writers tend to procrastinate when it comes to goodwill messages. Sending a ready-made card or picking up the telephone is easier than writing a message. Remember, though, that the personal sentiments of the sender are always more expressive and more meaningful to readers than are printed cards or oral messages. Taking the time to write gives more importance to our well wishes. Personal notes also provide a record that can be reread and treasured.

In expressing thanks, recognition, or sympathy, you should always do so promptly. These messages are easier to write when the situation is fresh in your mind. They also mean more to the recipient. Don't forget that a prompt thank-you note carries the hidden message that you care and that you consider the event to be important. The best goodwill messages—whether thanks, congratulations, praise, or sympathy—concentrate on the five Ss. Goodwill messages should be

- **Selfless.** Focus the message solely on the receiver, not the sender. Don't talk about yourself; avoid such comments as *I remember when I* . . . .
- **Specific.** Personalize the message by mentioning specific incidents or characteristics of the receiver. Telling a colleague *Great speech* is much less effective than *Great story about McDonald's marketing in Moscow.* Take care to verify names and other facts.
- **Sincere.** Let your words show genuine feelings. Rehearse in your mind how you would express the message to the receiver orally. Then transform that conversational language to your written message. Avoid pretentious, formal, or flowery language (*It gives me great pleasure to extend felicitations on the occasion of your firm's twentieth anniversary*).
- **Spontaneous.** Keep the message fresh and enthusiastic. Avoid canned phrases (*Congratulations on your promotion* or *Good luck in the future*). Strive for directness and naturalness, not creative brilliance.
- **Short.** Although goodwill messages can be as long as needed, try to accomplish your purpose in only a few sentences. What is most important is remembering an individual. Such caring does not require documentation or wordiness. Individuals and business organizations often use special note cards or stationery for brief messages.

Saying Thank You

A TD Bank study reinforced that the stereotype of polite Canadians is true. In fact the study showed that Canadians say "thank you" even more than they say "I'm sorry." Further, "the TD report says 85 percent of Canadians would rather be thanked in person, on the phone or via a personalized note versus on their mobile device."[18]

When someone has done you a favour or when an action merits praise, you need to extend thanks or show appreciation. Letters of appreciation may be written to past and present customers for their orders, to hosts for their hospitality, to individuals for kindnesses performed, and to employees for a job well done.

Because the receiver will be pleased to hear from you, you can open directly with the purpose of your message. The letter in Figure 8.11 thanks a speaker who addressed a group of marketing professionals. Although such thank-you notes can be quite short, this one is a little longer because the writer wants to lend importance to the receiver's efforts. Notice that every sentence relates to the receiver and offers enthusiastic praise. By using the receiver's name along with contractions and positive words, the writer makes the letter sound warm and conversational.

Written notes that show appreciation and express thanks are significant to their receivers. In expressing thanks you generally write a short note on special notepaper or heavy card stock. The following messages provide models for expressing thanks for a gift, for a favour, and for hospitality.

Expressing Thanks for a Gift. When expressing thanks, tell what the gift means to you. Use sincere, simple statements.

Thanks, Laura, to you and the other members of the department for honouring me with the crystal vase at my twentieth anniversary company party. The height and shape of the vase are perfect to hold roses from my garden. Each time I fill it, I'll think of your thoughtfulness.

Sending Thanks for a Favour. In showing appreciation for a favour, explain the importance of the gesture to you.

I sincerely appreciate your filling in for me last week when I was too ill to attend the planning committee meeting for the spring exhibition. Without your participation, much of my

FIGURE 8.11 Thank-You Letter for a Favour

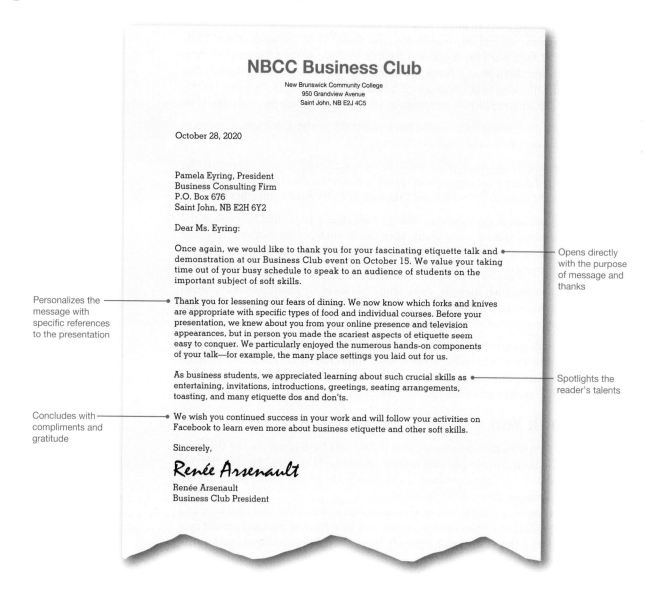

NBCC Business Club

New Brunswick Community College
950 Grandview Avenue
Saint John, NB E2J 4C5

October 28, 2020

Pamela Eyring, President
Business Consulting Firm
P.O. Box 676
Saint John, NB E2H 6Y2

Dear Ms. Eyring:

Once again, we would like to thank you for your fascinating etiquette talk and demonstration at our Business Club event on October 15. We value your taking time out of your busy schedule to speak to an audience of students on the important subject of soft skills.

Thank you for lessening our fears of dining. We now know which forks and knives are appropriate with specific types of food and individual courses. Before your presentation, we knew about you from your online presence and television appearances, but in person you made the scariest aspects of etiquette seem easy to conquer. We particularly enjoyed the numerous hands-on components of your talk—for example, the many place settings you laid out for us.

As business students, we appreciated learning about such crucial skills as entertaining, invitations, introductions, greetings, seating arrangements, toasting, and many etiquette dos and don'ts.

We wish you continued success in your work and will follow your activities on Facebook to learn even more about business etiquette and other soft skills.

Sincerely,

Renée Arsenault

Renée Arsenault
Business Club President

Opens directly with the purpose of message and thanks

Personalizes the message with specific references to the presentation

Spotlights the reader's talents

Concludes with compliments and gratitude

preparatory work would have been lost. Knowing that competent and generous individuals like you are part of our team, Jabari, is a great comfort. I'm grateful to you.

Extending Thanks for Hospitality. When you have been a guest, send a note that compliments the fine food, warm hospitality, excellent host, and good company.

Jeffrey and I want you to know how much we enjoyed the dinner party for our department that you hosted Saturday evening. Your warm hospitality, along with the lovely dinner, created a truly memorable evening. Most of all, though, we appreciate your kindness in cultivating togetherness in our department. Thanks, Jennifer.

Recognizing Employees for Their Contributions. A letter that recognizes specific employee contributions makes the person feel appreciated even if it is not accompanied by a bonus cheque.

Javinder, I am truly impressed by how competently you shepherded your team through the complex Horizon project. Thanks to your leadership, team members stayed on target, met their objectives, and kept the project on track. Most of all, I appreciate the long hours you put in to the final report.

Check out section 8-5a in MindTap, where you can watch a video featuring Phillip Nelson, a senior financial consultant, discuss sending personal but professional goodwill messages.

Replying to Goodwill Messages

Should you respond when you receive a congratulatory note or a written pat on the back? By all means! These messages are attempts to connect personally; they are efforts to reach out, to form professional or personal bonds. Failing to respond to notes of congratulations and most other goodwill messages is like failing to say *You're welcome* when someone says *Thank you.* Responding to such messages is simply the right thing to do. Do avoid, though, minimizing your achievements with comments that suggest you don't really deserve the praise or that the sender is exaggerating your good qualities.

Answering a Congratulatory Note. In responding to congratulations, keep it short and simple.

Thanks for your kind words regarding my award. I truly appreciate your warm wishes.

Responding to Praise. When acknowledging a pat-on-the-back note, use simple words in conveying your appreciation.

Your note about my work made me feel appreciated. I'm grateful for your thoughtfulness.

Expressing Sympathy

Most of us can bear misfortune and grief more easily when we know that others care. Notes expressing sympathy, though, are probably more difficult to write than any other kind of message. Commercial "In sympathy" cards make the task easier—but they are far less meaningful than personal notes.

Sending Condolences. In writing a sympathy note, (a) refer to the death or misfortune sensitively, using words that show you understand what a crushing blow it is; (b) in the case of a death, praise the deceased in a personal way; (c) offer assistance without going into excessive

CHECKLIST

Goodwill Messages

General Guidelines: The Five Ss

- **Be selfless.** Discuss the receiver, not the sender.
- **Be specific.** Instead of generic statements (You did a good job), include special details (*Your marketing strategy to target key customers proved to be outstanding*).
- **Be sincere.** Show your honest feelings with unpretentious language (*We are all very proud of your award*).
- **Be spontaneous.** Strive to make the message natural, fresh, and direct. Avoid canned phrases (*If I may be of service, please do not hesitate . . .*).
- **Keep the message short.** Remember that most goodwill messages are fairly short.

Giving Thanks

- **Cover three points in gift thank-yous.** (a) Identify the gift, (b) tell why you appreciate it, and (c) explain how you will use it.
- **Be sincere in sending thanks for a favour.** Tell what the favour means to you. Maintain credibility with sincere, simple statements.
- **Offer praise in expressing thanks for hospitality.** Compliment, as appropriate, the (a) fine food, (b) warm hospitality, (c) excellent host, and (d) good company.
- **Be specific when recognizing employees.** To make a note of appreciation meaningful, succinctly sum up the accomplishments for which you are grateful.

Responding to Goodwill Messages

- **Respond to congratulations.** Express your appreciation and how good the message made you feel.
- **Accept praise gracefully.** Don't make belittling comments (*I'm not really all that good!*) to reduce awkwardness or embarrassment.

Extending Sympathy

- **Refer to the loss or tragedy directly but sensitively.** In the first sentence, mention the loss and your personal reaction.
- **For deaths, praise the deceased.** Describe positive personal characteristics (*Howard was a forceful but caring leader*).
- **Offer assistance.** Suggest your availability, especially if you can do something specific.
- **End on a reassuring, positive note.** Refer to the strength the receiver finds in friends, family, or faith.

detail; and (d) end on a reassuring, forward-looking note. Sympathy messages may be typed, although handwriting seems more personal. In either case, use notepaper or personal stationery.

We are deeply saddened, Gayle, to learn of the death of your husband. Warren's kind nature endeared him to all who knew him. He will be missed. Although words seem empty in expressing our grief, we want you to know that your friends at QuadCom extend their profound sympathy to you. If we may help you in any way, please call.

We know that the treasured memories of your many happy years together, along with the support of your family and many friends, will provide strength and comfort in the months ahead.

Using E-mail for Goodwill Messages

In expressing thanks or responding to goodwill messages, handwritten notes are most impressive. However, if you frequently communicate with the receiver by e-mail and if you are sure your note will not get lost, then sending an e-mail goodwill message is acceptable. To express sympathy immediately after learning of a death or an accident, you might precede a phone call or a written condolence message with an e-mail. E-mail is a fast and nonintrusive way to show your feelings. However, immediately follow with a handwritten note. Your thoughtfulness is more lasting if you take the time to prepare a handwritten or printed message on notepaper or personal stationery.

Concept Check

1. Describe an occasion in which you should have written a goodwill message but failed to do so. Why was it difficult to write that message? What would make it easier for you to do so?
2. Why is it important to respond to a goodwill message?

SPOTLIGHT ON COMMUNICATION: PART 2

Raven Reads Revisited

CRITICAL THINKING

- If Raven Reads received a claim from a customer who didn't receive their subscription box, what are the three goals for Raven Reads to consider when composing an adjustment letter?
- If a customer writes to complain about something for which Raven Reads is not responsible (such as Canada Post soaking and destroying the subscription box), should the response letter contain an apology? Explain why or why not.

As the winner of the 2018 Startup Canada Indigenous Entrepreneur Award,[19] Nicole McLaren believes in giving back to the community. Proceeds from her sales have been donated to The First Nations Child & Family Caring Society, as well as the Dennis Franklin Cromarty Memorial Fund, which assists "Nishnawbe Aski Nation students' studies in Thunder Bay and at post-secondary institutions."[20]

Courtesy of Raven Reads

> I did about a year of research compiling my business plan so I knew the business model worked well but I was just really worried about the Indigenous specific content. When you choose to start a business that's very centric on anything to do with Indigenous, you need to just always be sensitive to how you're marketing your product. You want to be making sure that you're authentically supporting that issue and giving back to that issue as you go along.[21]

With every subscription, Raven Reads includes a membership to their Facebook Group Book Club to allow readers to connect. Subscribers can also follow the Raven Reads blog to learn about Indigenous cultures and literature.[22]

Summary of Learning Objectives

1 Understand the channels through which positive messages travel, and apply the 3-x-3 writing process.

- When writing neutral and positive messages, you can be direct because they convey routine, nonsensitive information.
- Apply the 3-x-3 writing process as you prewrite, draft, and revise messages.
- Use business letters when a permanent record is required, when formality and sensitivity are essential, and when confidentiality is critical.
- Write business letters on company stationery in block style with all lines starting at the left margin.

2 Compose direct messages that make requests, respond to inquiries online and offline, and deliver step-by-step instructions.

- In messages requesting information or action, state the purpose in the opening; explain the request in the body; express any questions in a parallel and grammatically balanced form; and close by telling the reader courteously what to do, while showing appreciation.
- In complying with requests, deliver the good news in the opening; explain and provide additional information in the body; and write a cordial, personalized closing that tells the reader how to proceed if action is needed.
- When writing instruction messages, divide the instructions into steps; list steps in the correct order; arrange the items vertically with bullets or numbers; begin each step with an action verb using the imperative; and ensure that the instructions don't sound dictatorial.
- When responding online, follow the example of businesses that strive to be positive, transparent, honest, timely, and helpful.

3 Prepare messages that make direct claims and voice complaints.

- When you compose a message to identify a wrong and request a correction, you are writing a claim.
- Begin by describing the problem or action to be taken; in the message body explain the request without emotion; in the closing summarize the request or action to be taken. Include an end date, if applicable, and express faith in future business if the problem is resolved.
- Include copies of relevant documents to support your claim.
- Take your complaint online only after exhausting all other options with the business in question; keep your post concise and clean; focus on your objective; and be prepared to support the facts.

4 Create adjustment messages that salvage customers' trust and promote further business.

- When granting a customer's claim, you are providing an adjustment, which has three goals: (a) rectifying the wrong, if one exists; (b) regaining the confidence of the customer; and (c) promoting further business.
- In the opening immediately grant the claim without sounding grudging. To regain the customer's trust, in the body explain what went wrong and how the problem will be corrected.

- In the closing express appreciation; extend thanks for past business; refer to a desire to be of service; and mention a new product, if appropriate.
- If you believe that an apology should be offered, present it early and briefly.

5 **Write special messages that convey kindness and goodwill.**

- Make sure that messages that deliver thanks, praise, or sympathy are selfless, specific, sincere, spontaneous, and short.
- When thanking someone for a gift, tell why you appreciate it, and explain how you will use the gift.
- When thanking someone for a favour, convey what the favour means to you, but don't gush.
- In expressions of sympathy, mention the loss tactfully; recognize good qualities in the deceased (in the case of a death); sincerely offer assistance; and conclude on a positive, reassuring note.

Chapter Review

1. Explain the types of positive messages and the strategy used when businesspeople write them. (Obj. 1)
2. What are the three benefits of using business letters instead of e-mail? (Obj. 1)
3. What is the best way to close a request message? (Obj. 2)
4. How should employees respond to an online post that violates company policy? (Obj. 2)
5. How should instructions be written? Give a brief original example. (Obj. 2)
6. What is the *imperative mood*, and why is it preferred over the indicative mood? (Obj. 2)
7. What is a *claim*? When should it be straightforward? (Obj. 3)
8. Why should a direct claim be made by letter rather than by e-mail or a telephone call? (Obj. 3)
9. What are a writer's three goals in composing adjustment messages? (Obj. 4)
10. When is it appropriate to use e-mail to send goodwill messages? (Obj. 5)

Critical Thinking

1. A writer compared letters and social media posts: "What is special about a letter is the time that is taken in creating a letter—that someone went to the trouble of finding a piece of paper, sitting down, crafting their thoughts, putting them on paper, and that they created this document really just for me. A letter is a very singular expression, it's a unique document, and for that reason, to get it in the mail feels almost like a gift. . . . It's a piece of paper that I can feel. . . . There's a physical connection."[23] How might these observations apply to business letters? What other special traits can you identify? (Obj. 1)
2. In promoting the value of letter writing, a well-known columnist recently wrote, "To trust confidential information to e-mail is to be a rube."[24] What did he mean? Do you agree? (Objs. 1, 3)
3. Why is it smart to keep your cool when making a claim, and how should you go about it? (Obj. 3)
4. Why is it important to regain the confidence of a customer in an adjustment message? How can it be done? (Obj. 4)
5. **Ethical Issue:** Assume that you have drafted a letter to a customer in which you apologize for the way the customer's personal information was breached by the Accounting Department. You show the letter to your boss, and she instructs you to remove the apology. It admits responsibility, she says, and the company cannot allow itself to be held liable. You are not a lawyer, but you can't see the harm in a simple apology. What should you do? (Obj. 4)

Activities

8.1 Short Responses to Online Comments (Objs. 1–5)

YOUR TASK Explain the positive and negative attributes of the following online posts.[25] Examine the companies' responses to them. Do they follow the guidelines in this chapter? How do the consumers' posts measure up?

Heather Jones **really really poor customer service by you guys. i am now looking into a new auto insurance provider....**

Yesterday at 8:57 am • Like • Comment

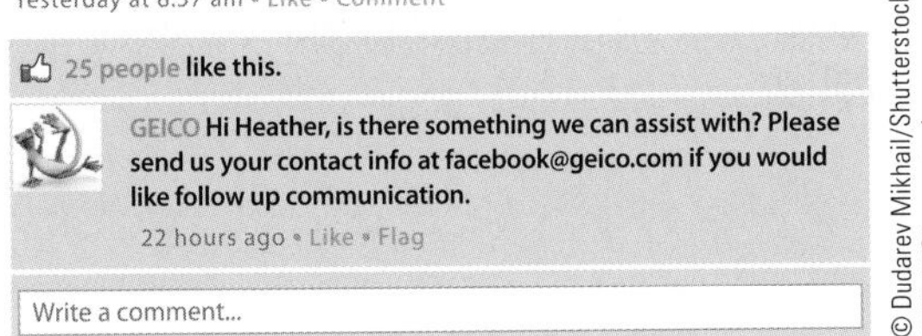

25 people like this.
GEICO Hi Heather, is there something we can assist with? Please send us your contact info at facebook@geico.com if you would like follow up communication.
22 hours ago • Like • Flag
Write a comment...

© Dudarev Mikhail/Shutterstock
© DM7/Shutterstock

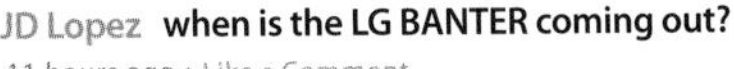

JD Lopez when is the LG BANTER coming out?

11 hours ago • Like • Comment

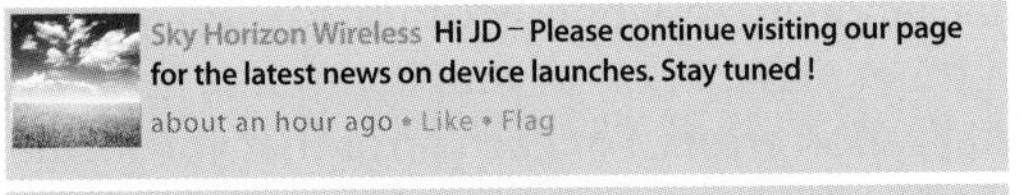

Sky Horizon Wireless Hi JD – Please continue visiting our page for the latest news on device launches. Stay tuned !
about an hour ago • Like • Flag
Write a comment...

© pk chai/Shutterstock
© gillmar/Shutterstock

Maria Daley **You should extend your 15% off since I tried to order things off the website and it crashed. Then I tried calling the 1 800 number and it is constantly busy. Very disappointed that I can not place my order!**

Monday at 11:09 pm • Like • Comment

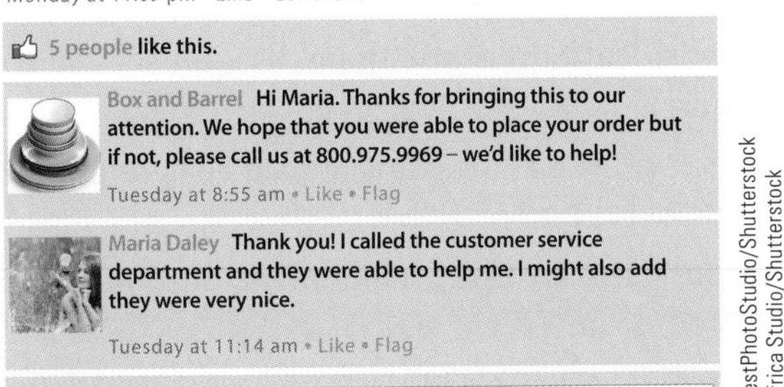

5 people like this.
Box and Barrel Hi Maria. Thanks for bringing this to our attention. We hope that you were able to place your order but if not, please call us at 800.975.9969 – we'd like to help!
Tuesday at 8:55 am • Like • Flag
Maria Daley Thank you! I called the customer service department and they were able to help me. I might also add they were very nice.
Tuesday at 11:14 am • Like • Flag
Write a comment...

© BestPhotoStudio/Shutterstock
© Africa Studio/Shutterstock

8.2 Direct Claim: The Real Thing (Obj. 3)

Like most consumers, you have probably occasionally been unhappy with service or with products you have used.

YOUR TASK Select a product or service that has disappointed you. Write a claim letter requesting a refund, replacement, explanation, or whatever seems reasonable. Generally, such letters are addressed to customer service departments. For claims about food products, be sure to include bar code identification from the package, if possible. Your instructor may ask you to mail this letter. Remember that smart companies want to know what their customers think, especially if a product could be improved. Give your ideas for improvement. When you receive a response, share it with your class.

8.3 Adjustment: We Can Restretch but Not Replace (Obj. 4)

E-mail

Your company, Art International, sells paintings through its website and catalogues. It specializes in workplace art intended for offices, executive suites, conference rooms, and common areas. To make shopping for office art easy, your art consultants preselect art, making sure that the finished product is framed and delivered in perfect shape. You are proud that Art International can offer fine works of original art at incredibly low prices. Recently, you received an e-mail from Gilmour Property Management claiming that a large oil painting that your company sent had arrived in damaged condition. The e-mail said, "This painting sags, and we can't possibly hang it in our executive offices." You were surprised at this message because the customer had signed for delivery and not mentioned any damage. The e-mail went on to demand a replacement.

> You find it difficult to believe that the painting is damaged because you are so careful about shipping. You give explicit instructions to shippers that large paintings must be shipped standing up, not lying down. You also make sure that every painting is wrapped in two layers of convoluted foam and one layer of Perf-Pack foam, which should be sufficient to withstand any bumps and scrapes that negligent shipping may cause. Nevertheless, you decide to immediately review your packing requirements with your shippers.
>
> It's against your company policy to give refunds or replace paintings that the receiver found acceptable when delivered. However, you could offer Gilmour Property Management the opportunity to take the painting to a local framing shop for restretching at your expense. The company could send the restretching bill to Art International at 216 Bloor Street West, Toronto, ON M5P 1K1.

YOUR TASK Compose an e-mail adjustment message that regains the customer's confidence. Send it to Trevor Gilmour at tgilmour@gilmourproperty.com.

8.4 Responding to Good Wishes: Saying Thank You (Obj. 5)

YOUR TASK Write a short note thanking a friend who sent you good wishes when you recently completed your degree.

8.5 Thanks for a Favour: Glowing Letter of Recommendation (Obj. 5)

One of your instructors has complied with your urgent request for a letter of recommendation and has given you an enthusiastic endorsement. Regardless of the outcome of your application, you owe thanks to all your supporters. Respond promptly after receiving this favour. Also, you can assume that your instructor is interested in your progress. Let him or her know whether your application was successful.

YOUR TASK Write an e-mail or, better yet, a letter thanking your instructor. Remember to make your thanks specific so that your words are meaningful. Once you know the outcome of your application, use the opportunity to build more goodwill by writing to your recommender again.

8.6 Extending Sympathy: For a Loss (Obj. 5)

YOUR TASK Imagine that your coworker's beloved family pet recently passed away. Write the coworker a letter of sympathy.

Grammar and Mechanics | *Review 8*

Capitalization

Review Guides 39 to 46 about capitalization in Appendix B, Grammar and Mechanics Guide, beginning on page B-1. On a sheet of paper or on your computer, revise the following sentences to correct capitalization errors. For each error that you locate, write the guide number that reflects this usage. Sentences may have more than one error. If a sentence is correct, write *C*. When you finish, compare your responses with the key in Appendix C.

EXAMPLE: Neither the Manager nor the Vice President would address hiring in the south.

REVISION: Neither the manager nor the vice president would address hiring in the South. [Guides 41, 43]

1. Sylvia's favourite Social Media Platform is Instagram, though she enjoys using facebook and Twitter as well.
2. All westjet airlines passengers must exit the plane at gate 2B in terminal 3 when they reach toronto international airport.
3. Professor mills assigned our class an Essay assignment on Canada's climate change accountability act.
4. My Cousin, who lives in the midwest, has a big mac and a dr. pepper for Lunch nearly every day.
5. Our Sales Manager and Director of Operations thought that the Company should purchase a new nordictrack treadmill for the Fitness room.
6. The World's Highest Tax Rate is in belgium, said professor du-babcock, who teaches at the city university of hong kong.
7. Rachel Warren, who heads our consumer services division, has a Master's Degree in Marketing from mcmaster university.
8. Please consult Figure 2.3 in Chapter 2 to obtain canadian census bureau population figures for the northeast.
9. Last Summer did you see the article titled "the global consequences of using crops for fuel"?
10. Kahee decided that he would return to college in the Winter to finish his diploma in graphic design.

Notes

[1] Raven Reads. (2019). *About us*. https://ravenreads.org/pages/about-us

[2] Ibid. Reprinted courtesy of Raven Reads.

[3] McCue, H. (2019, May 24). *Reconciliation through the arts: Indigenous subscription box opens up a safe space for dialogue*. Anishinabek News. https://anishinabeknews.ca/2019/05/24/reconciliation-through-the-arts-indigenous-subscription-box-opens-up-a-safe-space-for-dialogue/

[4] Ibid.

[5] CBC Radio. (2018, October 19). *The digital divide leaves more Canadians offline than you think*. Spark. https://www.cbc.ca/radio/spark/410-1.4868830/the-digital-divide-leaves-more-canadians-offline-than-you-think-1.4868857

[6] Ford, A. (2011, June 28). *Develop a comment monitoring policy . . . Or use this one*. Tymado Multimedia Solutions. http://tymado.com/2011/06/develop-a-comment-monitoring-policy-or-use-this-one

[7] Cited by permission from Ford, A. (2011, June 28). *Develop a comment monitoring policy . . . Or use this one*. Tymado Multimedia Solutions. http://tymado.com/2011/06/develop-a-comment-monitoring-policy-or-use-this-one

[8] Pilon, M. (2009, August 5). How to complain about a company. *Wall Street Journal*. http://blogs.wsj.com/wallet/2009/08/05/how-to-complain-about-a-company/tab/ print; Torabi, F. (2011, July 28). *Bad customer service? 3 smarter ways to complain*. CBS News. http://www.cbsnews.com/8301-505144_162-41542345/bad-customer-service-3-smarter-ways-to-complain; White, M. (2015, October 19). Lost bags, at 140 characters, and airlines respond. *The New York Times*. http://www.nytimes.com/2015/10/20/business/lost-bags-at-140-characters-and-airlines-respond.html

[9] Lewis, M. (2015, October 14). Fake app ratings net Bell Canada $1.25M fine. *Toronto Star*. https://www.thestar.com/business/2015/10/14/fake-app-ratings-net-bell-canada-125m-fine.html

[10] *New ways to complain: Airing your gripes can get you satisfaction—or trouble*. (2011, August). Consumer Reports. http://www.consumerreports.org/cro/money/consumer-protection/new-ways-to-complain/overview/index.htm

[11] Levesque, C. (2019, May 16). *Canada introducing digital charter to combat hate speech, misinformation*. Global News. https://www.ctvnews.ca/politics/canada-introducing-digital-charter-to-combat-hate-speech-misinformation-1.4424785

[12] Brach, B. (2016, January 10). *CBC News*. Online comments on news stories: a problem for everyone. http://www.cbc.ca/news/canada/british-columbia/syrian-refugees-online-new-comments-ban-1.3391961

[13] Government of Canada. (2019, June 25). *Canada's Digital Charter: Trust in a digital world*. https://www.ic.gc.ca/eic/site/062.nsf/eng/h_00108.html

[14] Ibid.

[15] Hiscock, M. (n.d.). Canadians love to say "sorry" so much, we had to make this law. *The Loop*. http://www.theloop.ca/canadians-love-to-say-sorry-so-much-we-had-to-make-this-law/

[16] Laidlaw, S. (2009, April 27). Saying "sorry" is a way back to grace. *Toronto Star*, pp. E1, E6

[17] Ibid.

[18] D'Souza, J. (2016, August 30). *Canadians tend to say "thank you" more than "sorry."* Huffington Post Canada. http://www.huffingtonpost.ca/2016/08/30/canadian-sayings_n_11725276.html

[19] McCue, H. (2019, May 24). *Reconciliation through the arts: Indigenous subscription box opens up a safe space for dialogue*. Anishinabek News. https://anishinabeknews.ca/2019/05/24/reconciliation-through-the-arts-indigenous-subscription-box-opens-up-a-safe-space-for-dialogue/

[20] Raven Reads. (2019). *About us*. https://ravenreads.org/pages/about-us.

[21] Futurpreneur Canada. (2019, June 21). *Indigenous businesses giving back to communities*. https://www.futurpreneur.ca/en/2019/indigenous-businesses-giving-back-to-canadian-communities/. Reprinted courtesy of Futurpreneur Canada.

[22] Raven Reads. (2019). *Why Raven Reads?* https://ravenreads.org/

[23] *A case for the dwindling art of letter writing in the 21st century*. (2014, June 5). Radio Boston WBUR. http://radioboston.wbur. org/2014/06/05/letter-writing-century

[24] Fallows, J. (2005, June 12). Enough keyword searches. Just answer my question. *New York Times*, p. BU3.

[25] Based on Buddy Media. (2010). *How do I respond to that? The definitive guide to Facebook publishing & moderation*. http://marketingcloud.buddymedia.com/whitepaper-form_the-definitive-guide-to-facebook-publishing-and-moderation_a

CHAPTER 9

Negative Messages

Syda Productions/Shutterstock

LEARNING OBJECTIVES

After studying this chapter, you should be able to

1 Understand the strategies of business communicators in conveying negative news, apply the 3-x-3 writing process, and avoid legal liability.

2 Distinguish between the direct and indirect strategies in conveying unfavourable news.

3 Explain the components of effective negative messages.

4 Apply effective techniques for refusing typical requests or claims and for presenting bad news to customers.

5 Describe and apply effective techniques for delivering bad news within organizations.

SPOTLIGHT ON COMMUNICATION: PART 1

Loblaw: Bread Price-Fixing Scandal

Established in 1919, Loblaw was the first self-serve grocery store in Ontario. Before then, a store clerk would collect items for customers. The concept of self-serve was so popular that 70 more Loblaw stores opened in Ontario within a decade of the first opening.[1]

Andrew Francis Wallace/Toronto Star/Getty Images

With over 2,000 stores across Canada, Loblaw was the top grocery store in the country, with its value placed at C$32.5 billion in the 2017 to 2018 fiscal year.[2]

Because of the store's popularity, consumers were shocked when they learned of Loblaw's involvement in the bread price-fixing scandal. According to news reports, Canada Bread and Weston Bakeries, two of Canada's largest bread-makers, conspired with retailers to inflate "the price of bread by at least $1.50 between 2001 and 2015."[3]

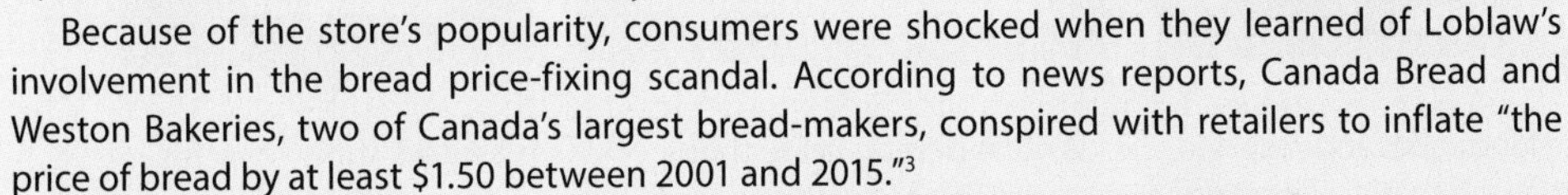

Because George Weston Inc. and Loblaw blew the whistle on the price-fixing scheme, they were granted immunity from prosecution by the Competition Bureau.[4] Even so, Loblaw lost the trust of its customers.

CRITICAL THINKING

- What are some techniques Loblaw could use to deliver bad news to its customers about its involvement in the scandal?
- What goals should Loblaw try to achieve when giving disappointing news to customers, employees, suppliers, or others?

Communicating Negative News Effectively

LEARNING OBJECTIVE 1

Understand the strategies of business communicators in conveying negative news, apply the 3-x-3 writing process, and avoid legal liability.

Bad things happen in all businesses. Goods are not delivered, products fail to perform as expected, service is poor, billing is fouled up, or customers are misunderstood. You may have to write messages ending business relationships, declining proposals, announcing price increases, refusing requests for donations, terminating employees, turning down invitations, or responding to unhappy customers. You might have to apologize for mistakes in orders or pricing, the rudeness of employees, substandard service, defective products, or jumbled instructions. As a company representative, you may have to respond to complaints voiced to the world on social media.

The truth is that everyone occasionally must deliver bad news in business. Because bad news disappoints, irritates, and sometimes angers the receiver, such messages must be written carefully. The bad feelings associated with disappointing news can generally be reduced if the receiver (a) knows the reasons for the rejection, (b) feels that the news was revealed sensitively, and (c) believes the matter was treated seriously and fairly.

In this chapter you will learn when to use the direct strategy and when to use the indirect strategy to deliver bad news. You will study the goals of business communicators in working with unfavourable news and learn techniques for achieving those goals.

Articulating Goals in Communicating Negative News

Delivering negative news is not the happiest communication task you may have, but doing it effectively can be gratifying. As a business communicator working with bad news, you will have many goals, the most important of which are summarized in Figure 9.1.

The strategies and techniques you are about to learn help in conveying disappointing news sensitively and safely. With experience, you will be able to vary these strategies and adapt them to your organization's specific communication tasks.

Applying the 3-x-3 Writing Process

Thinking through the entire writing process is especially important when writing bad-news messages because the way bad news is revealed often determines how it is accepted. You have probably heard people say, "I didn't mind the news so much, but I resented the way I was told!"

FIGURE 9.1 Goals in Conveying Unfavourable News

Explaining clearly and completely

- Readers understand and, in the best case, accept the bad news.
- Recipients do not have to call or write to clarify the message.

Conveying empathy and sensitivity

- Writers use language that respects the reader and attempts to reduce bad feelings.
- When appropriate, writers accept blame and apologize without creating legal liability for the organization or themselves.

Projecting a professional image

Writers stay calm, use polite language, and respond with clear explanations of why a negative message was necessary even when irate customers sound threatening and overstate their claims.

Maintaining friendly relations

Writers demonstrate their desire to continue pleasant relations with the receivers and to regain their confidence.

Being fair

Writers show that the decision was fair, impartial, and rational.

Certain techniques can help you deliver bad news sensitively, beginning with the familiar 3-x-3 writing process.

Analysis, Anticipation, and Adaptation. In Phase 1 (prewriting), you need to analyze the bad news and anticipate its effect on the receiver.

- Consider how the message will affect its receiver. If the disappointment will be mild, announce it directly—for example, a small rate increase in an online subscription.
- Use techniques to reduce the pain if the bad news is serious or personal.
- Choose words that show that you respect the reader as a responsible, valuable person.
- Select the best channel to deliver the bad news.
- Retain the goodwill of the customer. A letter on company stationery will be more impressive than an e-mail.

Research, Organization, and Drafting. In Phase 2 (drafting), you will gather information and brainstorm for ideas.

- Jot down all the reasons you have that explain the bad news. If four or five reasons prompted your negative decision, concentrate on the strongest and safest ones.
- Avoid presenting any weak reasons as readers may seize on them to reject the entire message. Include an ample explanation of the negative situation, and avoid fixing blame.
- Conduct research, if necessary, to help you explain what went wrong and why a decision or an action is necessary.

Editing, Proofreading, and Evaluating. In Phase 3 (revising), you will read over your message carefully to ensure that it says what you intend.

- Check your wording to be sure you are concise without being abrupt.
- Edit and improve coherence and tone. Readers are more likely to accept negative messages if the tone is friendly and respectful.

CENGAGE

MINDTAP

Check out section 9-1b in MindTap, where you can watch a video featuring Courtney Thorne, an editor, discuss how to convey negative news in an e-mail message.

- Proofread your message carefully.
- Evaluate your message. Is it too blunt? Too subtle? Have you delivered the bad news clearly but professionally?

Conveying Negative News Without Incurring Legal Liability

Before we examine the components of a negative message, let's look more closely at how you can avoid exposing yourself and your employer to legal liability when writing negative messages. Although we can't always anticipate the consequences of our words, we should be alert to three causes of legal difficulties: (a) abusive language, (b) careless language, and (c) the good-person syndrome.

Abusive Language. Calling people names (such as *thief*) can get you into trouble. *Defamation* is the legal term for any false statement that harms an individual's reputation. When the abusive language is written, it is called *libel*; when spoken, it is *slander*.

To be actionable (likely to result in a lawsuit), abusive language must be (a) false, (b) damaging to one's good name, and (c) "published"—that is, written or spoken in the presence of others. Therefore, if you were alone with Jane Doe and accused her of accepting bribes and selling company secrets to competitors, she couldn't sue because the defamation wasn't published. Her reputation was not damaged. However, if anyone heard the words or if they were written, you might be legally liable.

You may be prosecuted if you transmit a harassing or libellous message by e-mail or post it on social networking sites, such as Facebook and Twitter.[6] Such electronic transmissions are considered to be published. Moreover, a company may incur liability for messages sent through its computer system by employees. That's why many companies are increasing their monitoring of both outgoing and internal messages. Avoid making unproven charges in writing or letting your emotions prompt abusive language.

Careless Language. As the marketplace becomes increasingly litigious, we must be certain that our words communicate only what we intend. Take the case of a factory worker injured on the job. His lawyer subpoenaed company documents and discovered a seemingly harmless letter sent to a group regarding a plant tour. These words appeared in the letter: "Although we are honoured at your interest in our company, we cannot give your group a tour of the plant operations as it would be too noisy and dangerous." The court found in favour of the worker, inferring from the letter that working conditions were indeed hazardous.[7] The letter writer did not intend to convey the impression of dangerous working conditions, but the court accepted that interpretation.

The Good-Person Syndrome. Most of us hate to have to reveal bad news—that is, to be the bad person. To make ourselves look better, to make the receiver feel better, and to maintain good relations, we are tempted to make statements that are legally dangerous. Business communicators act as agents of their organizations. Their words, decisions, and opinions are assumed to represent those of the organization.

If you want to communicate your personal feelings or opinions, use your home computer or write on plain paper (rather than company letterhead) and sign your name without title or affiliation. Second, volunteering extra information can lead to trouble. Therefore, avoid supplying data that could be misused, and avoid making promises that can't be fulfilled. Don't admit or imply responsibility for conditions that caused damage or injury.

ETHICS CHECK

No References Policy

Some employers in Canada have adopted a "no references policy" for former employees. One reason cited was fear of lawsuits. Employees could potentially sue their employer for false or negative references or for sharing confidential information.[5] Do you think that a "no references policy" is a fair practice?

Concept Check

1. In what ways can you avoid the good-person syndrome when delivering bad news?
2. Consider a time when you received bad news. Was the direct or indirect strategy used? What about the message was effective, and what could have used improvement?

LEARNING OBJECTIVE 2

Distinguish between the direct and indirect strategies in conveying unfavourable news.

Analyzing Negative-News Strategies

To successfully convey bad news, writers must carefully consider the audience, purpose, and context. Approaches to negative news must be flexible.[8] Fortunately, you have two basic strategies for delivering negative news: direct and indirect.

Which approach is better suited for your particular message? One of the first steps you will take before delivering negative news is analyzing how your receiver will react to this news. In earlier chapters we discussed applying the direct strategy to positive messages. We suggested using the indirect strategy when the audience might be unwilling, uninterested, displeased, disappointed, or hostile. In this chapter we expand on that advice and suggest additional considerations that can help you decide which strategy to use.

When to Use the Direct Strategy

The direct strategy saves time and is preferred by some who consider it to be more professional and even more ethical than the indirect strategy. The direct strategy may be more effective in situations such as the following:

- **When the bad news is not damaging.** If the bad news is insignificant (such as a small increase in cost) and doesn't personally affect the receiver, then the direct strategy makes sense.
- **When the receiver may overlook the bad news.** Changes in service, new policy requirements, legal announcements—these critical messages may require boldness to ensure attention.
- **When the organization or receiver prefers directness.** Some companies and individuals expect all internal messages and announcements—even bad news—to be straightforward.
- **When firmness is necessary.** Messages that must demonstrate determination and strength should not use delaying techniques. For example, the last in a series of collection letters that seek payment on an overdue account may require a direct opener.

Notice in Figure 9.2 that the writer, Steven Ellis, is fairly direct in a letter announcing a security breach at Conectix Credit Union. Although he does not blurt out "your information has been compromised," he does announce a potential identity theft problem in the first sentence. He then explains that a hacker attack has compromised roughly a quarter of customer accounts. In the second paragraph, he recommends that Michael Arnush take specific corrective action to protect his identity and offers helpful contact information. The tone is respectful and serious. The credit union's letter is modelled on a template that was praised for achieving a balance between a direct and an indirect opening.[9]

Security breach messages provide a good example of how to employ the direct strategy in delivering bad news. Let's now explore when and how to use the indirect strategy in delivering negative news.

When to Use the Indirect Strategy

Some writing experts suggest that the indirect strategy "ill suits today's skeptical, impatient, even cynical audience."[10] To be sure, in social media, bluntness seems to dominate the public discourse. Directness is equated with honesty; hedging, with deceit. However, many communicators prefer to use the indirect strategy to present negative news. Whereas good news can be revealed quickly, bad news may be easier to accept when broken gradually. Even a direct bad-news message can benefit from sandwiching the negative news between positive statements.[11] Here are typical instances in which the indirect strategy works well:

- **When the bad news is personally upsetting.** If the negative news involves the receiver personally, such as a layoff notice, the indirect strategy makes sense. Telling

FIGURE 9.2 Announcing Bad News Directly: Security Breach Letter

CONECTIX™
CREDIT UNION

380 PARK STREET W, WINDSOR, ON N9A 3A8
www.conectix.com 203.448.2101

September 5, 2020

Mr. Michael Arnush
15 Queen Street
Chatham, ON N7M 2G5

Dear Mr. Arnush:

We are contacting you about a potential problem involving identity theft. On August 30, names, encrypted social insurance numbers, birth dates, and e-mail addresses of fewer than 25 percent of accounts were compromised in an apparent hacker attack on our website. Outside data security experts are working tirelessly to identify the causes of the breach as well as prevent future intrusions into our system. Immediately upon detecting the attack, we notified the local police authorities as well as the RCMP. We also alerted the three major credit-reporting agencies.

Uses modified direct strategy because urgent action is needed to prevent identity theft

We recommend that you place a fraud alert on your credit file. A fraud alert tells creditors to contact you before they open any new accounts or change your existing accounts. Please call any one of the three major credit bureaus. As soon as one credit bureau confirms your fraud alert, the others are notified to place fraud alerts. All three credit reports will be sent to you, free of charge.

Suggests recommended steps and provides helpful information about credit-reporting agencies

Equifax Canada	Experian	TransUnion Canada
1-800-465-7166	888-397-3742	1-866-525-0262

Even if you do not find any suspicious activity on your initial credit reports, the Canadian Anti-Fraud Centre (CAFC) recommends that you check your credit reports periodically. Victim information sometimes is held for use or shared among a group of thieves at different times. Checking your credit reports periodically can help you spot problems and address them quickly.

Gives reasons for the recommended action, provides contact information, and offers additional pointers

If you find suspicious activity on your credit reports or have reason to believe your information is being misused, call your local police department and file a police report. Get a copy of the report; many creditors want the information it contains to absolve you of the fraudulent debts. You also should file a complaint with the "CAFC" at www.antifraudcentre-centreantifraude.ca or at 1-888-654-9426.

Please visit our website at www.conectix.com/databreach for updates on the investigation, or call our privacy hotline at 800-358-4422. Affected customers will receive free credit-monitoring services for one year.

Ends by providing more helpful information, company phone number, and offer of one-year free credit monitoring

Sincerely,

Steven Ellis

Steven Ellis
Customer Service

employees that they no longer have a job is probably best done in person and by starting indirectly and giving reasons first. When a company has made a mistake that inconveniences or disadvantages a customer, the indirect strategy also makes sense.

- **When the bad news will provoke a hostile reaction.** When your message will irritate or infuriate the recipient, the indirect method may be best. It begins with a buffer and reasons, thus encouraging the reader to finish reading or hearing the message. A blunt announcement may make the receiver stop reading.
- **When the bad news threatens the customer relationship.** If the negative message may damage a customer relationship, the indirect strategy may help salvage the customer

FIGURE 9.3 Comparing the Direct and Indirect Strategies for Negative Messages

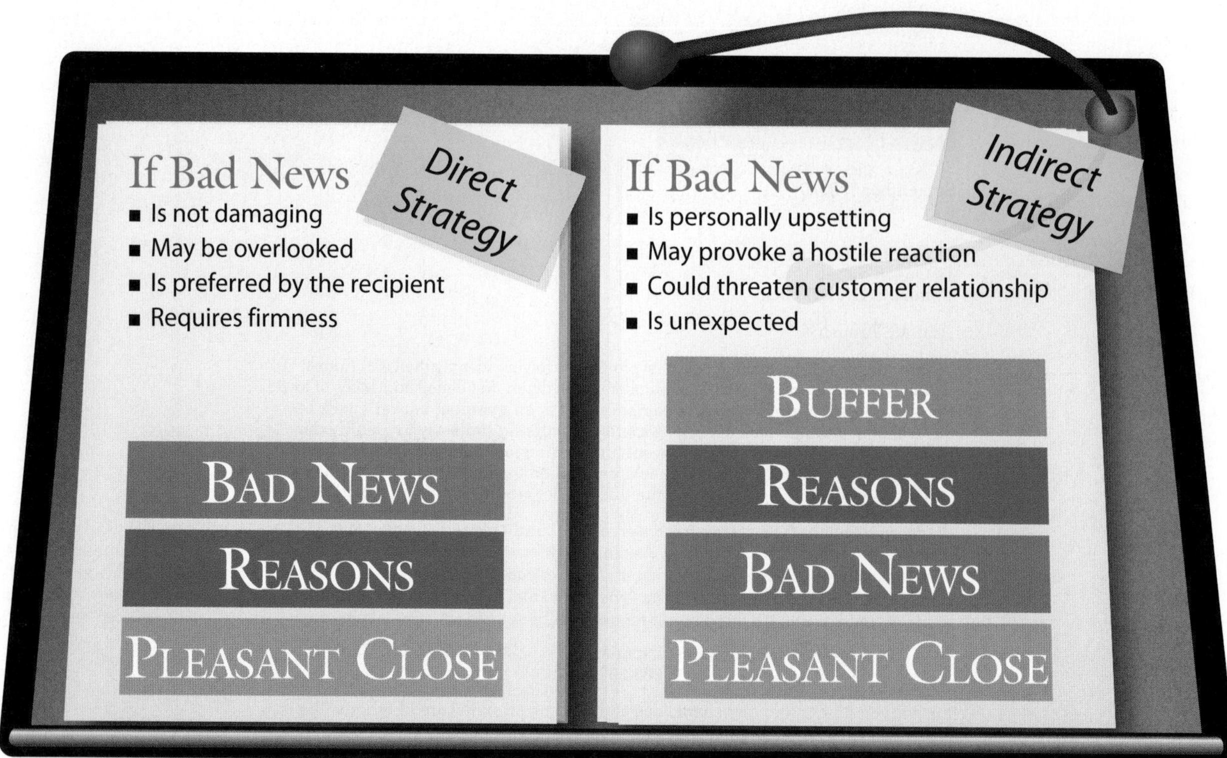

bond. Beginning slowly and presenting reasons that explain what happened can be more helpful than directly announcing bad news or failing to adequately explain the reasons.

- **When the bad news is unexpected.** Readers who are surprised by bad news tend to have a more negative reaction than those who expected it. If a company suddenly closes an office or a plant and employees had no inkling of the closure, that bad news would be better received if it were revealed cautiously with reasons first.

Whether to use the direct or indirect strategy depends largely on the situation, the reaction you expect from the audience, and your goals. As you can see in Figure 9.3, the major differences between the two strategies are whether you start with a buffer and how early you explain the reasons for the negative news.

Keeping the Indirect Strategy Ethical

You may worry that the indirect organizational strategy is unethical or manipulative because the writer deliberately delays the main idea. However, breaking bad news bluntly can cause pain and hard feelings. By delaying bad news, you soften the blow somewhat and ensure that your reasoning will be read while the receiver is still receptive. In using the indirect strategy, your motives are not to deceive the reader or to hide the news. Rather, your goal is to be a compassionate yet effective communicator.

The key to ethical communication lies in the motives of the sender. Unethical communicators *intend to deceive*. Although the indirect strategy provides a setting in which to announce bad news, it should not be used to avoid or misrepresent the truth. As you will see in Chapter 10, misleading, deceptive, and unethical claims are never acceptable.

CASE CONNECTIONS

Canadian Niceness

A stereotype about Canadians is that we are all nice. The Canada Project conducted a survey that revealed that "66 per cent of respondents" agree with this sentiment. Further research indicates that the "stereotype may lead Canadians to act nice" or to use nicer words online when compared to our American neighbours.[12] A survey of Twitter showed the following results:

> Canadians are in fact much nicer than Americans—at least on the social media platform. While Canadians commonly used words like "favourite", "gorgeous", "great", and "amazing", Americans favoured more negative words like "damn", "hate", "bored" and "annoying."[13]

This may indicate, however, that Canadians are perceived as nice because of how we speak, not necessarily as a reflection of our true personalities.[14]

TierneyMJ/Shutterstock

- How might Canadians' tendency to say nice things affect the delivery of negative news?

Concept Check

1. Many people say they prefer the direct approach when receiving bad news. What situational factors might cause you to use the indirect approach with these people?
2. When is it unethical to use the indirect strategy?

Composing Effective Negative Messages

LEARNING OBJECTIVE 3

Explain the components of effective negative messages.

Even though it may be impossible to make the receiver happy when delivering negative news, you can reduce bad feelings and resentment by structuring your message sensitively. Most negative messages contain some or all of these parts: buffer, reasons, bad news, and closing. This section also discusses apologies and how to convey empathy in delivering bad news.

Opening Indirect Messages With a Buffer

A buffer is a device to reduce shock or pain. To buffer the pain of bad news, begin with a neutral but meaningful statement that makes the reader continue reading. The buffer should be relevant and concise and provide a natural transition to the explanation that follows. The individual situation, of course, will help determine what you should put in the buffer. Avoid trite buffers such as *Thank you for your letter.*

Not all business communication authors agree that buffers increase the effectiveness of negative messages. However, in many cultures softening bad news is appreciated. Following are various buffer possibilities.

Best News. Start with the part of the message that represents the best news. For example, a message to workers announced new health plan rules limiting prescriptions to a 34-day supply and increasing co-payments. With home delivery, however, employees could save up to $24 on each prescription. To emphasize the good news, you might write, *You can now achieve significant savings and avoid trips to the drugstore by having your prescription drugs delivered to your home.*[15]

The Canadian Press/Tom Hanson

Canada has publicly apologized to Indigenous peoples for the residential school system, to Japanese Canadians for the internment camps during World War II, to Chinese Canadians for a head tax introduced in the 19th century, and to the Inuit of Inukjuak who were relocated from northern Québec and left near the North Pole without sufficient supplies.[16] Many of the Canadians who suffered are no longer living to hear the apology. What is the value of these apologies to their relatives, Canadian communities, and Canada as a whole?

Compliment. Praise the receiver's accomplishments, organization, or efforts, but do so with honesty and sincerity. For instance, in a letter declining an invitation to speak, you could write, *The Thalians have my sincere admiration for their fundraising projects on behalf of hungry children. I am honoured that you asked me to speak Friday, November 5.*

Appreciation. Convey thanks for doing business, for sending something, for showing confidence in your organization, for expressing feelings, or simply for providing feedback. Suppose you had to draft a letter that refuses employment. You could say, *I appreciated learning about the hospitality management program at Niagara College and about your qualifications in our interview last Friday.* Avoid thanking the reader, however, for something you are about to refuse.

Agreement. Make a relevant statement with which both reader and receiver can agree. A letter that rejects a loan application might read, *We both realize how much the export business has been affected by the relative weakness of the dollar in the past two years.*

Facts. Provide objective information that introduces the bad news. For example, in a memo announcing cutbacks in the hours of the employees' cafeteria, you might say, *During the past five years, the number of employees eating breakfast in our cafeteria has dropped from 32 percent to 12 percent.*

Understanding. Show that you care about the reader. Notice how in this letter to customers announcing a product defect, the writer expresses concern: *We know that you expect superior performance from all the products you purchase from OfficeCity. That's why we're writing personally about the Omega printer cartridges you recently ordered.*

Apologizing

You learned about making apologies in adjustment messages discussed in Chapter 8. We expand that discussion here because apologies are often part of negative-news messages. The truth is that sincere apologies work. Apologies to customers are especially important if you or your company erred. They cost nothing, and they go a long way in soothing hard feelings. For example, when the Royal Bank of Canada received backlash from an outsourcing arrangement it made for technical services, it posted an open letter to all Canadians. The letter addressed the concerns that were raised and apologized to the employees affected by the outsourcing, admitting that the company should have been more sensitive.[17]

Professional writer John Kador recommends what he calls "the 5Rs model" for effective apologies in business messages,[18] summarized in Figure 9.4. Consider these poor and improved apologies:

Poor apology: *We regret that you are unhappy with the price of frozen yogurt purchased at one of our self-serve scoop shops.*

Improved apology: *We are genuinely sorry that you were disappointed in the price of frozen yogurt recently purchased at one of our self-serve scoop shops. Your opinion is important to us, and we appreciate your giving us the opportunity to look into the problem you describe.*

Poor apology: *We apologize if anyone was affected.*

Improved apology: *I apologize for the frustration our delay caused you. As soon as I received your message, I began looking into the cause of the delay and realized that our delivery tracking system must be improved.*

FIGURE 9.4 Apologizing Effectively in the Digital Age: The 5Rs

Recognition
Acknowledge the specific offence.

- Organizations that apologize have better outcomes.
- Individuals who apologize well rise higher in management and have better relationships.

Responsibility
Accept personal responsibility.

- Accountability means taking responsibility and rejecting defensiveness.
- Accountability is an important skill.
- The cover-up is always worse than the crime.

Restitution
Explain exactly how you will fix it.

- A concrete explanation of what you will do to make things right is best.
- The remedy should be appropriate, adequate, and satisfying.

Remorse
Embrace *I apologize* and *I am sorry*.

- Apologies may become necessary unexpectedly.
- We can prevent automatic defensiveness by being prepared to apologize when the need arises.
- Apologies should be honest, sincere, and authentic.

Repeating
Say it won't happen again and mean it.

- Written apologies are more formal than spoken but work about the same.
- By communicating effectively over the long term, businesses gain the trust of employees, the public, as well as the media and are therefore better equipped to weather crises successfully.

Showing Empathy

One of the hardest things to do in negative messages is to convey sympathy and empathy. As discussed in Chapter 3, *empathy* is the ability to understand and enter into the feelings of another.

Here are some examples of ways to express empathy in written messages:

- In writing to an unhappy customer: We did not intentionally delay the shipment, and we sincerely regret the disappointment and frustration you must have suffered.
- In laying off employees: It is with great regret that we must take this step. Rest assured that I will be more than happy to write letters of recommendation for anyone who asks.
- In responding to a complaint: I am deeply saddened that our service failure disrupted your sale, and we will do everything in our power to. . . .
- In showing genuine feelings: You have every right to be disappointed. I am truly sorry that. . . .

Presenting the Reasons

Providing an explanation reduces feelings of ill will and improves the chances that readers will accept the bad news. Without sound reasons for denying a request, refusing a claim, or revealing other bad news, a message will fail, no matter how cleverly it is organized or written. For example, if you must deny a customer's request, as part of your planning before writing, you analyzed the request and decided to refuse it for specific reasons. Where do you place your reasons? In the indirect strategy, the reasons appear before the bad news. In the direct strategy, the reasons appear immediately after the bad news.

Explaining Clearly. If the reasons are not confidential and if they will not create legal liability, you can be specific: *Growers supplied us with a limited number of patio roses, and our demand this year was twice that of last year.* In refusing a speaking engagement, tell why the date is impossible: *On January 17 we have a board of directors meeting that I must attend.* Don't, however, make unrealistic or dangerous statements in an effort to be the "good person."

Citing Reader or Other Benefits, If Plausible. Readers are more open to bad news if in some way, even indirectly, it may help them. Readers also accept bad news more readily if they recognize that someone or something else benefits, such as other workers or the environment: *Although we would like to consider your application, we prefer to fill managerial positions from within.* Avoid trying to show reader benefits, though, if they appear insincere: *To improve our service to you, we are increasing our brokerage fees.*

Explaining Company Policy. Readers resent blanket policy statements prohibiting something: *Company policy requires us to promote from within.* Instead of hiding behind company policy, gently explain why the policy makes sense: *We prefer to promote from within because it rewards the loyalty of our employees.* By offering explanations, you demonstrate that you care about readers and are treating them as important individuals.

Choosing Positive Words. Because the words you use can affect a reader's response, choose carefully. Remember that the objective of the indirect strategy is holding the reader's attention until you have had a chance to explain the reasons justifying the bad news. To keep the reader in a receptive mood, avoid expressions with punitive, demoralizing, or otherwise negative connotations. Stay away from such words as *cannot, claim, denied, error, failure, fault, impossible, mistaken, misunderstand, never, regret, rejected, unable, unwilling, unfortunately,* and *violate.*

Showing Fairness and Serious Intent. In explaining reasons, show the reader that you take the matter seriously, have investigated carefully, and are making an unbiased decision. Receivers are more accepting of disappointing news when they feel that their requests have been heard and that they have been treated fairly. In cancelling funding for a program, board members provided this explanation: *As you know, the publication of* Rural Artist *was funded by a renewable annual grant from the Alberta Foundation for the Arts. Recent cutbacks in provincially sponsored city arts programs have left us with few funds. Because our grant has been discontinued, we have no alternative but to cease publication of* Rural Artist. *You have my assurance that the board has searched long and hard for some other viable funding, but every avenue of recourse has been closed before us. Accordingly, June's issue will be our last.*

Cushioning the Bad News

Although you can't prevent the disappointment that bad news brings, you can reduce the pain somewhat by breaking the news sensitively. Be especially considerate when the reader will suffer personally from the bad news. A number of thoughtful techniques can cushion the blow.

Positioning the Bad News Strategically. Instead of spotlighting it, sandwich the bad news between other sentences, perhaps among your reasons. Don't let the refusal begin or end a paragraph; the reader's eye will linger on these high-visibility spots. Another technique that reduces shock is putting a painful idea in a subordinate clause: *Although another candidate was hired, we appreciate your interest in our organization and wish you every success in your job search.* Subordinate clauses often begin with words such as *although, as, because, if,* and *since.*

Using the Passive Voice. Passive-voice verbs enable you to depersonalize an action. Whereas the active voice focuses attention on a person (*We don't give cash refunds*), the passive voice highlights the action (*Cash refunds are not given because . . .*). Use the passive voice for the bad news. In some instances you can combine passive-voice verbs and a subordinate clause: *Although franchise scoop shop owners cannot be required to lower their frozen yogurt prices, we are happy to pass along your comments for their consideration.*

Highlighting the Positive. As you learned earlier, messages are far more effective when you describe what you can do instead of what you can't do. Rather than *We will no longer allow credit card purchases,* try a more positive appeal: *We are now selling gasoline at discount cash prices.*

Implying the Refusal. It is sometimes possible to avoid a direct statement of refusal. Often, your reasons and explanations leave no doubt that a request has been denied. Explicit refusals may be unnecessary and at times cruel. In this refusal to contribute to a charity, for example, the writer never actually says *no: Because we will soon be moving into new offices in Edmonton, all our funds are earmarked for relocation costs. We hope that next year we will be able to support your worthwhile charity.* The danger of an implied refusal, of course, is that it is so subtle that the reader misses it. Be certain that you make the bad news clear, thus preventing the need for further correspondence.

Suggesting a Compromise or an Alternative. A refusal is not as depressing—for the sender or the receiver—if a suitable compromise, substitute, or alternative is available. In denying permission to a group of students to visit a historical private residence, for instance, this writer softens the bad news by proposing an alternative: *Although private tours of the grounds are not given, we do open the house and its gardens for one charitable event in the fall.* You can further reduce the impact of the bad news by refusing to dwell on it. Present it briefly (or imply it), and move on to your closing.

Go to section 9-3e in MindTap, where you can watch a video featuring Jason Allen John, a mortgage agent, discuss how to turn a negative into a positive.

Closing Pleasantly

After explaining the bad news sensitively, close the message with a pleasant statement that promotes goodwill. The closing should be personalized and may include a forward look, an alternative, good wishes, freebies, resale information, or a sales promotion. *Resale* refers to mentioning a product or service favourably to reinforce the customer's choice. For example, *you chose our best-selling model.*

Forward Look. Anticipate future relations or business. A letter that refuses a contract proposal might read: Thanks for your bid. We look forward to working with your talented staff when future projects demand your special expertise.

Alternative Follow-Up. If an alternative exists, end your letter with follow-through advice. For example, in reacting to an Internet misprint: Please note that our website contained an unfortunate misprint offering $850-per-night Whistler bungalows at $85. Although we cannot honour that rate, we are offering a special half-price rate of $425 to those who responded.

Good Wishes. A letter rejecting a job candidate might read: We appreciate your interest in our company, and we extend to you our best wishes in your search to find the perfect match between your skills and job requirements.

Freebies. When customers complain—primarily about food products or small consumer items—companies often send coupons, samples, or gifts to restore confidence and to promote future business. In response to a customer's complaint, you could write: *Your loyalty and your concern about our frozen entrées are genuinely appreciated. Because we want you to continue enjoying our healthy and convenient dinners, we are enclosing a coupon for your next Keybrand entrée.*

Resale or Sales Promotion. When the bad news is not devastating or personal, references to resale information or promotion may be appropriate: The computer workstations you ordered are unusually popular because of their scratch-resistant finishes. To help you locate hard-to-find accessories for these workstations, we invite you to visit our website for a huge selection of compatible devices and PC toolkits.

Avoid endings that sound canned, insincere, inappropriate, or self-serving. Don't invite further correspondence (*If you have any questions, do not hesitate . . .*), and don't refer to the bad news. Figure 9.5 reviews suggestions for delivering bad news sensitively.

FIGURE 9.5 Delivering Bad News Sensitively

1 Buffer	2 Reasons	3 Bad News	4 Closing
• Best news • Compliment • Appreciation • Agreement • Facts • Understanding • Apology	• Cautious explanation • Reader or other benefits • Company policy explanation • Positive words • Evidence that the matter was considered fairly and seriously	• Embedded placement • Passive voice • Implied refusal • Compromise • Alternative	• Forward look • Information about alternative • Good wishes • Freebies • Resale • Sales promotion

Concept Check

1. Which strategies have you used to soften the blow of significant bad news with your family and friends? If you haven't, imagine situations in which such strategic thinking might be wise.
2. Discuss your own examples of effective and ineffective apologies. Which elements determine whether we find an apology credible and sincere?

LEARNING OBJECTIVE 4

Apply effective techniques for refusing typical requests or claims and for presenting bad news to customers.

Refusing Typical Requests and Claims

Businesses must occasionally respond to disappointed customers in print and online. When you must refuse typical requests, you will first think about how the receiver will react to your refusal and decide whether to use the direct or the indirect strategy. If you have any doubt, use the indirect strategy.

Rejecting Requests for Favours, Money, Information, and Action

Requests for favours, money, information, and action may come from charities, friends, or business partners. Many are from people representing commendable causes, and you may wish you could comply. However, resources are usually limited. In a letter from Delta Management Associates, shown in Figure 9.6, the company must refuse a request for a donation to a charity. Following the indirect strategy, the letter begins with a buffer acknowledging the request. It also praises the good work of the charity and uses those words as a transition to the second paragraph. In the second paragraph, the writer explains why the company cannot donate. Notice that the writer reveals the refusal without actually stating it (*Because of internal restructuring and the economic downturn, we are forced to take a much harder look at funding requests that we receive this year*). This gentle refusal makes it unnecessary to be blunter in stating the denial.

In some donation refusal letters, the reasons may not be fully explained: Although we can't provide financial support at this time, we unanimously agree that the Make-A-Wish Foundation contributes a valuable service to sick children. The emphasis is on the foundation's good deeds rather than on an explanation for the refusal.

Messages that refuse requests for favours, money, information, and action can often be tactfully handled by showing appreciation for the inquiry and respect for the writer. Businesses that are required to write frequent refusals might prepare a form letter, changing a few variables as needed.

FIGURE 9.6 Refusing Donation Request

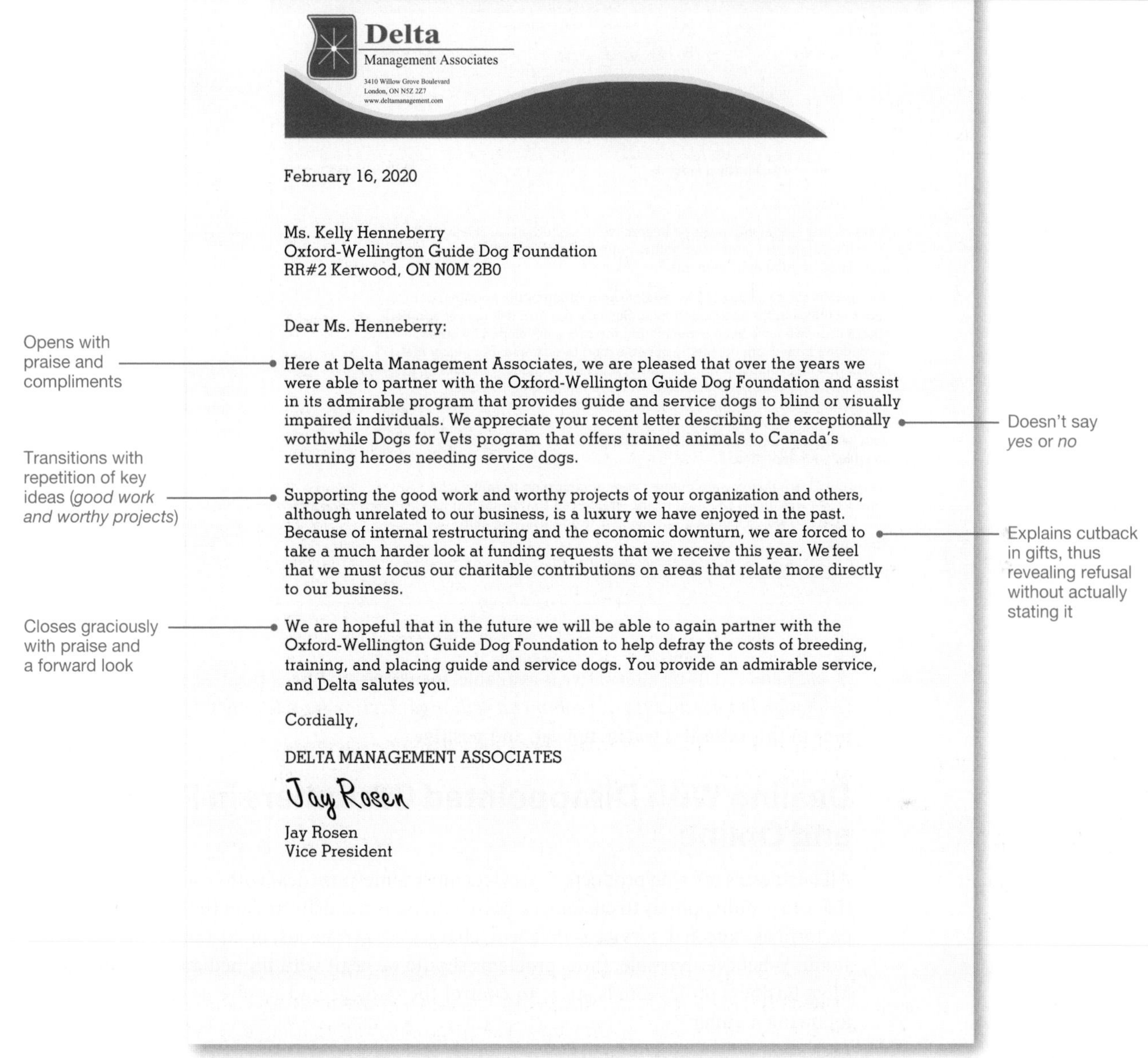

Delta
Management Associates
3410 Willow Grove Boulevard
London, ON N5Z 2Z7
www.deltamanagement.com
Opens with praise and compliments
Transitions with repetition of key ideas (*good work and worthy projects*)
Closes graciously with praise and a forward look
Doesn't say *yes* or *no*
Explains cutback in gifts, thus revealing refusal without actually stating it

February 16, 2020

Ms. Kelly Henneberry
Oxford-Wellington Guide Dog Foundation
RR#2 Kerwood, ON N0M 2B0

Dear Ms. Henneberry:

Here at Delta Management Associates, we are pleased that over the years we were able to partner with the Oxford-Wellington Guide Dog Foundation and assist in its admirable program that provides guide and service dogs to blind or visually impaired individuals. We appreciate your recent letter describing the exceptionally worthwhile Dogs for Vets program that offers trained animals to Canada's returning heroes needing service dogs.

Supporting the good work and worthy projects of your organization and others, although unrelated to our business, is a luxury we have enjoyed in the past. Because of internal restructuring and the economic downturn, we are forced to take a much harder look at funding requests that we receive this year. We feel that we must focus our charitable contributions on areas that relate more directly to our business.

We are hopeful that in the future we will be able to again partner with the Oxford-Wellington Guide Dog Foundation to help defray the costs of breeding, training, and placing guide and service dogs. You provide an admirable service, and Delta salutes you.

Cordially,

DELTA MANAGEMENT ASSOCIATES

Jay Rosen

Jay Rosen
Vice President

Declining Invitations

When you must decline an invitation to speak or make a presentation, you generally try to provide a response that says more than *I can't* or *I don't want to.* Unless the reasons are confidential or business secrets, try to explain them. Because responses to invitations are often taken personally, make a special effort to soften the refusal. In the e-mail shown in Figure 9.7, an accountant must say *no* to the invitation from a friend's son to speak before the young man's campus student association. This refusal starts with conviviality and compliments.

The writer then explains why he cannot accept. The refusal is embedded in a long paragraph and de-emphasized in a subordinate clause. (*Although your invitation must be declined*). The reader naturally concentrates on the main clause that follows (*I would like to*

FIGURE 9.7 Declining an Invitation

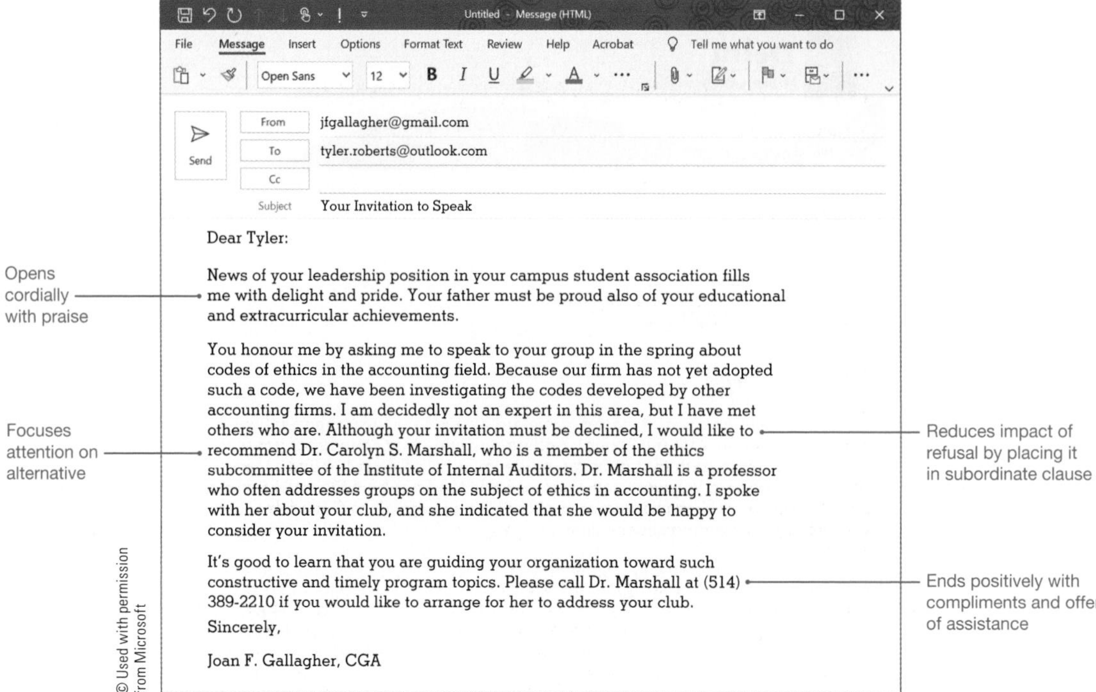
Untitled - Message (HTML)
File
Message
Insert
Options
Format Text
Review
Help
Acrobat
Tell me what you want to do
Send
From
jfgallagher@gmail.com
To
tyler.roberts@outlook.com
Cc
Subject
Your Invitation to Speak
Dear Tyler:
News of your leadership position in your campus student association fills me with delight and pride. Your father must be proud also of your educational and extracurricular achievements.
You honour me by asking me to speak to your group in the spring about codes of ethics in the accounting field. Because our firm has not yet adopted such a code, we have been investigating the codes developed by other accounting firms. I am decidedly not an expert in this area, but I have met others who are. Although your invitation must be declined, I would like to recommend Dr. Carolyn S. Marshall, who is a member of the ethics subcommittee of the Institute of Internal Auditors. Dr. Marshall is a professor who often addresses groups on the subject of ethics in accounting. I spoke with her about your club, and she indicated that she would be happy to consider your invitation.
It's good to learn that you are guiding your organization toward such constructive and timely program topics. Please call Dr. Marshall at (514) 389-2210 if you would like to arrange for her to address your club.
Sincerely,
Joan F. Gallagher, CGA
Opens cordially with praise
Focuses attention on alternative
Reduces impact of refusal by placing it in subordinate clause
Ends positively with compliments and offer of assistance
© Used with permission from Microsoft

recommend . . .). If no alternative is available, focus on something positive about the situation. (*Although I'm not an expert, I commend your organization for selecting this topic*). Overall, the tone of this refusal is warm, upbeat, and positive.

Dealing With Disappointed Customers in Print and Online

All businesses offering products or services must sometimes deal with troublesome situations that cause unhappiness to customers. Merchandise is not delivered on time, a product fails to perform as expected, service is deficient, charges are erroneous, or customers are misunderstood. Whenever possible, these problems should be dealt with immediately and personally. Most business professionals strive to control the damage and resolve such problems in the following manner:[19]

- Call or e-mail the individual or reply to the online post within 24 hours.
- Describe the problem and apologize.
- Explain why the problem occurred, what you are doing to resolve it, and how you will prevent it from happening again.
- Promote goodwill by following up with a message that documents the phone call or acknowledges the online exchange of posts.

Responding by E-mail and in Hard Copy. Written messages are important (a) when personal contact is impossible, (b) to establish a record of the incident, (c) to formally confirm follow-up procedures, and (d) to promote good relations. Dealing with problems immediately is very important in resolving conflict and retaining goodwill.

A bad-news follow-up letter is shown in Figure 9.8. Consultant Kimberly Haydn found herself in the embarrassing position of explaining why she had given out the name of her client to a salesperson. The client, C & C Resources International, had hired her firm, MKM

FIGURE 9.8 Bad-News Follow-Up Message

MKM CONSULTING ASSOCIATES

942 Lascelles Blvd.
Toronto, ON M4P 2BA

(416) 259-0971
www.mkmconsulting.com

May 7, 2020

Mr. Roger Martinez
Director, Administrative Operations
C & C Resources International
4208 Collins Avenue
Toronto, ON M3H 1A5

Dear Mr. Martinez:

Opens with agreement and apology

You have every right to expect complete confidentiality in your transactions with an independent consultant. As I explained in yesterday's telephone call, I am very distressed that you were called by a salesperson from ABS Payroll Services, Inc. This should not have happened, and I apologize to you again for inadvertently mentioning your company's name in a conversation with a potential vendor, ABS Payroll Services, Inc.

Explains what caused the problem and how it was resolved

Takes responsibility and promises to prevent recurrence

All clients of MKM Consulting are assured that their dealings with our firm are held in the strictest confidence. Because your company's payroll needs are so individual and because you have so many contract workers, I was forced to explain how your employees differed from those of other companies. Revealing your company name was my error, and I take full responsibility for the lapse. I can assure you that it will not happen again. I have informed ABS Payroll Services that it had no authorization to call you directly and that its actions have forced me to reconsider using its services for my future clients.

Closes with forward look

A number of other payroll services offer outstanding programs. I'm sure we can find the perfect partner to enable you to outsource your payroll responsibilities, thus allowing your company to focus its financial and human resources on its core business. I look forward to our next appointment when you may choose from a number of excellent payroll outsourcing firms.

Sincerely,

Kimberly Haydn

Kimberly Haydn
Partner

Tips for Resolving Problems and Following Up

- Whenever possible, call or see the individual involved.
- Describe the problem and apologize.
- Explain why the problem occurred.
- Take responsibility, if appropriate.
- Explain what you are doing to resolve it.
- Explain what you are doing to prevent recurrence.
- Follow up with a message that documents the personal contact.
- Look forward to positive future relations.

Consulting Associates, to help find an appropriate service for outsourcing its payroll functions. Without realizing it, Kimberly had mentioned to a potential vendor (ABS Payroll Services, Inc.) that her client was considering hiring an outside service to handle its payroll. An overeager salesperson from ABS Payroll Services immediately called on C & C Resources International, thus angering the client.

Kimberly Haydn first called her client to explain and apologize. She was careful to control her voice and rate of speaking. She also followed up with the letter shown in Figure 9.8. The letter not only confirms the telephone conversation but also adds the right touch of formality. It sends the nonverbal message that the writer takes the matter seriously and that it is important enough to warrant a hard-copy letter.

Many consumer problems are handled with letters, either written by consumers as complaints or by companies in response. However, e-mail and social networks are firmly established as channels for delivering complaints and negative messages.

Managing Negative News Online. Today's consumers eagerly embrace the idea of delivering their complaints to social networking sites rather than calling customer-service departments. Why rely on word of mouth or send a letter to a company about poor service or a defective product when you can shout your grievance to the entire world?

Airing gripes in public helps other consumers avoid the same problems and may improve the complainer's leverage in solving the problem. In addition, sending a 140-character tweet is much easier than writing a complaint e-mail or letter to a customer-service department or navigating endless telephone menus to reach an agent. Businesses can employ some of the following effective strategies to manage negative news on social networking sites and blogs:

- **Recognize social networks as an important communication channel.** Instead of fearing social networks as a disruptive force, smart companies greet these channels as opportunities to look into the true mindset of customers and receive free advice on how to improve.
- **Become proactive.** Company blogs and active websites with community forums help companies listen to their customers and to spread the word about their own good deeds.
- **Join the fun.** Wise companies have joined Twitter, Facebook, Flickr, YouTube, and LinkedIn so they can benefit from interacting with their customers and the public.
- **Monitor comments.** Many large companies employ social media managers and other digital media staff to monitor online traffic and respond immediately whenever possible. Teams listen online to what people are saying about their companies to engage the positive and address the negative. Because communicating effectively online is an important skill, several Canadian colleges and universities offer social media management programs.

Handling Problems With Orders

Not all customer orders can be filled as received. Suppliers may be able to send only part of an order or none at all. Substitutions may be necessary, or the delivery date may be delayed. Suppliers may suspect that all or part of the order is a mistake; the customer may actually want something else. In writing to customers about problem orders, it is generally wise to use the direct strategy if the message has some good-news elements. However, when the message is disappointing, the indirect strategy may be more appropriate.

Let's say you represent Live and Learn Toys, a large toy manufacturer, and you are scrambling for business in a slow year. A big customer, Child Land, calls in August and asks you to hold a block of your bestselling toy, the Space Station. Like most vendors, you require a deposit on large orders. September rolls around, and you still haven't received any money from Child Land. You must now write a tactful e-mail asking for the deposit—or else you will release the toy to other buyers. The problem, of course, is delivering the bad news without losing the customer's order and goodwill. Another challenge is making sure the reader understands the bad news. An effective message might begin with a positive statement that also reveals the facts:

You were smart to reserve a block of 500 Space Stations, which we have been holding for you since August. As the holidays approach, the demand for all our learning toys, including the Space Station, is rapidly increasing.

Next, the message should explain why the payment is needed and what will happen if it is not received:

Toy stores from St. John's to Victoria are asking us to ship these Space Stations. One reason the Space Station is moving out of our warehouses so quickly is its assortment of gizmos that children love, including a land rover vehicle, a shuttlecraft, a hovercraft, astronauts, and even a robotic arm. As soon as we receive your deposit of $4,000, we will have this popular item on its way to your stores. Without a deposit by September 20, though, we must release this block to other retailers.

The closing makes it easy to respond and motivates action:

For expedited service, please call our sales department at 800-358-4488 and authorize the deposit using your business credit card. You can begin showing the fascinating Live and Learn toy in your stores by November 1.

Denying Claims

Customers occasionally want something they are not entitled to or that you can't grant. They may misunderstand warranties or make unreasonable demands. Because these customers are often unhappy with a product or service, they are emotionally involved. Messages that say *no* to emotionally involved receivers will probably be your most challenging communication task. Fortunately, the reasons-before-refusal plan helps you be empathic and artful in breaking bad news. In denial letters, remember the following:

- Adopt the proper tone.
- Don't blame customers, even if they are at fault.
- Avoid you statements that sound preachy: You would have known that cash refunds are impossible if you had read your contract.
- Use neutral, objective language to explain why the claim must be refused.
- Consider offering resale information to rebuild the customer's confidence in your products or organization.

In Figure 9.9, the writer denies a customer's claim for the difference between the price the customer paid for speakers and the price he saw advertised locally (which would have resulted in a cash refund of $100). Although the catalogue service does match any advertised lower price, the price-matching policy applies *only* to exact models. This claim must be rejected because the advertisement the customer submitted showed a different, older speaker model.

The e-mail to Chris Dandron opens with a buffer that agrees with a statement in the customer's e-mail. It repeats the key idea of product confidence as a transition to the second paragraph. Next comes an explanation of the price-matching policy. The writer does not assume that the customer is trying to pull a fast one. Nor does he suggest that the customer didn't read or understand the price-matching policy. The safest path is a neutral explanation of the policy, along with precise distinctions between the customer's speakers and the older ones. The writer also gets a chance to resell the customer's speakers and demonstrate what a quality product they are. By the end of the third paragraph, it is evident to the reader that his claim is unjustified.

Refusing Credit

As much as companies want business, they can extend credit only when payment is likely to follow. Credit applications, from individuals or from businesses, are generally approved or disapproved based on the applicant's credit history. This record is supplied by a credit-reporting agency, such as Northern Credit Bureau, Equifax, or TransUnion. After reviewing the applicant's record, a credit manager applies the organization's guidelines and approves or disapproves the application.

If you must write a letter to a customer denying credit, you have four goals in conveying the refusal:

- Avoiding language that causes hard feelings
- Retaining the customer on a cash basis
- Preparing for possible future credit without raising false expectations
- Avoiding disclosures that could cause a lawsuit

Because credit applicants are likely to continue to do business with an organization even if they are denied credit, you will want to do everything possible to encourage that patronage.

FIGURE 9.9 E-mail Denying a Claim

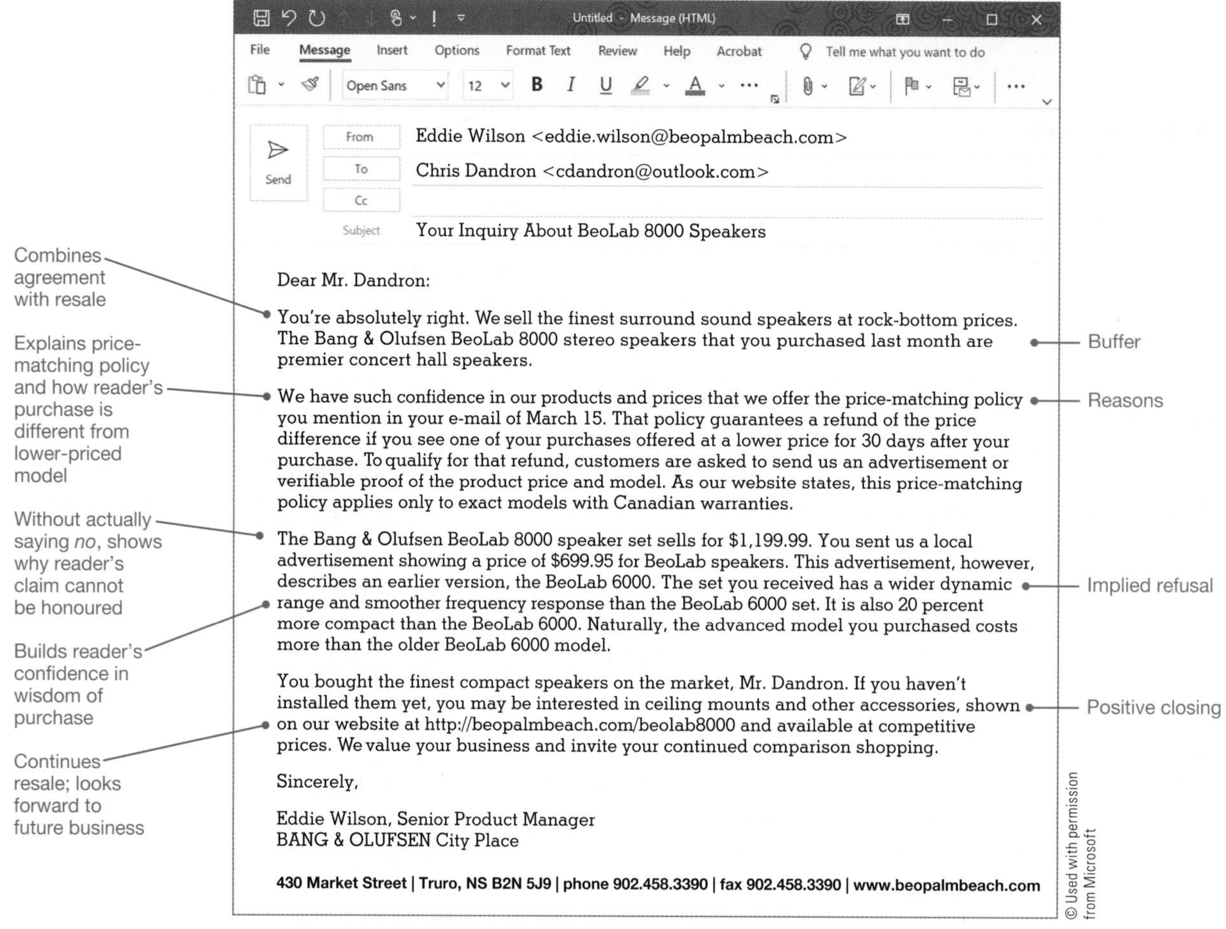

Untitled - Message (HTML)
File Message Insert Options Format Text Review Help Acrobat Tell me what you want to do
Open Sans 12
Send
From Eddie Wilson <eddie.wilson@beopalmbeach.com>
To Chris Dandron <cdandron@outlook.com>
Cc
Subject Your Inquiry About BeoLab 8000 Speakers
Dear Mr. Dandron:
You're absolutely right. We sell the finest surround sound speakers at rock-bottom prices. The Bang & Olufsen BeoLab 8000 stereo speakers that you purchased last month are premier concert hall speakers.
We have such confidence in our products and prices that we offer the price-matching policy you mention in your e-mail of March 15. That policy guarantees a refund of the price difference if you see one of your purchases offered at a lower price for 30 days after your purchase. To qualify for that refund, customers are asked to send us an advertisement or verifiable proof of the product price and model. As our website states, this price-matching policy applies only to exact models with Canadian warranties.
The Bang & Olufsen BeoLab 8000 speaker set sells for $1,199.99. You sent us a local advertisement showing a price of $699.95 for BeoLab speakers. This advertisement, however, describes an earlier version, the BeoLab 6000. The set you received has a wider dynamic range and smoother frequency response than the BeoLab 6000 set. It is also 20 percent more compact than the BeoLab 6000. Naturally, the advanced model you purchased costs more than the older BeoLab 6000 model.
You bought the finest compact speakers on the market, Mr. Dandron. If you haven't installed them yet, you may be interested in ceiling mounts and other accessories, shown on our website at http://beopalmbeach.com/beolab8000 and available at competitive prices. We value your business and invite your continued comparison shopping.
Sincerely,
Eddie Wilson, Senior Product Manager
BANG & OLUFSEN City Place
430 Market Street | Truro, NS B2N 5J9 | phone 902.458.3390 | fax 902.458.3390 | www.beopalmbeach.com
Combines agreement with resale
Explains price-matching policy and how reader's purchase is different from lower-priced model
Without actually saying *no*, shows why reader's claim cannot be honoured
Builds reader's confidence in wisdom of purchase
Continues resale; looks forward to future business
Buffer
Reasons
Implied refusal
Positive closing

Therefore, keep the refusal respectful, sensitive, and upbeat. A letter to a customer denying her credit application might begin as follows:

> *We genuinely appreciate your application on January 12 for a Fashion Express credit account.*

To avoid possible litigation, many companies offer no explanation of the reasons for a credit refusal. Instead, they provide the name of the credit-reporting agency and suggest that inquiries be directed to it. In the following example, notice the use of passive voice (*credit cannot be extended*) and a long sentence to de-emphasize the bad news:

> *After we received a report of your current credit record from Experian, it is apparent that credit cannot be extended at this time. To learn more about your record, you may call an Experian credit counsellor at (416) 356-0922.*

The cordial closing looks forward to the possibility of a future reapplication:

> *Thanks, Ms. Love, for the confidence you have shown in Fashion Express. We invite you to continue shopping at our stores, and we look forward to your reapplication in the future.*

Some businesses do provide reasons explaining credit denials (Credit cannot be granted because your firm's current and long-term credit obligations are nearly twice as great as your firm's total assets). They may also provide alternatives, such as deferred billing or cash discounts. When the letter denies a credit application that accompanies an order, the message may contain resale information. The writer tries to convert the order from credit to cash. For example, if a big order cannot be filled on a credit basis, perhaps part of the order could be filled on a cash basis.

Whatever form the bad-news message takes, it is a good idea to have the message reviewed by legal counsel because of the litigation land mines awaiting unwary communicators in this area.

Concept Check

1. Check out the Facebook or Twitter accounts for a large company, like Canadian Tire, TD Canada Trust, Enbridge Gas, or Giant Tiger. How do they manage negative news online? Find a specific response to a customer's complaint to discuss.
2. What are five strategies you should use when denying claims?

Managing Bad News Within Organizations

LEARNING OBJECTIVE 5

Describe and apply effective techniques for delivering bad news within organizations.

A tactful tone and a reasons-first approach help preserve friendly relations with customers. These same techniques are useful when delivering bad news within organizations. Interpersonal bad news might involve telling the boss that something went wrong or confronting an employee about poor performance. Organizational bad news might involve declining profits, lost contracts, harmful lawsuits, public relations controversies, and changes in policy. Within organizations, you may find yourself giving bad news in person or in writing.

Delivering Bad News in Person

Whether you are an employee or a supervisor, you may have the unhappy responsibility of delivering bad news. For example, you might have to tell the boss that the team's computer crashed, losing all its important files. Similarly, as a team leader or supervisor, you might be required to confront an underperforming employee. If you know that the news will upset the receiver, the reasons-first strategy is most effective. When the bad news involves one person or a small group nearby, you should generally deliver that news in person. Here are pointers on how to do so tactfully, professionally, and safely:[20]

- **Gather all the information.** Cool down and have all the facts before marching in on the boss or confronting someone. Remember that every story has two sides.
- **Prepare and rehearse.** Outline what you plan to say so that you are confident, coherent, and dispassionate.
- **Explain: past, present, future.** If you are telling the boss about a problem, such as the computer crash, explain what caused the crash, the current situation, and how and when you plan to fix it.
- **Consider taking a partner.** If you fear a "blame the messenger" reaction, especially from your boss, bring a colleague with you. Each person should have a consistent and credible part in the presentation. If possible, take advantage of your organization's internal resources. To lend credibility to your view, call on auditors, inspectors, or human resources experts.
- **Think about timing.** Don't deliver bad news when someone is already stressed or grumpy. Experts also advise against giving bad news on Friday afternoon when people have the weekend to dwell on it.
- **Be patient with the reaction.** Give the receiver time to vent, think, recover, and act wisely.

Check out section 9-5a in MindTap, where you can watch a video featuring Karen Richardson, a financial industry manager, discuss best practices for delivering bad news in a phone conversation.

Refusing Workplace Requests

Occasionally, managers must refuse requests from employees. In Figure 9.10, you see the first draft and revision of a message responding to a request from a key specialist, Luke Carson. He wants permission to attend a conference. However, he can't attend the conference because the timing is bad; he must be present at budget planning meetings scheduled for the same two weeks. Normally, this matter would be discussed in person. However, Luke has been travelling among branch offices, and he hasn't been in the office recently.

FIGURE 9.10 Refusing an Internal Request

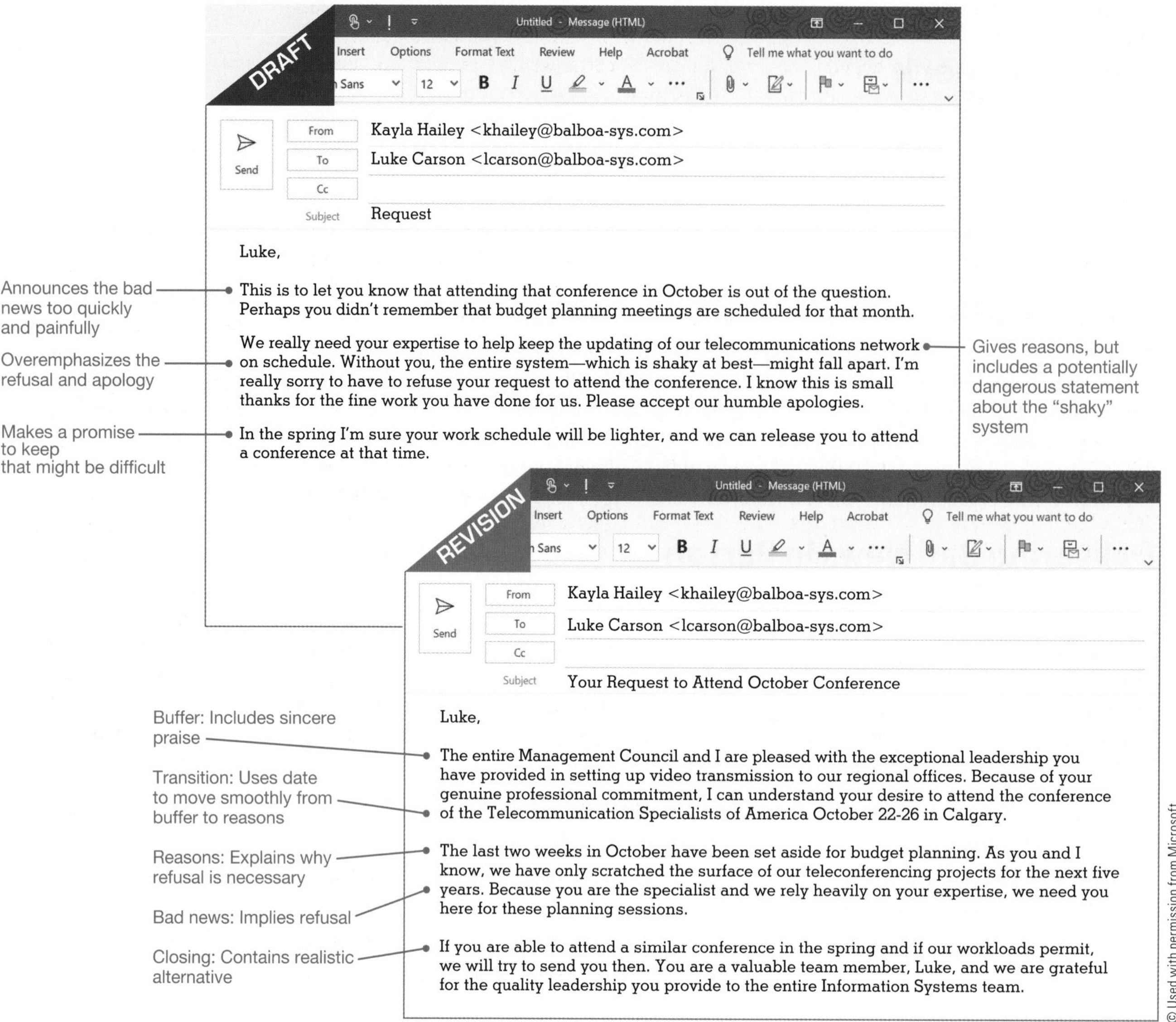

DRAFT
From
Kayla Hailey <khailey@balboa-sys.com>
To
Luke Carson <lcarson@balboa-sys.com>
Cc
Subject
Request
Luke,
This is to let you know that attending that conference in October is out of the question. Perhaps you didn't remember that budget planning meetings are scheduled for that month.
We really need your expertise to help keep the updating of our telecommunications network on schedule. Without you, the entire system—which is shaky at best—might fall apart. I'm really sorry to have to refuse your request to attend the conference. I know this is small thanks for the fine work you have done for us. Please accept our humble apologies.
In the spring I'm sure your work schedule will be lighter, and we can release you to attend a conference at that time.
Announces the bad news too quickly and painfully
Overemphasizes the refusal and apology
Makes a promise to keep that might be difficult
Gives reasons, but includes a potentially dangerous statement about the "shaky" system
REVISION
From
Kayla Hailey <khailey@balboa-sys.com>
To
Luke Carson <lcarson@balboa-sys.com>
Cc
Subject
Your Request to Attend October Conference
Luke,
The entire Management Council and I are pleased with the exceptional leadership you have provided in setting up video transmission to our regional offices. Because of your genuine professional commitment, I can understand your desire to attend the conference of the Telecommunication Specialists of America October 22-26 in Calgary.
The last two weeks in October have been set aside for budget planning. As you and I know, we have only scratched the surface of our teleconferencing projects for the next five years. Because you are the specialist and we rely heavily on your expertise, we need you here for these planning sessions.
If you are able to attend a similar conference in the spring and if our workloads permit, we will try to send you then. You are a valuable team member, Luke, and we are grateful for the quality leadership you provide to the entire Information Systems team.
Buffer: Includes sincere praise
Transition: Uses date to move smoothly from buffer to reasons
Reasons: Explains why refusal is necessary
Bad news: Implies refusal
Closing: Contains realistic alternative

The vice president's first inclination was to dash off a quick e-mail, as shown in the Figure 9.10 draft, and "tell it like it is." However, the vice president realized that this message was going to hurt and that it had possible danger areas. Moreover, the message misses a chance to give Luke positive feedback.

Buffer Includes a Compliment. An improved version of the e-mail starts with a buffer that delivers honest praise (*pleased with the exceptional leadership you have provided* and *your genuine professional commitment*). By the way, be generous with compliments; they cost you nothing. The buffer also includes the date of the meeting, used strategically to connect the reasons that follow.

Clear Reasons Provided. The middle paragraph provides reasons for the refusal. Notice that they focus on positive elements: Luke is the specialist; the company relies on his expertise; and everyone will benefit if he passes up the conference. In this section it becomes obvious that the request is being refused. The writer is not forced to say, *No, you may not attend.* Although the refusal is implied, the reader gets the message.

Closing Suggests Alternative. The closing suggests a qualified alternative (*if our workloads permit, we will try to send you then*). It also ends positively with gratitude for Luke's contributions to the organization and with another compliment (*you're a valuable player*). The improved version focuses on explanations and praise rather than on refusals and apologies. The success of this message depends on attention to the entire writing process, not just on using a buffer or scattering a few compliments throughout.

Announcing Bad News to Employees

In an age of social media, damaging information can rarely be contained for long. Executives can almost count on it to be leaked. Corporate officers who fail to communicate effectively and proactively may end up on the defensive and face an uphill battle trying to limit the damage. Many of the same techniques used to deliver bad news personally are useful when organizations face a crisis or must deliver bad news to employees. A crisis might involve serious performance problems, a major relocation, massive layoffs, a management shakeup, or public controversy. Instead of letting rumours distort the truth, managers ought to explain the organization's side of the story honestly and promptly.

Morale can be destroyed when employees learn of major events affecting their jobs through the grapevine or from news accounts—rather than from management. When bad news must be delivered to individual employees, management may want to deliver the news personally. With large groups, however, this is generally impossible. Instead, organizations deliver bad news through multiple channels ranging from hard-copy memos, which are formal and create a permanent record, to digital media.

Intranet Blog Post Draft. The intranet blog post shown in Figure 9.11 announces a substantial increase in the cost of employee health care benefits. However, this draft suffers from many problems. It announces jolting news bluntly in the first sentence. Worse, it offers little or no explanation for the steep increase in costs. It also sounds insincere (*We did everything possible . . .*) and arbitrary. In a final miscue, the writer fails to give credit to the company for absorbing previous health cost increases.

Revision Process. The revised message uses the indirect strategy, which improves the tone considerably.

- **Upbeat buffer.** Notice that it opens with a relevant, upbeat buffer regarding health care—but says nothing about increasing costs.
- **Smooth transition to reasons.** For a smooth transition, the second paragraph begins with a key idea from the opening (*comprehensive package*). The reasons section discusses rising costs with explanations and figures.
- **Embedded bad news.** The bad news (*you will be paying $119 a month*) is clearly presented but embedded within the paragraph. Throughout, the writer strives to show the fairness of the company's position.
- **Positive closing.** The ending, which does not refer to the bad news, emphasizes how much the company is paying and what a wise investment it is.
- **Kind approach.** Notice that the entire message demonstrates a kinder, gentler approach than that shown in the first draft.

Of prime importance in breaking bad news to employees is providing clear, convincing reasons that explain the decision. Parallel to this internal blog post, the message was also sent by e-mail. In smaller companies in which some workers do not have company e-mail, a hard-copy memo would be posted prominently on bulletin boards and in the lunchroom.

Saying No to Job Applicants

Being refused a job is one of life's major rejections. Tactless letters intensify the blow (*Unfortunately, you were not among the candidates selected for . . .*).

ETHICS CHECK

Fired via Skype

When Edmonton Oilers former coach Ralph Krueger was fired over Skype, he didn't see it coming. Krueger was at home in Switzerland when he received the call from the general manager. Because of the distance between them, the GM used Skype as a channel to deliver negative news for practicality.[21] Do you think it is fair or appropriate to be fired via a Skype call? Explain.

FIGURE 9.11 Announcing Bad News to Employees

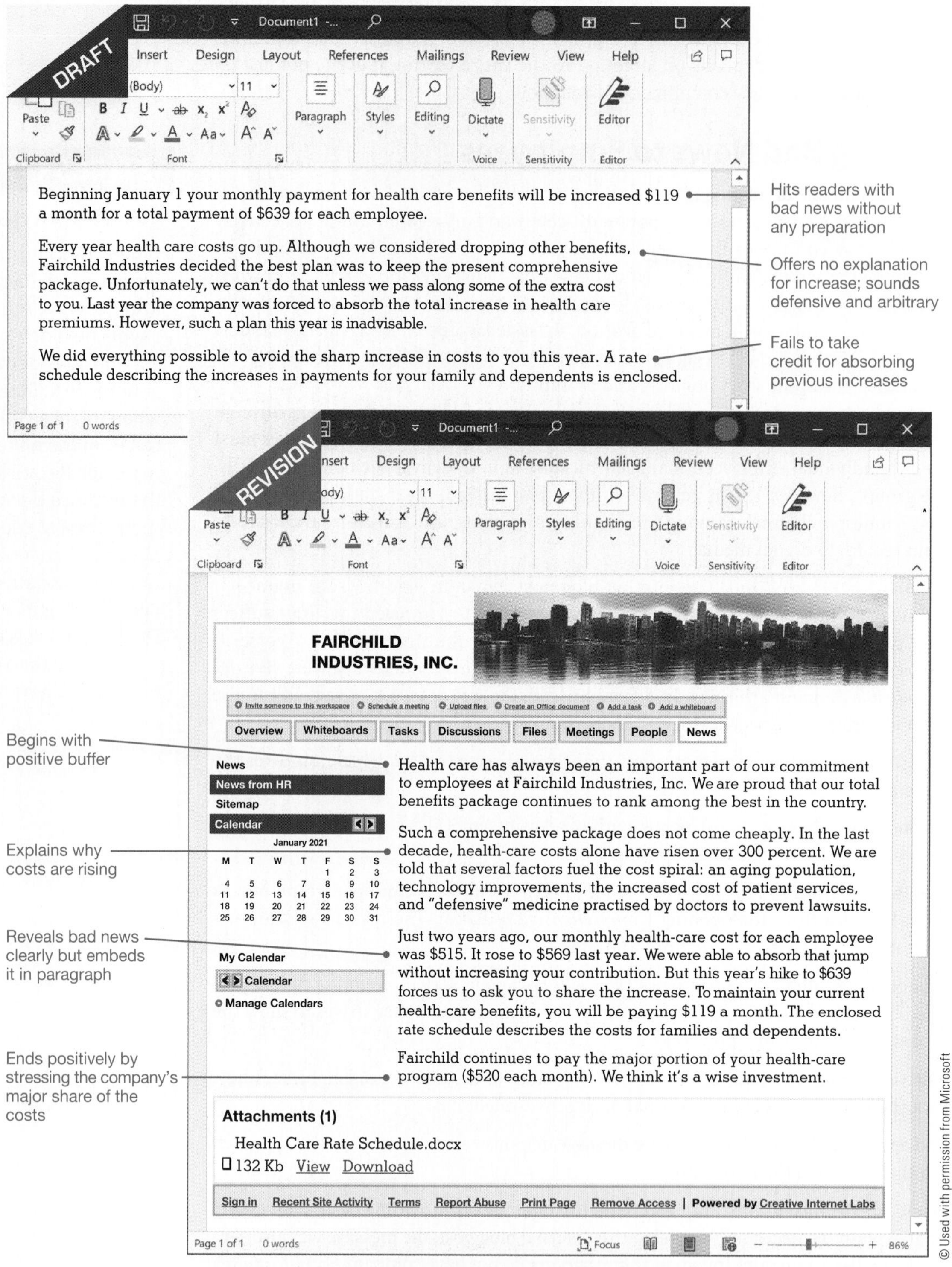

DRAFT
Beginning January 1 your monthly payment for health care benefits will be increased $119 a month for a total payment of $639 for each employee.
Every year health care costs go up. Although we considered dropping other benefits, Fairchild Industries decided the best plan was to keep the present comprehensive package. Unfortunately, we can't do that unless we pass along some of the extra cost to you. Last year the company was forced to absorb the total increase in health care premiums. However, such a plan this year is inadvisable.
We did everything possible to avoid the sharp increase in costs to you this year. A rate schedule describing the increases in payments for your family and dependents is enclosed.
Hits readers with bad news without any preparation
Offers no explanation for increase; sounds defensive and arbitrary
Fails to take credit for absorbing previous increases
REVISION
FAIRCHILD INDUSTRIES, INC.
Overview
Whiteboards
Tasks
Discussions
Files
Meetings
People
News
News
News from HR
Sitemap
Calendar
January 2021
My Calendar
Manage Calendars
Health care has always been an important part of our commitment to employees at Fairchild Industries, Inc. We are proud that our total benefits package continues to rank among the best in the country.
Such a comprehensive package does not come cheaply. In the last decade, health-care costs alone have risen over 300 percent. We are told that several factors fuel the cost spiral: an aging population, technology improvements, the increased cost of patient services, and "defensive" medicine practised by doctors to prevent lawsuits.
Just two years ago, our monthly health-care cost for each employee was $515. It rose to $569 last year. We were able to absorb that jump without increasing your contribution. But this year's hike to $639 forces us to ask you to share the increase. To maintain your current health-care benefits, you will be paying $119 a month. The enclosed rate schedule describes the costs for families and dependents.
Fairchild continues to pay the major portion of your health-care program ($520 each month). We think it's a wise investment.
Attachments (1)
Health Care Rate Schedule.docx
132 Kb View Download
Sign in Recent Site Activity Terms Report Abuse Print Page Remove Access | Powered by Creative Internet Labs
Begins with positive buffer
Explains why costs are rising
Reveals bad news clearly but embeds it in paragraph
Ends positively by stressing the company's major share of the costs

You can reduce the receiver's disappointment somewhat by using the indirect strategy—with one important variation. In the reasons section, it is wise to be vague in explaining why the candidate was not selected. First, giving concrete reasons may be painful to the receiver (*Your grade point average of 2.7 was low compared with the GPAs of other candidates*). Second,

FIGURE 9.12 Saying No to Job Candidates

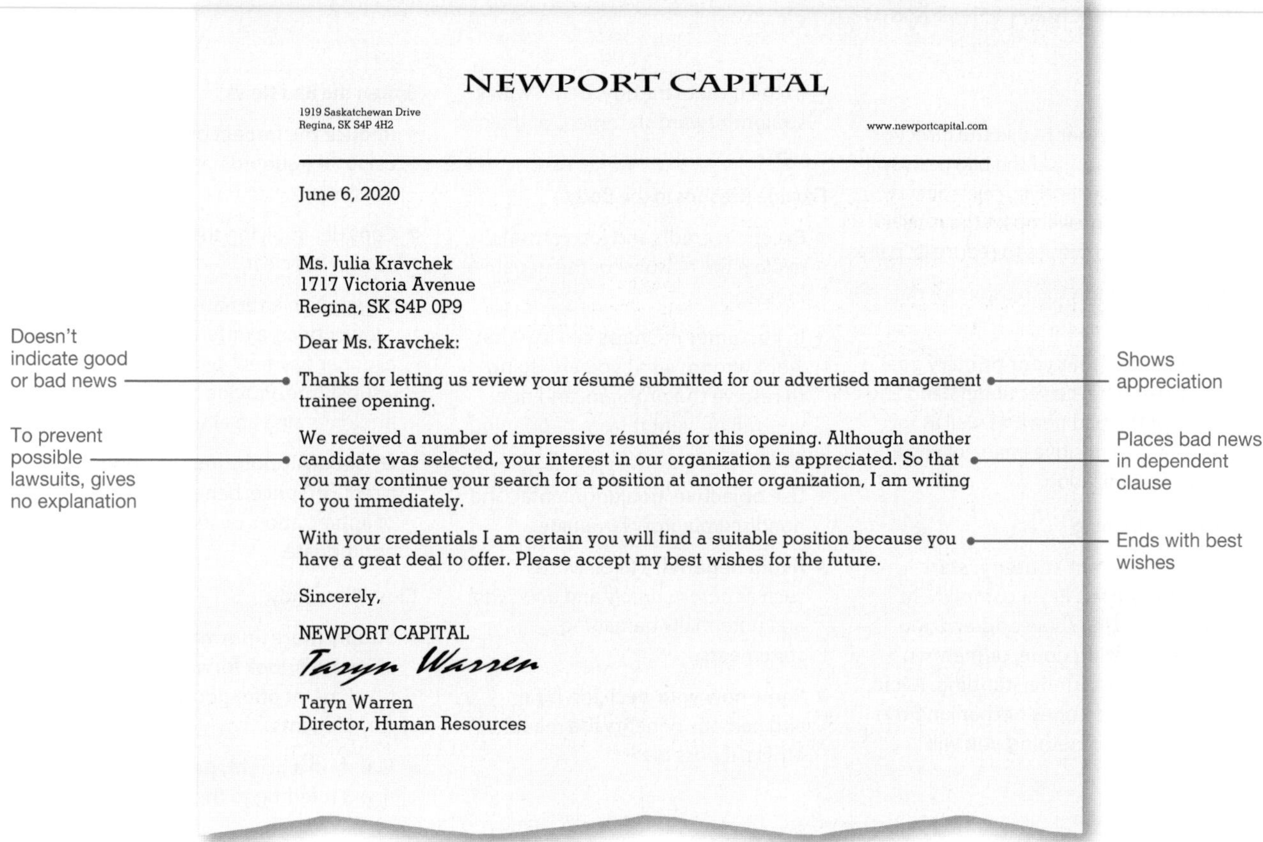

NEWPORT CAPITAL

1919 Saskatchewan Drive
Regina, SK S4P 4H2

www.newportcapital.com

June 6, 2020

Ms. Julia Kravchek
1717 Victoria Avenue
Regina, SK S4P 0P9

Dear Ms. Kravchek:

Thanks for letting us review your résumé submitted for our advertised management trainee opening.

We received a number of impressive résumés for this opening. Although another candidate was selected, your interest in our organization is appreciated. So that you may continue your search for a position at another organization, I am writing to you immediately.

With your credentials I am certain you will find a suitable position because you have a great deal to offer. Please accept my best wishes for the future.

Sincerely,

NEWPORT CAPITAL

Taryn Warren

Taryn Warren
Director, Human Resources

Doesn't indicate good or bad news
Shows appreciation
To prevent possible lawsuits, gives no explanation
Places bad news in dependent clause
Ends with best wishes

and more important, providing extra information may prove fatal in a lawsuit. Hiring and firing decisions generate considerable litigation today. To avoid charges of discrimination or wrongful actions, legal advisors warn organizations to keep employment rejection letters general, simple, and short.

The job refusal letter, shown in Figure 9.12, is tactful but intentionally vague. It implies that the applicant's qualifications don't match those needed for the position, but the letter doesn't reveal anything specific. The writer could have included this alternative closing: *We wish you every success in finding a position that exactly fits your qualifications.*

The Checklist on the next page summarizes tips on how to communicate negative news inside and outside your organization.

Concept Check

1. You are an executive at a company that suddenly has to lay off 400 employees within 3 days or risk financial disaster. You have to make the cuts quickly, but you don't want to be impersonal by announcing the cuts by e-mail. How would you announce the bad news?
2. In some cultures, using the direct approach for conveying negative news would be considered rude or inappropriate. Considering your culture, how is negative news normally conveyed? In what ways could the North American approach discussed in this chapter differ from other countries and cultures?

CHECKLIST

Conveying Negative News

Prewrite

- **Decide whether to use the direct or indirect strategy.** If the bad news will not upset the receiver, open directly. If the message will upset the receiver, consider techniques to reduce its pain.
- **Think through** the reasons for the bad news.
- **Remember that your primary goal** is to make the receiver understand and accept the bad news, as well as to maintain a positive image of you and your organization.

Plan the Opening

- **In the indirect strategy, start with a buffer.** Pay a compliment to the reader, show appreciation for something done, or mention some mutual understanding. Avoid raising false hopes or thanking the reader for something you will refuse.
- **In the direct strategy,** begin with a straightforward statement of the bad news.

Provide Reasons in the Body

- **Except in credit and job refusals,** explain the reasons for the negative message.
- **In customer mishaps clarify what went wrong,** what you are doing to resolve the problem, and how you will prevent it from happening again.
- **Use objective,** nonjudgmental, and nondiscriminatory language.
- **Avoid negativity** (e.g., words such as *unfortunately* and *unwilling*) and potentially damaging statements.
- **Show how your decision is fair** and perhaps benefits the reader or others, if possible.

Soften the Bad News

- **Reduce the impact of bad news** by using (a) a subordinate clause, (b) the passive voice, or (c) a long sentence.
- Consider implying the refusal, but be certain it is clear.
- **Suggest an alternative,** such as a lower price, a different product, a longer payment period, or a substitute. Provide help in implementing an alternative.
- **Offset disappointment** by offering a reduced price, benefits, tokens of appreciation, or something appropriate.

Close Pleasantly

- **Supply more information** about an alternative, look forward to future relations, or offer good wishes and compliments.
- **Maintain a bright, personal tone.** Avoid referring to the refusal.

SPOTLIGHT ON COMMUNICATION: PART 2

Loblaw Revisited

CRITICAL THINKING

- Consider the wording of the Loblaw Card Program website. What strategies is the company using to convey the negative news?
- Analysts have estimated that the inflated bread prices cost the average Canadian $400 over the price-fixing period.[25] Is the $25 gift card enough to restore faith in Loblaw? Explain why or why not.

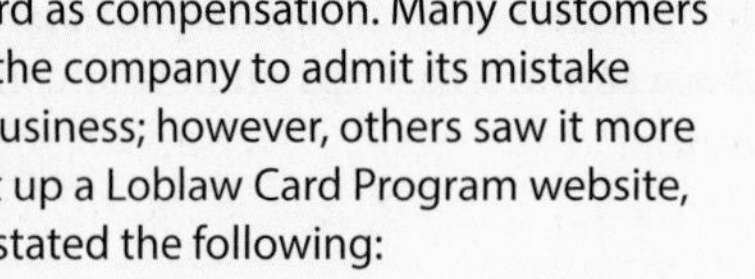

In response to the bread price-fixing scandal, Loblaw offered its customers a $25 gift card as compensation. Many customers felt it was honourable for the company to admit its mistake and work to regain their business; however, others saw it more as a gimmick.[22] Loblaw set up a Loblaw Card Program website, which is now closed, that stated the following:

Evan Mitsui/CBC Licensing

> $25 Loblaw Card
>
> Loblaw discovered that Canadians were overcharged for the cost of some packaged bread products in our stores and other grocery stores across Canada. In response, we offered eligible customers a $25 Loblaw Card that can be used to purchase items sold in our grocery stores across Canada.[23]

To be eligible for the card, Canadians needed to complete a form stating that they purchased qualifying bread products before March 1, 2015. They also needed to produce ID to show they were the age of majority, as minors were not eligible.[24]

Summary of Learning Objectives

1 Understand the strategies of business communicators in conveying negative news, apply the 3-x-3 writing process, and avoid legal liability.

- Explain clearly and completely while projecting a professional image.
- Convey empathy, sensitivity, and fairness.
- Be a mindful communicator who avoids careless and abusive language, which is defined as actionable language that is false, damaging to a person's reputation, and published (i.e., spoken in the presence of others or written).

2 Distinguish between the direct and indirect strategies in conveying unfavourable news.

- Use the direct strategy, with the bad news first, when the news is not damaging, when the receiver may overlook it, when the organization or receiver prefers directness, or when firmness is necessary.
- Use the indirect strategy, with a buffer and explanation preceding the bad news, when the bad news is personally upsetting, when it may provoke a hostile reaction, when it threatens the customer relationship, and when the news is unexpected.
- To avoid being unethical, never use the indirect method to deceive or manipulate the truth.

3 Explain the components of effective negative messages.

- To soften bad news, start with a buffer, such as the best news, a compliment, appreciation, agreement, facts, or understanding.
- Explain the reasons that necessitate the bad news, citing benefits to the reader or others. If you apologize, do so promptly and sincerely. Project empathy.
- Strive to cushion the bad news with strategic positioning.
- Close the message pleasantly.

4 Apply effective techniques for refusing typical requests or claims and for presenting bad news to customers.

- In rejecting requests for money, information, and action, follow the bad-news strategy: (a) buffer, (b) reasons, (c) explanation and possibly an alternative, and (d) positive close.
- To deal with a disappointed customer, (a) call or e-mail the individual immediately; (b) describe the problem and apologize (when the company is to blame); (c) explain why the problem occurred, what you are doing to resolve it, and how you will prevent it from happening again; and (d) promote goodwill with a follow-up message.
- To handle negative posts and reviews online, (a) verify the situation, (b) respond quickly and constructively, (c) consider giving freebies such as refunds or discounts, (d) learn from negative comments as though they were real-time focus group input, and (e) be prepared to accept the inevitable and move on.
- To deny claims, (a) use the reasons-before-refusal strategy, (b) don't blame customers, (c) use neutral objective language, and (d) consider offering resale information to rebuild the customer's confidence in your organization.
- When refusing credit, avoid language that causes hard feelings, strive to retain the customer on a cash basis, and avoid disclosures that could cause a lawsuit.

5 **Describe and apply effective techniques for delivering bad news within organizations.**

- To deliver workplace bad news in person, (a) gather all the information; (b) prepare and rehearse; (c) explain the past, present, and future; (d) consider taking a partner; (e) think about timing; and (f) be patient with the reaction.
- In announcing bad news to employees, strive to keep the communication open and honest, choose the best communication channel, and consider applying the indirect strategy, but give clear, convincing reasons.
- Be positive, but don't minimize the bad news; use objective language.
- In refusing job applicants, keep messages short, general, and tactful.

Chapter Review

1. Why is the indirect strategy appropriate for some negative-news messages? (Obj. 1)
2. When delivering bad news, how can a communicator reduce the bad feelings of the receiver? (Obj. 1)
3. Explain the differences between libel and slander. (Obj. 1)
4. What are the major differences between the direct and indirect strategies in delivering bad news? (Obj. 2)
5. What is a *buffer*? Name five or more techniques to buffer the opening of a bad-news message. (Obj. 3)
6. Name four or more techniques that cushion the delivery of bad news. (Obj. 3)
7. What are some strategies to effectively manage adverse news on social networking sites and blogs? (Obj. 4)
8. When denying customer claims, explain the benefits of using the reasons-before-refusal plan. (Obj. 4)
9. Why should you be especially careful to soften the refusal to an invitation? (Obj. 4)
10. For what reasons should a job refusal letter be intentionally vague? (Obj. 5)

Critical Thinking

1. Consider times when you have been aware that others were using the indirect strategy in writing or speaking to you. How did you react? (Obj. 2)
2. Does bad news travel faster and farther than good news? Why? What implications would this have for companies responding to unhappy customers? (Objs. 1–5)
3. If you had to give upsetting news to a colleague, would you use the direct or indirect strategy? Explain your personal decision. (Obj. 2)
4. Living in Pickering, Lauren Bossers worked virtually by e-mail and phone for a supply chain management software company in Winnipeg. Even though Bossers was a remote worker, she was shocked when her manager laid her off by phone. What might be some advantages and disadvantages to being let go remotely, if any? (Objs. 1, 5)
5. **Ethical Issue:** You work for a large corporation with headquarters in a small town. Recently, you received shoddy repair work and a huge bill from a local garage. Your car's transmission has the same problems that it did before you took it in for repair. You know that a complaint letter written on your corporation's stationery would be much more authoritative than one written on plain stationery. Should you use corporation stationery? (Obj. 1)

Activities

9.1 Organizational Strategies (Objs. 1–3)

YOUR TASK Identify which organizational strategy you would use for the following messages: direct or indirect.

a. A message from a car insurance company that it will no longer insure family members who drive the family car. Customers may expand their policies with more comprehensive coverage at a higher cost.

b. An announcement to employees that a financial specialist has cancelled a scheduled lunchtime talk and cannot reschedule.

c. An e-mail from the manager denying an employee's request for special parking privileges. The employee works closely with the manager on many projects.

9.2 Employing Passive-Voice Verbs (Obj. 3)

YOUR TASK Revise the following sentences to present the bad news with passive-voice verbs.

a. Our retail stores will no longer be accepting credit cards for purchases under $5.

b. We do not examine patients until they show their health cards.

c. Your car rental insurance coverage does not cover large SUVs.

9.3 Subordinating Bad News (Obj. 3)

YOUR TASK Revise the following sentences to position the bad news in a subordinate clause. (Hint: Consider beginning the clause with *Although.*) Use passive-voice verbs for the bad news.

a. Provincial law does not allow smoking within 3 metres of a postsecondary building. But the college has set aside 16 outdoor smoking areas.

b. We are sorry to report that we are unable to ship your complete order at this point in time. However, we are able to send two corner workstations now, and you should receive them within five days.

c. We appreciate your interest in our organization, but we are unable to extend an employment offer to you at this time.

9.4 Implying Bad News (Obj. 3)

YOUR TASK Revise the following statements to *imply* the bad news. If possible, use passive-voice verbs and subordinate clauses to further de-emphasize the bad news.

a. Unfortunately, we find it impossible to contribute to your excellent and worthwhile fundraising campaign this year. At present all the funds of our organization are needed to lease equipment and offices for our new branch in Moose Jaw. We hope to be able to support this commendable endeavour in the future.

b. We cannot ship our fresh fruit baskets COD. Your order was not accompanied by payment, so we are not shipping it. We have it ready, though, and will rush it to its destination as soon as you call us with your credit card number.

c. Because of the holiday period, all our billboard space was used this month. Therefore, we are sorry to say that we could not give your charitable group free display space. However, next month, after the holidays, we hope to display your message as we promised.

9.5 Bad News to Customers: Blunder in Scheduling Fairy Tale Cottage Wedding (Objs. 1–4)

As the wedding planner at the Bathurst Harbour Resort in New Brunswick, you just discovered a terrible mistake. Two weddings have been scheduled for the same Saturday in June. How could this happen? You keep meticulous records, but six months ago, you were away for two weeks. Another employee filled in for you. She apparently didn't understand the scheduling system and lined up two weddings for the Sacred Heart Cathedral on June 14. The month of June, of course, is the busiest month of the year. Weddings in the Sacred Heart Cathedral are usually booked two years in advance, and it can handle only one wedding a day.

It's now January, and Kellie Singer, one of the brides-to-be called to check on her arrangements. That's when you discovered the mistake. However, you didn't reveal the blunder to Kellie on the telephone. From experience, you know how emotional brides can be when their plans go awry. Now you must decide what to do. Your manager has given you complete authority in scheduling weddings, and you know he would back nearly any decision you make to rectify the mistake. Unfortunately, all of your harbour wedding venues are booked for June Saturdays. However, you do have some midweek openings for the Sacred Heart Cathedral in early June. If one of the brides could change to midweek, you might offer one free night in a sumptuous bridal suite as compensation.

Bathurst Harbour Resort offers dreamlike settings for unforgettable wedding celebrations. Couples and their guests can enjoy five-star resort services, a private coastline, glittering ballrooms, custom banquets, and alluringly wooded and landscaped strolling areas.

YOUR TASK Decide what course of action to take. The two brides-to-be are Kellie Singer, 3201 Peachtree Lane, Miramichi, New Brunswick E1N 6Y3, and Julie Brehm, 240 Lakeview Avenue, Rothesay, New Brunswick E2E 5X6. In a memo to your instructor, explain your response strategy. If you plan a phone call, outline what you plan to say. If your instructor requests, write a letter and copy your instructor.

9.6 Bad News to Employees: Nixing Social Media at Work (Objs. 1–5)

Social Media E-mail Web

Your boss at MarketingMatters, a hip midsized public relations agency, is concerned that the youngest employee generation may be oversharing on social media. Two supervisors have complained that they spotted inappropriate photos on Instagram posted by a small group of Gen-Zers on the company payroll. This group of twentysomethings is close-knit. Its members maintain friendships outside the office and in cyberspace. They are smart and plugged in, but they seem to have trouble recognizing boundaries of age and authority. They party every weekend, which is code for a lot of drinking, marijuana use, and even salacious escapades—all of which the young workers generously document with smartphone cameras on the spot and occasionally in real time. Sometimes they share snarky comments about their workplace, such as *Rough day at work* or *Talked to the most idiotic client ever!* On top of that, the young people think nothing of friending their colleagues and supervisors. Their friends rank in the hundreds; some in the group have exceeded 1,000 followers.

MarketingMatters maintains a permissive stance toward Internet use, but concern is growing that the young people are headed for trouble. The abuses continue despite the company's comprehensive Internet and social media use policy, which was widely disseminated. Probably the biggest risk MarketingMatters fears is the leaking of confidential information on social networking sites. After several meetings, the management decides to disallow social media use during work hours and to caution all employees against dangerous breaches of company policy and social media netiquette.

YOUR TASK Draft a message to be distributed by e-mail for the signature of your boss, Darcy M. Diamond, Director, Human Resources. Your message should remind all employees about the existing social networking policy and tactfully yet clearly announce the end of personal social media use at the office. The prohibition is effective immediately. Your message should also warn about the pitfalls of oversharing online.

Grammar and Mechanics | *Review 9*

Confusing Words and Frequently Misspelled Words

Review the lists of confusing words and frequently misspelled words in Appendix B, Grammar and Mechanics Guide, beginning on page B-1. On a sheet of paper or on your computer, revise the following sentences to correct errors in word use. Sentences may have more than one error. If a sentence is correct, write *C*. When you finish, compare your responses with the key in Appendix C.

EXAMPLE: He complained that his capitol investments had been aversely effected.

REVISION: He complained that his capital investments had been adversely affected.

1. Did you allready send an email to let the team know the meeting is canceled?
2. The principle part of the manager's response contained a complement and valuable advise.
3. In responding to the irate customer, Rachel made a conscience effort to show patients and present creditable facts.

4. In every day decision-making, the company trusts you to use your best judgement.
5. Before you procede with the report, please check those suprising statistics.
6. It's usally better to de-emphasize bad news rather then to spotlight it.
7. Incidently, passive-voice verbs can help you make a statement less personnel when neccessary.
8. Customers are more excepting of disapointing news if they are ensured that there requests were heard and treated fairly.
9. The customer's complaint illicited an immediate response that analized the facts carefully but was not to long.
10. Before apologizing to a customer, check with your superviser to review the liability questionairre.

Notes

[1] Loblaws. (2019). *About us*. https://www.loblaws.ca/about

[2] Statistica. (2018, March 22). *Loblaws—Statistics & facts*. https://www.statista.com/topics/3235/loblaws/

[3] Zochodne, G. (2018, June 29). Bread price-fixing scandal may have originated with PowerPoint presentation: Court documents. *Financial Post*. https://business.financialpost.com/news/retail-marketing/bread-price-fixing-scandal-may-have-originated-with-powerpoint-presentation-court-documents

[4] CBC News. (2017, December 22). *$1B class action filed against Loblaws for bread price-fixing*. https://www.cbc.ca/news/canada/sudbury/bread-price-fixing-class-action-1.4462416

[5] Mann Lawyers: Employment Law in Ottawa. (2015, January 13). *Letters of reference—bad idea?* https://employmentlawottawa.com/2015/01/13/letters-of-reference-bad-idea/

[6] Greenwald, J. (2009, June 1). *Layoffs may spark defamation suits*. http://businessinsurance.com

[7] McCord, E. A. (1991, April). The business writer, the law, and routine business communication: A legal and rhetorical analysis. *Journal of Business and Technical Communication*, 183.

[8] Creelman, V. (2012). The case for "living" models. *Business Communication Quarterly, 75*(2), 181.

[9] Veltsos, J. (2012). An analysis of data breach notifications as negative news. *Business Communication Quarterly, 75*(2), 198. https://doi.org/10.1177/1080569912443081

[10] Canavor, N. (2012). *Business writing in the digital age*. Sage, p. 62.

[11] Ibid., p. 16.

[12] McIntyre, C. (2017, June 28). Do Canadians deserve their reputation for being nice? *Maclean's*. https://www.macleans.ca/culture/do-canadians-deserve-their-reputation-for-being-nice/

[13] Ibid.

[14] Ibid.

[15] Shuit, D. P. (2003, September). Do it right or risk getting burned. *Workforce Management*, p. 80.

[16] MacDonald, N. (2016, May 19). *With our apologies: Canada makes "I'm sorry" a recurring policy*. CBC News. http://www.cbc.ca/news/politics/komagata-maru-official-apologies-1.3587870

[17] RBC. (2013). *An open letter to Canadians*. http://www.rbc.com/openletter/

[18] Cited in Canavor, N. (2012). *Business writing in the digital age*. Sage, p. 62.

[19] Mowatt, J. (2002, February). Breaking bad news to customers. *Agency Sales*, p. 30; Dorn, E. M. (1999, March). Case method instruction in the business writing classroom. *Business Communication Quarterly, 62*(1), 51–52.

[20] Ensall, S. (2007, January 30). Delivering bad news. *Personnel Today*, p. 31. Business Source Premier database; Lewis, B. (1999, September 13). To be an effective leader, you need to perfect the art of delivering bad news. *InfoWorld*, p. 124.

[21] *Edmonton Oilers coach fired over Skype, Ralph Krueger says he was "blindsided."* (2013, June 10). Huffington Post Alberta. http://www.huffingtonpost.ca/2013/06/10/oilers-coach-fired-skype-_n_3415954.html

[22] Harris, S. (2018, February 24). *Customers get their $25 Loblaw gift card as compensation for overpriced bread*. CBC News. https://www.cbc.ca/news/business/loblaw-25-gift-card-bread-price-fixing-1.4549723

[23] Loblaw Card Program. (2019). https://www.loblawcard.ca/

[24] Roseman, E. (2018, January 2). What you need to know about the $25 Loblaw card. *The Star*. https://www.thestar.com/business/personal_finance/2018/01/02/what-you-need-to-know-about-the-25-loblaw-card.html

[25] Markusoff, J. (2018, January 11). Loblaws' price-fixing may have cost you at least $400; Any way you slice it, Canadian bread shouldn't have cost this much. *Maclean's*. https://www.macleans.ca/economy/economicanalysis/14-years-of-loblaws-bread-price-fixing-may-have-cost-you-at-least-400/

CHAPTER

10

Persuasive and Sales Messages

LEARNING OBJECTIVES

After studying this chapter, you should be able to

1 Explain persuasion, identify effective persuasive techniques, and apply the 3-x-3 writing process to persuasive messages in print and online.

2 Describe the traditional four-part AIDA strategy for creating successful persuasive messages, and apply the four elements to draft effective and ethical business messages.

3 Craft persuasive messages that request actions, make claims, and deliver complaints.

4 Understand interpersonal persuasion at work and write persuasive messages within organizations.

5 Create effective and ethical direct-mail and e-mail sales messages.

6 Apply basic techniques in developing persuasive media releases.

SPOTLIGHT ON COMMUNICATION: PART 1

David Suzuki Foundation: One Nature

The David Suzuki Foundation, founded in 1990, works to preserve the natural world. The Foundation partners with communities to create and implement environmentally sustainable practices in Canada and around the world:[1]

Courtesy of David Suzuki Foundation

> Through evidence-based research, education and policy analysis, we work to conserve and protect the natural environment, and help create a sustainable Canada. We regularly collaborate with non-profit and community organizations, all levels of government, businesses and individuals.
>
> Our mission is to protect nature's diversity and the well-being of all life, now and for the future. Our vision is that we all act every day on the understanding that we are one with nature.[2]

David Suzuki is an award-winning geneticist and author and is well-known for hosting *The Nature of Things* television show on CBC. He has received honorary degrees and awards, and has been honoured by First Nation communities for his work to preserve Canada's waters, land, and ecosystems.[3]

As many countries, including Canada, declare a climate emergency, the David Suzuki Foundation's work is more important than ever.

CRITICAL THINKING

- Some Canadians are resistant to the idea that climate change is happening. How can the foundation take advantage of digital and print media to persuade Canadians to join its cause?
- Like all not-for-profit organizations, the Foundation relies heavily on donations. On its donation page it states: "Donate to protect the people and places you love."[4] What strategies are being used here? How does it motivate people to donate?

Persuading Effectively and Ethically in the Contemporary Workplace

LEARNING OBJECTIVE 1

Explain persuasion, identify effective persuasive techniques, and apply the 3-x-3 writing process to persuasive messages in print and online.

Contemporary businesses have embraced leaner corporate hierarchies, simultaneously relying on teams, eliminating division walls, and blurring the lines of authority. As teams and managers are abandoning the traditional command structure, sophisticated persuasive skills are becoming ever more important at work. Businesspeople must try to influence others.[5] Because many of us are poor persuaders or we don't always recognize persuasive tactics directed at us, the techniques outlined in this chapter are critical.

Although we are subjected daily to a barrage of print and electronic persuasive messages, many of us don't recognize the techniques of persuasion. To be smart consumers, we need to be alert to persuasive practices and how they influence behaviour. Being informed is our best defence.

This chapter focuses on messages that require deliberate and skilled persuasion in the workplace. This chapter also addresses selling, both offline and online.

What Is Persuasion?

As communication scholar Richard M. Perloff defines it, persuasion is "a symbolic process in which communicators try to convince other people to change their attitudes or behaviours regarding an issue through the transmission of a message in an atmosphere of free choice."[6] To help you understand how persuasion works, we will discuss its five components, which are outlined in the following sections.

Persuasion Is a Symbolic Process. *Symbols* are meaningful words, signs, and images infused with rich meaning—for example, words such as *peace*, signs such as national flags, and images such as the maple leaf for all things Canadian. An ethical persuader

Symbols, such as this Canada Organic logo, convey rich meaning to others and may be used to convey an organization's important values.

Canadian Food Inspection Agency (2014), Canada Organic Regime: A Certified Choice. Retrieved from http://www.inspection.gc.ca/food/organic-products/labelling-andgeneral-information/certified-choice/eng/1328082717777/1328082783032. Reproduced with the permission of the Canadian Food Inspection Agency, 2020.

understands the power of symbols and does not use them to trick others. Because people's attitudes change slowly, persuasion takes time.

Persuasion Involves an Attempt to Influence. Persuasion involves a conscious effort to influence another person with the understanding that change is possible.

Persuasion Is Self-Persuasion. Ethical communicators give others the choice to accept their arguments by making compelling, honest cases to support them. They plant the seed but do not coerce. They leave it to others to "self-influence," that is, to decide whether to make the change.

Persuasion Involves Transmitting a Message. Persuasive messages can be verbal or nonverbal, and they can be conveyed face to face or via the TV, radio, or social media. Persuasive messages are not always rational. They often appeal to our emotions. Consider the car commercial playing your favourite tune and showing pristine landscapes, not a gridlocked highway during rush hour.

Persuasion Requires Free Choice. Although *free* is a difficult term to define, we can perhaps agree that people are free when they are not forced to comply, when they can refuse the idea suggested to them, and when they are not pressured to act against their own preferences.

Many smart thinkers have tried to explain how powerful persuaders influence others. One model illustrating persuasion is shown in Figure 10.1. In the classic book *Influence*,[7] Robert B. Cialdini outlined six psychological triggers that prompt us to act and to believe: reciprocation, commitment, social proof, liking, authority, and scarcity. Each "weapon of automatic influence" motivates us to say *yes* or *no* without much thought or awareness. Our complex world forces us to resort to these shortcuts. Such automatic responses make us vulnerable to manipulation.

If you become aware of these gut-level mechanisms that trigger decisions, you will be able to resist unethical and manipulative persuasion more easily. Conversely, this knowledge might make you a successful persuader.

How Has Persuasion Changed in the Digital Age?

The preoccupation with persuasion is not new. However, persuasion in the 21st century is different from persuasion in previous historic periods in distinct ways.[8] The most striking developments are less than three decades old.

The Volume, Speed, and Reach of Persuasive Messages Have Exploded. In 2019 Canadians 18 years and older spent one hour and 32 minutes per day watching digital video. This number is steadily rising and will be one hours and 39 minutes daily by 2021.[9] With this rate of consumption, Canadians are increasingly exposed to persuasive messages.

Organizations of All Stripes Are in the Persuasion Business. Companies, ad agencies, PR firms, social activists, lobbyists, marketers, and more, spew persuasive messages. Although outspent by corporations that can sink millions into image campaigns, activists use social networks to galvanize their followers.

Persuasive Techniques Are More Subtle and Misleading. Instead of a blunt, pushy, hard-sell approach, persuaders play on emotions by using flattery, empathy, nonverbal cues, and likability appeals. They are selling an image or a lifestyle, not a product.[10] In this age of fake news, the media are increasingly infiltrated by partisan interests and spread messages masquerading as news.

Persuasion Is More Complex and Impersonal. North American consumers are diverse and don't necessarily think alike. To reach them, marketers carefully study various target groups and customize their appeals. Technology has increased the potential for distortion. People can "mash up" content, give it meanings the original source never intended, and blast it into the world in seconds.

You probably recognize how important it is not only to become a skilled persuader but also to identify devious messages and manipulation attempts directed at you. When you want

FIGURE 10.1 Six Basic Principles That Direct Human Behaviour

Reciprocation
"The Old Give and Take ... and Take"

Humans seem to be hardwired to give and take. If someone does us a favour, most of us feel obligated to return the favour. This rule is so binding that it may lead to a *yes* to a request we might otherwise refuse. This explains the "gifts" that accompany requests for money.

Commitment
"Hobgoblins of the Mind"

We believe in the correctness of a difficult choice once we make it. We want to keep our thoughts and beliefs consistent with what we have already decided. Fundraisers may ask for a small amount at first, knowing that we are likely to continue giving once we start.

Social Proof
"Truths Are Us"

To determine correct behaviour, we try to find out what other people think is correct. We see an action as more acceptable when others are doing it. Advertisers like to tell us that a product is "bestselling"; the message is that it must be good because others think so.

Liking
"The Friendly Thief"

We are more likely to accept requests of people we know and like or those who say they like us. Tupperware capitalizes on this impulse to buy from a friend. Strangers are persuasive if they are likable and attractive. Also, we favour people who are or appear to be like us.

Authority
"Directed Deference"

We tend to obey authority because we learn that a widely accepted system of authority is beneficial to the orderly functioning of society. People exuding authority, even con artists, can trigger our mechanical, blind compliance. Testimonials bank on this response to authority.

Scarcity
"The Rule of the Few"

We tend to regard opportunities as more valuable when their availability is restricted. Scarce items seem more appealing to us. The idea of potential loss greatly affects our decisions. Marketers may urge customers not to miss out on a "limited-time offer."

your ideas to prevail, start thinking about how to present them. Listeners and readers will be more inclined to accept what you are offering if you focus on important techniques, outlined in Figure 10.2 and further discussed throughout the chapter.

Applying the 3-x-3 Writing Process to Persuasive Messages

Changing people's views and overcoming their objections are difficult tasks. Pulling it off demands planning and perception. The 3-x-3 writing process provides a helpful structure for laying a foundation for persuasion. Of particular importance here are (a) analyzing the purpose, (b) adapting to the audience, (c) collecting information, and (d) organizing the message.

Analyzing the Purpose: Knowing What You Want to Achieve. The goal of a persuasive message is to convert the receiver to your ideas and motivate action. To accomplish this feat in the age of social media, persuaders seek to build relationships with their audiences. Even so, a message without a clear purpose is doomed. Too often, inexperienced writers reach the end of the first draft of a message before discovering exactly what they want the receiver to think or do.

FIGURE 10.2 Effective Persuasion Techniques

Establish credibility.

- Show that you are truthful, experienced, and knowledgeable.
- Use others' expert opinions and research to support your position.

Make a reasonable, specific request.

- Make your request realistic, doable, and attainable.
- Be clear about your objective. Vague requests are less effective.

Tie facts to benefits.

- Line up plausible support such as statistics, reasons, and analogies.
- Convert the supporting facts into specific audience benefits.

Recognize the power of loss.

- Show what others stand to lose if they don't agree.
- Know that people dread losing something they already possess.

Expect and overcome resistance.

- Anticipate opposition from conflicting beliefs, values, and attitudes.
- Be prepared to counter with well-reasoned arguments and facts.

Share solutions and compromise.

- Be flexible and aim for a solution that is acceptable to all parties.
- Listen to people and incorporate their input to create buy-in.

ETHICS CHECK

Fake News Phenomenon

With fake news being a global issue, Facebook and Google have rolled out tools designed to crack down on false or misleading messages. Even a Conservative Canadian politician admitted to spreading lies about the Liberal government, later admitting to *Maclean's* magazine that he did it to "make the left go nuts." Google introduced a "fact-check" tag into some news pages to help readers assess the legitimacy of the articles they're reading.[11] How else can Canadians guard against fake news?

As the author of the popular *Oh She Glows* cookbooks and blog, Angela Liddon understands contemporary persuasive techniques. Angela started her *Oh She Glows* blog out of her home in Oakville, Ontario, to write about the transformative role that healthful eating made in improving her life. Before long she was connecting with people all over the world, and now her blog has over one million unique readers each month.[12] She knows that to achieve success today, she must cultivate relationships, not just push products.[13] Angela engages her readers not only by maintaining a blog, but by tweeting updates and posting on her Facebook, Twitter, Instagram, and Pinterest pages. Readers can also sign up for the *Oh She Glows* newsletter.

CENGAGE MINDTAP

Go to section 10-1c in MindTap, where you can watch a video featuring Courtney Thorne, an editor, discuss how to use persuasion to achieve a goal.

Adapting to the Audience to Make Your Message Heard. In addition to identifying the purpose of a persuasive message, you also need to concentrate on the receiver. A persuasive message is futile unless it meets the needs of its audience. In a broad sense, you want to show how your request helps the receiver achieve some of life's major goals or fulfills key needs: money, power, comfort, confidence, importance, friends, peace of mind, and recognition, to name a few.

On a more practical level, you want to show how your request solves a problem, achieves a personal or work objective, or just makes life easier for your audience. When Angela Liddon introduced the Oh She Glows Recipe App, it was originally available only for Apple devices. However, because of consumer demand, she worked to develop and offer an Android option as well. She knew that convenient access to healthful recipes on the go would appeal to her readers. Liddon adapted the message to her audience by talking about the convenience of her app, as well as the family and budget-friendly filters.[14] See Figure 10.3 for an example.

When adapting persuasive requests to your audience, consider these questions that receivers will very likely be asking themselves:

Why should I?
What's in it for me?
What's in it for you?
Who cares?

Adapting to your audience means learning about audience members and analyzing why they might resist your proposal. It means searching for ways to connect your purpose with their needs. If completed before you begin writing, such analysis goes a long way toward overcoming resistance and achieving your goal.

Researching and Organizing Persuasive Data. After you have analyzed the audience and considered how to adapt your message to its needs, you are ready to collect data and organize it. You might brainstorm and prepare a rough outline of ideas.

The next step in a persuasive message is organizing data into a logical sequence. If you are asking for something that you know will be approved, little persuasion is required. In that

FIGURE 10.3 Angela Liddon Engages the Audience

Roman Odintsov

Contemporary persuaders understand that their audiences want to feel valued and to have their needs met. Consumers today are savvy and know that they have many choices. Angela Liddon uses popular social networks to engage her customers and to build a sincere relationship with them.

FIGURE 10.4 The AIDA Strategy for Persuasive Messages

STRATEGY	CONTENT	SECTION
Attention	Captures attention, creates awareness, makes a sales proposition, prompts audience to read on	Opening
Interest	Describes central selling points, focuses not on features of product/service but on benefits relevant to the reader's needs	Body
Desire	Reduces resistance, reassures the reader, elicits the desire for ownership, motivates action	Body
Action	Offers an incentive or a gift, limits the offer, sets a deadline, makes it easy for the reader to respond, closes the sale	Closing

case, you would make a direct request, as you studied in Chapter 8. However, when you expect resistance or when you need to educate the receiver, the indirect strategy often works better. The classic indirect strategy known by the acronym AIDA works well for many persuasive requests, not just in selling. Figure 10.4 summarizes this four-part strategy for overcoming resistance and crafting successful persuasive messages.

Concept Check

1. When have you had to persuade someone (a supervisor, a parent, an instructor, a friend, or a colleague) to do something or change a belief? What strategies did you use? Were they successful? How could you improve your technique?
2. In what ways has persuasion changed in the digital age?

LEARNING OBJECTIVE 2

Describe the traditional four-part AIDA strategy for creating successful persuasive messages, and apply the four elements to draft effective and ethical business messages.

Blending Four Major Elements in Successful Persuasive Messages

Although AIDA, the indirect strategy, appears to contain separate steps, successful persuasive messages actually blend the four steps into a seamless whole. The sequence of the steps may change depending on the situation and the emphasis. Regardless of where they are placed, the key elements in persuasive requests are (a) gaining your audience's attention, (b) building interest by convincing your audience that your proposal is worthy, (c) eliciting desire for the offer and reducing resistance, and (d) prompting action. Figure 10.5 summarizes the specific tools that writers use when following the AIDA strategy.

Gaining Attention in Persuasive Messages

To grab attention, the opening statement in a persuasive request should be brief, relevant, and engaging. When only mild persuasion is necessary, the opener can be low-key and factual. If, however, your request is substantial and you anticipate strong resistance, provide a thoughtful, provocative opening. Following are some examples:

- **Problem description.** In a recommendation to hire temporary employees: *Last month legal division staff members were forced to work 120 overtime hours, costing us $6,000 and causing considerable employee unhappiness.* With this opener you have presented a capsule of the problem your proposal will help solve.

FIGURE 10.5 Applying the Four-Part AIDA Strategy to Persuasive Documents

Attention	Interest	Desire	Action
Summary of problem	Facts, figures	Reduce resistance	Describe specific request
Unexpected statement	Expert opinions	Anticipate objections	Sound confident
Reader benefit	Examples	Offer counterarguments	Make action easy to take
Compliment	Specific details	Use *What if?* scenarios	Offer incentive or gift
Related facts	Direct benefits	Demonstrate competence	Don't provide excuses
Stimulating question	Indirect benefits	Show value of proposal	Repeat main benefits

- **Unexpected statement.** In a memo to encourage employees to attend an optional sensitivity seminar: *Men and women draw the line at decidedly different places in identifying what behaviour constitutes sexual harassment.* Note how this opener gets readers thinking immediately.
- **Reader benefit.** In a letter promoting Clear Card, a service that helps employees make credit card purchases without paying interest: *The average employee carries nearly $13,000 in revolving debt and pays $2,800 in interest and late fees. The Clear Card charges zero percent interest.* Employers immediately see the benefit of this offer to employees.
- **Compliment.** In a letter inviting a business executive to speak: *Because our members value your managerial expertise, they want you to be our speaker.* In offering praise or compliments, be careful to avoid obvious flattery. Be sincere.
- **Related facts.** In a message to company executives who are considering restricting cell phone use by employee drivers: *A recent study revealed that employers pay an average of $16,500 each time an employee is in a traffic accident.* This relevant fact sets the scene for the interest-building section that follows.
- **Stimulating question.** In a plea for funds to support environmental causes: *What do golden tortoise beetles, bark spiders, flounders, and Arctic foxes have in common?* Readers will be curious to find the answer to this intriguing question. (They all change colour depending on their surroundings.)

Building Interest in Persuasive Messages

After capturing attention, a persuasive request must retain that attention and convince the audience that the request is reasonable. To justify your request, be prepared to invest in a few paragraphs of explanation. Persuasive requests are likely to be longer than direct requests because the audience must be convinced rather than simply instructed. You can build interest and conviction through the use of the following:

- Facts, statistics
- Examples
- Expert opinion
- Specific details
- Direct benefits
- Indirect benefits

Showing how your request can benefit the audience directly or indirectly is a key factor in persuasion. If you were asking colleagues to donate to the Canadian Cancer Society, for example, you might promote *direct benefits,* such as a daffodil being permanently inscribed with the donor's message on the Society's donor wall.[15] Another direct benefit is a tax write-off for the contribution. An *indirect benefit* might be feeling good about helping the Society and knowing that Canadians with cancer will benefit from the gift. Nearly all charities rely in large part on indirect benefits to promote their causes.

Eliciting Desire and Reducing Resistance in Persuasive Requests

The best persuasive requests anticipate audience resistance. How will the receiver object to the request? When brainstorming, try *What if?* scenarios. Let's say you want to convince management that the employees' cafeteria should switch from disposable to ceramic dishes. What if managers say the change is too expensive? What if they argue that they recycle paper and plastic? What if they protest that ceramic is less hygienic? For each of these *What if?* scenarios, you need a counterargument.

Check out section 10-2c in MindTap, where you can watch a video featuring Jarrod Hann, vice president of sales at Xello, discuss how to use persuasion to influence behaviour.

Emphasize Benefits. Countering resistance and prompting desire in the receiver is important, but you must do it with finesse (*Although ceramic dishes cost more at first, they actually save money over time*). You can minimize objections by presenting your counterarguments in sentences that emphasize benefits: *Ceramic dishes may require a little more effort in cleaning, but they bring warmth and graciousness to meals. Most important, they help save the environment by requiring fewer resources and eliminating waste.* However, don't dwell on counterarguments, thus making them overly important. Finally, avoid bringing up objections that may never have occurred to the receiver in the first place.

Establish Credibility. Another factor that reduces resistance and elicits desire is credibility. Receivers are less resistant if your request is reasonable and if you are believable. When the receiver does not know you, you may have to establish your expertise, refer to your credentials, or demonstrate your competence. Even when you are known, you may have to establish your knowledge in a given area. If you are asking your manager for a new tablet computer, you might have to establish your credibility by providing articles about the latest tablets, their portability, low cost, battery life, and so on.

Prompting Action in Persuasive Messages

After gaining attention, building interest, eliciting desire, and reducing resistance, you will want to inspire the newly receptive audience to act. Knowing exactly what action you favour before you start to write enables you to point your arguments toward this important final paragraph. Here you make your recommendation as specifically and confidently as possible—without seeming pushy. Compare the following persuasive e-mail closings recommending training seminars in communication skills.

Too General

We are certain we can develop a series of training sessions that will improve the communication skills of your employees.

Too Timid

If you agree that our training proposal has merit, perhaps we could begin the series in June.

Too Pushy

Because we are convinced that you will want to begin improving the skills of your employees immediately, we have scheduled your series to begin in June.

Effective

You will see decided improvement in the communication skills of your employees. Please call me at 905-439-2201 by May 1 to give your approval so that training sessions may start in June, right after the completion of your internal restructuring.

Note how the last opening suggests a specific and easy-to-follow action. It also provides a deadline and a reason for that date.

Figure 10.6 exemplifies the AIDA persuasive strategy just discussed. Writing for her research firm, Danuta Hajek seeks to persuade other companies to complete a questionnaire revealing salary data. To most organizations, salary information is strictly confidential. What can she do to convince strangers to part with such private information?

To gain attention, Danuta poses two short questions that spotlight the need for salary information. To build interest and establish trust, she states that Herron & Hogan Research has been collecting business data for a quarter century and has received awards. She ties her reasonable request to audience benefits.

FIGURE 10.6 Persuasive Request

HERRON & HOGAN RESEARCH
1624 Fennel Street, Ottawa, ON K9J 6P7
Phone 613-349-2219
Fax 613-349-8967

May 18, 2020

Mr. Gregory S. Janssen
Mellon Wealth Management
2469 Langton Avenue
Thornhill, ON L3J 3M8

Dear Mr. Janssen:

Would you like access to more reliable salary data than Glassdoor has to offer? Has your company ever lost a valued employee to another organization that offered 20 percent more in salary for the same position?

To remain competitive in hiring and to retain qualified workers, companies rely on survey data showing current salaries. Herron & Hogan Research has been collecting business data for a quarter century and has been honoured by the Canadian Management Association for its accurate data. We need your help in collecting salary data for today's workers. Information from the enclosed questionnaire will supply companies like yours with such data.

Your information, of course, will be treated confidentially. The questionnaire takes but a few moments to complete, and it can provide substantial dividends for professional organizations just like yours that need comparative salary data.

To show our gratitude for your participation, we will send you free comprehensive salary surveys for your industry and your metropolitan area. Not only will you find basic salaries, but you will also learn about bonus and incentive plans, special pay differentials, expense reimbursements, and perquisites such as a company car and credit card.

Comparative salary data are impossible to provide without the support of professionals like you. Please complete the questionnaire and return it in the prepaid envelope before June 1, our spring deadline. Participating in this survey means that you will no longer be in the dark about how much your employees earn compared with others in your industry.

Sincerely yours,

HERRON & HOGAN RESEARCH

Danuta Hajek

Danuta Hajek
Director, Survey Research

Enclosures

Poses two short questions related to the reader

Gains attention

Presents reader benefit tied to request explanation; establishes credibility

Builds interest

Anticipates and counters resistance to confidentiality and time/effort objections

Elicits desire and reduces resistance

Offers free salary data as a direct benefit

Appeals to professionalism, an indirect benefit

Provides deadline and a final benefit to prompt action

Motivates action

Being an Ethical Persuader

Persuaders are effective only when they are believable. If receivers suspect that they are being manipulated or misled, or if they find any part of the argument untruthful, the total argument fails. Fudging the facts, exaggerating a point, omitting something crucial, or providing deceptive emphasis may seem tempting to some business communicators, but such schemes usually backfire.

Persuasion becomes unethical when facts are distorted, overlooked, or manipulated with an intent to deceive. Applied to language that manipulates, such distortion and twisting of the meaning is called *doublespeak*. Of course, persuaders naturally want to put forth their strongest case. However, that argument must be based on truth, objectivity, and fairness.

Consumers complain in blogs, tweets, and online posts about businesses resorting to aggressive sales tactics, manipulation, and outright lies.[16] Honest business communicators would not sacrifice their good reputation for short-term gain. Once lost, credibility is difficult to regain. As well, the Canadian Code of Advertising Standards, established in 1963, exists to promote the professional practice of advertising: "The *Code* is broadly supported by industry and is designed to help set and maintain standards of honesty, truth, accuracy, fairness and propriety in advertising."[17]

Concept Check

1. You might see advertisements that proclaim, *We make the world's best burger.* Called *puffery,* such promotional claims are not taken literally by reasonable consumers. Such subjective statements are accepted as puffery because they puff up, or exaggerate. Surprisingly, this kind of sales exaggeration is not illegal. However, when sales claims consist of objective statements that cannot be verified (*Our burgers were voted the best in town*), they become deceptive advertising. Consider your vast experience with TV and other advertising. Can you think of commercials or ads that seem to fall in the category of puffery or could even be considered deceptive? How do you know the difference between the two?
2. Many users resent advertising pop-ups and banner ads on social media sites. They go to Facebook, Instagram, Pinterest, and Twitter to socialize virtually, not to shop. How do you feel about sales pitches on your favourite social media sites?

LEARNING OBJECTIVE 3

Craft persuasive messages that request actions, make claims, and deliver complaints.

Writing Persuasive Requests, Making Claims, and Delivering Complaints

Convincing someone to change a belief or to perform an action when that person is reluctant requires planning and skill—and sometimes a little luck. A written, rather than face-to-face, request may require more preparation but can be more effective. Written messages require skill in persuasion. Persuasion is often more precise and controlled when you can think through your purpose and prepare a thoughtful message. AIDA, the indirect strategy, gives you an effective structure.

Writing Persuasive Requests

Persuading someone to do something that largely benefits you may not be the easiest task. Fortunately, many individuals and companies are willing to grant requests for time, money, information, cooperation, and special privileges. They comply for a variety of reasons. They may just happen to be interested in your project, or they may see goodwill potential for themselves. Professionals sometimes feel obligated to contribute their time or expertise to "give back." Often, though, businesses and individuals comply because they see that others will benefit from the request.

The persuasive action request shown in Figure 10.6 incorporates many of the techniques that are effective in persuasion: establishing credibility, making a reasonable and precise request, tying facts to benefits, and eliciting desire while overcoming resistance in the receiver.

Writing Persuasive Claims

Persuasive claims may involve damaged products, mistaken billing, inaccurate shipments, warranty problems, limited return policies, insurance mix-ups, or faulty merchandise. Generally, the direct strategy is best for requesting straightforward adjustments (see Chapter 8). When you feel your request is justified and will be granted, the direct strategy is most efficient. However, if a past request has been refused or ignored, or if you anticipate reluctance, then the indirect strategy is appropriate.

Developing a Logical Persuasive Argument. Strive for logical development in a claim message. You might open with sincere praise, an objective statement of the problem, a point of agreement, or a quick review of what you have done to resolve the problem. Then you can explain precisely what happened or why your claim is legitimate. Don't provide a blow-by-blow chronology of details; just hit the highlights. Be sure to enclose copies of relevant invoices, shipping orders, warranties, and payments. Close with a clear statement of what you want done: a refund, replacement, credit to your account, or other action. Be sure to think through the possibilities and make your request reasonable.

Using a Moderate Tone. The tone of your message is important. Don't suggest that the receiver intentionally deceived you or intentionally created the problem. Rather, appeal to the receiver's sense of responsibility and pride in the company's good name. Calmly express your disappointment in view of your high expectations of the product and of the company. Communicating your feelings without bitterness is often your strongest appeal.

Composing Effective Complaints

As their name suggests, complaints deliver bad news. Some complaint messages just vent anger. However, if the goal is to change something (and why bother to write except to motivate change?), then persuasion is necessary. An effective claim message makes a reasonable and valid request, presents a logical case with clear facts, and has a moderate tone. Anger and emotion are not effective persuaders.

Denise Blanchard's e-mail, shown in Figure 10.7, follows the persuasive pattern as she seeks credit for two VoIP (voice-over-Internet protocol) systems. She was quite upset because her company was counting on these new Internet systems to reduce its phone bills. Instead, the handsets produced so much static that incoming and outgoing calls were all but impossible to hear.

What's more, Denise was frustrated that the return merchandise authorization form she filled out at the company's website seemed to sink into a dark hole in cyberspace. However, she resolved to use a moderate tone in writing her complaint e-mail because she knew that a calm, unemotional tone would be more effective. She opted for a positive opening, a well-documented claim, and a request for specific action in the closing.

Concept Check

1. When have you had to complain to a company, an organization, or a person about something that went wrong or that offended you? Share your experience. What channel did you use for your complaint? How effective was your channel choice and strategy? What would you change in your method for future complaints?
2. Why is it important to use a moderate tone when writing a persuasive claim?

ETHICS CHECK

Changing Social Attitudes

As society's attitudes are changing, Canadian advertisers are faced with several crucial ethical decisions. With controversies surrounding contemporary issues, like human rights and the environment, advertising agencies need to be more ethically conscious than in the past.[18] For example, some advertisers may think twice before representing a company that uses genetically modified organisms (GMOs) in its products. Do you think that Canadian advertisers should adapt to changes in social mores?

Go to section 10-3c in MindTap, where you can watch a video featuring Jarrod Hann, vice president of sales at Xello, discuss approaches to making a formal complaint.

FIGURE 10.7 Persuasive Claim (Complaint) E-mail

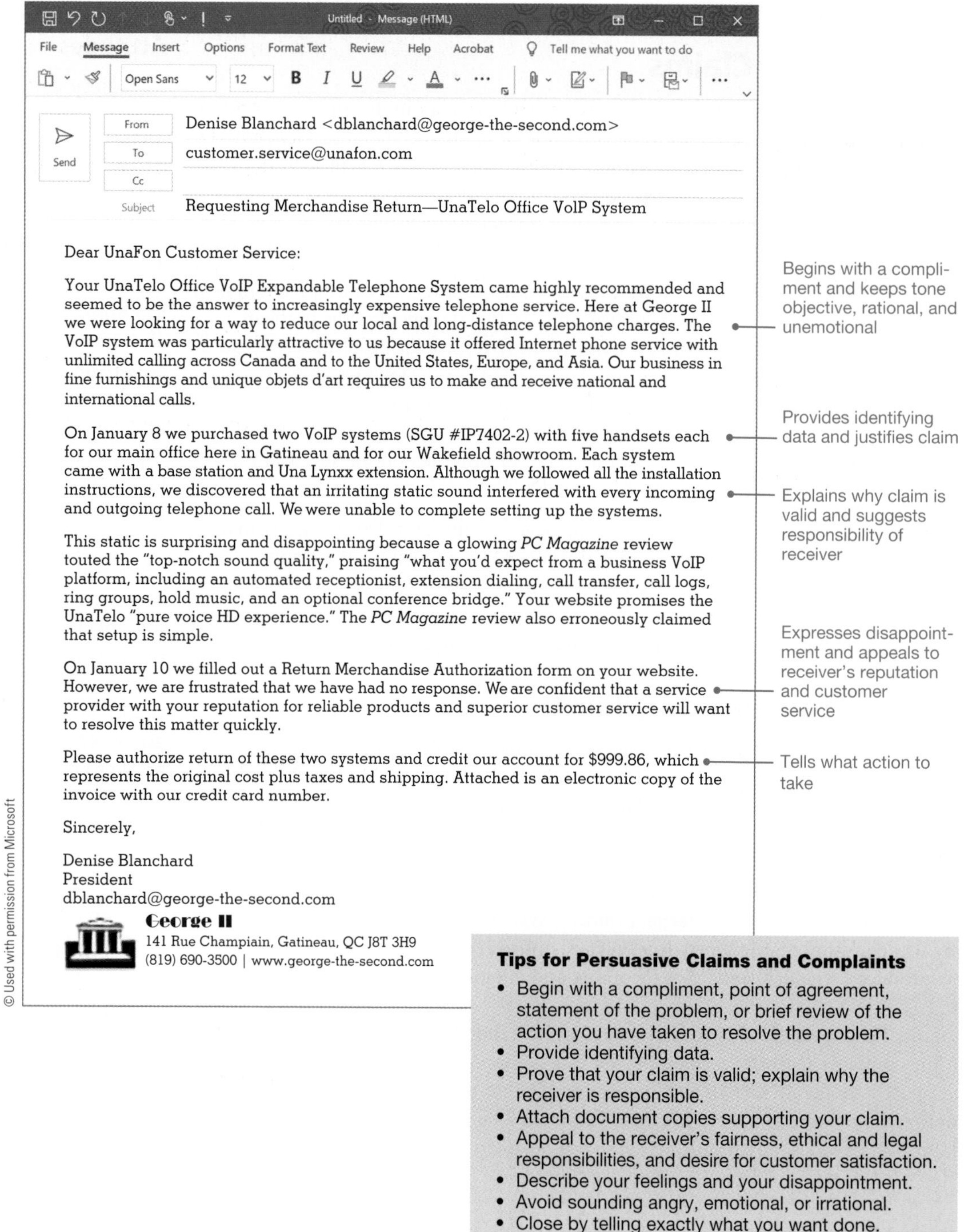

Untitled - Message (HTML)
File Message Insert Options Format Text Review Help Acrobat Tell me what you want to do
Open Sans 12
Send
From Denise Blanchard <dblanchard@george-the-second.com>
To customer.service@unafon.com
Cc
Subject Requesting Merchandise Return—UnaTelo Office VoIP System

Dear UnaFon Customer Service:

Your UnaTelo Office VoIP Expandable Telephone System came highly recommended and seemed to be the answer to increasingly expensive telephone service. Here at George II we were looking for a way to reduce our local and long-distance telephone charges. The VoIP system was particularly attractive to us because it offered Internet phone service with unlimited calling across Canada and to the United States, Europe, and Asia. Our business in fine furnishings and unique objets d'art requires us to make and receive national and international calls.

On January 8 we purchased two VoIP systems (SGU #IP7402-2) with five handsets each for our main office here in Gatineau and for our Wakefield showroom. Each system came with a base station and Una Lynxx extension. Although we followed all the installation instructions, we discovered that an irritating static sound interfered with every incoming and outgoing telephone call. We were unable to complete setting up the systems.

This static is surprising and disappointing because a glowing *PC Magazine* review touted the "top-notch sound quality," praising "what you'd expect from a business VoIP platform, including an automated receptionist, extension dialing, call transfer, call logs, ring groups, hold music, and an optional conference bridge." Your website promises the UnaTelo "pure voice HD experience." The *PC Magazine* review also erroneously claimed that setup is simple.

On January 10 we filled out a Return Merchandise Authorization form on your website. However, we are frustrated that we have had no response. We are confident that a service provider with your reputation for reliable products and superior customer service will want to resolve this matter quickly.

Please authorize return of these two systems and credit our account for $999.86, which represents the original cost plus taxes and shipping. Attached is an electronic copy of the invoice with our credit card number.

Sincerely,

Denise Blanchard
President
dblanchard@george-the-second.com
George II
141 Rue Champiain, Gatineau, QC J8T 3H9
(819) 690-3500 | www.george-the-second.com

Begins with a compliment and keeps tone objective, rational, and unemotional
Provides identifying data and justifies claim
Explains why claim is valid and suggests responsibility of receiver
Expresses disappointment and appeals to receiver's reputation and customer service
Tells what action to take

Tips for Persuasive Claims and Complaints

- Begin with a compliment, point of agreement, statement of the problem, or brief review of the action you have taken to resolve the problem.
- Provide identifying data.
- Prove that your claim is valid; explain why the receiver is responsible.
- Attach document copies supporting your claim.
- Appeal to the receiver's fairness, ethical and legal responsibilities, and desire for customer satisfaction.
- Describe your feelings and your disappointment.
- Avoid sounding angry, emotional, or irrational.
- Close by telling exactly what you want done.

LEARNING OBJECTIVE 4

Understand interpersonal persuasion at work and write persuasive messages within organizations.

Writing Persuasive Messages in Digital Age Organizations

As noted earlier, the lines of authority are blurry in today's workplaces, and the roles of executives are changing. Technology has empowered rank-and-file employees who can turn to their companies' intranets and don't need their managers to be information providers—formerly a crucial managerial role. This huge shift in authority is affecting the strategies for creating

CHECKLIST

Using the AIDA Strategy to Request Actions, Make Claims, and Deliver Complaints

Prewrite

- **Determine your purpose.** Know exactly what you want to achieve.
- **Anticipate the reaction of your audience.** Remember that the receiver is thinking, *Why should I? What's in it for me? What's in it for you? Who cares?*

Gain Attention

- **Use the indirect strategy** rather than blurting out the request immediately.
- **Begin with a problem description,** unexpected statement, reader benefit, compliment, related facts, or stimulating question to grab attention.

Build Interest

- **Convince the audience** that your request is reasonable.
- **Develop interest** by using facts, statistics, examples, testimonials, and specific details.
- **Establish your credibility,** if necessary, by explaining your background and expertise. Use testimonials, expert opinion, or research if needed.
- **Support your request** by tying facts to direct benefits (increased profits, better customer relations) or indirect benefits (helping the environment).
- **In claims and complaints,** be objective but prove the validity of your request.

Elicit Desire and Reduce Resistance

- **Anticipate objections** to your request by using *What if?* scenarios and provide compelling counterarguments.
- **Demonstrate credibility and competence.**
- **Use a moderate, unemotional tone.**

Motivate Action

- **Make a precise request** that spells out exactly what you want done. Add a deadline date if necessary.
- **Repeat a key benefit,** provide additional details, or offer an incentive. Express appreciation.
- **Be confident** without seeming pushy.

and the tone of workplace persuasive messages. Today's executives increasingly rely on persuasion to achieve buy-in from subordinates.[19]

This section focuses on messages flowing downward and upward within organizations. Horizontal messages exchanged among coworkers resemble those discussed earlier in requesting actions.

Persuading Employees: Messages Flowing Downward

Employees traditionally expected to be directed in how to perform their jobs; therefore, instructions or directives moving downward from superiors to subordinates usually required little persuasion. Messages such as information about procedures, equipment, or customer service still use the direct strategy, with the purpose immediately stated.

However, employees are sometimes asked to volunteer for projects outside of their work roles, such as tutoring disadvantaged children or helping at homeless shelters. Some organizations encourage employees to join programs to stop smoking, lose weight, or start exercising. In such cases, the four-part indirect AIDA strategy provides a helpful structure.

Because most employers care about retaining quality employees,[20] messages flowing downward require attention to tone. Warm words and a conversational tone convey a caring attitude. Persuasive requests coming from a trusted superior are more likely to be accepted than requests from a dictatorial executive who relies on threats and punishments to secure compliance. Because the words *should* and *must* sometimes convey a negative tone, be careful in using them.

Figure 10.8 shows a memo e-mailed by Gabriela Marrera, director of HR staffing and training at a large bank. Her goal is to persuade employees to participate in Helping Hands Day, a fundraising and community service event that the bank sponsors. In addition to volunteering their services for a day, employees also have to pay $30 to register! You can see that this is no small persuasion task for Gabriela.

FIGURE 10.8 Persuasive Organizational Message Flowing Downward

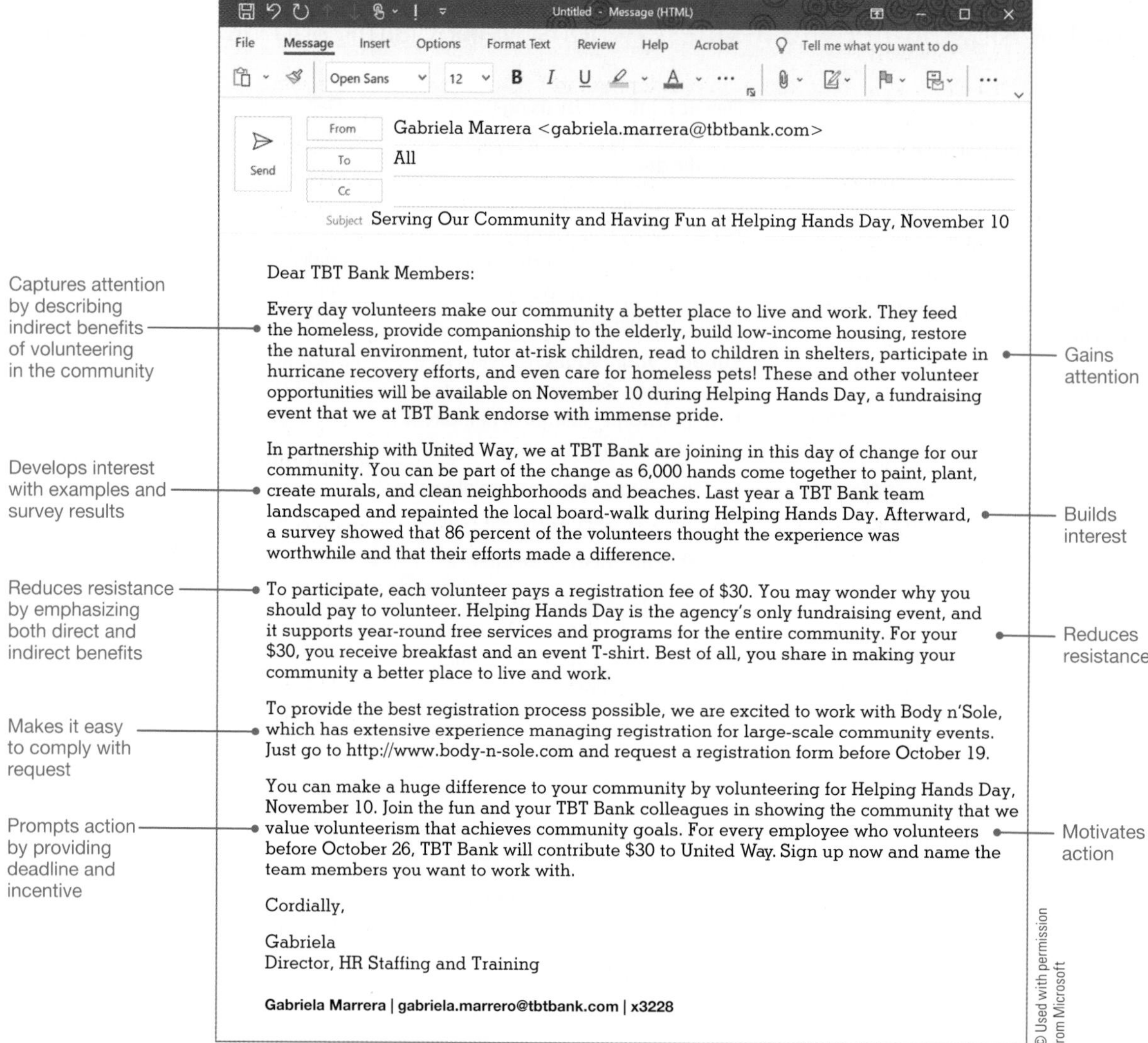

Untitled - Message (HTML)
File Message Insert Options Format Text Review Help Acrobat Tell me what you want to do
Open Sans 12
Send
From Gabriela Marrera <gabriela.marrera@tbtbank.com>
To All
Cc
Subject Serving Our Community and Having Fun at Helping Hands Day, November 10
Dear TBT Bank Members:
Every day volunteers make our community a better place to live and work. They feed the homeless, provide companionship to the elderly, build low-income housing, restore the natural environment, tutor at-risk children, read to children in shelters, participate in hurricane recovery efforts, and even care for homeless pets! These and other volunteer opportunities will be available on November 10 during Helping Hands Day, a fundraising event that we at TBT Bank endorse with immense pride.
In partnership with United Way, we at TBT Bank are joining in this day of change for our community. You can be part of the change as 6,000 hands come together to paint, plant, create murals, and clean neighborhoods and beaches. Last year a TBT Bank team landscaped and repainted the local board-walk during Helping Hands Day. Afterward, a survey showed that 86 percent of the volunteers thought the experience was worthwhile and that their efforts made a difference.
To participate, each volunteer pays a registration fee of $30. You may wonder why you should pay to volunteer. Helping Hands Day is the agency's only fundraising event, and it supports year-round free services and programs for the entire community. For your $30, you receive breakfast and an event T-shirt. Best of all, you share in making your community a better place to live and work.
To provide the best registration process possible, we are excited to work with Body n'Sole, which has extensive experience managing registration for large-scale community events. Just go to http://www.body-n-sole.com and request a registration form before October 19.
You can make a huge difference to your community by volunteering for Helping Hands Day, November 10. Join the fun and your TBT Bank colleagues in showing the community that we value volunteerism that achieves community goals. For every employee who volunteers before October 26, TBT Bank will contribute $30 to United Way. Sign up now and name the team members you want to work with.
Cordially,
Gabriela
Director, HR Staffing and Training
Gabriela Marrera | gabriela.marrero@tbtbank.com | x3228
Captures attention by describing indirect benefits of volunteering in the community
Gains attention
Develops interest with examples and survey results
Builds interest
Reduces resistance by emphasizing both direct and indirect benefits
Reduces resistance
Makes it easy to comply with request
Prompts action by providing deadline and incentive
Motivates action

Gabriela decides to follow the AIDA four-part indirect strategy beginning with gaining attention.

- She strives to capture attention by describing specific benefits of volunteering.
- The second paragraph builds interest by listing examples of what volunteers have accomplished during previous fundraising events.
- To reduce resistance, the third paragraph explains why the $30 fee makes sense.
- To motivate action in the closing, Gabriela states a strong indirect benefit. The bank will chip in an additional $30 for every employee who volunteers before the deadline. This significant indirect benefit combines with the direct benefits of having fun and joining colleagues in a community activity to create a strong persuasive message.

Persuading the Boss: Messages Flowing Upward

Convincing management to adopt a procedure or invest in a product or new equipment requires skillful communication. Managers are just as resistant to change as others are.

Providing evidence is critical when submitting a recommendation to your boss. Be ready to back up your request with facts, figures, and evidence. When selling an idea to management, strive to make a strong dollars-and-cents case.[21] A request that emphasizes how the proposal saves money or benefits the business is more persuasive than one that simply announces a good deal or tells how a plan works.

In describing an idea to your boss, state it confidently and fairly. Show that you have thought through the suggestion by describing the risks involved as well as the potential benefits. You may wonder whether you should even mention the downside of a suggestion. Most bosses will be relieved and impressed to know that you have considered the risks and the benefits of a proposal.[22] Two-sided arguments are generally more persuasive because they make you sound credible and fair. Presenting only one side of a proposal reduces its effectiveness because such a proposal seems biased, subjective, and flawed.

Persuasive messages travelling upward require a special sensitivity to tone. When asking superiors to change views or take action, use words such as *suggest* and *recommend* rather than *you must* and *we should*. Avoid sounding pushy or argumentative. Strive for a conversational, yet professional, tone that conveys warmth, competence, and confidence.

When marketing assistant Leonard Oliver wanted his boss to authorize the purchase of a multifunction colour laser copier, he knew he had to be persuasive. His memo, shown in Figure 10.9, illustrates an effective approach.

Notice that Leo's memo isn't short. A successful persuasive message typically takes more space than a direct message because proving a case requires evidence. In the end, Leo chose to send his memo as an e-mail attachment accompanied by a polite, short e-mail because he wanted to keep the document format in MS Word intact. He also felt that the message was too long to paste into his e-mail program. The subject line announces the purpose of the message but without disclosing the actual request. The strength of the persuasive document in Figure 10.9 is in the clear presentation of comparison figures showing how much money the company can save by purchasing a remanufactured copier.

Concept Check

1. Why are persuasive messages usually longer than direct messages?
2. Consider a time when an employer, a friend, or a family member asked you to volunteer your time. What persuasive techniques did they use to convince you to volunteer? In what ways was their approach effective or ineffective?

Creating Effective Sales Messages in Print and Online

LEARNING OBJECTIVE 5

Create effective and ethical direct-mail and e-mail sales messages.

Sales messages use persuasion to promote specific products and services. The best sales messages, whether delivered by direct mail or by e-mail, have much in common. In this section we look at how to apply the 3-x-3 writing process to sales messages. We also present techniques developed by experts to draft effective sales messages, both in print and online.

Applying the 3-x-3 Writing Process to Sales Messages

Marketing professionals analyze and perfect every aspect of a sales message to encourage consumers to read and act on the message. Like the experts, you will want to pay close attention to analysis and adaptation before writing the actual message.

Analyzing the Product. Before sitting down to write a sales message promoting a product, you must study the item carefully. What can you learn about its design and construction? What can you learn about its ease of use, efficiency, durability, and applications? Be sure to consider warranties, service, price, premiums, exclusivity, and special appeals.

FIGURE 10.9 Persuasive Message Flowing Upward

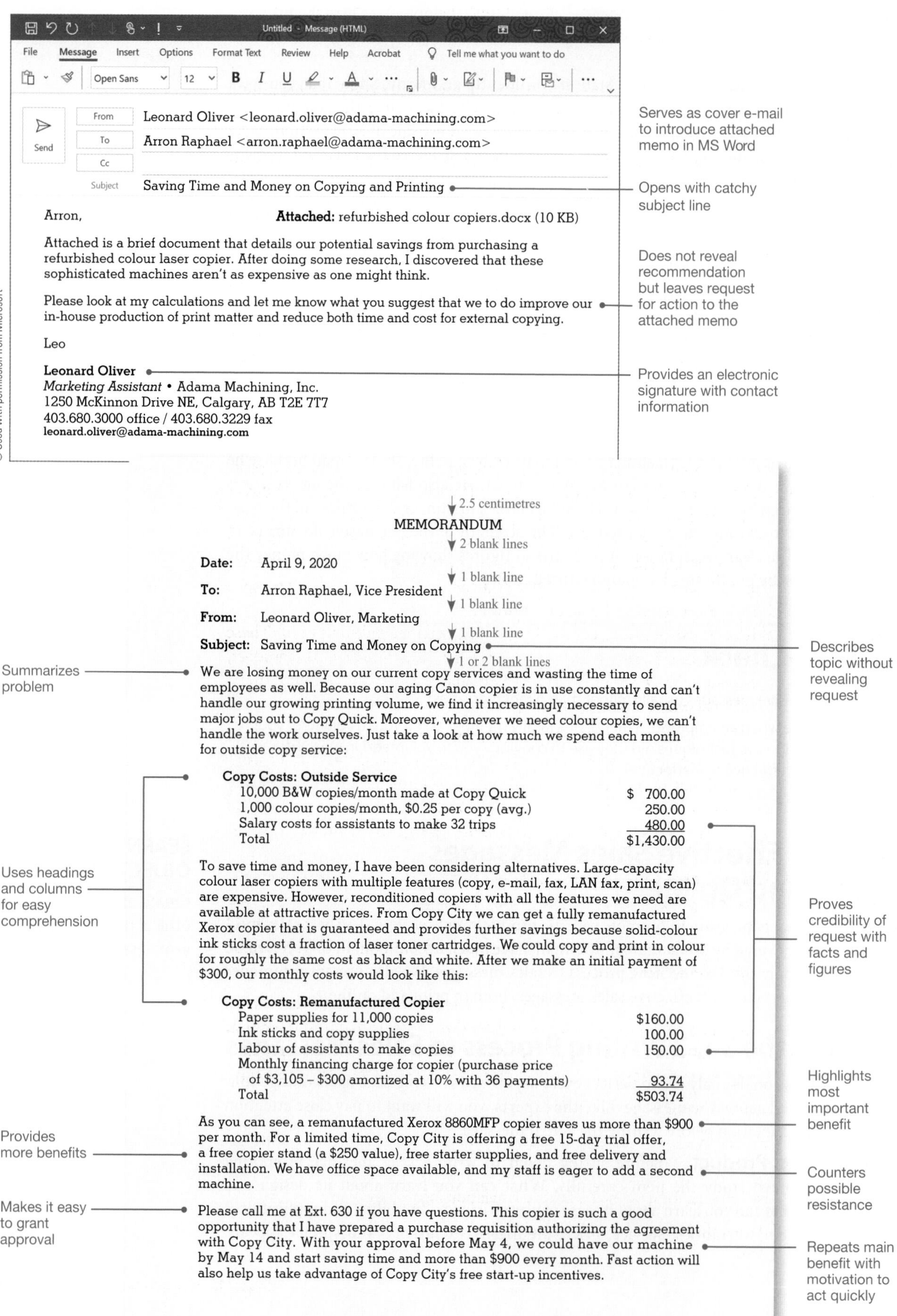

Untitled - Message (HTML)
File Message Insert Options Format Text Review Help Acrobat Tell me what you want to do
Open Sans 12
Send
From Leonard Oliver <leonard.oliver@adama-machining.com>
To Arron Raphael <arron.raphael@adama-machining.com>
Cc
Subject Saving Time and Money on Copying and Printing
Arron,
Attached: refurbished colour copiers.docx (10 KB)
Attached is a brief document that details our potential savings from purchasing a refurbished colour laser copier. After doing some research, I discovered that these sophisticated machines aren't as expensive as one might think.
Please look at my calculations and let me know what you suggest that we to do improve our in-house production of print matter and reduce both time and cost for external copying.
Leo
Leonard Oliver
Marketing Assistant • Adama Machining, Inc.
1250 McKinnon Drive NE, Calgary, AB T2E 7T7
403.680.3000 office / 403.680.3229 fax
leonard.oliver@adama-machining.com
Serves as cover e-mail to introduce attached memo in MS Word
Opens with catchy subject line
Does not reveal recommendation but leaves request for action to the attached memo
Provides an electronic signature with contact information
© Used with permission from Microsoft
2.5 centimetres
MEMORANDUM
2 blank lines
Date: April 9, 2020
1 blank line
To: Arron Raphael, Vice President
1 blank line
From: Leonard Oliver, Marketing
1 blank line
Subject: Saving Time and Money on Copying
1 or 2 blank lines
We are losing money on our current copy services and wasting the time of employees as well. Because our aging Canon copier is in use constantly and can't handle our growing printing volume, we find it increasingly necessary to send major jobs out to Copy Quick. Moreover, whenever we need colour copies, we can't handle the work ourselves. Just take a look at how much we spend each month for outside copy service:
Copy Costs: Outside Service
10,000 B&W copies/month made at Copy Quick $ 700.00
1,000 colour copies/month, $0.25 per copy (avg.) 250.00
Salary costs for assistants to make 32 trips 480.00
Total $1,430.00
To save time and money, I have been considering alternatives. Large-capacity colour laser copiers with multiple features (copy, e-mail, fax, LAN fax, print, scan) are expensive. However, reconditioned copiers with all the features we need are available at attractive prices. From Copy City we can get a fully remanufactured Xerox copier that is guaranteed and provides further savings because solid-colour ink sticks cost a fraction of laser toner cartridges. We could copy and print in colour for roughly the same cost as black and white. After we make an initial payment of $300, our monthly costs would look like this:
Copy Costs: Remanufactured Copier
Paper supplies for 11,000 copies $160.00
Ink sticks and copy supplies 100.00
Labour of assistants to make copies 150.00
Monthly financing charge for copier (purchase price of $3,105 – $300 amortized at 10% with 36 payments) 93.74
Total $503.74
As you can see, a remanufactured Xerox 8860MFP copier saves us more than $900 per month. For a limited time, Copy City is offering a free 15-day trial offer, a free copier stand (a $250 value), free starter supplies, and free delivery and installation. We have office space available, and my staff is eager to add a second machine.
Please call me at Ext. 630 if you have questions. This copier is such a good opportunity that I have prepared a purchase requisition authorizing the agreement with Copy City. With your approval before May 4, we could have our machine by May 14 and start saving time and more than $900 every month. Fast action will also help us take advantage of Copy City's free start-up incentives.
Summarizes problem
Uses headings and columns for easy comprehension
Provides more benefits
Makes it easy to grant approval
Describes topic without revealing request
Proves credibility of request with facts and figures
Highlights most important benefit
Counters possible resistance
Repeats main benefit with motivation to act quickly

At the same time, evaluate the competition so that you can compare your product's strengths against the competitor's weaknesses.

Now you are ready to identify your central selling point, the main theme of your appeal. Analyzing your product and studying the competition help you determine what to emphasize in your sales message.

Determining the Purpose of a Sales Message. Equally important is determining the specific purpose of your message. Do you want the reader to call for a free video and brochure? Listen to a podcast at your website? Fill out an order form? Send a credit card authorization? Before you write the first word of your message, know what response you want and what central selling point you will emphasize to achieve that purpose.

Adapting a Sales Message to Its Audience. Despite today's predominance of e-mail marketing over direct-mail letters, in terms of response rates, sales letters win. Direct mail achieves a 4.4 percent response rate compared with e-mail's paltry 0.12 percent.[23] The response rate can be increased dramatically by targeting the audience through selected database mailing lists. Let's say you are selling fitness equipment. A good mailing list might come from subscribers to fitness or exercise magazines, who you would expect to have similar interests, needs, and demographics (age, income, and other characteristics). With this knowledge you can adapt the sales message to a specific audience.

Crafting Successful Sales Letters

Direct mail is usually part of multichannel marketing campaigns. These messages are a powerful means to make sales, generate leads, boost retail traffic, solicit donations, and direct consumers to websites. Direct mail is a great channel for personalized, tangible, three-dimensional messages that are less invasive than telephone solicitations and less reviled than unsolicited e-mail. A recent study shows that tangible direct mail appears to have a greater emotional impact than virtual mail. Brain scans suggest that physical materials "engage a different (and presumably more retentive) part of the brain."[24]

You have probably received many direct-mail packages, often called junk mail. These packages typically contain a sales letter, a brochure, a price list, illustrations of the product, testimonials, and other persuasive appeals. Figure 10.10 juxtaposes the most relevant features of traditional direct-mail and online sales messages.

Considering the Value of Sales Letters. Because sales letters are generally written by specialists, you may never write one on the job. Why learn how to write a sales letter? Learning the techniques of sales writing will help you be more successful in any communication that requires persuasion and promotion. What's more, you will recognize sales strategies directed at you, which will make you a more perceptive consumer of ideas, products, and services.

Your primary goal in writing a sales message is to get someone to devote a few moments of attention to it. You may be promoting a product, a service, an idea, or yourself. In each case the most effective messages will follow the AIDA strategy and (a) gain attention, (b) build interest, (c) elicit desire and reduce resistance, and (d) motivate action. This is the same recipe we studied earlier, but the ingredients are different.

Gaining Attention in Sales Messages. One of the most critical elements of a sales message is its opening paragraph. This opener should be short (one to five lines), honest, relevant, and stimulating. Marketing pros have found that eye-catching typographical arrangements or provocative messages, such as the following, can hook a reader's attention:

- **Offer.** A free trip to Hawaii is just the beginning!
- **Promise.** Now you can raise your sales income by 50 percent or even more with the proven techniques found in . . .
- **Question.** Do you yearn for an honest, fulfilling relationship?
- **Quotation or proverb.** Necessity is the mother of invention.

FIGURE 10.10 Characteristics of Traditional Versus Online Sales Messages

Traditional Direct Mail (Sales Letter)	E-commerce (E-mail, Social Media Messages)
Creating static content (hard copy)	Creating dynamic digital content
Anticipating a single response (inquiry, sale)	Creating engagement instead of selling overtly
Resorting to "spray-and-pray" approach	Building one-to-one relationships and communities around brands
Single communication channel	Multiple communication channels
Limited response	Potentially unlimited responses
Monologue	Dialogue, potential for mass diffusion
Private response	Public, shared response
Asynchronous (delayed) response	Instant, real-time response possible
Passive	Interactive, participatory
Promoter-generated content	User-generated content
The needs of target groups must be anticipated and met in advance.	Consumers expect that brands understand their unique needs and deliver.
Direct mail is preferred for information about insurance, financial services, and health care; it's an excellent channel for offline customers.	**Savvy brands respond nimbly to customer participation; today's sophisticated consumers dislike a "hard sell."**

- **Fact.** The Greenland Inuit ate more fat than anyone in the world, and yet they had virtually no heart disease.
- **Product feature.** Volvo's snazzy new convertible ensures your safety with a roll bar that pops out when the car tips 40 degrees to the side.
- **Testimonial.** My name is Sheldon Schulman. I am a practising medical doctor. I am also a multimillionaire. I didn't make my millions by practising medicine, though. I made them by making investments in my spare time.
- **Startling statement.** Help improve the lives of impoverished Canadians. For just $100 you can.
- **Personalized action setting.** It's 4:30 p.m. and you have to make a decision. You need everybody's opinion, no matter where they are. Before you pick up your phone to call them one at a time, pick up this card: WebEx Teleconference Services.

Other openings calculated to capture attention might include a solution to a problem, an anecdote, a personalized statement using the receiver's name, or a relevant current event.

Building Interest With Rational and Emotional Appeals. In this phase of your sales message, you should describe clearly the product or service. In simple language emphasize the central selling points that you identified during your prewriting analysis. Those selling points can be developed using rational or emotional appeals.

Rational appeals are associated with reason and intellect. They translate selling points into references to making or saving money, increasing efficiency, or making the best use of resources. In general, rational appeals are appropriate when a product is expensive, long lasting, or important to health, security, and financial success.

Emotional appeals relate to status, ego, and sensual feelings. Appealing to the emotions is sometimes effective when a product is inexpensive, short-lived, or nonessential. Many clever sales messages, however, combine emotional and rational strategies for a dual appeal. Consider these examples:

Rational Appeal

You can buy the things you need and want, pay household bills, and pay off higher-cost loans and credit cards—as soon as you are approved and your ChoiceCredit card account is opened.

Emotional Appeal

Leave the urban bustle behind and escape to sun-soaked Bermuda! To recharge your batteries with an injection of sun and surf, all you need are your bathing suit, a little sunscreen, and your ChoiceCredit card.

Dual Appeal

New ChoiceCredit cardholders are immediately eligible for a $200 travel certificate and additional discounts at fun-filled resorts. Save up to 40 percent while lying on a beach in picturesque, sun-soaked Bermuda, the year-round resort island.

A physical description of your product is not enough, however. When you create warm feelings and highlight reader benefits, people buy because of product benefits.[25]

As the Case Connections feature shows, emotional appeal gains attention.

Reducing Resistance and Building Desire. Marketing specialists use a number of techniques to overcome resistance and build desire. When price is an obstacle, consider these suggestions:

- Delay mentioning price until after you've created a desire for the product.
- Show the price in small units, such as the price per issue of a magazine.
- Demonstrate how the reader saves money—for instance, by subscribing for two or three years.
- Compare your prices with those of a competitor.

CASE CONNECTIONS

President's Choice #EatTogether Campaign

Rawpixel.com/Shutterstock

In 2017 President's Choice, a Canadian label owned by Loblaw, launched its #EatTogether advertising campaign and now promotes June 14 as Eat Together Day.[26] According to Jared Smith, principal at Incite Marketing, there has been a "general decline in traditional advertising methods and a trend towards emotional storytelling" in Canada.[27] President's Choice's #EatTogether campaign is a success because it focused less on its products and more on bringing people together. Angus Tucker, executive creative director at john st., discussed the appeal of the campaign: "It's an opportunity for Canadians to reflect on who the country is and who we are as Canadians."[28]

Within a week of President's Choice launching its #EatTogether campaign, it had over a million views on YouTube.[29] Now, Eat Together Day Events take place yearly across Canada.[30]

- View President's Choice #EatTogether commercials on YouTube. Considering specific examples from the ads, how does this campaign effectively use emotional appeal?

In addition, you need to anticipate other objections and questions the receiver may have. When possible, translate these objections into selling points (*If you are worried about training your staff members on the new software, remember that our offer includes $1,000 worth of onsite one-on-one instruction*). Other techniques to overcome resistance and prove the credibility of the product include the following:

- **Testimonials.** "I never stopped eating, yet I lost 50 kilograms." —Tina Rivers, Woodstock, Ontario
- **Names of satisfied users (with permission, of course).** Enclosed is a partial list of private pilots who enthusiastically subscribe to our service.
- **Money-back guarantee or warranty.** We offer the longest warranties in the business—all parts and service onsite for five years!
- **Free trial or sample.** We are so confident that you will like our new accounting program that we want you to try it absolutely free.
- **Performance tests, polls, or awards.** Our TP-3000 was named Best Internet Phone, and Etown.com voted it Smartphone of the Year.

Motivating Action at the Conclusion of a Sales Message. All the effort put into a sales message goes to waste if the reader fails to act. To make it easy for readers to act, you can provide a reply card, a stamped and preaddressed envelope, a toll-free telephone number, an easy-to-scan website, or a promise of a follow-up call. Because readers often need an extra push, consider including additional motivators, such as the following:

- **Offer a gift.** You will receive a free cell phone with the purchase of any new car.
- **Promise an incentive.** With every new, paid subscription, we will plant a tree in one of Canada's National Forests.
- **Limit the offer.** Only the first 100 customers receive free travel mugs.
- **Set a deadline.** You must act before June 1 to get these low prices.
- **Guarantee satisfaction.** We will return your full payment if you are not entirely satisfied—no questions asked.

The final paragraph of the sales letter carries the punch. This is where you tell readers what you want them to do and give them reasons for doing it. Most sales letters also include postscripts because they make irresistible reading. Even readers who might skim over or bypass paragraphs are drawn to a P.S. Therefore, use a postscript to reveal your strongest motivator, to add a special inducement for a quick response, or to reemphasize a central selling point.

Putting Together All the Parts of a Sales Message. A direct-mail sales letter can be personalized, directed to target audiences, and filled with a more complete message than other advertising media can. However, direct mail is expensive. That's why crafting and assembling all the parts of a sales message are so critical.

Figure 10.11 shows a sales letter addressed to individuals and families who may need extended health insurance. To prompt the reader to respond to the mailing, the letter incorporates the effective four-part AIDA strategy. The writer first establishes the need for extended health coverage. Then she develops a rational central selling point (a variety of affordable extended health plans for every budget offered without sales pressure and medical jargon) and repeats this selling point in all the components of the letter. This sales letter saves its strongest motivator—a free heart-rate monitor for the first 30 callers—for the high-impact P.S. line.

Writing Successful E-mail Sales Messages

Much like traditional direct mail, e-mail marketing can attract new customers, keep existing ones, encourage future sales, cross-sell, and cut costs. However, e-marketers can create and send

FIGURE 10.11 ProHealth Sales Letter

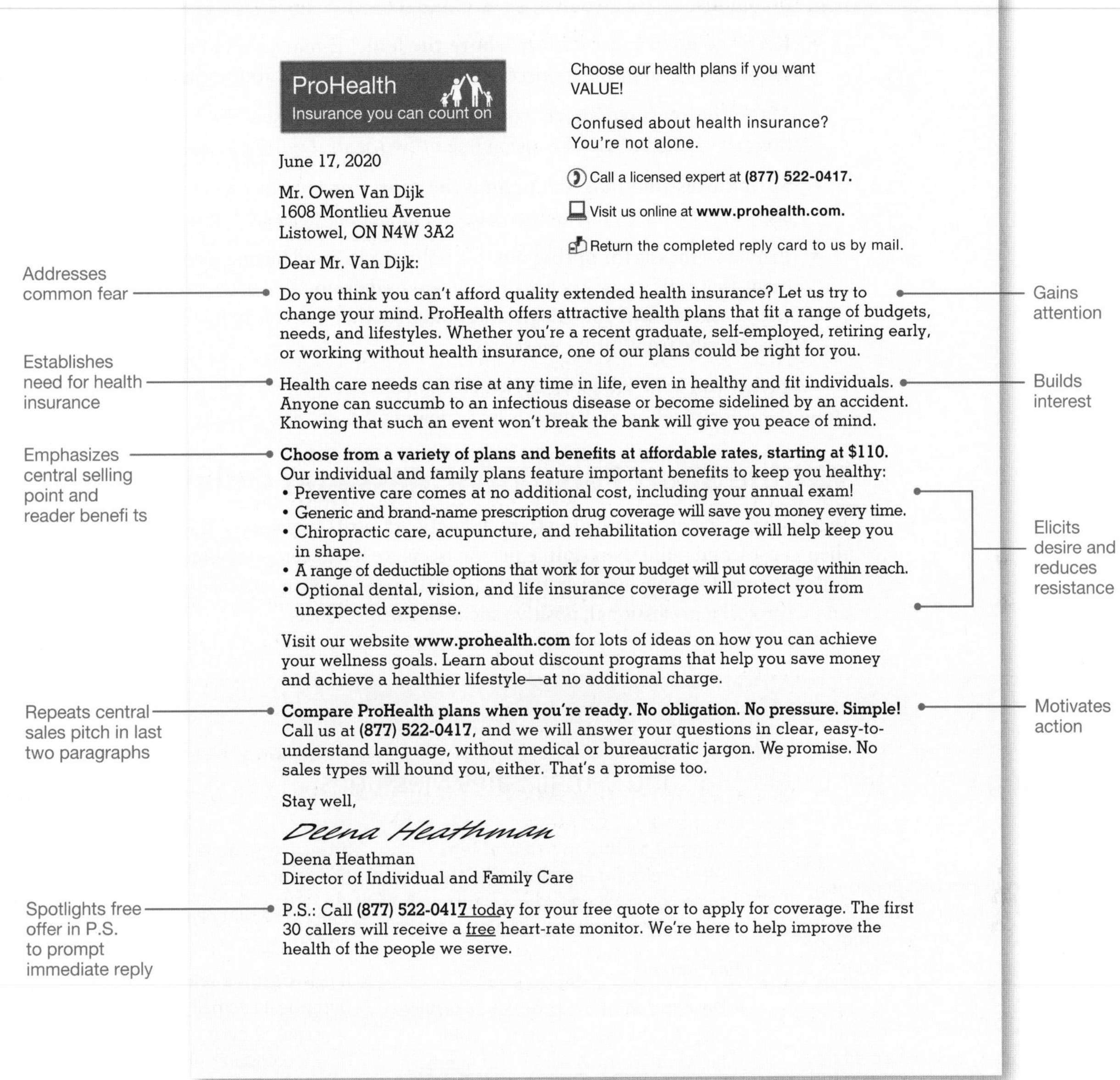

a promotion in half the time it takes to print and distribute a traditional message. To reach today's consumer, marketers must target their e-mails well if they want to have their messages opened.

ProHealth
Insurance you can count on
Choose our health plans if you want VALUE!
Confused about health insurance? You're not alone.
Call a licensed expert at **(877) 522-0417.**
Visit us online at **www.prohealth.com.**
Return the completed reply card to us by mail.
June 17, 2020
Mr. Owen Van Dijk
1608 Montlieu Avenue
Listowel, ON N4W 3A2
Dear Mr. Van Dijk:
Do you think you can't afford quality extended health insurance? Let us try to change your mind. ProHealth offers attractive health plans that fit a range of budgets, needs, and lifestyles. Whether you're a recent graduate, self-employed, retiring early, or working without health insurance, one of our plans could be right for you.
Health care needs can rise at any time in life, even in healthy and fit individuals. Anyone can succumb to an infectious disease or become sidelined by an accident. Knowing that such an event won't break the bank will give you peace of mind.
Choose from a variety of plans and benefits at affordable rates, starting at $110. Our individual and family plans feature important benefits to keep you healthy:
• Preventive care comes at no additional cost, including your annual exam!
• Generic and brand-name prescription drug coverage will save you money every time.
• Chiropractic care, acupuncture, and rehabilitation coverage will help keep you in shape.
• A range of deductible options that work for your budget will put coverage within reach.
• Optional dental, vision, and life insurance coverage will protect you from unexpected expense.
Visit our website **www.prohealth.com** for lots of ideas on how you can achieve your wellness goals. Learn about discount programs that help you save money and achieve a healthier lifestyle—at no additional charge.
Compare ProHealth plans when you're ready. No obligation. No pressure. Simple! Call us at **(877) 522-0417**, and we will answer your questions in clear, easy-to-understand language, without medical or bureaucratic jargon. We promise. No sales types will hound you, either. That's a promise too.
Stay well,
Deena Heathman
Deena Heathman
Director of Individual and Family Care
P.S.: Call **(877) 522-0417** today for your free quote or to apply for coverage. The first 30 callers will receive a free heart-rate monitor. We're here to help improve the health of the people we serve.
Addresses common fear
Establishes need for health insurance
Emphasizes central selling point and reader benefi ts
Repeats central sales pitch in last two paragraphs
Spotlights free offer in P.S. to prompt immediate reply
Gains attention
Builds interest
Elicits desire and reduces resistance
Motivates action

Selling by E-mail. If you will be writing online sales messages for your organization, try using the following techniques gleaned from the best-performing e-mails. Although much e-marketing dazzles receivers with colourful graphics, we focus on the words involved in persuasive sales messages. Earlier in the chapter, Figure 10.3 demonstrated many of the principles discussed here.

The first rule of e-marketing is to communicate only with those who have given permission. By sending messages only to "opt-in" folks, you greatly increase your "open rate"—those e-mails that will be opened. E-mail users detest spam. However, receivers are surprisingly receptive to offers tailored specifically for them. Here are a few guidelines that will help you create effective e-mail sales messages:

- **Craft a catchy subject line.** Include an audience-specific location (*Great Wolf Lodge opens in Niagara Falls!*); ask a meaningful question (*What's Your Dream Vacation?*); and use no more than 50 characters. Promise realistic solutions. Offer discounts or premiums.
- **Keep the main information "above the fold."** E-mails should be top heavy. Primary points should appear early in the message so that they capture the reader's attention.
- **Make the message short, conversational, and focused.** Because on-screen text is taxing to read, be brief. Focus on one or two central selling points only.
- **Sprinkle testimonials throughout the copy.** Consumers' own words are the best sales copy. These comments can serve as callouts or be integrated into the copy.
- **Provide a means for opting out.** It's polite and a good business tactic to include a statement that tells receivers how to be removed from the sender's mailing database. As well, Canada's anti-spam legislation requires that marketing materials include a way to unsubscribe from future messages.

Whether you write sales messages on the job or merely receive them, you will better understand their organization and appeals by reviewing this chapter and the tips in the Checklist.

Writing Short Persuasive Messages Online

Increasingly, writers are turning to social network posts to promote their businesses, further their causes, and build their online personas. As we have seen, social media are not primarily suited for overt selling; however, tweets and other online posts can be used to influence others and to project a professional, positive social online presence.

CHECKLIST

Preparing Persuasive Direct-Mail and E-mail Sales Messages

Prewrite

- **Analyze your product or service.** What makes it special? What central selling points should you emphasize? How does it compare with the competition?
- **Profile your audience.** How will this product or service benefit this audience?
- **Decide what you want** the audience to do at the end of your message.
- **For e-mails,** send only to those who have opted in.

Gain Attention

- **Describe a product feature,** present a testimonial, make a startling statement, or show the reader in an action setting.
- **Offer something valuable,** promise the reader a result, or pose a stimulating question.
- **Suggest a solution to a problem,** offer a relevant anecdote, use the receiver's name, or mention a meaningful current event.

Build Interest

- **Describe what the product or service** does for the reader. Connect cold facts with warm feelings and needs.
- **Use rational appeals** if the product or service is expensive, long-lasting, or important to health, security, or financial success. Use emotional appeals to suggest status, ego, or sensual feelings.
- **Explain how the product or service** can save or make money, reduce effort, improve health, produce pleasure, or boost status.

Elicit Desire and Reduce Resistance

- **Counter anticipated reluctance** with testimonials, money-back guarantees, attractive warranties, trial offers, or free samples.
- **Build credibility** with results of performance tests, polls, or awards.
- **If price is not a selling feature,** describe it in small units (99 cents an issue), show it as savings, or tell how it compares favourably with the competition.

Motivate Action

- **Close by repeating** a central selling point and describing an easy-to-take action.
- **Prompt the reader to act** immediately with a gift, an incentive, a limited offer, a deadline, or a guarantee of satisfaction.
- **Put the strongest motivator** in a postscript.
- **In e-mails** include an opportunity to opt out.

FIGURE 10.12 Analyzing Persuasive Tweets

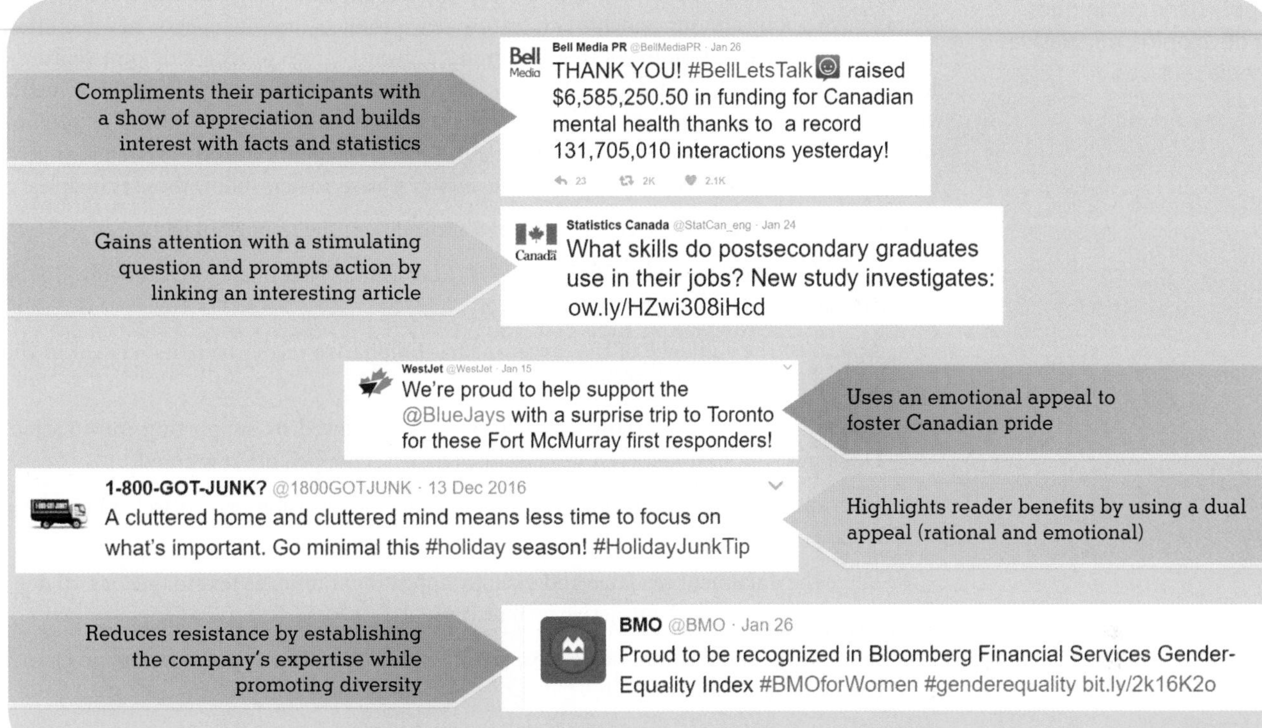

Typically, organizations and individuals with followers post updates of their events, exploits, thoughts, and experiences. In persuasive tweets and posts, writers try to pitch offers, prompt specific responses, or draw the attention of their audiences to interesting events and media links. Figure 10.12 displays a sampling of persuasive tweets.

Note that the compact format of a tweet requires extreme conciseness and efficiency. Don't expect the full four-part AIDA strategy to be represented in a 140-character Twitter message. Instead, you may see attention getters and calls for action, both of which must be catchy and intriguing. Regardless, many of the principles of persuasion apply even to micromessages.

Concept Check

1. Think of a product you have used and like. If you were trying to sell that product, what rational appeals would you use? What emotional appeals would you use? Try to sell that product to your classmates.
2. Being able to compose effective and concise micromessages and posts will positively contribute to your professional online persona. Brainstorm to identify a special skill you have, an event you want others to attend, a charitable cause dear to your heart, or a product you like. Applying what you have learned about short persuasive messages online, write your own 140-character persuasive tweet or post. Use Figure 10.12 as a starting point and model.

LEARNING OBJECTIVE 6

Apply basic techniques in developing persuasive media releases.

Developing Persuasive Media Releases

Media (news) releases announce important information to the media, whether traditional or digital. Such public announcements can feature new products, new managers, new facilities, sponsorships, participation in community projects, awards given or received, joint ventures, donations, or seminars and demonstrations. Naturally, organizations hope that the media will pick up this news and provide good publicity. However, purely self-serving or promotional information is not appealing to magazine and newspaper editors or to TV producers. To get them to read beyond the first sentence, media release writers follow these principles:

- Open with an attention-getting lead or a summary of the important facts.
- Include answers to the five Ws and one H (*who*, *what*, *when*, *where*, *why*, and *how*) in the article—but not all in the first sentence!
- Appeal to the audience of the target media. Emphasize reader benefits written in the style of the focus publication or newscast.
- Present the most important information early, followed by supporting information. Don't put your best ideas last because they may be chopped off or ignored.
- Insert intriguing and informative quotations of chief decision makers to lend the news release credibility.
- Make the document readable and visually appealing. Limit the text to one or two double-spaced pages with attractive formatting.
- Look and sound credible—no typos, no imaginative spelling or punctuation, no factual errors.

The most important ingredient of a press release, of course, is *news*. Articles that merely plug products end up in the circular file, or they languish unread on a company website. The press release in Figure 10.13 announced the launch of a unique breast cancer research study conducted by two reputable medical organizations, Dr. Susan Love Research Foundation and City of Hope. The announcement provides an appealing headline and describes the purpose and the process of the massive, long-term research project. The Health of Women Study is unusual in that it employs crowdsourcing and actively involves huge numbers of subjects online and by mobile devices. Moreover, data will be shared with all interested researchers and the participants themselves.

The best press releases focus on information that appeals to a targeted audience. A breast cancer study focusing on the potential causes and prevention of the disease is likely to generate keen and wide-ranging interest. The credibility of the study's sponsors discourages sensationalist coverage. Indirectly, the nonprofit organizations may also attract more research subjects and donations. Figure 10.13 illustrates many useful techniques for creating effective press releases.

Newspapers, magazines, and digital media are more likely to publish a media release that is informative, interesting, and helpful. The websites of many organizations today provide readily available media information including releases and photos.

Concept Check

1. What type of public announcements might a media (news) release announce?
2. Why is it important to carefully consider where to place the most important information in a news release?

FIGURE 10.13 Media Release With a Broad Appeal

DR. SUSAN LOVE RESEARCH FOUNDATION
Act with Love™
FOR A FUTURE WITHOUT BREAST CANCER

FOR IMMEDIATE RELEASE

MEDIA CONTACTS: Shirley Carr scarr@dslrf.org
Hanna Johnson hjohnson@dslrf.org
310-282-0600

"The key to ending breast cancer is to learn how to stop it before it starts."
--Dr. Susan Love, President, Dr. Susan Love Research Foundation

GROUNDBREAKING HEALTH OF WOMEN STUDY LAUNCHED

SANTA MONICA, Calif. – The Dr. Susan Love Research Foundation and Beckman Research Institute of City of Hope, today launch the Health of Women Study (HOW), a long-term cohort study tracking the health of women via online and mobile platforms. This new 21st-century research was designed to help find the root causes of breast cancer, leading to prevention. Any woman over 18 years old, as well as interested men, can join this revolutionary effort. HOW will study survivors and women who have not been diagnosed with breast cancer to investigate causes and new risk factors.

"The majority of women who get breast cancer have none of the known clinical risk factors for the disease," said Susan Love, MD, president and founder of the Dr. Susan Love Research Foundation. "We have made strides in how we treat breast cancer, but we still don't know how to prevent it. We believe this new kind of study that traces and involves healthy women and breast cancer patients will give us the data we need to find the cause and develop prevention."

"Cohort studies are most valuable in epidemiology, but they are extremely costly and difficult to manage," said Leslie Bernstein, PhD, Beckman Research Institute of City of Hope. "The HOW Study uses economical technology and will capture behaviour and lifestyle changes affecting women's cancer risk."

The HOW Study enables clinical researchers to pose questions rapidly, reaching a large sample population online and via mobile devices. Thus, researchers will capture more relevant data than has been feasible before and will empower consumers to become major stakeholders actively engaged in research. Study participants will be able to pose questions and play a tangible role in working to end breast cancer. "The important data collected as a part of HOW will be shared with researchers who can use it—a practice virtually unheard of in the research community," said Love.

In 2008 the Dr. Susan Love Research Foundation introduced the Love/Avon Army of Women to participate in breast cancer research studies looking into causes and prevention of the disease. Today the Army of Women has nearly 370,000 women ready to participate in research studies.

About the Study Sponsors
The mission of Dr. Susan Love Research Foundation is to eradicate breast cancer and improve the quality of women's health through innovative research, education and advocacy. Beckman Research Institute of City of Hope is known worldwide for its outstanding basic, translational and epidemiological research. For details, visit www.healthofwomenstudy.org

###

Annotations:
- Offers contacts for press inquiries
- Opens by explaining who, what, when, where, why, and how
- Quotes the chief investigators to add insight and credibility
- Addresses the recruitment of study subjects
- Offers means of obtaining additional information
- Provides optional headline
- Announces populations targeted by the study
- Explains in detail the unique features and benefits of the study
- Describes credentials of sponsoring organizations
- Uses pound symbols to signal end of release

SPOTLIGHT ON COMMUNICATION: PART 2

David Suzuki Foundation Revisited

CRITICAL THINKING

- Discuss the ways that David Suzuki builds interest in his speech. How are these strategies effective?
- How does he elicit desire and reduce resistance in his message?

In 2019 David Suzuki gave the following speech to student climate strikers in Vancouver:

Courtesy of David Suzuki Foundation

> I begin by recognizing that we are on the traditional, unceded territory of the Coast Salish people—Musqueam, Squamish and Tsleil-Waututh—and I thank you for caring for these lands and waters for thousands of years. It has been Indigenous people here and in many parts of the world who have taught me all about our responsibility to care for nature so she can continue to be abundant and generous for us. We all have to thank you for holding on to your values and culture and to be willing to share your knowledge with us.
>
> And thank you, youth of Vancouver, for inviting me to be part of your event and for the privilege of sharing a few thoughts with you. I am here today to speak as an elder, with no hidden agenda or vested interest in the status quo, and with a life of experience to give credence to my words.
>
> I also speak as a father and grandfather. Every parent hopes to leave their children better off than he or she was growing up, but my generation and the boomers that followed were too busy celebrating the recovery from the Great Depression of the 1930s and then victory in World War II and tried to keep the good times going through consumerism and economic growth.
>
> We didn't think about responsibility or long-term consequences of the way we were living; we just partied as if there was no tomorrow. Well, tomorrow has come. And we know that in the name of progress, we have mortgaged your futures by using up your rightful legacy:
>
> - land once covered in vast forests, wetlands and grasslands occupied by animals in great abundance and diversity,
> - oceans that were free of plastic and rich in biodiversity and fresh water that we could drink without treatment,
> - an atmosphere free of toxic chemicals and excess greenhouse gases.
>
> As a member of my generation, I thank you for leaving school today and gathering here to bring us to our senses in the realization that short-term profit, election to office and economic growth can no longer be society's highest priorities. Those priorities must be your future and the state of the world that you will inherit.[31]

You can find the speech in its entirety at the David Suzuki Foundation website at davidsuzuki.org.

Summary of Learning Objectives

1 Explain persuasion, identify effective persuasive techniques, and apply the 3-x-3 writing process to persuasive messages in print and online.

- *Persuasion* is the ability to use words and other symbols to influence an individual's attitudes and behaviours.

- Six psychological triggers prompt us to act and to believe: reciprocation, commitment, social proof, liking, authority, and scarcity.
- Effective persuaders establish credibility, make a specific request, tie facts to benefits, recognize the power of loss, expect and overcome resistance, share solutions, and compromise.
- Before writing, communicators decide what they want the receiver to do or think, they adapt their message to their audience, and they collect information and organize it into an appropriate strategy. They are indirect if the audience might resist the request.

2 Describe the traditional four-part AIDA strategy for creating successful persuasive messages, and apply the four elements to draft effective and ethical business messages.

- Include four major elements to craft a persuasive message: gain attention, build interest, elicit desire while reducing resistance, and motivate action.
- Gain attention by opening with a problem, unexpected statement, reader benefit, compliment, related fact, or stimulating question; build interest with facts, expert opinions, examples, details, and direct and indirect reader benefits.
- Elicit desire and reduce resistance by anticipating objections and presenting counterarguments; conclude by motivating a specific action and making it easy for the reader to respond.
- As an ethical persuader, avoid distortion, exaggeration, and doublespeak when making persuasive arguments.

3 Craft persuasive messages that request actions, make claims, and deliver complaints.

- Think through your purpose and prepare a thoughtful message; assume that receivers comply because they want to "give back" and because others may benefit.
- Make a logical argument, adopt an objective, unemotional tone, and prove that your request has merit.
- Open claims with sincere praise, an objective statement of the problem, a point of agreement, or a quick review of what you have done to resolve the problem; elicit desire and reduce resistance by anticipating objections and providing counterarguments.
- Motivate action by stating exactly what is to be done; add a deadline if necessary, and express appreciation.

4 Understand interpersonal persuasion at work and write persuasive messages within organizations.

- When asking subordinates to volunteer for projects or to make lifestyle changes, organizations may use the AIDA strategy to persuade.
- In messages flowing downward, good writers use a conversational tone and warm words; they focus on direct and indirect benefits.
- In messages flowing upward, such as recommendations from subordinates to supervisors, providing evidence is critical; making a strong dollars-and-cents appeal whenever appropriate strengthens the argument.
- Two-sided arguments are more persuasive because they make writers sound credible and fair.

5 **Create effective and ethical direct-mail and e-mail sales messages.**

- Sales messages must be preceded by careful analysis of the product or service until the central selling point can be identified.
- Effective sales messages begin with a short, honest, and relevant attention getter; simple language describing appropriate appeals builds interest.
- Testimonials, money-back guarantees, or free trials can reduce resistance and elicit desire; a gift, an incentive, or a deadline can motivate action.
- Tweets and other short persuasive social media posts can influence others and may even contain AIDA components.

6 **Apply basic techniques in developing persuasive media releases.**

- Open with an attention-getting lead or summary of the important facts.
- Answer the questions of who, what, when, where, why, and how.
- Write carefully to appeal to the audience of the target media.
- Present the most important information early, make your press release visually appealing, and make sure it looks and sounds credible.

Chapter Review

1. What is *persuasion*? (Obj. 1)
2. Explain four ways that persuasion has changed in the digital age. (Obj. 1)
3. What is the first element in the writing process for persuasive messages, and why is it important? (Obj. 2)
4. List six ways to build interest in a persuasive message and show that your request is reasonable. (Obj. 2)
5. Describe how you can develop a logical persuasive argument in a claim message (Obj. 3)
6. When is persuasion necessary in business messages flowing downward in an organization? (Obj. 4)
7. When might persuasion be necessary in messages flowing upward? (Obj. 4)
8. Name eight or more ways to attract attention in the opening of a sales message. (Obj. 5)
9. How can a writer motivate action in a sales letter? (Obj. 5)
10. What is the best way to open a media release? (Obj. 6)

Critical Thinking

1. The word *persuasion* turns some people off. What negative connotations can it have? (Obj. 1)
2. Have you ever believed a fake news story? What persuasive strategies did the writer use to make you believe the news was accurate? (Obj. 1)
3. In view of the burden that "junk" mail places on society (adding to landfills, using timber supplies, and overburdening the postal system), how can "junk" mail be justified? (Obj. 3)
4. Why are magazine and newspaper editors or TV producers wary of media (news) releases from businesses and reluctant to turn them into articles? (Obj. 6)
5. **Ethical Issue:** Two students at Cambridge University, England, charged businesses to have their logos painted on their own faces for a day. The students raised more than $40,000 toward their university tuition.[32] Companies such as Volvo adopted temporary tattoos in their promotions. Dunlop, however, went to the extreme by offering a set of free tires to those who would have the company's flying-D logo *permanently* tattooed somewhere on their bodies. Ninety-eight people complied.[33] Is it ethical for advertisers to resort to such extreme promotions, dubbed "skinvertising"? Do you think it's even effective? Would you participate? (Obj. 5)

Activities

10.1 Document for Analysis: Favour Request—Facebook Flub? (Objs. 1–3)

E-mail

A student chose Facebook to request a recommendation from his professor. The following message suffers from many writing faults, including poor tone and flawed persuasive strategy.

YOUR TASK Analyze the Facebook message and list at least five weaknesses. If your instructor directs, revise the message. Decide whether to use Facebook, of which the receiver is a member, or a conventional e-mail to make this request.

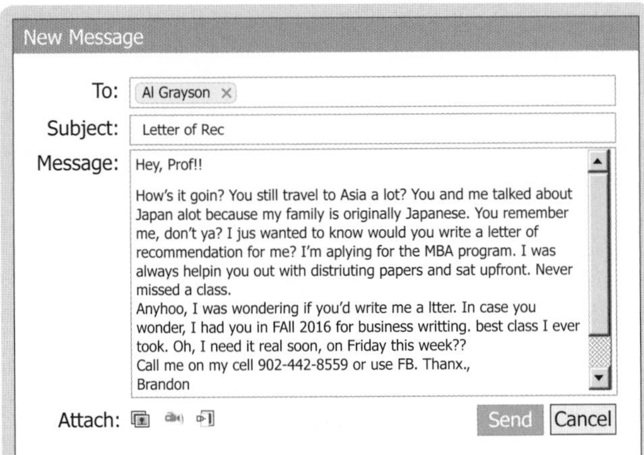

New Message

To: Al Grayson

Subject: Letter of Rec

Message: Hey, Prof!!

How's it goin? You still travel to Asia a lot? You and me talked about Japan alot because my family is originally Japanese. You remember me, don't ya? I jus wanted to know would you write a letter of recommendation for me? I'm aplying for the MBA program. I was always helpin you out with distriuting papers and sat upfront. Never missed a class.

Anyhoo, I was wondering if you'd write me a ltter. In case you wonder, I had you in FAll 2016 for business writting. best class I ever took. Oh, I need it real soon, on Friday this week??

Call me on my cell 902-442-8559 or use FB. Thanx.,

Brandon

Attach:

Send Cancel

10.2 Persuasive Organizational Message Flowing Downward: Fixing Atrocious Memo (Obj. 4)

The following memo (with names changed) was actually sent.

YOUR TASK Based on what you have learned in this chapter, improve the memo. Expect the staff to be somewhat resistant because they have never before had meeting restrictions.

Date: Current
To: All Managers and Employees
From: Nancy Nelson, CEO
Subject: Scheduling Meetings

Please be reminded that travel in the greater Toronto area is time consuming. In the future we are asking that you set up meetings that

1. Are of critical importance
2. Consider travel time for the participants
3. Consider phone conferences (or video or e-mail) in lieu of face-to-face meetings
4. Meetings should be at the location where most of the participants work and at the most opportune travel times
5. Travelling together is another way to save time and resources.

We all have our traffic horror stories. A recent one is that a certain manager was asked to attend a one-hour meeting in Waterloo. This required one hour travel in advance of the meeting, one hour for the meeting, and two and a half hours of travel through Toronto afterward. This meeting was scheduled for 4 p.m. Total time consumed by the manager for the one-hour meeting was four and a half hours.

Thank you for your consideration.

10.3 Persuasive Message Flowing Upward: We Want a Four-Day Workweek (Obj. 4)

E-mail Team

Some companies and municipalities are switching to a four-day workweek to reduce traffic congestion, air pollution, and stress for employees. Compressing the workweek into four 10-hour days sounds pretty good to you. You would much prefer having Friday free to schedule medical appointments and take care of family business, in addition to leisurely three-day weekends.

As a manager at Skin Essentials, a mineral-based skincare products and natural cosmetics company, you are convinced that the company's 200 employees could switch to a four-day workweek with many resulting benefits. For one thing, they would save on gasoline and commute time. You know that many cities and companies have already implemented a four-day workweek with considerable success. You took a quick poll of immediate employees and managers and found that 80 percent thought that a four-day workweek was a good idea.

YOUR TASK With a group of other students, conduct research on the Web and discuss your findings. What are the advantages of a four-day workweek? What organizations have already tried it? What appeals could be used to persuade management to adopt a four-day workweek?

What arguments could be expected, and how would you counter them? Individually or as a group, prepare a one-page persuasive e-mail or memo addressed to the Skin Essentials Management Council. Decide on a goal. Do you want to suggest a pilot study? Should you meet with management to present your ideas? How about starting a four-day workweek immediately?

10.4 Persuasive Request: Inviting an Alumna to Speak (Objs. 1–3)

E-mail

As public relations director for the Business and Accounting Association on your campus, you have been asked to find a keynote speaker for the first meeting of the school year. The owner of a successful local firm, TempHelp4You, is an alumna of your college. You think not only that many students would enjoy learning about how she started her business but also that some might like to sign up with her temporary help agency. She would need to prepare a 30-minute speech and take questions after the talk. The event will be held from noon until 1:30 p.m. on a date of your choosing in Branford Hall. You can offer her lunch at the event and provide her with a parking permit that she can pick up at the information kiosk at the main entrance to your campus. You need to have her response by a deadline you set.

YOUR TASK Write a direct-approach e-mail to Marion Minter in which you ask her to speak at your club's meeting. Send it to *mminter@temphelp4you.com*.

10.5 Using Reader Benefits to Sell (Objs. 1, 5)

Web

Audience benefits sell. People are more likely to be persuaded when they see a direct or indirect benefit of a product, service, idea, or cause. Features may describe a product or service, but they don't tell a story. To be persuasive, writers must convert features into benefits. They must tell the audience how they can best use the item to benefit from it.

YOUR TASK Online or offline find a product or service that you admire. Be sure to locate a detailed description of the item's unique features. Create a table and in the left column list the item's features. In the right column, convert the features into benefits by matching them to the needs of your target audience.

10.6 Writing Newsworthy Media Releases (Obj. 6)

You have been interviewed for a terrific job in corporate communications at an exciting organization. To test your writing skills, the organization asks you to rewrite one of its media releases for possible submission to your local newspaper. This means revising the information you find into a new media release that your local newspaper would be interested in publishing.

YOUR TASK Select an organization and study its media releases. You can also review this website for ideas: www.newswire.ca/news-releases.

Select one event or product that you think would interest your local newspaper. Although you can use the information from current media releases, don't copy the exact wording because the interviewer wants to see how you would present that information. Use the organization's format and submit the media release to your instructor with a cover note identifying the newspaper or other publication where you would like to see your media release published.

Grammar and Mechanics | *Review 10*

Number Use

Review Guides 47 to 50 about number usage in Appendix B, Grammar and Mechanics Guide, beginning on page B-1. On a sheet of paper or on your computer, revise the following sentences to correct errors in number usage. For each error that you locate, write the guide number that deals with this usage. Sentences may have more than one error. If a sentence is correct, write C. When you finish, compare your responses with the key in Appendix C.

EXAMPLE: 18 people posted notes on the Small Planet Facebook page.

REVISION: **Eighteen** people posted notes on the Small Planet Facebook page. [Guide 47]

1. Our manager reported receiving 7 messages from customers with the same 2 complaints.
2. 33 companies indicated that they were participating in renewable energy programs.

3. Consumers find that sending a one hundred forty character tweet is easier than writing a complaint letter.
4. UPS strives to make important deliveries before 10:00 o'clock a.m.
5. The meeting was rescheduled for March 7th at 2:00 p.m.
6. In the first 2 weeks of the year, we expect to hire at least 10 new employees.
7. With a birth occurring every 8 seconds, the Canadian population is currently estimated to be thirty five million.
8. One petition now has more than two hundred sixty, far and above the twenty five needed for an official House of Commons response.
9. You can burn one hundred fifty calories by walking as little as thirty minutes.
10. At least 9 prominent retail stores offer a thirty-day customer satisfaction return policy.

Notes

[1] David Suzuki Foundation. (2019). *Our story.* https://davidsuzuki.org/about/our-story/

[2] David Suzuki Foundation. (2019). *About.* https://davidsuzuki.org/about/. Reprinted courtesy of David Suzuki Foundation.

[3] David Suzuki Foundation. (2019). *David Suzuki.* https://davidsuzuki.org/expert/david-suzuki/

[4] David Suzuki Foundation. (2019). *Donate.* https://secure.e2rm.com/registrant/DonationPage.aspx?eventid=228533&_ga=2.50553450.2109776450.1573400406-691248279.1573400406

[5] Lovins, L. H. (n.d.). Natural Capitalism Solutions. http://www.natcapsolutions.org/index.php?option=com_content&view=article&id=247&Itemid=53

[6] Cialdini, R. B. (2009). *Influence: The psychology of persuasion.* HarperCollins e-books, p. x.

[7] Ibid., p. xiv.

[8] Discussion based on Perloff, R. M. (2010). *The dynamics of persuasion: Communication and attitudes in the twenty-first century* (4th ed.). Routledge, pp. 4–5.

[9] Chief Executive Officer. (2019). *Canada's changing media consumption.* https://www.ceo-na.com/business/industry/tipping-point-for-canadas-media-consumption/

[10] Perloff, R. M. (2010). *The dynamics of persuasion: Communication and attitudes in the twenty-first century* (4th ed.). Routledge, p. 9.

[11] Pedwell, T. (2017, January 24). *Google and Facebook working to bring fake news tools to Canada.* CBC News. http://www.cbc.ca/news/politics/google-facebook-fake-news-1.3950287

[12] Liddon, A. (2019). *Oh She Glows.* http://ohsheglows.com/

[13] *Harvard Business Review on reinventing your marketing.* (2011, May 7). Harvard Business Press Books.

[14] Liddon, A. (2016). Introducing Oh She Glows healthy plant-based recipes. *Oh She Glows.* http://ohsheglows.com/app/

[15] Canadian Cancer Society. (2017). *Single annual donations.* http://convio.cancer.ca/site/PageServer?pagename=GEN_SK_donor_recognition_single

[16] James, G. (2010, March 11). *Enterprise Rent-A-Car: When sales tactics backfire.* CBSNews.com/Moneywatch. http://www.cbsnews.com/8301-505183_162-28548988-10391735/enterprise-rent-a-car-when-sales-tactics-backfire; Strauss, S. (2010, May 24). Ask an expert: Do us a favour and avoid the hard sell, it's bad for business. *USAToday.* http://usatoday30.usatoday.com/money/smallbusiness/columnist/strauss/2010-05-23-hard-sell-tactics_N.htm; Salmon, J. (2010, May 12). *Barclays' hard sell tactics exposed.* ThisisMONEY.co.uk. http://www.thisismoney.co.uk/money/saving/article-1693952/Barclays-hard-sell-tactics-exposed.html

[17] Advertising Standards Canada. (n.d.). *The Canadian code of advertising standards.* http://www.adstandards.com/en/standards/canCodeOfAdStandards.aspx

[18] Media Experts. (2016). *Ethics in Canadian advertising—A conversation with Dr. Alan Middleton.* http://www.mediaexperts.com/ethics-in-canadian-advertising-a-conversation-with-dr-alan-middleton/

[19] McIntosh, P., & Luecke, R. A. (2011). *Increase your influence at work.* AMACOM, p. 2.

[20] Randstad Canada. (2019). *Reduce employee turnover and stop your best employees from quitting.* https://www.randstad.ca/employers/workplace-insights/corporate-culture/reduce-employee-turnover-and-stop-your-best-employees-from-quitting/

[21] Pollock, T. (2003, June). How to sell an idea. *SuperVision,* p. 15. http://search.proquest.com

[22] Communicating with the boss. (2006, May). *Communication Briefings,* p. 8.

[23] Pulcinella, S. (2017, August 30). Why direct mail marketing is far from dead. *Forbes.* https://www.forbes.com/sites/forbescommunicationscouncil/2017/08/30/why-direct-mail-marketing-is-far-from-dead/#64f71f43311d

[24] Lee, K. (2015, May 22). *Seven reasons to make direct mail part of your digital marketing.* ClickZ. https://www.clickz.com/clickz/column/2409287/seven-reasons-to-makedirect-mail-part-of-your-digital-marketing-plan; Millward Brown. (2009). *Using neuroscience to understand the role of direct mail,* p. 2. http://www.millwardbrown.com/Insights/CaseStudies/NeuroscienceDirectMail.aspx

[25] James, G. (2018). *Six ways to convince customers to buy.* Inc. https://www.inc.com/geoffrey-james/6-ways-to-convince-customers-to-buy.html

[26] President's Choice. (2019). *Let's celebrate eat together day!* https://eattogether.presidentschoice.ca/

[27] Mertz, E. (2017, January 9). *Emotional marketing: Get ready for more ads that move you in 2017.* Global News. http://globalnews.ca/news/3166942/emotional-marketing-get-ready-for-more-ads-that-move-you-in-2017/

[28] Ibid.

[29] Ibid.

[30] Ibid.

[31] David Suzuki Foundation. (2019, May 3). *Tomorrow has come: David Suzuki's speech to student climate strikers.* https://davidsuzuki.org/expert-article/tomorrow-has-come-david-suzukis-speech-to-student-climate-strikers/. Reprinted courtesy of David Suzuki Foundation.

[32] Edwards, L. (2012, March 5). *Are brands turning people into adverts with social media?* Socialmedia Today. http://socialmediatoday.com/laurahelen/462175/are-brands-turning-people-adverts-social-media

[33] Tong, V. (2007, November 26). *Tattoos: A new favorite of advertisers.* Boston.com. http://www.boston.com/news/education/higher/articles/2007/11/26/tattoos_a_new_favorite_of_advertisers/?page=full

fauxels

UNIT 4

Reports, Proposals, and Presentations

CHAPTER 11	CHAPTER 12	CHAPTER 13	CHAPTER 14
Reporting in the Workplace	Informal Business Reports	Proposals, Business Plans, and Formal Business Reports	Business Presentations

IN UNIT 4, YOU WILL DEVELOP THE FOLLOWING EMPLOYABILITY SKILLS:

EMPLOYABILITY AND SOFT SKILLS	
Oral and Written Communication	✓
Information Management	✓
Analyze and Present Numbers	✓
Critical Thinking	✓
Problem Solving	✓
Active Listening	✓
Professional Work Behaviours	✓
Goal-Setting	✓
Agility	✓
Adaptability	✓
Personal and Social Responsibility	✓
Ethical Decision Making	✓
Engagement	✓
Innovation and Creativity	✓
Learning Worker Attitude	✓
Team Building	✓
Accountability	✓
Project Collaboration	✓
Online Tools and Social Media[1]	✓

CHAPTER

11

Reporting in the Workplace

Pixabay

LEARNING OBJECTIVES

After studying this chapter, you should be able to

1 Explain informational and analytical report functions, organizational strategies, and writing styles, as well as typical report formats.

2 Apply the 3-x-3 writing process to contemporary business reports to create well-organized documents.

3 Locate and evaluate secondary sources, and understand how to conduct credible primary research.

4 Identify the purposes and techniques of citation and documentation in business reports, and avoid plagiarism.

5 Generate, use, and convert numerical data to visual aids, and create meaningful and attractive graphics.

SPOTLIGHT ON COMMUNICATION: PART 1

Statistics Canada—A Century of Trust, Safety, and Facts

The Internet has dramatically changed the way that people seek information. In only a few minutes and with minimal keystrokes, you can find thousands of possible sources of information. However, careful researchers know that quantity doesn't necessarily equal quality. To be sure of the value of the information, you must be convinced that the source is accurate, trustworthy, and reliable.

Adapted from Statistics Canada. No date. *Homepage*. Last updated July 30, 2020. https://www.statcan.gc.ca/eng/start (accessed December 1, 2019). This does not constitute an endorsement by Statistics Canada of this product.

One such source is the Statistics Canada website (www.statcan.gc.ca). There you will find statistics related to the economy, the environment, science, education, population, housing, labour, migration, health, and much more.[2] Much of the information is derived by a population census, which is compiled every five years. As of this writing, the most recent census was May 2016, with a 98.4 percent response rate, and over 13 million household questionnaires completed.[3]

Clearly, much has changed since the first census was conducted in 1666 by Jean Talon, who personally visited most of the 3215 inhabitants of the colony of New France to gather information about age, sex, marital status, and occupation. The initial census was driven by the need for information to help plan and develop the colony.[4]

In an effort to be more environmentally conscious, Statistics Canada sends letters that "provide a 16-digit access code to allow households to complete the census online, but also gives Canadians the option of having a paper version mailed to their homes." For the 2016 census, while most Canadians received the ten-question short survey, one in four households in Canada received the 36-page long-form questionnaire (National Household Survey). Both are mandatory, and failing to provide information or falsely answering is "liable to a summary conviction carrying a fine of up to $500, imprisonment of up to three months, or both."[5]

CRITICAL THINKING

- Why is it important for a country to conduct a census and collect data from its citizens?
- How can it benefit researchers to be familiar with the services offered by Statistics Canada?

Reporting in the Digital Age Workplace

LEARNING OBJECTIVE 1

Explain informational and analytical report functions, organizational strategies, and writing styles, as well as typical report formats.

Management decisions in many organizations are based on information submitted in the form of reports. Routine reports keep managers informed about completed tasks, projects, and work in progress. Reports help us understand and study systematically the challenges we encounter in business before we can outline the steps toward solving them. Business solutions are unthinkable without a thorough examination of the problems that prompted them.

The larger an organization is, the more vital the exchange and flow of information becomes. Business reports range from informal bulleted lists and half-page trip reports to formal 200-page financial forecasts. Reports may be internal or external documents. Their findings may be presented orally in front of a group or delivered and presented digitally—for instance, as e-mail messages, PDF (portable document format) files, or slide decks. These files can then be e-mailed, distributed on the company intranet, or posted on the Internet. In many organizations, however, reports still take the form of paper documents. Other reports, such as tax reports and profit-and-loss statements, present primarily numerical data.

This chapter examines the functions, strategies, writing style, and formats of typical business reports. It also introduces the report-writing process and discusses methods of collecting, documenting, and illustrating data. Some reports provide information only; others analyze and make recommendations. Although reports vary greatly in length, content, form, and formality level, they all have one or more of the following purposes: *to convey information*, *answer questions*, and *solve problems*.

Basic Report Functions

In terms of what they do, most reports fit into one of two broad categories: informational reports and analytical reports.

Informational Reports. Reports that present data without analysis or recommendations are primarily informational. For such reports, writers collect and organize facts, but they do not analyze the facts for readers. A trip report describing an employee's visit to a trade show, for example, presents information. Other reports that present information without analysis involve routine operations, compliance with regulations, and company policies and procedures.

Analytical Reports. Reports that provide data or findings, analyses, and conclusions are analytical. If requested, writers also supply recommendations. Analytical reports may intend to persuade readers to act or change their beliefs. For example, if you were writing a yardstick report that compares several potential manufacturing locations for a new automobile plant, you might conclude by recommending one site after discussing several criteria.

To distinguish among findings, conclusions, and recommendations, consider the example of an audit report. The auditor compiles facts and figures—the findings of the report—to meet the purpose or objective of the audit. Drawing inferences from the findings, the auditor arrives at conclusions. With the audit objectives in mind, the auditor may then propose corrective steps or actions as part of the recommendations.

Organizational Strategies

Like other business messages, reports may be organized directly or indirectly. The reader's expectations and the content of a report determine its development strategy, as illustrated in Figure 11.1. In long reports, such as corporate annual reports, some parts may be developed directly and others may be arranged indirectly.

FIGURE 11.1 Audience Analysis and Report Organization

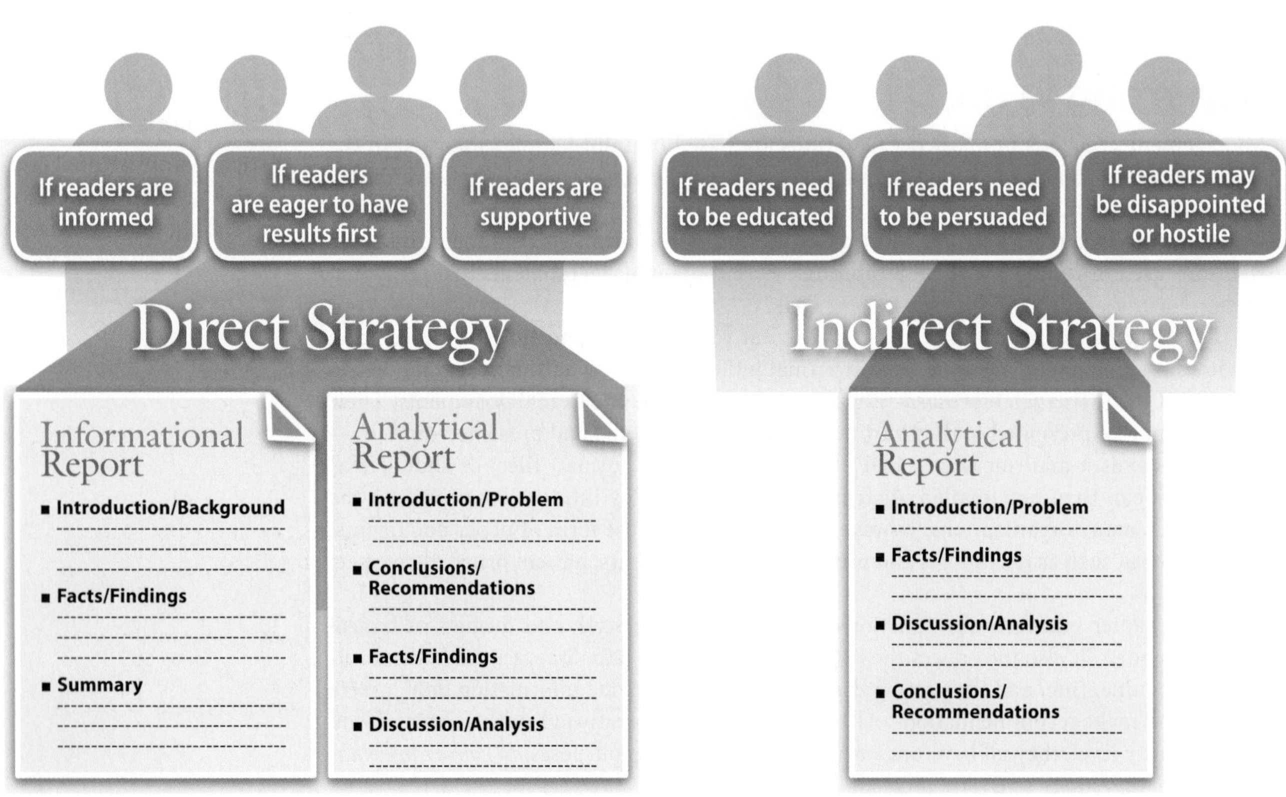

Direct Strategy. When the purpose for writing is presented close to the beginning of a report, the organizational strategy is direct. Informational reports, such as the letter report shown in Figure 11.2, are usually arranged directly. They open with an introduction, which is followed by the facts and a summary. In Figure 11.2, the writer explains a legal services plan using a letter report. The report begins with an introduction. The facts, divided into three subtopics and identified by descriptive headings, follow. The report ends with a summary and a complimentary close.

FIGURE 11.2 Informational Report—Letter Format

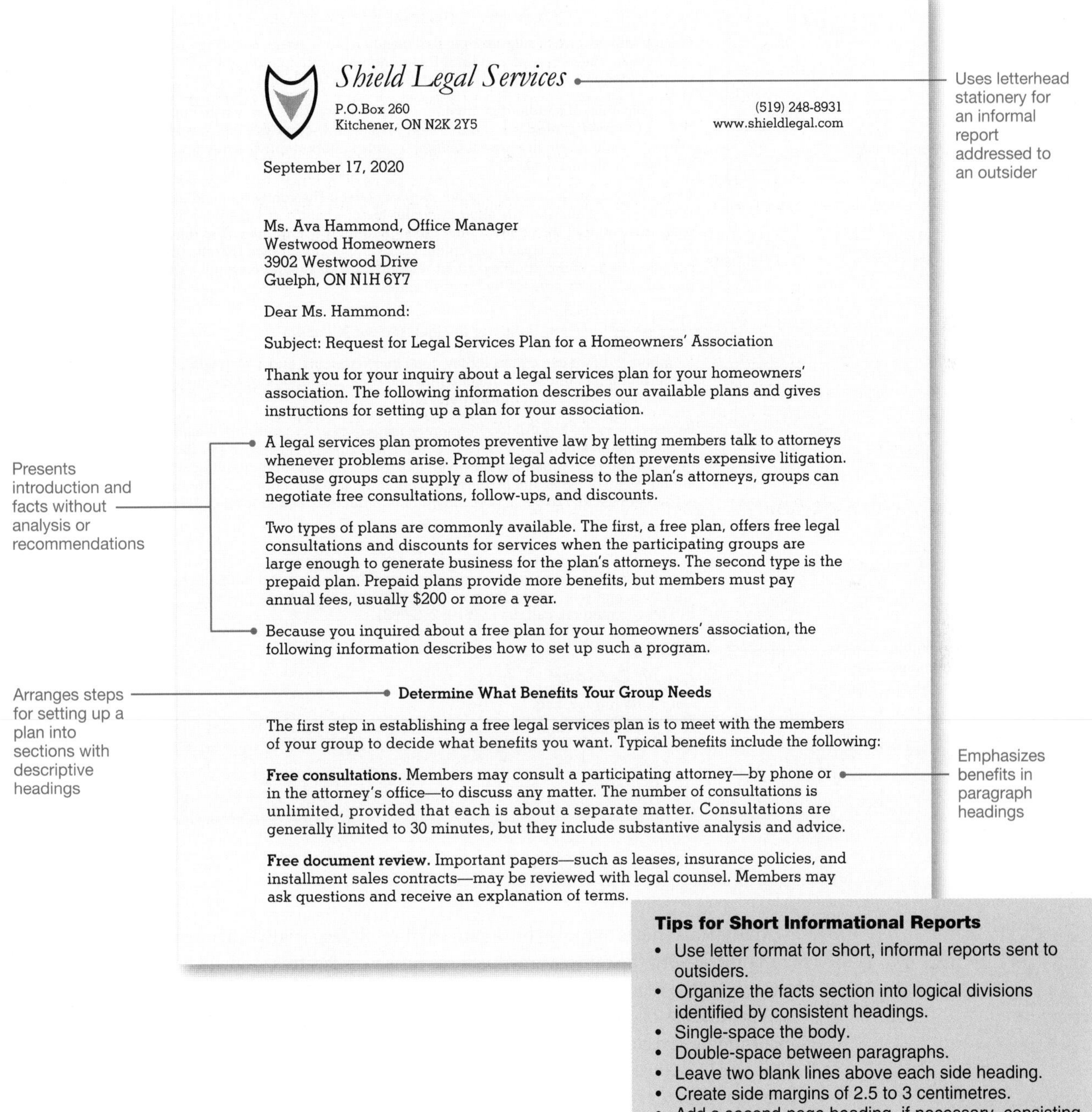

Shield Legal Services

P.O.Box 260
Kitchener, ON N2K 2Y5

(519) 248-8931
www.shieldlegal.com

September 17, 2020

Ms. Ava Hammond, Office Manager
Westwood Homeowners
3902 Westwood Drive
Guelph, ON N1H 6Y7

Dear Ms. Hammond:

Subject: Request for Legal Services Plan for a Homeowners' Association

Thank you for your inquiry about a legal services plan for your homeowners' association. The following information describes our available plans and gives instructions for setting up a plan for your association.

A legal services plan promotes preventive law by letting members talk to attorneys whenever problems arise. Prompt legal advice often prevents expensive litigation. Because groups can supply a flow of business to the plan's attorneys, groups can negotiate free consultations, follow-ups, and discounts.

Two types of plans are commonly available. The first, a free plan, offers free legal consultations and discounts for services when the participating groups are large enough to generate business for the plan's attorneys. The second type is the prepaid plan. Prepaid plans provide more benefits, but members must pay annual fees, usually $200 or more a year.

Because you inquired about a free plan for your homeowners' association, the following information describes how to set up such a program.

Determine What Benefits Your Group Needs

The first step in establishing a free legal services plan is to meet with the members of your group to decide what benefits you want. Typical benefits include the following:

Free consultations. Members may consult a participating attorney—by phone or in the attorney's office—to discuss any matter. The number of consultations is unlimited, provided that each is about a separate matter. Consultations are generally limited to 30 minutes, but they include substantive analysis and advice.

Free document review. Important papers—such as leases, insurance policies, and installment sales contracts—may be reviewed with legal counsel. Members may ask questions and receive an explanation of terms.

Uses letterhead stationery for an informal report addressed to an outsider
Presents introduction and facts without analysis or recommendations
Arranges steps for setting up a plan into sections with descriptive headings
Emphasizes benefits in paragraph headings

Tips for Short Informational Reports

- Use letter format for short, informal reports sent to outsiders.
- Organize the facts section into logical divisions identified by consistent headings.
- Single-space the body.
- Double-space between paragraphs.
- Leave two blank lines above each side heading.
- Create side margins of 2.5 to 3 centimetres.
- Add a second-page heading, if necessary, consisting of the addressee's name, the date, and the page number.

(Continued)

FIGURE 11.2 (*Continued*)

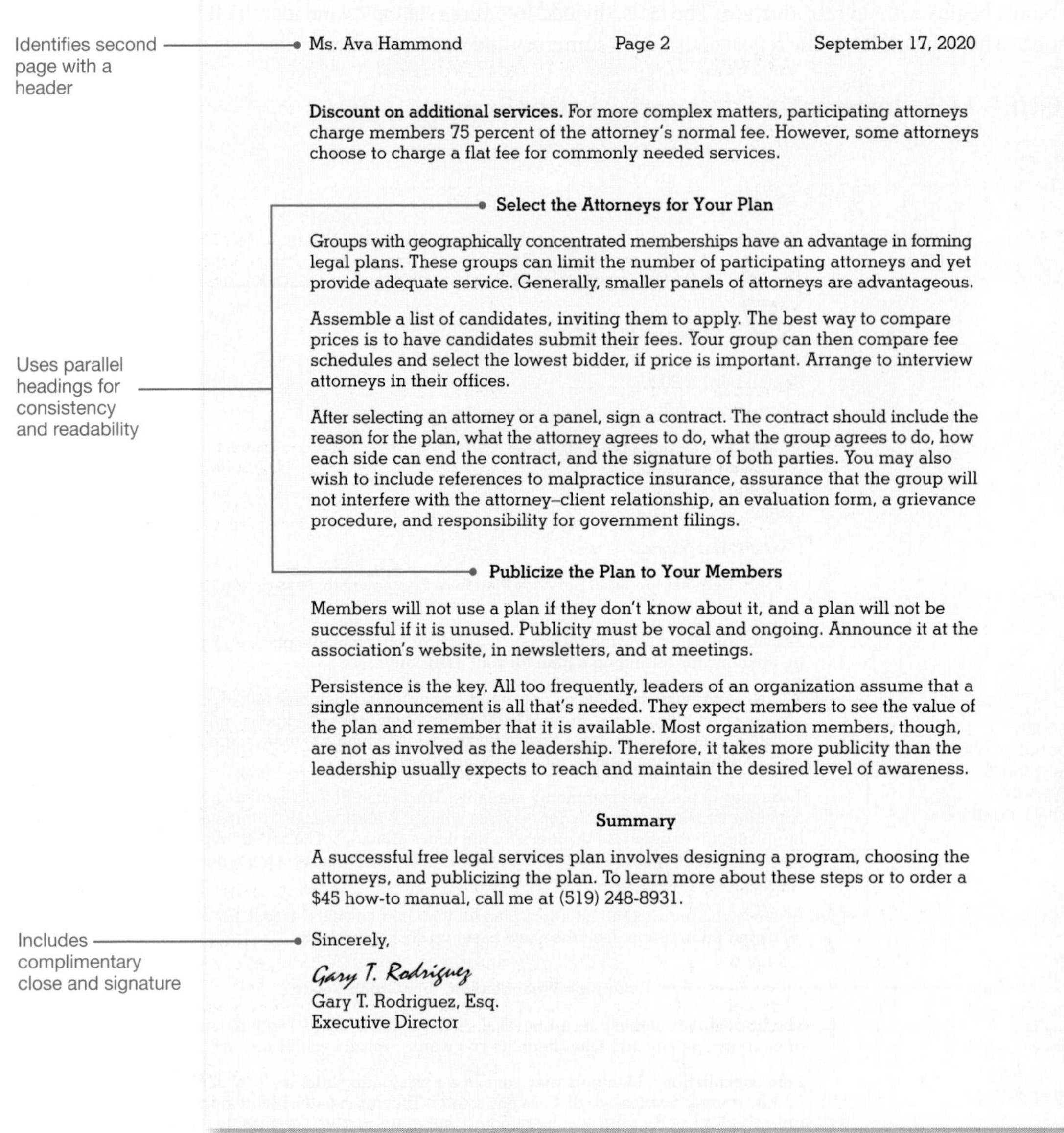

Identifies second page with a header
Uses parallel headings for consistency and readability
Includes complimentary close and signature

Ms. Ava Hammond Page 2 September 17, 2020

Discount on additional services. For more complex matters, participating attorneys charge members 75 percent of the attorney's normal fee. However, some attorneys choose to charge a flat fee for commonly needed services.

Select the Attorneys for Your Plan

Groups with geographically concentrated memberships have an advantage in forming legal plans. These groups can limit the number of participating attorneys and yet provide adequate service. Generally, smaller panels of attorneys are advantageous.

Assemble a list of candidates, inviting them to apply. The best way to compare prices is to have candidates submit their fees. Your group can then compare fee schedules and select the lowest bidder, if price is important. Arrange to interview attorneys in their offices.

After selecting an attorney or a panel, sign a contract. The contract should include the reason for the plan, what the attorney agrees to do, what the group agrees to do, how each side can end the contract, and the signature of both parties. You may also wish to include references to malpractice insurance, assurance that the group will not interfere with the attorney–client relationship, an evaluation form, a grievance procedure, and responsibility for government filings.

Publicize the Plan to Your Members

Members will not use a plan if they don't know about it, and a plan will not be successful if it is unused. Publicity must be vocal and ongoing. Announce it at the association's website, in newsletters, and at meetings.

Persistence is the key. All too frequently, leaders of an organization assume that a single announcement is all that's needed. They expect members to see the value of the plan and remember that it is available. Most organization members, though, are not as involved as the leadership. Therefore, it takes more publicity than the leadership usually expects to reach and maintain the desired level of awareness.

Summary

A successful free legal services plan involves designing a program, choosing the attorneys, and publicizing the plan. To learn more about these steps or to order a $45 how-to manual, call me at (519) 248-8931.

Sincerely,

Gary T. Rodriguez

Gary T. Rodriguez, Esq.
Executive Director

Analytical reports may also be organized directly, especially when readers are supportive of or familiar with the topic. Many busy executives prefer this strategy because it gives them the results of the report immediately. They don't have to spend time wading through the facts, findings, discussion, and analyses to get to the two items they are most interested in—the conclusions and recommendations.

Figure 11.3 illustrates such an arrangement. This analytical memo report describes environmental hazards of a property that a realtor has just listed. The realtor is familiar with the investigation and eager to find out the recommendations. Therefore, the memo is organized directly. You should be aware, though, that unless readers are familiar with the topic, they may find the direct strategy confusing. Many readers prefer the indirect strategy because it seems logical and mirrors the way they solve problems.

FIGURE 11.3 Analytical Report—Memo Format

Applies memo format for short, informal internal report

Uses first paragraph as introduction

Presents recommendations first (direct pattern) because reader is supportive and familiar with topic

Combines findings and analyses in short report

Diamond Environmental, Inc.

Interoffice Memo

DATE: March 7, 2020
TO: Paul Gregory, President
FROM: Izzie Edwards, Environmental Engineer I.E.
SUBJECT: Investigation of Mountain Park Commercial Site

For New River Realty, Inc., I've completed a preliminary investigation of its Mountain Park property listing. The following recommendations are based on my physical inspection of the site, official records, and interviews with officials and persons knowledgeable about the site.

Recommendations

To reduce its potential environmental liability, New River Realty should take the following steps in regard to its Mountain Park listing:

- Conduct an immediate asbestos survey at the site, including inspection of ceiling insulation material, floor tiles, and insulation around a gas-fired heater vent pipe at 2539 Mountain View Drive.
- Prepare an environmental audit of the generators of hazardous waste currently operating at the site, including Mountain Technology.
- Obtain lids for the dumpsters situated in the parking areas and ensure that the lids are kept closed.

Findings and Analyses

My preliminary assessment of the site and its immediate vicinity revealed rooms with damaged floor tiles on the first and second floors of 2539 Mountain View Drive. Apparently, in recent remodeling efforts, these tiles had been cracked and broken. Examination of the ceiling and attic revealed further possible contamination from asbestos. The insulation for the hot-water tank was in poor condition.

Located on the property is Mountain Technology, a possible hazardous waste generator. Although I could not examine its interior, this company has the potential for producing hazardous material contamination.

In the parking area, large dumpsters collect trash and debris from several businesses. These dumpsters were uncovered, thus posing a risk to the general public.

In view of the construction date of the structures on this property, asbestos-containing building materials might be present. Moreover, this property is located in an industrial part of the city, further prompting my recommendation for a thorough investigation. New River Realty can act immediately to eliminate one environmental concern: covering the dumpsters in the parking area.

Tips for Short Analytical Reports

- Use memo format for most short (ten or fewer pages) informal reports within an organization.
- Leave side margins of 2.5 to 3 centimetres.
- Sign your initials on the *From* line.
- Use an informal, conversational style.
- For direct analytical reports, put recommendations first.
- For indirect analytical reports, put recommendations last.

Indirect Strategy. The organizational strategy is indirect when the conclusions and recommendations, if requested, appear at the end of the report. Such reports usually begin with an introduction or a description of the problem, followed by facts and interpretations from the writer. They end with conclusions and recommendations. This strategy is helpful when readers are unfamiliar with the problem. This strategy is also useful when readers must be persuaded or when they may be disappointed in or hostile toward the report's findings. The writer is more likely to retain the reader's interest by first explaining, justifying, and analyzing the facts and then making recommendations. This strategy also seems most rational to readers because it follows the normal thought process: problem, alternatives (facts), solution.

Informal and Formal Writing Styles

Like other business messages, reports can range from informal to formal, depending on their purpose, audience, and setting. Research reports from consultants to their clients tend to be rather formal. Such reports must project objectivity, authority, and impartiality. However, depending on the industry, a report to your boss describing a trip to a conference would probably be informal.

Figure 11.4, which compares the characteristics of formal and informal report-writing styles, can help you decide which style is appropriate for your reports. Note that, increasingly, formal reports are written with contractions and in the active voice. Today report writers try to avoid awkward third-person references to themselves as *the researchers* or *the authors* because it sounds stilted and outdated.

Typical Report Formats

The format of a report depends on its length, topic, audience, and purpose. After considering these elements, you will probably choose from among the following formats.

Digital Formats and PDF Files. Writers routinely save and distribute reports as PDF files. This file type, invented by Adobe, condenses documents while preserving the formatting and graphics. A report created with Microsoft Word, Excel, or PowerPoint can easily be saved as a PDF file. A PDF report might include links to external websites, a nice advantage over printed reports. Web-based reports may feature engaging multimedia effects, such as interactive charts and video.

FIGURE 11.4 Report-Writing Styles

	Informal Writing Style	Formal Writing Style
Appropriate Use	• Short, routine reports • Reports for familiar audiences • Noncontroversial reports • Internal use reports • Internal announcements and invitations	• Lengthy, formal reports and proposals • Research studies • Controversial or complex reports • External use reports • Formal invitations
Overall Effect	• Friendly tone • Relationship building • Casual	• Objectivity and accuracy • Sense of professionalism and fairness • Professional distance between writer and reader
Writing Style Characteristics	• Use of first-person pronouns (*I, we, me, my, us, our*) • Use of contractions (*can't, don't*) • Emphasis on active-voice verbs (*I conducted the study*) • Shorter sentences • Familiar words • Conversational language	• Use of third person (*the researcher, the writer*, depending on the circumstances) • Absence of contractions (*cannot, do not*) • Use of passive-voice verbs (*the study was conducted*) • Professional, respectful language • Absence of humour and figures of speech • Elimination of "editorializing" (author's opinions and perceptions)

Digital Slide Decks. Many business writers deliver their report information in digital slideshows, also called slide decks. These slides can be sent by e-mail, embedded on the Internet, or posted on a company intranet. When used in reporting, slide decks may have more text than typical presentation slides. Photographs, tables, charts, and other visuals make slide decks more inviting to read than print pages of dense report text.

Infographics. Infographics, short for *information graphics*, are visual representations of data or information. They can display complex information quickly and clearly, and they are easier to understand than written text. Infographics are also affordable and easily shared on social media platforms. Infographics can tell compelling stories that help all types of businesses attract and inform consumers.

E-mail and Memo Formats. Many reports are attached to e-mails, posted online, or, if short, embedded in the body of e-mails. For short informal reports that stay within organizations, the memo format may still be appropriate. Memo reports begin with essential background information, using standard headings: *Date*, *To*, *From*, and *Subject*, as shown in Figure 11.3. Memo reports differ from regular memos in length, use of headings, and deliberate organization. Today, memo reports are rarely distributed in hard copy; more likely they are shared electronically as PDF files.

Forms and Templates. Office workers use digital forms that are usually made available on the company intranet or the Internet. Such electronic templates are suitable for repetitive data, such as monthly sales reports, performance appraisals, merchandise inventories, and personnel and financial reports. Employees can customize and fill in the templates and forms. Then they distribute them electronically or print them. Using standardized formats and headings saves a writer time and ensures that all necessary information is included.

Letter Format. The letter format for short informal reports (usually eight or fewer pages) addressed outside an organization can still be found in government agencies, real estate, and accounting firms. Prepared on office stationery, a letter report contains a date, inside address, salutation, and complimentary close, as shown in Figure 11.2. Although they may carry information similar to that found in correspondence, letter reports usually are longer and show more careful organization than typical letters. They also include headings to guide the reader through the content and may come with attachments. Like memo reports, letter reports are also likely to be sent to clients as PDF files.

Manuscript Format. For longer, more formal reports, business writers use the manuscript format. These reports are usually printed on plain paper without letterhead or memo forms. They too can be shared digitally as PDF files. They begin with a title followed by systematically displayed headings and subheadings. You will see examples of proposals and formal reports using the manuscript format in Chapter 13.

Concept Check

1. Visit the Statistics Canada website at www.statcan.gc.ca. Write a list of three interesting reports that are available. For you as a student, what is the value of having access to this information?
2. For the following reports, (a) name the report's primary function (informational or analytical), (b) recommend the direct or indirect strategy of development, and (c) select a report format (memo or e-mail, letter, or manuscript).
   a. A report to a grant-funding organization asking for continued funding for the humane removal and relocation of wildlife from homes and commercial buildings
   b. A yardstick report on the leisure industry put together by consultants who compare the potential of a future theme park at three different sites
   c. A report prepared by an outside consultant reviewing proposed components of a virtual municipal library and recommending the launch of its initial components

LEARNING OBJECTIVE 2

Apply the 3-x-3 writing process to contemporary business reports to create well-organized documents.

Applying the 3-x-3 Writing Process to Contemporary Reports

Because business reports are systematic attempts to compile often complex information, answer questions, and solve problems, the best reports are developed methodically. In earlier chapters the 3-x-3 writing process was helpful in guiding short projects, such as e-mails, memos, and letters. That same process is even more necessary when writers are preparing longer projects, such as reports and proposals. After all, an extensive project poses a greater organizational challenge than a short one and, therefore, requires a rigorous structure to help readers grasp the message. Let's channel the writing process into seven specific steps:

Step 1: Analyze the problem and purpose.

Step 2: Anticipate the audience and issues.

Step 3: Prepare a work plan.

Step 4: Conduct research.

Step 5: Organize, analyze, interpret, and illustrate the data.

Step 6: Compose the first draft.

Step 7: Edit, proofread, and evaluate.

How much time you spend on each step depends on your report task. A short informational report on a familiar topic might require a brief work plan, little research, and no data analysis. A complex analytical report, on the other hand, might demand a comprehensive work plan, extensive research, and careful data analysis. In this section we consider the first three steps in the process—analyzing the problem and purpose, anticipating the audience and issues, and preparing a work plan.

To illustrate the planning stages of a report, we will watch Emily Mason develop a report she's preparing for her boss, Joshua Nichols, at Pharmgen Laboratories. Joshua asked Emily to investigate the problem of transportation for sales representatives. Currently, some Pharmgen reps visit customers (mostly doctors and hospitals) using company-leased cars. A few reps drive their own cars, receiving reimbursements for use. In three months Pharmgen's leasing agreements for 14 cars expire, and Joshua is considering a major change. Emily's task is to investigate the choices and report her findings to Joshua.

Analyzing the Problem and Purpose

The first step in writing a report is understanding the problem or assignment clearly. For complex reports, prepare a written problem statement to clarify the task. In analyzing her report task, Emily had many questions: Is the problem that Pharmgen is spending too much money on leased cars? Does Pharmgen want to invest in owning a fleet of cars? Does Joshua suspect that reps are submitting inflated mileage figures? Before starting research for the report, Emily talked with Joshua to define the problem. She learned the several dimensions of the situation and wrote the following statement to clarify the problem—both for herself and for Joshua.

> **Problem statement:** *The leases on all company cars will be expiring in three months. Pharmgen must decide whether to renew them or develop a new policy regarding transportation for sales reps. Expenses and paperwork for employee-owned cars seem excessive.*

Emily further defined the problem by writing a specific question that she would try to answer in her report:

> **Problem question:** *What plan should Pharmgen follow in providing transportation for its sales reps?*

Now Emily was ready to concentrate on the purpose of the report. Again, she had questions: Exactly what did Joshua expect? Did he want a comparison of costs for buying and leasing cars? Should she conduct research to pinpoint exact reimbursement costs when employees drive their own cars? Did he want her to present her findings in a report and let him make a decision? Or did he want her to evaluate the choices and recommend a course of action? After talking with Joshua, Emily was ready to write a simple purpose statement for this assignment.

Simple statement of purpose: *To recommend a plan that provides sales reps with cars to be used in their calls.*

In writing useful purpose statements, choose action verbs telling what you intend to do: *analyze, choose, investigate, compare, justify, evaluate, explain, establish, determine,* and so on. Notice that Emily's statement begins with the action verb *recommend.*

Some reports require only a simple statement of purpose: to investigate expanded teller hours or to select a manager from among four candidates. Many assignments, though, demand additional focus to guide the project. An expanded statement of purpose considers three additional factors: scope, limitations, and significance.

Scope and Limitations. What issues or elements will be investigated? The scope statement prepares the audience by clearly defining which problem or problems will be analyzed and solved. To determine the scope, Emily brainstormed with Joshua and others to pin down her task. She learned that Pharmgen currently had enough capital to consider purchasing a fleet of cars outright. Joshua also told her that employee satisfaction was almost as important as cost-effectiveness. Moreover, he disclosed his suspicion that employee-owned cars were costing Pharmgen more than leased cars. Emily had many issues to sort out in setting the boundaries of her report.

What conditions affect the generalizability and utility of a report's findings? As part of the scope statement, the limitations further narrow the subject by focusing on constraints or exclusions. For this report Emily realized that her conclusions and recommendations might apply only to reps in her Edmonton sales district. Her findings would probably not be reliable for reps in Sudbury, Sault Ste. Marie, or Ottawa. Another limitation for Emily was time. She had to complete the report in four weeks, thus restricting the thoroughness of her research.

Significance. Why is the topic worth investigating at this time? Some topics, after initial examination, turn out to be less important than originally thought. Others involve problems that cannot be solved, making a study useless. For Emily and Joshua the problem had significance because Pharmgen's leasing agreement would expire shortly and decisions had to be made about a new policy for transportation of sales reps.

Emily decided to expand her statement of purpose to define the scope, describe the limitations of the report, and explain the significance of the problem.

Expanded statement of purpose: *The purpose of this report is to recommend a plan that provides sales reps with cars to be used in their calls. The report will compare costs for three plans: outright ownership, leasing, and compensation for employee-owned cars. It will also measure employee reactions to each plan. The report is significant because Pharmgen's current leasing agreement expires March 31 and an improved plan could reduce costs and paperwork. The study is limited to costs for sales reps in the Edmonton district.*

After expanding her statement of purpose, Emily checked it with Joshua Nichols to be sure she was on target.

Anticipating the Audience and Issues

After defining the purpose of a report, a writer must think carefully about who will read it. Concentrating solely on a primary reader is a major mistake. Although one individual may have solicited the report, others within the organization may eventually read it, including upper management and people in other departments. A report to an outside client may first be read by someone who is familiar with the problem and then be distributed to others less familiar with the topic. Moreover, candid statements to one audience may be offensive to another audience. Emily could make a major blunder, for instance, if she mentioned Joshua's suspicion that sales reps were padding their mileage statements. If the report were made public—as it probably would be to explain a new policy—the sales reps could feel insulted that their integrity was questioned.

As Emily considered her primary and secondary readers, she asked herself these questions:

- *What do my readers need to know about this topic?*
- *What do they already know?*
- *What is their educational level?*
- *How will they react to this information?*
- *Which sources will they trust?*
- *How can I make this information readable, believable, and memorable?*

Answers to these questions help writers determine how much background material to include, how much detail to add, whether to include jargon, what method of organization and presentation to follow, and what tone to use.

In the planning stages, a report writer must also break the major investigative problem into subproblems. This process, sometimes called *factoring*, identifies issues to be investigated or possible solutions to the main problem. In this case, Pharmgen must figure out the best way to transport sales reps. Each possible solution or issue that Emily considers becomes a factor or subproblem to be investigated. Emily came up with three tentative solutions to provide transportation to sales reps: (a) purchase cars outright, (b) lease cars, or (c) compensate employees for using their own cars. These three factors form the outline of Emily's study.

Emily continued to factor these main points into the following subproblems for investigation:

What plan should Pharmgen use to transport its sales reps?

I. Should Pharmgen purchase cars outright?
   A. How much capital would be required?
   B. How much would it cost to insure, operate, and maintain company-owned cars?
   C. Do employees prefer using company-owned cars?

II. Should Pharmgen lease cars?
   A. What is the best lease price available?
   B. How much would it cost to insure, operate, and maintain leased cars?
   C. Do employees prefer using leased cars?

III. Should Pharmgen compensate employees for using their own cars?
   A. How much has it cost in the past to compensate employees who used their own cars?
   B. How much paperwork is involved in reporting expenses?
   C. Do employees prefer being compensated for using their own cars?

Each subproblem would probably be further factored into additional subproblems. These issues may be phrased as questions, as Emily's are, or as statements. In factoring a complex problem, prepare an outline showing the initial problem and its breakdown into subproblems. Make sure your divisions are consistent (don't mix issues), exclusive (don't overlap categories), and complete (don't skip significant issues).

Preparing a Work Plan

After analyzing the problem, anticipating the audience, and factoring the problem, you are ready to prepare a work plan. A good work plan includes the following:

- Statement of the problem (based on key background/contextual information)
- Statement of the purpose including scope with limitations and significance

- Research strategy including a description of potential sources and methods of collecting data
- Tentative outline that factors the problem into manageable chunks
- Work schedule

Preparing a plan encourages you to evaluate your resources, set priorities, outline a course of action, and establish a schedule. Having a plan keeps you on track and provides management a means of measuring your progress.

A work plan gives a complete picture of a project. Because the usefulness and quality of any report rest primarily on its data, you will want to develop a clear research strategy, which includes allocating plenty of time to locate sources of information. For first-hand or primary information, you might interview people, prepare a survey, or even conduct a scientific experiment. For secondary information you will probably search electronic materials on the Internet and printed materials, such as books and magazines. Your work plan describes how you expect to generate or collect data. Because data collection is a major part of report writing, the next section of this chapter treats the topic in more detail.

Figure 11.5 shows a complete work plan for a proposal pitched by social marketing company BzzAgent's advertising executive Dave Balter to his client Lee Jeans. A work plan is useful because it outlines the issues to be investigated. Notice that considerable thought and discussion and even some preliminary research are necessary to be able to develop a useful work plan.

Although this tentative outline guides the investigation, it does not determine the content or order of the final report. You may, for example, study five possible solutions to a problem. If two prove to be useless, your report may discuss only the three winners. Moreover, you will organize the report to accomplish your goal and satisfy the audience. A busy executive who is familiar with a topic may prefer to read the conclusions and recommendations before a discussion of the findings. If someone authorizes the report, be sure to review the work plan with that person (your manager, client, or professor, for example) before proceeding with the project.

Concept Check

1. What are the seven steps when applying the 3-x-3 writing process to contemporary reports?
2. How does considering primary and secondary audiences help writers to plan their reports?

Identifying Secondary Sources and Conducting Primary Research

LEARNING OBJECTIVE 3

Locate and evaluate secondary sources, and understand how to conduct credible primary research.

Research, or the gathering of information, is one of the most important steps in writing a report. Think of your report as a tower. Because a report is only as good as its foundation—the questions you ask and the data you gather to answer those questions—the remainder of this chapter describes the fundamental work of finding, documenting, and illustrating data.

As you analyze a report's purpose and audience and prepare your research strategy, you will identify and assess the data you need to support your argument or explain your topic. As you do, you will answer questions about your objectives and audience: Will the audience need a lot of background or contextual information? Will your readers value or trust statistics, case studies, or expert opinions? Will they want to see data from interviews or surveys? Will summaries of focus groups be useful? Should you rely on organizational data? Figure 11.6 lists five forms of data and provides questions to guide you in making your research accurate and productive.

FIGURE 11.5 Work Plan for a Formal Report

Statement of Problem

Many women between the ages of 22 and 35 have trouble finding jeans that fit. Lee Jeans hopes to remedy that situation with its One True Fit line. We want to demonstrate to Lee that we can create a word-of-mouth campaign that will help it reach its target audience.

Statement of Purpose

Defines purpose, scope, limits, and significance of report

The purpose of this report is to secure an advertising contract from Lee Jeans. We will examine published accounts about the jeans industry and Lee Jeans in particular. In addition, we will examine published results of Lee's current marketing strategy. We will conduct focus groups of women in our company to generate campaign strategies for our pilot study of 100 BzzAgents. The report will persuade Lee Jeans that word-of-mouth advertising is an effective strategy to reach women in this demographic group and that BzzAgent is the right company to hire. The report is significant because an advertising contract with Lee Jeans would help our company grow significantly in size and stature.

Research Strategy (Sources and Methods of Data Collection)

Describes primary and secondary data

We will gather information about Lee Jeans and the product line by examining published marketing data and conducting focus group surveys of our employees. In addition, we will gather data about the added value of word-of-mouth advertising by examining published accounts and interpreting data from previous marketing campaigns, particularly those targeted toward similar age groups. Finally, we will conduct a pilot study of 100 BzzAgents in the target demographic.

Tentative Outline

Factors problem into manageable chunks

I. How effectively has Lee Jeans marketed to the target population (women ages 22 to 35)?
   A. Historically, who has typically bought Lee Jeans products? How often? Where?
   B. How effective are the current marketing strategies for the One True Fit line?

II. Is this product a good fit for our marketing strategy and our company?
   A. What do our staff members and our sample survey of BzzAgents say about this product?
   B. How well does our pool of BzzAgents correspond to the target demographic in terms of age and geographic distribution?

III. Why should Lee Jeans engage BzzAgent to advertise its One True Fit line?
   A. What are the benefits of word of mouth in general and for this demographic in particular?
   B. What previous campaigns have we engaged in that demonstrate our company's credibility?
   C. What are our marketing strategies, and how well did they work in the pilot study?

Work Schedule

Estimates time needed to complete report tasks

Task	Dates
Investigate Lee Jeans and One True Fit line's current marketing strategy	July 15–25
Test product using focus groups	
Create campaign materials for BzzAgents	
Run a pilot test with a selected pool of 100 BzzAgents	
Evaluate and interpret findings	
Compose draft of report	
Revise draft	
Submit final report	

Tips for Preparing a Work Plan

- Start early; allow plenty of time for brainstorming and preliminary research.
- Describe the problem motivating the report.
- Write a purpose statement that includes the report's scope, significance, and limitations.
- Describe the research strategy, including data collection sources and methods.
- Divide the major problem into subproblems stated as questions to be answered.
- Develop a realistic work schedule, citing dates for the completion of major tasks.
- Review the work plan with whoever authorized the report.

FIGURE 11.6 Gathering and Selecting Report Data

Form of Data	Questions to Ask
Background or historical	How much do my readers know about the problem?
	Has this topic/issue been investigated before?
	Are those sources current, relevant, and/or credible?
	Will I need to add to the available data?
Statistical	What or who is the source?
	How recent are the data?
	How were the figures derived?
	Will these data be useful in this form?
Expert opinion	Who are the experts?
	What are their biases?
	Are their opinions in print?
	Are they available for interviews?
	Do we have in-house experts?
Individual or group opinion	Whose opinion(s) would the readers value?
	Have surveys or interviews been conducted on this topic?
	If not, do questionnaires or surveys exist that I can modify and/or use?
	Would focus groups provide useful information?
Organizational	What are the proper channels for obtaining in-house data?
	Are permissions required?
	How can I learn about public and private companies?

Locating Secondary Sources

Data fall into two broad categories: primary and secondary. Primary data result from first-hand experience and observation. Secondary data come from reading what others have experienced or observed and written down. Secondary data are easier and cheaper to gather than primary data, which might involve interviewing large groups or sending out questionnaires.

We discuss secondary data first because that is where nearly every research project should begin. Often, something has already been written about your topic. Reviewing secondary sources can save time and effort and prevent you from reinventing the wheel. Most secondary material is available either in print or electronically.

Print Resources. Although we are seeing a steady movement away from print data and toward electronic data, some information is available only in print.

If you are an infrequent library user, begin your research by talking with a reference librarian about your project. Librarians won't do your research for you, but they will steer you in the right direction. Many librarians help you understand their computer, cataloguing, and retrieval systems by providing advice, brochures, handouts, and workshops. Several Canadian colleges and universities offer Ask Chat, an online or a texting service that connects students with a librarian. A consortium of librarians provide support for the service, and students are able to access this support from home.[8]

Books and E-books. Books and e-books provide excellent historical, in-depth data. Like most contemporary sources, books can be located through online listings.

milosk50/Shutterstock

Historically, cities have developed monikers based on global comparisons, such as "The Paris of Canada" for Montréal; shortened forms, such as "The Soo" for Sault Ste. Marie; significant characteristics or industries, such as "Steel Town" for Hamilton.[6] Recently, however, urban branding has become a strategy used by many cities to establish new brand identities. Charlottetown references both its historic past and its vibrant arts culture with "Great things happen here," and Whitehorse leaves no room for confusion with "The Wilderness City."[7] What types of research can be done to help cities evaluate their strengths and weaknesses?

- **Card catalogues.** Very few libraries still maintain card catalogues with all books indexed on 3-by-5 cards alphabetized by author, title, and subject.
- **Online catalogues.** Most libraries today have computerized their card catalogues. Most systems are fully automated, thus allowing users to learn not only whether a book is located in the library but also whether it is currently available. Moreover, online catalogues can help you trace and borrow items from other area libraries if your college or university doesn't own them. E-books can be conveniently downloaded and read from any device.

Periodicals. Magazines, pamphlets, and journals are called *periodicals* because of their recurrent, or periodic, publication. Journals are compilations of scholarly articles. Articles in journals and other periodicals are extremely useful because they are concise, limited in scope, and current. Publications are digitized and available in full text online, often as PDF documents.

Indexes. Contemporary business writers rely almost totally on electronic indexes and research databases to locate references, abstracts, and full-text articles from magazines, journals, and newspapers, such as *The Globe and Mail.*

When using Internet-based online indexes, follow the on-screen instructions or ask for assistance from a librarian. Beginning with a subject search such as *manufacturers' recalls* is helpful because it generally turns up more relevant citations than keyword searches—especially when searching for names of people (*Akio Toyoda*) or companies (*Toyota*). Once you locate usable references, print a copy of your findings, save them to a portable flash memory device or in a cloud-based storage location, or send them to your e-mail address.

Research Databases. As a writer of business reports today, you will probably begin your secondary research with electronic resources. Online databases have become the staple of secondary research. Most writers turn to them first because they are fast and easy to use. You can conduct detailed searches without ever leaving your office, home, or dorm room.

A *database* is a collection of information stored digitally so that it is accessible by computer or mobile electronic devices and searchable. Databases provide bibliographic information (titles of documents and brief abstracts) and full-text documents. Various databases contain a rich array of magazine, newspaper, and journal articles, as well as newsletters, business reports, company profiles, government data, reviews, and directories. The five databases most useful to Canadian business writers are Canadian Business and Current Affairs (CBCA) (ProQuest), Business Source Premier (EBSCO), Academic Search Premier (EBSCO), Conference Board of Canada e-Library, and Canadian Periodical Index (CPI.Q). Figure 11.7 shows the CBCA search menu.

Developing a search strategy and narrowing your search can save time. Think about the time frame for your search, the language of publication, and the types of materials you will need. Most databases enable you to focus a search easily. For example, if you were researching the Québec referendum and wanted to look at articles published in a specific year, most search tools would enable you to limit your search to that period. All databases and search engines allow you to refine your search and increase the precision of your hits.

Check out section 11-3a in MindTap, where you can watch a video featuring Ian McCleary, owner of Ian McCleary Insurance, discuss the importance of conducting good research.

FIGURE 11.7 CBCA (ProQuest) Search Result

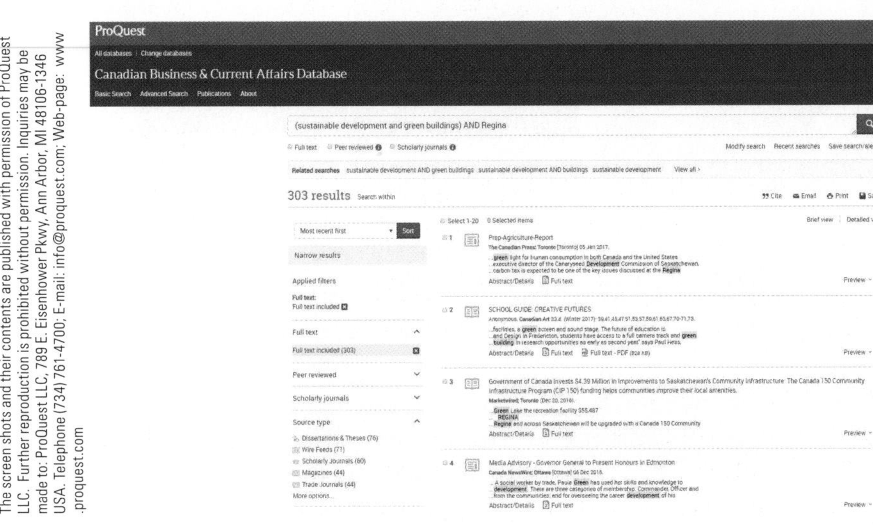

Canadian Business and Current Affairs database (ProQuest) indexes over 1,800 publications, offering a range of Canadian topics and perspectives. This figure shows that the search terms *sustainable development* and *energy efficiency* and *Regina* brought up 303 full-text search results. Savvy researchers further narrow their search to a more manageable number.

Efficient search strategies take time to master. Therefore, before wasting time and retrieving lots of useless material, talk to a librarian. Postsecondary and public libraries, as well as some employers, offer free access to several commercial databases, sparing you the high cost of individual subscriptions.

Go to section 11-3a in MindTap, where you can watch a video featuring Jason Allen John, a mortgage agent, discuss creating research-based reports.

The Internet

If you are like most adults today, you probably use the Internet for entertainment, socializing, and work every day. In this section we examine the Internet as an effective research tool.

Online Search Tools. Finding what you are looking for on the Internet is hopeless without powerful, specialized search tools. These search tools can be divided into two types: subject (or Web) directories and search engines. In addition, some search engines specialize in *metasearching*. This means they combine several powerful search engines into one (e.g., Infosearch, Dogpile, and Search.com).

Search engines differ in the way they trawl the vast amount of data on the Internet. Google uses automated software, "spiders" or bots, that crawl across the Internet at regular intervals to collect and index the information from each location visited. Some search tools use natural-language-processing technology to enable you to ask questions to gather information. Both search engines and subject directories will help you find specific information.

Applying Internet Search Strategies and Techniques. To conduct a thorough search for the information you need, build a (re)search strategy by understanding the tools available. Figure 11.8 outlines several effective search techniques.

To improve your odds of discovering more relevant sources, try these additional research strategies:

- **Learn basic Boolean search strategies.** You can save yourself a lot of time and frustration by narrowing your search with the following Boolean operators:

  AND — Identifies only documents containing all of the specified words: **employee AND productivity AND morale**

  OR — Identifies documents containing at least one of the specified words: **employee OR productivity OR morale**

  NOT — Excludes documents containing the specified word: **employee productivity NOT morale**

  NEAR — Finds documents containing target words or phrases within a specified distance, for instance, within ten words: **employee NEAR productivity.**

FIGURE 11.8 Useful Internet Search Techniques

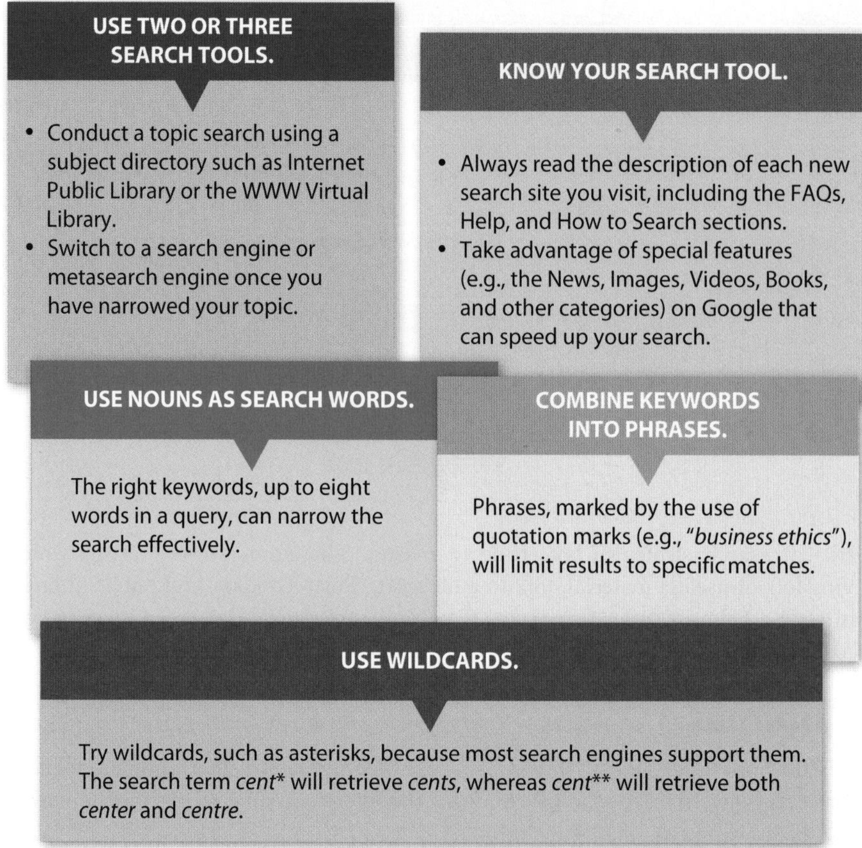

USE TWO OR THREE SEARCH TOOLS.
• Conduct a topic search using a subject directory such as Internet Public Library or the WWW Virtual Library.
• Switch to a search engine or metasearch engine once you have narrowed your topic.
KNOW YOUR SEARCH TOOL.
• Always read the description of each new search site you visit, including the FAQs, Help, and How to Search sections.
• Take advantage of special features (e.g., the News, Images, Videos, Books, and other categories) on Google that can speed up your search.
USE NOUNS AS SEARCH WORDS.
The right keywords, up to eight words in a query, can narrow the search effectively.
COMBINE KEYWORDS INTO PHRASES.
Phrases, marked by the use of quotation marks (e.g., "business ethics"), will limit results to specific matches.
USE WILDCARDS.
Try wildcards, such as asterisks, because most search engines support them. The search term cent* will retrieve cents, whereas cent** will retrieve both center and centre.

- **Keep trying.** If a search produces no results, check your spelling. If you are using Boolean operators, check the syntax of your queries. Try synonyms and variations on words. Try to be less specific in your search term. If your search produces too many hits, try to be more specific. Use the Advanced feature of your search engine to narrow your search. Use as many relevant keywords as possible.
- **Repeat your search a week later.** For the best results, return to your search a couple of days or a week later. The same keywords will probably produce additional results. That's because millions of new pages are being added every day. The ranking of hits can also change depending on how often a link is accessed by Internet users.

Credibility of Internet Sources. Most online users tend to assume that any information turned up by a search engine has somehow been evaluated as part of a valid selection process. However, unlike library-based research, information at many sites has not undergone the editing or scrutiny of scholarly publication procedures. The information we read in journals and most reputable magazines is reviewed, authenticated, and evaluated.

Information online is much less reliable than data from traditional sources. Wikis, blogs, and discussion forum entries illustrate this problem. They change constantly and may disappear fast so that your source can't be verified. Many don't provide any references or reveal sources that are either obscure or suspect. Academic researchers prefer lasting, scholarly sources.

Wikipedia and Other Encyclopedias. Postsecondary-level research requires you to use general encyclopedia information only as a starting point for more in-depth research. That means you will not cite Wikipedia, general encyclopedias, search engines, or similar reference works in your writing. Their information is too fluid and too general. However, these information-packed sites often provide their own references (bibliographies) that you can employ in your research. Locate the original sources of information rather than the condensed reference articles. Both the American Psychological Association (APA) and the Modern Language Association (MLA) favour the use of original source material.

Conducting Primary Research

Although you will start nearly every business report assignment by sifting through secondary sources, you will probably need primary data to give a complete picture. Business reports that solve specific, current problems typically rely on primary, first-hand data. Providing answers to business problems often means generating primary data through surveys, interviews, observation, or experimentation.

Surveys. Surveys collect data from groups of people. Before developing new products, for example, companies often survey consumers to learn their needs. The advantages of surveys are that they gather data economically and efficiently. Mail sent by Canada Post or e-mailed surveys reach big groups nearby or at great distances. Moreover, people responding to mailed or e-mailed surveys have time to consider their answers, thus improving the accuracy of the data.

PLUGGED IN

Staying on Top of Research Data

In collecting search results, you can easily lose track of websites and articles you quoted. To document online data that may change, as well as to manage all your other sources, you need a specific plan for saving the information. At the very least, you will want to create a working bibliography or list of *references* in which you record the URL of each electronic source. These techniques can help you stay in control of your data:

- Saving sources to a local drive or USB flash drive has advantages, including being able to open the document in a browser even if you don't have access to the Internet. More important, saving sources to disk or memory stick preserves information that may not be available later. Using either the **File** and **Save As** or the **File** and **Save Page As** menu command in your browser, you will be able to store the information permanently. Save images and other kinds of media by either right-clicking or command-clicking on the item, and selecting **Save Picture As** or **Save Image As**.
- Copying and pasting information you find online into MS Word is an easy way to save and store it. Copy and paste the URL into the file as well, and record the URL in your working bibliography. If you invest in Adobe's PDF Converter, you can save most files in the portable document format simply by choosing the **Print** command and selecting Adobe PDF in the **Printer** window of the **Print** menu. The URL, access date, and time stamp will be automatically saved on the document. You can keep your PDF documents as electronic files or print out paper copies later.
- Printing pages is a handy way to gather and store information. Doing so enables you to have copies of important data that you can annotate or highlight. Make sure the URL prints with the document (usually on the bottom of the page). If not, write it on the page.
- Bookmarking favourites is an option within browsers to enable you to record and store the URLs of important sources. The key to using this option is creating folders with relevant names and choosing concise and descriptive names for bookmarks.
- Cloud storage and e-mailing documents, URLs, or messages to yourself are also useful strategies. Many databases and online magazines permit you to e-mail information and sometimes the entire article to your account. A cloud storage account lets you access your files from any electronic device.

To use the Internet meaningfully, you must scrutinize what you find and check who authored and published it. Here are specific criteria to consider as you examine a site:

- **Currency.** What is the date of the Web page? Is some of the information obviously out of date? If the information is time sensitive and the site has not been updated recently, the site is probably not reliable.
- **Authority.** Who publishes or sponsors this Web page? What makes the presenter an authority? Is information about the author or creator available? Is a contact address available? Learn to be skeptical about data and assertions from individuals and organizations whose credentials are not verifiable.
- **Content.** Is the purpose of the page to entertain, inform, convince, or sell? How would you classify this page (e.g., news, personal, advocacy, reference)? Who is the intended audience, based on content, tone, and style? Can you judge the overall value of the content compared with the other resources on this topic?
- **Accuracy.** Do the facts presented seem reliable? Are there spelling, grammar, or usage errors? Do you see any evidence of bias? Are references provided? Errors and missing references should alert you that the data may be questionable.

Mailed or e-mailed surveys, of course, have disadvantages. Because most of us rank them with junk mail or spam, response rates may be low. Furthermore, respondents may not represent an accurate sample of the overall population, thus invalidating generalizations from the group. Let's say, for example, that an insurance company sends out a questionnaire asking about provisions in a new policy. If only older people respond, the questionnaire data cannot be used to generalize what people in other age groups might think. If a survey is only e-mailed, it may miss audiences that do not use the Internet.

A final problem with surveys has to do with truthfulness. Some respondents exaggerate their incomes or distort other facts, thus causing the results to be unreliable. Nevertheless, surveys may be the best way to generate data for business and student reports. In preparing print or electronic surveys, consider these pointers:

- **Select the survey population carefully.** Many surveys question a small group of people (a sample) and project the findings to a larger population. To be able to generalize from a survey, you need to make the sample large enough. In addition, you need to determine whether the sample represents the larger population. For important surveys you will want to learn sampling techniques.

- **Explain why the survey is necessary.** In a cover letter or an opening paragraph, describe the need for the survey. Suggest how someone or something other than you will benefit. If appropriate, offer to send recipients a copy of the findings.

- **Consider incentives.** If the survey is long, persuasive techniques may be necessary. Response rates can be increased by offering money (such as a loonie), coupons, gift certificates, books, or other gifts.

- **Limit the number of questions.** Resist the temptation to ask for too much. Request only information you will use. Don't, for example, include demographic questions (income, gender, age, and so forth) unless the information is necessary to evaluate responses.

- **Use questions that produce quantifiable answers.** Check-off, multiple-choice, yes-no, and scale (or rank-order) questions, illustrated in Figure 11.9, provide quantifiable data that are easily tabulated. Responses to open-ended questions (*What should the bookstore do about plastic bags?*) reveal interesting but difficult-to-quantify perceptions.[9] To obtain workable data, give interviewees a list of possible responses, as shown in Figure 11.9. For scale and multiple-choice questions, try to present all the possible answer choices. To be safe, add an *Other* or *Don't know* category in case the choices seem insufficient to the respondent. Many surveys use scale questions because they capture degrees of feelings. Typical scale headings are *Agree strongly*, *Agree somewhat*, *Neutral*, *Disagree somewhat*, and *Disagree strongly*.

- **Avoid leading or ambiguous questions.** The wording of a question can dramatically affect responses to it.[10] When respondents were asked, "Are we spending too much, too little, or about the right amount on *assistance to the poor*?" 13 percent responded *Too much*. When the same respondents were asked, "Are we spending too much, too little, or about the right amount on *welfare*?" 44 percent responded *Too much*. Because words have different meanings for different people, you must strive to use objective language and pilot test your questions with typical respondents. Ask neutral questions (*Do CEOs earn too much, too little, or about the right amount?*). Also, avoid queries that really ask two or more things (*Should the salaries of CEOs be reduced or regulated by government legislation?*). Instead, break them into separate questions (*Should the salaries of CEOs be reduced by government legislation? Should the salaries of CEOs be regulated by government legislation?*).

- **Make it easy for respondents to return the survey.** Researchers often provide prepaid self-addressed envelopes or business-reply envelopes. Low-cost Internet survey software, such as SurveyMonkey, help users develop simple, template-driven questions and allow survey takers to follow a link to take the survey.

- **Conduct a pilot study.** Try the questionnaire with a small group so that you can remedy any problems.

FIGURE 11.9 Preparing a Survey

1 Prewriting	2 Drafting	3 Revising
Analyze: The purpose is to help the bookstore decide whether it should replace plastic bags with cloth bags for customer purchases. **Anticipate:** The audience will be busy students who will be initially uninterested. **Adapt:** Because students will be unwilling to participate, the survey must be short and simple. Its purpose must be significant and clear. It must be easy to access online.	**Research:** Ask students how they would react to cloth bags. Use their answers to form response choices. **Organize:** Open by explaining the survey's purpose and importance. In the body ask clear questions that produce quantifiable answers. Conclude with appreciation and instructions. **Draft:** Write the first version of the online questionnaire.	**Edit:** Try out the questionnaire with a small representative group. Revise unclear questions. **Proofread:** Read for correctness. Be sure that answer choices do not overlap and that they are complete. Provide an *Other category* if appropriate. **Evaluate:** Is the survey clear, attractive, and easy to complete?

Greendale College Bookstore

STUDENT SURVEY

The Greendale College Bookstore wants to do its part in protecting the environment. Each year we give away 45,000 plastic bags for students to carry off their purchases. We are considering changing from plastic to cloth bags or some other alternative, but we need your views.

1. How many units are you currently carrying?

○ 15 or more units
○ 9 to 14 units
○ 8 to fewer units

2. How many times have you visited the bookstore this semester?

○ 0 times
○ 1 time
○ 2 times
○ 3 times
○ 4 or more times

3. Indicate your concern for the environment.

○ Very concerned
○ Concerned
○ Unconcerned

4. To protect the environment, would you be willing to change to another type of bag when buying books?

○ Yes
○ No

5. Indicate your feeling about the following alternatives.

For major purchases, the bookstore should:

	Agree	Undecided	Disagree
Continue to provide plastic bags.	○	○	○
Provide no bags; encourage students to bring their own bags.	○	○	○
Provide no bags; offer cloth bags at reduced price (about $3).	○	○	○

Interviews. Some of the best report information, particularly on topics about which little has been written, comes from individuals. These individuals are usually experts or veterans in their fields. Consider both in-house and outside experts for business reports. Tapping these sources will call for in-person, telephone, or online interviews. To elicit the most useful data, try these techniques:

- **Locate an expert.** Ask managers and individuals who are considered to be most knowledgeable in their areas. Check membership lists of professional organizations, and consult articles about the topic. Most people enjoy being experts or at least recommending them. You could also *crowdsource* your question in social media; that is, you could pose the query to your network to get input from your contacts.
- **Prepare for the interview.** Learn about the individual you are interviewing, and make sure you can pronounce the interviewee's name. Research the background and terminology of the topic. In addition, be prepared by making a list of questions that pinpoint your focus on the topic. Ask the interviewee if you may record the talk. Familiarize yourself with the recording device beforehand.
- **Maintain a professional attitude.** Call before the interview to confirm the arrangements, and then arrive on time. Be prepared to take notes if your recorder fails. Use your body language to convey respect.
- **Make your questions objective and friendly.** Adopt a courteous and respectful attitude. Don't get into a debating match with the interviewee, and don't interrupt. Remember that you are there to listen. Use open-ended questions to draw experts out.
- **Watch the time.** Tell interviewees in advance how much time you expect to need for the interview. Don't overstay your appointment. If your interviewees ramble, gently try to draw them back to the topic; otherwise, you may run out of time before asking all your questions.
- **End graciously.** Conclude the interview with a general question, such as *Is there anything you would like to add?* Express your appreciation, and ask permission to telephone later if you need to verify points.

Observation and Experimentation. Some kinds of primary data can be obtained only through first-hand observation and investigation. If you determine that you need observational data, then you need to plan carefully. Most important is deciding what or whom you are observing and how often those observations are necessary. For example, if you want to learn more about an organization's telephone customer service, you probably need to conduct an observation (along with interviews and perhaps even surveys). You will want to answer questions such as *How long does a typical caller wait before a customer-service rep answers the call?* and *Is the service consistent?* Recording 60-minute periods at various times throughout a week will give you a more accurate picture.

To observe, arrive early enough to introduce yourself and set up any equipment. If you are recording, secure permissions beforehand. In addition, take notes not only of the events or actions but also of the settings. Changes in environment often have an effect on actions of the participants.

Experimentation produces data suggesting causes and effects. Informal experimentation might be as simple as a pretest and posttest in a college or university course. Did students learn in the course? Scientists and professional researchers undertake more formal experimentation. They control variables to test their effects. Such experiments are not done haphazardly, however. Valid experiments require sophisticated research designs.

Concept Check

1. What are four criteria to consider when evaluating a website?
2. Why is it important to use survey questions that produce quantifiable results?

CASE CONNECTIONS

Contract Cheating on the Rise in Canada

Andriy Popov/Alamy Stock Photo

Contract cheating occurs when students pay a service to write assignments for them. These assignments are then submitted as the students' own work. In a CityNews exclusive investigation, they found that a man from Kenya, who chose to remain anonymous, wrote "hundreds of essays and assignments that have been submitted by Canadian university students over the last year."[11] This contract cheating is unethical not only because it violates academic integrity but also because of the treatment of the service's writers. The Kenyan man, who has a university education, says he received only $18 for an essay where a student paid $165. He was also "offered help with immigrating to Canada if he continued to work for a reduced fee for at least one year."[12] While unethical and problematic on many levels, contract cheating is not yet illegal in Canada:

> Education lawyer John Schuman says legally, there's not much that can be done to prevent students from plagiarizing or purchasing fully written essays outright.
>
> "There isn't much by way of the law in Canada that addresses this type of academic dishonesty. That's entirely within the universities and their own codes of conduct and their own disciplinary procedures," he says.
>
> If caught however, the discipline for these offences can range from a reduced grade to expulsion. At the University of Toronto, the penalty for buying an essay is expulsion, even if it is a first offence.[13]

Knowing that cheating has severe consequences, why would students pay for assignments and pass them off as their own? What can your college or university do to combat the rise in contract cheating?

Documenting Information

LEARNING OBJECTIVE 4

Identify the purposes and techniques of citation and documentation in business reports, and avoid plagiarism.

In writing business reports, you will often build on the ideas and words of others. In Western culture, whenever you "borrow" the ideas of others, you must give credit to your information sources. This is called *documentation*.

The Purposes of Documentation

As a careful writer, you should take pains to document report data properly for the following reasons:

- **To strengthen your argument.** Including good data from reputable sources will convince readers of your credibility and the logic of your reasoning.
- **To protect yourself against charges of plagiarism.** Acknowledging your sources keeps you honest. *Plagiarism*, which is unethical and in some cases illegal, is the act of using others' ideas without proper documentation.
- **To instruct the reader.** Citing references enables readers to pursue a topic further and make use of the information themselves.
- **To save time.** The world of business moves so quickly that words and ideas must often be borrowed—which is acceptable when you give credit to your sources.

ETHICS CHECK

Cribbing From References?

Doing last-minute research for a class or work project, you are in a hurry; therefore, you decide to copy some sources from the list of references that you found in an article on your topic to boost your number of works cited. Is it unethical to list sources you have not actually read?

Intellectual Theft: Plagiarism

Plagiarism of words or ideas is a serious offence and can lead to loss of a job. Famous historians, several high-level journalists, politicians, and educators have suffered grave consequences for copying from unnamed sources. Your instructor may use a commercial plagiarism detection service, such as Turnitin.com, which cross-references much of the information on the Internet, looking for documents with identical phrasing. The result, an "originality report," shows the instructor whether you have been accurate and honest. Many instructors also use the originality report as a learning tool for you; it may reveal unintentional weaknesses in your documentation that you can improve upon.

You can avoid charges of plagiarism and add clarity to your work by knowing what to document and by developing good research habits. First, however, let's consider the differences between business and academic writing with respect to documentation.

Academic Documentation and Business Practices

In the academic world, documentation is critical. Especially in the humanities and sciences, students are taught to cite sources by using quotation marks, parenthetical citations, footnotes, and bibliographies. Term papers require full documentation to demonstrate that a student has become familiar with respected sources and can cite them properly in developing an argument. Giving credit to the authors is extremely important. Students who plagiarize risk a failing grade in a class and even expulsion from school.

In business, however, documentation and authorship are sometimes viewed differently. Business communicators on the job may find that much of what is written does not follow the standards they learned in school. In many instances, individual authorship is unimportant. For example, employees may write for the signature of their bosses. The writer receives no credit. Similarly, teams turn out documents for which none of the team members receives individual credit. Internal business reports, which often include chunks of information from previous reports, also don't give credit.

Although both internal and external business reports are not as heavily documented as school assignments or term papers, business communication students are well advised to learn proper documentation methods. If facts are questioned, business writers must be able to produce their source materials.

What to Document

When you write reports, especially in college or university, you are continually dealing with other people's ideas. You are expected to conduct research, synthesize ideas, and build on the work of others. But you are also expected to give proper credit for borrowed material. To avoid plagiarism, you must give credit whenever you use the following:[14]

- Another person's ideas, opinions, examples, or theory
- Any facts, statistics, graphs, and drawings that are not common knowledge
- Quotations of another person's actual spoken or written words
- Paraphrases of another person's spoken or written words
- Visuals, images, and any kind of electronic media

Information that is common knowledge requires no documentation. For example, the statement *The Globe and Mail is a popular business newspaper* would require no citation. Statements that are not common knowledge, however, must be documented. For example, the following statement would require a citation because most people do not know these facts: *Five of the nation's top 15 cities are located in the Golden Horseshoe area in Ontario, on the densely populated shores of the Great Lakes.*[15] More important, someone went through the trouble and expense of assembling this original work and now *owns* it. Cite sources for such proprietary information—in this case, statistics reported by a newspaper or magazine. You probably know to use citations to document direct quotations, but you must also cite ideas that you summarize in your own words.

When in doubt about common knowledge, check to see whether the same piece of information is available in at least three sources in your topic's specific field and appears without citation. If what you borrow doesn't fall into one of the five categories listed earlier, for which you must give credit, you are safe in assuming it is common knowledge. Copyright and intellectual property are discussed in greater detail later in this chapter.

Good Research Habits

As they gather sources, report writers have two methods available for recording the information they find. The time-honoured manual method of notetaking works well because information is recorded on separate cards, which can then be conveniently arranged in the order needed to develop a thesis or an argument. Today, however, writers prefer to do their research online. Traditional notetaking may seem antiquated and laborious in comparison. Let's explore both methods.

Paper Note Cards. To make sure you know whose ideas you are using, train yourself to take excellent notes. If possible, know what you intend to find before you begin your research so that you won't waste time on unnecessary notes. Here are some pointers on taking good notes:

- Record all major ideas from various sources on separate note cards.
- Include all publication information (author, date, title, and so forth) along with precise quotations.
- Consider using one card colour for direct quotes and a different colour for your paraphrases and summaries.
- Put the original source material aside when you are summarizing or paraphrasing.

Digital Records. Instead of recording facts on note cards, savvy researchers today take advantage of digital media tools, as noted in the Plugged In box. Beware, however, of the risk of cutting and pasting your way into plagiarism. Here are some pointers on taking good virtual notes:

- Begin your research by setting up a folder on your local drive or cloud-based storage site.
- Create subfolders for major sections, such as introduction, body, and closing.
- When you find facts online or in research databases, highlight the material you want to record, copy it, and paste it into a document in an appropriate folder.
- Be sure to include all publication information in your references or works-cited lists.
- As discussed in the section on managing research data, consider archiving on a USB flash drive or external disk drive those Internet pages or articles used in your research in case the data must be verified.

The Fine Art of Paraphrasing In writing reports and using the ideas of others, you will probably rely heavily on *paraphrasing*, which means restating an original passage in your own words and in your own style. To do a good job of paraphrasing, follow these steps:

1. Read the original material intently to comprehend its full meaning.
2. Write your own version without looking at the original.
3. Avoid repeating the grammatical structure of the original and merely replacing words with synonyms.
4. Reread the original to be sure you covered the main points but did not borrow specific language.

To better understand the difference between plagiarizing and paraphrasing, study the following passages. Notice that the writer of the plagiarized version uses the same grammatical construction as the source and often merely replaces words with synonyms. Even the acceptable version, however, requires a reference to the source author.

Source

We have seen, in a short amount of time, the disappearance of a large number of household brands that failed to take sufficient and early heed of the software revolution that is upending traditional brick-and-mortar businesses and creating a globally pervasive digital economy.[16]

Plagiarized version

Many trusted household name brands disappeared very swiftly because they did not sufficiently and early pay attention to the software revolution that is toppling traditional physical businesses and creating a global digital economy (Saylor, 2012).

Acceptable paraphrase

Digital technology has allowed a whole new virtual global economy to blossom and very swiftly wipe out some formerly powerful companies that responded too late or inadequately to the disruptive force that has swept the globe (Saylor, 2012).

When and How to Quote

On occasion, you will want to use the exact words of a source, but beware of overusing quotations. Documents that contain pages of spliced-together quotations suggest that writers have few ideas of their own. Wise writers and speakers use direct quotations for three purposes only:

- To provide objective background data and establish the severity of a problem as seen by experts
- To repeat identical phrasing because of its precision, clarity, or aptness
- To duplicate exact wording before criticizing

When you must use a long quotation, try to summarize and introduce it in your own words. Readers want to know the gist of a quotation before they tackle it. For example, to introduce a quotation discussing the shrinking staffs of large companies, you could precede it with your words: *In predicting employment trends, Charles Waller believes the corporation of the future will depend on a small core of full-time employees.* To introduce quotations or paraphrases, use wording such as the following:

According to Waller, ...

Waller argues that . . . .

In his recent study, Waller reported . . . .

Use quotation marks to enclose exact quotations, as shown in the following: "The current image," says Charles Waller, "of a big glass-and-steel corporate headquarters on landscaped grounds directing a worldwide army of tens of thousands of employees may soon be a thing of the past" (2015, p. 51).

ETHICS CHECK

Permission for Performances

Before Canadian astronaut Chris Hadfield could perform David Bowie's song "Space Oddity" aboard the International Space Station (ISS), Bowie's permission had to be obtained, as the song is still under copyright entitling him to a fee when it is performed publicly.[18] Even after David Bowie's death, permission to use his work still has to be obtained from his estate. How can academic and business writers ensure that they obtain permission and credit as required?

Copyright Information

The Canadian *Copyright Act* protects creative endeavours by ensuring that the creators have the sole right to authorize their publication, performance, or reproduction. Copyright applies to all original literary or textual works, dramatic works, musical works, artistic works, and architectural works. The word *copyright* refers to the "right to copy," and a key provision is *fair dealing*, the exception to the exclusive rights of copyright holders. Fair dealing creates a limited number of exceptions, including private study, research, criticism, review, and news reporting. This list is exhaustive, such that fair dealing applies only to those categories of dealings that are specifically mentioned. The law of copyright also applies to the Internet, so most individual works found there are protected: using Internet text or graphics without the permission of the copyright holder, for instance, is an infringement of copyright law.[17]

How to Avoid Copyright Infringement. Whenever you borrow words, charts, graphs, photos, music, and other media—in short, any *intellectual property*—be sure you know what is legal and acceptable. The following guidelines will help:

- **Assume that all intellectual property is copyrighted.** Nearly everything created privately and originally after 1989 is copyrighted and protected whether or not it has a copyright notice.
- **Realize that Internet items and resources are NOT in the public domain.** No modern intellectual or artistic creation is in the public domain (free to be used by anyone) unless the owner explicitly says so.
- **Observe fair-dealing restrictions.** Avoid appropriating large amounts of outside material.
- **Ask for permission.** You are always safe if you obtain permission. Write to the source, identify the material you want to include, and explain where it will be used. Expect to pay for permission.
- **Don't assume that a footnote is all that is needed.** Including a footnote to a source prevents plagiarism but not copyright infringement. Anything copied beyond the boundaries of fair dealing requires permission.

For more information about *copyright law, fair dealing, public domain*, and *work for hire*, you can search online with these keywords.

Citation Formats

You can direct readers to your sources with parenthetical notes inserted into the text and with bibliographies. The most common citation formats are those presented by the Modern Language Association (MLA) and the American Psychological Association (APA). Learn more about how to use these formats in the Documentation and Formats section located in Appendix A.

Concept Check

1. The Internet has brought the paper mills to the masses. Some students pay to have their papers written by shady authors online. Discuss the views in your class regarding this practice and how it could be harmful to honest students. Is any harm done to colleges and universities? Society?
2. Research suggests that colleges with strong, explicit ethics codes and zero tolerance of cheating have the lowest incidence of academic dishonesty. Find the student handbook on your portal (or your school's website) for rules of conduct regarding cheating. Are they clear? What are the consequences for plagiarism?

Creating Effective Graphics

LEARNING OBJECTIVE 5

Generate, use, and convert numerical data to visual aids, and create meaningful and attractive graphics.

After collecting and interpreting information, you need to consider how best to present it. If your report contains complex data and numbers, you may want to consider graphics such as tables and charts. These graphics clarify data, create visual interest, and make numerical data meaningful. By simplifying complex ideas and emphasizing key data, well-constructed graphics make important information easier to remember. However, the same data can be shown in many forms; for example, in a chart, table, or graph. That's why you need to know how to match the appropriate graphic with your objective and how to incorporate it into your report.

Matching Graphics and Objectives

In developing the best graphics, you must decide what data you want to highlight and which graphics are most appropriate for use with your objectives. Figure 11.10 summarizes appropriate uses for each type of graphic. The following sections discuss each type in more detail.

Tables. Probably the most frequently used graphic in reports is the table. Because a table presents quantitative or verbal information in systematic columns and rows, it can clarify large quantities of data in small spaces. The disadvantage is that tables do not readily display

FIGURE 11.10 Matching Graphics to Objectives

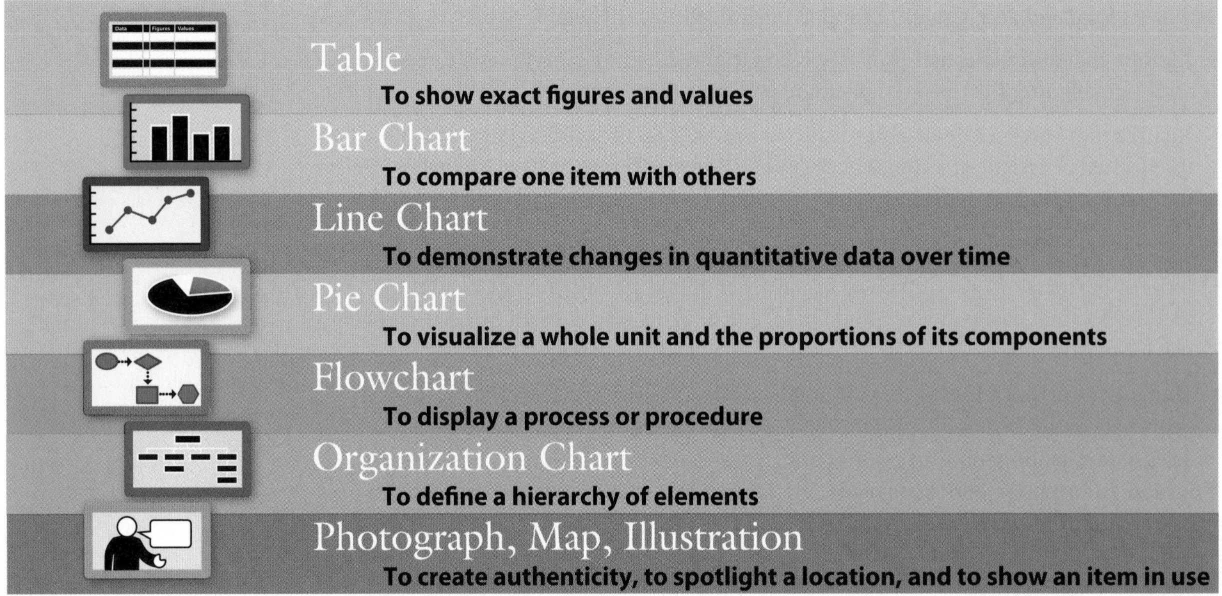
Table
To show exact figures and values
Bar Chart
To compare one item with others
Line Chart
To demonstrate changes in quantitative data over time
Pie Chart
To visualize a whole unit and the proportions of its components
Flowchart
To display a process or procedure
Organization Chart
To define a hierarchy of elements
Photograph, Map, Illustration
To create authenticity, to spotlight a location, and to show an item in use

trends. You may have made rough tables to help you organize the raw data collected from questionnaires or interviews. In preparing tables for your readers or listeners, however, you need to pay more attention to clarity and emphasis. Here are tips for making good tables, one of which is provided in Figure 11.11:

- Place titles and labels at the top of the table.
- Arrange items in a logical order (alphabetical, chronological, geographical, highest to lowest), depending on what you need to emphasize.
- Provide clear headings for the rows and columns.
- Make long tables easier to read by shading alternate lines or by leaving a blank line after groups of five.
- Place tables as close as possible to the place where they are mentioned in the text.
- Identify the units in which figures are given (percentages, dollars, units per worker hour) in the table title, in the column or row heading, with the first item in a column, or in a note at the bottom.
- Use *N/A* (*not available*) for missing data.

FIGURE 11.11 Table Summarizing Precise Data

Figure 1
MPM ENTERTAINMENT COMPANY
Income by Division (in millions of dollars)

	Theme Parks	Motion Pictures	DVDs & Blu-ray Discs	Total
2014	$15.8	$39.3	$11.2	$66.3
2015	18.1	17.5	15.3	50.9
2016	23.8	21.1	22.7	67.6
2017	32.2	22.0	24.3	78.5
2018 (projected)	35.1	21.0	26.1	82.2

Source: *Industry Profiles* (New York: DataPro, 2017), 225

PLUGGED IN

Telling a Story With Infographics

Although infographics seem to have burst onto the scene within the last decade, pictograms and ideograms (images and symbols visualizing an idea or action) date back thousands of years to cave paintings, hieroglyphs, and other writing systems.[19] Statistics Canada began using infographics "to help people, business owners, academics, and management at all levels, understand key information derived from the data."[20]

- **Purpose.** Good infographics tell a story and allow the reader to make sense of ever-growing amounts of data. The purpose of the best infographics, according to Statistics Canada, is "to quickly communicate a message, to simplify the presentation of large amounts of data, to see data patterns and relationships, and to monitor changes in variables over time."[21] Well-executed infographics illustrate often complex topics and data almost at one glance. Substituted for ho-hum, conventional visuals, good infographics can be stunning.
- **Infographics software.** Today even amateur designers can create captivating infographics. Any software that can merge text and visuals can help create infographics. However, no single piece of software is the ultimate tool.[22] Some come with a steep learning curve (e.g., Adobe Illustrator and Photoshop), whereas others are easier to use (Apple iWorks and MS Office). Some are cloud-based; others can be downloaded. Try out Google Public Data Explorer, StatSilk, or Creately.
- **Popular uses.** A few innovative companies have turned some reports and executive summaries into infographics. Résumés, advocacy documents such as white papers, decision trees, maps, flowcharts, instructions, rankings, brand messages, and more have been presented as infographics. Although infographics can tell a story with images and entertain while doing so, they can take up a lot of space and, therefore, are most appropriate online. There, viewers and readers can scroll unconstrained by the printed page. Smartphone apps allow users to track and share the numbers in their lives by creating personal infographics.

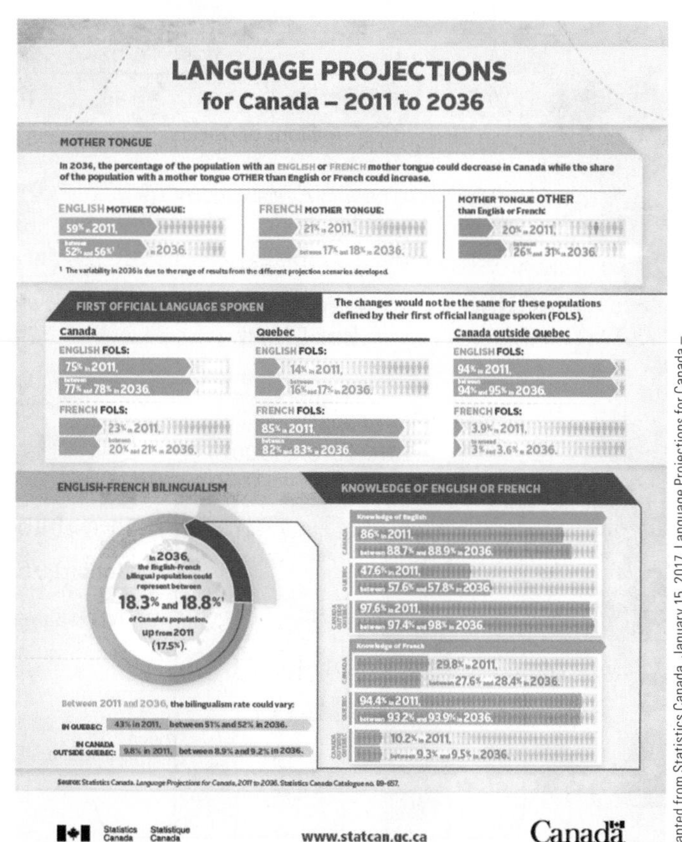

Adapted from Statistics Canada. January 15, 2017. Language Projections for Canada – 2011 to 2036. http://www.statcan.gc.ca/pub/11-627-m/11-627-m2017003-eng.htm (accessed September 30, 2020). This does not constitute an endorsement by Statistics Canada of this product.

The key to infographics is to present a concise and compelling story through images and graphical elements that encourages the reader or viewer to actively participate in the interpretation. Statistics Canada uses infographics to highlight recent census data, as well as statistical projections.

Tables, as illustrated in Figure 11.11, are especially suitable for illustrating exact figures in systematic rows and columns. The table in our figure is particularly useful because it presents data about the MPM Entertainment Company over several years, making it easy to compare several divisions. Figures 11.12 through 11.15 highlight some of the data shown in the MPM Entertainment Company table, illustrating vertical, horizontal, grouped, and segmented 100 percent bar charts, each of which creates a unique effect.

Bar Charts. Although they lack the precision of tables, bar charts enable you to make emphatic visual comparisons by using horizontal or vertical bars of varying lengths. Bar charts are useful for comparing related items, illustrating changes in data over time, and showing segments as a part of the whole. Note how the varied bar charts present information in differing ways.

FIGURE 11.12 Vertical Bar Chart

Figure 1
2019 MPM income by division

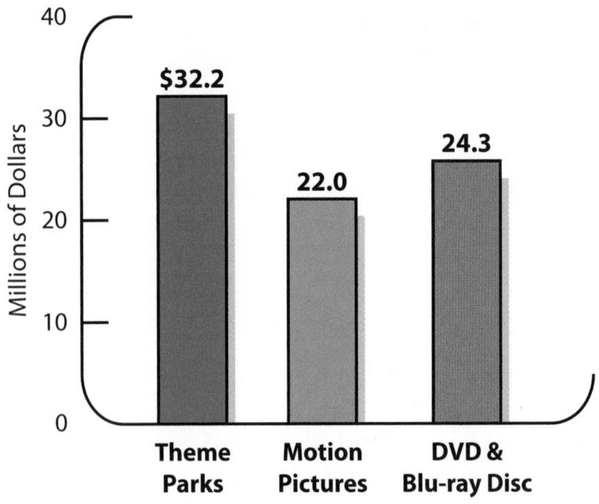

Millions of Dollars
40
30
20
10
0
$32.2
22.0
24.3
Theme Parks
Motion Pictures
DVD & Blu-ray Disc

Source: *Industry Profiles* (New York: DataPro, 2017).

FIGURE 11.13 Horizontal Bar Chart

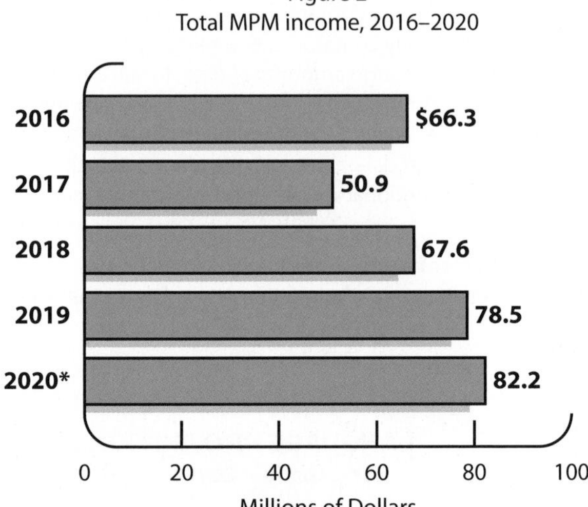

Figure 2
Total MPM income, 2016–2020

2016
$66.3
2017
50.9
2018
67.6
2019
78.5
2020*
82.2
0
20
40
60
80
100
Millions of Dollars

*Projected
Source: *Industry Profiles* (New York: DataPro, 2017).

FIGURE 11.14 Grouped Bar Chart

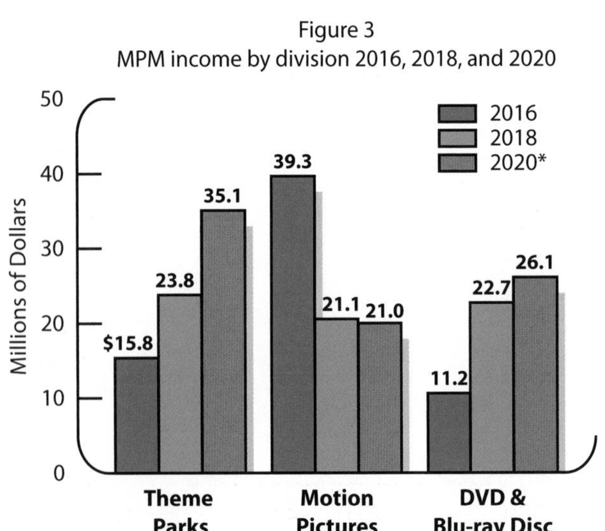

Figure 3
MPM income by division 2016, 2018, and 2020

Millions of Dollars
50
40
30
20
10
0
2016
2018
2020*
$15.8
23.8
35.1
39.3
21.1
21.0
11.2
22.7
26.1
Theme Parks
Motion Pictures
DVD & Blu-ray Disc

*Projected
Source: *Industry Profiles* (New York: DataPro, 2017).

FIGURE 11.15 Segmented 100 Percent Bar Chart

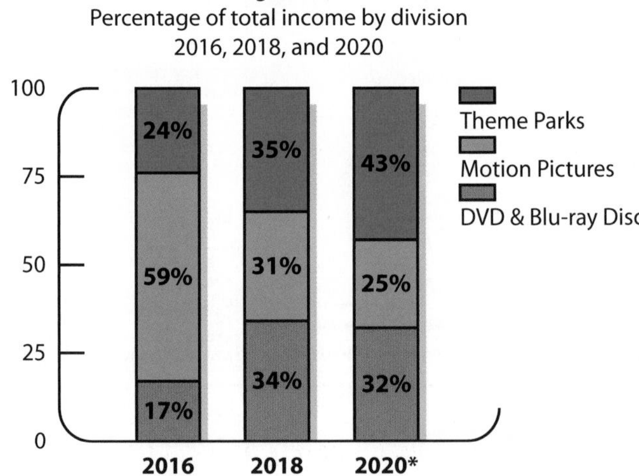

Figure 4
Percentage of total income by division
2016, 2018, and 2020

100
75
50
25
0
24%
59%
17%
35%
31%
34%
43%
25%
32%
2016
2018
2020*
Theme Parks
Motion Pictures
DVD & Blu-ray Disc

*Projected
Source: *Industry Profiles* (New York: DataPro, 2017).

Many techniques for constructing tables also hold true for bar charts. Here are a few additional tips:

- Keep the length and width of each bar and segment proportional.
- Include a total figure in the middle of the bar or at its end if the figure helps the reader and does not clutter the chart.
- Start dollar or percentage amounts at zero.
- Place the first bar at some distance (usually half the amount of space between bars) from the *y*-axis.
- Avoid showing too much information, thus avoiding clutter and confusion.
- Place each bar chart as close as possible to the place where it is mentioned in the text.

Line Charts. The major advantage of line charts is that they show changes over time, thus indicating trends. The vertical axis is typically the dependent variable; and the horizontal axis, the independent one. Simple line charts (Figure 11.16) show just one variable. Multiple line charts compare items, such as two or more data sets, using the same variable (Figure 11.17). Segmented line charts (Figure 11.18), also called surface charts, illustrate how the components of a whole change over time. To prepare a line chart, remember these tips:

- Begin with a grid divided into squares.
- Arrange the time component (usually years) horizontally across the bottom; arrange values for the other variable vertically.
- Draw small dots at the intersections to indicate each value at a given year.
- Connect the dots and add colour if desired.
- To prepare a segmented (surface) chart, plot the first value (say, DVD and Blu-ray disc income) across the bottom; add the next item (say, motion picture income) to the first figures for every increment; for the third item (say, theme park income), add its value to the total for the first two items. The top line indicates the total of the three values.

Pie Charts. Pie charts, or circle graphs, enable readers to see a whole and the proportion of its components, or wedges. Although less flexible than bar or line charts, pie charts are useful

FIGURE 11.16 Simple Line Chart

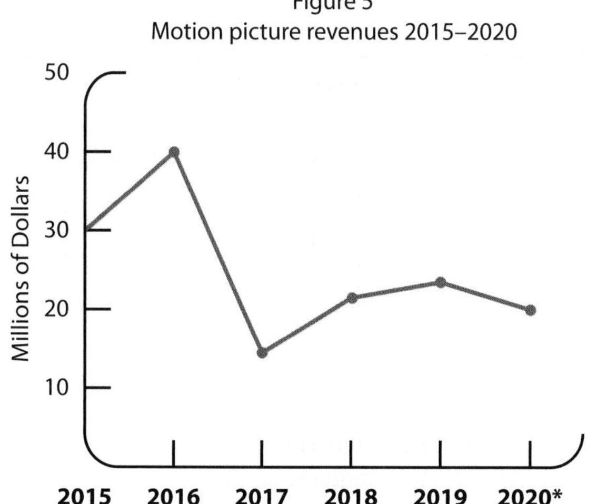

*Projected
Source: *Industry Profiles* (New York: DataPro, 2017).

FIGURE 11.17 Multiple Line Chart

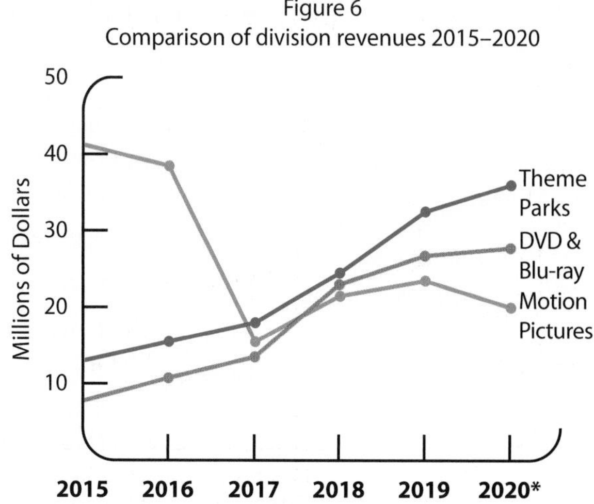

*Projected
Source: *Industry Profiles* (New York: DataPro, 2017).

FIGURE 11.18 Segmented Line (Area) Chart

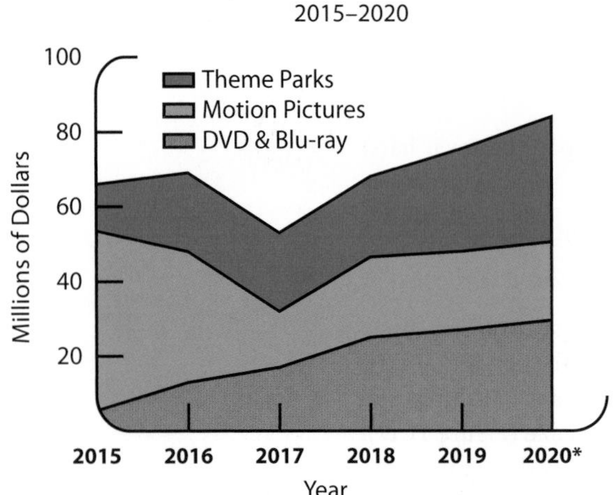

*Projected
Source: *Industry Profiles* (New York: DataPro, 2017).

FIGURE 11.19 Pie Chart

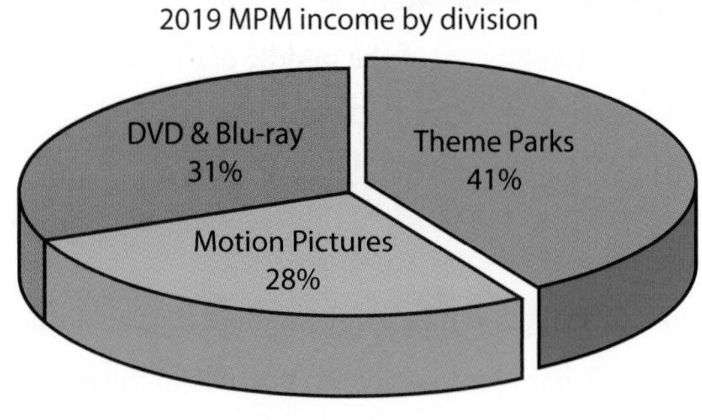

*Projected
Source: *Industry Profiles* (New York: DataPro, 2017).

for showing percentages, as Figure 11.19 illustrates. They are very effective for lay, or nonexpert, audiences. Notice that a wedge can be "exploded," or popped out, for special emphasis, as shown in Figure 11.19. MS Excel and other spreadsheet programs provide a selection of three-dimensional pie charts. For the most effective pie charts, follow these suggestions:

- Make the biggest wedge appear first. Computer spreadsheet programs correctly assign the biggest wedge first (beginning at the 12 o'clock position) and arrange the others in order of decreasing size as long as you list the data representing each wedge on the spreadsheet in descending order.
- Include, if possible, the actual percentage or absolute value for each wedge.
- Use four to six segments for best results; if necessary, group small portions into a wedge called *Other*.
- Draw radii from the centre.
- Distinguish wedges with colour, shading, or cross-hatching.
- Keep all the labels horizontal.

Flowcharts. Procedures are simplified and clarified by diagramming them in a flowchart, as shown in Figure 11.20. Whether you need to describe the procedure for handling a customer's purchase, highlight steps in solving a problem, or display a problem with a process, flowcharts help the reader visualize the process. Traditional flowcharts use the following symbols:

- Ovals to designate the beginning and end of a process
- Diamonds to designate decision points
- Rectangles to represent major activities or steps

Organization Charts. Many large organizations are so complex that they need charts to show the chain of command, from the boss down to the line managers and employees. Organization charts provide such information as who reports to whom, how many subordinates work for each manager (the span of control), and what channels of official communication exist. These charts may illustrate a company's structure—for example, by function, customer, or product. They may also be organized by the work being performed in each job or by the hierarchy of decision making.

FIGURE 11.20 Flowchart

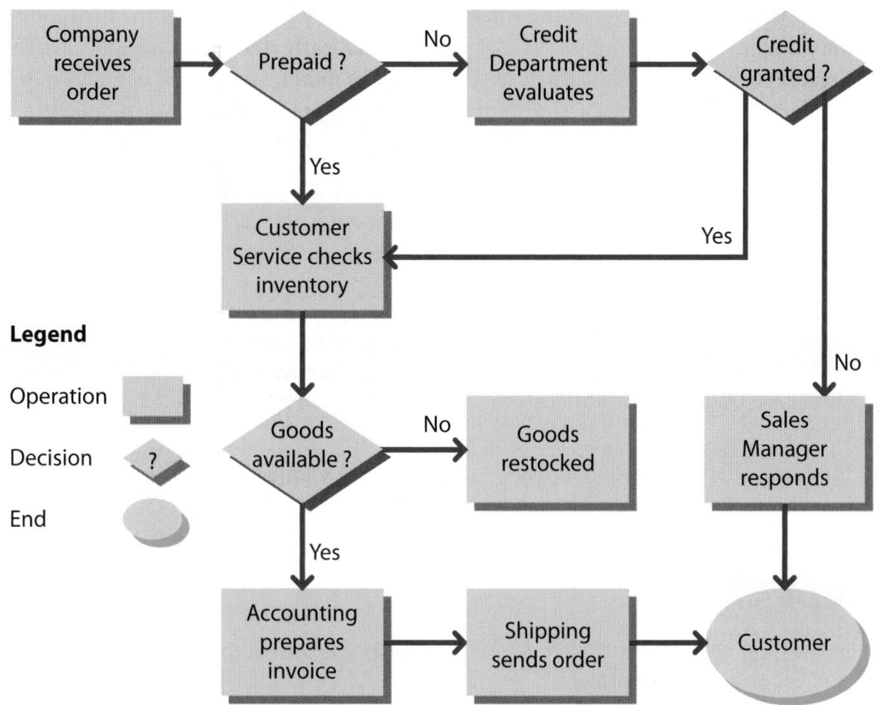

Photographs, Maps, and Illustrations. Some business reports include photographs, maps, and illustrations to serve specific purposes. Photos, for example, add authenticity and provide a visual record. An environmental engineer may use photos to document hazardous waste sites. Maps enable report writers to depict activities or concentrations geographically, such as dots indicating sales reps in cities across the country. Illustrations and diagrams are useful in indicating how an object looks or operates. A drawing showing the parts of a printer with labels describing their functions, for example, is more instructive than a photograph or verbal description.

With today's smart visualization tools as described in the Plugged In box, high-resolution photographs, maps, and illustrations can be inserted into business reports or accessed through hyperlinks within electronically delivered documents. Online they can be animated or appear in clusters as they do in infographics.

Incorporating Graphics in Reports

Used appropriately, graphics make reports more interesting and easier to understand. In putting graphics into your reports, follow these suggestions for best effects:

- **Evaluate the audience.** Consider the reader, the content, your schedule, and your budget. Graphics take time and can be costly to print in colour, so think carefully before deciding how many graphics to use. Six charts in an internal report to an executive may seem like overkill; however, in a long technical report to outsiders, six may be too few.
- **Use restraint.** Don't overuse colour or decorations. Although colour can effectively distinguish bars or segments in charts, too much colour can be distracting and confusing. Remember, too, that colours themselves sometimes convey meaning: reds suggest deficits or negative values; blues suggest calmness and authority; and yellow may suggest warning.
- **Be accurate and ethical.** Double-check all graphics for accuracy of figures and calculations. Be certain that your visuals aren't misleading—either accidentally or intentionally.

Manipulation of a chart scale can make trends look steeper and more dramatic than they really are. Moreover, be sure to cite sources when you use someone else's facts.

- **Introduce a graph meaningfully.** Refer to every graphic in the text, and place the graphic close to the point where it is mentioned. Help the reader understand the significance of the graphic by explaining what to look for or by summarizing the main point of the graphic. Don't assume the reader will automatically draw the same conclusions you reached from a set of data. Instead of saying, *The findings are shown in Figure 3*, tell the reader what to look for: *Two thirds of the responding employees, as shown in Figure 3, favour a flextime schedule.* The best introductions for graphics interpret them for readers.
- **Choose an appropriate caption or title style.** Like reports, graphics may use "talking" titles or generic, descriptive titles. Talking titles are more persuasive: they tell the reader what to think. Descriptive titles describe the facts more objectively. Examples of each follow.

Talking Title	Descriptive Title
Rising Workplace Drug Testing Unfair and Inaccurate	Workplace Drug Testing up 277 Percent
College Students' Diets Clogged With Fat	College Students and Nutrition

Concept Check

1. What are the most popular uses for infographics? How can you use infographics in your academic, professional, or personal life?
2. What are five ways to best incorporate graphics in a report?

SPOTLIGHT ON COMMUNICATION: PART 2

Statistics Canada Revisited

CRITICAL THINKING

- Visit Statistics Canada (www. statcan.gc.ca/eng/start) and select "Subjects" from the top menu bar. Which subjects will you find useful for your studies and why?
- "Statistics Canada has introduced infographics to help people, business owners, academics, and management at all levels understand key information derived from the data."[24] In what ways do infographics effectively communicate information?

While the census provides invaluable information, Statistics Canada also conducts over 350 surveys with individuals and organizations on virtually all aspects of Canadian life. Statistics Canada gathers information on "Canada's economy, society, and environment."[23]

Adapted from Statistics Canada. No date. *Subjects*. Last updated July 30, 2020. https://www150.statcan.gc.ca/n1/en/subjects?MM=1 (accessed December 1, 2019). This does not constitute an endorsement by Statistics Canada of this product.

If, for example, you wanted to start up a small retail business or had a new product you wanted to develop, you would need to develop an effective business plan. By visiting the Statistics Canada website, you could gather information about retail sales by type of product or type of store from surveys such as the Annual Retail and Wholesale Trade Survey, the Retail Chain Survey, or Direct Selling in Canada.[25] This information would be extremely beneficial to you.

The impact of the information collected by Statistics Canada affects all Canadians on a daily basis. It helps individuals and organizations manage their finances by reporting on the inflation rate; it analyzes medical treatments; and it analyzes the best environments for children.

Despite the wide range of information available, individual privacy and confidentiality of data are critical aspects. All personal information "created, held, or collected by Statistics Canada is protected by the *Privacy Act*"; survey respondents are protected by the *Statistics Act*.[26]

Summary of Learning Objectives

1 Explain informational and analytical report functions, organizational strategies, and writing styles, as well as typical report formats.

- Informational reports present data without analysis or recommendations.
- Analytical reports provide findings, analyses, conclusions, and recommendations when requested.
- Reports organized directly reveal the purpose and conclusions immediately; reports organized indirectly place the conclusions and recommendations last.
- Reports written in a formal style use third-person constructions, avoid contractions, and may include passive-voice verbs. Informal reports use first-person constructions, contractions, shorter sentences, familiar words, and active-voice verbs.

2 Apply the 3-x-3 writing process to contemporary business reports to create well-organized documents.

- Report writers begin by clarifying a problem and writing a problem statement, which may include the scope, significance, and limitations of the project.
- After analyzing the audience and defining major issues, report writers prepare a work plan, including a tentative outline and work schedule.
- Next, data must be collected, organized, interpreted, and illustrated.
- After composing the first draft, report writers edit (often many times), proofread, and evaluate.

3 Locate and evaluate secondary sources, and understand how to conduct credible primary research.

- Secondary data may be located by searching for books, periodicals, and newspapers, mostly through electronic indexes and online research databases; information retrieved from the Internet must be scrutinized for currency, authority, content, and accuracy.
- Researchers generate first-hand, primary data through surveys (in-person, online, and print), interviews, observation, and experimentation.
- Surveys are most efficient for gathering information from large groups of people; interviews are useful when working with experts in the field; and first-hand observation can produce rich data, but it must be objective.
- Experimentation produces data suggesting cause and effect; valid experiments require sophisticated research designs and careful matching of experimental and control groups.

4 Identify the purposes and techniques of citation and documentation in business reports, and avoid plagiarism.

- Documenting sources means giving credit to information sources to avoid plagiarism, strengthen an argument, and instruct readers.
- Report writers should document others' ideas, facts that are not common knowledge, quotations, and paraphrases; good notetaking is essential to giving accurate credit to sources.
- Paraphrasing involves putting another's ideas into your own words.
- Quotations may be used to provide objective background data, to repeat memorable phrasing, and to duplicate exact wording before criticizing.

5 **Generate, use, and convert numerical data to visual aids, and create meaningful and attractive graphics.**

- Graphics clarify data, add visual interest, and make complex data easy to understand; report writers work carefully to avoid distorting visual aids.
- Tables show quantitative information in systematic columns and rows; bar charts and line charts enable data to be compared visually.
- Pie charts show a whole and the proportion of its components; flowcharts diagram processes and procedures.
- Infographics combine images and graphic elements to illustrate information in an easy-to-understand format.

Chapter Review

1. Explain the difference between informational and analytical reports. (Obj. 1)
2. List five reasons for choosing an informal writing style over a formal style. (Obj.1)
3. What is the first step in writing a report? Provide a specific example. (Obj. 2)
4. What is a *work plan*, and why is it used? (Obj. 2)
5. Compare primary data and secondary data. Give an original example of each. (Obj. 3)
6. What are the advantages and disadvantages of online surveys? (Obj. 3)
7. In what way is documentation of sources different in colleges and universities than in business? (Obj. 4)
8. Why are your professors likely to discourage your use of Wikipedia and blogs as sources for your reports? (Obj. 4)
9. Briefly compare the advantages and disadvantages of illustrating data with charts (bar and line) versus tables. (Obj. 5)
10. What are five ways to best incorporate graphics in reports?

Critical Thinking

1. Information graphics, also called *infographics*, are popular online for reporting and illustrating complex data. Why do you think infographics continue to be popular? How could infographics be useful in your field? (Objs. 1, 4, 5)
2. Why do researchers often trust the reliability of information obtained from scholarly journals, major newspapers, and well-known magazines? Why should researchers use caution when accessing information from Wikipedia, online forums, and blogs? (Obj. 3)
3. Many individuals conduct surveys of interest on social media platforms, like Facebook. What are the potential issues with using these survey results in a report? (Obj. 3)
4. In what ways is documentation of sources different in colleges and universities than in business? (Obj. 4)
5. **Ethical Issue:** Consider this logical appeal under the heading "Reasons Students Hate Writing Essays or Term Papers" and evaluate its validity and ethics:

   Three term papers due tomorrow with three major tests from three of the classes as well as a long math assignment. What should a student do? This problem while in [*sic*] exaggeration often happens to students. It is like all the teachers decide to overwhelm the students in their classes with not only tests on the same day but also term papers, essays, or other writing assignments. This is the reason most students hate writing term papers or other types of writing. Other reasons for disliking writing assignments are poor English classes in high school, often instructors fail to explain different writing styles, unsure of topics to write, and instructors fail to read the writing assignments. . . . Don't be afraid to reach out and get help if it's needed! CustomPapers.com can assist you.[27] (Obj. 4)

Activities

11.1 Problem and Purpose Statements (Obj. 2)

YOUR TASK Identify a problem in your current job or a previous job, such as inadequate use of technology, inefficient procedures, spotty customer service, poor product quality, low morale, or a personnel problem. Assume that your boss agrees with your criticism and asks you to prepare a report. Write (a) a two- or three-sentence statement describing the problem, (b) a problem question, and (c) a simple statement of purpose for your report.

11.2 Plagiarism, Paraphrasing, and Citing Sources (Obj. 4)

One of the biggest challenges for student writers is paraphrasing secondary sources correctly to avoid plagiarism.

YOUR TASK For the following, read the original passage. Analyze the paraphrased version. List the weaknesses in relation to what you have learned about plagiarism and the use of references. Then write an improved version.

Original Passage

Developing casual online game titles can be much less risky than trying to create a game that runs on a console such as an Xbox. Casual games typically cost less than $200,000 to produce, and production cycles are only six months to a year. There's no shelf space, packaging, or CD production to pay for. Best of all, there's more room for innovation.[28]

Paraphrased Passage

The development of casual online games offers less risk than creating games running on Xbox and other consoles. Usually, casual games are cheaper, costing under $200,000 to create and 6 to 12 months to produce. Developers save on shelf space, packaging, and CD production too. Moreover, they have more freedom to innovate.

11.3 Types of Data and Research Questions (Obj. 3)

Researchers must identify or generate credible but also relevant data that will be suitable for their research tasks.

YOUR TASK In conducting research for the following reports, name at least one form of data you will need and questions you should ask to determine whether that set of data is appropriate (see Figure 11.6).

a. A report about the feasibility of an employer-provided preschool day-care program
b. A report on business attire in banking that you must submit to your company's executives, who want to issue a formal professional dress code on the job
c. A report examining the effectiveness of technology use policies in Canadian businesses

11.4 Exploring Campus Food Preferences With SurveyMonkey (Obj. 3)

Communication Technology | E-mail | Team | Web

Your Campus Business Club (CBC) is abuzz about a GrubHub study that analyzed the ordering habits of Canadian college students attending more than 50 schools across Canada. Not unexpectedly perhaps, the campus favourites would not qualify as health food. In addition, students tend to order late at night, order almost 50 percent more than nonstudents do, and tip 5 percent less than nonstudents do.[29] The current top three late-night snacks are frozen yogurt, waffle fries, and chicken souvlaki pita, followed by brownies, hibachi chicken, vegetarian spring rolls, sweet and sour chicken, and the obligatory cheese pizza. Buffalo chicken wings and spicy California rolls round out the top ten.

Your CBC wants to advocate for a new, small student-run restaurant in the campus food court. But what food should it dish out? Is it true that college students overwhelmingly prefer food high in salt, sugar, and fat? Your club colleagues have chosen you to create an online survey to poll fellow students, staff, and faculty about their preferences. You hope to generate data that will support the feasibility of the eatery and help CBC create winning menu choices.

The main provider of online survey software, SurveyMonkey, makes creating questionnaires fast, fun, and easy. After signing up for the free no-frills basic plan, you can create brief online questionnaires and e-mail the links to your targeted respondents. The programs analyze and display the results for you—at no charge.

YOUR TASK In pairs or teams of three, design a basic questionnaire to survey students on your campus about food options in the campus cafeteria. Visit SurveyMonkey and sign up for the basic plan. After creating the online survey, e-mail the survey link to as many members of the campus community as possible. For a smaller sample, start by polling students in your class. Interpret the results. As a team, write a memo that you will e-mail to the campus food services administrator advocating for a student-run eatery featuring the top-scoring national or regional foods. Your instructor may ask you to complete this activity as a report or proposal assignment after you study Chapter 12.

11.5 Seeking Business Infographics (Objs. 1, 4, 5)

Web

YOUR TASK Online or in print, find an infographic that visualizes intriguing business-relevant data. Look for sources within or below the infographic. Are they indicated? If yes, are they credible? How much hard statistical information is provided in relation to the space the infographic occupies? Does the infographic meet its objective: is the information clearly presented, easy to read, and insightful? Report your findings orally or in writing. Be prepared to show your chosen infographic to the class. Tip: In Google or a similar search engine, type the keyword *infographic* and among the search categories, select Images.

11.6 Creating a Bar Chart (Obj. 5)

The ability to create appropriate and relevant graphics is a sought-after skill in today's information-age workplace. Spreadsheet programs, such as Excel, make it easy to generate appealing visuals.

YOUR TASK Based on the statistics that follow, prepare (a) a bar chart comparing the latest tax rates in eight industrial countries and (b) a bar chart that shows the change from the previous year to the current year. The past-year data follow the current statistics in parentheses: Canada, 39 (33) percent; France, 52 (45) percent; Germany, 45 (41) percent; Japan, 34 (28) percent; the Netherlands, 46 (38) percent; Sweden, 52 (49) percent; the United Kingdom, 41 (38) percent; the United States, 22 (28) percent. These figures represent a percentage of the gross domestic product for each country. The current figures are largely estimates by the Central Intelligence Agency. The previous-year statistics were compiled by the Heritage Foundation. What should you emphasize in the chart and title? What trends do you recognize?

Grammar and Mechanics | *Review 11*

Total Review

The first ten chapters reviewed specific guides from Appendix B, Grammar and Mechanics Guide, beginning on page B-1. The exercises in this and the remaining chapters are total reviews, covering all the grammar and mechanics guides, plus the confusing words and frequently misspelled words. Each of the following sentences has **three** errors in grammar, punctuation, capitalization, usage, or spelling. On a sheet of paper or on your computer, write a correct version. Avoid adding new phrases, starting new sentences, or rewriting in your own words. When you finish, compare your responses with the key in Appendix C.

EXAMPLE: Many jobs in todays digital workplace are never advertised, there part of the hidden job market.

REVISION: Many jobs in **today's** digital workplace are never advertised; **they're** part of the hidden job market.

1. One creditable study revealed that thirty percent of jobs go to companies inside candidates.
2. Networking is said to be the key to finding a job, however, its easier said then done.
3. Some job seekers paid five hundred dollars each to attend twelve sessions that promised expert job-searching advise.
4. To excel at networking an easy to remember e-mail address is a must for a candidate.
5. My friend asked me if I had all ready prepared a thirty second elevator speech?
6. When Rachel and myself were collecting data for the report we realized that twitter and Facebook could be significant.

7. Todays workers must brush up their marketable skills otherwise they may not find another job after being laid off.
8. Being active on LinkedIn and building an impressive internet presence is important, but the looseness of these connections mean you shouldn't expect much from them.
9. Just between you and I, one of the best strategies in networking are distributing business cards with your personal tagline.
10. On February 1st our company President revealed that we would be hiring thirty new employees, which was excellent news for everyone.

Notes

[1] Based on Conference Board of Canada. (2020). *Employability skills*. https://www.conferenceboard.ca/edu/employability-skills.aspx

[2] Guide to Statistics Canada. (2009, July 17). UBC Library. http://toby.library.ubc.ca/webpage/webpage.cfm?id=773

[3] Jackson, H. (2016, May 2). *The long-form census is back, it's online—And this time, it's mandatory. CBC News*. http://www.cbc.ca/news/politics/mandatory-census-mail-out-1.3557511

[4] Statistics Canada. (2009, January 30). *History of the census of Canada*. http://www12.statcan.ca/census-recensement/2006/ref/about-apropos/hist-eng.cfm

[5] Jackson, H. (2016, May 2). *The long-form census is back, it's online—And this time, it's mandatory*. CBC News. http://www.cbc.ca/news/politics/mandatory-census-mail-out-1.3557511

[6] Rayburn, A. (2001). *Naming Canada: Stories about Canadian place names* (Rev. ed.). University of Toronto Press, p. 45.

[7] Heney, V. (2013, March 27). *Windsor's great rebrand. Hey receiver, conversations about communication*. http:// heyreceiver.com/windsors-great-rebrand/

[8] University of Guelph. (2017). *Ask: chat with a librarian*. http://www.lib.uoguelph.ca/ask-us

[9] Giorgetti, D., & Sebastiani, F. (2003, December). Automating survey coding by multiclass text categories. *Journal of the American Society for Information Science and Technology, 54*(14), 1269. http://search.proquest.com

[10] Goldsmith, B. (2002, June). The awesome power of asking the right questions. *OfficeSolutions*, 52; Bracey, G. W. (2001, November). Research-question authority. *Phi Delta Kappan*, p. 191.

[11] Sutherland, T. (2019, February 19). *Exclusive investigation: Kenyan man says he wrote essays for Canadian students*. CityNews. https://toronto.citynews.ca/2019/02/19/cheating-at-u-of-t/

[12] Ibid.

[13] Ibid.

[14] Writing Tutorial Services, Indiana University. (n.d.). *Plagiarism: What it is and how to recognize and avoid it*. http://www.indiana.edu/~wts/pamphlets/plagiarism.shtml. Courtesy of the Trustees of Indiana University.

[15] Bonoguore, T. (2007, March 13). Canadian census sees cities surging. *Globe and Mail*. https://theglobeandmail.com/news /national/canadian-census-sees-cities-surging / article20394056/

[16] Saylor, M. (2012). *The mobile wave: How mobile intelligence will change everything*. Vanguard Press, p. ix.

[17] *Canadian Copyright Act—Overview*. (2009). http://www.media-awareness.ca/english/resources/legislation/canadian_law/federal/copyright_act/cdn_copyright_ov.cfm

[18] Reid, D. (2013, May 15). *Why Hadfield's "Space Oddity" video almost didn't happen*. CTVnews. http://canadaam.ctvnews.ca/why-hadfield-s-space-oddity-video-almost-didn-t-happen-1.1282399

[19] Arafah, B. (2010, May 21). *Huge infographics design resources: Overview, principles, tips and examples*. Onextrapixel.com. http://www.onextrapixel.com/2010/05/21/ huge-infographics-design-resources-overview-principles-tips-and-examples

[20] Statistics Canada. (2017). *Infographics*. http://www.statcan.gc.ca/pub/11-627-m/index-eng.htm

[21] Ibid.

[22] Visually, Inc. (2012). *Infographics software*. http://visual.ly/learn/infographics-software

[23] Statistics Canada. (2019). *Statistics Canada*. https://www.statcan.gc.ca/eng/start

[24] Statistics Canada. (2019). *Infographics*. https://www150.statcan.gc.ca/n1/pub/11-627-m/index-eng.htm

[25] Statistics Canada. (2008, November 16). *Retail and wholesale*. http://cansim2.statcan.gc.ca/cgi-win/cnsmcgi.pgm?Lang=E&SP_Action=Result&SP_ID=60002&SP_TYP=1&SP_Sort=1&SP_Portal=2

[26] Statistics Canada. (2009, March 12). *Privacy notice*. http://www.statcan.gc.ca/reference/privacy-privee-eng.htm

[27] Custom Papers. (n.d.). *Reasons students hate writing essays or term papers*. http://custompapers.com/essay-not. Courtesy of CustomPapers.com.

[28] Reena, J. (2006, October 16). Enough with the shoot-'em-ups. *BusinessWeek*, p. 92.

[29] Based on Ledbetter, C. (2015, September 9). *The 10 foods college students order the most*. Huffington Post. http://www.huffingtonpost.com/entry/foods-college-students-order-the-most_us_55f0443be4b093be51bce93

CHAPTER 12

Informal Business Reports

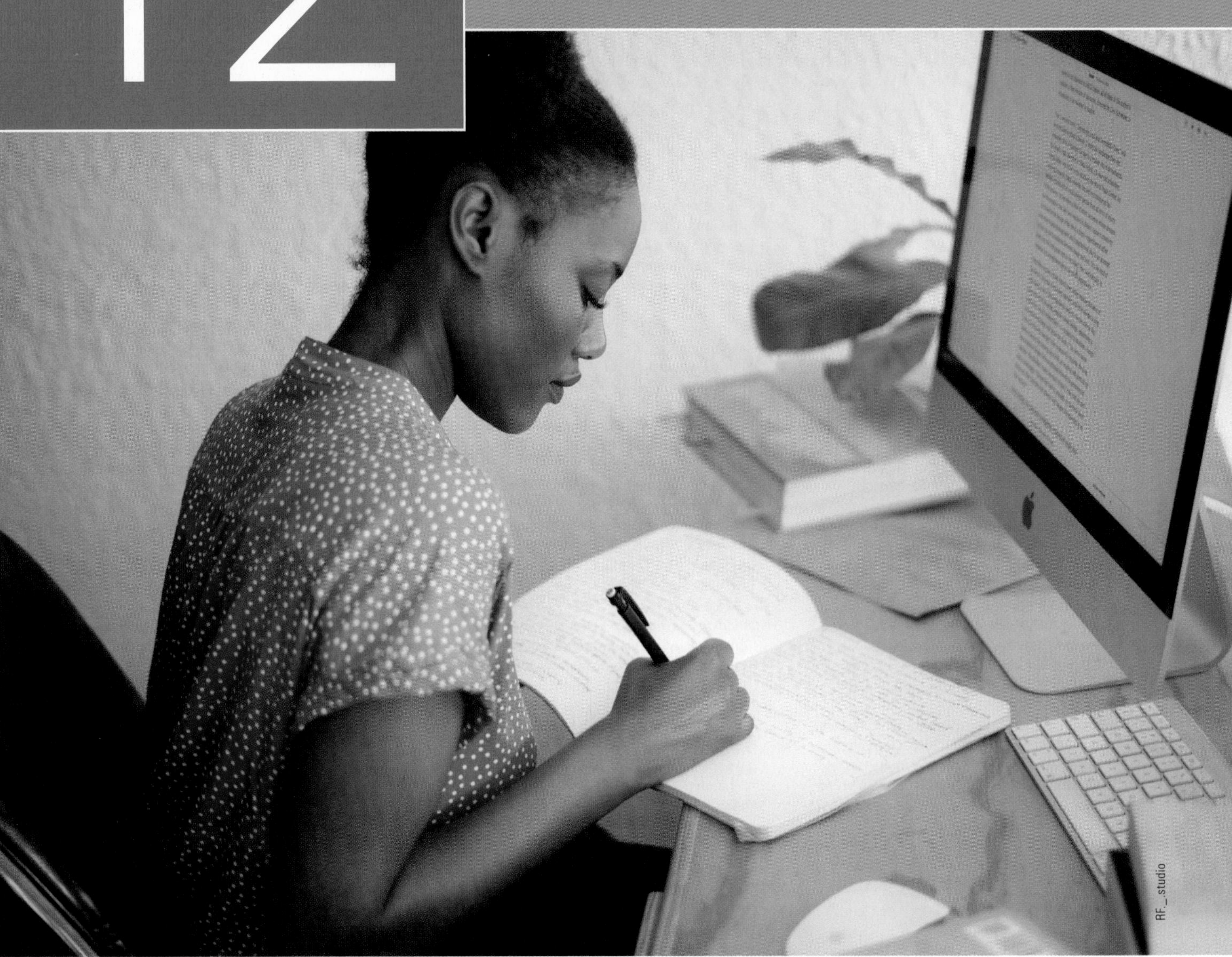
RF._.studio

LEARNING OBJECTIVES

After studying this chapter, you should be able to

1 Analyze, sort, and interpret statistical data and other information.

2 Draw meaningful conclusions and make practical report recommendations.

3 Organize report data logically and provide reader cues to aid comprehension.

4 Write short informational reports that describe routine tasks.

5 Prepare short analytical reports that solve business problems.

SPOTLIGHT ON COMMUNICATION: PART 1

Immersive Tech—Inspiring Teamwork

Courtesy of Fantasy 360 Technologies Inc. dba Immersive Tech

For everyone from small business owners to Fortune 500 companies, Immersive Tech designs custom escape rooms to meet every need. An *escape room* is "a game in which a group of people are locked in a room and have to escape by solving puzzles and using the clues provided."[1]

In 2014 cofounders Adrian Duke and Jeff Jang found that local Vancouver escape rooms were lacking in quality. They believe that "engaging and immersive experiences require an intense attention to detail and understanding of game design methodologies and believable theming."[2] With teamwork skills being more important than ever in the workplace, innovative team building training is also in demand:[3]

> Companies globally engage in team building regularly—scavenger hunts, go-kart racing and axe throwing are just a few of the many options available. Escape rooms in particular are fast becoming popular for small, medium and large corporations across the board. They offer an appealing package of teamwork, fun and small investment in terms of time that other activities don't necessarily offer.[4]

Because the global pandemic has more people working from home, Immersive Tech also offers innovative online options that use existing platforms to create puzzles for teams to complete together. Even when teams are virtual, teamwork can be honed and celebrated. Immersive Tech recommends that employers "find ways for [employees] to recognize that their accomplishment was done together and allow for ways for them to visually recognize that teamwork."[5]

Immersive Tech and its team also care about community. Duke, who was born in Meadow Lake, Saskatchewan, often returns home to offer mentorship to Indigenous youth. He also sits on the board of directors at Native Education College.[6] Jang, born and raised in Vancouver, volunteers his time to nonprofit organizations across the Lower Mainland.[7]

CRITICAL THINKING

- What type of information should Immersive Tech gather to help decide which companies may be interested in its escape rooms?
- If you were writing a report to your employer to request an escape room as part of your upcoming work conference, would you prepare an information or analytical report? Explain why. (Visit immersivetech.co and explore the website for more details.)

Analyzing Data

LEARNING OBJECTIVE 1

Analyze, sort, and interpret statistical data and other information.

Much of the information that allows decision makers to run their organizations comes to them in the form of reports. To respond to changing economic times, businesses need information to stay abreast of what is happening inside and outside their firms. This chapter focuses on interpreting and organizing data, drawing conclusions, providing reader cues, and writing informal business reports. You will also develop the Conference Board of Canada's Employability Skills 2000+ fundamental skill of using numbers to "observe and record data using appropriate methods, tools, and technology."[8]

Given the easy access to research databases, the Internet, and other sources of digitized information, collecting information is nearly effortless today. However, making sense of the massive amounts of data you may collect is much harder. You may feel overwhelmed as you look at a jumble of digital files, printouts, note cards, articles, interview notes, questionnaire results, and statistics. Unprocessed data become meaningful information through skillful and accurate sorting, analysis, combination, and recombination. You will be examining each item to see what it means by itself and what it means when connected with other data. You are looking for meanings, relationships, and answers to the research questions posed in your work plan.

Tabulating and Analyzing Data

After collecting numerical data and other information, you must tabulate and analyze them. Fortunately, several techniques can help you simplify, summarize, and classify large amounts

ETHICS CHECK

Good Corporate Citizens

According to Imagine Canada's survey of Canadian businesses, organizations donate to charities or accommodate employee volunteerism for four main reasons: (1) to build their company's brand or reputation, (2) to build strong communities that will support their business interests, (3) to build social capital and support among citizens and governments, and (4) to recruit and retain employees.[9] How do ethical considerations affect your opinions of companies or sway your buying decisions?

of data. The most helpful summarizing techniques are tables, statistical concepts (mean, median, and mode), correlations, grids, and decision matrices.

Tables. Tables usually help researchers summarize and simplify data. Using columns and rows, tables make quantitative information easier to comprehend. After assembling your data, you will want to prepare preliminary tables to enable you to see what the information means. Here is a table summarizing the response to one question from a campus survey about student parking:

Question: Should student fees be increased to build parking lots?

	Number	Percentage	
Strongly agree	76	11.5	**To simplify the table, combine these items: 50 percent support the proposal**
Agree	255	38.5	
No opinion	22	3.3	
Disagree	107	16.1	**To simplify the table, combine these items: 46.7 (nearly 47) percent oppose the proposal**
Strongly disagree	203	30.6	
Total	**663**	**100.0**	

Notice that this preliminary table includes a total number of responses and a percentage for each response. (To calculate a percentage, divide the figure for each response by the total number of responses and multiply by 100.)

Sometimes data become more meaningful when cross-tabulated. This process allows analysis of two or more variables together. By breaking down our student survey data into male and female responses, shown in the following table, we make an interesting discovery.

Question: Should student fees be increased to build parking lots?

	Total		Male			Female		
	Number	Percentage	Number	Percentage		Number	Percentage	
Strongly agree	76	11.5	8	2.2	**= 17.5 percent**	68	22.0	**= 87 percent support**
Agree	255	38.5	54	15.3		201	65.0	
No opinion	22	3.3	12	3.4		10	3.2	
Disagree	107	16.1	89	25.1	**= 79.1 percent**	18	5.8	**= 9.8 percent oppose**
Strongly disagree	203	30.6	191	54.0		12	4.0	
Total	**663**	**100.0**	**354**	**100.0**		**309**	**100.0**	

Although 50 percent of all student respondents supported the proposal, among females the approval rating was much stronger. You naturally wonder why such a disparity exists. Are female students unhappier than male students with the current parking situation? If so, why? Is safety a reason? Are male students more concerned with increased fees than female students are?

By cross-tabulating the findings, you sometimes uncover data that may help answer your problem question or that may prompt you to explore other possibilities. Do not, however, undertake cross-tabulation unless it serves more than merely satisfying your curiosity. Tables also help you compare multiple data collected from questionnaires and surveys. Figure 12.1 shows, in raw form, responses to several survey items. To convert these data into a more usable form, you need to calculate percentages for each item. Then you can arrange the responses in some rational sequence, such as largest percentage to smallest.

When the data are displayed in a table, you can more easily draw conclusions. As Figure 12.1 shows, North Shore College students apparently are not interested in public transportation or shuttle buses from satellite lots. They want to park on campus and restrict visitor parking, and only half are willing to pay for new parking lots.

FIGURE 12.1 Converting Survey Data Into Finished Tables

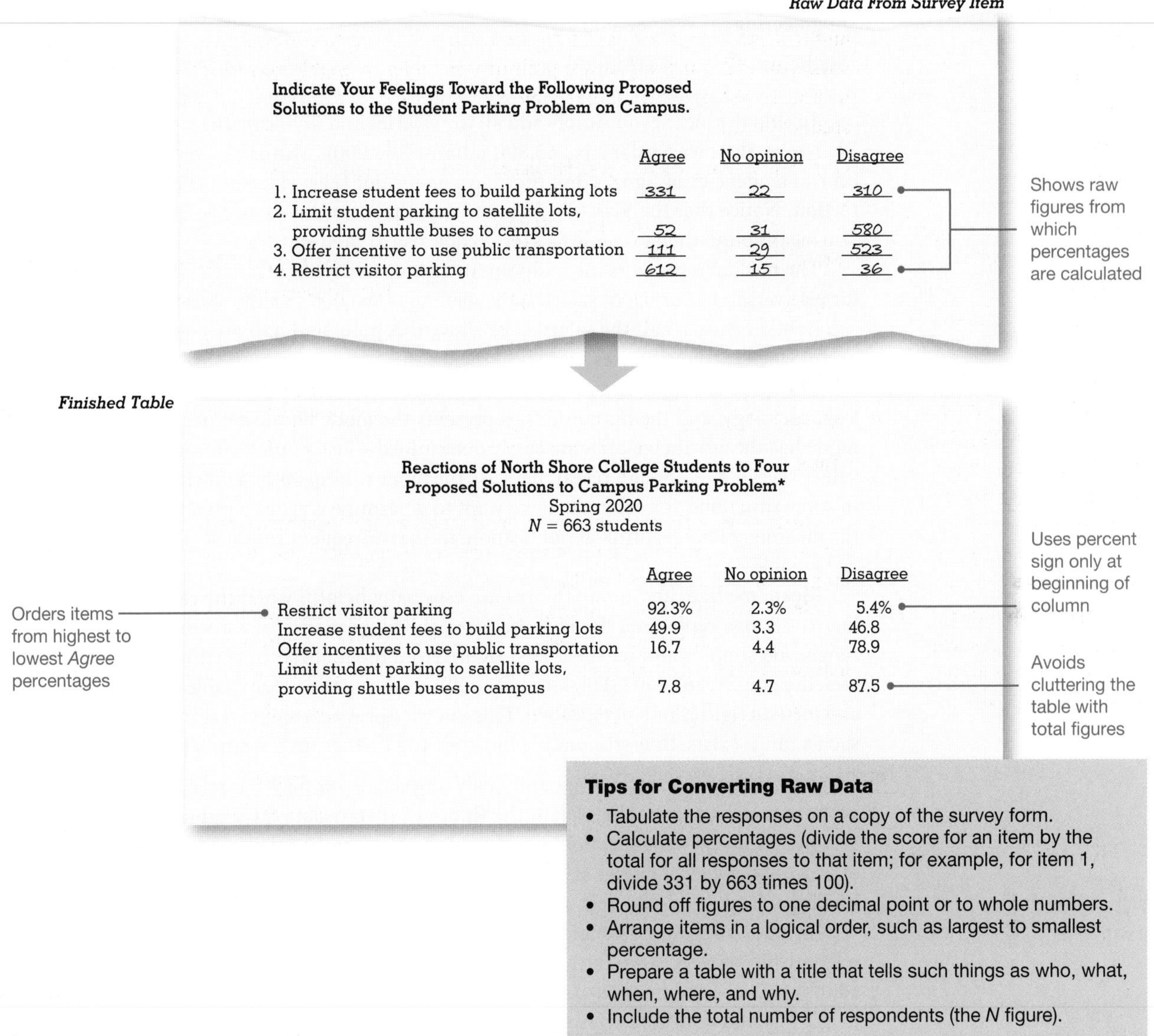
Raw Data From Survey Item

Indicate Your Feelings Toward the Following Proposed Solutions to the Student Parking Problem on Campus.

	Agree	No opinion	Disagree
1. Increase student fees to build parking lots	331	22	310
2. Limit student parking to satellite lots, providing shuttle buses to campus	52	31	580
3. Offer incentive to use public transportation	111	29	523
4. Restrict visitor parking	612	15	36

Shows raw figures from which percentages are calculated

Finished Table

Reactions of North Shore College Students to Four Proposed Solutions to Campus Parking Problem*
Spring 2020
N = 663 students

	Agree	No opinion	Disagree
Restrict visitor parking	92.3%	2.3%	5.4%
Increase student fees to build parking lots	49.9	3.3	46.8
Offer incentives to use public transportation	16.7	4.4	78.9
Limit student parking to satellite lots, providing shuttle buses to campus	7.8	4.7	87.5

Orders items from highest to lowest *Agree* percentages
Uses percent sign only at beginning of column
Avoids cluttering the table with total figures

Tips for Converting Raw Data

- Tabulate the responses on a copy of the survey form.
- Calculate percentages (divide the score for an item by the total for all responses to that item; for example, for item 1, divide 331 by 663 times 100).
- Round off figures to one decimal point or to whole numbers.
- Arrange items in a logical order, such as largest to smallest percentage.
- Prepare a table with a title that tells such things as who, what, when, where, and why.
- Include the total number of respondents (the *N* figure).

Measures of Central Tendency. Tables help you organize data, and the three M's—mean, median, and mode—help you describe data. These statistical terms are all occasionally used loosely to mean "average." To be safe, though, you should learn to apply these statistical terms precisely.

When people say *average*, they usually intend to indicate the *mean*, or arithmetic average. Let's say that you are studying the estimated starting salaries of graduates from various disciplines, ranging from education to medicine:

Education	$ 47,000	*Mode (figure occurring most frequently)*
Sociology	47,000	
Humanities	47,000	
Biology	53,000	
Health sciences	63,000	*Median (middle point in continuum)*

Business	66,000	*Mean (arithmetic average)*
Law	74,000	
Engineering	82,000	
Medicine	114,000	

To find the mean, you simply add all the salaries and divide by the total number of items. Therefore, the mean salary is $65,800 (almost $66,000). Means are very useful to indicate central tendencies of figures, but they have one major flaw: extremes at either end cause distortion. Notice that the $114,000 figure makes the mean salary of $66,000 deceptively high. Use means only when extreme figures do not distort the result.

The median represents the midpoint in a group of figures arranged from lowest to highest (or vice versa). In our list of salaries, the median is $63,000 (health sciences).

In other words, half the salaries are above this point and half are below it. The median is useful when extreme figures may warp the mean.

The *mode* is simply the value that occurs most frequently. In our list $47,000 (for education, sociology, and the humanities) represents the mode because it occurs three times. The mode has the advantage of being easily determined—just a quick glance at a list of arranged values reveals it. Although researchers use the mode infrequently, knowing the mode is useful in some situations; for example, if we want to determine a group's preferences. To remember the meaning of *mode*, think about fashion: the most frequent response, the mode, is the most fashionable.

Mean, median, and mode figures are especially helpful when the range of values is also known. Range represents the span between the highest and lowest values. To calculate the range, you simply subtract the lowest figure from the highest. In starting salaries for graduates, the range is $67,000 ($114,000 – $47,000). Knowing the range enables readers to put mean and median figures into perspective. This knowledge also prompts researchers to wonder why such a range exists, thus stimulating hunches and further investigation to solve problems.

Correlations. In tabulating and analyzing data, you may see relationships among two or more variables that help explain the findings. If your data for graduates' starting salaries also included years of education, you would doubtless notice that graduates with more years of education received higher salaries. A correlation may exist between years of education and starting salary.

Intuition suggests correlations that may or may not prove to be accurate. Is there a causal relationship between studying and good grades? Between electronic gadget use by supervising adults and increased injuries of children? The business researcher who sees a correlation needs to ask why and how the two variables are related. In this way apparent correlations stimulate investigation and present possible solutions to be explored.

In reporting correlations, you should avoid suggesting that a cause-and-effect relationship exists when none can be proved. Only sophisticated research methods can statistically prove correlations. Instead, present a correlation as a possible relationship (*The data suggest that beginning salaries are related to years of education*). Cautious statements followed by explanations gain you credibility and allow readers to make their own decisions.

Grids. Another technique for analyzing raw data—especially verbal data—is the grid. Let's say you have been asked by the CEO to collect opinions from all vice presidents about the CEO's four-point plan to build cash reserves. The grid shown in Figure 12.2 enables you to summarize the vice presidents' reactions to each point. Notice how this complex verbal information is transformed into concise, manageable data; readers can see immediately which points are supported and which are opposed. Imagine how long you could have struggled to comprehend the meaning of this verbal information without a grid.

Arranging data in a grid also works for projects, such as feasibility studies and yardstick reports, that compare many variables. *Consumer Reports* often uses grids to show information.

FIGURE 12.2 Grid to Analyze Complex Verbal Data About Building Cash Reserves

	Point 1	Point 2	Point 3	Point 4	Overall Reaction
VICE PRESIDENT 1	Disapproves. "Too little, too late."	Strong support. "Best of all points."	Mixed opinion. "Must wait and see market."	Indifferent.	Optimistic, but "hates to delay expansion for six months."
VICE PRESIDENT 2	Disapproves. "Creates credit trap."	Approves.	Strong disapproval.	Approves. "Must improve receivable collections."	Mixed support. "Good self-defence plan."
VICE PRESIDENT 3	Strong disapproval.	Approves. "Key to entire plan."	Indifferent.	Approves, but with "caveats."	"Will work only with sale of unproductive fixed assets."
VICE PRESIDENT 4	Disapproves. "Too risky now."	Strong support. "Start immediately."	Approves, "but may damage image."	Approves. "Benefits far outweigh costs."	Supports plan. Suggests focus on Pacific Rim markets.

Decision Matrices. A decision matrix is a special grid that helps managers make the best choice among complex options. Designed to eliminate bias and poor judgment, decision matrices are helpful in many fields. Assume you need to choose the most appropriate laptop for your sales representatives. You are most interested in weight, battery life, price, and hard drive size. You want to compare these features in four highly rated business laptop models. Figure 12.3 shows a simple decision matrix to help you make the choice. In Table 1, you evaluate each of the desired features on a scale of 1 to 5. Because the Apple MacBook Air weighs in at a very light 1.2 kilograms, you give it a score of 5 for weight. However, its hard drive capacity is much less desirable, and you give it a score of 1 for hard drive.

After you have evaluated all of the laptop models in Table 1, you assign relative weights to each feature. You decide to assign a factor of 5 to weight and to unit price because these two aspects are of average importance. However, your field sales reps want laptops with batteries that last. Therefore, battery life is twice as important; you assign it a factor of 10. You assign a factor of 7 to the size of the hard drive because this option is slightly more important than price, but somewhat less important than battery life. Then you multiply the scores in Table 1 with the weights and total them, as shown in Table 2. According to the weighted matrix and the rating system used, the Apple MacBook Air should be purchased for the sales reps because it received the highest score of 97 points, closely followed by the Lenovo ThinkPad and Acer TravelMate with 91 points.

Check out section 12-1a in MindTap, where you can watch a video featuring Jason Allen John, a mortgage agent, discuss how to use graphics in a report.

Concept Check

1. Nine homes recently sold in your community in the following order and for these amounts: \$260,000; \$360,000; \$260,000; \$280,000; \$260,000; \$320,000; \$280,000; \$420,000; and \$260,000. Your boss, Tom DiFranco, a realtor with Sanford & Associates, wants you to compute the mean, median, and mode for this real estate market. Compute the mean, median, and mode for the recently sold homes. Explain your analysis and the characteristics of each type of "average."
2. List six steps for creating a decision matrix. Provide an example of how a decision matrix could help you solve a problem.

FIGURE 12.3 Decision Matrix Used to Choose a Business Laptop for Sales Reps

Unweighted Decision Matrix—Table 1					
Features:	Weight	Battery Life	Price	Hard Drive	Total
Laptop Options					
Dell Precision: 2.8 GHz, 2.25 kg, 5 hrs, $1,500, 1.5 TB	1	2	2	5	
Lenovo ThinkPad: 2.3 GHz, 1.6 kg, 9:10 hrs, $1,300, 256 GB	2	4	4	3	
Apple MacBook Air: 1.6 GHz, 1.2 kg, 17:36 hrs, $1,400, 128 GB	5	5	3	1	
Acer TravelMate: 2.6 GHz, 1.5 kg, 7:30 hrs, $1,200, 265 GB	3	3	5	3	

Weighted Decision Matrix—Table 2					
Features:	Weight	Battery Life	Price	Hard Drive	Total
Laptop Options **Weights:**	**5**	**10**	**5**	**7**	
Dell Precision: 2.8 GHz, 2.25 kg, 5 hrs, $1,500, 1.5 TB	5	20	10	35	70
Lenovo ThinkPad: 2.3 GHz, 1.6 kg, 9:10 hrs, $1,300, 256 GB	10	40	20	21	91
Apple MacBook Air: 1.6 GHz, 1.2 kg, 17:36 hrs, $1,400, 128 GB	25	50	15	7	97
Acer TravelMate: 2.6 GHz, 1.5 kg, 7:30 hrs, $1,200, 265 GB	15	30	25	21	91

Tips for Creating a Decision Matrix

- **Select the most important criteria.** For a laptop computer, the criteria were weight, battery life, price, and hard drive size.
- **Create a matrix.** List each laptop model (Apple, Dell, and others) down the left side. Place the features across the top of the columns.
- **Evaluate the criteria.** Use a scale of 1 (lowest) to 5 (highest). Rate each feature for each option, as shown in Table 1.
- **Assign relative weights.** Decide how important each feature is, and give it a weight.
- **Multiply the scores.** For each feature in Table 1, multiply by the weights in Table 2 and write the score in the box.
- **Total the scores.** The total reveals the best choice.

LEARNING OBJECTIVE 2

Draw meaningful conclusions and make practical report recommendations.

Drawing Conclusions and Making Recommendations

The sections devoted to conclusions and recommendations are the most widely read portions of a report. Knowledgeable readers go straight to the conclusions to see what the report writer thinks the data mean. Because conclusions summarize and explain the findings, they represent the heart of a report.

Your value in an organization rises considerably if you can draw conclusions that analyze information logically and show how the data answer questions and solve problems. Solving problems requires research. Drawing logical conclusions from data is crucial to business success.

Analyzing Data to Arrive at Conclusions

Any set of data can produce a variety of meaningful conclusions. Always bear in mind, though, that the audience for a report wants to know how these data relate to the problem being studied. What do the findings mean in terms of solving the original report problem?

For example, the Marriott Corporation recognized a serious problem among its employees. Conflicting home and work requirements seemed to be causing excessive employee turnover and decreasing productivity. To learn the extent of the problem and to consider solutions, Marriott hired Hospitality Consultants to survey its staff. The hotel chain learned the following:

- Nearly 35 percent of its employees had children under age twelve, and 15 percent had children under age five.
- One third of its staff with young children took time off because of child-care difficulties, as shown in Figure 12.4.
- Many current employees left previous jobs because of work and family conflicts.
- Managers did not consider child-care or family problems to be appropriate topics for discussion at work.

FIGURE 12.4 Report Conclusions and Recommendations in Intranet Screen View

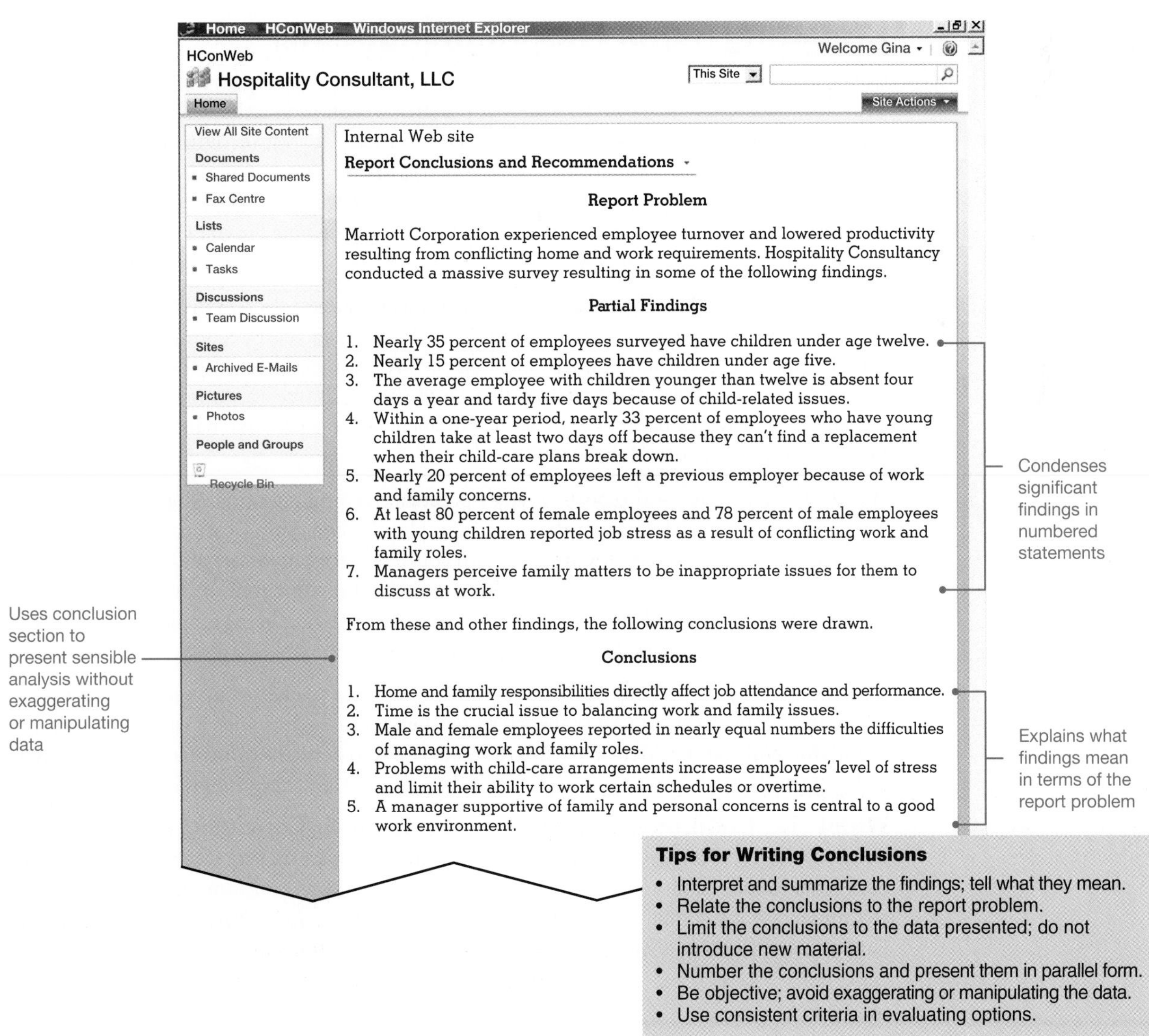

A sample of possible conclusions that a writer might draw from these findings is shown in Figure 12.4. Notice that each conclusion relates to the initial report problem. Although only a few possible findings and conclusions are shown here, you can see that the conclusions try to explain the causes for the home/work conflict among employees. Many report writers would expand the conclusion section by explaining each item and citing supporting evidence. Even for simplified conclusions, such as those shown in Figure 12.4, you will want to list each item separately and use parallel construction (balanced sentence structure).

Although your goal is to remain objective, drawing conclusions naturally involves a degree of subjectivity. Your goals, background, and frame of reference all colour the inferences you make. All writers interpret findings from their own perspectives, but they should not manipulate them to achieve a preconceived purpose. You can make your report conclusions more objective by using consistent evaluation criteria. Let's say you are comparing computers for an office equipment purchase. If you evaluate each by the same criteria (such as price, specifications, service, and warranty), your conclusions are more likely to be bias free.

You also need to avoid the temptation to sensationalize or exaggerate your findings or conclusions. Be careful of words such as *many*, *most*, and *all*. Instead of *many of the respondents felt*..., you might more accurately write *some of the respondents felt*.... Examine your motives before drawing conclusions. Do not let preconceptions or wishful thinking affect your reasoning.

Preparing Report Recommendations

Conclusions explain what the problem is whereas recommendations tell how to solve it. Typically, business readers prefer specific, practical recommendations. They want to know exactly how to implement the suggestions. The specificity of your recommendations depends on your authorization. What are you commissioned to do, and what does the reader expect? In the planning stages of your report project, you anticipate what the reader wants in the report. Your intuition and your knowledge of the audience indicate how far you should develop your recommendations.

Ideas for Implementation. In the recommendations section of the Marriott employee survey, shown in Figure 12.4, the consultants summarized their recommendations. In the actual report, the consultants would back up each recommendation with specifics and ideas for implementing them. For example, the child-care resource recommendation would be explained: it provides parents with names of agencies and professionals who specialize in locating child care across the country.

Agreeability. A good report provides practical recommendations that are agreeable to the audience. In the Marriott survey, for example, the consulting company knew that the Marriott wanted to help employees cope with conflicts between family and work obligations. As a result, the report's conclusions and recommendations focused on ways to resolve the conflict. If Marriott's goal had been merely to save money by reducing employee absenteeism, the recommendations would have been quite different.

Commands for Comprehension. If possible, make each recommendation a command. Note in Figure 12.4 that each recommendation begins with a verb. This structure sounds forceful and confident and helps the reader comprehend the information quickly. Avoid hedging words, such as *maybe* and *perhaps*; they reduce the strength of recommendations.

When to Combine Recommendations and Conclusions. Experienced writers may combine recommendations and conclusions. In short reports writers may omit conclusions and move straight to recommendations. An important point about recommendations is that they include practical suggestions for solving the report problem. Furthermore, they are always the result of prior logical analysis.

FIGURE 12.5 Understanding Findings, Conclusions, and Recommendations

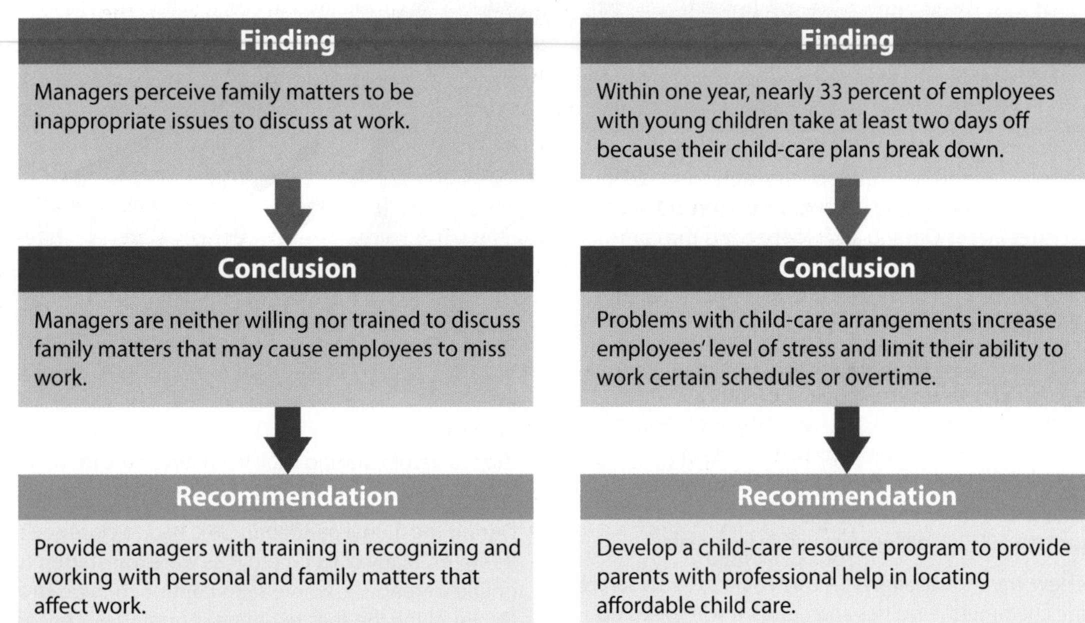

Moving From Findings to Recommendations

Recommendations evolve from the interpretation of the findings and conclusions. Consider the examples from the Marriott survey summarized in Figure 12.5.

Concept Check

1. What section is considered the heart of the report and why?
2. When does it make sense to combine conclusions and recommendations in a report?

Organizing Data

LEARNING OBJECTIVE 3

Organize report data logically and provide reader cues to aid comprehension.

After collecting sets of data, interpreting them, drawing conclusions, and thinking about the recommendations, you are ready to organize the parts of the report into a logical framework. Poorly organized reports lead to frustration. Readers will not understand, remember, or be persuaded. Wise writers know that reports rarely "just organize themselves." Instead, organization must be imposed on the data, and cues must be provided so the reader can follow the logic of the writer.

Informational reports, as you learned in Chapter 11, generally present data without interpretation. Informational reports typically consist of three parts. Analytical reports, which generally analyze data and draw conclusions, typically contain four parts. However, the parts in analytical reports do not always follow this sequence. For readers who know about the project, are supportive, or are eager to learn the results quickly, the direct strategy is appropriate. Conclusions and recommendations, if requested, appear up front. For readers who must be educated or persuaded, the indirect strategy works better. Conclusions and recommendations appear last, after the findings have been presented and analyzed.

Although every report is unique, the overall organizational strategies described here generally hold true. The real challenge, though, lies in (a) organizing the facts/findings and discussion/analysis sections and (b) providing reader cues.

CASE CONNECTIONS

SAIL Outdoors—Meeting Customer Demand

JHVEPhoto/Shutterstock

SAIL Outdoors, a sport and outdoor company founded in Québec, has been operating in Canada for 40 years. Even with branches across Ontario and Québec, it is the company's online market that has seen the most growth. To respond to online customer demand, SAIL opened their first online distribution warehouse:[10]

> This immense state-of-the-art warehouse is equipped with an ultra-modern inventory tracking system and . . . 700 feet of conveyor belt. This will enable the company to optimize the processing time for orders, to increase substantially the number of products in stock and . . . to process 500,000 online sales within four years.[11]

This new warehouse allows SAIL advisors to focus solely on online customers' inquiries and needs. It will speed up delivery and return processes, providing a seamless and pleasant shopping experience for its online customers.[12]

- SAIL's new venture focused on one type of customer: online shoppers. Consider the extent of research it conducted before making such a bold business move. What type of data do you think the company had to analyze?
- During the global pandemic, SAIL had to close several of its stores. Many of its employees were transferred to their online warehouse, where sales continued to be strong.[13] Do you think the shift to online shopping will become the norm? How will businesses need to adapt?

Ordering Information Logically

Whether you are writing informational or analytical reports, you must structure the data you have collected. Five common organizational methods are by time, component, importance, criteria, and convention. Regardless of the method you choose, be sure that it helps the reader understand the data. Reader comprehension should govern organization. For additional examples of organizational principles, please go to the section titled Knowing Your Audience, in Chapter 14.

Time. Ordering data by time means establishing a chronology of events. Agendas, minutes of meetings, progress reports, and procedures are usually organized by time. For example, a report describing an eight-week training program would most likely be organized by weeks. A plan for the step-by-step improvement of customer service would be organized by steps. A monthly trip report submitted by a sales rep might describe customers visited during Week 1, Week 2, and so on.

Beware of overusing chronologies (time) as an organizing method for reports, however. Although this method is easy and often mirrors the way data are collected, chronologies—like the sales rep's trip report—tend to be boring, repetitious, and lacking in emphasis. Readers cannot always pick out what is important.

Component. Especially for informational reports, data may be organized by components such as location, geography, division, product, or part. For instance, a report detailing company expansion might divide the plan into West Coast, East Coast, and Central expansion. The report could also be organized by divisions: personal products, consumer electronics, and household goods.

Importance. Organization by importance involves beginning with the most important item and proceeding to the least important—or vice versa. For example, the Marriott

FIGURE 12.6 Ordering Information Logically by Using Criteria

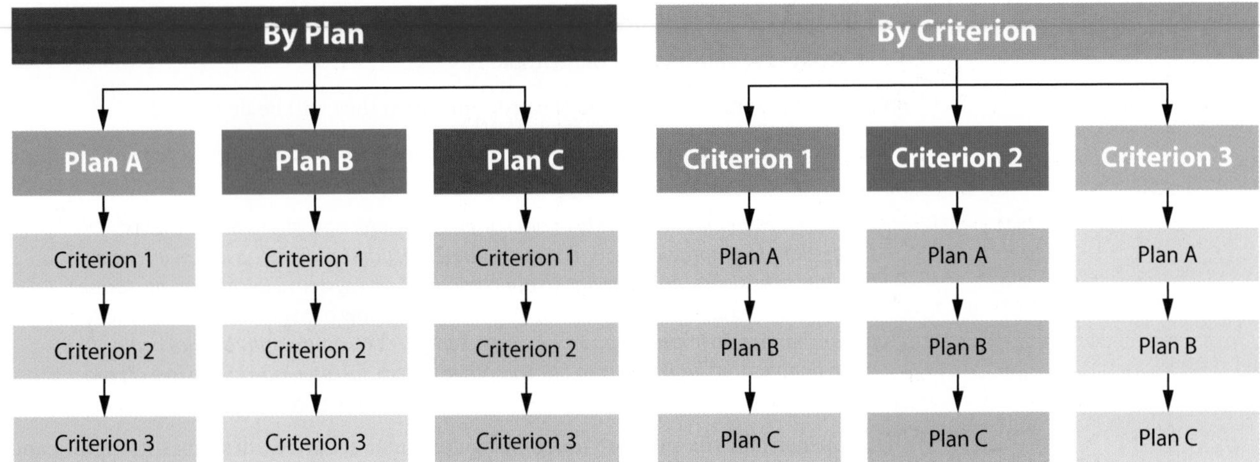

consultants' report describing work/family conflicts might begin by discussing child care, if the writer considered it the most important issue. Using importance to structure findings involves a value judgment. The writer must decide what is most important, always keeping in mind the readers' priorities and expectations. Busy readers appreciate seeing important points first; they may skim or skip other points.

On the other hand, building to a climax by moving from least important to most important enables the writer to focus attention at the end. Thus, the reader is more likely to remember the most important item. Of course, the writer also risks losing the reader's attention along the way.

Criteria. Establishing criteria by which to judge helps writers treat topics consistently. Let's say your report compares extended health plans A, B, and C. For each plan you examine the same standards: cost per employee, amount of deductible, and patient benefits. The resulting data could then be organized either by plans or by criteria, as Figure 12.6 illustrates.

Although you might favour organizing the data by plans (because that is the way you collected the data), the better way is by criteria. When you discuss patient benefits, for example, you would examine all three plans' benefits together. Organizing a report around criteria helps readers make comparisons, instead of forcing them to search through the report for similar data.

Convention. Many operational and recurring reports are structured according to convention. That is, they follow a prescribed plan that everyone understands. For example, an automotive parts manufacturer might ask all sales reps to prepare a weekly report with these headings: *Competitive observations* (competitors' price changes, discounts, new products, product problems, distributor changes, and product promotions), *Product problems* (quality, performance, and needs), and *Customer-service problems* (delivery, mailings, correspondence, social media, and Internet traffic). Management gets exactly the information it needs in an easy-to-read form.

Providing Reader Cues

When you finish organizing a report, you probably see a neat outline in your mind: major points, supported by subpoints and details. Readers, however, do not know the material as well as you do; they cannot see your outline. To guide them through the data, you need to provide the equivalent of a map and road signs. For both formal and informal reports, devices such as introductions, transitions, and headings prevent readers from getting lost.

Introduction. One of the best ways to point a reader in the right direction is to provide a report introduction that does three things:

- Tells the purpose of the report
- Describes the significance of the topic
- Previews the main points and the order in which they will be developed

The following paragraph includes all three elements in introducing a report on computer security:

> *This report examines the security of our current computer operations and presents suggestions for improving security. Lax computer security could mean loss of information, loss of business, and damage to our equipment and systems. Because many former employees released during recent downsizing efforts know our systems, we must make major changes. To improve security, I will present three recommendations: (a) begin using dongles that limit access to our computer system, (b) alter log-on and log-off procedures, and (c) move central computer operations to a more secure area.*

This opener tells the purpose (examining computer security), describes its significance (loss of information and business, damage to equipment and systems), and outlines how the report is organized (three recommendations). Good openers in effect set up a contract with the reader. The writer promises to cover certain topics in a specified order. Readers expect the writer to fulfill the contract. They want the topics to be developed as promised—using the same wording and presented in the order mentioned. For example, if in your introduction you state that you will discuss the use of *dongles* (a small plug-in security device), do not change the heading for that section to *security tokens.* Remember that the introduction provides a map to a report; switching the names on the map will ensure that readers get lost. To maintain consistency, delay writing the introduction until after you have completed the report. Long, complex reports may require introductions, brief internal summaries, and previews for each section.

Transitions. Expressions such as *on the contrary, at the same time*, and *however* show relationships and help reveal the logical flow of ideas in a report. These transitional expressions enable writers to tell readers where ideas are headed and how they relate. Notice how abrupt the following three sentences sound without any transition: *The iPad was the first mainstream tablet. [In fact] Reviewers say the iPad with Retina Display is still the best. [However] The display of the Google Nexus tablet trumps even the iPad's stunning screen.*

The following transitional expressions (see Figure 5.6 in Chapter 5 for a complete list) enable you to show readers how you are developing your ideas:

To present additional thoughts: *additionally, again, also, moreover, furthermore*

To suggest cause and effect: *accordingly, as a result, consequently, therefore*

To contrast ideas: *at the same time, but, however, on the contrary, though, yet*

To show time and order: *after, before, first, finally, now, previously, then, to conclude*

To clarify points: *for example, for instance, in other words, that is, thus*

In using these expressions, recognize that they do not always have to sit at the head of a sentence. Listen to the rhythm of the sentence, and place the expression where a natural pause occurs. Used appropriately, transitional expressions serve readers as guides; misused or overused, they can be as distracting and frustrating as too many road signs on a highway.

Headings. Good headings are another structural cue that assists readers in comprehending the organization of a report. They highlight major ideas, allowing busy readers to see the big picture at a glance. Moreover, headings provide resting points for the mind and for the eye, breaking up large chunks of text into manageable and inviting segments.

Report writers may use functional or talking headings, examples of which are summarized in Figure 12.7. Functional headings show the outline of a report but provide little insight for readers. Functional headings are useful for routine reports. They are also appropriate for

FIGURE 12.7 Distinguishing Among Functional, Talking, and Combination Headings

Functional Headings	Talking Headings	Combination Headings
• Background • Findings • Personnel • Production Costs	• Lack of Space and Cost Compound Parking Program • Survey Shows Support for Parking Fees	• Introduction: Lack of Parking Reaches Crisis Proportions • Parking Recommendations: Shuttle and New Structures

sensitive topics that might provoke emotional reactions. By keeping the headings general, experienced writers hope to minimize reader opposition or response to controversial subjects.

Talking headings provide more information and spark interest. Unless carefully written, however, talking headings can fail to reveal the organization of a report. With some planning, though, headings can combine the best attributes of both functional and talking, as Figure 12.7 shows.

The best strategy for creating helpful talking headings is to write a few paragraphs first and then generate a talking heading that covers both paragraphs. To create the most effective headings, follow a few basic guidelines:

- **Use appropriate heading levels.** The position and format of a heading indicate its level of importance and relationship to other points. Figure 12.8 illustrates and discusses a commonly used heading format for business reports. For an overview of an alphanumeric outline, please see Figure 5.3 in Chapter 5.
- **Capitalize and emphasize carefully.** Most writers use all capital letters (without underlines) for main titles, such as the report, chapter, and unit titles. For first- and second-level headings, they capitalize only the first letter of main words such as nouns, verbs, adjectives, adverbs, names, and so on. Articles (*a*, *an*, *the*), conjunctions (*and*, *but*, *or*, *nor*), and prepositions with three or fewer letters (*in*, *to*, *by*, *for*) are not capitalized unless they appear at the beginning or end of the heading. For additional emphasis, most writers use a bold font, as shown in Figure 12.8.
- **Try to balance headings within levels.** Although it may not always be possible, attempt to create headings that are grammatically parallel at a given level. For example, *Developing Product Teams* and *Presenting Plan to Management* are balanced, but *Development of Product Teams* and *Presenting Plan to Management* are not.
- **For short reports use first-level or first- and second-level headings.** Many business reports contain only one or two levels of headings. For such reports use first-level headings (centred, bolded) and, if needed, second-level headings (flush left, bolded). See Figure 12.8.
- **Include at least one heading per report page, but don't end the page with a heading.** Headings increase the readability and attractiveness of report pages. Use at least one per page to break up blocks of text. Move a heading that is separated from the text that follows from the bottom of the page to the top of the following page.
- **Apply punctuation correctly.** Omit end punctuation in first- and second-level headings. End punctuation is required in third-level headings because they are capitalized and punctuated like sentences. Proper nouns (names) are capitalized in third-level headings as they would be in a sentence.
- **Keep headings short but clear.** One-word headings are emphatic but not always clear. For example, the heading *Budget* does not adequately describe figures for a summer

FIGURE 12.8 Styles for Heading Levels

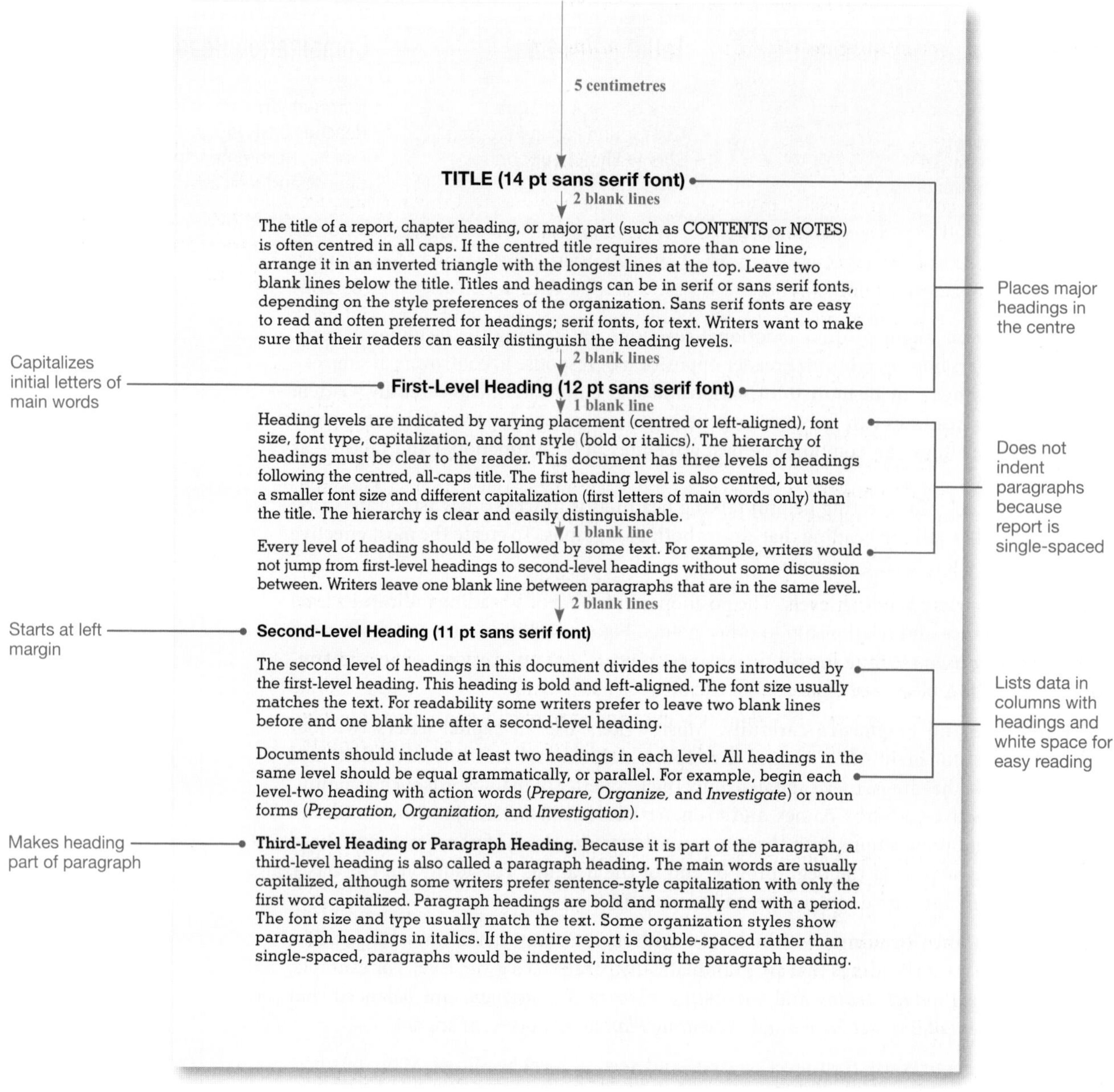

5 centimetres
TITLE (14 pt sans serif font)
2 blank lines
The title of a report, chapter heading, or major part (such as CONTENTS or NOTES) is often centred in all caps. If the centred title requires more than one line, arrange it in an inverted triangle with the longest lines at the top. Leave two blank lines below the title. Titles and headings can be in serif or sans serif fonts, depending on the style preferences of the organization. Sans serif fonts are easy to read and often preferred for headings; serif fonts, for text. Writers want to make sure that their readers can easily distinguish the heading levels.
2 blank lines
First-Level Heading (12 pt sans serif font)
1 blank line
Heading levels are indicated by varying placement (centred or left-aligned), font size, font type, capitalization, and font style (bold or italics). The hierarchy of headings must be clear to the reader. This document has three levels of headings following the centred, all-caps title. The first heading level is also centred, but uses a smaller font size and different capitalization (first letters of main words only) than the title. The hierarchy is clear and easily distinguishable.
1 blank line
Every level of heading should be followed by some text. For example, writers would not jump from first-level headings to second-level headings without some discussion between. Writers leave one blank line between paragraphs that are in the same level.
2 blank lines
Second-Level Heading (11 pt sans serif font)
The second level of headings in this document divides the topics introduced by the first-level heading. This heading is bold and left-aligned. The font size usually matches the text. For readability some writers prefer to leave two blank lines before and one blank line after a second-level heading.
Documents should include at least two headings in each level. All headings in the same level should be equal grammatically, or parallel. For example, begin each level-two heading with action words (Prepare, Organize, and Investigate) or noun forms (Preparation, Organization, and Investigation).
Third-Level Heading or Paragraph Heading. Because it is part of the paragraph, a third-level heading is also called a paragraph heading. The main words are usually capitalized, although some writers prefer sentence-style capitalization with only the first word capitalized. Paragraph headings are bold and normally end with a period. The font size and type usually match the text. Some organization styles show paragraph headings in italics. If the entire report is double-spaced rather than single-spaced, paragraphs would be indented, including the paragraph heading.
Places major headings in the centre
Capitalizes initial letters of main words
Does not indent paragraphs because report is single-spaced
Starts at left margin
Lists data in columns with headings and white space for easy reading
Makes heading part of paragraph

project involving student interns for an oil company in Alberta. Try to keep your headings brief (no more than eight words) and understandable. Experiment with headings that concisely tell who, what, when, where, and why.

Concept Check

1. Identify the following report headings and titles as functional, talking, or combination. Discuss the usefulness and effectiveness of each.
   a. Project Costs
   b. How to Prevent Identity Theft

c. Disadvantages
d. Balancing Worker Productivity and Social Media Use
e. Recommendations: Solving Our Applicant-Tracking Problem

2. What are five different ways to order information logically in a report?

Writing Short Informational Reports

LEARNING OBJECTIVE 4

Write short informational reports that describe routine tasks.

Now that we have covered the basics of gathering, interpreting, and organizing data, we are ready to put it all together into short informational or analytical reports. Informational reports often describe periodic, recurring activities (such as monthly sales or weekly customer calls), as well as situational, nonrecurring events (such as trips, conferences, and progress on special projects). Short informational reports may also include summaries of longer publications. What all these reports have in common is delivering information to readers who do not have to be persuaded. Informational report readers usually are neutral or receptive.

You can expect to write many informational reports as an entry-level or middle-management employee. Because these reports generally deliver nonsensitive data and, therefore, will not upset the reader, they are organized directly. Often, they need little background material or introductory comments because readers are familiar with the topics. Although they are generally conversational and informal, informational reports should not be so casual that the reader struggles to find the important points.

Main points must be immediately visible. Headings, lists, bulleted items, and other graphic design elements, as well as clear organization, enable readers to grasp major ideas immediately.

The lessons that you have learned about conciseness, clarity, courtesy, and effective writing in general throughout earlier chapters apply to report writing as well. After all, competent reports can boost your visibility in the company and promote your advancement. The following pointers on design features and techniques can assist you in improving your reports.

Effective Document Design

Desktop publishing packages, sophisticated word processing programs, and high-quality laser printers now make it possible for you to turn out professional-looking documents and promotional materials. Resist the temptation, however, to overdo it by incorporating too many features in one document. The top ten design tips summarized in Figure 12.9 will help you apply good sense and solid design principles in "publishing" your documents.

Summaries

A summary compresses the main points from a book, a report, an article, a website, a meeting, or a convention. A summary saves time by reducing a report or an article by 85 to 95 percent. Employees are sometimes asked to write summaries that condense technical reports, periodical articles, or books so that their staff or superiors may grasp the main ideas quickly. Students may be asked to write summaries of articles, chapters, or books to sharpen their writing skills and to confirm their knowledge of reading assignments. In writing a summary, follow these general guidelines:

- Present the goal or purpose of the document being summarized. Why was it written?
- Highlight the research methods (if appropriate), findings, conclusions, and recommendations.
- Omit illustrations, examples, and references.
- Organize for readability by including headings and bulleted or enumerated lists.
- Include your reactions or an overall evaluation of the document if asked to do so.

FIGURE 12.9 The Top Ten Tips for Designing Better Documents

1 Analyze your audience.
Give readers what they need. Avoid flashiness in traditional documents. Use headings and lists to suit a busy audience.

2 Avoid amateurish effects.
Strive for simple, clean, and forceful effects. Do not overwhelm readers with cluttered documents.

3 Choose an appropriate font size.
Use body text that is 11 to 12 points tall. Larger type looks amateurish. Smaller type is hard to read.

4 Use a consistent typeface.
Stay with a single family of type within one document. For emphasis and contrast, vary the font size and weight with bold, italic, and other selections.

5 Do not justify right margins.
Opt for ragged-right margins to add white space. Slower readers find ragged-right text more legible.

6 Separate paragraphs and sentences properly.
Skip a line between single-spaced paragraphs. Indent five spaces in double-spaced text. Don't skip a line. Be consistent.

7 Design readable headings.
For high readability, show most headings in upper- and lowercase and choose sans-serif type such as Arial or Calibri.

8 Strive for an attractive page layout.
Balance print and white space. Provide a focal point three lines above the centre of the page. Expect readers to scan a page in a Z pattern.

9 Use graphics and clip art with restraint.
You can import, copy, or scan charts, drawings, photos, and clip art into documents. Use only images that are well drawn, relevant, and appropriately sized.

10 Develop expertise.
Use the desktop publishing features of your current word processing program, or learn software such as PagePlus or Adobe InDesign.

An *executive summary* summarizes a long report, proposal, or business plan. It concentrates on what management needs to know from a longer report. How to prepare an executive summary is covered in Chapter 13.

Periodic (Activity) Reports

Most businesses—especially larger ones—require *periodic reports* (sometimes called *activity reports*) to keep management informed of operations. These recurring reports are written at regular intervals—weekly, monthly, yearly—so that management can monitor business strategies and, if necessary, remedy any problems. Some periodic reports simply contain figures, such as sales volume, number and kind of customer-service calls, shipments delivered, accounts payable, and personnel data. More challenging periodic reports require descriptions and discussions of activities. In preparing a narrative description of their activities, employees writing periodic reports usually do the following:

- Summarize regular activities and events performed during the reporting period
- Describe irregular events deserving the attention of management
- Highlight special needs and problems

FIGURE 12.10 Periodic (Activity) Report

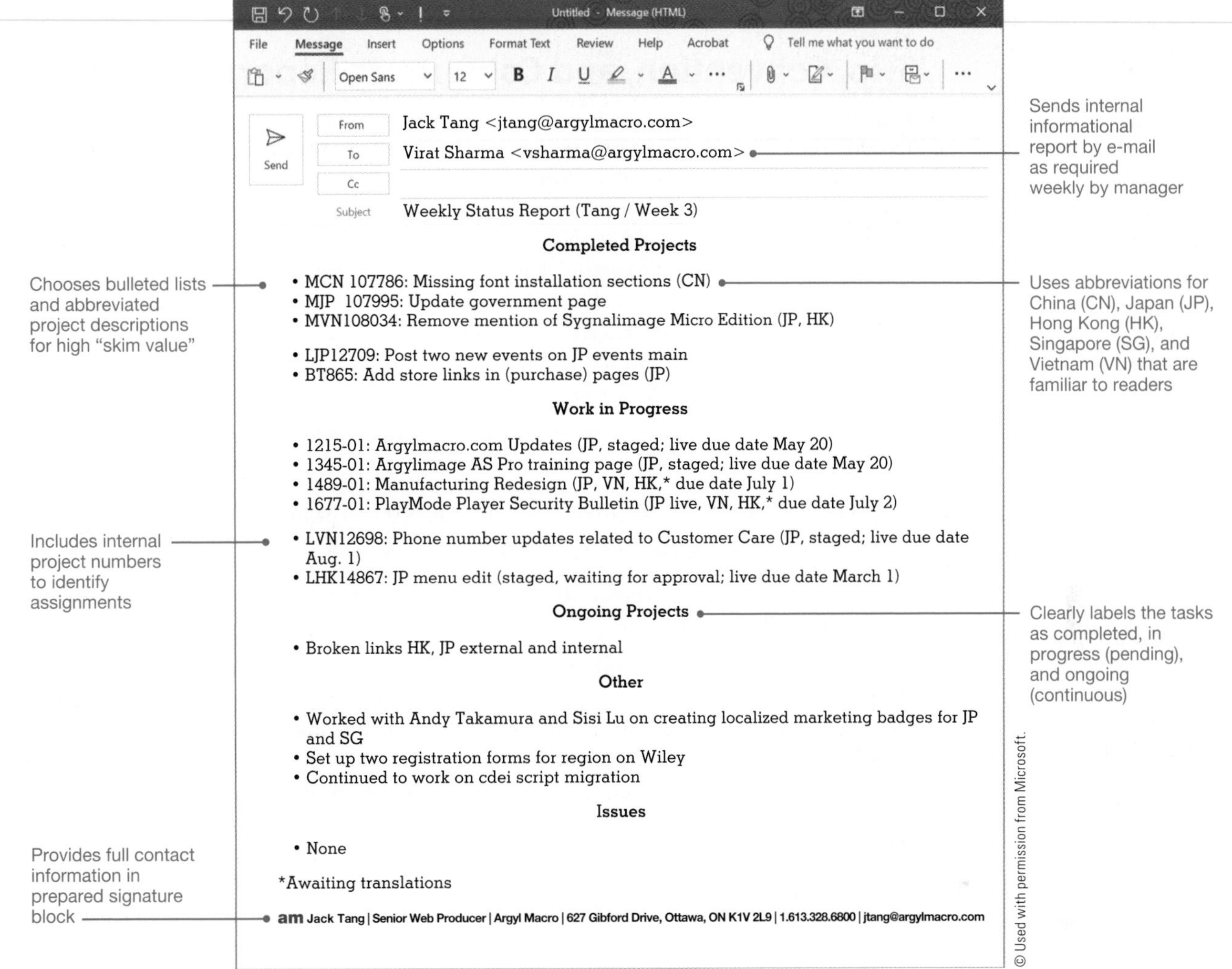

Untitled - Message (HTML)
File Message Insert Options Format Text Review Help Acrobat Tell me what you want to do
Open Sans 12
Send
From Jack Tang <jtang@argylmacro.com>
To Virat Sharma <vsharma@argylmacro.com>
Cc
Subject Weekly Status Report (Tang / Week 3)
Completed Projects
• MCN 107786: Missing font installation sections (CN)
• MJP 107995: Update government page
• MVN108034: Remove mention of Sygnalimage Micro Edition (JP, HK)
• LJP12709: Post two new events on JP events main
• BT865: Add store links in (purchase) pages (JP)
Work in Progress
• 1215-01: Argylmacro.com Updates (JP, staged; live due date May 20)
• 1345-01: Argylimage AS Pro training page (JP, staged; live due date May 20)
• 1489-01: Manufacturing Redesign (JP, VN, HK,* due date July 1)
• 1677-01: PlayMode Player Security Bulletin (JP live, VN, HK,* due date July 2)
• LVN12698: Phone number updates related to Customer Care (JP, staged; live due date Aug. 1)
• LHK14867: JP menu edit (staged, waiting for approval; live due date March 1)
Ongoing Projects
• Broken links HK, JP external and internal
Other
• Worked with Andy Takamura and Sisi Lu on creating localized marketing badges for JP and SG
• Set up two registration forms for region on Wiley
• Continued to work on cdei script migration
Issues
• None
*Awaiting translations
am Jack Tang | Senior Web Producer | Argyl Macro | 627 Gibford Drive, Ottawa, ON K1V 2L9 | 1.613.328.6800 | jtang@argylmacro.com
Sends internal informational report by e-mail as required weekly by manager
Chooses bulleted lists and abbreviated project descriptions for high "skim value"
Uses abbreviations for China (CN), Japan (JP), Hong Kong (HK), Singapore (SG), and Vietnam (VN) that are familiar to readers
Includes internal project numbers to identify assignments
Clearly labels the tasks as completed, in progress (pending), and ongoing (continuous)
Provides full contact information in prepared signature block

Managers naturally want to know that routine activities are progressing normally. Routine reports are typically sent by e-mail and may take the form of efficient bulleted lists without commentary.

Figure 12.10 shows a weekly activity report prepared by Jack Tang, a senior Web producer at the information technology firm Argyl Macro in Ottawa. Jack is responsible for his firm's online presence in Asian countries or territories, mainly Japan, China, Hong Kong, and Vietnam. In his weekly reports to his supervisor, Virat Sharma, Jack neatly divides his projects into three categories: *completed*, *in progress*, and *ongoing*. In progress means the task is not yet completed or is pending. Ongoing refers to continuous tasks, such as regular maintenance. Virat, the manager, then combines the activity reports from all his subordinates into a separate periodic report detailing the department's activities to send to his superiors.

Jack justifies the use of jargon, the lack of a salutation and complimentary close, and ultrashort bulleted items as follows: "We e-mail our reports internally, so some IT jargon can be expected. The readers will understand it. Virat and upper management all want reporting to be brief and to the point. Bullets fit us just fine." Periodic reports ensure that information within the company flows steadily and that supervisors know the status of current and pending projects. This efficient information flow is all the more important because Jack works at home two days a week. Several of his coworkers also telecommute.

Trip, Convention, and Conference Reports

Employees sent on business trips or to conventions and conferences typically must submit reports when they return. Organizations want to know that their money was well spent in funding the travel. These reports inform management about new procedures, equipment, and laws, as well as supplying information that affects products, operations, and service.

The hardest parts of writing these reports are selecting the most relevant material and organizing it coherently. Generally, it is best not to use chronological sequencing (*in the morning we did X, at lunch we heard Y, and in the afternoon we did Z*). Instead, focus on three to five topics in which your reader will be interested. These items become the body of the report. Then simply add an introduction and a closing, and your report is organized. Here is a general outline for trip, conference, and convention reports:

- Begin by identifying the event (exact date, name, and location) and previewing the topics to be discussed.
- Summarize in the body three to five main points that might benefit the reader.
- Itemize your expenses, if requested, on a separate sheet.
- Close by expressing appreciation, suggesting action to be taken, or synthesizing the value of the trip or event.

Madison Gardner was recently hired as marketing specialist in the Marketing Department of a wireless devices and consumer electronics store in Toronto, Ontario. Recognizing her lack of experience in online customer service, the marketing manager gave her permission to attend a two-day training conference titled Social Customer Service. Her boss, Bryce Corliss, encouraged Madison to attend, saying, "We are serious about increasing our social media involvement, and we want to build solid relationships with our customers while promoting our products. Come back and tell us what you learned." When she returned, Madison wrote the conference report shown in Figure 12.11. Here is how she described its preparation: "I know my boss values brevity, so I worked hard to make my report no more than a page. The conference saturated me with great ideas, far too many to cover in one brief report. So, I decided to discuss two topics that would most benefit our staff. By the third draft, I had compressed my ideas into a manageable size without sacrificing any of the meaning."

Progress and Interim Reports

Continuing projects often require progress or interim reports to describe their status. These reports may be external (advising customers regarding the headway of their projects) or internal (informing management of the status of activities). Progress reports typically follow this pattern of development:

- Specify in the opening the purpose and nature of the project.
- Provide background information if the audience requires filling in.
- Describe the work completed.
- Explain the work currently in progress, including personnel, activities, methods, and locations.
- Describe current problems and anticipate future problems and possible remedies.
- Discuss future activities and provide the expected completion date.

As a location manager for Maple Leaf Productions in Toronto, Ellie Harper frequently writes progress reports, such as the one shown in Figure 12.12. Producers want to know

FIGURE 12.11 Conference Report

Date: February 25, 2020

To: Bryce Corliss, Marketing Manager BC

From: Madison Gardner, Marketing Specialist

Subject: Conference on Social Customer Service–January 2020

I attended the Social Customer Service conference in Toronto, Ontario, on January 28-29, sponsored by Social Solutions Inc. The conference emphasized the importance of delivering excellent customer service in social spaces (social media gathering places). As we prepare to increase our social media involvement, this report summarizes two topics that would benefit our employees: (a) the rising expectations of customers in social media networks, and (b) the role of customer service specialists.

Identifies the topic and previews the report's contents

The Rising Expectations of Customers in Social Spaces

Conference presenters emphasized the following customer service expectations:

- Customers expect social business connections to be helpful and friendly—always.
- Online customers expect that you're listening and will remember what they said to you last time.
- Before buying, customers are powerfully influenced by user reviews, Facebook comments, Twitter feeds, and forum messages.
- Customers expect honest and prompt responses when they have questions and complaints.

Sets off major topics with bold headings in the same font

The Role of Customer Service Specialists

Whether a company hires a social media management service or uses in-house personnel, the responsibilities of social customer service specialists are the same:

- Monitor customer feedback and respond promptly to questions and complaints.
- Check social media platforms for mention of their businesses. Send text message responses to the right people immediately.
- Examine the company's Facebook activity and create dialogue on Twitter.
- When problems occur, own up to them and explain publicly what you're doing to make things right.

Covers the main ideas that will benefit the reader

Sharing Conference Highlights

Companies realize the importance of communicating with customers promptly and personally, especially in social spaces. Since our company is heavily invested in social media platforms, the conference topics seemed especially relevant. I would be happy to share highlights from the conference at our next management meeting. Let me know what date and time work best.

Concludes with an offer to share information

what she is doing, and a phone call does not provide a permanent record. Here is how she described the reasoning behind her progress report: "I usually include background information in my reports because a director does not always know or remember exactly what specifications I was given for a location search. Then I try to hit the high points of what I have completed and what I plan to do next, without getting bogged down in tiny details. Although it would be easier to skip them, I have learned to be up front with any problems that I anticipate. I do not tell how to solve the problems, but I feel duty-bound to at least mention them."

Investigative Reports

Investigative reports deliver data for specific situations—without offering interpretations or recommendations. These nonrecurring reports are generally arranged by using the direct

FIGURE 12.12 Progress Report

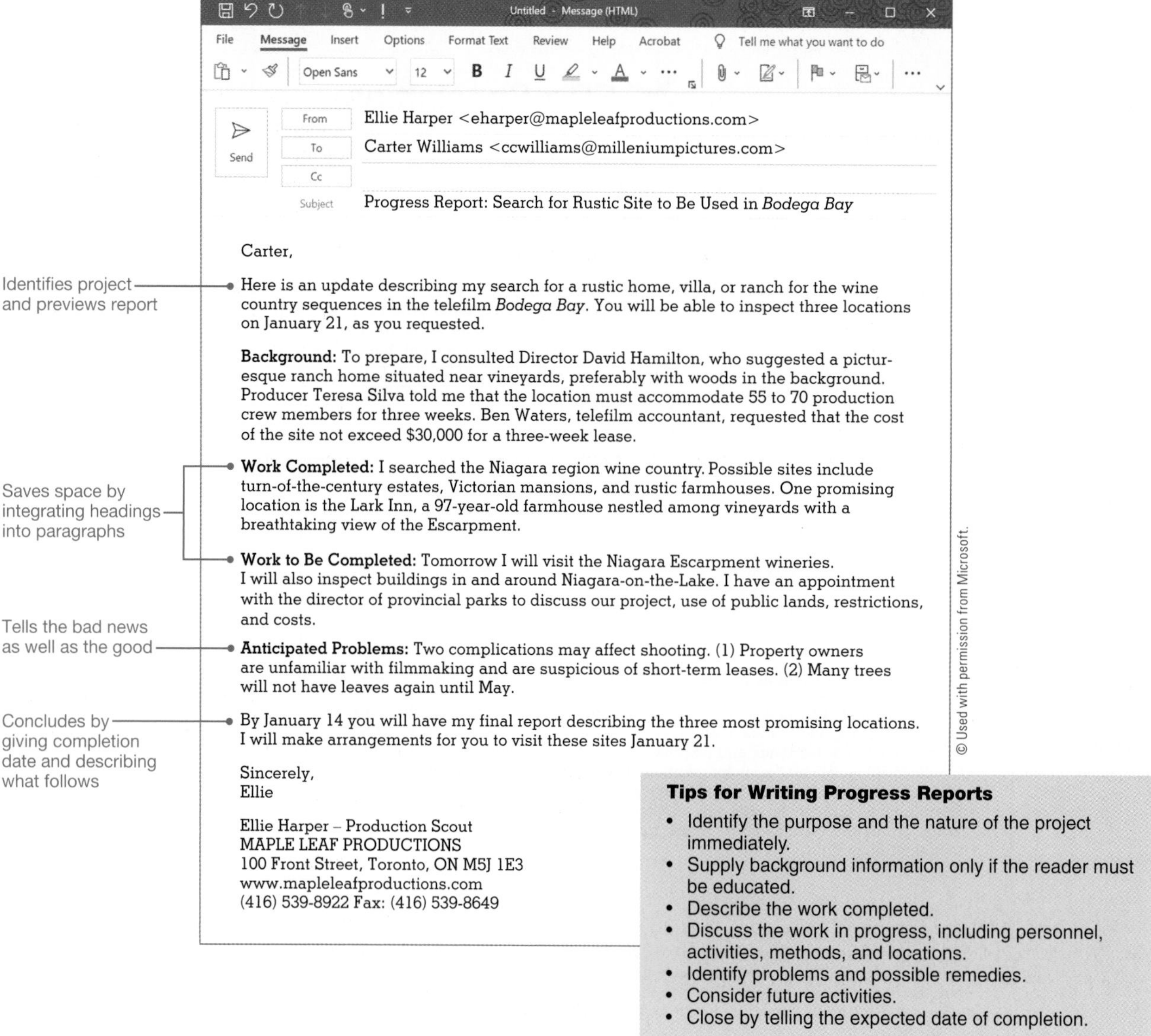

From: Ellie Harper <eharper@mapleleafproductions.com>

To: Carter Williams <ccwilliams@milleniumpictures.com>

Cc:

Subject: Progress Report: Search for Rustic Site to Be Used in *Bodega Bay*

Carter,

Here is an update describing my search for a rustic home, villa, or ranch for the wine country sequences in the telefilm *Bodega Bay*. You will be able to inspect three locations on January 21, as you requested.

Background: To prepare, I consulted Director David Hamilton, who suggested a picturesque ranch home situated near vineyards, preferably with woods in the background. Producer Teresa Silva told me that the location must accommodate 55 to 70 production crew members for three weeks. Ben Waters, telefilm accountant, requested that the cost of the site not exceed $30,000 for a three-week lease.

Work Completed: I searched the Niagara region wine country. Possible sites include turn-of-the-century estates, Victorian mansions, and rustic farmhouses. One promising location is the Lark Inn, a 97-year-old farmhouse nestled among vineyards with a breathtaking view of the Escarpment.

Work to Be Completed: Tomorrow I will visit the Niagara Escarpment wineries. I will also inspect buildings in and around Niagara-on-the-Lake. I have an appointment with the director of provincial parks to discuss our project, use of public lands, restrictions, and costs.

Anticipated Problems: Two complications may affect shooting. (1) Property owners are unfamiliar with filmmaking and are suspicious of short-term leases. (2) Many trees will not have leaves again until May.

By January 14 you will have my final report describing the three most promising locations. I will make arrangements for you to visit these sites January 21.

Sincerely,
Ellie

Ellie Harper – Production Scout
MAPLE LEAF PRODUCTIONS
100 Front Street, Toronto, ON M5J 1E3
www.mapleleafproductions.com
(416) 539-8922 Fax: (416) 539-8649

Untitled - Message (HTML)
File Message Insert Options Format Text Review Help Acrobat Tell me what you want to do
Send
Identifies project and previews report
Saves space by integrating headings into paragraphs
Tells the bad news as well as the good
Concludes by giving completion date and describing what follows

Tips for Writing Progress Reports

- Identify the purpose and the nature of the project immediately.
- Supply background information only if the reader must be educated.
- Describe the work completed.
- Discuss the work in progress, including personnel, activities, methods, and locations.
- Identify problems and possible remedies.
- Consider future activities.
- Close by telling the expected date of completion.

strategy with three segments: introduction, body, and summary. The body—which includes the facts, findings, or discussion—may be organized by time, component, importance, criteria, or convention. The subject matter of the report usually suggests the best way to divide or organize it. What is important is dividing the topic into logical segments—say, three to five areas that are roughly equal and do not overlap.

Whether you are writing a periodic, a trip, a conference, a progress, or an investigative report, you will want to review the suggestions found in the following Checklist.

Concept Check

1. What pattern of development do progress and interim reports usually follow?
2. What is the best way to organize the introduction of an informational report?

CHECKLIST

Writing Informational Reports

Introduction

- **Begin directly.** Identify the report and its purpose.
- **Provide a preview.** If the report is over a page long, give the reader a brief overview of its organization.
- **Supply background data selectively.** When readers are unfamiliar with the topic, briefly fill in the necessary details.
- **Divide the topic.** Strive to group the facts or findings into three to five roughly equal segments that do not overlap.

Body

- **Arrange the subtopics logically.** Consider organizing by time, component, importance, criteria, or convention.
- **Use clear headings.** Supply functional or talking headings (at least one per page) that describe each important section.
- **Determine degree of formality.** Use an informal, conversational writing style unless the audience expects a more formal tone.
- **Enhance readability with graphic highlighting.** Make liberal use of bullets, numbered and lettered lists, headings, underlined items, and white space.

Summary/Concluding Remarks

- **When necessary, summarize the report.** Briefly review the main points and discuss what action will follow.
- **Offer a concluding thought.** If relevant, express appreciation or describe your willingness to provide further information.

Preparing Short Analytical Reports

LEARNING OBJECTIVE 5

Prepare short analytical reports that solve business problems.

Analytical reports differ significantly from informational reports. Although both seek to collect and present data clearly, analytical reports also evaluate the data and typically try to persuade the reader to accept the conclusions and act on the recommendations. Informational reports emphasize facts; analytical reports emphasize reasoning and conclusions.

For some readers you may organize analytical reports directly with the conclusions and recommendations near the beginning. Directness is appropriate when the reader has confidence in the writer, based on either experience or credentials. Frontloading the recommendations also works when the topic is routine or familiar and the reader is supportive.

Directness can backfire, though. If you announce the recommendations too quickly, the reader may immediately object to a single idea. Once the reader is opposed, changing an unfavourable mindset may be difficult or impossible. A reader may also believe that you have oversimplified or overlooked something significant if you lay out all the recommendations before explaining how you arrived at them. When you must lead the reader through the process of discovering the solution or recommendation, use the indirect strategy: present conclusions and recommendations last.

Most analytical reports answer questions about specific problems and aid in decision making. How can we use social media most effectively? Should we close the Bradford plant? Should we buy or lease company cars? How can we improve customer service? Three categories of analytical reports answer business questions: justification/recommendation reports, feasibility reports, and yardstick reports. Because these reports all solve problems, the categories are not mutually exclusive. What distinguishes them are their goals and organization.

Justification/Recommendation Reports

Both managers and employees must occasionally write reports that justify or recommend something, such as buying equipment, changing a procedure, hiring an employee, consolidating departments, or investing funds. These reports may also be called *internal proposals* because their persuasive nature is similar to that of external proposals (presented in Chapter 13). Large organizations sometimes prescribe how these reports should be organized; they use forms with conventional headings. When you are free to select an organizational plan yourself, however, let your audience and topic determine your choice of the direct or indirect strategy.

Direct Strategy. For nonsensitive topics and recommendations that will be agreeable to readers, you can organize directly according to the following sequence:

- Identify the problem or need briefly.
- Announce the recommendation, solution, or action concisely and with action verbs.
- Explain more fully the benefits of the recommendation or steps necessary to solve the problem.
- Include a discussion of pros, cons, and costs.
- Conclude with a summary specifying the recommendation and necessary action.

Indirect Strategy. When a reader may oppose a recommendation or when circumstances suggest caution, do not rush to reveal your recommendation.

Consider using the following sequence for an indirect approach to your recommendations:

- Refer to the problem in general terms, not to your recommendation, in the subject line.
- Describe the problem or need your recommendation addresses. Use specific examples, supporting statistics, and authoritative quotations to lend credibility to the seriousness of the problem.
- Discuss alternative solutions, beginning with the least likely to succeed.
- Present the most promising alternative (your recommendation) last.
- Show how the advantages of your recommendation outweigh its disadvantages.
- Summarize your recommendation. If appropriate, specify the action it requires.
- Ask for authorization to proceed if necessary.

Cheyenne St. Marie, an executive assistant at a large petroleum and mining company in Calgary, Alberta, received a challenging research assignment. Her boss, the director of Human Resources, asked her to investigate ways to persuade employees to quit smoking. Here is how Cheyenne described her task: "We banned smoking many years ago inside our buildings and on the premises, but we never tried very hard to get smokers to actually kick their habits. My job was to gather information about the problem and learn how other companies have helped workers stop smoking. The report would go to my boss, but I knew he would pass it along to the management council for approval."

Continuing her explanation, Cheyenne said, "If the report were just for my boss, I would put my recommendation right up front, because I'm sure he would support it. But the management council is another story. They need persuasion because of the costs involved—and because some of them are smokers. Therefore, I put the alternative I favoured last. To gain credibility, I footnoted my sources. I had enough material for a ten-page report, but I kept it to two pages in keeping with our company report policy." Cheyenne chose MLA style to document her sources. A long report that uses APA style is shown in Chapter 13.

Cheyenne single-spaced her report, shown in Figure 12.13, because her company prefers this style. Some companies prefer the readability of double spacing. Be sure to check with your organization for its preference before printing your reports.

Feasibility Reports

Feasibility reports examine the practicality and advisability of following a course of action. They answer this question: Will this plan or proposal work? Feasibility reports typically are internal reports written to advise on matters, such as consolidating departments, offering a wellness program to employees, or hiring an outside firm to handle a company's accounting or social media presence. These reports may also be written by consultants called in to investigate a problem. The focus of these reports is on the decision: rejecting or proceeding with the proposed option. Because your role is not to persuade the reader to accept the decision, you will want to present the decision immediately. In writing feasibility reports, consider these suggestions:

- Announce your decision immediately.
- Provide a description of the background and problem necessitating the proposal.
- Discuss the benefits of the proposal.
- Describe the problems that may result.
- Calculate the costs associated with the proposal, if appropriate.
- Show the time frame necessary for implementing the proposal.

FIGURE 12.13 Justification/Recommendation Report, MLA Style

DATE: October 11, 2020

TO: Austin Sebastian, Director, Human Resources

CC: Louise Dumont, Assistant Director, Human Resources

FROM: Cheyenne St. Marie, Executive Assistant *C.S.M.*

SUBJECT: Smoking Cessation Programs for Employees

At your request, I have examined measures that encourage employees to quit smoking. As company records show, approximately 23 percent of our employees still smoke, despite the antismoking and clean-air policies we adopted in 2019. To collect data for this report, I studied professional and government publications; I also inquired at companies and clinics about stop-smoking programs.

Introduces purpose of report, tells method of data collection, and previews organization

Avoids revealing recommendation immediately

This report presents data describing the significance of the problem, three alternative solutions, and a recommendation based on my investigation.

Uses headings that combine function and description

Significance of Problem: Health Care and Productivity Losses

Employees who smoke are costly to any organization. The following statistics show the effects of smoking for workers and for organizations:

- Absenteeism is 40 to 50 percent greater among smoking employees.
- Accidents are two to three times greater among smokers.
- Bronchitis, lung and heart disease, cancer, and early death are more frequent among smokers (Arhelger 4).

Documents data sources for credibility, uses MLA style citing author and page number in the text

Although our clean-air policy prohibits smoking in the building, shop, and office, we have done little to encourage employees to stop smoking. Many workers still go outside to smoke at lunch and breaks. Other companies have been far more proactive in their attempts to stop employee smoking. Many companies have found that persuading employees to stop smoking was a decisive factor in reducing their health insurance premiums. Below is a discussion of three common stop-smoking measures tried by other companies, along with a projected cost factor for each (Rindfleisch 4).

Alternative Solutions

Discusses least effective alternative first

Alternative 1: Literature and Events

The least expensive and easiest stop-smoking measure involves the distribution of literature, such as "The Ten-Step Plan" from Smokefree Enterprises and government pamphlets citing smoking dangers. Some companies have also sponsored events such as the Great Canadian Smoke-Out, a one-day occasion intended to develop group spirit in spurring smokers to quit. "Studies show, however," says one expert, "that literature and company-sponsored events have little permanent effect in helping smokers quit" (Mendel 108).

Cost: Negligible

(Continued)

FIGURE 12.13 (*Continued*)

Austin Sebastian October 11, 2020 Page 2

Alternative 2: Stop-Smoking Programs Outside the Workplace

Local clinics provide treatment programs in classes at their centres. Here in Fairbanks we have the Smokers' Treatment Centre, ACC Motivation Centre, and New-Choice Program for Stopping Smoking. These behaviour-modification stop-smoking programs are acknowledged to be more effective than literature distribution or incentive programs. However, studies of companies using off-workplace programs show that many employees fail to attend regularly and do not complete the programs.

Cost: $1,200 per employee, three-month individual program (New-Choice Program)
$900 per employee, three-month group session

Highlights costs for easy comparison

Alternative 3: Stop-Smoking Programs at the Workplace

Many clinics offer workplace programs with counsellors meeting employees in company conference rooms. These programs have the advantage of keeping a firm's employees together so that they develop a group spirit and exert pressure on each other to succeed. The most successful programs are on company premises and also on company time. Employees participating in such programs had a 72 percent greater success record than employees attending the same stop-smoking program at an outside clinic (Honda 35). A disadvantage of this arrangement, of course, is lost work time—amounting to about two hours a week for three months.

Arranges alternatives so that most effective is last

Cost: $900 per employee, two hours per week of release time for three months

Conclusions

Summarizes findings

Smokers require discipline, counselling, and professional assistance in kicking the nicotine habit, as explained at the Canadian Cancer Society website ("Guide to Quitting Smoking"). Workplace stop-smoking programs on company time are more effective than literature, incentives, and off-workplace programs. If our goal is to reduce health care costs and lead our employees to healthful lives, we should invest in a workplace stop-smoking program with release time for smokers. Although the program temporarily reduces productivity, we can expect to recapture that loss in lower health care premiums and healthier employees.

Recommendation

Therefore, I recommend that we begin a stop-smoking treatment program on company premises with two hours per week of release time for participants for three months.

Reveals recommendation only after discussing all alternatives

Page 3

Works Cited

Magazine — Arhelger, Zack. "The End of Smoking." *The World of Business*, 5 Nov. 2019, pp. 3–8.

Website article — "Guide to Quitting Smoking." *The Canadian Cancer Society.org*, 27 Oct. 2019, www.cancer.org/healthy/stayawayfromtobacco/guidetoquittingsmoking/guide-to-quitting-smoking-toc.

Journal article — Honda, Emeline M. "Managing Anti-Smoking Campaigns: The Case for Company Programs." *Management Quarterly*, vol. 32, 2018, pp. 29–47.

Book — Mendel, I. A. *The Puff Stops Here*. Science Publications, 2018.

Newspaper article — Rindfleisch, Terry. "Smoke-Free Workplaces Can Help Smokers Quit, Expert Says." *Evening Chronicle*, 4 Dec. 2019, pp. 4+.

FIGURE 12.14 Feasibility Report

APEX CPA SERVICES LLP
MEMORANDUM

Date: May 12, 2020

To: Astrid Oliver-Leone, Vice President

From: Cora Hidalgo, Human Resources Manager C.H.

Subject: Feasibility of a Social Media and Internet Monitoring Program

The plan calling for implementing an employee social media and Internet monitoring program is workable and could be fully implemented by July 2. This report discusses the background, benefits, problems, costs, and time frame.

Background: Current Misuse of Social Media and the Internet

We allow employees Internet access for job-related tasks. Many of us use social media, specifically Facebook, Twitter, and Instagram, to communicate with our clients and the public. However, we know that many employees are using their access for personal reasons, resulting in lowered productivity, higher costs, and a strain on our network. We hired an outside consultant who suggested an Internet monitoring program.

Benefits of Plan: Appropriate Use of Social Media and the Internet

The proposed plan calls for installing Internet monitoring software such as EmployeeMonitoring, Perfect Keylogger, or Spector CNE. We would fully disclose to employees that this software will be tracking their online activity. We will also teach employees what social media and Internet use is appropriate. In addition to increased productivity, lowered costs, and improved network performance, this software will produce numerous other benefits. It can help protect our company against loss of intellectual property, trade secrets, and confidential information. The software will limit any liability for sexual harassment, workplace harassment, or cyberstalking. It will shield us against copyright infringement from employees who illegally download digital content.

Employee Acceptance

One of the biggest problems will be convincing employees to accept this new policy without feeling as if their privacy is being violated. However, our consultant can help us communicate the reasons for this policy in a way that employees will understand. In addition, adequate training will help employees understand the appropriate use of social media and the Internet.

Costs

Implementing the monitoring plan involves two direct costs. The first is the initial software cost of $400 to $900, depending on the package we choose. The second cost involves employee training and trainer fees. Initial training will cost about $1,000. However, the expenditures are within the project's budget.

Time Frame

Selecting the software package will take about two weeks. Preparing a training program will require another three weeks. Once the program is started, I expect a breaking-in period of at least three months. By July 2 the Internet monitoring program will be fully functional, resulting in increased productivity, decreased costs, lowered liability, and improved network performance.

Please let me know by May 21 whether you would like additional information about social media and Internet monitoring programs.

Outlines organization of the report

Reveals decision immediately

Describes problem and background

Evaluates positive and negative aspects of proposal objectively

Presents costs and schedule; omits unnecessary summary

Cora Hidalgo, human resources manager for a large public accounting firm, wrote the feasibility report shown in Figure 12.14. Because she discovered that the company was losing time and money as a result of personal e-mail and Internet use by employees, she talked with the vice president, Astrid Oliver-Leone, about the problem. Astrid didn't want Cora to take time away from her job to investigate what other companies were doing to prevent this type of problem. Instead, she suggested that they hire a consultant to investigate what other companies were doing to prevent or limit personal e-mail and Internet use. The vice president then wanted to know whether the consultant's plan was feasible. Although Cora's report is only one page long, it provides all the necessary information: background, benefits, employee acceptance, costs, and time frame.

Yardstick Reports

Yardstick reports examine problems with two or more solutions. To determine the best solution, the writer establishes criteria by which to compare the alternatives. The criteria then act as a yardstick against which all the alternatives are measured, as shown in Figure 12.15. The yardstick approach is effective for companies that must establish specifications for equipment purchases and then compare each manufacturer's product with the established specs. The yardstick approach is also effective when exact specifications cannot be established.

FIGURE 12.15 Yardstick Report

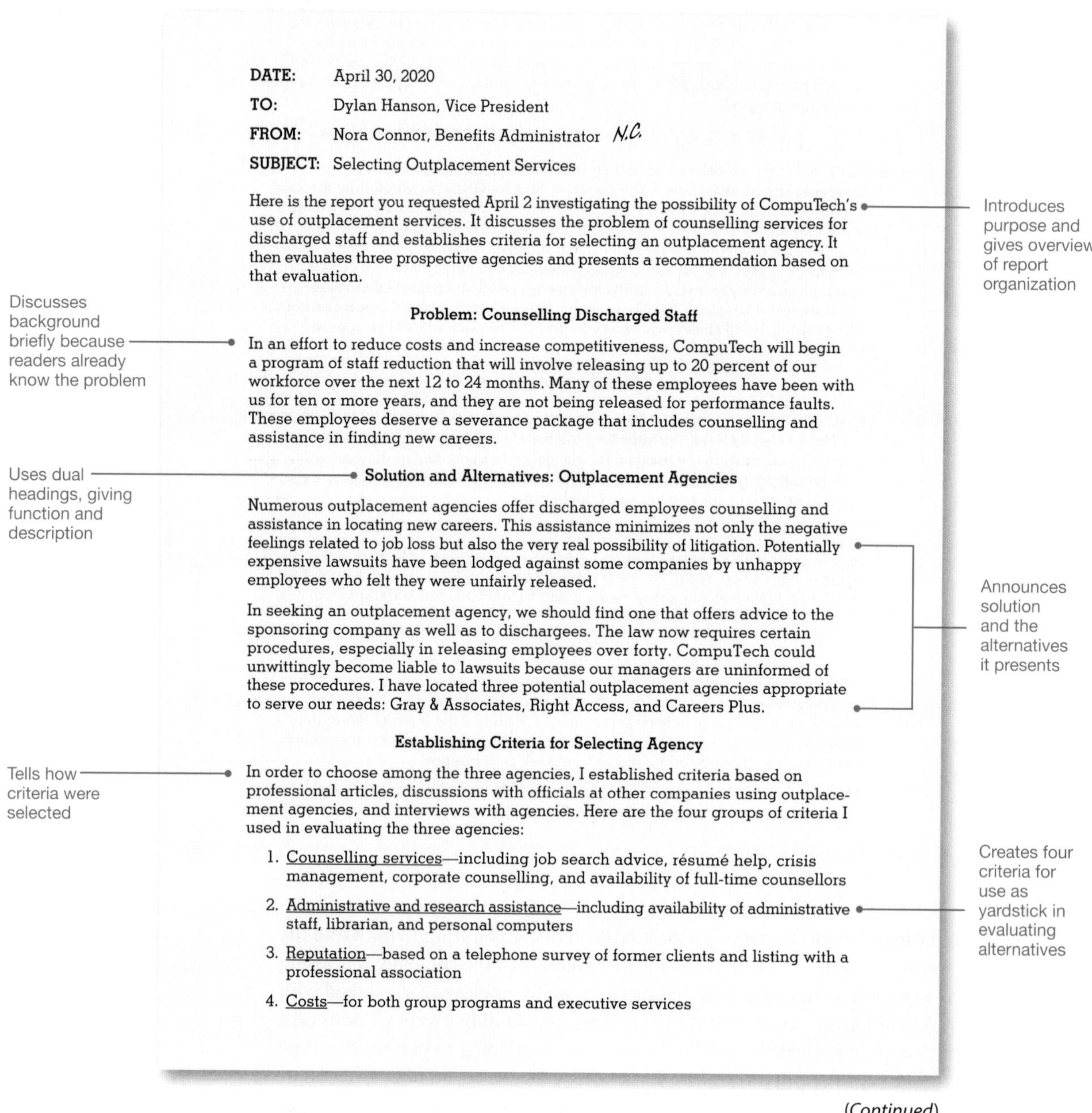

DATE: April 30, 2020

TO: Dylan Hanson, Vice President

FROM: Nora Connor, Benefits Administrator *N.C.*

SUBJECT: Selecting Outplacement Services

Here is the report you requested April 2 investigating the possibility of CompuTech's use of outplacement services. It discusses the problem of counselling services for discharged staff and establishes criteria for selecting an outplacement agency. It then evaluates three prospective agencies and presents a recommendation based on that evaluation.

Problem: Counselling Discharged Staff

In an effort to reduce costs and increase competitiveness, CompuTech will begin a program of staff reduction that will involve releasing up to 20 percent of our workforce over the next 12 to 24 months. Many of these employees have been with us for ten or more years, and they are not being released for performance faults. These employees deserve a severance package that includes counselling and assistance in finding new careers.

Solution and Alternatives: Outplacement Agencies

Numerous outplacement agencies offer discharged employees counselling and assistance in locating new careers. This assistance minimizes not only the negative feelings related to job loss but also the very real possibility of litigation. Potentially expensive lawsuits have been lodged against some companies by unhappy employees who felt they were unfairly released.

In seeking an outplacement agency, we should find one that offers advice to the sponsoring company as well as to dischargees. The law now requires certain procedures, especially in releasing employees over forty. CompuTech could unwittingly become liable to lawsuits because our managers are uninformed of these procedures. I have located three potential outplacement agencies appropriate to serve our needs: Gray & Associates, Right Access, and Careers Plus.

Establishing Criteria for Selecting Agency

In order to choose among the three agencies, I established criteria based on professional articles, discussions with officials at other companies using outplacement agencies, and interviews with agencies. Here are the four groups of criteria I used in evaluating the three agencies:

1. Counselling services—including job search advice, résumé help, crisis management, corporate counselling, and availability of full-time counsellors
2. Administrative and research assistance—including availability of administrative staff, librarian, and personal computers
3. Reputation—based on a telephone survey of former clients and listing with a professional association
4. Costs—for both group programs and executive services

Introduces purpose and gives overview of report organization
Discusses background briefly because readers already know the problem
Uses dual headings, giving function and description
Announces solution and the alternatives it presents
Tells how criteria were selected
Creates four criteria for use as yardstick in evaluating alternatives

(Continued)

FIGURE 12.15 *(Continued)*

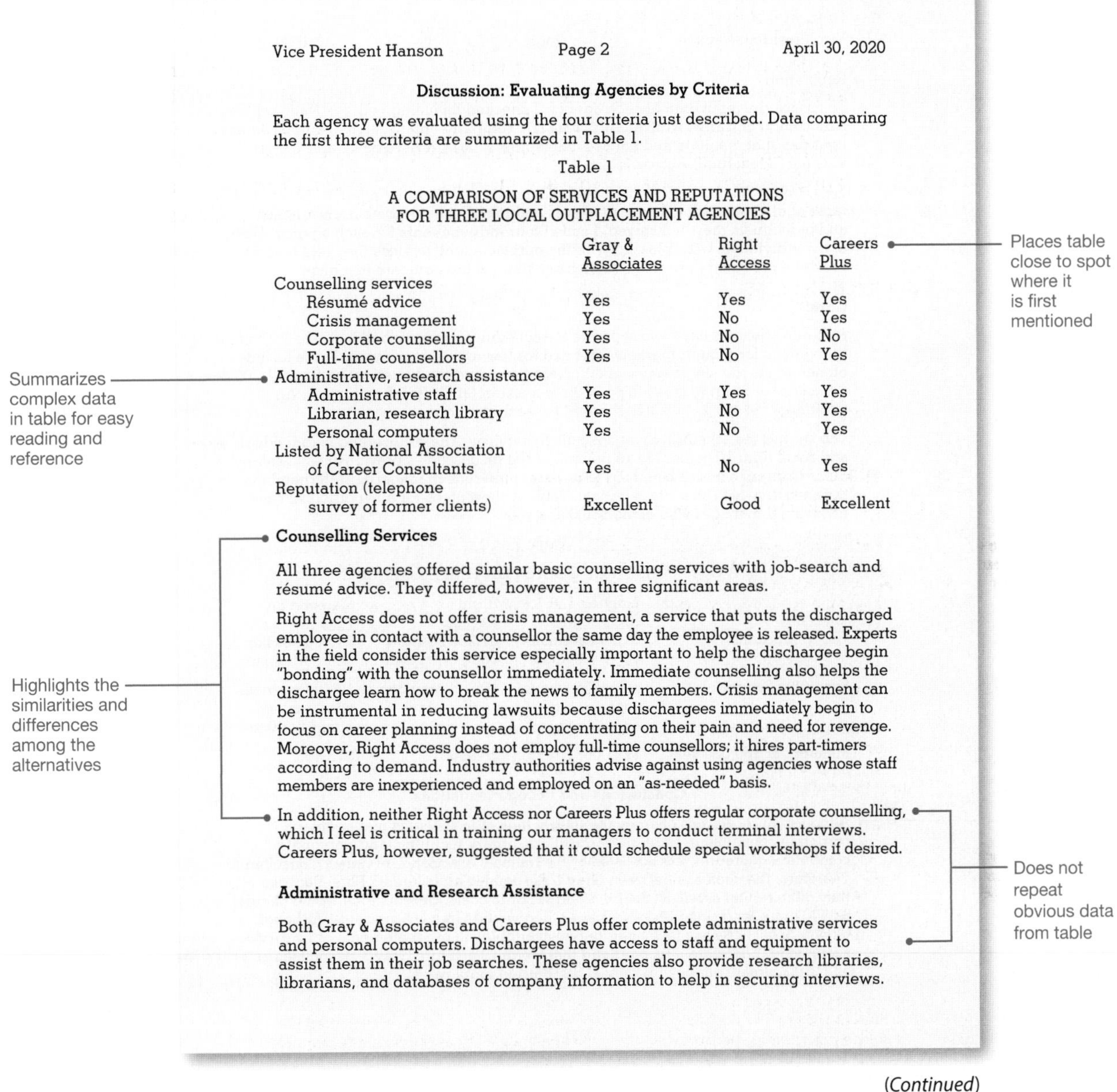

Vice President Hanson | Page 2 | April 30, 2020

Discussion: Evaluating Agencies by Criteria

Each agency was evaluated using the four criteria just described. Data comparing the first three criteria are summarized in Table 1.

Table 1

A COMPARISON OF SERVICES AND REPUTATIONS FOR THREE LOCAL OUTPLACEMENT AGENCIES

	Gray & Associates	Right Access	Careers Plus
Counselling services			
Résumé advice	Yes	Yes	Yes
Crisis management	Yes	No	Yes
Corporate counselling	Yes	No	No
Full-time counsellors	Yes	No	Yes
Administrative, research assistance			
Administrative staff	Yes	Yes	Yes
Librarian, research library	Yes	No	Yes
Personal computers	Yes	No	Yes
Listed by National Association of Career Consultants	Yes	No	Yes
Reputation (telephone survey of former clients)	Excellent	Good	Excellent

Counselling Services

All three agencies offered similar basic counselling services with job-search and résumé advice. They differed, however, in three significant areas.

Right Access does not offer crisis management, a service that puts the discharged employee in contact with a counsellor the same day the employee is released. Experts in the field consider this service especially important to help the dischargee begin "bonding" with the counsellor immediately. Immediate counselling also helps the dischargee learn how to break the news to family members. Crisis management can be instrumental in reducing lawsuits because dischargees immediately begin to focus on career planning instead of concentrating on their pain and need for revenge. Moreover, Right Access does not employ full-time counsellors; it hires part-timers according to demand. Industry authorities advise against using agencies whose staff members are inexperienced and employed on an "as-needed" basis.

In addition, neither Right Access nor Careers Plus offers regular corporate counselling, which I feel is critical in training our managers to conduct terminal interviews. Careers Plus, however, suggested that it could schedule special workshops if desired.

Administrative and Research Assistance

Both Gray & Associates and Careers Plus offer complete administrative services and personal computers. Dischargees have access to staff and equipment to assist them in their job searches. These agencies also provide research libraries, librarians, and databases of company information to help in securing interviews.

Places table close to spot where it is first mentioned
Summarizes complex data in table for easy reading and reference
Highlights the similarities and differences among the alternatives
Does not repeat obvious data from table

(Continued)

The real advantage to yardstick reports is that alternatives can be measured consistently by using the same criteria. Writers using a yardstick approach typically do the following:

- Begin by describing the problem or need.
- Explain possible solutions and alternatives.
- Establish criteria for comparing the alternatives; tell how the criteria were selected or developed.
- Discuss and evaluate each alternative in terms of the criteria.
- Draw conclusions and make recommendations.

Nora Connor, benefits administrator for computer manufacturer CompuTech, was called on to write the report in Figure 12.15 comparing outplacement agencies. These agencies

FIGURE 12.15 (*Continued*)

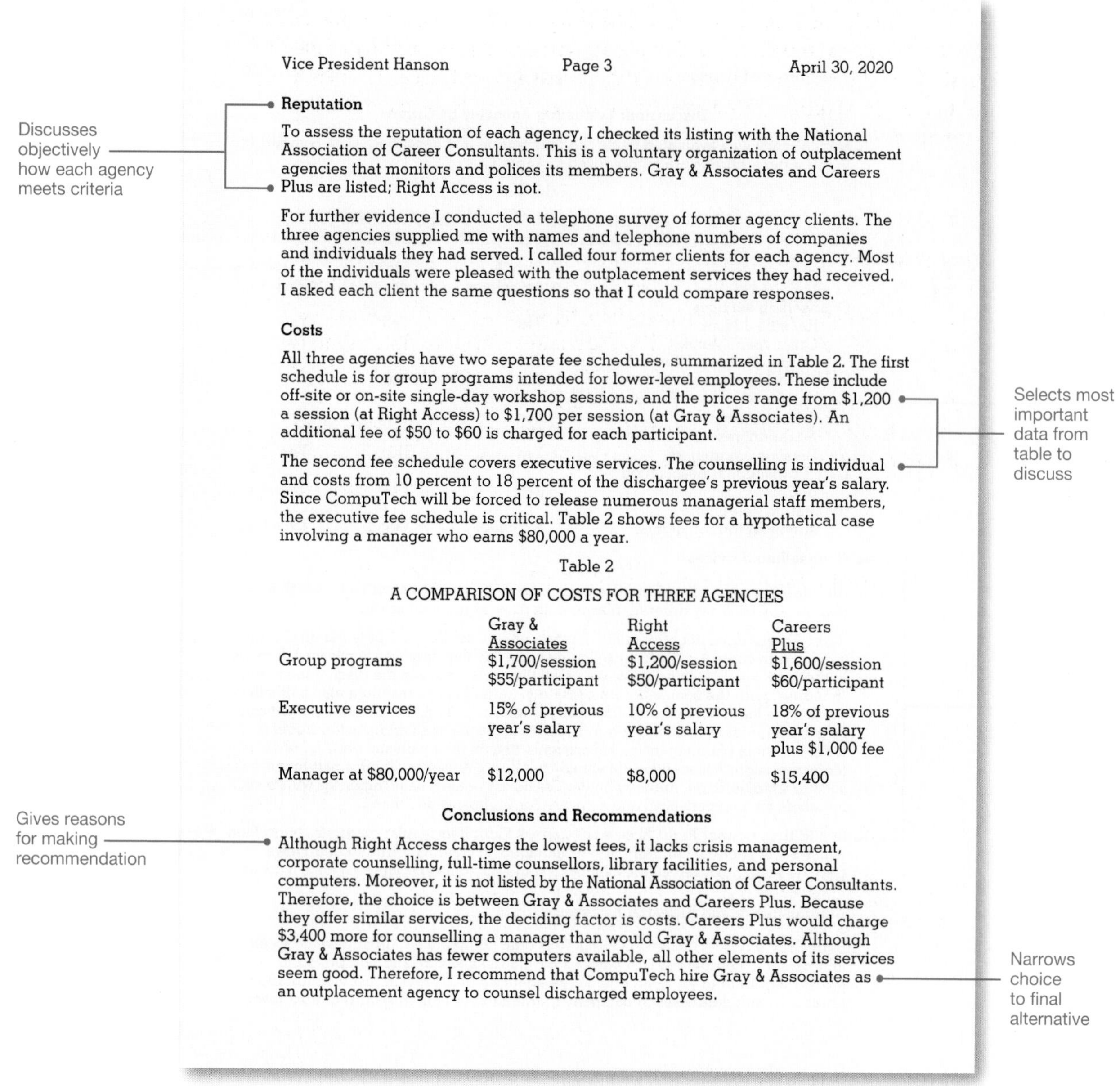

Discusses objectively how each agency meets criteria
Selects most important data from table to discuss
Gives reasons for making recommendation
Narrows choice to final alternative

Vice President Hanson   Page 3   April 30, 2020

Reputation

To assess the reputation of each agency, I checked its listing with the National Association of Career Consultants. This is a voluntary organization of outplacement agencies that monitors and polices its members. Gray & Associates and Careers Plus are listed; Right Access is not.

For further evidence I conducted a telephone survey of former agency clients. The three agencies supplied me with names and telephone numbers of companies and individuals they had served. I called four former clients for each agency. Most of the individuals were pleased with the outplacement services they had received. I asked each client the same questions so that I could compare responses.

Costs

All three agencies have two separate fee schedules, summarized in Table 2. The first schedule is for group programs intended for lower-level employees. These include off-site or on-site single-day workshop sessions, and the prices range from $1,200 a session (at Right Access) to $1,700 per session (at Gray & Associates). An additional fee of $50 to $60 is charged for each participant.

The second fee schedule covers executive services. The counselling is individual and costs from 10 percent to 18 percent of the dischargee's previous year's salary. Since CompuTech will be forced to release numerous managerial staff members, the executive fee schedule is critical. Table 2 shows fees for a hypothetical case involving a manager who earns $80,000 a year.

Table 2

A COMPARISON OF COSTS FOR THREE AGENCIES

	Gray & Associates	Right Access	Careers Plus
Group programs	$1,700/session $55/participant	$1,200/session $50/participant	$1,600/session $60/participant
Executive services	15% of previous year's salary	10% of previous year's salary	18% of previous year's salary plus $1,000 fee
Manager at $80,000/year	$12,000	$8,000	$15,400

Conclusions and Recommendations

Although Right Access charges the lowest fees, it lacks crisis management, corporate counselling, full-time counsellors, library facilities, and personal computers. Moreover, it is not listed by the National Association of Career Consultants. Therefore, the choice is between Gray & Associates and Careers Plus. Because they offer similar services, the deciding factor is costs. Careers Plus would charge $3,400 more for counselling a manager than would Gray & Associates. Although Gray & Associates has fewer computers available, all other elements of its services seem good. Therefore, I recommend that CompuTech hire Gray & Associates as an outplacement agency to counsel discharged employees.

counsel discharged employees and help them find new positions; fees are paid by the former employer. Nora knew that times were bad for CompuTech and that extensive downsizing would take place in the next two years. Her task was to compare outplacement agencies and recommend one to CompuTech.

After collecting information, Nora found that her biggest problem was organizing the data and developing a system for making comparisons. All the outplacement agencies she investigated seemed to offer the same basic package of services.

With the information she gathered about three outplacement agencies, she made a big grid listing the names of the agencies across the top. Down the side she listed general categories—such as services, costs, and reputation. Then she filled in the information for each agency. This grid, which began to look like a table, helped her organize all the pieces of information. After studying the grid, she saw that all the information could be grouped into four categories: counselling services, administrative and research assistance, reputation, and costs. She made these the criteria she would use to compare agencies.

Next, Nora divided her grid into two parts, which became Table 1 and Table 2. In writing the report, she could have made each agency a separate heading, followed by a discussion of how it measured up to the criteria. Immediately, though, she saw how repetitious that would become. Therefore, she used the criteria as headings and discussed how each agency met each criterion—or failed to meet it. Making a recommendation was easy once Nora had made the tables and could see how the agencies compared.

Digital Slide Decks

In addition to using print, many business writers deliver their reports as digital slideshows, also called slide decks. These slides can be sent by e-mail, embedded on websites, or posted on a company intranet. If you research business topics online, look up Internet statistics, or, for example, visit certain WordPress blogs, you may see slide decks or sliders. When used in reporting, slide decks are heavier on text than bulleted presentation slides (see Figure 12.16). However, any text typically appears in small chunks and in large print. Lively, copious photographs and other visuals make slide decks more inviting to read than print pages of dense report text are. See Chapter 14 for a discussion of slide presentations delivered orally.

FIGURE 12.16 Informal Reports Delivered as Slide Decks

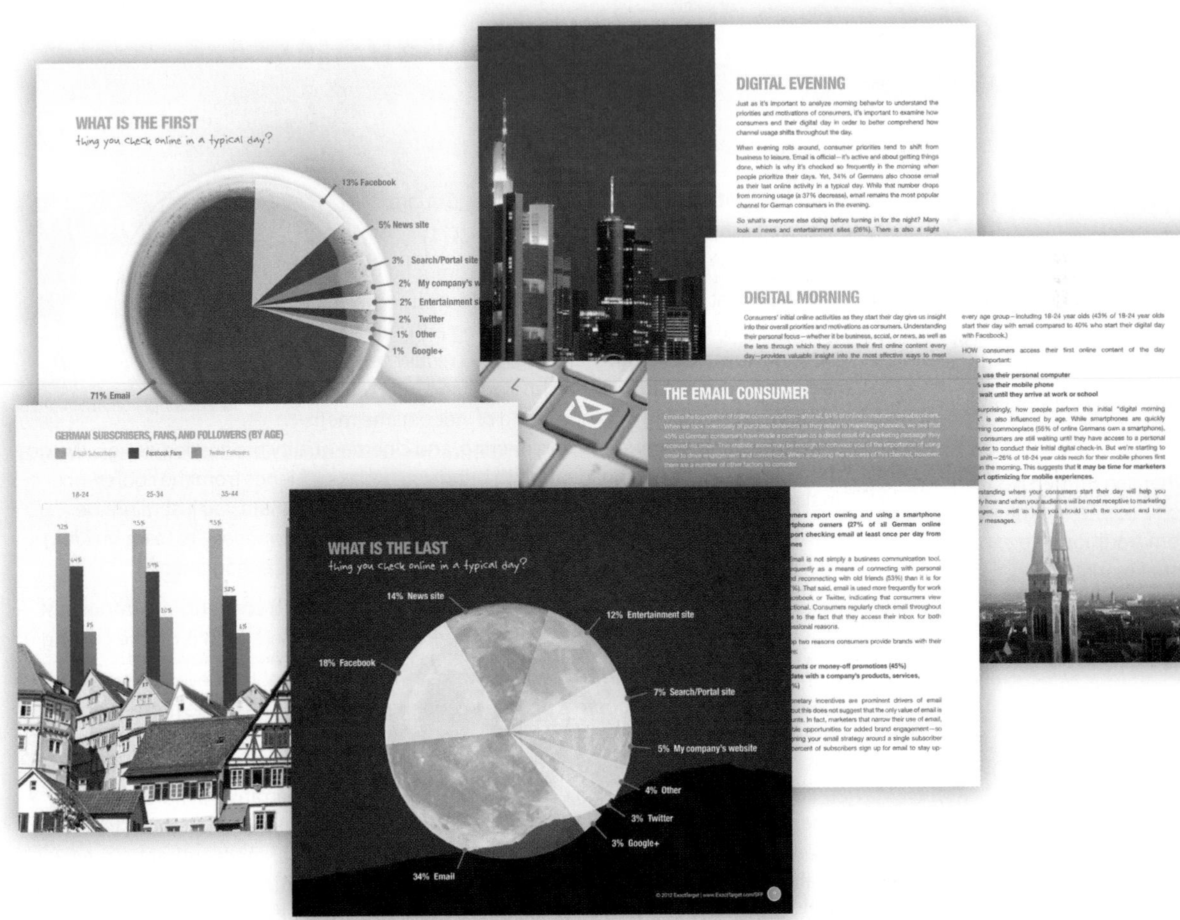

©exacttarget

Source: http://www.exacttarget.com/resource-center/digital-marketing/infographics/sff-german-digital-republic.

CHECKLIST

Writing Analytical Reports

Introduction

- **Identify the purpose of the report.** Explain why the report is being written.
- **Describe the significance of the topic.** Explain why the report is important.
- **Preview the organization of the report.** Especially for long reports, explain how the report will be organized.
- **Summarize the conclusions and recommendations for receptive audiences.** Use the direct strategy only if you have the confidence of the reader.

Findings

- **Discuss pros and cons.** In recommendation/justification reports, evaluate the advantages and disadvantages of each alternative. For unreceptive audiences consider placing the recommended alternative last.
- **Establish criteria to evaluate alternatives.** In yardstick reports, create criteria to use in measuring each alternative consistently.
- **Support the findings with evidence.** Supply facts, statistics, expert opinion, survey data, and other proof from which you can draw logical conclusions.
- **Organize the findings for logic and readability.** Arrange the findings around the alternatives or the reasons leading to the conclusion. Use headings, enumerations, lists, tables, and graphics for emphasis.

Conclusions/Recommendations

- **Draw reasonable conclusions from the findings.** Develop conclusions that answer the research question. Justify the conclusions with highlights from the findings.
- **Make recommendations, if asked.** For multiple recommendations prepare a list. Use action verbs. Explain fully the benefits of the recommendation or steps necessary to solve the problem or answer the question.

SPOTLIGHT ON COMMUNICATION: PART 2

Immersive Tech—Revisited

CRITICAL THINKING

- Regarding gameplay and technology, in what ways are the collection, organization, and distribution of up-to-date information important to Immersive Tech?
- What can Immersive Tech do to accelerate the shift from traditional to experiential marketing?

Courtesy of Fantasy 360 Technologies Inc. dba Immersive Tech

In an interview with James Graham of Victory Square, cofounder Jeff Jang discussed Immersive Tech's philosophy:

> When we introduce Immersive Tech to someone new, we tell them that we live and breathe a philosophy that experiences need to be high impact, engaging and authentic to leave impressions worth sharing. Our creative team is a powerhouse of gameplay, technology, and interaction designers leveraging a unique blend of video game methodologies, amusement park engineering, and cinema-quality production design. We go beyond surface-level engagement to bring you and your friends from the conference hall, board room, or music festival to a bespoke adventure where you just might be the hero to save the world. From product launches, brand awareness, to team building across the world, we've perfected the use of play to drive real engagement.[14]

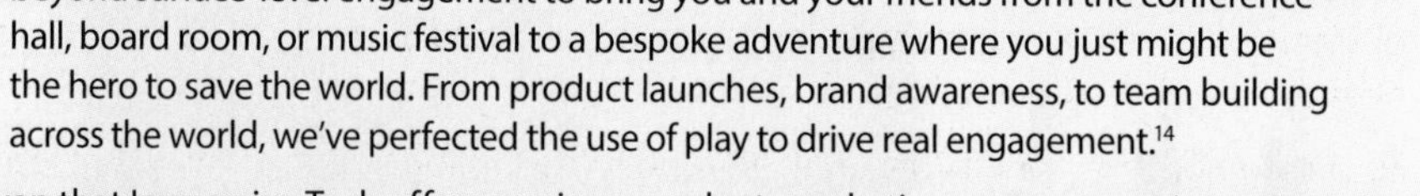

Given that Immersive Tech offers a unique product, marketing concepts are important. As marketing moves from traditional strategies to experiential, Immersive Tech is on the cutting edge:

> Experiential marketing in 2019 and onward is more important than ever as we're beginning to see across the board a decline in engagement with a lot of the more "traditional" marketing channels such as Facebook, Twitter and Youtube. This is especially the case with millennials, with a lot of it feeling very disingenuous and clearly a marketing piece. Engagement through experiences and compelling narrative is more impactful and the only way for brands to leave a lasting impression unique enough to stand out. Working together with your friends to solve a challenge is far more authentic, memorable and impactful than posing with a passive installation, for example. Brands are catching on to this slowly but we want to accelerate that shift even faster.[15]

Concept Check

1. What is the correct sequence for organizing a justification/recommendation report using an indirect strategy?
2. What is the difference between a feasibility report and a yardstick report?

Summary of Learning Objectives

1 Analyze, sort, and interpret statistical data and other information.

- To make sense of report information, writers sort it into tables or analyze it by mean (the arithmetic average), median (the midpoint in a group of figures), and mode (the most frequent response); range represents a span between the highest and lowest figures.
- Grids help organize complex data into rows and columns; a decision matrix, a special grid with weights, assists decision makers in choosing objectively among complex options.
- Writers need to maintain accuracy in applying statistical techniques to gain and maintain credibility with their readers.

2 Draw meaningful conclusions and make practical report recommendations.

- Writers explain what the survey data mean in a conclusion—especially in relation to the original report problem
- Reports that call for recommendations require writers to make specific suggestions for actions that can solve the report problem.
- Recommendations should be feasible, practical, and potentially agreeable to the audience; they should relate to the initial report problem and may be combined with conclusions.

3 Organize report data logically and provide reader cues to aid comprehension.

- Reports may be organized in many ways, including by (a) time (establishing a chronology), (b) component (discussing a problem by geography, division, or product), (c) importance (arranging data from most important to least important, or vice versa), (d) criteria (comparing items by standards), or (e) convention (using an already established grouping).
- To help guide the reader through the text, introductions, transitions, and headings serve as cues.

4 Write short informational reports that describe routine tasks.

- Typical informational reports include periodic, trip, convention, progress, and investigative reports.
- The introduction in informational reports previews the purpose and supplies background data, if necessary.
- The body of an informational report is generally divided into three to five segments that may be organized by time, component, importance, criteria, or convention; clear headings make the body easy to scan. Unless formality is expected, an informal, conversational style is used.

- In the conclusion writers review the main points and discuss actions that will follow; the report may conclude with a final thought, appreciation, or an offer to provide more information.

5 Prepare short analytical reports that solve business problems.

- Typical analytical reports include justification/recommendation reports, feasibility reports, and yardstick reports.
- Justification/recommendation reports may be organized directly or indirectly. They describe a problem, discuss alternative solutions, prove the superiority of one solution, and explain the action to be taken.
- Feasibility reports, generally organized directly, study the advisability of following a course of action.
- Yardstick reports compare two or more solutions to a problem by measuring each against a set of established criteria, thus ensuring consistency.

Chapter Review

1. What type of data is best analyzed by using a grid? (Obj. 1)
2. What are *correlations*? (Obj. 1)
3. How can you make report conclusions more objective? Provide an example. (Obj. 2)
4. What is the difference between conclusions and recommendations, and what do business readers expect from a report writer's recommendations? (Obj. 2)
5. What three devices can report writers use to prevent readers from getting lost in the text? (Obj. 3)
6. Explain three types of report headings, as well as their characteristics and uses. (Obj. 3)
7. Name typical short informational reports and their overall purpose. (Obj. 4)
8. List five tips for designing effective report documents (Obj. 4)
9. When is the indirect pattern appropriate for justification/recommendation reports? (Obj. 5)
10. What are *digital slide decks*, and why are they becoming popular? (Obj. 5)

Critical Thinking

1. How can you take unprocessed data and create meaningful information? (Objs. 1–5)
2. When tabulating and analyzing data, you may discover relationships among two or more variables that help explain the findings. Can you trust these correlations and assume that their relationship is one of cause and effect? Explain. (Obj. 1)
3. How can you increase your chances that your report recommendations will be implemented? (Obj. 2)
4. Why is it important to carefully decide on the direct or indirect strategy when writing a justification/recommendation report? (Obj. 5)
5. **Ethical Issue:** As *The New York Times* reported, "Every day, on average, a scientific paper is retracted because of misconduct." Two percent of scientists are willing to admit that they have manipulated their data to suit their purposes. Considering that researchers publish about 2 million articles each year, 2 percent is not a negligible number.[16] What might motivate such misconduct, and why is it a serious offence? (Obj. 2)

Activities

12.1 Analyzing Survey Results (Obj. 1)

Team

Your business communication class at North Shore College was asked by the college bookstore manager, Jim Duff, to conduct a survey. Concerned about the environment, Duff wants to learn students' reactions to eliminating plastic bags, of which the bookstore gives away 45,000 annually. Students answered questions about a number of proposals, resulting in the following raw data:

For major purchases the bookstore should

	Agree	Undecided	Disagree
1. Continue to provide plastic bags	132	17	411
2. Provide no bags; encourage students to bring their own bags	414	25	121
3. Provide no bags; offer cloth bags at a reduced price (about $3)	357	19	184
4. Give a cloth bag with each major purchase; the cost will be included in registration fees	63	15	482

YOUR TASK In groups of four or five, do the following:

a. Convert the data into a table (see Figure 12.1) with a descriptive title. Arrange the items in a logical sequence.

b. How could these survey data be cross-tabulated? Would cross-tabulation serve any purpose?

c. Given the conditions of this survey, name at least three conclusions that researchers could draw from the data.

d. Prepare three to five recommendations to be submitted to Mr. Duff. How could the bookstore implement them?

e. Role-play a meeting in which the recommendations and implementation plan are presented to Jim Duff. One student plays the role of Duff; the remaining students play the role of the presenters.

12.2 Using a Decision Matrix to Buy a Car (Objs. 1, 2)

Sherveen, an outrigger canoe racer, needs to buy a new car. He wants a vehicle that will carry his disassembled boat and outrigger. At the same time, he will need to travel long distances on business. His passion is soft-top sports cars, but he is also concerned about gas mileage. These four criteria are impossible to find in one vehicle. Sherveen has the following choices:

- Station wagon
- SUV with or without a sunroof
- Four-door sedan, a high-kilometres-per-gallon family car
- Sports car, convertible

He wants to consider the following criteria:

- Price
- Ability to carry cargo such as a canoe
- Fuel efficiency
- Comfort over long distances
- Good looks and fun
- Quality build/manufacturer's reputation

YOUR TASK Follow the steps outlined in Figure 12.3 to determine an assessment scale and to assign a score to each feature. Then, consider which weights are probably most important to Sherveen, given his needs. Calculate the totals to find the vehicle that's most suitable for Sherveen.

12.3 Periodic Report: Keeping the Boss in the Loop (Obj. 4)

E-mail

You work hard at your job, but you rarely see your boss. They have asked to be informed of your activities and accomplishments and any problems you are encountering.

YOUR TASK For a job that you currently hold or a previous one, describe your regular activities, discuss irregular events that management should be aware of, and highlight any special needs or problems you are having. If you don't have a job, communicate to your instructor your weekly or monthly activities as they are tied to your classes, homework, and writing assignments. Establish components or criteria such as those in the bulleted e-mail in Figure 12.10. Use the memo format or write an e-mail report in bullet form, as shown in Figure 12.10. Address the memo or the e-mail report to your boss or, alternatively, to your instructor.

12.4 Progress Report: Providing a Project Update (Obj. 4)

E-mail

If you are writing a long report either for another course or for the long report assignment described in Chapter 13, you will want to keep your instructor informed of your progress.

YOUR TASK Write a progress report informing your instructor of your work. Briefly describe the project (its purpose, scope, limitations, and methodology), work completed, work yet to be completed, problems encountered, future activities, and expected completion date. Address the e-mail report to your instructor. If your instructor allows, try your hand at the bulleted e-mail report introduced in Figure 12.10.

12.5 Informational or Analytical Report: Examining Tweets and Other Social Media Posts (Objs. 4, 5)

E-mail | Social Media | Web

Select a Canadian company that appeals to you and search recent tweets and Facebook posts about it. Soon you will recognize trends and topic clusters that may help you organize the report content by criteria. For example, if you conduct a search using the hashtag #MolsonCoors, you will obtain a huge number of tweets about the company and brand. Many returned tweets will be only marginally interesting because they show up just because #MolsonCoors is mentioned.

> If you explore Facebook, you will mostly find official pages and fan sites, most of which display favourable posts. You would have to look hard to find negative posts, partly also because companies moderate discussions and often remove offensive posts according to their user agreements.

YOUR TASK Write either an informational or an analytical report about the company you chose. In an informational report to your instructor, you could summarize your findings in memo form or as an e-mail. Describe how the tweets about the company are trending. Are they overwhelmingly positive or negative? Organize the report around the subject areas you identify (criteria). Alternatively, you could write an analytical report analyzing the strategies your chosen company adopts in responding to tweets and Facebook posts. Your analytical report would evaluate the organization's social media responses and provide specific examples to support your claims.

12.6 Yardstick Report: Improving Workplace Procedures (Obj. 5)

YOUR TASK Identify a problem or procedure that must be changed at your work or in an organization you know. Consider challenges such as poor scheduling of employees, outdated equipment, slow order processing, failure to encourage employees to participate fully, restrictive rules, inadequate training, or disappointed customers. Consider several solutions or courses of action (retaining the present status could be one alternative). Develop criteria that you could use to evaluate each alternative. Write a report measuring each alternative by the yardstick you have created. Recommend a course of action to your boss or to the organization head.

Grammar and Mechanics | *Review 12*

Total Review

The first ten chapters reviewed specific guides from Appendix B, Grammar and Mechanics Guide, beginning on page B-1. The exercise in this chapter is a total review, covering all the grammar and mechanics guides, plus confusing words and frequently misspelled words. Each of the following sentences has **three** errors in grammar, punctuation, capitalization, usage, or spelling. On a sheet of paper or on your computer, write a correct version. Avoid adding new phrases, starting new sentences, or rewriting in your own words. When you finish, compare your responses with the key in Appendix C.

EXAMPLE: The auditors report, which my boss and myself read very closely, contained three main flaws, factual inaccuracies, omissions, and incomprehensible language.

REVISION: The auditor's report, which my boss and I read very closely, contained three main flaws: factual inaccuracies, omissions, and incomprehensible language.

1. After our supervisor and her returned from their meeting at 2:00 p.m. we were able to sort the customers names more quickly.
2. 6 of the 18 workers in my department were released, as a result we had to work harder to achieve our goals.

3. Toyota, the market-leading japanese carmaker continued to enjoy strong positive ratings despite a string of much publicized recalls.
4. Michaels presentation to a nonprofit group netted him only three hundred dollars, a tenth of his usual honorarium but he believes in pro bono work.
5. To reflect our guiding principals and our commitment to executive education we offer financial support to more than sixty percent of our current MBA candidates.
6. Our latest press release which was written in our Corporate Communication Department announces the opening of three asian offices.
7. In his justification report dated September first, Justin argued that expansion to 12 branch offices could boost annual revenue to 22 million dollars.
8. The practicality and advisability of opening twelve branch offices is what will be discussed in the consultants feasability report.
9. The President, who had went to a meeting in the Midwest, delivered a report to Jeff and I when he returned.
10. Because some organizations prefer single spaced reports be sure to check with your organization to learn it's preference.

Notes

[1] Macmillan Dictionary. (2020). Escape room. In *Macmillan.com dictionary*. Retrieved April 23, 2020, from https://www.macmillandictionary.com/dictionary/british/escape-room

[2] Immersive Tech. (2020). *About us*. https://immersivetech.co/about-us

[3] Ibid.

[4] Fantasy 360 Technologies Inc. dba Immersive Tech. (2019, September 16). *Top 5 reasons you should consider a mobile escape room*. https://immersivetech.co/news/2019/9/15/top-5-reasons-you-should-consider-a-mobile-escape-room. Reprinted courtesy of Fantasy 360 Technologies Inc. dba Immersive Tech.

[5] Immersive Tech. (2020, March 13). *When engagement moves inside—Our top 5 best practices*. https://immersivetech.co/news/2020/3/6/e21ajdllacd28cc8s7xp2r1b4aaqir

[6] Adrian Duke. (2020). *LinkedIn profile*. https://ca.linkedin.com/in/adrianduke

[7] Jeff Jang. (2020). *LinkedIn profile*. https://ca.linkedin.com/in/jeffreyjang

[8] Conference Board of Canada. (2016). *Employability skills 2000+*. http://www.conferenceboard.ca/Libraries/EDUC_PUBLIC/esp2000.sflb

[9] Imagine Canada. (n.d.). *Research and public policy: Corporate citizenship*. http://www.imaginecanada.ca/node/33

[10] Cision. (2019, November 19). *SAIL Outdoors unveils its first distribution centre exclusive to online orders* [Press release]. https://www.newswire.ca/news-releases/sail-outdoors-unveils-its-first-distribution-centre-in-longueuil-805449342.html

[11] Ibid.

[12] Ibid.

[13] CP24 News. (2020, June 5). *Sail to close six stores in Ontario and Quebec, affecting 500 employees*. https://www.cp24.com/news/sail-to-close-six-stores-in-ontario-and-quebec-affecting-500-employees-1.4970501

[14] Graham, J. (2019, May). *In conversation: Jeff Jang of Immersive Tech*. Victory Square. https://victorysquare.com/blog/in-conversation-jeff-jang-of-immersive-tech. Reprinted courtesy of Fantasy 360 Technologies Inc. dba Immersive Tech.

[15] Ibid. Reprinted courtesy of Fantasy 360 Technologies Inc. dba Immersive Tech.

[16] Marcus, A., & Oransky, I. (2015, May 22). What's behind big science frauds? *New York Times*. Retrieved from http://www.nytimes.com/2015/05/23/opinion/whats-behind-bigscience-frauds.html?_r=0

CHAPTER 13

Proposals, Business Plans, and Formal Business Reports

fauxels

LEARNING OBJECTIVES

After studying this chapter, you should be able to

1 Understand the importance and purpose of proposals, and name the basic components of informal proposals.

2 Discuss the components of formal and grant proposals.

3 Identify the components of typical business plans.

4 Describe the components and purpose of the front matter in formal business reports.

5 Understand the body and back matter of formal business reports.

6 Specify final writing tips that aid authors of formal business reports.

SPOTLIGHT ON COMMUNICATION: PART 1

Egale Canada—Fostering Inclusion

Angyalosi Beata/Shutterstock

Egale Canada is an advocacy organization based in Toronto, Ontario. "Egale promotes and fosters the human rights and equitable inclusion of lesbian, gay, bisexual, trans, queer, intersex and Two Spirit (LGBTQI2S) people in community, schools, and work through consultation, programs and services, training & development and community engagement."[1] Egale envisions a world free of oppression, hatred, and bias. Its work aims to transform attitudes—and lives—through awareness to promote inclusion for LGBTQI2S people. Much of this work begins in the workplace:

- 30 percent of LGBTQ employees in Canada report experiencing discrimination in the workplace compared to only 3 percent of non-LGBTQ employees.
- 49 percent of trans people are turned down or suspect they were turned down for a job because they are trans.
- 30 percent of openly LGBTQI2S people leave their workplaces because they feel unwelcome or unsupported by management.
- 92 percent of the top 50 Fortune 500 companies feel that diversity policies (including sexual orientation and gender identity) are good for business.[2]

Egale offers a range of workshops for public, private, and not-for-profit sector workplaces. With a focus on human rights and inclusion, Egale's training reaches all organizational levels to create a safer workplace for every employee.[3]

CRITICAL THINKING

- Organizations like Egale write proposals to generate workshop and training contract opportunities. Given that some companies might be resistant to change, what persuasive strategies could Egale use in the introduction of its proposals to secure contracts?
- In what ways can a well-written grant proposal help nonprofit organizations like Egale? What could Egale detail in the body of a grant proposal to increase its chances for funding? Visit egale.ca to learn more about the organization.

Informal Proposals

LEARNING OBJECTIVE 1

Understand the importance and purpose of proposals, and name the basic components of informal proposals.

Proposals can mean life or death for an organization. Why are they so important? Let's begin by defining what they are. A *proposal* may be defined as a written offer to solve problems, provide services, or sell equipment. Profit-making organizations depend on proposals to compete for business. A well-written proposal can generate millions of dollars of income. Smaller organizations also depend on proposals to sell their products and services. Equally dependent on proposals are many nonprofit organizations. Their funding depends on grant proposals, to be discussed shortly.

Some proposals are internal, often taking the form of justification and recommendation reports. You learned about these persuasive reports in Chapter 12. Most proposals, however, are external and respond to requests for proposals. When government organizations or businesses know exactly what they want, they prepare a *request for proposal* (RFP), specifying their requirements. Government agencies and private businesses use RFPs to solicit competitive bids from vendors. RFPs ensure that bids are comparable and that funds are awarded fairly, using consistent criteria. Several websites, like RFP.ca, provide search engines to locate RFP opportunities in Canada.[4]

Proposals may be further divided into two categories: solicited and unsolicited. Enterprising companies looking for work might submit unsolicited proposals and are watchful for business opportunities. Although many kinds of proposals exist, we'll focus on informal, formal, and grant proposals.

Components of Informal Proposals

Informal proposals may be presented in short (two- to four-page) letters. Sometimes called *letter proposals*, they usually contain six principal components: introduction, background, proposal,

FIGURE 13.1 Components of Informal and Formal Proposals

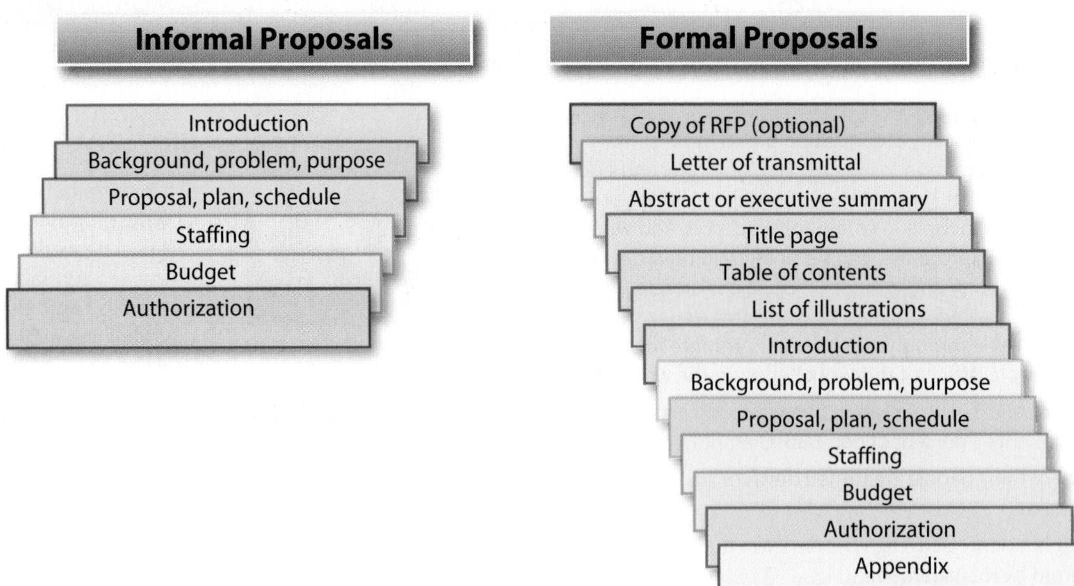

staffing, budget, and authorization request. As you can see in Figure 13.1, both informal and formal proposals contain these six basic parts.

Figure 13.2 illustrates a letter proposal to a dentist who sought to improve patient satisfaction. Notice that this letter proposal contains all six components of an informal proposal.

Introduction. Most proposals begin by briefly explaining the reasons for the proposal and highlighting the writer's qualifications. To make your introduction more persuasive, you should strive to provide a hook, such as the following:

- Hint at extraordinary results with details to be revealed shortly.
- Promise low costs or speedy results.
- Mention a remarkable resource (well-known authority, new computer program, well-trained staff) available exclusively to you.
- Identify a serious problem and promise a solution, to be explained later.
- Specify a key issue or benefit that you feel is the heart of the proposal.

In the proposal introduction shown in Figure 13.2, Ronald Bridger focused on what the customer wanted. The researcher analyzed the request of Toronto dentist Louisa Canto and decided that she was most interested in specific recommendations for improving service to her patients. However, Ronald did not hit on this hook until he had written a first draft and had come back to it later. It's often helpful to put off writing the proposal introduction until after you have completed other parts. In longer proposals the introduction also describes the scope and limitations of the project, as well as outlining the organization of the material to come.

Background, Problem, and Purpose. The background section identifies the problem and discusses the goals or purposes of the project. In an unsolicited proposal, your goal is to convince the reader that a problem exists. Therefore, you must present the problem in detail, discussing such factors as monetary losses, failure to comply with government regulations, or loss of customers. In a solicited proposal, your aim is to persuade the reader that you understand the problem completely. Therefore, if you are responding to an RFP, this means repeating its language. For example, if the RFP asks for the *design of a maintenance program for mobile communication equipment*, you would use the same language in explaining the

FIGURE 13.2 Informal Letter Proposal

1 Prewriting	**2 Drafting**	**3 Revising**
Analyze: The purpose of this letter proposal is to persuade the reader to accept this proposal. **Anticipate:** The reader expects this proposal but must be convinced that this survey project is worth its hefty price. **Adapt:** Because the reader will be resistant at first, use a persuasive approach that emphasizes benefits.	**Research:** Collect data about the reader's practice and other surveys of patient satisfaction. **Organize:** Identify four specific purposes (benefits) of this proposal. Specify the survey plan. Promote the staff, itemize the budget, and ask for approval. **Draft:** Prepare a first draft, expecting to improve it later.	**Edit:** Revise to emphasize benefits. Improve readability with functional headings and lists. Remove jargon and wordiness. **Proofread:** Check spelling of client's name. Verify dates and calculation of budget figures. Recheck all punctuation. **Evaluate:** Is this proposal convincing enough to sell the client?

235-2 Lombard St.
Toronto, ON M5C 1M1
phone 416.457.7332
fax 416.457.8614
email: info@quintileresearch.com

May 30, 2020

Louisa Canto, D.D.S.
400-181 Bay Street
Toronto, ON M5J 2T3

Dear Dr. Canto:

Understanding the views of your patients is the key to meeting their needs. Quintile Research is pleased to propose a plan to help you become even more successful by learning what patients expect of your practice, so that you can improve your services.

[Uses opening paragraph in place of introduction] *[Grabs attention with hook that focuses on key benefit]*

Background and Goals

We know that you have been incorporating a total quality management system in your practice. Although you have every reason to believe that your patients are pleased with your services, you may want to give them an opportunity to discuss what they like and possibly don't like about your office. Specifically, your purposes are to survey your patients to (a) determine the level of their satisfaction with you and your staff, (b) elicit their suggestions for improvement, (c) learn more about how they discovered you, and (d) compare your preferred and standard patients.

[Identifies four purposes of survey]

Proposed Plan

[Announces heart of proposal]

On the basis of our experience in conducting many local and national customer satisfaction surveys, Quintile proposes the following plan:

Survey. We will develop a short but thorough questionnaire probing the data you desire. Although the survey instrument will include both open-ended and close-ended questions, it will concentrate on the latter. Close-ended questions enable respondents to answer easily; they also facilitate systematic data analysis. The questionnaire will gauge patients' views of courtesy, professionalism, billing accuracy, friendliness, and waiting time. After you approve it, the questionnaire will be sent to a carefully selected sample of 300 patients whom you have separated into groupings of preferred and standard.

Analysis. Survey data will be analyzed by demographic segments, such as patient type, age, and gender. Using state-of-the art statistical tools, our team of seasoned experts will study (a) satisfaction levels, (b) the reasons for satisfaction or dissatisfaction, and (c) the responses of your preferred compared to standard patients. Moreover, our team will give you specific suggestions for making patient visits more pleasant.

[Describes procedure for solving problem or achieving goals]

Report. You will receive a final report with the key findings clearly spelled out, Dr. Canto. Our expert staff will draw conclusions based on the results. The report will include tables summarizing all responses, divided into preferred and standard clients.

[Divides total plan into logical segments for easy reading]

(*Continued*)

FIGURE 13.2 (*Continued*)

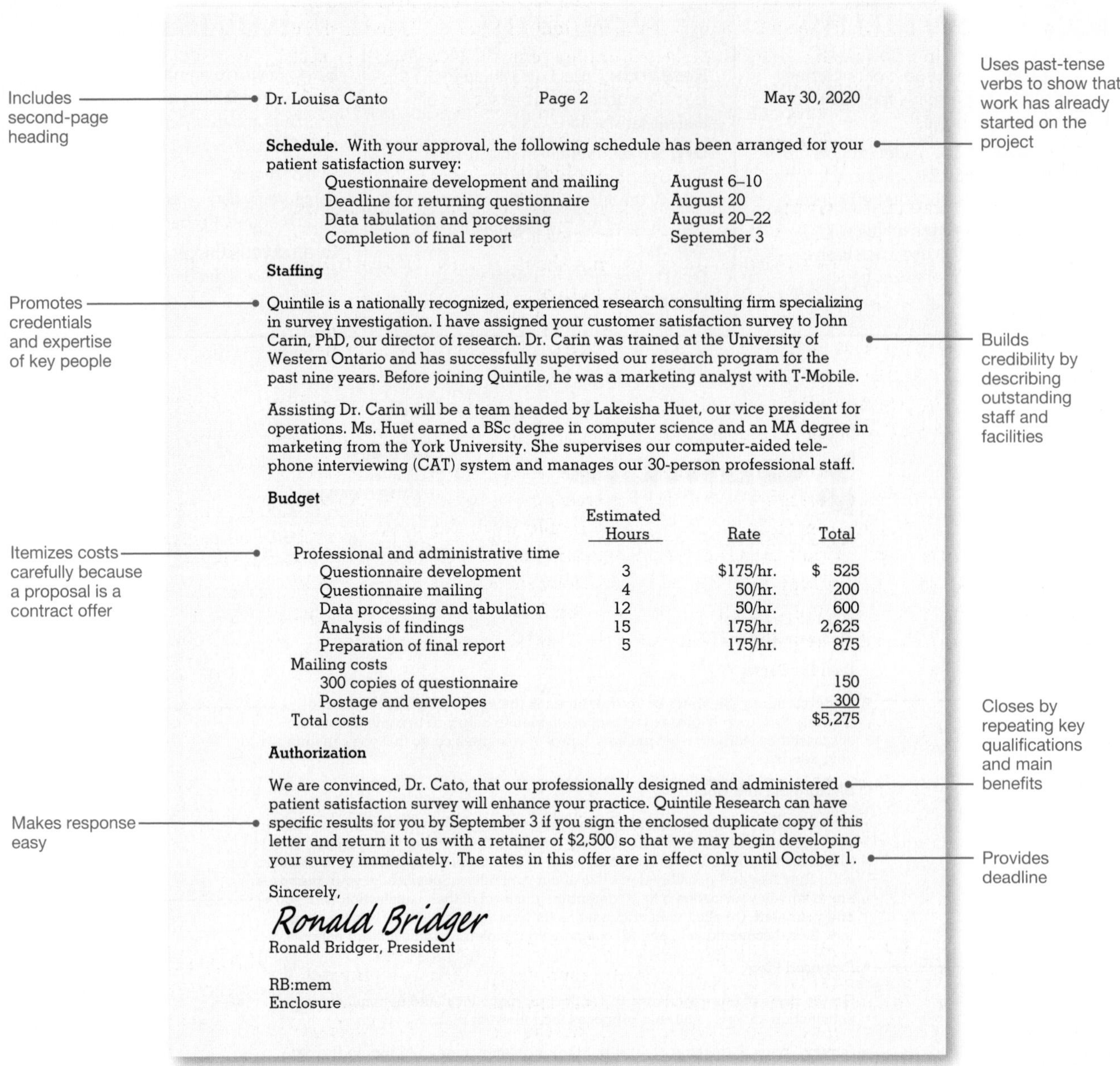
Includes second-page heading
Uses past-tense verbs to show that work has already started on the project
Promotes credentials and expertise of key people
Builds credibility by describing outstanding staff and facilities
Itemizes costs carefully because a proposal is a contract offer
Closes by repeating key qualifications and main benefits
Makes response easy
Provides deadline

Dr. Louisa Canto   Page 2   May 30, 2020

Schedule. With your approval, the following schedule has been arranged for your patient satisfaction survey:

Questionnaire development and mailing	August 6–10
Deadline for returning questionnaire	August 20
Data tabulation and processing	August 20–22
Completion of final report	September 3

Staffing

Quintile is a nationally recognized, experienced research consulting firm specializing in survey investigation. I have assigned your customer satisfaction survey to John Carin, PhD, our director of research. Dr. Carin was trained at the University of Western Ontario and has successfully supervised our research program for the past nine years. Before joining Quintile, he was a marketing analyst with T-Mobile.

Assisting Dr. Carin will be a team headed by Lakeisha Huet, our vice president for operations. Ms. Huet earned a BSc degree in computer science and an MA degree in marketing from the York University. She supervises our computer-aided telephone interviewing (CAT) system and manages our 30-person professional staff.

Budget

	Estimated Hours	Rate	Total
Professional and administrative time			
Questionnaire development	3	$175/hr.	$ 525
Questionnaire mailing	4	50/hr.	200
Data processing and tabulation	12	50/hr.	600
Analysis of findings	15	175/hr.	2,625
Preparation of final report	5	175/hr.	875
Mailing costs			
300 copies of questionnaire			150
Postage and envelopes			300
Total costs			$5,275

Authorization

We are convinced, Dr. Cato, that our professionally designed and administered patient satisfaction survey will enhance your practice. Quintile Research can have specific results for you by September 3 if you sign the enclosed duplicate copy of this letter and return it to us with a retainer of $2,500 so that we may begin developing your survey immediately. The rates in this offer are in effect only until October 1.

Sincerely,

Ronald Bridger

Ronald Bridger, President

RB:mem
Enclosure

purpose of your proposal. This section might include segments titled Basic Requirements, Critical Tasks, or Important Secondary Problems.

Proposal, Plan, and Schedule. In the proposal section itself, you should discuss your plan for solving the problem. In some proposals this is tricky because you want to disclose enough of your plan to secure the contract without giving away so much information that your services aren't needed. Without specifics, though, your proposal has little chance, so you must decide how much to reveal. Tell what you propose to do and how it will benefit the reader. Remember, however, that a proposal is a sales presentation. Sell your methods, product, and *deliverables* (items that will be left with the client). In this section some writers specify how the project will be managed and how its progress will be audited. Most writers also include a schedule of activities or timetable showing when events will take place.

Staffing. The staffing section of a proposal describes the credentials and expertise of the project leaders. It may also identify the size and qualifications of the support staff, along with other resources, such as computer facilities and special programs for analyzing statistics. The staffing section is a good place to endorse and promote your staff and to demonstrate to the client that your company can do the job. Some firms follow industry standards and include staff qualifications in an appendix. They may also feature the résumés of the major project participants, such as the program manager and team leaders. If key contributors must be replaced during the project, the proposal writer may commit to providing only individuals with equivalent qualifications. The first rule is to give clients exactly what they asked for regarding staff qualifications, the number of project participants, and proposal details.

Budget. A central item in most proposals is the budget, a list of proposed project costs. You need to prepare this section carefully because it represents a contract; you cannot raise the price later—even if your costs increase. You can—and should—protect yourself from rising costs with a deadline for acceptance. In the budget section, some writers itemize hours and costs; others present a total sum only. Ronald Bridger felt that he needed to justify the budget for his firm's patient satisfaction survey, so he itemized the costs line by line, as shown in Figure 13.2. However, the budget for a proposal to conduct a one-day seminar to improve employee communication skills might be a lump sum only. Your analysis of the project will help you decide what kind of budget to prepare.

Authorization Request. Informal proposals often close with a request for approval or authorization. In addition, the closing should remind the reader of key benefits and motivate action. It might also include a deadline beyond which the offer is invalid. Authorization information can be as simple as naming in the letter of transmittal the company official who would approve the contract resulting from the proposal. However, in most cases, a *model contract* is sent along that responds to the requirements specified by the RFP. This model contract almost always results in negotiations before the final project contract is awarded.

Check out section 13-2a in MindTap, where you can watch a video featuring Jason Allen John, a mortgage agent, discuss best practices when writing proposals.

Concept Check

1. What are the six common components of informal and formal proposals?
2. How can you make the introduction of a proposal more persuasive? Provide three specific examples.

Preparing Formal Proposals

LEARNING OBJECTIVE 2

Discuss the components of formal and grant proposals.

Formal proposals differ from informal proposals not in style but in size and format. Formal proposals respond to big projects and may range from 5 to 200 or more pages. Because proposals are vital to the success of many organizations, larger businesses may use specialists who do nothing but write proposals. Smaller firms rely on in-house staff to develop proposals. Proposals use standard components that enable companies receiving bids to compare "apples with apples." Writers must know the parts of proposals and how to develop those parts effectively.

Components of Formal Proposals

To help readers understand and locate the parts of a formal proposal, writers organize the project into a typical structure, as shown in Figure 13.1. In addition to the six basic components described for informal proposals, formal proposals may contain some or all of the following front matter and back matter components.

Copy of the RFP. A copy of the request for proposal may be included in the front matter of a formal proposal. Large organizations may have more than one RFP circulating, and identification is necessary.

Letter of Transmittal. A letter of transmittal, usually found inside formal proposals, addresses the person who is designated to receive the proposal or who will make the final decision. The letter describes how you learned about the problem or confirms that the proposal responds to the enclosed RFP. This persuasive letter briefly presents the major features and benefits of your proposal. Here, you should assure the reader that you are authorized to make the bid and mention the time limit for which the bid stands. You may also offer to provide additional information and ask for action, if appropriate.

Abstract or Executive Summary. An abstract is a brief summary (typically one page) of a proposal's highlights intended for specialists or technical readers. An executive summary also reviews the proposal's highlights, but it is written for managers and should be less technically oriented. An executive summary tends to be longer than an abstract, up to 10 percent of the original text. In reports and proposals, the executive summary typically represents a nutshell version of the entire document and addresses all its sections or chapters. Formal proposals may contain either an abstract or an executive summary, or both. For more information about writing executive summaries in formal reports, see the section Writing Formal Business Reports later in the chapter.

Title Page. The title page includes the following items, generally in this order: title of proposal, name of client organization, RFP number or other announcement, date of submission, and the authors' names and the name of their organization.

Table of Contents. Because most proposals do not contain an index, the table of contents becomes quite important. A table of contents should include all headings and their beginning page numbers. Items that appear before the contents (copy of RFP, letter of transmittal, abstract, and title page) typically are not listed in the contents. However, any appendixes should be listed.

List of Illustrations. Proposals with many tables and figures often contain a list of illustrations. This list includes each figure or table title and its page number. If you have just a few figures or tables, however, you may omit this list.

Appendixes. Ancillary material of interest to only some readers goes in appendixes. Appendix A might include résumés of the principal investigators or testimonial letters. Appendix B might include examples or a listing of previous projects. Other appendixes could include audit procedures, technical graphics, or professional papers cited in the body of the proposal.

Grant Proposals

A *grant proposal* is a formal proposal submitted to a government or civilian organization that explains a project, outlines its budget, and requests money in the form of a grant. Every year governments, private foundations, and public corporations make available billions of dollars in funding for special projects. These funds, or grants, require no repayment, but the funds must be used for the purposes outlined in the proposal. Grants are often made to charities, educational facilities, and especially to nonprofits.

Many of the parts of a grant proposal are similar to those of a formal proposal and include the following:

- An abstract and a needs statement that explain a problem or situation that the grant project proposes to address
- A detailed body to explain that the problem is significant enough to warrant funding and that the proposal can solve the problem, as well as short- and long-term goals, which must be reasonable, measurable, and attainable within a specific time frame
- An action plan to explain what will be done by whom and when
- The budget to outline how the money will be spent
- A plan for measuring progress toward completion of its goal

Skilled grant writers are among the most in-demand professionals today. A grant writer is the vital connecting link between a funder and the grant seeker. Large projects may require a team of writers to produce various sections of a grant proposal. Then one person does the final editing and proofreading. Effective grant proposals require careful organization, planning, and

CHECKLIST

Writing Proposals

Introduction

- **Indicate the purpose.** Specify why you are making the proposal.
- **Develop a persuasive hook.** Suggest excellent results, low costs, or exclusive resources. Identify a serious problem or name a key issue or benefit.

Background, Problem, Purpose

- **Provide necessary background.** Discuss the significance of the proposal and the goals or purposes that matter to the client.
- **Introduce the problem.** For unsolicited proposals convince the reader that a problem exists. For solicited proposals show that you fully understand the customer's problem and its ramifications.

Proposal, Plan, Schedule

- **Explain the proposal.** Present your plan for solving the problem or meeting the need.
- **Discuss plan management and evaluation.** If appropriate, tell how the plan will be implemented and evaluated.
- **Outline a timetable.** Furnish a schedule showing what will be done and when.

Staffing

- **Promote the qualifications of your staff.** Explain the specific credentials and expertise of the key personnel for the project.
- **Mention special resources and equipment.** Show how your support staff and resources are superior to those of the competition.

Budget

- **Show project costs.** For most projects, itemize costs. Remember that proposals are contracts.
- **Include a deadline.** Here or in the conclusion, present the date beyond which the bid figures are no longer valid.

Authorization

- **Ask for approval.** Make it easy for the reader to authorize the project (e.g., *Sign and return the duplicate copy*).

writing. Skillful writing is particularly important because funding organizations may receive thousands of applications for a single award.

Well-written proposals win contracts and sustain the business life of many companies, individuals, and nonprofit organizations. The Checklist above summarizes key elements to remember in writing proposals.

Concept Check

1. If you had control over a big company's philanthropic budget, which causes would you support and why? What kind of appeal in a grant proposal would you consider persuasive?
2. Some consulting firms use experienced managers, but they also employ inexperienced, lower-paid staff to lower costs. How would you write the staffing section of a proposal with experienced managers but inexperienced staff?

Creating Effective Business Plans

LEARNING OBJECTIVE 3

Identify the components of typical business plans.

Another form of proposal is a business plan. Let's say you want to start your own business. In most cases, you will need financial backing, such as a bank loan, seed money from an individual angel investor, or funds supplied by venture capitalists. A business plan is critical for securing financial support of any kind. Such a plan also ensures that you have done your homework and know what you are doing in launching your business. It provides you with a detailed strategy for success.

Creating a business plan for an entirely new concept takes time. Estimates range from 100 to 200 hours to research and write a start-up plan.[5] Classic software, such as Business Plan Pro, can help those who have done their research, assembled the relevant data, and just want formatting help. Enloop, a business plan app, makes it quick and easy to provide a financial forecast for bankers and investors.[6] However, business plan apps provide a cookie-cutter plan that doesn't work for everyone.

Components of Typical Business Plans

For people who are serious about starting a business, the importance of a comprehensive, thoughtful business plan cannot be overemphasized. A *business plan* may be defined as a description of a proposed company that explains how it expects to achieve its marketing, financial, and operational goals. The Government of Canada's *Canada Business Network* reinforces the importance of a well-written business plan and provides the following tips:

- A business plan is a valuable tool for every business owner, whether you are starting up, have been in business for years, or are ready to grow.
- Think of your business plan as a sales document. It must convince readers that your venture has the potential to be successful.
- Your enthusiasm, dedication, and confidence in the project should be evident to the reader.
- Know what elements are considered essential in any business plan and the key points that should be included in each section of your plan.[7]

If you are considering becoming an entrepreneur, your business plan is more likely to secure the funds it needs if it is carefully written and includes the following elements.

Letter of Transmittal. A letter of transmittal provides contact information for all principals and explains your reason for writing. If you are seeking venture capital or an angel investor, the transmittal letter may become a pitch letter. In that case you would want to include a simple description of your idea and a clear statement of what's in it for the investor. The letter should include a summary of the market, a brief note about the competition, and an explanation of why your business plan is worthy of investment.

Mission Statement. A business plan mission statement explains the purpose of your business and why it will succeed. Because potential investors will be looking for this mission statement, consider highlighting it with a paragraph heading (*Mission Statement*) or using bolding or italics. Some consultants say that you should be able to write your mission statement in eight or fewer words.[8] Others think that one or two short paragraphs might be more realistic. Regardless, mission statements should be simple, concise, memorable, and unique.

Executive Summary. Your executive summary, which is written last, highlights the main points of your business plan and should not exceed two pages. It should conclude by introducing the parts of the plan and asking for financial backing. Some business plans combine the mission statement and executive summary.

Table of Contents and Company Description. List the page numbers and topics included in your plan. Identify the form of your business (proprietorship, partnership, or corporation) and its type (merchandising, manufacturing, or service). For existing companies, describe the company's founding, growth, sales, and profit.

Product or Service Description. In jargon-free language, explain what you are providing, how it will benefit customers, and why it is better than existing products or services. For start-ups, explain why the business will be profitable. Investors aren't always looking for a unique product or service. Instead, they are searching for a concept whose growth potential distinguishes it from others competing for funds.

Market Analysis. Discuss market characteristics, trends, projected growth, customer behaviour, complementary products and services, and barriers to entry. Identify your customers and how you will attract, hold, and increase your market share. Discuss the strengths and weaknesses of your direct and indirect competitors.

Operations and Management. Explain specifically how you will run your business, including location, equipment, personnel, and management. Highlight experienced and well-trained members of the management team and your advisors. Many investors consider this the most important factor in assessing business potential. Can your management team implement this business plan?

ETHICS CHECK

Honesty Is Key

A business plan's purpose is to help manage a company and raise capital; hence, it is a persuasive document that must be accurate and honest. Whether the goal is to persuade a lender or investors or whether it is the blueprint for running operations, the business plan must be realistic. What are the risks of manipulating numbers or downplaying potential challenges?

Financial Analysis. Outline a realistic start-up budget that includes fees for legal and professional services, occupancy, licences and permits, equipment, insurance, supplies, advertising and promotions, salaries and wages, accounting, income, and utilities. Also present an operating budget that projects costs for personnel, insurance, rent, depreciation, loan payments, salaries, taxes, repairs, and so on. Explain how much money you have, how much you will need to start up, and how much you will need to stay in business.

Appendixes. Provide necessary extras, such as managers' résumés, promotional materials, and product photos. Most appendixes contain tables that exhibit the sales forecast, a personnel plan, anticipated cash flow, profit and loss, and a balance sheet.

Sample Business Plans on the Internet

Writing a business plan is easier if you can see examples and learn from experts' suggestions. On the Internet you will find many sites devoted to business plans. Some sites want to sell you something; others offer free advice. The Canadian government provides a link at https://sbs-spe.feddevontario.canada.ca/en/sample-business-plans-and-templates to sample business plans and templates. A quick Google search will reveal many other sites offering free and pay-for-service advice.

The Business Development Bank of Canada (BDC), a financial institution owned by the Government of Canada, provides financial and consulting services to small and medium-sized Canadian businesses. At the BDC website (www.bdc.ca/en), you will find business plan advice and templates. In addition to suggestions for writing and using a business plan, the BDC site provides tools for self-assessments, continuity planning, and information about marketing and financing. The site provides a wide range of resources and tools for the budding entrepreneur.

Concept Check

1. Why do experts refer to a business plan as a "living document"? Some have said that a business plan needs constant review and adjustment. What might account for such a short shelf life?
2. What information should you include in the Market Analysis section of a business plan?

Writing Formal Business Reports

LEARNING OBJECTIVE 4

Describe the components and purpose of the front matter in formal business reports.

A *formal report* may be defined as a document in which a writer analyzes findings, draws conclusions, and makes recommendations intended to solve a problem. Formal business reports are similar to formal proposals in length, organization, and serious tone. Instead of making an offer, however, formal reports represent the end product of thorough investigation and analysis. They present ordered information to decision makers in business, industry, government, and education. In many ways formal business reports are extended versions of the analytical business reports presented in Chapter 12. If you are preparing a formal business report, be sure to review the work plan that appeared in Chapter 11.

Informal and formal business reports have similar components, as shown in Figure 13.3, but, as you might expect, formal reports have more sections.

Front Matter Components of Formal Business Reports

A number of front matter and back matter items lengthen formal reports but enhance their professional tone and serve their multiple audiences. Formal reports may be read by many levels of managers, along with technical specialists and financial consultants. Therefore, breaking a long, formal report into small segments makes its information more accessible and easier to understand for all readers. The segments in the front of the report, called front matter or preliminaries, are discussed in this section. They are also illustrated in Figure 13.4, the model formal report shown in this chapter. This analytical report studies the economic impact of an industrial park on Winnipeg, Manitoba, and makes recommendations for increasing the city's revenues.

FIGURE 13.3 Components of Informal and Formal Reports

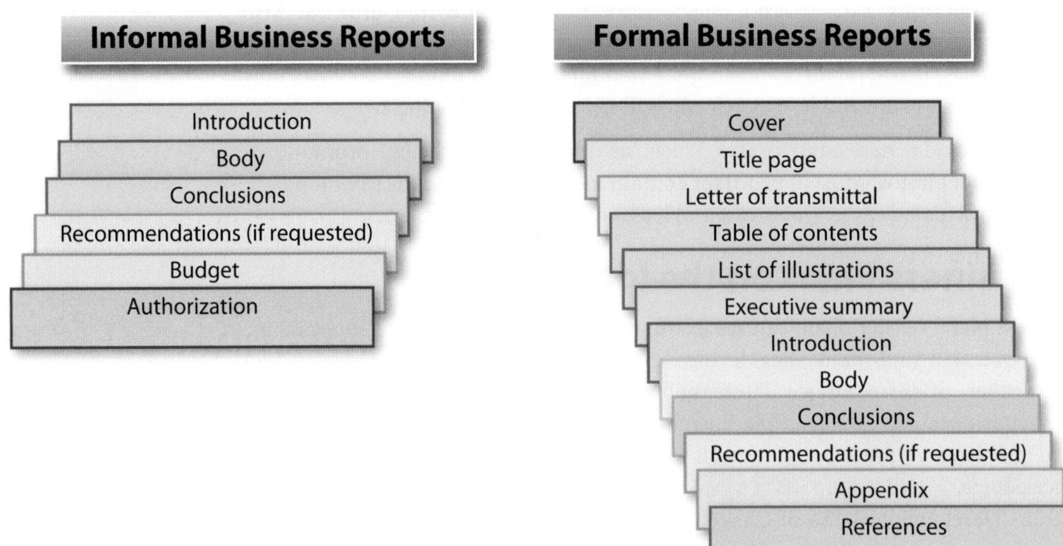

Cover. Traditional formal reports are usually enclosed in vinyl or heavy paper binders to protect the pages and to give a professional, finished appearance. Some companies have binders imprinted with their name and logo. The title of the report may appear through a cut-out window or may be applied with an adhesive label. Electronic formal reports may present an attractive title with the company logo.

Title Page. A report title page, as illustrated in the Figure 13.4 model report, begins with the name of the report typed in uppercase letters (no underscore and no quotation marks). Next comes *Presented to* (or *Submitted to*) and the name, title, and organization of the individual receiving the report. Lower on the page is *Prepared by* (or *Submitted by*) and the author's name plus any necessary identification. The last item on the title page is the date of submission. All items after the title are typed in a combination of upper- and lowercase letters.

Letter or Memo of Transmittal. Generally written on organization stationery, a letter or memorandum of transmittal introduces a formal report. You will recall that letters are sent to outsiders and memos to insiders. A transmittal letter or memo uses the direct strategy and is usually less formal than the report itself (e.g., the letter or memo may use contractions and the first-person pronouns *I* and *we*). The transmittal letter or memo typically (a) announces the topic of the report and tells how it was authorized; (b) briefly describes the project; (c) highlights the report's findings, conclusions, and recommendations, if the reader is expected to be supportive; and (d) closes with appreciation for the assignment, instruction for the reader's follow-up actions, acknowledgement of help from others, or offers of assistance in answering questions. If a report is going to various readers, a special transmittal letter or memo should be prepared for each, anticipating how each reader will use the report.

Table of Contents. The table of contents shows the headings in the report and their page numbers. It gives an overview of the report topics and helps readers locate them. You should wait to prepare the table of contents until after you have completed the report. For short reports you should include all headings. For longer reports you might want to list only first- and second-level headings. Leaders (spaced or unspaced dots) help guide the eye from the heading to the page number. Items may be indented in outline form or typed flush with the left margin.

FIGURE 13.4 Model Formal Report With APA Citation Style

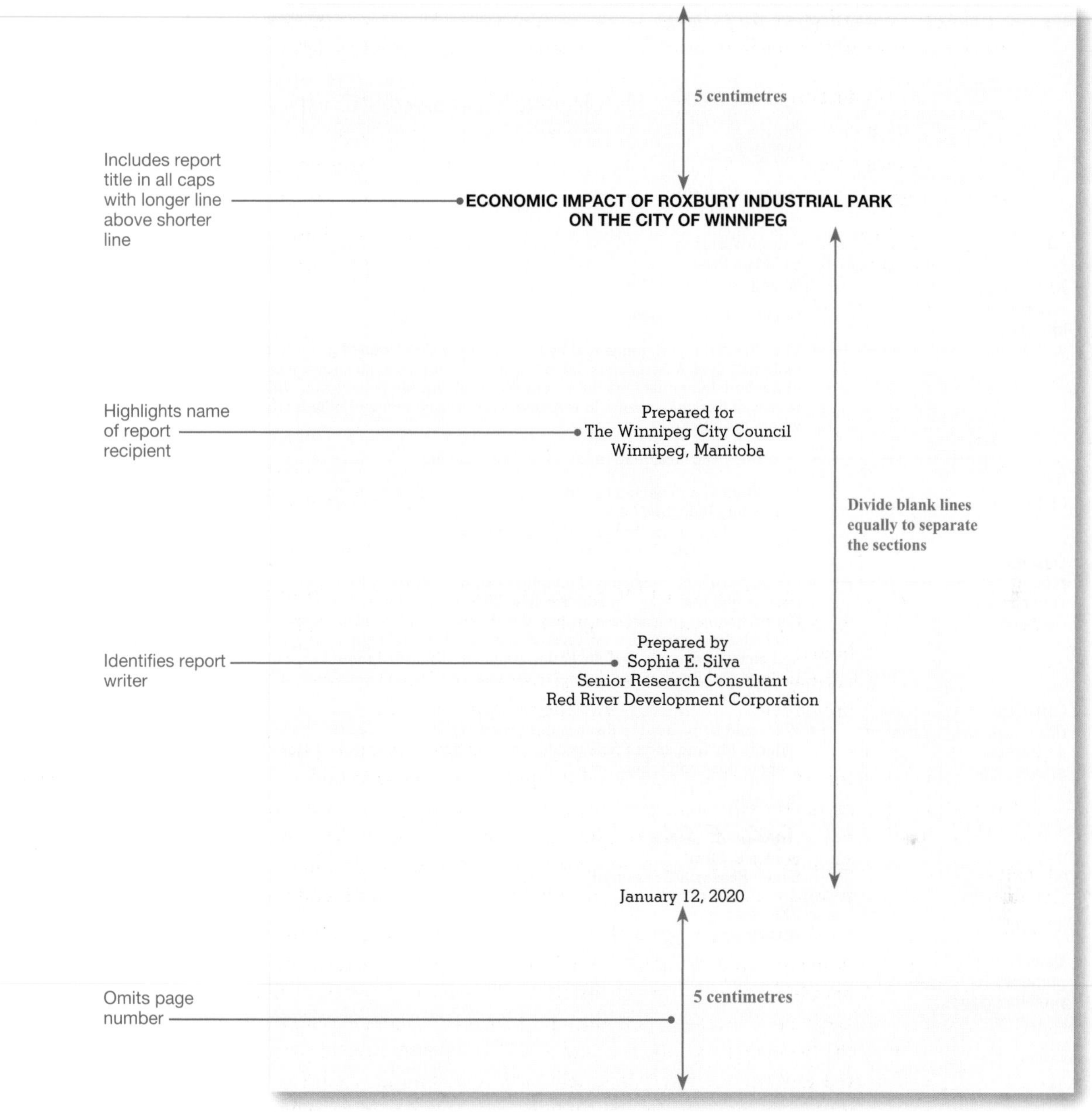

The title page is usually arranged in four evenly balanced areas. If the report is to be bound on the left, move the left margin and centre point 0.5 cm to the right (i.e., set the left margin to 2.5 cm). Notice in this business example that no page number appears on the title page, although it counts as page i. However, the recommended format for APA style includes a running head and page number beginning on the title page.

In designing the title page, be careful to avoid anything unprofessional—such as too many typefaces or fonts, italics, oversized print, and inappropriate graphics. Keep the title page simple and professional. This model report uses APA documentation style. However, it does not use double-spacing, the recommended format for research papers using APA style. Instead, this model uses single-spacing, which saves space and is more appropriate for business reports.

(Continued)

FIGURE 13.4 (*Continued*) Letter of Transmittal

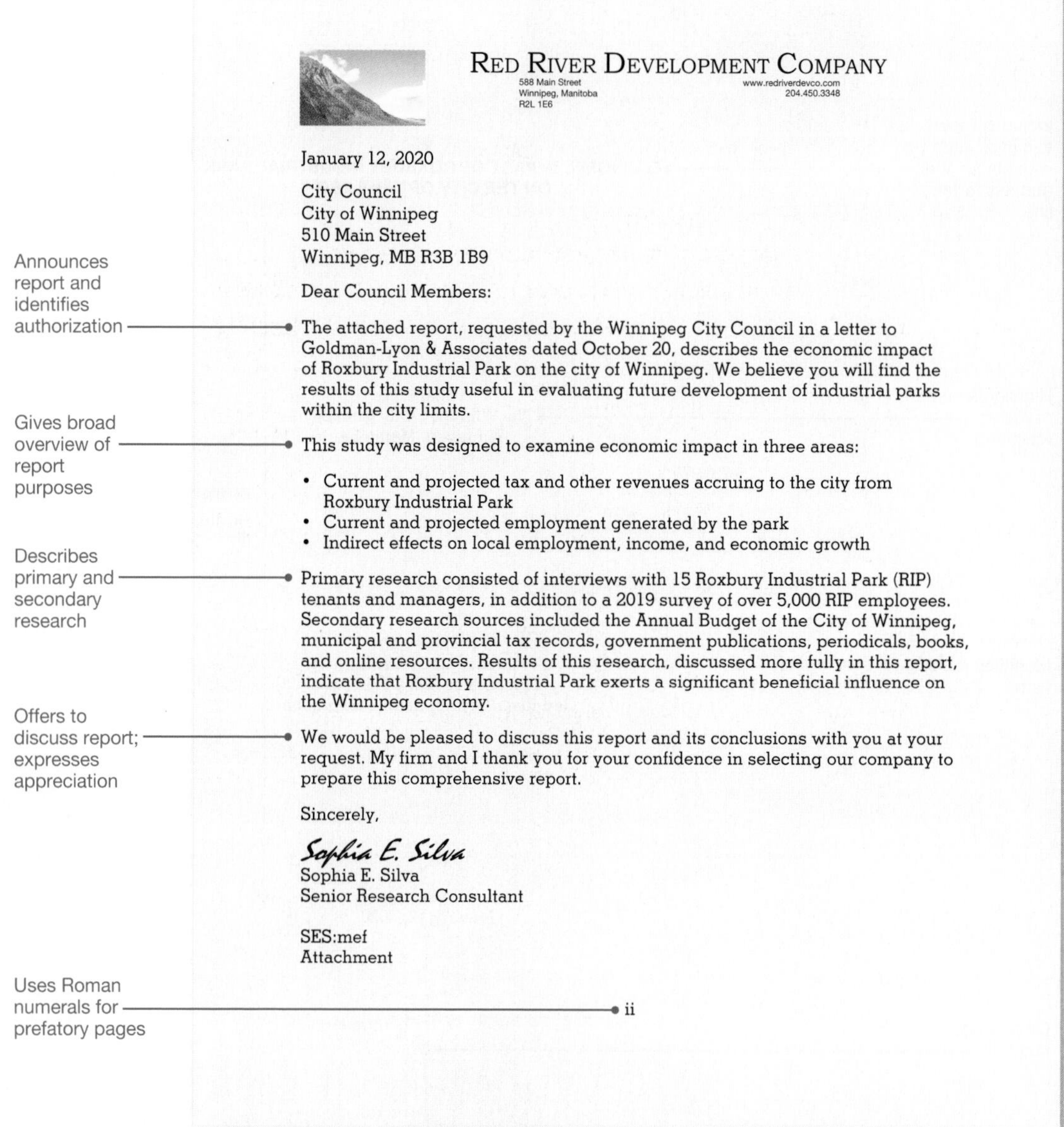

RED RIVER DEVELOPMENT COMPANY
588 Main Street
Winnipeg, Manitoba
R2L 1E6
www.redriverdevco.com
204.450.3348

January 12, 2020

City Council
City of Winnipeg
510 Main Street
Winnipeg, MB R3B 1B9

Dear Council Members:

The attached report, requested by the Winnipeg City Council in a letter to Goldman-Lyon & Associates dated October 20, describes the economic impact of Roxbury Industrial Park on the city of Winnipeg. We believe you will find the results of this study useful in evaluating future development of industrial parks within the city limits.

This study was designed to examine economic impact in three areas:

- Current and projected tax and other revenues accruing to the city from Roxbury Industrial Park
- Current and projected employment generated by the park
- Indirect effects on local employment, income, and economic growth

Primary research consisted of interviews with 15 Roxbury Industrial Park (RIP) tenants and managers, in addition to a 2019 survey of over 5,000 RIP employees. Secondary research sources included the Annual Budget of the City of Winnipeg, municipal and provincial tax records, government publications, periodicals, books, and online resources. Results of this research, discussed more fully in this report, indicate that Roxbury Industrial Park exerts a significant beneficial influence on the Winnipeg economy.

We would be pleased to discuss this report and its conclusions with you at your request. My firm and I thank you for your confidence in selecting our company to prepare this comprehensive report.

Sincerely,

Sophia E. Silva
Sophia E. Silva
Senior Research Consultant

SES:mef
Attachment

ii

A letter or memo of transmittal announces the report topic and explains who authorized it. It briefly describes the project and previews the conclusions, if the reader is supportive. Such messages generally close by expressing appreciation for the assignment, suggesting follow-up actions, acknowledging the help of others, or offering to answer questions. The margins for the transmittal should be the same as for the report, about 2 to 2.5 cm on all sides. The letter should be left-justified. A page number is optional.

(*Continued*)

FIGURE 13.4 (*Continued*) Table of Contents and List of Figures

Uses leaders to guide eye from heading to page number

Indents secondary headings to show levels of outline

Includes tables and figures in one list for simplified numbering

TABLE OF CONTENTS

LIST OF FIGURES

iii

Because the table of contents and the list of figures for this report are small, they are combined on one page. Notice that the titles of major section headings are in all caps, while other headings are a combination of upper- and lowercase letters. This duplicates the style within the report. Advanced word processing capabilities enable you to generate a contents page automatically, including leaders and accurate page numbering—no matter how many times you revise. Notice that the page numbers are right justified. Multiple-digit page numbers must line up properly (say, the number 9 under the 0 of 10).

(*Continued*)

FIGURE 13.4 (*Continued*) Executive Summary

Opens directly with major research findings

Identifies data sources

Summarizes organization of report

Condenses recommendations

EXECUTIVE SUMMARY

The city of Winnipeg can benefit from the development of industrial parks like the Roxbury Industrial Park. Both direct and indirect economic benefits result, as shown by this in-depth study conducted by Red River Development Company. The study was authorized by the Winnipeg City Council when Goldman-Lyon & Associates sought the City Council's approval for the proposed construction of a G-L industrial park. The City Council requested evidence demonstrating that an existing development could actually benefit the city.

Our conclusion that the city of Winnipeg benefits from industrial parks is based on data supplied by a survey of 5,000 Roxbury Industrial Park employees, personal interviews with managers and tenants of RIP, municipal and provincial documents, and professional literature.

Analysis of the data revealed benefits in three areas:

- **Revenues.** The city of Winnipeg earned over $3 million in tax and other revenues from the Roxbury Industrial Park in 2018. By 2025, this income is expected to reach $5.4 million (in constant 2018 dollars).
- **Employment.** In 2019, RIP businesses employed a total of 7,035 workers, who earned an average wage of $56,579. By 2025, RIP businesses are expected to employ directly nearly 15,000 employees who will earn salaries totaling over $998 million.
- **Indirect benefits.** Because of the multiplier effect, by 2025, Roxbury Industrial Park will directly and indirectly generate a total of 38,362 jobs in the Winnipeg metropolitan area.

On the basis of these findings, it is recommended that development of additional industrial parks be encouraged to stimulate local economic growth. The city would increase its tax revenues significantly, create much-needed jobs, and thus help stimulate the local economy in and around Winnipeg.

iv

For readers who want a quick overview of the report, the executive summary presents its most important elements. Executive summaries focus on the information the reader requires for making a decision related to the issues discussed in the report. The summary may include some or all of the following elements: purpose, scope, research methods, findings, conclusions, and recommendations. Its length depends on the report it summarizes. A 100-page report might require a 10-page summary. Shorter reports may contain one-page summaries, as shown here. Unlike letters of transmittal (which may contain personal pronouns and references to the writer), the executive summary of a long report is formal and impersonal. It uses the same margins as the body of the report. See the discussion of executive summaries in this chapter.

(*Continued*)

FIGURE 13.4 (*Continued*) Page 1

Uses a bulleted list for clarity and ease of reading

Lists three problem questions

Describes authorization for report and background of study

Includes APA citation with author name and date

INTRODUCTION: ROXBURY AND THE LOCAL ECONOMY

This study was designed to analyze the direct and indirect economic impact of Roxbury Industrial Park on the city of Winnipeg. Specifically, the study seeks answers to these questions:

- What current tax and other revenues result directly from this park? What tax and other revenues may be expected in the future?
- How many and what kinds of jobs are directly attributable to the park? What is the employment picture for the future?
- What indirect effects has Roxbury Industrial Park had on local employment, incomes, and economic growth?

BACKGROUND: THE ROLE OF RIP IN COMMERCIAL DEVELOPMENT

The development firm of Goldman-Lyon & Associates commissioned this study of Roxbury Industrial Park at the request of the Winnipeg City Council. Before authorizing the development of a proposed Goldman-Lyon industrial park, the city council requested a study examining the economic effects of an existing park. Members of the city council wanted to determine to what extent industrial parks benefit the local community, and they chose Roxbury Industrial Park as an example.

For those who are unfamiliar with it, Roxbury Industrial Park is a 400-acre industrial park located in the city of Winnipeg about 6.5 kilometres from the centre of the city. Most of the land lies within a specially designated area known as Redevelopment Project No. 2, which is under the jurisdiction of the Winnipeg Redevelopment Agency. Planning for the park began in 2004; construction started in 2006.

The original goal for Roxbury Industrial Park was development for light industrial users. Land in this area was zoned for uses such as warehousing, research and development, and distribution. Like other communities, Winnipeg was eager to attract light industrial users because such businesses tend to employ a highly educated workforce, are relatively quiet, and do not pollute the environment (Cohen, 2019). The city of Winnipeg recognized the need for light industrial users and widened an adjacent highway to accommodate trucks and facilitate travel by workers and customers coming from Winnipeg.

1

Titles for major parts of a report are centred in all caps. In this model document we show several combination headings. As the name suggests, combination heads are a mix of functional headings, such as *INTRODUCTION*, *BACKGROUND*, *DISCUSSION*, and *CONCLUSIONS*, and talking heads that reveal the content. Most business reports would use talking heads or a combination, such as *FINDINGS REVEAL REVENUE,* and *EMPLOYMENT BENEFITS*. First-level headings (such as *Revenues* on page 2) are printed with bold upper- and lowercase letters. Second-level headings (such as *Distribution* on page 3) begin at the side, are bolded, and are written in upper- and lowercase letters. See Figure 12.8 for an illustration of heading formats.

(*Continued*)

FIGURE 13.4 (*Continued*) Page 2

The park now contains 14 building complexes with over 1.25 million square feet of completed building space. The majority of the buildings are used for office, research and development, marketing and distribution, or manufacturing uses. Approximately 20 hectares of the original area are yet to be developed.

Provides specifics for data sources

Data for this report came from a 2019 survey of over 5,000 Roxbury Industrial Park employees; interviews with 15 RIP tenants and managers; the annual budget of the city of Winnipeg; municipal and provincial tax records; and current books, articles, journals, and online resources. Projections for future revenues resulted from analysis of past trends and "Estimates of Revenues for Debt Service Coverage, Redevelopment Project Area 2" (Miller, 2018, p. 79).

Uses combination heads

DISCUSSION: REVENUES, EMPLOYMENT, AND INDIRECT BENEFITS

Previews organization of report

The results of this research indicate that major direct and indirect benefits have accrued to the city of Winnipeg and surrounding areas as a result of the development of Roxbury Industrial Park. The research findings presented here fall into three categories: (a) revenues, (b) employment, and (c) indirect benefits.

Revenues

Roxbury Industrial Park contributes a variety of tax and other revenues to the city of Winnipeg, as summarized in Figure 1. Current revenues are shown, along with projections to the year 2027. At a time when the economy is unstable, revenues from an industrial park such as Roxbury can become a reliable income stream for the city of Winnipeg.

Places figure close to textual reference

Figure 1

REVENUES RECEIVED BY THE CITY OF WINNIPEG
FROM ROXBURY INDUSTRIAL PARK

Current Revenues and Projections to 2027

	2018	2027
Sales and use taxes	$1,966,021	$3,604,500
Revenues from licences	532,802	962,410
Franchise taxes	195,682	220,424
Provincial gas tax receipts	159,420	211,134
Licences and permits	86,213	201,413
Other revenues	75,180	206,020
Total	$3,015,318	$5,405,901

Source: City of Winnipeg Chief Financial Officer. *2018 Annual Financial Report*. Winnipeg: City Printing Office, 2019, p. 12.

2

Notice that this formal report is single-spaced. Many businesses prefer this space-saving format. However, some organizations prefer double-spacing, especially for preliminary drafts. If you single-space, do not indent paragraphs. If you double-space, do indent the paragraphs. Page numbers may be centred 2.5 cm from the bottom of the page or placed 2.5 cm from the upper right corner at the margin. Your word processor can insert page numbers automatically. Strive to leave a minimum of 2.5 cm for top, bottom, and side margins. References follow the parenthetical citation style (or in-text citation style) of the American Psychological Association (APA). Notice that the author's last name, the year of publication, and the page number appear in parentheses. The complete bibliographic entry for any in-text citation appears at the end of the report in the references section.

(*Continued*)

FIGURE 13.4 (*Continued*) Page 3

Sales and Use Revenues

Continues interpreting figures in table

As shown in Figure 1, the city's largest source of revenues from RIP is the sales and use tax. Revenues from this source totaled $1,966,021 in 2018, according to figures provided by the City of Winnipeg Chief Financial Officer (2019, p. 28). Sales and use taxes accounted for more than half of the park's total contribution to the total income of $3,015,318.

Other Revenues

Other major sources of city revenues from RIP in 2018 include alcohol licences, motor vehicle in lieu fees, trailer coach licences ($532,802), franchise taxes ($195,682), and provincial gas tax receipts ($159,420). Although not shown in Figure 1, other revenues may be expected from the development of recently acquired property. The Canadian Economic Development Administration has approved a grant worth $975,000 to assist in expanding the current park eastward on an undeveloped parcel purchased last year. Revenues from leasing this property may be sizable.

Projections

Includes ample description of electronic reference

Total city revenues from RIP will nearly double by 2027, producing an income of $5.4 million. This estimate is based on an annual growth rate of 0.65 percent, as projected by Statistics Canada.

Employment

Sets stage for next topic to be discussed

One of the most important factors to consider in the overall effect of an industrial park is employment. In Roxbury Industrial Park the distribution, number, and wages of people employed will change considerably in the next six years.

Distribution

A total of 7,035 employees currently work in various industry groups at Roxbury Industrial Park. The distribution of employees is shown in Figure 2. The largest number of workers (58 percent) is employed in manufacturing and assembly operations. The next largest category, computer and electronics, employs 24 percent of the workers. Some overlap probably exists because electronics assembly could be included in either group. Employees also work in publishing (9 percent), warehousing and storage (5 percent), and other industries (4 percent).

Although the distribution of employees at Roxbury Industrial Park shows a wide range of employment categories, it must be noted that other industrial parks would likely generate an entirely different range of job categories.

3

Only the most important research findings are interpreted and discussed for readers. The depth of discussion depends on the intended length of the report, the goal of the writer, and the expectations of the reader. Because the writer wants this report to be formal in tone, she avoids *I* and *we* in all discussions.

As you type a report, avoid widows and orphans (ending a page with the first line of a paragraph or carrying a single line of a paragraph to a new page). Strive to start and end pages with at least two lines of a paragraph, even if a slightly larger bottom margin results.

(*Continued*)

FIGURE 13.4 (*Continued*) Page 4

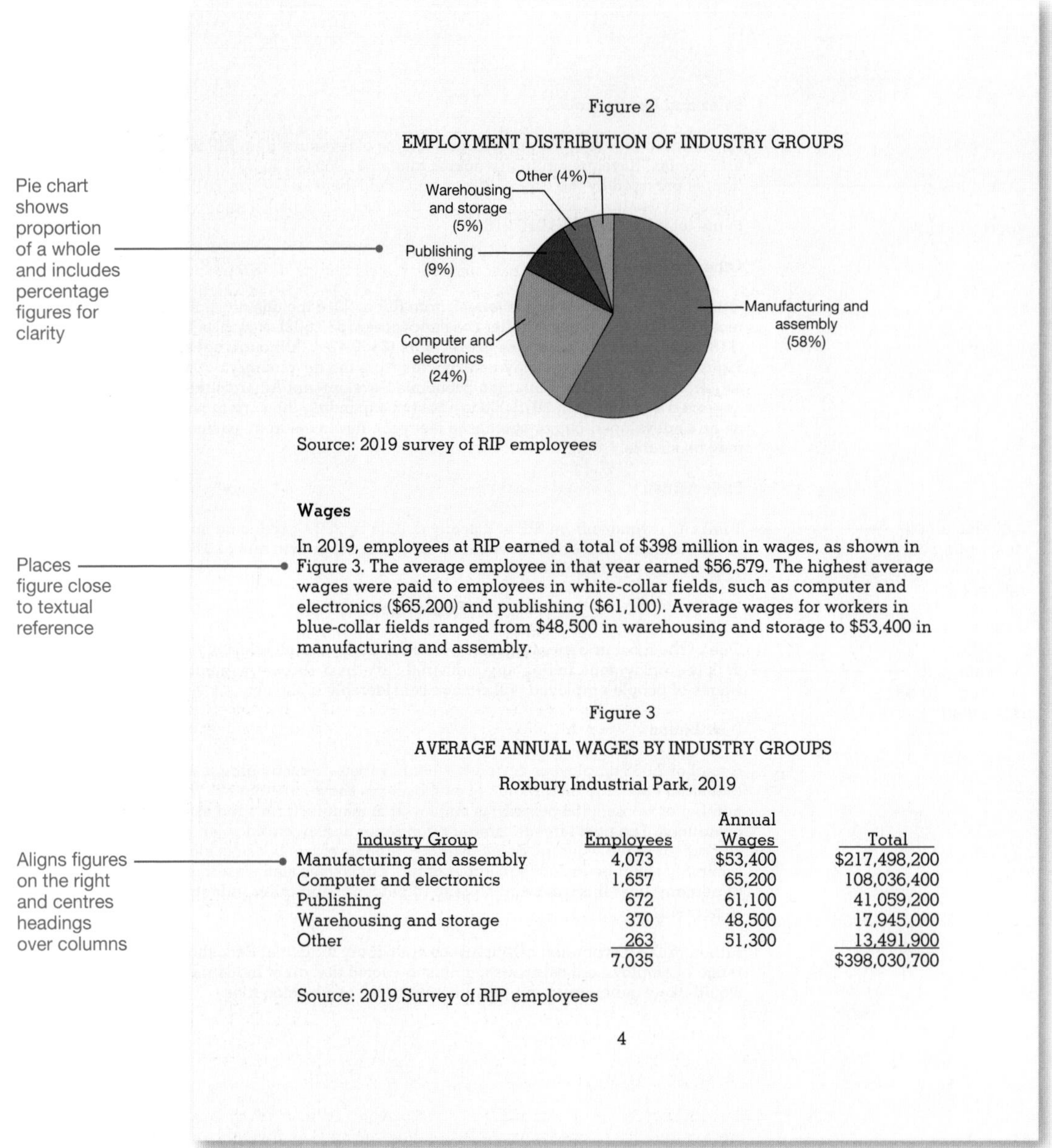
Pie chart shows proportion of a whole and includes percentage figures for clarity
Places figure close to textual reference
Aligns figures on the right and centres headings over columns

Figure 2

EMPLOYMENT DISTRIBUTION OF INDUSTRY GROUPS

Other (4%)
Warehousing and storage (5%)
Publishing (9%)
Computer and electronics (24%)
Manufacturing and assembly (58%)

Source: 2019 survey of RIP employees

Wages

In 2019, employees at RIP earned a total of $398 million in wages, as shown in Figure 3. The average employee in that year earned $56,579. The highest average wages were paid to employees in white-collar fields, such as computer and electronics ($65,200) and publishing ($61,100). Average wages for workers in blue-collar fields ranged from $48,500 in warehousing and storage to $53,400 in manufacturing and assembly.

Figure 3

AVERAGE ANNUAL WAGES BY INDUSTRY GROUPS

Roxbury Industrial Park, 2019

Industry Group	Employees	Annual Wages	Total
Manufacturing and assembly	4,073	$53,400	$217,498,200
Computer and electronics	1,657	65,200	108,036,400
Publishing	672	61,100	41,059,200
Warehousing and storage	370	48,500	17,945,000
Other	263	51,300	13,491,900
	7,035		$398,030,700

Source: 2019 Survey of RIP employees

4

If you use figures or tables, be sure to introduce them in the text (e.g., *as shown in Figure 3*). Although it is not always possible, try to place them close to the spot where they are first mentioned. To save space, you can print the title of a figure at its side. Because this report contains few tables and figures, the writer named them all "Figures" and numbered them consecutively. Graphics that serve for reference only and aren't discussed in the text belong in the appendix.

(*Continued*)

FIGURE 13.4 (*Continued*) Page 5

Clarifies information and tells what it means in relation to original research questions

Projections

By 2027 Roxbury Industrial Park is expected to more than double its number of employees, bringing the total to over 15,000 workers. The total payroll in 2027 will also more than double, producing over $998 million (using constant 2018 dollars) in salaries to RIP employees. These projections are based on a 9 percent growth rate (Miller, 2018, p. 78), along with anticipated increased employment as the park reaches its capacity.

Future development in the park will influence employment and payrolls. One RIP project manager stated in an interview that much of the remaining 50 acres is planned for medium-rise office buildings, garden offices, and other structures for commercial, professional, and personal services (I. M. Novak, personal communication, November 30, 2019). Average wages for employees are expected to increase because of an anticipated shift to higher-paying white-collar jobs. Industrial parks often follow a similar pattern of evolution (Badri, Rivera, & Kusak, 2016, p. 41). Like many industrial parks, RIP evolved from a warehousing centre into a manufacturing complex.

CONCLUSIONS

Analysis of tax revenues, employment data, personal interviews, and professional literature leads to the following conclusions and recommendations about the economic impact of Roxbury Industrial Park on the city of Winnipeg:

Uses a numbered list for clarity and ease of reading

1. Sales tax and other revenues produced over $3 million in income to the city of Winnipeg in 2018. By 2027 sales tax and other revenues are expected to produce $5.4 million in city income.
2. RIP currently employs 7,035 employees, the majority of whom are working in manufacturing and assembly. The average employee in 2019 earned $56,579.
3. By 2027, RIP is expected to employ more than 15,000 workers producing a total payroll of over $998 million.
4. Employment trends indicate that by 2027 more RIP employees will be engaged in higher-paying white-collar positions.

RECOMMENDATIONS

On the basis of these findings, we recommend that the City Council Winnipeg authorize the development of additional industrial parks to stimulate local economic growth. The direct and indirect benefits of Roxbury Industrial Park strongly suggest that future commercial development would have a positive impact on the Winnipeg community and the surrounding region as population growth and resulting greater purchasing power would trigger higher demand.

As the Roxbury example shows, gains in tax revenue, job creation, and other direct and indirect benefits would follow the creation of additional industrial parks in and around Winnipeg.

5

After discussing and interpreting the research findings, the writer articulates what she considers the most important conclusions and recommendations.

(*Continued*)

FIGURE 13.4 (*Continued*) References

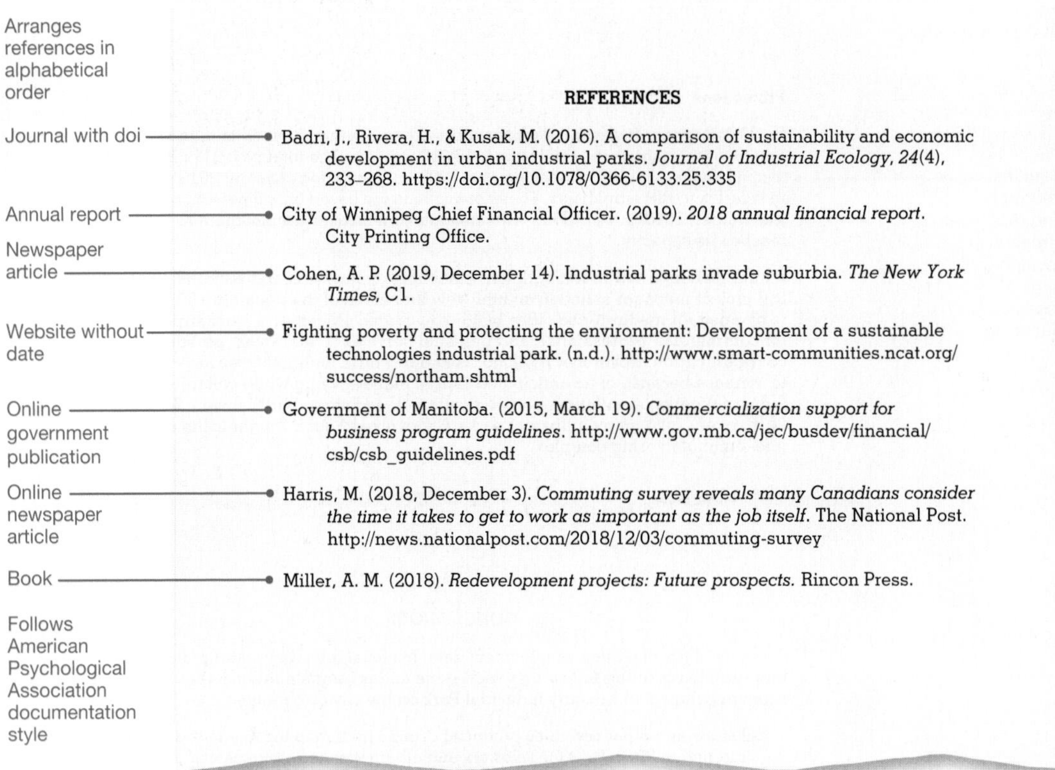

REFERENCES

Badri, J., Rivera, H., & Kusak, M. (2016). A comparison of sustainability and economic development in urban industrial parks. *Journal of Industrial Ecology, 24*(4), 233–268. https://doi.org/10.1078/0366-6133.25.335

City of Winnipeg Chief Financial Officer. (2019). *2018 annual financial report.* City Printing Office.

Cohen, A. P. (2019, December 14). Industrial parks invade suburbia. *The New York Times,* C1.

Fighting poverty and protecting the environment: Development of a sustainable technologies industrial park. (n.d.). http://www.smart-communities.ncat.org/success/northam.shtml

Government of Manitoba. (2015, March 19). *Commercialization support for business program guidelines.* http://www.gov.mb.ca/jec/busdev/financial/csb/csb_guidelines.pdf

Harris, M. (2018, December 3). *Commuting survey reveals many Canadians consider the time it takes to get to work as important as the job itself.* The National Post. http://news.nationalpost.com/2018/12/03/commuting-survey

Miller, A. M. (2018). *Redevelopment projects: Future prospects.* Rincon Press.

On this page the writer lists all references cited in the text, as well as others that she examined during her research. The writer lists these citations following the APA referencing style. Notice that all entries are arranged alphabetically. Book and periodical titles are italicized. When referring to online items, she shows the full name of the citation and then identifies the URL. This references page is shown with single-spacing, which is preferable for business reports. However, APA style recommends double-spacing for research reports, including the references page. APA style also shows "References" in upper- and lowercase letters. However, the writer preferred to use all caps to be consistent with other headings in this business report.

List of Illustrations. For reports with several figures or tables, you may want to include a list to help readers locate them. This list may appear on the same page as the table of contents, space permitting. For each figure or table, include a title and page number. Some writers distinguish between tables and all other illustrations, which they call figures. If you make the distinction, you should prepare separate lists of tables and figures. Because the model report in Figure 13.4 has few illustrations, the writer labelled them all *figures*, a method that simplifies numbering.

Executive Summary. The purpose of an executive summary is to present an overview of a longer report to people who may not have time to read the entire document. Generally, an executive summary is prepared by the author of the report. However, occasionally you may be asked to write an executive summary of a published report or article written by someone else. In either case, your goal will be to summarize the important points. The best way to prepare an executive summary is to do the following:

- **Look for strategic words and sentences.** Read the completed report carefully. Pay special attention to the first and last sentences of paragraphs, which often contain summary statements. Look for words that enumerate (*first, next, finally*) and words that express causation (*therefore, as a result*). Also, look for words that signal essentials (*basically, central, leading, principal, major*) and words that contrast ideas (*however, consequently*).

- **Prepare an outline with headings.** At a minimum, include headings for the purpose, findings, and conclusions/recommendations. What kernels of information would your reader want to know about these topics?
- **Fill in your outline.** Some writers cut and paste important parts of the text. Then they condense with careful editing. Others find it more efficient to create new sentences as they prepare the executive summary.
- **Begin with the purpose.** The easiest way to begin an executive summary is with the words *The purpose of this report is to* . . . . Experienced writers may be more creative.
- **Follow the report sequence.** Present all your information in the order in which it is found in the report.
- **Eliminate nonessential details.** Include only main points. Do not include anything not in the original report. Use minimal technical language.
- **Control the length.** An executive summary is usually no longer than 10 percent of the original document. Thus, a 100-page report might require a 10-page summary. A 10-page report might need only a 1-page summary—or no summary at all. The executive summary for a long report may also include graphics to adequately highlight main points.

To see a representative executive summary, look at Figure 13.4. Although it is only one page long, this executive summary includes headings to help the reader see the main divisions immediately. Let your organization's practices guide you in determining the length and format of an executive summary.

Introduction. Formal reports begin with an introduction that sets the scene and announces the subject. Because they contain many parts that serve different purposes, formal reports are somewhat redundant. The same information may be included in the letter of transmittal, summary, and introduction. To avoid sounding repetitious, try to present the data slightly differently. However, do not skip the introduction because you have included some of its information elsewhere. You cannot be sure that your reader saw the information earlier. A good report introduction typically covers the following elements, although not necessarily in this order:

- **Background.** Describe events leading up to the problem or need.
- **Problem or purpose.** Explain the report topic and specify the problem or need that motivated the report.
- **Significance.** Tell why the topic is important. You may want to quote experts or cite newspapers, journals, books, online resources, and other secondary sources to establish the importance of the topic.
- **Scope.** Clarify the boundaries of the report, defining what will be included or excluded.
- **Organization.** Orient readers by giving them a road map that previews the structure of the report.

Beyond these minimal introductory elements, consider adding any of the following information that may be relevant to your readers:

- **Authorization.** Identify who commissioned the report. If no letter of transmittal is included, also tell why, when, by whom, and to whom the report was written.
- **Literature review.** Summarize what other authors and researchers have published on this topic, especially for academic and scientific reports.
- **Sources and methods.** Describe your secondary sources (periodicals, books, databases). Also explain how you collected primary data, including the survey size, sample design, and statistical programs you used.
- **Definitions of key terms.** Define words that may be unfamiliar to the audience. Also define terms with special meanings, such as *small businesses* if it refers to a specific number of employees.

CASE CONNECTIONS

NWT Brewing Company

Courtesy of NWT Brewing Company

Located in Yellowknife, NWT Brewing Company is the only microbrewery in the Northwest Territories. In addition to its 500 mL bottled beer, the brewery offers refillable growler jugs and kegs of various sizes.[9]

In January 2014, Fletcher and Miranda quit their fulltime jobs to become business owners. With Fletcher as Brewmaster and Miranda as General Manager, the two make up the heart of NWT Brewing Company and Woodyard Brewhouse and Eatery. The two paved their way through an untapped industry in the far North that posed many challenges but . . . local beer was eventually flowing in Yellowknife.

Within the first year of operation, their crowd-pleasing beer, Kicksled Cream Ale, won a bronze medal at the Canadian Brewing awards landing the NWT on the Canadian beer map. The Woodyard Brewhouse & Eatery has not only become a pillar in the Yellowknife community but was named one of the top 50 bars in Canada in 2018. Fletcher hopes to continue the success of the business and looks forward to expanding operations in the near future with a larger, second brewing facility.[10]

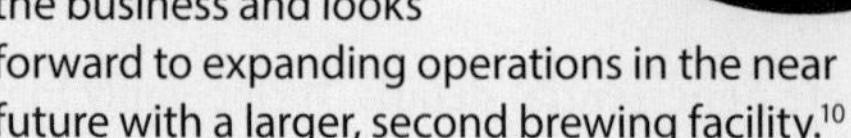

For these new business owners, operations haven't always been easy. In 2018, when their equipment supplier went into receivership, NWT Brewing Co. lost a sizable investment. They persevered, however, and focused their sites on future growth.[11]

- As NWT Brewing Co. gets ready to expand, how can an effective business plan help the company to reach its goals? Because it is already an established business, what components of the business plan should the owners give extra attention to?

Concept Check

1. Discuss the pros and cons of the following two methods for completing the outline of the executive summary of a formal report: (a) cutting and pasting existing report sentences, or (b) creating new sentences.
2. What is the purpose of a letter or memo of transmittal in a formal business report?

LEARNING OBJECTIVE 5

Understand the body and back matter of formal business reports.

Body and Back Matter Components of Formal Business Reports

The body of a formal business report is the longest and most substantive section of the text. The author or team discusses the problem and findings before reaching conclusions and making recommendations. Extensive and bulky materials that don't fit in the text belong in the appendix. Although some very long reports may have additional components, the back matter usually concludes with a list of sources. The body and back matter of formal business reports are discussed in this section. Look back to Figure 13.3, which shows the parts of typical reports, the order in which they appear, and the elements usually found only in formal reports.

Because formal business reports can be long and complex, they usually include more sections than routine informal business reports do. These components are standard and conventional; that is, the audience expects to see them in a professional report. Documents that conform to such expectations are easier to read and deliver their message more effectively. You will find most of the components addressed here in the model report in Figure 13.4, the formal analytical report studying the economic impact of an industrial park on Winnipeg, Manitoba.

Body

The principal section in a formal report is the body. It discusses, analyzes, interprets, and evaluates the research findings or solution to the initial problem. This is where you show the evidence that justifies your conclusions. Organize the body into main categories following your original outline or using one of the organizational methods described in Chapter 12 (i.e., time, component, importance, criteria, or convention).

Although we refer to this section as the body, it does not carry that heading. Instead, it contains clear headings that explain each major section. Headings may be functional, talking, or a combination, as discussed in Chapter 12. The model report in Figure 13.4 uses combination headings that divide the body into smaller parts.

Conclusions

This important section tells what the findings mean, particularly in terms of solving the original problem. Some writers prefer to intermix their conclusions with the analysis of the findings—instead of presenting the conclusions separately. Other writers place the conclusions before the body so that busy readers can examine the significant information immediately. Still others combine the conclusions and recommendations. Most writers, though, present the conclusions after the body because readers expect this structure. In long reports this section may include a summary of the findings. To improve comprehension, you may present the conclusions in a numbered or bulleted list. See Chapter 12 for more suggestions on drawing conclusions.

Recommendations

When asked, you should submit recommendations that make precise suggestions for actions to solve the report problem. Recommendations are most helpful when they are practical, reasonable, feasible, and ethical. Naturally, they should evolve from the findings and conclusions. Do not introduce new information in the conclusions or recommendations sections. As with conclusions, the position of recommendations is somewhat flexible. They may be combined with conclusions, or they may be presented before the body, especially when the audience is eager and supportive. Generally, though, in formal reports they come last.

Recommendations require an appropriate introductory sentence, such as *The findings and conclusions in this study support the following recommendations.* When making many recommendations, you can number them and phrase each as a command, such as *Begin an employee fitness program with a workout room available five days a week*, or present them in a paragraph. If appropriate, add information describing how to implement each recommendation. Some reports include a timetable describing the who, what, when, where, why, and how for putting each recommendation into operation. Chapter 12 provides more information about writing recommendations.

Appendixes

Incidental or supporting materials belong in appendixes at the end of a formal report. These materials are relevant to some readers but not to all. They may also be too bulky to include in the text. Appendixes may include survey forms, copies of other reports, tables of data, large graphics, and related correspondence.

If multiple appendixes are necessary, they are named Appendix A, Appendix B, and so forth.

Works Cited or References

If you use the MLA (Modern Language Association) referencing format, list all sources of information alphabetically in a section titled *Works Cited.* If you use the APA (American Psychological Association) format, your list is called *References.* Your listed sources must correspond to in-text citations in the report whenever you are borrowing words or ideas from published and unpublished resources.

ETHICS CHECK

Cheater on the Team

If one of your teammates cowriting a formal report with you has been found to have plagiarized a portion of your writing project, typically the instructor will punish the entire group, assuming ownership by the entire team. After all, researchers are expected to deliver a product that they have jointly prepared. Is this fair? Explain.

CHECKLIST

Preparing Formal Business Reports: Report Process

- **Analyze the report and purpose.** Develop a problem question (*Could expanded development of the Roxbury Industrial Park benefit the City of Winnipeg?*) and a purpose statement (*The purpose of this report is to investigate the expansion of Roxbury Industrial Park and possible benefits accruing to the City of Winnipeg in the area of revenues, employment, and other indirect benefits*).
- **Anticipate the audience and issues.** Consider primary and secondary audiences. What do they already know? What do they need to know? Divide the major problem into subproblems for investigation.
- **Prepare a work plan.** Include problem and purpose statements, as well as a description of the sources and methods of collecting data. Prepare a tentative project outline and work schedule with anticipated dates of completion for all segments of the project.
- **Collect data.** Begin by searching secondary sources for information on your topic. Then, if necessary, gather primary data.
- **Document data sources.** When saving files from business databases or the Internet, be sure to record the complete publication information. Prepare electronic folders or note cards citing all references (author, date, source, page, and quotation). Select a documentation format and use it consistently.
- **Interpret and organize the data.** Arrange the collected information in tables, grids, or outlines to help you visualize relationships and interpret meanings. Organize the data into an outline.
- **Prepare graphics.** Make tables, charts, graphs, and illustrations—but only if they serve a function. Use graphics to help clarify, condense, simplify, or emphasize your data.
- **Compose the first draft.** Type the first draft from your outline. Use appropriate headings and transitional expressions to guide the reader through the report.
- **Revise and proofread.** Revise to eliminate wordiness, ambiguity, and redundancy. Look for ways to improve readability, such as bulleted or numbered lists. Proofread three times for (a) word and content meaning; (b) grammar, punctuation, and usage errors; and (c) formatting.
- **Evaluate the final product.** Will it achieve its purpose? Encourage feedback so that you can learn how to improve future reports.

Regardless of the documentation format, you must include the author, title, publication, date of publication, page number, and other significant data for all ideas or quotations used in your report. For electronic references include the preceding information plus the Internet address or URL leading to the citation. For model electronic and other citations, examine the list of references at the end of Figure 13.4. Note that double-spacing is used in academic papers, assignments, and unpublished manuscripts for the ease of reading and to allow for feedback. However, double-spacing is unnecessary in completed work reports, as shown in Figure 13.4. Appendix A contains additional documentation models and information.

Concept Check

1. What materials might you include as appendixes in a formal business report?
2. Before writing a work plan, what are the first two steps in preparing a formal business report? Why are these steps crucial to the report writing process?

LEARNING OBJECTIVE 6

Specify final writing tips that aid authors of formal business reports.

Final Writing Tips

Formal business reports are not undertaken lightly. They involve considerable effort in all three phases of writing, beginning with analysis of the problem and anticipation of the audience (as discussed in Chapter 4). Researching the data, organizing it into a logical presentation, and composing the first draft (Chapter 5) make up the second phase of writing. Editing, proofreading, and evaluating (Chapter 6) are completed in the third phase. Although everyone approaches the writing process somewhat differently, the following tips offer advice in problem areas faced by most writers of formal reports:

- **Allow sufficient time.** Develop a realistic timetable and stick to it.
- **Finish data collection.** Do not begin writing until you have collected all the data and drawn the primary conclusions. For reports based on survey data, complete the tables and figures first.
- **Work from a good outline.** A big project, such as a formal report, needs the order and direction provided by a clear outline, even if the outline has to be revised as the project unfolds.
- **Back up your work often.** Save your document frequently and keep backup copies on disks or other devices. Print out important materials so that you have a hard copy. Take these precautions to guard against the grief caused by lost files, power outages, and computer malfunctions.
- **Save difficult sections.** If some sections are harder to write than others, save them until you have developed confidence and a rhythm from working on easier topics.
- **Use bias-free language.** Use bias-free language to "avoid perpetuating prejudicial beliefs or demeaning attitudes" in your writing.[12] Instead, use specific language that avoids generalizations about "age, disability, gender, participation in research, race and ethnicity, sexual orientation, socioeconomic status, and intersectionality."[13] Review Chapter 4 for more on bias-free language and visit https://apastyle.apa.org/ for more examples.
- **Be consistent in verb tense.** Use past-tense verbs to describe completed actions (e.g., *the respondents said* or *the survey showed*). Use present-tense verbs, however, to explain current actions (*the purpose of the report is, this report examines, the table shows*). When citing references, use past-tense verbs (*Jones reported that*). Do not switch back and forth between present- and past-tense verbs in describing related data.
- **Generally avoid *I* and *we*.** To make formal reports seem as objective and credible as possible, most writers omit first-person pronouns. This formal style sometimes results in the overuse of passive-voice verbs (e.g., *periodicals were consulted* and *the study was conducted*). Look for alternative constructions (*periodicals indicated* and *the study revealed*). It is also possible that your organization may allow first-person pronouns, so check before starting your report.
- **Let the first draft sit.** After completing the first version, put it aside for a day or two. Return to it with the expectation of revising and improving it. Do not be afraid to make major changes.
- **Revise for clarity, coherence, and conciseness.** Read a printed copy out loud. Do the sentences make sense? Do the ideas flow together naturally? Can wordiness be cut? Make sure that your writing is so clear that a busy manager does not have to reread any part.
- **Proofread the final copy three times.** First, read a printed copy slowly for word meanings and content. Then read the copy again for spelling, punctuation, grammar, and other mechanical errors. Finally, scan the entire report to check its formatting and consistency (page numbering, indenting, spacing, headings, and so forth).

Putting It All Together

Formal reports in business generally aim to study problems and recommend solutions. Sophia Silva, senior research consultant with Red Rock Development Company, was asked to study the economic impact of a local industrial park on the City of Winnipeg, Manitoba, resulting in the formal report shown in Figure 13.4.

As shown in Figure 13.4, the Winnipeg City Council hired consultants to evaluate Roxbury Industrial Park and to assess whether future commercial development would stimulate further

CHECKLIST

Preparing Formal Business Reports: Report Components

- **Title page.** Balance the following lines on the title page: (a) name of the report (in all caps); (b) name, title, and organization of the individual receiving the report; (c) author's name, title, and organization; and (d) date submitted.
- **Letter of transmittal.** Announce the report topic and explain who authorized it. Briefly describe the project and preview the conclusions, if the reader is supportive. Close by expressing appreciation for the assignment, suggesting follow-up actions, acknowledging the help of others, or offering to answer questions.
- **Table of contents.** Show the page number where each report heading appears in the report. Connect the page numbers and headings with leaders (spaced dots) using your word processing software. The major headings in a report parts are in all caps, and other headings are a combination of upper- and lowercase letters.
- **List of illustrations.** Include a list of tables, illustrations, or figures showing the title of the item and its page number. If space permits, put these lists on the same page as the table of contents. The title of this section should reflect what is listed; for example, if you have tables and figures or illustrations, list them separately and title the section *List of Illustrations*. If you have chosen to refer to tables and graphics as figures, title the section *List of Figures*.
- **Executive summary.** Summarize the report purpose, findings, conclusions, and recommendations. Gauge the length of the summary by the length of the report and by your organization's practices.
- **Introduction.** Explain the problem motivating the report; describe its background and significance. Clarify the scope and limitations of the report. Optional items include a review of the relevant literature and a description of data sources, methods, and key terms. Close by previewing the report's organization.
- **Body.** Discuss, analyze, and interpret the research findings or the proposed solution to the problem. Arrange the findings in logical segments following your outline. Use clear, descriptive headings. Major section headings appear in all caps.
- **Conclusions and recommendations.** Explain what the findings mean in relation to the original problem. If requested, make recommendations that suggest actions for solving the problem. Conclusions and recommendations may be enumerated or explained in paragraphs, as appropriate for the report.
- **Appendixes.** Include items of interest to some, but not all, readers, such as questionnaires, transcripts of interviews, data sheets, and other information that is not essential to explain your findings, but that supports your analysis. Add large graphics—pictures, maps, figures—that are not discussed directly in the text.
- **Works cited or references.** If footnotes are not provided in the text, list all references in a section called *Works Cited* or *References*.

economic growth. Sophia Silva subdivided the economic impact into three aspects: Revenues, Employment, and Indirect Benefits. The report was compiled from survey data and from secondary sources that Sophia consulted.

Sophia's report illustrates many of the points discussed in this chapter. Although it is a good example of the typical report format and style, it should not be viewed as the only way to present a report. Wide variation exists in business and academic reports.

The Checklist above summarizes the report components in one handy list.

Concept Check

1. When composing a title page for a formal business report, what are four unprofessional design elements to avoid?
2. How many times should you proofread a formal business report, and what should you be proofreading for each time?

SPOTLIGHT ON COMMUNICATION: PART 2

Egale Revisited

LightField Studios/Shutterstock

As part of its mission, Egale invests in supporting the aging LGBTQI2S population. Seniors are "vulnerable to multiple and intersecting forms of discrimination based on age, including abuse, abandonment, negligence, mistreatment and violence because of their sexual orientation, gender identity, diverse bodies and/or physical characteristics."[14] Egale's studies have found the following:

- 52 percent of LGBTQI2S seniors fear being forced back into the closet in residential care.
- 53 percent of older LGBTQI2S seniors feel isolated.
- 40 percent of LGBTQI2S seniors have not disclosed their sexual orientation or gender identity to their primary healthcare provider because of the fear of discrimination.
- 80 percent of LGBTQI2S seniors are interested in LGBTQI2S-friendly housing.[15]

To gather information about seniors' experiences and to identify issues, Egale hosted a LGBTQI2S Seniors Knowledge Sharing Forum in Toronto, as well as online consultations and individual interviews. The information gathered will help with advocacy and building resources for seniors.[16]

CRITICAL THINKING

- Imagine that you work at an assisted living residence for seniors. You've identified that there is a need to overhaul the living space to make it inclusive for LGBTQI2S residents. You will need to convince the owner to make these changes. What component of the formal business reports will be most important and why?
- For this formal report, why is it important to have a works cited or references page?

Summary of Learning Objectives

1 Understand the importance and purpose of proposals, and name the basic components of informal proposals.

- Proposals are important to organizations because they generate business or funding.
- A *proposal* is a written offer to solve problems, provide services, or sell equipment; requests for proposals (RFPs) specify what a proposal should include.
- Standard parts of informal proposals include (a) a persuasive introduction explaining the purpose of the proposal; (b) background identifying the problem and project goals; (c) a proposal, plan, or schedule outlining the project; (d) a section describing staff qualifications; (e) expected costs; and (f) a request for approval or authorization.

2 Discuss the components of formal and grant proposals.

- Formal proposals may include additional parts not found in informal proposals: (a) a copy of the RFP (request for proposals); (b) a letter of transmittal; (c) an abstract or executive summary; (d) a title page; (e) a table of contents; (f) a list of illustrations; and (g) an appendix.
- A *grant proposal* is a formal document submitted to a government agency or funding organization that explains a project, outlines its budget, and requests grant money that requires no repayment.
- Grants are made to charities, educational facilities, and especially to nonprofits.

3 Identify the components of typical business plans.

- A business plan describes a proposed business and explains how it expects to achieve its marketing, financial, and operational goals.

- Typical business plans include a letter of transmittal, a mission statement, an executive summary, a table of contents, a company description, a product or service description, market analysis, a description of operations and management, financial analysis, and appendixes.
- Startup businesses seeking financial backing must pay particular attention to the product or service description, as well as to the operations and management analyses. Startups must prove growth potential and present a team capable of implementing the business plan.

4 Describe the components and purpose of the front matter in formal business reports.

- In a formal report, the author analyzes findings, draws conclusions, and makes recommendations intended to solve a problem.
- The front matter may include a cover, a title page, a letter or memo of transmittal, a table of contents, a list of illustrations, and an executive summary that explains key points.
- In the introduction the writer typically discusses the significance, scope, and organization of the report, as well as its authorization, relevant literature, sources, methods of research, and definitions of key terms.

5 Understand the body and back matter of formal business reports.

- The body of the report discusses, analyzes, interprets, and evaluates the research findings or solution to a problem.
- The conclusion states what the findings mean and how they relate to the report's purpose.
- The recommendations explain how to solve the report problem.
- The last portions of a formal report are the appendixes and references or works cited.

6 Specify final writing tips that aid authors of formal business reports.

- Before writing, develop a realistic timetable and collect all the necessary data.
- While writing, work from a good outline, and use the features of your computer wisely.
- As you write, use verb tenses consistently, use bias-free language, and generally avoid *I* and *we*
- After completing the first draft, wait a few days before you edit to improve clarity, coherence, and conciseness; proofread the final copy three times.

Chapter Review

1. What is the difference between solicited and unsolicited proposals? (Objs. 1, 2)
2. Why do government agencies make requests for proposals (RFPs)? (Objs. 1, 2)
3. Why does an entrepreneur need to write a business plan? (Obj. 3)
4. What should a business plan mission statement include and how long should it be? (Obj. 3)
5. Name eight components of a typical business plan. (Obj. 3)
6. Why are formal reports written in business? Give an original example of a business-related formal report. (Obj. 4)
7. How long should a typical executive summary be? (Obj. 4)
8. What should the writer strive to do in the body of a formal business report? (Obj. 5)
9. What is the purpose of references or works cited? (Obj. 5)
10. In your view what are six of the most important tips for the writer of a formal report? Explain each of your choices. (Obj. 6)

Critical Thinking

1. In what ways is a proposal similar to a persuasive sales message? (Obj. 1)
2. Which category of proposal, solicited or unsolicited, is more likely to succeed and why? (Obj. 1)
3. If you were about to launch a new business, would you write your business plan from scratch or use a software program to do it? What are the pros and cons of each method? (Obj. 3)
4. Some people say that business reports shouldn't contain footnotes. If you were writing your first business report and did considerable research, what would you do about documenting your sources? (Obj. 5)
5. **Ethical Issue:** Is it ethical for a student team to substantially revise a report from a team that wrote about the same topic during the previous semester? What does your school say about such a practice? (Objs. 2, 4)

Activities

13.1 Proposal: What Workplace Problem Deserves Serious Investigation? (Obj. 1)

The ability to spot problems before they turn into serious risks is prized by most managers. Draw on your internship and work experience. Can you identify a problem that could be solved with a small to moderate financial investment? Look for issues such as missing lunch or break rooms for staff; badly needed health initiatives, such as gyms or sport club memberships; low-gas-mileage, high-emission company vehicles; or a lack of recycling efforts.

YOUR TASK Discuss with your instructor the workplace problem that you have identified. Make sure you choose a relatively weighty problem that can be lessened or eliminated with a minor expenditure. Be sure to include a cost–benefit analysis. Address your unsolicited letter or memo proposal to your current or former boss and copy your instructor.

13.2 Business Plan: Would You Survive the Shark Tank? (Obj. 3)

Team | Web

Business plans at many schools are more than classroom writing exercises. They have won regional, national, and worldwide prizes. Although some contests are part of MBA programs, other contests are available for undergraduates. As part of a business plan project, you and your team are challenged to come up with an idea for a new business or service. For example, you might want to offer a lunch service with fresh sandwiches or salads delivered to office workers' desks. You might propose building a better website for an organization. You might want to start a document preparation business that offers production, editing, and printing services. You might have a terrific idea for an existing business to expand with a new product or service.

YOUR TASK Working in teams, explore entrepreneurial ventures based on your experience and expertise. Conduct team meetings to decide on a product or service, develop a work plan, assign responsibilities, and create a schedule. Your goal is to write a business plan that will convince potential investors (sometimes your own management) that you have an excellent business idea and that you can pull it off. Check out sample business plans online. The two deliverables from your project will be your written business plan and an oral presentation. Your written plan should include a cover, transmittal document (letter or memo), title page, table of contents, executive summary, proposal (including introduction, body, and conclusion), appendix items, glossary (optional), and sources. In the body of the document, be sure to explain your mission and vision, the market, your marketing strategy, operations, and financials. Address your business plan to your instructor.

13.3 Service Learning: Write Away! (Objs. 1, 2, 4, 5)

E-mail | Web

Your school may be one that encourages service learning, a form of experiential learning. You could receive credit for a project that bridges academic and nonacademic communities. Because writing skills are in wide demand, you may have an opportunity to simultaneously apply your skills, contribute to the community, and expand your résumé. The National Service-Learning Clearinghouse describes service learning as "a teaching and learning strategy that integrates meaningful community service with instruction and reflection to enrich the learning experience, teach civic responsibility, and strengthen communities."[17] The Internet offers many sites devoted to examples of students engaging in service-learning projects.

YOUR TASK Research possible service-learning projects in this class or another. Your instructor may ask you to submit a memo or an e-mail message analyzing your findings. Describe at least four completed service-learning projects that you found online. Draw conclusions about what made them successful or beneficial. What kinds of similar projects might be possible for you or students in your class? Your instructor may use this as a research project or turn it into a hands-on project by having you find a service organization in your community that needs trained writers.

13.4 Unsolicited Proposal: Keeping Gizmos Safe in Residence (Objs. 1, 2)

Team

As an enterprising college student, you recognized a problem as soon as you arrived on campus. Residence rooms filled with pricey digital doodads were very attractive to thieves. Some students move in with more than $3,000 in gear, including laptops, tablets, flat-screen TVs, digital cameras, MP3 players, video game consoles, smartphones, and hoards of other digital delights. You solved the problem by buying an extra-large steel footlocker in which to stash your valuables. However, shipping the footlocker was expensive (nearly $100), and you had to wait for it to arrive from a catalogue company. Your bright idea is to propose to the Student Administrative Council (SAC) that it allow you to offer these steel footlockers to students at a reduced price and with campus delivery. Your footlocker, which you found by searching online, is extremely durable and works great as a coffee table, nightstand, or card table. It comes with a smooth interior liner and two compartments.

YOUR TASK Working individually or with a team, imagine that you have made arrangements with a manufacturer to act as an intermediary selling footlockers on your campus at a reduced price. Consult online for manufacturers and make up your own figures. How can you get the SAC's permission to proceed? Give that organization a cut? Use your imagination in deciding how this plan might work on a college campus. Then prepare an unsolicited proposal to your SAC. Outline the problem and your goals of protecting students' valuables and providing convenience. Check online for statistics regarding on-campus burglaries. Such figures should help you develop one or more persuasive hooks. Then explain your proposal, project possible sales, discuss a timetable, and describe your staffing. Submit your proposal to Anthony Johnson, president, Student Administrative Council.

13.5 Unsolicited Proposal: Requesting Funding for Your Campus Business Organization (Obj. 1)

Let's say you are a member of a campus business or sports club. Your organization has managed its finances well, and, therefore, it is able to fund monthly activities. However, membership dues are insufficient to cover any extras. Identify a need, such as for a hardware or software purchase, a special one-time event that would benefit a great number of students, or officer training.

YOUR TASK Request one-time funding to cover what you need by writing an unsolicited letter or memo proposal to your assistant dean, who oversees student business clubs. Identify your need or problem, show the benefit of your request, support your claims with evidence, and provide a budget (if necessary).

Grammar and Mechanics | *Review 13*

Total Review

The first ten chapters reviewed specific guides from Appendix B, Grammar and Mechanics Guide, beginning on page B-1. The exercise in this chapter is a total review, covering all the grammar and mechanics guides plus confusing words and frequently misspelled words. Each of the following sentences has **three** errors in grammar, punctuation, capitalization, usage, or spelling. On a sheet of paper or on your computer, write a correct version. Avoid adding new phrases, starting new sentences, or rewriting in your own words. When you finish, compare your responses with the key in Appendix C.

EXAMPLE: If you face writers block you should review the 3 main reasons for writing.

REVISION: If you face **writer's** block**,** you should review the **three** main reasons for writing.

1. Our CEO and President both worked on the thirty page proposal. Which was due immediately.
2. Managers in 2 departments' complained that their departments should have been consulted.

3. The RFP and it's attachments arrived to late for my manager and I to complete the necessary research.
4. Although we worked everyday on the proposal, we felt badly that we could not meet the May 15th deadline.
5. If the program and staff is to run smooth we must submit an effective grant proposal.
6. Although short a successful mission statement should capture the businesses goals and values. In a few succinct sentences.
7. A proposal budget cannot be changed if costs raise later, consequently, it must be written careful.
8. A good eight-word mission statement is a critical tool for funding, it helps start-up company's evolve there big idea without being pulled off track.
9. Entrepreneur Stephanie Rivera publisher of a urban event callendar, relies on social media to broadcast her message.
10. Stephanie asked Jake and myself to help her write a business plan. That would guide her new company and garner permanent funding

Notes

[1] Egale Canada. (2020). *About*. https://egale.ca/about/
[2] Egale Canada. (2020). *Inclusive workplaces*. https://egale.ca/training-workshops/inclusive-workplaces/
[3] Ibid.
[4] RFP.ca. (2017). *Find public sector contract opportunities*. http://www.rfp.ca/
[5] Score Association. (2014). *How long does it take to create a business plan?* http://youngstown.score.org/node/834797
[6] Lewis, H. (2013, January 5). Hassle-free business plans. *New York Post*. http://www.nypost.com/p/news/business/hassle_free_business_plans_4tqWOfXU9hmWrsLUKgFECO
[7] Government of Canada. (2017). *Why do you need a business plan?* Canada Business Network. http://canadabusiness.ca/business-planning/why-do-you-need-a-business-plan/
[8] Starr, K. (2012, September 18). The eight-word mission statement. *Stanford Social Innovation Review*. http://www.ssireview.org/blog/entry/the_eight_word_mission_statement
[9] NWT Brewing Company. (2020). *About*. https://nwtbrewingco.com/pages/about
[10] Ibid. Reprinted courtesy of NWT Brewing Company.
[11] Panza-Beltrandi, G. (2018, November 30). *N.W.T.'s only microbrewery out $100K after equipment supplier goes out of business*. CBC News. https://www.cbc.ca/news/canada/north/nwt-brewing-out-100k-supplier-recievership-1.4926769
[12] American Psychological Association. (2020). *Bias-free language*. https://apastyle.apa.org/style-grammar-guidelines/bias-free-language
[13] Ibid.
[14] Egale Canada. (2019). *Get her on Ellen*. http://getheronellen.com/
[15] Egale Canada. (2019). *Helen Kennedy's letter to Ellen*. http://jptghoellen.wpengine.com/wp-content/uploads/2019/10/Egale-Canada-Helen-Kennedys-Letter-to-Ellen.pdf
[16] Egale Canada. (2019, November 29). *LGBTQI2S seniors community consult*. https://egale.ca/awareness/lgbtqi2s-seniors-community-consult/
[17] Office of Civic Engagement & Service. (n.d.). *Definition of service learning*. Fayetteville State University. Retrieved from http://www.uncfsu.edu/civic-engagement/service-learning/definition-of-service-learning

CHAPTER 14

Business Presentations

Atstock Productions/Shutterstock

LEARNING OBJECTIVES

After studying this chapter, you should be able to

1. Recognize various types of business presentations, and discuss preparing for any of these presentations.
2. Explain how to organize your business presentation, build audience rapport, and understand contemporary visual aids.
3. Create an impressive, error-free multimedia presentation that shows a firm grasp of basic visual design principles.
4. Specify delivery techniques for use before, during, and after a presentation.
5. Organize presentations for intercultural audiences and in teams.
6. List techniques for improving telephone skills to project a positive image.

SPOTLIGHT ON COMMUNICATION: PART 1

Universal Design for Learning—Creating Accessible Presentations

bongkarn thanyakij

Universal Design for Learning (UDL) is a teaching framework that makes learning accessible for everyone. Within today's diverse classrooms and workplaces, people have different ways they learn. "[UDL] is a framework to improve and optimize teaching and learning for all people based on scientific insights into how humans learn."[1] UDL has its origins in architecture. For example, when ramps are planned for people who use wheelchairs, other people benefit, like those who use strollers, bicycles, rolling suitcases, or walkers. When UDL is used in a teaching setting, multiple learners will benefit as well.[2]

UDL has three guiding principles for its design: multiple means of *representation*, to give learners various ways of acquiring information and knowledge; multiple means of *expression*, to provide learners with alternatives for demonstrating what they know; and multiple means of *engagement*, to tap into learners' interests, challenge them appropriately, and motivate them to learn.[3] As part of UDL, consider how you share information during your presentation:

> Display information in a flexible format so that the following perceptual features can be varied:
>
> - The size of text, images, graphs, tables, or other visual content
> - The contrast between background and text or image
> - The colour used for information or emphasis
> - The volume or rate of speech or sound
> - The speed or timing of video, animation, sound, simulations, etc.
> - The layout of visual or other elements
> - The font used for print materials[4]

CRITICAL THINKING

- If you aren't familiar with your audience, how can UDL help to make your presentation accessible for everyone?
- Consider how you normally present information to groups. What aspects of UDL are you already using? What changes do you need to make so that your material is fully accessible?

Creating Effective Business Presentations

LEARNING OBJECTIVE 1

Recognize various types of business presentations, and discuss preparing for any of these presentations.

At some point, all businesspeople have to inform others or sell an idea. Such information and persuasion are often conveyed in person and involve audiences of various sizes. If you are like most people, you have some apprehension when speaking in public. That's normal. Good speakers are made, not born. The good news is that you can conquer the fear of public speaking and hone your skills with instruction and practice.

Speaking Skills and Your Career

The savviest future businesspeople take advantage of opportunities in college or university to develop their speaking skills. Such skills often play an important role in a successful career. In fact, the No. 1 predictor of success and upward mobility, according to one study, is how much you enjoy public speaking and how effective you are at it.[5] Another study revealed that Canadian employers value speaking skills as one of their top five important soft skills, ranking second only to dependability.[6]

This chapter prepares you to use speaking skills in making effective oral presentations, whether alone or as part of a team, whether face to face or virtually. You will learn what to do before, during, and after your presentation, as well as how to design effective visual aids and multimedia presentations. Before diving into specifics on how to become an excellent presenter, consider the types of business presentations you may encounter in your career.

Understanding Presentation Types

A common part of a business professional's life is making presentations. Some presentations are informative while others may be persuasive. Some are face to face, and increasingly, since the global pandemic, others are virtual. Some are performed before big audiences, whereas others are given to smaller groups. Some presentations are elaborate; others, simple. Figure 14.1 shows a sampling of business presentations you may encounter in your career.

Knowing Your Purpose

Regardless of the type of presentation, you must prepare carefully if you expect it to be effective. The most important part of your preparation is deciding what you want to accomplish. Do you want to persuade management to increase the marketing budget? Do you want to inform customer-service reps of three important ways to prevent miscommunication? Whether your goal is to persuade or to inform, you must have a clear idea of where you are going. At the end of your presentation, what do you want your listeners to remember or do?

Sandra Castleman, a loan officer at Dominion Trust, faced such questions as she planned a talk for a class in small business management. Sandra's former business professor had asked her to return to campus and give the class advice about borrowing money from banks to start new businesses. Because Sandra knew so much about this topic, she found it difficult to extract a specific purpose statement for her presentation. After much thought she narrowed her purpose to this: *To inform potential entrepreneurs about three important factors that loan officers consider before granting start-up loans to launch small businesses.* Her entire presentation focused on ensuring that the class members understood and remembered three principal ideas.

Knowing Your Audience

A second key element in preparation is analyzing your audience, anticipating its reactions, and adjusting to its needs if necessary. Audiences may fall into four categories, as summarized in Figure 14.2. By anticipating your audience, you have a better idea of how to organize your

FIGURE 14.1 Types of Business Presentations

- Overview or summary of an issue, a proposal, or a problem
- Delivery of information, discussion of questions, collection of feedback

- Oral equivalent of business reports and proposals
- Informational or persuasive oral account, simple or elaborate

- Online, prerecorded audio clip delivered over the Web
- Opportunity to launch products, introduce and train employees, and sell products and services

- Collaboration facilitated by technology (telepresence or Web)
- Real-time meeting online with remote colleagues

- Web-based presentation, lecture, workshop, or seminar
- Digital transmission with or without video to train employees, interact with customers, or promote products

FIGURE 14.2 Succeeding With Four Audience Types

Audience Members	Organizational Pattern	Delivery Style	Supporting Material
Friendly They like you and your topic.	Use any pattern. Try something new. Involve the audience.	Be warm, pleasant, and open. Use lots of eye contact and smiles.	Include humour, personal examples, and experiences.
Neutral They are calm, rational; their minds are made up, but they think they are objective.	Present both sides of the issue. Use pro/con or problem/solution patterns. Save time for audience questions.	Be controlled. Do nothing showy. Use confident, small gestures.	Use facts, statistics, expert opinion, and comparison and contrast. Avoid humour, personal stories, and flashy visuals.
Uninterested They have short attention spans; they may be there against their will.	Be brief—include no more than three points. Avoid topical and pro/con patterns that seem lengthy to the audience.	Be dynamic and entertaining. Move around, if possible. Use large gestures.	Use humour, cartoons, colourful visuals, powerful quotations, and startling statistics.
	Avoid darkening the room, being motionless, passing out handouts, using boring visuals, or expecting the audience to participate.		
Hostile They want to take charge or to ridicule the speaker; they may be defensive, emotional.	Organize using a noncontroversial pattern, such as a topical, chronological, or geographical strategy.	Be calm and controlled. Speak evenly and slowly.	Include objective data and expert opinion. Avoid anecdotes and humour.
	Avoid a question-and-answer period, if possible; otherwise, use a moderator or accept only written questions.		

presentation. Regardless of the type of audience, however, remember to plan your presentation so that it focuses on audience benefits. The members of your audience will want to know what's in it for them.

Other elements, such as age, gender, education level, experience, and the size of the audience will affect your style and message. Analyze the following questions to determine your organizational pattern, delivery style, and supporting material.

- How will this topic appeal to this audience?
- How can I relate this information to my listeners' needs?
- How can I earn respect so that they accept my message?
- What would be most effective in making my point? Facts? Statistics? Personal experiences? Expert opinion? Humour? Cartoons? Graphic illustrations? Demonstrations? Case histories? Analogies?
- What measures must I take to ensure that this audience remembers my main points?

Go to section 14-1d in MindTap, where you can watch a video featuring Mike Draper, a partner at Growth Advisors Inc., discuss how to know your audience.

Check out section 14-1d in MindTap, where you can watch a video featuring Courtney Appleby, a campaign manager, discuss strategies for presenting to senior team members.

If you have agreed to speak to an audience with which you are unfamiliar, ask for the names of a half-dozen people who will be in the audience. Contact them and learn about their backgrounds and expectations for the presentation. This information can help you answer questions about what they want to hear and how deeply you should explore the subject. You will want to thank these people when you start your speech. Doing this kind of homework will impress the audience.

Concept Check

1. Remember some of the speeches or oral presentations you have witnessed. What were some of the elements that made them stand out, whether positively or negatively?
2. How would you classify your classmates as an audience for student presentations: friendly, neutral, uninterested, or hostile? Why?

LEARNING OBJECTIVE 2

Explain how to organize your business presentation, build audience rapport, and understand contemporary visual aids.

Connecting With Audiences by Organizing Content and Using Visual Aids

Once you have determined your purpose and analyzed the audience, you are ready to collect information and organize it logically. Good organization and intentional repetition are the two most powerful keys to audience comprehension and retention. In fact, many speech experts recommend the following admittedly repetitious, but effective, plan:

Step 1: Tell them what you are going to tell them.

Step 2: Tell them.

Step 3: Tell them what you have told them.

In other words repeat your main points in the introduction, body, and conclusion of your presentation. Although it is redundant, this strategy is necessary in oral presentations. Let's examine how to construct the three parts of an effective presentation: introduction, body, and conclusion.

Capturing Attention in the Introduction

How many times have you heard a speaker begin with *It's a pleasure to be here*, Or *I'm honoured to be asked to speak*, or the all-too-common *Today I'm going to talk about....* Boring openings such as these get speakers off to a dull start. Avoid such banalities by striving to accomplish three goals in the introduction to your presentation:

- Capture listeners' attention and get them involved.
- Identify yourself and establish your credibility.
- Preview your main points.

If you are able to appeal to listeners and involve them in your presentation right from the start, you are more likely to hold their attention until the finish. Consider some of the same techniques that you used to open sales letters: a question, a startling fact, a joke, a story, or a quotation. Some speakers achieve involvement by opening with a question or command that requires audience members to raise their hands or stand up. Additional techniques to gain and keep audience attention are presented in the next Career Coach box.

To establish your credibility, you need to describe your position, knowledge, education, or experience—whatever qualifies you to speak. The way you dress, the self-confidence you display, and your direct eye contact can also build credibility. In addition, try to connect with your audience. Listeners respond particularly well to speakers who reveal something of themselves and identify with them. Use humour if you can pull it off (not everyone can); self-effacing humour may work best for you.

CAREER COACH

Gaining and Keeping Audience Attention

Experienced speakers know how to capture the attention of an audience and how to maintain that attention throughout a presentation. You can spruce up your presentations by trying these 12 proven techniques.

- **A promise.** Begin with a realistic promise that keeps the audience expectant (e.g., *By the end of this presentation, you will know how you can increase your sales by 50 percent!*).
- **Drama.** Open by telling an emotionally moving story or by describing a serious problem that involves the audience. Throughout your talk include other dramatic elements, such as a long pause after a key statement. Change your vocal tone or pitch. Professionals use high-intensity emotions, such as anger, joy, sadness, and excitement.
- **Eye contact.** As you begin, command attention by surveying the entire audience to take in all listeners. Give yourself two to five seconds to linger on individuals to avoid fleeting, unconvincing eye contact. Don't just sweep the room and the crowd.
- **Movement.** Leave the lectern area, if possible. Move around the conference table or down the aisles of the presentation room, if it's feasible. Try to move toward your audience, especially at the beginning and end of your talk.
- **Questions.** Keep listeners active and involved with rhetorical questions. Ask for a show of hands to get each listener thinking. The response will also give you a quick gauge of audience attention.
- **Demonstrations.** Include a member of the audience in a demonstration. Ask for a volunteer.
- **Samples/props.** If you are promoting a product, consider using items to toss out to the audience or to award as prizes to volunteer participants. You can also pass around product samples or promotional literature. Be careful, though, to maintain control.
- **Visuals.** Give your audience something to look at besides you. Use a variety of visual aids in a single session. Also consider writing the concerns expressed by your audience on a flipchart or on a whiteboard or smart board as you go along.
- **Dress.** Enhance your credibility with your audience by dressing professionally for your presentation. Professional attire will help you look competent and qualified, making your audience more likely to listen and take you seriously.
- **Current events/statistics.** Mention a current event or statistic (the more startling, the better) that is relevant to your topic and to which the audience can relate.
- **A quotation.** Quotations, especially those made by well-known individuals, can be powerful attention-getting devices. The quotation should be pertinent to your topic, short, and interesting.
- **Self-interest.** Review your entire presentation to ensure that it meets the critical *What's-in-it-for-me* audience test. Remember that people are most interested in things that benefit them.

After capturing your audience's attention and effectively establishing your credibility using humour or some other technique, you will want to preview the main points of your topic, perhaps with a visual aid.

Take a look at Sandra Castleman's introduction, shown in Figure 14.3, to see how she integrated all the elements necessary for a good opening.

Organizing the Body of the Presentation

The most effective oral presentations focus on a few principal ideas. Therefore, the body of your short presentation (20 or fewer minutes) should include a limited number of main points, say, two to four. Develop each main point with adequate, but not excessive, explanation and details. Too many details can obscure the main message, so keep your presentation simple and logical. Remember, listeners have no pages to refer to should they become confused.

When Sandra Castleman began planning her presentation, she realized immediately that she could talk for hours on her topic. She also knew that listeners are not good at separating major and minor points, so she sorted out a few main ideas. In the banking industry, loan officers generally ask the following three questions of each applicant for a small business loan: (a) Are you ready to "hit the ground running" in starting your business? (b) Have you done your homework? and (c) Have you made realistic projections of potential sales, cash flow, and equity investment? These questions would become her main points, but Sandra wanted to streamline them further so that her audience would be sure to remember them. She encapsulated the questions in three words: *experience*, *preparation*, and *projection*. As you can see in Figure 14.3,

FIGURE 14.3 Outlining an Oral Presentation

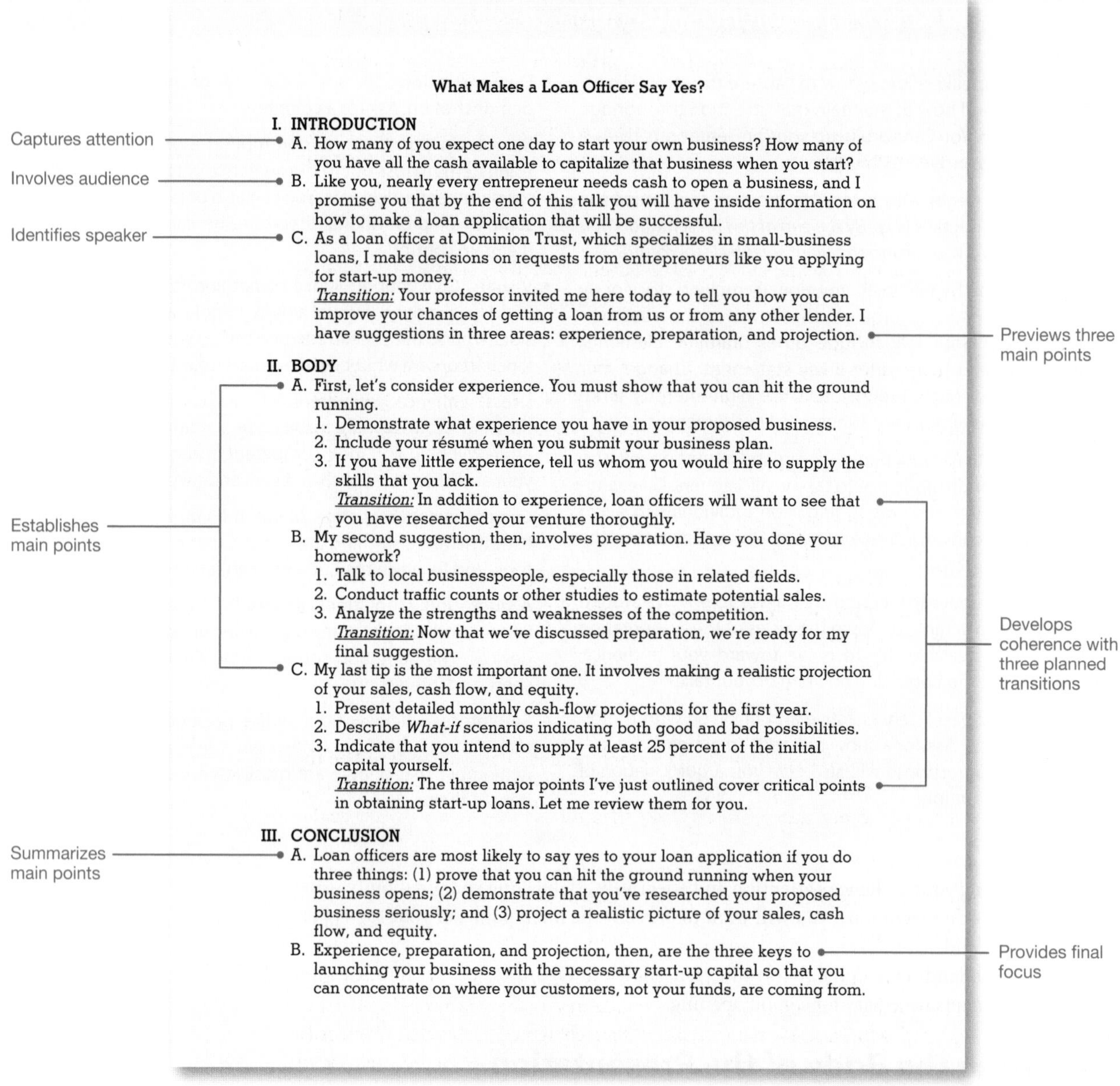

What Makes a Loan Officer Say Yes?
I. INTRODUCTION
Captures attention
A. How many of you expect one day to start your own business? How many of you have all the cash available to capitalize that business when you start?
Involves audience
B. Like you, nearly every entrepreneur needs cash to open a business, and I promise you that by the end of this talk you will have inside information on how to make a loan application that will be successful.
Identifies speaker
C. As a loan officer at Dominion Trust, which specializes in small-business loans, I make decisions on requests from entrepreneurs like you applying for start-up money.
Transition: Your professor invited me here today to tell you how you can improve your chances of getting a loan from us or from any other lender. I have suggestions in three areas: experience, preparation, and projection.
Previews three main points
II. BODY
Establishes main points
A. First, let's consider experience. You must show that you can hit the ground running.
1. Demonstrate what experience you have in your proposed business.
2. Include your résumé when you submit your business plan.
3. If you have little experience, tell us whom you would hire to supply the skills that you lack.
Transition: In addition to experience, loan officers will want to see that you have researched your venture thoroughly.
B. My second suggestion, then, involves preparation. Have you done your homework?
1. Talk to local businesspeople, especially those in related fields.
2. Conduct traffic counts or other studies to estimate potential sales.
3. Analyze the strengths and weaknesses of the competition.
Transition: Now that we've discussed preparation, we're ready for my final suggestion.
C. My last tip is the most important one. It involves making a realistic projection of your sales, cash flow, and equity.
1. Present detailed monthly cash-flow projections for the first year.
2. Describe What-if scenarios indicating both good and bad possibilities.
3. Indicate that you intend to supply at least 25 percent of the initial capital yourself.
Transition: The three major points I've just outlined cover critical points in obtaining start-up loans. Let me review them for you.
Develops coherence with three planned transitions
III. CONCLUSION
Summarizes main points
A. Loan officers are most likely to say yes to your loan application if you do three things: (1) prove that you can hit the ground running when your business opens; (2) demonstrate that you've researched your proposed business seriously; and (3) project a realistic picture of your sales, cash flow, and equity.
B. Experience, preparation, and projection, then, are the three keys to launching your business with the necessary start-up capital so that you can concentrate on where your customers, not your funds, are coming from.
Provides final focus

Sandra prepared a sentence outline showing these three main ideas. Each is supported by examples and explanations.

How to organize and sequence main ideas may not be immediately obvious when you begin working on a presentation. The following methods, which review and amplify those discussed in Chapter 12, provide many possible strategies and examples to help you organize a presentation:

- **Chronology.** Example: A presentation describing the history of a problem is organized from the first sign of trouble to the present.
- **Geography/space.** Example: A presentation about the changing diversity of the workforce is organized by regions in the country (East Coast, West Coast, and so forth).
- **Topic/function/conventional grouping.** Example: A report discussing mishandled airline baggage is organized by names of airlines.

- **Comparison (pro/con).** Example: A report compares organic farming methods with those of modern industrial farming.
- **Journalistic pattern (the five Ws and an H).** Example: A report describing how identity thieves can ruin your good name is organized by *who, what, when, where, why,* and *how.*
- **Value/size.** Example: A report describing fluctuations in housing costs is organized by prices of homes.
- **Importance.** Example: A report describing five reasons a company should move its headquarters to a specific city is organized from the most important reason to the least important.
- **Problem/solution.** Example: A company faces a problem, such as declining sales. A solution, such as reducing the staff, is offered.
- **Simple/complex.** Example: A report explaining genetic modification of plants such as corn is organized from simple seed production to complex gene introduction.
- **Best case/worst case.** Example: A report analyzing whether two companies should merge is organized by the best-case result (improved market share, profitability, employee morale) as opposed to the worst-case result (devalued stock, lost market share, employee malaise).

In the presentation shown in Figure 14.3, Sandra arranged the main points by importance, placing the most important point last, where it had maximum effect. When organizing any presentation, prepare a little more material than you think you will actually need. Savvy speakers always have something useful in reserve, such as an extra handout, slide, or idea—just in case they finish early. At the same time, most speakers go about 25 percent over the allotted time as opposed to their practice runs at home in front of the mirror. If your speaking time is limited, as it usually is in your classes, aim for less than the limit when rehearsing so that you don't take time away from the next presenters.

Summarizing in the Conclusion

Nervous speakers often rush to wrap up their presentations because they can't wait to flee the stage. However, listeners will remember the conclusion more than any other part of a speech. That's why you should spend some time to make it most effective. Strive to achieve three goals:

- Summarize the main themes of the presentation.
- Leave the audience with a specific and noteworthy takeaway.
- Include a statement that allows you to leave the podium gracefully.

A conclusion is akin to a punch line and must be memorable. Think of it as the high point of your presentation, a valuable kernel of information to take away. The takeaway should tie in with the opening or present a forward-looking idea. Avoid merely rehashing, in the same words, what you said before, but ensure that the audience will take away very specific information or benefits and a positive impression of you and your company. The takeaway is the value of the presentation to the audience and the benefit audience members believe they have received. The tension that you built in the early parts of the talk now culminates in the close. Compare these poor and improved conclusions:

Poor conclusion: *Well, I guess that's about all I have to say. Thanks for your time.*

Improved: *In bringing my presentation to a close, I will restate my major purpose. . . .*

Improved: *In summary, my major purpose has been to. . . .*

Improved: *In conclusion, let me review my three major points. They are. . . .*

Notice how Sandra Castleman, in the conclusion shown in Figure 14.3, summarized her three main points and provided a final focus to listeners.

If you are promoting a recommendation, you might end as follows: In conclusion, I recommend that we retain Matrixx Marketing to conduct a telemarketing campaign beginning September 1 at a cost of X dollars. To complete this recommendation, I suggest that we (a) finance this campaign from our operations budget, (b) develop a persuasive message describing our new product, and (c) name Hélène Beck to oversee the project.

In your conclusion you could use an anecdote, an inspiring quotation, or a statement that ties in the opener and offers a new insight. Whatever you choose, be sure to include a closing thought that indicates you are finished.

Establishing Audience Rapport

Good speakers are adept at building audience rapport, and they think about how they are going to build that rapport as they organize their presentations. Building rapport means that speakers form a bond with the audience; they entertain as well as inform. How do they do it? Based on observations of successful and unsuccessful speakers, we learn that the good ones use a number of verbal and nonverbal techniques to connect with the audience. Their helpful techniques include providing effective imagery, supplying verbal signposts, and using body language strategically.

Effective Imagery. You will lose your audience quickly if you fill your talk with abstractions, generalities, and dry facts. To enliven your presentation and enhance comprehension, try using some of the techniques shown in Figure 14.4. However, beware of exaggeration or distortion. Keep your imagery realistic and credible.

Verbal Signposts. Speakers must remember that listeners, unlike readers of a report, cannot control the rate of presentation or reread pages to review main points. As a result,

FIGURE 14.4 Effective Imagery Engages the Audience

METAPHOR
Comparison between dissimilar things without the words *like* or *as*

- Our competitor's CEO is a snake when it comes to negotiating.
- My desk is a garbage dump.

ANALOGY
Comparison of similar traits between dissimilar things

- Product development is similar to conceiving, carrying, and delivering a baby.
- Downsizing is comparable to a gardener's regimen of pruning and trimming.

PERSONALIZED STATISTICS
Facts that affect the audience

- Look around you. Only three out of five graduates will find a job right after graduation.
- One typical meal at a fast food restaurant contains all the calories you need for an entire day.

SCENARIOS
The worst or best that could happen

- If we don't back up now, a crash could wipe out all customer data.
- If we fix the system now, we can expand our customer files and also increase sales.

ANECDOTE
A personal story

- Let me share a few personal blunders online and what I learned from my mistakes.
- I always worried about my pets while I was away. That's when I decided to start a pet hotel.

SIMILE
Comparison that includes the words *like* or *as*

- This report is a like a corn maze—long, winding, and confusing.
- She's as happy as someone who just won the lottery.

listeners get lost easily. Knowledgeable speakers help the audience recognize the organization and main points in an oral message with verbal signposts. They keep listeners on track by including helpful previews, summaries, and transitions such as these:

Previewing

The next segment of my talk presents three reasons for. . . .

Let's now consider the causes of. . . .

Summarizing

Let me review with you the major problems I have just discussed. . . .

You see, then, that the most significant factors are. . . .

Switching directions

Thus far we have talked solely about. . . . Now, let's move to. . . .

I have argued that . . . and . . . , but an alternative view holds that. . . .

You can further improve any oral presentation by including appropriate transitional expressions, such as *first, second, next, then, therefore, moreover, on the other hand, on the contrary,* and *in conclusion.* These transitional expressions, which you learned about in Figure 5.6 in Chapter 5, build coherence, lend emphasis, and tell listeners where you are headed. Notice in Sandra Castleman's outline, shown in Figure 14.3, the specific transitional elements designed to help listeners recognize each new principal point.

Nonverbal Messages. Although what you say is most important, the nonverbal messages you send can also have a potent effect on how well your audience receives your message. How you look, how you move, and how you speak can make or break your presentation. The following suggestions focus on nonverbal tips to ensure that your verbal message resonates with your audience.

- **Look terrific!** Like it or not, you will be judged by your appearance. For everything but small in-house presentations, be sure you dress professionally. The rule of thumb is that you should dress at least as well as the best-dressed person in the audience.
- **Animate your body.** Be enthusiastic and let your body show it. Emphasize ideas to enhance points about size, number, and direction. Use a variety of gestures, but don't consciously plan them in advance.
- **Punctuate your words.** You can keep your audience interested by varying your tone, volume, pitch, and pace. Use pauses before and after important points. Allow the audience to take in your ideas.
- **Get out from behind the lectern.** Avoid staying rigidly behind a lectern or table. Movement makes you look natural and comfortable. You might pick a few places in the room to move to. Even if you must stay close to your visual aids, make a point of leaving them occasionally so that the audience can see your whole body.
- **Vary your facial expression.** Begin with a smile, but change your expressions to correspond with the thoughts you are voicing.

Whenever possible, beginning presenters should have an experienced speaker watch them and give them tips as they rehearse. Your instructor is an important coach who can provide you with invaluable feedback. In the absence of helpers, record yourself and watch your nonverbal behaviour on camera. Are you doing what it takes to build rapport?

Understanding Contemporary Visual Aids

Before you make a business presentation, consider this wise proverb: "Tell me, I forget. Show me, I remember. Involve me, I understand." Your goals as a speaker are to make listeners understand, remember, and act on your ideas. To get them interested and involved, include effective visual aids. Some experts claim that we acquire 85 percent of all our knowledge visually.[7] Therefore, an oral presentation that incorporates visual aids is far more likely to be understood and retained than one lacking visual enhancement.

Good visual aids serve many purposes. They emphasize and clarify main points, thus improving comprehension and retention. They increase audience interest, and they make the presenter appear more professional, better prepared, and more persuasive. Well-designed visual aids illustrate and emphasize your message more effectively than words alone; therefore, they may help shorten a meeting or achieve your goal faster. Visual aids are particularly helpful for inexperienced speakers because the audience concentrates on the visual aid rather than on the speaker. However, experienced speakers work hard at not being eclipsed or upstaged by their slideshows. Good visual aids also serve to jog the memory of a speaker, thus improving self-confidence, poise, and delivery.

Types of Visual Aids

Speakers have many forms of visual media readily available if they want to enhance their presentations. Figure 14.5 describes the pros and cons of a number of visual aids that can guide you

FIGURE 14.5 Pros and Cons of Visual Aid Options

Medium: High Tech	Pros	Cons
Multimedia slides 	Create professional appearance with many colour, art, graphic, and font options. Allow users to incorporate video, audio, and hyperlinks. Offer ease of use and transport via removable storage media, Web download, or e-mail attachment. Are inexpensive to update.	Present potential incompatibility issues. Require costly projection equipment and practice for smooth delivery. Tempt user to include razzle-dazzle features that may fail to add value. Can be too one-dimensional and linear.
Nonlinear presentations 	Enable presenter to zoom in on and out of content to show the big picture or specific details in nonlinear, 3D quality. Provide attractive templates. Allow users to insert rich media. Offer an interactive, cinematic, and dynamic experience.	Require Internet access because they are cloud based. Don't allow editing of images. Offer limited font choices. Can be difficult to operate for some presenters used to individual slides; can make moving around the canvas challenging. Zooming can be distracting and even nauseating.
Video 	Gives an accurate representation of the content; strongly indicates forethought and preparation.	Creates potential for compatibility issues related to computer video formats. Is generally expensive to create and update.
Medium: Low Tech		
Handouts 	Encourage audience participation. Are easy to maintain and update. Enhance recall because audience keeps reference material.	Increase risk of unauthorized duplication of speaker's material. Can be difficult to transport. May cause speaker to lose audience's attention.
Flipcharts or whiteboards 	Provide inexpensive option available at most sites. Enable users to (a) create, (b) modify or customize on the spot, (c) record comments from the audience, and (d) combine with more high-tech visuals in the same presentation.	Require graphics talent. Can be difficult for larger audiences to see. Can be cumbersome to transport. Easily wear with use.
Props 	Offer a realistic reinforcement of message content. Increase audience participation with close observation.	Lead to extra work and expense in transporting and replacing worn objects. Are of limited use with larger audiences.

Photos (top to bottom): Andrey Yurlov/Shutterstock.com; Elena Elisseeva/Shutterstock.com; HotVector/Shutterstock.com; Marko Rupena/Shutterstock.com; Mykola Komarovskyy/Shutterstock.com; Andrey_Popov/Shutterstock.com

in selecting the best one for any speaking occasion. Two of the most popular visuals for business presentations are multimedia slides and handouts. Nonlinear (or dynamic) presentations, an alternative to multimedia slides, are also growing in popularity.

Multimedia Slides. With today's excellent software programs—such as Microsoft PowerPoint, Apple Keynote, and Adobe Presenter—you can create dynamic, colourful presentations with your desktop, laptop, tablet, or smartphone. The output from these programs is generally shown on a computer screen, a TV monitor, an LCD (liquid crystal display) panel, or a screen. With a little expertise and the right equipment, you can create multimedia presentations that include audio, videos, images, animation, and hyperlinks, as described shortly in the discussion of multimedia presentations. Multimedia slides can also be uploaded to a website or broadcast live over the Internet.

Handouts. You can enhance and complement your presentations by distributing pictures, outlines, brochures, articles, charts, summaries, or other supplements. Speakers who use presentation software often prepare a set of their slides along with notes to hand out to viewers. Timing the distribution of any handout, though, is tricky. If given out during a presentation, your handouts tend to distract the audience, causing you to lose control. Therefore, you should discuss handouts during the presentation but delay distributing them until after you finish. If you do this, tell audience members at the beginning of your presentation that you will be distributing handouts at the end.

Nonlinear Presentations. Many business presenters feel limited by multimedia slides, which tend to be too linear. As a result, some communicators are starting to create more dynamic visual aids. Using software such as Prezi, which is a cloud-based presentation and storytelling tool, businesspeople can design 3D presentations. These 3D presentations allow the speaker to *move* out of and into images to help the audience better understand and remember content, details, and relationships.[8] Nonlinear presentations allow presenters to communicate their ideas in a more exciting, creative way. Audience members also seem to appreciate the cinematic, interactive quality of these presentations.

Moving Beyond PowerPoint Bullets. Electronic slideshows, created using PowerPoint in particular, are a staple of business presentations. However, overuse or misuse may be the downside of the ever-present PowerPoint slideshow. Over more than two decades of the software program's existence, millions of poorly created and badly delivered presentations have tarnished PowerPoint's reputation as an effective communication tool. Tools are helpful only when used properly.

In the last few years, several communication consultants have tried to show business how it can move beyond bullet points. The experts recommend creating slideshows that tell a story and send a powerful message with much less text and more images.[9] Some businesspeople who are ready to explore highly visual, less text-laden design choices are turning to nonlinear presentations and other media-rich presentations designed using software such as Prezi. However, before breaking with established rules and expectations, you first need to understand design basics.

Even much-touted alternatives to PowerPoint, such as Prezi and emaze, require some knowledge of the sound design principles covered in the next section. The goal is to abandon boring bulleted lists.

Check out section 14-2f in MindTap, where you can watch a video featuring Courtney Appleby, a campaign manager, discuss tips for using PowerPoint.

Concept Check

1. With reference to the Career Coach box, what are the top three strategies for gaining and keeping audience attention when you are delivering a presentation in class? Considering your audience of peers, explain why these strategies are best.
2. What do you feel is the most effective visual aid to use during a presentation? Explain how the visual aid enhances a presentation.

LEARNING OBJECTIVE 3

Create an impressive, error-free multimedia presentation that shows a firm grasp of basic visual design principles.

Preparing Engaging Multimedia Presentations

When operated by proficient designers and skillful presenters, PowerPoint, Keynote, or Prezi can add visual impact to any presentation. In the sections that follow, you will learn to create an impressive multimedia presentation using the most widely used presentation software program, PowerPoint. You will also learn how Prezi can be used to create nonlinear presentations as an alternative to PowerPoint. With any software program, of course, gaining expertise requires an investment of time and effort. You could take a course, or you could teach yourself through an online tutorial.

Applying the 3-x-3 Writing Process to Multimedia Presentations

The following sections explain how to adjust your visuals to the situation and your audience. We review the three phases of the writing process and show how they help you develop a visually appealing PowerPoint or Prezi presentation.

Analyzing the Situation and Purpose

Making the best content and design choices for your presentation depends greatly on your analysis of the situation. Will your slides be used during a live presentation? Will they be part of a self-running presentation, such as in a store kiosk? Will they be sent as a PowerPoint show or a PDF document to a client instead of a hard-copy report? Are you converting your presentation for viewing on smartphones or tablets?

If you are e-mailing the presentation or posting it online as a self-contained file, or slide deck, it will typically feature more text than if you were delivering it orally. If, on the other hand, you are creating slides for a live presentation, you will likely rely more on images than on text.

Adjusting Slide Design to Your Audience

Think about how you can design your presentation to get the most positive response from your audience. Audiences respond, for example, to the colours, images, and special effects you use. Primary ideas are generally best conveyed with bold colours, such as blue, green, and purple. Because the messages that colours convey can vary from culture to culture, choose colours carefully.

The Meaning of Colour. In North America, blue is the colour of credibility, tranquility, conservatism, and trust. Therefore, it is the background colour of choice for many business presentations. Green relates to interaction, growth, money, and stability. It can work well as a background or an accent colour. Purple can also work as a background or an accent colour. It conveys spirituality, royalty, dreams, and humour.[10] As for text, adjust the colour in such a way that it provides high contrast and is readable as a result. White or yellow, for example, usually works well on dark backgrounds.

Adapt the slide colours based on where the presentation will be given. Use light text on a dark background for presentations in darkened rooms. Use dark text on a light background for presentations in lighted rooms. Avoid using a dark font on a dark background, such as red text on a dark-blue background. In the same way, avoid using a light font on a light background, such as white text on a pale-blue background.

The Power of Images. Adapt the amount of text on your slide to how your audience will use the slides. As a general guideline, most graphic designers encourage the 6-x-6 rule: "Six bullets per screen, max; six words per bullet, max."[11] You may find, however, that breaking this rule is sometimes necessary, particularly when your users will be viewing the presentation on their own with no speaker assistance. For most purposes, though, strive to minimize the use of text.

When using PowerPoint or other presentation software, try to avoid long, boring bulleted lists. You can alter layouts by repositioning, resizing, or changing the fonts for the placeholders in which your title, bulleted list, organization chart, video clip, photograph, or other elements

FIGURE 14.6 Using Images and Illustrations for Greater Impact

Before Revision

Reasons for Selling Online

- Your online business can grow globally.
- Customer convenience.
- You can conduct your business 24/7.
- No need for renting a retail store or hiring employees.
- Reduce inquiries by providing policies and a privacy statement.
- Customers can buy quickly and easily.

After Revision

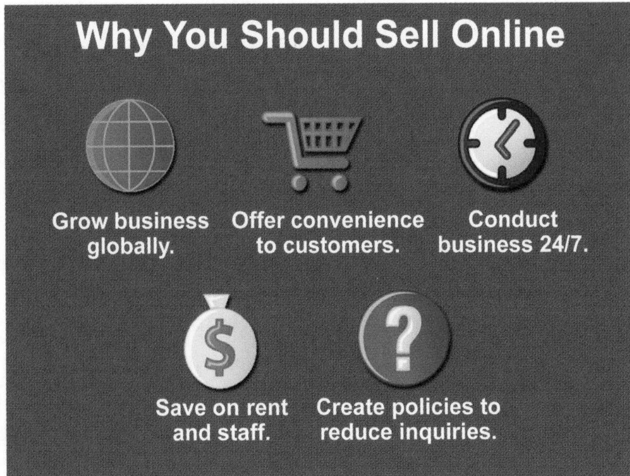

The slide on the left contains bullet points that are not parallel and that overlap in meaning. The second and sixth bullet points say the same thing. Moreover, some bullet points are too long. After revision, the slide on the right has a more convincing title illustrating the "you" view. The bullet points are shorter, and each begins with a verb for parallelism and an emphasis on action. The illustrations add interest.

appear. Figure 14.6 shows how to make your slides visually more appealing and memorable even with relatively small changes.

Notice that the bulleted items on the Before slide in Figure 14.6 are not parallel. The wording looks as if the author had been brainstorming or freewriting a first draft. The second and sixth bullet points express the same thought, that shopping online is convenient and easy for customers. Some bullet points are too long. The bullets on the After slide are short and well within the 6-x-6 rule, although they are complete sentences. The illustrations in the revised slide add interest and illustrate the points. You may use royalty-free stock photos that you can download from the Internet for personal or school use without penalty, or consider taking your own digital pictures.

You can also use other PowerPoint features, such as SmartArt, to add variety and pizzazz to your slides. Converting pure text and bullet points to graphics, charts, and other images will keep your audience interested and help them retain the information you are presenting.

The Impact of Special Effects. Just as you anticipate audience members' reactions to colour, you can usually anticipate their reactions to special effects. Using animation and sound effects—flying objects, swirling text, clashing cymbals, and the like—only because they are available is not a good idea. Special effects distract your audience, drawing attention away from your main points. Add animation features only if doing so helps convey your message or adds interest to the content. When your audience members leave, they should be commenting on the ideas you conveyed—not the cool swivels and sound effects. The zooming effect of Prezi presentations can add value to your presentation as long as it can make your audience understand connections and remember content.

Building Your Business Presentation

After considering design principles and their effects, you are ready to start putting together your presentation. In this section you will learn how to organize and compose your presentation, which templates to choose, and how to edit, proofread, and evaluate your work.

Organizing Your Presentations. When you prepare your presentation, translate the major headings in your outline into titles for slides. Then build bullet points using short phrases. In Chapter 5 you learned to improve readability by using graphic highlighting techniques, including bullets, numbers, and headings. In preparing a PowerPoint or Prezi presentation, you will use those same techniques.

The slides (or canvas) you create to accompany your spoken ideas can be organized with visual elements that will help your audience understand and remember what you want to communicate. Let's say, for example, that you have three points in your presentation. You can create a blueprint slide that captures the three points in a visually appealing way, and then you can use that slide several times throughout your presentation. Near the beginning, the blueprint slide provides an overview of your points. Later, it will provide transitions as you move from point to point. For transitions, you can direct your audience's attention by highlighting the next point you will be talking about. Finally, the blueprint slide can be used near the end to provide a review of your key points.

Composing Your Presentation. During the composition stage, many users fall into the trap of excessive formatting and programming. They fritter away precious time fine-tuning their slides or canvas. They don't spend enough time on what they are going to say and how they will say it. To avoid this trap, set a limit for how much time you will spend making your slides or canvas visually appealing. Your time limit will be based on how many "bells and whistles" (a) your audience expects and (b) your content requires to make it understandable.

Remember that not every point or every thought requires a visual. In fact, it's smart to switch off the presentation occasionally and direct the focus to you. Darkening the screen while you discuss a point, tell a story, give an example, or involve the audience will add variety to your presentation.

Create a slide or canvas only if it accomplishes at least one of the following purposes:

- Generates interest in what you are saying and helps the audience follow your ideas
- Highlights points you want your audience to remember
- Introduces or reviews your key points
- Provides a transition from one major point to the next
- Illustrates and simplifies complex ideas

Consider perusing the Help articles built into your presentation software or purchasing one of many inexpensive guides to electronic slide presentations. Your presentations will be more appealing, and you will save time if you know, for example, how to design with master slides and how to create your own templates. In a later section of this chapter, you will find very specific steps to follow as you create your presentation.

Working With Templates. All presentation programs require you to (a) select or create a template that will serve as the background for your presentation and (b) make each individual slide by selecting a layout that best conveys your message. Novice and even advanced users often use existing templates because they are designed by professionals who know how to combine harmonious colours, borders, bullet styles, and fonts for pleasing visual effects. If you prefer, you can alter existing templates so they better suit your needs. Adding a corporate logo, adjusting the colour scheme to better match the colours used on your organization's website, or selecting a different font are just some of the ways you can customize existing templates. One big advantage of templates is that they get you started quickly.

Be careful, though, of what one expert has labelled "visual clichés."[12] Overused templates and even clip art that come preinstalled with PowerPoint and Prezi can weary viewers who have seen them repeatedly in presentations. Instead of using a standard template, search for a *PowerPoint template* or *Prezi template* in your favourite online search tool. You will see hundreds of template options available as free downloads. Unless your employer requires that presentations all have the same look, your audience will appreciate fresh templates that complement the purpose of your presentation and provide visual variety.

Revising and Proofreading Your Presentation. Use the PowerPoint slide sorter view to rearrange, insert, and delete slides during the revision process. You can also use the Prezi editor to make any necessary changes to your canvas. This is the time to focus on

FIGURE 14.7 Designing More Effective Slides

Before Revision

DESIGN TIPS FOR SLIDE TEXT

1. STRIVE TO HAVE NO MORE THAN SIX BULLETS PER SLIDE AND NO MORE THAN SIX WORDS PER BULLET.
2. IF YOU USE UPPER- AND LOWERCASE TEXT, IT IS EASIER TO READ.
3. IT IS BETTER TO USE PHRASES RATHER THAN SENTENCES.
4. USING A SIMPLE HIGH-CONTRAST TYPEFACE IS EASIER TO READ AND DOES NOT DISTRACT FROM YOUR PRESENTATION.
5. BE CONSISTENT IN YOUR SPACING, CAPITALIZATION, AND PUNCTUATION.

After Revision

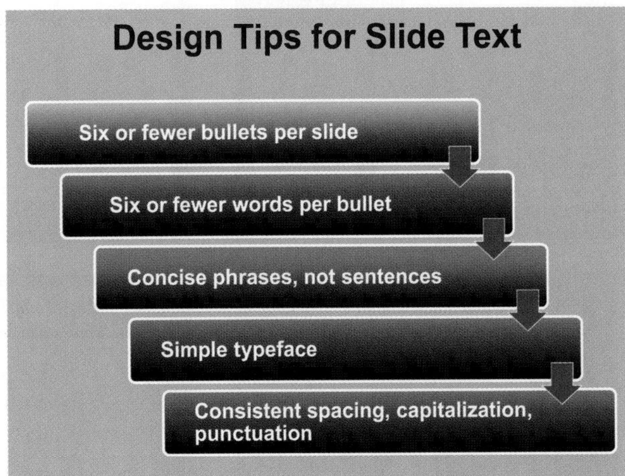

Design Tips for Slide Text
Six or fewer bullets per slide
Six or fewer words per bullet
Concise phrases, not sentences
Simple typeface
Consistent spacing, capitalization, punctuation

The slide on the left uses a difficult-to-read font style. In addition, the slide includes too many words per bullet and violates most of the slide-making rules it covers. After revision, the slide on the right provides a pleasing colour combination, uses short bullet points in a readable font style, and creates an attractive list using PowerPoint SmartArt features.

making your presentation as clear and concise as possible. If you are listing items, be sure that they all use parallel grammatical form. Figure 14.7 shows how to revise a PowerPoint slide to improve it for conciseness, parallelism, and other features. Study the design tips described in the first slide and determine which suggestions were not followed. Then compare it with the revised slide.

As you are revising, check carefully to find spelling, grammar, punctuation, and other errors. Use the spell-check feature, but don't rely on it without careful proofing, preferably from a printed copy of the slideshow. Nothing is as embarrassing as projecting errors on a huge screen in front of an audience. Also, check for consistency in how you capitalize and punctuate points throughout the presentation.

Evaluating Your Presentation. The final stage in applying the 3-x-3 writing process to developing a PowerPoint or Prezi presentation involves evaluation. Is your message presented in a visually appealing way? Have you tested your presentation on the equipment and in the room you will be using during your presentation? Do the colours you selected work in this new setting? Are the font styles and sizes readable from the back of the room? Figure 14.8 shows examples of PowerPoint slides that incorporate what you have learned in this discussion.

The dark purple background and the complementary hues in the slideshow shown in Figure 14.8 are standard choices for many business presentations. With an unobtrusive dark background, white fonts are a good option for maximum contrast and, hence, readability. The creator of the presentation varied the slide design to break the monotony of bulleted or numbered lists. Images and animated diagrams add interest and zing to the slides.

Courtesy of Kiva

When the founders of the microlending nonprofit organization Kiva make business presentations around the world, audiences respond with enthusiastic applause and even tears. Kiva's online lending platform connects personal lenders with individuals living in poverty in developing nations, enabling villagers to start tomato farms, carpet kiosks, and other small ventures that improve their lives. Kiva's presentations include heartwarming stories and videos about village entrepreneurs to show that small loans can make a big difference. What tips can communicators follow to deliver powerful, inspirational presentations?

FIGURE 14.8 PowerPoint Slides That Illustrate Multimedia Presentations

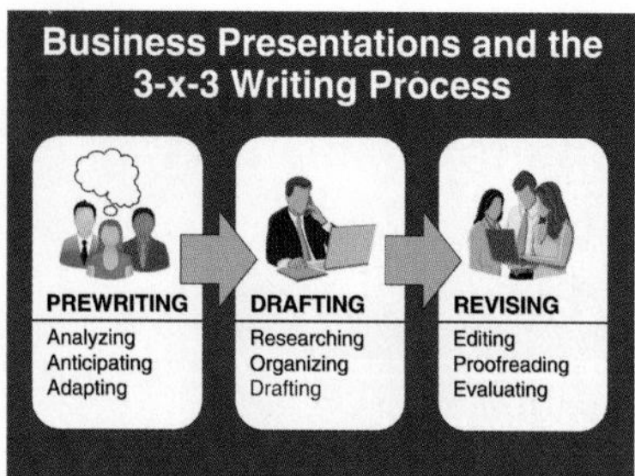

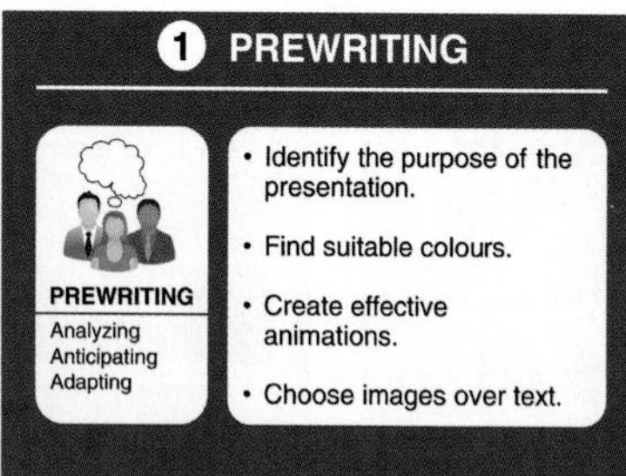

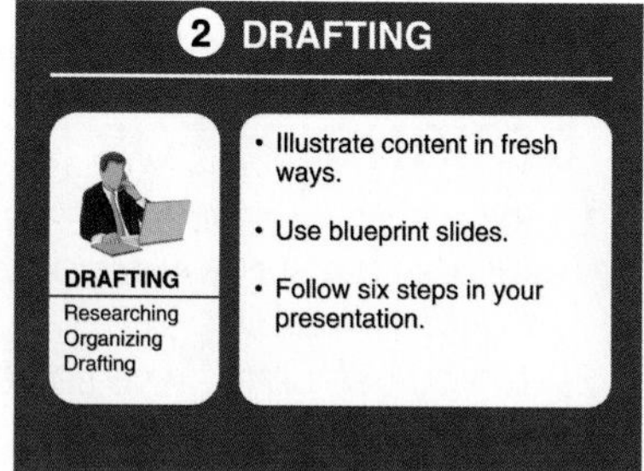

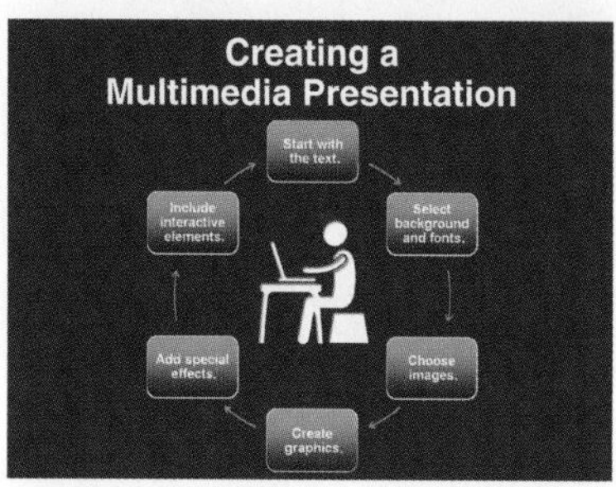

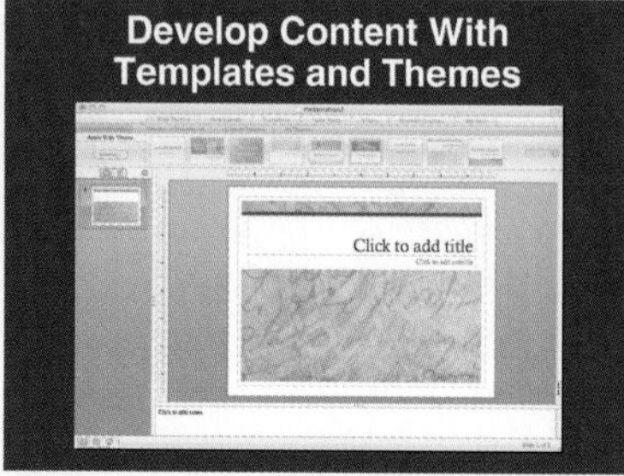

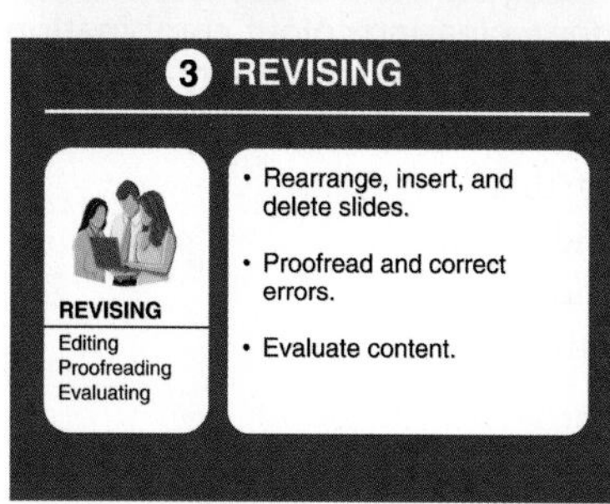

Preparing and Anticipating

Solid preparation and practice are crucial. One expert advises presenters to complete their PowerPoint slides or Prezi canvases a week before the actual talk and rehearse several times each day before the presentation.[13] Allow plenty of time before your presentation to set up and test your equipment. Confirm that the places you plan to stand or sit are not in the line of the projected image. Audience members don't appreciate having part of the slide displayed on your body. Make sure that all video or Web links are working and that you know how to operate all features the first time you try.

No matter how much time you put into preshow setup and testing, you still have no guarantee that all will go smoothly. Therefore, you should always bring a backup of your presentation. Handouts of your presentation provide a good substitute. Copying your presentation to a USB flash drive that could run from any available computer might prove useful as well. Copying your presentation to the cloud (e.g., Dropbox or Google Drive) or sending it to yourself as an e-mail attachment can also prove beneficial.

Some presenters allow their PowerPoint slides or Prezi canvases to overpower their presentations. In developing a presentation, don't expect your visuals to carry the show. Avoid being upstaged by not relying totally on your slides or canvas. Remember that you are the main attraction!

FIGURE 14.9 Seven Steps to a Powerful Multimedia Presentation

1 Start with the text.

What do you want your audience to believe, do, or remember? Organize your ideas into an outline with major and minor points.

2 Select background and fonts.

Choose a template or create your own. Focus on consistent font styles, sizes, colours, and backgrounds. Try to use no more than two font styles in your presentation. The point size should be between 24 and 36, and title fonts should be larger than text font.

3 Choose images that help communicate your message.

Use relevant clip art, infographics, photographs, maps, or drawings to illustrate ideas. Access Microsoft Office Online in PowerPoint and choose from thousands of images and photographs, most of which are in the public domain and require no copyright permissions. Before using images from other sources, determine whether permission from the copyright holder is required.

4 Create graphics.

Use software tools to transform boring bulleted items into appealing graphics and charts. PowerPoint's SmartArt feature can be used to create organization charts, cycles and radials, time lines, pyramids, matrixes, and Venn diagrams. Use PowerPoint's Chart feature to develop types of charts including line, pie, and bar charts. But don't overdo the graphics!

5 Add special effects.

To keep the audience focused, use animation and transition features to control when text or objects appear. With motion paths, 3D, and other animation options, you can move objects to various positions on the slide and zoom in on and out of images and text on your canvas. To minimize clutter, you can dim or remove them once they have served their purpose.

6 Create hyperlinks.

Make your presentation more interactive and intriguing by connecting to videos, spreadsheets, or websites.

7 Move your presentation online.

Make your presentation available by posting it to the Internet or an organization's intranet. Even if you are giving a face-to-face presentation, attendees appreciate these electronic handouts. The most complex option for moving your multimedia presentation to the Web involves a Web conference or broadcast. To discourage copying, convert your presentations to PDF documents—with a watermark and in black and white, if needed.

Image: Viorel Sima/Shutterstock.com

Seven Steps to a Powerful Multimedia Presentation

We have now discussed many suggestions for making effective PowerPoint and Prezi presentations, but you may still be wondering how to put it all together. Figure 14.9 presents a step-by-step process for creating a powerful multimedia presentation.

Concept Check

1. When working with templates, how can you avoid a clichéd presentation?
2. Not every point or every thought of your presentation requires a visual. What are five reasons to create a slide or canvas for your presentation?

CASE CONNECTIONS

Hooked on Tech

fauxels

Do you feel dependent on social media or newsfeeds? The majority of Canadians will answer a resounding *yes*. It's not just because we like to feel connected to friends and current events; it's also because the devices and apps are designed not only to engage us but to hook us.

According to Nir Eyal, author of *Hooked: How to Build Habit-Forming Products*, "these devices and apps are hacking our attention. That's what they're designed to do."[14]

Designers use principles of behavioural psychology based on the work of B.F. Skinner. Through rewards systems, like notifications, likes, and pleasing sounds, habits are formed as our online behaviours are being positively reinforced. And when rewards are intermittent, Skinner's research on conditioning shows that responses increase.[15] This means that we click more to increase our chances of a rewarding outcome.

Eyal notes that if we are going to change our behaviours, we need to discover the root of our dependency:

> The root cause is what's called an internal trigger, not the external triggers that we tend to blame—the pings, the dings, the rings. Those are external triggers. It's these internal triggers—uncertainty, loneliness, fatigue, anxiety, stress—this is the reason we keep reaching for one distraction or another.[16]

While it isn't realistic to give up technology altogether, understanding why we rely on technology and taking steps to limit our access will decrease distraction and dependency.[17]

- Increasingly, we are presenting to distracted audiences. While it is impolite to use a device during someone's presentation, many audience members have developed dependence on their smartphones. What are some creative ways that you can have the audience use their devices to engage with your content?

LEARNING OBJECTIVE 4

Specify delivery techniques for use before, during, and after a presentation.

Polishing Your Delivery and Following Up

Once you have organized your presentation and prepared visuals, you are ready to practise delivering it. You will feel more confident and appear more professional if you know more about various delivery methods and techniques to use before, during, and after your presentation.

Choosing a Delivery Method

Inexperienced speakers often hold on to myths about public speaking. They may believe that they must memorize an entire presentation or read from a manuscript to be successful. Let's debunk the myths and focus on effective delivery techniques.

Avoid Memorizing Your Presentation. Unless you are an experienced performer, you will sound robotic and unnatural if you try to recite your talk by heart. What's more, forgetting your place can be disastrous! That is why we don't recommend memorizing an entire oral presentation. However, memorizing significant parts—the introduction, the conclusion, and perhaps a meaningful quotation—can make your presentation dramatic and impressive.

Don't Read From Your Notes. Reading your business presentation to an audience from notes or a manuscript is boring, and listeners will quickly lose interest. Because reading suggests that you don't know your topic well, the audience loses confidence in your expertise. Reading also prevents you from maintaining eye contact. You can't see audience reactions; consequently, you can't benefit from feedback.

Deliver Your Presentation Extemporaneously. The best plan for delivering convincing business presentations, by far, is to speak *extemporaneously*, especially when you are displaying a multimedia presentation such as a PowerPoint slideshow or Prezi canvas. Extemporaneous delivery means speaking freely, generally without notes, after preparing and rehearsing. Reading from notes or a manuscript in addition to a PowerPoint slideshow or a Prezi canvas will damage your credibility.

Know When Notes Are Appropriate. If you give a talk without multimedia technology, you may use note cards or an outline containing key sentences and major ideas, but beware of reading from a script. By preparing and then practising with your notes, you can use them while also talking to your audience in a conversational manner. Your notes should be neither entire paragraphs nor single words. Instead, they should contain a complete sentence or two to introduce each major idea. Below the topic sentence(s), outline subpoints and illustrations. Note cards will keep you on track and prompt your memory but only if you have rehearsed the presentation thoroughly.

Familiarize Yourself With Online Software Functions. When delivering your presentation using videoconferencing platforms like Zoom or WebEx, take time to familiarize yourself with the software functions. Do you know how to view and respond to participants' comments? Are you comfortable with audio and video functions and how to share your screen? Review online tutorials to improve your online proficiency before your presentation.

Combating Stage Fright

Nearly everyone experiences some degree of stage fright when speaking before a group. Being afraid is quite natural and results from actual physiological changes occurring in your body. Faced with a frightening situation, your body reacts with the fight-or-flight response, discussed more fully in the next Career Coach box. You can learn to control and reduce stage fright, as well as to incorporate techniques for effective speaking, by using the following strategies and techniques before, during, and after your presentation.

Before Your Presentation

Speaking in front of a group will become less daunting if you allow for adequate preparation, sufficient practice, and rehearsals. Interacting with the audience and limiting surprises, such as malfunctioning equipment, will also enhance your peace of mind. Review the following tips for a smooth start:

- **Prepare thoroughly.** One of the most effective strategies for reducing stage fright is knowing your subject thoroughly. Research your topic diligently and prepare a careful sentence outline. Those who try to wing it usually suffer the worst butterflies—and give the worst presentations.
- **Rehearse repeatedly.** When you rehearse, practise your entire presentation, not just the first half. In PowerPoint you may print out speaker's notes, an outline, or a handout featuring miniature slides, which are excellent for practice. If you don't use an electronic slideshow, place your outline sentences on separate note cards. You may also want to include transitional sentences to help you move to the next topic as you practise. Rehearse alone or before friends and family. Also consider making an audio or a video recording of your rehearsals so you can evaluate your effectiveness.
- **Time yourself.** Most audiences tend to get restless during longer talks. Therefore, try to complete your presentation in no more than 20 minutes. If you have a time limit, don't go over it. Set a simple kitchen timer during your rehearsal to keep track of time. Better yet, PowerPoint offers a function called Rehearse Timings in the Slide Show tab that can measure the length of your talk as you practise. Other presentation software packages offer similar features.
- **Dress professionally.** Dressing professionally for a presentation will make you look more credible to your audience. You will also feel more confident. If you are not used to professional attire, practise wearing it or you may appear uncomfortable in formal wear.
- **Check the room and the equipment.** If you are using a computer, a projector, or sound equipment, be certain they are operational. Before you start, check electrical outlets and the position of the viewing screen. Ensure that the seating arrangement is appropriate to your needs.

Go to section 14-4c in MindTap, where you can watch a video featuring Jarrod Hann, VP sales, discuss rehearsing business presentations.

CAREER COACH

How to Avoid Stage Fright

Ever get nervous before making a presentation? Everyone does! And it's not all in your head, either. When you face something threatening or challenging, your body reacts in what psychologists call the fight-or-flight response. This physical reflex provides your body with increased energy to deal with threatening situations. It also creates those sensations—dry mouth, sweaty hands, increased heart rate, and stomach butterflies—that we associate with stage fright. The fight-or-flight response prepares your body for action—in this case, making a presentation.

Because everyone feels some form of apprehension before speaking, it's impossible to eliminate the physiological symptoms altogether. However, you can reduce their effects with the following techniques:

- **Breathe deeply.** Use deep breathing to ease your fight-or-flight symptoms. Inhale to a count of ten, hold this breath to a count of ten, and exhale to a count of ten. Concentrate on your counting and your breathing; both activities reduce your stress.
- **Convert your fear.** Don't view your sweaty palms and dry mouth as evidence of fear. Interpret them as symptoms of exuberance, excitement, and enthusiasm to share your ideas.
- **Know your topic and come prepared.** Feel confident about your topic. Select a topic that you know well and that is relevant to your audience. Prepare thoroughly and practise extensively.
- **Use positive self-talk.** Remind yourself that you know your topic and are prepared. Tell yourself that the audience is on your side—because it is! Moreover, most speakers appear to be more confident than they feel. Make this apparent confidence work for you.
- **Take a sip of water.** Drink some water to alleviate your dry mouth and constricted voice box, especially if you're talking for more than 15 minutes.
- **Shift the spotlight to your visuals.** At least some of the time the audience will be focusing on your slides, handouts, or whatever you have prepared—and not totally on you.
- **Ignore any stumbles.** Realize that it is okay to make an occasional mistake. Don't apologize or confess your nervousness. If you make a mistake, ignore the stumble and keep going. The audience will forget any mistakes quickly.
- **Feel proud when you finish.** You will be surprised at how good you feel when you finish. Take pride in what you have accomplished, and your audience will reward you with applause and congratulations. Your body, of course, will call off the fight-or-flight response and return to normal!

CENGAGE

MINDTAP

Check out section 14-4c in MindTap, where you can watch a video featuring Karen Richardson, an associate marketing manager, discuss being prepared for presentations.

- **Greet members of the audience.** Try to make contact with a few members of the audience when you enter the room, while you are waiting to be introduced, or when you go to the podium. Your body language should convey friendliness, confidence, and enjoyment.
- **Practise stress reduction.** If you feel tension and fear while you are waiting your turn to speak, use stress-reduction techniques, such as deep breathing. Additional techniques to help you conquer stage fright are presented in the Career Coach box.

During Your Presentation

To stay in control during your talk, to build credibility, and to engage your audience, follow these time-tested guidelines for effective speaking:

- **Begin with a pause and present your first sentence from memory.** When you first approach the audience, take a moment to make yourself comfortable. Establish your control of the situation. By memorizing your opening, you can immediately establish rapport with the audience through eye contact. You will also sound confident and knowledgeable.
- **Maintain eye contact.** If the size of the audience overwhelms you, pick out two individuals on the right and two on the left. Talk directly to these people. Don't ignore listeners in the back of the room. Even when presenting to a large audience, try to make genuine, not fleeting eye contact with as many people as possible during your presentation.

- **Control your voice and vocabulary.** This means speaking in moderated tones but loudly enough to be heard. Eliminate verbal static, such as *ah, er, like, you know*, and *um*. Silence is preferable to meaningless fillers when you are thinking of your next idea.
- **Use a microphone.** When possible, use a microphone so everyone can hear you clearly, especially in a large or busy room. If offered a microphone, never decline by saying your voice is loud enough. Microphones provide a clear and distinct sound, enabling people with hearing loss to fully engage in your presentation.[18]
- **Show enthusiasm.** If you are not excited about your topic, how can you expect your audience to be? Show passion for your topic through your tone, facial expressions, and gestures. Adding variety to your voice also helps to keep your audience alert and interested.
- **Skip the apologies.** Don't begin with a weak opening, such as I know you have heard this before, but we need to review it anyway. Or I had trouble with my computer and the slides, so bear with me. Unless the issue is blatant, such as not being able to load the presentation or make the projector work, apologies are counterproductive. Focus on your presentation.
- **Slow down and know when to pause.** Many novice speakers talk too rapidly, displaying their nervousness and making it very difficult for audience members to understand their ideas. Put the brakes on and listen to what you are saying. Pauses give the audience time to absorb an important point. Silence can be effective, especially when you are transitioning from one point to another.
- **Move naturally.** If you have a lectern, don't hide behind it. Move about casually and naturally. Avoid fidgeting with your clothing, hair, or items in your pockets. Do not roll up your sleeves or put your hands in your pockets. Learn to use your body to express a point.
- **Control visual aids with clickers, pointers, and blank screens.** Discuss and interpret each visual aid for the audience. Move aside as you describe it so that people can see it fully. Learn to use a clicker to advance your slides remotely. Use a laser pointer if necessary, but steady your hand if it is shaking. Dim the slideshow when not discussing the slides. In Slide Show view in PowerPoint, press B on the keyboard to blacken the screen or W to turn the screen white. In Prezi, remember to zoom back out when necessary.
- **Avoid digressions.** Stick to your outline and notes. Don't suddenly include clever little anecdotes or digressions that occur to you on the spot. If it is not part of your rehearsed material, leave it out so you can finish on time.
- **Summarize your main points and drive home your message.** Conclude your presentation by reiterating your main points or by emphasizing what you want the audience to think or do. Once you have announced your conclusion, proceed to it directly.

After Your Presentation

As you are concluding your presentation, handle questions and answers competently and provide handouts if appropriate. Try the following techniques:

- **Distribute handouts.** If you prepared handouts with data the audience will need, pass them out after you finish to prevent any distraction during your talk.
- **Encourage questions but keep control.** If the situation permits a question-and-answer period, announce it at the beginning of your presentation. Then, when you finish, ask for questions. Set a time limit for questions and answers. If you don't know the answer to a question, don't make one up or panic. Instead offer to find the answer within a day or two. If you make such a promise, be sure to follow through. Don't allow one individual to dominate the Q & A period. Keep the entire audience involved.
- **Repeat questions.** Although you may hear the question, some audience members may not have. Begin each answer with a repetition of the question. This also gives you thinking time. Then, direct your answer to the entire audience.

- **Reinforce your main points.** You can use your answers to restate your primary ideas (*I'm glad you brought that up because it gives me a chance to elaborate on . . .*). In answering questions, avoid becoming defensive or debating the questioner.
- **Avoid *Yes, but* answers.** The word *but* immediately cancels any preceding message. Try replacing it with *and*. For example, *Yes, X has been tried. And Y works even better because. . . .*
- **End with a summary and appreciation.** To signal the end of the session before you take the last question, say something like, *We have time for just one more question.* As you answer the last question, try to work it into a summary of your main points. Then, express appreciation to the audience for the opportunity to talk with them.

CHECKLIST

Preparing and Organizing Oral Presentations

Getting Ready to Speak

- **Identify your purpose.** Decide what you want your audience to believe, remember, or do when you finish. Aim all parts of your talk toward this purpose.
- **Analyze the audience.** Consider how to adapt your message (its organization, appeals, and examples) to your audience's knowledge and needs.

Organizing the Introduction

- **Connect with the audience.** Capture the audience's attention by opening with a promise, story, startling fact, question, quotation, relevant problem, or self-effacing joke.
- **Establish your authority.** Demonstrate your credibility by identifying your position, expertise, knowledge, or qualifications.
- **Preview your main points.** Introduce your topic and summarize its principal parts.

Organizing the Body

- **Develop two to four main points.** Streamline your topic so that you can concentrate on its major issues.
- **Arrange the points logically.** Sequence your points chronologically, from most important to least important, by comparison, or by some other strategy.
- **Prepare transitions.** Between major points write bridge statements that connect the previous item to the next one. Use transitional expressions as verbal signposts (*first, second, then, however, consequently*).
- **Have extra material ready.** Be prepared with more information and visuals in case you have additional time to fill.

Organizing the Conclusion

- **Review your main points.** Emphasize your main ideas in the closing so your audience will remember them.
- **Provide a strong, final focus.** Tell how your listeners can use this information, why you have spoken, or what you want them to do. End with a specific audience benefit or thought-provoking idea (a takeaway), not just a boring rehash.

Designing Visual Aids

- **Select your medium carefully.** Consider the pros and cons of each alternative.
- **Highlight main ideas.** Use visual aids to illustrate major concepts only. Keep them brief and simple.
- **Try to replace bullets whenever possible.** Use flowcharts, diagrams, timelines, and images to substitute for bulleted lists when suitable.
- **Use aids skillfully.** Talk to the audience, not to the visuals. Paraphrase their content.

Developing Multimedia Presentations

- **Learn to use your software program.** Study template and layout designs to see how you can adapt them to your purposes.
- **Select colours based on the light level in the room.** Consider how mixing light and dark fonts and backgrounds affects their visibility. Use templates and preset layouts if you are new to your presentation software.
- **Use bulleted points for major ideas.** Make sure your points are all parallel, and observe the 6-x-6 rule.
- **Include multimedia options that will help you convey your message.** Use moderate animation features and hyperlinks to make your talk more interesting and to link to files with related content in the same document, in other documents, or on the Internet. Use Prezi's zooming feature to help audience members focus on details.
- **Make speaker's notes.** Jot down the narrative supporting each visual, and use these notes to practise your presentation. Do not read from notes while speaking to an audience, however.
- **Maintain control.** Don't let your slides or canvas upstage you. Engage your audience by using additional techniques to help them visualize your points.

Concept Check

1. Why do some presenters avoid making steady eye contact? What might these individuals do to correct this problem?
2. What are the ways you can design and deliver your presentation to make it accessible for everyone?

Developing Intercultural and Team Presentations

LEARNING OBJECTIVE 5

Organize presentations for intercultural audiences and in teams.

Most of the information presented thus far assumes you are a single presenter before a traditional audience. However, in this increasingly digital and global workplace, presentations take on myriad forms and purposes. Now we'll explore effective techniques for adapting presentations to intercultural audiences and participating in team-based presentations.

Adapting Presentations to Intercultural Audiences

Every good speaker adapts to the audience, and intercultural presentations call for special adjustments and sensitivity. Most people understand that they must speak slowly, choose simple English, avoid jargon and clichés, use short sentences, and pause frequently when communicating with people for whom English is an additional language (EAL).

Beyond these basic language adaptations, however, more fundamental sensitivity is often necessary. In organizing a presentation for an intercultural audience, you may need to anticipate and adapt to various speaking conventions, values, and nonverbal behaviours. You may also need to contend with limited language skills and a certain reluctance to voice opinions openly.

Understanding Different Values and Nonverbal Behaviours. In addressing intercultural audiences, anticipate expectations and perceptions that may differ significantly from your own.

- **Indirect approach.** North American emphasis on getting to the point quickly is not equally prized around the globe. Therefore, think twice about delivering your main idea up front. Many people (notably those in Japanese, Latin American, and Arabic cultures) consider such directness to be brash and inappropriate. Others may not share our cultural emphasis on straightforwardness.
- **Language and pace.** When working with an interpreter or speaking before individuals whose English is limited, you must be very careful about your language. For example, you will need to express ideas in small chunks to give the interpreter time to translate. You may need to slow down as you speak and stop after each thought to allow time for the translation that will follow. Even if your presentation or speech is being translated simultaneously, remember to speak slowly and to pause after each sentence to ensure that your message is rendered correctly in the target language.
- **Organization.** You may want to divide your talk into distinct topics, developing each separately and encouraging a discussion period after each one. Such organization enables participants to ask questions and digest what has been presented. This technique is especially effective in cultures in which people communicate in "loops." In the Middle East, for example, Arab speakers "mix circuitous, irrelevant (by North American standards) conversations with short dashes of information that go directly to the point." Presenters who are patient, tolerant, and "mature" (in the eyes of the audience) will make the sale or win the contract.[19]
- **Formality.** Remember, too, that some cultures prefer greater formality than North Americans exercise. When communicating with people from such cultures, instead of first names, use only honorifics (*Mr.*, *Ms.*, or Mx.) and last names, as well as academic

ETHICS CHECK

Fast Talkers

CBC News reported that technology may be turning us into faster talkers. Studies show that Canadians are speaking faster, often too fast for our brains to fully process. The average rate of speech used to be 145 words per minute (wpm), and now it is being measured at 160 to 180 wpm.[22] In one of your courses, you are watching a PowerPoint presentation during which the presenter talks so rapidly that it is difficult to keep up. How should the instructor and the class handle the evaluation of such a presentation?

or business titles—such as *doctor* or *director*. Writing on a flipchart seems natural and spontaneous in this country. Abroad, though, such informal techniques may suggest that the speaker does not value the audience enough to prepare proper visual aids in advance.[20]

Adjusting Visual Aids to Intercultural Audiences. Although you may have to exercise greater caution with culturally diverse audiences, you still want to use visual aids to help communicate your message. Find out from your international contact whether you can present in English or will need an interpreter. In many countries listeners are too polite or too proud to speak up when they don't understand you. One expert advises explaining important concepts in several ways by using different words and then requesting members of the audience to relay their understanding of what you have just said back to you. Another expert suggests packing more text on to PowerPoint slides and staying closer to the literal meaning of words. After all, most EAL speakers understand written text much better than they comprehend spoken English. In North America presenters may spend 90 seconds on a slide, whereas in other countries they may need to slow down to two minutes per slide.[21]

To ensure clarity and show courtesy, provide handouts in English and the target language. Distribute translated handouts, summarizing your important information, when you finish. Never use numbers without projecting or writing them out for all to see. If possible, say numbers in both languages, but only if you can pronounce or even speak the target language well enough to avoid embarrassment.

Preparing Collaborative Presentations With Teams

For many reasons increasing numbers of organizations are using teams, as discussed in Chapter 2. While the goals of each team presentation will vary, the outcome of any team effort is often (a) a written report, (b) a multimedia slideshow or presentation, or (c) an oral presentation delivered live. The boundaries are becoming increasingly blurred between flat, two-dimensional hard-copy reports and multimedia, hyperlinked slideshows, and nonlinear presentations. Both hard-copy reports and multimedia presentations are delivered to clients in business today.

Preparing to Work Together. Before any group begins to talk about a specific project, members should get together and establish basic ground rules. One of the first tasks is naming a meeting leader to conduct meetings, a recorder to keep a record of group decisions, and an evaluator to determine whether the group is on target and meeting its goals. The group should decide whether it will be governed by consensus (everyone must agree), by majority rule, or by some other method.

Another important topic to discuss during team formation is how to deal with team members who are not carrying their share of the load. Teams should decide whether they will "fire" members who are not contributing or take some other action in dealing with slackers.

The most successful teams make meetings a priority. They compare schedules to set up the best meeting times, and they meet often, either in person or virtually. Today's software makes meeting and collaborating online efficient and productive. Team members can use tools such as Google Drive to collaboratively create and edit documents and presentations. Prezi offers a tool called Meeting that allows team members to collaborate live on a Prezi canvas. Team members who learn to use these tools can work on presentations with others from anywhere in the world at any time of day, synchronously or asynchronously.

Planning and Preparing the Presentation. Once teams have established ground rules, members are ready to discuss the presentation. During these discussions, they must be sure to keep a record of all decisions. They should establish the specific purpose for the presentation and identify the main issues involved. They should consider how the presentation will be delivered—in person, online, or by e-mail. The team should decide on its parts, length, and graphics. They should profile the audience and focus on the questions audience members will want answered. If the presentation involves persuasion, they must decide what appeals will achieve the team's purpose.

Next the team should develop a work plan (see Chapter 11), assign jobs, and set deadlines. If time is short, members should work backward from the due date. Teams must schedule time for content and creative development, as well as for a series of rehearsals. The best-planned presentations can fall apart if they are poorly rehearsed.

All team members should have written assignments. These assignments should detail each member's specific responsibilities for researching content, producing visuals, developing handout materials, building transitions between segments, and showing up for rehearsals.

Collecting Information. One of the most challenging jobs for team projects is generating and collecting information. Unless facts are accurate, the most high-powered presentation will fail. Brainstorm for ideas, assign topics, and decide who will be responsible for gathering what information. Establishing deadlines for collecting information is important if a team is to remain on schedule. Team members should also discuss ways to ensure the accuracy of the information collected.

Organizing, Writing, and Revising. When a project progresses into the organizing and writing stages, a team may need to modify some of its earlier decisions. Team members may review the proposed organization of the final presentation and adjust it if necessary. In composing the first draft of a presentation, team members will probably write separate segments. As they work on these segments, they should use the same version of a presentation graphics program to facilitate combining files. They can also use tools such as Google Drive to edit documents.

As individuals work on separate parts of an oral presentation, team members must try to make logical connections between segments. Each presenter builds a bridge to the next member's topic to create a smooth transition. Team members should also agree to use the same template, and they should allow only one person to make global changes in colour, font, and other formatting on the slide and title masters.

Editing, Rehearsing, and Evaluating. The last stage in a collaborative project involves editing, rehearsing, and evaluating. One person should merge all the files, run a spell-checker, and be certain that the files are consistent in design, format, and vocabulary. Teams making presentations should practise together several times. If that is not feasible, experts say that teams must schedule at least one full real-time rehearsal with the entire group. Whenever possible, practise in a room[23] that is similar to the location of your talk. Consider video recording one of the rehearsals so that all presenters can critique their own performance. Schedule a dress rehearsal with an audience at least two days before the actual presentation. Practise fielding questions.

Successful group presentations emerge from thoughtful preparation, clear definitions of contributors' roles, commitment to a group-approved plan, and a willingness to take responsibility for the final product.

Concept Check

1. Discuss four effective ways to design and deliver your presentation for intercultural audiences.
2. When team members divide tasks to work on separate parts of a presentation, how can the team ensure all of the parts come together for a seamless delivery?

Improving Speaking Skills for Effective Phone Calls

LEARNING OBJECTIVE 6

List techniques for improving telephone skills to project a positive image.

One form of business presentation involves presenting yourself on the telephone, a skill that is still very important in today's workplace. Despite the heavy reliance on e-mail, the telephone remains an extremely important piece of equipment in offices. With today's wireless technology, it doesn't matter whether you are in or out of the office. You can usually be reached by phone. This section focuses on traditional telephone techniques as well as smartphone use and voice mail—all opportunities to make a good impression. As a business communicator, you can be more productive, efficient, and professional by following some simple suggestions.

Making Telephone Calls Professionally

Before making a telephone call, decide whether the intended call is really necessary. Could you find the information yourself? If you wait a while, will the problem resolve itself? Perhaps your message could be delivered more efficiently by some other means. Some companies have found that telephone calls are often less important than the work they interrupt. Alternatives to telephone calls include instant messaging, texting, e-mail, memos, and calls to automated voice mail systems. If you must make a telephone call, consider using the following suggestions to make it fully productive:

- **Plan a mini-agenda.** To avoid having to make a second telephone call, jot down notes regarding all the topics you need to discuss.
- **Use a three-point introduction.** When placing a call, immediately (a) name the person you are calling, (b) identify yourself and your affiliation, and (c) give a brief explanation of your reason for calling. For example: *May I speak to Larry Lieberman? This is Hillary Dahl of Sebastian Enterprises, and I'm seeking information about a software program called ZoneAlarm Internet Security.*
- **Be brisk if you are rushed.** For business calls when your time is limited, avoid questions such as *How are you?* Instead, say, *Lisa, I knew you would be the only one who could answer these two questions for me.* Another efficient strategy is to set a contract with the caller: *Lisa, I have only ten minutes, but I really wanted to get back to you.*
- **Be cheerful and accurate.** Let your voice show the same kind of animation that you radiate when you greet people in person. In your mind try to envision the individual answering the telephone. A smile can certainly affect the tone of your voice, so smile at that person.
- **Be professional and courteous.** Remember that you are representing yourself and your company when you make phone calls. Use professional vocabulary and courteous language. Say *thank you* and *please* during your conversations. Don't eat, drink, or chew gum while talking on the phone: these activities can often be heard on the other end.
- **Bring it to a close.** The responsibility for ending a call lies with the caller. This is sometimes difficult to do if the other person rambles on. You may need to use suggestive closing language, such as the following: (a) *I have certainly enjoyed talking with you*; (b) *Thanks for your help*; or (c) *I must go now, but should we talk again in a few weeks?*
- **Avoid telephone tag.** If you call someone who's not in, ask when it would be best to call again. State that you will call at a specific time—and do it. If you ask a person to call you, give a time when you can be reached—and then be sure you are available at that time.
- **Leave complete voice mail messages.** Always enunciate clearly and speak slowly when giving your telephone number or spelling your name. Be sure to provide a complete message, including your name, telephone number, and the time and date of your call. Explain your purpose so that the receiver can be ready with the required information when returning your call.

Receiving Telephone Calls Professionally

With a little forethought you can project a professional image and make your telephone a productive, efficient work tool. Developing good telephone manners and techniques, such as the following, will also reflect well on you and on your organization.

- **Identify yourself immediately.** In answering your telephone or someone else's, provide your name, title or affiliation, and, possibly, a greeting. For example, *Larry Lieberman, Digital Imaging Corporation. How may I help you?* Force yourself to speak clearly and slowly. Remember that the caller may be unfamiliar with what you are saying and fail to recognize slurred syllables.
- **Be responsive and helpful.** If you are in a support role, be sympathetic to callers' needs. Instead of *I don't know,* try *That's a good question; let me investigate.* Instead of *We can't do that,* try *That's a tough one; let's see what we can do.* Avoid *no* at the beginning of a sentence. It sounds especially abrasive and displeasing because it suggests total rejection.

- **Practise telephone confidentiality.** When answering calls for others, be courteous and helpful, but don't give out confidential information. Better to say, *She's away from her desk* or *He's out of the office* than to report a colleague's exact whereabouts. Also, be tight-lipped about sharing company information with strangers.
- **Take messages carefully.** Few things are as frustrating as receiving a potentially important phone message that is illegible. Repeat the spelling of names and verify telephone numbers. Write messages legibly and record their time and date. Promise to give the messages to intended recipients, but don't guarantee return calls.
- **Leave the line respectfully.** If you must put a call on hold, let the caller know and give an estimate of how long you expect the call to be on hold. Give the caller the option of holding. Say, *Would you prefer to hold, or would you like me to call you back?*

Using Smartphones for Business

Today's smartphones are very sophisticated mobile devices. They enable you to conduct business from virtually anywhere at any time. The smartphone has become an essential part of communication in the workplace, and the number of Canadian cell phone users has continued to increase. More than 91 percent of Canadians own a cell phone, compared to only 41 percent owning a landline. This indicates that "approximately one third of Canadian households rely exclusively on wireless services."[24] Because so many people depend on their smartphones, it is important to understand proper use and etiquette. Most of us have experienced thoughtless and rude smartphone behaviour. Researchers say that the rampant use of mobile electronic devices has increased workplace incivility. Some employees consider texting and compulsive e-mail checking while working and during meetings disruptive, even insulting. To avoid offending, smart business communicators practise smartphone etiquette, as outlined in Figure 14.10.

Making the Best Use of Voice Mail

Because telephone calls can be disruptive, many businesspeople make extensive use of voice mail to intercept and screen incoming calls on their landlines and smartphones. Here are some ways to make voice mail work most effectively for you.

On the Receiver's End. Your voice mail should project professionalism and should provide an easy way for your callers to leave messages for you. Here are some voice mail etiquette tips:

- **Don't overuse voice mail.** Don't use voice mail to avoid taking phone calls. It is better to answer calls yourself than to let voice mail messages build up.
- **Prepare a professional, concise, friendly greeting.** Make your voice mail greeting sound warm and inviting, both in tone and content. Identify yourself, thank the caller, and briefly explain that you are unavailable. Invite the caller to leave a message or, if appropriate, call back. Here's a typical voice mail greeting: *Hi! This is Larry Lieberman of Proteus Software, and I appreciate your call. You have reached my voice mail because I'm either working with customers or talking on another line at the moment. Please leave your name, number, and reason for calling so that I can be prepared when I return your call.*
- **Respond to messages promptly.** Check your messages regularly, and try to return all voice mail messages within one business day.
- **Plan for vacations and other extended absences.** If you will not be picking up voice mail messages for an extended period, let callers know how they can reach someone else if needed.

On the Caller's End. When leaving a voice mail message, you should follow these tips:

- **Be prepared to leave a message.** Before calling someone, be prepared for voice mail. Decide what you are going to say and what information you are going to include in your message. If necessary, write your message down before calling.

FIGURE 14.10 Adopting Courteous and Responsible Cell Phone Practices

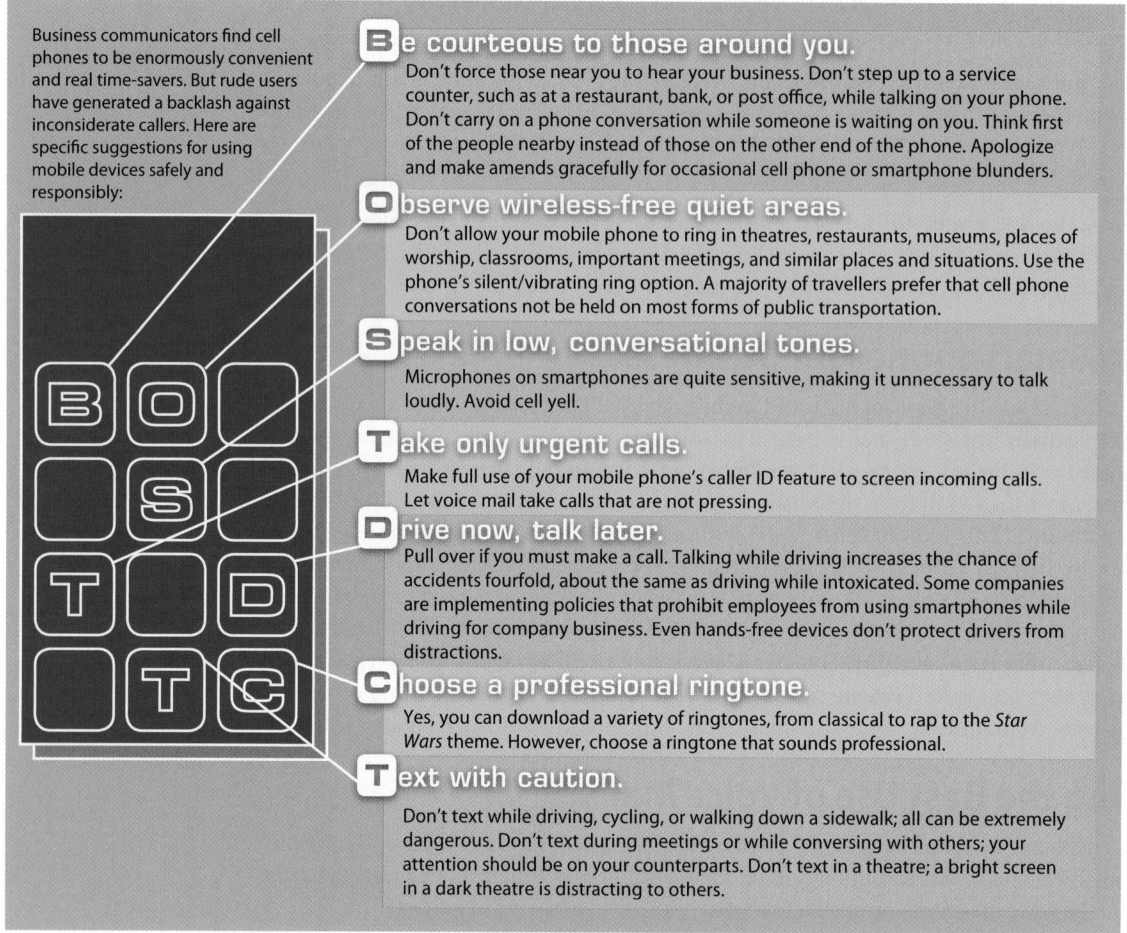

Business communicators find cell phones to be enormously convenient and real time-savers. But rude users have generated a backlash against inconsiderate callers. Here are specific suggestions for using mobile devices safely and responsibly:
Be courteous to those around you.
Don't force those near you to hear your business. Don't step up to a service counter, such as at a restaurant, bank, or post office, while talking on your phone. Don't carry on a phone conversation while someone is waiting on you. Think first of the people nearby instead of those on the other end of the phone. Apologize and make amends gracefully for occasional cell phone or smartphone blunders.
Observe wireless-free quiet areas.
Don't allow your mobile phone to ring in theatres, restaurants, museums, places of worship, classrooms, important meetings, and similar places and situations. Use the phone's silent/vibrating ring option. A majority of travellers prefer that cell phone conversations not be held on most forms of public transportation.
Speak in low, conversational tones.
Microphones on smartphones are quite sensitive, making it unnecessary to talk loudly. Avoid cell yell.
Take only urgent calls.
Make full use of your mobile phone's caller ID feature to screen incoming calls. Let voice mail take calls that are not pressing.
Drive now, talk later.
Pull over if you must make a call. Talking while driving increases the chance of accidents fourfold, about the same as driving while intoxicated. Some companies are implementing policies that prohibit employees from using smartphones while driving for company business. Even hands-free devices don't protect drivers from distractions.
Choose a professional ringtone.
Yes, you can download a variety of ringtones, from classical to rap to the *Star Wars* theme. However, choose a ringtone that sounds professional.
Text with caution.
Don't text while driving, cycling, or walking down a sidewalk; all can be extremely dangerous. Don't text during meetings or while conversing with others; your attention should be on your counterparts. Don't text in a theatre; a bright screen in a dark theatre is distracting to others.
B O S T D T C

- **Leave a concise, thorough message.** When leaving a message, always identify yourself by using your complete name and affiliation. Mention the date and time you called and a brief explanation of your reason for calling. Always leave a complete phone number, including the area code. Tell the receiver the best time to return your call. Don't ramble.
- **Speak slowly and articulate.** You want to make sure that your receiver will be able to understand your message. Speak slowly and pronounce your words carefully, especially when providing your phone number. The receiver should be able to write information down without having to replay your message.
- **Be careful with confidential information.** Don't leave confidential or private information in a voice mail message. Remember that anyone could gain access to this information.

Concept Check

1. Do your own informal tally in your class to find out what you and your classmates consider acceptable cell phone use in various settings—when walking down the street, in a restaurant, in a place of worship, in class, on a date, and more.
2. When is it acceptable not to return a call when a callback was requested?

SPOTLIGHT ON COMMUNICATION: PART 2

Universal Design for Learning—Revisited

Within a classroom or workplace setting, you will be required to present or facilitate content to others. Your audience may have invisible challenges that affect the way they learn. For example, you may not know that there are people with hearing difficulties in your audience:

Christina Morillo

> Sound is a particularly effective way to convey the impact of information, which is why sound design is so important in movies and why the human voice is particularly effective for conveying emotion and significance. However, information conveyed solely through sound is not equally accessible to all learners and is especially inaccessible for learners with hearing disabilities, for learners who need more time to process information, or for learners who have memory difficulties. In addition, listening itself is a complex strategic skill that must be learned. To ensure that all learners have access to learning, options should be available for any information, including emphasis, presented aurally.[25]

- Use text equivalents in the form of captions or automated speech-to-text (voice recognition) for spoken language.
- Provide visual diagrams, charts, notations of music or sound.
- Provide written transcripts for videos or auditory clips.
- Provide American Sign Language (ASL) for spoken English.
- Use visual analogues to represent emphasis and prosody (e.g., emoticons, symbols, or images).
- Provide visual or tactile (e.g., vibrations) equivalents for sound effects or alerts.
- Provide visual and/or emotional description for musical interpretation.[26]

CRITICAL THINKING

- In what ways can building in accessibility for students who have visual or hearing challenges benefit those who don't?
- How can you incorporate the options for alternatives to sound in your class presentations?

Summary of Learning Objectives

1 Recognize various types of business presentations, and discuss preparing for any of these presentations.

- Speaking skills rank high on employers' wish lists and are crucial to career success.
- Presentations can be informative or persuasive, face to face or virtual, performed in front of big audiences or smaller groups, and elaborate or simple.
- Business professionals give a variety of business presentations, including briefings, reports, podcasts, virtual presentations, and webinars.
- Once speakers know what they want to accomplish with their presentation, they must identify the purpose and the audience.

2 Explain how to organize your business presentation, build audience rapport, and understand contemporary visual aids.

- The introduction should capture the listener's attention, identify the speaker, establish credibility, and preview the main points.

- The body should discuss two to four main points, with appropriate explanations, details, and verbal signposts to guide listeners.
- The conclusion should review the main points, provide a memorable takeaway, and allow the speaker to leave the podium gracefully.
- Contemporary visual aids—such as multimedia slides, handouts, and nonlinear presentations—illustrate and emphasize main points, draw audience interest, and make the presenter look more professional, better prepared, and more persuasive.

3 Create an impressive, error-free multimedia presentation that shows a firm grasp of basic visual design principles.

- Before creating a presentation, effective speakers analyze its purpose, delivery, and distribution; presenters organize their work by translating the major headings in the outline into slide titles.
- Expert presenters adjust their slide design to their audiences and demonstrate that they understand the meaning of colour, the power of images, and the impact of special effects.
- The final stage of creating a slideshow requires revising and proofreading, as well as evaluating.
- Presenters must anticipate potential technical difficulties, rehearse, and create backups of their presentations.

4 Specify delivery techniques for use before, during, and after a presentation.

- Effective public speaking techniques include avoiding memorizing, refraining from reading from notes, and delivering the presentation extemporaneously.
- Before the talk, speakers prepare a sentence outline, rehearse repeatedly, time themselves, dress professionally, check the room, greet audience members, and practise stress reduction.
- During the talk, speakers present the first sentence from memory, maintain eye contact, control their voice, use a microphone, show enthusiasm, skip apologies, pace themselves, use pauses, move naturally, control visuals competently, avoid digressions, and summarize their main points.
- After the talk, presenters distribute handouts and answer questions; they repeat questions, reinforce main points, avoid *yes, but* answers; and end with a summary and appreciation.

5 Organize presentations for intercultural audiences and in teams.

- Businesspeople adapt language to intercultural audiences and understand different conventions.
- In intercultural environments, presenters speak slowly, use simple English, avoid directness, break the presentation into short chunks, respect formality, and adapt visuals to their audiences.
- Teams of presenters should name a leader, discuss decision making, work out a schedule, determine how to rein in uncooperative members, and decide on the purpose and procedures for preparing the final presentation.
- Teams coordinate their assigned contributions and edit, rehearse, and evaluate their presentations.

6 List techniques for improving telephone skills to project a positive image.

- Efficient callers plan a mini-agenda, use a three-point introduction (name, affiliation, and purpose), practise sounding cheerful and courteous, and use closing language.
- Workers need to follow proper etiquette when using their smartphones for business.
- Skilled businesspeople prepare a concise, friendly voice mail greeting, respond to messages promptly, and plan for extended absences.
- Callers should be prepared to leave a concise message, speak slowly and clearly, and not reveal confidential information.

Chapter Review

1. Why is it important to know your audience and purpose before you start planning your oral presentation? (Obj. 1)
2. What are five types of business presentations that you may encounter in the workplace? (Obj. 1)
3. In the introduction of an oral presentation, you can establish your credibility by using what two methods? (Obj. 2)
4. Why are visual aids particularly useful to inexperience speakers? (Obj. 3)
5. How is the 6-x-6 rule applied in preparing bulleted points in a multimedia slideshow? (Obj. 3)
6. Why should speakers deliver the first sentence from memory? (Obj. 4)
7. Why is it important not to read directly from your notes during a presentation? (Obj. 4)
8. Discuss five ways to avoid stage fright. (Obj. 4)
9. How might presentations before intercultural audiences be altered to be most effective? (Obj. 5)
10. Discuss five tips for using smartphones courteously, safely, and responsibly. (Obj. 6)

Critical Thinking

1. Careful business writers always document their sources in written reports; however, when the report findings are presented by using PowerPoint, the sources are often omitted. Should information in PowerPoint presentations be sourced? If so, how? Is omitting this information unethical? (Obj. 2)
2. Why do many communication consultants encourage businesspeople to move beyond bullet points? What do they recommend instead and why? (Objs. 2, 3)
3. How can speakers prevent multimedia presentation software from overpowering their presentations? (Obj. 3)
4. What is extemporaneous speaking, and what makes it the best delivery method for business presentations? (Obj. 4)
5. **Ethical Issue:** Critics of PowerPoint claim that flashy graphics, sound effects, and animation often conceal thin content. Consider, for example, the findings regarding the space shuttle *Challenger* accident that killed seven astronauts. Report authors charged that NASA scientists had used PowerPoint presentations to make it look as though they had done analyses that they hadn't. An overreliance on presentations instead of focusing on analysis may have contributed to the shuttle disaster.[27] What lessons about ethical responsibilities when using PowerPoint can be learned from this catastrophe in communication? (Objs. 1–3)

Activities

14.1 The Importance of Oral Communication Skills in Your Field (Objs. 1, 4)

YOUR TASK Interview one or two individuals in your professional field. How is oral communication important in this profession? Does the need for oral skills change as one advances? What suggestions can these people make to newcomers to the field for developing proficient oral communication skills? Discuss your findings with your class.

14.2 Outlining an Oral Presentation (Objs. 1, 2)

One of the hardest parts of preparing an oral presentation is developing the outline.

YOUR TASK Select an oral presentation topic from a list provided by your instructor, or suggest an original topic. Prepare an outline for your presentation by using the following format:

Title
Purpose

	I. INTRODUCTION
State your name	A.
Gain attention and involve audience	B.
Establish credibility	C.
Preview main points	D.
Transition	
	II. BODY
Main point	A.
Illustrate, clarify, contrast	1.
	2.
	3.
Transition	
Main point	B.
Illustrate, clarify, contrast	1.
	2.
	3.
Transition	
Main point	C.
Illustrate, clarify, contrast	1.
	2.
	3.
Transition	
	III. CONCLUSION
Summarize main points	A.
Provide final focus or takeaway	B.
Encourage questions	C.

14.3 Observing and Outlining a TEDTalk (Objs. 1–3)

Communication Technology | E-mail | Web

To learn from the presentation skills of the best speakers today, visit the TED channel on YouTube or the TED website. Watch one or more of the 2,400+ TED talks (motto: Ideas worth spreading) available online. Standing at over one billion views worldwide, the presentations cover topics from the fields of technology, entertainment, and design (TED).

YOUR TASK If your instructor directs, select and watch one of the TED talks and outline it. You may also be asked to focus on the speaker's presentation techniques based on the guidelines you have studied in this chapter. Jot down your observations either as notes for a classroom discussion or to serve as a basis for an informative memo or e-mail. If directed by your instructor, compose a concise yet informative tweet directing Twitter users to your chosen TED Talk and commenting on it.

14.4 Taming Stage Fright (Obj. 4)

What scares you the most about making a presentation in front of your class? Being tongue-tied? Fearing all eyes on you? Messing up? Forgetting your ideas and looking unprofessional?

YOUR TASK Discuss the previous questions as a class. Then, in groups of three or four, talk about ways to overcome these fears. Your instructor may ask you to write a memo, an e-mail, or a discussion board post (individually or collectively) summarizing your suggestions, or you may break out of your small groups and report your best ideas to the entire class.

14.5 Something to Talk About: Topics for an Oral Presentation (Objs. 1–5)

Communication Technology | Team | Web

YOUR TASK Select a topic from the following list, or additional topics provided by your instructor. Individually or as a team, prepare a short oral presentation. Consider yourself an expert or a team of experts called in to explain some aspect of the topic before a group of interested people. Because your time is limited, prepare a concise yet forceful presentation with effective visual aids.

If this is a group presentation, form a team of three or four members and conduct thorough research on one of the following topics, as directed by your instructor. Follow the tips on team presentations in this chapter. Divide the tasks fairly, meet for discussions and rehearsals, and crown your achievement with a 10- to 15-minute presentation to your class. Make your multimedia presentation interesting and dynamic.

How can businesses benefit from Facebook, Instagram, Twitter, or LinkedIn? Cite specific examples in your chosen field.

What kind of marketing works best with students on college or university campuses? Word of mouth? Internet advertising? Free samples? How do students prefer to get information about goods and services?

How can your organization appeal to its members to prevent them from texting while driving or from driving under the influence?

How can students and other citizens contribute to conserving gasoline and other fossil fuel to save money and help slow global climate change?

What is the economic outlook for a given product, such as electric cars, laptop computers, digital cameras, fitness equipment, or a product of your choice?

What is telecommuting, and for what kinds of workers is it an appropriate work alternative?

What should a guide to proper smartphone etiquette include?

Why should a company have a written e-mail, Web use, and social media policy?

What are the pros and cons of using Prezi zoom presentations? Would they be appropriate in your field?

What smartphone apps are available that will improve a businessperson's productivity?

14.6 Presenting Yourself Professionally on the Telephone and in Voice Mail (Obj. 6)

YOUR TASK Practising the phone skills you learned in this chapter, leave your instructor a professional voice mail message. Prepare a mini-agenda before you call. Introduce yourself. If necessary, spell your name and indicate the course and section. Speak slowly and clearly, especially when leaving your phone number. Think of a comment you could make about an intriguing fact, a peer discussion, or your business communication class.

Grammar and Mechanics | *Review 14*

Total Review

The first ten chapters reviewed specific guides from Appendix B, Grammar and Mechanics Guide, beginning on page B-1. The exercise in this chapter is a total review, covering all the grammar and mechanics guides plus confusing words and frequently misspelled words. Each of the following sentences has **three** errors in grammar, punctuation, capitalization, usage, or spelling. On a sheet of paper or on your computer, write a correct version. Avoid adding new phrases, starting new sentences, or rewriting in your own words. When you finish, compare your responses with the key in Appendix C.

EXAMPLE: My accountant and me are greatful to be asked to make a short presentation, however, we may not be able to cover the entire budget.

REVISION: My accountant and **I** are **grateful** to be asked to make a short presentation**;** however, we may not be able to cover the entire budget.

1. The CEOs assistant scheduled my colleague and I for a twenty minute presentation to explain the new workplace sustainability initiative.
2. PowerPoint presentations, claims one expert should be no longer then twenty minutes and have no more than ten slides.
3. The introduction to a presentation should accomplish 3 goals, (a) capture attention, (b) establish credibility and (c) preview main points.
4. In the body of a short presentation speakers should focus on no more than 3 principle points.

5. A poll of two thousand employees revealed that 4/5 of them said they feared giving a presentation more then anything else they could think of.
6. A list of tips for inexperienced speakers are found in the article titled "Forty Quick Tips For Speakers."
7. The Director of operations made a fifteen-minute presentation giving step by step instructions on achieving our sustainability goals.
8. In the Spring our companies stock value is expected to raise at least 10 percent.
9. The appearance and mannerisms of a speaker definately effects a listeners evaluation of the message.
10. Because the bosses daughter was a dynamic speaker who had founded a successful company she earned at least twenty thousand dollars for each presentation.

Notes

[1] CAST. (2020). *About universal design for learning.* http://www.cast.org/our-work/about-udl.html#.XmPmiKhKhPY

[2] Ibid.

[3] Government of Alberta. (2010). *Making a difference: Meeting diverse learning needs with differentiated instruction.* https://education.alberta.ca/media/384968/makingadifference_2010.pdf

[4] CAST. (2020). *Offer ways of customizing the display of information.* http://udlguidelines.cast.org/representation/perception/customize-display

[5] Hooey, B. (2005). *Speaking for success!* Toastmasters International. http://membersshaw.ca/toasted/speaking_success.htm

[6] Workopolis. (2014, September). *The most sought after soft skills by Canadian employers.* http://careers.workopolis.com/advice/the-most-sought-after-soft-skills-by-canadian-employers/

[7] Dr. John J. Medina as quoted by Reynolds, G. (2010). *Presentation zen design.* Berkeley, CA: New Riders, p. 97.

[8] Monroe, K. (2018, July 7). *Basics of using Prezi.* https://prezi.com/0ayes0ryabus/basics-of-using-prezi/

[9] Atkinson, C. (2008). *Beyond bullet points* (2nd ed.). Microsoft Press.

[10] Booher, D. (2003). *Speak with confidence: Powerful presentations that inform, inspire, and persuade.* McGraw-Hill Professional, p. 126. See also Paradi, D. (2009, March 3). *Choosing colours for your presentation slides.* Indezine. http://www.indezine.com/ideas/prescolours.html

[11] Bates, S. (2005). *Speak like a CEO: Secrets for commanding attention and getting results.* McGraw-Hill Professional, p. 113.

[12] Sommerville, J. (n.d.). *The seven deadly sins of PowerPoint presentations.* About.com. http://entrepreneurs.about.com/cs/marketing/a/7sinsofppt.htm

[13] Kupsh, J. (2011, January 21). *Presentation delivery guidelines to remember.* Training.http://www.trainingmag.com/article/presentation-delivery-guidelines-remember

[14] CBC Radio. (2020, January 10). *Designing for dependence: How your devices and apps are built to get you hooked.* https://www.cbc.ca/radio/day6/mourning-iran-crash-victims-former-weinstein-aide-zelda-perkins-watching-cats-while-high-design-20-more-1.5421075/designing-for-dependence-how-your-devices-and-apps-are-built-to-get-you-hooked-1.5421078

[15] Ibid.

[16] Ibid.

[17] Ibid.

[18] Ramey, J. B. (2019, March 20). A note from your colleagues with hearing loss: Just use a microphone already. *The Chronicle of Higher Education.* https://www.chronicle.com/article/A-Note-From-Your-Colleagues/245916

[19] Wunderle, W. (2007, March/April). How to negotiate in the Middle East. *U.S. Army Professional Writing Collection, 5*(7). http://www.army.mil/professionalwriting/volumes/volume5/july_2007/7_07_4.html. See also Marks, S. J. (2001, September). Nurturing global workplace connections. *Workforce*, p. 76.

[20] Dulek, R. E., Fielden, J. S., & Hill, J. S. (1991, January/February). International communication: An executive primer. *Business Horizons*, p. 22.

[21] Davidson, R., & Rosen, M. Cited in Brandel, M. (2006, February 20). Sidebar: Don't be the ugly American. *Computerworld.* http://www.computerworld.com/s/article/108772/Sidebar_Don_t_Be_the_Ugly_American

[22] Ross, C. (2011, October 31). *How technology is turning us into faster talkers. CBC News.* http://www.cbc.ca/news/canada/how-technology-is-turning-us-into-faster-talkers-1.1111667

[23] Peterson, R. (n.d.). *Presentations: Are you getting paid for overtime?* Presentation Coaching Institute. http://www.passociates.com/getting_paid_for_overtime.shtml; Marken Communications. (2001, March 14). *The sales presentation: The bottom line is selling.* http://www.markencom.com/docs/01mar14.htm

[24] CWTA. (2019). *Facts and figures.* Retrieved from https://www.cwta.ca/facts-figures/

[25] CAST. (2020). *Offer alternatives for auditory information.* http://udlguidelines.cast.org/representation/perception/alternatives-auditory

[26] Ibid.

[27] Vergano, D. (2004, August 31). Computers: Scientific friend or foe? *USA Today*, p. D6.

UNIT 5

Employment Communication

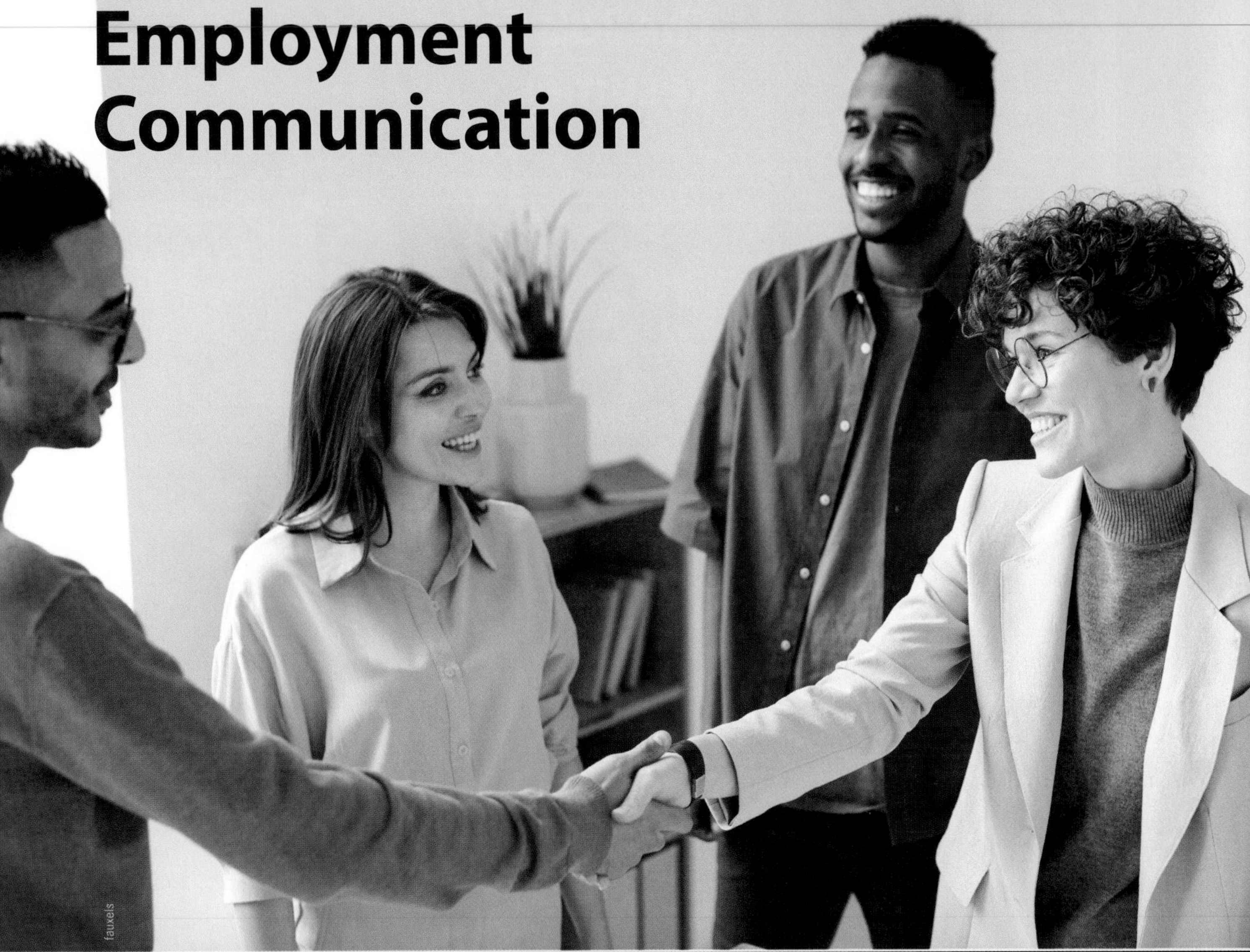

CHAPTER 15
The Job Search and Résumés

CHAPTER 16
Interviewing and Following Up

IN UNIT 5, YOU WILL DEVELOP THE FOLLOWING EMPLOYABILITY SKILLS:

EMPLOYABILITY AND SOFT SKILLS	
Oral and Written Communication	✓
Information Management	✓
Critical Thinking	✓
Problem Solving	✓
Active Listening	✓
Professional Work Behaviours	✓
Goal-setting	✓
Agility	✓
Adaptability	✓
Personal and Social Responsibility	✓
Ethical Decision Making	✓
Engagement	✓
Innovation and Creativity	✓
Learning Worker Attitude	✓
Team Building	✓
Accountability	✓
Project Collaboration	✓
Online Tools and Social Media[1]	✓

CHAPTER 15

The Job Search and Résumés

SFIO CRACHO/Shutterstock

LEARNING OBJECTIVES

After studying this chapter, you should be able to

1 Begin a job search by recognizing emerging trends and technologies, exploring your interests, evaluating your qualifications, and investigating career opportunities.

2 Develop effective search strategies to explore the open job market.

3 Expand your job-search strategies by pursuing the hidden job market.

4 Organize your qualifications and information to create a winning, customized résumé.

5 Optimize your job search and résumé by taking advantage of today's digital tools.

6 Understand the value of cover messages and how to draft and submit a customized message.

SPOTLIGHT ON COMMUNICATION: PART 1

Rocky Mountaineer—Careers With a View

Courtesy of Rocky Mountaineer

Customers who book with Rocky Mountaineer enjoy scenic rail routes from British Columbia to Alberta through the Canadian Rockies.[2] Established in 1990, Rocky Mountaineer now has major Canadian hiring locations in Vancouver, Whistler, Quesnel, and Kamloops, British Columbia, as well as Banff and Jasper, Alberta. Rocky Mountaineer was voted one of BC's top employers in 2020 for the following reasons:[3]

- Rocky Mountaineer's onboard employees enjoy a unique rolling work environment through some of the country's most spectacular scenery, while head office employees can take advantage of an onsite fitness facility with free memberships.
- Along with in-house training initiatives, Rocky Mountaineer supports longer term employee development with tuition subsidies for courses both related and not directly related to their current position.
- Along with three weeks of starting paid vacation, employees at Rocky Mountaineer can take advantage of a discounted rail pass program that extends to their family members and friends.[4]

The hiring opportunities for trains, stations, and guest experience centres include hospitality, business, culinary, managerial positions, and more.[5] Rocky Mountaineer attributes its success to its passionate and dedicated employees:[6]

> We are committed to providing our employees a fantastic environment where coming to work doesn't feel like work. We are committed to an employee experience that parallels that of our guests and we believe that our people are Rocky Mountaineer's number one asset.[7]

CRITICAL THINKING

- Rocky Mountaineer's rail routes run from April to October. What are the benefits and drawbacks of seasonal employment?
- In addition to salary considerations, what other work benefits do you value? For example, Rocky Mountaineer offers discounted rail packages for employees and their families.

Job Searching in the Digital Age

LEARNING OBJECTIVE 1

Begin a job search by recognizing emerging trends and technologies, exploring your interests, evaluating your qualifications, and investigating career opportunities.

Whether you are actively looking for a position now or hope to do so later, becoming aware of job trends and requirements is important so that you can tailor your education for success when you enter the market. This chapter presents cutting-edge advice regarding job searching, résumé writing, and cover messages to give you an advantage in a labour market that is more competitive, more mobile, and more dependent on technology than ever before.

A successful job search today requires a blend of old and new job-hunting skills. Traditional techniques are still effective, but savvy job candidates must also be ready to act on emerging trends, some of which are presented in Figure 15.1. Job boards, social networks, and mobile technologies have all become indispensable tools in hunting for a job. Surprisingly, however, even in this digital age, personal networking, referrals, and who you know continue to be primary routes to hiring.

If you are fearful of entering a highly competitive job market, think of the many advantages you have: your recent training, current skills, and enthusiasm. Remember, too, that you are less expensive to hire than experienced candidates. In addition, you have this book with the latest research, invaluable advice, and model documents to guide you in your job search. Think positively!

Using Technology to Aid Your Job Search

Technology is increasingly an integral part of the job-search process. Nearly every job hunter today has at least one mobile device, and the number of apps for these devices is overwhelming. You can download apps to plan your career, organize the job-search process, scour numerous job boards, and receive immediate job alerts.

FIGURE 15.1 Looking at the Latest Trends in Job Searching and Résumés

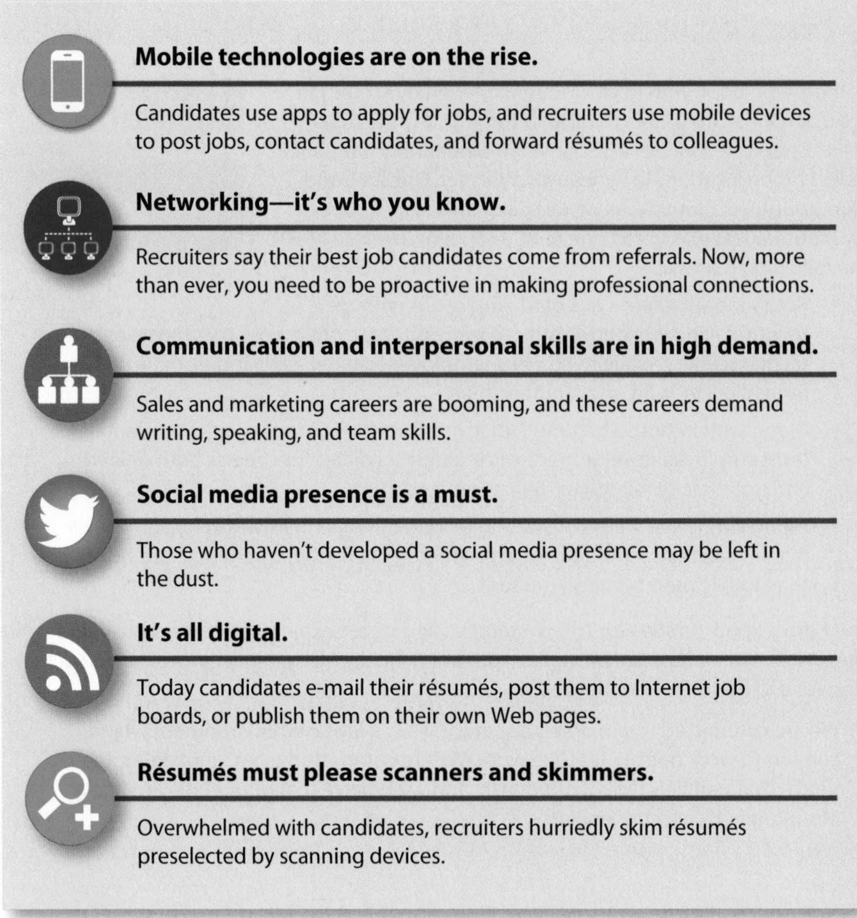

Mobile technologies are on the rise.
Candidates use apps to apply for jobs, and recruiters use mobile devices to post jobs, contact candidates, and forward résumés to colleagues.
Networking—it's who you know.
Recruiters say their best job candidates come from referrals. Now, more than ever, you need to be proactive in making professional connections.
Communication and interpersonal skills are in high demand.
Sales and marketing careers are booming, and these careers demand writing, speaking, and team skills.
Social media presence is a must.
Those who haven't developed a social media presence may be left in the dust.
It's all digital.
Today candidates e-mail their résumés, post them to Internet job boards, or publish them on their own Web pages.
Résumés must please scanners and skimmers.
Overwhelmed with candidates, recruiters hurriedly skim résumés preselected by scanning devices.

Organizations Bet on Technology. Beyond mobile devices, technology has greatly affected the way organizations announce jobs, select candidates, screen résumés, and conduct interviews. Big (and increasingly medium-sized) companies tend to use applicant tracking systems (ATS) to automatically post openings, select résumés, rank candidates, and generate interview requests. In this chapter, you'll learn to craft your job search and résumé to take advantage of tracking systems and other technologies flooding the job-search market.

It's an Employers' Market. At the same time as technology is revolutionizing the job scene, other significant changes in the labour market will affect your job search and subsequent employment. In years past the emphasis was on what the applicant wanted. Today it's on what the employer wants.[8] Employers are most interested in how candidates will add value to their organizations. That's why today's most successful candidates customize their résumés to highlight their qualifications for each opening. In addition, career paths are no longer linear; most new hires will not begin a job and steadily rise through the ranks. Jobs are more short-lived, and people are constantly relearning and retraining.

The Résumé Is Not Dead. The résumé is still important, but it may not be the document that introduces the job seeker these days. Instead, the résumé may come only after the candidate has established a real-world relationship. What's more, chances are that your résumé and cover message will be read digitally rather than in print. Although some attention-grabbing publications scream that the print résumé is dead, the truth is that every job hunter needs one. Whether offered online or in print, your résumé should be always available and current.

FIGURE 15.2 Four Steps in a Successful Job Search

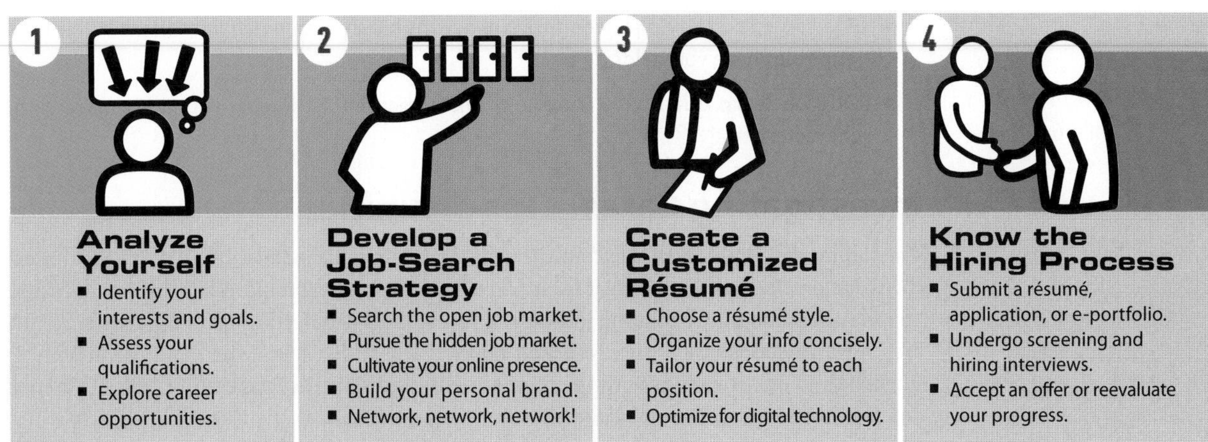

1
Analyze Yourself
■ Identify your interests and goals.
■ Assess your qualifications.
■ Explore career opportunities.
2
Develop a Job-Search Strategy
■ Search the open job market.
■ Pursue the hidden job market.
■ Cultivate your online presence.
■ Build your personal brand.
■ Network, network, network!
3
Create a Customized Résumé
■ Choose a résumé style.
■ Organize your info concisely.
■ Tailor your résumé to each position.
■ Optimize for digital technology.
4
Know the Hiring Process
■ Submit a résumé, application, or e-portfolio.
■ Undergo screening and hiring interviews.
■ Accept an offer or reevaluate your progress.

The job-search process begins long before you are ready to prepare your résumé. Regardless of the kind of employment you seek, you must invest time and effort in getting ready. Your best plan for completing a successful job search involves a four-step process: (1) analyzing yourself, (2) developing a job-search strategy, (3) preparing a résumé, and (4) knowing the hiring process, as illustrated in Figure 15.2.

Launching Your Job Search With Self-Analysis

The first step in a job search is analyzing your interests and goals and evaluating your qualifications. This means exploring what you like and dislike so that you can make good employment choices. For guidance in choosing a career that eventually proves to be satisfying, consider the following questions:

- What are you passionate about? Can you turn this passion into a career?
- Do you enjoy working with people, data, or things?
- Would you like to work for someone else or be your own boss?
- How important are salary, benefits, technology support, and job stability?
- How important are working environment, colleagues, and job stimulation?
- Must you work in a specific city, geographical area, or climate?
- Are you looking for security, travel opportunities, money, power, or prestige?
- How would you describe the perfect job, boss, and coworkers?

Evaluating Your Qualifications

Beyond your interests and goals, take a good look at your qualifications. What assets do you have to offer? Your responses to the following questions will target your thinking and prepare a foundation for your résumé. Always keep in mind, though, that employers seek more than empty assurances: they will want proof of your qualifications.

- What technology skills can you present? What specific software programs are you familiar with? What Internet experience do you have, and what social media skills can you offer?
- Do you communicate well in speech and in writing? Do you know another language?
- How can you verify these talents?
- What other skills have you acquired in school, on the job, or through activities? How can you demonstrate these skills?

- Do you work well with people? Do you enjoy teamwork? What proof can you offer? Consider extracurricular activities, clubs, class projects, and jobs.
- Are you a leader, self-starter, or manager? What evidence can you offer? What leadership roles have you held?
- Do you learn quickly? Can you think critically? How can you demonstrate these characteristics?

Investigating Career Opportunities

The job market in Canada is extraordinarily dynamic and flexible. Individuals just entering the workforce will likely make at least three to four career changes in their lives.[9] Although you may be frequently changing jobs in the future, you still need to train for a specific career area now. In choosing an area, you will make the best decisions when you can match your interests and qualifications with the requirements and rewards in specific careers. Where can you find the best career data? Here are some suggestions:

- **Visit your campus career centre.** Most campus career centres have career counsellors, workshops, literature, inventories, career-related software programs, and employment or internship databases that allow you to explore such fields as accounting, finance, office technology, information systems, and hotel management.
- **Search for apps and online help.** Many job-search sites—such as Monster, CareerBuilder, and Workopolis—offer career-planning information and resources.
- **Use your library.** Print and online resources in your library are especially helpful. Consult *The Blue Book of Canadian Business*, *Canadian Key Business Directory*, and *The Financial Post 100 Best Companies to Work for in Canada* for information about job requirements, qualifications, salaries, and employment trends.
- **Take a summer job, internship, or part-time position in your field.** Nothing is better than trying out a career by actually working in it or in a related area. Many companies offer internships and temporary or part-time jobs to begin training college and university students and to develop relationships with them. Unsurprisingly, many of those internships turn into full-time positions. One study revealed that 60 percent of students who completed paid internships were offered full-time jobs.[10]
- **Interview someone in your chosen field.** People are usually flattered when asked to describe their careers. Inquire about needed skills, required courses, financial and other rewards, benefits, working conditions, future trends, and entry requirements.
- **Volunteer with a nonprofit organization.** Many colleges and universities encourage service learning. In volunteering their services, students gain valuable experience, and nonprofits appreciate the expertise and fresh ideas that students bring.
- **Monitor the classified ads.** Early in your postsecondary career, begin monitoring want ads and the websites of companies in your career area. Check job availability, qualifications sought, duties, and salary ranges. Don't wait until you are about to graduate to see how the job market looks.

Concept Check

1. A study by career website The Ladders found that candidates need to apply to a job within 72 hours after it has been posted online. After that the chances of being hired drop by more than 50 percent. Does this sound reasonable to you? How can job candidates apply so quickly?
2. Why is it important to familiarize yourself with online application systems, mobile apps, and other job search technologies?

Developing a Job-Search Strategy Focused on the Open Job Market

LEARNING OBJECTIVE 2

Develop effective search strategies to explore the open job market.

Once you have analyzed what you want in a job and what you have to offer, you are ready to focus on a job-search strategy. You're probably most interested in how job seekers today are finding their jobs. What methods did they use? A study, summarized in Figure 15.3, reveals how 1,303 workers found their "best" jobs. When the first two categories are combined, you see that a resounding 61 percent of respondents used some form of networking, whether person-to-person or online, to locate their best jobs. Despite the explosion of digital job-search apps and online job boards, networking remains the No. 1 tool for finding a desirable position. Technology, however, plays an increasingly weighty role in the job search. As that happens, the line between online and traditional networking blurs.

Searching the Open Job Market

The open job market consists of positions that are advertised or listed publicly. Most job seekers start searching by using Google to look for positions in their fields and within their commute areas.

Searching online is a common, but not always rewarding, approach. Both recruiters and job seekers complain about online job boards. Corporate recruiters say that the big job boards bring a flood of candidates, many of whom are not suited for the listed jobs. Job candidates report that listings are frequently outdated and fail to produce leads.

Although the Internet may seem like a giant swamp that swallows résumés, job boards can provide valuable job-search information such as résumé, interviewing, and salary tips. Job boards also serve as a jumping-off point in most searches. They inform candidates about the kinds of jobs available and the skill sets required. Even though social media sites like

FIGURE 15.3 How Did Job Seekers Find Their Best Jobs?

Personal networking	40%
Online social networking (Facebook, 10%; LinkedIn, 6%; Twitter, 5%)	21%
Online job board	20%
Classified advertisement	19%
Recruiter	10%
Career fair	7%
College or university connection	7%

LinkedIn and Twitter have taken the recruitment world by storm, many job seekers will begin their search with job boards.

Exploring the Big Boards. As Figure 15.3 indicates, a number of jobs are still found through online job boards. We suggest a few general sites as well as sites for postsecondary graduates.

- **Career Builder** claims to be one of the top 30 trafficked websites in the world.
- **Monster.ca** boasts 2 million unique visitors per month[11]
- **Wowjobs.ca** claims to be Canada's largest search engine.
- **Workopolis** promotes itself as Canada's largest and most popular online job site.
- **Charity Village** is a resource for finding careers at not-for-profit organizations.
- **TalentEgg** is a career hub for students and new graduates.
- **Jobbank.gc.ca** is Service Canada's one-stop job listing website whose mandate is helping workers and employers connect.
- **Indeed.ca** markets itself as the No. 1 job site in the world and aggregates job listings from thousands of websites, including company career pages, job boards, newspaper advertisements, associations, and blogs.

Pursuing Company Leads. Probably the best way to find a job online is at a company's own website. Many companies post job openings only at their own sites to avoid being inundated by the volume of applicants responding to postings at online job boards. A company's website is the first place to go if you have a specific employer in mind. You might find vision and mission statements, a history of the organization, and the names of key hiring managers. If a company isn't currently hiring, don't be afraid to send a résumé and cover message expressing your desire to be considered for future jobs.

Checking Niche Sites. If you seek a job in a specialized field, look for a niche site, such as HealthCareJobs.ca, Political Job Hunt, or Jeff Gaulin's Journalism Job Board.

Taking Advantage of Mobile Apps. Job seekers are eagerly embracing smartphone apps to gain an edge in the job search. With many of the following mobile apps, you can access and vet job openings as soon as they are listed—even when you are on the go.[12] Like its full website, the Indeed Job Search app lets you filter your search results based on your field, desired salary, and location. Monster, Simply Hired, and Snagajob all offer mobile links to job listings from a variety of sources.

Checking Newspapers, Career Fairs, and Other Sources. Despite the rush to mobile technology, some organizations still list openings in newspapers. Don't overlook this possibility, especially for local jobs. Plenty of jobs can also be found through career fairs and university and college alumni contacts.

When posting job-search information online, it's natural to want to put your best foot forward and openly share information that will get you a job. The challenge is striking a balance between supplying enough information and protecting your privacy. To avoid some of the risks involved, see Figure 15.4.

Concept Check

1. Write a list of companies or organizations where you would like to work. Do you know anyone with personal connections to these workplaces? For example, an acquaintance, a peer, a friend of a friend, or an instructor? If not, how can you create networking opportunities to connect with people who work there?
2. What are seven ways to protect yourself when using online boards for your job search?

FIGURE 15.4 Protecting Yourself When Posting on Online Job Boards

- **Use reputable, well-known sites** and never pay to post your résumé.
- **Don't divulge personal data** such as your date of birth, social insurance number, or home address. Use your city and province or territory in place of your home address.
- **Set up a separate e-mail account** with a professional-sounding e-mail address for your job search.
- **Post privately** if possible. Doing so means that you can control who has access to your e-mail address and other information.
- **Keep careful records** of every site on which you posted. At the end of your job search, remove all posted résumés.
- **Don't include your references** or reveal their contact information without permission.
- **Don't respond to blind job postings** (those without company names or addresses). Unfortunately, scammers use online job boards to post fake job ads to gather your personal information.

Unlocking the Hidden Job Market With Networking

LEARNING OBJECTIVE 3

Expand your job-search strategies by pursuing the hidden job market.

Not all available positions are announced or advertised in the open job market. Between 50 and 80 percent are estimated to be in the hidden job market.[13] More jobs today are found through referrals and person-to-person contacts than through any other method. That's because people trust what they know. Therefore, your goal is to become known to a large network of people, and this means going beyond close friends.

Building a Personal Network

Because most candidates find jobs today through networking, be prepared to work diligently to build your personal networks. This effort involves meeting people and talking to them about your field or industry so that you can gain information and locate possible job vacancies. Not only are many jobs never advertised, but some positions aren't even contemplated until the right person appears. See the Career Coach box on the next page with tips to help you establish your own network.

Targeting Social Media in a Job Search

As digital technology continues to change our lives, job candidates have a powerful new tool at their disposal: social media networks. These networks have become critical in a job search. If you have a referral, your chances of landing an interview multiply. Today's expansion of online networks has produced an additional path to developing those coveted referrals.

Letting LinkedIn Help You Find a Job. If you are seriously looking for a job, it's extremely important that you list yourself at LinkedIn. This social media site dominates

CAREER COACH

Network Your Way to a Job in the Hidden Market

Companies do not always announce openings publicly because interviewing all the applicants, many of whom aren't qualified, is time consuming. What's more, even when a job is advertised, companies dislike hiring "strangers." The key to finding a good job, then, is converting yourself from a "stranger" into a known quantity through networking. You can use either traditional methods or online resources.

Traditional Networking

- **Develop a list.** Make a list of anyone who would be willing to talk with you about finding a job. List your friends, relatives, former employers, former coworkers, members of your religious group, people in social and athletic clubs, present and former teachers, neighbours, friends of your parents. Also consider asking your campus career centre for alumni contacts who will talk with students. Figure 15.5 suggests possibilities.
- **Make contacts.** Call the people on your list or, even better, try to meet with them in person. To set up a meeting, say, *I'm looking for a job, and I wonder if you could give me some advice.* During your visit be friendly, well organized, polite, and interested in what your contact has to say. Provide a copy of your résumé, and try to keep the conversation centred on your job-search area. Your goal is to get two or more referrals. In pinpointing your request, ask, *Do you know of anyone who might have an opening for a person with my skills?* If the person does not, ask, *Do you know of anyone else who might know of someone who would?*
- **Follow up on your referrals.** Call the people whose names are on your referral list. You might say something like, *Hello. I'm Eric Rivers, a friend of Meredith Medcalf's. She suggested that I call you. I'm looking for a position as a marketing trainee, and she thought you might be willing to spare a few minutes and steer me in the right direction.* Don't ask for a job. During your referral interview, ask how the individual got started in this line of work, what he or she likes best (or least) about the work, what career paths exist in the field, and what problems must be overcome by a newcomer. Most important, ask how a person with your background and skills might get started in the field. Send an informal thank-you note to anyone who helps you in your job search, and stay in touch with the most promising contacts.

Online Networking

- **Join a career networking group.** Build your own professional network by joining sites like LinkedIn.com or ryze.com. Some of these sites are fee based whereas others are free. Once you connect with an individual, the content of your discussions and the follow-up is similar to that of traditional networking.
- **Locate a relevant blog.** Blogs are the latest trend for networking and sharing information. A quick Internet search will reveal hundreds of career-related blogs and blogs in your field of study. Consider blogs like job-hunt.org, talentegg.ca/incubator/, and workology.com. Once you locate a relevant blog, you can read recent postings, search archives, and reply to postings.

Career Application

Begin developing your network. Conduct at least one referral interview or join one online networking group. Record the results you experienced and the information you learned from the networking option you chose. Report to the class your reactions and findings.

FIGURE 15.5 Whom to Contact in Networking

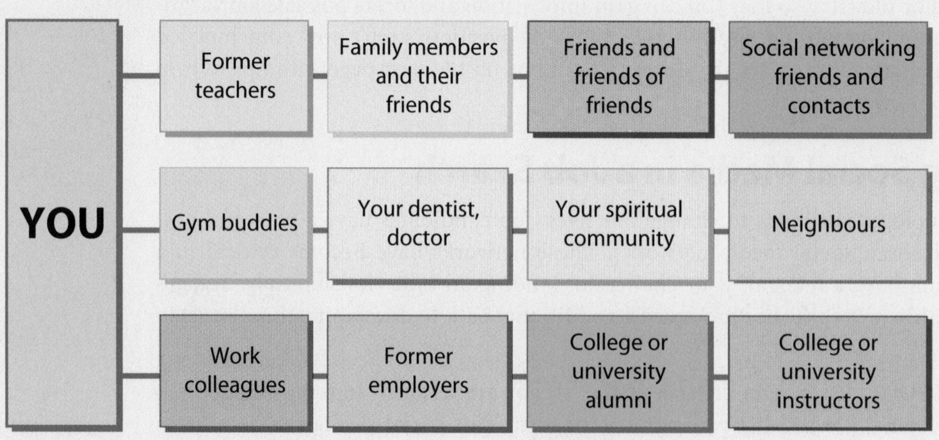

FIGURE 15.6 Harnessing the Power of LinkedIn

Five Ways College Students Can Use LinkedIn to Help Them Find a Job

1. **Receiving Job Alerts.** LinkedIn notifies you of recommended jobs.
2. **Leveraging Your Network.** You may start with two connections, but you can leverage those connections to thousands.
3. **Researching a Company.** Before applying to a company, you can check it out on LinkedIn and locate valuable inside information.
4. **Getting Recommendations.** LinkedIn helps you take the awkwardness out of asking for recommendations. It's so easy!
5. **Helping Companies Find You.** Many companies are looking for skilled postsecondary graduates, and your strong profile on LinkedIn can result in inquiries.

JuliusKielaitis/Shutterstock.com

the world of job searching and recruiting: "With more than 20 million companies listed on the site and 14 million open jobs, it's no surprise to find out that 90% of recruiters regularly use LinkedIn."[14] It's truly the place to find and be found, especially for new graduates. It lists well over a million and a half student jobs and internships in addition to millions of full-time jobs.[15] Developing an online presence at LinkedIn enables you to post information about yourself in one central place where it's available to potential employers, graduate schools, future colleagues, and people you will want to stay connected to. A LinkedIn page tells the working world that you are a professional, and it remains significant even after you obtain a position. LinkedIn can aid your job search in at least five ways, as shown in Figure 15.6.

Enlisting Other Social Networks in a Job Hunt. In addition to LinkedIn, job seekers can join Facebook and Twitter to find job opportunities, market themselves to companies, showcase their skills, highlight their experience, and possibly land that dream job. Because organizations may post open jobs to their Facebook or Twitter pages prior to advertising them elsewhere, you might gain a head start on submitting an application by following them on these sites. If you have a Facebook account, examine your profile and decide what you want prospective employers to see—or not see. Create a simple profile with minimal graphics, widgets, and photos to present yourself professionally. Post only content relevant to your job search or career, and choose your friends wisely.

Employers often use these social media sites to check the online presence of a candidate. One report revealed that nine out of ten recruiters use social media to search, monitor, and vet candidates before the interview.[16] You can make it easy for your potential employer to learn more about you by including an informative bio in your Twitter or Facebook profile that has a link to your LinkedIn profile. You can also make yourself more discoverable by posting thoughtful blog posts and tweets on topics related to your career goal.

ThisIsEngineering

A recent study found that sharing employment interests on Facebook generates useful job leads. What are pros and cons of using social media to network professionally?[17]

Creating Your Personal Brand

A large part of your job-search strategy involves building a brand for yourself. You may be thinking, *Who me? A brand?* Yes, absolutely! Before you get into the thick of the job hunt, focus on developing your brand so that you know what you want to emphasize.

Personal branding involves deciding what makes you special and desirable in the job market. What is your unique selling point? What special skill set makes you stand out among all job applicants? What would your instructors or employers say is your greatest strength? Think about your intended audience. What are you promoting about yourself?

Experts suggest that you create a tagline that describes what you do, who you are, and what's special about you. A nurse wrote this fetching tagline:

> *Tireless, caring registered nurse who helps pediatric cancer patients and their families feel at ease throughout treatment and recovery*

If you prefer a shorter tagline for your business card, consider the sample taglines for new graduates in Figure 15.7. It's okay to shed a little modesty and strut your stuff. However, do keep your tagline simple, short, and truthful so that it's easy to remember.

Once you have a tagline, prepare a professional-looking business card with your name and tagline. Include an easy-to-remember e-mail address, such as *firstname.lastname@domain.com.*

Now that you have your tagline and business card, work on an elevator speech. This is a pitch that you can give in 60 seconds or less describing who you are and what you can offer. Tweak your speech for your audience, and practise until you can say it naturally. Here are suggestions to help you prepare your own authentic elevator speech depending on your situation:

> *Hi, my name is __________ I am about to graduate from __________ with a degree in __________. I'm looking to __________ because I enjoy __________. I recently __________ where I was able to develop such skills as __________. I'm looking for a position in __________. Do you have any suggestions or advice on how I can __________?*

FIGURE 15.7 Branding YOU

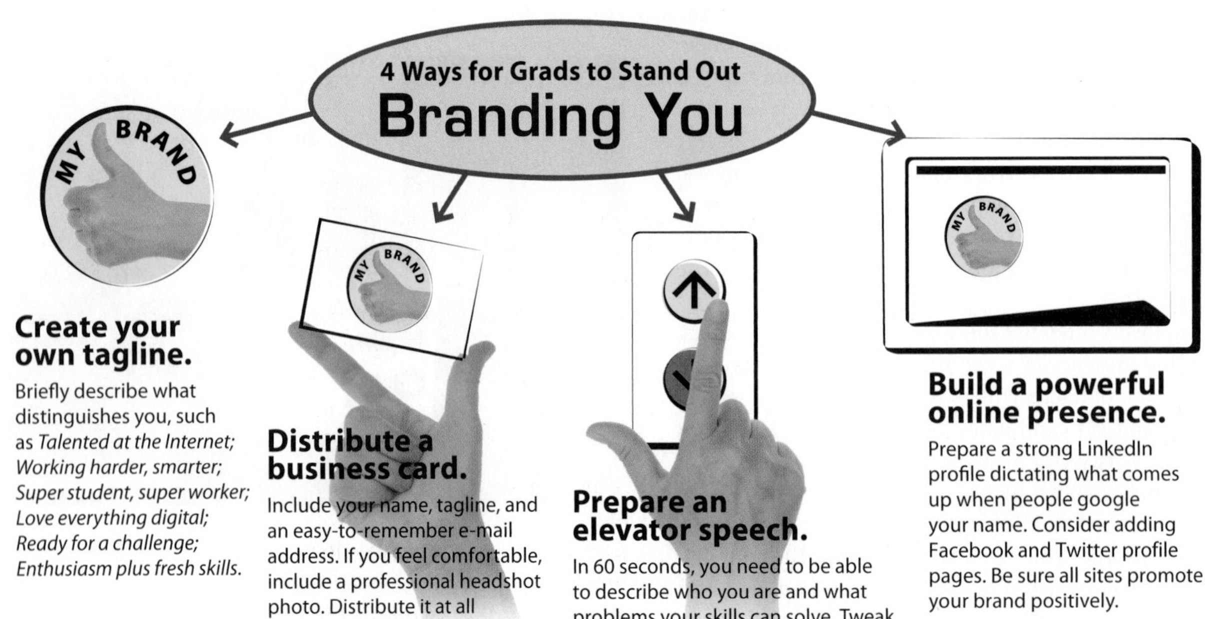

4 Ways for Grads to Stand Out
Branding You
MY BRAND
Create your own tagline.
Briefly describe what distinguishes you, such as Talented at the Internet; Working harder, smarter; Super student, super worker; Love everything digital; Ready for a challenge; Enthusiasm plus fresh skills.
Distribute a business card.
Include your name, tagline, and an easy-to-remember e-mail address. If you feel comfortable, include a professional headshot photo. Distribute it at all opportunities.
Prepare an elevator speech.
In 60 seconds, you need to be able to describe who you are and what problems your skills can solve. Tweak your speech for your audience, and practise until it feels natural.
Build a powerful online presence.
Prepare a strong LinkedIn profile dictating what comes up when people google your name. Consider adding Facebook and Twitter profile pages. Be sure all sites promote your brand positively.
John Smith Design/Shutterstock.com

Concept Check

1. How has the global pandemic affected the job-search process? What skills do job seekers need to develop in order to thrive during challenging times?
2. Write three taglines for yourself. In groups, share your taglines and discuss which one would sound best on a business card.

Creating a Customized Résumé

LEARNING OBJECTIVE 4

Organize your qualifications and information to create a winning, customized résumé.

In today's highly competitive job market, the focus is not so much on what you want but on what the employer needs. That's why you will want to prepare a tailored résumé for every position you seek. The competition is so stiff today that you cannot get by with a generic, all-purpose résumé. Although you can start with a basic résumé, you should customize it to fit each company and position if you want it to stand out from the crowd.

The Internet has made it so easy to apply for jobs that recruiters are swamped with applications. As a job seeker, you have about five seconds to catch the recruiter's eye—if your résumé is even read by a person. It may very well first encounter an *applicant tracking system* (ATS). This software helps businesses automatically post openings, screen résumés, rank candidates, and generate interview requests. These automated systems make writing your résumé doubly challenging. Although your goal is to satisfy a recruiter or hiring manager, that person will never see your résumé unless it is selected by the ATS. You will learn more about applicant tracking systems shortly.

You may not be in the job market at this moment, but preparing a résumé now has advantages. Having a current résumé makes you look well organized and professional should an unexpected employment opportunity arise. Moreover, preparing a résumé early may reveal weaknesses and give you time to address them. If you have accepted a position, it's still a good idea to keep your résumé up-to-date. You never know when an opportunity might come along!

Choosing a Résumé Style

The first step in preparing a winning, customized résumé that appeals to both the human reader and the ATS screening device is to decide what style to use. Résumés usually fall into two categories: chronological and functional. This section presents basic information and insider tips on how to choose an appropriate résumé style, determine its length, and arrange its parts. You will also learn about adding a summary of qualifications, which many busy recruiters welcome. Models of the résumés in the following discussion are shown in our Résumé Gallery.

What Is a Chronological Résumé? The most popular résumé format is the chronological résumé, shown in Figures 15.10, 15.11, and 15.13 in our Résumé Gallery. The chronological résumé lists work history job by job but in reverse order, starting with the most recent position. Recruiters favour the chronological format because they are familiar with it and because it quickly reveals a candidate's education and experience. The chronological style works well for candidates who have experience in their field of employment and for those who show steady career growth, but it is less appropriate for people who have changed jobs frequently or who have gaps in their employment records. For postsecondary students and others who lack extensive experience, the functional résumé format may be preferable.

What Is a Functional Résumé? The functional résumé, shown in Figure 15.12, focuses on a candidate's skills rather than on past employment. Like a chronological résumé, the functional résumé begins with the candidate's name, contact information, job objective, and education. Instead of listing jobs, though, the functional résumé groups skills and accomplishments in special categories, such as Supervisory and Management Skills or Retailing and Marketing Experience. This résumé style highlights accomplishments and can de-emphasize a negative employment history.

Check out section 15-4a in MindTap, where you can watch a video featuring Karen Richardson, an associate marketing manager, discuss creative versus templated résumés.

People who have changed jobs frequently, who have gaps in their employment records, or who are entering an entirely different field may prefer the functional résumé. Recent graduates with little or no related employment experience often find the functional résumé useful. Older job seekers who want to downplay a long job history and job hunters who are afraid of appearing overqualified may also prefer the functional format. Be aware, though, that online job boards may insist on the chronological format. In addition, some recruiters are suspicious of functional résumés, thinking the candidate is hiding something.

How Long Should a Résumé Be? Experts disagree on how long a résumé should be. Conventional wisdom has always held that recruiters prefer one-page résumés. However, recruiters who are serious about candidates often prefer the kind of details that can be provided in a two-page or longer résumé. The best advice is to make your résumé as long as needed to present your skills to recruiters and hiring managers. Individuals with more experience will naturally have longer résumés. Those with fewer than ten years of experience, those making a major career change, and those who have had only one or two employers will likely have one-page résumés.

Organizing Your Information Into Effective Résumé Categories

Although résumés have standard categories, their arrangement and content should be strategically planned. A customized résumé emphasizes skills and achievements aimed at a particular job or company. It shows a candidate's most important qualifications first, and it de-emphasizes weaknesses. In organizing your qualifications and information, try to create as few headings as possible; more than six looks cluttered. No two résumés are ever exactly alike, but most writers consider including all or some of these categories: Main Heading, Career Objective, Summary of Qualifications, Education, Experience, Capabilities and Skills, and Awards and Activities.

Main Heading. Your résumé, whether chronological or functional, should start with an uncluttered and simple main heading. The first line should always be your name; add your middle initial for an even more formal look. Format your name so that it stands out on the page. Following your name, list your contact information, including your complete address,

CASE CONNECTIONS

Canadian Red Cross—The Value of Volunteering

AFP Contributor/Getty Images

Many not-for-profit organizations rely heavily on the generosity of their volunteers. The Red Cross depends on volunteers to help with its mission "to prevent and alleviate human suffering wherever it may be found."[18] And volunteers are not only providing invaluable service, they are gaining essential employability skills, networking opportunities, and job experience for future employment.

Volunteers make up more than 70 percent of the Canadian Red Cross. Whether you want to learn a new skill, meet new people, experience something meaningful, or simply help where help is needed, volunteer opportunities at the Canadian Red Cross are as diverse as the people who fill them.[19] All volunteers have to fill out an application and complete an interview, including screening and reference checks.[20] The Red Cross provides an orientation training for all of its volunteers so they are ready to help where needed.

- What specific skills can you develop while volunteering? Why is volunteer experience valuable to have on your résumé?

area code and phone number, and e-mail address. Your telephone should be one where you can receive messages. The outgoing message at this number should be in your voice, it should state your full name, and it should be concise and professional. If you include your cell phone number and are expecting an important call from a recruiter, pick up only when you are in a quiet environment and can concentrate.

For your e-mail address, be sure it sounds professional instead of something like *toosexy4you@gmail.com* or *sixpackguy@yahoo.com*. Also be sure that you are using a personal e-mail address. Putting your work e-mail address on your résumé announces to prospective employers that you are using your current employer's resources to look for another job. If you have a LinkedIn profile or a website where an e-portfolio or samples of your work can be viewed, include the links in the main heading.

Career Objective. Opinion is divided about the effectiveness of including a career objective on a résumé. Recruiters think such statements indicate that candidates have made a commitment to a career and are sure about what they want to do. Yet some career coaches today say objectives "feel outdated" and too often are all about what the candidate wants instead of what the employer wants.[21] Regardless, a well-written objective—customized for the job opening—makes sense, especially for new graduates with fresh training and relevant skills. The objective can include strategic keywords for ATS. If you decide to include an objective, focus on what you can contribute to the organization, not on what the organization can do for you.

> **Poor objective:** *To obtain a position with a well-established organization that will lead to a lasting relationship in the field of marketing.* (It sounds vague and self-serving.)
>
> **Improved objective:** *To obtain a marketing position in which I use my recent training in writing and computer skills to increase customer contacts and expand brand penetration using social media.* (It names specific skills and includes many nouns that might activate an ATS.)

Avoid the words *entry level* in your objective, as these words emphasize lack of experience. If you omit a career objective, be sure to discuss your career goals in your cover message.

Optional Summary of Qualifications. Over the past decade, the biggest change in résumés has been a switch from a career objective to a summary of qualifications at the top.[22] Once a job is advertised, a hiring manager may get hundreds or even thousands of résumés in response. A summary ensures that your most impressive qualifications are not overlooked by a recruiter who is skimming résumés quickly. A summary also enables you to present a concentrated list of many relevant keywords for an ATS to pick up, thus boosting your chance of selection.[23] Additionally, because résumés today may be viewed on tablets and smartphones, the summary spotlights your most compelling qualifications in a highly visible spot.

A summary of qualifications (also called *career profile*, *job summary*, or *professional highlights*) should include three to eight bulleted statements that prove you are the ideal candidate for the position. When formulating these statements, consider your experience in the field, your education, your unique skills, awards you have won, certifications, and any other accomplishments that you want to highlight. Include numbers wherever possible. Target the most important qualifications an employer will be looking for in the person hired for this position. Focus on nouns that might be selected as keywords by an ATS. Examples appear in Figures 15.10 and 15.13.

Education. The next component in a chronological résumé is your education—if it is more noteworthy than your work experience. In this section you should include the name and location of schools, dates of attendance, major fields of study, and diplomas or degrees received. By the way, once you have attended college or university, you don't need to list high school information on your résumé.

Your grade point average or class ranking may be important to prospective employers. One way to enhance your GPA is to calculate it in your major courses only (for example, *3.6/4.0 in major*). It is not unethical so long as you clearly show that your GPA is in the major only.

Under Education you might be tempted to list all the courses you took, but such a list makes for dull reading and consumes valuable space. Refer to courses only if you can relate them to the position sought. When relevant, include certificates earned, seminars attended, workshops completed, scholarships awarded, and honours earned. If your education is incomplete, include such statements as *BSc degree expected 6/18* or *80 units completed in 120-unit program*. Title this section Education, Academic Preparation, or Professional Training. If you are preparing a functional résumé, you will probably put the Education section below your skills summaries, as Dallas Dayal has done in Figure 15.12.

Work Experience or Employment History. When your work or volunteer experience is significant and relevant to the position sought, this information should appear before your education. List your most recent employment first and work backward, including only those jobs that you think will help you win the targeted position. A job application form may demand a full employment history, but your résumé may be selective. Be aware, though, that time gaps in your employment history will probably be questioned in the interview. For each position show the following:

- Employer's name, city, and province or territory
- Dates of employment (month and year)
- Most important job title
- Significant duties, activities, accomplishments, and promotions

Be sure to include relevant volunteer work. A survey conducted by LinkedIn revealed that 41 percent of LinkedIn hiring managers consider volunteer work experience as respectable as paid work experience when evaluating candidates.[24]

Your employment achievements and job duties will be easier to read if you place them in bulleted lists. Rather than list every single thing you have done, customize your information so that it relates to the target job. Your bullet points should be concise but not complete sentences, and they usually do not include personal pronouns (*I, me, my*). Strive to be specific:

Poor: *Worked with customers*

Improved: *Developed customer-service skills by successfully interacting with 40+ customers daily*

Whenever possible, quantify your achievements:

Poor: *Did equipment study and report*

Improved: *Conducted research and wrote final study analyzing equipment needs of 100 small businesses in St. Catharines*

Poor: *Was successful in sales*

Improved: *Personally generated orders for sales of $90,000 annually*

In addition to technical skills, employers seek individuals with communication, management, and interpersonal capabilities. This means you will want to select work experiences and achievements that illustrate your initiative, dependability, responsibility, resourcefulness, flexibility, and leadership. Employers also want people who can work in teams.

Poor: *Worked effectively in teams*

Improved: *Collaborated with interdepartmental team in developing ten-page handbook for temporary workers*

Poor: *Joined in team effort on campus*

Improved: *Headed student government team that conducted the most successful voter registration in campus history*

Statements describing your skills and work experience should include many nouns relevant to the job you seek. These nouns may match keywords sought by the ATS. To appeal to human readers, your statements should also include action verbs, such as those in Figure 15.8.

FIGURE 15.8 Action Verbs for Powerful Résumés

Communication Skills	Teamwork, Supervision Skills	Management, Leadership Skills	Research Skills	Clerical, Detail Skills	Creative Skills
clarified	advised	analyzed	assessed	activated	acted
collaborated	coordinated	authorized	collected	approved	conceptualized
explained	demonstrated	coordinated	critiqued	classified	designed
interpreted	developed	directed	diagnosed	edited	fashioned
integrated	evaluated	headed	formulated	generated	founded
persuaded	expedited	implemented	gathered	maintained	illustrated
promoted	facilitated	improved	interpreted	monitored	integrated
resolved	guided	increased	investigated	proofread	invented
summarized	motivated	organized	reviewed	recorded	originated
translated	set goals	scheduled	studied	streamlined	revitalized
wrote	trained	strengthened	systematized	updated	shaped

Starting each of your bullet points with an action verb will help ensure that your bulleted lists are parallel.

Capabilities and Skills. Recruiters want to know specifically what you can do for their companies. Therefore, list your special skills. In this section be sure to include many nouns that relate to the targeted position. Include your ability to use the Internet, search engines, software programs, social media, office equipment, and communication technology tools. Use expressions such as *proficient in*, *competent in*, *experienced in*, and *ability to*, as illustrated in the following:

Poor: *Have payroll experience*

Improved: *Proficient in preparing federal, provincial, and local payroll tax returns, as well as franchise and personal property tax returns*

Poor: *Trained in computer graphics*

Improved: *Certified in graphic design including infographics through an intensive 350-hour classroom program*

Poor: *Have writing skills*

Improved: *Competent in writing, editing, and proofreading reports, tables, letters, memos, e-mails, manuscripts, and business forms*

You will also want to highlight exceptional aptitudes, such as working well under stress, learning computer programs quickly, and interacting with customers. If possible, provide details and evidence that back up your assertions. Include examples of your writing, speaking, management, organizational, interpersonal, and presentation skills—particularly those talents that are relevant to your targeted job. For recent graduates, this section can be used to give recruiters evidence of your potential and to address successful college or university projects.

Awards, Honours, and Activities. If you have three or more awards or honours, highlight them by listing them under a separate heading. If not, put them in the Education or Work Experience section if appropriate. Include awards, scholarships (financial and other), fellowships, dean's list, honours, recognition, commendations, and certificates. Be sure to identify items clearly. Your reader may be unfamiliar with different groups or awards; tell what they mean.

Poor: *Recipient of Star award*

Improved: *Recipient of Star award given by Mt. Allison University to outstanding graduates who combine academic excellence and extracurricular activities*

It's also appropriate to include school, community, volunteer, and professional activities. Employers are interested in evidence that you are a well-rounded person. This section provides an opportunity to demonstrate leadership and interpersonal skills. Strive to use action statements.

Poor: *Treasurer of business club*

Improved: *Collected dues, kept financial records, and paid bills while serving as treasurer of 35-member business management club*

Personal Data. Today's résumés omit personal data, such as birth date, marital status, height, weight, national origin, health, disabilities, and religious affiliation. Such information doesn't relate to genuine occupational qualifications, and recruiters are legally barred from asking for such information. Some job seekers do, however, include hobbies or interests (such as skiing or photography) that might grab the recruiter's attention or serve as conversation starters. You could also indicate your willingness to travel or to relocate since many companies will be interested.

References. Listing references directly on a résumé takes up valuable space. Moreover, references are not normally instrumental in securing an interview—few companies check them before the interview. Instead, recruiters prefer that you bring to the interview a list of individuals willing to discuss your qualifications. Therefore, you should prepare a separate list, such as that in Figure 15.9, when you begin your job search. Consider three to five individuals, such as instructors, your current employer or previous employers, colleagues or subordinates, and other professional contacts. Ask whether they would be willing to answer inquiries regarding your qualifications for employment. Be sure, however, to provide them with an opportunity to refuse. No reference is better than a negative one. Better yet, to avoid rejection and embarrassment, ask only those contacts who will give you a glowing endorsement.

Do not include personal or character references, such as friends, family, or neighbours, because recruiters rarely consult them. Companies are more interested in the opinions of objective individuals who know how you perform professionally and academically. One final note: most recruiters see little reason for including the statement *References available upon request.* It is unnecessary and takes up precious space.

FIGURE 15.9 Sample Reference List

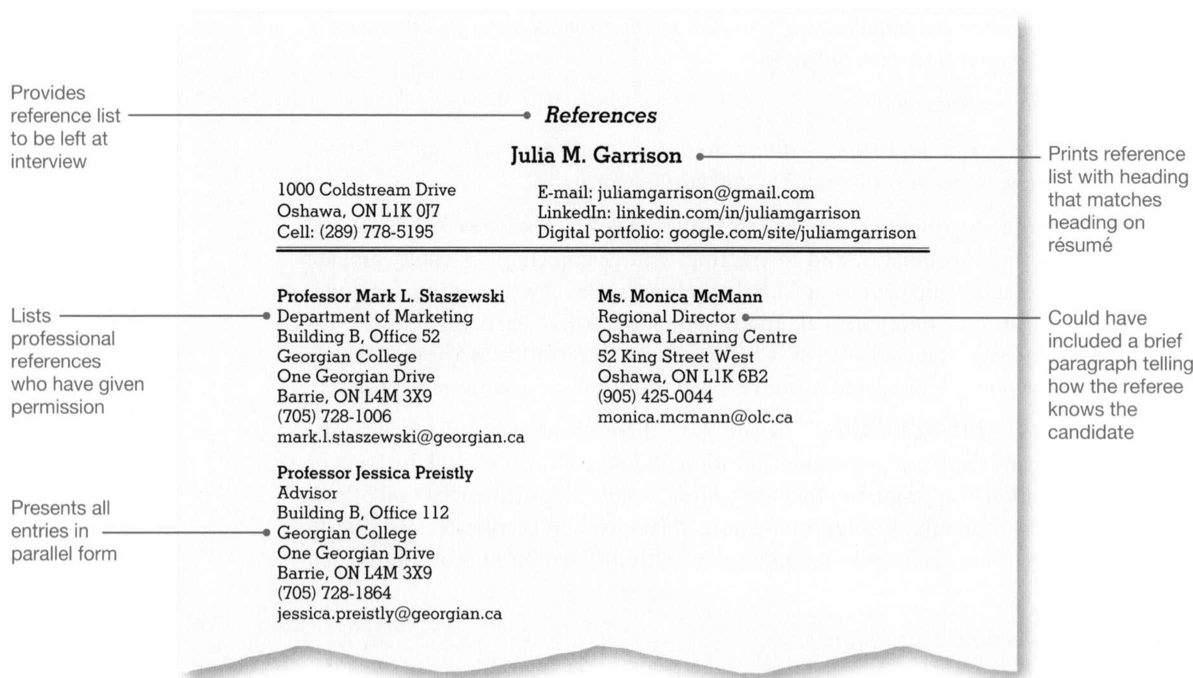
References

Julia M. Garrison

1000 Coldstream Drive
Oshawa, ON L1K 0J7
Cell: (289) 778-5195

E-mail: juliamgarrison@gmail.com
LinkedIn: linkedin.com/in/juliamgarrison
Digital portfolio: google.com/site/juliamgarrison

Professor Mark L. Staszewski
Department of Marketing
Building B, Office 52
Georgian College
One Georgian Drive
Barrie, ON L4M 3X9
(705) 728-1006
mark.l.staszewski@georgian.ca

Ms. Monica McMann
Regional Director
Oshawa Learning Centre
52 King Street West
Oshawa, ON L1K 6B2
(905) 425-0044
monica.mcmann@olc.ca

Professor Jessica Preistly
Advisor
Building B, Office 112
Georgian College
One Georgian Drive
Barrie, ON L4M 3X9
(705) 728-1864
jessica.preistly@georgian.ca

From Guffey/Loewy, *Essentials of Business Communication* (with www.meguffey.com Printed Access Card), 9E.

Résumé Gallery

FIGURE 15.10 Chronological Résumé: Recent University Graduate With Limited Experience

Haley Hawkins used Microsoft Word to design a traditional chronological résumé that she plans to give to recruiters at campus job fairs or during interviews. The two-column formatting enables recruiters and hiring managers to immediately follow the chronology of her education and experience. This formatting is easy to create by using the Word table feature and removing the borders so that no lines show.

Haley includes an objective that is specific in describing what she seeks but broad enough to encompass many possible positions. Her summary of qualifications emphasizes the highlights of her experience and education. Because she has so little experience, she includes a brief list of related courses to indicate her areas of interest and training. Although she has limited paid experience that relates to the position she seeks, she is able to capitalize on her intern experience by featuring accomplishments and transferable skills.

Haley M. Hawkins

680 Mountain View Lane
Victoria, BC V8Z 4C4
Cell: 614-479-1982

E-mail: haleymhawkins@gmail.com
LinkedIn: linkedin.com/in/haleymhawkins
Digital portfolio: google.com/site/haleymhawkins

OBJECTIVE

Position in sales, marketing, or e-marketing in which my marketing, communication, and social media expertise helps an organization expand its brand penetration.

SUMMARY OF QUALIFICATIONS

- Graduated with honours in e-marketing from University of Victoria
- Applied e-marketing and public relations training as a successful intern
- Experienced in posting to Twitter, Facebook, YouTube, and other platforms
- Keep up-to-date with constantly evolving technologies in online social networking
- Developed strong work ethic with part-time jobs that financed more than 50 percent of my education
- Honed leadership skills as vice president of award-winning chapter of Canadian Marketing Association

EDUCATION AND RELATED COURSE WORK

BA in Business Administration, University of Victoria, May 2020
Major: Business Administration with e-marketing emphasis
Minor: Organizational Communication
GPA: Major, 3.7; overall 3.5 (A = 4.0)

Marketing Research and Analysis
Social Relations in the Workplace
Writing for the Web and Social Media
Marketing Communication
Professional Public Relations
Organizational Behaviour

PROFESSIONAL EXPERIENCE

Social Media Intern 09/2019–02/2020
Pacific Media Consultants, Victoria, BC
- Collaborated with 5-person team to develop social media presence for Centre for LifeLong Learning
- Introduced clients to LinkedIn and established Facebook and Twitter accounts for LifeLong Learning staff
- Demonstrated how to boost social media presence with announcements and tweets of upcoming activities
- Prepared brochure, handouts, name tags, and press kit to promote one Saturday event
- Handled over 40 client calls with the account management team, ranging from project check-ins to inbound client inquiries in a professional and personable manner

Manager 06/2017–08/2019
Juice Zone, Victoria, BC
- Developed management skills in assuming all responsibilities in absence of store owners, including finances, scheduling, and oversight
- Supervised daily store operations, maintained store security, and managed a team of 5 to 10 employees to ensure productivity and profitability

HONOURS

- Received Brooks Award as the outstanding graduate in marketing based on academic excellence and service to the community

ACTIVITIES

- Served as vice president of University of Victoria chapter of the Canadian Marketing Association, providing monthly marketing forums, events, and competitions, helping our chapter earn national recognition

FIGURE 15.11 Chronological Résumé: Student Seeking Internship

Although Amy has had one internship, she is seeking another as she is about to graduate. To aid her search, she prepared a chronological résumé that emphasizes her education and related course work. She elected to omit her home address because she prefers that all communication take place digitally or by telephone. Instead of a career objective, she states exactly the internship position she seeks.

Notice that her résumé uses standard headings that would be easily recognized by an applicant tracking system. She decided not to start with a summary of qualifications because she has little to offer. Instead, she focused on her experience and related it to the position she seeks.

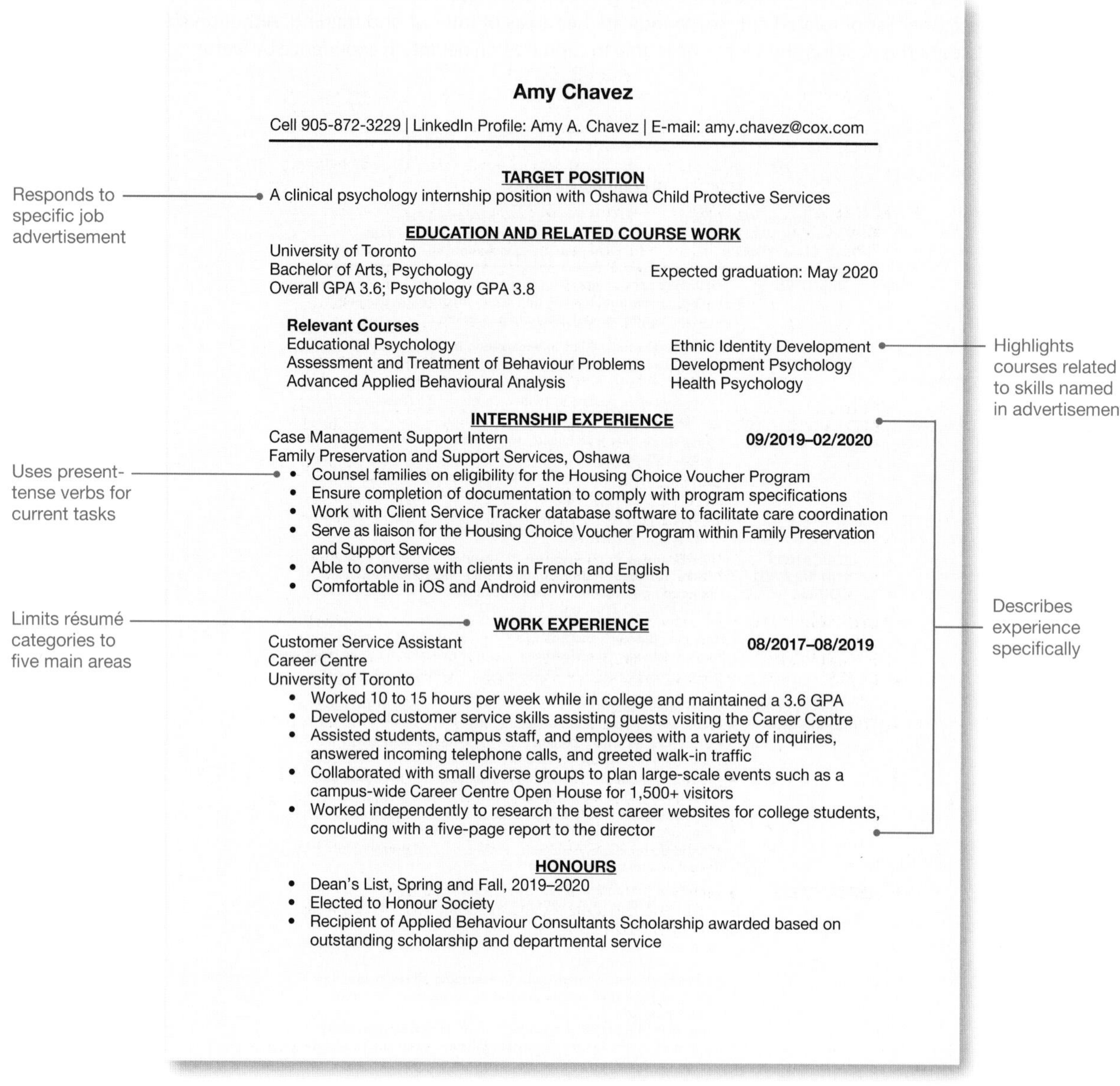
Amy Chavez

Cell 905-872-3229 | LinkedIn Profile: Amy A. Chavez | E-mail: amy.chavez@cox.com

TARGET POSITION

A clinical psychology internship position with Oshawa Child Protective Services

EDUCATION AND RELATED COURSE WORK

University of Toronto
Bachelor of Arts, Psychology — Expected graduation: May 2020
Overall GPA 3.6; Psychology GPA 3.8

Relevant Courses

Educational Psychology
Assessment and Treatment of Behaviour Problems
Advanced Applied Behavioural Analysis
Ethnic Identity Development
Development Psychology
Health Psychology

INTERNSHIP EXPERIENCE

Case Management Support Intern — **09/2019–02/2020**
Family Preservation and Support Services, Oshawa

- Counsel families on eligibility for the Housing Choice Voucher Program
- Ensure completion of documentation to comply with program specifications
- Work with Client Service Tracker database software to facilitate care coordination
- Serve as liaison for the Housing Choice Voucher Program within Family Preservation and Support Services
- Able to converse with clients in French and English
- Comfortable in iOS and Android environments

WORK EXPERIENCE

Customer Service Assistant — **08/2017–08/2019**
Career Centre
University of Toronto

- Worked 10 to 15 hours per week while in college and maintained a 3.6 GPA
- Developed customer service skills assisting guests visiting the Career Centre
- Assisted students, campus staff, and employees with a variety of inquiries, answered incoming telephone calls, and greeted walk-in traffic
- Collaborated with small diverse groups to plan large-scale events such as a campus-wide Career Centre Open House for 1,500+ visitors
- Worked independently to research the best career websites for college students, concluding with a five-page report to the director

HONOURS

- Dean's List, Spring and Fall, 2019–2020
- Elected to Honour Society
- Recipient of Applied Behaviour Consultants Scholarship awarded based on outstanding scholarship and departmental service

Responds to specific job advertisement
Highlights courses related to skills named in advertisement
Uses present-tense verbs for current tasks
Describes experience specifically
Limits résumé categories to five main areas

FIGURE 15.12 Functional Résumé: Recent College Graduate With Unrelated Part-Time Experience

Recent graduate Dallas Dayal chose this functional format to de-emphasize his meagre work experience and emphasize his potential in sales and marketing. This version of his résumé is more generic than one targeted for a specific position. Nevertheless, it emphasizes his strong points with specific achievements and includes an employment section to satisfy recruiters. The functional format presents ability-focused topics. It illustrates what the job seeker can do for the employer instead of narrating a history of previous jobs. Although recruiters prefer chronological résumés, the functional format is a good choice for new graduates, career changers, and those with employment gaps.

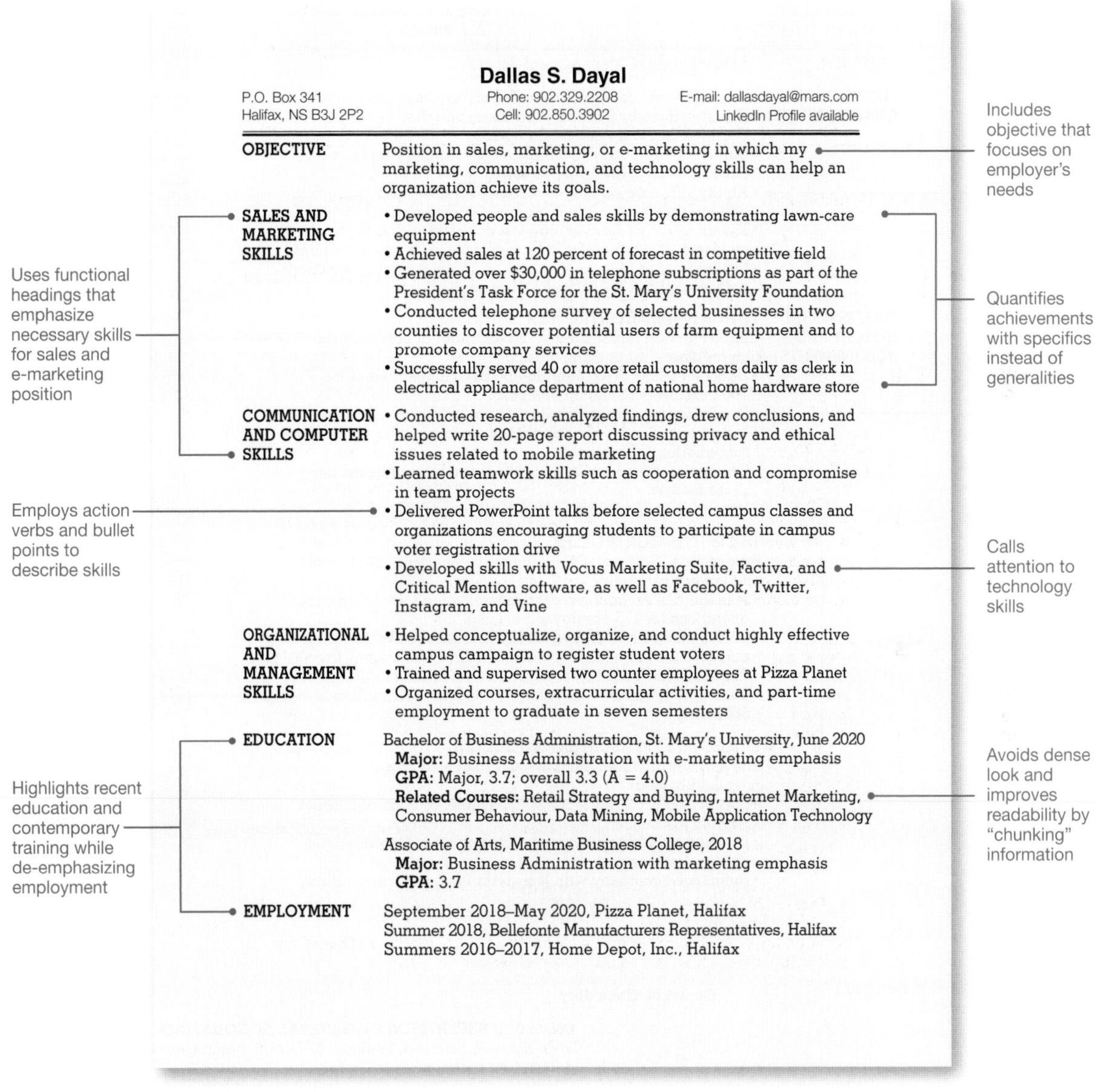

Dallas S. Dayal

P.O. Box 341
Halifax, NS B3J 2P2

Phone: 902.329.2208
Cell: 902.850.3902

E-mail: dallasdayal@mars.com
LinkedIn Profile available

OBJECTIVE
Position in sales, marketing, or e-marketing in which my marketing, communication, and technology skills can help an organization achieve its goals.

SALES AND MARKETING SKILLS
- Developed people and sales skills by demonstrating lawn-care equipment
- Achieved sales at 120 percent of forecast in competitive field
- Generated over $30,000 in telephone subscriptions as part of the President's Task Force for the St. Mary's University Foundation
- Conducted telephone survey of selected businesses in two counties to discover potential users of farm equipment and to promote company services
- Successfully served 40 or more retail customers daily as clerk in electrical appliance department of national home hardware store

COMMUNICATION AND COMPUTER SKILLS
- Conducted research, analyzed findings, drew conclusions, and helped write 20-page report discussing privacy and ethical issues related to mobile marketing
- Learned teamwork skills such as cooperation and compromise in team projects
- Delivered PowerPoint talks before selected campus classes and organizations encouraging students to participate in campus voter registration drive
- Developed skills with Vocus Marketing Suite, Factiva, and Critical Mention software, as well as Facebook, Twitter, Instagram, and Vine

ORGANIZATIONAL AND MANAGEMENT SKILLS
- Helped conceptualize, organize, and conduct highly effective campus campaign to register student voters
- Trained and supervised two counter employees at Pizza Planet
- Organized courses, extracurricular activities, and part-time employment to graduate in seven semesters

EDUCATION
Bachelor of Business Administration, St. Mary's University, June 2020
Major: Business Administration with e-marketing emphasis
GPA: Major, 3.7; overall 3.3 (A = 4.0)
Related Courses: Retail Strategy and Buying, Internet Marketing, Consumer Behaviour, Data Mining, Mobile Application Technology

Associate of Arts, Maritime Business College, 2018
Major: Business Administration with marketing emphasis
GPA: 3.7

EMPLOYMENT
September 2018–May 2020, Pizza Planet, Halifax
Summer 2018, Bellefonte Manufacturers Representatives, Halifax
Summers 2016–2017, Home Depot, Inc., Halifax

FIGURE 15.13 Chronological Résumé: University Graduate With Substantial Experience

Because Rachel has many years of experience and seeks executive-level employment, she highlighted her experience by placing it before her education. Her summary of qualifications highlighted her most impressive experience and skills. This chronological two-page résumé shows the steady progression of her career to executive positions, a movement that impresses and reassures recruiters.

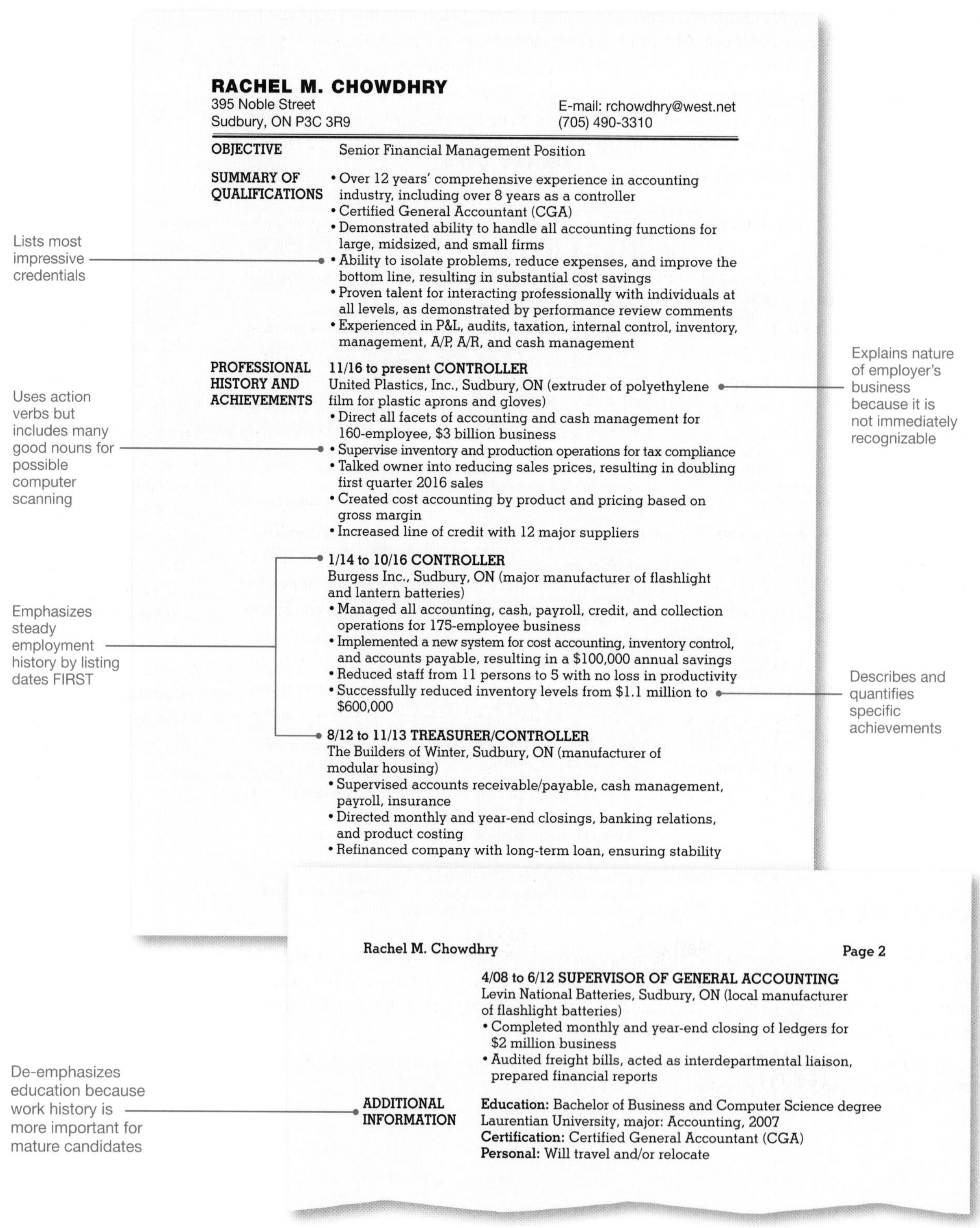

RACHEL M. CHOWDHRY
395 Noble Street
Sudbury, ON P3C 3R9
E-mail: rchowdhry@west.net
(705) 490-3310

OBJECTIVE Senior Financial Management Position

SUMMARY OF QUALIFICATIONS
- Over 12 years' comprehensive experience in accounting industry, including over 8 years as a controller
- Certified General Accountant (CGA)
- Demonstrated ability to handle all accounting functions for large, midsized, and small firms
- Ability to isolate problems, reduce expenses, and improve the bottom line, resulting in substantial cost savings
- Proven talent for interacting professionally with individuals at all levels, as demonstrated by performance review comments
- Experienced in P&L, audits, taxation, internal control, inventory, management, A/P, A/R, and cash management

PROFESSIONAL HISTORY AND ACHIEVEMENTS

11/16 to present CONTROLLER
United Plastics, Inc., Sudbury, ON (extruder of polyethylene film for plastic aprons and gloves)
- Direct all facets of accounting and cash management for 160-employee, $3 billion business
- Supervise inventory and production operations for tax compliance
- Talked owner into reducing sales prices, resulting in doubling first quarter 2016 sales
- Created cost accounting by product and pricing based on gross margin
- Increased line of credit with 12 major suppliers

1/14 to 10/16 CONTROLLER
Burgess Inc., Sudbury, ON (major manufacturer of flashlight and lantern batteries)
- Managed all accounting, cash, payroll, credit, and collection operations for 175-employee business
- Implemented a new system for cost accounting, inventory control, and accounts payable, resulting in a $100,000 annual savings
- Reduced staff from 11 persons to 5 with no loss in productivity
- Successfully reduced inventory levels from $1.1 million to $600,000

8/12 to 11/13 TREASURER/CONTROLLER
The Builders of Winter, Sudbury, ON (manufacturer of modular housing)
- Supervised accounts receivable/payable, cash management, payroll, insurance
- Directed monthly and year-end closings, banking relations, and product costing
- Refinanced company with long-term loan, ensuring stability

Rachel M. Chowdhry **Page 2**

4/08 to 6/12 SUPERVISOR OF GENERAL ACCOUNTING
Levin National Batteries, Sudbury, ON (local manufacturer of flashlight batteries)
- Completed monthly and year-end closing of ledgers for $2 million business
- Audited freight bills, acted as interdepartmental liaison, prepared financial reports

ADDITIONAL INFORMATION
Education: Bachelor of Business and Computer Science degree Laurentian University, major: Accounting, 2007
Certification: Certified General Accountant (CGA)
Personal: Will travel and/or relocate

Lists most impressive credentials
Uses action verbs but includes many good nouns for possible computer scanning
Emphasizes steady employment history by listing dates FIRST
De-emphasizes education because work history is more important for mature candidates
Explains nature of employer's business because it is not immediately recognizable
Describes and quantifies specific achievements

Polishing Your Résumé and Keeping It Honest

Because your résumé is probably the most important message you will ever write, you will revise it many times. With so much information in concentrated form and with so much riding on its outcome, your résumé demands careful polishing, proofreading, and critiquing.

As you continue to work on your résumé, look for ways to improve it. For example, consider consolidating headings. By condensing your information into as few headings as possible, you will produce a clean, professional-looking document. Study other résumés for valuable formatting ideas. Ask yourself what graphic highlighting techniques you can use to improve readability: capitalization, underlining, indenting, and bulleting. Experiment with headings and styles to achieve a pleasing, easy-to-read message. Moreover, look for ways to eliminate wordiness. For example, instead of *Supervised two employees who worked at the counter*, try *Supervised two counter employees*. Review Chapter 5 for more tips on writing concisely.

As you revise, be certain to verify all the facts, particularly those involving your previous employment and education. Don't be caught in a mistake, or worse, a distortion of previous jobs and dates of employment. These items likely will be checked, and the consequences of puffing up a résumé with deception or flat-out lies are simply not worth the risk.

A résumé is expected to showcase a candidate's strengths and minimize weaknesses. For this reason, recruiters expect a certain degree of self-promotion. Some résumé writers, however, step over the line that separates honest self-marketing from deceptive half-truths and lies. Distorting facts on a résumé is unethical; lying may be illegal. Most important, either practice can destroy a career.

Go to section 15-4d in MindTap, where you can watch a video featuring Candice Wong, a registered physiotherapist, discuss how to use graphic elements on your résumé to stand out.

ETHICS CHECK

Are Canadians Lying on Their Résumés?

Given today's competitive job market, it might be tempting to exaggerate on your résumé. A study revealed that Canadian employers have caught applicants fibbing about their skill set, job titles, academic degrees, and the companies they worked for.[25] If a candidate has lied on her résumé but has made it through the interview process and is offered a position, does she have anything to worry about?

Proofreading Your Résumé

After revising your résumé, you must proofread, proofread, and proofread again for spelling, grammar, mechanics, content, and format. Then have a knowledgeable friend or relative proofread it yet again. This is one document that must be perfect. Because the job market is so competitive, one typo, misspelled word, or grammatical error could eliminate you from consideration.

If you are thinking that you'd like to hire someone to write your résumé, don't! First, you know yourself better than anyone else could know you. Second, you will end up with either a generic or a one-time résumé. A generic résumé in today's highly competitive job market will lose out to a customized résumé nine times out of ten. Equally useless is a one-time résumé aimed at a single job. What if you don't get that job? Because you will need to revise your résumé many times as you seek a variety of jobs, be prepared to write (and rewrite) it yourself.

Concept Check

1. Why do you think it is so important to customize your résumé for each employer and each job for which you apply? How do you think employers will respond to a customized résumé versus a generic résumé? Is creating a customized résumé for each position worth your time and effort? Share your opinions with your classmates.
2. In your opinion, what is the difference between honest self-marketing and deception? What are some examples from your experience?

Check out section 15-4e in MindTap, where you can watch a video featuring Taylor Roberts, a general manager, discuss elements of successful résumés.

LEARNING OBJECTIVE 5

Optimize your job search and résumé by taking advantage of today's digital tools.

Enhancing Your Job Search With Today's Digital Tools

Just as electronic media have changed the way candidates seek jobs, these same digital tools have changed the way employers select qualified candidates. This means that the first reader of your résumé may very well be an ATS. Estimates suggest that as many as 90 percent of large companies use these systems.[26] In addition, résumé databases such as Monster and CareerBuilder use similar screening techniques to filter applications. The primary goal of your résumé is pleasing a human reader. However, it must first get past the ATS gatekeeper to be selected and put in the right category.

Maximizing the Rank of Your Résumé

The higher your résumé ranks when it is evaluated by an ATS, the more likely it will be reviewed by a recruiter or hiring manager. In the past candidates tried to game the system by stuffing their résumés with keywords. Newer screening systems are not so easily fooled. Although keywords are important, your résumé must qualify in other ways to be selected. The following techniques, in addition to those cited earlier, can boost the probability that your résumé will rank high enough to qualify for review by a human reader.

- **Include specific keywords or keyword phrases.** Study carefully any advertisements and job descriptions for the position you want. Describe your experience, education, and qualifications in terms associated with the job advertisement or job description for this position. However, don't just plop a keyword into your résumé; use it in context to ensure ATS recognition (e.g., collaborated within four-member team to create a pilot business plan).
- **Focus on nouns.** Although action verbs will make your résumé appeal to a recruiter, the ATS will often be looking for nouns in three categories: (a) a job title, position, or role (e.g., *accountant, Web developer, team leader*); (b) a technical skill or specialization (e.g., *JavaScript, e-newsletter editor*); and (c) a certification, tool used, or specific experience (e.g., *Certified Financial Analyst, experience with WordPress*).[27]
- **Use variations of the job title.** ATS may seek a slightly different job title from what you list. To be safe, include variations and abbreviations (e.g., *occupational therapist, certified occupational therapist*, or *COTA*). If you don't have experience in your targeted area, use the job title you seek in your objective.
- **Concentrate on the Skills section.** A majority of keywords sought by employers are for some specialized or technical skill requirement. Therefore, be sure the Skills section of your résumé is loaded with nouns that describe your skills and qualifications.
- **Keep the formatting simple.** Stay away from logos, pictures, symbols, and shadings.
- **Use conventional headings.** Include familiar headings, such as Skills, Qualifications, and Education. ATS software may not recognize headings such as Professional Engagement or Core Competencies.

Showcasing Your Qualifications in a Career E-portfolio

As the workplace becomes increasingly digital, you have yet another way to display your qualifications to prospective employers—the career e-portfolio. This is a collection of digital files that can be navigated with the help of menus and hyperlinks much like a personal website.

What Goes in a Career E-portfolio? An e-portfolio provides viewers with a snapshot of your talents, accomplishments, and technical skills. It may include a copy of your résumé, reference letters, commendations for special achievements, awards, certificates, work

FIGURE 15.14 Making a Career E-portfolio

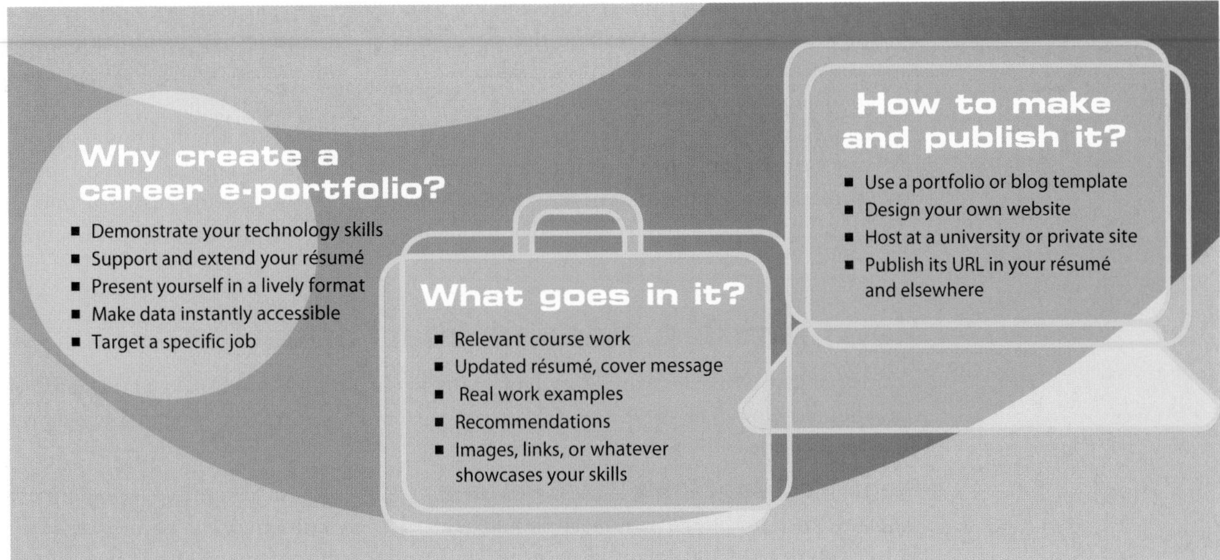

samples, a complete list of your courses, thank-you letters, and other items that tout your accomplishments. An e-portfolio could also offer links to digital copies of your artwork, film projects, videos, blueprints, documents, photographs, multimedia files, and blog entries that might otherwise be difficult to share with potential employers.

Why create a career e-portfolio?
Demonstrate your technology skills
Support and extend your résumé
Present yourself in a lively format
Make data instantly accessible
Target a specific job
What goes in it?
Relevant course work
Updated résumé, cover message
Real work examples
Recommendations
Images, links, or whatever showcases your skills
How to make and publish it?
Use a portfolio or blog template
Design your own website
Host at a university or private site
Publish its URL in your résumé and elsewhere

Because e-portfolios offer a variety of resources in one place, they have many advantages, as seen in Figure 15.14. When they are posted on websites, they can be viewed at an employer's convenience. Let's say you are talking on the phone with an employer in another city who wants to see a copy of your résumé. You can simply refer the employer to the website where your résumé resides. E-portfolios can also be seen by many individuals in an organization without circulating a paper copy.

However, the real reason for preparing an e-portfolio is that it shows off your talents and qualifications more thoroughly than a print résumé does.

Some recruiters may be skeptical about e-portfolios because they fear that such presentations will take more time to view than paper-based résumés do. Nontraditional job applications may end up at the bottom of the pile or be ignored. That's why some applicants submit a print résumé in addition to an e-portfolio.

How Are E-portfolios Accessed? E-portfolios are generally accessed at websites, where they are available around the clock to employers. If the websites are not password protected, however, you should remove personal information. Some colleges and universities make website space available for student e-portfolios. In addition, institutions may provide instruction and resources for scanning photos, digitizing images, and preparing graphics.

Expanding Employment Chances With a Video Résumé

Still another way to expand your employment possibilities is with a video résumé. Video résumés enable job candidates to present their experience, qualifications, and interests in video form. This format has many benefits. It allows candidates to demonstrate their public speaking, interpersonal, and technical skills more impressively than they can in traditional print résumés. Both employers and applicants can save recruitment and travel costs by using video résumés. Instead of flying distant candidates to interviews, organizations can see them digitally.

Video résumés are becoming more prevalent with the emergence of YouTube, inexpensive webcams, and widespread broadband. With simple edits on a computer, you can customize a video message to a specific employer and tailor your résumé for a particular job opening. In making a video résumé, dress professionally in business attire, just as you would for an in-person interview. Keep your video to three minutes or less. Explain why you would be a good employee and what you can do for the company that hires you.

Before committing time and energy to a video résumé, decide whether it is appropriate for your career field. Such presentations make sense for online, media, social, and creative professions. Traditional organizations, however, may be less impressed. Done well, a video résumé might give you an edge. Done poorly, however, it could bounce you from contention.

How Many Résumés and What Format?

At this point you may be wondering how many résumés you should make and what format they should follow. The good news is that you need only one basic résumé that you can customize for various job prospects and formats.

Preparing a Basic Print-Based Résumé. The one basic résumé you should prepare is a print-based traditional résumé. It should be attractively formatted to maximize readability. This résumé is useful (a) during job interviews, (b) for person-to-person networking situations, (c) for recruiters at career fairs, and (d) when you are competing for a job that does not require an electronic submission.

You can create a basic, yet professional-looking, résumé by using your word processing program. The Résumé Gallery in this chapter provides ideas for simple layouts that are easily duplicated and adapted. You can also examine résumé templates for design and format ideas. Their inflexibility, however, may be frustrating as you try to force your skills and experience into a predetermined template sequence. What's more, recruiters who read hundreds of résumés can usually spot a template-based résumé. Instead, create your own original résumé that reflects your unique qualifications.

Converting to a Plain-Text Résumé for Digital Submission. After preparing a basic résumé, you can convert it to a plain-text résumé so that it is available for e-mailing or pasting into online résumé submission forms. Employers prefer plain-text documents because they avoid possible e-mail viruses and word processing incompatibilities. Usually included in the body of an e-mail message, a plain-text résumé is immediately searchable. To make a plain-text résumé, create a new document in which you incorporate the following changes:

- Use basic fonts such as Helvetica or Arial. Eliminate the use of italics, boldface, and underlining, which cause some scanners to glitch or choke.
- Consider using capital letters rather than boldface type to emphasize words—but don't overdo the caps.
- Remove images, designs, colours, and any characters not on a standard keyboard.
- Punctuate and capitalize correctly so that the software knows where to begin and end a field. Avoid the lowercase expression frequently seen in texting.
- If you use a header or footer feature to place your name at the top of your résumé, be sure that your name and contact information also appear in the body of the résumé.
- In Microsoft Word save the document with Plain Text (*.txt) as the file type.
- Send yourself a copy embedded in an e-mail message to check its appearance. Also send it to a friend to try it out.

Submitting Your Résumé

The format you choose for submitting your résumé depends on what is required. If you are responding to a job advertisement, be certain to read the listing carefully to learn how the employer wants you to submit your résumé. Not following the prospective employer's instructions can eliminate you from consideration before your résumé is even reviewed. If you have any doubt about what format is desired, send an e-mail inquiry to a company representative or call and ask. Most organizations will request one of the following submission formats:

- **Word document.** Some organizations ask candidates to send their résumés and cover messages by surface mail. Organizations may also request that résumés be submitted as Word documents attached to e-mail messages, despite the fear of viruses.

CHECKLIST

Creating and Submitting a Customized Résumé

Preparation

- **Analyze your strengths.** Determine what aspects of your education, experience, and personal characteristics will be assets to prospective employers.
- **Research job listings.** Learn about available jobs, common qualifications, and potential employers. The best résumés are customized for specific jobs with specific companies.

Heading, Objective, and Summary of Qualifications

- **Identify yourself.** List your name, address, telephone numbers, and possibly links to your e-portfolio and LinkedIn profile.
- **Include a career objective for a targeted job.** Use an objective only if it is intended for a specific job (*Objective: Junior cost accountant position in the petroleum industry*).
- **Prepare a summary of qualifications.** Include a list of three to eight bulleted statements that highlight your qualifications for the targeted position.

Education

- **Name your degree/diploma, date of graduation, and institution.** Emphasize your education if your experience is limited.
- **List your major and GPA.** Give information about your studies, but don't inventory all your courses.

Work Experience

- **Itemize your jobs.** Start with your most recent job. Give the employer's name and city, dates of employment (month, year), and most significant job title.
- **Describe your experience.** Use action verbs and specific nouns to summarize achievements and skills relevant to your targeted job.
- **Promote your soft skills.** Give evidence of communication, management, and interpersonal talents. Employers want more than empty assurances; try to quantify your skills and accomplishments (*Developed teamwork skills while collaborating with six-member task force in producing 20-page mission statement*).

Special Skills, Achievements, and Awards

- **Highlight your technology skills.** Remember that nearly all employers seek employees who are proficient in using the Internet, e-mail, word processing, social media, spreadsheets, and presentation programs.
- **Show that you are a well-rounded individual.** List awards, experiences, and extracurricular activities—particularly if they demonstrate leadership, teamwork, reliability, loyalty, industry, initiative, efficiency, and self-sufficiency.

Final Tips

- **Look for ways to condense your data.** Omit all street addresses except your own. Consolidate your headings. Study models and experiment with formats to find the most readable and efficient groupings.
- **Omit references.** Have a list of references available for the interview, but don't include them on your résumé unless requested.
- **Resist the urge to inflate your qualifications.** Be accurate in listing your education, grades, honours, job titles, employment dates, and job experience.
- **Proofread, proofread, proofread!** Make this important document perfect by proofreading at least three times. Ask a friend to check it too.

Submitting

- **Follow instructions for submitting.** Learn whether the employer wants candidates to send a print résumé, e-mail résumé, plain-text version, or PDF file.
- **Practise sending a plain-text résumé.** Before submitting a plain-text résumé, try sending it to yourself or friends. Perfect your skill in achieving an attractive format.

- **Plain-text document.** As discussed earlier, many employers expect applicants to submit résumés and cover letters as plain-text documents. This format is also widely used for posting to an online job board or for sending by e-mail. Plain-text résumés may be embedded within or attached to e-mail messages.
- **PDF document.** For safety reasons some employers prefer PDF files. A PDF résumé looks exactly like the original and cannot be altered. Most computers have Adobe Acrobat Reader installed for easy reading of PDF files. Convert your résumé by saving it as a PDF file in Word's "save as" option.
- **Company database.** Larger organizations and the government may prefer that you complete an online form with your résumé information. This enables them to plug your data into their template categories for rapid searching. You might be able to cut and paste the information from your résumé into the form; however, uploading the information is less likely to cause problems for a scanning device.[28]

Concept Check

1. What techniques can you use to increase the chances of an ATS giving your résumé a high ranking? Which of these techniques also make your résumé appealing to a human reader?
2. Name four reasons why it is important to prepare a basic print-based résumé.

LEARNING OBJECTIVE 6

Understand the value of cover messages and how to draft and submit a customized message.

Cover Letters—Do They Still Matter?

A cover message, also known as a cover letter or letter of application, has always been a graceful way of introducing your résumé. However, with the steady movement toward online recruiting and digitized applicant tracking systems, cover letters are losing significance for recruiters. A recent survey by JobVite revealed that 63 percent of the 1,404 recruiter respondents thought that cover messages were unimportant.[29] Hiring managers present a different story though. They often seek as much information as they can obtain to avoid expensive bad hires, and cover letters reveal writing skills, as well as key evidence missing in a résumé.[30]

Given the stiff competition for jobs today, candidates can set themselves apart with well-written cover messages. If you are required to apply via software that limits your input, how can you get your cover message and résumé to key decision makers? Use LinkedIn or the company website to learn the names of those involved with hiring, and send your résumé and cover letter directly to these individuals, calling attention to your candidacy.

Creating a Customized Cover Letter

Especially in today's competitive employment scene, candidates must make themselves stand out. Cover messages reveal to employers your ability to put together complete sentences and to sound intelligent. In addition, many employers still prefer that you e-mail a résumé and a cover letter because it's more convenient for them than going online.[31] A cover message also can be more personal, and it showcases your special talents without relying on a chronology of your education and employment.

Recruiting professionals disagree about the length of a cover letter. Some prefer short messages with no more than two paragraphs embedded in an e-mail message.[32] Other recruiters desire longer messages that supply more information, thus giving them a better opportunity to evaluate a candidate's qualifications and writing skills. Regardless of its length, a cover message should have three primary parts: (a) an opening that captures attention, introduces the message, and identifies the position; (b) a body that sells the candidate and focuses on the employer's needs; and (c) a closing that requests an interview and motivates action.

When putting your cover message together, remember that the biggest mistake job seekers make when writing cover messages is making them sound too generic. You should, therefore, write a personalized, customized cover message for every position that interests you.

Gaining Attention in the Opening

Your cover message will be more appealing—and more likely to be read—if it begins by addressing the reader by name. Rather than sending your letter to the *Hiring Manager* or *Human Resources Department*, try to identify the name of the appropriate individual by studying the company's website. You could also call the human resources department and ask for the name of the person in charge of hiring. Another possibility is using LinkedIn to find someone working in the same department as the position in the posted job. This person may know the name of the hiring manager. If you still cannot find the name of any person to address, you might replace the salutation of your letter with a descriptive subject line such as Application for Marketing Specialist Position.

How you open your cover message depends largely on whether the application is solicited or unsolicited. If an employment position has been announced and applicants are being solicited, you can use a direct approach. If you do not know whether a position is open and you are prospecting for a job, use an indirect approach. Whether direct or indirect, the opening should attract the attention of the reader. Strive for openings that are more imaginative than *Please consider this letter an application for the position of*. . . or *I would like to apply for*. . . .

Openings for Solicited Jobs. When applying for a job that has been announced, consider some of the following techniques to open your cover message:

- **Refer to the name of an employee in the company.** Remember that employers always hope to hire known quantities rather than complete strangers.

  Brendan Borello, a member of your Customer Service Department, told me that Alliance Resources is seeking an experienced customer service representative. The enclosed summary of my qualifications demonstrates my preparation for this position.

- **Refer to the source of your information precisely.** If you are answering an advertisement, include the exact position advertised and the name and date of the publication. If you are responding to a position listed on an online job board, include the website name and the date the position was posted.

  My talent for interacting with people coupled with more than five years of customer service experience make me an ideal candidate for the director of customer relations position you advertised on the CareerJournal website on August 3.

- **Refer to the job title and describe how your qualifications fit the requirements.** Hiring managers are looking for a match between an applicant's credentials and the job needs.

  Ceradyne Company's marketing assistant opening is an excellent match with my qualifications. As a recent graduate of Western University with a major in marketing, I offer solid academic credentials, as well as industry experience gained from an internship at Flotek Industries.

Openings for Unsolicited Jobs. If you are unsure whether a position actually exists, you might use a more persuasive opening. Because your goal is to convince this person to read on, try one of the following techniques:

- **Demonstrate an interest in and knowledge of the reader's business.** Show the hiring manager that you have done your research and that this organization is more than a mere name to you.

  Because Signa HealthNet, Inc. is organizing a new information management team for its recently established group insurance division, could you use the services of a well-trained information systems graduate who seeks to become a professional systems analyst?

- **Show how your special talents and background will benefit the company.** Human resources managers need to be convinced that you can do something for them.

  Could your rapidly expanding publications division use the services of an editorial assistant who offers exceptional language skills, an honours degree from the University of Saskatchewan, and two years' experience in producing a campus literary publication?

In applying for an advertised job, Sophia Williams wrote the solicited cover letter shown in Figure 15.15. Notice that her opening identifies the position advertised on the company's website so that the reader knows exactly what advertisement Sophia means. Using features on her word processing program, Sophia designed her own letterhead that uses her name and looks like professionally printed letterhead paper.

More challenging are unsolicited cover messages, such as the letter of Jared Chen shown in Figure 15.16. Because he hopes to discover or create a job, his opening must grab the reader's attention immediately. To do that, he capitalizes on company information appearing in an online article. Jared purposely kept his cover letter short and to the point because he anticipated that a busy executive would be unwilling to read a long, detailed letter. Jared's unsolicited letter prospects for a job. Some job candidates feel that such letters may be even more productive than efforts to secure advertised jobs, since prospecting candidates face less competition and show initiative. Notice that Jared's letter uses a personal business letter format with his return address above the date.

FIGURE 15.15 Solicited Cover Letter

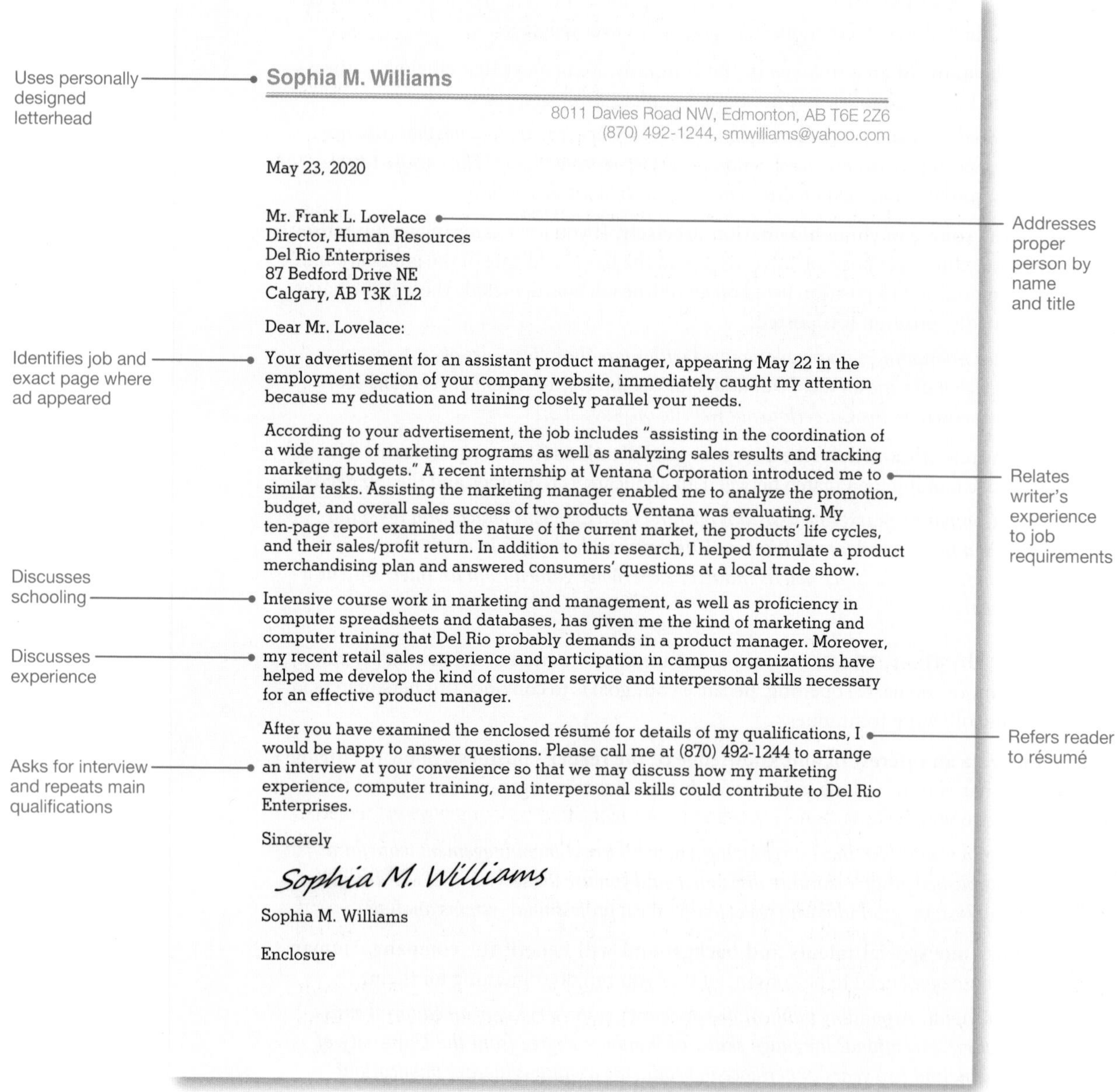
Uses personally designed letterhead
Addresses proper person by name and title
Identifies job and exact page where ad appeared
Relates writer's experience to job requirements
Discusses schooling
Discusses experience
Refers reader to résumé
Asks for interview and repeats main qualifications

Sophia M. Williams

8011 Davies Road NW, Edmonton, AB T6E 2Z6
(870) 492-1244, smwilliams@yahoo.com

May 23, 2020

Mr. Frank L. Lovelace
Director, Human Resources
Del Rio Enterprises
87 Bedford Drive NE
Calgary, AB T3K 1L2

Dear Mr. Lovelace:

Your advertisement for an assistant product manager, appearing May 22 in the employment section of your company website, immediately caught my attention because my education and training closely parallel your needs.

According to your advertisement, the job includes "assisting in the coordination of a wide range of marketing programs as well as analyzing sales results and tracking marketing budgets." A recent internship at Ventana Corporation introduced me to similar tasks. Assisting the marketing manager enabled me to analyze the promotion, budget, and overall sales success of two products Ventana was evaluating. My ten-page report examined the nature of the current market, the products' life cycles, and their sales/profit return. In addition to this research, I helped formulate a product merchandising plan and answered consumers' questions at a local trade show.

Intensive course work in marketing and management, as well as proficiency in computer spreadsheets and databases, has given me the kind of marketing and computer training that Del Rio probably demands in a product manager. Moreover, my recent retail sales experience and participation in campus organizations have helped me develop the kind of customer service and interpersonal skills necessary for an effective product manager.

After you have examined the enclosed résumé for details of my qualifications, I would be happy to answer questions. Please call me at (870) 492-1244 to arrange an interview at your convenience so that we may discuss how my marketing experience, computer training, and interpersonal skills could contribute to Del Rio Enterprises.

Sincerely

Sophia M. Williams

Sophia M. Williams

Enclosure

FIGURE 15.16 Unsolicited Cover Letter

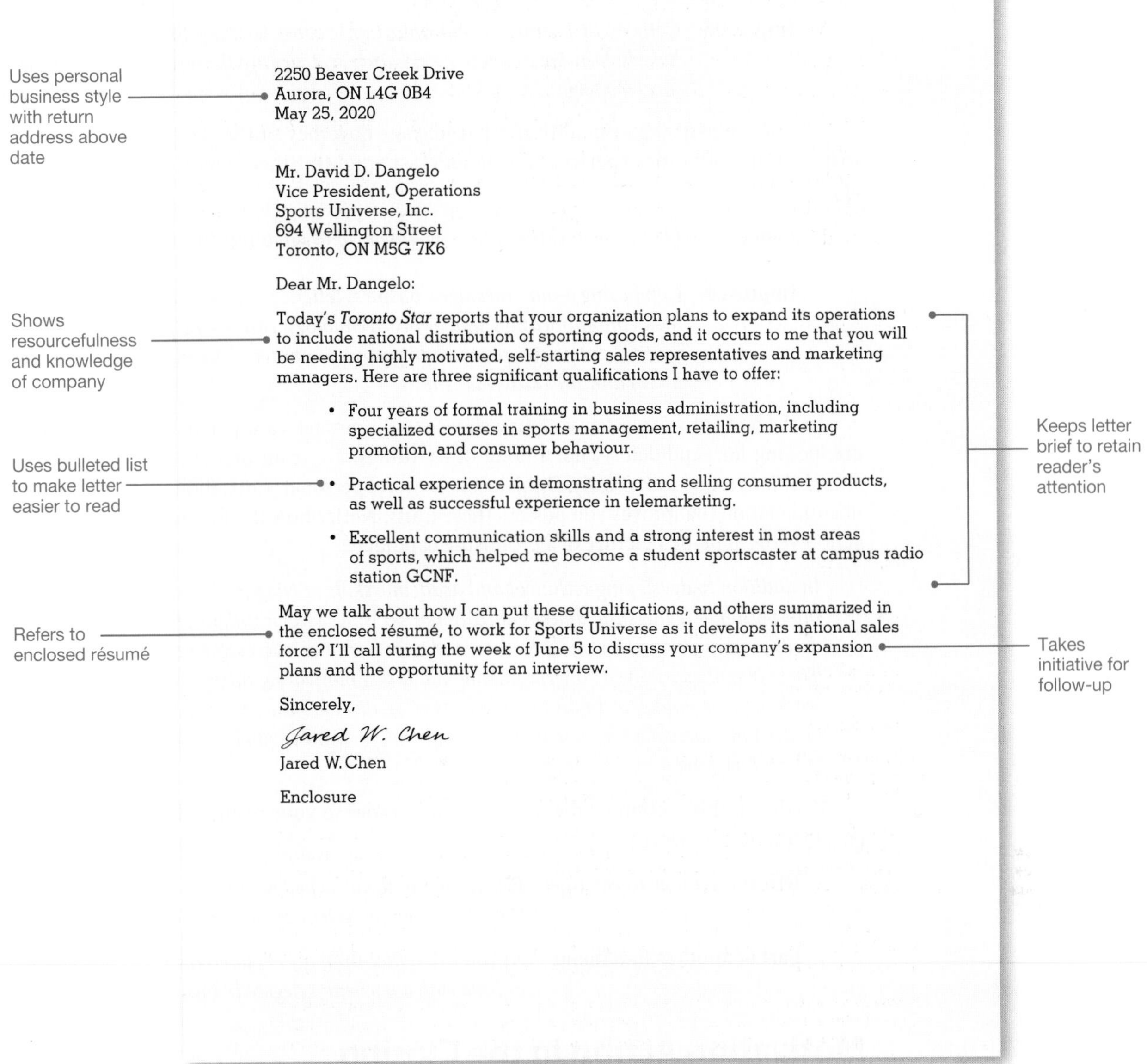
Uses personal business style with return address above date
Shows resourcefulness and knowledge of company
Uses bulleted list to make letter easier to read
Refers to enclosed résumé
Keeps letter brief to retain reader's attention
Takes initiative for follow-up

2250 Beaver Creek Drive
Aurora, ON L4G 0B4
May 25, 2020

Mr. David D. Dangelo
Vice President, Operations
Sports Universe, Inc.
694 Wellington Street
Toronto, ON M5G 7K6

Dear Mr. Dangelo:

Today's *Toronto Star* reports that your organization plans to expand its operations to include national distribution of sporting goods, and it occurs to me that you will be needing highly motivated, self-starting sales representatives and marketing managers. Here are three significant qualifications I have to offer:

- Four years of formal training in business administration, including specialized courses in sports management, retailing, marketing promotion, and consumer behaviour.
- Practical experience in demonstrating and selling consumer products, as well as successful experience in telemarketing.
- Excellent communication skills and a strong interest in most areas of sports, which helped me become a student sportscaster at campus radio station GCNF.

May we talk about how I can put these qualifications, and others summarized in the enclosed résumé, to work for Sports Universe as it develops its national sales force? I'll call during the week of June 5 to discuss your company's expansion plans and the opportunity for an interview.

Sincerely,

Jared W. Chen

Jared W. Chen

Enclosure

Promoting Your Strengths in the Message Body

After you have captured the attention of the reader and identified your purpose in the letter opening, you should use the body of the letter to plug your qualifications for this position. If you are responding to an advertisement, you will want to explain how your preparation and experience fulfill the stated requirements. If you are prospecting for a job, you may not know the exact requirements. Your employment research and knowledge of your field, however, should give you a reasonably good idea of what is expected for this position.

It is also important to stress reader benefits. In other words, you should describe your strong points in relation to the needs of the employer. Hiring officers want you to tell them what you can do for their organizations. This is more important than telling what courses you took in university or college or what duties you performed in your previous jobs.

Poor: *I have completed courses in business communication, report writing, and technical writing.*

Improved: *Courses in business communication, report writing, and technical writing have helped me develop the research and writing skills required of your technical writers.*

Choose your strongest qualifications and show how they fit the targeted job. Remember that students with little experience are better off spotlighting their education and its practical applications:

Poor: *I have taken classes that prepare me to be an administrative assistant.*

Improved: *Composing e-mail messages, business letters, memos, and reports in my business communication and office technology courses helped me develop the writing, language, proofreading, and computer skills mentioned in your ad for an administrative assistant.*

In the body of your letter, you may choose to discuss relevant personal traits. Employers are looking for candidates who, among other things, are team players, take responsibility, show initiative, and learn easily. Don't just list several personal traits, though; instead, include documentation that proves you possess these traits. Notice how the following paragraph uses action verbs to paint a picture of a promising candidate:

In addition to developing technical and academic skills at Niagara College, I have gained interpersonal, leadership, and organizational skills. As vice president of the business students' organization, I helped organize and supervise two successful fundraising events. These activities involved conceptualizing the tasks, motivating others to help, scheduling work sessions, and coordinating the efforts of 35 diverse students in reaching our goal. I enjoyed my success with these activities and look forward to applying such experience in your management trainee program.

Finally, in this section or the next, refer the reader to your résumé. Do so directly or as part of another statement.

Direct reference to résumé: *Please refer to the attached résumé for additional information regarding my education, experience, and references.*

Part of another statement: *As you will notice from my enclosed résumé, I will graduate in June with a bachelor's degree in business administration.*

Motivating Action in the Closing

After presenting your case, you should conclude by asking confidently for an interview. Don't ask for the job. To do so would be presumptuous and naive. In requesting an interview, you might suggest reader benefits or review your strongest points. Sound sincere and appreciative. Remember to make it easy for the reader to agree by supplying your telephone number and the best times to call you. In addition, keep in mind that some hiring officers prefer that you take the initiative to call them. Avoid expressions such as *I hope*, which weaken your closing. Here are possible endings:

Poor: *I hope to hear from you soon.*

Improved: *This brief description of my qualifications and the additional information on my résumé demonstrate my genuine desire to put my skills in accounting to work for McLellan and Associates. Please call me at (905) 488-2291 before 10 a.m. or after 3 p.m. to arrange an interview.*

Poor: *I look forward to a call from you.*

Improved: *To add to your staff an industrious, well-trained administrative assistant with proven Internet and communication skills, call me at (504) 492-1433 to arrange an interview. I look forward to meeting with you to discuss my qualifications further.*

Poor: *Thanks for looking over my qualifications.*

Improved: *I look forward to the opportunity to discuss my qualifications for the financial analyst position more fully in an interview. I can be reached at (613) 458-4030.*

Sending Your Résumé and Cover Message

How you submit your résumé depends on the employer's instructions, which usually involve one of the following methods:

- Submit both your cover letter and résumé in an e-mail message. Convert both to plain text.
- Send your cover letter as an e-mail message and attach your résumé (plain text, Word document, or PDF).
- Send a short e-mail message with both your cover letter and résumé attached.
- Send your cover letter and résumé as printed Word documents by Canada Post.

If you are serious about landing the job, take the time to prepare a professional cover message. If you are e-mailing your résumé, use the same cover message you would send by surface mail, but shorten it a bit, as illustrated in Figure 15.17. Just below your name, include your address, e-mail address, and phone number. For résumés submitted as PDF files, send the cover message as a PDF also.

FIGURE 15.17 E-mail Cover Message

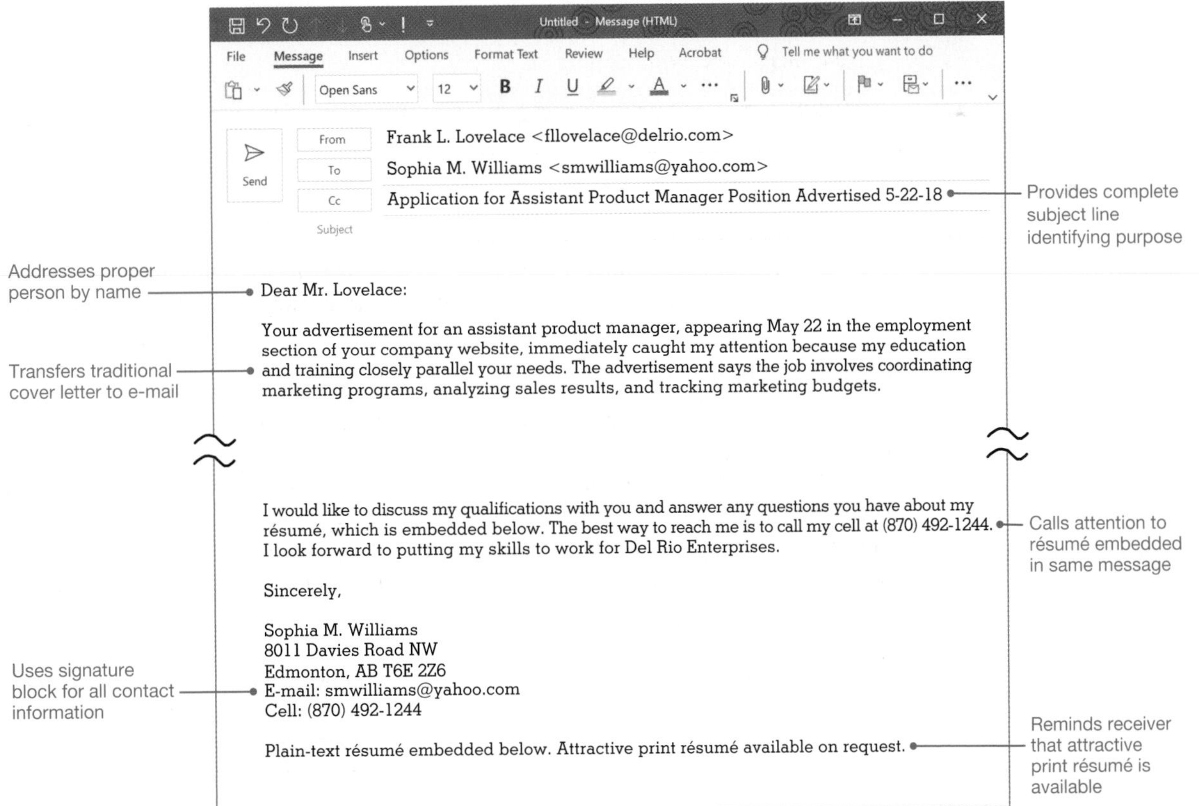

Final Tips for Successful Cover Messages

As you revise your cover message, notice how many sentences begin with *I*. Although it is impossible to talk about yourself without using *I*, you can reduce "I" domination with a number of thoughtful techniques. Make activities and outcomes, and not you, the subjects of sentences. Sometimes you can avoid *I* domination by focusing on the "you" view. Another way to avoid starting sentences with *I* is to move phrases from within the sentence to the beginning.

Poor: *I took classes in business communication and computer applications.*

Improved: *Classes in business communication and computer applications prepared me to . . . . (Make activities the subject.)*

Poor: *I enjoyed helping customers, which taught me to . . . .*

Improved: *Helping customers was a real pleasure and taught me to . . . . (Make outcomes the subject.)*

Poor: *I am a hardworking team player who . . . .*

Improved: *You are looking for a hardworking team player who . . . . (Use "you" view.)*

Poor: *I worked to support myself all through college, thus building . . . .*

Improved: *All through college, I worked to support myself, thus building . . . . (Move phrases to the beginning.)*

However, strive for a comfortable style. In your effort to avoid sounding self-centred, don't write unnaturally.

Like your résumé, your cover message must look professional and suggest quality. This means using a traditional letter style, such as block format. Also, be sure to print it on the same quality paper as your résumé. As with your résumé, proofread it several times yourself; then have a friend read it for content and mechanics. Don't rely on spell-check to find all the errors. Just like your résumé, your cover message must be perfect.

CHECKLIST

Preparing and Sending a Customized Cover Letter

Opening

- **Use the receiver's name.** Whenever possible, address the proper individual by name.
- **Identify the position, where you found it, and your information source, if appropriate.** Specify the advertised position, date, and publication name. If someone referred you, name that person.
- **Gain the reader's attention.** Use one of these techniques: (a) tell how your qualifications fit the job specifications, (b) show knowledge of the reader's business, (c) describe how your special talents will be assets to the company, or (d) use an original and relevant expression.

Body

- **Describe what you can do for the reader.** Demonstrate how your background and training fill the job requirements.
- **Highlight your strengths.** Summarize your principal assets in terms of education, experience, and special skills. Avoid repeating specific wording from your résumé.
- **Refer to your résumé.** In this section or the closing, direct the reader to the attached résumé. Do so directly or incidentally as part of another statement.

Closing

- **Ask for an interview.** Also consider reviewing your strongest points or suggesting how your assets will benefit the company.
- **Make it easy to respond.** Tell when you can be reached during office hours, or announce when you will call the reader. Note that some recruiters prefer that you call them.

Sending

- **Include a cover message with your résumé.** Send your cover message along with your résumé as a Word attachment, embedded in an e-mail message, as a plain-text attachment, as a PDF file, or as a fax.
- **If you e-mail your cover message, put your contact information in the signature area.** Move your return address from the top of the letter to the signature block. Include your phone number and e-mail address.

Concept Check

1. A blogger recently wrote that "cover letters probably don't matter, but you still need one." How can you justify cover letters?
2. Why is it important to reduce the number of times you use *I* in your cover letter? What are some techniques to reduce this usage?

SPOTLIGHT ON COMMUNICATION: PART 2

Rocky Mountaineer—Revisited

Courtesy of Rocky Mountaineer

Rocky Mountaineer's train routes provide unobstructed, beautiful views of Canadian landscapes and wildlife. As part of its corporate giving efforts, Rocky Mountaineer has "a team member-led social purpose council, which informs and guides [its] approach to supporting meaningful impact in communities and the environment."[33] Each year, their team decides which causes to support:

> For 2020, our team selected two causes to support: reducing hunger in the communities where we work around the world; and protecting wildlife where our train travels in Western Canada. We have partnered with Critter Care Wildlife Society to support the treatment, care and release of sick, injured and orphaned wildlife in British Columbia. Our team contributes to these causes through fundraising, in-kind donations, and volunteer activities.
>
> To honour our team members' employment anniversaries, we contribute annually to Tree Canada's National Greening Program. To date, more than 13,500 trees have been planted in BC thanks to our contributions.[34]

To aid their fundraising initiatives, Rocky Mountaineer also donates rail packages to not-for-profit organizations. For the service the company provides, its reputation for giving back to the community, and the quality of jobs it provides for employees, Rocky Mountaineer has received numerous awards, including Canada's Top Employers and Canada's Best Managed Companies.[35] They have also been "named as one of the World's Greatest Trips" by *National Geographic*.[35]

CRITICAL THINKING

- Consider your own personal values. Why is it important to seek work at an organization or company that shares your values?
- If you were preparing a cover letter to work at Rocky Mountaineer, how would you gain attention in the opening paragraph and promote your strengths in the message body?

Summary of Learning Objectives

1 Begin a job search by recognizing emerging trends and technologies, exploring your interests, evaluating your qualifications, and investigating career opportunities.

- Recognize that searching for a job now includes such indispensable tools as job boards, social networks, and mobile technologies.
- Start the process by learning about yourself, your field of interest, and your qualifications. How do your skills match what employers seek?
- To investigate career opportunities, visit a campus career centre, search for apps and online help, take a summer job, interview someone in your field, volunteer, or join professional organizations.
- Identify job availability, the skills and qualifications required, duties, and salaries.

2 Develop effective search strategies to explore the open job market.

- Research reveals that job seekers found their best jobs through personal networking, online social networking, online job boards, classified advertisements, recruiters, college fairs, and other connections.
- In searching the open job market—that is, jobs that are listed and advertised—explore the big job boards, such as Indeed, CareerBuilder, Monster, and Workopolis.
- To find a job with a specific company, go directly to that company's website and check its openings and possibilities.
- Take advantage of mobile apps to access and vet job openings as soon as they are listed.

3 Expand your job-search strategies by pursuing the hidden job market.

- Estimates suggest that as many as 80 percent of jobs are in the hidden job market—that is, never advertised. Successful job candidates find jobs in the hidden job market through networking.
- An effective networking procedure involves (a) developing a contact list, (b) reaching out to these contacts in person and online in search of referrals, and (c) following up on referrals.
- Because electronic media and digital tools continue to change our lives, savvy candidates use social media networks—especially LinkedIn—to extend their networking efforts.
- Effective networking strategies include building a personal brand, preparing a professional business card with a tagline, composing a 60-second elevator speech that describes what you can offer, and building a powerful online presence.

4 Organize your qualifications and information to create a winning, customized résumé.

- Because of intense competition, you must customize your résumé to appeal to an applicant tracking system (ATS) and to a human reader.
- Chronological résumés, which list work and education by dates, rank highest with recruiters. Functional résumés, which highlight skills instead of jobs, may be helpful for people with little experience, those changing careers, and those with negative employment histories.
- Arrange your skills and achievements to aim at a particular job or company.
- The most effective résumés include action verbs to appeal to human readers and job-specific nouns that become keywords selected by ATS.

5 Optimize your job search and résumé by taking advantage of today's digital tools.

- To maximize the rank of your résumé when it is evaluated by an ATS, include specific keywords, such as nouns that name job titles, technical skills, and tools used or specific experience.
- Consider preparing a career e-portfolio to showcase your qualifications. This collection of digital files can feature your talents, accomplishments, and technical skills.
- A video résumé enables you to present your experience, qualifications, and interests in video form.
- Start with a basic print-based résumé from which you can make a plain-text résumé stripped of formatting to be embedded within e-mail messages and submitted online.

6 **Understand the value of cover messages and how to draft and submit a customized message.**

- Cover messages help recruiters make decisions, and they enable candidates to set themselves apart from others.
- In the opening of a cover message, gain attention by addressing the receiver by name and identifying the job. You might also identify the person who referred you.
- In the body of the message, build interest by stressing your strengths in relation to the stated requirements. Explain what you can do for the targeted company.
- In the body or closing, refer to your résumé, request an interview, and make it easy for the receiver to respond.

Chapter Review

1. As a recent graduate of college or university, what advantages do you have as you enter the job market? (Obj. 1)
2. Although you may not actually find a job on the Internet, how can the big job boards be helpful to job hunters? (Obj. 2)
3. What is the *hidden job market*, and how can candidates find jobs in it? (Obj. 3)
4. How can attending a job fair help you access the hidden job market? (Obj. 3)
5. How do chronological and functional résumés differ, and what are the advantages and disadvantages of each? (Obj. 4)
6. What kind of information should you include in the summary of qualifications on your résumé? (Obj. 4)
7. What changes must be made to a typical résumé to make it effective for computer scanning? (Obj. 5)
8. What is a *career e-portfolio*? How can having one benefit you? (Obj. 5)
9. What information should you include in the introduction of a cover letter? (Obj. 6)
10. Why is it important to include a cover message with all résumés you send, even if you send them by e-mail? (Obj. 6)

Critical Thinking

1. How has job searching for candidates and job placement for hiring managers changed in the digital age? In your opinion, have the changes had a positive or a negative effect? Why? (Obj. 1)
2. How can networking, even with people who aren't in your field, aid you in your job search? (Obj. 3)
3. If an employer requests a résumé, should you also include a cover letter even though the employer didn't specifically ask for one? Explain. (Obj. 4)
4. Why might it be more effective to apply for unsolicited jobs than for advertised jobs? Discuss the advantages and disadvantages of letters that "prospect" for jobs. (Obj. 6)
5. **Ethical Issue:** Some jobs are advertised even when a leading candidate has the position nailed down. The candidate could be an internal applicant or someone else with an inside track. Although not required by law, management policies and human resources departments at many companies demand that hiring managers list all openings on job boards or career sites. Often, hiring managers have already selected candidates for these phantom jobs. Do you believe it is ethical to advertise jobs that are not really available?[37] (Objs. 1–3)

Activities

15.1 Evaluating Your Qualifications (Objs. 1–3)

YOUR TASK Prepare four worksheets that inventory your qualifications in these areas: employment, education, capabilities and skills, and honours and activities. Use active verbs when appropriate and specific nouns that describe job titles and skills.

a. **Employment.** Begin with your most recent job or internship. For each position list the following information: employer; job title; dates of employment; and three to five duties, activities, or accomplishments. Emphasize activities related to your job goal. Strive to quantify your achievements.

b. **Education.** List degrees/diplomas, certificates, and training accomplishments. Include courses, seminars, and skills that are relevant to your job goal. Calculate your grade point average in your major.

c. **Capabilities and skills.** List all capabilities and skills that qualify you for the job you seek. Use words and phrases such as *skilled, competent, trained, experienced,* and *ability to.* Also list five or more qualities or interpersonal skills necessary for success in your chosen field. Write action statements demonstrating that you possess some of these qualities. Empty assurances aren't good enough; try to show evidence (*Developed teamwork skills by working with a committee of eight to produce a . . .*).

d. **Awards, honours, and activities.** Explain any awards so that the reader will understand them. List campus, community, and professional activities that suggest you are a well-rounded individual or possess traits relevant to your target job.

15.2 Beginning Your Job Search With Self-Analysis (Obj. 1)

E-mail

YOUR TASK In an e-mail or a memo addressed to your instructor, answer the questions in the earlier section titled Launching Your Job Search With Self-Analysis. Draw a conclusion from your answers. What kind of career, company, position, and location seem to fit your self-analysis?

15.3 Searching the Job Market (Obj. 1)

Web

Where are the jobs? Even though you may not be in the market at the moment, become familiar with the kinds of available positions because job awareness should be an important part of your education.

YOUR TASK Clip or print a job advertisement or announcement from (a) the classified section of a newspaper, (b) an online job board, (c) a company website, or (d) a professional association listing. Select an advertisement or announcement describing the kind of employment you are seeking now or plan to seek when you graduate. Save this advertisement or announcement to attach to the résumé you will write in **Activity 15.5.**

15.4 Using LinkedIn in Your Job Search (Obj. 2)

Social Media | Web

LinkedIn is the acknowledged No. 1 site for job seekers and recruiters. It's free and easy to join. Even if you are not in the job market yet, becoming familiar with LinkedIn can open your eyes to the kinds of information employers seek and also give you practice in filling in templates such as those that applicant tracking systems employ.

YOUR TASK To become familiar with LinkedIn, set up an account and complete a profile. This consists of a template with categories to fill in. The easiest way to begin is to view a LinkedIn video taking you through the steps of creating a profile. Search for LinkedIn Profile Checklist. It discusses how to fill in information in categories such as the following:

- **Photo.** Have a friend or a professional take a photo that shows your head and shoulders. No selfies! Wear work-appropriate attire and a smile.
- **Headline.** Use a tagline to summarize your professional goals.
- **Summary.** Explain what motivates you, what you are skilled at, and where you want to go in the future.
- **Experience.** List the jobs you have held and be sure to enter the information precisely in the template categories. You can even include photos and videos of your work.

You can fill in other categories such as Organizations, Honours, and Publications. After completing a profile, discuss your LinkedIn experience with classmates. If you already have an account set up, discuss how it operates and your opinion of its worth. How can LinkedIn help students now and in the future?

15.5 Writing Your Résumé (Obj. 4)

YOUR TASK Using all the tips presented in this chapter, write your résumé. Aim it at a full-time job, part-time position, or internship that you researched online. Attach the job listing to your résumé. Also prepare a list of references. Revise your résumé until it is perfect.

15.6 Preparing Your Cover Message (Obj. 6)

E-mail

YOUR TASK Using the job listing from Activity 15.3, write a cover message introducing your résumé. Decide whether it should be a letter or an e-mail. Again, revise until it is perfect.

Total Review

The first ten chapters reviewed specific guides from Appendix B, Grammar and Mechanics Guide, beginning on page B-1. The exercise in this chapter is a total review, covering all the grammar and mechanics guides plus confusing words and frequently misspelled words. Each of the following sentences has **three** errors in grammar, punctuation, capitalization, usage, or spelling. On a sheet of paper or on your computer, write a correct version. Avoid adding new phrases, starting new sentences, or rewriting in your own words. When you finish, compare your responses with the key in Appendix C.

EXAMPLE: If you have 10 or fewer years' of experience, its customary to prepare a one-page résumé.

REVISION: If you have **ten** or fewer **years** of experience, **it's** customary to prepare a one-page résumé.

1. To conduct a safe online job search, you should: (a) Use only reputable job boards, (2) keep careful records, and (c) limit the number of sites on which you post your résumé.
2. Todays employers use sights such as Facebook to learn about potential employees. Which means that a job seeker must maintain a professional online presence.
3. When searching for jobs candidates discovered that the résumé is more likely to be used to screen candidate's then for making hiring decisions.
4. If I was you I would shorten my résumé to 1 page and include a summary of qualifications.
5. Mitchell wondered whether it was alright to ask his professor for employment advise?
6. At last months staff meeting team members examined several candidates résumés.
7. Rather then schedule face to face interviews the team investigated videoconferencing.
8. 11 applicants will be interviewed on April 10th, consequently, we may need to work late to accommodate them.
9. Although as many as twenty-five percent of jobs are found on the Internet the principle source of jobs still involves networking.
10. If Troy had went to the companies own website he might have seen the position posted immediately.

Notes

[1] Based on Conference Board of Canada. (2020). *Employability skills.* https://www.conferenceboard.ca/edu/employability-skills.aspx

[2] Rocky Mountaineer. (2020). *About us.* https://www.rockymountaineer.com/about-us

[3] Media Corp Canada, Inc. (2020). *Rocky Mountaineer: Recognized as one of BC's top employers (2020).* https://reviews.canadastop100.com/top-employer-rocky-mountaineer

[4] Ibid.

[5] Rocky Mountaineer. (2020). *Seasonal positions.* https://www.rockymountaineer.com/careers/seasonal-positions

[6] Rocky Mountaineer. (2020). *Why Rocky Mountaineer?* https://www.rockymountaineer.com/careers/why-rocky-mountaineer

[7] Ibid. Reprinted courtesy of Rocky Mountaineer.

[8] Waldman, J. (2014, February 16). *10 things you need to know about today's job search.* Careerrealism. Retrieved from http://www.careerealism.com/todays-job-search

[9] Catano, V. M. (2009). *Recruitment and selection in Canada* (4th ed.). Nelson Education, p. 149.

[10] Adams, S. (2012, July 25). Odds are that your internship will get you a job. *Forbes.* http://www.forbes.com/sites/susanadams/2012/07/25/odds-are-your-internship-will-get-you-a-job

[11] Job Board Finder. (2018, May 28). *Top 10 job boards in Canada.* https://www.jobboardfinder.com/news/top-10-job-boards-in-canada/

[12] Nuckles, B. (2015, January 8). 12 best job search apps. *Business News Daily*. Retrieved from http://www.businessnewsdaily.com/5992-best-job-search-apps.html

[13] CBC News. (2017, May 4). *Get offline and get out more: Tips for tapping into Calgary's 'hidden' job market.* https://www.cbc.ca/news/canada/calgary/summer-jobs-youth-tips-calgary-employment-1.4099259

[14] Kinsta. (2020). *Mind-blowing LinkedIn statistics and facts.* https://kinsta.com/blog/linkedin-statistics/

[15] Garriott, O. (2015, February 6). *10 LinkedIn tips for students and new grads.* LinkedIn Pulse. Retrieved from https://www.linkedin.com/pulse/10-tips-students-new-grads-linkedin-omar-garriott

[16] Singer, M. (2015, September 22). *Welcome to the 2015 recruiter nation, formerly known as the social recruiting survey.* Jobvite. http://www.jobvite.com/blog/welcome-to-the-2015-recruiter-nation-formerly-known-as-the-social-recruiting-survey

[17] Photo essay based on Albanesius, C. (2013, March 15). Need a job? Tap into your Facebook network, study finds. *PC Mag.* http://www.pcmag.com

[18] Canadian Red Cross. (2020). *Why volunteer with us?* https://www.redcross.ca/volunteer/why-volunteer-with-us

[19] Ibid.

[20] Canadian Red Cross. (2020). *Apply now.* https://www.redcross.ca/volunteer/apply-now

[21] Green, A. (2012, June 20). *10 things to leave off your résumé.* http://money.usnews.com/money/blogs/outside-voices-careers/2012/06/20/10-things-to-leave-off-your-resume

[22] Korkki, P. (2007, July 1). So easy to apply, so hard to be noticed. *New York Times.* http://www.nytimes.com/2007/07/01/business/yourmoney/01career.html

[23] Slack, M. (n.d.). *How to write a qualifications summary.* Résumé Genius. https://resumegenius.com/how-to-write-a-resume/qualifications-summary-writing-guide

[24] LinkedIn for Volunteers. (n.d.). *Use your skills to make a positive impact.* https://volunteer.linkedin.com

[25] Lloyd, M. (2015, August 13). *How often Canadians lie on their resumes and what they're lying about.* News 1130. Retrieved from http://www.news1130.com/2015/08/13/how-often-canadians-lie-on-their-resumes-and-what-theyre-lying-about/

[26] Struzik, E., IBM expert quoted in Weber, L. (2012, January 24). Your résumé vs. oblivion. *The Wall Street Journal*, p. B6.

[27] Optimalresume.com. (n.d.). *Optimizing your résumé for scanning and tracking.* http://www.montclair.edu/CareerServices/OptimalsScannedresumes.pdf

[28] Vaas, L. (n.d.). *Résumé, meet technology: Making your résumé format machine-friendly.* The Ladders. Retrieved from http://www.theladders.com/career-advice/resume-technology-resume-format-machine-friendly

[29] JobVite. (2015, July). *The JobVite recruiter national survey 2015.* https://www.jobvite.com/wp-content/uploads/2015/09/jobvite_recruiter_nation_2015.pdf

[30] Crispo, V. (2015, April 22). *So . . . do cover letters matter?* Idealist Careers. http://idealistcareers.org/so-do-cover-letters-matter

[31] Cavazos, N. (2014, April 15). *Do cover letters matter?* ZipRecruiter. https://www.ziprecruiter.com/blog/do-cover-letters-still-matter

[32] Balderrama, S. (2009, February 26). *Do you still need a cover letter?* http://msn.careerbuilder.com/Article/MSN-1811-Cover-Letters-Resumes-Do-You-Still-Need-a-Cover-Letter

[33] Rocky Mountaineer. (2020). *Corporate giving.* https://www.rockymountaineer.com/about-us/corporate-giving

[34] Ibid. Reprinted courtesy of Rocky Mountaineer.

[35] Rocky Mountaineer. (2020). *Rocky Mountaineer: Awards and accolades.* https://www.rockymountaineer.com/sites/default/files/2019-10/media_kit_awards_2018.pdf

[36] Rocky Mountaineer. (2020). *Awards and accolades.* https://www.rockymountaineer.com/about-us/awards-accolades

[37] Weber, L., & Kwoh, L. (2013, January 9). Beware the phantom job listing. *The Wall Street Journal*, pp. B1, B6.

Interviewing and Following Up

CHAPTER 16

mavo/Shutterstock

LEARNING OBJECTIVES

After studying this chapter, you should be able to

1. Explain the purposes, sequence, and types of job interviews.
2. Describe what to do *before* an interview, including using professional phone techniques, researching the target company, rehearsing success stories, cleaning up digital dirt, and fighting fear.
3. Describe what to do *during* an interview, including controlling nonverbal messages and answering typical interview questions.
4. Describe what to do *after* an interview, including thanking the interviewer, contacting references, and writing follow-up messages.
5. Prepare additional employment documents.

SPOTLIGHT ON COMMUNICATION: PART 1

Ubisoft—A Top Canadian Employer

Pe3k/Shutterstock

Ubisoft is a thriving Canadian software company, employing over 5,000 Canadians.[1] It is a "leading producer, publisher and distributor of interactive entertainment."[2] It has over 40 development studios that span five continents and employees who represent "95 nationalities and 55 spoken languages."[3] Ubisoft's franchises and games include Assassin's Creed, Rayman, Far Cry, Just Dance, Rabbids, the Tom Clancy series, and more. In addition, the Ubisoft Club boasts over 140 million registered members.[4]

In 2020 Ubisoft was voted as one of Montréal's top employers.[5] The following highlights some of the reasons:

- Home to approximately one third of the company's worldwide workforce, Ubisoft's Canadian Studios were designed with employee feedback and include many unique features to inspire creativity and encourage a little fun in the workplace—the Mile End studio houses video games and foosball tables, food truck–themed kitchenettes, and even fully staffed onsite fitness facilities with a variety of instructor-led classes.
- Ubisoft encourages employees to become owners through a share purchase plan (available to all employees) and also enables employees to reap the benefits of the company's financial success through a profit-sharing plan.
- Ubisoft invests in long-term employee development, offering tuition subsidies for job-related courses, a variety of in-house and online training programs, and a unique mentorship "café"—employees can even apply for "Missions," temporary assignments to other Ubisoft studios worldwide for a designated period of time (with additional costs covered).[6]

Ubisoft not only offers careers in art, design, and animation but also hires for finance, human resources, sales, communications, information systems, and quality control.[7]

CRITICAL THINKING

- Before you apply for a job, why must you carefully investigate the background of any company that interests you?
- How would you craft a résumé and cover letter so that it would stand out when it arrives at Ubisoft?

LEARNING OBJECTIVE 1

Explain the purposes, sequence, and types of job interviews.

Interviewing Effectively in Today's Competitive Market

Whether you are completing your education and searching for your first serious position or are in the workforce and striving to change jobs—a job interview can be life changing. Because employment is a major part of everyone's life, the job interview takes on enormous importance.

Most people consider job interviews extremely stressful. However, the more you learn about the process and the more prepared you are, the less stress you will feel. Moreover, a job interview is a two-way street. It is not just about being judged by the employer. You, the applicant, will be using the job interview to evaluate the employer. Do you really want to work for this organization?

To be successful in a highly competitive market, you must keep up with the latest trends and techniques that recruiters use to choose the very best candidates. Figure 16.1 illustrates six hot trends in today's employment scene. To help you respond to these trends, this chapter presents the latest tips and other traditional techniques that will improve your interviewing skills and boost your confidence.

Yes, job interviews can be intimidating and stressful. However, you can expect to ace an interview when you know what's coming and when you prepare thoroughly. Remember, preparation often determines who gets the job. First, though, you need to know the purposes and sequencing of employment interviews and the types of interviews you might encounter in your job search.

FIGURE 16.1 Latest Trends in Interviewing

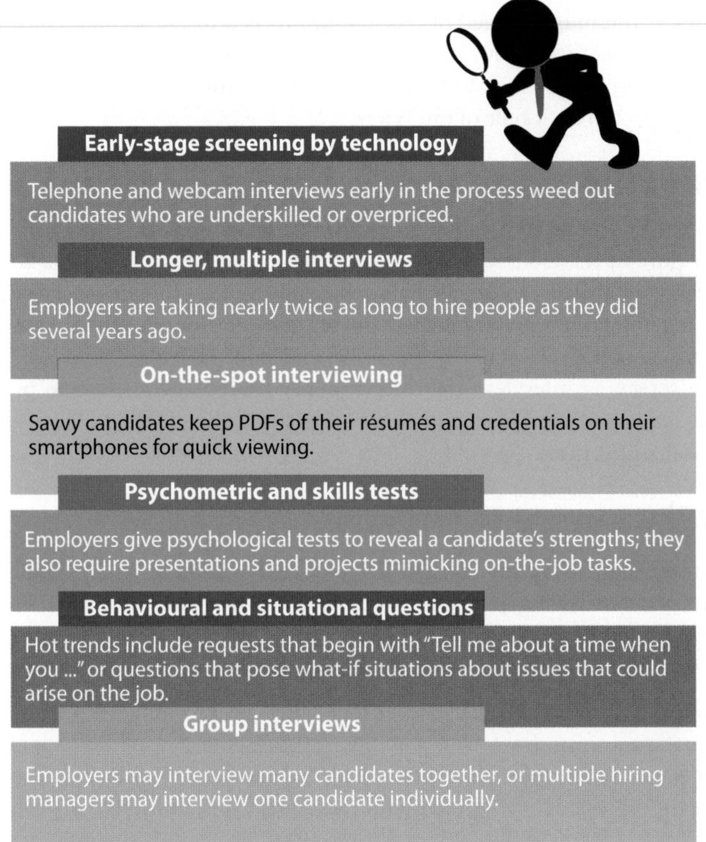

Early-stage screening by technology
Telephone and webcam interviews early in the process weed out candidates who are underskilled or overpriced.
Longer, multiple interviews
Employers are taking nearly twice as long to hire people as they did several years ago.
On-the-spot interviewing
Savvy candidates keep PDFs of their résumés and credentials on their smartphones for quick viewing.
Psychometric and skills tests
Employers give psychological tests to reveal a candidate's strengths; they also require presentations and projects mimicking on-the-job tasks.
Behavioural and situational questions
Hot trends include requests that begin with "Tell me about a time when you ..." or questions that pose what-if situations about issues that could arise on the job.
Group interviews
Employers may interview many candidates together, or multiple hiring managers may interview one candidate individually.

Purposes and Sequencing of Employment Interviews

An interview has several purposes for you as a job candidate. It is an opportunity to (a) convince the employer of your potential, (b) learn more about the job and the company, and (c) expand on the information in your résumé. This is the time for you to gather information about whether you would fit into the company culture. You should also be thinking about whether this job suits your career goals.

From the employer's perspective, the interview is an opportunity to (a) assess your abilities in relation to the requirements for the position; (b) discuss your training, experience, knowledge, and abilities in more detail; (c) see what drives and motivates you; and (d) decide whether you would fit into the organization.

The hiring process often follows a six-stage sequence, as illustrated in Figure 16.2. Following the application, interviews proceed from screening interviews to hiring interviews.

FIGURE 16.2 Six Stages of the Hiring Process

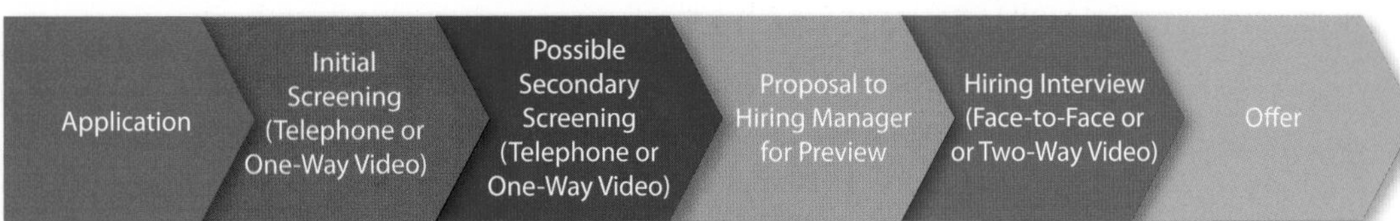

Types of Employment Interviews

Job applicants generally face two kinds of interviews: screening interviews and hiring/placement interviews. You must succeed in the first to proceed to the second. Once you make it to the hiring/placement interview, you will find a variety of interview styles, including one-on-one, panel, group, sequential, and video interviews. You will be better prepared if you know what to expect in each type of interview.

Screening Interviews

Screening interviews do just that—they screen candidates to eliminate those who fail to meet minimum requirements. Companies use screening interviews to save time and money by weeding out less-qualified candidates before scheduling face-to-face interviews. Although some screening interviews are conducted during job fairs or on school campuses, many screening interviews take place on the telephone, and some take place online.[8]

During a screening interview, the interviewer will probably ask you to provide details about the education and experience listed on your résumé; therefore, you must be prepared to promote your qualifications.

Hiring/Placement Interviews

The most promising candidates selected from screening interviews are invited to hiring/placement interviews. Hiring managers want to learn whether candidates are motivated, qualified, and a good fit for the position. Their goal is to learn how the candidate would fit into their organization. Conducted in depth, hiring/placement interviews take many forms.

One-on-One Interviews. In one-on-one interviews, which are the most common type, you can expect to sit down with a company representative and talk about the job and your qualifications. If the representative is the hiring manager, questions will be specific and job related. If the representative is from human resources, the questions will probably be more general.

Panel Interviews. Panel interviews are typically conducted by people who will be your supervisors and colleagues. Usually seated around a table, interviewers take turns asking questions. If possible before these interviews, try to gather basic biographical information about each panel member. This information may be available on the company website or LinkedIn. Try to take notes during the interview so that you can remember each person's questions and what was important to that individual. Don't take notes on a laptop or other digital device as interviewers may think you are checking incoming texts.

Group Interviews. Group interviews occur when a company interviews several candidates for the same position at the same time. Some employers use this technique to measure leadership skills and communication styles. During a group interview, stay focused on the interviewer, and treat the other candidates with respect. Even if you are nervous, try to remain calm, take your time when responding, and express yourself clearly. The key during a group interview is to make yourself stand out from the other candidates in a positive way.[9]

Sequential Interviews. In a sequential interview, you meet individually with two or more interviewers one on one over several hours or days. You must listen carefully and respond positively to all interviewers. Promote your qualifications to each one; don't assume that any interviewer knows what was said in a previous interview. Keep your responses fresh, even when repeating yourself many times. Subsequent interviews also tend to be more in-depth than first interviews, which means that you need to be even more prepared and know even more about the company.

Video Interviews. Perhaps the hottest trend in interviewing is conducting video interviews. And, with the COVID-19 pandemic, there has been a large shift to online

PLUGGED IN

Preparing for a Video Job Interview

Both one-way and two-way video interviews enable job seekers to connect with potential employers without travelling. However, because video interviews present many potential pitfalls, preparation is essential. The following tips can help you make sure you are ready.

- **Do your homework.** Using the Internet, learn all that you can about the target company including its competitors, its products, and its goals.
- **Plan your answers.** For one-way interviews, you have the questions in advance, giving you a marvellous opportunity to prepare perfect responses. For two-way interviews, practise your answers to typical questions until you can recite them flawlessly by looking straight into the camera.
- **Check your tech.** Be sure you know how your webcam and microphone work so that your audio and video are clear and free of glitches. Position the camera at eye level.
- **Look at your lighting.** Place a light behind your computer so that your face is not in the shadows.
- **Control your surroundings.** The room you sit in should be neat, attractive, and quiet. Avoid distractions, such as barking dogs, crying children, flushing toilets, or ringing cell phones.
- **Dress to impress.** Just as you would prepare for a face-to-face interview, be well groomed. If you are interviewing for a professional position, wear a suit. Avoid distracting prints, disturbingly bright colours, and loud jewellery.
- **Practise, practise, practise.** Know your answers well enough to be natural and comfortable in saying them, but avoid sounding mechanical. This requires a lot of practice.
- **Be the best you can be.** Sit up straight, look interested by leaning forward slightly, and don't let your gaze drop, suggesting you are reading from a script. Don't mumble or fidget. Focus on answers and stories that demonstrate why you are the best fit for the job.

interviews. One-way (asynchronous) video interviewing enables a candidate to respond to a list of pre-scripted questions prepared by the hiring organization. When convenient, the candidate creates a video recording of the answers. The interviewer can view the job seeker, but the job seeker cannot see the interviewer. One-way interviewing benefits employers by cutting the time needed to meet many candidates; it benefits candidates by enabling them to be interviewed at their leisure without travelling to distant locations. Candidates also can practise and perfect their responses by rerecording.

Two-way video interviewing is similar to regular face-to-face interviewing, but it is typically conducted through video chat. A key advantage of two-way interviewing is that it provides an interactive forum enabling hiring companies to better assess a candidate's communication skills, body language, and personality. Preparing for either a one-way or a two-way video interview is extremely important; check out the accompanying Plugged In for tips to help you succeed.

Concept Check

1. Conduct an Internet search to see how the COVID-19 pandemic has affected interviewing practices. Have many employers moved to video interviews? Is a handshake still appropriate during a face-to-face interview?
2. Think about job interviews you've had in the past. Did the interview move through all six stages of the hiring process, or did the process differ for a part-time position? What did you learn from the interviewing process? In groups, discuss the experiences you've had. If you haven't had a job interview yet, take notes about your peers' experiences.

LEARNING OBJECTIVE 2

Describe what to do *before* an interview, including using professional phone techniques, researching the target company, rehearsing success stories, cleaning up digital dirt, and fighting fear.

Before the Interview

After you have sent out at least one résumé or filled out at least one job application, you must consider yourself an active job seeker. Being active in the job market means that you should be prepared to be contacted by potential employers. As discussed earlier, employers often use screening interviews to narrow the list of candidates. If you do well in the screening interview, you will be invited to an in-person or video meeting.

Using Professional Phone Techniques

Even with the popularity of e-mail, most employers contact job applicants by phone to set up interviews. Employers can judge how well applicants communicate by hearing their voices and expressions over the phone. Therefore, once you are actively looking for a job, anytime the phone rings, it could be a potential employer. Don't make the mistake of letting an unprofessional voice mail message or a lazy roommate or a sloppy cell phone manner ruin your chances. To make the best impression, try these tips:

- On your answering device, make sure that your outgoing message is concise and professional, with no distracting background sounds. It should be in your own voice and include your full name for clarity. You can find more tips for creating professional telephone messages in Chapter 14.
- Tell those who might answer your phone at home about your job search. Explain to them the importance of acting professionally and taking complete messages. Family members or roommates can affect the first impression an employer has of you.
- If you have children, prevent them from answering the phone during your job search. Children of all ages are not known for taking good messages.
- If you have put your cell phone number on your résumé, don't answer unless you are in a good location to carry on a distraction-free conversation with an employer.
- Use voice mail to screen calls. By screening incoming calls, you can be totally in control when you return a prospective employer's call.

Making the First Conversation Impressive

Whether you answer the phone directly or return an employer's call, make sure you are prepared for the conversation. Remember that how you conduct yourself on the phone will create a lasting impression. To make that first impression a positive one, follow these tips:

- Treat any call from an employer just like an interview. Use a professional tone and businesslike language. Be polite and enthusiastic, and sell your qualifications.
- If caught off guard by the call, ask whether you can call back in a few minutes. Take that time to organize your materials and yourself.
- Have a copy of your résumé available so that you can answer any questions that come up. Also have your list of references, a calendar, and a notepad handy.
- Be prepared for a screening interview. As discussed earlier, this might occur during the first phone call.
- Take good notes during the phone conversation. Obtain accurate directions, and verify the spelling of your interviewer's name. If you will be interviewed by more than one person, get all their names.
- If given a chance, ask for an interview on Tuesday at 10:30 a.m. This is considered the most opportune time. Avoid the start of the day on Monday and the end of the day on Friday.[10]
- Before you hang up, reconfirm the date and time of your interview. You could say something like *I look forward to meeting with you next Wednesday at 2 p.m.*

Researching the Target Company

Once you have scheduled an in-person or online interview, you need to start preparing for it. One of the most important steps in effective interviewing is gathering detailed information about a prospective employer. Never enter an interview cold. Recruiters are impressed by candidates who have done their homework.

Scouring the Internet for Important Company Data. Search the potential employer's website, news sources, trade journals, and industry directories. Unearth information about the job, the company, and the industry. Learn all you can about the company's history, mission and goals, size, geographic locations, and number of employees. Check out its customers, competitors, culture, management structure, reputation in the community, financial condition, strengths and weaknesses, and future plans, as well as the names of its leaders. Analyze its advertising, including sales and marketing brochures.

Check out section 16-2c in MindTap, where you can watch a video featuring Candice Wong, a registered physiotherapist, discuss the importance of researching your industry before an interview.

Locating Inside Information. To locate inside information, use social media sources, such as LinkedIn, Facebook, and Twitter. Beyond these sites, LinkedIn's Job Insider toolbar can help you discover whether you know someone who already works at the company.

Try to connect with someone who is currently employed—but not working in the immediate area where you want to be hired. Be sure to seek out someone who is discreet. Blogs are also excellent sources for insider information and company research. One marketing specialist calls them "job posting gold mines."[11] In addition, don't forget to Google the interviewer. Employers are pleased when job candidates take an interest in them.

Rehearsing Success Stories

Go to section 16-2d in MindTap, where you can watch a video featuring Courtney Appleby, a campaign manager, discuss how to prepare for an interview.

To feel confident and be ready to sell your qualifications, prepare and practise success stories. These stories are specific examples of your educational and work-related experience that demonstrate your qualifications and achievements. Look over the job description and your résumé to determine what skills, training, personal characteristics, and experience you want to emphasize during the interview. Then prepare a success story for each one. Incorporate numbers, such as dollars saved or percentage of sales increased, whenever possible. Your success stories should be detailed but brief. Think of them as 30-second sound bites.

Practise telling your success stories until they fluently roll off your tongue and sound natural. Then in the interview be certain to find places to insert them. Tell stories about (a) dealing with a crisis, (b) handling a tough interpersonal situation, (c) successfully juggling many priorities, (d) changing course to deal with changed circumstances, (e) learning from a mistake, (f) working on a team, and (g) going beyond expectations.[12]

Cleaning Up Digital Dirt

Potential employers definitely screen a candidate's online presence by using Google and social media sites, such as Facebook, LinkedIn, and Twitter.[13] The top reasons cited for not considering an applicant after an online search were that the candidate (a) posted provocative or inappropriate photographs or information; (b) posted content about drinking or doing drugs; (c) talked negatively about current or previous employers, colleagues, or clients; (d) exhibited poor communication skills; (e) made discriminatory comments; (f) lied about qualifications; or (g) revealed a current or previous employer's confidential information.[14]

A recent study by York University revealed that not only does a poor online presence affect your chances of being hired, but it can also affect your starting salary. The researchers were surprised to learn that employers ranked women who consciously presented a professional online image higher than men who did. Most importantly, the research revealed that not everyone is managing their social media presence.[15]

Think about cleaning up your online presence by following these steps:

- **Remove questionable content.** Remove any incriminating, provocative, or distasteful photos, content, and links that could make you look unprofessional to potential employers.

Laura Stanley

Removing questionable content from social media sites should be the first step of any job search. Unsuitable material may include your own photos or posts but may also come from someone else's comments about your content. Remember to view your social media presence the same way a future employer would, and ask yourself whether the personal information you share would be embarrassing if it were publicly known. Why is it a good idea to Google yourself?[16]

- **Stay positive.** Don't complain about things in your professional or personal life online. Even negative reviews you have written on sites such as Amazon.ca can turn employers off.
- **Be selective about who is on your list of friends.** You don't want to miss an opportunity because you seem to associate with negative, immature, or unprofessional people. Your best bet is to make your personal social networking pages private.
- **Avoid joining groups or fan pages that may be viewed negatively.** If you think an online group or activity you are involved in might show poor judgment, remove yourself immediately.
- **Don't discuss your job search if you are still employed.** Employees can find themselves in trouble with their current employers by writing status updates or sending tweets about their job searches.

Dressing for, Travelling to, and Arriving at Your Interview

The big day has arrived! Ideally, you are fully prepared for your interview. Now you need to make sure that everything goes smoothly. On the morning of your interview, give yourself plenty of time to groom and dress.

Deciding What to Wear. What to wear may worry you because business attire today ranges from ultracasual to formal suits. When in doubt, ask the person requesting the interview.[17]

Here's what you definitely should not wear, according to Monster.com:[18] (a) ill-fitting clothes; (b) overly casual attire, such as jeans, tennis shoes, shorts, T-shirts, hats, flip-flops, and any item promoting messages or brands; (c) distracting items; (d) excessive accessories; or (e) something very different from what the interviewer suggested.

Make sure you can arrive at the employer's office without being rushed. If something unexpected happens that will cause you to be late, such as an accident or a bridge closure, call the interviewer right away to explain what is happening. Most interviewers will understand, and your call will show that you are responsible. On the way to the interview, don't smoke, don't eat anything messy or smelly, and don't wear perfume or cologne. Arrive at the interview five or ten minutes early, but not earlier. If you are very early, wait in the car or in a café nearby. If possible, check your appearance before going in.

Being Polite and Pleasant. When you enter the office, be courteous and congenial to everyone. Remember that you are being judged not only by the interviewer but also by the receptionist and anyone else who sees you before and after the interview. They will notice how you sit, what you read, and how you look. Introduce yourself to the receptionist, and wait to be invited to sit. You may be asked to fill out a job application while you are waiting. You will find tips for doing this effectively later in this chapter.

Greeting the Interviewer and Making a Positive First Impression. Greet the interviewer confidently, and don't be afraid to initiate a handshake. Doing so exhibits professionalism and confidence. Extend your hand, look the interviewer directly in the eye, smile pleasantly, and say, *I'm pleased to meet you, Mr. Thomas. I am Constance Ferraro.* In this culture a firm, not crushing, handshake sends a nonverbal message of poise and assurance. Once introductions have taken place, wait for the interviewer to offer you a chair. Make small talk with upbeat comments such as *This is a beautiful headquarters* or *I'm very impressed with the facilities you have here.* Don't immediately begin rummaging in your briefcase for your résumé. Being at ease and unrushed suggest that you are self-confident.

Fighting Fear

Expect to be nervous before and during the interview. It's natural! One of the best ways to overcome fear is to know what happens in a typical interview. You can further reduce your fears by following these suggestions:

- **Practise interviewing.** Try to get as much interviewing practice as you can—especially with real companies. The more times you experience the interview situation, the less nervous you will be. However, don't schedule interviews unless you are genuinely interested in the organization. If offered, campus mock interviews also provide excellent practice, and the interviewers will offer tips for improvement.
- **Prepare thoroughly.** Research the company. Know how you will answer the most frequently asked questions. Be ready with success stories. Rehearse your closing statement. Knowing that you have done all you can to be ready for the interview is a tremendous fear preventive.
- **Understand the process.** Find out ahead of time how the interview will be structured. Will you be meeting with an individual, or will you be interviewed by a panel? Is this the first of a series of interviews? Don't be afraid to ask about these details before the interview so that an unfamiliar situation won't catch you off guard.
- **Dress professionally.** If you know you look sharp, you will feel more confident.
- **Breathe deeply.** Plan to take deep breaths, particularly if you feel anxious while waiting for the interviewer. Deep breathing makes you concentrate on something other than the interview and also provides much-needed oxygen.
- **Know that you are not alone.** Everyone feels some anxiety during a job interview. Interviewers expect some nervousness, and a skilled interviewer will try to put you at ease.
- **Remember that an interview is a two-way street.** The interviewer isn't the only one who is gleaning information. You have come to learn about the job and the company. In fact, during some parts of the interview, you will be in charge. This should give you courage.

Concept Check

1. If you are interviewing for a company where most of the employees are dressed very casually, should you wear similar clothes to a job interview with that company? Why or why not?
2. Why is it important to be aware of your online presence during the job search process? What are ways to clean up your digital dirt?

CASE CONNECTIONS

Making the Most of Job Fairs

Courtesy of Denise Bissonnette

Denise Bissonnette, based in Winnipeg, Manitoba, "is one of North America's most sought-after trainers and speakers on career development, job development, workforce development, and 'true livelihood.'"[19] She offers the following tips for before, during, and after the job fair:

What to do BEFORE the job fair

- Research the employers that plan to attend. Information can be found on the company's website or at the local library or in business papers.

(Continued)

- Prepare questions for the employers.
- Prepare an introduction and a personal summary statement.
- Practise your responses to typical interview questions.
- Prepare a résumé that presents your background clearly and concisely. Estimate the number of employers that you plan to visit and bring twice that many résumés.

What to do DURING the job fair

- Prepare to make a good first impression by dressing appropriately.
- Be prepared to approach and talk to someone at every exhibit.
- Use your waiting time wisely. While standing in line at an exhibit, introduce yourself to the folks ahead of or behind you, taking the opportunity to connect with your peers.
- Make the most of your time with recruiters. Be responsive to the employer's questions while maintaining a positive attitude that exudes professionalism.
- Always ask about the next step before wrapping up.
- Thank employers for their time and consideration.
- Take notes of your conversations.
- Take breaks so that you can maintain a positive and upbeat attitude.
- Network, network, network!

What to do AFTER the job fair

- Follow-up by sending a thank-you letter to those you met at the fair![20]
- At job fairs, employers and recruiters often conduct on-the-spot screening interviews. How can you best prepare before attending a job fair?

LEARNING OBJECTIVE 3

Describe what to do *during* an interview, including controlling nonverbal messages and answering typical interview questions.

CENGAGE

MINDTAP

Go to section 16-3a in MindTap, where you can watch a video featuring Taylor Roberts, a general manager, discuss the importance of soft skills in an interview.

During the Interview

Throughout the interview you will be answering questions and asking your own questions. Your demeanour, body language, and other nonverbal cues will also be on display. The interviewer will be trying to learn more about you, and you should be learning more about the job and the organization. Although you may be asked some unique questions, many interviewers ask standard, time-proven questions, which means that you can prepare your answers ahead of time.

Sending Positive Nonverbal Messages and Acting Professionally

You have already sent nonverbal messages to your interviewer by arriving on time, being courteous, dressing professionally, and greeting the receptionist confidently. You will continue to send nonverbal messages throughout the interview. Remember that what comes out of your mouth and what is written on your résumé are not the only messages an interviewer receives from you. Nonverbal messages also create powerful impressions on people. You can send positive nonverbal messages during face-to-face and online interviews by following these tips:

- **Control your body movements.** Keep your hands, arms, and elbows to yourself. Don't lean on a desk. Keep your feet on the floor. Don't cross your arms in front of you. Keep your hands out of your pockets.
- **Exhibit good posture.** Sit erect, leaning forward slightly. Don't slouch in your chair; at the same time, don't look too stiff and uncomfortable. Good posture demonstrates confidence and interest.
- **Practise appropriate eye contact.** A direct eye gaze, at least in North America, suggests interest and trustworthiness. If you are being interviewed by a panel, remember to maintain eye contact with all interviewers. Alternatively, be aware of cultural differences, and match the level of eye contact during the interview.
- **Use gestures effectively.** Nod to show agreement and interest. Gestures should be used as needed but not overused.
- **Smile enough to convey a positive attitude.** Have a friend give you honest feedback on whether you generally smile too much or not enough.

- **Listen attentively.** Show the interviewer you are interested and attentive by listening carefully to the questions being asked. This will also help you answer questions appropriately.
- **Turn off your cell phone or other electronic devices.** Avoid the embarrassment of having your smartphone ring, or even as much as buzz, during an interview. Turn off your electronic devices completely; don't just switch them to vibrate.
- **Don't chew gum.** Chewing gum during an interview is distracting and unprofessional.
- **Sound enthusiastic and interested—but sincere.** The tone of your voice has an enormous effect on the words you say. Avoid sounding bored, frustrated, or sarcastic during an interview. Employers want employees who are enthusiastic and interested.
- **Avoid empty words.** Filling your answers with verbal pauses such as *um*, *uh*, *like*, and *basically* communicates that you are not prepared. Also avoid annoying distractions, such as clearing your throat repeatedly or sighing deeply.
- **Be confident but not conceited.** Most recruiters want candidates who are self-assured but not too casual and not arrogant. Let your body language, posture, dress, and vocal tone prove your confidence. Speak at a normal volume and enunciate words clearly without mumbling.[21]

Naturally, hiring managers make subjective decisions based on intuition, but they need to ferret out pleasant people who fit in. To that end some recruiters apply "the airport test" to candidates: "Would I want to be stuck in the airport for 12 hours with this person if my flight were delayed?"[22]

Preparing to Answer Interview Questions

One way you can compensate for lack of experience is to have carefully prepared and well-rehearsed responses to typical interview questions. In addition, the way you answer questions can be almost as important as what you say. Use the interviewer's name and title from time to time when you answer. *Yes, Ms. Luna, I would be pleased to tell you about* . . . . People like to hear their own names. Be sure you are pronouncing the name correctly, and don't overuse this technique. Avoid answering questions with a simple *yes* or *no*; elaborate on your answers to better promote yourself and your assets. Keep your answers positive; don't criticize anything or anyone.

During the interview it may be necessary to occasionally refocus and clarify vague questions. Some interviewers are inexperienced and ill at ease in the role. You may even have to ask your own question to understand what was asked, *By ______, do you mean ______?* Consider closing out some of your responses with *Does that answer your question?* or *Would you like me to elaborate on any particular experience?*

Always aim your answers at the key characteristics interviewers seek: expertise, competence, motivation, interpersonal skills, decision-making skills, enthusiasm for the company and the job, and a pleasing personality. Remember to stay focused on your strengths. Don't reveal weaknesses, even if you think they make you look human. You won't be hired for your weaknesses, only for your strengths.

As you respond, be sure to use good English and enunciate clearly. Avoid slurred words such as *gonna*, as well as slang expressions such as *yeah* and *like*. As you practise answering expected interview questions, it is always a good idea to make a recording. Is your speech filled with verbal static?

You can't expect to be perfect in an employment interview. No one is. But you can avert disaster by avoiding certain topics and behaviours, such as those described in Figures 16.3 and 16.4.

The following sections present questions that may be asked during employment interviews. To get you thinking about how to respond, we have provided an answer for, or a discussion of, one or more of the questions in each group. As you read the remaining questions in each group, think about how you could respond most effectively. For additional questions, contact your campus career centre, or consult one of the career websites discussed in Chapter 15.

FIGURE 16.3 Ten Interview Actions to Avoid

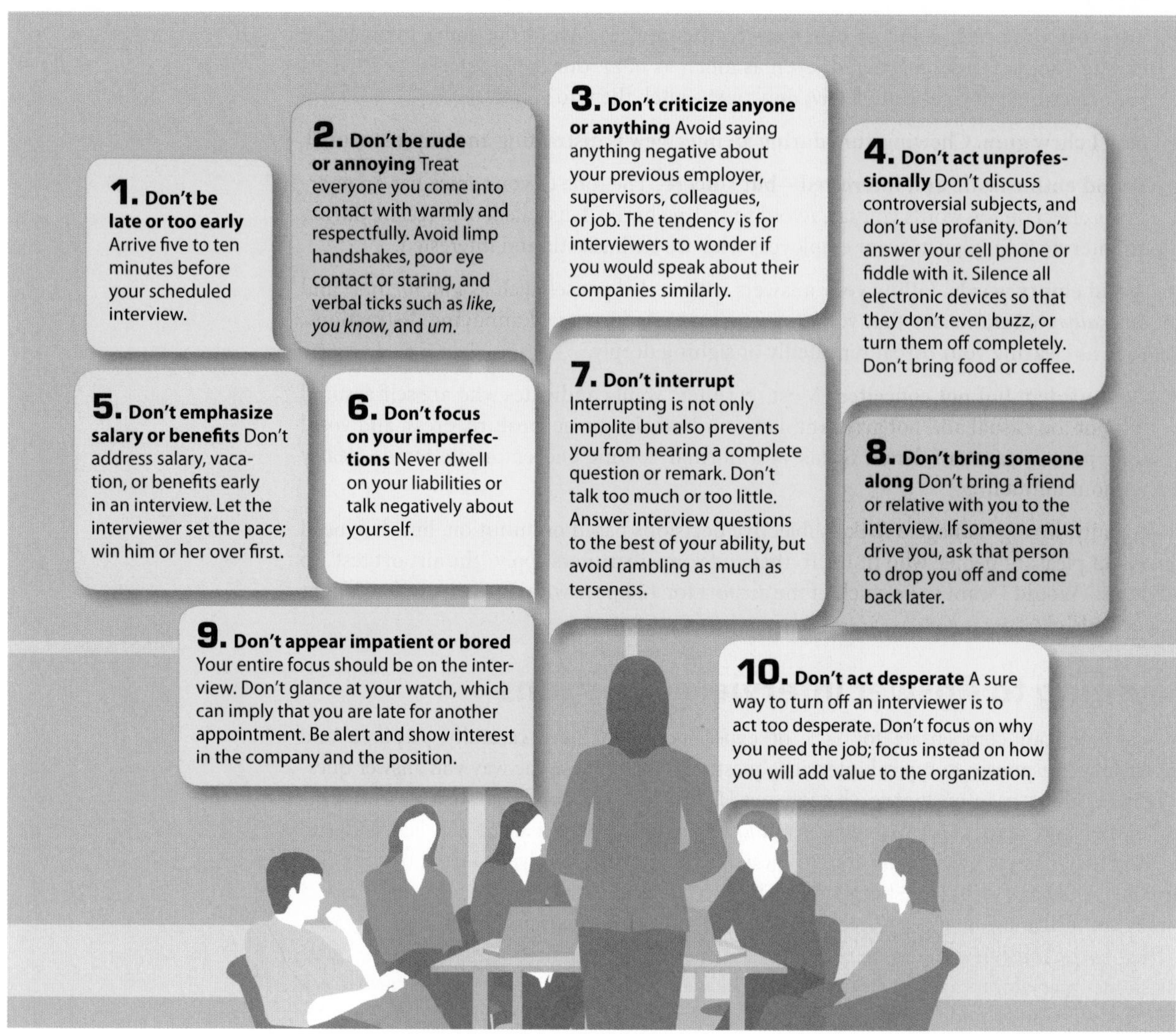

1. Don't be late or too early Arrive five to ten minutes before your scheduled interview.
2. Don't be rude or annoying Treat everyone you come into contact with warmly and respectfully. Avoid limp handshakes, poor eye contact or staring, and verbal ticks such as like, you know, and um.
3. Don't criticize anyone or anything Avoid saying anything negative about your previous employer, supervisors, colleagues, or job. The tendency is for interviewers to wonder if you would speak about their companies similarly.
4. Don't act unprofessionally Don't discuss controversial subjects, and don't use profanity. Don't answer your cell phone or fiddle with it. Silence all electronic devices so that they don't even buzz, or turn them off completely. Don't bring food or coffee.
5. Don't emphasize salary or benefits Don't address salary, vacation, or benefits early in an interview. Let the interviewer set the pace; win him or her over first.
6. Don't focus on your imperfections Never dwell on your liabilities or talk negatively about yourself.
7. Don't interrupt Interrupting is not only impolite but also prevents you from hearing a complete question or remark. Don't talk too much or too little. Answer interview questions to the best of your ability, but avoid rambling as much as terseness.
8. Don't bring someone along Don't bring a friend or relative with you to the interview. If someone must drive you, ask that person to drop you off and come back later.
9. Don't appear impatient or bored Your entire focus should be on the interview. Don't glance at your watch, which can imply that you are late for another appointment. Be alert and show interest in the company and the position.
10. Don't act desperate A sure way to turn off an interviewer is to act too desperate. Don't focus on why you need the job; focus instead on how you will add value to the organization.

Questions to Get Acquainted

After opening introductions, recruiters generally try to start the interview with personal questions designed to put you at ease. They are also striving to gain an overview to see whether you will fit into the organization's culture. When answering these questions, keep the employer's needs in mind and try to incorporate your success stories.

1. Tell me about yourself.
   Experts agree that you must keep this answer short (one to two minutes tops) but on target. Use this chance to promote yourself. Stick to educational, professional, or business-related strengths; avoid personal or humorous references. Be ready with at least three success stories illustrating characteristics important to this job. Demonstrate responsibility you have been given; describe how you contributed as a team player. Try practising this formula: *I have completed a ______ degree/diploma with a major in ______. Recently I worked for ______ as a ______. Before that I worked for as a ______. My strengths are ______ (interpersonal) and ______ (technical).* Try rehearsing your response in 30-second segments devoted to your education, work experience, qualifications, and skills.

FIGURE 16.4 How to Bomb a Job Interview

Emiliano Rodriguez/Shutterstock.com; Aila Images/Shutterstock.com

Source: Based on 2015 Career Builder survey of more than 2,500 hiring and human resource managers. Retrieved from http://www.careerbuilder.com/share/aboutus/pressreleasesdetail.aspx?sd=1%2F14%2F2016&id=pr929&ed=12%2F31%2F2016.

2. What are your greatest strengths?
   Stress your strengths that are related to the position, such as *I am well organized, thorough, and attentive to detail.* Tell success stories and give examples that illustrate these qualities: *My supervisor says that my research is exceptionally thorough. For example, I recently worked on a research project in which I. . . .*
3. Do you prefer to work by yourself or with others? Why?
   This question can be tricky. Provide a middle-of-the-road answer that not only suggests your interpersonal qualities but also reflects an ability to make independent decisions and work without supervision.
4. What was your college/university major, and why did you choose it?
5. What are some things you do in your spare time?

Questions to Gauge Your Interest

Interviewers want to understand your motivation for applying for a position. Although they will realize that you are probably interviewing for other positions, they still want to know why you are interested in this particular position with this organization. These types of questions help them determine your level of interest.

1. Why do you want to work for [name of company]?
   Questions like this illustrate why you must research an organization thoroughly before the interview. The answer to this question must prove that you understand the company and its culture. This is the perfect place to bring up the company research you did before the interview. Show what you know about the company, and discuss why you want to become a part of this organization. Describe your desire to work for this organization not only from your perspective but also from its point of view. What do you have to offer that will benefit the organization?
2. Why are you interested in this position?
3. What do you know about our company?
4. Why do you want to work in the ____ industry?
5. What interests you about our products (or services)?

Questions About Your Experience and Accomplishments

After questions about your background and education and questions that measure your interest, the interview generally becomes more specific with questions about your experience and accomplishments. Remember to show confidence when you answer these questions. If you are not confident in your abilities, why should an employer be?

1. Why should we hire you when we have applicants with more experience or better credentials?
   In answering this question, remember that employers often hire people who present themselves well instead of others with better credentials. Emphasize your personal strengths that could be an advantage with this employer. Are you a hard worker? How can you demonstrate it? Have you had recent training? Some people have had more years of experience but actually have less knowledge because they have done the same thing over and over. Stress your experience using the latest methods and equipment. Be sure to mention your computer training and use of the Internet. Tell success stories. Emphasize that you are open to new ideas and learn quickly. Above all, show that you are confident in your abilities.
2. Describe the most rewarding experience of your career so far.
3. How have your education and professional experiences prepared you for this position?
4. What were your major accomplishments in each of your past jobs?
5. What was a typical workday like?
6. What job functions did you enjoy most? Least? Why?
7. Tell me about your computer skills.
8. Who was the toughest boss you ever worked for and why?
9. What were your major achievements in college?
10. Why did you leave your last position? *OR* Why are you leaving your current position?

Questions About the Future

Questions that look into the future tend to stump some candidates, especially those who have not prepared adequately. Employers ask these questions to see whether you are goal-oriented and to determine whether your goals are realistic.

1. Where do you expect to be five (or ten) years from now?
   Formulate a realistic plan with respect to your present age and situation. The important thing is to be prepared for this question. It is a sure kiss of death to respond that you

would like to have the interviewer's job! Instead, show an interest in the current job and in making a contribution to the organization. Talk about the levels of responsibility you would like to achieve. One employment counsellor suggests showing ambition but not committing to a specific job title. Suggest that you hope to have learned enough to have progressed to a position in which you will continue to grow. Keep your answer focused on educational and professional goals, not personal goals.

2. Do you plan to continue your education?
3. What do you predict for future of the ____ industry?
4. What would you most like to accomplish if you get this position?
5. How do you keep current with what is happening in your profession?

Challenging Questions

The following questions may make you uncomfortable, but the important thing to remember is to answer truthfully without dwelling on your weaknesses. As quickly as possible, convert any negative response into a discussion of your strengths.

1. What is your greatest weakness?
   It is amazing how many candidates knock themselves out of the competition by answering this question poorly. Actually, you have many choices. You can present a strength as a weakness (*Some people complain that I'm a workaholic or too attentive to details*). You can mention a corrected weakness (*Because I needed to learn about designing websites, I took a course*). You could cite an unrelated skill (*I really need to brush up on my French*). You can cite a learning objective (*One of my long-term goals is to learn more about international management. Does your company have any plans to expand overseas?*). Another possibility is to reaffirm your qualifications (*I have no weaknesses that affect my ability to do this job*). Be careful that your answer doesn't sound too cliché (*I tend to be a perfectionist*) and instead shows careful analysis of your abilities.
2. What type of people do you have no patience for?
   Avoid letting yourself fall into the trap of sounding overly critical. One possible response is I have always gotten along well with others. But I confess that I can be irritated by complainers who don't accept responsibility.
3. How would your former (or current) supervisor describe you as an employee?
4. What do you want the most from your job?
5. Are you currently using illegal drugs?
6. Who in your life has influenced you the most and why?
7. What are you reading right now?
8. Describe your ideal work environment.
9. Is the customer always right?
10. How do you define success?

Questions About Salary

Nearly all salaries are negotiable, depending on your qualifications. Knowing the typical salary range for the target position is very important in this negotiation. The recruiter can tell you the salary ranges—but you will have to ask. If you have had little experience, you will probably be offered a salary somewhere between the low point and the midpoint in the range. With more experience, you can negotiate for a higher figure. A word of caution, though. One personnel manager warns that candidates who emphasize money are suspect because they may leave if offered a few thousand dollars more elsewhere. See the

CAREER COACH

Let's Talk Money: Salary Negotiation Dos and Don'ts

Nearly all salaries are negotiable. The following dos and don'ts can guide you to a better starting salary.

- **Do** make sure you have done your research on the salary you should expect for the position you are seeking. Understand how geographic location affects salary ranges.
- **Don't** bring up salary before the employer does. Delay salary negotiations until you know exactly what the position entails.
- **Do** be aware of your strengths and achievements. Demonstrate the value you will bring to the employer.
- **Don't** tell the employer the salary you need to pay your bills or meet personal obligations.
- **Do** let the employer make the first salary offer. If asked, say you expect a salary that is competitive with the market, or give a salary range that you find acceptable.
- **Don't** inflate your current earnings just to get a higher salary offer.
- **Do** thank the employer for the offer when it is made.
- **Don't** feel obligated to accept the first salary offer. Take the time to consider all factors before negotiating salary or making any job offer decisions.
- **Don't** be overly aggressive when negotiating or focus solely on salary. Consider the entire compensation package.
- **Do** try to obtain other concessions (shorter review time, better title, better workspace) or benefits (bonuses, vacation time) if you aren't successful at negotiating a salary you want.
- **Don't** agree to the first acceptable salary offer you receive if you are not sure about the job or the company.
- **Do** get the offer in writing.

accompanying Career Coach box for dos and don'ts in negotiating a starting salary. Here are typical salary-related questions:

1. What salary are you looking for?
   One way to handle salary questions is to ask politely to defer the discussion until it is clear that a job will be offered to you (*I'm sure when the time comes, we will be able to work out a fair compensation package. Right now, I'd rather focus on whether we have a match*). Another possible response is to reply candidly that you can't know what to ask until you know more about the position and the company. If you continue to be pressed for a dollar figure, give a salary range with an annual dollar amount. Be sure to do research before the interview so that you know what similar jobs are paying in your geographic region. For example, check the Government of Canada's Job Bank has a page where you can explore current wages by occupation and region (jobbank.gc.ca/trend-analysis). When citing salary expectations, you will sound more professional if you cite an annual salary range rather than a dollar-per-hour amount.
2. How much are you presently earning?
3. How much do you think you are worth?
4. How much money do you expect to earn within the next ten years?
5. Are you willing to take a pay cut from your current (or previous) job?

Situational Questions

Questions related to situations help employers test your thought processes and logical thinking. When using situational questions, interviewers describe a hypothetical situation and ask how you would handle it. Situational questions differ based on the type of position for which you are interviewing. Knowledge of the position and the company culture will help you respond favourably to these questions. Even if the situation sounds negative, keep your response positive. Here are just a few examples with possible answers for the first two:

1. How would you respond if your fellow team members strongly resisted a proposal you made in a meeting?

You might explain the rationale behind your proposal with specific examples of the benefits that the recommendation could bring to the team. If the team continues to oppose your proposal, you should let it go and move on.

2. What would you do if you knew that your boss gave your team data that was totally wrong?
   Let's say, for example, that in a team meeting your boss provided data that had not been updated, and you recognized the error immediately. Before responding, you should confirm that your figures are correct. Then you might tactfully share the correct data in a private conversation with your boss. You could suggest that the error was an oversight perhaps caused by figures that were released after an initial report, and say that you know that your boss would want to base the team project on accurate data. You would not correct your boss in front of the team, and you would try to understand why the mistake was made.
3. Your supervisor has told you to do something a certain way, and you think that way is wrong and that you know a far better way to complete the task. What would you do?
4. Assume that you are hired for this position. You soon learn that one of the staff is extremely resentful because she applied for your position and was turned down. As a result, she is being unhelpful and obstructive. How would you handle the situation?
5. A colleague has told you in confidence that she suspects another colleague of stealing. What would your actions be?

Behavioural Questions

Instead of traditional interview questions, you may be asked to tell stories. The interviewer may say, *Describe a time when ...* or *Tell me about a time when ....* To respond effectively, learn to use the storytelling, or STAR, technique, as illustrated in Figure 16.5. Ask yourself what the Situation or Task was, what Action you took, and what the Results were.[23] Practise using this method to recall specific examples of your skills and accomplishments. To be fully prepared, develop a coherent and articulate STAR narrative for every bullet point on your résumé. When answering behavioural questions, describe only educational and work-related situations or tasks, and try to keep them as current as possible. Here are a few examples of behavioural questions.

1. Tell me about a time when you solved a difficult problem.
   Tell a concise story explaining the situation or task, what you did, and the result. For example, When I was at Ace Products, we continually had a problem of excessive back

FIGURE 16.5 Using the STAR Technique to Answer Behavioural Interview Questions

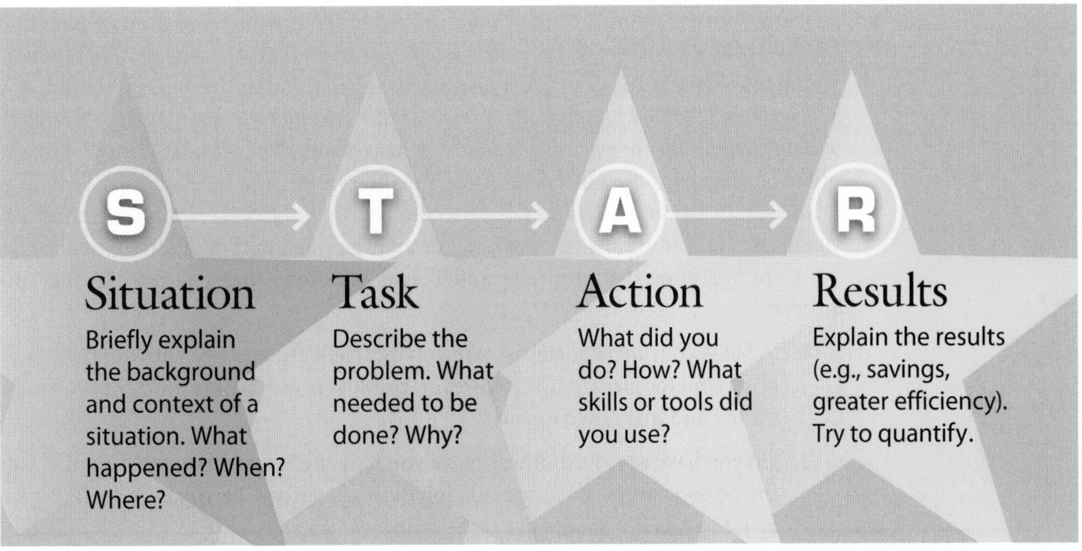

S
T
A
R
Situation
Briefly explain the background and context of a situation. What happened? When? Where?
Task
Describe the problem. What needed to be done? Why?
Action
What did you do? How? What skills or tools did you use?
Results
Explain the results (e.g., savings, greater efficiency). Try to quantify.

orders. After analyzing the situation, I discovered that orders went through many unnecessary steps. I suggested that we eliminate much of the paperwork. As a result, we reduced back orders by 30 percent. Go on to emphasize what you learned and how you can apply that learning to this job. Practise your success stories in advance so that you will be ready.

2. Describe a situation in which you were able to use persuasion to convince someone to see things your way.
   The recruiter is interested in your leadership and teamwork skills. You might respond, I have learned to appreciate the fact that the way you present an idea is just as important as the idea itself. When trying to influence people, I put myself in their shoes and find some way to frame my idea from their perspective. I remember when I . . . .
3. Describe a time when you had to analyze information and make a recommendation.
4. Describe a time that you worked successfully as part of a team.
5. Tell me about a time that you dealt with confidential information.
6. Give me an example of a time when you were under stress to meet a deadline.
7. Tell me about a time when you had to go beyond the call of duty to get a job done.
8. Tell me about a time you were able to deal with another person successfully even though that individual did not like you personally (or vice versa).
9. Give me an example of when you showed initiative and took the lead.
10. Tell me about a recent situation in which you had to deal with an upset customer or coworker.

Illegal and Inappropriate Questions

In Canada employment laws that prohibit discrimination in the workplace also apply to interviews. Questions regarding race, national origin, sexual orientation, religion, age, marital status, family situation, arrest record, medical conditions, personal information (such as height or weight), or disabilities are not allowed in an interview. Therefore, it is inappropriate for interviewers to ask any question related to these areas. These questions become illegal, though, only when a court of law determines that the employer is asking them with the intent to discriminate. Most illegal interview questions are asked innocently by inexperienced interviewers. Some are only trying to be friendly when they inquire about your personal life or family. Regardless of the intent, how should you react?

If you find the question harmless and if you want the job, go ahead and answer it. If you think that answering it would damage your chance to be hired, try to deflect the question tactfully with a response such as *Could you tell me how my marital status relates to the responsibilities of this position?* or *I prefer to keep my personal and professional lives separate.* If you are uncomfortable answering a question, try to determine the reason behind it; you might answer, *I don't let my personal life interfere with my ability to do my job,* or *Are you concerned with my availability to work overtime?* Another option, of course, is to respond to any inappropriate or illegal question by confronting the interviewer and threatening a lawsuit or refusing to answer. However, you could not expect to be hired under these circumstances. In any case, you might want to reconsider working for an organization that sanctions such procedures.

Here are some inappropriate and illegal questions that you may or may not want to answer:[24]

11. What is your marital status? Are you married? Do you live with anyone? Do you have a boyfriend (or girlfriend)? (However, employers can ask your marital status after hiring for tax and insurance forms.)
12. Do you have any disabilities? Have you had any recent illnesses? (But it is legal to ask if the person can perform specific job duties, such as *Can you carry a 22.5-kilogram sack up a three-metre ladder five times daily?*)

13. I notice you have an accent. Where are you from? What is the origin of your last name? What is your first language? (However, it is legal to ask what languages you speak fluently if language ability is related to the job.)
14. Have you ever filed a workers' compensation claim or been injured on the job?
15. Have you ever had a drinking problem or been addicted to drugs? (But it is legal to ask if a person currently uses illegal drugs.)
16. Have you ever been arrested? (But it is legal to ask, *Have you ever been convicted of* ___? when the crime is related to the job.)
17. How old are you? What is your date of birth? When did you graduate from high school? (But it is legal to ask, *Are you 16 years [or 18 years or 21 years] old or older?* depending on the age requirements for the position.)
18. Of what country are you a citizen? Are you a Canadian citizen? Where were you born? (But it is legal to ask, *Are you authorized to work in Canada*?)
19. What is your maiden name? (But it is legal to ask, What is your full name? or, Have you worked under another name?)
20. Do you have any religious beliefs that would prevent you from working weekends or holidays? (An employer can, however, ask you if you are available to work weekends and holidays or otherwise within the company's required schedule.)
21. Do you have children? Do you plan to have children? Do you have adequate child-care arrangements? (However, employers can ask for dependant information for tax and insurance purposes after you are hired. Also, they can ask if you would be able to travel or work overtime on occasion.)
22. How much do you weigh? How tall are you? (However, employers can ask you about your height and weight if minimum standards are necessary to safely perform a job.)[25]

Asking Your Own Questions

At some point in the interview, usually near the end, you will be asked whether you have any questions. The worst thing you can do is say *no*, which suggests that you are not interested in the position. Instead, ask questions that will help you gain information and will impress the interviewer with your thoughtfulness and interest in the position. Remember that this interview is a two-way street. You must be happy with the prospect of working for this organization. You want a position that matches your skills and personality. Use this opportunity to learn whether this job is right for you. Be aware that you don't have to wait for the interviewer to ask you for questions. You can ask your own questions throughout the interview to learn more about the company and position. Here are some questions you might ask:

1. What will my duties be (if not already discussed)?
2. Tell me what it is like working here in terms of the people, management practices, workloads, and expected performance.
3. What training programs are available from this organization? What specific training will be given for this position?
4. Who would be my immediate supervisor?
5. What is the organizational structure, and where does this position fit in?
6. Is travel required in this position?
7. How is job performance evaluated?
8. What are the major challenges for a person in this position?
9. What do you like best about working for this organization?
10. May I have a tour of the facilities?

ETHICS CHECK

Poor Credit Rating?

As part of the hiring process, many Canadian companies are now requesting credit checks, in addition to criminal record checks. If applicants have substantial debt, or a bad credit rating, a study has shown that they could be at a higher risk for committing in-store theft.[26] Do you agree with this study? Should employers be allowed to deny employment based on an applicant's poor credit rating? How should an applicant handle a request for a credit check?

Ending Positively

After you have asked your questions, the interviewer will signal the end of the interview, usually by standing up or by expressing appreciation that you came. If not addressed earlier, you should at this time find out what action will follow. Demonstrate your interest in the position by asking when it will be filled or what the next step will be. Too many candidates leave the interview without knowing their status or when they will hear from the recruiter.

Before you leave, summarize your strongest qualifications, show your enthusiasm for obtaining this position, and thank the interviewer for a constructive interview and for considering you for the position. Ask the interviewer for a business card, which will provide the information you need to write a thank-you letter. You might also ask if you may stay in touch through LinkedIn.

Shake the interviewer's hand with confidence, and acknowledge anyone else you see on the way out. Be sure to thank the receptionist. Departing gracefully and enthusiastically will leave a lasting impression on those responsible for making the final hiring decision.

Concept Check

1. What is your greatest fear of what you might do or what might happen to you during an employment interview? How can you overcome your fears?
2. Should job candidates be required to give their social media passwords to recruiters when asked? Explain your view. What does your province or territory allow in this regard?

LEARNING OBJECTIVE 4

Describe what to do *after* an interview, including thanking the interviewer, contacting references, and writing follow-up messages.

After the Interview

After leaving the interview, immediately make notes of what was said in case you are called back for a second interview. Write down key points that were discussed, the names of people you spoke with, and other details of the interview. Ask yourself what went really well and what you could improve. Note your strengths and weaknesses during the interview so that you can work to improve in future interviews.

Sending a Thank-You Message

After a job interview, you should always send a thank-you note, e-mail, or letter. This courtesy sets you apart from other applicants, most of whom will not bother. Your message also reminds the interviewer of your visit and shows your good manners and genuine enthusiasm for the job.

Follow-up thank-you messages are most effective if sent immediately after the interview. Generally, you have three options for your message: a handwritten note card, a word-processed letter on bond paper, or an e-mail. No texts. Handwritten cards are always impressive. However, 89 percent of the managers in one survey said that sending a thank-you note in the form of an e-mail was altogether acceptable.[27] If you choose e-mail, make sure that you use professional language, standard capitalization, and proper punctuation.

Your message will be most effective if sent immediately after your interview. In your message refer to the date of the interview, the exact title of the job for which you were interviewed, and specific topics discussed. Try to mention something you liked about the interview such as *Job interviews can be stressful, but you made me feel comfortable, and I am grateful for that.* Avoid worn-out phrases such as *Thank you for taking the time to interview me.* Be careful, too, about overusing *I*, especially to begin sentences. Most important, show that you really want the job and that you are qualified for it. Notice how the letter in Figure 16.6 conveys enthusiasm and confidence.

If you have been interviewed by more than one person, send a separate thank-you message to each interviewer.

FIGURE 16.6 Interview Follow-Up Message

Todd D. Delgado

2250 Tupper Street
Thunder Bay, ON P7A 4A5
(807) 627-4362, toddddelgado@gmail.com

June 1, 2020

Ms. Tiffany Escalante
iDesign Marketing & Media
246 Maitland Street
London, ON N6B 2Y2

Dear Ms. Escalante:

Talking with you Wednesday, May 31, about the graphic designer position in London was both informative and interesting.

Thanks for describing the position in such detail and for introducing me to Ms. Dangelo, the senior designer. Her current project designing an annual report in four colours sounds fascinating as well as quite challenging.

Now that I've learned in greater detail the specific tasks of your graphic designers, I'm more than ever convinced that my computer and creative skills can make a genuine contribution to your graphic productions. My training in design and layout using PhotoShop and InDesign ensures that I could be immediately productive on your staff.

You will find me an enthusiastic and hardworking member of any team effort. As you requested, I'm enclosing additional samples of my work. I'm eager to join the graphics staff at your London headquarters, and I look forward to hearing from you soon.

Sincerely,

Todd D. Delgado

Todd D. Delgado
Enclosures

Uses customized letterhead but could have merely typed street and city address above dateline

Mentions the interview date and specific job title

Personalizes the message by referring to topics discussed in the interview

Highlights specific skills for the job

Shows good manners, appreciation, and perseverance—traits that recruiters value

Reminds reader of interpersonal skills as well as enthusiasm and eagerness for this job

Contacting Your References

Once you have thanked your interviewer, it is time to alert your references that they may be contacted by the employer. You might also have to request a letter of recommendation to be sent to the employer by a certain date. As discussed in Chapter 15, you should have already asked permission to use these individuals as references, and you should have supplied them with a copy of your résumé and information about the types of positions you are seeking.

To provide the best possible recommendation, your references need information. What position have you applied for with what company? What should they stress to the prospective employer? Write your referent an e-mail or a letter describing the position, its requirements, and the recommendation deadline. Include copies of your résumé, transcript, and, if applicable, the job posting or ad with detailed information about the opening. You might remind her of a positive experience with you that she could use in the recommendation. Remember that recommenders need evidence to support generalizations, so give them appropriate facts and information.

Following Up

If you don't hear from the interviewer within five days, or at the specified time, consider following up. The standard advice to job candidates is to call a few days after the interview. However, some experts suggest that calling a hiring manager is risky. You may put a busy recruiter on the spot and force him or her to search for your application. An e-mail to find out how the decision process is going may be your best bet because such a message is much less intrusive. If you asked about it in the interview, you might follow up with the interviewer through LinkedIn.

If you believe it is safe to follow up by phone or if the recruiter suggested it, practise saying something like, *I'm wondering what else I can do to convince you that I'm the right person for this job*, or *I'm calling to find out the status of your search for the ___ position.* When following up, it is important to sound professional and courteous. Sounding desperate, angry, or frustrated that you have not been contacted can ruin your chances.

Depending on the response you get to your first follow-up request, you may have to follow up additional times.[28] Keep in mind, though, that some employers won't tell you about their hiring decision unless you are the one hired. Don't harass the interviewer, and don't force a decision. If you don't hear back from an employer within several weeks after following up, it is best to assume that you didn't get the job and to continue with your job search.

CENGAGE

MINDTAP

Check out section 16-4c in MindTap, where you can watch a video featuring Candice Wong, a registered physiotherapist, discuss sending a thank-you e-mail after an interview.

Concept Check

1. If over a week has passed since your interview, what is the best way to follow up with the hiring manager or recruitment team?
2. When is it appropriate to send a thank-you message after an interview?

LEARNING OBJECTIVE 5

Prepare additional employment documents.

Preparing Additional Employment Documents

Although the résumé and cover letter are your major tasks, other important documents and messages are often required during the job-search process. You may need to complete an employment application form and write follow-up letters. You might also have to write a letter of resignation when leaving a job. Because each of these tasks reveals something about you and your communication skills, you will want to put your best foot forward. These documents often subtly influence company officials to offer a job.

Application Form

Some organizations require job candidates to fill out application forms instead of, or in addition to, submitting résumés. This practice permits them to gather and store standardized data about each applicant. Whether the application is on paper or online, follow the directions carefully and provide accurate information. The following suggestions can help you be prepared:

- Carry a card summarizing vital statistics not included on your résumé. If you are asked to fill out an application form in an employer's office, you will need a handy reference to the following data: graduation dates; beginning and ending dates of all employment; salary history; full names, titles, and present work addresses of former supervisors; full addresses and phone numbers of current and previous employers; and full names, occupational titles, occupational addresses, and telephone numbers of people who have agreed to serve as references.

- Look over all the questions before starting.
- Fill out the form neatly, using blue or black ink. Many career counsellors recommend printing your responses; cursive handwriting can be difficult to read.
- Answer all questions honestly. Write *Not applicable* or *N/A* if appropriate. Don't leave any sections blank.
- Use accurate spelling, grammar, capitalization, and punctuation.
- If asked for the position desired, give a specific job title or type of position. Don't say, *Anything* or *Open*. These answers make you look unfocused; moreover, they make it difficult for employers to know what you are qualified for or interested in.
- Be prepared for a salary question. Unless you know what comparable employees are earning in the company, the best strategy is to suggest a salary range or to write *Negotiable*.
- Be prepared to explain the reasons for leaving previous positions. Use positive or neutral phrases such as *Relocation*, *Seasonal*, *To accept a position with more responsibility*, *Temporary position*, *To continue education*, or *Career change*. Avoid words or phrases such as *Fired*, *Quit*, *Didn't get along with supervisor*, or *Pregnant*.
- Look over the application before submitting to make sure it is complete and that you have followed all instructions. Sign and date the application.

Application or Résumé Follow-Up Message

If your résumé or application generates no response within a reasonable time, you may decide to send a short follow-up e-mail or letter, such as outlined in the following situations. Doing so (a) jogs the memory of the personnel officer, (b) demonstrates your serious interest, and (c) allows you to emphasize your qualifications or to add new information.

Rejection Follow-Up Message

If you didn't get the job and you think it was perfect for you, don't give up. Employment specialists encourage applicants to respond to a rejection. The candidate who was offered the position may decline, or other positions may open up. In a rejection follow-up e-mail or letter, it is acceptable to admit that you are disappointed. Be sure to add, however, that you are still interested and will contact the company again in a month in case a job opens up. Then follow through for a couple of months—but don't overdo it. You should be professional and persistent, not annoying.

Job Acceptance and Rejection Message

When all your hard work pays off, you will be offered the position you want. Although you will likely accept the position over the phone, it is a good idea to follow up with an acceptance e-mail or letter to confirm the details and to formalize the acceptance.

If you must turn down a job offer, show your professionalism by writing a sincere letter. This letter should thank the employer for the job offer and explain briefly that you are turning it down. Taking the time to extend this courtesy could help you in the future if this employer has a position you really want.

Resignation Letter

After you have been in a position for a time, you may find it necessary to leave. Perhaps you have been offered a better position, or maybe you have decided to return to school full-time. Whatever the reason, you should leave your position gracefully and tactfully. Although you will likely discuss your resignation in person with your supervisor, it is a good idea to document your resignation by writing a formal letter. Some resignation letters are brief while others contain great detail. Remember that many resignation letters are placed in personnel files; therefore, you should format and write yours using the professional business letter-writing techniques you learned earlier.

The amount of time that you have been with a company may also dictate the amount of notice you should provide. The higher and more responsible your position, the longer the notice you should give your employer. You should, however, always give some notice as a courtesy.

Writing job acceptance, job rejection, and resignation letters requires effort. That effort, however, is worth it because you are building bridges that may carry you to even better jobs in the future.

Concept Check

1. You confide in a friend that you don't feel confident about going to job interviews. She tells you that you need more practice, and she suggests that you apply for jobs that you know you don't want and accept interviews with companies in which you are not genuinely interested just so you can develop your interviewing skills. She says that interviewers expect some shopping. Do you agree? Should you take her advice? Why or why not?
2. Why is it a smart strategy to thank an interviewer, to follow up, and even to send a rejection follow-up message? What are the risks associated with this strategy?

SPOTLIGHT ON COMMUNICATION: PART 2

Ubisoft Revisited

CRITICAL THINKING

- How does thorough preparation help a candidate reduce the stress and butterflies most people feel during an interview?
- How can you inquire about a company's training opportunities without sounding inexperienced?

In 2020 Ubisoft was selected as one of Canada's top employers for young people.[29] The company offers co-op opportunities and paid internships for students. Other reasons for the recognition as a top employer include the following:

Courtesy of Mediacorp Canada

- Ubisoft created a Game Lab Competition, which challenges students to develop playable 3D video game prototypes in 10 weeks. Winners are determined for various categories, with prizes of up to $22,000 in scholarships as well as internships or employment opportunities.
- Ubisoft nurtures the development of high-potential employees through a dedicated graduate program—the two-year initiative features a one-year placement at its Toronto studio and a one-year placement in Europe or an alternative studio in North America
- Ubisoft Toronto runs NXT, an annual competition for video game development students in their final year at postsecondary schools in Ontario—students and recent graduates have an opportunity to showcase their portfolio and receive feedback from industry veterans and a chance to win a three-month apprenticeship at the company (with the possibility of a contract extension or permanent role).[30]

Ubisoft is also seeking new graduates. In addition to offering tuition subsidies for further training, the company offers "subsidies for professional accreditation, [an] orientation program, online training, in-house training, mentoring, in-house career planning services, [and] leadership training."[31]

Summary of Learning Objectives

1 Explain the purposes, sequence, and types of job interviews.

- As a job candidate, you have the following purposes in an interview: (a) convince the employer of your potential, (b) learn more about the job and the company, and (c) expand on the information in your résumé.
- From the employer's perspective, the interview is an opportunity to (a) assess your abilities in relation to the requirements for the position; (b) discuss your training, experience, knowledge, and abilities in more detail; (c) see what drives and motivates you; and (d) decide whether you would fit into the organization.
- Screening interviews, conducted by telephone or video, seek to eliminate less qualified candidates.
- Hiring/placement interviews may be one on one, panel, group, sequential, or video.

2 Describe what to do *before* an interview, including using professional phone techniques, researching the target company, rehearsing success stories, cleaning up digital dirt, and fighting fear.

- Make the first conversation impressive by using professional, businesslike language, and having your résumé, a calendar, and a list of your references handy.
- Research the target company by scouring the Internet and the company's advertising to learn about its products, history, mission, goals, size, geographic locations, employees, customers, competitors, culture, management structure, reputation in the community, finances, strengths, weaknesses, and future plans.
- Rehearse 30-second success stories that demonstrate your qualifications and achievements.
- Check your online presence and strive to clean up any digital dirt.

3 Describe what to do *during* an interview, including controlling nonverbal messages and answering typical interview questions.

- During your interview send positive nonverbal messages by controlling body movements, showing good posture, maintaining eye contact, using gestures effectively, and smiling enough to convey a positive, professional attitude.
- Practise answering typical questions, such as why you want to work for the organization, why you should be hired, and how your education and experience have prepared you for the position.
- Be ready for situational questions that ask you to respond to hypothetical situations; expect behavioural questions that begin with *Tell me about a time when you . . . .*
- End the interview positively by summarizing your strongest qualifications, showing enthusiasm for obtaining the position, thanking the interviewer, asking what the next step is, and requesting permission to follow up.

4 Describe what to do *after* an interview, including thanking the interviewer, contacting references, and writing follow-up messages.

- After leaving the interview, immediately make notes of the key points discussed; note your strengths and weaknesses during the interview so that you can work to improve in future interviews.
- Write a thank-you letter, card, or e-mail including the date of the interview, the exact job title for which you were interviewed, specific topics discussed, and gratitude for the interview.

- Alert your references that they may be contacted.
- If you don't hear from the interviewer when expected, call or send an e-mail to follow up.

5 **Prepare additional employment documents.**

- When filling out an application form, look over all the questions before starting.
- If you don't get the job, consider writing a letter that expresses your disappointment but also your desire to be contacted in case a job opens up.
- If you are offered a job, write a letter that confirms the details and formalizes your acceptance.
- Upon resigning from a position, write a letter that confirms the date of resignation, offers assistance to prepare for your resignation, and expresses thanks.

Chapter Review

1. What are the main purposes of a job interview for the applicant and for the employer? (Obj. 1)
2. What is a *screening interview*, and why is it so important? (Obj. 1)
3. Briefly describe the types of hiring/placement interviews candidates may encounter. (Obj. 1)
4. What should a job candidate learn about a company before going to a job interview? (Obj. 2)
5. When an interviewer asks about marital status, how should a candidate reply? (Obj. 3)
6. What are situational and behavioural interview questions, and how can a candidate craft responses that will make a favourable impression on the interviewer? (Obj. 3)
7. What is the best way to handle questions about salary expectations? (Obj. 3)
8. List the steps candidates should take immediately following a job interview. (Obj. 4)
9. If a candidate is offered a position, why is it important for that person to write an acceptance letter, and what should it include? (Obj. 4)
10. When applying to job positions, why is it smart to carry a card with vital statistics not included on your résumé? (Obj. 5)

Critical Thinking

1. What can you do to improve the first impression you make at an interview? (Objs. 2, 3)
2. Online psychometric and skills tests with multiple-choice questionnaires have become a hot trend in interviewing today. Employers may ask not only how applicants would handle tricky situations, but also how happy they are or how much they have stolen from their previous employer. The multiple-choice format poses a dilemma for applicants because they don't know whether to be truthful or say what the employer might want to hear. Is this practice fair? What are some advantages and disadvantages of this practice? (Objs. 1, 2)
3. Most job seekers are thrilled to be offered a job, and they fear haggling over salary. Yet employment specialists say that failing to negotiate can be a mistake that reverberates for years. Do you agree or disagree with this statement? Why? (Obj. 3)

4. Like criminal background checks and drug tests, social media background checks have become commonplace in today's recruiting. What are the pros and cons of conducting such checks as a primary or sole means of screening applicants? (Objs. 2, 3)

5. **Ethical Issue:** A recruiter for an organization has an outstanding prospect for a position. As part of his screening process, the recruiter checks the online presence of the candidate and discovers from her social networks that she is 18 weeks pregnant—and happily so. He knows that the target position involves a big project that will go live just about the time she will be taking maternity leave. He decides not to continue the hiring process with this candidate. Is his action legal? Ethical? What lesson could be learned about posting private information online? (Objs. 2, 3)

Activities

16.1 Employing Social Media to Investigate Jobs (Obj. 2)

Social Media Web

Blogs and social media sites, such as Facebook and Twitter, are becoming important tools in the job-search process. By accessing blogs, company Facebook pages, and Twitter feeds, job seekers can locate much insider information about a company's culture and day-to-day activities.

YOUR TASK Using the Internet, locate a blog that is maintained by an employee of a company where you might like to work. Monitor the blog for at least a week. Also, access the company's Facebook page and monitor Twitter feeds for at least a week. Prepare a short report summarizing what you learned about the company through reading the blog postings, status updates, and tweets. Include a statement of whether this information would be valuable during your job search.

16.2 Digging for Digital Dirt: Keeping a Low Profile Online (Obj. 2)

Social Media Web

Before embarking on your job hunt, you should find out what employers might find if they searched your personal life in cyberspace, specifically on Facebook, Twitter, and so forth. Running your name through Google and other search engines, particularly enclosed in quotation marks to lower the number of hits, is usually the first step.

YOUR TASK Use Google to explore the Internet for your full name, enclosed in quotation marks. In Google don't forget to run an *Images* search at www.google.ca/images to find any photos of questionable taste. If your instructor requests, share your insights with the class—not the salacious details, but general observations—or write a short memo summarizing the results.

16.3 Building Interview Skills With Worksheets (Obj. 3)

Successful interviews require diligent preparation and repeated practice. To be well prepared, you need to know what skills are required for your targeted position. In addition to computer and communication skills, employers generally want to know whether you work well with a team, accept responsibility, solve problems, are efficient, meet deadlines, show leadership, save time and money, and are a hard worker.

YOUR TASK Consider a position for which you are eligible now or one for which you will be eligible when you complete your education. Identify the skills and traits necessary for this position. If you prepared a résumé in Chapter 15, be sure that it addresses these targeted areas. Now prepare interview worksheets listing at least ten technical and other skills or traits you think a recruiter will want to discuss in an interview for your targeted position.

16.4 Telling Success Stories (Obj. 3)

You can best showcase your talents if you are ready with your own success stories that illustrate how you have developed the skills or traits required for your targeted position.

YOUR TASK Using the worksheets you prepared in **Activity 16.3**, prepare success stories that highlight the required skills or traits. Select three to five stories to develop into answers to potential interview questions. For example, here is a typical question: *How does your background relate to the position we have open?* A possible response: *As you know, I have just completed my program in ______________. In addition, I have over three years of part-time work experience in a variety of retail settings. In one position I was selected to supervise the front end in the absence of the owner. I developed responsibility and customer service skills by scheduling cashiers, resolving customers' issues, and monitoring store activities. When the owner returned from a* *vacation, I was commended for the smooth running of the store and was given additional responsibilities in recognition of my efforts.* People relate to and remember stories. Try to shape your answers into memorable stories.

16.5 Polishing Answers to Interview Questions (Obj. 3)

Team

Practice makes perfect in interviewing. The more often you rehearse responses to typical interview questions, the closer you are to getting the job.

YOUR TASK Select three questions from each of these question categories discussed in this chapter: questions to get acquainted, questions to gauge your interest, questions about your experience and accomplishments, questions about the future, and challenging questions. Write your answers to each set of questions. Try to incorporate skills and traits required for the targeted position, and include success stories where appropriate. Polish these answers and your delivery technique by practising in front of a mirror or by making an audio or a video recording. Your instructor may choose this assignment as a group activity in class.

16.6 Embracing Mock Interviews (Obj. 3)

Team

One of the best ways to understand interview dynamics and to develop confidence is to role-play the parts of interviewer and candidate in a mock interview.

YOUR TASK Choose a partner for this activity. Each partner makes a list of two interview questions for each of the eight interview question categories presented in this chapter. In team sessions you and your partner role-play an actual interview. One acts as interviewer; the other is the candidate. Before the interview the candidate tells the interviewer the job they are applying for and the name of the company. For the interview the interviewer and candidate should dress appropriately and sit in chairs facing each other. The interviewer greets the candidate and makes the candidate comfortable. The candidate gives the interviewer a copy of their résumé. The interviewer asks three questions (or more, depending on your instructor's time schedule) from the candidate's list. The interviewer may also ask follow-up questions, if appropriate. When finished, the interviewer ends the meeting graciously. After one interview, partners reverse roles and repeat.

Grammar and Mechanics | *Review 16*

Total Review

The first ten chapters reviewed specific guides from Appendix B, Grammar and Mechanics Guide, beginning on page B-1. The exercise in this chapter is a total review, covering all the grammar and mechanics guides plus confusing words and frequently misspelled words. Each of the following sentences has **three** errors in grammar, punctuation, capitalization, usage, or spelling. On a sheet of paper or on your computer, write a correct version. Avoid adding new phrases, starting new sentences, or rewriting in your own words. When you finish, compare your responses with the key in Appendix C.

1. Most interviews usualy cover the same kinds of questions, therefore smart candidates prepare for them.
2. Rodney wondered how many companys use social media to check candidates backgrounds?
3. Despite the heavy use of e-mail most employers' use the telephone to reach candidates and set up there interviews.
4. In interviewing job candidates recruiters have the following three purposes, assessing their skills, discussing their experience and deciding whether they are a good fit for the organization.
5. If your job history has gaps in it be prepared to explain what you did during this time, and how you kept up to date in your field.
6. Interviewing is a two way street and candidates should be prepared with there own meaningful questions.

7. Emma was asked whether she had a bachelors degree, and whether she had three years experience.
8. If you are consentious and want to create a good impression be sure to write a thank you message after a job interview.
9. When Marias interview was over she told friends that she had done good.
10. Maria was already to send a thank-you message, when she realized she could not spell the interviewers name.

Notes

[1] Yerema, R., & Leung, K. (2020). *Ubisoft Canadian Studios*. Canadastop 100. https://reviews.canadastop100.com/top-employer-ubisoft-canada#%23winner

[2] Ubisoft. (2020). *Facts and figures*. https://ubistatic-a.akamaihd.net/0090/PROD/ubigroup/PressKit/20180611/2019_09_Press_Kit_Facts_Figures-EN_new.pdf

[3] Ibid.

[4] Ibid.

[5] Yerema, R., & Leung, K. (2020, January 29). *Ubisoft Canadian Studios: Recognized as one of Montreal's top employers (2020)*. Mediacorp Canada. https://reviews.canadastop100.com/top-employer-ubisoft-canada#%23winner

[6] Ibid. Reprinted courtesy of Mediacorp Canada.

[7] Ubisoft. (2020). *Careers*. https://www.ubisoft.com/en-US/careers/experience.aspx

[8] Bergey, B. (2009, December 10). *Online job interviews becoming more popular*. WKOW.com. http://www.wkowtv.com/Global/story.asp?S=11655389; Kennedy, J. L. (2008). *Job interviews for dummies*. Wiley, p. 20.

[9] Cristante, D. (2009, June 15). *How to succeed in a group interview*. CareerFAQs. http://www.careerfaqs.com.au/job-interview-tips/1116/How-to-succeed-in-a-group-interview

[10] Breslin, S. (2011, November 25). 7 weird job tips. *Forbes*. http://www.forbes.com/sites/susannahbreslin/2012/11/25/7-weird-job-interview-tips

[11] Gold, T. (2010, November 28). *How social media can get you a job*. Marketing Trenches. http://www.marketingtrenches.com/marketing-careers/how-social-media-can-get-you-a-job

[12] Ryan, L. (2007, May 6). *Job seekers: Prepare your stories*. Ezine Articles. http://practicaljobsearchadvice.blogspot.com/2007/05/job-seekers-prepare-your-stories.html

[13] Haefner, R. (2009, June 10). *More employers screening candidates via social networking sites*. CareerBuilder. http://www.careerbuilder.com/Article/CB-1337-Getting-Hired-More-Employers-Screening-Candidates-via-Social-Networking-Sites

[14] Ibid.

[15] Why job hunters should pay close attention to their online presence. (2016). *York University Magazine*, p. 7.

[16] George Washington University. (2015, December 8). *E-professionalism: Social media resources: Cleaning up your digital dirt*. Himmelfarb Health Sciences Library. http://libguides.gwumc.edu/php?g=27787&p=170414

[17] Ryan, L. (2015, March 21). What to wear to a job interview. *Forbes*. http://www.forbes.com/sites/lizryan/2015/03/21/what-to-wear-to-a-job-interview/#325cf0117605

[18] Conlan, C. (n.d.). *The 6 worst things to wear to a job interview*. Monster.com. http://www.monster.com/career-advice/article/worst-things-to-wear-to-job-interview

[19] Bissonnette, D. (2017). *Introducing Denise to your audience: Short bio*. http://www.denisebissonnette.com/bio.htm

[20] Bissonnette, D. (2011). *Making the most of a job fair: Tips for before, during, and after*. http://www.denisebissonnette.com/docs/SevenGreatReasons.pdf

[21] Korkki, P. (2009, September 13). Subtle cues can tell an interviewer "pick me." *The New York Times*. https://www.nytimes.com/2009/09/13/jobs/13search.html

[22] Susan L. Hodas as cited in Korkki, P. (2009, September 13). Subtle cues can tell an interviewer "pick me." *The New York Times*. https://www.nytimes.com/2009/09/13/jobs/13search.html

[23] Tyrell-Smith, T. (2011, January 25). *Tell a story that will get you hired. Money/U.S. News & World Report*. http://money.usnews.com/money/blogs/outside-voices-careers/2011/01/25/tell-a-story-that-will-get-you-hired

[24] HR World editors. (n.d.). *30 interview questions you can't ask and 30 sneaky, legal alternatives to get the same info*. HR World. http://www.hrworld.com/features/30-interview-questions-111507

[25] Ibid.

[26] Lum, Z. (2015, April 21). *Use of credits checks to screen job applicants growing in Canada as U.S. clamps down*. Huffington Post. http://www.huffingtonpost.ca/2015/04/21/td-bank-credit-rating-jobs_n_7057312.html

[27] CareerBuilder. (2011, December 31). More than one-in-five hiring managers say they are less likely to hire a candidate who didn't send a thank-you note, finds new CareerBuilder survey. http://www.careerbuilder.com/share/aboutus/pressreleasesdetail.aspx?id=pr631&sd=4/14/2011&ed =12/31/2011

[28] Korkki, P. (2009, August 23). No response after an interview? What to do. *The New York Times*. Retrieved from https://www.nytimes.com/2009/08/23/jobs/25searchweb.html

[29] Yerema, R., & Leung, K. (2020, January 29). *Ubisoft Canadian Studios: Recognized as one of Montreal's top employers (2020)*. Mediacorp Canada. https://reviews.canadastop100.com/top-employer-ubisoft-canada#%23winner

[30] Ibid. Reprinted courtesy of Mediacorp Canada.

[31] Ibid.

APPENDIX A

Documentation Formats

For many reasons business writers are careful to properly document report data. Citing sources strengthens a writer's argument, as you learned in Chapter 11, while also shielding the writer from charges of plagiarism. Moreover, good references help readers pursue further research. As a business writer, you can expect to routinely borrow ideas and words to show that your ideas are in sync with the rest of the business world, to gain support from business leaders, or simply to save time in developing your ideas. To be ethical, however, you must show clearly what you borrowed and from whom.

Source notes tell where you found your information. For quotations, paraphrases, graphs, drawings, or online images you have borrowed, you need to cite the original authors' names, full titles, and the dates and facts of publication. The purpose of source notes, which appear at the end of your report, is to direct your readers to the complete references. Many systems of documentation are used by businesses, but they all have one goal: to provide clear, consistent documentation.

Rarely, business writers use content notes, which are identified with a raised number at the end of the quotation. At the bottom of the page, the number is repeated with a remark, clarification, or background information.

During your business career, you may use a variety of documentation systems. The two most common systems in the academic world are those of the American Psychological Association (APA) and the Modern Language Association (MLA). Each organization has its own style for text references and bibliographic lists. The APA style is increasingly the standard in business communication. This book uses a modified APA style. However, some business organizations use their own documentation systems.

Before starting any research project, whether for a class or in a business, inquire about the preferred documentation style. For school assignments ask about specifics. For example, should you include uniform resource locator (URLs) and dates of retrieval for online sources? For workplace assignments ask to see a previous report either in hard-copy version or as an e-mail attachment.

In your business and class writing, you will usually provide a brief citation in parentheses that refers readers to the complete reference that appears in a references or works-cited section at the end of your document. Following is a summary of APA and MLA formats with examples.

AMERICAN PSYCHOLOGICAL ASSOCIATION FORMAT

First used primarily in the social and physical sciences, the APA documentation format uses the author-date method of citation. This method, with its emphasis on current information, is especially appropriate for business. Within the text, the date of publication of the referenced work appears immediately after the author's name (*Rivera, 2020*), as illustrated in the brief APA example in Figure A.1. At the end of the report, all references appear alphabetically on a page labelled References. The APA format does not require a date of retrieval for most online sources, but you should check with your instructor or supervisor about the preferred format for your class or organization. For more information about the APA format, see the *Publication Manual of the American Psychological Association*, Seventh Edition (Washington, D.C.: American Psychological Association, 2020).

FIGURE A.1 Portions of APA Text Page and References

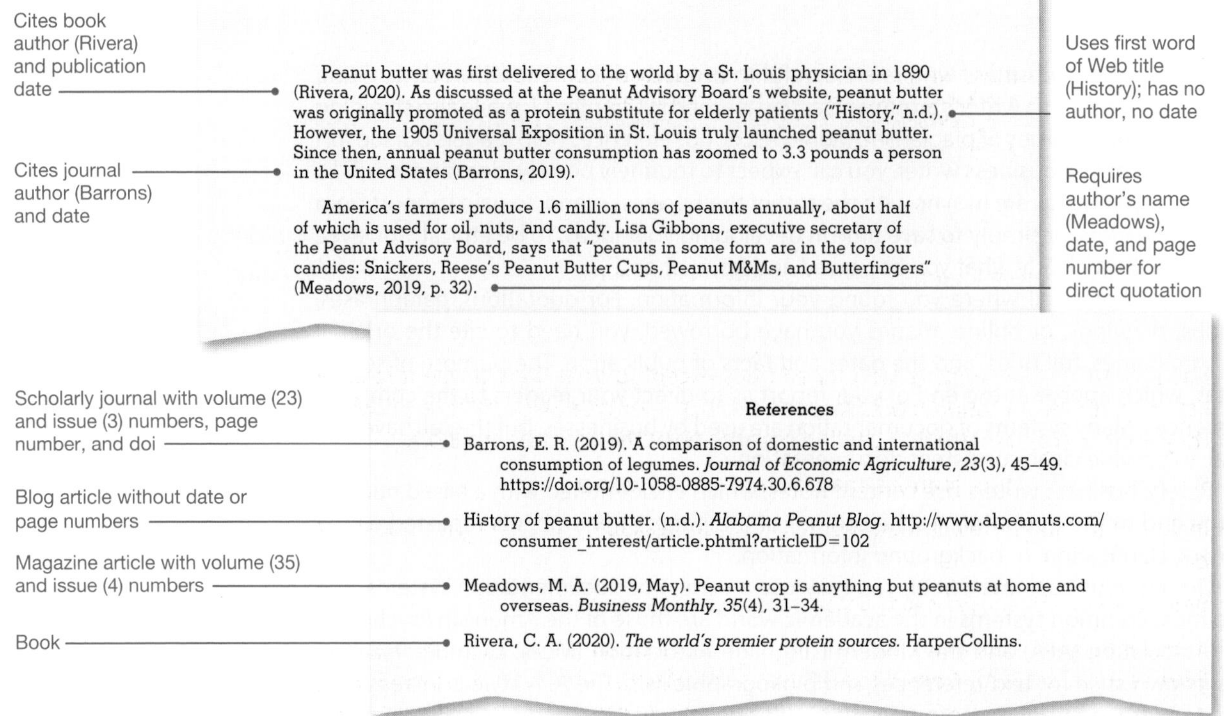

Cites book author (Rivera) and publication date
Cites journal author (Barrons) and date
Uses first word of Web title (History); has no author, no date
Requires author's name (Meadows), date, and page number for direct quotation
Peanut butter was first delivered to the world by a St. Louis physician in 1890 (Rivera, 2020). As discussed at the Peanut Advisory Board's website, peanut butter was originally promoted as a protein substitute for elderly patients ("History," n.d.). However, the 1905 Universal Exposition in St. Louis truly launched peanut butter. Since then, annual peanut butter consumption has zoomed to 3.3 pounds a person in the United States (Barrons, 2019).
America's farmers produce 1.6 million tons of peanuts annually, about half of which is used for oil, nuts, and candy. Lisa Gibbons, executive secretary of the Peanut Advisory Board, says that "peanuts in some form are in the top four candies: Snickers, Reese's Peanut Butter Cups, Peanut M&Ms, and Butterfingers" (Meadows, 2019, p. 32).
Scholarly journal with volume (23) and issue (3) numbers, page number, and doi
Blog article without date or page numbers
Magazine article with volume (35) and issue (4) numbers
Book
References
Barrons, E. R. (2019). A comparison of domestic and international consumption of legumes. Journal of Economic Agriculture, 23(3), 45–49. https://doi.org/10-1058-0885-7974.30.6.678
History of peanut butter. (n.d.). Alabama Peanut Blog. http://www.alpeanuts.com/consumer_interest/article.phtml?articleID=102
Meadows, M. A. (2019, May). Peanut crop is anything but peanuts at home and overseas. Business Monthly, 35(4), 31–34.
Rivera, C. A. (2020). The world's premier protein sources. HarperCollins.

APA In-Text Format

Within your text, document each text, figure, or personal source with a short description in parentheses. Following are selected guidelines summarizing the important elements of APA style.

- For a direct quotation, include the last name of the author(s), if available, the year of publication, and the page number or other locator; for example, (*Meadows, 2020, p. 32*). If no author is shown in the text or on a website, use a shortened title or a heading that can be easily located on the References page; for example, *("History," n.d.).*
- If you mention the author in the text, do not use the name again in the parenthetical reference. Just cite the date; for example, *According to Meadows (2020).*
- Search for dates on the home page or at the bottom of website pages. If no date is available for a source, use *n.d.*

APA References Format

At the end of your report, in a section called References, list all references alphabetically by author or by title if no author is available. To better understand the anatomy of an APA scholarly journal article reference, see Figure A.2.

As with all documentation methods, APA has specific capitalization, punctuation, and sequencing rules, some of which are summarized here:

- Include the last name of the author(s) followed by initials. APA is gender neutral, so first and middle names are not spelled out; for example, (*Aten, K.*).
- Show the date of publication in parentheses immediately after the author's name. A magazine or newspaper citation will also include the month and day in the parentheses.

FIGURE A.2 Anatomy of an APA Journal Article Reference

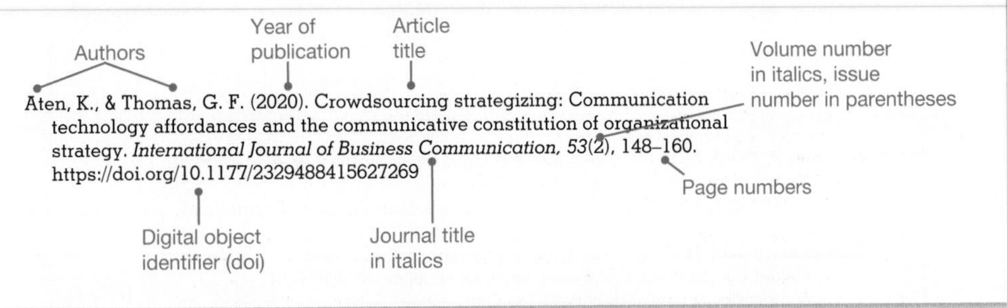

- Use sentence-style capitalization for all titles except journal titles. In the reference list, do not use quotation marks for article, chapter, or Web page titles, even when they appear in a parenthetical citation because no author name is available.
- Italicize titles of books, journals, magazines, and newspapers.
- Include the digital object identifier (DOI) when available for online periodicals or books.
- Break a URL or DOI only before a mark of punctuation, such as a slash.
- If the website content may change, as in a wiki, include a retrieval date; for example, *Retrieved July 7, 2020, from https://encyclopediaofmath.org/wiki/Main_Page*. Please note, however, that many instructors require that all Internet references in student papers be identified by their URLs.

For a comprehensive list of APA documentation format examples, see Figure A.3.

MODERN LANGUAGE ASSOCIATION FORMAT

Writers in the humanities and the liberal arts frequently use the Modern Language Association (MLA) documentation format, illustrated briefly in Figure A.4. In parentheses close to the textual reference, include the author's name and page cited (*Rivera 25*). At the end of your writing on a page titled Works Cited, list all the sources alphabetically. Some writers include all of the sources consulted. For more information, consult the *MLA Handbook*, Eighth Edition (New York: The Modern Language Association of America, 2016).

MLA In-Text Format

Following any borrowed material in your text, provide a short parenthetical description. Here are selected guidelines summarizing important elements of MLA style:

- For a direct quotation, enclose in parentheses the last name of the author(s), if available, and the page number without a comma; for example, (*Rivera 25*). If the source has no author, use a shortened title of the page or a heading that is easily found on the works-cited page; for example, *("History")*.
- If you mention the author in the text, do not use the name again in parentheses; for example, *According to Rivera, ". . ." (27)*.

MLA Works-Cited Format

In a section called Works Cited, list all references alphabetically by author or, if no author is available, by title. As with all documentation methods, MLA has specific capitalization and sequencing rules. Some of the most significant are summarized here:

- Include the author's last name first, followed by the first name and initial, as in Rivera, Charles A.

FIGURE A.3 APA Sample References

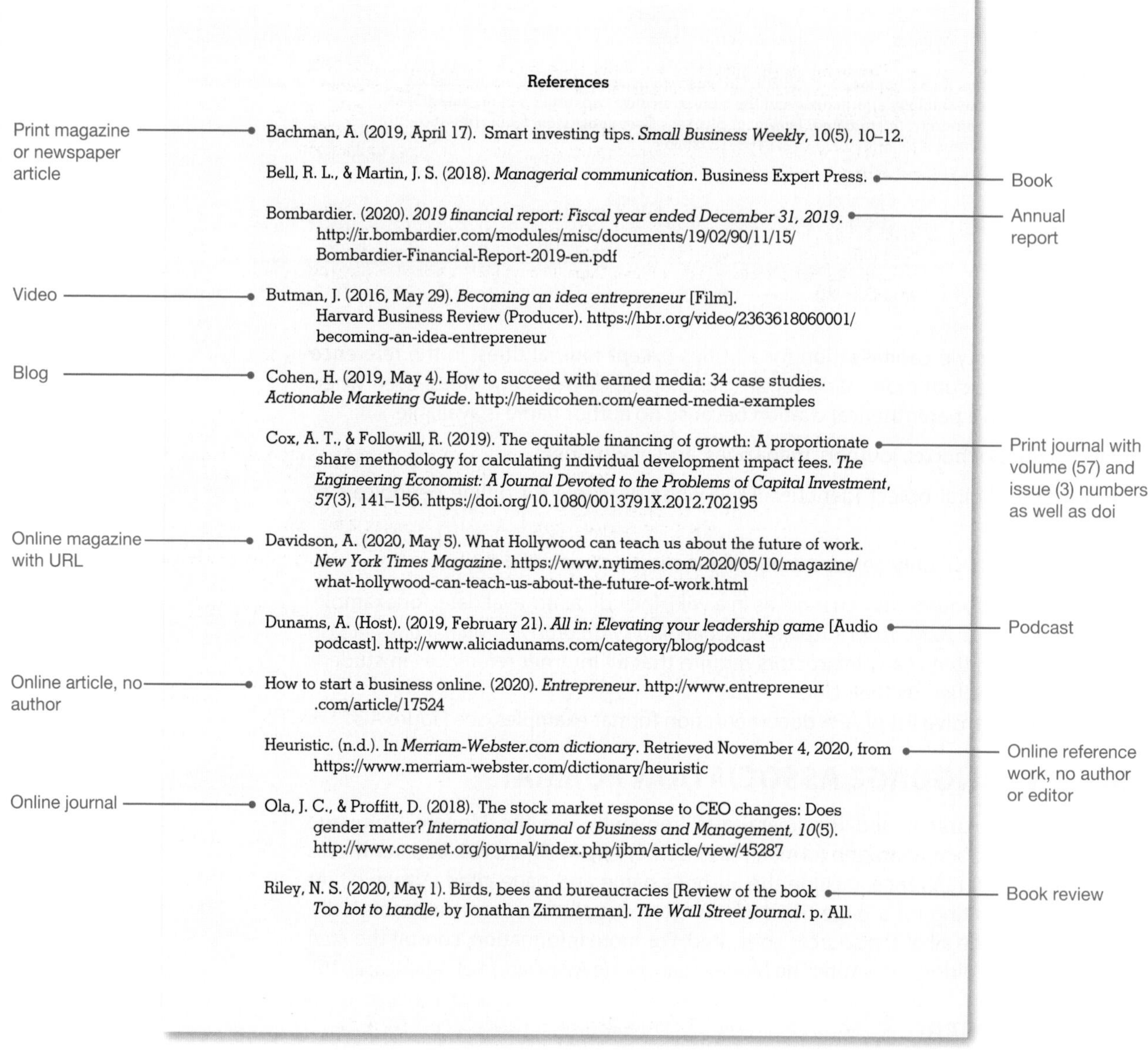

References
Print magazine or newspaper article
Bachman, A. (2019, April 17). Smart investing tips. *Small Business Weekly*, 10(5), 10–12.
Bell, R. L., & Martin, J. S. (2018). *Managerial communication*. Business Expert Press.
Book
Bombardier. (2020). *2019 financial report: Fiscal year ended December 31, 2019*. http://ir.bombardier.com/modules/misc/documents/19/02/90/11/15/Bombardier-Financial-Report-2019-en.pdf
Annual report
Video
Butman, J. (2016, May 29). *Becoming an idea entrepreneur* [Film]. Harvard Business Review (Producer). https://hbr.org/video/2363618060001/becoming-an-idea-entrepreneur
Blog
Cohen, H. (2019, May 4). How to succeed with earned media: 34 case studies. *Actionable Marketing Guide*. http://heidicohen.com/earned-media-examples
Cox, A. T., & Followill, R. (2019). The equitable financing of growth: A proportionate share methodology for calculating individual development impact fees. *The Engineering Economist: A Journal Devoted to the Problems of Capital Investment, 57*(3), 141–156. https://doi.org/10.1080/0013791X.2012.702195
Print journal with volume (57) and issue (3) numbers as well as doi
Online magazine with URL
Davidson, A. (2020, May 5). What Hollywood can teach us about the future of work. *New York Times Magazine*. https://www.nytimes.com/2020/05/10/magazine/what-hollywood-can-teach-us-about-the-future-of-work.html
Dunams, A. (Host). (2019, February 21). *All in: Elevating your leadership game* [Audio podcast]. http://www.aliciadunams.com/category/blog/podcast
Podcast
Online article, no author
How to start a business online. (2020). *Entrepreneur*. http://www.entrepreneur.com/article/17524
Heuristic. (n.d.). In *Merriam-Webster.com dictionary*. Retrieved November 4, 2020, from https://www.merriam-webster.com/dictionary/heuristic
Online reference work, no author or editor
Online journal
Ola, J. C., & Proffitt, D. (2018). The stock market response to CEO changes: Does gender matter? *International Journal of Business and Management, 10*(5). http://www.ccsenet.org/journal/index.php/ijbm/article/view/45287
Riley, N. S. (2020, May 1). Birds, bees and bureaucracies [Review of the book *Too hot to handle*, by Jonathan Zimmerman]. *The Wall Street Journal*. p. All.
Book review

Note: Although APA style prescribes double-spacing for the references page, we show single-spacing to conserve space and to represent preferred business usage.

- Enclose in quotation marks the titles of articles, essays, stories, chapters of books, pages in websites, articles in blogs, individual episodes of television and radio broadcasts, and short musical compositions.
- Italicize the titles of books, magazines, newspapers, websites, blogs, and journals.
- Include website URLs and access dates unless your instructor or organization asks that this information not be provided.
- Do not include identification of the medium (such as *Web, Print, Video*) as had been required in the *MLA Handbook*, Seventh Edition.

To better understand the anatomy of the format of an MLA scholarly journal article reference, see Figure A.5. For a comprehensive list of MLA documentation format examples, see Figure A.6.

FIGURE A.4 Portions of MLA Text Page and Works Cited

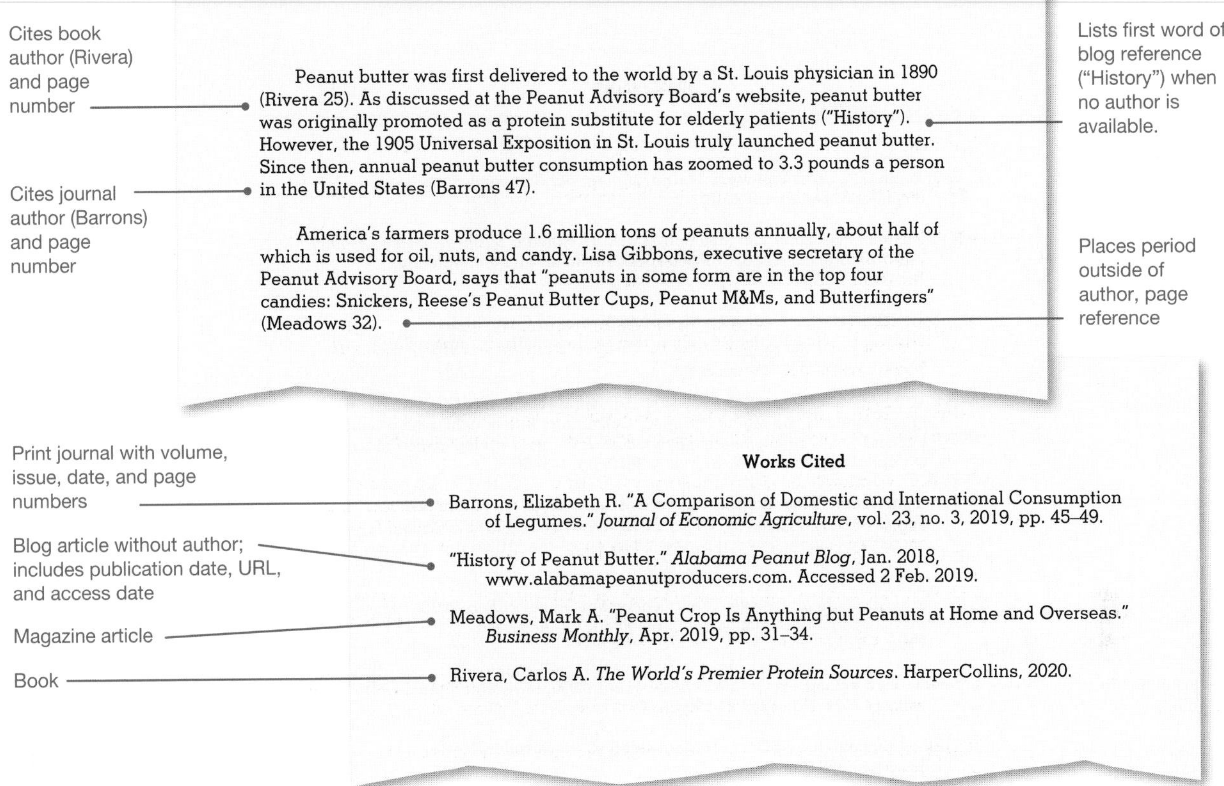

Cites book author (Rivera) and page number
Lists first word of blog reference ("History") when no author is available.
Cites journal author (Barrons) and page number
Places period outside of author, page reference
Peanut butter was first delivered to the world by a St. Louis physician in 1890 (Rivera 25). As discussed at the Peanut Advisory Board's website, peanut butter was originally promoted as a protein substitute for elderly patients ("History"). However, the 1905 Universal Exposition in St. Louis truly launched peanut butter. Since then, annual peanut butter consumption has zoomed to 3.3 pounds a person in the United States (Barrons 47).
America's farmers produce 1.6 million tons of peanuts annually, about half of which is used for oil, nuts, and candy. Lisa Gibbons, executive secretary of the Peanut Advisory Board, says that "peanuts in some form are in the top four candies: Snickers, Reese's Peanut Butter Cups, Peanut M&Ms, and Butterfingers" (Meadows 32).
Print journal with volume, issue, date, and page numbers
Blog article without author; includes publication date, URL, and access date
Magazine article
Book
Works Cited
Barrons, Elizabeth R. "A Comparison of Domestic and International Consumption of Legumes." *Journal of Economic Agriculture*, vol. 23, no. 3, 2019, pp. 45–49.
"History of Peanut Butter." *Alabama Peanut Blog*, Jan. 2018, www.alabamapeanutproducers.com. Accessed 2 Feb. 2019.
Meadows, Mark A. "Peanut Crop Is Anything but Peanuts at Home and Overseas." *Business Monthly*, Apr. 2019, pp. 31–34.
Rivera, Carlos A. *The World's Premier Protein Sources*. HarperCollins, 2020.

FIGURE A.5 Anatomy of an MLA Journal Article Reference

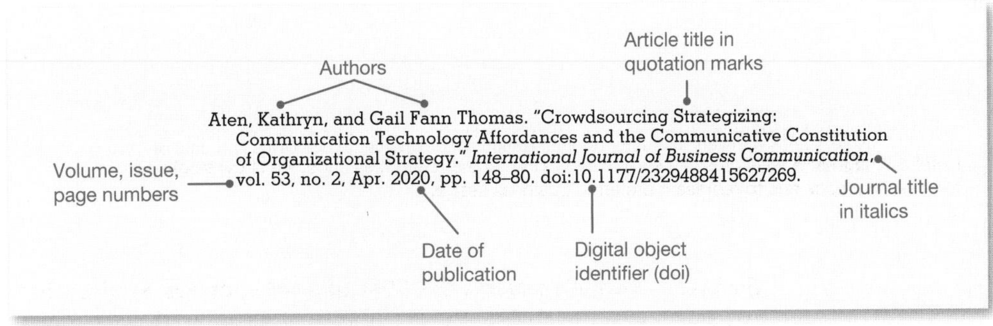

FIGURE A.6 MLA Sample References

Works Cited

Print magazine or newspaper article — Bachman, Alicia. "Smart Investing Tips." *Small Business Weekly*, 17 Apr. 2019, pp. 10–12.

Bell, Reginald L., and Jeanette S. Martin. *Managerial Communication.* Business Expert Press, 2018. — Book

Online video. Note: MLA style omits *http://* in URLs — Butman, John. "Becoming an Idea Entrepreneur." *Harvard Business Review*, 29 May 2016, hbr.org/video/2363618060001/becoming-an-idea-entrepreneur. Accessed 19 Aug. 2020.

Blog — Cohen, Heidi. "How to Succeed with Earned Media: 34 Case Studies." *Media PR*, 4 May 2019, heidicohen.com/earned-media-examples. Accessed 26 Sept. 2020.

Cox, Arthur T., and Robert Followill. "The Equitable Financing of Growth: A Proportionate Share Methodology for Calculating Individual Development Impact Fees." *The Engineering Economist: A Journal Devoted to the Problems of Capital Investment*, vol. 57, no. 3, 2019, pp. 141–56. — Print journal with volume (57) and issue (3) numbers

Online magazine — Davidson, Adam. "What Hollywood Can Teach Us about the Future of Work." *New York Times Magazine*, 5 May 2020, www.nytimes.com/2020/05/10/magazine/what-hollywood-can-teach-us-about-the-future-of-work.html?ref=business. Accessed 9 July 2020.

Dunams, Alicia. *All In: Elevating Your Leadership Game*. 21 Feb. 2019, www.aliciadunams.com/category/blog/podcast. Accessed 5 Mar. 2020. — Podcast

Online article, no author — "How to Start a Business Online." *Entrepreneur*, 2020, www.entrepreneur.com/article/17524. Accessed 23 May 2020.

Hunter, Douglas. "Re: CEOs' exorbitant salaries." Received by Hector Sotomeyor, 23 June 2019. — E-mail message

Online journal with volume (10) and issue (5) numbers as well as doi — Ola, J. Christian, and Dennis Proffitt. "The Stock Market Response to CEO Changes: Does Gender Matter?" *International Journal of Business and Management*, vol. 10, no. 5, 2018. doi:10.5539/ijbm.v10n5p1.

Riley, Naomi Schaefer. "Birds, Bees and Bureaucracies." Review of *Too Hot to Handle*, by Jonathan Zimmerman. *The Wall Street Journal*, 1 May 2020, p. 11. — Book review

2019 financial report: Fiscal year ended December 31, 2019. Bombardier, Inc., 2020, ir.bombardier.com/modules/misc/documents/19/02/90/11/15/Bombardier-Financial-Report-2019-en.pdf. — Annual report from website

Note: Check with your instructor or organization about whether to cite URLs and date of access.

APPENDIX B

Grammar and Mechanics Guide

In the business world, people are often judged by the way they speak and write. Using the language competently can mean the difference between success and failure. Often a speaker sounds accomplished; but when that same individual puts ideas in print, errors in language usage destroy that person's credibility. One student observed, "When I talk, I get by on my personality; but when I write, the flaws in my communication show through. That's why I'm in this class."

HOW THIS GRAMMAR AND MECHANICS GUIDE CAN HELP YOU

This grammar and mechanics guide contains 54 guidelines covering sentence structure, grammar, usage, punctuation, capitalization, and number style. These guidelines focus on the most commonly used—and abused—language elements. Numerous checkpoint exercises enable you to try your skills immediately. In addition to the 54 language guides in this section, you will find a list of 165 frequently misspelled words and a quick review of selected confusing words.

The concentrated materials in this guide help novice business communicators concentrate on the major areas of language use. The guide focuses on a limited number of language guidelines and troublesome words. Your objective should be mastery of these language principles and words, which represent a majority of the problems typically encountered by business writers.

HOW TO USE THIS GRAMMAR AND MECHANICS GUIDE

Your instructor may give you the short language diagnostic test (located on the Instructor's Resource Centre website) to help you assess your competency. After taking the diagnostic test, read and work your way through the 54 guidelines. Concentrate on areas in which you are weak. Memorize the spellings and definitions of the confusing words at the end of this section.

In *Business Communication: Process and Product*, you will find two kinds of exercises for your practice. (a) *Checkpoints*, located in this appendix, focus on a small group of language guidelines. Use them to test your comprehension as you complete each section. (b) *Grammar and Mechanics exercises*, located at the end of each chapter of the textbook, help reinforce your language skills at the same time you are learning about the processes and products of business communication. As you complete the review exercises, you may want to use the standard proofreading marks shown on the inside front cover.

- **Reference books.** More comprehensive treatment of grammar and punctuation guidelines can be found in Clark and Clark's *HOW 13: A Handbook for Office Professionals*, ISBN 978-1-111-82086-2; Jack Finnbogason and Al Valleau's *A Canadian Writer's Pocket Guide* (5th ed.), ISBN 978-0-17-653161-4; Joanne Buckley's *Checkmate: A Writing Reference for Canadians* (3rd ed.), ISBN 978-0-17-650256-0; and John Hodges and Andrew Stubbs's *The Harbrace Handbook for Canadians* (6th ed.), ISBN 978-0-17-622509-4.

GRAMMAR AND MECHANICS GUIDELINES

Sentence Structure

GUIDE 1: Avoid sentence fragments. A fragment is an incomplete sentence. You can recognize a complete sentence because it (a) includes a subject (a noun or pronoun that interacts with a verb), (b) includes a verb (a word expressing action or describing a condition), and (c) makes sense (comes to a close). A complete sentence is an independent clause. One of the most serious errors a writer can make is punctuating a fragment as if it were a complete sentence.

FRAGMENT	IMPROVED
Because 90 percent of all business transactions involve written messages. Good writing skills are critical.	Because 90 percent of all business transactions involve written messages, good writing skills are critical.
The recruiter requested a writing sample. Even though the candidate seemed to communicate well.	The recruiter requested a writing sample, even though the candidate seemed to communicate well.

Tip. Fragments often can be identified by the words that introduce them—words such as *although, as, because, even, except, for example, if, instead of, since, so, such as, that, which,* and *when*. These words introduce dependent clauses. Make sure such clauses are always connected to independent clauses.

DEPENDENT CLAUSE — INDEPENDENT CLAUSE

Since she had become supervisor, she had to write more memos and reports.

GUIDE 2: Avoid run-on (fused) sentences. A sentence with two independent clauses must be joined by a coordinating conjunction (*and, or, nor, but*) or by a semicolon (;). Without a conjunction or a semicolon, a run-on sentence results.

RUN-ON	IMPROVED
Rachel considered an internship she also thought about graduate school.	Rachel considered an internship, and she also thought about graduate school.
	Rachel considered an internship; she also thought about graduate school.

GUIDE 3: Avoid comma-splice sentences. A comma splice results when a writer joins (splices together) two independent clauses—without using a coordinating conjunction (*and, or, nor, but*).

COMMA SPLICE	IMPROVED
Disney World operates in Orlando, EuroDisney serves Paris.	Disney World operates in Orlando; EuroDisney serves Paris.
Visitors wanted a resort vacation, however they were disappointed.	Disney World operates in Orlando, and EuroDisney serves Paris.
	Visitors wanted a resort vacation; however, they were disappointed.

Tip. In joining independent clauses, beware of using a comma and words such as *consequently, furthermore, however, therefore, then, thus,* and so on. These conjunctive adverbs require semicolons.

Note: Sentence structure is also covered in Chapter 5.

✓Checkpoint

Revise the following to correct sentence fragments, comma splices, and run-ons.

1. Although it began as a side business for Disney. Destination weddings now represent a major income source.
2. About 2,000 weddings are held yearly. Which is twice the number just ten years ago.

3. Weddings may take place in less than one hour, however the cost may be as much as $5,000.
4. Limousines line up outside Disney's wedding pavilion, they are scheduled in two-hour intervals.
5. Most couples prefer a traditional wedding, others request a fantasy experience.

For all the Checkpoint sentences, compare your responses with the Key to Checkpoint Exercises near the end of this appendix.

Verb Tense

GUIDE 4: Use present-tense, past-tense, and past-participle verb forms correctly.

Present Tense	Past Tense	Past Participle
(Today I ___)	(Yesterday I ___)	(I have ___)
am	was	been
begin	began	begun
break	broke	broken
bring	brought	brought
choose	chose	chosen
come	came	come
do	did	done
give	gave	given
go	went	gone
know	knew	known
pay	paid	paid
see	saw	seen
steal	stole	Stolen
take	took	taken

The package *came* yesterday, and Kevin *knew* what it contained.

If I *had seen* the shipper's bill, I *would have paid* it immediately.

I *know* the answer now; I wish I *had known* it yesterday.

Tip. Probably the most frequent mistake in tenses results from substituting the past-participle form for the past tense. Notice that the past-participle tense requires auxiliary verbs, such as *has, had, have, would have*, and *could have*.

FAULTY	CORRECT
When he *come* over last night, he *brung* pizza.	When he *came* over last night, he *brought* pizza.
If he *had came* earlier, we *could have saw* the video.	If he *had come* earlier, we *could have seen* the video.

Verb Mood

GUIDE 5: Use the subjunctive mood to express hypothetical (untrue) ideas. The most frequent misuse of the subjunctive mood involves using *was* instead of *were* in clauses introduced by *if* and *as though* or containing *wish*.

If I *were* (not *was*) you, I would take a business writing course.

Sometimes I wish I *were* (not *was*) the manager of this department.

He acts as though he *were* (not *was*) in charge of this department.

Tip. If the statement could possibly be true, use *was.*

If I *was* to blame, I accept the consequences.

✓Checkpoint

Correct faults in verb tenses and mood.

6. If I was you, I would have went to the ten o'clock meeting.
7. Kevin could have wrote a better report if he had began earlier.
8. When the project manager seen the report, he immediately come to my office.
9. I wish the project manager was in my shoes for just one day.
10. If the manager had knew all that we do, I'm sure he would have gave us better reviews.

Verb Voice

For a discussion of active- and passive-voice verbs, see Chapter 5.

Verb Agreement

GUIDE 6: Make subjects agree with verbs despite intervening phrases and clauses. Become a detective in locating true subjects. Don't be deceived by prepositional phrases and parenthetical words that often disguise the true subject.

Our study of annual budgets, five-year plans, and sales proposals *is* (not *are*) progressing on schedule. (The true subject is *study.*)

The budgeted item, despite additions proposed yesterday, *remains* (not *remain*) as submitted. (The true subject is *item.*)

A vendor's evaluation of the prospects for a sale, together with plans for follow-up action, *is* (not *are*) what we need. (The true subject is *evaluation.*)

Tip. Subjects are nouns or pronouns that control verbs. To find subjects, cross out prepositional phrases beginning with words such as *about, at, by, for, from, of,* and *to.* Subjects of verbs are not found in prepositional phrases. Also, don't be tricked by expressions introduced by *together with, in addition to,* and *along with.*

GUIDE 7: With subjects joined by *and*, use plural verbs. Watch for true subjects joined by the conjunction *and.* They require plural verbs.

The CEO and one of his assistants *have* (not *has*) ordered a limo.

Considerable time and money *were* (not *was*) spent on remodelling.

Exercising in the gym and jogging every day *are* (not *is*) how he keeps fit.

GUIDE 8: Subjects joined by *or* or *nor* may require singular or plural verbs. The verb should agree with the closer subject.

Either the software or the printer *is* (not *are*) causing the glitch. (The verb is controlled by the closer subject, *printer.*)

Neither Montréal nor Calgary *has* (not *have*) a chance of winning. (The verb is controlled by *Calgary.*)

Tip. In joining singular and plural subjects with *or* or *nor,* place the plural subject closer to the verb. Then, the plural verb sounds natural. For example, *Either the manufacturer or the distributors are responsible.*

GUIDE 9: Use singular verbs for most indefinite pronouns. The following pronouns all take singular verbs: *anyone, anybody, anything, each, either, every, everyone, everybody, everything, neither, nobody, nothing, someone, somebody,* and *something.*

Everyone in both offices *was* (not *were*) given a bonus.

Each of the employees *is* (not *are*) being interviewed.

GUIDE 10: Use singular or plural verbs for collective nouns, depending on whether the members of the group are operating as a unit or individually. Words such as *faculty, administration, class, crowd,* and *committee* are considered *collective* nouns. If the members of the collective are acting as a unit, treat them as singular subjects. If they are acting individually, it is usually better to add the word *members* and use a plural verb.

CORRECT	IMPROVED
The finance committee *is* working harmoniously. (*Committee* is singular because its action is unified.)	
The planning committee *are* having difficulty agreeing. (*Committee* is plural because its members are acting individually.)	The planning committee members *are* having difficulty agreeing. (Add the word *members* if a plural meaning is intended.)

Tip. In North America collective nouns are generally considered singular. In Britain these collective nouns are generally considered plural.

✓Checkpoint

Correct the errors in subject–verb agreement.

11. The agency's time and talent was spent trying to develop a blockbuster ad campaign.
12. Your e-mail message, along with both of its attachments, were not delivered to my computer.
13. Each of the *Fortune* 500 companies are being sent a survey regarding women in management.
14. A full list of names and addresses are necessary before we can begin.
15. Either the judge or the lawyer have asked for a recess.

Pronoun Case

GUIDE 11: Learn the three cases of pronouns and how each is used. Pronouns are substitutes for nouns. Every business writer must know the following pronoun cases.

Subjective (Nominative) Case Used for subjects of verbs and subject complements	Objective Case Used for objects of prepositions and objects of verbs	Possessive Case Used to show possession
I	me	my, mine
we	us	our, ours
you	you	you, yours
he	him	his
she	her	her, hers
it	it	its
they	them	their, theirs
who, whoever it	whom, whomever	whose

GUIDE 12: Use subjective-case pronouns as subjects of verbs and as complements. Complements are words that follow linking verbs (such as *am, is, are, was, were, be, being,* and *been*) and rename the words to which they refer.

Bryan and *I* (not *Bryan* and *me*) are looking for entry-level jobs. (Use subjective-case pronouns as the subjects of the verb phrase *are looking*.)

We hope that Marci and *he* (not *him*) will be hired. (Use a subjective-case pronoun as the subject of the verb phrase *will be hired*.)

It must have been *she* (not *her*) who called last night. (Use a subjective-case pronoun as a subject complement.)

Tip. If you feel awkward using subjective pronouns after linking verbs, rephrase the sentence to avoid the dilemma. Instead of *It is she who is the boss*, say, *She is the boss*.

GUIDE 13: Use objective-case pronouns as objects of prepositions and verbs.

Send the e-mail to *her* and *me* (not *she* and *I*). (The pronouns *her* and *me* are objects of the preposition *to*.)

The CEO appointed Rick and *him* (not *he*) to the committee. (The pronoun *him* is the object of the verb *appointed*.)

Tip. When a pronoun appears in combination with a noun or another pronoun, ignore the extra noun or pronoun and its conjunction. Then, the case of the pronoun becomes more obvious.

Jason asked Jennifer and *me* (not *I*) to lunch. (Ignore *Jennifer and*.)

The server brought hamburgers to Jason and *me* (not *I*). (Ignore *Jason and*.)

Tip. Be especially alert to the following prepositions: *except*, *between*, *but*, and *like*. Be sure to use objective pronouns as their objects.

Just between you and *me* (not *I*), that mineral water comes from the tap.

Everyone except Robert and *him* (not *he*) responded to the invitation.

GUIDE 14: Use possessive pronouns to show ownership. Possessive pronouns (such as *hers*, *yours*, *whose*, *ours*, *theirs*, and *its*) require no apostrophes.

All reports except *yours* (not *your's*) have to be rewritten.

The apartment and *its* (not *it's*) contents are *hers* (not *her's*) until June.

Tip. Don't confuse possessive pronouns and contractions. Contractions are shortened forms of subject–verb phrases (such as *it's* for *it is*, *there's* for *there is*, *who's* for *who is*, and *they're* for *they are*).

✓Checkpoint

Correct errors in pronoun case.

16. My partner and me have looked at many apartments, but your's has the best location.
17. We thought the car was her's, but it's licence plate does not match.
18. Just between you and I, do you think there printer is working?
19. Theres not much the boss or me can do if its broken, but its condition should have been reported to him or I earlier.
20. We received several applications, but your's and her's were missing.

GUIDE 15: Use pronouns ending in *-self* only when they refer to previously mentioned nouns or pronouns.

The president *himself* ate all the M&Ms.

Send the package to Mike or *me* (not *myself*).

Tip. Trying to sound less egocentric, some radio and TV announcers incorrectly substitute *myself* when they should use *I*. For example, "Jimmy and *myself* (should be *I*) are cohosting the telethon."

GUIDE 16: Use *who* or *whoever* for subjective-case constructions and *whom* or *whomever* for objective-case constructions. In determining the correct choice, it is helpful to substitute *he* for *who* or *whoever* and *him* for *whom* or *whomever*.

For *whom* was this software ordered? (The software was ordered for *him*.)

Who did you say called? (You did say *he* called?)

Give the supplies to *whoever* asked for them. (In this sentence the clause *whoever asked for them* functions as the object of the preposition *to*. Within the clause *whoever* is the subject of the verb *asked*. Again, try substituting *he*: *he asked for them*.)

✓Checkpoint

Correct any errors in the use of *who* or *whom* and pronouns ending in *-self*.

21. The boss herself is willing to call whoever we decide to honour.
22. Who have you asked to develop ads for our new products?
23. I have a pizza for whomever placed the telephone order.
24. The meeting is set for Wednesday; however, Matt and myself cannot attend.
25. Incident reports must be submitted by whomever experiences a personnel problem.

Pronoun Reference

GUIDE 17: Make pronouns agree in number and gender with the words to which they refer (their antecedents) when gender is known. When the gender of the antecedent is known, gendered pronouns are acceptable.

One of the men failed to fill in *his* name on the application. (The singular pronoun *his* refers to the singular *One*.)

Somebody on the girls' team left *her* car's headlights on. (The singular pronoun *her* and singular noun *car* are necessary because they refer to the singular subject *Somebody*.)

According to APA style, use the singular *they* when pronouns are unknown:

When referring to individuals whose identified pronouns are not known or when the gender of a generic or hypothetical person is irrelevant within the context, use the singular *they* to avoid making assumptions about an individual's gender. Use the forms *they*, *them*, *theirs*, and so forth.[1]

The employee raised the most money for the food bank, so *they* were given a certificate of appreciation. (The singular pronoun *they* refers to the singular *employee*.)

FAULTY	IMPROVED
Every employee should receive *his* cheque Friday. (The pronoun *his* assumes gender.)	All employees should receive *their* cheques Friday. (Make the subject plural to avoid bias. This option is preferred by many writers today.) Every employee should receive *their* cheque Friday. (Use the singular *they* to achieve bias-free language.) All employees should receive cheques Friday. (Omit the possessive pronoun entirely.) Every employee should receive *a* cheque Friday. (Substitute *a* for a pronoun.)

GUIDE 18: Be sure that pronouns, such as *it*, *which*, *this*, and *that*, refer to clear antecedents. Vague pronouns confuse the reader because they have no clear single antecedent. The most troublesome are *it*, *which*, *this*, and *that*. Replace vague pronouns with concrete nouns, or provide these pronouns with clear antecedents.

FAULTY	IMPROVED
Our office recycles as much paper as possible because *it* helps the environment. (Does *it* refer to *paper*, *recycling*, or *office*?)	Our office recycles as much paper as possible because *such an effort* helps the environment. (*Effort* supplies a concrete noun for the vague pronoun *it*.)
The disadvantages of some mobile apps can offset their advantages. *That* merits further evaluation. (What merits evaluation: advantages, disadvantages, or the offsetting of one by the other?)	The disadvantages of some mobile apps can offset their advantages. That fact merits further evaluation. (*Fact* supplies a concrete noun for the vague pronoun *that*.)
Negotiators announced an expanded wellness program, reductions in dental coverage, and a proposal to move child-care facilities off site. *This* ignited employee protests. (What exactly ignited employee protests?)	Negotiators announced an expanded wellness program, reductions in dental coverage, and a proposal to move child-care facilities off site. *This* change in child-care facilities ignited employee protests. (The pronoun *This* now has a clear reference.)

Tip. Whenever you use the words *this*, *that*, *these*, and *those* by themselves, a red flag should pop up. These words are dangerous when they stand alone. Inexperienced writers often use them to refer to an entire previous idea, rather than to a specific antecedent, as shown in the preceding examples. You can usually solve the problem by adding another idea to the pronoun (such as *this change*).

✓Checkpoint

Correct the faulty and vague pronoun references in the following sentences. Numerous remedies exist.

26. Every employee must wear their picture identification badge.
27. Flexible working hours may mean slower career advancement, but it appeals to many workers.
28. Any renter must pay his rent by the first of the month.
29. Someone in this office reported that his computer had a virus.
30. Obtaining agreement on job standards, listening to coworkers, and encouraging employee suggestions all helped to open lines of communication. This is particularly important in team projects.

Adjectives and Adverbs

GUIDE 19: Use adverbs, not adjectives, to describe or limit the action of verbs. Use adjectives after linking verbs.

Andrew said he did *well* (not *good*) on the exam. (The adverb *well* describes how he did.)

After its tune-up, the engine is running *smoothly* (not *smooth*). (The adverb *smoothly* describes the verb *is running*.)

Don't take the manager's criticism *personally* (not *personal*). (The adverb *personally* tells how to take the criticism.)

She finished her homework *more quickly* (not *quicker*) than expected. (The adverb *more quickly* explains how she finished her homework.)

Liam felt *bad* (not *badly*) after he heard the news. (The adjective *bad* follows the linking verb *felt*.)

GUIDE 20: Hyphenate two or more adjectives that are joined to create a compound modifier before a noun.

You need an *easy-to-remember* e-mail address and a *one-page* résumé.

Person-to-person networking continues to be the best way to find a job.

Tip. Don't confuse adverbs ending in *-ly* with compound adjectives: *newly enacted* law and *highly regarded* CEO would not be hyphenated.

✓Checkpoint

Correct any problems in the use of pronouns, adjectives, and adverbs.

31. My manager and me could not resist the once in a lifetime opportunity.
32. Because John and him finished their task so quick, they made a fast trip to the recently opened snack bar.
33. If I do good on the exam, I qualify for many part time jobs and a few full time positions.
34. The vice president told him and I not to take the announcement personal.
35. In the not too distant future, we may enjoy more practical uses of robots.

Commas

GUIDE 21: Use commas to separate three or more items (words, phrases, or short clauses) in a series (Comma Series: CmSer).

Downward communication delivers job instructions, procedures, and appraisals.

In preparing your résumé, try to keep it brief, make it easy to read, and include only job-related information.

The new ice cream flavours include cookie dough, chocolate raspberry truffle, cappuccino, and almond amaretto.

Tip. Some professional writers omit the comma before *and*. However, most business writers prefer to retain that comma because it prevents misreading the last two items as one item. Notice in the previous example how the final two ice cream flavours could have been misread if the comma had been omitted.

GUIDE 22: Use commas to separate introductory clauses and certain phrases from independent clauses (Comma Introductory: CmIntro). This guideline describes the comma most often omitted by business writers. Sentences that open with dependent clauses (frequently introduced by words such as *since*, *when*, *if*, *as*, *although*, and *because*) require commas to separate them from the main idea. The comma helps readers recognize where the introduction ends and the big idea begins. Introductory phrases of four or more words or phrases containing verbal elements also require commas.

If you recognize introductory clauses, you will have no trouble placing the comma. (A comma separates the introductory dependent clause from the main clause.)

When you have mastered this rule, half the battle with commas will be won.

As expected, additional explanations are necessary. (Use a comma even if the introductory clause omits the understood subject: *As we expected*.)

In the spring of last year, we opened our franchise. (Use a comma after a phrase containing four or more words.)

Having considered several alternatives, we decided to invest. (Use a comma after an introductory verbal phrase.)

To invest, we needed $100,000. (Use a comma after an introductory verbal phrase, regardless of its length.)

Tip. Short introductory prepositional phrases (three or fewer words) require no commas. Don't clutter your writing with unnecessary commas after introductory phrases such as *by 2017*, *in the fall*, or *at this time*.

GUIDE 23: Use a comma before the coordinating conjunction in a compound sentence (Comma Conjunction: CmConj). The most common coordinating conjunctions are *and*, *or*, *nor*, and *but*. Occasionally, *for*, *yet*, and *so* may also function as coordinating conjunctions. When coordinating conjunctions join two independent clauses, commas are needed.

> The investment sounded too good to be true, *and* many investors were dubious about it. (Use a comma before the coordinating conjunction *and* in a compound sentence.)
>
> Niagara Falls is the honeymoon capital of the world, *but* some newlyweds prefer more exotic destinations.

Tip. Before inserting a comma, test the two clauses. Can each of them stand alone as a complete sentence? If either is incomplete, skip the comma.

> Promoters said the investment offer was for a limited time and could not be extended by even one day. (Omit a comma before *and* because the second part of the sentence is not a complete independent clause.)
>
> Lease payments are based largely on your down payment and on the value of the car at the end of the lease. (Omit a comma before *and* because the second half of the sentence is not a complete clause.)

✓Checkpoint

Add appropriate commas.

36. Before she enrolled in this class Erin used to sprinkle her writing with commas semicolons and dashes.
37. After studying punctuation she learned to use commas more carefully and to reduce her reliance on dashes.
38. At this time Erin is engaged in a serious yoga program but she also finds time to enlighten her mind.
39. Next fall Erin may enroll in communication and merchandising courses or she may work for a semester to earn money.
40. When she completes her junior year she plans to apply for an internship in Montréal Edmonton or Toronto.

GUIDE 24: Use commas appropriately in dates, addresses, geographical names, degrees, and long numbers (Comma Date: CmDate).

> September 30, 1993, is his birthday. (For dates use commas before and after the year.)
>
> Send the application to James Kirby, 2045 120th Avenue NW, Edmonton, AB T5W 1M3, as soon as possible. (For addresses use commas to separate all units except the two-letter province or territory abbreviation and the postal code.)
>
> Lisa expects to move from Calgary, Alberta, to Sarnia, Ontario, next fall. (For geographical areas use commas to enclose the second element.)
>
> Karen Munson, CGA, and Richard B. Larsen, PhD, were the speakers. (Use commas to enclose professional designations and academic degrees following names.)
>
> The latest census figures show the city's population to be 342,000. (In figures use commas to separate every three digits, counting from the right. Note that in many countries, including Canada, a space separator is often used instead of a comma.)

GUIDE 25: Use commas to set off internal sentence interrupters (Comma Internal: CmIn). Sentence interrupters may be verbal phrases, dependent clauses, contrasting elements, or parenthetical expressions (also called transitional phrases). These interrupters often provide information that is not grammatically essential.

> Medical researchers, *working steadily for 18 months,* developed a new cancer therapy. (Use commas to set off an internal interrupting verbal phrase.)
>
> The new therapy, *which applies a genetically engineered virus,* raises hopes among cancer specialists. (Use commas to set off nonessential dependent clauses.)
>
> Dr. James C. Morrison, *who is one of the researchers,* made the announcement. (Use commas to set off nonessential dependent clauses.)
>
> It was Dr. Morrison, *not Dr. Arturo,* who led the team effort. (Use commas to set off a contrasting element.)
>
> This new therapy, *by the way,* was developed from a herpes virus. (Use commas to set off a parenthetical expression.)

Tip. Parenthetical (transitional) expressions are helpful words that guide the reader from one thought to the next. Here are typical parenthetical expressions that require commas:

as a matter of fact	in addition	of course
as a result	in the meantime	on the other hand
consequently	nevertheless	therefore
for example		

Tip. Always use *two* commas to set off an interrupter, unless it begins or ends a sentence.

✓Checkpoint

Insert necessary commas.

41. James listed 222 George Henry Blvd. Toronto ON M2J 1E6 as his forwarding address.
42. This report is not however one that must be classified.
43. Employment of paralegals which is expected to decrease 12 percent next year is contracting because of the slow economy.
44. The contract was signed May 15 2014 and remains in effect until May 15 2020.
45. As a matter of fact the average North American drinks enough coffee to require five kilograms of coffee beans annually.

GUIDE 26: Avoid unnecessary commas (Comma Unnecessary: CmNo). Do not use commas between sentence elements that belong together. Do not automatically insert commas before every *and* or at points where your voice might drop if you were saying the sentence out loud.

FAULTY

> Growth will be spurred by the increasing complexity of business operations, and by large employment gains in trade and services. (A comma unnecessarily precedes *and.*)
>
> All students with high grades, are eligible for the honour society. (A comma unnecessarily separates the subject and verb.)
>
> One of the reasons for the success of the business honour society is, that it is very active. (A comma unnecessarily separates the verb and its complement.)
>
> Our honour society has, at this time, over 50 members. (Commas unnecessarily separate a prepositional phrase from the sentence.)

✓**Checkpoint**

Remove unnecessary commas. Add necessary ones.

46. Car companies promote leasing because it brings customers back into their showrooms sooner, and gives dealers a steady supply of late-model used cars.
47. When shopping for a car you may be offered a fantastic leasing deal.
48. The trouble with many leases is, that the value of the car at the end of the lease may be less than expected.
49. We think on the other hand, that you should compare the costs of leasing and buying, and that you should talk to a tax adviser.
50. North American and Japanese automakers are, at this time, offering intriguing lease deals.

Semicolons, Colons

GUIDE 27: Use a semicolon to join closely related independent clauses. Experienced writers use semicolons to show readers that two thoughts are closely associated. If the ideas are not related, they should be expressed in separate sentences. Often, but not always, the second independent clause contains a conjunctive adverb (such as *however, consequently, therefore,* or *furthermore*) to show the relation between the two clauses. Use a semicolon before a conjunctive adverb of two or more syllables (such as *however, consequently, therefore,* or *furthermore*) and a comma after it.

> Learning history is easy; learning its lessons is almost impossible. (A semicolon joins two independent clauses.)
>
> He was determined to complete his degree; consequently, he studied diligently. (A semicolon precedes the conjunctive adverb, and a comma follows it.)
>
> Serena wanted a luxury apartment located near campus; however, she couldn't afford the rent. (A semicolon precedes the conjunctive adverb, and a comma follows it.)

Tip. Don't use a semicolon unless each clause is truly independent. Try the sentence test. Omit the semicolon if each clause could not stand alone as a complete sentence.

FAULTY	IMPROVED
There is no point in speaking; unless you can improve on silence. (The second half of the sentence is a dependent clause. It could not stand alone as a sentence.)	There is no point in speaking unless you can improve on silence.
Although I cannot change the direction of the wind; I can adjust my sails to reach my destination. (The first clause could not stand alone.)	Although I cannot change the direction of the wind, I can adjust my sails to reach my destination.

GUIDE 28: Use a semicolon to separate items in a series when one or more of the items contains internal commas.

> Representatives from as far away as Longueuil, Québec; Vancouver, British Columbia; and Whitehorse, Yukon, attended the conference.
>
> Stories circulated about Henry Ford, founder, Ford Motor Company; Lee Iacocca, former CEO, Chrysler Motor Company; and Shoichiro Toyoda, founder, Toyota Motor Company.

GUIDE 29: Use a colon after a complete thought that introduces a list of items. Words such as *these, the following,* and *as follows* may introduce the list or they may be implied.

> The following cities are on the tour: Toronto, Ottawa, and Winnipeg.

An alternative tour includes several West Coast cities: Vancouver, Nanaimo, and Victoria.

Tip. Be sure that the statement before a colon is grammatically complete. An introductory statement that ends with a preposition (such as *by*, *for*, *at*, and *to*) or a verb (such as *is*, *are*, or *were*) is incomplete. The list following a preposition or a verb actually functions as an object or as a complement to finish the sentence.

FAULTY	IMPROVED
Three Big Macs were ordered by: Pam, Jim, and Lee. (Do not use a colon after an incomplete statement.)	Three Big Macs were ordered by Pam, Jim, and Lee.
Other items that they ordered were: fries, Cokes, and salads. (Do not use a colon after an incomplete statement.)	Other items that they ordered were fries, Cokes, and salads.

GUIDE 30: Use a colon after business letter salutations and to introduce long quotations.

Dear Mr. Duran: Dear Lisa:

In discussing social media conversations, the consultant said: "Finding the right balance will take time, if it is ever achieved. Unlike face-to-face conversations, there's really no good way yet for people to let one another know when they are revealing too much."

Tip. Use a comma to introduce short quotations. Use a colon to introduce long one-sentence quotations and quotations of two or more sentences.

✓Checkpoint

Add appropriate semicolons and colons.

51. Marco's short-term goal is an entry-level job his long-term goal however is a management position.
52. Speakers included the following professors Rebecca Hilbrink University of Western Ontario Lora Lindsey McGill University and Michael Malone Durham College.
53. The recruiter was looking for three qualities loyalty initiative and enthusiasm.
54. Microsoft seeks experienced individuals however it will hire recent graduates who are skilled.
55. Mississauga is an expanding region therefore many business opportunities are available.

Apostrophe

GUIDE 31: If an ownership word does not end in an *s* sound, add an apostrophe and *s*, whether the word is singular or plural.

We hope to show a profit in one year's time. (Add *'s* because the ownership word *year* is singular and does not end in *s*.)

The children's teacher allowed free time on the computer. (Add *'s* because the ownership word *children*, although it is plural, does not end in *s*.)

GUIDE 32: If an ownership word does end in an *s* sound and is singular, add an apos trophe and *s*.

The witness's testimony was critical. (Add *'s* because the ownership word *witness* is singular and ends in *s*.)

The boss's cell phone rang during the meeting. (Add *'s* because the ownership word *boss* is singular and ends in *s*.

If the ownership words ends in an *s* sound and is plural, add only an apostrophe.

> Both investors' portfolios showed diversification. (Add only an apostrophe because the ownership word *investors* is plural and ends in *s*.)

> Some workers' benefits will cost more. (Add only an apostrophe because the ownership word *workers* is plural and ends in *s*.)

Tip. To determine whether an ownership word ends in *s*, use it in an *of* phrase. For example, *one month's salary* becomes *the salary of one month*. By isolating the ownership word without its apostrophe, you can decide whether it ends in *s*.

GUIDE 33: Use a possessive pronoun or add an apostrophe and *s* to make a noun possessive when it precedes a gerund (a verb form used as a noun).

> We all protested *Laura's* (not *Laura*) smoking. (Add an apostrophe and *s* to the noun preceding the gerund.)

> *His* (not *Him*) talking on his cell phone angered moviegoers. (Use a possessive pronoun before the gerund.)

> I appreciate *your* (not *you*) answering the telephone while I was gone. (Use a possessive pronoun before the gerund.)

✓Checkpoint

Correct any problems with possessives.

56. Both companies executives received huge bonuses, even when employees salaries were falling.
57. In just one weeks time, we promise to verify all members names and addresses.
58. The manager and I certainly appreciate you bringing this matter to our CGAs attention.
59. All beneficiaries names must be revealed when insurance companies write policies.
60. Is your sister-in-laws job downtown?

Other Punctuation

GUIDE 34: Use one period to end a statement, a command, an indirect question, or a polite request. Never use two periods.

> Matt worked at BioTech, Inc. (Statement. Use only one period.)

> Deliver it before 5 p.m. (Command. Use only one period.)

> Stacy asked whether she could use the car next weekend. (Indirect question)

> Will you please send me an employment application. (Polite request)

Tip. Polite requests often sound like questions. To determine the punctuation, apply the action test. If the request prompts an action, use a period. If it prompts a verbal response, use a question mark.

FAULTY	IMPROVED
Could you please correct the balance on my next statement? (This polite request prompts an action rather than a verbal response.)	Could you please correct the balance on my next statement.

Tip. To avoid the punctuation dilemma with polite requests, do not phrase the request as a question. Phrase it as a command: *Please correct the balance on my next statement*. It still sounds polite, and the punctuation problem disappears.

GUIDE 35: Use a question mark after a direct question and after statements with questions appended.

Are they hiring at BioTech, Inc.?

Most of their training is in-house, isn't it?

GUIDE 36: Use a dash to (a) set off parenthetical elements containing internal commas, (b) emphasize a sentence interruption, or (c) separate an introductory list from a summarizing statement. The dash has legitimate uses. However, some writers use it whenever they know that punctuation is necessary, but they are not sure exactly what. The dash can be very effective, if not misused.

Three top students—Gene Engle, Donna Hersh, and Mika Sato—won awards. (Use dashes to set off elements with internal commas.)

Executives at IBM—despite rampant rumours in the stock market—remained quiet regarding dividend earnings. (Use dashes to emphasize a sentence interruption.)

Japan, Taiwan, and Turkey—these were areas hit by recent earthquakes. (Use a dash to separate an introductory list from a summarizing statement.)

GUIDE 37: Use parentheses to set off nonessential sentence elements, such as explanations, directions, questions, and references.

Researchers find that the office grapevine (see Chapter 1 for more discussion) carries surprisingly accurate information.

Only two dates (February 15 and March 1) are suitable for the meeting.

Tip. Careful writers use parentheses to de-emphasize and the dash to emphasize parenthetical information. One expert said, "Dashes shout the news; parentheses whisper it."

GUIDE 38: Use quotation marks to (a) enclose the exact words of a speaker; (b) enclose the titles of articles, chapters, or other short works; and (c) enclose specific definitions of words or expressions.

"If you make your job important," said the consultant, "it's quite likely to return the favour." (Quotation marks enclose the exact words of a speaker.)

The recruiter said that she was looking for candidates with good communication skills. (Omit quotation marks because the exact words of the speaker are not quoted.)

In *The Financial Post*, I saw an article titled "Communication for Global Markets." (Quotation marks enclose the title of an article. Italics identify the name of newspapers, magazines, and books.)

The term *tweet* refers to "a post made on the microblogging site Twitter." (Quotation marks enclose the definition of a word.)

For jargon, slang, words used in a special sense such as humour, irony, and words following *stamped* or *marked*, some writers use italics. Other writers use quotation marks.

Computer criminals are often called *hackers* (OR "hackers"). (Jargon)

My teenager said that the film *The Hunger Games* is *sick* (OR "sick"). (Slang)

Justin claimed that he was *too ill* (OR "too ill") to come to work yesterday. (Irony)

The package was stamped *Fragile* (OR "Fragile"). (Words following *stamped*)

Tip. Never use quotation marks arbitrarily, as in *Our "spring" sale starts April 1.*

✓Checkpoint

Add appropriate punctuation.

61. Will you please send your print catalogue as soon as possible
62. (Direct quotation) Our Stanley Cup promotion said the CEO will cost nearly $500,000
63. (De-emphasize) Two kinds of batteries see page 16 of the instruction booklet may be used in this camera.
64. Tim wondered whether sentences could end with two periods
65. Stephanie plans to do a lot of chillaxing during her vacation.

Capitalization

GUIDE 39: Capitalize proper nouns and proper adjectives. Capitalize the *specific* names of persons, places, institutions, buildings, religions, holidays, months, organizations, laws, races, languages, and so forth. Do not capitalize seasons, and do not capitalize common nouns that make *general* references.

Proper Nouns	Common Nouns
Michelle Deluca	the manufacturer's rep
Algonquin Provincial Park	the wilderness park
College of the Rockies	the community college
CN Tower	the downtown building
Canadian Environmental Assessment Agency	the federal agency
Persian, Armenian, Hindi	modern foreign languages
Annual Spring Festival	in the spring
Proper Adjectives	
Hispanic markets	Italian dressing
Xerox copy	Japanese executives
Swiss chocolates	Reagan economics

GUIDE 40: Capitalize only specific academic courses and degrees.

Professor Donna Howard, PhD, will teach Accounting 121 next spring.

James Barker, who holds bachelor's and master's degrees, teaches marketing.

Jessica enrolled in classes in management, English, and business law.

GUIDE 41: Capitalize courtesy, professional, religious, government, family, and business titles when they precede names.

Mr. Jameson, Mrs. Alvarez, and Ms. Robinson (Courtesy titles)

Professor Andrews, Dr. Lee (Professional titles)

Rabbi Cohen, Pastor Williams, Pope Benedict (Religious titles)

Senator Tom Harrison, Mayor Jackson (Government titles)

Uncle Edward, Aunt Teresa, Cousin Vinney (Family titles)

Vice President Morris, Budget Director Lopez (Business titles)

Do not capitalize a title when it is followed by an appositive (i.e., when the title is followed by a noun that renames or explains it).

Only one professor, Jonathan Marcus, favoured a tuition hike.

Local candidates counted on their premier, Lee Jones, to help raise funds.

Do not capitalize titles following names unless they are part of an address:

Mark Yoder, president of Yoder Enterprises, hired all employees.

Paula Beech, director of Human Resources, interviewed all candidates.

Send the package to Amanda Harr, Advertising Manager, Cambridge Publishers, 20 Park Plaza, Saint John, NB E2L 1G2. (Title in an address)

Generally, do not capitalize a title that replaces a person's name.

Only the prime minister, his chief of staff, and one senator made the trip.

The director of marketing and the sales manager will meet at 1 p.m.

Do not capitalize family titles used with possessive pronouns.

my mother, his father, your cousin

GUIDE 42: Capitalize the main words in titles, subject lines, and headings. *Main* words are all words except (a) the articles *a*, *an*, and *the*; (b) the conjunctions *and*, *but*, *or*, and *nor*; (c) prepositions containing two or three letters (e.g., *of*, *for*, *in*, *on*, *by*); (d) the word *to* in infinitives (such as *to work*, *to write*, and *to talk*); and (e) the word *as*—unless any of these words are the first or last words in the title, subject line, or heading.

I enjoyed the book *A Customer Is More Than a Name*. (Book title)

Team Meeting to Discuss Deadlines Rescheduled for Friday (Subject line)

We liked the article titled "Advice From a Pro: How to Say It With Pictures." (Article)

Check the Advice and Resources link at the CareerBuilder website.

(Note that the titles of books are italicized, but the titles of articles are enclosed in quotation marks.)

GUIDE 43: Capitalize names of geographic locations. Capitalize *north*, *south*, *east*, *west*, and their derivatives only when they represent specific geographical regions.

from the Pacific Northwest	heading northwest on the highway
living in the West	west of the city

GUIDE 44: Capitalize the main words in the specific names of departments, divisions, or committees within business organizations. Do not capitalize general references.

All forms are available from our Department of Human Resources.

The Consumer Electronics Division launched an upbeat marketing campaign.

We volunteered for the Employee Social Responsibility Committee.

You might send an application to their personnel department.

GUIDE 45: Capitalize product names only when they refer to trademarked items. Do not capitalize the common names following manufacturers' names.

Dell laptop computer	Skippy peanut butter	NordicTrack treadmill
Eveready Energizer	Norelco razor	Canon colour copier
Coca-Cola	Panasonic plasma television	Big Mac sandwich

GUIDE 46: Capitalize most nouns followed by numbers or letters (except in page, paragraph, line, and verse references).

Room 14	Exhibit A	Flight 12, Gate 43

✓**Checkpoint**

Capitalize all appropriate words.

66. vice president moore bought a new droid smartphone before leaving for the east coast.
67. when you come on tuesday, travel west on highway 5 and exit at mt. pleasant street.
68. The director of our human resources department called a meeting of the company's building security committee.
69. our manager and president are flying on air canada flight 34 leaving from gate 69 at the toronto international airport.
70. my father read a businessweek article titled can you build loyalty with bricks and mortar?

Number Usage

GUIDE 47: Use word form to express (a) numbers ten and under and (b) numbers beginning sentences. General references to numbers *ten* and under should be expressed in word form. Also use word form for numbers that begin sentences. If the resulting number involves more than two words, however, recast the sentence so that the number does not fall at the beginning.

We answered *six* text messages for the *four* sales reps.

Fifteen customers responded to our *three* cell phone ads today.

A total of 155 smartphones were awarded as prizes. (Avoid beginning the sentence with a long number such as *one hundred fifty-five.*)

GUIDE 48: Use figures to express most references to numbers 11 and over.

Over *150* people from *53* companies attended the two-day workshop.

A *120* mL serving of Häagen-Dazs toffee crunch ice cream contains *300* calories and *19* grams of fat.

GUIDE 49: Use figures to express money, dates, clock time, decimals, and percentages.

One item costs only *$1.95*; most, however, were priced between *$10* and *$35*. (Omit the decimals and zeros in even sums of money.)

We scheduled a meeting for May 12. (Notice that we do NOT write May 12th.)

We expect deliveries at 10:15 a.m. and again at 4 p.m. (Use lowercase *a.m.* and *p.m.*)

All packages must be ready by 4 o'clock. (Do NOT write 4:00 o'clock.)

When sales dropped *4.7* percent, net income fell *9.8* percent. (In contextual material use the word *percent* instead of the symbol %.)

GUIDE 50: Use a combination of words and figures to express sums of 1 million and over. Use words for small fractions.

Orion lost *$62.9 million* in the latest fiscal year on revenues of *$584 million*. (Use a combination of words and figures for sums of 1 million and over.)

Only one half of the registered voters turned out. (Use words for small fractions.)

Tip. To ease your memory load, concentrate on the numbers normally expressed in words: numbers *ten* and under, numbers at the beginning of a sentence, and small fractions. Nearly everything else in business is generally written with figures.

✓**Checkpoint**

Correct any inappropriate expression of numbers.

71. Although he budgeted fifty dollars, Jake spent 94 dollars and 34 cents for supplies.
72. Is the meeting on November 7th or November 14th?
73. UPS deliveries arrive at nine AM and again at four fifteen PM.
74. The company applied for a fifty thousand dollar loan at six%.
75. The Canadian population is just over 35,000,000, and the world population is estimated to be nearly 7,300,000,000.

Abbreviations

Abbreviations should be used only when they are clear and appropriate. Be aware that every field (such as technology and engineering) has its own specialized abbreviations. Therefore, be certain before you use such abbreviations that the receiver of your information is familiar with them.

GUIDE 51: Use abbreviations for titles before and after proper names.

Mr. Peter Mansbridge	Joshua Paul, *Jr.*
Rev. Simon Brownsley	*Hon.* Diane Finley
Samford Amhas, *MD*	Ronny Muntroy, *PhD*

GUIDE 52: Learn when to use periods with abbreviations.

Use a period with conventional abbreviations.

Mrs. Ms. Mr. Dr. Hon. Prof.

Acronyms (shortened forms), which are pronounced as a word, do not have periods.

AIDS scuba laser UNICEF NAFTA

Latin abbreviations have periods.

e.g. i.e. etc. vs.

GUIDE 53: Use abbreviations for familiar institutions, organizations, associations, corporations, and people.

INSTITUTIONS

UBC UWO WLU CNIB

ORGANIZATIONS AND ASSOCIATIONS

NDP	CIA	YMCA	CAW	CAPIC	CMA
OPEC	G8	OSSTF	NHLPA	CHRP	CSIS

CORPORATIONS

IBM CTW CBC

PEOPLE

PET FDR LBJ JFK

GUIDE 54: Remember your audience when using abbreviations. If the short form or abbreviation is not well known, spell it out before using it throughout the discussion.

> The CBE (Council of Biology Editors) documentation style is used primarily in the sciences. Consult a reference text for information about how to use CBE documentation.

✓**Checkpoint**

Correct any inappropriate use of abbreviations.

76. My dr., Samnik Shanban, md, has wonderful credentials.
77. To save both money and time, the specialist recommended l.a.s.e.r. surgery.
78. The question was addressed to Prof Antle.
79. You should remember to use a large-sized font when preparing overheads, eg, 24-point or larger.
80. Mrs. Cathrick was n.a. for comment.

Key to Checkpoint Exercises

This key shows all corrections. If you marked anything else, double-check the appropriate guideline.

1. Disney, destination
2. yearly, which
3. hour; however,
4. pavilion;
5. wedding;
6. If I were you, I would have gone . . .
7. could have written . . . had begun earlier.
8. project manager saw . . . immediately came
9. project manager were
10. manager had known . . . would have given
11. time and talent were spent (Note that two subjects require a plural verb.)
12. attachments, was (Note that the subject is *message*.)
13. Each of . . . companies is (Note that the subject is *Each*.)
14. list of names and addresses is (Note that the subject is *list*.)
15. lawyer has
16. My partner and I . . . but yours
17. was hers, but its
18. you and me . . . their printer
19. There's not much the boss or I can do if it's broken, . . . reported to him or me earlier.
20. but yours and hers
21. whomever
22. Whom have you asked . . .
23. for whoever
24. Matt and I
25. by whoever
26. Every employee must wear a picture identification badge, OR All employees must wear picture identification badges.
27. slower career advancement, but flexible scheduling appeals to many workers. (Revise to avoid the vague pronoun it.)
28. Any renter must pay the rent . . . OR All renters must pay their rent . . .
29. reported that a computer . . . OR reported that their computer . . .
30. communication. These techniques are particularly important (Revise to avoid the vague pronoun This.)
31. My manager and I could not resist the once-in-a-lifetime opportunity.
32. John and he finished their task so quickly (Do not hyphenate recently opened.)
33. do well . . . part-time jobs and a few full-time
34. told him and me . . . personally.
35. not-too-distant future
36. class, Erin . . . with commas, semicolons,
37. studying punctuation,
38. program,
39. merchandising courses,
40. junior year, . . . in Montréal, Edmonton,
41. Blvd., Toronto, ON M2J 1E6,
42. not, however,
43. paralegals, . . . next year,
44. May 15, 2014, . . . May 15, 2020.
45. fact,
46. sooner [delete comma]
47. car,
48. is [delete comma]
49. think, on the other hand, . . . buying [delete comma]
50. automakers are [delete comma] at this time [delete comma]

51. entry-level job; his long-term goal, however,
52. professors: Rebecca Hilbrink, University of Western Ontario; Lora Lindsey, McGill University; and Michael Malone, Durham College.
53. qualities: loyalty, initiative,
54. individuals; however,
55. region; therefore,
56. companies'... employees'
57. one week's time, ... members'
58. appreciate your ... CGA's
59. beneficiaries'
60. sister-in-law's
61. possible.
62. "Our Stanley Cup promotion," said the CEO, "will cost nearly $500,000."
63. Two kinds of batteries (see page 16 of the instruction booklet)
64. two periods.
65. *chillaxing* or "chillaxing"
66. Vice President Moore ... Droid ... East Coast
67. When . . . Tuesday, . . . Highway 5 . . . Mt. Pleasant Street.
68. Human Resources Department ... Building Security Committee
69. Our . . . Air Canada Flight 34 . . . Gate 69 at the Toronto International Airport
70. My . . . *BusinessWeek* article titled "Can You Build Loyalty With Bricks and Mortar?"
71. $50 ... $94.34
72. November 7 or November 14 [delete th]
73. 9 a.m. ... 4:15 p.m. (Note only one period at the end of the sentence.)
74. 50,000 loan at 6 percent.
75. 35 million ... 7.3 billion
76. doctor ... MD,
77. laser
78. Professor
79. e.g.
80. not available

Confusing Words

accede:	to agree or consent
exceed:	to go over a limit
accept:	to receive
except:	to exclude; (prep) but
adverse:	opposing; antagonistic
averse:	unwilling; reluctant
advice:	suggestion, opinion
advise:	to counsel or recommend
affect:	to influence
effect:	(n) outcome, result; (v) to bring about, to create
all ready:	prepared
already:	by this time
all right:	satisfactory
alright:	unacceptable variant spelling
altar:	structure for worship
alter:	to change
appraise:	to estimate
apprise:	to inform
ascent:	(n) rising or going up
assent:	(v) to agree or consent
assure:	to promise
ensure:	to make certain
insure:	to protect from loss
capital:	(n) city that is seat of government; wealth of an individual; (adj) chief
capitol:	building that houses U.S. state or national lawmakers
cereal:	breakfast food
serial:	arranged in sequence
cite:	to quote; to summon
sight:	a view; to see
site:	location
coarse:	rough texture
course:	a route; part of a meal; a unit of learning
complement:	that which completes
compliment:	(n) praise, flattery; (v) to praise or flatter
conscience:	regard for fairness
conscious:	aware
council:	governing body
counsel:	(n) advice, lawyer, consultant; (v) to give advice
credible:	believable
creditable:	good enough for praise or esteem; reliable
desert:	(n) arid land; (v) to abandon

dessert:	sweet food	miner:	person working in a mine
device:	invention or mechanism	minor:	(adj) lesser; (n) a person under age
devise:	to design or arrange	patience:	calm perseverance
disburse:	to pay out	patients:	people receiving medical treatment
disperse:	to scatter widely	personal:	private, individual
elicit:	to draw out	personnel:	employees
illicit:	unlawful	plaintiff:	(n) one who initiates a lawsuit
envelop:	(v) to wrap, surround, or conceal	plaintive:	(adj) expressive of suffering or woe
envelope:	(n) a container for a written message	populace:	(n) the masses; population of a place
every day:	each single day	populous:	(adj) densely populated
everyday:	ordinary	precede:	to go before
farther:	a greater distance	proceed:	to continue
further:	additional	precedence:	priority
formally:	in a formal manner	precedents:	events used as an example
formerly:	in the past	principal:	(n) capital sum; school official; (adj) chief
grate:	(v) to reduce to small particles; to cause irritation; (n) a frame of crossed bars blocking a passage	principle:	rule of action
		stationary:	immovable
great:	(adj) large in size; numerous; eminent or distinguished	stationery:	writing material
		than:	conjunction showing comparison
hole:	an opening	then:	adverb meaning "at that time"
whole:	complete	their:	possessive form of they
imply:	to suggest indirectly	there:	at that place or point
infer:	to reach a conclusion	they're:	contraction of they are
lean:	(v) to rest against; (adj) not fat	to:	a preposition; the sign of the infinitive
lien:	(n) a legal right or claim to property	too:	an adverb meaning "also" or "to an excessive extent"
liable:	legally responsible	two:	a number
libel:	damaging written statement	waiver:	abandonment of a claim
loose:	not fastened	waver:	to shake or fluctuate
lose:	to misplace		

165 Frequently Misspelled Words

absence
accommodate
achieve
acknowledgment
across
adequate
advisable
analyze
annually
appointment
argument
automatically
bankruptcy
becoming
beneficial
budget
business
calendar
cancelled
catalogue
centre
changeable
column
committee
congratulate
conscience
conscious
consecutive
consensus
consistent
control
convenient
correspondence
courteous
criticize
decision
deductible
defendant
definitely
dependant (n)
dependent (adj)
describe
desirable
destroy
development
disappoint
dissatisfied
division
efficient
embarrass
emphasis
emphasize
employee
envelope
equipped
especially
evidently
exaggerate
excellent
exempt
existence
extraordinary
familiar
fascinate
feasible
February
fibre
fiscal
foreign
forty

fourth
friend
genuine
government
grammar
grateful
guarantee
harass
height
hoping
immediate
incidentally
incredible
independent
indispensable
interrupt
irrelevant
itinerary
judgment
knowledge
legitimate
library
licence (n)
license (v)
maintenance
manageable
manufacturer
mileage
miscellaneous
mortgage
necessary
nevertheless
ninety
ninth
noticeable
occasionally
occurred
offered
omission
omitted
opportunity
opposite
ordinarily
paid
pamphlet
permanent
permitted
pleasant
practical
prevalent
privilege
probably
procedure
profited
prominent
qualify
quantity
questionnaire
receipt
receive
recognize
recommendation
referred
regarding
remittance
representative
restaurant
schedule
secretary
separate
similar
sincerely
software
succeed
sufficient
supervisor
surprise
tenant
therefore
thorough
though
through
truly
undoubtedly
unnecessarily
usable
usage
using
usually
valuable
vigorous (*but* vigour)
volume
weekday
writing
yield

Notes

1 American Psychological Association. (2020). *Bias-free language: Gender*. https://apastyle.apa.org/style-grammar-guidelines/bias-free-language/gender

APPENDIX C

Key to Grammar and Mechanics

Chapter 1

1. Because you will be entering a fast-paced competitive, and highly connected digital **environment, communication** and technology skills are critical to your career success. [b, Guide 1, Fragment]
2. Such skills are particularly significant **now when** jobs are scarce and competition is keen. [b, Guide 1, Fragment]
3. Many qualified people will apply for **openings; however,** candidates with exceptional communication skills will immediately stand out. [c, Guide 3, Comma splice. Use a semicolon or start a new sentence with *However*.]
4. Although we cannot predict the kinds of future jobs that will be available, they will undoubtedly require brainpower and education. [a, Correctly punctuated]
5. In traditional companies decisions must move through many levels of **managers; in** flat organizations decisions can be made more quickly. [c, Guide 3, Comma splice. Use a semicolon or start a new sentence with *In*.]
6. Millions of workers no longer report to nine-to-five **jobs thanks** largely to advances in new technologies and wireless Internet access. [b, Guide 1, Fragment]
7. Nearly all potential employers said that being able to think critically, communicate clearly, and solve complex problems is more important than a candidate's program of study. [a, Correctly punctuated]
8. The grapevine can be a powerful source of **information, although** it increasingly operates informally through social media. [b, Guide 1, Fragment]
9. Ethical companies experience less litigation, and they also are the target of less government regulation. [a, Correctly punctuated]
10. Even when an action is **legal, it** may violate generally accepted principles of right and wrong. [b, Guide 1, Fragment]

Chapter 2

1. Have you **spoken** with the other member of the virtual team? [Guide 4]
2. During job interviews one of the most frequently requested soft skills **is** writing proficiency. [Guide 6]
3. Jeremy said he wished he **were** president for just one day. [Guide 5]
4. Better decisions and faster response time **explain** why companies are using teams. [Guide 7]
5. Either the team leader or the manager **is** going to schedule the meeting. [Guide 8]
6. Conflict and disagreement **are** normal and should be expected in team interactions. [Guide 7]
7. Everything in the company's e-mails and written records **was** made public during the trial. [Guide 9]
8. A committee of faculty and students **is** examining strategies to improve campus interviewing. [Guide 10]
9. Each of the employees was given the opportunity to **choose** a team to join. [Guide 4]
10. When two candidates have equal qualifications, the one who appears to be more polished and professional is more likely to be hired and promoted. C [Guide 11]

Chapter 3

1. Please send texts to my manager and **me** so that she and I both understand the situation. [Guide 13]
2. Except for Mark and **me,** all the sales reps attended the team meeting. [Guide 13]
3. Google encourages developers to create apps and games for families and children using **its** new program [Guide 14]
4. Most of **us** consumers remember when fruits and vegetables were available only in season. [Guide 13]
5. Send the report to the administrative assistant or **me** when it's finished. [Guide 15]
6. All employees have a right to see **their** personnel folder. [Guide 17]
7. Lunches will be delivered to **whoever** ordered them. [Guide 16]
8. Most reservations were made in time, but **yours** and **hers** missed the deadline. [Guide 14]
9. C [Guide 13]
10. It must have been **she** who sent the e-mail to Jason and me. [Guide 12]

Chapter 4

1. The ability to prepare a purposeful, concise, and audience-centred message does not come **naturally** to most people. [Guide 19]
2. Christie thought she had done **well** in her performance review. [Guide 19]
3. The team wiki enables everyone to see the most **up-to-the-minute** status information. [Guide 20]
4. All of our **newly created** team documents can be posted quickly to the wiki. [Guides 20 and 19]
5. We all felt **bad** when one member lost her laptop and had no backup. [Guide 19]
6. The 3-x-3 writing process provides **step-by-step** instructions for preparing messages. [Guide 20]
7. Everyone likes the **newly revamped** website and its up-to-date links. [Guide 20]
8. Our project ran **smoothly** after Justin reorganized the team. [Guide 19]
9. Locally installed online collaboration tools are **easy to use** and work well. [Guide 20]
10. **Well-written** business messages sound conversational but professional. [Guide 20]

Chapter 5

1. Informal research methods include looking in the **files,** talking with your **boss,** and interviewing the target audience. [Guide 21, CmSer]
2. When we use company **e-mail,** we realize that our messages are monitored. [Guide 22, CmIntr]
3. By learning to distinguish between dependent and independent **clauses,** you will be able to avoid serious sentence faults. [Guide 22, CmIntr]
4. Active-voice verbs are best in most business **messages,** but passive-voice verbs are useful when sensitivity is required [Guide 23, CmConj]
5. We hired Davida **Michaels,** who was the applicant with the best **qualifications,** as our new social media manager. [Guide 25, CmIn]
6. Our business was incorporated on August 1, **2008,** in **Calgary,** Alberta. [Guide 24, CmDate]
7. The new social media **business,** by the **way,** is flourishing and is expected to show a profit soon. [Guide 25, CmIn]
8. After he **graduates,** Dustin plans to move to Victoria and find work there. [Guide 22, CmIntr]
9. Last fall our company introduced policies regulating the use of cell **phones, texting,** and e-mail on the job. [Guide 21, CmSer]
10. C [Guide 26, CmNo]

Chapter 6

1. Companies find it difficult to name new **products; consequently,** they often hire specialists. [Guide 27]
2. New product names must be **interesting; however,** many of the best names are already taken. [Guide 27]
3. Branding a product is a creative **endeavour;** the name becomes a product's shorthand. [Guide 27]
4. Global names must be appealing in such faraway places as **Beijing, China; Montréal, Canada;** and Dubai **City,** United Arab Emirates. [Guide 28]
5. One naming expert warned companies with the following **comment:** "Be aware of global consequences. For example, Bimbo is the name of a Mexican baking conglomerate. However, the word in English has an unsavoury meaning." [Guide 30]
6. Product and company names are developed by combining the following three linguistic **elements:** morphemes, phonemes, and syntax. [Guide 29]
7. One of the reasons company names such as Google and Apple work is that they are **catchy; however,** they are also backed by high-quality products. [Guide 27]
8. Some English sounds (such as L, V, F, and W) are considered **feminine;** others (such as X, M, and Z) are viewed as masculine. [Guide 27]
9. Among the company officers judging new names were Anthony Simmons, vice **president;** Rachel Lohr, **CFO;** and Lavonne Jones, manager. [Guide 28]
10. Tech specialists created a snazzy new **app; however,** it lacked an exciting name. [Guide 27]

Chapter 7

1. In just one **year's** time, James increased the number of his blog followers by 20 percent. [Guide 31]
2. Many followers of **James's** blog commented on the overuse of the *Reply All* button. [Guide 32]
3. Would you please give me directions to your downtown **headquarters.** [Guide 34]
4. Success often depends on an **individual's** ability to adapt to change. [Guide 31]
5. My friend recommended an article titled **"Ten** Tools for Building Your Own Mobile **App."** [Guide 38]
6. You must replace the ink cartridge **(see** page 8 in the **manual)** before printing. [Guide 37]
7. Tyler wondered whether all sales **managers'** databases needed to be updated. [Guide 32]
8. (Direct quotation) **"The** death of e-**mail,"** said Mike Song, **"has** been greatly **exaggerated."** [Guide 38]
9. In just two **years'** time, the number of people e-mailing on mobile devices nearly doubled. [Guide 32]
10. The staffing meeting starts at 10 a.m. sharp, doesn't **it?** [Guide 35]

Chapter 8

1. Sylvia's favourite **social media platform** is Instagram, though she enjoys using **Facebook** and Twitter as well. [Guides 39]
2. All **WestJet Airlines** passengers must exit the plane at **Gate** 2B in **Terminal** 3 when they reach **Toronto International Airport**. [Guides 39, 46]
3. Professor **Mills** assigned our class an **essay** assignment on **Canada's Climate Change Accountability Act**. [Guides 39, 41]
4. My **cousin**, who lives in the **Midwest**, has a **Big Mac** and a **Dr. Pepper** for **lunch** nearly every day. [Guides 41, 43, 45]
5. Our **sales manager** and **director** of **operations** thought that the **company** should purchase a new **NordicTrack** treadmill for the **fitness** room. [Guides 41, 39, 45]
6. The world's highest tax rate is in Belgium, said Professor Du-Babcock, who teaches at the City University of Hong Kong. [Guides 39, 41]
7. Rachel Warren, who heads our Consumer Services Division, has a master's degree in marketing from McMaster University. [Guides 44, 40, 39]
8. Please consult Figure 2.3 in Chapter 2 to obtain **Canadian Census Bureau** population figures for the **Northeast**. [Guides 46, 39, 43]
9. Last **summer** did you see the article titled "**The Global Consequences of Using Crops for Fuel**"? [Guides 39, 42]
10. Kahee decided that he would return to college in the **winter** to finish his diploma in graphic design. [Guides 39, 40]

Chapter 9

1. Did you **already** send an email to let the team know the meeting is **cancelled**?
2. The **principal** part of the manager's response contained a **compliment** and valuable **advice**.
3. In responding to the irate customer, Rachel made a **conscious** effort to show **patience** and present **credible** facts.
4. In **everyday** decision-making, the company trusts you to use your best **judgment**.
5. Before you **proceed** with the report, please check those **surprising** statistics.
6. It's **usually** better to de-emphasize bad news rather **than** to spotlight it.
7. **Incidentally**, passive-voice verbs can help you make a statement less **personal** when **necessary**.
8. Customers are more **accepting** of **disappointing** news if they are **assured** that **their** requests were heard and treated fairly.
9. The customer's complaint **elicited** an immediate response that **analyzed** the facts carefully but was not **too** long.
10. Before apologizing to a customer, check with your **supervisor** to review the liability **questionnaire**.

Chapter 10

1. Our manager reported receiving **seven** messages from customers with the same **two** complaints. [Guide 47]
2. **Thirty-three** companies indicated that they were participating in renewable energy programs. [Guide 47]
3. Consumers find that sending a **140-character** tweet is easier than writing a complaint letter. [Guide 48]
4. UPS strives to make important deliveries before **10 a.m.** [Guide 49]
5. The meeting was rescheduled for **March 7** at **2 p.m.** [Guide 49]
6. In the first **two** weeks of the year, we expect to hire at least **ten** new employees. [Guide 47]
7. With a birth occurring every **eight** seconds, the Canadian population is currently estimated to be **35 million.** [Guides 47, 50]
8. One petition now has more than **260** signatures, far and above the **25** needed for an official House of Commons response. [Guide 48]
9. You can burn **150** calories by walking as little as **30** minutes. [Guide 48]
10. At least **nine** prominent retail stores offer a **30-day** customer satisfaction return policy. [Guides 47, 48]

Chapter 11

1. One **credible** study revealed that **30** percent of jobs go to **companies'** inside candidates.
2. Networking is said to be the key to finding a **job;** however, **it's** easier said **than** done.
3. Some job seekers paid **$500** each to attend **12** sessions that promised expert job-searching **advice**.
4. To excel at **networking, a candidate** must have an **easy-to-remember** e-mail address.
5. My friend asked me if I had **already** prepared a **30-second** elevator **speech.**
6. When Rachel and **I** were collecting data for the **report,** we realized that **Twitter** and Facebook could be significant.

7. **Today's** workers must brush up their marketable **skills; otherwise,** they may not find another job after being laid off.
8. Being active on LinkedIn and building an impressive **Internet** presence **are** important, but the looseness of these connections **means** you shouldn't expect much from them.
9. Just between you and **me**, one of the best strategies in networking **is** distributing business cards with your personal tagline.
10. On **February 1** our company **president** revealed that we would be hiring **30** new employees, which was excellent news for everyone.

Chapter 12

1. After our supervisor and **she** returned from their meeting at **2 p.m.,** we were able to sort the **customers'** names more quickly.
2. **Six** of the 18 workers in my department were **released**; as a **result,** we had to work harder to achieve our goals.
3. Toyota, the market-leading **Japanese carmaker,** continued to enjoy strong positive ratings despite a string of **much-publicized** recalls.
4. **Michael's** presentation to a nonprofit group netted him only **$300,** a tenth of his usual **honorarium,** but he believes in pro bono work.
5. To reflect our guiding **principles** and our commitment to executive **education,** we offer financial support to more than **60** percent of our current MBA candidates.
6. Our latest press **release,** which was written in our Corporate Communication **Department,** announces the opening of three **Asian** offices.
7. In his justification report dated September **1,** Justin argued that expansion to **12** branch offices could boost annual revenue to **$22 million.**
8. The practicality and advisability of opening 12 branch offices **are** what will be discussed in the **consultant's feasibility** report.
9. The **president**, who had **gone** to a meeting in the Midwest, delivered a report to Jeff and **me** when he returned.
10. Because some organizations prefer **single-spaced reports,** be sure to check with your organization to learn **its** preference.

Chapter 13

1. Our CEO and **president** both worked on the **30-page proposal, which** was due immediately.
2. Managers in **two departments** [delete apostrophe] complained that their departments should have been consulted.
3. The RFP and **its** attachments arrived **too** late for my manager and **me** to complete the necessary research.
4. Although we worked **every day** on the proposal, we felt **bad** that we could not meet the May **15** deadline.
5. If the program and staff **are** to run **smoothly,** we must submit an effective grant proposal.
6. Although **short,** a successful mission statement should capture the **business's** goals and values [delete period] **in** a few succinct sentences.
7. A proposal budget cannot be changed if costs **rise later;** consequently, it must be written **carefully.**
8. A good eight-word mission statement is a critical tool for **funding;** it helps start-up **companies** evolve **their** big idea without being pulled off track.
9. Entrepreneur Stephanie **Rivera**, publisher of **an** urban event **calendar**, relies on social media to broadcast her message.
10. Stephanie asked Jake and **me** to help her write a business **plan that** would guide her new company and garner **permanent** funding**.**

Chapter 14

1. The **CEO's** assistant scheduled my colleague and **me** for a **20**-minute presentation to explain the new workplace sustainability initiative.
2. PowerPoint presentations, claims one **expert,** should be no longer **than 20** minutes and have no more than ten slides.
3. The introduction to a presentation should accomplish **three goals:** (a) capture attention, (b) establish **credibility,** and (c) preview main points.
4. In the body of a short **presentation,** speakers should focus on no more than **three principal** points.
5. A poll of **2,000** employees revealed that **four fifths** of them said they feared giving a presentation more **than** anything else they could think of.
6. A list of tips for inexperienced speakers **is** found in the article titled **"40** Quick Tips **for** Speakers."
7. The **director** of operations made a **15**-minute presentation giving **step-by-step** instructions on achieving our sustainability goals.
8. In the **spring** our **company's** stock value is expected to **rise** at least 10 percent.
9. The appearance and mannerisms of a speaker **definitely affect** a **listener's** evaluation of the message.
10. Because the **boss's** daughter was a dynamic speaker who had founded a successful **company,** she earned at least **$20,000** for each presentation.

Chapter 15

1. To conduct a safe online job search, you **should** [delete colon] (a) **use** only reputable job boards, **(b)** keep careful records, and (c) limit the number of sites on which you post your résumé.
2. **Today's** employers use **sites** such as Facebook to learn about potential **employees, which** means that a job seeker must maintain a professional online presence.
3. When searching for **jobs,** candidates discovered that the résumé is more likely to be used to screen **candidates than** for making hiring decisions.
4. If I **were you,** I would shorten my résumé to **one** page and include a summary of qualifications.
5. Mitchell wondered whether it was **all right** to ask his professor for employment **advice.**
6. At last **month's** staff **meeting,** team members examined several **candidates'** résumés.
7. Rather **than** schedule **face-to-face interviews,** the team investigated videoconferencing.
8. **Eleven** applicants will be interviewed on April **10;** consequently, we may need to work late to accommodate them.
9. Although as many as **25** percent of jobs are found on the **Internet,** the **principal** source of jobs still involves networking.
10. If Troy had **gone** to the **company's** own **website,** he might have seen the position posted immediately.

Chapter 16

1. Most interviews **usually** cover the same kinds of **questions; therefore,** smart candidates prepare for them.
2. Rodney wondered how many **companies** use the Internet to check **candidates' backgrounds.**
3. Despite the heavy use of **e-mail,** most **employers** use the telephone to reach candidates and set up **their** interviews.
4. In interviewing job **candidates,** recruiters have the following three **purposes:** assessing their skills, discussing their **experience,** and deciding whether they are a good fit for the organization.
5. If your job history has gaps in **it,** be prepared to explain what you did during this **time** [delete comma] and how you kept **up-to-date** in your field.
6. Interviewing is a **two-way street,** and candidates should be prepared with **their** own meaningful questions.
7. Emma was asked whether she had a **bachelor's degree** [delete comma] and whether she had three **years'** experience.
8. If you are **conscientious** and want to create a good **impression,** be sure to write a **thank-you** message after a job interview.
9. When **Maria's** interview was **over,** she told friends that she had done **well.**
10. Maria was **all ready** to send a thank-you **message** [omit comma] when she realized she could not spell the **interviewer's** name.

Index

Italic page numbers indicate illustrative information in figures.

C

D

E

F

G

H

I

J

K

L

S

T